Mergent's
DIVIDEND
ACHIEVERS

Spring 2004

Mergent's DIVIDEND ACHIEVERS

Mergent, Inc.

JONATHAN WORRALL
Publisher

THOMAS WECERA
Associate Publisher

JOHN PEDERNALES
Director of Global Fundamental Data

Index Department

ROBY MUNTONI
Director of Index Operations

KEVIN HECKERT
Editor of Index and Publication Operations

John Wiley & Sons, Inc.

SUE LEWIS
Publisher

JOAN O'NEIL
Publisher

JO-ANN WASSERMAN
Associate Publisher

DAVID PUGH
Editor

COLLEEN SCOLLANS
Senior Marketing Manager

MICHAEL GREGORY
Director, Production & Operations

JENNIFER CHINWORTH
Production Editor

MERGENT'S DIVIDEND ACHIEVERS (ISSN 1547-8335; electronic ISSN 1548-2839) is published quarterly by Mergent, Inc. and Wiley Subscription Services, Inc., a Wiley Company, 111 River Street, Hoboken, NJ 07030-5774.

SUBSCRIPTION PRICE: Print only: $165.00 in U.S., Canada, and Mexico and $189.00 outside of North America for individuals, and $165.00 in U.S., $205.00 in Canada and Mexico, and $239.00 outside North America for institutions, agencies, and libraries. Prices subject to change. Payment must be made in U.S. dollars drawn on a U.S. bank. Claims for undelivered copies will be accepted only after the following issue has been received. Please enclose a copy of the mailing label. Missing copies will be supplied when losses have been sustained in transit and where reserve stock permits. Please allow four weeks for processing a change of address. Address subscription inquiries to Subscription Manager, Jossey-Bass, a Wiley Company, 989 Market Street, San Francisco, CA 94103-1741; Tel.: (888) 378-2537, (415) 433-1740 (International); E-mail: jbsubs@jbp.com.

POSTMASTER: Send address changes to *Mergent's Dividend Achievers*, Jossey-Bass, 989 Market Street, San Francisco, CA 94103-1741.

ADVERTISING SALES: Inquiries concerning advertising should be forwarded to the Advertising Sales Manager, c/o John Wiley & Sons, Inc., 111 River Street, Hoboken, NJ 07030-5774; (201) 748-8832. Advertising Sales, European Contact: Jackie Sibley, c/o John Wiley & Sons, Ltd., The Atrium, Southern Gate, Chichester, West Sussex, PO19 8SQ, England; Tel.: 44 1243 770 351; Fax: 44 1243 770 432; E-mail: adsales@wiley.co.uk.

www.wiley.com/go/mergent

TABLE OF CONTENTS
U.S. Dividend Achievers

Canadian Dividend Achievers

Notes From The Editor

In this edition of Mergent's Dividend Achievers, Mergent is featuring full-page profiles of the Canadian Dividend Achievers. After researching its universe of more than 3,500 Canadian companies, Mergent has identified 27 companies that have consistently increased their dividends for the last five or more consecutive years. This elite group represents less than 1.0% of all Canadian companies. Canadian Utilities Ltd., a provider of natural gas and electric energy in the Province of Alberta, leads the group with 21 years of dividend increases.

As of March 31, 2004, the average yield for Mergent's Canadian Dividend Achievers was 2.2%. The highest yield of 3.4% belonged to Enbridge Inc., which is engaged in the transportation and distribution of energy. The five-year average annual compound dividend growth rate amounted to 14.8%. BMTC Group, which is engaged in retail sales of furniture and household and electronic appliances in Quebec, recorded the highest five-year average annual compound dividend growth rate of 29.2%.

In the U.S., for the first quarter ended March 31, 2004, the strength of the financial markets began to wane as investors turned their attention to geo-political uncertainty. The markets were also impacted by unimpressive employment reports in January and February and what many investors termed as "overbought" conditions creating a "mini bubble".

Despite the economic environment, Mergent's Dividend Achiever Index price appreciation was 1.99% for the quarter ended March 31, 2004 compared to -0.92% for the Dow Jones Industrial Average (DJIA) and 1.29% for the S&P500.

Year-to-date, the Dividend Achiever Index total return was 2.54%, which is particularly striking when considering the tax legislation changes of 2003. With the new tax rate, investors gain up to an additional 30% on dividend income, making dividend-paying securities an attractive alternative to fixed-income securities. Total return for the DJIA fell 0.43%, while the S&P 500 posted a gain of 1.69%.

Mergent's Dividend Achiever Index uses a market-capitalization-weighted scheme. The real-time price appreciation performance is calculated and published by the American Stock Exchange under the ticker symbol DAA. The Index is reconstituted annually and changes are effective on the last trading day of January.

For the trailing ten years ended March 31, 2004, annualized total returns were as follows:

Mergent's Dividend Achievers	15.13%
Dow Jones Industrial Average	13.28%
S&P 500	11.68%

In 2004, Mergent, Inc. achieved another milestone through the successful licensing of its Dividend Achiever selection methodology to BlackRock, Inc., one of the largest investment management firms in the United States with more than $309 billion in assets under management (as of 12/31/03). The new closed-end fund named "BlackRock Strategic Dividend Achievers Trust," which began trading on the New York Stock Exchange (NYSE) under the ticker symbol BDT on March 26, 2004, focuses on small to mid capitalized companies.

Mergent's foray into the closed-end market was achieved through the initial public offering of the BlackRock Dividend Achievers Trust on December 19, 2003. This closed-end fund, which raised more than $720 million and trades on the NYSE under the ticker symbol BDV, reflects the top yielding constituents of Mergent's Dividend Achievers. One should note that the pre-tax yield for BDV, an impressive 6%, excludes the new tax benefits associated with the reduced taxes on dividend income.

As of March 31, 2004, BlackRock, Inc. had more than $1.2 billion in assets under management on the Dividend Achievers selection methodology. Mergent plans to continue licensing the Dividend Achievers Index for the creation of additional investment products. For more information on the Fund visit www.Blackrock.com.

In 2004, Mergent continuing its 26 year tradition identified 303 "Dividend Achievers". These companies are profiled in the spring 2004 edition, expanded to include performance and statistical information on

Mergent's Dividend Achievers Index.

This edition includes companies that have increased dividends for 50 years, such as Procter and Gamble, a manufacturer and marketer of nearly 300 products to more than five billion consumers in 140 countries, Diebold, Inc., a provider of self-service delivery systems such as automatic teller machines and electronic security, and American States Water Company, a supplier of water and electrical service to customers in California and Arizona. Newcomers to the Dividend Achievers include companies such as Harley-Davidson, Inc., Caterpillar Inc, and Brown & Brown, Inc.

Kevin B. Heckert

Kevin B. Heckert
Editor of Index and
Publication Operations

Timeline

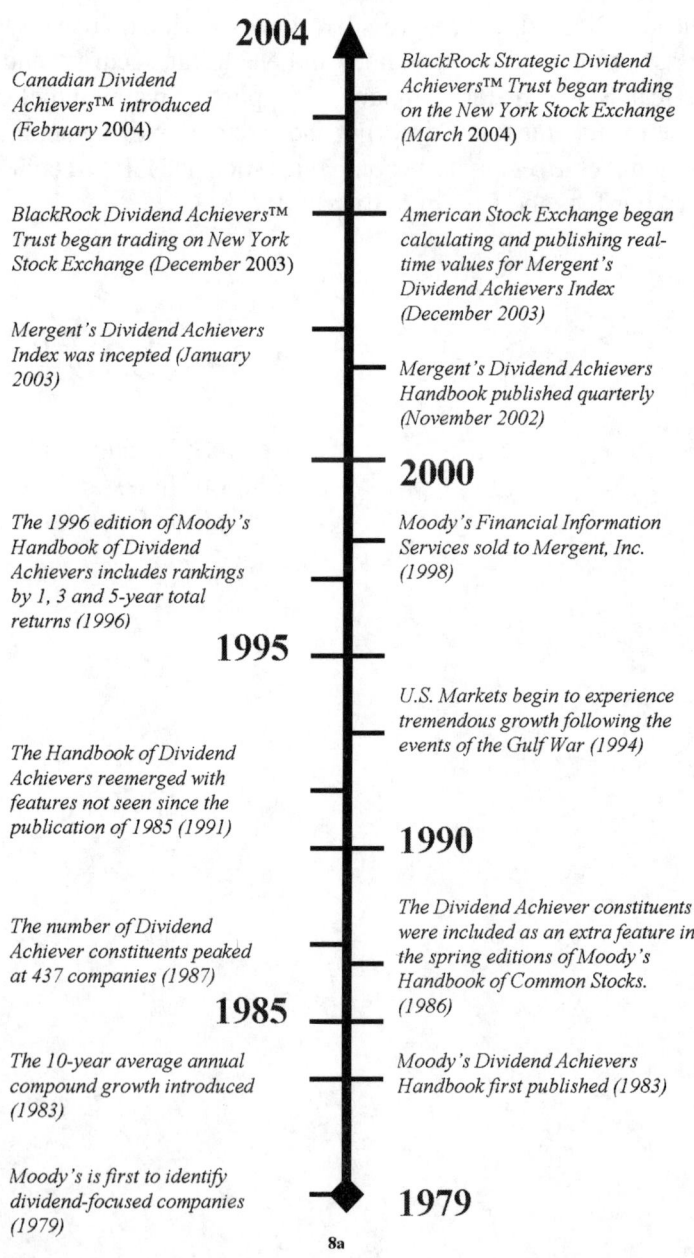

2004

Canadian Dividend Achievers™ introduced (February 2004)

BlackRock Strategic Dividend Achievers™ Trust began trading on the New York Stock Exchange (March 2004)

BlackRock Dividend Achievers™ Trust began trading on New York Stock Exchange (December 2003)

American Stock Exchange began calculating and publishing real-time values for Mergent's Dividend Achievers Index (December 2003)

Mergent's Dividend Achievers Index was incepted (January 2003)

Mergent's Dividend Achievers Handbook published quarterly (November 2002)

2000

The 1996 edition of Moody's Handbook of Dividend Achievers includes rankings by 1, 3 and 5-year total returns (1996)

Moody's Financial Information Services sold to Mergent, Inc. (1998)

1995

U.S. Markets begin to experience tremendous growth following the events of the Gulf War (1994)

The Handbook of Dividend Achievers reemerged with features not seen since the publication of 1985 (1991)

1990

The number of Dividend Achiever constituents peaked at 437 companies (1987)

The Dividend Achiever constituents were included as an extra feature in the spring editions of Moody's Handbook of Common Stocks. (1986)

1985

The 10-year average annual compound growth introduced (1983)

Moody's Dividend Achievers Handbook first published (1983)

Moody's is first to identify dividend-focused companies (1979)

1979

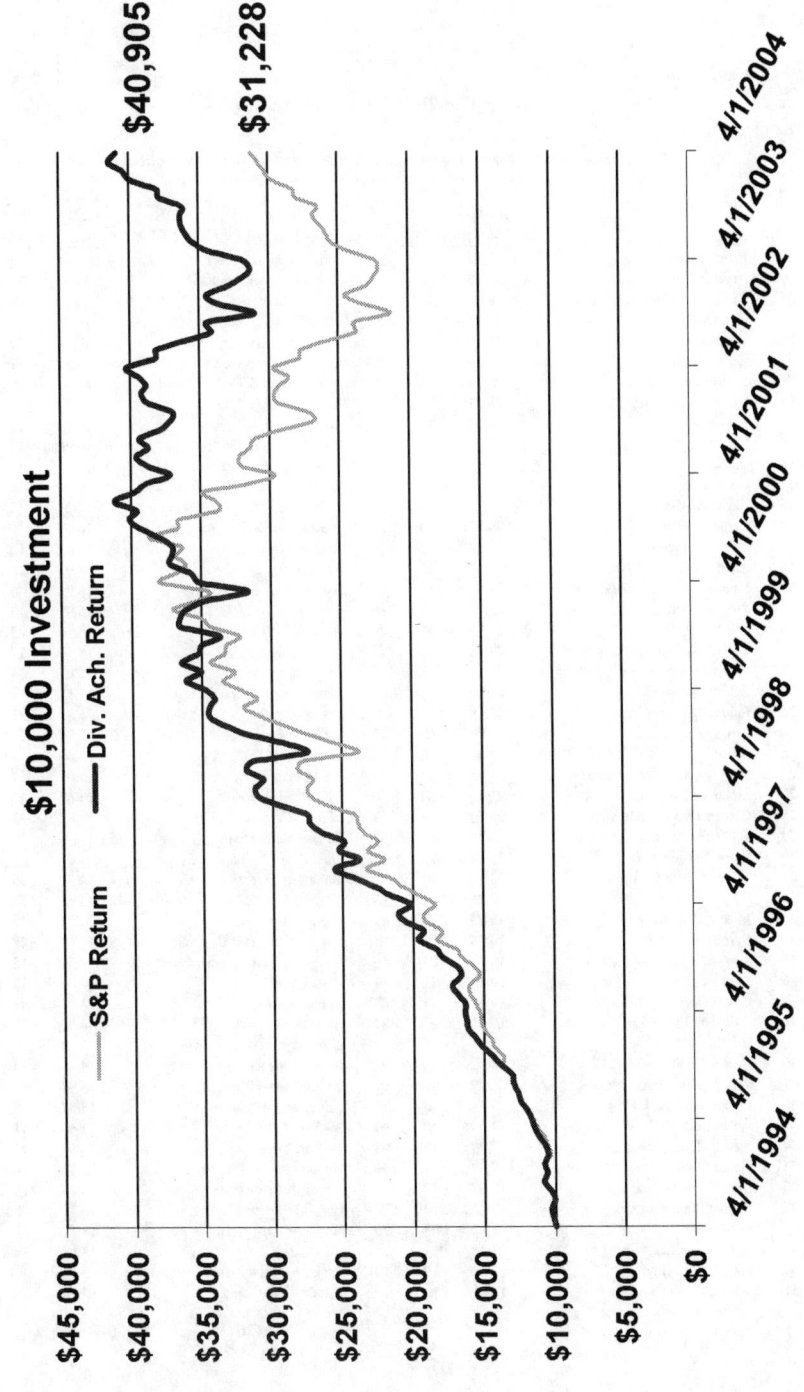

$10,000 Investment

— S&P Return
— Div. Ach. Return

$40,905

$31,228

4/1/1994 · 4/1/1995 · 4/1/1996 · 4/1/1997 · 4/1/1998 · 4/1/1999 · 4/1/2000 · 4/1/2001 · 4/1/2002 · 4/1/2003 · 4/1/2004

$0 · $5,000 · $10,000 · $15,000 · $20,000 · $25,000 · $30,000 · $35,000 · $40,000 · $45,000

Ranking The 2004 Dividend Achievers

Companies are listed by the 10-year average annual compound growth of their dividends.
Also shown are total numbers of consecutive years of dividend growth

Rank	Name	10-Year Growth Rate	Years
1	People's Bank	43.97	10
2	Paychex Inc	39.78	15
3	Cullen/Frost Bankers, Inc.	38.01	10
4	Courier Corp.	35.65	10
5	Hibernia Corp.	35.59	10
6	Citigroup Inc	29.70	17
7	Harley-Davidson, Inc.	29.24	10
8	Doral Financial Corp.	28.21	14
9	Home Depot, Inc.	26.39	16
10	SWS Group, Inc.	26.20	11
11	Chittenden Corp.	25.35	11
12	Caterpillar Inc.	25.20	10
13	BancFirst Corp.	24.71	10
14	Camden Property Trust	24.67	10
15	Linear Technology Corp.	24.24	11
16	Anchor BanCorp Wisconsin	24.22	10
17	Pinnacle West Capital Corp.	24.04	10
18	Stryker Corp.	23.11	11
18	SEI Investments Co.	23.11	12
20	CVB Financial Corp.	23.06	13
21	Roper Industries, Inc.	22.77	11
22	TCF Financial Corp.	22.43	12
23	Fidelity National Financial	22.29	16
24	Pier 1 Imports Inc.	22.08	12
25	Franklin Electric Co., Inc.	22.05	10
26	National Commerce Financial	21.65	29
27	Medtronic, Inc.	21.43	26
28	Charter One Financial, Inc.	20.90	15
29	Wolverine World Wide, Inc.	20.85	10
30	Eaton Vance Corp	20.64	22
31	T Rowe Price Group Inc.	20.54	17
32	Washington Mutual Inc.	20.29	14
33	M & T Bank Corp	20.24	23
34	Sysco Corp.	20.18	27
35	Synovus Financial Corp.	19.67	27
36	Meridian Bioscience Inc.	19.53	11
37	Cintas Corporation	19.19	21
38	Fifth Third Bancorp	18.85	31
39	Wal-Mart Stores, Inc.	18.75	22
40	Archer Daniels Midland Co.	18.62	29
41	WestAmerica Bancorporation	18.49	14
42	Independent Bank Corp.	18.14	15
43	AptarGroup Inc.	17.92	10
44	First Federal Capital Corp.	17.72	12
45	Nucor Corp.	17.69	31
46	Jack Henry & Associates, Inc.	17.67	12
47	Sterling Bancshares, Inc.	17.61	10
48	SLM Corp.	17.42	23
49	Corus Bankshares, Inc.	17.42	17
50	F.N.B. Corp (FL)	17.38	19
51	Whitney Holding Corp.	17.25	10
52	Arrow International,Inc.	16.98	11
53	Superior Industries Intl.	16.92	18
54	Freddie Mac	16.80	13
55	Pacific Capital Bancorp	16.75	34
56	Commerce Bancorp, Inc	16.74	12
57	Republic Bancorp, Inc.	16.71	11
58	Wells Fargo & Co.	16.71	16
59	Hudson United Bancorp	16.64	13
60	AFLAC Inc.	16.59	21
61	Tanger Factory Outlet Cntrs.	16.47	10
62	Applebee's International	16.23	12
63	General Growth Properties	16.23	10
63	Community First Bankshares	16.23	10
65	Healthcare Realty Trust, Inc.	16.19	10
66	Danaher Corp.	16.09	10
67	Popular Inc.	16.03	11
68	Tootsie Roll Industries Inc	16.02	40
69	Mercury General Corp.	15.97	17
70	State Street Corp.	15.76	23
71	S & T Bancorp, Inc.	15.70	14
72	Pfizer Inc.	15.67	36
73	Harleysville National Corp.	15.58	17
74	SouthTrust Corp.	15.33	33
75	First Indiana Corp.	15.22	12
76	Sigma-Aldrich Corp.	15.07	22
77	First Financial Holdings, Inc.	15.02	11
78	McGrath RentCorp	14.87	13
79	MBNA Corp.	14.87	12
80	Glacier Bancorp, Inc.	14.76	12
81	Golden West Financial Corp.	14.71	20
82	Gallagher (Arthur J.) & Co.	14.70	19
83	Leggett & Platt, Inc.	14.66	32
84	Brady Corp.	14.64	19
85	Automatic Data Processing	14.63	28
86	Simmons First National Corp.	14.36	12
87	BB&T Corp.	14.32	32
88	Illinois Tool Works, Inc.	14.27	41
89	McDonald's Corp	14.24	27
90	Legg Mason, Inc.	14.18	20
91	Irwin Financial Corp.	14.08	14
92	Park National Corp.	13.88	16
93	American International Group	13.87	18
94	Johnson & Johnson	13.86	41
95	Praxair, Inc.	13.85	11
96	Fannie Mae	13.83	18
97	Brown & Brown, Inc.	13.78	10
98	General Electric Co.	13.73	28
99	Northern Trust Corp.	13.71	18
100	Trustmark Corp.	13.68	30
101	Bank of America Corp.	13.39	26
102	Teleflex Incorporated	13.24	26

Rank	Name	10-Year Growth Rate	Years	Rank	Name	10-Year Growth Rate	Years
103	Old Republic International	13.19	22	161	Dover Corp.	9.74	48
104	Artesian Resources Corp.	13.08	11	162	Valley National Bancorp	9.72	12
105	Transatlantic Holdings, Inc.	12.93	13	163	United Technologies Corp.	9.69	10
106	National Penn Bancshares	12.84	25	164	Nordson Corp.	9.69	23
107	Wiley (John) & Sons Inc.	12.84	10	165	Mine Safety Appliances Co	9.64	33
108	Compass Bancshares Inc.	12.84	22	166	Protective Life Corp.	9.57	14
109	Webster Financial Corp.	12.69	11	167	First Merchants Corp.	9.55	19
110	Badger Meter, Inc.	12.61	11	168	Carlisle Companies Inc.	9.53	27
111	Associated Banc-Corp.	12.47	33	169	Sherwin-Williams Co.	9.51	24
112	Heinz (H.J.) Co.	12.44	40	169	First Commonwealth Fin.	9.51	16
113	Alberto-Culver Co.	12.44	19	171	Regions Financial Corp.	9.42	32
114	Avery Dennison Corp.	12.41	28	172	Unizan Financial Corp	9.39	19
115	Franklin Resources, Inc.	12.39	14	173	Anheuser-Busch Cos., Inc.	9.34	29
116	Raven Industries, Inc.	12.33	16	174	Becton, Dickinson and Co.	9.26	31
117	Chemical Financial Corp.	12.13	28	175	Pentair, Inc.	9.20	27
118	Commerce Bancshares, Inc.	12.02	35	176	Meredith Corp.	9.04	10
119	ConAgra Foods, Inc.	12.01	26	177	Community Trust Bancorp	8.97	15
120	SunTrust Banks, Inc.	11.99	18	178	National City Corp	8.96	11
121	First Charter Corp.	11.94	11	179	Sterling Financial Corp.	8.94	16
122	Lancaster Colony Corp.	11.94	34	180	Vulcan Materials Co.	8.84	11
123	First Midwest Bancorp, Inc.	11.87	11	180	Community Bank System	8.84	12
124	Ecolab, Inc.	11.81	11	182	Wrigley (William) Jr. Co.	8.72	23
125	ABM Industries, Inc.	11.76	39	183	Citizens Banking Corp	8.66	20
126	Mercantile Bankshares Corp.	11.70	27	184	Federal Signal Corp.	8.66	16
127	First Financial Corp.	11.65	11	185	Hillenbrand Industries	8.53	33
128	Myers Industries Inc.	11.61	27	185	FirstMerit Corp	8.53	21
129	Altria Group Inc	11.61	38	187	TEPPCO Partners, L.P.	8.46	11
130	Nuveen Investments Inc	11.61	11	188	Sara Lee Corp.	8.45	27
131	Family Dollar Stores, Inc.	11.61	27	188	Alfa Corp	8.45	18
132	Procter & Gamble Co.	11.45	50	190	Washington Federal Inc.	8.43	20
133	Abbott Laboratories	11.38	31	191	RLI Corp.	8.40	27
134	Holly Corp.	11.36	10	192	Bemis, Inc.	8.40	20
135	Cincinnati Financial Corp.	11.33	43	193	Harleysville Group, Inc.	8.37	17
136	Jefferson-Pilot Corp.	11.19	36	194	Beckman Coulter, Inc.	8.31	12
137	Comerica, Inc.	11.01	20	195	Lilly (Eli) & Co.	8.28	36
138	1st Source Corp.	10.92	16	196	Clorox Co.	8.28	27
139	Merck & Co., Inc	10.91	20	197	Old National Bancorp	8.26	20
140	General Dynamics Corp.	10.84	12	198	Wilmington Trust Corp.	8.13	22
140	Ambac Financial Group, Inc.	10.84	12	199	KeyCorp (New)	8.10	24
142	United Mobile Homes, Inc.	10.78	13	200	United Bankshares, Inc.	8.07	22
143	Valspar Corp.	10.55	25	201	Weyco Group, Inc	8.06	23
144	BancorpSouth Inc.	10.55	17	202	Emerson Electric Co.	7.94	47
145	Rouse Co.	10.48	11	203	PepsiCo Inc.	7.89	32
146	Colgate-Palmolive Co.	10.39	41	204	Banta Corporation	7.81	25
147	AmSouth Bancorporation	10.35	33	205	Johnson Controls Inc	7.79	28
148	Pitney Bowes, Inc.	10.31	20	206	Midland Co.	7.75	17
149	State Auto Financial Corp.	10.22	12	207	Susquehanna Bancshares, Inc	7.69	33
150	Fulton Financial Corp.	10.13	30	208	McCormick & Co., Inc.	7.65	17
151	Lowe's Cos., Inc.	10.13	42	209	Grainger (W.W.) Inc.	7.62	32
152	Marsh & McLennan Cos., Inc.	10.12	42	210	Walgreen Co.	7.60	28
153	Pennichuck Corp.	10.10	10	211	Farmer Bros. Co.	7.33	15
154	Second Bancorp, Inc.	10.10	16	212	Air Products & Chemicals, Inc.	7.06	21
155	HON Industries Inc.	10.03	15	213	Avon Products, Inc.	7.05	13
156	MBIA Inc.	10.01	16	214	West Pharmaceutical Svcs.	7.05	11
157	Coca-Cola Co (The)	9.98	41	215	Bandag, Inc.	7.01	27
158	Kimco Realty Corp.	9.96	11	216	Target Corp	6.91	32
159	Marshall & Ilsley Corp.	9.93	31	217	La-Z-Boy Inc.	6.83	22
160	Hershey Foods Corp.	9.75	29	218	NACCO Industries Inc.	6.76	20

Rank	Name	10-Year Growth Rate	Years	Rank	Name	10-Year Growth Rate	Years
219	Bank of Hawaii Corp	6.76	26	262	Kimberly-Clark Corp.	4.50	29
220	Diebold, Inc.	6.70	50	263	Stanley Works	4.39	36
221	Hormel Foods Corp.	6.68	36	264	NICOR Inc.	4.37	16
222	National Security Group, Inc	6.65	13	265	Gannett Co., Inc.	4.16	32
223	Rohm & Haas Co.	6.61	26	266	Briggs & Stratton Corp.	4.14	12
224	McGraw-Hill Cos., Inc.	6.60	30	267	Progressive Corp.	4.14	34
225	Wesbanco, Inc.	6.54	18	268	Vectren Corp	3.96	28
226	Stepan Co.	6.53	37	269	MDU Resources Group Inc.	3.87	13
227	Frisch's Restaurants, Inc.	6.36	20	270	Questar Corp.	3.65	24
228	Cedar Fair, L.P.	6.31	16	271	SJW Corp.	3.62	37
229	EastGroup Properties, Inc.	6.28	11	272	Wesco Financial Corp.	3.61	32
230	Sonoco Products Co.	6.23	20	273	Gorman-Rupp Co.	3.54	31
231	SBC Communications, Inc.	6.21	19	274	Black Hills Corporation	3.47	32
232	Telephone and Data Systems	6.19	29	275	Atmos Energy Corp.	3.43	16
233	Health Care Property Investors	6.05	18	276	Quaker Chemical Corp.	3.42	32
234	Masco Corp.	5.96	45	277	National Fuel Gas Co. (NJ)	3.38	32
235	Aqua America Inc	5.90	12	278	Florida Public Utilities Co.	3.37	35
236	Haverty Furniture Cos., Inc.	5.90	33	279	Supervalu Inc.	3.31	31
237	Lincoln National Corp.	5.83	20	280	Energen Corp.	3.25	21
238	ALLTEL Corp.	5.76	43	281	Progress Energy, Inc.	3.17	15
239	Parker-Hannifin Corp.	5.66	47	282	Exxon Mobil Corp.	3.13	21
240	Piedmont Natural Gas Co., Inc.	5.48	24	283	Helmerich & Payne, Inc.	2.92	27
241	Chubb Corp.	5.40	39	284	Tennant Co.	2.76	31
242	RPM International Inc	5.39	30	285	Smith (A.O.) Corp	2.65	11
243	Genuine Parts Co.	5.37	47	286	Otter Tail Corp.	2.54	28
244	St. Paul Companies, Inc.	5.26	17	287	UGI Corp. (New)	2.53	16
245	Bard (C.R.), Inc.	5.24	32	288	Middlesex Water Co.	2.51	31
246	PPG Industries, Inc.	5.22	32	289	Cleco Corp. (New)	2.47	22
247	Fuller (H.B.) Company	5.18	36	290	Federal Realty Investment Tr.	2.33	36
248	VF Corp.	5.17	31	291	WPS Resources Corp.	2.07	45
249	Brown-Forman Corp.	5.16	19	292	Clarcor Inc.	1.93	23
250	Washington REIT	5.15	42	293	Peoples Energy Corp.	1.74	20
251	Quixote Corp.	5.14	10	294	Universal Health Realty Inc. Tr.	1.68	16
252	United Dominion Realty Trust	5.08	18	295	WGL Holdings, Inc.	1.65	27
253	Universal Corp.	5.05	33	296	California Water Service Group	1.60	36
254	ChevronTexaco Corp.	5.03	16	297	Commercial Net Lease Realty	1.53	14
255	Hilb, Rogal and Hamilton Co.	5.03	17	298	EnergySouth, Inc.	1.46	26
256	Weingarten Realty Investors	4.97	15	299	Consolidated Edison, Inc.	1.45	29
257	May Department Stores Co.	4.84	28	300	Connecticut Water Service	1.25	28
258	CenturyTel, Inc.	4.79	30	301	American States Water Co.	1.11	50
259	ServiceMaster Co. (The)	4.76	33	302	MGE Energy Inc	0.95	28
260	3M Co	4.75	45	303	Donnelley (R.R.) & Sons Co.	0.82	34
261	Bowl America Inc.	4.74	31				

Longest Records Of Dividend Achievement

These Dividend Achievers boast the longest records of consecutive annual dividend increases.

Rank	Years	Name	Ticker	Rank	Years	Name	Ticker
1	50	American States Water Co.	AWR		34	Progressive Corp.	PGR
	50	Diebold, Inc.	DBD	41	33	AmSouth Bancorporation	ASO
	50	Procter & Gamble Co.	PG		33	Associated Banc-Corp.	ASBC
4	48	Dover Corp.	DOV		33	Haverty Furniture Cos., Inc.	HVT
5	47	Emerson Electric Co.	EMR		33	Hillenbrand Industries, Inc.	HB
	47	Genuine Parts Co.	GPC		33	Mine Safety Appliances Co	MSA
	47	Parker-Hannifin Corp.	PH		33	ServiceMaster Co. (The)	SVM
8	45	3M Co	MMM		33	SouthTrust Corp.	SOTR
	45	Masco Corp.	MAS		33	Susquehanna Bancshares, Inc	SUSQ
	45	WPS Resources Corp.	WPS		33	Universal Corp.	UVV
11	43	ALLTEL Corp.	AT	50	32	Bard (C.R.), Inc.	BCR
	43	Cincinnati Financial Corp.	CINF		32	BB&T Corp. (Lumberton, NC)	BBT
13	42	Lowe's Cos., Inc.	LOW		32	Black Hills Corporation	BKH
	42	Marsh & McLennan Cos., Inc.	MMC		32	Gannett Co., Inc.	GCI
	42	Washington R.E.I.T	WRE		32	Grainger (W.W.) Inc.	GWW
16	41	Coca-Cola Co (The)	KO		32	Leggett & Platt, Inc.	LEG
	41	Colgate-Palmolive Co.	CL		32	National Fuel Gas Co.	NFG
	41	Illinois Tool Works, Inc.	ITW		32	PepsiCo Inc.	PEP
	41	Johnson & Johnson	JNJ		32	PPG Industries, Inc.	PPG
20	40	Heinz (H.J.) Co.	HNZ		32	Quaker Chemical Corp.	KWR
	40	Tootsie Roll Industries Inc	TR		32	Regions Financial Corp.	RF
22	39	ABM Industries, Inc.	ABM		32	Target Corp	TGT
	39	Chubb Corp.	CB		32	Wesco Financial Corp.	WSC
24	38	Altria Group Inc	MO	63	31	Abbott Laboratories	ABT
25	37	SJW Corp.	SJW		31	Becton, Dickinson and Co.	BDX
	37	Stepan Co.	SCL		31	Bowl America Inc.	BWLA
27	36	California Water Service Group	CWT		31	Fifth Third Bancorp	FITB
	36	Federal Realty Investment Trust	FRT		31	Gorman-Rupp Co.	GRC
	36	Fuller (H.B.) Company	FUL		31	Marshall & Ilsley Corp.	MI
	36	Hormel Foods Corp.	HRL		31	Middlesex Water Co.	MSEX
	36	Jefferson-Pilot Corp.	JP		31	Nucor Corp.	NUE
	36	Lilly (Eli) & Co.	LLY		31	Supervalu Inc.	SVU
	36	Pfizer Inc.	PFE		31	Tennant Co.	TNC
	36	Stanley Works	SWK		31	VF Corp.	VFC
35	35	Commerce Bancshares, Inc.	CBSH	74	30	CenturyTel, Inc.	CTL
	35	Florida Public Utilities Co.	FPU		30	Fulton Financial Corp.	FULT
37	34	Donnelley (R.R.) & Sons Co.	RRD		30	McGraw-Hill Cos., Inc. (The)	MHP
	34	Lancaster Colony Corp.	LANC		30	RPM International Inc	RPM
	34	Pacific Capital Bancorp	PCBC		30	Trustmark Corp.	TRMK

Dividend Achiever Arrivals

The following companies, which recorded at least ten consecutive years
of dividend increases in 2003, mark their debut as Dividend Achievers.

Anchor Bancorp Wisconsin, Inc.
AptarGroup Inc.
Artesian Resources Corp.
BancFirst Corp.
Brown & Brown, Inc.
Camden Property Trust
Caterpillar Inc.
Courier Corp.
Cullen/Frost Bankers, Inc.
Danaher Corp.
Farmer Bros. Co.
First Merchants Corp.
Franklin Electric Co., Inc.
General Growth Properties, Inc.
Harley-Davidson, Inc.
Healthcare Realty Trust, Inc.
Helmerich & Payne, Inc.
Hibernia Corp.

Holly Corp.
Independent Bank Corporation
Meredith Corp.
Meridian Bioscience Inc.
Parker-Hannifin Corp.
Pennichuck Corp.
People's Bank
Pinnacle West Capital Corp.
Quixote Corp.
Second Bancorp, Inc.
Simmons First National Corp.
Sterling Bancshares, Inc.
SWS Group, Inc.
Tanger Factory Outlet Centers, Inc.
United Technologies Corp.
Whitney Holding Corp.
Wiley (John) & Sons Inc.
Wolverine World Wide, Inc.

Dividend Achiever Departures

The following former Dividend Achievers have not increased their regular cash dividends in 2003.

American National Insurance Co.
Bank of New York Co., Inc.
Bristol-Myers Squibb Co.
Donegal Group Inc.
El Paso Corp.
Energy West Inc.
First Financial Bancorp
FleetBoston Financial Corp.

GATX Corp.
J.P. Morgan Chase & Co.
Northwestern Corp.
TECO Energy Inc.
Trustco Bank Corp. (N.Y.)
Unitrin, Inc.
Virco Mfg. Corp.

The following former Dividend Achievers have been acquired in 2003.

First Virginia Banks, Inc.

Household International, Inc.

The following former Canadian Dividend Achievers have been acquired in 2000.

Cara Operations Ltd.

Dividend Achiever Name Changes

The following Dividend Achiever companies have changed their name.

Old Name

Nuveen (John) Company (The)
Philadelphia Suburban Corporation
Philip Morris Companies, Inc.
St. Paul Companies, Inc.

New Name

Nuveen Investments, Inc.
Aqua America, Inc.
Altria Group, Inc.
St Paul Travelers Companies Inc.

Top 20 by Return on Equity

Based on latest available year-end information. Ratios determined using net income.

Rank	Company	R.O.E.	Rank	Company	R.O.E.
1	Avon Products, Inc.	179.05%	11	Altria Group Inc	36.70%
2	Colgate-Palmolive Co.	160.22%	12	Hershey Foods Corp.	35.75%
3	Anheuser-Busch Cos., Inc.	76.55%	13	Sysco Corp.	35.42%
4	Sara Lee Corp.	65.29%	14	Fannie Mae	35.33%
5	SLM Corp.	58.31%	15	Procter & Gamble Co.	32.04%
6	Heinz (H.J.) Co.	47.22%	16	Nuveen Investments Inc	31.04%
7	Pitney Bowes, Inc.	45.81%	17	Coca-Cola Co (The)	30.85%
8	Merck & Co., Inc	43.85%	18	3M Co	30.48%
9	Clorox Co.	40.58%	19	PepsiCo Inc.	29.99%
10	SEI Investments Co.	39.31%	20	Florida Public Utilities Co.	29.96%

Top 20 by Return on Assets

Based on latest available year-end information. Ratios determined using net income.

Rank	Company	R.O.A	Rank	Company	R.O.A
1	SEI Investments Co.	24.13%	11	Nuveen Investments Inc	15.09%
2	Colgate-Palmolive Co.	19.00%	12	Johnson & Johnson	14.91%
3	Avon Products, Inc.	18.66%	13	T Rowe Price Group Inc.	14.71%
4	Wrigley (William) Jr. Co.	17.69%	14	Applebee's International, Inc.	14.53%
5	Raven Industries, Inc.	17.40%	15	Stryker Corp.	14.36%
6	Lancaster Colony Corp.	16.86%	16	Anheuser-Busch Cos., Inc.	14.13%
7	Merck & Co., Inc	16.83%	17	PepsiCo Inc.	14.09%
8	Eaton Vance Corp	16.11%	18	3M Co	13.65%
9	Coca-Cola Co (The)	15.90%	19	Clorox Co.	13.50%
10	Harley-Davidson, Inc.	15.46%	20	Pier 1 Imports Inc.	13.37%

Top 20 by Current Yield

Based on closing prices at March 31, 2004

Rank	Company	Yield	Rank	Company	Yield
1	Commercial Net Lease Realty, Inc.	6.48%	11	NICOR Inc.	5.28%
2	TEPPCO Partners, L.P.	6.19%	12	Cedar Fair, L.P.	5.15%
3	United Dominion Realty Trust	5.96%	13	Consolidated Edison, Inc.	5.12%
4	Healthcare Realty Trust, Inc.	5.90%	14	SBC Communications, Inc.	5.09%
5	Health Care Property Investors	5.87%	15	Altria Group Inc	5.00%
6	Universal Health Realty Inc. Trust	5.85%	16	Progress Energy, Inc.	4.89%
7	United Mobile Homes, Inc.	5.77%	17	Peoples Energy Corp.	4.84%
8	Camden Property Trust	5.65%	18	Weingarten Realty Investors	4.80%
9	Tanger Factory Outlet Centers	5.43%	19	Atmos Energy Corp.	4.77%
10	EastGroup Properties, Inc.	5.41%	20	Cleco Corp.	4.73%

Highest Price/Earnings Ratios

Based on latest available year-end information. Ratios determined using net income.

Rank	Company	P/E Ratio	Rank	Company	P/E Ratio
1	Meredith Corp.	505.60	11	RPM International Inc	55.13
2	Farmer Bros. Co.	276.50	12	Pennichuck Corp.	53.75
3	First Indiana Corp.	125.94	13	Stepan Co.	50.76
4	SWS Group, Inc.	105.35	14	EastGroup Properties, Inc.	50.71
5	United Dominion Realty Trust	93.43	15	Linear Technology Corp.	50.03
6	Helmerich & Payne, Inc.	81.86	16	Paychex Inc	45.64
7	Nucor Corp.	76.85	17	People's Bank	45.14
8	Telephone and Data Systems	67.50	18	First Charter Corp.	44.79
9	Pfizer Inc.	64.91	19	Stryker Corp.	39.70
10	Camden Property Trust	63.31	20	Tanger Factory Outlet Centers	38.74

Lowest Price/Earnings Ratios

Based on latest available year-end information. Ratios determined using net income.

Rank	Company	P/E Ratio	Rank	Company	P/E Ratio
1	Florida Public Utilities Co.	6.47	11	Holly Corp.	11.06
2	Fidelity National Financial, Inc.	7.03	12	MBIA Inc.	11.18
3	Fannie Mae	9.40	13	National Fuel Gas Co. (NJ)	11.18
4	SBC Communications, Inc.	9.59	14	Bank of America Corp.	11.36
5	Old Republic International	9.78	15	CenturyTel, Inc.	11.55
6	ABM Industries, Inc.	9.92	16	Universal Corp.	11.71
7	Washington Mutual Inc.	10.14	17	ALLTEL Corp.	11.74
8	National City Corp	10.37	18	Altria Group Inc	12.05
9	Freddie Mac	10.47	19	Sterling Bancshares, Inc. (TX)	12.17
10	Irwin Financial Corp.	11.01	20	Protective Life Corp.	12.20

Highest Seven-Year Price Scores

Scores cover a seven-year period ending 3/31/04

Rank	Company	Price Score	Rank	Company	Price Score
1	Doral Financial Corp.	239.3	11	CVB Financial Corp.	167.4
2	Raven Industries, Inc.	228.9	12	Lowe's Cos., Inc.	166.0
3	Courier Corp.	211.9	13	Weyco Group, Inc	164.5
4	Holly Corp.	187.3	14	UGI Corp.	164.2
5	Applebee's International, Inc.	184.9	15	Clarcor Inc.	164.2
6	Independent Bank Corporation	181.9	16	General Growth Properties, Inc.	161.5
7	SLM Corp.	181.2	17	Progressive Corp.	159.1
8	Golden West Financial Corp.	175.0	18	Harleysville National Corp.	158.1
9	Fidelity National Financial, Inc.	170.5	19	Family Dollar Stores, Inc.	158.0
10	Hilb, Rogal and Hamilton Co.	169.3	20	Legg Mason, Inc.	157.5

Highest Twelve-Month Price Scores

Scores cover a twelve-month period ending 3/31/04.

Rank	Company	Price Score	Rank	Company	Price Score
1	Mine Safety Appliances	131.14	11	Raven Industries, Inc.	113.80
2	Haverty Furniture Cos.	121.02	12	Caterpillar Inc.	112.77
3	NACCO Industries Inc.	117.59	13	McDonald's Corp	112.77
4	Harleysville National	116.22	14	Carlisle Companies Inc.	112.70
5	West Pharm. Scvs.	115.40	15	Supervalu Inc.	112.35
6	Jack Henry & Assoc.	114.68	16	National Security Group	111.79
7	HON Industries Inc.	114.64	17	General Growth Properties	111.78
8	Briggs & Stratton Corp.	114.36	18	Frisch's Restaurants, Inc.	111.71
9	Irwin Financial Corp.	114.31	19	Nordson Corp.	111.34
10	Roper Industries, Inc.	114.04	20	Applebee's International	110.63

Top 20 By Revenues

Based on latest available year-end information

Rank	Name	Revenues	Rank	Name	Revenues
1	Wal-Mart Stores, Inc.	$246,525,000,000	11	Pfizer Inc	$45,188,000,000
2	Exxon Mobil Corp.	$237,992,000,000	12	Target Corp	$43,917,000,000
3	General Electric Co.	$132,797,000,000	13	Procter & Gamble Co.	$43,377,000,000
4	ChevronTexaco Corp.	$119,703,000,000	14	Johnson & Johnson	$41,862,000,000
5	Citigroup Inc	$94,713,000,000	15	SBC Communications	$40,843,000,000
6	American International	$84,169,000,000	16	Freddie Mac	$35,927,000,000
7	Altria Group Inc	$81,832,000,000	17	Walgreen Co.	$32,505,400,000
8	Home Depot, Inc.	$58,247,000,000	18	Wells Fargo & Co.	$31,800,000,000
9	Fannie Mae	$53,768,000,000	19	United Technologies	$31,034,000,000
10	Bank of America Corp.	$48,065,000,000	20	Archer Daniels Midland	$30,708,033,000

Top 20 By Net Income

Based on latest available year-end information

Rank	Name	Net Income	Rank	Name	Net Income
1	Exxon Mobil Corp.	$21,510,000,000	11	Johnson & Johnson	$7,197,000,000
2	Citigroup Inc	$17,853,000,000	12	Merck & Co., Inc	$6,830,900,000
3	General Electric Co.	$15,002,000,000	13	Wells Fargo & Co.	$6,202,000,000
4	Bank of America Corp.	$10,810,000,000	14	Procter & Gamble Co.	$5,186,000,000
5	American International	$9,274,000,000	15	Coca-Cola Co (The)	$4,347,000,000
6	Altria Group Inc	$9,204,000,000	16	Freddie Mac	$4,147,000,000
7	SBC Communications	$8,505,000,000	17	Pfizer Inc	$3,910,000,000
8	Wal-Mart Stores, Inc.	$8,039,000,000	18	Washington Mutual Inc	$3,880,000,000
9	Fannie Mae	$7,905,000,000	19	Home Depot, Inc.	$3,664,000,000
10	ChevronTexaco Corp.	$7,230,000,000	20	PepsiCo Inc.	$3,568,000,000

Top 20 by Market Capitalization

Based on closing prices at 3/31/04

Rank	Name	Current Value	Rank	Name	Current Value
1	General Electric Co.	$306,447,036,457	11	Altria Group Inc	$110,597,313,658
2	Exxon Mobil Corp.	$274,901,589,985	12	Merck & Co., Inc	$98,322,622,733
3	Pfizer Inc.	$267,484,874,701	13	Wells Fargo & Co.	$95,887,286,604
4	Citigroup Inc	$266,703,600,486	14	ChevronTexaco Corp.	$93,833,218,913
5	Wal-Mart Stores, Inc.	$258,325,239,772	15	PepsiCo Inc.	$92,446,826,381
6	American International	$186,076,945,958	16	Home Depot, Inc.	$85,002,064,978
7	Johnson & Johnson	$150,544,218,235	17	SBC Communications	$81,243,843,763
8	Procter & Gamble Co.	$136,000,731,955	18	Lilly (Eli) & Co.	$75,122,281,882
9	Coca-Cola Co (The)	$123,311,056,819	19	Fannie Mae	$72,243,442,045
10	Bank of America Corp.	$120,320,493,435	20	3M Co	$64,258,371,865

Bottom 20 by Market Capitalization

Based on closing prices at 3/31/04

Rank	Name	Current Value	Rank	Name	Current Value
1	National Security Group	$56,987,700	11	Quixote Corp.	$183,654,990
2	Pennichuck Corp.	$67,163,850	12	Stepan Co.	$207,478,560
3	Bowl America Inc.	$75,690,300	13	Weyco Group, Inc	$216,108,830
4	Florida Public Utilities Co.	$80,196,000	14	Gorman-Rupp Co.	$221,289,600
5	Artesian Resources Corp.	$112,496,550	15	Connecticut Water Svc.	$226,711,300
6	Badger Meter, Inc.	$123,595,500	16	Quaker Chemical Corp.	$243,255,800
7	United Mobile Homes, Inc.	$127,349,550	17	Raven Industries, Inc.	$282,529,800
8	Frisch's Restaurants, Inc.	$139,370,000	18	Middlesex Water Co.	$299,425,500
9	Meridian Bioscience Inc.	$154,597,470	19	SWS Group, Inc.	$306,529,650
10	EnergySouth, Inc.	$169,902,103	20	Second Bancorp, Inc.	$310,596,800

Top 20 by Total Assets

Based on latest available year-end information

Rank	Name	Total Assets	Rank	Name	Current Value
1	Citigroup Inc	$1,264,032,000,000	11	Pfizer Inc	$116,775,000,000
2	Fannie Mae	$1,009,569,000,000	12	National City Corp	$113,933,460,000
3	Bank of America Corp.	$736,445,000,000	13	Lincoln National Corp.	$106,744,868,000
4	American Intl. Group	$678,346,000,000	14	SBC Communications	$100,166,000,000
5	General Electric Co.	$647,483,000,000	15	Altria Group Inc	$96,175,000,000
6	Freddie Mac	$617,340,000,000	16	Wal-Mart Stores, Inc.	$94,685,000,000
7	Wells Fargo & Co.	$387,798,000,000	17	Fifth Third Bancorp	$91,143,000,000
8	Washington Mutual Inc.	$275,178,000,000	18	BB&T Corp.	$90,466,613,000
9	Exxon Mobil Corp.	$174,278,000,000	19	State Street Corp.	$87,534,000,000
10	SunTrust Banks, Inc.	$125,393,153,000	20	KeyCorp	$84,487,000,000

About Total Return

Total return represents one of the best measures of how well an investor in any given stock has fared because it reflects both dividend payments and price appreciation. Mergent has calculated total return for each Dividend Achiever company on the basis that cash dividends of each stock were reinvested in that company's shares on the ex-dividend date of each dividend paid. Thus the preceding table demonstrates the effect of compounding as well as each stock's performance and the level of dividends paid. Figures have been adjusted for splits, stock dividends and spin-offs. In the case of a spin-off, shares in the spun-off company were assumed to be converted to cash and reinvested in the original company's stock.

How to read the rankings: On the following pages, the Dividend Achiever companies are listed alphabetically with their respective total returns and rankings over a trailing one, three and five year period ending 3/31/04. For example, an investor who bought shares at the end of March, 2003 in 1st Source Corp., and sold them at the end of March, 2004, would have realized a 95.313% gain on the original investment. Following each company's one-year total return is its three-year total return and ranking and five-year total return and ranking. The three-year total return is based on an investment made at the end of March, 2001, and the five-year total return on an investment made at the end of March, 1999. The three- and five-year total-return percentages represent cumulative totals. Thus an investment made in 1st Source at the end of March, 2001, would have increased 13.052% if the stock were sold at the end of March, 2004. If an investor had bought shares in 1st Source at the end of March, 1999, and sold them at the end of March, 2004, his investment would have slipped 0.472%.

Ranking The Dividend Achievers By Total Returns

Based on the 1, 3 & 5 year periods ending 3/31/04.

Name	1-Year Tot. Ret.	1 Year Rank	3-Year Tot. Ret.	3-Year Rank	5-Year Tot. Ret.	5-Year Rank
1st Source Corp.	95.313%	5	13.052%	143	-0.472%	283
3M Co	27.736%	182	18.154%	81	19.991%	36
Abbott Laboratories	11.885%	265	-2.410%	279	-0.655%	284
ABM Industries, Inc.	39.536%	103	6.806%	216	5.190%	229
AFLAC Inc.	24.508%	210	14.105%	128	8.662%	166
Air Products & Chemicals, Inc.	23.196%	217	11.115%	168	9.598%	156
Alberto-Culver Co.	-10.349%	293	4.033%	236	14.017%	87
Alfa Corp	19.972%	234	15.316%	114	13.250%	101
ALLTEL Corp.	14.678%	254	1.000%	261	-1.924%	291
Altria Group Inc	90.688%	8	9.266%	186	13.353%	97
Ambac Financial Group, Inc.	46.892%	69	5.720%	227	15.981%	64
American International Group Inc	44.777%	80	-3.679%	284	2.338%	262
American States Water Co.	5.791%	281	6.981%	211	12.195%	118
AmSouth Bancorporation	22.988%	222	15.958%	110	-1.750%	289
Anchor BanCorp Wisconsin, Inc	18.360%	241	24.328%	42	12.094%	121
Anheuser-Busch Cos., Inc.	11.253%	268	5.102%	230	7.467%	189
Applebee's International, Inc.	45.845%	76	37.833%	7	30.430%	8
AptarGroup Inc.	19.536%	237	8.705%	192	8.740%	164
Aqua America Inc	26.276%	192	15.147%	115	15.394%	68
Archer Daniels Midland Co.	58.565%	41	11.905%	158	7.142%	192
Arrow International,Inc.	48.414%	64	17.292%	92	23.274%	25
Artesian Resources Corp.	44.676%	81	21.991%	54	13.827%	92
Associated Banc-Corp.	42.747%	88	17.084%	96	13.859%	90
Atmos Energy Corp.	25.964%	196	6.980%	212	4.988%	233
Automatic Data Processing Inc.	38.097%	111	-7.224%	293	1.299%	270
Avery Dennison Corp.	8.522%	274	8.302%	196	3.554%	250
Avon Products, Inc.	33.530%	139	25.136%	38	10.883%	139
Badger Meter, Inc.	24.658%	207	12.288%	152	6.477%	200
BancFirst Corp. (Oklahoma City, Ok)	27.885%	181	13.761%	134	11.182%	136
BancorpSouth Inc.	22.609%	224	17.224%	93	9.161%	160
Bandag, Inc.	60.113%	38	26.000%	29	14.486%	81
Bank of America Corp.	25.703%	200	17.501%	88	5.622%	216
Bank of Hawaii Corp (DE)	53.604%	55	36.920%	9	19.169%	44
Banta Corporation	59.294%	39	25.749%	32	21.053%	33
Bard (C.R.), Inc.	54.953%	48	30.224%	24	15.098%	73
BB&T Corp. (Lumberton, NC)	16.290%	249	3.231%	243	2.204%	265
Beckman Coulter, Inc.	60.233%	34	11.732%	161	20.540%	34
Becton, Dickinson and Co.	42.218%	90	12.104%	157	5.675%	215
Bemis, Inc.	-37.606%	.302	-6.607%	292	-2.015%	292
Black Hills Corporation	20.335%	232	-8.185%	297	11.976%	123
Bowl America Inc.	32.217%	151	19.611%	74	23.981%	23
Brady Corp.	37.553%	115	6.248%	222	14.818%	76
Briggs & Stratton Corp.	77.085%	17	22.947%	48	8.377%	169
Brown & Brown, Inc.	24.609%	208	31.689%	17	36.734%	4
Brown-Forman Corp.	26.034%	193	17.200%	94	12.146%	120
California Water Service Group (DE)	14.238%	256	3.439%	242	6.677%	197
Camden Property Trust	46.574%	72	16.442%	101	18.122%	49
Carlisle Companies Inc.	42.072%	92	21.984%	55	5.358%	225
Caterpillar Inc.	63.638%	29	23.354%	44	13.341%	98
Cedar Fair, L.P.	45.393%	78	21.674%	60	11.135%	137
CenturyTel, Inc.	0.408%	286	-0.727%	270	-9.455%	302
Charter One Financial, Inc.	31.526%	154	13.953%	132	10.526%	145
Chemical Financial Corp.	39.031%	105	23.778%	43	7.811%	183
ChevronTexaco Corp.	40.247%	99	3.082%	245	2.679%	260
Chittenden Corp. (Burlington, Vt.)	29.304%	171	12.315%	150	11.526%	132

Name	1-Year Tot. Ret.	1 Year Rank	3-Year Tot. Ret.	3-Year Rank	5-Year Tot. Ret.	5-Year Rank
Chubb Corp.	60.221%	36	0.617%	263	5.464%	222
Cincinnati Financial Corp.	24.580%	209	6.823%	215	5.545%	218
Cintas Corporation	33.070%	144	3.967%	238	0.510%	278
Citigroup Inc	53.846%	53	6.517%	218	11.619%	129
Citizens Banking Corp	42.972%	87	10.502%	173	1.082%	274
Clarcor Inc.	23.329%	216	25.449%	35	21.426%	30
Cleco Corp. (New)	58.805%	40	-1.515%	276	9.462%	157
Clorox Co.	8.165%	275	17.982%	82	-1.891%	290
Coca-Cola Co (The)	26.507%	190	5.328%	229	-2.488%	294
Colgate-Palmolive Co.	2.976%	283	1.320%	258	5.003%	231
Comerica, Inc.	48.733%	63	-0.776%	272	0.243%	279
Commerce Bancorp, Inc. (NJ)	67.501%	25	4.129%	233	28.408%	12
Commerce Bancshares, Inc.	32.765%	146	13.719%	135	9.860%	153
Commercial Net Lease Realty, Inc.	39.272%	104	25.930%	30	18.422%	48
Community Bank System, Inc.	51.225%	59	20.266%	69	16.812%	54
Community First Bankshares, Inc.	29.393%	170	19.673%	72	12.337%	115
Community Trust Bancorp, Inc.	34.099%	137	34.694%	12	16.038%	61
Compass Bancshares Inc.	36.305%	119	27.777%	26	15.021%	74
ConAgra Foods, Inc.	34.399%	136	17.831%	84	4.189%	242
Connecticut Water Service, Inc.	9.708%	271	11.810%	159	15.112%	72
Consolidated Edison, Inc.	20.470%	231	11.026%	170	3.993%	245
Corus Bankshares, Inc.	3.614%	282	-6.280%	290	5.793%	212
Courier Corp.	-8.498%	291	30.549%	22	27.186%	14
Cullen/Frost Bankers, Inc.	43.910%	84	9.898%	178	14.388%	82
CVB Financial Corp.	9.485%	272	29.285%	25	20.232%	35
Danaher Corp.	42.138%	91	19.730%	71	12.410%	113
Diebold, Inc.	43.827%	85	22.213%	50	16.433%	58
Donnelley (R.R.) & Sons Co.	70.742%	20	8.207%	198	1.690%	267
Doral Financial Corp.	0.783%	285	21.832%	57	24.394%	22
Dover Corp.	62.490%	33	4.094%	235	4.702%	235
EastGroup Properties, Inc.	46.342%	75	20.407%	67	22.378%	29
Eaton Vance Corp	44.257%	82	7.498%	206	31.465%	7
Ecolab, Inc.	16.907%	245	11.473%	164	10.959%	138
Emerson Electric Co.	35.623%	126	1.381%	257	4.965%	234
Energen Corp.	28.788%	174	7.124%	208	24.524%	21
EnergySouth, Inc.	36.291%	120	22.282%	49	14.366%	83
Exxon Mobil Corp.	21.860%	226	3.135%	244	5.522%	219
F.N.B. Corp (FL)	-15.494%	296	5.861%	225	6.418%	201
Family Dollar Stores, Inc.	17.422%	243	12.687%	146	10.097%	149
Fannie Mae	16.542%	248	-0.349%	266	3.184%	254
Farmer Bros. Co.	18.315%	242	15.745%	112	13.716%	93
Federal Realty Investment Trust	58.561%	42	38.530%	5	21.112%	32
Federal Signal Corp.	44.014%	83	4.105%	234	2.436%	261
Fidelity National Financial, Inc.	47.604%	68	32.198%	16	33.030%	6
Fifth Third Bancorp (Cincinnati, OH)	12.600%	263	3.022%	246	6.343%	202
First Charter Corp.	25.808%	198	14.310%	125	5.332%	226
First Commonwealth Financial Corp.	32.275%	149	13.202%	139	10.771%	140
First Federal Capital Corp.	7.061%	277	17.739%	86	15.016%	75
First Financial Corp. (IN)	27.000%	185	15.978%	109	9.127%	161
First Financial Holdings, Inc.	24.483%	211	17.058%	97	13.018%	107
First Indiana Corp.	31.709%	153	1.561%	255	8.530%	168
First Merchants Corp.	14.893%	253	9.302%	185	5.892%	209
First Midwest Bancorp, Inc.	35.451%	127	17.293%	91	13.092%	105
FirstMerit Corp	46.855%	70	3.719%	240	3.566%	248
Florida Public Utilities Co.	43.665%	86	25.458%	34	16.030%	62
Franklin Electric Co., Inc.	36.739%	117	22.131%	52	15.249%	70
Franklin Resources, Inc.	70.161%	22	13.086%	141	15.191%	71
Freddie Mac	13.258%	260	-1.540%	277	1.978%	266
Frisch's Restaurants, Inc.	55.891%	44	31.467%	18	24.904%	18
Fuller (H.B.) Company	24.957%	205	12.212%	153	0.750%	276
Fulton Financial Corp. (PA)	27.955%	179	17.646%	87	11.540%	131
Gallagher (Arthur J.) & Co.	35.886%	123	7.623%	203	25.231%	17

Name	1-Year Tot. Ret.	1 Year Rank	3-Year Tot. Ret.	3-Year Rank	5-Year Tot. Ret.	5-Year Rank
Gannett Co., Inc.	26.551%	189	15.069%	116	8.029%	176
General Dynamics Corp.	62.675%	31	13.991%	130	8.120%	173
General Electric Co.	22.745%	223	-7.883%	294	-1.715%	288
General Growth Properties, Inc.	-33.290%	301	2.765%	249	3.814%	246
Genuine Parts Co.	11.127%	269	11.808%	160	5.902%	208
Glacier Bancorp, Inc. (New)	35.665%	125	36.961%	8	19.327%	43
Golden West Financial Corp.	56.152%	43	20.270%	68	28.913%	10
Gorman-Rupp Co.	34.924%	132	14.650%	122	13.252%	100
Grainger (W.W.) Inc.	13.613%	259	14.007%	129	3.367%	252
Harley-Davidson, Inc.	34.928%	131	12.365%	148	13.498%	94
Harleysville Group, Inc. (PA)	-22.665%	299	-2.555%	280	2.212%	264
Harleysville National Corp.	46.434%	73	27.485%	27	19.769%	37
Haverty Furniture Cos., Inc.	100.186%	4	17.023%	98	11.998%	122
Health Care Property Investors, Inc.	-10.157%	292	-0.735%	271	4.645%	237
Healthcare Realty Trust, Inc.	85.053%	11	27.482%	28	23.393%	24
Heinz (H.J.) Co.	31.404%	155	1.036%	260	-1.265%	285
Helmerich & Payne, Inc.	13.076%	261	-13.868%	299	5.859%	210
Hershey Foods Corp.	34.635%	133	7.798%	202	9.454%	158
Hibernia Corp.	42.394%	89	21.844%	56	14.735%	77
Hilb, Rogal and Hamilton Co.	23.143%	218	30.820%	20	36.308%	5
Hillenbrand Industries, Inc.	35.210%	129	13.618%	137	9.413%	159
Holly Corp.	12.849%	262	41.598%	3	38.312%	2
Home Depot, Inc.	54.475%	51	-4.086%	285	-1.580%	287
HON Industries Inc.	32.246%	150	18.971%	78	12.496%	112
Hormel Foods Corp.	40.564%	96	16.157%	106	11.877%	125
Hudson United Bancorp	27.532%	183	22.197%	51	7.870%	182
Illinois Tool Works, Inc.	37.885%	112	12.970%	145	6.158%	204
Independent Bank Corporation	55.711%	45	38.149%	6	30.251%	9
Irwin Financial Corp. (Columbus, IN)	39.918%	101	9.591%	180	6.501%	199
Jack Henry & Associates, Inc.	83.239%	12	-6.007%	289	16.669%	57
Jefferson-Pilot Corp.	46.388%	74	9.017%	188	6.022%	206
Johnson & Johnson	-10.696%	294	6.762%	217	3.085%	256
Johnson Controls Inc	-17.228%	298	-0.628%	268	0.011%	281
KeyCorp (New)	39.694%	102	9.534%	181	3.556%	249
Kimberly-Clark Corp.	41.927%	93	-0.459%	267	7.568%	188
Kimco Realty Corp.	49.858%	61	25.916%	31	19.650%	38
Lancaster Colony Corp.	7.591%	276	12.977%	144	10.569%	144
La-Z-Boy Inc.	28.241%	177	8.792%	191	4.630%	238
Legg Mason, Inc.	91.506%	7	30.776%	21	22.993%	26
Leggett & Platt, Inc.	32.713%	147	9.503%	182	5.436%	223
Lilly (Eli) & Co.	19.440%	238	-2.673%	281	-3.053%	295
Lincoln National Corp. (ID)	73.839%	19	6.433%	220	1.590%	269
Linear Technology Corp.	20.764%	230	-3.299%	282	8.108%	174
Lowe's Cos., Inc.	37.776%	113	24.503%	41	13.323%	99
M & T Bank Corp	15.996%	250	10.084%	174	14.550%	80
Marsh & McLennan Cos., Inc.	11.447%	267	1.387%	256	6.769%	195
Marshall & Ilsley Corp.	50.743%	60	14.609%	123	8.017%	177
Masco Corp.	66.702%	26	9.988%	175	3.138%	255
May Department Stores Co. (The)	78.695%	16	1.806%	254	0.074%	280
MBIA Inc.	64.441%	28	6.445%	219	11.276%	134
MBNA Corp.	80.839%	15	8.983%	189	12.730%	110
McCormick & Co., Inc.	40.886%	94	18.278%	79	19.605%	39
McDonald's Corp	100.346%	3	3.492%	241	-8.045%	299
McGrath RentCorp	38.451%	109	14.259%	127	13.031%	106
McGraw-Hill Cos., Inc. (The)	38.964%	106	9.945%	176	8.276%	172
MDU Resources Group Inc.	29.800%	166	-10.743%	298	11.713%	128
Medtronic, Inc.	6.449%	278	1.970%	253	6.328%	203
Mercantile Bankshares Corp.	30.495%	161	8.001%	200	5.610%	217
Merck & Co., Inc	-16.648%	297	-13.879%	300	-8.664%	301
Mercury General Corp.	35.152%	130	18.159%	80	9.726%	154
Meredith Corp.	33.486%	140	13.966%	131	10.718%	141
Meridian Bioscience Inc.	34.535%	135	64.488%	2	13.129%	103
MGE Energy Inc	21.604%	228	14.264%	126	13.974%	88

Name	1-Year Tot. Ret.	1 Year Rank	3-Year Tot. Ret.	3-Year Rank	5-Year Tot. Ret.	5-Year Rank
Middlesex Water Co.	-3.426%	288	3.894%	239	7.958%	180
Midland Co.	40.468%	97	17.093%	95	16.402%	59
Mine Safety Appliances Co	-15.478%	295	6.085%	223	36.746%	3
Myers Industries Inc.	30.890%	158	9.486%	183	0.797%	275
NACCO Industries Inc.	82.163%	14	11.246%	165	3.229%	253
National City Corp	32.298%	148	13.609%	138	4.547%	240
National Commerce Financial Corp.	23.966%	213	7.262%	207	6.670%	198
National Fuel Gas Co. (NJ)	17.421%	244	-19.712%	302	8.581%	167
National Penn Bancshares, Inc.	28.181%	178	16.217%	104	12.346%	114
National Security Group, Inc	70.199%	21	23.257%	47	17.168%	52
NICOR Inc.	35.761%	124	2.991%	248	4.124%	243
Nordson Corp.	52.912%	56	14.691%	120	7.632%	186
Northern Trust Corp.	55.369%	46	-8.018%	295	2.290%	263
Nucor Corp.	63.191%	30	16.141%	107	7.785%	184
Nuveen Investments Inc	27.248%	184	17.807%	85	16.716%	56
Old National Bancorp	9.032%	273	8.912%	190	0.518%	277
Old Republic International Corp.	-4.001%	289	-2.274%	278	8.329%	171
Otter Tail Corp.	6.197%	279	1.287%	259	9.675%	155
Pacific Capital Bancorp	31.954%	152	24.853%	39	19.426%	42
Park National Corp. (Newark, Oh.)	25.102%	204	12.294%	151	6.962%	193
Parker-Hannifin Corp.	47.806%	66	13.912%	133	11.896%	124
Paychex Inc	31.270%	156	-0.646%	269	12.147%	119
Pennichuck Corp.	26.360%	191	13.110%	140	15.457%	67
Pentair, Inc.	69.279%	23	33.995%	14	13.155%	102
People's Bank (Bridgeport, CT)	90.297%	9	25.460%	33	12.315%	116
Peoples Energy Corp.	30.780%	159	9.419%	184	11.184%	135
PepsiCo Inc.	36.225%	121	8.198%	199	7.695%	185
Pfizer Inc.	14.474%	255	-3.613%	283	-4.173%	296
Piedmont Natural Gas Co., Inc.	23.128%	219	9.856%	179	7.370%	191
Pier 1 Imports Inc.	51.324%	58	23.302%	45	24.843%	19
Pinnacle West Capital Corp.	23.646%	215	-1.154%	275	5.304%	227
Pitney Bowes, Inc.	37.265%	116	9.931%	177	-5.376%	297
Popular Inc.	29.979%	164	15.837%	111	8.786%	163
PPG Industries, Inc.	31.092%	157	10.588%	171	5.376%	224
Praxair, Inc.	-33.239%	300	-4.933%	287	1.248%	271
Procter & Gamble Co.	19.168%	239	20.582%	66	2.787%	259
Progress Energy, Inc.	26.015%	194	7.087%	209	7.870%	181
Progressive Corp. (OH)	47.867%	65	39.323%	4	12.985%	109
Protective Life Corp.	33.415%	142	8.570%	193	1.224%	272
Quaker Chemical Corp.	28.627%	175	16.402%	102	15.845%	65
Questar Corp.	25.938%	197	12.179%	155	18.779%	47
Quixote Corp.	35.253%	128	-0.189%	265	14.698%	78
Raven Industries, Inc.	85.227%	10	72.267%	1	46.956%	1
Regions Financial Corp.	16.888%	246	12.204%	154	4.076%	244
Republic Bancorp, Inc. (MI)	34.593%	134	17.422%	89	13.863%	89
RLI Corp.	45.218%	79	24.803%	40	22.458%	27
Rohm & Haas Co.	36.702%	118	11.178%	167	5.507%	220
Roper Industries, Inc.	68.488%	24	11.219%	166	15.840%	66
Rouse Co.	60.145%	37	31.180%	19	22.398%	28
RPM International Inc (DE)	62.667%	32	21.045%	65	7.447%	190
S & T Bancorp, Inc. (Indiana, PA.)	21.588%	229	12.571%	147	12.621%	111
Sara Lee Corp.	19.733%	236	3.013%	247	-0.065%	282
SBC Communications, Inc.	25.971%	195	-14.337%	301	-8.633%	300
Second Bancorp, Inc. (OH)	49.255%	62	25.341%	36	8.355%	170
SEI Investments Co.	26.565%	188	2.290%	251	16.810%	55
ServiceMaster Co. (The)	24.300%	212	5.655%	228	-7.180%	298
Sherwin-Williams Co.	47.806%	67	16.468%	100	7.987%	178
Sigma-Aldrich Corp.	25.691%	201	5.742%	226	14.365%	84
Simmons First National Corp.	53.918%	52	34.949%	11	13.386%	96
SJW Corp.	-53.408%	303	-22.267%	303	-9.604%	303
SLM Corp.	15.029%	251	21.168%	63	25.425%	15
Smith (A.O.) Corp	10.224%	270	16.159%	105	10.710%	142
Sonoco Products Co.	20.019%	233	7.568%	204	4.249%	241
SouthTrust Corp.	33.294%	143	15.603%	113	14.246%	85

Name	1-Year Tot. Ret.	1 Year Rank	3-Year Tot. Ret.	3-Year Rank	5-Year Tot. Ret.	5-Year Rank
St. Paul Companies, Inc.	29.465%	169	-0.785%	273	7.594%	187
Stanley Works	82.222%	13	11.496%	163	13.116%	104
State Auto Financial Corp.	53.639%	54	19.979%	70	19.596%	41
State Street Corp.	66.646%	27	4.720%	232	5.716%	214
Stepan Co.	0.876%	284	0.626%	262	3.452%	251
Sterling Bancshares, Inc. (TX)	14.172%	257	5.987%	224	15.391%	69
Sterling Financial Corp. (PA)	16.662%	247	17.838%	83	5.071%	230
Stryker Corp.	29.162%	172	19.377%	76	28.697%	11
SunTrust Banks, Inc.	35.916%	122	4.961%	231	4.573%	239
Superior Industries International, Inc.	-1.585%	287	2.191%	252	10.110%	148
Supervalu Inc.	100.758%	2	34.235%	13	10.073%	150
Susquehanna Bancshares, Inc	27.896%	180	16.005%	108	9.901%	152
SWS Group, Inc.	23.716%	214	3.981%	237	-1.526%	286
Synovus Financial Corp.	40.404%	98	-0.927%	274	5.736%	213
Sysco Corp.	55.307%	47	14.878%	117	25.279%	16
T Rowe Price Group Inc.	101.143%	1	21.260%	62	10.585%	143
Tanger Factory Outlet Centers, Inc	54.778%	50	36.631%	10	24.636%	20
Target Corp	54.853%	49	7.546%	205	6.755%	196
TCF Financial Corp.	29.752%	167	13.081%	142	16.149%	60
Teleflex Incorporated	40.140%	100	7.892%	201	8.702%	165
Telephone and Data Systems, Inc.	74.774%	18	-8.071%	296	5.483%	221
Tennant Co.	28.603%	176	-0.087%	264	4.989%	232
TEPPCO Partners, L.P.	40.708%	95	23.285%	46	15.994%	63
Tootsie Roll Industries Inc	29.099%	173	-4.953%	288	-2.122%	293
Transatlantic Holdings, Inc.	33.699%	138	-4.811%	286	12.246%	117
Trustmark Corp.	25.463%	202	14.330%	124	10.196%	147
UGI Corp. (New)	11.794%	266	30.442%	23	28.026%	13
United Bankshares, Inc.	13.718%	258	14.704%	119	8.922%	162
United Dominion Realty Trust, Inc.	29.912%	165	21.803%	59	19.597%	40
United Mobile Homes, Inc.	21.607%	227	14.717%	118	17.107%	53
United Technologies Corp.	51.506%	57	6.859%	214	6.104%	205
Universal Corp.	38.480%	108	11.712%	162	17.573%	50
Universal Health Realty Income Trust	37.722%	114	25.137%	37	17.217%	51
Unizan Financial Corp	38.483%	107	21.415%	61	5.955%	207
Valley National Bancorp	23.076%	220	14.681%	121	14.064%	86
Valspar Corp.	21.891%	225	21.154%	64	10.518%	146
Vectren Corp	19.898%	235	9.257%	187	1.094%	273
VF Corp.	26.814%	187	12.354%	149	1.591%	268
Vulcan Materials Co.	60.222%	35	2.408%	250	4.687%	236
Walgreen Co.	12.337%	264	-6.447%	291	3.577%	247
Wal-Mart Stores, Inc.	14.895%	252	6.318%	221	5.816%	211
Washington Federal Inc.	22.995%	221	11.032%	169	13.017%	108
Washington Mutual Inc.	25.432%	203	8.235%	197	11.870%	126
Washington R.E.I.T.	30.689%	160	16.263%	103	19.105%	45
Webster Financial Corp.	46.782%	71	21.819%	58	13.392%	95
Weingarten Realty Investors	-5.453%	290	13.619%	136	11.394%	133
Wells Fargo & Co. (New)	29.629%	168	6.928%	213	11.798%	127
Wesbanco, Inc.	33.447%	141	22.056%	53	3.028%	258
Wesco Financial Corp.	30.319%	163	8.389%	195	3.080%	257
West Pharmaceutical Services, Inc.	95.000%	6	19.393%	75	5.215%	228
WestAmerica Bancorporation	30.362%	162	12.150%	156	11.573%	130
Weyco Group, Inc	26.868%	186	33.264%	15	19.030%	46
WGL Holdings, Inc.	18.460%	240	7.040%	210	9.959%	151
Whitney Holding Corp.	25.731%	199	19.654%	73	13.847%	91
Wiley (John) & Sons Inc.	32.826%	145	17.301%	90	7.966%	179
Wilmington Trust Corp. (DE)	38.309%	110	10.580%	172	8.104%	175
Wolverine World Wide, Inc.	45.433%	77	19.234%	77	21.336%	31
WPS Resources Corp.	24.925%	206	16.662%	99	14.576%	79
Wrigley (William) Jr. Co.	6.195%	280	8.471%	194	6.864%	194

Ranking the Dividend Achievers by Total Return

Based on the 1 year period ending 3/31/04.

Rank	Name	Ticker	1-Year Tot. Ret	Rank	Name	Ticker	1-Year Tot. Ret
1	T Rowe Price Group Inc.	TROW	101.14%	11	Healthcare Realty Trust	HR	85.05%
2	Supervalu Inc.	SVU	100.76%	12	Jack Henry & Associates	JKHY	83.24%
3	McDonald's Corp	MCD	100.35%	13	Stanley Works	SWK	82.22%
4	Haverty Furniture Cos., Inc.	HVT	100.19%	14	NACCO Industries Inc.	NC	82.16%
5	1st Source Corp.	SRCE	95.31%	15	MBNA Corp.	KRB	80.84%
6	West Pharmaceutical Services	WST	95.00%	16	May Department Stores Co	MAY	78.70%
7	Legg Mason, Inc.	LM	91.51%	17	Briggs & Stratton Corp.	BGG	77.09%
8	Altria Group Inc	MO	90.69%	18	Telephone and Data Sys.	TDS	74.77%
9	People's Bank	PBCT	90.30%	19	Lincoln National Corp.	LNC	73.84%
10	Raven Industries, Inc.	RAVN	85.23%	20	Donnelley (R.R.) & Sons	RRD	70.74%

Based on the 3 year period ending 3/31/04.

Rank	Name	Ticker	3-Year Tot. Ret	Rank	Name	Ticker	3-Year Tot. Ret
1	Raven Industries, Inc.	RAVN	72.27%	11	Simmons First National	SFNC	34.95%
2	Meridian Bioscience Inc.	VIVO	64.49%	12	Community Trust Bancorp	CTBI	34.69%
3	Holly Corp.	HOC	41.60%	13	Supervalu Inc.	SVU	34.24%
4	Progressive Corp.	PGR	39.32%	14	Pentair, Inc.	PNR	33.99%
5	Federal Realty Invest. Trust	FRT	38.53%	15	Weyco Group, Inc	WEYS	33.26%
6	Independent Bank Corp.	IBCP	38.15%	16	Fidelity National Financial	FNF	32.20%
7	Applebee's International, Inc.	APPB	37.83%	17	Brown & Brown, Inc.	BRO	31.69%
8	Glacier Bancorp, Inc.	GBCI	36.96%	18	Frisch's Restaurants, Inc.	FRS	31.47%
9	Bank of Hawaii Corp	BOH	36.92%	19	Rouse Co.	RSE	31.18%
10	Tanger Factory Outlet Ctrs.	SKT	36.63%	20	Hilb, Rogal and Hamilton	HRH	30.82%

Based on the 5 year period ending 3/31/04.

Rank	Name	Ticker	5-Year Tot. Ret	Rank	Name	Ticker	5-Year Tot. Ret
1	Raven Industries, Inc.	RAVN	46.96%	11	Stryker Corp.	SYK	28.70%
2	Holly Corp.	HOC	38.31%	12	Commerce Bancorp, Inc.	CBH	28.41%
3	Mine Safety Appliances Co	MSA	36.75%	13	UGI Corp.	UGI	28.03%
4	Brown & Brown, Inc.	BRO	36.73%	14	Courier Corp.	CRRC	27.19%
5	Hilb, Rogal and Hamilton Co.	HRH	36.31%	15	SLM Corp.	SLM	25.42%
6	Fidelity National Financial	FNF	33.03%	16	Sysco Corp.	SYY	25.28%
7	Eaton Vance Corp	EV	31.47%	17	Gallagher (Arthur J.) & Co.	AJG	25.23%
8	Applebee's International, Inc.	APPB	30.43%	18	Frisch's Restaurants, Inc.	FRS	24.90%
9	Independent Bank Corp.	IBCP	30.25%	19	Pier 1 Imports Inc.	PIR	24.84%
10	Golden West Financial Corp.	GDW	28.91%	20	Tanger Factory Outlet Ctrs.	SKT	24.64%

Web Site & Dividend Reinvestment Plan Information

Company	Web Site	DRIP
1st Source Corp.	www.1stsource.com	No
3M Company	www.3m.com	Yes
Abbott Laboratories	www.abbott.com	Yes
ABM Industries Inc.	www.abm.com	No
AFLAC Inc.	www.aflac.com	Yes
Air Products & Chemicals	www.airproducts.com	Yes
Alberto-Culver Co.	www.alberto.com	No
Alfa Corp.	www.alfains.com	Yes
ALLTEL Corp.	www.alltel.com	Yes
Altria Group, Inc.	www.altria.com	Yes
Ambac Financial Group, Inc.	www.ambac.com	No
American International Group	www.aig.com	No
American States Water Co.	www.aswater.com	Yes
AmSouth Bancorporation	www.amsouth.com	Yes
Anchor BanCorp Wisconsin, Inc.	www.anchorbank.com	No
Anheuser-Busch Cos., Inc.	www.anheuser-busch.com	Yes
Applebee's International, Inc.	www.applebees.com	No
AptarGroup Inc.	www.aptargroup.com	No
Aqua America Inc	www.aquaamerica.com	Yes
Archer-Daniels-Midland Co.	www.admworld.com	Yes
Arrow International, Inc.	www.arrowintl.com	No
Artesian Resources Corp.	www.artesianwater.com	Yes
Associated Banc-Corp.	www.associatedbank.com	Yes
Atmos Energy Corp.	www.atmosenergy.com	Yes
Automatic Data Processing	www.adp.com	No
Avery Dennison Corp.	www.averydennison.com	Yes
Avon Products, Inc.	www.avon.com	Yes
Badger Meter, Inc.	www.badgermeter.com	Yes
BancFirst Corp.	www.bancfirst.com	No
BancorpSouth, Inc.	www.bancorpsouth.com	Yes
Bandag, Inc.	www.bandag.com	Yes
Bank of America Corp.	www.bankofamerica.com	Yes
Bank of Hawaii Corp.	www.boh.com	Yes
Banta Corp.	www.banta.com	Yes
Bard (C.R.) Inc.	www.crbard.com	Yes
BB&T Corp.	www.bbandt.com	Yes
Beckman Coulter, Inc.	www.beckmancoulter.com	Yes
Becton, Dickinson & Co.	www.bd.com	Yes
Bemis Co., Inc.	www.bemis.com	Yes
Black Hills Power, Inc.	www.blackhillscorp.com	Yes
Bowl America Inc.	----	No
Brady Corp.	www.bradycorp.com	Yes
Briggs & Stratton Corp.	www.briggsandstratton.com	Yes
Brown & Brown, Inc.	www.brown-n-brown.com	No
Brown-Forman Corp.	www.brown-forman.com	Yes
California Water Service Co.	www.calwater.com	Yes
Camden Property Trust	www.camdenliving.com	Yes
Carlisle Companies Inc.	www.carlisle.com	Yes
Caterpillar Inc.	www.cat.com	Yes
Cedar Fair, L.P.	www.cedarfair.com	Yes
CenturyTel, Inc.	www.centurytel.com	Yes
Charter One Financial, Inc.	www.charterone.com	Yes
Chemical Financial Corp.	www.chemicalbankmi.com	Yes
ChevronTexaco Corp.	www.chevrontexaco.com	Yes
Chittenden Corp.	www.chittenden.com	Yes
Chubb Corp.	www.chubb.com	Yes
Cincinnati Financial Corp.	www.cinfin.com	Yes
Cintas Corp.	www.cintas.com	No

Web Site & Dividend Reinvestment Plan Information

Company	Web Site	DRIP
Citigroup Inc.	www.citigroup.com	No
Citizens Banking Corp.	www.cbclientsfirst.com	Yes
Clarcor Inc.	www.clarcor.com	Yes
CLECO Corp.	www.cleco.com	Yes
Clorox Co. (The)	www.clorox.com	Yes
Coca-Cola Co. (The)	www.coca-cola.com	Yes
Colgate-Palmolive Co.	www.colgate.com	Yes
Comerica, Inc.	www.comerica.com	Yes
Commerce Bancorp, Inc.	www.commerceonline.com	No
Commerce Bancshares, Inc.	www.commercebank.com	Yes
Commercial Net Lease Realty	www.cnlreit.com	Yes
Community Bank System, Inc.	www.communitybankna.com	Yes
Community First Bankshares, Inc.	www.communityfirst.com	Yes
Community Trust Bancorp, Inc.	www.ctbi.com	No
Compass Bancshares, Inc.	www.compassweb.com	Yes
ConAgra Foods, Inc.	www.conagra.com	Yes
Connecticut Water Service, Inc.	www.ctwater.com	Yes
Consolidated Edison, Inc.	www.conedison.com	Yes
Corus Bankshares, Inc.	www.corusbank.com	No
Courier Corp.	www.courier.com	No
Cullen/Frost Bankers, Inc.	www.frostbank.com	No
CVB Financial Corp.	www.cvbcorp.com	No
Danaher Corp.	www.danaher.com	No
Diebold, Inc.	www.diebold.com	Yes
Donnelley (R.R.) & Sons Co.	www.rrdonnelley.com	Yes
Doral Financial Corp.	www.doralfinancial.com	No
Dover Corp.	www.dovercorporation.com	Yes
Eastgroup Properties, Inc.	www.eastgroup.net	No
Eaton Vance Corp.	www.eatonvance.com	No
Ecolab Inc.	www.ecolab.com	Yes
Emerson Electric Co.	www.gotoemerson.com	Yes
Energen Corp.	www.energen.com	Yes
EnergySouth, Inc.	www.energysouth.com	Yes
Exxon Mobil Corp.	www.exxonmobil.com	Yes
F.N.B. Corp.	www.fnbcorporation.com	Yes
Family Dollar Stores, Inc.	www.familydollar.com	No
Fannie Mae	www.fanniemae.com	Yes
Farmer Bros. Co.	----	No
Federal Realty Invest. Trust	www.federalrealty.com	Yes
Federal Signal Corp.	www.federalsignal.com	Yes
Fidelity National Financial, Inc.	www.fnf.com	No
Fifth Third Bancorp	www.53.com	Yes
First Charter Corp.	www.firstcharter.com	Yes
First Commonwealth Financial	www.fcfbank.com	Yes
First Federal Capital Corp	www.firstfed.com	Yes
First Financial Corp.	www.first-online.com	No
First Financial Holdings, Inc.	www.firstfinancialholdings.com	Yes
First Indiana Corp.	www.firstindiana.com	Yes
First Merchants Corp.	www.firstmerchants.com	Yes
First Midwest Bancorp, Inc.	www.firstmidwest.com	Yes
FirstMerit Corp.	www.firstmerit.com	Yes
Florida Public Utilities Co.	www.fpuc.com	Yes
Franklin Electric Co., Inc.	www.fele.com	No
Franklin Resources, Inc.	www.franklintempleton.com	Yes
Freddie Mac	www.freddiemac.com	Yes
Frisch's Restaurants, Inc.	www.frischs.com	No
Fuller (H.B.) Co.	www.hbfuller.com	Yes
Fulton Financial Corp.	www.fult.com	Yes
Gallagher (Arthur J.) & Co.	www.ajg.com	No
Gannett Co., Inc.	www.gannett.com	Yes
General Dynamics Corp.	www.generaldynamics.com	No
General Electric Co.	www.ge.com	Yes

Web Site & Dividend Reinvestment Plan Information

Company	Web Site	DRIP
General Growth Properties, Inc.	www.generalgrowth.com	Yes
Genuine Parts Co.	www.genpt.com	Yes
Glacier Bancorp, Inc.	www.glacierbancorp.com	Yes
Golden West Financial Corp.	www.worldsavings.com	No
Gorman-Rupp Co. (The)	www.gormanrupp.com	Yes
Grainger, (W.W.) Inc.	www.grainger.com	No
Harley-Davidson, Inc.	www.harley-davidson.com	Yes
Harleysville Group Inc.	www.harleysvillegroup.com	Yes
Harleysville National Corp.	www.hncbank.com	Yes
Haverty Furniture Cos., Inc.	www.havertys.com	No
Health Care Property Investors	www.hcpi.com	Yes
Healthcare Realty Trust, Inc.	www.healthcarerealty.com	Yes
Heinz (H.J.) Co.	www.heinz.com	Yes
Helmerich & Payne, Inc.	www.hpinc.com	No
Hershey Foods Corp.	www.hersheys.com	Yes
Hibernia Corp.	www.hibernia.com	No
Hilb, Rogal & Hamilton Co.	www.hrh.com	No
Hillenbrand Industries, Inc.	www.hillenbrand.com	Yes
Holly Corp.	www.hollycorp.com	No
Home Depot, Inc. (The)	www.homedepot.com	Yes
Hon Industries Inc.	www.honi.com	No
Hormel Foods Corp.	www.hormel.com	Yes
Hudson United Bancorp	www.hudsonunitedbank.com	Yes
Illinois Tool Works Inc.	www.itw.com	Yes
Independent Bank Corporation	www.ibcp.com	Yes
Irwin Financial Corp.	www.irwinfinancial.com	Yes
Jack Henry & Associates, Inc.	www.jackhenry.com	Yes
Jefferson-Pilot Corp.	www.jpfinancial.com	Yes
Johnson & Johnson	www.jnj.com	Yes
Johnson Controls, Inc.	www.johnsoncontrols.com	Yes
KeyCorp	www.key.com	Yes
Kimberly-Clark Corp.	www.kimberly-clark.com	Yes
Kimco Realty Corp.	www.kimcorealty.com	Yes
Lancaster Colony Corp.	www.lancastercolony.com	Yes
La-Z-Boy Inc.	www.la-z-boy.com	Yes
Legg Mason, Inc.	www.leggmason.com	No
Leggett & Platt, Inc.	www.leggett.com	No
Lilly (Eli) & Co.	www.lilly.com	Yes
Lincoln National Corp.	www.lfg.com	Yes
Linear Technology Corp.	www.linear.com	No
Lowe's Cos., Inc.	www.lowes.com	Yes
M&T Bank Corp.	www.mandtbank.com	Yes
Marsh & McLennan Cos., Inc.	www.mmc.com	Yes
Marshall & Ilsley Corp.	www.micorp.com	Yes
Masco Corp.	www.masco.com	Yes
May Department Stores (The)	www.maycompany.com	Yes
MBIA Inc.	www.mbia.com	No
MBNA Corp.	www.mbna.com	No
McCormick & Co., Inc.	www.mccormick.com	Yes
McDonald's Corp.	www.mcdonalds.com	Yes
McGrath Rentcorp	www.mgrc.com	No
McGraw-Hill Cos., Inc. (The)	www.mcgraw-hill.com	Yes
MDU Resources Group, Inc.	www.mdu.com	Yes
Medtronic, Inc.	www.medtronic.com	Yes
Mercantile Bankshares Corp.	www.mrbk.com	Yes
Merck & Co., Inc.	www.merck.com	Yes
Mercury General Corp.	www.mercuryinsurance.com	Yes
Meredith Corp.	www.meredith.com	Yes
Meridian Bioscience Inc.	www.meridianbioscience.com	Yes
MGE Energy, Inc.	www.mge.com	Yes
Middlesex Water Co.	www.middlesexwater.com	Yes
Midland Co. (The)	www.midlandcompany.com	Yes
Mine Safety Appliances Co.	www.msanet.com	No

Web Site & Dividend Reinvestment Plan Information

Company	Web Site	DRIP
Myers Industries, Inc.	www.myersind.com	Yes
NACCO Industries, Inc.	www.nacco.com	No
National City Corp.	www.nationalcity.com	Yes
National Commerce Financial	www.ncbccorp.com	Yes
National Fuel Gas Co.	www.natfuel.com	Yes
National Penn Bancshares, Inc.	www.nationalpennbancshares.com	Yes
National Security Group (The)	www.nationalsecuritygroup.com	No
NICOR Inc.	www.nicorinc.com	Yes
Nordson Corp.	www.nordson.com	Yes
Northern Trust Corp.	www.northerntrust.com	No
Nucor Corp.	www.nucor.com	Yes
Nuveen Investments, Inc.	www.nuveen.com	No
Old National Bancorp	www.oldnational.com	Yes
Old Republic International Corp.	www.oldrepublic.com	Yes
Otter Tail Corp.	www.ottertail.com	Yes
Pacific Capital Bancorp	www.pcbancorp.com	No
Park National Corp.	www.parknationalcorp.com	Yes
Parker-Hannifin Corp.	www.parker.com	Yes
Paychex, Inc.	www.paychex.com	Yes
Pennichuck Corp.	www.pennichuck.com	Yes
Pentair, Inc.	www.pentair.com	Yes
People's Bank	www.peoples.com	Yes
Peoples Energy Corp.	www.pecorp.com	Yes
PepsiCo, Inc.	www.pepsico.com	Yes
Pfizer Inc.	www.pfizer.com	Yes
Piedmont Natural Gas Co., Inc.	www.piedmontng.com	Yes
Pier 1 Imports, Inc.	www.pier1.com	Yes
Pinnacle West Capital Corp.	www.pinnaclewest.com	Yes
Pitney Bowes Inc.	www.pb.com	Yes
Popular, Inc.	www.popularinc.com	Yes
PPG Industries, Inc.	www.ppg.com	Yes
Praxair, Inc.	www.praxair.com	Yes
Procter & Gamble Co. (The)	www.pg.com	Yes
Progress Energy, Inc.	www.progress-energy.com	Yes
Progressive Corp. (The)	www.progressive.com	No
Protective Life Corp.	www.protective.com	Yes
Quaker Chemical Corp.	www.quakerchem.com	Yes
Questar Corp.	www.questar.com	Yes
Quixote Corp.	www.quixotecorp.com	No
Raven Industries, Inc.	www.ravenind.com	Yes
Regions Financial Corp.	www.regionsbank.com	Yes
Republic Bancorp Inc.	www.republicbancorp.com	Yes
RLI Corp.	www.rlicorp.com	Yes
Rohm & Haas Co.	www.rohmhaas.com	Yes
Roper Industries, Inc.	www.roperind.com	No
Rouse Company (The)	www.therousecompany.com	Yes
RPM International Inc.	www.rpminc.com	Yes
S&T Bancorp, Inc.	www.stbank.com	Yes
Sara Lee Corp.	www.saralee.com	Yes
SBC Communications Inc.	www.sbc.com	Yes
Second Bancorp, Inc.	www.secondbancorp.com	Yes
SEI Investments Co.	www.seic.com	No
ServiceMaster Co. (The)	www.servicemaster.com	Yes
Sherwin-Williams Co. (The)	www.sherwin.com	Yes
Sigma-Aldrich Corp.	www.sigma-aldrich.com	No
Simmons First National Corp.	www.simmonsfirst.com	No
SJW Corp.	www.sjwater.com	No
SLM Corporation	www.salliemae.com	Yes
Smith (A.O.) Corp.	www.aosmith.com	Yes
Sonoco Products Co.	www.sonoco.com	Yes
SouthTrust Corp.	www.southtrust.com	Yes
St. Paul Cos., Inc. (The)	www.stpaul.com	Yes
Stanley Works (The)	www.stanleyworks.com	Yes
State Auto Financial Corp.	www.stauto.com	Yes

Web Site & Dividend Reinvestment Plan Information

Company	Web Site	DRIP
State Street Corp.	www.statestreet.com	Yes
Stepan Co.	www.stephan.com	No
Sterling Bancshares, Inc.	www.banksterling.com	No
Sterling Financial Corp.	www.sterlingfi.com	Yes
Stryker Corp.	www.strykercorp.com	No
SunTrust Banks, Inc.	www.suntrust.com	Yes
Superior Industries Int'l, Inc.	www.supind.com	Yes
SuperValu Inc.	www.supervalu.com	Yes
Susquehanna Bancshares, Inc.	www.susqbanc.com	Yes
SWS Group, Inc.	www.swsgroupinc.com	No
Synovus Financial Corp.	www.synovus.com	Yes
Sysco Corp.	www.sysco.com	Yes
T. Rowe Price Group, Inc.	www.troweprice.com	Yes
Tanger Factory Outlet Centers, Inc.	www.tangeroutlet.com	Yes
Target Corp.	www.target.com	Yes
TCF Financial Corp.	www.tcfbank.com	Yes
Teleflex Inc.	www.teleflex.com	Yes
Telephone & Data Systems	www.teldta.com	Yes
Tennant Co.	www.tennantco.com	Yes
TEPPCO Partners, L.P.	www.teppco.com	No
Tootsie Roll Industries, Inc.	www.tootsie.com	No
Transatlantic Holdings, Inc.	www.transre.com	No
Trustmark Corp.	www.trustmark.com	Yes
UGI Corp.	www.ugicorp.com	Yes
United Bankshares, Inc.	www.ubsi-wv.com	Yes
United Dominion Realty Trust	www.udrt.com	Yes
United Mobile Homes, Inc.	www.umh.com	Yes
United Technologies Corp.	www.utc.com	Yes
Universal Corp.	www.universalcorp.com	Yes
Universal Health Realty Inc. Trust	www.uhrit.com	Yes
Unizan Financial Corp.	www.unbcorp.com	Yes
Valley National Bancorp	www.valleynationalbank.com	Yes
Valspar Corp. (The)	www.valspar.com	Yes
Vectren Corporation	www.vectren.com	Yes
VF Corp.	www.vfc.com	Yes
Vulcan Materials Co.	www.vulcanmaterials.com	Yes
Walgreen Co.	www.walgreens.com	Yes
Wal-Mart Stores, Inc.	www.wal-mart.com	Yes
Washington Federal, Inc.	www.washingtonfederal.com	No
Washington Mutual, Inc.	www.wamu.com	Yes
Washington R.E.I.T.	www.writ.com	Yes
Webster Financial Corp.	www.websterbank.com	Yes
Weingarten Realty Investors	www.weingarten.com	Yes
Wells Fargo & Co.	www.wellsfargo.com	Yes
WesBanco, Inc.	www.wesbanco.com	Yes
Wesco Financial Corp.	----	No
West Pharmaceutical Services	www.westpharma.com	Yes
WestAmerica Bancorporation	www.westamerica.com	Yes
Weyco Group, Inc.	www.weycogroup.com	No
WGL Holdings, Inc.	www.washgas.com	Yes
Whitney Holding Corp.	www.whitneybank.com	Yes
Wiley (John) & Sons Inc.	www.wiley.com	No
Wilmington Trust Corp.	www.wilmingtontrust.com	Yes
Wolverine World Wide, Inc.	www.wolverineworldwide.com	No
WPS Resources Corp.	www.wpsr.com	Yes
Wrigley (Wm.) Jr. Co.	www.wrigley.com	Yes

NAICS Classification of Companies By Industry

Accommodation and Food Services
Applebee's International, Inc.
Frisch's Restaurants, Inc.
* McDonald's Corporation

Administrative & Support and Waste Management
Administrative and Support Services
ServiceMaster Company (The)

Waste Management and Remediation Services
* Johnson Controls, Inc.

Arts, Entertainment, and Recreation
Bowl America Inc.
* Cedar Fair, L.P.

Construction
ABM Industries Incorporated
* MDU Resources Group, Inc.

Finance and Insurance
Commercial Banking
1st Source Corp.
* AmSouth Bancorporation
* Associated Banc-Corp.
BancFirst Corp.
* BancorpSouth, Inc.
* Bank of America Corporation
* Bank of Hawaii Corporation
* BB&T Corporation
* Chemical Financial Corp.
* Chittenden Corporation
* Citizens Banking Corp.
* Comerica, Inc.
* Commerce Bancorp, Inc.
* Commerce Bancshares, Inc.
* Community Bank System, Inc.
* Community First Bankshares, Inc.
Community Trust Bancorp, Inc.
* Compass Bancshares Inc.
Corus Bankshares, Inc.
Cullen/Frost Bankers, Inc.
CVB Financial Corp.
* F.N.B. Corp.
* Fifth Third Bancorp
* First Charter Corp.
* First Commonwealth Financial
First Financial Corp.
* First Merchants Corp.
* First Midwest Bancorp, Inc.
* FirstMerit Corp.
* Fulton Financial Corp.
* Harleysville National Corp.
* Hibernia Corporation
* Hudson United Bancorp
* Independent Bank Corporation
* Irwin Financial Corp.
* KeyCorp

* M&T Bank Corporation
* Marshall & Ilsley Corporation
MBNA Corporation
* Mercantile Bankshares Corp.
* National Commerce Financial
* National Penn Bancshares, Inc.
Northern Trust Corp.
* Old National Bancorp
Pacific Capital Bancorp
* Park National Corp.
* People's Bank
* Popular, Inc.
* Regions Financial Corporation
* Republic Bancorp, Inc.
* S&T Bancorp, Inc.
* Second Bancorp, Inc.
Simmons First National Corp.
* SouthTrust Corp.
* State Street Corporation
Sterling Bancshares, Inc.
* Sterling Financial Corp.
* SunTrust Banks, Inc.
* Susquehanna Bancshares, Inc.
SWS Group, Inc.
* Synovus Financial Corporation
* TCF Financial Corp.
* Trustmark Corp.
* United Bankshares, Inc.
* Unizan Financial Corp.
* Valley National Bancorp
* Wells Fargo & Company
* WesBanco, Inc.
* WestAmerica Bancorporation
* Whitney Holding Corp.
* Wilmington Trust Corporation

Direct Health and Medical Insurance Carriers
* AFLAC Incorporated

Direct Life Insurance Carriers
* Jefferson-Pilot Corp.
* Lincoln National Corporation
National Security Group, Inc.
* Protective Life Corporation

Direct Property and Casualty Insurance Carriers
* Alfa Corp.
American International Group
* Chubb Corporation (The)
* Cincinnati Financial Corp.
* Harleysville Group, Inc.
Mercury General Corporation
* Midland Company (The)
Progressive Corporation (The)
* RLI Corp.
* State Auto Financial Corp.
Transatlantic Holdings, Inc.
Wesco Financial Corp.

NAICS Classification of Companies By Industry

Direct Title Insurance Carriers
Fidelity National Financial, Inc.

Insurance Agencies and Brokerages
Brown & Brown, Inc.
Gallagher (Arthur J.) & Company
Hilb, Rogal & Hamilton Company
* Marsh & McLennan Companies

Nondepository Credit Intermediation
Doral Financial Corporation
* Fannie Mae
* Freddie Mac
SLM Corporation

Real Estate Investment Trusts
Camden Property Trust
* Commercial Net Lease Realty
* EastGroup Properties, Inc.
* Federal Realty Investment Trust
* General Growth Properties, Inc.
* Health Care Property Investors
* Healthcare Realty Trust, Inc.
* Kimco Realty Corp.
* Tanger Factory Outlet Centers, Inc.
* United Dominion Realty Trust
* United Mobile Homes, Inc.
* Universal Health Realty Inc. Trust
* Washington Real Est. Invst Trust
* Weingarten Realty Investors

Reinsurance Carriers
Ambac Financial Group, Inc.
MBIA Inc.
* Old Republic International Corp.
* St. Paul Companies, Inc. (The)

Savings Institutions
Anchor BanCorp Wisconsin, Inc.
* Charter One Financial, Inc.
* First Federal Capital Corp.
* First Financial Holdings, Inc.
* First Indiana Corp.
* Glacier Bancorp, Inc.
Golden West Financial Corp.
Washington Federal, Inc.
* Washington Mutual, Inc.
* Webster Financial Corp.

Securities and Other Financial Investments
* Citigroup Inc.
Eaton Vance Corporation
* Franklin Resources, Inc.
Legg Mason, Inc.
Nuveen Investments, Inc.
SEI Investments Co.
* T. Rowe Price Group, Inc.

Information
Information Services and Data Processing
Automatic Data Processing, Inc.
* Jack Henry & Associates, Inc.
* Paychex, Inc.

Publishing Industries
Courier Corp.
* Gannett Co., Inc.
* McGraw-Hill Companies, Inc.
Meredith Corporation
Wiley (John) & Sons Inc.

Telecommunications
* ALLTEL Corporation
* CenturyTel, Inc.
* Telephone and Data Systems, Inc.

Management of Companies & Enterprises
* National City Corporation
* SBC Communications Inc.
* Universal Corporation

Manufacturing
Beverage and Tobacco Product Manufacturing
* Altria Group, Inc.
* Anheuser-Busch Companies
* Brown-Forman Corporation
* Coca-Cola Company (The)
Farmer Bros. Co.
* PepsiCo Inc.

Chemical Manufacturing
* 3M Company
* Air Products & Chemicals, Inc.
Alberto-Culver Company
* Avon Products, Inc.
* Clorox Company (The)
* Colgate-Palmolive Company
* Ecolab, Inc.
* Fuller (H.B.) Company
* PPG Industries, Inc.
* Praxair, Inc.
* Procter & Gamble Company
* Rohm & Haas Company
* RPM International Inc.
* Sherwin-Williams Company
Sigma-Aldrich Corp.
Stepan Company
* Valspar Corporation (The)

Computer and Electronic Product Manufacturing
* Badger Meter, Inc.
* Beckman Coulter, Inc.
* Emerson Electric Co.
Linear Technology Corp.
* Medtronic, Inc.

NAICS Classification of Companies By Industry

Elec. Eqpmt., Appliance, and Component Mfg.
Franklin Electric Co., Inc.
* General Electric Company
* Gorman-Rupp Co.
* Smith (A.O.) Corporation

Fabricated Metal Product Manufacturing
Danaher Corporation
* Parker-Hannifin Corp.
* Stanley Works

Food Manufacturing
* Archer Daniels Midland Co.
* ConAgra Foods, Inc.
* Heinz (H.J.) Company
* Hershey Foods Corporation
* Hormel Foods Corporation
* Lancaster Colony Corp.
* McCormick & Company, Inc.
* Sara Lee Corporation
Tootsie Roll Industries, Inc.
* Wrigley (Wm.) Jr. Company

Furniture and Related Product Manufacturing
HON Industries Incorporated
* La-Z-Boy Incorporated
Leggett & Platt, Incorporated
* Masco Corporation

Machinery Manufacturing
* Briggs & Stratton Corporation
* Caterpillar Inc.
* Diebold, Inc.
* Dover Corporation
NACCO Industries, Inc.
* Nordson Corp.
* Pentair, Inc.
Roper Industries, Inc.
* Tennant Company

Medical Equipment and Supplies Manufacturing
Arrow International, Inc.
* Bard (C.R.), Inc.
* Becton, Dickinson and Company
* Meridian Bioscience Inc.
Stryker Corporation
* Teleflex Inc.

Paper and Wood Product Manufacturing
* Avery Dennison Corporation
* Bemis Company, Inc.
* Kimberly-Clark Corporation
* Sonoco Products Company

Petroleum and Coal Products Manufacturing
* ChevronTexaco Corp.
* Exxon Mobil Corporation
Holly Corp.
* Quaker Chemical Corporation

Pharmaceutical Preparation Manufacturing
* Abbott Laboratories
* Johnson & Johnson
* Lilly (Eli) & Company
* Merck & Co., Inc.
* Pfizer Inc.

Plastics and Rubber Products Manufacturing
AptarGroup Inc.
* Bandag, Inc.
* Carlisle Companies Incorporated
* Illinois Tool Works, Incorporated
* Myers Industries, Inc.
* West Pharmaceutical Services

Primary Metal Manufacturing
* Nucor Corporation

Printing and Related Support Activities
* Banta Corporation
* Donnelley (R.R.) & Sons Co.

Textiles, Apparel, and Leather Manufacturing
* VF Corporation
Weyco Group, Inc.
Wolverine World Wide, Inc.

Transportation Equipment Manufacturing
* Clarcor Inc.
* Federal Signal Corp.
General Dynamics Corporation
* Harley-Davidson, Inc.
Superior Industries International, Inc.
* United Technologies Corp.

Other Manufacturing
* Brady Corporation
* Hillenbrand Industries, Inc.
Mine Safety Appliances Co.
Quixote Corp.
* Raven Industries, Inc.

Mining
Helmerich & Payne, Inc.
* Vulcan Materials Company

Real Estate and Rental and Leasing
Real Estate
* Rouse Company (The)

Rental and Leasing Services
Cintas Corp.
McGrath RentCorp

Retail Trade
Building Material and Supplies Dealers
* Home Depot (The), Inc.
* Lowe's Companies, Inc.

NAICS Classification of Companies By Industry

Furniture and Consumer Electronics
Haverty Furniture Companies
* Pier 1 Imports, Inc.

General Merchandise Stores
Family Dollar Stores, Inc.
* May Department Stores Co.
* Target Corporation
* Wal-Mart Stores, Inc.

Health and Personal Care Stores
* Walgreen Co.

Transportation and Warehousing
* Atmos Energy Corporation
* EnergySouth, Inc.
  TEPPCO Partners, L.P.

Utilities
Utilities - Electric
* Black Hills Corporation
* Cleco Corporation
* Consolidated Edison, Inc.
* MGE Energy Inc.
* Otter Tail Corp.
* Pinnacle West Capital Corp.
* Progress Energy, Inc.
* WPS Resources Corporation

Utilities - Natural Gas
* Energen Corporation
* Florida Public Utilities Co.
* National Fuel Gas Company
* NICOR Inc.
* Peoples Energy Corporation
* Piedmont Natural Gas Company, Inc.
* Questar Corporation
* UGI Corporation
* Vectren Corporation
* WGL Holdings, Inc.

Utilities - Water
* American States Water Co.
* Aqua America, Inc.
* Artesian Resources Corp.
* California Water Service Group
* Connecticut Water Service, Inc.
* Middlesex Water Co.
* Pennichuck Corp.
  SJW Corp.

Wholesale Trade
* Genuine Parts Company
  Grainger (W.W.), Inc.
* Pitney Bowes Inc.
* Supervalu Inc.
* Sysco Corporation

* Designates companies offering dividend reinvestment plans.

Ranking the 2004 Canadian Dividend Achievers

Companies are listed by the five-year average annual compound growth rate of their dividends.

Rank	Company	Ticker	5-Year Growth Rate	Rank	Company	Ticker	5-Year Growth Rate
1	BMTC Group Inc.	GBT A	26.191	15	Atco Ltd.	ACO X	13.485
2	Loblaw Cos. Ltd.	L	24.573	16	Thomson Corp.	TOC	12.939
3	Weston (George) Limited	WN	24.356	17	Melcor Developments Ltd.	MRD	12.888
4	Empire Ltd.	EMP A	22.698	18	Leon's Furniture Ltd.	LNF	12.196
5	Investors Group Inc.	IGI	21.673	19	Buhler Industries, Inc.	BUI	11.382
5	Jean Coutu Group	PJC A	21.673	20	National Bank of Canada	NA	10.351
7	Great-West Lifeco Inc.	GWO	20.654	21	Toromont Industries Ltd.	TIH	10.301
8	Metro Inc.	MRU A	20.546	22	Bank of Montreal	BMO	8.774
9	Power Financial Corp	PWF	19.551	23	Enbridge Inc.	ENB	8.188
10	AGF Management Ltd.	AGF B	17.808	24	Terasen Inc.	TER	7.017
11	Quebecor World Inc.	IQW	16.724	25	West Fraser Timber Co.	WFT	4.554
12	Power Corp. du Canada	POW	16.466	26	Canadian Utilities Ltd.	CU	4.462
13	Royal Bank of Canada	RY	14.343	27	Imperial Oil Ltd.	IMO	3.144
14	Canadian Nat'l.Railway	CNI	13.539				

Ranking the 2004 Canadian Dividend Achievers By Current Yield

Based on closing prices at 3/31/04

Rank	Company	Yield	Rank	Company	Yield
1	Enbridge Inc.	3.43	15	Buhler Industries, Inc.	2.06
2	Canadian Utilities Ltd.	3.39	16	Leon's Furniture Ltd.	1.85
3	Royal Bank of Canada	3.33	17	Power Corp. du Canada	1.81
4	Terasen Inc.	3.20	18	Metro Inc.	1.55
5	Investors Group Inc.	3.08	19	Canadian Nat'l. Railway Co.	1.50
5	Bank of Montreal	2.95	20	Imperial Oil Ltd.	1.49
7	National Bank of Canada	2.88	21	Weston (George) Limited	1.47
8	Quebecor World Inc.	2.84	22	Empire Ltd.	1.44
9	Atco Ltd.	2.64	23	West Fraser Timber Co.	1.40
10	Great-West Lifeco Inc.	2.54	24	Toromont Industries Ltd.	1.36
11	Thomson Corp.	2.41	25	Loblaw Cos. Ltd.	1.21
12	Melcor Developments Ltd.	2.34	26	BMTC Group Inc.	0.84
13	Power Financial Corp	2.34	27	Jean Coutu Group	0.70
14	AGF Management Ltd.	2.33			

Ranking the the 2004 Canadian Dividend Achievers by Total Return

Based on the 1 year period ending 3/31/04.

Rank	Name	Ticker	1-Year Tot. Ret	Rank	Name	Ticker	1-Year Tot. Ret
1	Toromont Industries Ltd.	TIH	90.00%	15	Enbridge Inc.	ENB	25.18%
2	AGF Management Ltd.	AGF B	64.57%	16	Jean Coutu Group	PJC A	24.06%
3	Investors Group Inc.	IGI	49.49%	17	Loblaw Cos. Ltd.	L	19.21%
4	Power Corp. du Canada	POW	48.44%	18	Leon's Furniture Ltd.	LNF	18.35%
5	Power Financial Corp	PWF	46.52%	19	Quebecor World Inc.	IQW	18.23%
6	National Bank of Canada	NA	45.29%	20	Empire Ltd.	EMP A	16.74%
7	Great-West Lifeco Inc.	GWO	41.96%	21	Buhler Industries, Inc.	BUI	16.04%
8	Bank of Montreal	BMO	38.56%	22	West Fraser Timber Co.	WFT	13.45%
9	Canadian Utilities Ltd.	CU	36.81%	23	Royal Bank of Canada	RY	12.58%
10	Terasen Inc.	TER	36.35%	24	Thomson Corp.	TOC	7.87%
11	Melcor Developments	MRD	31.14%	25	Weston (George) Limited	WN	7.32%
12	Atco Ltd.	ACO X	26.66%	26	Canadian National Railway	CNI	-6.48%
13	Metro Inc.	MRU A	26.39%	27	BMTC Group Inc.	GBT A	-17.69%
14	Imperial Oil Ltd.	IMO	26.19%				

Based on the 3 year period ending 3/31/04.

Rank	Name	Ticker	3-Year Tot. Ret	Rank	Name	Ticker	3-Year Tot. Ret
1	BMTC Group Inc.	GBT A	38.87%	15	Bank of Montreal	BMO	13.60%
2	Melcor Developments	MRD	30.19%	16	Great-West Lifeco Inc.	GWO	13.45%
3	Toromont Industries Ltd.	TIH	28.27%	17	Royal Bank of Canada	RY	12.57%
4	Metro Inc.	MRU A	25.40%	18	Jean Coutu Group	PJC A	11.93%
5	Buhler Industries, Inc.	BUI	24.70%	19	Enbridge Inc.	ENB	11.04%
6	Investors Group Inc.	IGI	24.12%	20	Canadian Utilities Ltd.	CU	10.30%
7	Empire Ltd.	EMP A	21.50%	21	Loblaw Cos. Ltd.	L	9.11%
8	National Bank of Canada	NA	20.68%	22	Weston (George) Limited	WN	4.59%
9	Power Financial Corp	PWF	19.80%	23	Canadian National Railway	CNI	2.99%
10	Terasen Inc.	TER	17.81%	24	Atco Ltd.	ACO X	2.47%
11	Imperial Oil Ltd.	IMO	16.90%	25	AGF Management Ltd.	AGF B	-2.24%
12	West Fraser Timber Co.	WFT	16.26%	26	Thomson Corp.	TOC	-6.38%
13	Leon's Furniture Ltd.	LNF	15.74%	27	Quebecor World Inc.	IQW	-9.55%
14	Power Corp. du Canada	POW	15.70%				

Based on the 5 year period ending 3/31/04.

Rank	Name	Ticker	5-Year Tot. Ret	Rank	Name	Ticker	5-Year Tot. Ret
1	BMTC Group Inc.	GBT A	35.17%	15	Investors Group Inc.	IGI	14.92%
2	Bank of Montreal	BMO	31.69%	16	Power Corp. du Canada	POW	14.71%
3	Royal Bank of Canada	RY	31.47%	17	Leon's Furniture Ltd.	LNF	14.24%
4	Melcor Developments	MRD	25.18%	18	Enbridge Inc.	ENB	12.61%
5	Toromont Industries Ltd.	TIH	20.12%	19	Weston (George) Limited	WN	9.96%
6	Buhler Industries, Inc.	BUI	20.06%	20	Loblaw Cos. Ltd.	L	9.45%
7	Metro Inc.	MRU A	19.18%	21	Canadian Utilities Ltd.	CU	8.97%
8	Empire Ltd.	EMP A	17.86%	22	West Fraser Timber Co.	WFT	8.45%
9	National Bank of Canada	NA	17.51%	23	Atco Ltd.	ACO X	7.34%
10	Jean Coutu Group	PJC A	17.02%	24	Thomson Corp.	TOC	1.03%
11	Imperial Oil Ltd.	IMO	17.02%	25	AGF Management Ltd.	AGF B	0.63%
12	Great-West Lifeco Inc.	GWO	15.80%	26	Canadian National Railway	CNI	0.00%
13	Power Financial Corp	PWF	15.63%	27	Quebecor World Inc.	IQW	-5.16%
14	Terasen Inc.	TER	15.31%				

NAICS Classification Of Canadian Companies By Industry

Company	Description
AGF Management Ltd.	Investment Advice
Atco Ltd.	Electric Power Distribution
Bank of Montreal	Commercial Banking
BMTC Group Inc.	Furniture Stores
Buhler Industries, Inc.	Farm and Garden Machinery and Equipment Merchant Wholesalers
Canadian National Railway Co.	Line-Haul Railroads
Canadian Utilities Ltd.	Electric Bulk Power Transmission and Control
Empire Ltd	Other Grocery and Related Products Merchant Wholesalers
Enbridge Inc.	All Other Pipeline Transportation
Great-West Lifeco Inc.	Direct Life Insurance Carriers
Imperial Oil Ltd.	Crude Petroleum and Natural Gas Extraction
Investors Group Inc.	Investment Advice
Jean Coutu Group (PJC) Inc. (The)	Pharmacies and Drug Stores
Leon's Furniture Ltd.	Institutional Furniture Manufacturing
Loblaw Cos. Ltd.	Warehouse Clubs and Supercenters
Melcor Developments Ltd.	Land Subdivision
Metro Inc	General Line Grocery Merchant Wholesalers
National Bank of Canada	Commercial Banking
Power Corp. du Canada	Offices of Other Holding Companies
Power Financial Corp.	Direct Life Insurance Carriers
Quebecor World Inc.	Commercial Screen Printing
Royal Bank of Canada	Commercial Banking
Terasen Inc.	Natural Gas Distribution
Thomson Corp.	Book Publishers
Toromont Industries Ltd.	Air-Conditioning and Warm Air Heating Equipment
West Fraser Timber Co., Ltd.	Logging
Weston (George) Limited	Commercial Bakeries

Web Site & Dividend Reinvestment Plan Information

Company	Web Site	DRIP
AGF Management Ltd.	www.agf.com	No
Atco Ltd.	www.atco.com	No
Bank of Montreal	www.bmo.com	Yes
BMTC Group Inc.	www.braultetmartineau.com	No
Buhler Industries, Inc.	www.buhler.com	No
Canadian National Railway Co.	www.cn.ca	No
Canadian Utilities Ltd.	www.canadian-utilities.com	No
Empire Ltd	www.empireco.ca	No
Enbridge Inc.	www.enbridge.com	Yes
Great-West Lifeco Inc.	www.greatwestlifeco.com	No
Imperial Oil Ltd.	www.imperialoil.ca	Yes
Investors Group Inc.	www.investorsgroup.com	No
Jean Coutu Group (PJC) Inc. (The)	www.jeancoutu.com	No
Leon's Furniture Ltd.	www.leons.ca	No
Loblaw Cos. Ltd.	www.loblaw.com	No
Melcor Developments Ltd.	www.melcor.ca	No
Metro Inc.	www.metro.ca	No
National Bank of Canada	www.nbc.ca	No
Power Corp. du Canada	www.powercorp.com	No
Power Financial Corp	www.powerfinancial.com	No
Quebecor World Inc.	www.quebecorworld.com	No
Royal Bank of Canada	www.rbc.com	No
Terasen Inc.	www.bcgas.com	No
Thomson Corp.	www.thomcorp.com	No
Toromont Industries Ltd.	www.toromont.com	No
West Fraser Timber Co., Ltd.	www.westfraser.com	No
Weston (George) Limited	www.weston.ca	No

Frequently Asked Questions

Topics Questions:

- How does a dividend-paying company become a Dividend Achiever?
- What percentage of dividend-paying companies classified as Dividend Achievers?
- How many economic sectors and industries are represented by Dividend Achievers?
- What distinguishes Dividend Achievers from other U.S. listed companies?
- How often is the Dividend Achievers Index reconstituted?
- How are corporate actions handled?
- What type of information is available on the Dividend Achievers constituents?

Q: How does a dividend-paying company become a Dividend Achiever?

A: A publicly-traded company that has increased its dividends for the last ten or more consecutive years will be classified as a Dividend Achiever. Depending on the industry, companies must also meet certain capitalization requirements in order to be considered a Dividend Achiever.

Q: What percentage of dividend-paying companies classified as Dividend Achievers?

A: Just 3.0.% of 10,000-plus North American-listed, dividend-paying common stocks are classified as Dividend Achievers.

Q: How many economic sectors and industries are represented by Dividend Achievers?

A: Dividend Achievers represent five economic sectors and more than 50 industries.

Q: What distinguishes Dividend Achievers from other U.S. listed companies?

A: Dividend Achievers have demonstrated the ability to consistently increase dividend payments over a substantial period of time, through volatile markets and challenging political climates.

Q: Does Mergent Inc. offer a Dividend Achiever Index?

A: Mergent currently offers an Index that tracks the daily performance of Dividend Achiever constituents. The inception date was January 17, 2003. The real time price appreciation values are published by the American Stock Exchange under the Symbol ^DAA.

Q: How often is the Index reconstituted?

A: The Dividend Achievers Index is reconstituted annually.

Q: How are corporate actions handled?

A: If an Index constituent is acquired and is no longer actively traded, the company will cease classification as a Dividend Achiever. If an Index constituent spins off a portion of its business or merges with another company, it will be handled on a case by case basis.

HOW TO USE THIS BOOK

MERGENT'S Dividend Achievers is a compact, easy-to-use reference that provides basic financial and business information on 303 companies that have increased their cash dividend payments for at least ten consecutive years, adjusting for splits. The presentation of background information plus current and historical data provides the answers to four basic questions for each company:

1. What does the company do?
   (See G.)
2. How has it done in the past?
   (See B, J.)
3. How is it doing now?
   (See C, D, H.)
4. How will it fare in the future?
   (See I.)

A. CAPSULE STOCK INFORMATION shows where the stock is traded and its symbol, a recent price and price/earnings ratio, plus the yield afforded by the indicated dividend based on a recent price. The indicated dividend is the current annualized dividend based on the most recent regular cash payment. Also shown is the 52-week range of the Company's stock price.

B. LONG-TERM PRICE CHART illustrates the pattern of monthly stock price movements, fully adjusted for stock dividends and splits. The chart points out the degree of volatility in the price movement of the company's stock and what its long-term trend has been, and shows how it has performed versus the S&P 500 Index. It indicates areas of price support and resistance, plus other technical points to be considered by the investor. The bars at the base of the long-term price chart indicate the monthly trading volume. Monthly trading volume offers the individual an opportunity to recognize at what periods stock accumulation occurs and what percent of a company's outstanding shares are traded.

PRICE SCORES – Above each company's price/volume chart are its *Mergent's Price Scores*. These are basic measures of the stock's performance. Each stock is measured against the New York Stock Exchange Composite Index.

A score of 100 indicates that the stock did well as the New York Stock Exchange Composite Index during the time period. A score of less than 100 means that the stock did not do as well; a score of more than 100 means that the stock outperformed the NYSE Composite Index. All stock prices are adjusted splits and stock dividends. The time period measured for each company conclude with the date of the recent price shown in the top line of each company's profile.

The *7 YEAR PRICE SCORE* mirrors the common stock's price growth over the previous seven years. The higher the price score the better the relative performance. It is based on the ratio of the latest 12-month average price to the current seven year average. This ratio is then indexed against the same ratio for the market as a whole (the New York Stock Exchange Composite Index), which is taken as 100.

The *12 MONTH PRICE SCORE* is a similar measurement but for a shorter period of time. It is based on the ratio of the latest two-month average price to the current 12-month average. As was done for the Long-Term Price Score, this ratio is also indexed to the same ratio for the market as a whole.

C. INTERIM EARNINGS (Per Share) – Figures are reported before effect of extraordinary items, discontinued operations and cumulative effects of accounting changes. Each figure is for the quarterly period indicated. These figures are essentially as reported by the company, although all figures are adjusted for all stock dividends and splits.

D. INTERIM DIVIDENDS (Per Share) – The cash dividends are the actual dollar amounts declared by the company. No adjustments have been made for stock dividends and splits. **Ex-Dividend Date**: a stockholder must purchase the stock prior to this date in order to be entitled to the dividend. The **Record Date** indicates the date on which the

ILLUSTRATIVE, INC. **A**

Exchange	Symbol	Price	52Wk Range	Yield	P/E
NYS	ILL	$35.70 (2/20/2004)	37.45-21.46	0.78	20.40

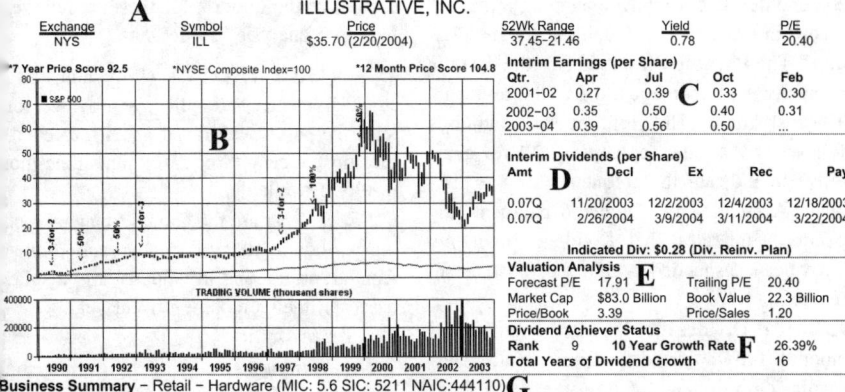

*7 Year Price Score 92.5   *NYSE Composite Index=100   *12 Month Price Score 104.8

Interim Earnings (per Share) **C**

Qtr.	Apr	Jul	Oct	Feb
2001-02	0.27	0.39	0.33	0.30
2002-03	0.35	0.50	0.40	0.31
2003-04	0.39	0.56	0.50	...

B

Interim Dividends (per Share) **D**

Amt	Decl	Ex	Rec	Pay
0.07Q	11/20/2003	12/2/2003	12/4/2003	12/18/2003
0.07Q	2/26/2004	3/9/2004	3/11/2004	3/22/2004

Indicated Div: $0.28 (Div. Reinv. Plan)

Valuation Analysis **E**

Forecast P/E	17.91	Trailing P/E	20.40
Market Cap	$83.0 Billion	Book Value	22.3 Billion
Price/Book	3.39	Price/Sales	1.20

Dividend Achiever Status **F**

Rank	9	10 Year Growth Rate	26.39%
Total Years of Dividend Growth			16

TRADING VOLUME (thousand shares)

Business Summary – Retail – Hardware (MIC: 5.6 SIC: 5211 NAIC:444110) **G**

Illustrative, Inc. operated 1,607 retail warehouse stores as of Aug 3 2003 in the United States, Canada and Mexico that offer a wide assortment of building materials and home improvement products. The average Illustrative store has about 108,000 square feet of interior floor space and is stocked with approximately 40,000 to 50,000 separate items. Most stores have about 22,000 square feet of additional outdoor selling area for landscaping supplies. Co. operates 53 Illustrative Design Center stores that sell products and services primarily for home decorating and remodeling projects, five Illustrative Supply stores, nine Illustrative Landscape Supply stores and one Illustrative, Inc. Floor Store outlet.

Recent Developments **H**

For the three months ended Nov 2 2003, net earnings advanced 22.0% to $1.15 billion from $940.0 million in the corresponding prior–year period. Net sales increased 14.7% to $16.60 billion from $14.48 billion a year earlier. Comparable–store sales were up 7.8% year over year, while average sale per customer transaction rose to $52.10 from $49.66 in the third quarter of 2002. Gross profit totaled $5.19 billion, or 31.3% of net sales, compared with $4.58 billion, or 31.6% of net sales, the year before. Operating income climbed 21.9% to $1.82 billion from $1.50 billion the previous year. During the quarter, Co. opened 36 new stores.

Prospects **I**

Co. is projecting sales growth of between 9.0% and 12.0% and earnings growth of 15.0% to 17.0% during the current fiscal year. Results are being positively affected by Co.'s efforts to remodel many of its older stores and improve customer service through the installation of self–checkout stations, which have been installed in 760 stores as of Nov 2 2003. Separately, Co. is taking steps to expand its services business through acquisitions. On Nov 10 2003, Co. signed a definitive agreement to acquire RMA Home Services, Inc., an Atlanta, GA–based contract installer of replacement windows and siding. In September 2003, Co. acquired IPUSA, a Tampa, FL–based contract installer of roofing.

Financial Data **J**

(US$ in Thousands)	11/02/2003	08/03/2003	05/04/2003	02/02/2003	02/03/2002	01/28/2001	01/30/2000	01/31/1999	02/01/1998	02/02/1997
Earnings Per Share	1.46	0.95	0.39	1.56	1.29	1.10	1.00	0.70	0.51	0.43
Cash Flow Per Share	2.67	2.00	1.20	2.04	2.53	1.18	1.04	0.82	0.45	0.50
Tang. Book Val. Per Share	...	...	8.75	8.38	7.52	6.32	5.22	3.82	3.16	2.71
Dividends Per Share	0.25	0.23	0.22	0.21	0.17	0.16	0.11	0.08	0.06	0.05
Dividend Payout %	17.12	24.21	56.41	13.46	13.18	14.55	11.00	11.43	11.76	11.63
Income Statement										
Total Revenues	49,691,000	33,093,000	15,104,000	58,247,000	53,553,000	45,738,000	38,434,000	30,219,000	24,156,000	19,535,503
Total Indirect Exp.	10,290,000	6,920,000	3,381,000	12,278,000	11,215,000	9,490,000	7,616,000	5,944,000	4,869,000	3,900,430
Depreciation & Amort.	786,000	505,000	248,000	903,000	764,000	601,000	463,000	373,000	283,000	232,340
Operating Income	5,337,000	3,514,000	1,448,000	5,830,000	4,932,000	4,191,000	3,795,000	2,661,000	1,912,000	1,533,650
Net Interest Inc./(Exp.)	(7,000)	(7,000)	(6,000)	42,000	25,000	26,000	9,000	(7,000)	2,000	9,490
Income Before Income Taxes	5,330,000	3,507,000	1,442,000	5,872,000	4,957,000	4,217,000	3,804,000	2,654,000	1,898,000	1,534,769
Income Taxes	1,977,000	1,301,000	535,000	2,208,000	1,913,000	1,636,000	1,484,000	1,040,000	738,000	597,030
Net Income	3,353,000	2,206,000	907,000	3,664,000	3,044,000	2,581,000	2,320,000	1,614,000	1,160,000	937,739
Average Shs. Outstg.	2,295,000	2,300,000	2,297,000	2,344,000	2,353,000	2,352,000	2,342,000	2,320,000	2,286,000	2,194,884
Balance Sheet										
Cash & Cash Equivalents	4,944,000	5,209,000	4,264,000	2,253,000	2,546,000	177,000	176,000	62,000	174,000	558,436
Total Current Assets	15,697,000	15,567,000	15,309,000	11,917,000	10,361,000	7,777,000	6,390,000	4,933,000	4,460,000	3,709,373
Net Property	18,876,000	18,263,000	17,654,000	17,168,000	15,375,000	13,068,000	10,227,000	8,160,000	6,509,000	5,437,046
Total Assets	35,374,000	34,612,000	33,847,000	30,011,000	26,394,000	21,385,000	17,081,000	13,465,000	11,229,000	9,341,710
Total Current Liabilities	10,972,000	10,389,000	10,925,000	8,035,000	6,501,000	4,385,000	3,656,000	2,857,000	2,456,000	1,842,126
Long–Term Obligations	847,000	1,327,000	1,321,000	1,321,000	1,250,000	1,545,000	750,000	1,566,000	1,303,000	1,246,593
Net Stockholders' Equity	22,261,000	21,933,000	20,678,000	19,802,000	18,082,000	15,004,000	12,341,000	8,740,000	7,098,000	5,955,186
Net Working Capital	4,725,000	5,178,000	4,384,000	3,882,000	3,860,000	3,392,000	2,734,000	2,076,000	2,004,000	1,867,247
Year–end Shs. Outstg.	2,273,000	2,365,000	2,294,000	2,293,000	2,345,888	2,323,747	2,304,317	2,213,178	2,196,324	2,162,317
Statistical Record										
Operating Profit Margin %	10.74	10.61	9.58	10.00	9.20	9.16	9.87	8.80	7.91	7.85
Return on Equity %	15.06	10.05	4.38	18.50	16.83	17.20	18.79	18.46	16.34	15.74
Return on Assets %	9.47	6.37	2.68	12.20	11.53	12.06	13.58	11.98	10.33	10.03
Debt/Total Assets %	2.39	3.83	3.91	4.40	4.73	7.22	4.39	11.63	11.60	13.34
Price Range	37.43-20.52	34.41-20.52	28.34-20.52	51.31-20.35	52.32-32.28	67.06-34.21	67.26-35.25	40.00-19.95	19.60-10.59	12.43-8.98
P/E Ratio	25.64-14.05	36.22-21.60	72.67-52.62	32.89-13.04	40.71-25.02	60.96-31.10	67.26-35.25	57.14-28.50	38.43-20.76	28.91-20.88
Average Yield %	0.84	0.82	0.91	0.60	N/A	0.32	0.24	0.14	0.39	N/A

Address: 2455 Paces Ferry Road N.W., Atlanta, GA 30339–4024, United States **K** Telephone: (770) 433–8211 Fax: (770) 431-2707 Web Site: www.illusinc.com	Officers: Robert L. Nardelli – Chmn. Pres., C.E.O. Francis S. Blake – Exec. V.P., Bus. Devel., Strategy, Corp. Oper. Transfer Agents:EquiServe Trust Company, N.A., Providence, Auditors:KPMG LLP	Investor Contact:Investor Relations, 770–384–4388 Legal Counsel:Smith, Cohen, Ringel, Kohler &Martin Institutional Holdings **L** No of Institutions: 10 Shares: 5,387,488

shareholder had to have been a holder of record in order to have qualified for the dividend. The **Payable Date** indicates the date the company paid or intends to pay the dividend. The cash amount shown in the first column is followed by a letter (example "Q" for quarterly) to indicate the frequency of the dividend. A notation of 'Dividend payment suspended' indicates that dividend payments have been suspended within the most recent ten years.

Indicated Dividend – This is the annualized amount (fully adjusted for splits) of the latest regular cash dividend. Companies with Dividend Reinvestment Plans are indicated here.

E. VALUATION ANALYSIS is a tool for evaluating a company's stock. Included are: Forecast Price/Earnings, Trailing Price/Earnings, Market Capitalization, Book Value, Price/Book and Price/Sales.

F. DIVIDEND ACHIEVER STATUS – The company's rank among the Dividend Achievers for dividend growth is indicated. Each company is ranked by its ten-year compound annual average cash dividend growth rate, which is also shown here, along with the total consecutive years of increases.

G. BUSINESS SUMMARY explains what a company does in terms of the products or services it sells, its markets, and the position the company occupies in its industry. For a quick reference, included are the Company's Standard Industrial Classification (SIC), North American Industry Classification (NAIC) and Mergent's Industry Classification (MIC).

H. RECENT DEVELOPMENTS – This section captures what has happened in which results are available. It provides analysis of recently released sales and earnings figures, including special charges and credits, and may also include results by sector, expense trends and ratios, and other current information.

I. PROSPECTS – This section focuses on what is anticipated for the immediate future,

as well as the outlook for the next few ye based on analysis by Mergent.

J. FINANCIAL DATA (fully adjusted stock dividends and splits) is provided for least the past seven fiscal years, preceded the most recent three-, six- and nine-mo results if available.

Fiscal Years are the annual financial repo ing periods as determined by each compar Annual prices and dividends are display based on the Company's fiscal year.

Per Share Data:

The Earnings Per Share figure essentia is what has been reported by the compar Earnings per share, and all per share figure are adjusted for subsequent stock dividen and splits. Earnings per share reported aft 12/15/97 are presented on a diluted basis, described by Financial Accounting Standarc Board Statement 128. Prior to that date, earr ings per share are presented on a primar basis.

Cash Flow Per Share is computed by divid ing the cash flow from operating activities b average shares outstanding.

Tangible Book Value Per Share is calcu lated as stockholders equity (the value o common shares, paid-in capital and retainec earnings) minus preferred stock and intangibles such as goodwill, patents anc excess acquisition costs, divided by year-enc shares outstanding. It demonstrates the under lying cash value of each common share if the company were to be liquidated as of that date.

Dividends Per Share is the total of cash payments made per share to shareholders for the trailing 12-month period.

Dividend Payout % is the proportion of earnings available for common stock that is paid to common shareholders in the form of cash dividends. It is significant because it indicates what percentage of earnings is being reinvested in the business for internal growth.

INCOME STATEMENT, BALANCE SHEET AND STATISTICAL RECORD – Includes pertinent earnings and balance sheet information essential to analyzing a corporation's performance. The comparisons are shown as originally reported, provide the necessary historical perspective to intelligently review the various operating and financial trends. Generic definitions follow.

Income Statement:

Total Revenues figure is the total of gross revenues, gross sales, or equivalent items of income from operations.

Total Indirect Expenses consists of development costs than material and labor costs which are directly related to the construction of improvements, including administrative and office expenses, commissions, architectural, engineering and financing costs.

Depreciation and Amortization includes all non-cash charges such as depletion and amortization as well as depreciation.

Operating Income is the profit remaining after deducting depreciation as well as all operating costs and expenses from the company's net sales and revenues. This figure is *before* interest expenses, extraordinary gains and charges, and income and expense items of a non-operating nature.

Net Interest Income/(Expense) is the net amount of interest paid and received by a company during the fiscal year.

Income Before Income Taxes is the remaining income *after* deducting all costs, expenses, property charges, interest, etc. but *before* deducting income taxes.

Equity Earnings/Minority Interest is the net amount of profits allocated to minority owners or affiliates.

Income Taxes are shown as reported by the company and include both the amount of current taxes actually paid out and the amount deferred to future years.

Income From Continuing Operations is the amount remaining from total revenues after provisions for all operating and non-operating costs and expenses, including interest and taxes, have been deducted. Generally, extraordinary gains and losses and discontinued operations are excluded. Non-extraordinary charges such as restructuring or asset impairment charges are included in net income figures, as is income from minority interests in other companies.

Net Income is the amount remaining from total revenues after provisions for all operating and non-operating costs and expenses, including interest and taxes, have been deducted. Net income includes gains and losses from extraordinary items, accounting changes and discontinued operations. Non-extraordinary items such as restructuring or asset impairments are also included, as is income from minority interests in other companies. Net income is usually shown before preferred dividends have been deducted.

Average Shares Outstanding is the weighted average number of shares including common equivalent shares outstanding during the year, as reported by the corporation and fully adjusted for all stock dividends and splits. The use of *average shares* minimizes the distortion in *earnings per share* which could result from issuance of a large amount of stock or the company's purchase of a large amount of its own stock during the year.

Balance Sheet:

All balance sheet items are shown as reported by the corporation in its annual report. Because of the limited amount of space available and in an effort to simplify and standardize accounts, some items have been combined.

Cash & Cash Equivalents comprise unrestricted cash and temporary investments in marketable securities, such as U.S. Government securities, certificates of deposit and short-term investments.

Total Current Assets are all of the company's short-term assets, including cash, marketable securities, inventories, certain receivables, etc., as reported.

Net Property is total fixed assets, including all property, land, plants, buildings, equipment, fixtures, etc., less accumulated depreciation.

Total Assets represent the sum of the company's tangible and intangible property, as stated on its annual audited balance sheet.

HOW TO USE THIS BOOK (Continued)

Total Current Liabilities are all of the obligations the company due within one year, as reported.

Long-term Obligations are total long-term debts (due beyond one year) reported by the company, including bonds, capital lease obligations, notes, mortgages, debentures, etc.

Net Stockholders' Equity is the sum of all capital stock accounts – stated values of preferred and common stock, paid-in capital, earned surplus (retained earnings), etc., net of all treasury stock.

Net Working Capital is derived by subtracting Current Liabilities from Current Assets.

Year-end Shares Outstanding are the number of shares outstanding as of the date of the company's quarterly/annual report, exclusive of treasury stock and adjusted for subsequent stock dividends and splits.

Statistical Record:

Operating Profit Margin indicates operating profit as a percentage of net sales or revenues.

Net Profit % is the ratio of income from continuing operations to total revenues, expressed as a percentage.

Return on Equity % is the ratio of income from continuing operations to stockholders' equity, expressed as a percentage. This ratio illustrates how effectively the investment of the stockholders is being utilized to earn a profit.

Return on Assets % represents the ratio of income from continuing operations to total assets. This ratio indicates how effectively assets are being used to produce profit.

Debt/Total Assets represents the ratio of long-term obligations to total assets as a percentage.

Price Ranges are based on each Company's fiscal year. Where actual stock sales did not take place, a range of lowest bid and highest asked prices is shown.

Price/Earnings Ratio is shown as a range. The figures are calculated by dividing the

stock's highest price for the year and its l⦁est price by the year's earnings per sh⦁. Growth stocks tend to command higher P than cyclical stocks.

Average Yield % is the ratio of annual d⦁dends to the real average of the prices over fiscal year.

EDITOR'S NOTE: In order to preserve ⦁ historical relationships between prices, ea⦁ings and dividends, figures are not restated reflect subsequent events. Figures a⦁ presented in U.S. dollars unless otherw⦁ indicated.

K. ADDITIONAL INFORMATION ⦁ each stock includes the officers of the co⦁pany, investor relations contact, address, tel phone and fax numbers, website, transf⦁ agents, auditors, legal counsel and instit⦁ tional holdings.

L. INSTITUTIONAL HOLDINGS indicate the number of investment companies, insu⦁ ance companies, mutual funds, bank trust an⦁ college endowment funds holding the stoc and the total number of shares held as la⦁ reported.

OTHER DEFINITIONS

FACTORS PERTAINING ESPECIALLY TO UTILITIES

Net Income/Net Property % is the ratio of income from continuing operations to net plant (including construction work in figure⦁ indicates the realized rate of return on book value of properties.

Net Income/Total Capitalization % is the ratio between net income and capitalization, which includes all long-term debt obligations and shareholders' equity.

Accumulated Depreciation/Gross Property % reflects the percentage of properties that have been depreciated. A lower percentage indicates a higher book value of properties.

FACTORS PERTAINING ESPECIALLY TO BANKS

Net Interest Income is interest income less interest expenses. It represents the amount of income generated by a bank's primary interest-related business. This figure is presented before any credit loss provisions.

Non-interest Income is any income that is not interest-related. Such income could include, among other things, credit card in income, advisory and other bank fees and gains on securities sales.

Total Deposits are total time and demand deposits entrusted to a bank.

Net Loans are all promissory notes held, including agricultural, commercial, personal, real estate and other loans outstanding, after deducting unearned discount and allowance for possible loan losses.

Equity/Assets % represents the amount of assets that are retained in the Company, or the amount of assets that are not obligated to outside parties.

Non Interest Expense/Total Income % is a measure of how effectively a bank is operating. It is the ratio of non-interest expense to total income.

FACTORS PERTAINING ESPECIALLY TO INSURANCE COMPANIES

Premium Income is the amount of insurance premiums received. This is the primary revenue source for insurance companies.

Net Investment Income is the amount received from investments during a reporting period.

Total Investments represents the invested assets of an insurance company. Certain invested assets may include, among other things, fixed maturities (such as bonds), common equity securities, mortgage loans and short-term investments.

Return on Revenues % (similar to Net Profit %) is the percentage of total revenues remaining after the deduction of all non-extraordinary costs, including interest and taxes.

FACTORS PERTAINING ESPECIALLY TO REAL ESTATE INVESTMENT TRUSTS

Total Income (similar to Total Revenues) is all income from operations. Total Income could include, among other things, rental income, mortgage income and certain interest income.

Net Income + Depreciation/Assets % represents the ratio of income from continuing operations and non-cash depreciation to total assets. This measures how effectively assets are being used to produce cash profits.

HOW TO USE THIS BOOK (Continued)

ABBREVIATIONS
AND
SYMBOLS

(Div. Reinv. Plan)....Dividend Reinvestment Plan Offered

A... Annual

ASE .... American Stock Exchange

( )...Deficit

E... Extra

M ....Monthly

N/A............................. Not Applicable

N.M........................... Not Meaningful

NYS .... New York Stock Exchange

OTC ....Over-The-Counter Market

p .... Preliminary

Q.....................................Quarterly

S .... Semi-annual

Sp...........................Special Dividend

U.........................Frequency Unknown

1ST SOURCE CORP.

Exchange	Symbol	Price	52Wk Range	Yield	P/E
NMS	SRCE	$24.75 (3/31/2004)	24.75-12.70	1.62	27.20

*7 Year Price Score 83.8   *NYSE Composite Index=100   *12 Month Price Score 107.5

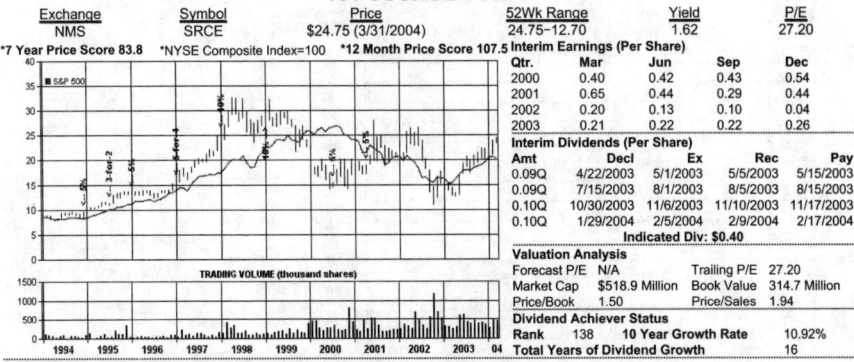

Interim Earnings (Per Share)

Qtr.	Mar	Jun	Sep	Dec
2000	0.40	0.42	0.43	0.54
2001	0.65	0.44	0.29	0.44
2002	0.20	0.13	0.10	0.04
2003	0.21	0.22	0.22	0.26

Interim Dividends (Per Share)

Amt	Decl	Ex	Rec	Pay
0.09Q	4/22/2003	5/1/2003	5/5/2003	5/15/2003
0.09Q	7/15/2003	8/1/2003	8/5/2003	8/15/2003
0.10Q	10/30/2003	11/6/2003	11/10/2003	11/17/2003
0.10Q	1/29/2004	2/5/2004	2/9/2004	2/17/2004
		Indicated Div: $0.40		

Valuation Analysis

Forecast P/E	N/A	Trailing P/E	27.20
Market Cap	$518.9 Million	Book Value	314.7 Million
Price/Book	1.50	Price/Sales	1.94

Dividend Achiever Status

Rank	138	10 Year Growth Rate	10.92%
Total Years of Dividend Growth			16

Business Summary: Commercial Banking (MIC: 8.1 SIC: 6022 NAIC:522110)

1st Source is a registered bank holding company, with $3.33 billion in assets as of Dec 31 2003. Through its subsidiary, 1st Source Bank, Co. provides consumer and commercial banking services to individual and business customers through 60 banking locations in 15 counties in the northern Indiana-southwestern Michigan market area. Co. also competes for business nationwide by offering specialized financing services for used private and cargo aircraft, automobiles for leasing and rental agencies, medium and heavy duty trucks, construction and environmental equipment.

Recent Developments: For the year ended Dec 31 2003, net income jumped 90.8% to $19.2 million compared with $10.0 million in 2002. Total interest income fell 18.6% to $162.3 million from $199.5 million the year before. Total interest expense dropped 26.9% to $59.1 million versus $80.8 million a year earlier. Net interest income declined 13.0% to $103.3 million from $118.7 million a year earlier. Provision for loan losses fell 56.2% to $17.4 million from $39.7 million in 2002. Total non-interest income advanced 9.7% to $80.2 million, reflecting growth in mortgage loan servicing, trust and deposit fees and insurance commission income. Total non-interest expense slid 1.3% to $138.9 million.

Prospects: In the near term, net interest margin may continue to be pressured by a slight change in the mix of Co.'s earning assets and the decrease in the overall level of interest rates. In addition, fees on loans may continue to decrease due to the recognition of these fees over the life of the loans. Meanwhile, Co. is experiencing improvement in the quality of its loan portfolio, evidenced by lower nonperforming assets ratios and lower net charge offs. The ratio of nonperforming assets to net loans and leases was 1.59% on Dec 31 2003 versus 2.79% on Dec 31 2002. Meanwhile, customer acceptance of Co.'s new personal on-line banking product, *InfoSource Online*, bodes well for Co.

Financial Data

(US$ in Thousands)	12/31/2003	12/31/2002	12/31/2001	12/31/2000	12/31/1999	12/31/1998	12/31/1997	12/31/1996
Earnings Per Share	0.91	0.47	1.82	1.79	1.68	1.45	1.23	1.19
Tang. Book Val. Per Share	15.01	14.60	14.58	13.72	12.63	11.32	10.13	11.25
Dividends Per Share	0.370	0.360	0.350	0.330	0.280	0.250	0.220	0.190
Dividend Payout %	40.65	76.59	19.30	18.69	16.81	17.37	18.35	15.97
Income Statement								
Total Interest Income	162,322	199,503	242,183	235,392	200,429	196,148	173,316	148,820
Total Interest Expense	59,070	80,817	123,397	130,425	100,726	102,227	87,324	73,429
Net Interest Income	103,252	118,686	118,786	104,967	99,703	93,921	85,992	75,391
Provision for Loan Losses	17,361	39,657	28,623	14,877	7,442	9,156	6,052	4,649
Non-Interest Income	80,196	73,117	92,836	73,914	63,260	51,521	35,656	25,479
Non-Interest Expense	138,904	137,735	121,232	104,003	99,023	85,500	72,977	60,622
Income Before Taxes	27,183	14,411	61,767	60,001	56,498	50,786	42,619	35,599
Income from Cont Ops	...	13,045	40,708	39,971	38,027	33,241	28,227	...
Net Income	19,154	10,039	38,498	37,573	35,768	31,020	26,489	23,203
Average Shs. Outstg.	21,150	21,310	21,170	20,982	21,210	21,356	21,546	19,401
Balance Sheet								
Cash & Due from Banks	109,787	120,894	129,431	118,123	101,911	132,514	90,864	137,588
Securities Avail. for Sale	1,527,526	1,308,581	1,280,956	1,067,032	1,017,270	983,390	714,841	725,698
Net Loans & Leases	2,160,955	2,266,874	2,477,740	2,264,418	2,022,979	1,840,767	1,761,357	1,323,685
Total Assets	3,330,153	3,407,468	3,562,691	3,182,181	2,872,945	2,732,021	2,418,154	2,079,767
Total Deposits	2,487,215	2,712,905	2,882,806	2,462,724	2,127,452	2,177,107	1,891,791	1,633,978
Long-Term Obligations	79,246	16,878	11,939	12,060	12,174	13,189	16,656	18,596
Total Liabilities	3,015,462	3,098,039	3,211,751	2,866,859	2,589,375	2,471,412	2,178,451	1,907,934
Net Stockholders' Equity	314,691	309,429	306,190	270,572	238,820	215,859	194,953	171,833
Shares Outstanding	20,962	21,188	20,994	19,714	18,901	19,063	19,231	15,268
Statistical Record								
Return on Equity %	6.08	4.21	13.29	14.77	15.92	15.39	14.47	13.50
Return on Assets %	0.57	0.38	1.14	1.25	1.32	1.21	1.16	1.11
Equity/Assets %	9.44	9.08	8.59	8.50	8.31	7.90	8.06	8.26
Non-Int. Exp./Tot. Inc. %	57.27	50.52	36.18	33.62	37.55	34.52	34.92	34.78
Price Range	22.40-12.70	26.68-10.95	28.00-17.08	22.68-14.23	32.43-21.77	32.78-22.86	24.92-14.39	15.29-12.44
P/E Ratio	24.62-13.96	56.77-23.30	15.38-9.39	12.67-7.95	19.30-12.96	22.60-15.77	20.26-11.70	12.85-10.46
Average Yield %	2.09	1.82	1.70	1.88	1.03	0.90	1.14	1.41

Address: 100 North Michigan Street, South Bend, IN 46601
Telephone: (574) 235-5000
Web Site: www.1stsource.com

Officers: Christopher J. Murphy III - Chmn., Pres., C.E.O., Wellington D. Jones III - Exec. V.P.

Investor Contact: (574) 235-2702
Institutional Holding
No of Institutions: 3
Shares: 5,238 **% Held:** -

3M CO

Exchange	Symbol	Price	52Wk Range	Yield	P/E
NYS	MMM	$81.87 (3/31/2004)	85.48–60.80	1.76	27.11

*7 Year Price Score 135.1   *NYSE Composite Index=100   *12 Month Price Score 104.5

Interim Earnings (Per Share)

Qtr.	Mar	Jun	Sep	Dec
2000	0.60	0.59	0.62	0.51
2001	0.56	0.25	0.49	0.49
2002	0.57	0.59	0.69	0.64
2003	0.63	0.78	0.83	0.78

Interim Dividends (Per Share)

Amt	Decl	Ex	Rec	Pay
0.33Q	8/11/2003	8/20/2003	8/22/2003	9/12/2003
100%	8/11/2003	9/30/2003	9/22/2003	9/29/2003
0.33Q	11/10/2003	11/19/2003	11/21/2003	12/12/2003
0.36Q	2/9/2004	2/18/2004	2/20/2004	3/12/2004
			Indicated Div: $1.44	

Valuation Analysis

Forecast P/E	N/A	Trailing P/E	27.11
Market Cap	$31.9 Billion	Book Value	7.9 Billion
Price/Book	8.39	Price/Sales	3.63

Dividend Achiever Status

Rank	260	10 Year Growth Rate	4.75%
Total Years of Dividend Growth			45

Business Summary: Chemicals (MIC: 11.1 SIC: 2891 NAIC:325520)

3M is a diversified technology company with positions in health care, industrial, display and graphics, consumer and office, safety, security and protection services, electronics, telecommunications and electrical, and transportation. In the U.S., Co. has 12 sales offices in 10 states and operates 61 manufacturing facilities in 23 states. Internationally, Co. has 185 sales offices, and operates 75 manufacturing and converting facilities in 28 countries. Co.'s brands include icons such as *Scotch, Post–it, Scotchgard, Thinsulate, Scotch–Brite, Filtrete, Dyneon* and *O–Cel–O*.

Recent Developments: For the year ended Dec 31 2003, net income rose 21.7% to $2.40 billion from $1.97 billion the year before. Earnings for 2003 and 2002 included after–tax charges of $58.0 million and $108.0 million, respectively, related to restructuring and other one–time charges. Net sales grew 11.6% to $18.23 billion. Health care sales improved 12.2% to $4.00 billion, while industrial sales rose 6.6% to $3.35 billion. Display and graphics sales advanced 32.9% to $2.96 billion, and consumer and office sales increased 6.7% to $2.61 billion. Safety, security and protection services sales grew 14.4% to $1.93 billion, while transportation sales rose 10.8% to $1.54 billion.

Prospects: After weathering a difficult business environment through much of 2003, Co. believes that it is well positioned for solid business growth in the coming year as corporate initiatives are helping to drive improvements in productivity, cash flow and top–line growth. For 2004, Co. expects earnings per share to range from $0.80 to $0.82 in the first quarter and between $3.46 and $3.52 for the full year. Sales volumes are expected to grow between 5.0% and 8.0% in 2004. Separately, on Jan 12 2003, Co. entered into an agreement to acquire Hornell International, a global supplier of protective equipment for welding applications based in Sweden, in a cash transaction valued at about $100.0 million.

Financial Data

(US$ in Millions)	12/31/2003	12/31/2002	12/31/2001	12/31/2000	12/31/1999	12/31/1998	12/31/1997	12/31/1996
Earnings Per Share	3.02	2.49	1.79	2.32	2.17	1.48	2.53	1.81
Cash Flow Per Share	4.74	3.78	3.84	2.90	3.73	2.90	2.03	2.64
Tang. Book Val. Per Share	6.62	4.90	6.17	7.16	7.06	7.40	7.31	7.53
Dividends Per Share	1.320	1.240	1.200	1.160	1.120	1.100	1.060	0.960
Dividend Payout %	43.70	49.69	67.03	50.00	51.61	74.07	41.89	53.03
Income Statement								
Total Revenues	18,232	16,332	16,054	16,724	15,659	15,021	15,070	14,236
Total Indirect Exp.	5,234	4,790	5,032	4,879	3,851	4,238	3,815	3,646
Depreciation & Amort.	964	954	1,089	1,025	900	866	870	883
Operating Income	3,713	3,046	2,273	3,058	2,956	2,039	2,675	2,491
Net Interest Inc./(Exp.)	(56)	(41)	(87)	(111)	(109)	(139)	(94)	(79)
Income Taxes	1,202	966	702	1,025	1,032	685	1,241	886
Eqty Earns/Minority Int.	(52)	(65)	(54)	(92)	(85)	(54)	(78)	(77)
Income from Cont Ops	...	...	...	1,857	...	1,213	...	1,516
Net Income	2,403	1,974	1,430	1,782	1,763	1,175	2,121	1,526
Average Shs. Outstg.	795	791	799	799	813	816	838	844
Balance Sheet								
Cash & Cash Equivalents	1,836	618	616	302	441	448	477	744
Total Current Assets	7,720	6,059	6,296	6,379	6,066	6,318	6,168	6,486
Total Assets	17,600	15,329	14,606	14,522	13,896	14,153	13,238	13,364
Total Current Liabilities	5,082	4,457	4,509	4,754	3,819	4,386	3,983	3,606
Long–Term Obligations	1,805	2,140	1,520	971	1,480	1,614	1,015	851
Net Stockholders' Equity	7,885	5,993	6,086	6,531	6,289	5,936	5,926	6,284
Net Working Capital	2,638	1,602	1,787	1,625	2,247	1,932	2,185	2,880
Shares Outstanding	784	780	782	792	797	802	810	834
Statistical Record								
Operating Profit Margin %	20.36	18.65	14.15	18.28	18.87	13.57	17.75	17.49
Return on Equity %	30.47	32.93	23.49	28.43	28.03	20.43	35.79	24.12
Return on Assets %	13.65	12.87	9.79	12.78	12.68	8.57	16.02	11.34
Debt/Total Assets %	10.25	13.96	10.40	6.68	10.65	11.40	7.66	6.36
Price Range	85.25–60.51	65.49–51.85	62.75–43.49	60.97–39.50	51.41–34.94	48.72–34.00	51.75–40.50	42.75–31.31
P/E Ratio	28.23–20.03	26.30–20.82	35.06–24.30	26.28–17.03	23.69–16.10	32.92–22.97	20.45–16.01	23.62–17.30
Average Yield %	1.92	2.04	2.16	2.52	2.56	2.64	2.32	2.76

Address: 3M Center, St. Paul, MN 55144–1000	Officers: W. James McNerney – Chmn., C.E.O., Joseph A. Giordano – Exec. V.P., Intl. Oper.	Investor Contact:651–733–8206
Telephone: (651) 733–1110	Transfer Agents:Wells Fargo Shareowner Services,	Institutional Holding
Web Site: www.3m.com	St. Paul,	No of Institutions: 5
		Shares: 222,885 % Held: –

ABBOTT LABORATORIES

Exchange	Symbol	Price	52Wk Range	Yield	P/E
NYS	ABT	$41.10 (3/31/2004)	47.15–37.85	2.53	23.49

*7 Year Price Score 99.6   *NYSE Composite Index=100   *12 Month Price Score 96.3

Interim Earnings (Per Share)

Qtr.	Mar	Jun	Sep	Dec
2000	0.44	0.44	0.42	0.48
2001	(0.14)	0.34	0.40	0.39
2002	0.54	0.38	0.46	0.40
2003	0.51	0.16	0.48	0.60

Interim Dividends (Per Share)

Amt	Decl	Ex	Rec	Pay
0.245Q	6/20/2003	7/11/2003	7/15/2003	8/15/2003
0.245Q	9/12/2003	10/10/2003	10/15/2003	11/15/2003
0.245Q	12/12/2003	1/13/2004	1/15/2004	2/15/2004
0.26Q	2/20/2004	4/13/2004	4/15/2004	5/15/2004
	Indicated Div: $1.04 (Div. Reinv. Plan)			

Valuation Analysis

Forecast P/E	16.68	Trailing P/E	23.49
Market Cap	$64.2 Billion	Book Value	13.1 Billion
Price/Book	5.57	Price/Sales	3.70

Dividend Achiever Status

Rank	133	10 Year Growth Rate	11.38%
Total Years of Dividend Growth		31

Business Summary: Pharmaceuticals (MIC: 9.1 SIC: 2834 NAIC:325412)

Abbott Laboratories' principal business is the discovery, development, manufacture, and sale of health care products has five reportable revenue segments. The Pharmaceutical Products segment's products include a line of adult and pediatric pharmaceuticals. The Diagnostic Products segment's products include diagnostic systems and tests. The Hospital Products segment's products include acute care injectable drugs and systems. The Ross Products segment's products include a line of pediatric and adult nutritionals. The International segment's products include products marketed and primarily manufactured outside the U.S.

Recent Developments: For the year ended Dec 31 2003, net earnings declined 1.4% to $2.75 billion compared with $2.79 billion the previous year. Results for 2003 and 2002 included pre–tax acquired in–process research and development charges of $100.2 million and $107.7 million, respectively. Net sales increased 11.3% to $19.68 billion from $17.68 billion the prior year. The increase in sales was primarily attributed to a 22.3% improvement in U.S. pharmaceutical sales, largely due to strong sales growth of *Humira*. Sales growth was also fueled by the creation of a new operating model in the Medical Products Group, designed to focus on higher–growth, higher–margin products and businesses.

Prospects: Going forward, Co. will place emphasis on the continued worldwide launch of *Humira*, the launch of several new products in its U.S. immunoassay business and the spin–off of Hospira. Co. expects to complete the spin–off of Hospira in the first half of 2004. Meanwhile, Co. expect earnings for full–year 2004 to range from $2.40 to $2.48 per share. Separately, Co. announced that it has agreed to acquire TheraSense, Inc. for approximately $1.20 billion. TheraSense is a developer, manufacturer and marketer of FreeStyle®blood glucose self–monitoring systems. Co. expects to complete the transaction during the second quarter of 2004.

Financial Data

(US$ in Thousands)

	12/31/2003	12/31/2002	12/31/2001	12/31/2000	12/31/1999	12/31/1998	12/31/1997	12/31/1996
Earnings Per Share	1.75	1.78	0.99	1.78	1.57	1.51	1.34	1.20
Cash Flow Per Share	2.38	2.65	2.27	1.97	1.88	1.76	1.68	1.52
Tang. Book Val. Per Share	2.89	1.92	1.13	4.53	3.78	2.87	2.54	2.47
Dividends Per Share	0.970	0.910	0.820	0.740	0.660	0.580	0.520	0.460
Dividend Payout %	55.42	51.40	82.82	41.57	42.03	38.74	39.17	38.33
Income Statement								
Total Revenues	19,680,561	17,684,663	16,285,246	13,745,916	13,177,625	12,477,845	11,883,462	11,013,460
Total Indirect Exp.	6,884,613	5,648,268	6,642,832	3,968,188	4,051,067	3,965,481	3,987,358	3,664,401
Depreciation & Amort.	1,273,991	1,177,345	1,168,018	827,431	828,006	784,243	727,754	686,085
Operating Income	3,322,532	3,530,141	1,894,032	3,400,575	3,149,375	3,117,923	2,850,426	2,617,061
Net Interest Inc./(Exp.)	(146,213)	(205,220)	(234,759)	(23,221)	(81,765)	(104,118)	(86,802)	(50,924)
Income Taxes	981,532	881,634	333,945	1,029,879	948,931	910,487	856,064	787,517
Income from Cont Ops	2,752,880	2,791,779	1,549,203	2,786,528	2,447,957	2,330,112	2,093,882	...
Net Income	2,753,233	2,793,703	1,550,390	2,785,977	2,445,759	2,333,231	2,094,462	1,882,033
Average Shs. Outstg.	1,571,869	1,573,293	1,565,963	1,565,579	1,557,655	1,545,658	1,561,462	1,562,494
Balance Sheet								
Cash & Cash Equivalents	1,286,421	966,127	713,540	1,156,718	723,296	383,317	259,010	123,084
Total Current Assets	10,290,415	9,121,772	8,419,189	7,376,241	6,419,754	5,553,136	5,038,208	4,480,902
Total Assets	26,715,342	24,259,102	23,296,423	15,283,254	14,471,044	13,216,213	12,061,068	11,125,600
Total Current Liabilities	7,639,535	7,002,202	7,926,817	4,297,540	4,516,711	4,962,126	5,034,468	4,343,717
Long–Term Obligations	3,452,329	4,273,973	4,335,493	1,076,368	1,336,789	1,339,694	937,983	932,898
Net Stockholders' Equity	13,072,258	10,664,553	9,059,432	8,570,906	7,427,595	5,713,661	4,998,677	4,820,182
Net Working Capital	2,650,880	2,119,570	492,372	3,078,701	1,903,043	591,010	3,740	137,185
Shares Outstanding	1,564,517	1,563,068	1,554,530	1,545,934	1,547,019	1,516,063	1,528,188	1,548,898
Statistical Record								
Operating Profit Margin %	16.88	19.96	11.63	24.73	23.89	24.98	23.98	23.76
Return on Equity %	21.05	26.17	17.10	32.51	32.95	40.78	41.88	39.04
Return on Assets %	10.30	11.50	6.64	18.23	16.91	17.63	17.36	16.91
Debt/Total Assets %	12.92	17.61	18.61	7.04	9.23	10.13	7.77	8.38
Price Range	47.15–34.38	57.70–31.00	56.77–42.06	55.75–29.63	52.94–33.38	49.75–32.78	34.31–25.19	28.50–19.38
P/E Ratio	26.94–19.65	32.42–17.42	57.34–42.49	31.32–16.64	33.72–21.26	32.95–21.71	25.61–18.80	23.75–16.15
Average Yield %	2.35	1.98	1.64	1.78	1.51	1.42	1.69	2.03

Address: 100 Abbott Park Road, Abbott Park, IL 60064–6400	Officers: Miles D. White – Chmn., C.E.O., Richard A. Gonzalez – Pres., C.O.O., Medical Products	Investor Contact:847–937–3923
Telephone: (847) 937–6100	Transfer Agents:EquiServe, Providence, RI	Institutional Holding
Web Site: www.abbott.com		No of Institutions: 1,079
		Shares: 979,957,364 % Held: 62.80%

ABM INDUSTRIES, INC.

Exchange	Symbol	Price	52Wk Range	Yield	P/E
NYS	ABM	$17.95 (3/31/2004)	18.80–13.01	2.23	24.59

*7 Year Price Score 107.8 *NYSE Composite Index=100 *12 Month Price Score 96.0

Interim Earnings (Per Share)

Qtr.	Jan	Apr	Jul	Oct
1999–00	0.16	0.20	0.26	0.30
2000–01	0.17	0.24	0.26	(0.02)
2001–02	0.16	0.27	0.25	0.24
2002–03	0.09	0.20	0.21	0.23

Interim Dividends (Per Share)

Amt	Decl	Ex	Rec	Pay
0.095Q	6/10/2003	7/10/2003	7/14/2003	8/4/2003
0.095Q	9/9/2003	10/8/2003	10/13/2003	11/3/2003
0.10Q	12/9/2003	1/8/2004	1/12/2004	2/2/2004
0.10Q	3/9/2004	4/7/2004	4/12/2004	5/3/2004

Indicated Div: $0.40

Valuation Analysis

Forecast P/E	17.47	Trailing P/E	N/A
Market Cap	$884.8 Million	Book Value	N/A
Price/Book	N/A	Price/Sales	N/A

Dividend Achiever Status

Rank	125	10 Year Growth Rate	11.76%
Total Years of Dividend Growth			39

Business Summary: Miscellaneous Business Services (MIC: 12.8 SIC: 7349 NAIC:238210)

ABM Industries and its subsidiaries provide janitorial, parking, engineering, security, lighting and mechanical services for commercial, industrial, institutional and retail facilities in the United States and British Columbia, Canada. Co. conducts business through a number of subsidiaries, which are grouped into seven segments based on the nature of the business operations. Referred to collectively as the ABM Family of Services,at Oct 31 2003 the seven segments were: Janitorial, Parking, Engineering, Security, Lighting, Mechanical and Facility Services.

Recent Developments: For the year ended Oct 31 2003, income from continuing operations fell 17.4% to $36.4 million, before a gain from discontinued operations of $54.1 million, compared with net income of $46.7 million 2002. Earnings for 2002 benefited from the inclusion of a $10.0 million gain from two partial settlements on the World Trade Center insurance claim, and a $2.0 million tax benefit from the adjustment of prior-year estimated tax liabilities. Total revenues climbed 8.9% to $2.26 billion from $2.08 billion a year earlier, reflecting acquisitions completed in 2003 as well as a full year of revenue generated from Lakeside Building Maintenance, acquired in July 2002.

Prospects: On Oct 20 2003, Co. announced that it had acquired the operations of HGO, a provider of janitorial services based in King of Prussia, PA. Assets acquired by Co. include contracts in the greater Philadelphia metropolitan area, including sites in New Jersey and Delaware. Annual revenues from the acquisition are about $40.0 million. At Oct 31 2003, Co. held $111.0 million in cash and had no debt. As a result, Co. is positioned to continue to make acquisitions in its core services. In addition, Co.'s businesses are experiencing solid increases in activity. Consequently, Co. expects fiscal year 2004 income from continuing operations to be in the range of $0.80 to $0.90 per diluted share.

Financial Data
(US$ in Thousands)

	10/31/2003	10/31/2002	10/31/2001	10/31/2000	10/31/1999	10/31/1998	10/31/1997	10/31/1996
Earnings Per Share	0.73	0.92	0.65	0.92	0.82	0.72	0.61	0.52
Cash Flow Per Share	1.20	2.17	1.31	0.39	0.74	0.69	0.63	0.43
Tang. Book Val. Per Share	5.00	4.46	5.08	4.48	3.82	3.11	2.38	2.25
Dividends Per Share	0.370	0.350	0.320	0.300	0.270	0.230	0.190	0.160
Dividend Payout %	51.36	38.31	50.00	32.70	32.72	31.94	31.76	32.14
Income Statement								
Total Revenues	2,262,476	2,191,957	1,950,038	1,807,557	1,629,716	1,501,827	1,252,472	1,086,925
Total Indirect Exp.	172,651	176,931	177,361	164,186	150,902	149,361	132,105	111,105
Depreciation & Amort.	14,829	15,182	26,328	23,524	20,698	19,593	16,118	13,651
Operating Income	54,852	69,328	52,945	72,693	67,232	57,508	46,964	38,105
Net Interest Inc./(Exp.)	(758)	(1,052)	(2,602)	(3,320)	(1,959)	(3,465)	(2,675)	(2,581)
Income Taxes	18,454	22,600	20,119	28,350	27,565	23,578	19,725	16,385
Income from Cont Ops	36,398	...	...	...	...	...	...	...
Net Income	90,458	46,728	32,826	44,343	39,667	33,930	27,239	21,720
Average Shs. Outstg.	50,004	51,015	50,020	47,418	47,496	46,322	43,744	40,482
Balance Sheet								
Cash & Cash Equivalents	110,947	19,427	3,052	2,000	2,139	1,844	1,783	1,567
Total Current Assets	500,648	437,785	465,541	436,819	367,589	324,308	294,417	233,755
Total Assets	795,983	704,939	683,100	641,985	563,384	501,363	467,152	379,770
Total Current Liabilities	256,691	227,090	235,999	212,620	183,310	157,824	156,660	113,798
Long-Term Obligations	...	...	942	36,811	28,903	33,720	38,402	33,664
Net Stockholders' Equity	444,036	386,670	361,177	309,909	270,551	231,134	191,413	157,893
Net Working Capital	243,957	210,695	229,542	224,199	184,279	166,484	137,757	119,957
Shares Outstanding	48,367	48,997	48,778	45,998	44,814	43,202	40,928	38,978
Statistical Record								
Operating Profit Margin %	2.42	3.16	2.71	4.02	4.12	3.82	3.74	3.50
Return on Equity %	8.19	12.08	9.08	14.01	14.32	14.28	13.77	13.22
Return on Assets %	4.57	6.62	4.80	6.90	7.04	6.76	5.83	5.71
Debt/Total Assets %	...	...	0.13	5.73	5.13	6.72	8.22	8.86
Price Range	16.44–12.72	19.43–13.05	19.10–12.50	13.97–9.69	17.31–11.00	18.41–12.63	14.53–7.75	10.09–6.56
P/E Ratio	22.52–17.42	21.12–14.18	29.38–19.23	15.18–10.53	21.11–13.41	25.56–17.53	23.82–12.70	19.41–12.62
Average Yield %	2.49	2.16	2.02	2.49	1.87	1.56	1.85	1.96

Address: 160 Pacific Avenue, San Francisco, CA 94111	Officers: Martin H. Mandles – Chmn., Chief Admin. Officer, Henrik C. Slipsager – Pres., C.E.O.	Institutional Holding No of Institutions: 18
Telephone: (415) 733-4000	Transfer Agents:Mellon Investor Services LLC San Francisco, CA	Shares: 1,114,212 % Held: –
Web Site: www.abm.com		

4

AFLAC INC.

Exchange	Symbol	Price	52Wk Range	Yield	P/E
NYS	AFL	$40.14 (3/31/2004)	41.17–30.10	0.95	26.41

*7 Year Price Score 137.6 *NYSE Composite Index=100 *12 Month Price Score 97.1

Interim Earnings (Per Share)

Qtr.	Mar	Jun	Sep	Dec
2000	0.28	0.37	0.30	0.31
2001	0.33	0.28	0.36	0.31
2002	0.34	0.40	0.45	0.36
2003	0.45	0.48	0.45	0.14

Interim Dividends (Per Share)

Amt	Decl	Ex	Rec	Pay
0.07Q	4/23/2003	5/13/2003	5/15/2003	6/2/2003
0.08Q	7/23/2003	8/12/2003	8/14/2003	9/2/2003
0.08Q	10/22/2003	11/10/2003	11/13/2003	12/1/2003
0.095Q	2/2/2004	2/11/2004	2/13/2004	3/1/2004

Indicated Div: $0.38 (Div. Reinv. Plan)

Valuation Analysis

Forecast P/E	15.26	Trailing P/E	26.41
Market Cap	$20.8 Billion	Book Value	6.6 Billion
Price/Book	2.77	Price/Sales	1.61

Dividend Achiever Status

Rank	60	10 Year Growth Rate	16.59%
Total Years of Dividend Growth	21		

TRADING VOLUME (thousand shares)

Business Summary: Insurance (MIC: 8.2 SIC: 6321 NAIC:524114)

AFLAC is an international insurance organization whose principal subsidiary is American Family Life Assurance Company of Columbus. In addition to life, and health & accident insurance, Co. has pioneered cancer–expense and intensive–care insurance coverage. Co.'s subsidiary Communicorp specializes in printing, advertising, audio–visuals, sales incentives, business meetings and mailings. As of Jul 23 2003, Co. insured more than 40.0 million people worldwide, and offered policies to employees through 271,200 payroll accounts. Also, Co. insures one out of four Japanese households and is the second largest life insurer in Japan in terms of individual policies in force.

Recent Developments: For the year ended Dec 31 2003, net income decreased 3.1% to $795.0 million compared with $821.0 million in 2002. Results for 2003 and 2002 included after–tax realized investment losses of $191.0 million and $15.0 million, and an accounting change charge of $3.0 million and gain of $37.0 million, respectively. Results for 2002 included policyholder protection fund losses of $26.0 million. The decline in earnings reflected lower–than–expected new sales in the U.S. and significant investment losses, partially offset by strong sales increases in Co.'s Japan business and improved brand recognition. Total revenues grew 11.6% to $11.45 billion from $10.26 billion in 2002.

Prospects: Co. will remain focused on writing accounts for smaller businesses as well as increasingly heading toward major corporations. Also, in Japan, Co. expects sales growth to continue to be strong with the second half of the year improving over the first half. For 2004, Co. expects to generate total new annualized premium sales growth in Japan and the U.S. in the range of range of 5.0% to 10.0% in yen terms and of between 10.0% to 12.0% in dollar terms. In addition, for 2004 and 2005, Co. anticipates operating earnings per diluted share growth of 17.0% and 15.0%, respectively, excluding foreign currency translation.

Financial Data

(US$ in Thousands)	12/31/2003	12/31/2002	12/31/2001	12/31/2000	12/31/1999	12/31/1998	12/31/1997	12/31/1996
Earnings Per Share	1.52	1.55	1.28	1.26	1.03	0.88	1.04	0.68
Tang. Book Val. Per Share	13.03	12.42	10.40	8.86	7.27	7.09	6.43	3.57
Dividends Per Share	0.300	0.230	0.190	0.160	0.140	0.120	0.110	0.090
Dividend Payout %	19.73	14.83	15.03	13.09	14.00	14.34	10.69	13.24
Income Statement								
Total Premium Income	9,921,000	8,595,000	8,061,000	8,239,000	7,264,000	5,943,000	5,873,661	5,910,036
Other Income	1,526,000	1,662,000	1,537,000	1,481,000	1,376,000	1,161,000	842,595	1,069,639
Total Revenues	11,447,000	10,257,000	9,598,000	9,720,000	8,640,000	7,104,000	6,716,256	6,979,675
Total Indirect Exp.	543,000	510,000	396,000	273,000	387,000	386,000	286,591	323,147
Inc. Before Inc. Taxes	1,225,000	1,259,000	1,081,000	1,012,000	778,000	551,000	597,597	589,737
Income Taxes	430,000	438,000	394,000	325,000	207,000	64,000	279,797	255,638
Income from Cont Ops	...	...	...	...	...	...	317,800	334,099
Net Income	795,000	821,000	687,000	687,000	571,000	487,000	585,023	394,363
Average Shs. Outstg.	522,138	528,326	537,380	544,906	550,846	551,744	563,192	578,048
Balance Sheet								
Cash & Cash Equivalents	1,052,000	1,379,000	852,000	609,000	616,000	374,000	235,675	...
Premiums Due	1,003,000	849,000	728,000	681,000	639,000	588,000	480,609	480,831
Invst. Assets: Total	42,999,000	37,768,000	31,941,000	31,558,000	31,408,000	26,610,000	22,600,891	20,484,855
Total Assets	50,964,000	45,058,000	37,860,000	37,232,000	37,041,000	31,183,000	29,454,005	25,022,812
Long–Term Obligations	1,409,000	1,312,000	1,207,000	1,079,000	1,111,000	596,000	523,209	353,533
Net Stockholders' Equity	6,646,000	6,394,000	5,425,000	4,694,000	3,868,000	3,770,000	3,430,472	2,125,569
Shares Outstanding	509,892	514,439	521,615	529,209	531,482	531,368	532,872	578,048
Statistical Record								
Return on Equity %	11.96	12.84	12.66	14.63	14.76	12.91	9.26	15.71
Return on Assets %	1.55	1.82	1.81	1.84	1.84	1.54	1.56	1.07
Price Range	36.67-30.08	33.17-23.12	34.83-23.01	36.53-17.19	27.81-19.88	22.00-11.73	14.19-9.38	10.81-7.13
P/E Ratio	24.13-19.79	21.40-14.92	27.21-17.98	28.99-13.64	27.00-19.30	25.00-13.33	13.64-9.01	15.90-10.48
Average Yield %	0.92	0.78	0.66	0.60	0.59	0.74	0.92	1.06

Address: 1932 Wynnton Road, Columbus, GA 31999 **Telephone:** (706) 323–3431 **Web Site:** www.aflac.com	**Officers:** Daniel P. Amos – Chmn., C.E.O., Kriss Cloninger III – Pres., C.F.O., Treas. **Transfer Agents:** AFLAC Incorporated, Columbus, GA	**Investor Contact:** 706–596–3264 **Institutional Holding** **No of Institutions:** 41 **Shares:** 5,225,868 **% Held:** –

5

AIR PRODUCTS & CHEMICALS, INC.

Exchange	Symbol	Price	52Wk Range	Yield	P/E
NYS	APD	$50.12 (3/31/2004)	55.00–40.86	1.84	28.00

*7 Year Price Score 112.7   *NYSE Composite Index=100   *12 Month Price Score 98.0

Interim Earnings (Per Share)

Qtr.	Dec	Mar	Jun	Sep
2000–01	0.62	0.43	0.60	0.68
2001–02	0.52	0.57	0.63	0.64
2002–03	0.58	0.51	0.12	0.58
2003–04	0.58	...	...	...

Interim Dividends (Per Share)

Amt	Decl	Ex	Rec	Pay
0.23Q	5/15/2003	6/27/2003	7/1/2003	8/11/2003
0.23Q	9/18/2003	9/29/2003	10/1/2003	11/10/2003
0.23Q	11/20/2003	12/30/2003	1/2/2004	2/9/2004
0.23Q	3/18/2004	3/30/2004	4/1/2004	5/10/2004
		Indicated Div: $0.92 (Div. Reinv. Plan)		

Valuation Analysis

Forecast P/E	18.26	Trailing P/E	28.00
Market Cap	$11.4 Billion	Book Value	4.0 Billion
Price/Book	3.00	Price/Sales	1.83

Dividend Achiever Status

Rank	212	10 Year Growth Rate	7.06%
Total Years of Dividend Growth	21	

Business Summary: Chemicals (MIC: 11.1 SIC: 2813 NAIC:325120)

Air Products & Chemicals is engaged in the business of industrial gas and related industrial process equipment and is a producer of certain chemicals. The gases business segment recovers and distributes industrial gases such as oxygen, nitrogen, argon, hydrogen, carbon monoxide, carbon dioxide, synthesis gas and helium. The chemicals business segment produces and markets performance materials and chemical intermediates. The equipment business segment designs and manufactures equipment for cryogenic air separation, gas processing, natural gas liquefaction, and hydrogen purification.

Recent Developments: For the three months ended Dec 31 2003, net income climbed 2.4% to $131.8 million compared with income of $128.7 million, before an accounting change charge of $2.9 million, in 2002. Sales amounted to $1.68 billion, up 16.4% from $1.45 billion in the prior–year period. Revenues benefited from higher volumes in the gases and chemicals segments, acquisitions, and favorable currency effects. Operating income increased 2.5% to $198.8 million compared with $194.0 million the year before. Operating income reflected higher volumes and positive acquisition and currency effects, partially offset by higher operating costs.

Prospects: Co. reaffirmed earnings per share for full–year fiscal 2004 in the range of $2.35 to $2.65. Assuming the positive trend in the first quarter of fiscal 2004 continues, Co. expects to achieve the mid to upper end of this range. However, Co. remains cautious about higher raw material costs, economic growth in Europe, and the timing of equipment orders. Meanwhile, Co. expects earnings per share for the second quarter of fiscal 2004 in the range of $0.58 to $0.62. Separately, Co. plans to continue to focus on cost–reduction initiatives and drive portfolio management. Consequently, upfront costs related to these actions could reduce Co.'s earnings outlook for fiscal 2004.

Financial Data

(US$ in Thousands)	3 Mos	09/30/2003	09/30/2002	09/30/2001	09/30/2000	09/30/1999	09/30/1998	09/30/1997
Earnings Per Share	0.58	1.79	2.36	2.33	0.57	2.09	2.48	1.91
Cash Flow Per Share	0.90	4.63	4.77	4.94	5.43	5.04	4.42	4.69
Tang. Book Val. Per Share	13.64	12.99	13.33	13.67	12.30	11.38	11.07	20.07
Dividends Per Share	0.880	0.860	0.810	0.770	0.730	0.690	0.620	0.560
Dividend Payout %	151.72	48.04	34.32	33.04	128.07	33.01	25.00	29.45
Income Statement								
Total Revenues	1,684,900	6,297,300	5,401,200	5,683,700	5,419,100	5,015,000	4,876,000	4,574,400
Total Indirect Exp.	255,900	1,042,900	757,700	894,000	857,000	832,800	1,250,900	1,189,500
Depreciation & Amort.	170,400	10,300	3,800	38,800	35,800	38,200	37,200	49,000
Operating Income	198,800	604,500	774,900	725,900	792,600	712,300	816,100	681,600
Net Interest Inc./(Exp.)	(30,900)	(119,700)	(117,400)	(191,200)	(196,700)	(159,100)	(162,800)	(161,300)
Income Taxes	51,300	147,200	240,800	219,000	(13,700)	203,400	276,900	201,100
Eqty Earns/Minority Int.	15,200	66,400	57,900	76,100	80,000	46,400	38,000	66,300
Income from Cont Ops	...	400,200	...	493,400	86,000	438,100	517,900	385,500
Net Income	131,800	397,300	525,400	465,600	124,200	450,500	546,800	429,300
Average Shs. Outstg.	227,000	223,600	222,700	219,300	216,200	216,000	220,100	224,900
Balance Sheet								
Cash & Cash Equivalents	92,900	76,200	253,700	66,200	94,100	61,600	61,500	52,500
Total Current Assets	2,214,700	2,067,900	1,909,300	1,684,800	1,805,000	1,782,400	1,641,700	1,624,300
Total Assets	9,786,600	9,431,900	8,495,000	8,084,100	8,270,500	8,235,500	7,489,600	7,244,100
Total Current Liabilities	1,441,400	1,581,200	1,256,200	1,352,400	1,374,800	1,857,800	1,265,600	1,124,600
Long–Term Obligations	2,373,700	2,168,600	2,041,000	2,027,500	2,615,800	1,961,600	2,274,300	2,291,700
Net Stockholders' Equity	3,982,500	3,782,500	3,460,400	3,105,800	2,821,300	2,961,600	2,667,300	2,648,100
Net Working Capital	773,300	486,700	653,100	332,400	430,200	(75,400)	376,100	499,700
Shares Outstanding	227,265	227,265	227,219	227,186	229,305	229,304	211,500	119,500
Statistical Record								
Operating Profit Margin %	11.79	9.59	14.34	12.72	14.52	14.16	16.63	14.75
Return on Equity %	3.30	10.58	15.18	15.88	3.04	14.79	19.41	14.55
Return on Assets %	1.34	4.24	6.18	6.10	1.03	5.31	6.91	5.32
Debt/Total Assets %	24.25	22.99	24.02	25.08	31.62	23.81	30.36	31.63
Price Range	53.07–44.50	48.64–37.49	53.05–36.82	48.00–32.94	39.00–24.19	49.00–27.94	45.13–29.75	44.09–29.13
P/E Ratio	91.50–76.72	27.17–20.94	22.48–15.60	20.60–14.14	68.42–42.43	23.44–13.37	18.20–12.00	23.09–15.25
Average Yield %	1.83	1.99	1.74	1.90	2.32	1.85	1.58	1.51

Address: 7201 Hamilton Boulevard, Allentown, PA 18195–1501 **Telephone:** (610) 481–4911 **Web Site:** www.airproducts.com	**Officers:** John P. Jones III – Chmn., Pres., C.E.O., Mark L. Bye – Exec. V.P., Gases & Equipment **Transfer Agents:**American Stock Transfer &Trust Company, New York, NY	**Investor Contact:**610–481–5775 **Institutional Holding** **No of Institutions:** 4 **Shares:** 107,686 **% Held:** –

ALBERTO-CULVER CO.

Exchange	Symbol	Price	52Wk Range	Yield	P/E
NYS	ACV	$43.87 (3/31/2004)	45.82-31.73	0.91	30.89

*7 Year Price Score 151.3   *NYSE Composite Index=100   *12 Month Price Score 101.2

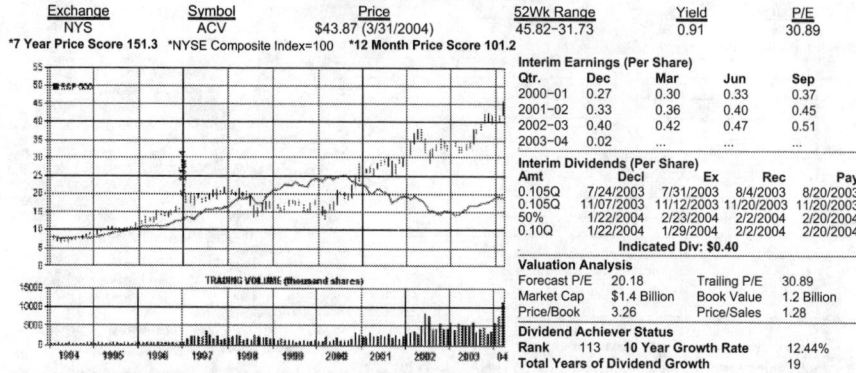

Interim Earnings (Per Share)

Qtr.	Dec	Mar	Jun	Sep
2000-01	0.27	0.30	0.33	0.37
2001-02	0.33	0.36	0.40	0.45
2002-03	0.40	0.42	0.47	0.51
2003-04	0.02	...	...	...

Interim Dividends (Per Share)

Amt	Decl	Ex	Rec	Pay
0.105Q	7/24/2003	7/31/2003	8/4/2003	8/20/2003
0.105Q	11/07/2003	11/12/2003	11/20/2003	11/20/2003
50%	1/22/2004	2/23/2004	2/2/2004	2/20/2004
0.10Q	1/22/2004	1/29/2004	2/2/2004	2/20/2004
	Indicated Div: $0.40			

Valuation Analysis

Forecast P/E	20.18	Trailing P/E	30.89
Market Cap	$1.4 Billion	Book Value	1.2 Billion
Price/Book	3.26	Price/Sales	1.28

Dividend Achiever Status

Rank	113	10 Year Growth Rate	12.44%
Total Years of Dividend Growth			19

Business Summary: Chemicals (MIC: 11.1 SIC: 2844 NAIC:325620)

Alberto-Culver operates under two business segments. The Global Consumer Products segment develops, manufactures, and markets beauty, health care, food and household products to the U.S., Canada and internationally. Major products include *Alberto V05*, *St. Ives*, *TRESemme*, *Motions*, *Just for Me*, *Mrs. Dash* and *Molly McButter*. Co.'s second business, Sally Beauty Company, is comprised of two operations: Sally Beauty Supply, a chain of cash-and-carry outlets offering professional beauty supplies to both salon professionals and retail consumers, and Beauty Systems Group, a full-service beauty products distributor offering professional brands to salons and through professional-only stores.

Recent Developments: For the quarter ended Dec 31 2003, net income dropped 95.2% to $1.7 million from $36.0 million in the equivalent prior-year quarter. Results for 2003 included a non-cash charge of $63.2 million related to Co.'s conversion to one class of common stock. Net sales increased 9.8% to $764.8 million from $696.8 million the previous year, supported by solid results in both its consumer packaged goods and professional beauty supply distribution businesses, the inclusion of the West Coast Beauty Supply acquisition for one month in the quarter, and stronger overseas currency exchange rates. Gross profit improved 10.9% to $382.0 million versus $344.5 million in 2002.

Prospects: Looking ahead, prospects appear promising, supported by good sales and profit growth at Sally Beauty stores, the Beauty Systems Group and the sustainability of Co.'s beauty care businesses. Meanwhile, Co. announced that it will outsource its grocery production to specialty contractors to boost efficiency and to gain access to better research and development facilities for new product development. Separately, Co. noted that due to its conversion to one class of common stock, it will recognize additional pre-tax non-cash charges of $23.6 million during the remainder of fiscal year 2004 and $19.1 million over the next three fiscal years in diminishing amounts.

Financial Data

(US$ in Thousands)	3 Mos	09/30/2003	09/30/2002	09/30/2001	09/30/2000	09/30/1999	09/30/1998	09/30/1997
Earnings Per Share	0.02	1.80	1.54	1.27	1.22	1.00	0.91	0.94
Cash Flow Per Share	0.30	2.42	2.60	1.90	1.49	1.04	1.17	0.92
Tang. Book Val. Per Share	6.79	7.03	5.03	4.60	3.44	3.87	3.83	3.71
Dividends Per Share	0.28	0.27	0.23	0.21	0.19	0.17	0.15	0.13
Dividend Payout %	14.00	14.81	14.94	16.80	15.85	16.67	16.85	13.48
Income Statement								
Total Revenues	764,751	2,891,417	2,650,976	2,494,180	2,247,163	1,975,928	1,834,711	1,775,258
Total Indirect Exp.	373,975	1,168,376	1,060,018	1,087,685	967,923	855,724	791,631	750,483
Depreciation & Amort.	12,553	48,827	47,214	51,405	49,638	42,174	38,105	38,937
Operating Income	8,058	273,791	234,428	189,066	173,490	146,502	140,985	144,359
Net Interest Inc./(Exp.)	(5,380)	(22,391)	(22,636)	(21,830)	(19,209)	(12,719)	(8,607)	(8,238)
Income Taxes	937	89,247	74,127	56,860	51,097	47,493	49,311	50,704
Net Income	1,741	162,153	137,665	110,376	103,184	86,290	83,067	85,417
Average Shs. Outstg.	91,199	89,956	88,821	86,757	84,615	85,743	93,630	95,455
Balance Sheet								
Cash & Cash Equivalents	252,213	370,148	217,485	202,839	114,951	57,816	73,305	87,600
Total Current Assets	1,126,887	1,165,489	984,217	876,949	740,537	645,554	591,565	580,259
Total Assets	2,025,617	1,945,609	1,729,491	1,516,501	1,389,819	1,184,534	1,068,184	1,000,059
Total Current Liabilities	453,597	465,509	460,447	390,303	340,789	336,401	313,625	311,252
Long-Term Obligations	320,564	320,587	320,181	321,183	340,948	225,173	171,760	149,441
Net Stockholders' Equity	1,158,647	1,062,129	862,459	736,009	636,481	568,820	533,991	497,004
Net Working Capital	673,290	699,980	523,770	486,646	399,748	309,153	277,940	269,007
Shares Outstanding	90,032	88,460	87,268	85,242	83,909	83,588	85,815	84,213
Statistical Record								
Operating Profit Margin %	1.05	9.46	8.84	7.58	7.72	7.41	7.68	8.13
Return on Equity %	0.15	15.26	15.96	14.99	16.21	15.17	15.55	17.18
Return on Assets %	0.08	8.33	7.95	7.27	7.42	7.28	7.77	8.54
Debt/Total Assets %	15.82	16.47	18.51	21.17	24.53	19.00	16.07	14.94
Price Range	42.64-39.21	39.39-31.45	38.19-25.61	30.28-19.12	21.08-13.04	18.46-14.71	21.71-13.33	20.96-14.42
P/E Ratio	N.M.	21.88-17.47	24.80-16.63	23.84-15.06	17.28-10.69	18.46-14.71	23.86-14.65	22.30-15.34
Average Yield %	1.02	1.16	1.09	1.22	1.68	1.49	1.19	1.07

Address: 2525 Armitage Avenue, Melrose Park, IL 60160	Officers: Leonard H. Lavin – Chmn., Bernice E. Lavin – Vice-Chmn., Treas., Sec.	Investor Contact:708-450-3000
Telephone: (708) 450-3000	Transfer Agents:EquiServe L.P., Providence, RI	Institutional Holding
Web Site: www.alberto.com		No of Institutions: 13
		Shares: 710,299 % Held: –

ALFA CORP

Exchange	Symbol	Price	52Wk Range	Yield	P/E
NMS	ALFA	$13.61 (3/31/2004)	14.00-12.15	2.35	13.89

*7 Year Price Score 126.9 ***NYSE Composite Index=100** ***12 Month Price Score 91.3**

TRADING VOLUME (thousand shares)

Interim Earnings (Per Share)

Qtr.	Mar	Jun	Sep	Dec
2000	0.20	0.26	0.17	0.22
2001	0.18	0.22	0.23	0.25
2002	0.23	0.20	0.22	0.25
2003	0.23	0.24	0.23	0.28

Interim Dividends (Per Share)

Amt	Decl	Ex	Rec	Pay
0.08Q	4/24/2003	5/13/2003	5/15/2003	5/30/2003
0.08Q	7/23/2003	8/13/2003	8/15/2003	8/29/2003
0.08Q	10/27/2003	11/12/2003	11/14/2003	12/1/2003
0.08Q	1/26/2004	2/11/2004	2/13/2004	3/1/2004
	Indicated Div: $0.32 (Div. Reinv. Plan)			

Valuation Analysis

Forecast P/E	13.52	Trailing P/E	13.89
Market Cap	$1.1 Billion	Book Value	638.5 Million
Price/Book	1.67	Price/Sales	1.73

Dividend Achiever Status

Rank	188	10 Year Growth Rate	8.45%
Total Years of Dividend Growth			18

Business Summary: Insurance (MIC: 8.2 SIC: 6331 NAIC:524126)

Alfa is a financial services holding company that operates predominantly in the insurance industry through its wholly owned subsidiaries Alfa Life Insurance Corporation, Alfa Insurance Corporation, Alfa General Insurance Corporation, Alfa Agency Mississippi, Inc. and Alfa Agency Georgia, Inc. Co.'s insurance subsidiaries write life insurance in Alabama, Georgia and Mississippi, and property and casualty insurance in Georgia and Mississippi. Co. has five non-insurance subsidiaries that are engaged in consumer financing, commercial leasing, residential and commercial construction and real estate sales.

Recent Developments: For the year ended Dec 31 2003, net income grew 9.4% to $78.5 million from $71.7 million the previous year. Total revenues increased 5.2% to $618.0 million from $587.5 million in 2002. Property and casualty insurance premiums rose 7.2% to $459.1 million, due to rate increases in homeowner and auto insurance. Life insurance premiums grew 6.9% to $33.6 million, while revenues from life insurance policy charges increased 3.2% to $32.5 million. Net investment income fell 5.6% to $83.5 million. Operating income was $74.4 million, up 8.8% from $68.4 million the year before.

Prospects: Property and casualty premiums and policy charges should continue to grow, following rate increases in homeowner in February 2003 and in auto in August 2003. Approximately 80.0% of the benefit of the rate increase in auto, which accounts for over 60.0% of Co.'s personal lines written premiums, will occur in 2004. Meanwhile, Co. is experiencing a continuing shift in business mix in favor of term life insurance versus whole life insurance and an increase in mortality to 105.0% from 92.0% in 2002. In January 2004, Co. introduced a new interest-sensitive life insurance product that has been well received and should help improve its growth, especially in traditional life products.

Financial Data

(US$ in Thousands)	12/31/2003	12/31/2002	12/31/2001	12/31/2000	12/31/1999	12/31/1998	12/31/1997	12/31/1996
Earnings Per Share	0.98	0.90	0.88	0.85	0.80	0.69	0.64	0.39
Tang. Book Val. Per Share	7.95	7.09	6.49	6.04	5.16	5.31	4.82	3.96
Dividends Per Share	0.310	0.290	0.280	0.250	0.230	0.210	0.199	0.191
Dividend Payout %	32.14	33.05	31.92	30.00	29.53	31.70	31.05	48.97
Income Statement								
Total Premium Income	525,229	491,105	452,869	429,197	405,330	391,838	370,965	337,186
Net Investment Income	83,509	88,519	84,714	72,891	67,807	62,512	57,529	54,194
Other Income	9,309	7,925	8,713	8,225	9,124	6,636	5,516	4,955
Total Revenues	618,047	587,548	546,296	510,313	482,261	460,986	434,010	396,336
Total Indirect Exp.	143,155	138,085	131,843	116,229	105,274	96,584	87,967	80,115
Inc. Before Inc. Taxes	106,597	99,345	98,094	94,746	92,077	83,265	76,800	45,854
Income Taxes	28,128	27,637	28,133	27,925	27,520	26,549	24,006	13,665
Income from Cont Ops	...	...	69,962	...	...	...	...	...
Net Income	78,469	71,708	69,506	66,821	64,557	56,716	52,794	32,189
Average Shs. Outstg.	80,390	79,546	78,963	78,814	80,471	82,296	81,861	81,573
Balance Sheet								
Cash & Cash Equivalents	10,893	9,762	10,225	4,476	6,650	5,948	5,821	4,424
Premiums Due	40,278	34,044	39,821	36,596	30,158	37,573	26,224	23,930
Invst. Assets: Total	1,421,077	1,308,867	1,202,289	1,182,519	1,058,712	990,378	967,141	813,304
Total Assets	2,045,075	1,884,055	1,697,604	1,546,303	1,335,347	1,246,659	1,170,066	1,019,330
Net Stockholders' Equity	638,512	566,098	509,112	473,561	408,667	423,622	382,931	323,312
Shares Outstanding	80,217	79,278	78,359	78,297	79,084	79,736	79,375	81,573
Statistical Record								
Return on Equity %	12.28	12.66	13.74	14.11	15.79	13.38	13.78	9.95
Return on Assets %	3.83	3.80	4.12	4.32	4.83	4.54	4.51	3.15
Price Range	13.50-10.92	16.05-10.75	12.35-9.06	9.69-7.31	12.13-7.50	12.13-8.13	9.00-5.63	7.25-5.31
P/E Ratio	13.78-11.14	17.83-11.94	14.03-10.30	11.40-8.60	15.16-9.38	17.57-11.78	14.06-8.79	18.59-13.62
Average Yield %	2.46	2.25	2.66	2.87	2.57	2.15	2.70	3.09

Address: 2108 East South Boulevard, Montgomery, AL 36116-2015 **Telephone:** (334) 288-3900 **Web Site:** www.alfains.com	**Officers:** Jerry A. Newby - Chmn., Pres., C. Lee Ellis - Exec. V.P., Oper., Treas.	**Investor Contact:** (334) 288-3900 **Institutional Holding** **No of Institutions:** 18 **Shares:** 245,737,144 **% Held:** -

ALLTEL CORP.

Exchange	Symbol	Price	52Wk Range	Yield	P/E
NYS	AT	$49.89 (3/31/2004)	53.25-43.99	2.97	16.36

*7 Year Price Score 90.6 *NYSE Composite Index=100 ***12 Month Price Score 86.8**

Interim Earnings (Per Share)

Qtr.	Mar	Jun	Sep	Dec
2000	0.68	3.15	1.53	0.84
2001	1.19	0.70	0.71	0.74
2002	0.68	0.69	0.76	0.83
2003	0.73	0.72	0.78	0.82

Interim Dividends (Per Share)

Amt	Decl	Ex	Rec	Pay
0.35Q	4/24/2003	6/5/2003	6/9/2003	7/3/2003
0.35Q	7/24/2003	9/4/2003	9/8/2003	10/3/2003
0.37Q	10/23/2003	12/4/2003	12/8/2003	1/3/2004
0.37Q	1/22/2004	2/20/2004	2/24/2004	4/3/2004

Indicated Div: $1.48 (Div. Reinv Plan)

Valuation Analysis

Forecast P/E	15.05	Trailing P/E	16.36
Market Cap	$15.5 Billion	Book Value	N/A
Price/Book	N/A	Price/Sales	N/A

Dividend Achiever Status

Rank	238	10 Year Growth Rate	5.76%
Total Years of Dividend Growth			43

Business Summary: Communications (MIC: 10.1 SIC: 4813 NAIC:517310)

ALLTEL is a provider of wireless and wireline local, long–distance, network access and Internet services. Telecommunications products are warehoused and sold by Co.'s distribution subsidiary. A subsidiary also publishes telephone directories for affiliates and other independent telephone companies. In addition, a subsidiary provides billing, customer care and other data processing and outsourcing services to telecommunications companies. As of Dec 31 2003, Co. provided wireless communications service to more than 8.0 million customers in 23 states, and local wireline telephone service to nearly 3.1 million customers primarily located in rural areas in 15 states.

Recent Developments: For the twelve months ended Dec 31 2003, income from continuing operations was $953.5 million compared with income of $850.1 million a year earlier. Results for 2003 and 2002 included integration expenses and other charges of $19.0 million and $69.9 million, and gains of $17.9 million and $1.0 million on the disposal of assets, writedown of investments and other non–recurring items, respectively. Total revenues and sales advanced 12.2% to $7.98 billion, reflecting growth in Co.'s communications customer base resulting primarily from acquisitions and the corresponding increase in access revenues. Operating income was $1.90 billion, 10.4% higher than the year before.

Prospects: Co.'s near–term outlook appears good, reflecting decent growth prospects from its wireless segment and mostly stable conditions from its wireline operations. For instance, for the year ended Dec 31 2003, Co. had 7.83 million average wireless customers, a gain of 10.4% from last year. Also, average revenue per customer per month rose 1.1% to $47.51, while average post–pay churn, or the average monthly rate of customer disconnects, improved to 2.09% versus 2.23% in 2002. Meanwhile, although total wireline customers slipped 2.3% to 3.1 million for the quarter ended Dec 31 2003, Co. ended the quarter with 153,028 digital subscriber line (DSL) customers versus 70,182 DSL customers a year earlier.

Financial Data

(US$ in Thousands)	12/31/2003	12/31/2002	12/31/2001	12/31/2000	12/31/1999	12/31/1998	12/31/1997	12/31/1996
Earnings Per Share	3.05	2.96	3.34	6.20	2.47	1.89	2.70	1.52
Cash Flow Per Share	7.91	8.30	6.60	4.72	4.73	4.49	4.25	4.23
Tang. Book Val. Per Share	2.65	N.M	6.86	5.91	7.02	5.81	8.67	8.87
Dividends Per Share	1.400	1.360	1.320	1.280	1.220	1.160	1.100	1.040
Dividend Payout %	45.90	45.94	39.52	20.64	49.39	61.37	40.74	68.42
Income Statement								
Total Revenues	7,979,900	7,983,400	7,598,900	7,067,000	6,302,271	5,194,008	3,263,563	3,192,418
Total Indirect Exp.	2,764,800	2,804,900	1,259,900	1,013,800	952,692	1,014,129	467,636	544,395
Depreciation & Amort.	1,247,700	1,178,600	1,167,900	988,400	862,172	707,129	450,762	424,115
Operating Income	1,898,000	1,815,600	1,664,700	1,667,500	1,525,107	889,026	747,024	591,625
Net Interest Inc./(Exp.)	(378,600)	(349,400)	(288,900)	(310,800)	(280,175)	(263,669)	(130,181)	(130,832)
Income Taxes	580,600	541,200	704,300	1,385,300	547,218	446,864	320,815	169,703
Eqty Earns/Minority Int.	64,400	65,800	57,000	120,500	105,025	114,859	...	...
Income from Cont Ops	953,500	...	1,047,500	1,965,400	...	...	...	...
Net Income	1,330,100	924,300	1,067,000	1,928,800	783,634	525,475	507,886	291,737
Average Shs. Outstg.	312,800	312,300	313,500	317,200	316,814	277,276	187,689	190,370
Balance Sheet								
Cash & Cash Equivalents	657,800	155,500	85,300	67,200	17,595	55,472	16,212	13,874
Total Current Assets	1,729,100	1,646,000	1,767,800	1,780,700	1,167,179	980,831	665,844	709,468
Total Assets	16,661,100	16,389,100	12,609,000	12,182,000	10,774,203	9,374,226	5,633,445	5,359,183
Total Current Liabilities	1,492,700	1,819,200	1,285,100	1,515,900	1,193,967	1,206,508	637,281	590,696
Long–Term Obligations	5,581,200	6,145,500	3,861,500	4,611,700	3,750,413	3,491,755	1,874,172	1,756,142
Net Stockholders' Equity	7,022,200	5,998,100	5,565,800	5,095,400	4,205,737	3,270,822	2,208,506	2,097,107
Net Working Capital	236,400	(173,200)	482,700	264,800	(26,788)	(225,677)	28,563	118,772
Shares Outstanding	312,643	311,182	310,529	312,983	314,257	281,198	183,673	187,200
Statistical Record								
Operating Profit Margin %	23.78	22.74	21.90	23.59	24.19	17.11	22.88	18.53
Return on Equity %	13.57	15.40	18.82	38.57	18.63	16.06	22.99	13.91
Return on Assets %	5.72	5.63	8.30	16.13	7.27	5.60	9.01	5.44
Debt/Total Assets %	33.49	37.49	30.62	37.85	34.80	37.24	33.26	32.76
Price Range	56.05-41.15	62.58-36.93	68.25-50.49	82.69-47.94	91.38-57.06	61.13-39.38	41.38-30.00	35.38-27.00
P/E Ratio	18.38-13.49	21.14-12.48	20.43-15.12	13.34-7.73	36.99-23.10	32.34-20.83	15.32-11.11	23.27-17.76
Average Yield %	2.99	2.74	2.25	2.05	1.72	3.46	3.24	3.38

Address: One Allied Drive, Little Rock, AR 72202	Officers: Joe T. Ford – Chmn., Scott T. Ford – Pres., C.E.O.	Investor Contact:501–905–8991
Telephone: (501) 905–8000	Transfer Agents:Wachovia Bank, Charlotte, NC	Institutional Holding
Web Site: www.alltel.com		No of Institutions: 20
		Shares: 61,697,073 % Held: –

ALTRIA GROUP INC

Exchange	Symbol	Price	52Wk Range	Yield	P/E
NYS	MO	$54.45 (3/31/2004)	58.44–28.10	5.00	12.05

*7 Year Price Score 102.6 *NYSE Composite Index=100 *12 Month Price Score 110.2

Interim Earnings (Per Share)

Qtr.	Mar	Jun	Sep	Dec
2000	0.87	0.95	1.03	0.90
2001	0.80	1.03	1.06	0.99
2002	1.09	1.21	2.06	0.85
2003	1.07	1.20	1.22	1.03

Interim Dividends (Per Share)

Amt	Decl	Ex	Rec	Pay
0.64Q	5/28/2003	6/11/2003	6/13/2003	7/8/2003
0.68Q	8/27/2003	9/11/2003	9/15/2003	10/9/2003
0.68Q	12/10/2003	12/18/2003	12/22/2003	1/9/2004
0.68Q	2/25/2004	3/11/2004	3/15/2004	4/12/2004

Indicated Div: $2.72

Valuation Analysis

Forecast P/E	9.24	Trailing P/E	12.05
Market Cap	$115.1 Billion	Book Value	N/A
Price/Book	N/A	Price/Sales	N/A

Dividend Achiever Status

Rank	129	10 Year Growth Rate	11.61%
Total Years of Dividend Growth			38

Business Summary: Tobacco Products (MIC: 4.2 SIC: 2111 NAIC:312221)

Altria Group, through its wholly-owned subsidiaries, Philip Morris USA Inc., Philip Morris International Inc. and its 84.6% majority-owned subsidiary, Kraft Foods Inc., is engaged in the manufacture and sale of various consumer products, including cigarettes, packaged grocery products, snacks, beverages, cheese and convenient meals. Philip Morris USA's major premium brands are *Marlboro*, *Virginia Slims* and *Parliament*. Its principal discount brand is *Basic*. Philip Morris Capital Corporation, another wholly-owned subsidiary, is primarily engaged in leasing activities.

Recent Developments: For the year ended Dec 31 2003, net earnings were $9.20 billion versus $11.10 billion in 2002. Results for 2003 and 2002 included asset impairment and exit costs of $86.0 million and $223.0 million, partially offset by gains on sales of businesses of $31.0 million and $80.0 million, respectively. Results for 2003 also included a legal settlement charge of $202.0 million and relocation charges of $69.0 million. Results for 2002 included a provision of $290.0 million for airline industry exposure and a gain of $2.63 billion on the sale of Co.'s Miller Brewing Co. business. Net revenue rose 1.8% to $81.83 billion, aided by favorable currency and higher food and international tobacco revenues.

Prospects: Co.'s near-term prospects are mixed. On one hand, Co.'s results should benefit from recent retail gains from its domestic tobacco operations, as well as additional market share gains from its international tobacco unit, Philip Morris International. However, Co.'s outlook is somewhat restrained by the recent sluggish performance of its worldwide Kraft food business, due in part to a weak cookie category that has been hurt by consumers' increased health and wellness focus and lower contributions from new products. Accordingly, Co. is projecting full-year 2004 diluted earnings of between $4.57 and $4.67 per share, which includes $0.23 per share related to Kraft's restructuring program.

Financial Data
(US$ in Thousands)

	12/31/2003	12/31/2002	12/31/2001	12/31/2000	12/31/1999	12/31/1998	12/31/1997	12/31/1996
Earnings Per Share	4.52	5.21	3.88	3.75	3.19	2.20	2.58	2.56
Cash Flow Per Share	5.30	4.98	4.02	4.86	4.73	3.31	3.41	3.08
Dividends Per Share	2.600	2.380	2.170	1.970	1.800	1.640	1.600	1.400
Dividend Payout %	57.52	45.68	55.92	52.53	56.42	74.54	62.01	54.69
Income Statement								
Total Revenues	81,832,000	80,408,000	89,924,000	80,356,000	78,596,000	74,391,000	72,055,000	69,204,000
Total Indirect Exp.	12,893,000	12,753,000	23,975,000	19,449,000	18,700,000	21,016,000	17,762,000	16,224,000
Depreciation & Amort.	9,000	7,000	1,014,000	591,000	582,000	584,000	585,000	594,000
Operating Income	15,910,000	16,601,000	15,702,000	14,679,000	13,490,000	9,977,000	11,663,000	11,769,000
Net Interest Inc./(Exp.)	(1,150,000)	(1,134,000)	(1,418,000)	(719,000)	(795,000)	(890,000)	(1,052,000)	(1,086,000)
Income Taxes	5,151,000	6,424,000	5,407,000	5,450,000	5,020,000	3,715,000	4,301,000	4,380,000
Eqty Earns/Minority Int.	(405,000)	(572,000)	(311,000)	...	...	...	...	...
Income from Cont Ops	...	...	8,566,000	...	...	...	...	...
Net Income	9,204,000	11,102,000	8,560,000	8,510,000	7,675,000	5,372,000	6,310,000	6,303,000
Average Shs. Outstg.	2,038,000	2,129,000	2,210,000	2,272,000	2,403,000	2,446,000	2,442,000	2,463,327
Balance Sheet								
Cash & Cash Equivalents	3,777,000	565,000	453,000	937,000	5,100,000	4,081,000	2,282,000	240,000
Total Current Assets	21,382,000	17,441,000	17,275,000	17,238,000	20,895,000	20,230,000	17,440,000	15,190,000
Total Assets	96,175,000	87,540,000	84,968,000	79,067,000	61,381,000	59,920,000	55,947,000	54,871,000
Total Current Liabilities	21,393,000	19,082,000	20,141,000	25,949,000	18,017,000	16,379,000	15,071,000	14,867,000
Long-Term Obligations	21,163,000	21,355,000	19,163,000	20,181,000	12,226,000	12,615,000	12,430,000	13,134,000
Net Stockholders' Equity	25,077,000	19,478,000	19,620,000	15,005,000	15,305,000	16,197,000	14,920,000	14,218,000
Net Working Capital	(11,000)	(1,641,000)	(2,866,000)	(8,711,000)	2,878,000	3,851,000	2,369,000	323,000
Shares Outstanding	2,037,263	2,039,229	2,152,503	2,208,896	2,338,519	2,430,535	2,425,487	2,431,347
Statistical Record								
Operating Profit Margin %	19.44	20.64	17.46	18.26	17.16	13.41	16.18	17.00
Return on Equity %	36.70	56.99	43.65	56.71	50.14	33.16	42.29	44.33
Return on Assets %	9.57	12.68	10.08	10.76	12.50	8.96	11.27	11.48
Debt/Total Assets %	22.00	24.39	22.55	25.52	19.91	21.05	22.21	23.93
Price Range	54.92–28.10	57.72–36.17	52.96–40.13	45.25–18.88	55.13–22.06	58.31–35.19	47.38–37.12	39.62–28.79
P/E Ratio	12.15–6.22	11.08–6.94	13.65–10.34	12.07–5.03	17.28–6.92	26.51–15.99	18.36–14.39	15.48–11.25
Average Yield %	6.29	4.99	4.59	7.14	4.94	3.70	3.78	4.34

Address: 120 Park Avenue, New York, NY 10017	**Officers:** Louis C. Camilleri – Chmn., C.E.O., Nancy J. De Lisi – Sr. V.P., Mergers & Acquisitions	**Investor Contact:**917–663–3460
Telephone: (917) 663–5000	**Transfer Agents:**First Chicago Trust Company, Jersey City, NJ	**Institutional Holding** No of Institutions: 21
Web Site: www.philipmorris.com		**Shares:** 1,428,928 **% Held:** –

AMBAC FINANCIAL GROUP, INC.

Exchange	Symbol	Price	52Wk Range	Yield	P/E
NYS	ABK	$73.78 (3/31/2004)	79.25-51.61	0.60	15.37

*7 Year Price Score 139.3   *NYSE Composite Index=100   ***12 Month Price Score 99.5**

TRADING VOLUME (thousand shares)

1994 1995 1996 1997 1998 1999 2000 2001 2002 2003 04

Interim Earnings (Per Share)

Qtr.	Mar	Jun	Sep	Dec
2000	0.80	0.86	0.84	0.91
2001	0.90	0.99	1.02	1.06
2002	1.07	1.09	1.21	0.60
2003	1.27	1.48	1.45	1.54

Interim Dividends (Per Share)

Amt	Decl	Ex	Rec	Pay
0.10Q	5/6/2003	5/15/2003	5/19/2003	6/4/2003
0.11Q	7/17/2003	8/7/2003	8/11/2003	9/3/2003
0.11Q	10/16/2003	11/6/2003	11/10/2003	12/3/2003
0.11Q	1/28/2004	2/6/2004	2/10/2004	3/3/2004

Indicated Div: $0.44

Valuation Analysis

Forecast P/E	11.50	Trailing P/E	15.37
Market Cap	$7.8 Billion	Book Value	4.1 Billion
Price/Book	1.67	Price/Sales	5.27

Dividend Achiever Status

Rank	140	10 Year Growth Rate	10.84%
Total Years of Dividend Growth		12	

Business Summary: Insurance (MIC: 8.2 SIC: 6351 NAIC:524130)

Ambac Financial Group is a holding company whose subsidiaries provide financial guarantee products and other financial services to clients in both the public and private sectors. Co. provides financial guarantees for public finance and structured finance obligations through its principal operating subsidiary, Ambac Assurance. Through its financial services subsidiaries, Co. provides financial and investment products including investment agreements, interest rate and total return swaps and funding conduits, principally to its clients which include municipalities and their authorities, school districts, health care organizations and asset-backed issuers.

Recent Developments: For the year ended Dec 31 2003, income was $628.1 million, before a loss from discontinued operations of $9.2 million, versus income of $431.9 million, before income from discontinued operations of $666,000, in 2002. Total revenues increased 32.7% to $1.27 billion. Revenues included a net realized investment gain of $38.4 million in 2003 and a net realized investment loss of $91.7 million in 2002. Net premiums earned and other credit enhancement fees climbed 31.6% to $667.3 million, reflecting increased activity across all markets. Net premiums for Public, Structured and International Finance increased 18.0%, 30.6% and 47.6%, respectively. Net investment income rose 9.1% to $328.1 million.

Prospects: Prospects appear promising across all of Co.'s business. Specifically, the international market, particularly Europe, continues to offer solid growth opportunities, evidenced by continued strong growth in premiums written. Meanwhile, public finance, Co.'s most mature market segment, is benefiting from solid issuance volume and pricing conditions. For the full-year 2004, Co. expects state and local government budget pressures will continue to serve as a catalyst for substantial new and creative insurance opportunities. Accordingly, Co. is targeting 14.0% to 16.0% earnings growth, excluding refundings and investment items.

Financial Data

(US$ in Thousands)	12/31/2003	12/31/2002	12/31/2001	12/31/2000	12/31/1999	12/31/1998	12/31/1997	12/31/1996
Earnings Per Share	5.74	3.97	3.97	3.41	2.87	2.37	2.08	2.63
Tang. Book Val. Per Share	39.70	34.20	28.25	24.59	19.23	19.97	17.84	15.34
Dividends Per Share	0.420	0.380	0.340	0.300	0.280	0.250	0.230	0.200
Dividend Payout %	7.31	9.57	8.56	8.99	9.74	10.67	11.02	7.60
Income Statement								
Total Premium Income	620,317	471,534	378,734	311,276	264,426	113,920	54,289	63,843
Net Investment Income	321,089	297,297	267,847	241,047	209,284	186,190	159,709	144,941
Other Income	330,802	202,987	78,339	68,987	59,607	58,162	68,053	(15,270)
Total Revenues	1,272,208	971,818	724,920	621,310	533,317	358,272	282,051	193,514
Total Indirect Exp.	14,562	7,170	...	...	...	...	...	...
Inc. Before Inc. Taxes	849,589	564,190	568,727	482,124	404,658	230,148	186,285	280,834
Income Taxes	221,490	131,596	135,821	115,952	96,741	74,918	62,966	99,189
Eqty Earns/Minority Int.	...	...	...	...	...	...	...	627
Income from Cont Ops	628,099	...	...	...	...	...	...	...
Net Income	618,915	432,594	432,906	366,172	307,917	155,230	123,319	181,645
Average Shs. Outstg.	109,409	109,066	108,948	107,415	107,049	106,995	106,840	104,895
Balance Sheet								
Cash & Cash Equivalents	328,846	682,395	502,782	554,733	337,484	380,062	231,000	321,414
Premiums Due	7,455	11,947	15,282	9,680	778,787	843,013	293,506	51,766
Invst. Assets: Total	13,776,289	12,539,310	10,287,850	8,323,872	8,962,535	8,748,377	6,915,122	5,200,542
Total Assets	16,747,314	15,355,538	12,267,695	10,120,300	11,345,096	11,212,311	8,249,722	5,875,965
Long-Term Obligations	791,775	616,715	619,315	424,061	423,995	423,929	223,864	223,798
Net Stockholders' Equity	4,254,558	3,625,179	2,983,688	2,596,114	2,018,450	2,096,090	1,872,482	1,615,016
Shares Outstanding	107,144	105,990	105,584	105,550	104,936	104,913	104,920	105,270
Statistical Record								
Return on Revenues %	49.37	44.51	59.71	58.93	57.73	43.32	43.72	93.86
Return on Equity %	14.76	11.93	14.50	14.10	15.25	7.40	6.58	11.24
Return on Assets %	3.75	2.81	3.52	3.61	2.71	1.38	1.49	3.09
Price Range	72.19-44.51	69.69-49.90	63.43-45.50	58.31-26.13	40.92-30.08	43.79-27.54	31.54-21.00	23.00-15.29
P/E Ratio	12.58-7.75	17.55-12.57	15.98-11.46	17.10-7.66	14.26-10.48	18.48-11.62	15.16-10.10	8.75-5.81
Average Yield %	0.68	0.63	0.61	0.75	0.76	0.69	0.90	1.12

Address: One State Street Plaza, New York, NY 10004
Telephone: (212) 668-0340
Web Site: www.ambac.com

Officers: Phillip B. Lassiter – Chmn., Howard C. Pfeffer – Vice–Chmn., Sr. Managing Dir., Public Fin., Investment & Fin. Serv.
Transfer Agents: Citibank, N.A., New York, NY

Investor Contact: (800) 221-1854
Institutional Holding
No of Institutions: 6
Shares: 2,334,020   **% Held:** –

AMERICAN INTERNATIONAL GROUP INC

Exchange	Symbol	Price	52Wk Range	Yield	P/E
NYS	AIG	$71.35 (3/31/2004)	75.12-50.60	0.36	20.21

*7 Year Price Score 95.5   *NYSE Composite Index=100   *12 Month Price Score 93.9

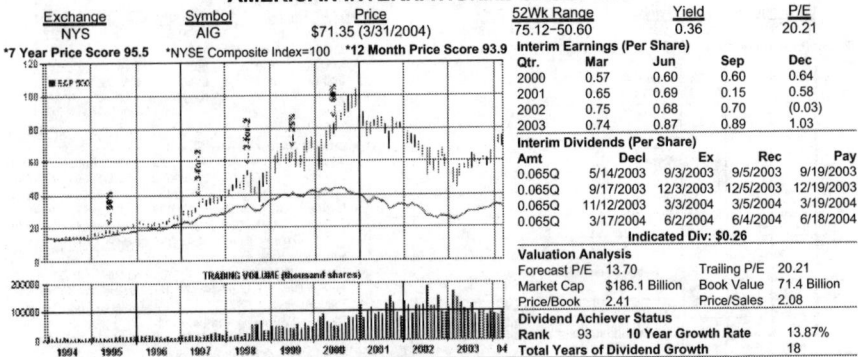

Interim Earnings (Per Share)

Qtr.	Mar	Jun	Sep	Dec
2000	0.57	0.60	0.60	0.64
2001	0.65	0.69	0.15	0.58
2002	0.75	0.68	0.70	(0.03)
2003	0.74	0.87	0.89	1.03

Interim Dividends (Per Share)

Amt	Decl	Ex	Rec	Pay
0.065Q	5/14/2003	9/3/2003	9/5/2003	9/19/2003
0.065Q	9/17/2003	12/3/2003	12/5/2003	12/19/2003
0.065Q	11/12/2003	3/3/2004	3/5/2004	3/19/2004
0.065Q	3/17/2004	6/2/2004	6/4/2004	6/18/2004

Indicated Div: $0.26

Valuation Analysis

Forecast P/E	13.70	Trailing P/E	20.21
Market Cap	$186.1 Billion	Book Value	71.4 Billion
Price/Book	2.41	Price/Sales	2.08

Dividend Achiever Status

Rank	93	10 Year Growth Rate	13.87%
Total Years of Dividend Growth		18

Business Summary: Insurance (MIC: 8.2 SIC: 6331 NAIC:524126)

American International Group is a holding company. Through its subsidiaries, Co. is engaged in a broad range of insurance and insurance–related activities in the United States and abroad. AIG's primary activities include both General and Life Insurance operations. Other activities include Financial Services, and Retirement Services & Asset Management. General Insurance Operations: AIG's General Insurance subsidiaries are multiple line companies writing substantially all lines of property and casualty insurance. Premiums are earned primarily on a pro rata basis over the term of the related coverage.

Recent Developments: For the year ended Dec 31 2003, net income climbed 68.0% to $9.27 billion from $5.52 billion the prior year. Results for 2003 included an accounting charge of $9.0 million and an investment charge of $76.0 million. Results for 2002 included a charge of $1.80 billion from an increase in claim reserves in Co.'s property-casualty insurance group. General insurance premiums grew 30.8% to $31.73 billion. Life insurance premiums rose 12.6% to $22.88 billion. Financial services operating income increased 12.6% to $2.46 billion, while retirement services and asset management operating income rose 25.1% to $1.27 billion. Realized capital losses narrowed to $950.9 million from $1.60 billion in 2002.

Prospects: Going forward, premium rates in the General Insurance business should continue to be strong both domestically and in key international markets, although some lines may begin to moderate. In the Life Insurance segment, Co. expects continued growth through the acquisition of GE Edison in Japan, and its investment in, and agreement to market accident and health products with, the People's Insurance Company of China. Domestically, Co. expects continued strong operating growth, fueled by its expanded distribution and new products. Meanwhile, Co. expects both its Retirement Services operations and its Asset Management operations to continue to benefit

Financial Data

(US$ in Millions)	12/31/2003	12/31/2002	12/31/2001	12/31/2000	12/31/1999	12/31/1998	12/31/1997	12/31/1996
Earnings Per Share	3.53	2.10	2.07	2.41	2.15	1.90	1.68	1.45
Tang. Book Val. Per Share	24.38	20.31	19.93	16.98	14.33	13.78	12.19	11.13
Dividends Per Share	0.220	0.170	0.150	0.140	0.120	0.110	0.100	0.080
Dividend Payout %	6.34	8.47	7.63	5.83	5.87	5.93	5.99	...
Income Statement								
Total Premium Income	54,613	44,589	38,608	31,017	27,486	24,345	22,347	20,833
Other Income	29,556	27,775	16,851	11,423	10,265	6,507	5,601	5,041
Total Revenues	84,169	72,364	55,459	42,440	37,751	30,852	27,947	25,874
Total Indirect Exp.	67,395	59,340	...	...	...	...	...	...
Inc. Before Inc. Taxes	15,341	10,583	8,139	8,349	7,512	5,472	4,617	3,957
Income Taxes	4,264	2,328	2,339	2,458	2,219	1,594	1,367	1,116
Eqty Earns/Minority Int.	(379)	(295)	(301)	(255)	(238)	(112)	82	56
Income from Cont Ops	10,698	7,960	5,499	...	...	...	...	...
Net Income	9,274	5,519	5,363	5,636	5,055	3,766	3,332	2,897
Average Shs. Outstg.	2,628	2,634	2,650	2,343	2,350	1,978	1,982	1,987
Balance Sheet								
Cash & Cash Equivalents	78,869	70,517	65,150	53,692	43,995	36,784	28,972	22,964
Premiums Due	62,285	63,613	60,594	42,012	37,898	35,652	33,109	29,937
Invst. Assets: Total	386,830	308,378	279,763	161,281	140,070	106,279	87,051	79,820
Total Assets	678,346	561,229	492,982	306,577	268,238	194,398	163,971	148,431
Long–Term Obligations	56,003	47,923	37,447	20,672	2,344	1,620	13,885	13,299
Net Stockholders' Equity	71,061	56,950	49,948	38,272	32,411	26,731	23,601	21,644
Shares Outstanding	2,608	2,609	2,615	2,332	2,323	1,968	1,967	1,980
Statistical Record								
Return on Equity %	15.01	13.46	10.54	14.22	15.17	13.88	13.88	13.14
Return on Assets %	1.57	1.41	1.11	1.83	1.88	1.93	2.03	1.95
Price Range	66.28-44.47	79.61-51.10	96.88-67.05	103.7-54.29	74.46-51.53	54.44-35.50	39.80-25.51	27.29-20.89
P/E Ratio	18.78-12.60	37.91-24.33	46.80-32.39	43.02-22.53	34.63-23.97	28.65-18.68	23.69-15.19	18.82-14.41
Average Yield %	0.38	0.26	0.18	0.17	0.19	0.24	0.30	0.34

Address: 70 Pine Street, New York, NY 10270	Officers: Maurice R. Greenberg – Chmn., C.E.O., Thomas R. Tizzio – Sr. Vice–Chmn., Gen. Insurance	Investor Contact:212–770–6293
Telephone: (212) 770-7000	Transfer Agents:EquiServe Trust Company, N.A.	Institutional Holding No of Institutions: 9
Web Site: www.aig.com	Providence RI	Shares: 2,522,843 % Held: –

AMERICAN STATES WATER CO.

Exchange	Symbol	Price	52Wk Range	Yield	P/E
NYS	AWR	$24.40 (3/31/2004)	28.71–23.37	3.62	31.28

*7 Year Price Score 122.7   *NYSE Composite Index=100   *12 Month Price Score 88.3

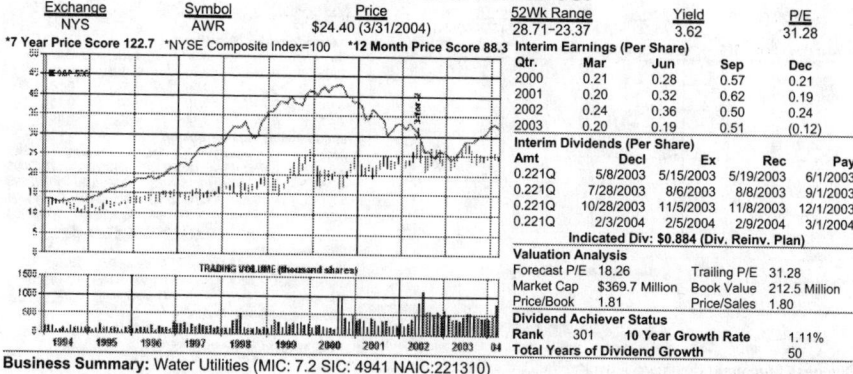

Interim Earnings (Per Share)

Qtr.	Mar	Jun	Sep	Dec
2000	0.21	0.28	0.57	0.21
2001	0.20	0.32	0.62	0.19
2002	0.24	0.36	0.50	0.24
2003	0.20	0.19	0.51	(0.12)

Interim Dividends (Per Share)

Amt	Decl	Ex	Rec	Pay
0.221Q	5/8/2003	5/15/2003	5/19/2003	6/1/2003
0.221Q	7/28/2003	8/6/2003	8/8/2003	9/1/2003
0.221Q	10/28/2003	11/5/2003	11/8/2003	12/1/2003
0.221Q	2/3/2004	2/5/2004	2/9/2004	3/1/2004

Indicated Div: $0.884 (Div. Reinv. Plan)

Valuation Analysis

Forecast P/E 18.26		Trailing P/E 31.28
Market Cap $369.7 Million		Book Value 212.5 Million
Price/Book 1.81		Price/Sales 1.80

Dividend Achiever Status

Rank 301	10 Year Growth Rate	1.11%
Total Years of Dividend Growth		50

Business Summary: Water Utilities (MIC: 7.2 SIC: 4941 NAIC:221310)

American States Water is a public utility that purchases, produces, distributes, and sells water, and distributes electricity through its primary subsidiary Southern California Water Company (SCW). SCW is organized into one electric customer service area and three water service regions operating within 75 communities in 10 counties in California and provides water service in 21 customer service areas. Through its American States Utility Services subsidiary, Co. performs non–regulated, water related services and operations on a contract basis. Co.'s subsidiary, Chaparral City Water Company, is an Arizona public utility company serving Fountain Hills, AZ and and a portion of Scottsdale, AZ.

Recent Developments: For the year ended Dec 31 2003, net income decreased 41.5% to $11.9 million compared with $20.3 million in 2002. The decline in earnings was primarily attributed to lack of timely approval of revenue increases by the public utilities commission of the state of California, a decrease in water demand due to unfavorable weather conditions, and a charge of $6.2 million for refund of water right lease revenues. Operating revenues rose 1.7% to $212.7 million from $209.2 million a year earlier. Total operating expenses grew 4.4% to $179.1 million. Net operating income declined 10.7% to $33.6 million versus $37.6 million a year earlier.

Prospects: On Mar 16 2004, the California Public Utilities Commission (CPUC) authorized an annualized increase of about $8.1 million, or 12.1%, in revenues for Co.'s Southern California Water Company's Region III service area. In addition, Co. was authorized by the CPUC to implement additional rate increases effective during 2004 and 2005 of $4.7 million in the aggregate, subject to CPUC earnings tests. Meanwhile, American States Utility Services is pursuing growth and new business development for Co., most specifically in the area of privatization of water and wastewater systems at military bases.

Financial Data

(US$ in Thousands)	12/31/2003	12/31/2002	12/31/2001	12/31/2000	12/31/1999	12/31/1998	12/31/1997	12/31/1996
Earnings Per Share	0.78	1.34	1.33	1.27	1.19	1.08	1.04	1.12
Cash Flow Per Share	3.07	1.70	2.59	2.18	2.90	2.34	2.14	2.64
Tang. Book Val. Per Share	13.96	14.04	13.22	12.75	11.82	11.48	11.24	11.01
Dividends Per Share	0.880	0.870	0.860	0.850	0.850	0.840	0.830	0.810
Dividend Payout %	113.33	65.02	65.00	67.27	71.43	77.78	79.81	72.32
Income Statement								
Total Revenues	212,669	209,205	197,514	183,960	173,421	148,060	153,755	151,529
Total Indirect Exp.	68,374	55,993	60,612	48,615	48,816	40,649	39,372	36,750
Costs & Expenses	179,064	171,557	160,822	151,653	144,907	123,049	130,297	128,100
Depreciation & Amort.	39,584	36,604	35,902	30,678	27,300	25,076	21,904	20,204
Operating Income	33,605	37,648	36,692	32,307	28,514	25,011	23,458	23,429
Net Interest Inc./(Exp.)	(18,070)	(17,699)	(15,735)	(14,122)	(12,945)	(11,207)	(10,157)	(10,500)
Income Taxes	3,285	12,949	15,379	15,127	13,345	10,130	9,830	10,283
Income from Cont Ops	...	...	...	...	...	14,573	...	...
Net Income	11,892	20,339	20,447	18,086	16,101	14,623	14,059	13,460
Average Shs. Outstg.	15,227	15,157	15,256	14,116	13,437	13,437	13,435	11,836
Balance Sheet								
Net Property	602,298	563,311	539,842	509,096	449,595	414,753	383,623	357,776
Total Assets	757,475	701,650	683,764	616,646	533,181	484,671	457,074	430,922
Long–Term Obligations	229,799	231,089	245,692	176,452	167,363	120,809	115,286	107,190
Net Stockholders' Equity	212,487	213,279	201,582	194,323	160,446	155,899	152,653	148,366
Shares Outstanding	15,212	15,180	15,119	15,113	13,436	13,437	13,437	13,329
Statistical Record								
Operating Profit Margin %	15.80	17.99	18.57	17.56	16.44	16.89	15.25	15.46
Net Inc./Net Property %	1.97	3.61	3.78	3.55	3.58	3.52	3.66	3.76
Net Inc./Tot. Capital %	2.35	4.06	4.06	4.26	4.25	4.48	4.48	4.49
Return on Equity %	5.59	9.53	10.14	9.30	10.03	9.34	9.20	9.07
Accum. Depr./Gross Prop. %	26.98	26.86	26.09	25.40	25.23	25.02	24.57	24.17
Price Range	28.71–21.80	28.85–21.01	25.32–19.35	24.75–17.00	26.50–14.87	19.42–14.50	16.92–13.67	15.92–12.67
P/E Ratio	36.81–27.95	21.53–15.68	19.04–14.55	19.49–13.39	22.27–12.50	17.98–13.43	16.27–13.14	14.21–11.31
Average Yield %	3.54	3.54	3.83	4.17	4.18	5.03	5.52	5.71

Address: 630 East Foothill Blvd., San Dimas, CA 91773–1212	Officers: Lloyd E. Ross – Chmn., Floyd E. Wicks – Pres., C.E.O.	Investor Contact:909–394–3633
Telephone: (909) 394–3600	Transfer Agents:ChaseMellon Shareholder Services, L.L.C., Ridgefield Park, NJ	Institutional Holding No of Institutions: 3
Web Site: www.aswater.com		Shares: 11,514 % Held: –

AMSOUTH BANCORPORATION

Exchange	Symbol	Price	52Wk Range	Yield	P/E
NYS	ASO	$23.51 (3/31/2004)	26.00-19.09	4.08	13.28

*7 Year Price Score 105.5 *NYSE Composite Index=100 *12 Month Price Score 98.2

TRADING VOLUME (thousand shares)

1994 1995 1996 1997 1998 1999 2000 2001 2002 2003 04

Interim Earnings (Per Share)

Qtr.	Mar	Jun	Sep	Dec
2000	0.35	0.26	(0.10)	0.35
2001	0.34	0.36	0.37	0.38
2002	0.40	0.42	0.43	0.43
2003	0.44	0.44	0.45	0.44

Interim Dividends (Per Share)

Amt	Decl	Ex	Rec	Pay
0.23Q	4/17/2003	6/13/2003	6/17/2003	7/1/2003
0.23Q	7/17/2003	9/15/2003	9/17/2003	10/1/2003
0.24Q	10/15/2003	12/17/2003	12/19/2003	1/2/2004
0.24Q	1/15/2004	3/16/2004	3/18/2004	4/1/2004

Indicated Div: $0.96 (Div. Reinv. Plan)

Valuation Analysis

Forecast P/E	11.87	Trailing P/E	13.28
Market Cap	$8.4 Billion	Book Value	2.5 Billion
Price/Book	3.48	Price/Sales	2.93

Dividend Achiever Status

Rank	147	10 Year Growth Rate	10.35%
Total Years of Dividend Growth			33

Business Summary: Commercial Banking (MIC: 8.1 SIC: 6022 NAIC:522110)

AmSouth Bancorporation is a regional bank holding company headquartered in Birmingham, AL. As of Dec 31 2003, Co. had assets of $44.87 billion and operated more than 650 branch banking offices and over 1,200 ATMs in the following southeastern states: Alabama, Florida, Tennessee, Mississippi, Georgia, and Louisiana. Co., through its affiliates, provides a full line of traditional and nontraditional financial services including consumer and commercial banking, small business banking, mortgage lending, equipment leasing, annuity and mutual fund sales, and trust and investment management services.

Recent Developments: For the year ended Dec 31 2003, net income totaled $626.1 million, up 2.8% compared with $609.1 million in the prior year. Net interest income slipped 3.9% to $1.41 billion from $1.47 billion a year earlier. Provision for loan losses fell 18.7% to $173.7 million from $213.6 million the year before. Non-interest revenues climbed 15.7% to $855.8 million from $739.4 million the previous year, stemming from continuing investments in branch expansion and other revenue producing initiatives. Non-interest expenses were $1.21 billion, up 7.0% versus $1.13 billion in 2002. Income before income taxes grew 2.2% to $891.1 million from $871.8 million in the prior year.

Prospects: Results are being positively affected by strong deposit growth and increased demand for commercial, small business, home equity and residential mortgage loans. Meanwhile, earnings are benefiting from growth in non-interest revenues, including increases in deposit service fees, income from trust services, mortgage income and securities gains, along with improving trends in credit quality. Separately, net interest income should continue to benefit from a slower pace of loan and investment prepayments. Looking ahead, Co. is targeting full-year 2004 earnings of between $1.87 and $1.92 per share.

Financial Data

(US$ in Thousands)	12/31/2003	12/31/2002	12/31/2001	12/31/2000	12/31/1999	12/31/1998	12/31/1997	12/31/1996
Earnings Per Share	1.77	1.68	1.45	0.86	0.86	1.44	1.21	0.95
Tang. Book Val. Per Share	9.17	8.81	8.13	7.52	7.56	8.04	7.64	7.38
Dividends Per Share	0.920	0.880	0.840	0.800	0.670	0.530	0.490	0.470
Dividend Payout %	51.97	52.38	57.93	93.02	78.29	36.86	41.02	49.47
Income Statement								
Total Interest Income	2,086,451	2,254,116	2,634,540	3,070,426	2,932,750	1,462,541	1,377,788	1,353,821
Total Interest Expense	671,816	781,476	1,239,656	1,691,323	1,424,804	763,571	701,511	701,440
Net Interest Income	1,414,635	1,472,640	1,394,884	1,379,103	1,507,946	698,970	676,277	652,381
Provision for Loan Losses	173,700	213,550	187,100	227,600	165,626	58,134	67,399	65,171
Non-Interest Income	855,778	739,361	748,222	669,494	847,557	346,626	266,004	235,274
Non-Interest Expense	1,205,577	1,126,622	1,185,394	1,366,435	1,648,506	582,117	526,192	534,232
Income Before Taxes	891,136	871,829	770,612	454,562	541,371	405,345	348,690	288,252
Net Income	626,121	609,147	536,346	329,127	340,468	262,712	226,167	182,676
Average Shs. Outstg.	354,308	362,329	370,948	384,677	396,515	181,921	186,178	191,041
Balance Sheet								
Cash & Due from Banks	1,163,986	1,221,985	1,441,561	1,278,691	1,563,335	619,599	658,500	648,494
Securities Avail. for Sale	7,125,971	4,744,866	4,829,512	1,908,917	5,964,703	3,029,372	2,507,690	2,290,478
Net Loans & Leases	28,205,790	26,969,339	24,760,886	23,764,250	25,903,283	12,586,184	12,058,471	11,901,197
Total Assets	44,866,066	40,571,272	38,600,414	38,464,227	43,406,554	19,794,075	18,622,256	18,407,264
Total Deposits	30,440,353	27,315,624	26,167,017	26,623,304	27,912,443	13,283,804	12,945,197	12,467,599
Long-Term Obligations	7,852,434	6,889,283	6,102,255	5,883,405	5,603,486	3,239,759	1,633,224	1,435,675
Total Liabilities	42,385,847	37,455,275	35,645,315	36,122,571	40,447,349	18,474,050	17,237,011	17,011,435
Net Stockholders' Equity	3,229,669	3,115,997	2,955,099	2,813,407	2,959,205	1,427,629	1,385,245	1,395,829
Shares Outstanding	351,891	353,424	363,035	373,806	391,374	177,376	181,208	189,081
Statistical Record								
Return on Equity %	19.38	19.54	18.14	11.69	11.50	18.40	16.32	13.08
Return on Assets %	1.39	1.50	1.38	0.85	0.78	1.32	1.21	0.99
Equity/Assets %	7.19	7.68	7.65	7.31	6.81	7.21	7.43	7.58
Non-Int. Exp./Tot. Inc. %	40.97	37.63	35.04	36.53	43.60	32.17	32.01	33.61
Price Range	24.58-19.09	22.88-18.28	20.15-15.13	19.88-11.88	34.00-19.00	30.42-21.42	25.11-14.07	14.81-10.33
P/E Ratio	13.89-10.79	13.62-10.88	13.90-10.43	23.11-13.81	39.53-22.09	21.12-14.87	20.75-11.63	15.59-10.88
Average Yield %	4.23	4.19	4.70	5.02	2.58	2.05	2.67	3.89

Address: 1900 Fifth Avenue North, Birmingham, AL 35203
Telephone: (205) 320-7151
Web Site: www.amsouth.com

Officers: C. Dowd Ritter — Chmn., Pres., C.E.O., Candice W. Bagby — Sr. Exec. V.P., Consumer Banking, Mktg.
Transfer Agents:The Bank of New York, New York, NY

Investor Contact:205-801-0265
Institutional Holding
No of Institutions: 26
Shares: 2,232,489 % Held: –

ANCHOR BANCORP WISCONSIN, INC

Exchange	Symbol	Price	52Wk Range	Yield	P/E
NMS	ABCW	$25.29 (3/31/2004)	27.10–22.20	1.74	11.60

*7 Year Price Score 133.3   *NYSE Composite Index=100   *12 Month Price Score 94.1

Interim Earnings (Per Share)

Qtr.	Jun	Sep	Dec	Mar
2000–01	0.29	0.28	0.28	0.31
2001–02	0.35	0.37	0.37	0.46
2002–03	0.42	0.49	0.55	0.56
2003–04	0.59	0.48	0.43	...

Interim Dividends (Per Share)

Amt	Decl	Ex	Rec	Pay
0.10Q	4/21/2003	4/29/2003	5/1/2003	5/15/2003
0.11Q	7/22/2003	7/30/2003	8/1/2003	8/15/2003
0.11Q	10/20/2003	10/29/2003	10/31/2003	11/14/2003
0.11Q	1/20/2004	1/28/2004	1/30/2004	2/15/2004

Indicated Div: $0.44

Valuation Analysis

Forecast P/E	12.90	Trailing P/E	11.60
Market Cap	$632.1 Million	Book Value	293.0 Million
Price/Book	N/A	Price/Sales	N/A

Dividend Achiever Status

Rank	16	10 Year Growth Rate	24.22%
Total Years of Dividend Growth			10

Business Summary: Other Depository Banking (MIC: 8.5 SIC: 6036 NAIC:522120)

Anchor BanCorp Wisconsin is engaged in the savings and loan business through its wholly-owned banking subsidiary, AnchorBank, fsb. Co. also has a non-banking subsidiary, Investment Directions, Inc., which invests in real estate partnerships. Through AnchorBank, Co. offers checking, savings, money market accounts, mortgages, home equity and other consumer loans, student loans, credit cards, annuities and related consumer financial services. AnchorBank also offers banking services to businesses, including checking accounts, lines of credit, secured loans and commercial real estate loans. As of Mar 31 2003, total assets were $3.54 billion and total deposits amounted to $2.57 billion.

Recent Developments: For the quarter ended Dec 31 2003, net income fell 25.9% to $9.9 million versus $13.4 million in the same period of 2002. This decrease was due to lower interest income, partially offset by a decline in interest expense, an increase in non-interest income, and a decrease in income tax expense. Results for 2003 and 2002 included net gains on the sale of loans of $1.7 million and $7.6 million, respectively. Results for 2003 also included a gain of $11.9 million from real estate investment partnership home sales. Net interest income slid 7.4% to $27.5 million. Non-interest income advanced 92.7% to $17.3 million, while non-interest expense grew 70.6% to $28.2 million.

Prospects: Co expects earnings to continue to be negatively affected by a decline in refinance activity. However, asset growth will remain a strategic part of Co.'s business plan. Going forward, Co.'s strategy for asset and liability management is to maintain an interest rate gap that minimizes the impact of interest rate movements on the net interest margin. This strategy includes Co. selling substantially all new originations of long-term, fixed-rate, single-family residential mortgage loans in the secondary market, and invest in adjustable-rate or medium-term, fixed-rate, single-family residential mortgage loans, medium-term mortgage-related securities and consumer loans.

Financial Data

(US$ in Thousands)	9 Mos	6 Mos	3 Mos	03/31/2003	03/31/2002	03/31/2001	03/31/2000	03/31/1999
Earnings Per Share	1.96	2.08	2.19	2.02	1.55	1.16	0.78	1.28
Tang. Book Val. Per Share	12.16	11.80	11.70	11.40	11.12	9.62	9.01	5.68
Dividends Per Share	0.420	0.400	0.380	0.360	0.320	0.290	0.250	0.190
Dividend Payout %	21.43	19.23	17.35	17.94	20.80	25.43	32.05	15.23
Income Statement								
Total Interest Income	144,169	96,928	49,042	209,605	225,701	228,647	202,065	155,966
Total Interest Expense	60,637	40,886	20,582	92,856	128,454	148,096	119,393	93,548
Net Interest Income	83,532	56,042	28,460	116,749	97,247	80,551	82,672	62,418
Provision for Loan Losses	1,350	900	450	1,800	2,485	945	1,306	815
Non–Interest Income	56,530	20,965	13,066	31,018	20,469	15,215	11,946	9,260
Non–Interest Expense	81,533	35,005	18,150	68,004	59,531	51,450	59,985	41,405
Income Before Taxes	57,179	41,102	22,926	79,698	56,846	41,659	35,098	38,214
Eqty Earns/Minority Int.	3,301	...	...	...	...	...	...	...
Net Income	35,231	25,293	14,093	49,563	36,367	26,977	19,502	23,544
Average Shs. Outstg.	23,507	23,669	23,771	24,592	23,462	23,207	25,159	18,379
Balance Sheet								
Securities Avail. for Sale	282,486	513,690	335,766	282,943	211,286	196,184	92,212	79,073
Net Loans & Leases	14,448	49,211	61,666	2,770,988	2,627,248	2,414,976	2,302,721	1,724,242
Total Assets	3,665,544	3,661,558	3,622,614	3,538,621	3,507,076	3,127,474	2,911,152	2,141,688
Total Deposits	2,552,279	2,579,353	2,633,503	2,574,188	2,553,987	2,119,320	1,897,369	1,505,990
Long–Term Obligations	750,729	721,994	607,614	595,816	621,590	712,650	664,446	428,395
Total Liabilities	3,366,904	3,368,541	3,322,915	3,245,617	3,229,564	2,907,862	2,693,937	1,999,449
Net Stockholders' Equity	298,640	293,017	299,699	293,004	277,512	219,612	217,215	142,239
Shares Outstanding	22,910	23,137	23,907	23,942	24,950	22,814	24,088	24,999
Statistical Record								
Return on Equity %	11.79	8.63	4.70	16.91	13.10	12.28	8.97	16.55
Return on Assets %	0.96	0.69	0.38	1.40	1.03	0.86	0.66	1.09
Equity/Assets %	8.14	8.00	8.27	8.28	7.91	7.02	7.46	6.64
Non–Int. Exp./Tot. Inc. %	40.62	29.69	29.22	28.26	24.18	21.09	28.02	25.05
Price Range	26.12–21.95	26.12–21.95	24.46–21.95	24.25–17.99	21.64–13.13	16.75–12.88	20.00–12.75	24.13–15.38
P/E Ratio	17.41–14.63	24.41–20.51	41.46–37.20	12.00–8.91	13.96–8.47	14.44–11.10	25.64–16.35	18.85–12.01
Average Yield %	1.73	1.67	1.63	1.68	1.92	1.89	1.54	0.93

Address: 25 West Main Street, Madison, WI 53703 **Telephone:** (608) 252–8700 **Web Site:** www.anchorbank.com	**Officers:** Douglas J. Timmerman – Chmn., Pres., C.E.O., Michael W. Helser – C.F.O., Treas.	**Investor Contact:** (608) 252–1810 **Institutional Holding** **No of Institutions:** 42 **Shares:** 2,705,026 **% Held:** –

ANHEUSER–BUSCH COS., INC.

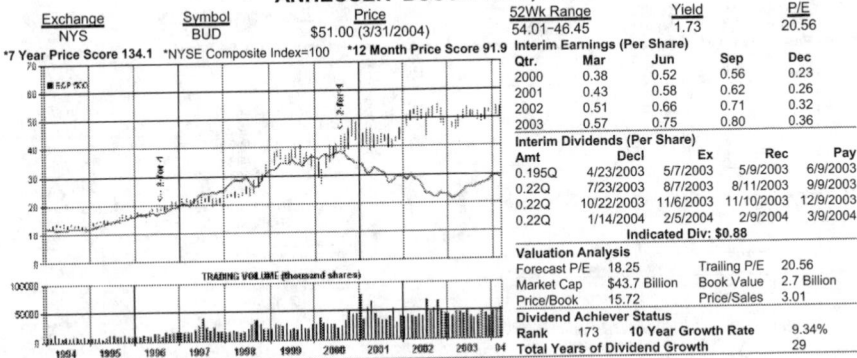

Exchange	Symbol	Price	52Wk Range	Yield	P/E
NYS	BUD	$51.00 (3/31/2004)	54.01–46.45	1.73	20.56

*7 Year Price Score 134.1   *NYSE Composite Index=100   *12 Month Price Score 91.9

Interim Earnings (Per Share)

Qtr.	Mar	Jun	Sep	Dec
2000	0.38	0.52	0.56	0.23
2001	0.43	0.58	0.62	0.26
2002	0.51	0.66	0.71	0.32
2003	0.57	0.75	0.80	0.36

Interim Dividends (Per Share)

Amt	Decl	Ex	Rec	Pay
0.195Q	4/23/2003	5/7/2003	5/9/2003	6/9/2003
0.22Q	7/23/2003	8/7/2003	8/11/2003	9/9/2003
0.22Q	10/22/2003	11/6/2003	11/10/2003	12/9/2003
0.22Q	1/14/2004	2/5/2004	2/9/2004	3/9/2004

Indicated Div: $0.88

Valuation Analysis

Forecast P/E	18.25	Trailing P/E	20.56
Market Cap	$43.7 Billion	Book Value	2.7 Billion
Price/Book	15.72	Price/Sales	3.01

Dividend Achiever Status

Rank	173	10 Year Growth Rate	9.34%
Total Years of Dividend Growth		29

Business Summary: Food (MIC: 4.1 SIC: 2082 NAIC:312120)

Anheuser–Busch Companies is the parent holding company of Anheuser–Busch, Inc., the world's largest brewer of beer. Co.'s beer is sold under brand names including *Budweiser*, *Michelob*, *Busch*, and *Natural Light*. Worldwide sales of Co.'s beer brands aggregated 111.0 million barrels in 2003. Additionally, theme park operations are conducted through Co.'s subsidiary, Busch Entertainment Corporation, which owned nine theme parks as of Dec 31 2003. Co. also engages in packaging, malt and rice production, international beer, non–beer beverages, real estate development, marketing communications, and transportation services.

Recent Developments: For the year ended Dec 31 2003, net income climbed 7.3% to $2.08 billion compared with $1.93 billion the previous year. Net sales grew 4.3% to $14.15 billion from $13.57 billion a year earlier. Domestic beer net sales rose 3.9% to $10.98 billion, reflecting higher revenue per barrel and increased beer volume. International net sales increased 9.4% to $636.6 million, mainly due to volume growth in China. Packaging net sales climbed 2.5% to $1.22 billion, reflecting increased demand for Co.'s can, bottle and label packaging products. Entertainment net sales advanced 7.6% to $923.9 million, largely due to higher admissions pricing and increased in–park spending.

Prospects: In the near term, Co. expects industry volume growth to remain positive. Co. continues to benefit from the favorable pricing environment in the U.S. beer market. Notably, Co.'s low carbohydrate, super–premium *Michelob ULTRA* brand is providing a positive portfolio mix benefit boosting revenue per barrel results. Also, Co.'s *Bud Light* brand continues to increase it share of the premium light segment. Meanwhile, Co. continues to focus on its international growth strategy, which includes growing its business in China and its interest in Mexico's largest brewer, Modelo. Going forward, Co. continues to expect earnings per share growth of 12.0% for 2004.

Financial Data
(US$ in Thousands)

	12/31/2003	12/31/2002	12/31/2001	12/31/2000	12/31/1999	12/31/1998	12/31/1997	12/31/1996
Earnings Per Share	2.48	2.20	1.89	1.69	1.47	1.26	1.18	1.13
Cash Flow Per Share	3.54	3.14	2.61	2.45	2.18	2.23	1.81	1.99
Tang. Book Val. Per Share	2.73	3.19	4.15	4.11	3.79	3.95	3.61	4.05
Dividends Per Share	0.830	0.750	0.690	0.630	0.580	0.540	0.500	0.460
Dividend Payout %	33.46	34.09	36.50	37.27	39.45	42.68	42.37	40.52
Income Statement								
Total Revenues	14,146,700	13,566,400	12,911,500	12,261,800	11,703,700	11,245,800	11,066,200	10,883,700
Total Indirect Exp.	2,498,300	2,455,400	2,220,300	2,174,400	2,147,000	1,958,000	1,916,300	1,780,600
Depreciation & Amort.	877,200	847,300	834,500	803,500	777,000	738,400	683,700	593,900
Operating Income	3,199,300	2,979,700	2,723,000	2,494,700	2,302,300	2,125,300	2,053,000	2,083,800
Net Interest Inc./(Exp.)	(375,400)	(349,700)	(333,200)	(313,800)	(285,300)	(259,700)	(211,200)	(187,900)
Income Taxes	1,093,300	1,041,500	913,200	828,300	762,900	704,300	703,600	736,800
Eqty Earns/Minority Int.	344,900	351,700	240,100	200,000	157,500	85,000	50,300	...
Income from Cont Ops	...	...	...	...	...	...	1,179,200	1,156,100
Net Income	2,075,900	1,933,800	1,704,500	1,551,600	1,402,200	1,233,300	1,169,200	1,189,900
Average Shs. Outstg.	837,000	878,900	901,600	919,700	953,600	975,000	999,400	1,021,200
Balance Sheet								
Cash & Cash Equivalents	191,100	188,900	162,600	159,900	152,100	224,800	147,300	93,600
Total Current Assets	1,630,300	1,504,700	1,550,400	1,547,900	1,600,600	1,640,400	1,583,900	1,465,800
Total Assets	14,689,500	14,119,500	13,862,000	13,084,500	12,640,400	12,484,300	11,727,100	10,463,600
Total Current Liabilities	1,857,200	1,787,700	1,732,300	1,675,700	1,987,200	1,730,300	1,500,700	1,430,900
Long–Term Obligations	7,285,400	6,603,200	5,983,900	5,374,500	4,880,600	4,718,600	4,365,600	3,270,900
Net Stockholders' Equity	2,711,700	3,052,300	4,061,500	4,128,900	3,921,500	4,216,000	4,041,800	4,029,100
Net Working Capital	(226,900)	(283,000)	(181,900)	(127,800)	(386,600)	(89,900)	83,200	34,900
Shares Outstanding	813,100	846,600	879,100	903,600	922,200	953,200	974,040	994,714
Statistical Record								
Operating Profit Margin %	22.61	21.96	21.08	20.34	19.67	18.89	18.55	19.14
Return on Equity %	76.55	63.35	41.96	37.57	35.75	29.25	29.17	28.69
Return on Assets %	14.13	13.69	12.29	11.85	11.09	9.87	10.05	11.04
Debt/Total Assets %	49.59	46.76	43.16	41.07	38.61	37.79	37.22	31.25
Price Range	53.69–45.92	54.97–44.00	46.51–38.50	49.81–27.53	40.94–32.56	34.13–21.69	23.94–19.75	21.56–16.22
P/E Ratio	21.65–18.52	24.99–20.00	24.61–20.37	29.47–16.29	27.85–22.15	27.08–17.21	20.29–16.74	19.08–14.35
Average Yield %	1.65	1.49	1.62	1.62	1.59	2.11	2.32	2.50

Address: One Busch Place, St. Louis, MO 63118	Officers: August A. Busch III – Chmn., Patrick T. Stokes – Pres., C.E.O.	Investor Contact:314–577–9629 Institutional Holding
Telephone: (314) 577–2000	Transfer Agents:Mellon Investor Services, LLC, Ridgefield Park, NJ	No of Institutions: 14
Web Site: www.anheuser-busch.com		Shares: 1,107,435 % Held: –

16

APPLEBEE'S INTERNATIONAL, INC.

Exchange	Symbol	Price	52Wk Range	Yield	P/E
NMS	APPB	$41.28 (3/31/2004)	42.03–27.40	0.17	25.85

*7 Year Price Score 184.9   ***NYSE Composite Index=100**   ***12 Month Price Score 110.6**

Interim Earnings (Per Share)

Qtr.	Mar	Jun	Sep	Dec
2000	0.24	0.27	0.26	0.29
2001	0.29	0.31	0.29	0.26
2002	0.35	0.37	0.37	0.37
2003	0.43	0.35	0.45	0.41

Interim Dividends (Per Share)

Amt	Decl	Ex	Rec	Pay
0.053A	12/14/2001	12/21/2001	12/26/2001	1/29/2002
3-for-2	5/9/2002	6/12/2002	5/24/2002	6/11/2002
0.06A	12/12/2002	12/24/2002	12/27/2002	1/30/2003
0.07A	12/12/2003	12/23/2003	12/26/2003	1/23/2004

Indicated Div: $0.07

Valuation Analysis

Forecast P/E	17.21	Trailing P/E	25.85
Market Cap	$2.3 Billion	Book Value	434.4 Million
Price/Book	N/A	Price/Sales	N/A

Dividend Achiever Status

Rank	62	10 Year Growth Rate 16.23%
Total Years of Dividend Growth		12

Business Summary: Hospitality &Tourism (MIC: 5.1 SIC: 5812 NAIC:722110)

Applebee's International develops, franchises and operates a national chain of casual dining restaurants under the trademark of "Applebee's Neighborhood Grill & Bar." Each of the restaurants is designed as a neighborhood establishment featuring a selection of moderately-priced food and beverage items with full-service luncheon and evening dining. The restaurants feature a selection of entrees, including beef, chicken, seafood and pasta items prepared in a variety of cuisines, as well as appetizers, salads, sandwiches, specialty drinks and desserts. As of Dec 28 2003, there were 1,585 Applebee's restaurants in 49 states and nine countries.

Recent Developments: For the year ended Dec 28 2003, net earnings increased 12.7% to $93.6 million versus $83.0 million in the previous year. Results for 2003 and 2002 included losses on disposition of restaurants and equipment of $699,000 and $1.1 million, respectively. Total revenues advanced 19.4% to $990.1 million from $829.5 million a year earlier. Company restaurant sales jumped 19.7% to $867.2 million, due to restaurant openings and an increase in weighted average weekly sales of 4.6%, as well as the acquisition of franchise restaurants. Franchise royalties and fees rose 7.5% to $109.8 million, while other franchise income surged 389.1% to $13.1 million. Comparable company restaurant sales rose 5.2%.

Prospects: Co.'s franchisees are continuing to implement the "Carside to Go™" program, which should be a significant driver of sales and traffic growth in 2004. Meanwhile, Co. is pleased with early results of several new items being tested in conjunction with an alliance with Weight Watchers. This strategic initiative should contribute to results in the second half of 2004 and beyond. In 2004, Co. anticipates at least 100 new restaurant openings, including 28 company restaurants and between 70 and 80 franchise restaurants. Co. expects capital expenditures for 2004 to range from $80.0 million to $90.0 million, while earnings for 2004 are expected in the range of $1.98 to $2.02 per diluted share.

Financial Data
(US$ in Thousands)

	12/28/2003	12/29/2002	12/30/2001	12/31/2000	12/26/1999	12/27/1998	12/28/1997	12/29/1996
Earnings Per Share	1.64	1.46	1.15	1.06	0.84	0.74	0.63	0.54
Cash Flow Per Share	3.08	2.37	1.84	1.86	1.56	1.35	1.22	0.92
Tang. Book Val. Per Share	6.40	5.45	4.38	3.44	2.70	2.89	3.35	3.08
Dividends Per Share	0.070	0.060	0.053	0.049	0.044	0.040	0.036	0.031
Dividend Payout %	4.27	4.11	4.61	4.62	5.24	5.41	5.71	5.74
Income Statement								
Total Revenues	990,138	826,796	744,344	690,152	669,584	647,562	515,820	413,131
Total Indirect Exp.	109,472	83,795	81,770	73,524	80,549	65,486	58,255	52,816
Depreciation & Amort.	364	381	5,851	5,934	5,997	5,538	3,258	2,293
Operating Income	153,647	129,708	112,427	107,207	94,910	88,562	71,283	58,833
Net Interest Inc./(Exp.)	(1,733)	(2,168)	(7,456)	(9,304)	(10,814)	(9,922)	(1,705)	(1,571)
Income Taxes	52,627	47,109	38,227	36,777	31,537	29,753	26,710	22,711
Income from Cont Ops	...	...	65,650	...	...	50,656	...	...
Net Income	93,558	83,027	64,041	63,161	54,198	50,015	45,091	38,014
Average Shs. Outstg.	56,939	56,922	56,877	59,170	64,352	68,366	71,190	70,173
Balance Sheet								
Cash & Cash Equivalents	17,867	15,169	22,048	10,763	1,427	1,767	8,908	17,346
Total Current Assets	86,622	69,579	67,999	53,181	34,211	34,909	43,954	83,992
Total Assets	644,001	566,114	500,411	471,707	442,216	510,904	377,474	314,111
Total Current Liabilities	149,332	115,186	97,746	93,835	77,662	65,951	62,488	41,843
Long-Term Obligations	20,670	52,186	74,525	90,461	106,293	145,522	22,579	24,435
Net Stockholders' Equity	459,732	392,581	325,183	281,718	253,873	296,053	290,443	244,764
Net Working Capital	(62,710)	(45,607)	(29,747)	(40,654)	(43,451)	(31,042)	(18,534)	42,149
Shares Outstanding	55,192	55,388	55,814	56,744	59,843	66,465	70,834	70,422
Statistical Record								
Operating Profit Margin %	15.51	15.68	15.10	15.53	14.17	13.67	13.81	14.24
Return on Equity %	20.35	21.14	20.18	22.41	21.34	17.11	15.52	15.53
Return on Assets %	14.52	14.66	13.11	13.38	12.25	9.91	11.94	12.10
Debt/Total Assets %	3.20	9.21	14.89	19.17	24.03	28.48	5.98	7.77
Price Range	39.89–23.09	27.27–19.63	24.36–12.75	16.61–9.83	15.33–9.00	11.47–7.22	13.50–8.33	14.89–8.17
P/E Ratio	24.32–14.08	18.68–13.45	21.18–11.09	15.67–9.28	18.25–10.71	15.50–9.76	21.43–13.23	27.57–15.12
Average Yield %	0.20	0.21	0.22	0.32	0.32	0.32	0.27	0.17

Address: 4551 W. 107th Street, Overland Park, KS 66207 **Telephone:** (913) 967–4000 **Web Site:** www.applebees.com	**Officers:** Lloyd L. Hill – Chmn., Pres., C.E.O., Steven K. Lumpkin – Exec. V.P., C.F.O., Treas.	**Investor Contact:** (913) 967–4109 **Institutional Holding** No of Institutions: 24 Shares: 7,829,537 % Held: –

APTARGROUP INC.

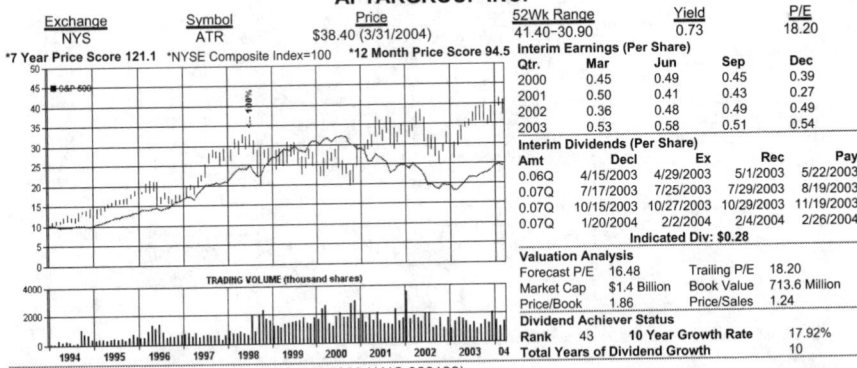

Exchange	Symbol	Price	52Wk Range	Yield	P/E
NYS	ATR	$38.40 (3/31/2004)	41.40-30.90	0.73	18.20

*7 Year Price Score 121.1 *NYSE Composite Index=100 *12 Month Price Score 94.5

Interim Earnings (Per Share)

Qtr.	Mar	Jun	Sep	Dec
2000	0.45	0.49	0.45	0.39
2001	0.50	0.41	0.43	0.27
2002	0.36	0.48	0.49	0.49
2003	0.53	0.58	0.51	0.54

Interim Dividends (Per Share)

Amt	Decl	Ex	Rec	Pay
0.06Q	4/15/2003	4/29/2003	5/1/2003	5/22/2003
0.07Q	7/17/2003	7/25/2003	7/29/2003	8/19/2003
0.07Q	10/15/2003	10/27/2003	10/29/2003	11/19/2003
0.07Q	1/20/2004	2/2/2004	2/4/2004	2/26/2004

Indicated Div: $0.28

Valuation Analysis

Forecast P/E	16.48	Trailing P/E	18.20
Market Cap	$1.4 Billion	Book Value	713.6 Million
Price/Book	1.86	Price/Sales	1.24

Dividend Achiever Status

Rank	43	10 Year Growth Rate	17.92%
Total Years of Dividend Growth		10

Business Summary: Plastics (MIC: 11.7 SIC: 3089 NAIC:326199)

AptarGroup is an international company that designs, manufactures and sells consumer product dispensing systems for the personal care, fragrance/cosmetic, pharmaceutical, household and food/beverage markets. Operations are divided into two segments, Dispensing Systems and SeaquistPerfect. The dispensing segment focuses on providing value-added dispensing systems (pumps, closures and aerosol valves), while SeaquistPerfect sells primarily aerosol valves and certain pumps to the personal care, household, and to a lesser degree, the food/beverage markets. Co. has manufacturing facilities located throughout the world, including North America, Europe, Asia and South America.

Recent Developments: For the year ended Dec 31 2003, net income advanced 19.6% to $79.7 million compared with $66.6 million in 2002. Results for 2003 included an acquired research and development charge of $1.3 million. Results for 2002 included a patent dispute settlement charge of $4.2 million and severance and other charges of $1.1 million. Net sales climbed 20.3% to $1.11 billion from $926.7 million a year earlier. The improvement in sales was primarily attributed to favorable foreign currency exchange as well as stronger sales of custom tooling to customers. Operating income grew 15.8% to $123.9 million versus $107.1 million the year before.

Prospects: Looking ahead, Co. is cautiously optimistic with regard to the coming fiscal year as its outlook continues to be hampered by short-term sales visibility. Presently, Co. expects a slow start to 2004 as increased demand from the pharmaceutical and food/beverage markets may be partially offset by continued soft demand from the fragrance/cosmetic market. For the first quarter of 2004, Co. anticipates diluted earnings per share to be equal or slightly exceed the $0.53 recorded in the corresponding prior-year period. Longer-term, operating results should benefit from the diversity of Co.'s product range, markets served and geographic presence.

Financial Data
(US$ in Thousands)

	12/31/2003	12/31/2002	12/31/2001	12/31/2000	12/31/1999	12/31/1998	12/31/1997	12/31/1996
Earnings Per Share	2.16	1.82	1.61	1.78	1.59	1.65	1.27	1.04
Cash Flow Per Share	3.78	4.21	3.52	3.58	3.20	2.30	2.36	1.88
Tang. Book Val. Per Share	16.75	12.11	9.00	8.54	8.02	10.13	8.37	8.05
Dividends Per Share	0.260	0.240	0.220	0.200	0.180	0.160	0.150	0.140
Dividend Payout %	12.03	13.18	13.66	11.23	11.32	9.69	11.76	13.46
Income Statement								
Total Revenues	1,114,689	926,691	891,986	883,481	834,317	713,506	655,390	615,808
Total Indirect Exp.	258,705	225,895	227,304	215,949	206,177	173,733	158,289	152,158
Depreciation & Amort.	85,851	72,141	73,584	70,949	68,670	54,446	49,917	47,876
Operating Income	123,946	107,073	101,868	113,890	108,436	95,158	78,991	63,996
Net Interest Inc./(Exp.)	(6,901)	(8,612)	(13,750)	(17,238)	(13,076)	(5,305)	(4,121)	(5,198)
Income Taxes	37,591	31,711	29,447	33,256	33,066	38,368	32,067	22,625
Eqty Earns/Minority Int.	928	191	(248)	506	(918)	219	1,991	691
Income from Cont Ops	...	...	58,908	...	...	...	...	...
Net Income	79,679	66,647	58,844	64,666	58,712	60,821	46,529	37,548
Average Shs. Outstg.	36,901	36,623	36,529	36,369	36,913	36,799	36,518	35,800
Balance Sheet								
Cash & Cash Equivalents	164,982	90,205	48,013	55,559	32,416	25,159	17,717	16,386
Total Current Assets	602,454	447,196	374,915	407,549	351,234	316,649	256,161	237,231
Total Assets	1,264,334	1,047,671	915,327	952,239	863,298	714,673	585,433	576,136
Total Current Liabilities	283,220	162,688	154,151	203,102	159,905	167,433	125,397	116,259
Long-Term Obligations	125,196	219,182	239,387	252,752	235,649	80,875	70,740	76,569
Net Stockholders' Equity	783,051	594,467	469,204	440,540	420,269	415,508	342,055	335,699
Net Working Capital	319,234	284,508	220,764	204,447	191,329	149,216	130,764	120,972
Shares Outstanding	37,700	37,200	37,000	36,600	36,500	36,100	36,000	35,800
Statistical Record								
Operating Profit Margin %	11.11	11.55	11.42	12.89	12.99	13.33	12.05	10.39
Return on Equity %	10.17	11.21	12.55	14.67	13.97	14.63	13.60	11.18
Return on Assets %	6.30	6.36	6.43	6.79	6.80	8.51	7.94	6.51
Debt/Total Assets %	9.90	20.92	26.15	26.54	27.29	11.31	12.08	13.29
Price Range	39.48-26.51	38.70-25.12	36.90-27.38	30.00-19.88	30.81-22.75	32.94-20.25	29.38-16.44	21.44-15.13
P/E Ratio	18.28-12.27	21.26-13.80	22.92-17.00	16.85-11.17	19.38-14.31	19.96-12.27	23.13-12.94	20.61-14.54
Average Yield %	0.75	0.75	0.69	0.80	0.66	0.56	0.64	0.78

Address: 475 West Terra Cotta Avenue, Crystal Lake, IL 60014 **Telephone:** (815) 477-0424 **Web Site:** www.aptargroup.com	**Officers:** King Harris – Chmn., Peter Pfeiffer – Vice-Chmn. **Transfer Agents:**National City Bank Corporate Trust Operations., Cleveland, OH	**Institutional Holding** No of Institutions: 31 Shares: 997,090 % Held: –

AQUA AMERICA INC

Exchange	Symbol	Price	52Wk Range	Yield	P/E
NYS	WTR	$21.68 (3/31/2004)	22.55–17.36	2.21	27.44

*7 Year Price Score 139.9   *NYSE Composite Index=100   *12 Month Price Score 99.9

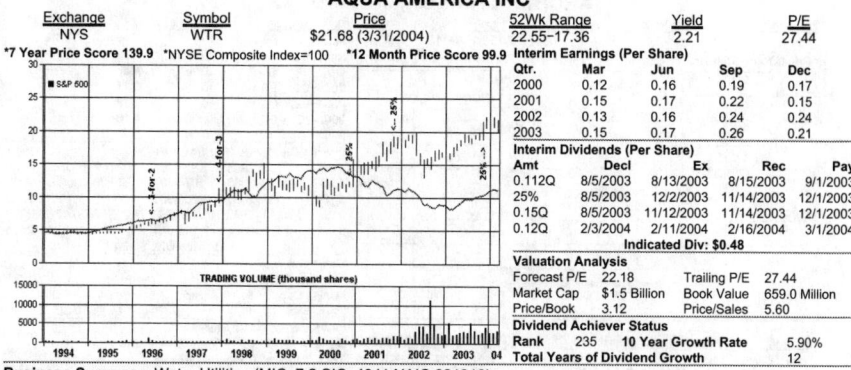

Interim Earnings (Per Share)

Qtr.	Mar	Jun	Sep	Dec
2000	0.12	0.16	0.19	0.17
2001	0.15	0.17	0.22	0.15
2002	0.13	0.16	0.24	0.24
2003	0.15	0.17	0.26	0.21

Interim Dividends (Per Share)

Amt	Decl	Ex	Rec	Pay
0.112Q	8/5/2003	8/13/2003	8/15/2003	9/1/2003
25%	8/5/2003	12/2/2003	11/14/2003	12/1/2003
0.15Q	8/5/2003	11/12/2003	11/14/2003	12/1/2003
0.12Q	2/3/2004	2/11/2004	2/16/2004	3/1/2004

Indicated Div: $0.48

Valuation Analysis

Forecast P/E	22.18	Trailing P/E	27.44
Market Cap	$1.5 Billion	Book Value	659.0 Million
Price/Book	3.12	Price/Sales	5.60

Dividend Achiever Status

Rank	235	10 Year Growth Rate	5.90%
Total Years of Dividend Growth			12

Business Summary: Water Utilities (MIC: 7.2 SIC: 4941 NAIC:221310)

Aqua America is a holding company for regulated utilities providing water or wastewater services to approx. 2,500,000 people in 15 states. Co.'s two primary subsidiaries are Pennsylvania Suburban Water Company, a regulated public utility that provides water or wastewater services to about 1,300,000 residents in the suburban areas north and west of the City of Philadelphia and in ten other counties in PA, and Consumers Water Company, a holding company for several regulated public utility companies that provide water or wastewater service to about 700,000 residents in various communities in four states.

Recent Developments: For the year ended Dec 31 2003, net income grew 5.3% to $70.8 million compared with $67.2 million in 2002. Results for 2003 included five months of financial results for the AquaSource operations that were acquired on Jul 31 2003. Results for 2003 and 2002 included gains on the sale of other assets of $5.7 million and $2.1 million, respectively. Results for 2002 also included gains on the sale of water systems of $5.7 million. Operating revenues advanced 14.0% to $367.2 million from $322.0 million a year earlier. The improvement in revenues was primarily attributed to increased customer base due to acquisitions and higher water rates at several of Co.'s operating companies.

Prospects: Going forward, Co. plans to implement management systems that will allow it to further control costs and improve efficiencies. However, in 2004, Co.'s operating expense ratio is expected to increase from the levels experienced during the past five years due to the AquaSource operations, which have relatively higher fixed operating costs in contrast to the rest of Co.'s operations. Consequently, Co. expects its return on revenues to be lower in 2004 than in the past four years also as a result of the acquisition of AquaSource.

Financial Data

(US$ in Thousands)	12/31/2003	12/31/2002	12/31/2001	12/31/2000	12/31/1999	12/31/1998	12/31/1997	12/31/1996
Earnings Per Share	0.79	0.77	0.69	0.64	0.45	0.52	0.45	0.53
Cash Flow Per Share	1.60	1.40	1.18	1.06	0.91	1.01	0.81	1.00
Tang. Book Val. Per Share	7.11	5.80	5.52	5.13	4.58	4.27	3.56	4.78
Dividends Per Share	0.480	0.430	0.400	0.370	0.350	0.340	0.310	0.300
Dividend Payout %	61.51	55.41	57.98	58.11	79.53	64.55	70.73	56.60
Income Statement								
Total Revenues	367,233	322,028	307,280	275,538	257,326	150,977	136,171	122,503
Total Indirect Exp.	73,070	63,789	61,055	55,484	57,523	26,124	23,473	21,598
Costs & Expenses	213,672	181,524	172,940	157,225	156,281	84,298	79,372	73,213
Depreciation & Amort.	51,463	44,322	40,168	34,100	31,903	16,089	14,580	13,333
Operating Income	153,561	140,504	134,340	118,313	101,045	66,679	56,799	49,290
Net Interest Inc./(Exp.)	(44,662)	(40,396)	(39,859)	(40,360)	(33,698)	(18,975)	(17,890)	(15,311)
Income Taxes	45,923	42,046	38,976	34,105	26,531	19,605	15,873	13,971
Income from Cont Ops	...	...	...	...	...	...	...	19,778
Net Income	70,795	67,206	60,111	52,890	36,384	28,819	23,188	20,743
Average Shs. Outstg.	89,244	86,538	85,943	81,767	80,673	54,445	51,314	37,212
Balance Sheet								
Net Property	1,824,291	1,486,703	1,368,115	1,251,427	1,135,364	609,808	534,483	502,938
Total Assets	2,069,736	1,717,069	1,560,339	1,414,010	1,280,805	701,450	618,472	582,944
Long–Term Obligations	696,666	582,910	516,520	468,769	413,752	261,826	232,471	217,518
Net Stockholders' Equity	659,030	493,097	473,833	432,347	368,901	234,759	194,745	180,015
Shares Outstanding	92,589	84,895	85,483	83,868	80,102	54,154	53,712	36,984
Statistical Record								
Operating Profit Margin %	41.81	43.63	43.71	42.93	39.26	44.16	41.71	40.23
Net Inc./Net Property %	3.88	4.52	4.39	4.22	3.20	4.72	4.33	4.12
Net Inc./Tot. Capital %	5.22	6.24	6.06	5.86	4.64	5.80	5.42	5.16
Return on Equity %	10.74	13.62	12.68	12.23	9.86	12.27	11.90	10.98
Accum. Depr./Gross Prop. %	20.76	19.06	18.42	18.53	18.49	18.20	18.52	17.92
Price Range	22.25–15.77	19.98–13.02	19.39–12.80	15.88–8.64	15.14–10.30	15.23–9.76	11.30–6.00	7.63–5.25
P/E Ratio	28.16–19.96	25.95–16.91	28.10–18.55	24.81–13.50	33.64–22.90	29.29–18.77	25.12–13.33	14.40–9.90
Average Yield %	2.58	2.54	2.49	3.28	2.95	2.87	3.85	4.84

Address: 762 W. Lancaster Avenue, Bryn Mawr, PA 19010–3489 **Telephone:** (610) 524–8000 **Web Site:** www.suburbanwater.com	**Officers:** Nicholas DeBenedictis – Chmn., Pres., Roy H. Stahl – Exec. V.P., Sec., Gen. Couns. **Transfer Agents:** BankBoston, N.A., Boston, MA	**Investor Contact:** 610–525–1400 **Institutional Holding** **No of Institutions:** 11 **Shares:** 333,830 **% Held:** –

ARCHER DANIELS MIDLAND CO.

Exchange	Symbol	Price	52Wk Range	Yield	P/E
NYS	ADM	$16.87 (3/31/2004)	17.59–10.78	1.78	18.74

*7 Year Price Score 95.6   *NYSE Composite Index=100   *12 Month Price Score 101.7

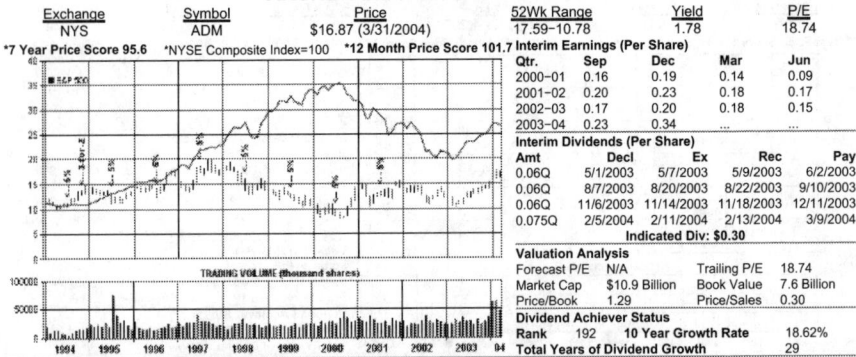

Interim Earnings (Per Share)

Qtr.	Sep	Dec	Mar	Jun
2000-01	0.16	0.19	0.14	0.09
2001-02	0.20	0.23	0.18	0.17
2002-03	0.17	0.20	0.18	0.15
2003-04	0.23	0.34	...	

Interim Dividends (Per Share)

Amt	Decl	Ex	Rec	Pay
0.06Q	5/1/2003	5/7/2003	5/9/2003	6/2/2003
0.06Q	8/7/2003	8/20/2003	8/22/2003	9/10/2003
0.06Q	11/6/2003	11/14/2003	11/18/2003	12/11/2003
0.075Q	2/5/2004	2/11/2004	2/13/2004	3/9/2004

Indicated Div: $0.30

Valuation Analysis

Forecast P/E	N/A	Trailing P/E	18.74
Market Cap	$10.9 Billion	Book Value	7.6 Billion
Price/Book	1.29	Price/Sales	0.30

Dividend Achiever Status

Rank	192	10 Year Growth Rate	18.62%
Total Years of Dividend Growth			29

Business Summary: Food (MIC: 4.1 SIC: 2075 NAIC:311225)

Archer Daniels Midland is engaged in procuring, transporting, storing, processing and merchandising agricultural commodities and products. Co. processes soybeans, cottonseed, sunflower seeds, canola, peanuts, flaxseed and corn germ into vegetable oils and meals primarily for the food and feed industries. In addition, Co.'s corn milling operations produce products for the food and beverage industry, along with ethyl alcohol, or ethanol, which is used as a gasoline additive. Co. also processes wheat, corn and milo into flour.

Recent Developments: For the three months ended Dec 31 2003, net earnings totaled $220.8 million, up 68.3% compared with $131.2 million in the corresponding prior–year period. Results benefited from improved market conditions across many of Co.'s business segments. Net sales and other operating income climbed 17.7% to $9.19 billion from $7.81 billion the year before. Gross profit was $604.3 million, or 6.6% of net sales and other operating income, versus $490.9 million, or 6.3% of net sales and other operating income, a year earlier. Operating profit increased 66.5% to $495.1 million from $297.4 million the year before due to increased ethanol and corn sweetener volumes and strong worldwide demand for grains.

Prospects: Earnings are being positively affected by higher oilseed crushing margins in North America and Asia, increased ethanol sales volumes, and strong worldwide demand for grains and feedstuffs. Oilseeds Processing results are being bolstered by increased demand for protein meal by the poultry and livestock industry, and vegetable oil from the food industry. Meanwhile, Corn Processing sales growth is being driven by increased demand for ethanol, primarily by gasoline refiners in the northeast U.S., higher sweetener and ethanol selling prices and lower net corn costs.

Financial Data

(US$ in Thousands)	6 Mos	3 Mos	06/30/2003	06/30/2002	06/30/2001	06/30/2000	06/30/1999	06/30/1998
Earnings Per Share	0.57	0.23	0.70	0.78	0.58	0.44	0.40	0.58
Cash Flow Per Share	(0.73)	0.26	1.67	2.30	1.30	1.21	1.77	0.89
Tang. Book Val. Per Share	11.20	10.63	10.42	10.39	9.55	9.39	9.13	9.47
Dividends Per Share	0.240	0.240	0.240	0.190	0.180	0.170	0.170	0.160
Dividend Payout %	42.10	104.34	34.28	25.33	32.44	40.04	41.82	27.57
Income Statement								
Total Revenues	17,156,406	7,967,902	30,708,033	23,453,561	20,051,421	12,876,817	14,283,335	16,108,630
Total Indirect Exp.	497,437	231,796	947,694	826,922	731,029	729,358	701,075	660,692
Depreciation & Amort.	340,878	167,114	648,726	614,070	621,974	647,639	622,181	560,110
Operating Income	560,611	221,958	779,444	856,534	700,769	490,217	530,954	720,268
Net Interest Inc./(Exp.)	...	...	(359,971)	(355,956)	(398,131)	(377,404)	(326,207)	(293,220)
Income Taxes	166,681	67,473	179,829	207,844	138,615	52,334	138,545	206,403
Eqty Earns/Minority Int.	...	...	65,991	61,532	104,909	88,206	(4,273)	20,364
Income from Cont Ops	...	...	451,144	...	...	...	281,288	...
Net Income	371,002	150,181	451,145	511,093	383,284	300,903	265,964	403,609
Average Shs. Outstg.	645,992	645,132	646,086	656,955	664,507	669,279	685,328	686,047
Balance Sheet								
Cash & Cash Equivalents	1,247,952	1,364,991	1,309,628	978,661	817,758	931,449	903,569	725,494
Total Current Assets	11,027,823	9,095,264	8,421,857	7,363,231	6,150,301	6,162,367	5,789,588	5,451,714
Total Assets	19,938,630	17,686,389	17,182,879	15,416,273	14,339,931	14,423,100	14,029,881	13,833,534
Total Current Liabilities	7,242,308	5,481,256	5,147,472	4,719,297	3,866,981	4,332,945	3,840,265	3,717,303
Long–Term Obligations	3,865,124	3,855,306	3,872,287	3,111,294	3,351,067	3,277,218	3,191,883	2,847,130
Net Stockholders' Equity	7,605,882	7,217,029	7,069,197	6,754,821	6,331,683	6,110,243	6,240,640	6,504,912
Net Working Capital	3,785,515	3,614,008	3,274,385	2,643,934	2,283,320	1,829,422	1,949,323	1,734,411
Shares Outstanding	647,992	646,664	644,855	649,993	662,378	650,682	683,340	686,611
Statistical Record								
Operating Profit Margin %	3.26	2.78	2.53	3.65	3.49	3.80	3.71	4.47
Return on Equity %	4.87	2.08	6.38	7.56	6.05	4.92	4.50	6.20
Return on Assets %	1.86	0.84	2.62	3.31	2.67	2.08	2.00	2.91
Debt/Total Assets %	19.38	21.79	22.53	20.18	23.36	22.72	22.75	20.58
Price Range	15.22–12.08	14.06–12.08	14.28–10.54	15.60–12.00	15.20–7.92	13.34–8.22	16.25–11.99	19.90–15.32
P/E Ratio	26.70–21.19	61.13–52.52	20.40–15.06	20.00–15.38	26.21–13.65	30.31–18.68	40.62–29.96	34.31–26.42
Average Yield %	1.75	1.83	1.98	1.39	1.58	1.57	1.23	0.89

Address: 4666 Faries Parkway,	Officers: G. Allen Andreas – Chmn., C.E.O., Paul B.	Investor Contact:217–424–4586
Decatur, IL 62525	Mulhollem – Pres., C.O.O.	Institutional Holding
Telephone: (217) 424–5200	Transfer Agents:Hickory Point Bank &Trust, fsb,	No of Institutions: 14
Web Site: www.admworld.com	Decatur, IL	Shares: 3,927,928 % Held: –

ARROW INTERNATIONAL,INC.

Exchange	Symbol	Price	52Wk Range	Yield	P/E
NMS	ARRO	$29.89 (3/31/2004)	29.89–20.40	1.20	25.12

*7 Year Price Score 131.4   *NYSE Composite Index=100   ***12 Month Price Score 102.3**

Interim Earnings (Per Share)

Qtr.	Nov	Feb	May	Aug
2000–01	0.25	0.26	0.27	0.27
2001–02	0.27	0.29	0.25	0.08
2002–03	0.26	0.27	0.33	0.18
2003–04	0.33	0.35	...	...

Interim Dividends (Per Share)

Amt	Decl	Ex	Rec	Pay
2–for–1	7/16/2003	8/18/2003	8/1/2003	8/15/2003
0.08Q	7/16/2003	8/27/2003	8/29/2003	9/12/2003
0.08Q	11/14/2003	11/25/2003	11/28/2003	12/12/2003
0.09Q	2/13/2004	2/25/2004	2/27/2004	3/12/2004

Indicated Div: $0.36

Valuation Analysis

Forecast P/E	N/A	Trailing P/E	25.12
Market Cap	$656.7 Million	Book Value	390.6 Million
Price/Book	N/A	Price/Sales	N/A

Dividend Achiever Status

Rank	52	10 Year Growth Rate	16.98%
Total Years of Dividend Growth			11

Business Summary: Medical Instruments &Equipment (MIC: 9.6 SIC: 3841 NAIC:339112)

Arrow International, Inc. develops, manufactures and markets a broad range of clinically advanced, disposable catheters and related products for critical and cardiac care. Co.'s critical care products are used principally for central vascular access in the administration of fluids, drugs, and blood products, patient monitoring and diagnostic purposes. Co.'s cardiac care products include cardiac assist products, such as intra-aortic balloon pumps and catheters, which are used primarily to augment temporarily the pumping capability of the heart following cardiac surgery, serious heart attack or balloon angioplasty.

Recent Developments: For the three months ended Feb 29 2004, net income improved 29.6% to $15.4 million compared with $11.9 million in the corresponding quarter of the previous year. Net sales increased 16.8% to $108.3 million from $92.8 million in the year-earlier period. The increase in sales was primarily due to favorable currency exchange rates and recent acquisitions. Sales of critical care products climbed 17.2% to $92.0 million from $78.5 million, while sales of cardiac care products advanced 14.0% to $16.3 million from $14.3 million in the prior-year quarter. Operating income jumped 30.6% to $23.0 million versus $17.6 million the year before.

Prospects: Co. will continue to focus on its strategy to grow its core business. Co.'s core growth rate for the first six months of fiscal 2004 was 9.7%, which is slightly below its goal of double-digit growth. The growth reflects continued growth of sharps protection kits for Central Venous Catheters, continued growth of the StimuCath® regional anesthesia catheter, new leadership and stronger sales and marketing in Europe. In 2004, Co. expects sales to range from $424.0 million to $428.0 million and diluted earnings from $1.35 to $1.40 per share. Co.'s sales and earnings targets reflect additional spending on the introduction of the AutoCAT® 2 WAVE™ and support of the LionHeart™ program.

Financial Data

(US$ in Thousands)	3 Mos	08/31/2003	08/31/2002	08/31/2001	08/31/2000	08/31/1999	08/31/1998	08/31/1997
Earnings Per Share	1.11	1.04	0.89	1.05	1.02	0.77	0.18	0.79
Cash Flow Per Share	0.54	1.79	1.76	0.96	1.26	1.22	0.86	0.69
Tang. Book Val. Per Share	8.41	6.90	6.69	5.48	4.66	4.53	4.16	3.71
Dividends Per Share	0.190	0.150	0.130	0.120	0.110	0.100	0.090	0.080
Dividend Payout %	17.12	14.42	15.16	11.90	11.21	13.63	51.35	10.75
Income Statement								
Total Revenues	103,101	380,376	340,759	334,042	320,340	295,946	260,890	245,889
Total Indirect Exp.	32,582	125,524	112,576	103,708	98,322	104,585	117,598	73,315
Depreciation & Amort.	5,676	23,226	21,693	22,696	20,931	18,606	15,623	15,552
Operating Income	21,616	64,606	58,558	71,761	71,595	52,120	29,220	61,763
Net Interest Inc./(Exp.)	(109)	1,203	(392)	(1,897)	(1,945)	(975)	(328)	(3)
Income Taxes	6,944	21,248	18,777	22,925	23,266	19,646	19,010	22,997
Net Income	14,424	45,670	39,000	46,545	46,184	35,695	8,572	36,735
Average Shs. Outstg.	43,982	43,773	44,211	44,240	45,037	46,390	46,451	46,454
Balance Sheet								
Cash & Cash Equivalents	62,948	46,975	33,103	2,968	3,959	3,939	4,652	6,276
Total Current Assets	266,824	241,880	224,873	203,985	179,651	166,627	154,617	135,973
Total Assets	519,746	493,897	425,680	417,710	385,814	357,484	322,881	320,373
Total Current Liabilities	87,322	77,966	50,425	78,429	89,601	58,726	54,361	54,513
Long–Term Obligations	2,000	3,735	300	600	900	11,105	11,686	12,043
Net Stockholders' Equity	408,261	390,646	360,356	326,089	285,204	278,167	247,868	245,917
Net Working Capital	179,502	163,914	174,448	125,556	90,050	107,901	100,256	81,460
Shares Outstanding	43,429	43,285	43,941	44,002	44,001	46,115	46,448	46,452
Statistical Record								
Operating Profit Margin %	20.96	16.98	17.18	21.48	22.34	17.61	11.20	25.11
Return on Equity %	3.53	11.69	10.82	14.27	16.19	12.83	3.45	14.93
Return on Assets %	2.77	9.24	9.16	11.14	11.97	9.98	2.65	11.46
Debt/Total Assets %	0.38	0.75	0.07	0.14	0.23	3.10	3.61	3.75
Price Range	27.10–22.43	25.80–15.75	24.20–16.93	20.16–17.06	19.81–11.88	15.69–9.44	20.38–13.00	17.63–13.00
P/E Ratio	82.12–67.97	24.81–15.14	27.19–19.02	19.20–16.25	19.42–11.64	20.37–12.26	113.2–72.22	22.31–16.46
Average Yield %	0.75	0.73	0.64	0.64	0.69	0.76	0.53	0.53

Address: 2400 Bernville Road, Reading, PA 19605 **Telephone:** (610) 378–0131 **Web Site:** www.arrowintl.com	**Officers:** Carl G. Anderson – Chmn, C.E.O., Philip B. Fleck – Pres., C.O.O.

Investor Contact:610–478–3116
Institutional Holding
No of Institutions: 24
Shares: 42,645,770   **% Held:** –

ARTESIAN RESOURCES CORP.

Exchange	Symbol	Price	52Wk Range	Yield	P/E
OTC	ARTN B	$28.23 (3/31/2004)	29.50-19.90	2.87	29.41

*7 Year Price Score 141.4 *NYSE Composite Index=100 *12 Month Price Score 102.3

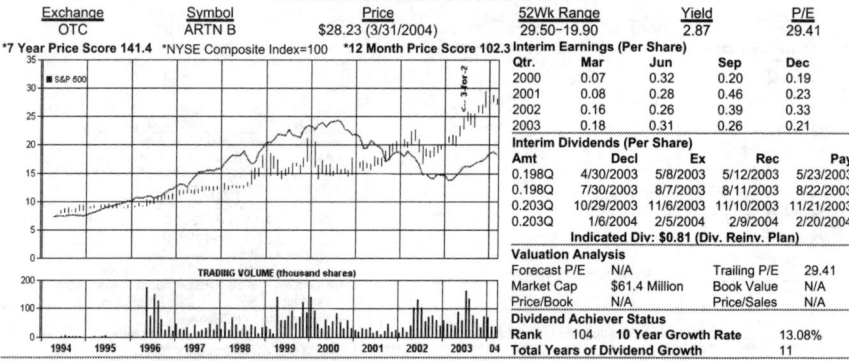

Interim Earnings (Per Share)

Qtr.	Mar	Jun	Sep	Dec
2000	0.07	0.32	0.20	0.19
2001	0.08	0.28	0.46	0.23
2002	0.16	0.26	0.39	0.33
2003	0.18	0.31	0.26	0.21

Interim Dividends (Per Share)

Amt	Decl	Ex	Rec	Pay
0.198Q	4/30/2003	5/8/2003	5/12/2003	5/23/2003
0.198Q	7/30/2003	8/7/2003	8/11/2003	8/22/2003
0.203Q	10/29/2003	11/6/2003	11/10/2003	11/21/2003
0.203Q	1/6/2004	2/5/2004	2/9/2004	2/20/2004
	Indicated Div: $0.81 (Div. Reinv. Plan)			

Valuation Analysis

Forecast P/E	N/A	Trailing P/E	29.41
Market Cap	$61.4 Million	Book Value	N/A
Price/Book	N/A	Price/Sales	N/A

Dividend Achiever Status

Rank	104	10 Year Growth Rate	13.08%
Total Years of Dividend Growth			11

Business Summary: Water Utilities (MIC: 7.2 SIC: 4941 NAIC:221310)

Artesian Resources distributes and sells water to residential, commercial, industrial, governmental, municipal and utility customers throughout Delaware. As of Dec 31 2003, Co. had approximately 70,000 metered customers and served a population of approximately 230,000 (including contract services), representing about 29.0% of Delaware's total population. Co. also provides water for public and private fire protection to customers in its service territories. Co.'s gross water sales revenue by major customer classifications for 2003 were 62.0% for residential, 32.0% for commercial, industrial, governmental, municipal and utility, and 6.0% for fire protection and other.

Recent Developments: For the year ended Dec 31 2003, net income decreased 6.0% to $3.9 million compared with $4.2 million the previous year. The decrease in net income was primarily attributed to reduced customer water usage, an increase in purchased water expense and higher interest expense. Operating revenues rose 4.9% to $36.3 million from $34.6 million a year earlier, reflecting an increase in water sales of 4.5% due to customer growth and rate increases. Total operating expenses were $27.8 million, up 5.1% from $26.4 million in 2002. Operating income climbed 4.3% to $8.5 million versus $8.2 million the prior year.

Prospects: Going forward, Co. will continue to place emphasis on increasing its source of supply. Co.'s focus to develop additional sources of supply as needed should enhance its ability to readily meet increasing customer demand. Meanwhile, Co. is benefiting from its efforts to keep controllable expense increases to a minimum. Separately, Co. plans to invest approximately $25.4 million in its utility plant. The largest portion of the projected investment will result from efforts to identify, develop, treat and protect sources of water supply. Also, Co. plans to invest about $7.7 million in new treatment facilities, equipment and wells.

Financial Data

(US$ in Thousands)	12/31/2003	12/31/2002	12/31/2001	12/31/2000	12/31/1999	12/31/1998	12/31/1997	12/31/1996
Earnings Per Share	0.96	1.14	1.05	0.78	0.97	0.96	0.71	0.70
Cash Flow Per Share	3.53	0.76	2.86	1.28	2.48	2.71	1.54	...
Tang. Book Val. Per Share	13.50	13.25	11.16	10.78	10.70	10.22	9.85	9.71
Dividends Per Share	0.790	0.770	0.740	0.720	0.700	0.640	0.610	0.590
Dividend Payout %	83.07	67.83	70.25	93.58	72.60	66.89	85.98	84.29
Income Statement								
Total Revenues	36,295	34,597	31,987	27,551	26,777	25,466	22,340	20,892
Total Indirect Exp.	8,276	8,263	7,145	6,120	6,224	5,754	5,405	4,883
Costs & Expenses	27,766	26,422	24,586	21,340	20,687	19,799	17,933	16,791
Depreciation & Amort.	3,635	3,392	3,001	2,706	2,417	2,183	2,441	2,193
Operating Income	8,529	8,175	7,401	6,211	6,090	5,667	4,407	4,101
Net Interest Inc./(Exp.)	(4,889)	(4,388)	(4,537)	(4,055)	(3,298)	(3,162)	(2,580)	(2,536)
Net Income	3,917	4,167	3,321	2,451	2,980	2,720	1,985	1,659
Average Shs. Outstg.	3,993	3,612	3,108	3,066	2,994	2,724	2,662	...
Balance Sheet								
Net Property	187,893	167,338	152,356	134,038	122,481	109,780	97,694	88,993
Total Assets	216,324	183,072	163,534	144,407	132,482	119,376	107,867	99,708
Long-Term Obligations	80,558	63,970	49,370	50,717	34,529	32,053	32,103	26,259
Net Stockholders' Equity	52,691	51,176	34,445	32,829	32,356	27,933	26,587	25,759
Shares Outstanding	3,900	3,861	3,059	3,019	2,997	2,705	2,670	2,622
Statistical Record								
Operating Profit Margin %	23.49	23.62	23.13	22.54	22.74	22.25	19.72	19.62
Net Inc./Net Property %	2.08	2.49	2.17	1.82	2.43	2.47	2.03	1.86
Net Inc./Tot. Capital %	2.70	3.38	3.70	2.78	4.25	4.39	3.33	3.13
Return on Equity %	7.43	8.14	9.64	7.46	9.21	9.73	7.46	6.43
Price Range	29.33-19.71	22.67-16.76	20.63-15.50	21.00-14.00	21.17-14.00	18.25-12.17	12.67-10.83	11.33-8.92
P/E Ratio	30.55-20.53	19.88-14.70	19.64-14.76	26.92-17.95	21.82-14.43	19.01-12.67	17.84-15.26	16.19-12.74
Average Yield %	3.34	3.90	4.22	4.46	4.26	4.71	5.11	5.72

Address: 664 Churchmans Road, Newark, DE 19702 Telephone: (302) 453-6900 Web Site: www.artesianwater.com	Officers: Dian C. Taylor - Chmn., Pres., C.E.O., Joseph A. DiNunzio - Sr. V.P., Sec.	Investor Contact: (800) 332-5114 Institutional Holding No of Institutions: 6 Shares: 908,604 % Held: -

ASSOCIATED BANC-CORP.

Exchange	Symbol	Price	52Wk Range	Yield	P/E
NMS	ASBC	$44.79 (3/31/2004)	45.55-32.15	3.04	14.59

*7 Year Price Score 124.2 *NYSE Composite Index=100 *12 Month Price Score 100.9

TRADING VOLUME (thousand shares)

Interim Earnings (Per Share)

Qtr.	Mar	Jun	Sep	Dec
2000	0.61	0.57	0.55	0.50
2001	0.57	0.62	0.61	0.65
2002	0.69	0.68	0.70	0.72
2003	0.77	0.76	0.79	0.75

Interim Dividends (Per Share)

Amt	Decl	Ex	Rec	Pay
0.34Q	4/23/2003	4/29/2003	5/1/2003	5/15/2003
0.34Q	7/23/2003	7/30/2003	8/1/2003	8/15/2003
0.34Q	10/22/2003	10/30/2003	11/3/2003	11/17/2003
0.34Q	1/28/2004	1/30/2004	2/2/2004	2/16/2004

Indicated Div: $1.36 (Div. Reinv. Plan)

Valuation Analysis

Forecast P/E	12.35	Trailing P/E	14.59
Market Cap	$3.4 Billion	Book Value	1.3 Billion
Price/Book	2.34	Price/Sales	3.25

Dividend Achiever Status

Rank	111	10 Year Growth Rate	12.47%
Total Years of Dividend Growth			33

Business Summary: Commercial Banking (MIC: 8.1 SIC: 6022 NAIC:522110)

Associated Banc-Corp. is a multi-bank holding company headquartered in Green Bay, WI. Co. provides advice and specialized services to its affiliates in banking policy and operations, including auditing, data processing, marketing/advertising, investing, legal/compliance, personnel services, trust services, risk management, facilities management, and other financial services functionally related to banking. Through its affiliates, Co. provides a wide range of banking services to individuals and small- to medium-sized businesses. As of Dec 31 2002, Co. had total assets of $15.25 billion and 217 banking offices serving over 151 communities in Wisconsin, Illinois and Minnesota.

Recent Developments: For the year ended Dec 31 2003, net income rose 8.5% to $228.7 million from $210.7 million the year before. Results for 2003 and 2002 included net asset sale gains of $1.6 million and $657,000, respectively. Net interest income grew 1.9% to $510.8 million. Provision for loan losses decreased 7.7% to $46.8 million. Total non-interest income climbed 14.2% to $246.5 million, primarily due to increases in mortgage banking revenue, retail commission income and service charges on deposit accounts. Total non-interest expense rose 5.0% to $388.7 million. Total loans inched up 0.1% to $10.29 billion, while total deposits rose 7.3% to $9.79 billion.

Prospects: Although commercial loan demand is not as strong as Co. anticipated, it is experiencing healthy growth in its mortgage business and in consumer deposits. Co. continues to focus on its long-term goal of increasing its annual earnings per share by 10.0%. In 2004, Co. expects growth from more diverse revenue sources, including consumer banking, small business banking and wealth management, as well as the traditional commercial business to help replace reduced mortgage revenue. Co. also anticipates overall asset quality to improve. Looking ahead, Co. expects earnings per share of $3.25 for 2004.

Financial Data

(US$ in Thousands)	12/31/2003	12/31/2002	12/31/2001	12/31/2000	12/31/1999	12/31/1998	12/31/1997	12/31/1996
Earnings Per Share	3.07	2.79	2.45	2.23	2.12	2.03	0.67	1.71
Tang. Book Val. Per Share	14.45	13.71	16.38	13.31	11.89	11.54	10.67	11.79
Dividends Per Share	1.330	1.210	1.100	1.000	0.950	0.860	0.730	0.620
Dividend Payout %	43.32	43.43	45.18	45.01	45.13	42.43	108.98	36.26
Income Statement								
Total Interest Income	727,364	792,106	880,622	931,157	814,520	785,765	787,244	311,732
Total Interest Expense	216,602	290,840	458,637	547,590	418,775	411,028	411,637	142,477
Net Interest Income	510,762	501,266	421,985	383,567	395,745	374,737	375,607	169,255
Provision for Loan Losses	46,813	50,699	28,210	20,206	19,243	14,740	31,668	4,665
Non-Interest Income	246,435	220,308	195,603	184,196	165,906	167,951	95,976	65,083
Non-Interest Expense	388,668	374,549	338,369	317,736	305,092	294,985	323,647	140,385
Income Before Taxes	321,716	296,326	251,009	229,821	237,316	232,963	116,268	89,288
Net Income	228,657	210,719	179,522	167,983	164,943	157,020	52,359	57,244
Average Shs. Outstg.	74,507	75,493	73,167	75,251	77,513	77,184	77,361	33,327
Balance Sheet								
Cash & Due from Banks	389,140	430,691	587,994	368,186	284,652	331,532	288,021	236,314
Securities Avail. for Sale	3,773,784	3,362,669	3,197,021	2,891,647	2,841,498	2,356,960	2,167,694	437,440
Net Loans & Leases	10,114,188	10,140,684	8,891,660	8,793,147	8,244,752	7,173,020	6,983,845	3,112,431
Total Assets	15,247,894	15,043,275	13,604,374	13,128,394	12,519,902	11,250,667	10,691,439	4,419,079
Total Deposits	9,792,843	9,124,852	8,612,611	9,291,646	8,691,829	8,557,819	8,364,137	3,508,041
Long-Term Obligations	1,852,219	1,906,845	1,103,395	122,420	24,283	26,004	15,270	21,130
Total Liabilities	13,899,467	13,771,092	12,533,958	12,159,698	11,610,113	10,371,946	9,877,746	4,025,934
Net Stockholders' Equity	1,348,427	1,272,183	1,070,416	968,696	909,789	878,721	813,693	393,145
Shares Outstanding	73,360	74,280	65,335	72,727	76,472	76,093	76,193	33,324
Statistical Record								
Return on Equity %	16.95	16.56	16.77	17.34	18.12	17.86	6.43	14.56
Return on Assets %	1.49	1.40	1.31	1.27	1.31	1.39	0.48	1.29
Equity/Assets %	8.84	8.45	7.86	7.37	7.26	7.81	7.61	8.89
Non-Int. Exp./Tot. Inc. %	39.91	37.00	31.44	28.49	31.12	30.93	36.44	37.26
Price Range	43.13-32.15	38.25-27.20	33.55-27.05	28.31-18.44	35.59-25.05	36.45-22.11	38.84-27.87	24.10-19.42
P/E Ratio	14.05-10.47	13.71-9.75	13.70-11.04	12.69-8.27	16.79-11.82	17.95-10.89	57.97-34.13	14.10-11.36
Average Yield %	3.57	3.56	3.54	4.41	3.22	2.72	2.64	2.88

Address: 1200 Hansen Road, Green Bay, WI 54304 Telephone: (920) 491-7000 Web Site: www.associatedbank.com	Officers: Robert C. Gallagher - Chmn., Pres., C.E.O., John C. Seramur - Vice-Chmn.	Investor Contact:920-491-7120 Institutional Holding No of Institutions: 16 Shares: 2,293,825 % Held: -

ATMOS ENERGY CORP.

Exchange	Symbol	Price	52Wk Range	Yield	P/E
NYS	ATO	$25.57 (3/31/2004)	26.86–21.43	4.77	15.22

*7 Year Price Score 100.7   *NYSE Composite Index=100   ***12 Month Price Score 92.6**

Interim Earnings (Per Share)

Qtr.	Dec	Mar	Jun	Sep
2000–01	0.70	1.13	(0.08)	(0.28)
2001–02	0.50	1.01	0.08	(0.14)
2002–03	0.60	1.24	0.00	(0.13)
2003–04	0.57	...	...	...

Interim Dividends (Per Share)

Amt	Decl	Ex	Rec	Pay
0.30Q	5/13/2003	5/22/2003	5/27/2003	6/10/2003
0.30Q	8/13/2003	8/21/2003	8/25/2003	9/10/2003
0.305Q	11/11/2003	11/21/2003	11/25/2003	12/10/2003
0.305Q	2/10/2004	2/23/2004	2/25/2004	3/10/2004

Indicated Div: $1.22

Valuation Analysis

Forecast P/E	15.69	Trailing P/E	15.22
Market Cap	$1.1 Billion	Book Value	879.4 Million
Price/Book	1.46	Price/Sales	0.41

Dividend Achiever Status

Rank	276	10 Year Growth Rate	3.43%
Total Years of Dividend Growth		16

Business Summary: Gas Utilities (MIC: 7.4 SIC: 4922 NAIC:486210)

Atmos Energy is engaged in the natural gas utility business as well as certain non–regulated natural gas businesses. Co. distributes natural gas through sales and transportation arrangements to about 1.7 million residential, commercial public authority and industrial customers through its regulated utility operations in twelve states. Co. also transports natural gas through its distribution system. Co.'s non–regulated businesses provide natural gas storage services and own an interest in storage fields in Kansas, Kentucky, Louisiana and Mississippi. Co. also provides energy management and gas marketing services and electrical power generation to wholesale customers in Texas and Louisiana.

Recent Developments: For the first quarter ended Dec 31 2003, net income advanced 14.5% to $29.5 million from $25.8 million in the corresponding prior–year quarter. Net revenues increased 12.2% to $763.6 million from $680.4 million a year earlier. On a segment basis, Utility revenues climbed 15.1% to $460.5 million, while Natural Gas Marketing revenues rose 8.8% to $373.8 million. Other non–utility revenues jumped 25.1% to 3.6 million. Gross profit grew 16.0% to $159.1 million from $137.2 million the year before. Total utility gas throughput decreased 3.8% to 68.2 billion cubic feet, while the average cost of gas per thousand cubic feet increased 26.2% to $6.35.

Prospects: On Mar 1 2004, Co. announced that it has completed the acquisition of the natural gas assets of ComFurT Gas, Inc., a natural gas utility and propane distributor based in Buena Vista, CO. Co. paid $2.0 million cash for ComFurT Gas' 49–mile natural gas distribution system which serves approximately 1,800 customers. Separately, the steps taken by Co.'s non–utility operations during the past year are driving improved margins. In addition, recently approved rate increases in two of Co.'s jurisdictions should add approximately $8.4 million a year to future revenues. As a result, Co. expects earnings for fiscal 2004 to range from $1.55 to $1.60 per diluted share.

Financial Data

(US$ in Thousands)	3 Mos	09/30/2003	09/30/2002	09/30/2001	09/30/2000	09/30/1999	09/30/1998	09/30/1997
Earnings Per Share	1.68	1.71	1.45	1.47	1.14	0.58	1.84	0.81
Cash Flow Per Share	0.22	1.06	7.18	2.16	1.71	2.74	3.05	2.33
Tang. Book Val. Per Share	11.67	11.34	9.18	12.42	12.28	12.08	12.20	11.04
Dividends Per Share	1.205	1.200	1.180	1.160	1.140	1.100	1.060	1.000
Dividend Payout %	71.73	70.17	81.37	78.91	100.00	189.65	57.60	123.46
Income Statement								
Total Revenues	763,616	2,799,916	950,849	1,442,275	850,152	690,196	848,208	906,835
Total Indirect Exp.	38,596	142,046	40,614	104,343	92,493	91,599	77,343	77,388
Costs & Expenses	700,075	2,612,076	795,518	1,311,994	764,836	635,957	735,329	840,226
Depreciation & Amort.	23,473	87,001	81,469	67,664	63,855	56,874	47,555	45,257
Operating Income	63,541	187,840	155,331	130,281	85,316	54,239	112,879	66,609
Net Interest Inc./(Exp.)	(17,335)	(63,660)	(59,174)	(47,011)	(43,823)	(36,298)	(30,149)	(28,185)
Income Taxes	17,872	46,910	35,180	33,368	20,319	9,555	31,806	14,298
Income from Cont Ops	...	79,461	...	...	...	...	...	...
Net Income	29,541	71,688	59,656	56,090	35,918	17,744	55,265	23,838
Average Shs. Outstg.	51,861	46,496	41,250	38,247	31,594	30,819	30,031	29,409
Balance Sheet								
Net Property	1,538,224	1,515,989	1,300,320	1,335,398	982,346	965,782	917,860	849,127
Total Assets	2,812,946	2,518,508	1,980,221	2,036,180	1,348,758	1,230,537	1,141,390	1,088,311
Long–Term Obligations	860,705	863,918	670,463	692,399	363,198	377,483	398,548	302,981
Net Stockholders' Equity	879,352	857,517	573,235	583,864	392,466	377,663	371,158	327,260
Shares Outstanding	51,797	51,475	41,675	40,791	31,952	31,247	30,398	29,642
Statistical Record								
Operating Profit Margin %	8.32	6.70	16.33	9.03	10.03	7.85	13.30	7.34
Net Inc./Net Property %	1.92	4.72	4.58	4.20	3.65	1.83	6.02	2.80
Net Inc./Tot. Capital %	1.48	3.68	4.32	3.96	4.04	2.04	6.50	3.31
Return on Equity %	3.35	9.26	10.40	9.60	9.15	4.69	14.88	7.28
Accum. Depr./Gross Prop. %	39.03	38.87	38.88	36.70	37.81	37.66	36.54	36.28
Price Range	24.99–21.02	25.45–20.70	24.46–18.37	26.25–19.31	25.00–14.75	32.69–23.06	31.06–24.63	27.63–22.00
P/E Ratio	43.84–42.00	14.88–12.11	16.87–12.67	17.86–13.14	21.93–12.94	56.36–39.76	16.88–13.38	34.10–27.16
Average Yield %	4.89	5.21	5.37	5.08	5.85	4.11	3.74	4.16

Address: Three Lincoln Centre, Dallas, TX 75240	**Officers:** Robert W. Best – Chmn., Pres., C.E.O., John P. Reddy – Sr. V.P., C.F.O.
Telephone: (972) 934 9227	**Transfer Agents:** EquiServe Trust Company,
Web Site: www.atmosenergy.com	Providence, RI

Investor Contact: (972) 855–3729
Institutional Holding
No of Institutions: 2
Shares: 58,796 **% Held:** –

24

AUTOMATIC DATA PROCESSING INC.

Exchange	Symbol	Price	52Wk Range	Yield	P/E
NYS	ADP	$42.00 (3/31/2004)	44.54-31.13	1.33	26.09

*7 Year Price Score 86.8   *NYSE Composite Index=100   ***12 Month Price Score 96.2**

Interim Earnings (Per Share)

Qtr.	Sep	Dec	Mar	Jun
2000-01	0.27	0.32	0.45	0.40
2001-02	0.31	0.42	0.56	0.46
2002-03	0.34	0.43	0.54	0.37
2003-04	0.32	0.38	...	...

Interim Dividends (Per Share)

Amt	Decl	Ex	Rec	Pay
0.12Q	5/13/2003	6/11/2003	6/13/2003	7/1/2003
0.12Q	8/11/2003	9/10/2003	9/12/2003	10/1/2003
0.14Q	11/11/2003	12/10/2003	12/12/2003	1/1/2004
0.14Q	1/29/2004	3/11/2004	3/15/2004	4/1/2004

Indicated Div: $0.56

Valuation Analysis

Forecast P/E	22.57	Trailing P/E	N/A
Market Cap	$26.0 Billion	Book Value	N/A
Price/Book	N/A	Price/Sales	N/A

Dividend Achiever Status

Rank	85	10 Year Growth Rate	14.63%
Total Years of Dividend Growth		28

Business Summary: IT &Technology (MIC: 10.2 SIC: 7374 NAIC:518210)

Automatic Data Processing provides computerized transaction processing, data communication, and information services. Co.'s Employer Services group offers payroll processing, human resource and benefits administration products and services. Co.'s Brokerage Services group provides transaction processing systems, desktop productivity applications and investor communications services to the financial services industry. Co.'s Dealer Services group provides dealer management computer systems to automotive retailers and their manufacturers. Co.'s Claims Services group offers business solutions for clients in the property and casualty insurance, auto collision repair and auto recycling industries.

Recent Developments: For the three months ended Dec 31 2003, net earnings slipped 12.7% to $228.6 million compared with $261.7 million in the second quarter of 2002. Results were hampered by lower interest rates, Co.'s incremental investment activity and by dilution from last year's acquisitions. Total revenues climbed 8.6% to $1.83 billion versus $1.68 billion in the prior-year period. Brokerage Services' revenues improved 6.6% to $340.0 million, primarily due to an increase in investor communications activity. Revenue in the Dealer Services segment rose 8.5%, while Employer Services' revenues rose 8.9%. Claims Services revenues decreased

Prospects: Looking ahead, near-term results are expected to benefit from better momentum in the brokerage markets, improving economic conditions and the assumption that there will be further interest rate declines. As a result, Co. has narrowed its earnings per share guidance for fiscal 2004 to $1.53 to $1.58 versus its previous guidance of $1.50 to $1.60. In addition, Co. continues to forecast mid-single digit revenue growth, and anticipates stronger sales growth in the Employer Services segment during the second half of fiscal 2004 due to investments in products and a larger U.S. sales force. Also, Co. is on track to spend about $130.0 million to $145.0 million for fiscal 2004 on investments.

Financial Data

(US$ in Thousands)	6 Mos	3 Mos	06/30/2003	06/30/2002	06/30/2001	06/30/2000	06/30/1999	06/30/1998
Earnings Per Share	0.71	0.32	1.68	1.75	1.44	1.31	1.10	0.99
Cash Flow Per Share	0.92	0.27	2.58	2.42	2.30	1.65	1.34	1.37
Tang. Book Val. Per Share	4.64	4.64	4.57	5.25	4.96	4.70	3.96	2.90
Dividends Per Share	0.480	0.470	0.470	0.430	0.380	0.320	0.280	0.240
Dividend Payout %	67.60	148.43	27.97	24.85	26.38	25.00	25.90	25.00
Income Statement								
Total Revenues	3,547,677	1,720,277	7,147,017	7,004,263	7,017,570	6,287,512	5,540,141	4,798,061
Total Indirect Exp.	2,903,926	1,427,599	2,532,227	2,360,610	2,500,582	2,387,917	2,060,379	1,826,674
Depreciation & Amort.	148,335	74,726	274,682	279,077	320,856	284,282	272,807	244,616
Operating Income	643,751	292,678	1,518,071	1,673,008	1,616,864	1,335,099	1,103,590	908,242
Net Interest Inc./(Exp.)	35,741	17,449	97,575	97,508	(14,260)	(13,140)	(19,090)	(24,042)
Income Taxes	252,980	116,420	627,050	686,200	600,290	448,800	387,660	278,900
Net Income	423,430	194,850	1,018,150	1,100,770	924,720	840,800	696,840	605,300
Average Shs. Outstg.	599,242	600,849	605,917	630,579	645,989	646,098	636,892	620,822
Balance Sheet								
Cash & Cash Equivalents	1,394,791	1,859,427	2,005,384	1,475,815	1,790,601	1,824,429	1,092,494	897,176
Total Current Assets	2,946,252	3,325,867	3,675,501	2,817,257	3,083,460	3,524,452	2,194,257	1,829,304
Total Assets	24,700,123	18,714,386	19,833,671	18,276,522	17,889,090	16,850,816	5,824,820	5,175,355
Total Current Liabilities	1,665,296	1,707,534	1,998,783	1,411,102	1,336,273	1,296,668	1,286,393	1,221,041
Long-Term Obligations	84,585	84,713	84,674	90,648	110,227	132,017	145,765	192,063
Net Stockholders' Equity	5,374,413	5,349,633	5,371,473	5,114,205	4,700,997	4,582,818	4,007,941	3,406,451
Net Working Capital	1,280,956	1,618,333	1,676,718	1,406,155	1,747,187	1,767,784	907,864	608,263
Shares Outstanding	589,910	594,438	594,839	616,317	623,936	628,746	623,627	604,212
Statistical Record								
Operating Profit Margin %	18.14	17.01	21.24	23.88	23.04	21.23	19.91	18.92
Return on Equity %	7.87	3.64	18.95	21.52	19.67	18.34	17.38	17.76
Return on Assets %	1.71	1.04	5.13	6.02	5.16	4.98	11.96	11.69
Debt/Total Assets %	0.34	0.45	0.42	0.49	0.61	0.78	2.50	3.71
Price Range	40.49-33.86	40.49-33.86	44.70-27.25	60.27-43.10	68.88-49.56	57.69-38.00	46.19-31.88	36.44-22.56
P/E Ratio	57.03-47.69	126.5-105.8	26.61-16.22	34.44-24.63	47.83-34.42	44.04-29.01	41.99-28.98	36.81-22.79
Average Yield %	1.27	1.25	1.29	0.81	0.65	0.67	0.71	0.83

Address: One ADP Boulevard, Roseland, NJ 07068-1728	**Officers:** Arthur F. Weinbach – Chmn., C.E.O., Gary C. Butler – Pres., C.O.O.	**Investor Contact:**973-974-5858 **Institutional Holding**
Telephone: (973) 974-5000	**Transfer Agents:**Mellon Investor Services,	**No of Institutions:** 4
Web Site: www.adp.com	Ridgefield Park, NJ	**Shares:** 11,920,277 **% Held:** –

25

AVERY DENNISON CORP.

Exchange	Symbol	Price	52Wk Range	Yield	P/E
NYS	AVY	$62.21 (3/31/2004)	64.50-47.75	2.38	25.60

*7 Year Price Score 103.5   *NYSE Composite Index=100   *12 Month Price Score 88.1

Interim Earnings (Per Share)

Qtr.	Mar	Jun	Sep	Dec
2000	0.70	0.73	0.73	0.68
2001	0.65	0.61	0.63	0.58
2002	0.66	0.74	0.64	0.55
2003	0.71	0.70	0.65	0.37

Interim Dividends (Per Share)

Amt	Decl	Ex	Rec	Pay
0.36Q	4/24/2003	6/2/2003	6/4/2003	6/18/2003
0.36Q	7/24/2003	8/29/2003	9/3/2003	9/17/2003
0.37Q	10/23/2003	12/1/2003	12/3/2003	12/17/2003
0.37Q	1/29/2004	3/1/2004	3/3/2004	3/17/2004

Indicated Div: $1.48 (Div. Reinv. Plan)

Valuation Analysis

Forecast P/E	16.75	Trailing P/E	25.60
Market Cap	$6.8 Billion	Book Value	1.3 Billion
Price/Book	4.65	Price/Sales	1.29

Dividend Achiever Status

Rank	114	10 Year Growth Rate 12.41%
Total Years of Dividend Growth		28

Business Summary: Paper Products (MIC: 11.11 SIC: 2672 NAIC:322222)

Avery Dennison is a worldwide manufacturer of pressure-sensitive adhesives and materials, office products and converted products. A portion of self-adhesive material is converted into labels and other products through embossing, printing, stamping and die-cutting, and some are sold in unconverted form as base materials, tapes and reflective sheeting. Co. also manufactures and sells a variety of office products and other items not involving pressure-sensitive components, such as notebooks, three-ring binders, organization systems, felt-tip markers, glues, fasteners, business forms, tickets, tags, and imprinting equipment.

Recent Developments: For the twelve months ended Dec 27 2003, income from continuing operations slipped 2.8% to $242.8 million compared with $249.8 million in 2002. Challenging economic conditions hampered most of Co.'s core businesses. Results for 2003 and 2002 included expenses of $30.5 million and $32.1 million, respectively, primarily for asset impairments, restructuring and lease cancellation costs. Results for 2003 and 2002 excluded after-tax gains of $25.1 million and $7.4 million, respectively, from discontinued operations. Net sales were $4.76 billion, up 14.6% from $4.16 billion in the prior year. Sales benefited from the favorable effect of currency exchange rates and acquisitions.

Prospects: Co. expects earnings per share for the first quarter of 2004 in the range of $0.60 to $0.67 and for full-year 2004 in the range of $2.75 to $3.10, excluding restructuring charges. Also, Co. expects to record final charges of $30.0 million to $35.0 million related to the Jackstadt integration during the first half of 2004, which is expected to have a negative effect on earnings per share. Co.'s outlook for 2004 reflects improved economic trends and is based on other key assumptions, including revenue growth of 4.0% to 6.0% in the first quarter and 3.5% to 6.5% for full-year 2004, and operating margin in the range of 8.0% to 9.0% in the first quarter and 9.0% to 10.0% for full-year 2004

Financial Data

(US$ in Thousands)	12/27/2003	12/28/2002	12/29/2001	12/30/2000	01/01/2000	01/02/1999	12/27/1997	12/28/1996
Earnings Per Share	2.43	2.59	2.47	2.84	2.13	2.15	1.93	1.62
Cash Flow Per Share	3.34	5.25	3.80	4.10	4.29	4.06	3.47	2.89
Tang. Book Val. Per Share	4.52	2.53	4.69	3.93	4.17	6.88	6.87	6.71
Dividends Per Share	1.450	1.350	1.230	1.110	0.990	0.870	0.720	0.620
Dividend Payout %	59.67	52.12	49.79	39.08	46.47	40.46	37.30	38.27
Income Statement								
Total Revenues	4,762,600	4,206,900	3,803,300	3,893,500	3,768,200	3,459,900	3,345,700	3,222,500
Total Indirect Exp.	1,034,900	913,100	830,500	851,300	907,600	773,200	739,800	712,400
Depreciation & Amort.	179,300	152,800	156,000	156,900	150,400	127,200	116,800	113,400
Operating Income	423,100	440,600	409,700	480,900	373,800	371,300	342,900	305,900
Net Interest Inc./(Exp.)	(57,700)	(43,700)	(50,200)	(54,600)	(43,400)	(34,600)	(31,700)	(37,400)
Income Taxes	92,100	107,600	116,400	142,800	115,000	113,400	106,400	94,700
Income from Cont Ops	242,800	...	243,400	...	...	...	...	171,700
Net Income	267,900	257,200	243,200	283,500	215,400	223,300	204,800	175,900
Average Shs. Outstg.	100,000	99,400	98,600	99,800	101,300	104,100	106,100	108,300
Balance Sheet								
Cash & Cash Equivalents	29,500	22,800	19,100	11,400	6,900	18,500	3,300	3,800
Total Current Assets	1,440,900	1,215,500	982,500	982,400	956,000	802,000	793,500	804,500
Total Assets	4,105,300	3,652,400	2,819,200	2,699,100	2,592,500	2,142,600	2,046,500	2,036,700
Total Current Liabilities	1,496,000	1,296,100	951,300	800,700	850,400	664,300	629,900	693,900
Long-Term Obligations	887,700	837,200	626,700	772,900	617,500	465,900	404,100	370,700
Net Stockholders' Equity	1,318,700	1,056,400	929,400	828,100	809,900	833,300	837,200	832,000
Net Working Capital	(55,100)	(80,600)	31,200	181,700	105,600	137,700	163,600	110,600
Shares Outstanding	99,569	110,467	109,890	110,245	98,800	100,000	102,400	103,600
Statistical Record								
Operating Profit Margin %	8.88	10.47	10.77	12.35	9.91	10.73	10.24	9.49
Return on Equity %	18.41	24.34	26.18	34.23	26.59	26.79	24.46	20.63
Return on Assets %	5.91	7.04	8.63	10.50	8.30	10.42	10.00	8.43
Debt/Total Assets %	21.62	22.92	22.22	28.63	23.81	21.74	19.74	18.20
Price Range	63.51-47.75	69.49-52.86	60.24-44.39	78.00-43.31	72.88-39.75	60.75-40.88	44.13-33.38	35.88-23.88
P/E Ratio	26.14-19.65	26.83-20.41	24.39-17.97	27.46-15.25	34.21-18.66	28.26-19.01	22.86-17.29	22.15-14.74
Average Yield %	2.64	2.19	2.34	1.88	1.71	1.74	1.81	2.18

Address: 150 North Orange Grove Boulevard, Pasadena, CA 91103 **Telephone:** (626) 304-2000 **Web Site:** www.averydennison.com	**Officers:** Philip M. Neal - Chmn., C.E.O., Dean A. Scarborough - Pres., C.O.O. **Transfer Agents:** EquiServe Trust Company, N.A., Jersey City, NJ	**Investor Contact:** 626-304-2204 **Institutional Holding** **No of Institutions:** 5 **Shares:** 122,175 **% Held:** -

26

AVON PRODUCTS, INC.

Exchange	Symbol	Price	52Wk Range	Yield	P/E
NYS	AVP	$75.87 (3/31/2004)	75.87–56.89	0.74	27.29

*7 Year Price Score 141.4 *NYSE Composite Index=100   ***12 Month Price Score 98.0**

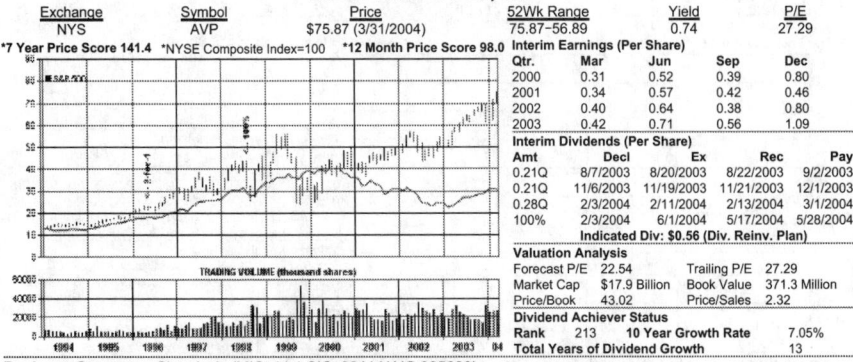

Interim Earnings (Per Share)

Qtr.	Mar	Jun	Sep	Dec
2000	0.31	0.52	0.39	0.80
2001	0.34	0.57	0.42	0.46
2002	0.40	0.64	0.38	0.80
2003	0.42	0.71	0.56	1.09

Interim Dividends (Per Share)

Amt	Decl	Ex	Rec	Pay
0.21Q	8/7/2003	8/20/2003	8/22/2003	9/2/2003
0.21Q	11/6/2003	11/19/2003	11/21/2003	12/1/2003
0.28Q	2/3/2004	2/11/2004	2/13/2004	3/1/2004
100%	2/3/2004	6/1/2004	5/17/2004	5/28/2004
		Indicated Div: $0.56 (Div. Reinv. Plan)		

Valuation Analysis

Forecast P/E	22.54	Trailing P/E	27.29
Market Cap	$17.9 Billion	Book Value	371.3 Million
Price/Book	43.02	Price/Sales	2.32

Dividend Achiever Status

Rank	213	10 Year Growth Rate	7.05%
Total Years of Dividend Growth			13

Business Summary: Chemicals (MIC: 11.1 SIC: 2844 NAIC:325620)

Avon Products is a global manufacturer and marketer of beauty and related products. Co.'s products fall into four product categories: Beauty, which consists of cosmetics, fragrance and toiletries; Beauty Plus, which consists of jewelry, watches and apparel and accessories; Beyond Beauty, which consists of home products, gifts and candles; and women's health and wellness, which consists of vitamins and nutrition supplements, exercise and fitness items, and self-care and stress relief products. As of Apr 25, 2003, Co. had operations in 58 countries and its products were distributed in 85 more for coverage in 143 countries.

Recent Developments: For the year ended Dec 31 2003, net income grew 24.4% to $664.8 million from $534.6 million the previous year. Results for 2002 included special after-tax charges of $25.2 million for business transformation initiatives. Total revenue increased 10.4% to $6.88 billion from $6.23 billion the prior year. Sales of beauty products increased 15.0%, active representatives rose 12.0% to 4.4 million, and units increased 5.0%, with all geographic regions contributing. Cost of sales rose 7.2% to $2.61 billion. Marketing, distribution and administrative expense climbed 11.5% to $3.22 billion. Operating income amounted to $1.04 billion, up 20.8% from $863.5 million the year before.

Prospects: Going forward, Co. expects to benefit from continuing growth in beauty sales, strong performances in international operations and positive foreign currency effects. For 2004, local currency sales should increase 10.0%, with little or no currency impact. Co. expects that the U.S. will resume healthy sales growth in the mid-single digits, with operating profit forecasted to be in the range of 8.0% to 10.0%. Internationally, Co. expects sales and operating profit to increase at rates similar to those of 2003. Earnings in 2004 are projected to increase 10.0% to 12.0% from 2003 levels.

Financial Data
(US$ in Thousands)

	12/31/2003	12/31/2002	12/31/2001	12/31/2000	12/31/1999	12/31/1998	12/31/1997	12/31/1996
Earnings Per Share	2.78	2.22	1.79	2.02	1.17	1.02	1.27	1.19
Cash Flow Per Share	3.08	2.30	3.06	1.33	1.79	1.21	1.18	1.44
Tang. Book Val. Per Share	1.57	N.M	N.M	N.M	N.M	1.08	1.08	0.90
Dividends Per Share	0.840	0.800	0.760	0.740	0.720	0.680	0.630	0.580
Dividend Payout %	30.21	36.03	42.45	36.63	61.53	66.66	49.60	48.74
Income Statement								
Total Revenues	6,876,000	6,228,300	5,994,500	5,714,600	5,289,100	5,212,700	5,079,400	4,814,200
Total Indirect Exp.	3,224,000	2,979,600	2,906,200	2,803,200	2,603,000	2,570,000	2,490,600	2,348,200
Depreciation & Amort.	133,200	142,900	124,000	97,100	83,000	72,000	72,100	64,500
Operating Income	1,042,800	870,000	749,400	788,700	549,400	473,200	537,800	544,800
Net Interest Inc./(Exp.)	(34,800)	(43,500)	(56,700)	(76,200)	(32,100)	(18,800)	(18,800)	(25,500)
Income Taxes	318,900	292,300	230,900	201,700	204,200	190,800	197,900	191,400
Eqty Earns/Minority Int.	(9,800)	(8,700)	(4,500)	(4,200)	...	4,900	1,800	(1,100)
Income from Cont Ops	...	...	430,000	485,100	...	...	...	...
Net Income	664,800	534,600	430,000	478,400	302,400	270,000	338,800	317,900
Average Shs. Outstg.	241,570	245,470	246,050	242,950	259,370	265,950	267,000	267,400
Balance Sheet								
Cash & Cash Equivalents	694,000	606,800	508,500	122,700	117,400	105,600	141,900	184,500
Total Current Assets	2,226,100	2,048,200	1,889,100	1,545,700	1,337,800	1,341,400	1,344,000	1,349,600
Total Assets	3,562,300	3,327,500	3,193,100	2,826,400	2,528,600	2,433,500	2,272,900	2,222,400
Total Current Liabilities	1,587,700	1,975,500	1,461,000	1,359,300	1,712,800	1,329,500	1,355,900	1,391,300
Long-Term Obligations	877,700	767,000	1,236,300	1,108,200	701,400	201,000	102,200	104,500
Net Stockholders' Equity	371,300	(127,700)	(74,600)	(215,800)	(406,100)	285,100	285,000	241,700
Net Working Capital	638,400	72,700	428,100	186,400	(375,000)	11,900	(11,900)	(41,700)
Shares Outstanding	235,298	235,257	236,681	238,162	237,895	262,520	263,628	265,640
Statistical Record								
Operating Profit Margin %	15.16	13.96	12.50	13.80	10.38	9.07	10.58	11.31
Return on Equity %	179.04	N.M	N.M	N.M	N.M	94.70	118.87	131.52
Return on Assets %	18.66	16.06	13.47	17.16	11.95	11.09	14.90	14.30
Debt/Total Assets %	24.63	23.05	38.71	39.20	27.73	8.25	4.49	4.70
Price Range	69.35–49.16	56.96–43.72	49.59–36.77	49.56–25.38	56.19–23.81	46.19–25.38	38.34–25.50	29.44–18.25
P/E Ratio	24.95–17.68	25.66–19.69	27.70–20.54	24.54–12.56	48.02–20.35	45.28–24.88	30.19–20.08	24.74–15.34
Average Yield %	1.38	1.58	1.71	1.94	1.69	1.82	1.99	2.48

Address: 1345 Avenue of the Americas, New York, NY 10105-0196	**Officers:** Andrea Jung – Chmn., C.E.O., Susan J. Kropf – Pres., C.O.O.	**Investor Contact:** 212-282-5320
Telephone: (212) 282-5000	**Transfer Agents:** EquiServe Trust Company, N.A.	**Institutional Holding**
Web Site: www.avon.com	Providence, RI	**No of Institutions:** 14
		Shares: 430,086 **% Held:** –

27

BADGER METER, INC.

Exchange	Symbol	Price	52Wk Range	Yield	P/E
ASE	BMI	$37.25 (3/31/2004)	39.75-25.75	2.90	16.20

*7 Year Price Score 104.6 *NYSE Composite Index=100 *12 Month Price Score 104.0

Interim Earnings (Per Share)

Qtr.	Mar	Jun	Sep	Dec
2000	0.67	0.44	0.56	0.33
2001	0.28	0.16	0.29	0.30
2002	0.49	0.70	0.70	0.31
2003	0.21	0.78	0.80	0.51

Interim Dividends (Per Share)

Amt	Decl	Ex	Rec	Pay
0.26Q	5/2/2003	5/28/2003	5/30/2003	6/13/2003
0.27Q	8/15/2003	8/27/2003	8/29/2003	9/15/2003
0.27Q	11/14/2003	11/26/2003	12/1/2003	12/15/2003
0.27Q	2/13/2004	2/25/2004	2/27/2004	3/15/2004

Indicated Div: $1.08 (Div. Reinv. Plan)

Valuation Analysis

Forecast P/E	14.90	Trailing P/E	16.20
Market Cap	$118.9 Million	Book Value	55.2 Million
Price/Book	2.26	Price/Sales	0.68

Dividend Achiever Status

Rank	110	10 Year Growth Rate	12.61%
Total Years of Dividend Growth			11

Business Summary: Instruments and Related Products (MIC: 11.15 SIC: 3824 NAIC:334514)

Badger Meter is a global marketer and manufacturer of products, and a provider of services, using flow measurement and control technologies. Co.'s products are used to measure and control the flow of liquids in a range of applications. Residential and commercial water meters are generally sold to water utilities. Industrial sales comprise the remainder of the sales and include automotive fluid meters and systems, small precision valves, electromagnetic meters, impeller flow meters and industrial process meters. Co.'s products are primarily manufactured and assembled in Wisconsin, Oklahoma, Arizona, Mexico and Czech Republic facilities.

Recent Developments: For the twelve months ended Dec 31 2003, net earnings climbed 4.2% to $7.6 million compared with $7.3 million in 2002. Earnings benefited from increased sales of automatic meter reading products, decreased sales of lower-margin local-read meters, cost containment efforts, reduced interest expense, a decrease in expenditures and currency translation gains. Net sales rose 10.0% to $184.0 million from $167.3 million in the prior year. Sales increased in both the utility and industrial markets and benefited from two acquisitions completed in 2002. Gross margin increased 8.1% to $60.5 million compared with $56.0 million in the previous year.

Prospects: Earnings improvement in 2003 was negatively affected by foreign operating losses related to Co.'s operations in France, which caused Co. to increase its foreign tax reserves. As a result, Co. has implemented a number of actions to improve profitability at this facility, including reducing the workforce and lowering operating expenses. Co. expects these steps will position this business for improved performance in the near future. Going forward, Co. will continue to invest in research and development efforts, with an emphasis on expanding its product line to meet the needs of market segments Co. has not served in the past.

Financial Data

(US$ in Thousands)	12/31/2003	12/31/2002	12/31/2001	12/31/2000	12/31/1999	12/31/1998	12/31/1997	12/31/1996
Earnings Per Share	2.30	2.20	1.03	2.00	2.60	2.12	1.65	1.36
Cash Flow Per Share	4.26	3.70	2.62	3.81	4.12	3.76	1.30	2.67
Tang. Book Val. Per Share	14.19	12.81	13.28	13.16	12.54	12.72	11.43	10.06
Dividends Per Share	1.060	1.020	1.000	0.860	0.720	0.600	0.480	0.430
Dividend Payout %	46.08	46.36	97.08	43.00	27.69	28.30	29.16	31.61
Income Statement								
Total Revenues	183,989	167,317	138,537	146,389	150,877	143,813	130,771	116,018
Total Indirect Exp.	46,419	42,805	38,430	41,995	42,495	43,317	37,769	33,774
Depreciation & Amort.	7,832	7,980	6,801	6,073	5,633	4,675	3,953	4,119
Operating Income	14,100	13,195	6,065	11,019	16,660	13,994	10,968	8,755
Net Interest Inc./(Exp.)	(1,737)	(1,849)	(1,381)	(2,206)	(1,256)	(630)	(455)	(368)
Income Taxes	5,774	4,166	1,646	3,786	5,959	5,117	3,683	3,040
Net Income	7,577	7,271	3,364	6,941	9,700	8,247	6,522	5,127
Average Shs. Outstg.	3,299	3,304	3,275	3,470	3,728	3,896	3,961	3,781
Balance Sheet								
Cash & Cash Equivalents	2,089	3,779	3,410	4,237	3,752	2,371	1,055	1,123
Total Current Assets	62,998	55,380	44,364	44,517	47,979	45,652	42,539	35,046
Total Assets	133,851	126,463	98,836	98,710	103,086	96,945	82,297	66,133
Total Current Liabilities	37,052	48,555	23,782	37,695	36,829	34,876	28,669	17,400
Long-Term Obligations	24,450	13,046	20,498	5,944	11,493	2,600	928	1,091
Net Stockholders' Equity	55,171	48,095	43,002	43,319	43,009	47,848	41,467	36,638
Net Working Capital	25,946	6,825	20,582	6,822	11,150	10,776	13,870	17,645
Shares Outstanding	3,292	3,220	3,179	3,207	3,339	3,645	3,571	3,551
Statistical Record								
Operating Profit Margin %	7.66	7.88	4.37	7.52	11.04	9.73	8.38	7.54
Return on Equity %	13.73	15.11	7.82	16.02	22.55	17.23	15.72	13.99
Return on Assets %	5.66	5.74	3.40	7.03	9.40	8.50	7.92	7.75
Debt/Total Assets %	18.26	10.31	20.73	6.02	11.14	2.68	1.12	1.64
Price Range	39.75-25.75	34.00-22.30	32.00-20.00	36.75-23.00	40.31-29.69	40.75-25.00	55.50-18.25	20.63-12.38
P/E Ratio	17.28-11.20	15.45-10.14	31.07-19.42	18.38-11.50	15.50-11.42	19.22-11.79	33.64-11.06	15.17-9.10
Average Yield %	3.30	3.49	3.85	2.96	2.12	1.73	1.44	2.79

Address: 4545 W. Brown Deer Road, Milwaukee, WI 53223 Telephone: (414) 355-0400 Web Site: www.badgermeter.com	Officers: James L. Forbes - Chmn., Richard A. Meeusen - Pres., C.E.O.	Investor Contact:414-371-5702 Institutional Holding No of Institutions: 12 Shares: 609,646 % Held: -

BANCFIRST CORP.

Exchange	Symbol	Price	52Wk Range	Yield	P/E
NMS	BANF	$55.44 (3/31/2004)	59.80–44.15	1.80	13.86

*7 Year Price Score 135.9   *NYSE Composite Index=100   ***12 Month Price Score 100.1**

Interim Earnings (Per Share)
Qtr.	Mar	Jun	Sep	Dec
2000	0.75	0.78	0.85	0.81
2001	0.85	0.84	0.82	0.83
2002	0.96	1.02	1.07	1.01
2003	1.07	1.02	0.93	0.98

Interim Dividends (Per Share)
Amt	Decl	Ex	Rec	Pay
0.22Q	5/22/2003	6/26/2003	6/30/2003	7/15/2003
0.25Q	8/28/2003	9/26/2003	9/30/2003	10/15/2003
0.25Q	11/20/2003	12/29/2003	12/31/2003	1/15/2004
0.25Q	2/26/2004	3/29/2004	3/31/2004	4/15/2004

Indicated Div: $1.00

Valuation Analysis
Forecast P/E	12.39	Trailing P/E	13.86
Market Cap	$449.9 Million	Book Value	249.3 Million
Price/Book	N/A	Price/Sales	N/A

Dividend Achiever Status
Rank	13	10 Year Growth Rate	24.71%
Total Years of Dividend Growth			10

Business Summary: Commercial Banking (MIC: 8.1 SIC: 6021 NAIC:522110)

BancFirst is a bank holding company that provides a range of commercial banking services to retail customers and small to medium-sized businesses both in the non-metropolitan trade centers of Oklahoma and the metropolitan markets of Oklahoma City, Tulsa, Lawton, Muskogee, Norman and Shawnee. Retail and commercial banking services include commercial, real estate, agricultural and consumer lending; depository and funds transfer services; collections; safe deposit boxes; cash management services; retail brokerage services; and other services tailored for both individual and corporate customers. As of Dec 31 2003, total assets were $2.92 billion and deposits amounted to $2.59 billion.

Recent Developments: For the year ended Dec 31 2003, net income slipped 5.0% to $31.9 million from $33.6 million the year before. Results for 2003 included a loss on the extinguishment of debt of $2.4 million. Total interest income decreased 10.3% to $141.0 million. Total interest expense fell 33.2% to $31.9 million. Net interest income slid 0.2% to $109.1 million, primarily due to low interest rates, partially offset by loan growth and changes in the mix of deposits. Provision for loan losses declined 29.5% to $3.7 million. Total noninterest income slid 8.0% to $48.8 million. Total noninterest expense climbed 7.1% to $105.4 million, mainly due to an operational loss and provisions for uncollectible receivables.

Prospects: Looking ahead, continued low interest rates could further negatively impact Co.'s net interest margin, whiles slow economic Looking ahead, continued low interest rates could further negatively impact Co.'s net interest margin, whiles slow economic growth could have an adverse effect on loan growth and asset quality. Additionally, complying with changes in corporate governance, reporting and other regulatory requirements will result in higher costs. Separately, in Nov 2003, Co. completed the acquisition of the Hobart and Lone Wolf, Oklahoma branches of Gold Bank. As a result of the transaction, Co. acquired approximately $16.3 million of loans and other assets, and assumed approximately $40.5 million of deposits, for a premium of approximately $2.73 million.

Financial Data
(US$ in Thousands)	12/31/2003	12/31/2002	12/31/2001	12/31/2000	12/31/1999	12/31/1998	12/31/1997	12/31/1996
Earnings Per Share	4.00	4.06	3.34	3.19	2.75	2.27	2.41	2.33
Tang. Book Val. Per Share	28.51	28.24	24.33	21.17	17.33	19.13	17.40	15.19
Dividends Per Share	0.910	0.760	0.720	0.640	0.560	0.480	0.400	0.320
Dividend Payout %	22.75	18.71	21.55	20.06	20.36	21.14	16.59	13.73
Income Statement								
Total Interest Income	141,032	157,139	182,643	182,389	159,384	161,042	97,990	87,843
Total Interest Expense	31,915	47,809	77,711	80,054	66,149	68,290	40,291	34,059
Net Interest Income	109,117	109,330	104,932	102,335	93,235	92,752	57,699	53,784
Provision for Loan Losses	3,722	5,276	1,780	4,045	2,521	2,211	982	994
Non-Interest Income	48,820	45,212	36,908	29,902	28,707	24,019	15,821	14,999
Non-Interest Expense	105,382	98,380	96,620	87,724	81,453	80,482	48,537	43,270
Income Before Taxes	48,833	50,886	43,440	40,468	37,968	34,078	24,001	24,519
Net Income	31,882	33,562	27,961	26,217	23,949	21,550	15,749	15,088
Average Shs. Outstg.	7,972	8,260	8,371	8,224	8,699	9,510	6,533	6,483
Balance Sheet								
Cash & Due from Banks	155,367	152,239	152,577	162,455	126,691	132,286	69,652	76,877
Securities Avail. for Sale	564,735	565,225	544,291	560,551	596,715	582,649	310,343	283,857
Net Loans & Leases	1,921,075	1,790,495	1,692,902	1,640,958	1,432,933	1,319,220	845,612	751,614
Total Assets	2,921,369	2,796,862	2,757,045	2,570,255	2,335,807	2,335,883	1,345,789	1,235,711
Total Deposits	2,585,690	2,428,648	2,401,328	2,267,397	2,082,696	2,024,800	1,175,110	1,105,453
Long-Term Obligations	36,063	34,087	24,090	26,613	26,392	12,966	7,051	6,636
Total Liabilities	2,665,997	2,545,354	2,533,877	2,373,297	2,171,093	2,133,966	1,222,855	1,123,615
Net Stockholders' Equity	255,372	251,508	223,168	196,958	164,714	201,917	122,934	112,096
Shares Outstanding	7,822	8,136	8,260	8,112	8,112	9,291	6,345	6,400
Statistical Record								
Return on Equity %	12.48	13.34	12.52	13.31	14.53	10.67	12.81	13.45
Return on Assets %	1.09	1.19	1.01	1.02	1.02	0.92	1.17	1.22
Equity/Assets %	8.74	8.99	8.09	7.66	7.05	8.64	9.13	9.07
Non-Int. Exp./Tot. Inc. %	55.50	48.61	44.00	41.32	43.30	43.48	42.64	42.07
Price Range	59.80–42.85	51.74–34.45	43.25–33.75	40.25–24.88	37.13–30.50	48.25–32.88	34.75–27.06	27.25–19.00
P/E Ratio	14.95–10.71	12.74–8.49	12.95–10.10	12.62–7.80	13.50–11.09	21.26–14.48	14.42–11.23	11.70–8.15
Average Yield %	1.77	1.73	1.86	2.04	1.63	1.19	1.30	1.45

Address: 101 North Broadway, Oklahoma City, OK 73102−8401 Telephone: (405) 270−1086 Web Site: www.bancfirst.com	Officers: H. E. Rainbolt − Chmn., James R. Daniel − Vice−Chmn.	Institutional Holding No of Institutions: 16 Shares: 42,480 % Held: −

29

BANCORPSOUTH INC.

Exchange	Symbol	Price	52Wk Range	Yield	P/E
NYS	BXS	$21.88 (3/31/2004)	24.45-18.56	3.29	13.02

*7 Year Price Score N/A   *NYSE Composite Index=100   *12 Month Price Score 101.3

Interim Earnings (Per Share)

Qtr.	Mar	Jun	Sep	Dec
2000	0.32	0.32	0.11	0.13
2001	0.27	0.28	0.26	0.38
2002	0.36	0.38	0.33	0.32
2003	0.50	0.37	0.43	0.38

Interim Dividends (Per Share)

Amt	Decl	Ex	Rec	Pay
0.16Q	4/23/2003	6/11/2003	6/13/2003	7/1/2003
0.16Q	7/16/2003	9/11/2003	9/15/2003	10/1/2003
0.18Q	10/22/2003	12/11/2003	12/15/2003	1/2/2004
0.18Q	1/28/2004	3/11/2004	3/15/2004	4/1/2004

Indicated Div: $0.72 (Div. Reinv. Plan)

Valuation Analysis

Forecast P/E	13.81	Trailing P/E	13.02
Market Cap	$1.8 Billion	Book Value	868.9 Million
Price/Book	2.15	Price/Sales	2.60

Dividend Achiever Status

Rank 144   10 Year Growth Rate 10.55%
Total Years of Dividend Growth 17

Business Summary: Commercial Banking (MIC: 8.1 SIC: 6022 NAIC:522110)

BancorpSouth is a bank holding company headquartered in Tupelo, MS with assets of $10.31 billion and total deposits of $8.60 as of Dec 31 2003. Co. operates 246 commercial banking, insurance, trust, broker/dealer and consumer finance locations in Mississippi, Tennessee, Alabama, Arkansas, Texas and Louisiana. Co. and its subsidiaries provide a range of financial services to individuals and small-to-medium size businesses. Co. operates investment services, consumer finance, credit insurance and insurance agency subsidiaries. Co.'s trust department offers a variety of services including personal trust and estate services, and certain employee benefit accounts and plans.

Recent Developments: For the year ended Dec 31 2003, net income climbed 17.1% to $131.1 million from $112.0 million in the corresponding period a year earlier. Net interest revenue slipped 5.5% to $351.1 million from $371.5 million the prior year. Provision for credit losses declined 14.6% to $25.1 million from $29.4 million the year before. Total non-interest revenue advanced 52.3% to $190.1 million from $124.8 million the previous year. Total non-interest expense rose 5.8% to $322.6 million from $305.0 million in 2002. As of Dec 31 2003, total assets was $10.31 billion, up 1.1% versus $10.19 billion on Dec 31 2002.

Prospects: Earnings are benefiting from strong growth in non-interest revenue, driven by substantial gains in mortgage loan originations, increased service charges, as well as from sharply higher insurance commissions stemming from the 2003 acquisitions of Ramsey, Krug, Farrell & Lensing, Inc. and Wright & Percy Insurance. Meanwhile, net interest revenue is being hampered by low interest rate levels and weak loan demand, despite improving loan demand during the latter part of 2003.Going forward, Co. will continue to evaluate opportunities to expand its products and services through both acquisitions and internal growth.

Financial Data

(US$ in Thousands)	12/31/2003	12/31/2002	12/31/2001	12/31/2000	12/31/1999	12/31/1998	12/31/1997	12/31/1996
Earnings Per Share	1.68	1.39	1.19	0.88	1.20	1.01	1.01	1.01
Tang. Book Val. Per Share	10.38	10.39	9.91	9.39	8.68	8.47	8.09	7.50
Dividends Per Share	0.640	0.600	0.560	0.520	0.480	0.440	0.380	0.340
Dividend Payout %	38.09	43.16	47.05	59.09	40.00	43.56	37.43	33.66
Income Statement								
Total Interest Income	526,911	590,418	665,835	738,791	414,187	383,519	307,094	277,919
Total Interest Expense	175,805	218,892	331,093	346,883	196,686	187,412	144,055	126,505
Net Interest Income	351,106	371,526	334,742	391,908	217,501	196,107	163,039	151,414
Provision for Loan Losses	25,130	29,411	22,259	26,166	14,689	15,014	9,008	8,804
Non-Interest Income	190,086	132,239	128,633	85,578	79,331	53,018	43,667	40,745
Non-Interest Expense	322,594	312,398	295,313	274,227	183,000	152,084	131,988	118,472
Income Before Taxes	193,468	161,956	145,803	177,093	99,143	82,027	65,710	64,883
Income from Cont Ops	...	...	...	139,152	...	...	...	...
Net Income	131,134	112,018	98,463	74,396	68,953	54,477	45,350	42,883
Average Shs. Outstg.	78,164	80,481	82,979	84,811	57,524	53,871	44,788	42,426
Balance Sheet								
Cash & Due from Banks	369,699	356,976	341,513	314,888	217,270	175,354	286,307	153,148
Securities Avail. for Sale	1,989,690	1,642,172	1,083,191	857,400	345,284	549,767	406,212	230,739
Net Loans & Leases	6,140,955	6,301,510	5,990,050	6,013,585	3,997,975	3,419,083	2,719,150	2,432,062
Total Assets	10,305,035	10,189,247	9,395,429	9,044,034	5,776,926	5,203,741	4,180,143	3,617,239
Total Deposits	8,599,128	8,548,918	7,856,840	7,480,920	4,815,415	4,441,963	3,540,255	3,161,379
Long-Term Obligations	267,364	139,757	140,939	152,049	138,560	178,318	47,539	55,778
Total Liabilities	9,436,129	9,256,424	8,590,026	8,254,458	5,279,526	4,747,384	3,819,721	3,301,915
Net Stockholders' Equity	868,906	807,823	805,403	789,576	497,400	456,357	360,422	315,324
Shares Outstanding	77,926	77,680	81,225	84,043	57,304	53,833	44,542	42,026
Statistical Record								
Return on Equity %	15.09	13.86	12.22	17.62	13.86	11.93	12.58	13.59
Return on Assets %	1.27	1.09	1.04	1.53	1.19	1.04	1.08	1.18
Equity/Assets %	8.43	7.92	8.57	8.73	8.61	8.76	8.62	8.71
Non-Int. Exp./Tot. Inc. %	44.99	43.22	37.17	33.26	37.08	34.83	37.62	37.17
Price Range	24.45-17.72	22.00-16.30	17.00-12.88	17.13-11.88	19.13-15.50	23.75-17.00	23.75-14.25	...
P/E Ratio	14.55-10.55	15.83-11.73	14.29-10.82	19.46-13.49	15.94-12.92	23.51-16.83	23.51-14.11	...
Average Yield %	3.03	3.06	3.40	3.54	2.85	2.14	2.21	N/A

Address: One Mississippi Plaza, Tupelo, MS 38804 Telephone: (662) 680-2000 Web Site: www.bancorpsouth.com	Officers: Aubrey B. Patterson - Chmn., C.E.O., James V. Kelley - Pres., C.O.O. Transfer Agents:SunTrust Bank, Atlanta, GA	Institutional Holding No of Institutions: 11 Shares: 167,669 % Held: -

BANDAG, INC.

Exchange	Symbol	Price	52Wk Range	Yield	P/E
NYS	BDG	$49.77 (3/31/2004)	49.77-31.76	2.61	16.00

*7 Year Price Score 99.4 *NYSE Composite Index=100 *12 Month Price Score 99.7

Interim Earnings (Per Share)

Qtr.	Mar	Jun	Sep	Dec
2000	0.48	0.85	0.86	0.71
2001	0.11	0.46	0.71	0.84
2002	0.06	0.57	1.02	0.87
2003	0.12	0.45	1.03	1.51

Interim Dividends (Per Share)

Amt	Decl	Ex	Rec	Pay
0.32Q	5/13/2003	6/16/2003	6/18/2003	7/18/2003
0.32Q	8/26/2003	9/16/2003	9/18/2003	10/17/2003
0.325Q	11/11/2003	12/17/2003	12/19/2003	1/16/2004
0.325Q	3/9/2004	3/17/2004	3/19/2004	4/19/2004

Indicated Div: $1.30 (Div. Reinv. Plan)

Valuation Analysis

Forecast P/E N/A	Trailing P/E 20.15
Market Cap $454.8 Million	Book Value 449.5 Million
Price/Book 0.69	Price/Sales 0.37

Dividend Achiever Status

Rank 215   10 Year Growth Rate   7.01%
Total Years of Dividend Growth 27

Business Summary: Rubber Products (MIC: 11.6 SIC: 3011 NAIC:326211)

Bandag is engaged in the manufacture of pre-cured tread rubber, equipment, and supplies primarily for the re-treading of truck and bus tires by a patented cold-bonding reaction process. Co. also does some custom processing of rubber compounds. As of Dec 31 2003, revenues were generated by more than 1,000 franchised dealers in the U.S. and abroad who are licensed to produce and market cold process retreads utilizing the Bandag process. Co.'s wholly-owned subsidiary, Tire Management Solutions, Inc., provides tire management systems outsourcing for commercial truck fleets. Tire Distribution Systems, Inc., also a wholly-owned subsidiary, sells and services new and retread tires.

Recent Developments: For the year ended Dec 31 2003, net income declined 20.3% to $60.2 million compared with income of $50.1 million, before an accounting change charge of $47.3 million, in the previous year. Net sales decreased 9.3% to $816.4 million from $900.5 million a year earlier. Sales for Tire Distribution Systems, Inc. fell 34.3% to $239.7 million, primarily due to the divestitures and closures of 71 locations in 2003 and 2002. Sales for Co.'s traditional retread business advanced 7.7% to $576.7 million. Tire retread volume decreased 5.0% in the North America and 8.0% in the International business units and rose 3.0% in the Europe business unit. Cost of products sold decreased 9.9% to $508.1 million.

Prospects: On Feb 13 2004, Co. announced the acquisition of an 87.5% majority interest in Speedco, Inc. from its founders and Equilon Enterprises, LLC, a Royal Dutch Shell Group company. Speedco provides quick-service truck lubrication nationwide through 26 company-owned and six licensed on-highway locations. Co. paid approximately $56.0 million for its stake and to assume and retire $20.1 million of debt. Speedco's nationwide presence provides a solid platform for the expanded delivery of en-route maintenance services both now and in the years ahead. Together, Co. and Speedco expect to improve the efficiency and costs of delivering vehicle services to the commercial trucking industry.

Financial Data

(US$ in Thousands)	12/31/2003	12/31/2002	12/31/2001	12/31/2000	12/31/1999	12/31/1998	12/31/1997	12/31/1996
Earnings Per Share	3.11	2.52	2.12	2.90	2.40	2.63	5.33	3.44
Cash Flow Per Share	4.03	6.60	5.63	4.77	5.16	3.83	3.11	4.80
Tang. Book Val. Per Share	24.60	21.96	21.21	20.02	18.61	17.84	16.99	17.84
Dividends Per Share	1.280	1.260	1.220	1.180	1.140	1.100	1.000	0.900
Dividend Payout %	41.15	50.00	57.54	40.68	47.50	41.82	18.76	26.16
Income Statement								
Total Revenues	828,186	911,953	982,209	1,013,426	1,027,878	1,079,498	741,528	768,999
Total Indirect Exp.	233,744	269,889	301,434	283,964	292,635	316,642	226,560	194,834
Depreciation & Amort.	27,179	32,333	46,155	50,465	53,764	51,410	36,857	34,595
Operating Income	86,303	78,375	73,881	108,107	101,817	110,285	111,168	132,016
Net Interest Inc./(Exp.)	(2,403)	(6,857)	(7,376)	(8,732)	(9,727)	(10,772)	(3,339)	(1,236)
Income Taxes	23,700	21,465	22,673	39,042	39,760	40,194	80,922	49,176
Income from Cont Ops	...	50,053	...	...	...	...	26,907	...
Net Income	60,200	2,793	43,832	60,333	52,330	59,319	121,994	81,604
Average Shs. Outstg.	19,369	19,888	20,686	20,778	21,764	22,559	22,908	23,746
Balance Sheet								
Cash & Cash Equivalents	200,784	143,673	155,019	93,385	60,094	47,633	197,975	33,542
Total Current Assets	466,286	416,082	450,174	427,179	428,118	439,124	598,994	341,700
Total Assets	660,529	617,827	718,572	714,549	722,421	755,729	899,904	588,342
Total Current Liabilities	148,193	147,861	186,075	132,735	154,053	174,909	306,542	139,214
Long-Term Obligations	22,857	28,571	94,286	100,000	100,000	100,000	100,000	...
Net Stockholders' Equity	477,077	424,593	488,996	474,157	454,075	467,297	463,414	410,867
Net Working Capital	318,093	268,221	264,099	294,444	274,065	264,215	292,452	202,486
Shares Outstanding	19,268	19,151	20,641	20,561	20,770	21,955	22,813	22,923
Statistical Record								
Operating Profit Margin %	10.42	8.59	7.52	10.66	9.90	10.21	13.28	17.16
Return on Equity %	12.61	11.78	8.96	12.72	11.52	12.69	5.80	19.86
Return on Assets %	9.11	8.10	6.09	8.44	7.24	7.84	2.98	13.87
Debt/Total Assets %	3.46	4.62	13.12	13.99	13.84	13.23	11.11	...
Price Range	42.30-28.67	41.16-26.47	46.19-25.34	42.63-22.38	41.31-23.63	59.50-28.38	55.00-45.75	55.50-44.75
P/E Ratio	13.60-9.22	16.33-10.50	21.79-11.95	14.70-7.72	17.21-9.84	22.62-10.79	10.32-8.58	16.13-13.01
Average Yield %	3.56	3.62	3.95	4.07	3.59	2.50	1.99	1.83

Address: 2905 North Highway 61, Muscatine, IA 52761-5886 **Telephone:** (563) 262-1400 **Web Site:** www.bandag.com	**Officers:** Martin G. Carver - Chmn., Pres., C.E.O., Warren W. Heidbreder - V.P., C.F.O., Sec. **Transfer Agents:** Bank Boston, NA, Boston, MA	**Investor Contact:** (319) 262-1260 **Institutional Holding** No of Institutions: 12 Shares: 6,030 % Held: -

BANK OF AMERICA CORP.

Exchange	Symbol	Price	52Wk Range	Yield	P/E
NYS	BAC	$80.98 (3/31/2004)	83.53-68.00	3.95	11.36

*7 Year Price Score 121.1 *NYSE Composite Index=100 *12 Month Price Score 91.0

Interim Earnings (Per Share)

Qtr.	Mar	Jun	Sep	Dec
2000	1.33	1.23	1.10	0.86
2001	1.15	1.24	0.52	1.27
2002	1.38	1.40	1.45	1.68
2003	1.59	1.80	1.92	1.82

Interim Dividends (Per Share)

Amt	Decl	Ex	Rec	Pay
0.64Q	4/30/2003	6/4/2003	6/6/2003	6/27/2003
0.80Q	6/25/2003	9/3/2003	9/5/2003	9/26/2003
0.80Q	10/22/2003	12/3/2003	12/5/2003	12/26/2003
0.80Q	1/28/2004	3/3/2004	3/5/2004	3/26/2004
		Indicated Div: $3.20		

Valuation Analysis

Forecast P/E	11.51	Trailing P/E	11.36
Market Cap	$121.2 Billion	Book Value	47.9 Billion
Price/Book	2.50	Price/Sales	2.49

Dividend Achiever Status

Rank	101	10 Year Growth Rate	13.39%
Total Years of Dividend Growth			26

Business Summary: Commercial Banking (MIC: 8.1 SIC: 6021 NAIC:522110)

Bank of America, with $736.45 billion in total assets as of Dec 31 2003, is a bank holding and financial holding company. Co.'s Consumer and Commercial Banking segment provides banking products and services. Co.'s Asset Management segment offers investment, fiduciary and banking and credit expertise; asset management services; and investment, securities and financial planning services. Co.'s Global Corporate and Investment Banking segment provides capital raising, advisory services, derivatives capabilities, equity and debt sales and trading. Equity Investments includes Principal Investing, which is comprised of investments in privately–held and publicly–traded companies.

Recent Developments: For the year ended Dec 31 2003, net income advanced 16.9% to $10.81 billion versus $9.25 billion in 2002. Co.'s ability to grow deposits and increase market share coupled with strong performance in mortgage, credit/debit card and investment banking operations and a significant improvement in credit quality drove earnings in 2003. Net interest income increased 2.6% to $21.46 billion from $20.92 billion a year earlier. Non–interest income climbed 21.0% to $16.42 billion, while non–interest expense rose 9.2% to $20.13 billion. Co. grew consumer checking accounts by 1.2 million and opened 4.3 million new credit card accounts in 2003.

Prospects: On Oct 27 2003, Co. announced an agreement to acquire FleetBoston Financial Corporation in a stock–for–stock transaction valued at nearly $47.00 billion. The combined bank will serve approximately 33.0 million consumer relationships, with leading market shares throughout the Northeast, Southeast, Midwest, Southwest and West regions of the United States. After the transaction is completed, Co. will feature an extensive delivery network through almost 5,700 retail banking offices, 16,500 automated teller machines, on–line and electronic bill–pay services and 24–hour telephone banking. For 2004, Co. expects to meet earnings projections of approximately $7.12 per share.

Financial Data

(US$ in Millions)	12/31/2003	12/31/2002	12/31/2001	12/31/2000	12/31/1999	12/31/1998	12/31/1997	12/31/1996
Earnings Per Share	7.13	5.91	4.18	4.52	4.48	2.90	4.17	3.92
Tang. Book Val. Per Share	22.76	23.76	20.79	18.99	15.66	16.68	14.85	18.43
Dividends Per Share	2.880	2.440	2.280	2.060	1.850	1.590	1.370	1.200
Dividend Payout %	40.39	41.28	54.54	45.57	41.29	54.82	32.85	30.61
Income Statement								
Total Interest Income	31,643	32,161	38,293	43,258	37,323	38,588	16,579	13,796
Total Interest Expense	10,179	11,238	18,003	24,816	19,086	20,290	8,681	7,467
Net Interest Income	21,464	20,923	20,290	18,442	18,237	18,298	7,898	6,329
Provision for Loan Losses	...	...	2,535	1,820	2,920	800	605	
Non–Interest Income	16,422	13,571	14,348	14,514	14,309	13,206	5,155	3,713
Non–Interest Expense	20,127	18,436	20,709	18,083	17,986	18,741	7,447	5,665
Income Before Taxes	15,861	12,991	10,117	11,788	12,215	8,048	4,796	3,634
Net Income	10,810	9,249	6,792	7,517	7,882	5,165	3,077	2,375
Average Shs. Outstg.	1,515	1,565	1,625	1,664	1,760	1,775	737	603
Balance Sheet								
Securities Avail. for Sale	67,993	68,122	84,450	64,651	81,647	78,590	46,047	12,277
Net Loans & Leases	365,300	335,904	322,278	385,355	363,834	350,206	141,010	120,315
Total Assets	736,445	660,458	621,764	642,191	632,574	617,679	264,562	185,794
Total Deposits	414,113	386,458	373,495	364,244	347,273	357,260	138,194	106,498
Long–Term Obligations	75,343	61,145	62,496	67,547	55,486	45,888	27,204	22,985
Total Liabilities	688,465	610,139	573,244	594,563	588,142	571,741	243,225	172,085
Net Stockholders' Equity	47,980	50,319	48,520	47,628	44,432	45,938	21,337	13,709
Shares Outstanding	1,441	1,500	1,559	1,613	1,677	1,724	712	573
Statistical Record								
Return on Equity %	22.53	18.38	13.99	15.78	17.73	11.24	14.42	17.32
Return on Assets %	1.46	1.40	1.09	1.17	1.24	0.83	1.16	1.27
Equity/Assets %	6.51	7.61	7.80	7.41	7.02	7.43	8.06	7.37
Non–Int. Exp./Tot. Inc. %	41.87	40.31	39.34	31.30	34.83	36.18	34.26	32.35
Price Range	83.53-65.63	76.90-54.15	65.00-46.75	60.81-38.00	75.75-48.06	87.88-47.81	71.19-48.69	52.13-32.63
P/E Ratio	11.72-9.20	13.01-9.16	15.55-11.18	13.45-8.41	16.91-10.73	30.30-16.49	17.07-11.68	13.30-8.32
Average Yield %	3.82	3.61	3.61	4.23	2.88	2.35	2.25	2.88

Address: Bank of America Corporate Center, Charlotte, NC 28255 Telephone: (704) 386–8486 Web Site: www.bankofamerica.com	Officers: Kenneth D. Lewis – Chmn., Pres., C.E.O., James H. Hance – Vice–Chmn., C.F.O. Transfer Agents:Mellon Investor Services LLC, South Hakensack, NJ	Investor Contact:704–386–5681 Institutional Holding No of Institutions: 46 Shares: 4,388,253 % Held: –

BANK OF HAWAII CORP (DE)

Exchange	Symbol	Price	52Wk Range	Yield	P/E
NYS	BOH	$46.33 (3/31/2004)	47.15-31.02	2.59	20.96

*7 Year Price Score 145.4 *NYSE Composite Index=100 *12 Month Price Score 106.0

Interim Earnings (Per Share)

Qtr.	Mar	Jun	Sep	Dec
2000	0.50	0.08	0.44	0.40
2001	0.42	0.32	0.37	0.35
2002	0.41	0.42	0.43	0.44
2003	0.47	0.48	0.61	0.65

Interim Dividends (Per Share)

Amt	Decl	Ex	Rec	Pay
0.19Q	1/27/2003	2/20/2003	2/24/2003	3/14/2003
0.19Q	7/28/2003	8/20/2003	8/22/2003	9/15/2003
0.30Q	10/27/2003	11/19/2003	11/21/2003	12/12/2003
0.30Q	1/23/2004	2/26/2004	3/1/2004	3/12/2004

Indicated Div: $1.20 (Div. Reinv. Plan)

Valuation Analysis

Forecast P/E	N/A	Trailing P/E	20.96
Market Cap	$3.0 Billion	Book Value	793.2 Million
Price/Book	3.01	Price/Sales	3.74

Dividend Achiever Status

Rank	219	10 Year Growth Rate	6.76%
Total Years of Dividend Growth	26		

TRADING VOLUME (thousand shares)

Business Summary: Commercial Banking (MIC: 8.1 SIC: 6022 NAIC:522110)

Bank of Hawaii, with assets of $9.46 billion as of Dec 31 2003, is a bank holding company. Co. operates in Hawaii, the West Pacific, and American Samoa. The Retail banking segment offers loan, lease and deposit products to consumers and small businesses. The Commercial banking segment provides corporate banking and commercial real estate loans, lease financing, auto dealer financing, deposit and cash management products to mid–to–large sized companies. The Investment Services group includes private banking, trust services, asset management, institutional investment advice and retail brokerage. The Treasury and Other Corporate segment provides corporate asset and liability management.

Recent Developments: For the year ended Dec 31 2003, net income increased 11.6% to $135.2 million compared with $121.2 million in the previous year. Results for 2003 and 2002 included information technology replacement charges of $21.9 million and $13.6 million, respectively. Results for 2002 also included provision for loan losses of $11.6 million and a restructuring charge of $2.4 million. Net interest income decreased 1.2% to $365.9 million from $370.2 million a year earlier. Net interest margin was 4.23% versus 3.99% the year before.Total non–interest income inched up 0.2% to $198.7 million, while total non–interest expense declined 3.1% to $357.9 million.

Prospects: Entering 2004, Hawaii's economy continues its strong pace, and Co. is in a position to build on its successes. Co. has a plan to execute over the next three years to continue its momentum and provide guidance through 2006. The new plan is expected to accelerate revenue growth in island markets, better integrate business segments, develop management teams, improve efficiency and maintain a discipline of dependable risk and capital management. Looking ahead to 2004, Co. expects net income to be approximately $157.0 million, or $2.76 per diluted share. Return on average equity is expected to rise to 20.0% in 2004.

Financial Data

(US$ in Thousands)	12/31/2003	12/31/2002	12/31/2001	12/31/2000	12/31/1999	12/31/1998	12/31/1997	12/31/1996
Earnings Per Share	2.21	1.70	1.46	1.42	1.64	1.32	1.72	1.63
Tang. Book Val. Per Share	13.37	15.08	16.16	13.93	12.57	12.06	11.46	12.13
Dividends Per Share	0.870	0.730	0.720	0.710	0.680	0.650	0.620	0.580
Dividend Payout %	39.36	42.94	49.31	50.00	41.46	49.81	36.33	35.58
Income Statement								
Total Interest Income	442,521	516,538	828,262	1,057,493	1,026,519	1,099,786	1,062,576	982,056
Total Interest Expense	76,579	146,307	368,584	501,262	451,776	523,185	526,278	499,773
Net Interest Income	365,942	370,231	459,678	556,231	574,743	576,601	536,298	482,283
Provision for Loan Losses	...	11,616	74,339	142,853	60,915	84,014	30,338	22,227
Non–Interest Income	198,720	199,921	452,619	263,429	265,581	211,751	187,789	164,477
Non–Interest Expense	357,875	370,835	597,616	496,430	553,238	540,279	474,261	419,816
Income Before Taxes	206,787	187,701	66,533	179,990	225,686	163,613	218,000	203,273
Income from Cont Ops	...	...	(55,631)	...	...	...	...	...
Net Income	135,195	121,180	117,795	113,661	132,957	106,964	139,488	133,124
Average Shs. Outstg.	61,085	71,447	80,577	79,813	80,044	81,142	80,946	82,425
Balance Sheet								
Cash & Due from Banks	363,495	374,352	405,981	523,969	639,895	564,243	795,322	581,221
Securities Avail. for Sale	1,991,116	2,287,201	2,001,420	2,507,076	2,542,232	3,018,403	2,651,270	2,306,586
Net Loans & Leases	5,637,331	5,256,265	5,966,530	9,168,140	9,280,848	9,416,809	9,114,325	8,347,905
Total Assets	9,461,672	9,515,797	10,644,079	14,013,816	14,440,315	15,016,563	14,995,464	14,009,167
Total Deposits	7,332,779	6,920,161	6,673,596	9,080,581	9,394,218	9,576,342	9,621,275	8,684,079
Long–Term Obligations	227,563	275,004	469,735	997,152	727,657	585,616	705,789	932,143
Total Liabilities	8,668,515	8,500,659	9,380,785	12,712,460	13,227,985	13,830,969	13,878,257	12,943,045
Net Stockholders' Equity	793,132	1,015,759	1,247,012	1,301,356	1,212,330	1,185,594	1,117,207	1,066,122
Shares Outstanding	54,928	63,015	73,218	79,612	80,036	80,326	79,685	79,918
Statistical Record								
Return on Equity %	17.04	11.92	N.M.	8.73	10.96	9.02	12.48	12.48
Return on Assets %	1.42	1.27	N.M.	0.81	0.92	0.71	0.93	0.95
Equity/Assets %	8.38	10.67	11.71	9.28	8.39	7.89	7.45	7.61
Non–Int. Exp./Tot. Inc. %	55.81	51.76	46.66	37.58	42.82	41.19	37.93	36.62
Price Range	42.72-29.43	30.75-23.88	27.88-16.94	22.94-11.25	24.69-17.38	25.44-14.75	28.00-20.38	21.88-16.63
P/E Ratio	19.33-13.32	18.09-14.05	19.10-11.60	16.15-7.92	15.05-10.59	19.27-11.17	16.28-11.85	13.42-10.20
Average Yield %	2.54	2.62	3.13	4.26	3.25	3.00	2.61	3.12

Address: 130 Merchant Street, Honolulu, HI 96813
Telephone: (808) 538-4727
Web Site: www.boh.com

Officers: Michael E. ONeill – Chmn., C.E.O., Alton T. Kuioka – Vice–Chair, Commercial Banking
Transfer Agents: Continental Stock Transfer &Trust Company, New York, NY; or Pacific Century Trust, a division of Bank of Hawaii, Honolulu, HI

Investor Contact: (808) 537-8037
Institutional Holding
No of Institutions: 4
Shares: 34,080 **% Held:** –

BANTA CORPORATION

Exchange	Symbol	Price	52Wk Range	Yield	P/E
NYS	BN	$46.29 (3/31/2004)	46.29-29.42	1.47	25.57

*7 Year Price Score N/A *NYSE Composite Index=100 *12 Month Price Score 104.5

Interim Earnings (Per Share)

Qtr.	Apr	Jul	Sep	Dec
2000	0.39	0.50	0.78	0.68
2001	0.11	0.50	0.75	0.65
2002	0.41	0.52	0.76	0.02
2003	0.44	0.28	0.62	0.47

Interim Dividends (Per Share)

Amt	Decl	Ex	Rec	Pay
0.17Q	4/29/2003	7/16/2003	7/18/2003	8/1/2003
0.17Q	7/29/2003	10/15/2003	10/17/2003	11/3/2003
0.17Q	12/9/2003	1/21/2004	1/23/2004	2/2/2004
0.17Q	1/27/2004	4/14/2004	4/16/2004	5/3/2004

Indicated Div: $0.68 (Div. Reinv. Plan)

Valuation Analysis

Forecast P/E	14.51	Trailing P/E	25.57
Market Cap	$1.2 Billion	Book Value	489.4 Million
Price/Book	1.87	Price/Sales	0.67

Dividend Achiever Status

Rank	204	10 Year Growth Rate	7.81%
Total Years of Dividend Growth	25

Business Summary: Printing (MIC: 13.4 SIC: 2759 NAIC:323119)

Banta provides a broad range of printing and digital imaging services. Co. operates in three business segments: print, turnkey services, and healthcare. The print segment provides products and services to publishers of educational and general books and special interest magazines. The print segment also supplies direct marketing materials and consumer and business catalogs. The turnkey services segment provides supply–chain management, product assembly, fulfillment and product localization services to technology companies. The healthcare products are primarily engaged in the production of disposable products used in outpatient clinics, dental offices and hospitals.

Recent Developments: For the twelve months ended Jan 3 2004, net income climbed 6.4% to $46.6 million compared with $43.8 million in 2002. Earnings benefited from Co.'s business diversity, market niche focus, productivity gains and operating efficiencies. Results for 2003 included after–tax restructuring and litigation settlement charges of $13.5 million, while results for 2002 included an after–tax asset impairment charge of $16.3 million. Net sales were $1.42 billion, up 3.8% from $1.37 billion in the prior year. Sales reflected double–digit increases from Co.'s supply-chain management business. Earnings from operations were unchanged at $81.6 million.

Prospects: Looking ahead, Co. expects commercial print market to improve over 2003, which should help its catalog and direct marketing businesses. Co.'s literature management business is also well–positioned to accelerate its growth with expanded capacity and capabilities. However, educational printing could be difficult in 2004 as many states struggle with budget deficits. As a result, improvement in educational spending is not expected until 2005. The supply–chain management sector should continue to benefit from Co.'s strong bonds with technology companies, prospects for increased technology spending and outsourcing trends.

Financial Data

(US$ in Thousands)	01/03/2004	12/28/2002	12/29/2001	12/30/2000	01/01/2000	01/02/1999	01/03/1998	12/28/1996
Earnings Per Share	1.81	1.71	2.01	2.35	0.59	1.80	1.44	1.63
Cash Flow Per Share	4.29	5.79	7.18	5.04	4.62	4.60	3.84	3.54
Tang. Book Val. Per Share	17.35	15.46	13.88	12.41	12.31	11.82	11.79	12.29
Dividends Per Share	0.660	0.640	0.610	0.600	0.560	0.510	0.470	0.430
Dividend Payout %	36.46	37.42	30.34	25.53	94.91	28.33	32.63	26.38
Income Statement								
Total Revenues	1,418,497	1,366,457	1,457,935	1,537,729	1,278,278	1,335,796	1,202,483	1,083,763
Total Indirect Exp.	223,770	221,846	189,704	195,682	217,992	167,932	159,019	126,855
Depreciation & Amort.	63,848	78,430	75,378	75,744	68,212	66,862	62,107	58,270
Operating Income	81,614	81,643	108,409	114,793	48,370	97,545	79,544	92,172
Net Interest Inc./(Exp.)	(8,420)	(11,343)	(13,720)	(16,754)	(12,362)	(10,825)	(11,062)	(10,214)
Income Taxes	27,800	28,002	32,200	37,900	18,600	33,150	27,500	33,300
Net Income	46,614	43,799	49,997	58,743	16,010	52,940	43,323	50,907
Average Shs. Outstg.	25,742	25,565	24,857	24,980	27,177	29,474	30,113	31,249
Balance Sheet								
Cash & Cash Equivalents	181,112	154,836	65,976	27,660	27,651	26,584	16,432	57,417
Total Current Assets	523,166	460,150	373,616	406,675	355,861	354,620	365,676	347,455
Total Assets	886,023	805,264	788,046	854,524	773,344	769,966	781,216	719,218
Total Current Liabilities	223,851	185,782	184,750	240,319	245,353	196,491	200,368	127,825
Long–Term Obligations	87,712	111,489	130,981	179,202	113,520	120,628	130,065	133,696
Net Stockholders' Equity	513,429	453,113	407,278	370,912	353,775	409,931	414,103	420,592
Net Working Capital	299,315	274,368	188,866	166,356	110,508	158,129	165,308	219,630
Shares Outstanding	25,791	25,247	24,729	24,566	23,942	28,260	29,793	30,969
Statistical Record								
Operating Profit Margin %	5.75	5.97	7.43	7.46	3.78	7.30	6.61	8.50
Return on Equity %	9.07	9.66	12.27	15.83	4.52	12.91	10.46	12.10
Return on Assets %	5.26	5.43	6.34	6.87	2.07	6.87	5.54	7.07
Debt/Total Assets %	9.89	13.84	16.62	20.97	14.67	15.66	16.64	18.58
Price Range	40.93-27.34	38.91-29.30	30.92-22.93	25.42-17.56	27.00-17.25	27.38-24.69	...	...
P/E Ratio	22.61-15.10	22.75-17.13	15.38-11.41	10.82-7.47	45.76-29.24	15.21-13.72	...	...
Average Yield %	1.95	1.90	2.23	2.92	2.46	1.96	N/A	N/A

Address: 225 Main Street, Menasha, WI 54952–8003	Officers: Donald D. Belcher – Chmn., Stephanie A. Streeter – Pres., C.E.O.	Investor Contact: (920) 751–7777
Telephone: (920) 751–7777	Transfer Agents:American Stock Transfer &Trust Company, New York, NY	Institutional Holding No of Institutions: 23
Web Site: www.banta.com		Shares: 420,071 % Held: –

BARD (C.R.), INC.

Exchange	Symbol	Price	52Wk Range	Yield	P/E
NYS	BCR	$97.64 (3/31/2004)	97.64–60.13	0.94	30.51

*7 Year Price Score 142.1   *NYSE Composite Index=100   *12 Month Price Score 102.3

Interim Earnings (Per Share)

Qtr.	Mar	Jun	Sep	Dec
2000	0.62	0.65	0.66	0.16
2001	0.65	0.68	0.68	0.74
2002	0.65	0.83	0.57	0.89
2003	0.89	0.94	0.98	0.39

Interim Dividends (Per Share)

Amt	Decl	Ex	Rec	Pay
0.22Q	4/16/2003	4/24/2003	4/28/2003	5/9/2003
0.23Q	7/9/2003	7/17/2003	7/21/2003	8/1/2003
0.23Q	10/8/2003	10/16/2003	10/20/2003	10/31/2003
0.23Q	12/10/2003	1/14/2004	1/19/2004	1/30/2004

Indicated Div: $0.92 (Div. Reinv. Plan)

Valuation Analysis

Forecast P/E	17.15	Trailing P/E	30.51
Market Cap	$5.0 Billion	Book Value	1.0 Billion
Price/Book	3.99	Price/Sales	2.91

Dividend Achiever Status

Rank	245	10 Year Growth Rate	5.24%
Total Years of Dividend Growth	32		

Business Summary: Medical Instruments &Equipment (MIC: 9.6 SIC: 3841 NAIC:339112)

Bard (C.R.) is a major multinational developer, manufacturer and marketer of health care products. Co. engages in the design, manufacture, packaging, distribution and sale of medical, surgical, diagnostic and patient–care devices. Co. holds strong positions in the fields of vascular, urology, oncology and surgical specialty products. Co.'s products are marketed worldwide to hospitals, individual health care professionals, extended care facilities, alternate site facilities and the home, employing a combination of direct delivery and medical specialty distributors.

Recent Developments: For the year ended Dec 31 2003, net income climbed 8.7% to $168.5 million compared with $155.0 million the previous year. Net sales increased 12.5% to $1.43 billion from $1.27 billion a year earlier, reflecting higher domestic and international sales. Vascular net sales advanced 18.3% to $307.3 million from $259.7 million, while urology net sales rose 7.6% to $451.5 million from $419.7 million the year before. Oncology net sales improved 12.5% to $336.3 million from $299.0 million, while surgery net sales jumped 18.6% to $272.3 million from $229.5 million the prior year.

Prospects: Co. is benefiting from stronger contributions across the majority of its businesses and geographies as well as from key new products. Recent sales have been notably higher in both Co.'s U.S. and international markets. Much of this improvement is attributable to the progress of strategic initiatives designed to achieve an increased level of sustainable revenue growth. Co. is funding these initiatives through significant improvements in its gross margin. Looking ahead, Co. will continue to place emphasis on strategic investing and achieving 12.0% annual growth in earnings per share.

Financial Data

(US$ in Thousands)	12/31/2003	12/31/2002	12/31/2001	12/31/2000	12/31/1999	12/31/1998	12/31/1997	12/31/1996
Earnings Per Share	3.20	2.94	2.75	2.09	2.28	4.51	1.26	1.62
Cash Flow Per Share	4.99	5.15	4.77	4.03	1.74	3.71	1.71	2.14
Tang. Book Val. Per Share	10.70	9.67	2.05	N.M	N.M	N.M	N.M	2.70
Dividends Per Share	0.900	0.860	0.840	0.820	0.780	0.740	0.700	0.660
Dividend Payout %	28.12	29.25	30.54	39.23	34.21	16.40	55.55	40.74
Income Statement								
Total Revenues	1,433,100	1,273,800	1,181,300	1,098,800	1,036,500	1,164,700	1,213,500	1,194,400
Total Indirect Exp.	560,500	464,100	446,000	413,000	404,500	(153,700)	542,100	568,700
Depreciation & Amort.	44,700	42,300	53,200	49,600	49,100	58,700	57,300	57,400
Operating Income	275,700	239,600	199,000	190,400	179,800	461,500	131,500	102,700
Net Interest Inc./(Exp.)	(5,900)	(6,100)	(8,000)	(15,600)	(17,200)	(20,400)	(29,400)	(26,400)
Income Taxes	54,700	56,000	61,700	47,100	55,200	212,100	32,600	10,200
Net Income	168,500	155,000	143,200	106,900	118,100	252,300	72,300	92,500
Average Shs. Outstg.	52,600	52,800	52,000	51,221	51,881	55,970	57,273	57,090
Balance Sheet								
Cash & Cash Equivalents	422,000	383,200	271,000	119,700	95,900	42,400	60,700	78,000
Total Current Assets	875,100	758,000	647,400	526,600	529,100	488,500	563,500	576,900
Total Assets	1,692,000	1,416,700	1,539,400	1,469,100	1,476,700	1,435,700	1,670,100	1,332,500
Total Current Liabilities	421,900	316,900	234,500	224,500	352,500	302,800	310,600	336,200
Long–Term Obligations	151,500	152,200	156,400	204,300	158,400	160,000	340,700	342,800
Net Stockholders' Equity	1,045,500	880,400	788,700	613,900	574,300	567,600	573,100	601,500
Net Working Capital	453,200	441,100	412,900	302,100	176,600	185,700	252,900	240,700
Shares Outstanding	51,754	51,602	52,383	50,908	50,781	51,497	56,785	56,986
Statistical Record								
Operating Profit Margin %	19.23	18.80	16.84	17.32	17.34	39.62	10.83	8.59
Return on Equity %	16.11	17.60	18.15	17.41	20.56	44.45	12.61	15.37
Return on Assets %	9.95	10.94	9.30	7.27	7.99	17.57	4.32	6.94
Debt/Total Assets %	8.95	10.74	10.15	13.90	10.72	11.14	20.39	25.72
Price Range	81.25–54.82	64.50–46.25	64.51–41.99	54.69–35.25	59.13–42.25	49.50–28.69	38.00–26.50	37.13–26.50
P/E Ratio	25.39–17.13	21.94–15.73	23.46–15.27	26.17–16.87	25.93–18.53	10.98–6.36	30.16–21.03	22.92–16.36
Average Yield %	1.33	1.57	1.62	1.82	1.55	1.95	2.22	2.05

Address: 730 Central Avenue, Murray Hill, NJ 07974	**Officers:** Timothy M. Ring – Chmn., C.E.O., John H. Weiland – Pres., C.O.O.	**Investor Contact:** (908) 277–8139	
Telephone: (908) 277–8000	**Transfer Agents:**EquiServe Trust Company, N.A., Providence, RI	**Institutional Holding** No of Institutions: 11	
Web Site: www.crbard.com		**Shares:** 365,188 **% Held:** –	

BB&T CORP.

Exchange	Symbol	Price	52Wk Range	Yield	P/E
NYS	BBT	$35.30 (3/31/2004)	39.66-31.75	3.63	17.05

*7 Year Price Score 110.2 *NYSE Composite Index=100 *12 Month Price Score 97.9

TRADING VOLUME (thousand shares)

Interim Earnings (Per Share)

Qtr.	Mar	Jun	Sep	Dec
2000	0.46	0.48	0.12	0.49
2001	0.53	0.54	0.48	0.57
2002	0.64	0.68	0.68	0.70
2003	0.69	0.67	0.21	0.50

Interim Dividends (Per Share)

Amt	Decl	Ex	Rec	Pay
0.32Q	6/24/2003	7/9/2003	7/11/2003	8/1/2003
0.32Q	8/26/2003	10/15/2003	10/17/2003	11/3/2003
0.32Q	12/16/2003	1/14/2004	1/16/2004	2/2/2004
0.32Q	2/24/2004	4/14/2004	4/16/2004	5/3/2004

Indicated Div: $1.28 (Div. Reinv. Plan)

Valuation Analysis

Forecast P/E	12.35	Trailing P/E	17.05
Market Cap	$16.8 Billion	Book Value	9.9 Billion
Price/Book	2.12	Price/Sales	3.43

Dividend Achiever Status

Rank	87	10 Year Growth Rate	14.32%
Total Years of Dividend Growth			32

Business Summary: Commercial Banking (MIC: 8.1 SIC: 6021 NAIC:522110)

BB&T, a multi-bank holding company with assets of $80.44 billion as of June 30 2003, operates more than 1,100 banking offices in the Carolinas, Virginia, West Virginia, Tennessee, Kentucky, Georgia, Maryland, Florida, Alabama, Indiana and Washington, D.C. Co.'s largest subsidiary is Branch Banking and Trust Company (BB&T–NC). BB&T–NC's subsidiaries include BB&T Leasing Corp., BB&T Investment Services, and BB&T Insurance Services. Co.'s other subsidiaries include Branch Banking and Trust Co. of South Carolina, Branch Banking and Trust Co. of Virginia, and Fidelity Service Corporation.

Recent Developments: For the twelve months ended Dec 31 2003, net income totaled $1.06 billion, down 17.7% compared with income of $1.29 billion, before a $9.8 million accounting change charge, in the prior year. Results for 2003 and 2002 included after–tax merger–related charges of $358.9 million and $24.7 million, respectively. Net interest income climbed 12.2% to $3.08 billion from $2.75 billion the year before. Provision for loan and lease losses slipped 6.0% to $248.0 million from $263.7 million the previous year. Non–interest income increased 18.6% to $1.89 billion from $1.59 billion, while non–interest expense jumped 35.9% to $3.11 billion from $2.29 billion a year earlier.

Prospects: Earnings are being hurt by weak commercial loan demand and costs stemming from the integration of recent acquisitions. On Feb 2 2004, Co. announced that its wholly–owned subsidiary BB&T Insurance Services completed its acquisition of McGriff, Seibels & Williams Inc., a Birmingham, AL insurance broker, for about $300.0 million of stock and $50.0 million of cash. On Dec 2 2003, Co. announced plans to acquire Republic Bancshares Inc., an operator of 71 banking offices in Florida with assets of $2.80 billion, for about $436.0 million. The transaction is expected to be completed during the second quarter of 2004. Separately, Co. is targeting earnings of between $2.81 and $2.91 per share in 2004.

Financial Data

(US$ in Thousands)	12/31/2003	12/31/2002	12/31/2001	12/31/2000	12/31/1999	12/31/1998	12/31/1997	12/31/1996
Earnings Per Share	2.07	2.70	2.12	1.55	1.83	1.71	1.30	1.27
Tang. Book Val. Per Share	10.91	12.04	13.49	11.91	9.66	9.50	8.22	7.91
Dividends Per Share	1.220	1.100	0.980	0.860	0.750	0.660	0.580	0.500
Dividend Payout %	58.93	40.74	46.22	55.48	40.98	38.59	44.61	39.37
Income Statement								
Total Interest Income	4,354,792	4,434,044	4,849,538	4,339,674	3,115,780	2,481,182	2,122,940	1,606,613
Total Interest Expense	1,272,787	1,686,584	2,415,053	2,322,046	1,534,065	1,233,778	1,023,415	778,120
Net Interest Income	3,082,005	2,747,460	2,434,485	2,017,628	1,581,715	1,247,404	1,099,525	828,493
Provision for Loan Losses	248,000	263,700	224,318	127,431	92,097	80,310	89,850	53,661
Non–Interest Income	1,889,135	1,692,475	1,378,691	777,022	761,356	528,002	474,914	297,389
Non–Interest Expense	3,106,110	2,385,538	2,228,430	1,761,539	1,346,904	961,374	937,150	654,053
Income Before Taxes	1,509,952	1,620,597	1,238,215	1,124,211	909,201	725,970	545,163	414,962
Income from Cont Ops	957,825	1,123,129	851,425	844,973	617,978	494,073	357,666	280,458
Net Income	1,064,903	1,303,009	973,638	626,442	612,847	501,825	359,942	283,664
Average Shs. Outstg.	514,082	478,792	459,269	398,915	335,298	293,571	276,440	223,672
Balance Sheet								
Cash & Due from Banks	2,217,961	1,929,650	1,871,437	1,471,035	1,138,820	938,797	839,579	638,748
Securities Avail. for Sale	16,256,773	17,747,965	16,719,359	13,878,582	10,575,265	8,031,796	6,549,393	5,136,789
Net Loans & Leases	60,794,990	50,416,621	44,891,339	38,932,351	28,524,467	22,350,692	19,516,871	14,180,663
Total Assets	90,466,613	80,216,816	70,869,945	59,340,228	43,480,996	34,427,227	29,177,600	21,246,562
Total Deposits	59,349,785	51,280,016	44,733,275	38,014,501	27,251,142	23,046,907	20,210,116	14,953,914
Long–Term Obligations	10,807,700	13,587,841	11,721,076	8,354,672	5,491,734	4,736,934	3,282,958	2,051,767
Total Liabilities	80,531,882	72,828,902	64,719,736	54,554,303	40,281,837	31,668,679	26,939,963	19,517,393
Net Stockholders' Equity	9,934,731	7,387,914	6,150,209	4,785,925	3,199,159	2,758,548	2,237,637	1,729,169
Shares Outstanding	541,942	470,452	455,682	401,678	331,170	290,211	272,104	218,594
Statistical Record								
Return on Equity %	9.64	15.20	13.84	17.65	19.31	17.91	15.98	16.21
Return on Assets %	1.05	1.40	1.20	1.42	1.42	1.43	1.22	1.32
Equity/Assets %	10.98	9.20	8.67	8.06	7.35	8.01	7.66	8.13
Non–Int. Exp./Tot. Inc. %	49.74	38.93	35.77	34.42	34.73	31.94	36.07	34.35
Price Range	39.66-31.15	39.23-31.26	38.48-31.42	38.25-22.00	40.44-27.31	40.63-27.31	32.50-17.63	18.38-12.94
P/E Ratio	19.16-15.05	14.53-11.58	18.15-14.82	24.68-14.19	22.10-14.92	23.76-15.97	25.00-13.56	14.47-10.19
Average Yield %	3.46	2.99	2.75	3.06	2.11	1.98	2.47	3.26

Address: 200 West Second Street, Winston–Salem, NC 27102	Officers: John A. Allison IV – Chmn., C.E.O., Kelly S. King – Pres.	Investor Contact:336-733-3058
Telephone: (336) 733–2000	Transfer Agents:Branch Banking &Trust Company, Wilson, NC	Institutional Holding
Web Site: www.bbandt.com		No of Institutions: 25
		Shares: 1,025,218 % Held: –

BECKMAN COULTER, INC.

Exchange	Symbol	Price	52Wk Range	Yield	P/E
NYS	BEC	$54.54 (3/31/2004)	55.18–33.87	0.81	20.50

*7 Year Price Score 128.1 *NYSE Composite Index=100 *12 Month Price Score 108.7

TRADING VOLUME (thousand shares)

Interim Earnings (Per Share)

Qtr.	Mar	Jun	Sep	Dec
2000	0.35	0.52	0.46	0.70
2001	0.37	0.58	0.52	0.74
2002	0.43	0.64	0.49	0.52
2003	0.70	0.82	0.62	1.07

Interim Dividends (Per Share)

Amt	Decl	Ex	Rec	Pay
0.09Q	4/10/2003	5/7/2003	5/9/2003	5/29/2003
0.11Q	7/31/2003	8/13/2003	8/15/2003	9/4/2003
0.11Q	10/7/2003	10/14/2003	10/16/2003	11/6/2003
0.11Q	...	2/18/2004	2/20/2004	3/11/2004

Indicated Div: $0.44 (Div. Reinv. Plan)

Valuation Analysis

Forecast P/E	15.29	Trailing P/E	20.50
Market Cap	$3.4 Billion	Book Value	738.5 Million
Price/Book	3.76	Price/Sales	1.29

Dividend Achiever Status

Rank	194	10 Year Growth Rate	8.31%
Total Years of Dividend Growth			12

Business Summary: Instruments and Related Products (MIC: 11.15 SIC: 3826 NAIC:334516)

Beckman Coulter designs, manufactures, and markets systems, which consist of instruments, chemistries, software and supplies that are designed to meet a variety of biomedical laboratory needs. Co.'s products are used in a range of applications from instruments used for medical research, clinical research and drug discovery to diagnostic systems. Co. operates in two segments: clinical diagnostics and biomedical research. Clinical diagnostics offers products that aid in the detection and monitoring of disease by means of laboratory evaluation and analysis of substances from patients. Biomedical research provides products for a wide range of applications based on the study of life processes.

Recent Developments: For the twelve months ended Dec 31 2003, net earnings jumped 52.9% to $207.2 million compared with $135.5 million in 2002. Growth in 2003 benefited from the successful introduction of a number of new products. Results for 2003 and 2002 included a credit of $49.9 million and an expense of $39.3 million, respectively, for litigation settlements. Results for 2003 also included a restructuring charge of $18.5 million. Sales rose 6.5% to $2.19 billion from $2.06 billion in the prior year. Gross profit increased 12.1% to $1.05 billion from $934.5 million in the previous year. Operating income jumped 47.4% to $329.5 million compared with $223.5 million the year before.

Prospects: Co. expects sales for full-year 2004 to grow 7.0% to 8.0% with 7.0% to 9.0% growth in Clinical Diagnostics and 5.0% o 6.0% growth in Biomedical Research, depending on currency translation. Net earnings for 2004 are expected to grow 13.0% to 15.0% and earnings per share should grow 11.0% to 13.0%, excluding unusual items in 2003. The tax rate is expected to increase from 27.0% in 2003 to 28.0% in 2004. For the first quarter of 2004, Co. expects sales to grow 8.0% to 10.0% due to continued strength in the Clinical Diagnostics Division and the specialty testing product area. Earnings per share for the first quarter are expected to be in the range of $0.48 to $0.52.

Financial Data

(US$ in Thousands)	12/31/2003	12/31/2002	12/31/2001	12/31/2000	12/31/1999	12/31/1998	12/31/1997	12/31/1996
Earnings Per Share	3.21	2.08	2.21	2.03	1.78	0.57	(4.79)	1.29
Cash Flow Per Share	3.49	4.86	4.32	3.38	3.57	(0.03)	2.49	2.40
Tang. Book Val. Per Share	2.99	N.M	N.M	N.M	N.M	N.M	N.M	7.12
Dividends Per Share	0.400	0.350	0.340	0.325	0.320	0.303	0.300	0.260
Dividend Payout %	12.46	16.82	15.38	16.01	17.92	53.16	N.M.	20.15
Income Statement								
Total Revenues	2,192,500	2,059,400	1,984,000	1,886,900	1,808,700	1,718,200	1,198,000	1,028,000
Total Indirect Exp.	718,200	711,000	686,000	658,700	650,100	682,800	825,300	427,700
Depreciation & Amort.	106,800	109,800	126,400	136,100	143,700	152,400	109,100	87,800
Operating Income	329,500	223,500	239,600	232,600	216,500	114,800	(237,000)	122,500
Net Interest Inc./(Exp.)	(30,300)	(37,900)	(46,900)	(65,600)	(66,000)	(74,400)	(23,300)	(12,300)
Income Taxes	65,600	43,400	63,500	56,400	48,700	13,100	12,500	36,800
Income from Cont Ops	...	...	141,500	...	...	...	...	...
Net Income	207,200	135,500	138,400	125,500	106,000	33,500	(264,400)	74,700
Average Shs. Outstg.	64,493	65,060	64,011	61,800	59,400	58,600	55,200	57,800
Balance Sheet								
Cash & Cash Equivalents	74,600	91,400	36,000	29,600	34,400	24,700	33,500	42,700
Total Current Assets	1,161,200	1,056,200	1,035,600	927,800	966,400	956,600	976,700	579,400
Total Assets	2,558,200	2,263,600	2,178,000	2,018,200	2,110,800	2,133,300	2,331,000	960,100
Total Current Liabilities	578,200	611,600	509,900	501,100	575,900	719,300	894,900	279,300
Long–Term Obligations	625,600	626,600	760,300	862,800	980,700	982,200	1,181,300	176,600
Net Stockholders' Equity	897,700	592,100	518,200	343,900	227,900	126,900	81,800	398,900
Net Working Capital	583,000	444,600	525,700	426,700	390,500	237,300	81,800	300,100
Shares Outstanding	62,000	61,000	61,200	59,700	58,000	56,800	55,200	55,952
Statistical Record								
Operating Profit Margin %	15.02	10.85	12.07	12.32	11.96	6.68	N.M.	11.91
Return on Equity %	23.08	22.88	27.30	36.49	46.51	26.39	N.M.	18.72
Return on Assets %	8.09	5.98	6.49	6.21	5.02	1.57	N.M.	7.78
Debt/Total Assets %	24.45	27.68	34.90	42.75	46.46	46.04	50.67	18.39
Price Range	51.31–28.50	52.47–25.78	47.01–34.50	41.94–23.66	27.56–20.00	31.81–20.00	26.06–18.78	20.38–16.25
P/E Ratio	15.98–8.88	25.23–12.39	21.27–15.61	20.66–11.65	15.48–11.24	55.81–35.09	N/A	15.79–12.60
Average Yield %	0.98	0.84	0.83	0.99	1.34	1.13	1.39	1.41

Address: 4300 N. Harbor Boulevard, Fullerton, CA 92834–3100	Officers: John P. Wareham – Chmn., C.E.O., Scott Garrett – Pres., C.O.O.	Investor Contact: (714) 773–7620
Telephone: (714) 871–4848	Transfer Agents: EquiServe Trust Company, N.A. Providence, RI	Institutional Holding
Web Site: www.beckmancoulter.com		No of Institutions: 20
		Shares: 394,969 % Held: –

BECTON, DICKINSON AND CO.

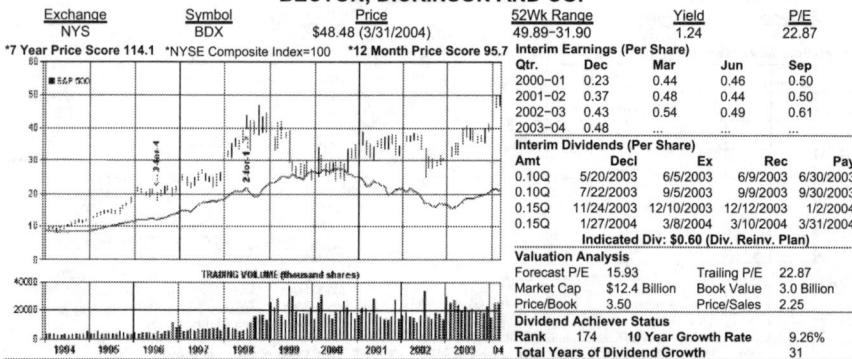

Exchange	Symbol	Price	52Wk Range	Yield	P/E
NYS	BDX	$48.48 (3/31/2004)	49.89-31.90	1.24	22.87

*7 Year Price Score 114.1   *NYSE Composite Index=100   *12 Month Price Score 95.7

Interim Earnings (Per Share)

Qtr.	Dec	Mar	Jun	Sep
2000–01	0.23	0.44	0.46	0.50
2001–02	0.37	0.48	0.44	0.50
2002–03	0.43	0.54	0.49	0.61
2003–04	0.48	...	...	...

Interim Dividends (Per Share)

Amt	Decl	Ex	Rec	Pay
0.10Q	5/20/2003	6/5/2003	6/9/2003	6/30/2003
0.10Q	7/22/2003	9/5/2003	9/9/2003	9/30/2003
0.15Q	11/24/2003	12/10/2003	12/12/2003	1/2/2004
0.15Q	1/27/2004	3/8/2004	3/10/2004	3/31/2004

Indicated Div: $0.60 (Div. Reinv. Plan)

Valuation Analysis

Forecast P/E	15.93	Trailing P/E	22.87
Market Cap	$12.4 Billion	Book Value	3.0 Billion
Price/Book	3.50	Price/Sales	2.25

Dividend Achiever Status

Rank	174	10 Year Growth Rate	9.26%
Total Years of Dividend Growth			31

Business Summary: Medical Instruments &Equipment (MIC: 9.6 SIC: 3841 NAIC:339112)

Becton, Dickinson and Co. is engaged principally in the manufacture and sale of a broad range of medical supplies, devices, laboratory equipment and diagnostic products used by healthcare institutions, life science researchers, clinical laboratories, industry and the general public. Co.'s operations consist of three worldwide business segments: BD Medical, BD Diagnostics and BD Biosciences. BD Medical include products such as hypodermic syringes and needles for injection. BD Diagnostics include products such as clinical and industrial microbiology, and sample collection products. BD Biosciences include products and services for a variety of applications in life sciences.

Recent Developments: For the three months ended Dec 31 2003, net income advanced 10.4% to $125.4 million compared with $113.6 million in the corresponding quarter the previous year. Revenues increased 14.1% to $1.20 billion from $1.05 billion in the year–earlier period. The increase is revenue growth was primarily attributed to favorable foreign currency translation, particularly with respect to the Euro. Revenues for BD Medical climbed 9.7% to $626.9 million from $571.6 million, while revenues for BD Diagnostics improved 20.9% to $400.9 million in the prior–year quarter. Revenues for BD Biosciences jumped 15.7% to $171.7 million from $148.4 million the year before.

Prospects: Co. is benefiting from strong revenue growth and continued improvement in operating efficiency. Sales growth is being fueled by increased sales of respiratory and flu diagnostic tests, as well as Co.'s broad line of safety–engineered products, immunocytometry instruments and reagents, and the the ProbeTec™ET system. Co. is also benefiting from favorable foreign currency translation, particularly in Japan and Europe. Meanwhile, Co. recently announced that it will focus its sales and marketing efforts on the Logic™and Paradigm Link™blood glucose meters, and will discontinue supply of the Latitude™system product offering in the U.S.

Financial Data

(US$ in Thousands)	3 Mos	09/30/2003	09/30/2002	09/30/2001	09/30/2000	09/30/1999	09/30/1998	09/30/1997
Earnings Per Share	0.48	2.07	1.79	1.63	1.49	1.04	0.90	1.15
Cash Flow Per Share	0.81	3.43	3.11	2.89	2.33	1.63	1.91	1.80
Tang. Book Val. Per Share	7.15	6.63	4.94	5.35	3.80	2.74	3.30	4.10
Dividends Per Share	0.400	0.400	0.390	0.380	0.450	0.340	0.290	0.260
Dividend Payout %	83.33	19.32	21.79	23.31	30.20	31.49	31.38	21.95
Income Statement								
Total Revenues	1,199,531	4,527,940	4,033,069	3,754,302	3,618,334	3,418,412	3,116,873	2,810,523
Total Indirect Exp.	390,273	1,442,524	1,252,229	1,195,130	1,197,684	1,185,945	1,079,464	946,697
Depreciation & Amort.	90,316	344,456	304,865	305,700	288,255	258,863	228,749	209,771
Operating Income	168,374	749,126	675,663	645,880	514,804	445,248	405,432	450,515
Net Interest Inc./(Exp.)	(8,929)	(36,560)	(33,304)	(55,414)	(74,197)	(72,052)	(56,340)	(39,373)
Income Taxes	33,997	162,650	148,607	138,348	127,070	96,936	104,298	122,566
Income from Cont Ops	...	...	...	438,402	...	...	...	...
Net Income	125,402	547,056	479,982	401,652	392,897	275,719	236,568	300,074
Average Shs. Outstg.	261,872	263,635	268,183	268,833	263,239	264,580	262,128	259,586
Balance Sheet								
Cash & Cash Equivalents	534,640	519,886	244,965	86,700	54,757	64,592	90,641	140,955
Total Current Assets	2,367,343	2,338,569	1,928,707	1,762,942	1,660,677	1,683,725	1,542,762	1,312,609
Total Assets	5,608,919	5,572,253	5,040,460	4,802,287	4,505,096	4,436,958	3,846,038	3,080,252
Total Current Liabilities	940,815	1,043,374	1,252,453	1,264,676	1,353,538	1,329,322	1,091,913	678,197
Long–Term Obligations	1,164,923	1,184,031	802,867	782,996	779,569	954,169	765,176	665,449
Net Stockholders' Equity	3,045,015	2,896,954	2,487,974	2,328,767	1,955,998	1,768,688	1,613,820	1,385,433
Net Working Capital	1,426,528	1,295,195	676,254	498,266	307,139	354,403	450,849	634,412
Shares Outstanding	252,705	251,133	255,529	259,236	253,496	250,797	247,843	244,168
Statistical Record								
Operating Profit Margin %	14.03	16.54	16.75	17.20	14.22	13.02	13.00	16.02
Return on Equity %	4.11	18.88	19.29	18.82	20.08	15.58	14.65	21.65
Return on Assets %	2.23	9.81	9.52	9.12	8.72	6.21	6.15	9.74
Debt/Total Assets %	20.76	21.24	15.93	16.30	17.30	21.50	19.89	21.60
Price Range	41.45-35.71	40.43-28.40	38.47-25.01	39.00-26.56	34.13-23.88	46.88-25.44	43.75-21.81	27.63-19.50
P/E Ratio	86.35-74.40	19.53-13.72	21.49-13.97	23.93-16.30	22.90-16.02	45.07-24.46	48.61-24.24	24.02-16.96
Average Yield %	1.05	1.14	0.85	1.12	1.64	0.90	0.84	1.05

Address: 1 Becton Drive, Franklin Lakes, NJ 07417–1880 **Telephone:** (201) 847–6800 **Web Site:** www.bd.com	**Officers:** Edward J. Ludwig – Chmn., Pres., C.E.O., John R. Considine – Exec. V.P., C.F.O. **Transfer Agents:**First Chicago Trust Company of New York, Jersey City, NJ	**Investor Contact:**800–284–6845 **Institutional Holding** **No of Institutions:** 4 **Shares:** 285,650 **% Held:** –

BEMIS, INC.

Exchange	Symbol	Price	52Wk Range	Yield	P/E
NYS	BMS	$26.00 (3/31/2004)	26.12-21.27	2.46	18.98

*7 Year Price Score 112.5   *NYSE Composite Index=100   *12 Month Price Score 91.9

Interim Earnings (Per Share)

Qtr.	Mar	Jun	Sep	Dec
2000	0.27	0.33	0.30	0.32
2001	0.28	0.33	0.34	0.37
2002	0.32	0.41	0.40	0.41
2003	0.33	0.36	0.32	0.36

Interim Dividends (Per Share)

Amt	Decl	Ex	Rec	Pay
0.14Q	7/31/2003	8/11/2003	8/13/2003	9/2/2003
0.14Q	10/29/2003	11/12/2003	11/14/2003	12/1/2003
0.16Q	1/29/2004	2/12/2004	2/17/2004	3/1/2004
100%	1/29/2004	3/2/2004	2/17/2004	3/1/2004

Indicated Div: $0.64 (Div. Reinv. Plan)

Valuation Analysis

Forecast P/E	14.15	Trailing P/E	18.98
Market Cap	$1.4 Billion	Book Value	1.1 Billion
Price/Book	2.29	Price/Sales	0.99

Dividend Achiever Status

Rank	192	10 Year Growth Rate 8.40%
Total Years of Dividend Growth		20

Business Summary: Paper Products (MIC: 11.11 SIC: 2671 NAIC:322221)

Bemis Company is a manufacturer of flexible packaging products and pressure–sensitive materials used by food, consumer products, manufacturing, and other companies worldwide. Flexible packaging products include a broad range of consumer and industrial packaging consisting of high–barrier products that include advanced multi–layer coextruded, coated and laminated film structures; polyethylene products; and paper products. Pressure–Sensitive Materials include roll label products, graphics and distribution products, and technical and industrial products. As of Jul 23 2003, Co. manufactured from 56 facilities in ten countries.

Recent Developments: For the year ended Dec 31 2003, net income decreased 11.1% to $147.1 million compared with $165.5 million in 2002. The decline in earnings reflected costs for restructuring items, legal fees, and higher selling expenses associated with acquisitions, sales force coordination and the introduction of new products. Results for 2003 included restructuring and related charges of $0.19 per diluted share. Net sales advanced 11.2% to $2.64 billion, reflecting acquisitions made during the latter half of 2002 and favorable foreign currency translation. Flexible packaging segment sales grew 12.3% to $2.10 billion. Pressure–sensitive materials segment sales climbed 7.0% to $534.1 million.

Prospects: The flexible packaging segment should continue to build its sales by seeking new market expansion in North America and Europe for its existing technology as well as investing in new technologies. Co. expects to launch the *ICE*®film product line in Finland during the summer of 2004. Meanwhile, the pressure sensitive materials segment launched a new product in December 2003 and after the completion of its restructuring efforts, Co. expects to significantly improve its capacity utilization and reduce fixed costs in that product line. Meanwhile, in 2004, Co. expects earnings in the range of $3.15 to $3.30 per diluted share, including restructuring charges of $0.02 per diluted share.

Financial Data

(US$ in Thousands)	12/31/2003	12/31/2002	12/31/2001	12/31/2000	12/31/1999	12/31/1998	12/31/1997	12/31/1996
Earnings Per Share	1.37	1.54	1.32	1.22	1.09	1.04	1.00	0.95
Cash Flow Per Share	2.88	2.66	2.99	1.96	1.75	2.07	1.33	1.27
Tang. Book Val. Per Share	5.80	4.10	4.39	4.76	5.51	4.87	4.61	4.37
Dividends Per Share	0.560	0.520	0.500	0.480	0.460	0.440	0.400	0.360
Dividend Payout %	40.87	33.76	37.87	39.34	42.20	42.10	40.00	37.89
Income Statement								
Total Revenues	2,635,018	2,369,038	2,293,104	2,164,583	1,918,025	1,848,004	1,877,237	1,655,431
Total Indirect Exp.	278,143	246,771	217,471	202,355	205,477	198,065	201,602	206,474
Depreciation & Amort.	128,189	119,231	124,147	108,130	97,717	88,910	78,856	66,192
Operating Income	255,338	282,152	260,191	244,969	218,194	208,548	195,270	175,387
Net Interest Inc./(Exp.)	(12,564)	(15,445)	(30,343)	(31,609)	(21,218)	(21,866)	(18,893)	(13,397)
Income Taxes	92,100	101,500	87,100	80,900	71,100	70,500	67,400	61,700
Net Income	147,145	165,515	140,325	130,602	114,775	111,432	107,584	101,081
Average Shs. Outstg.	107,733	107,492	106,243	107,106	105,314	106,648	107,760	106,504
Balance Sheet								
Cash & Cash Equivalents	76,476	56,401	35,101	28,910	18,187	23,738	13,827	10,223
Total Current Assets	751,906	721,655	586,897	639,959	583,581	517,939	516,393	466,921
Total Assets	2,292,534	2,256,650	1,922,974	1,888,643	1,532,143	1,453,054	1,362,567	1,168,795
Total Current Liabilities	315,586	325,853	238,182	495,097	253,268	242,788	251,187	214,445
Long–Term Obligations	583,399	718,277	595,249	437,952	372,267	371,363	316,791	241,077
Net Stockholders' Equity	1,138,733	958,974	886,148	798,757	725,895	670,807	639,885	567,097
Net Working Capital	436,320	395,802	348,715	144,862	330,313	275,151	265,206	252,476
Shares Outstanding	106,242	105,887	105,739	105,204	104,378	104,538	105,936	104,722
Statistical Record								
Operating Profit Margin %	9.69	11.90	11.34	11.31	11.37	11.28	10.40	10.59
Return on Equity %	12.92	17.25	15.83	16.35	15.81	16.61	16.81	17.82
Return on Assets %	6.41	7.33	7.29	6.91	7.49	7.66	7.89	8.64
Debt/Total Assets %	25.44	31.82	30.95	23.18	24.29	25.55	23.24	20.62
Price Range	25.53-19.89	29.04-19.94	26.08-14.41	19.25-12.03	19.97-15.22	23.47-16.97	23.59-17.91	18.56-13.06
P/E Ratio	18.64-14.52	18.85-12.95	19.76-10.91	15.78-9.86	18.32-13.96	22.57-16.32	23.59-17.91	19.54-13.75
Average Yield %	2.47	2.03	2.50	2.93	2.57	2.16	1.91	2.20

Address: 222 South 9th Street, Minneapolis, MN 55402–4099 **Telephone:** (612) 376–3000 **Web Site:** www.bemis.com	**Officers:** John H. Roe – Chmn., Jeffrey H. Curler – Pres., C.E.O. **Transfer Agents:** Wells Fargo Bank Minnesota, South St. Paul, MN	**Investor Contact:** 612–376–3000 **Institutional Holding** **No of Institutions:** 2 **Shares:** 18,146 **% Held:** –

BLACK HILLS CORPORATION

Exchange	Symbol	Price	52Wk Range	Yield	P/E
NYS	BKH	$31.87 (3/31/2004)	33.35-27.26	3.89	17.32

*7 Year Price Score 109.7 *NYSE Composite Index=100 *12 Month Price Score 94.7

Interim Earnings (Per Share)

Qtr.	Mar	Jun	Sep	Dec
2000	0.42	0.38	0.71	0.86
2001	...	1.34	0.61	1.47
2002	0.52	0.54	0.64	0.63
2003	0.62	0.54	0.54	0.14

Interim Dividends (Per Share)

Amt	Decl	Ex	Rec	Pay
0.30Q	4/29/2003	5/16/2003	5/20/2003	6/1/2003
0.30Q	8/4/2003	8/13/2003	8/15/2003	9/1/2003
0.30Q	10/21/2003	11/12/2003	11/14/2003	12/1/2003
0.31Q	2/4/2004	2/12/2004	2/17/2004	3/1/2004

Indicated Div: $1.24 (Div. Reinv. Plan)

Valuation Analysis

Forecast P/E	13.63	Trailing P/E	17.32
Market Cap	$746.3 Million	Book Value	707.4 Million
Price/Book	0.99	Price/Sales	0.56

Dividend Achiever Status

Rank	247	10 Year Growth Rate	3.47%
Total Years of Dividend Growth			32

Business Summary: Electricity (MIC: 7.1 SIC: 4911 NAIC:221121)

Black Hills is an energy and communications company with three segments. Co.'s Wholesale Energy group generates and sells electricity, produces coal, natural gas and crude oil primarily in the Rocky Mountain region, and markets and transports fuel products. Co.'s Electric Utility group engages in the generation, transmission and distribution of electricity to about 61,000 customers in South Dakota, Wyoming and Montana. Co.'s Communications group offers broadband telecommunications services, including local and long distance telephone, expanded cable television, cable modem Internet access and high-speed data and video services to residential and business customers in part of South Dakota.

Recent Developments: For the year ended Dec 31 2003, income from continuing operations before accounting changes decreased 2.7% to $57.0 million compared with $58.6 million in the previous year. Results for 2003 included contract termination revenue of $114.0 million and an impairment of long-lived assets charge of $117.2 million. Total revenues advanced 37.6% to $1.25 billion from $908.5 million a year earlier. Higher revenues reflected improved crude oil marketing volumes and prices and increased power generation capacity in the Wholesale group, higher off-system wholesale sales volume and prices at the Electric Utility group, and a larger customer base at the Communications group.

Prospects: On Mar 4 2004, Co. announced that the Public Utilities Commission of Nevada approved a long-term tolling contract to provide capacity and energy from its Las Vegas Cogeneration II power plant to Nevada Power Company. The contract, effective on Apr 1 2004, expires Dec 31 2013. The 224 megawatt combined-cycle plant will be fully dispatchable by Nevada Power to serve its retail load. Separately, Co. has agreed to acquire Cheyenne Light, Fuel & Power. Cheyenne Light is a regulated utility serving residential, commercial and industrial energy consumers in Cheyenne, WY. Cheyenne Light's 38,000 electric customers and 30,000 gas customers will add significantly to Co.'s retail presence in Wyoming.

Financial Data

(US$ in Thousands)	12/31/2003	12/31/2002	12/31/2001	12/31/2000	12/31/1999	12/31/1998	12/31/1997	12/31/1996
Earnings Per Share	1.84	2.33	3.42	2.37	1.73	1.19	1.49	1.40
Cash Flow Per Share	5.49	8.05	6.88	3.34	3.52	2.52	2.58	2.55
Tang. Book Val. Per Share	19.54	15.41	14.67	10.44	10.13	9.51	9.46	8.91
Dividends Per Share	1.200	1.160	1.120	1.080	1.040	1.000	0.940	0.920
Dividend Payout %	65.21	49.78	32.74	45.56	60.11	84.03	63.53	65.71
Income Statement								
Total Revenues	1,250,052	423,919	1,558,558	1,623,836	791,875	679,254	313,662	162,588
Total Indirect Exp.	289,759	148,207	157,679	92,191	56,219	65,802	45,938	43,745
Costs & Expenses	1,113,295	291,318	1,388,379	1,509,086	729,984	630,021	254,752	108,283
Depreciation & Amort.	80,791	69,738	54,051	32,864	25,067	24,037	22,311	22,794
Operating Income	136,757	132,601	170,179	114,750	61,891	49,233	58,910	54,305
Net Interest Inc./(Exp.)	(51,953)	(40,605)	(37,248)	(23,267)	(11,846)	(11,846)	(11,799)	(12,219)
Income Taxes	29,920	29,662	50,544	30,358	15,789	11,708	14,326	13,578
Eqty Earns/Minority Int.	5,747	1,426	(4,186)	(11,273)	...	...	...	...
Income from Cont Ops	56,995	63,193	...	...	...	...	...	...
Net Income	61,222	61,452	88,077	52,848	37,067	25,808	32,359	30,252
Average Shs. Outstg.	31,015	27,167	25,771	22,281	21,482	21,665	21,706	21,660
Balance Sheet								
Net Property	628,036	932,516	539,234	794,281	464,189	389,607	401,127	400,434
Total Assets	2,063,225	2,236,783	1,658,767	1,320,320	674,806	559,417	508,741	467,354
Long-Term Obligations	868,459	618,862	415,798	307,092	160,700	162,030	163,360	164,691
Net Stockholders' Equity	709,747	535,163	515,164	282,346	216,606	206,666	205,403	193,175
Shares Outstanding	32,297	27,102	26,890	22,921	21,371	21,719	21,705	21,675
Statistical Record								
Operating Profit Margin %	10.94	31.27	10.91	7.06	7.81	7.24	18.78	33.40
Net Inc./Net Property %	9.74	6.58	16.33	6.65	7.98	6.62	8.06	7.55
Net Inc./Tot. Capital %	3.58	4.75	8.58	7.65	8.49	6.08	7.67	7.44
Return on Equity %	8.03	11.80	17.09	18.71	17.11	12.48	15.75	15.66
Accum. Depr./Gross Prop. %	48.44	21.37	44.50	28.89	37.32	37.11	32.95	31.14
Price Range	33.35-22.26	36.84-19.15	58.05-26.35	45.13-20.56	26.38-20.50	27.38-20.75	24.21-17.50	18.92-15.25
P/E Ratio	18.13-12.10	15.81-8.22	16.97-7.70	19.04-8.68	15.25-11.85	23.00-17.44	16.25-11.74	13.51-10.89
Average Yield %	4.08	3.99	2.86	4.17	4.51	4.21	4.85	5.54

Address: 625 Ninth Street, Rapid City, SD 57701	**Officers:** Daniel P. Landguth – Chmn., David R. Emery – Pres., C.E.O.	**Investor Contact:**605-721-1700
Telephone: (605) 721-1700	**Transfer Agents:**Wells Fargo Shareowner Services,	**Institutional Holding**
Web Site: www.blackhillscorp.com	St. Paul, MN	**No of Institutions:** 146
		Shares: 11,707,176 **% Held:** 43.60%

BOWL AMERICA INC.

Exchange	Symbol	Price	52Wk Range	Yield	P/E
ASE	BWL A	$14.70 (3/31/2004)	15.15-11.12	3.67	15.81

*7 Year Price Score 141.1   *NYSE Composite Index=100   *12 Month Price Score 98.9

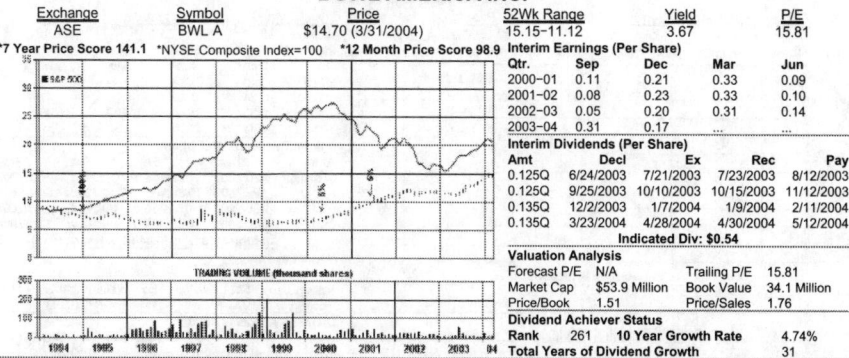

Interim Earnings (Per Share)

Qtr.	Sep	Dec	Mar	Jun
2000–01	0.11	0.21	0.33	0.09
2001–02	0.08	0.23	0.33	0.10
2002–03	0.05	0.20	0.31	0.14
2003–04	0.31	0.17	...	...

Interim Dividends (Per Share)

Amt	Decl	Ex	Rec	Pay
0.125Q	6/24/2003	7/21/2003	7/23/2003	8/12/2003
0.125Q	9/25/2003	10/10/2003	10/15/2003	11/12/2003
0.135Q	12/2/2003	1/7/2004	1/9/2004	2/11/2004
0.135Q	3/23/2004	4/28/2004	4/30/2004	5/12/2004
	Indicated Div: $0.54			

Valuation Analysis

Forecast P/E	N/A	Trailing P/E	15.81
Market Cap	$53.9 Million	Book Value	34.1 Million
Price/Book	1.51	Price/Sales	1.76

Dividend Achiever Status

Rank	261	10 Year Growth Rate	4.74%
Total Years of Dividend Growth		31

Business Summary: Sporting &Recreational (MIC: 13.5 SIC: 7933 NAIC:713950)

Bowl America, through its wholly–owned subsidiaries, operates bowling centers. Co. operates in the greater metropolitan area of Washington, D.C., the greater metropolitan area of Baltimore, MD, Orlando, FL, the greater metropolitan area of Jacksonville, FL, and the greater metropolitan area of Richmond, VA. These establishments are fully air–conditioned with facilities for service of food and beverages, game rooms, rental lockers, and playroom facilities. All centers provide shoes for rental, and bowling balls are provided free. In addition, each center retails bowling accessories. Most locations are equipped for glow–in–the–dark bowling, popular for parties and non–league bowling.

Recent Developments: For the thirteen weeks ended Dec 28 2003, net income fell 10.9% to $911,860 compared with $1.0 million in the corresponding prior–year period. Operating revenues dropped 2.9% to $7.3 million from $7.5 million a year earlier. Bowling and other revenues slid 1.9% to $5.2 million, while food, beverage and merchandise sales declined 5.3% to $2.1 million. Revenues were negatively affected by the operation of fewer locations, and slowed open play bowling. Also, Co.'s Florida centers appear to have been adversely affected by the newly imposed indoor smoking ban.

Prospects: During the thirteen weeks ended Sep 28 2003, Co. disposed of a property that housed a money–losing bowling center. Co. plans to use the proceeds from the sale to acquire property for a new bowling center, which may qualify for a deferral of the tax on the profit if the acquisition is closed within six months of the disposal. In the event such qualification does not take place, the tax would be paid in 2003. League bowling at comparable centers during October would have been flat, except for declines from a year ago in Co.'s Florida centers. Those facilities were subject to a new smoking ban. Meanwhile, mild and sunny weather in Maryland and Virginia has depressed daytime open play.

Financial Data

(US$ in Thousands)	6 Mos	3 Mos	06/29/2003	06/30/2002	07/01/2001	07/02/2000	06/27/1999	06/28/1998
Earnings Per Share	0.48	0.31	0.70	0.74	0.74	0.75	0.55	0.48
Cash Flow Per Share	0.62	0.20	1.05	1.16	0.91	1.18	0.88	0.84
Tang. Book Val. Per Share	6.63	6.54	6.41	6.34	6.66	6.78	6.12	5.65
Dividends Per Share	0.490	0.480	0.480	0.460	0.420	0.390	0.370	0.360
Dividend Payout %	102.08	156.45	68.57	62.16	57.91	51.83	67.21	74.07
Income Statement								
Total Revenues	13,453	6,145	29,376	29,810	29,401	28,902	27,547	27,087
Total Indirect Exp.	3,139	(579)	2,532	2,662	3,551	2,919	3,105	3,179
Depreciation & Amort.	787	395	1,613	1,764	1,940	2,100	2,268	2,323
Operating Income	3,713	2,401	5,113	5,394	4,893	5,751	4,552	4,103
Net Interest Inc./(Exp.)	...	...	476	599	1,036	823	685	675
Income Taxes	1,427	923	2,005	2,174	2,060	2,361	1,902	1,716
Net Income	2,486	1,574	3,583	3,819	3,868	4,213	3,335	3,062
Average Shs. Outstg.	5,138	5,138	5,145	5,132	5,222	5,587	6,026	6,240
Balance Sheet								
Cash & Cash Equivalents	12,132	11,210	1,503	1,634	1,338	1,523	1,557	1,944
Total Current Assets	15,232	14,643	12,608	11,538	9,613	11,495	10,453	11,194
Total Assets	39,973	38,842	37,537	36,563	37,598	40,711	41,748	40,435
Total Current Liabilities	4,051	3,454	2,711	1,820	2,407	2,165	2,064	1,968
Net Stockholders' Equity	34,069	33,652	32,953	32,682	32,703	34,868	35,477	35,292
Net Working Capital	11,181	11,189	9,897	9,718	7,206	9,330	8,389	9,226
Shares Outstanding	5,138	5,138	5,138	5,149	4,908	5,139	5,793	6,236
Statistical Record								
Operating Profit Margin %	27.60	39.07	17.40	18.09	16.64	19.89	16.52	15.14
Return on Equity %	7.29	4.67	10.87	11.68	11.82	12.08	9.40	8.67
Return on Assets %	6.21	4.05	9.54	10.44	10.28	10.34	7.98	7.57
Price Range	14.00-11.75	13.00-11.75	12.15-11.12	12.25-10.01	9.90-7.26	7.50-6.24	8.16-5.78	8.50-6.12
P/E Ratio	29.17-24.48	41.94-37.90	17.36-15.89	16.55-13.53	13.38-9.81	10.00-8.31	14.84-10.51	17.72-12.76
Average Yield %	3.79	3.83	4.12	4.16	4.93	5.94	5.56	4.76

Address: 6446 Edsall Road, Alexandria, VA 22312 Telephone: (703) 941–6300 Web Site: N/A	Officers: Leslie H. Goldberg – Pres., C.E.O., C.O.O., Ruth E. Macklin – Sr. V.P., Treas.	Institutional Holding No of Institutions: 11 Shares: 476,509 % Held: 9.30%

BRADY CORP.

Exchange	Symbol	Price	52Wk Range	Yield	P/E
NYS	BRC	$38.08 (3/31/2004)	42.50-29.10	2.21	18.13

*7 Year Price Score 110.0 *NYSE Composite Index=100 *12 Month Price Score 104.1

TRADING VOLUME (thousand shares)

Interim Earnings (Per Share)

Qtr.	Oct	Jan	Apr	Jul
2000-01	0.49	0.37	0.44	1.03
2001-02	0.34	0.26	0.36	1.41
2002-03	0.35	0.12	0.37	0.95
2003-04	0.44	0.34	...	...

Interim Dividends (Per Share)

Amt	Decl	Ex	Rec	Pay
0.20Q	5/20/2003	7/8/2003	7/10/2003	7/31/2003
0.21Q	9/9/2003	10/8/2003	10/10/2003	10/31/2003
0.21Q	11/20/2003	1/7/2004	1/9/2004	1/30/2004
0.21Q	2/6/2004	4/6/2004	4/9/2004	4/30/2004

Indicated Div: $0.84 (Div. Reinv. Plan)

Valuation Analysis

Forecast P/E	21.07	Trailing P/E	18.13
Market Cap	$811.3 Million	Book Value	366.1 Million
Price/Book	2.52	Price/Sales	1.56

Dividend Achiever Status

Rank	84	10 Year Growth Rate	14.64%
Total Years of Dividend Growth			19

Business Summary: Consumer Accessories (MIC: 4.6 SIC: 3993 NAIC:339950)

Brady is an international manufacturer and marketer of identification products and specialty materials. Co.'s products include labels and signs, printing systems and software, label–application and data–collection systems, safety devices and precision die–cut materials. Co.'s major products include identification applications and specialty tape products, including wire and cable markers, high–performance labels, laboratory identification products, stand–alone printing systems, bar–code and other software, graphics and workplace applications. Co. serves more than 300,000 customers in electronics, telecommunications, manufacturing, electrical, construction, education and other industries.

Recent Developments: For the three months ended Jan 31 2004, net income totaled $8.0 million compared with $2.8 million in the corresponding prior–year period. Results for the recent period included a pre–tax restructuring charge of $66,000. Net sales climbed 18.0% to $152.9 million from $129.6 million a year earlier, fueled primarily by acquisitions and favorable foreign currency exchange rates. Cost of products sold increased 13.4% to $74.7 million from $65.9 million the year before, while selling, general and administrative expenses grew 10.9% to $60.5 million from $54.5 million the previous year. Operating income more than doubled to $12.1 million from $4.5 million the year before.

Prospects: Sales and earnings are being positively affected by improved conditions in several key markets in the U.S. and Europe, along with strong telecom and electronics markets in Asia. In addition, results are benefiting from cost–savings generated by Co.'s restructuring initiatives. Co. anticipates further market improvements, as well as ongoing benefits from acquisitions and exchange rates, should continue to boost results during the remainder of fiscal 2004. Co. is targeting sales of between $615.0 million and $645.0 million for the current fiscal year, along with net income in the range of $37.0 million to $41.0 million.

Financial Data
(US$ in Thousands)

	6 Mos	3 Mos	07/31/2003	07/31/2002	07/31/2001	07/31/2000	07/31/1999	07/31/1998
Earnings Per Share	2.10	1.88	1.79	2.37	2.33	4.07	3.43	2.43
Cash Flow Per Share	0.92	0.43	1.18	1.16	1.15	1.05	1.35	1.04
Tang. Book Val. Per Share	8.61	8.63	8.93	9.22	8.88	8.25	8.17	7.86
Dividends Per Share	.820	0.810	0.800	0.760	0.720	0.680	0.640	0.600
Dividend Payout %	39.05	43.09	44.65	32.07	30.90	16.71	18.66	24.69
Income Statement								
Total Revenues	304,854	151,906	554,866	516,962	545,944	541,077	470,862	455,150
Total Indirect Exp.	129,172	63,005	248,124	219,273	244,109	242,179	204,887	204,325
Depreciation & Amort.	10,162	4,783	17,771	16,630	22,646	17,833	15,149	13,288
Operating Income	27,821	15,758	32,149	41,503	44,522	69,291	63,772	45,930
Net Interest Inc./(Exp.)	(31)	(30)	(121)	(82)	(418)	(578)	(445)	(403)
Income Taxes	9,263	5,216	11,035	14,982	17,244	28,930	25,198	18,129
Net Income	18,386	10,353	21,420	28,253	27,546	47,201	39,584	28,036
Average Shs. Outstg.	23,787	23,334	46,754	46,679	46,214	45,866	45,365	45,203
Balance Sheet								
Cash & Cash Equivalents	58,211	60,105	76,088	75,969	62,811	60,784	75,466	65,609
Total Current Assets	218,375	215,932	215,157	210,026	194,993	203,183	203,169	184,053
Total Assets	485,990	469,057	449,519	420,525	392,476	398,134	351,120	311,824
Total Current Liabilities	99,926	95,248	91,279	74,262	71,163	87,099	73,285	58,667
Long–Term Obligations	48	581	568	3,751	4,144	4,157	1,402	3,716
Net Stockholders' Equity	366,099	353,069	338,961	324,242	302,579	291,224	260,564	233,373
Net Working Capital	118,449	120,684	123,878	135,764	123,830	116,084	129,884	125,386
Shares Outstanding	23,643	23,470	23,309	23,121	22,914	22,731	22,604	22,496
Statistical Record								
Operating Profit Margin %	9.12	10.37	5.79	8.02	8.15	12.80	13.54	10.10
Return on Equity %	5.02	2.93	6.31	8.71	9.10	16.20	15.19	12.01
Return on Assets %	3.78	2.20	4.76	6.71	7.01	11.85	11.27	8.99
Debt/Total Assets %	0.01	0.12	0.12	0.89	1.05	1.04	0.39	1.19
Price Range	42.50-31.81	36.20-31.81	35.40-25.78	40.60-27.30	38.94-27.75	35.81-24.75	35.00-16.38	35.50-20.00
P/E Ratio	55.19-41.31	82.27-72.30	19.78-14.40	17.13-11.52	16.71-11.91	8.80-6.08	10.20-4.77	14.61-8.23
Average Yield %	2.77	2.31	2.50	2.20	2.20	1.68	3.23	1.91

Address: 6555 West Good Hope Road, Milwaukee, WI 53223-0571 Telephone: (414) 358-6600 Web Site: www.bradycorp.com	Officers: Katherine M. Hudson – Chmn., Frank M. Jaehnert – Pres., C.E.O. Transfer Agents:Wells Fargo Shareowner Services, St. Paul, MN	Investor Contact:414-438-6940 Institutional Holding No of Institutions: 90 Shares: 16,562,950 % Held: 72%

BRIGGS & STRATTON CORP.

Exchange	Symbol	Price	52Wk Range	Yield	P/E
NYS	BGG	$67.47 (3/31/2004)	70.35-39.11	1.96	15.58

*7 Year Price Score 115.4 *NYSE Composite Index=100 *12 Month Price Score 114.4

Interim Earnings (Per Share)

Qtr.	Sep	Dec	Mar	Jun
2000-01	(0.29)	0.92	1.38	0.20
2001-02	(0.81)	0.11	1.58	1.48
2002-03	(0.32)	0.53	1.81	1.47
2003-04	0.18	0.87	...	...

Interim Dividends (Per Share)

Amt	Decl	Ex	Rec	Pay
0.32Q	4/16/2003	5/29/2003	6/2/2003	6/27/2003
0.33Q	8/6/2003	8/19/2003	8/21/2003	10/1/2003
0.33Q	10/15/2003	11/26/2003	12/1/2003	1/2/2004
0.33Q	1/21/2004	2/26/2004	3/1/2004	4/1/2004

Indicated Div: $1.32 (Div. Reinv. Plan)

Valuation Analysis

Forecast P/E	14.75	Trailing P/E	15.58
Market Cap	$1.5 Billion	Book Value	549.1 Million
Price/Book	2.77	Price/Sales	0.84

Dividend Achiever Status

Rank	266	10 Year Growth Rate	4.14%
Total Years of Dividend Growth		12	

Business Summary: Industrial Machinery and Equipment (MIC: 11.5 SIC: 3519 NAIC:333618)

Briggs & Stratton is a producer of air cooled gasoline engines for outdoor power equipment. Co. designs, manufactures, markets and services these products for original equipment manufacturers (OEMs) worldwide. These engines are primarily aluminum alloy gasoline engines ranging from 3 to 31 horsepower. Co. engines are marketed under various brand names including Classic™Sprint™, Quattro™, Quantum®, INTEK™, I/C®, Industrial Plus™and Vanguard™. Additionally, through its wholly owned subsidiary, Briggs & Stratton Power Products Group, LLC, Co. designs, manufactures and markets portable generators, pressure washers and related accessories.

Recent Developments: For the three months ended Dec 28 2003, net income increased 75.7% to $20.6 million compared with $11.7 million in the corresponding year-earlier period. Net sales climbed 18.0% to $416.0 million from $352.6 million the year before. Co. attributed the net sales improvement to volume increases from both its engine and power products business segments, a mix of engine shipments that favored higher priced product and a benefit from more favorable exchange rates on Euro denominated engine sales. Income from operations was $38.7 million, 46.1% higher than the prior-year quarter.

Prospects: Healthy top line growth trends strengthen Co.'s near-term outlook. Co. noted that major retailers of power equipment are all projecting growth over last year's performance and expect original equipment manufacturers (OEM's) to have adequate inventory to meet the spring demand. So, certain OEM's have moved up their production schedules, thus making their engine purchases earlier than in previous years. Also, Co.'s power product segment is seeing strong growth, fueled by increased promotional activities and Co.'s introduction of a new pressure washer product. As a result, Co. has again raised its full-year fiscal 2004 net income forecast to between $105.0 million and $110.0 million.

Financial Data

(US$ in Thousands)	6 Mos	3 Mos	06/29/2003	06/30/2002	07/01/2001	07/02/2000	06/27/1999	06/28/1998
Earnings Per Share	1.08	0.18	3.49	2.36	2.21	5.97	4.52	2.85
Cash Flow Per Share	(8.40)	(4.39)	6.83	8.17	3.09	3.39	4.85	5.50
Tang. Book Val. Per Share	17.66	16.96	16.30	13.33	11.53	18.51	15.44	12.86
Dividends Per Share	1.290	1.280	1.280	1.260	1.240	1.200	1.160	1.120
Dividend Payout %	119.44	711.11	36.67	53.38	56.10	20.10	25.66	39.29
Income Statement								
Total Revenues	747,379	331,395	1,657,633	1,529,372	1,312,446	1,590,557	1,501,726	1,327,610
Total Indirect Exp.	98,070	45,900	178,078	153,731	141,000	134,225	125,219	129,986
Depreciation & Amort.	32,290	15,846	112	112	2,104	51,370	49,604	47,716
Operating Income	52,971	14,295	152,404	118,358	99,106	205,229	180,136	124,688
Net Interest Inc./(Exp.)	(19,428)	(9,832)	(37,889)	(42,244)	(28,596)	(19,687)	(15,031)	(16,632)
Income Taxes	11,600	1,890	37,940	27,390	23,860	80,150	63,670	42,500
Eqty Earns/Minority Int.	...	...	(56)	70,015	4,433	14,364	5,442	5,232
Income from Cont Ops	...	...	...	116,120	...	...	...	...
Net Income	24,651	4,016	80,638	53,120	48,013	136,473	106,101	70,645
Average Shs. Outstg.	25,096	22,105	24,480	24,452	21,966	22,842	23,459	24,775
Balance Sheet								
Cash & Cash Equivalents	119,323	238,556	324,815	215,945	88,743	16,989	60,806	84,527
Total Current Assets	871,817	795,484	807,147	669,944	613,430	471,997	459,146	382,046
Total Assets	1,523,601	1,454,036	1,475,193	1,349,039	1,296,195	930,245	875,885	793,409
Total Current Liabilities	314,521	266,119	301,395	266,023	242,182	312,778	282,502	222,945
Long-Term Obligations	501,356	501,063	503,397	499,022	508,134	98,512	113,307	128,102
Net Stockholders' Equity	549,090	530,393	514,987	449,646	422,752	409,465	365,910	316,488
Net Working Capital	557,296	529,365	505,752	403,921	371,248	159,219	176,644	159,101
Shares Outstanding	22,365	22,183	21,785	21,639	21,599	21,746	23,200	23,824
Statistical Record								
Operating Profit Margin %	7.08	4.31	9.19	7.73	7.55	12.90	11.99	9.39
Return on Equity %	4.48	0.75	15.65	25.82	11.35	33.32	28.99	22.32
Return on Assets %	1.61	0.27	5.46	8.60	3.70	14.67	12.11	8.90
Debt/Total Assets %	32.90	34.46	34.12	36.99	39.20	10.58	12.93	16.14
Price Range	68.50-50.50	60.76-50.50	50.80-31.18	48.12-30.24	48.00-30.88	63.00-31.31	68.25-33.69	52.63-37.00
P/E Ratio	63.43-46.76	337.6-280.6	14.56-8.93	20.39-12.81	21.72-13.97	10.55-5.24	15.10-7.45	18.46-12.98
Average Yield %	2.14	2.30	3.16	3.12	3.10	2.44	2.35	2.37

Address: 12301 West Wirth Street, Wauwatosa, WI 53222	Officers: Frederick P. Stratton – Chmn. Emeritus, John S. Shiely – Chmn., Pres., C.E.O.	Investor Contact:414-259-5333
Telephone: (414) 259-5333	Transfer Agents:U.S. Bank, N.A., Milwaukee, WI	Institutional Holding No of Institutions: 76
Web Site: www.briggsandstratton.com		Shares: 721,582 % Held: –

43

BROWN & BROWN, INC.

Exchange	Symbol	Price	52Wk Range	Yield	P/E
NYS	BRO	$38.76 (3/31/2004)	39.30–29.71	0.72	24.23

*7 Year Price Score N/A   *NYSE Composite Index=100   *12 Month Price Score 88.0

TRADING VOLUME (thousand shares)

Interim Earnings (Per Share)

Qtr.	Mar	Jun	Sep	Dec
2000	0.15	0.24	0.15	0.04
2001	0.20	0.20	0.21	0.24
2002	0.31	0.31	0.29	0.31
2003	0.44	0.41	0.38	0.37

Interim Dividends (Per Share)

Amt	Decl	Ex	Rec	Pay
0.058Q	4/24/2003	5/6/2003	5/8/2003	5/22/2003
0.058Q	7/23/2003	8/4/2003	8/6/2003	8/20/2003
0.07Q	10/22/2003	11/3/2003	11/5/2003	11/19/2003
0.07Q	1/21/2004	2/2/2004	2/4/2004	2/18/2004
				Indicated Div: $0.28

Valuation Analysis

Forecast P/E	16.98	Trailing P/E	24.23
Market Cap	$2.7 Billion	Book Value	498.0 Million
Price/Book	4.52	Price/Sales	4.08

Dividend Achiever Status

Rank	97	10 Year Growth Rate	13.78%
Total Years of Dividend Growth			10

Business Summary: Insurance (MIC: 8.2 SIC: 6411 NAIC:524210)

Brown & Brown is primarily engaged in the property and casualty business. Co.'s business is divided into four divisions. The Retail Division sells insurance products to commercial, professional and individual clients. The National Programs Division is comprised of two units: Professional Programs, which provides professional liability and related package products; and Special Programs, which markets targeted products and services for specific industries, trade groups and market niches. The Service Division provides third–party administration for workers' compensation and employee benefit markets. The Brokerage Division sells commercial insurance through independent agents and brokers.

Recent Developments: For the year ended Dec 31 2003, net income increased 32.7% to $110.3 million from $83.1 million the previous year. Total revenues advanced 20.9% to $551.0 million from $455.7 million the prior year. Revenues benefited from new business production and revenues from agencies acquired. Commissions and fees increased 20.7% to $545.3 million. Investment income fell 51.5% to $1.4 million, while other income jumped to $4.3 million from $508,000 a year earlier. Employee compensation and benefits expenses grew 19.4% to $268.4 million. Other operating expenses rose 12.1% to $74.6 million, while interest expense fell 22.2% to $3.6 million.

Prospects: Co. is seeing stronger interest in the acquisition and merger arena, as more and more entrepreneurs seem to be recognizing the value of joining with larger, stronger partners. Recently, Co. announced the acquisitions of Pashley Insurance Agency, a New Jersey–based commercial property and casualty agency, and Niagara Insurance Group, a retail insurance agency which focuses on commercial property and casualty and employee benefits throughout the Northeast. Looking ahead, Co. believes it is on track to achieve its intermediate term goal of $1.00 billion in revenues and a 40.0% operating profit margin.

Financial Data

(US$ in Thousands)	12/31/2003	12/31/2002	12/31/2001	12/31/2000	12/31/1999	12/31/1998	12/31/1997	12/31/1996
Earnings Per Share	1.60	1.22	0.85	0.58	0.49	0.43	0.37	0.31
Tang. Book Val. Per Share	0.39	0.16	N.M	0.34	0.20	0.08	0.52	0.32
Dividends Per Share	0.240	0.200	0.160	0.130	0.110	0.100	0.088	0.082
Dividend Payout %	15.15	16.39	18.82	23.27	23.23	23.83	23.87	25.81
Income Statement								
Net Investment Income	1,428	2,945	3,686	3,890	2,560	3,308	4,085	3,230
Other Income	549,612	452,797	361,343	205,816	173,853	150,483	125,106	115,450
Total Revenues	551,040	455,742	365,029	209,706	176,413	153,791	129,191	118,680
Total Indirect Exp.	368,662	312,596	266,864	155,138	131,521	115,746	91,576	85,919
Inc. Before Inc. Taxes	176,482	134,664	90,478	53,978	44,208	37,485	31,638	27,046
Income Taxes	66,160	49,271	34,834	20,792	17,036	14,432	12,251	10,548
Eqty Earns/Minority Int.	...	(2,271)	(1,731)	...	...	...	...	...
Net Income	110,322	83,122	53,913	33,186	27,172	23,053	19,387	16,498
Average Shs. Outstg.	68,897	68,043	63,222	57,326	54,944	53,724	52,350	52,098
Balance Sheet								
Cash & Cash Equivalents	57,308	91,693	16,499	31,686	37,940	42,920	49,025	32,873
Premiums Due	146,672	144,244	101,449	83,199	67,783	69,186	62,148	62,940
Invst. Assets: Total	11,227	9,031	9,434	6,125	9,930	11,229	12,779	12,375
Total Assets	865,854	754,349	488,737	276,719	235,163	230,513	194,129	179,743
Long–Term Obligations	41,107	57,585	78,195	2,736	3,909	17,207	4,093	5,300
Net Stockholders' Equity	498,035	391,590	175,285	121,911	103,026	84,208	77,142	67,286
Shares Outstanding	68,561	68,178	63,194	57,398	54,880	53,992	52,428	51,936
Statistical Record								
Return on Equity %	22.15	21.22	30.75	27.22	26.37	27.37	25.13	24.51
Return on Assets %	12.74	11.01	11.03	11.99	11.55	10.00	9.98	9.17
Price Range	37.44–27.29	36.13–24.74	30.81–15.45	17.72–7.81	10.03–7.42	10.42–7.24	7.82–6.83	...
P/E Ratio	23.40–17.06	29.61–20.28	36.25–18.18	30.55–13.47	20.47–15.15	24.24–16.84	21.14–18.47	...
Average Yield %	0.75	0.63	0.71	1.05	1.25	1.12	1.11	N/A

Address: 220 South Ridgewood Ave., Daytona Beach, FL 32114	Officers: J. Hyatt Brown – Chmn., C.E.O., Jim W. Henderson – Pres., C.O.O., Asst. Treas.	Investor Contact: 904–239–7250
Telephone: (368) 252–9601	Transfer Agents: Wachovia Bank N.A., Charlotte, NC	Institutional Holding
Web Site: www.bbinsurance.com		No of Institutions: 193
		Shares: 41,567,275 % Held: 61.10%

BROWN-FORMAN CORP.

Exchange	Symbol	Price	52Wk Range	Yield	P/E
NYS	BF A	$47.66 (3/31/2004)	49.95-37.77	1.78	22.80

*7 Year Price Score 126.2 *NYSE Composite Index=100 *12 Month Price Score 102.7

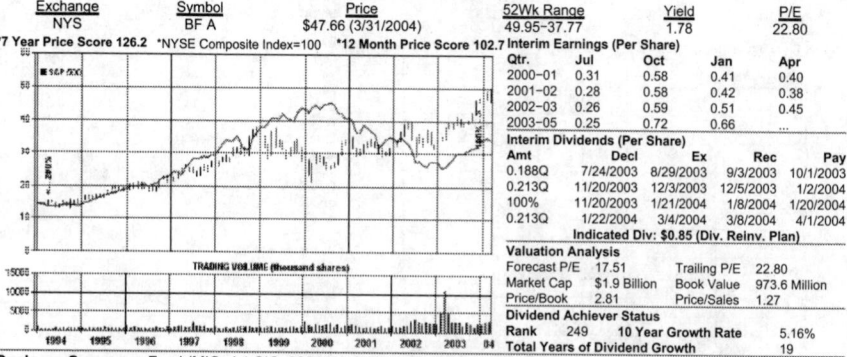

Interim Earnings (Per Share)

Qtr.	Jul	Oct	Jan	Apr
2000-01	0.31	0.58	0.41	0.40
2001-02	0.28	0.58	0.42	0.38
2002-03	0.26	0.59	0.51	0.45
2003-05	0.25	0.72	0.66	...

Interim Dividends (Per Share)

Amt	Decl	Ex	Rec	Pay
0.188Q	7/24/2003	8/29/2003	9/3/2003	10/1/2003
0.213Q	11/20/2003	12/3/2003	12/5/2003	1/2/2004
100%	11/20/2003	1/21/2004	1/8/2004	1/20/2004
0.213Q	1/22/2004	3/4/2004	3/8/2004	4/1/2004

Indicated Div: $0.85 (Div. Reinv. Plan)

Valuation Analysis

Forecast P/E	17.51	Trailing P/E	22.80
Market Cap	$1.9 Billion	Book Value	973.6 Million
Price/Book	2.81	Price/Sales	1.27

Dividend Achiever Status

Rank	249	10 Year Growth Rate	5.16%
Total Years of Dividend Growth		19

Business Summary: Food (MIC: 4.1 SIC: 2084 NAIC:312130)

Brown-Forman, with assets of $2.28 billion as of Jul 31 2003, operates in two business segments: wines and spirits and consumer durables. The wines and spirits segment includes the production, importing and marketing of wines and distilled spirits under brand names of *Jack Daniel's, Southern Comfort, Finlandia* Vodka, *Canadian Mist, Korbel California* champagnes, and *Fetzer, Bolla* and *Bel Arbor California* wines. The consumer durables segment includes tableware and flatware sold under the *Lenox, Gorham* and *Dansk* brand names, as well as *Hartmann* luggage.

Recent Developments: For the quarter ended Jan 31 2004, net income improved 15.0% to $80.5 million compared with $70.0 million in the corresponding period of the year before. Net sales grew 9.7% to $697.0 million from $635.6 million the year before. Sales for the beverages segment rose 12.3% to $531.0 million, driven by the benefits of a weaker U.S. dollar, the addition of new markets to Co.'s distribution arrangement for Finlandia Vodka Worldwide, and continued volume and pricing growth for Co.'s spirits brands. Sales for the consumer durables segment inched up 2.0% to $166.0 million, reflecting slight improvements in the direct-to-consumer channel and Co.'s retail outlet stores.

Prospects: Looking ahead, Co. expects the environment to remain challenging for its wine and consumer durables businesses in the fourth quarter of fiscal 2004. However, Co. is encouraged by the opportunities and trends for its spirits brands. As a result, Co. will be significantly increasing its advertising investments behind its spirits brands in the fourth quarter. This increased level of advertising investment, coupled with higher pension expenses and Co.'s ongoing focus on lowering wholesale and retail inventories on a global basis, is expected to temper earnings growth in the fourth quarter. Earnings per share is anticipated to range from $2.09 to $2.13 for fiscal 2004.

Financial Data

(US$ in Thousands)	9 Mos	6 Mos	3 Mos	04/30/2003	04/30/2002	04/30/2001	04/30/2000	04/30/1999
Earnings Per Share	1.64	0.98	0.25	1.81	1.66	1.70	1.59	1.46
Cash Flow Per Share	2.03	0.45	0.31	1.79	1.82	1.68	1.75	1.55
Tang. Book Val. Per Share	3.38	3.09	2.34	2.42	7.79	6.74	5.67	4.76
Dividends Per Share	0.770	0.750	0.730	0.720	0.680	0.640	0.600	0.570
Dividend Payout %	47.25	76.53	289.21	39.94	40.84	37.64	38.05	39.24
Income Statement								
Total Revenues	1,681,900	1,087,900	460,800	2,060,000	1,958,000	1,924,000	1,877,000	1,776,000
Total Indirect Exp.	664,300	446,200	220,200	800,000	780,000	779,000	755,000	723,000
Depreciation & Amort.	41,700	27,400	13,100	55,000	55,000	64,000	62,000	55,000
Operating Income	317,800	190,900	52,100	378,000	353,000	374,000	348,000	322,000
Net Interest Inc./(Exp.)	(15,000)	(10,000)	(5,000)	(5,000)	(5,000)	(8,000)	(5,000)	(4,000)
Income Taxes	102,900	61,500	16,000	128,000	120,000	133,000	125,000	116,000
Net Income	199,900	119,400	31,100	245,000	228,000	233,000	218,000	202,000
Average Shs. Outstg.	121,886	121,774	121,710	135,126	137,000	137,200	137,000	137,400
Balance Sheet								
Cash & Cash Equivalents	110,100	74,500	71,900	72,000	116,000	86,000	180,000	171,000
Total Current Assets	1,107,900	1,217,000	1,077,000	1,068,000	1,029,000	994,000	1,020,000	999,000
Total Assets	2,331,900	2,429,700	2,280,600	2,264,000	2,016,000	1,939,000	1,802,000	1,735,000
Total Current Liabilities	485,600	621,700	574,500	548,000	495,000	538,000	522,000	517,000
Long-Term Obligations	629,800	629,200	629,000	629,000	40,000	40,000	41,000	53,000
Net Stockholders' Equity	973,600	928,900	834,200	840,000	1,311,000	1,187,000	1,048,000	917,000
Net Working Capital	622,300	595,300	502,500	520,000	534,000	456,000	498,000	482,000
Shares Outstanding	121,431	121,356	121,287	121,134	136,696	136,918	137,024	137,012
Statistical Record								
Operating Profit Margin %	18.89	17.54	11.30	18.34	18.02	19.43	18.54	18.13
Return on Equity %	20.53	12.85	3.72	29.16	17.39	19.62	20.80	22.02
Return on Assets %	8.57	4.91	1.36	10.82	11.30	12.01	12.09	11.64
Debt/Total Assets %	27.00	25.89	27.58	27.78	1.98	2.06	2.27	3.05
Price Range	47.81-37.77	42.75-37.77	41.21-37.77	40.03-29.66	39.31-29.72	35.09-25.00	37.75-21.22	38.63-27.59
P/E Ratio	29.15-23.03	43.62-38.54	164.8-151.1	22.11-16.38	23.68-17.90	20.64-14.71	23.74-13.35	26.46-18.90
Average Yield %	1.85	1.88	1.86	2.03	2.07	2.17	2.00	1.75

Address: 850 Dixie Highway, Louisville, KY 40210 Telephone: (502) 585-1100 Web Site: www.brown-forman.com	Officers: Owsley Brown II - Chmn., C.E.O., Phoebe A. Wood - Exec. V.P., C.F.O. Transfer Agents:First Chicago Trust Company of New York, Jersey City, NJ	Institutional Holding No of Institutions: 2 Shares: 10,000 % Held: -

CALIFORNIA WATER SERVICE GROUP

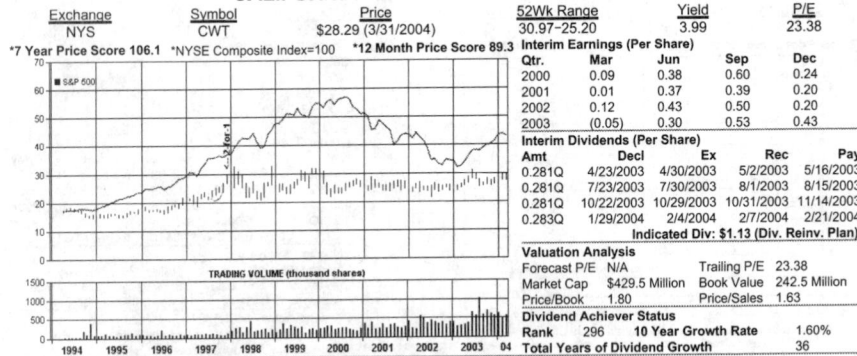

Exchange	Symbol	Price	52Wk Range	Yield	P/E
NYS	CWT	$28.29 (3/31/2004)	30.97-25.20	3.99	23.38

*7 Year Price Score 106.1   *NYSE Composite Index=100   *12 Month Price Score 89.3

Interim Earnings (Per Share)

Qtr.	Mar	Jun	Sep	Dec
2000	0.09	0.38	0.60	0.24
2001	0.01	0.37	0.39	0.20
2002	0.12	0.43	0.50	0.20
2003	(0.05)	0.30	0.53	0.43

Interim Dividends (Per Share)

Amt	Decl	Ex	Rec	Pay
0.281Q	4/23/2003	4/30/2003	5/2/2003	5/16/2003
0.281Q	7/23/2003	7/30/2003	8/1/2003	8/15/2003
0.281Q	10/22/2003	10/29/2003	10/31/2003	11/14/2003
0.283Q	1/29/2004	2/4/2004	2/7/2004	2/21/2004

Indicated Div: $1.13 (Div. Reinv. Plan)

Valuation Analysis

Forecast P/E N/A	Trailing P/E 23.38
Market Cap $429.5 Million	Book Value 242.5 Million
Price/Book 1.80	Price/Sales 1.63

Dividend Achiever Status

Rank 296	10 Year Growth Rate	1.60%
Total Years of Dividend Growth		36

Business Summary: Water Utilities (MIC: 7.2 SIC: 4941 NAIC:221310)

California Water Service Group is a utility water company that provides regulated and non–regulated water utility services to over 2.0 million customers in 99 communities in California, Washington, New Mexico and Hawaii as of Dec 31 2003. Co. is the parent company of California Water Service Company, Washington Water Service Company, New Mexico Water Service Company, Hawaii Water Service Company and CWS Utility Services. The sole business of Co. consists of the production, purchase, storage, purification, distribution and sale of water for domestic, industrial, public, and irrigation uses, and for fire protection. Annual water production totaled nearly 132.00 billion gallons for 2003.

Recent Developments: For the year ended Dec 31 2003, net income advanced 1.8% to $19.4 million compared with $19.! million in 2002. Operating revenue grew 5.3% to $277.1 million from $263.2 million a year earlier, reflecting rate increases of $12.6 million and $6.0 million in revenues from sales to new customers. This was offset by decreased revenues of $4.6 million from sales to existing customers, primarily due to increased rainfall in the first half of 2003. Net operating income slid 1.7% to $30.2 million versus $30.7 million the year before. Net non–regulated income fell 4.1% to $2.1 million from $2.2 million in 2002.

Prospects: Future results will benefit from the California Public Utilities Commission's (CPUC) approval of Co.'s numerous prior pending applications. In 2003, Co. received approval for rate increases that are likely to add $26.0 million in annual revenues, as well as $9.0 million in surcharges collected over a 24–month period. However, since the rate increases are not collected retroactively, it will take time to see their full effect. Further, in January 2004, CPUC approved an additional rate increase of $4.2 million, which became effective in January 2004.

Financial Data

(US$ in Thousands)	12/31/2003	12/31/2002	12/31/2001	12/31/2000	12/31/1999	12/31/1998	12/31/1997	12/31/1996
Earnings Per Share	1.21	1.25	0.97	1.31	1.53	1.45	1.83	1.50
Cash Flow Per Share	2.79	2.20	2.52	2.28	...	2.97	3.12	2.63
Tang. Book Val. Per Share	14.44	13.12	12.95	13.12	13.69	13.37	13.00	12.22
Dividends Per Share	1.120	1.120	1.110	1.100	1.080	1.070	1.050	1.040
Dividend Payout %	92.97	89.60	114.94	83.96	70.59	73.79	57.65	69.33
Income Statement								
Total Revenues	277,128	263,151	246,820	244,806	206,440	186,273	195,324	182,764
Total Indirect Exp.	122,919	112,901	115,234	111,114	95,482	85,647	87,039	80,491
Costs & Expenses	246,894	232,854	221,669	211,610	175,830	156,199	160,975	152,397
Depreciation & Amort.	23,256	21,238	19,226	18,368	15,802	14,563	13,670	12,665
Operating Income	30,234	30,297	25,151	33,196	30,610	30,074	34,349	30,367
Net Interest Inc./(Exp.)	(17,517)	(16,841)	(16,029)	(14,646)	(13,201)	(12,446)	(11,902)	(11,907)
Income Taxes	8,506	8,797	...	...	...	...	...	...
Net Income	19,417	19,073	14,965	19,963	19,919	18,395	23,305	19,067
Average Shs. Outstg.	15,893	15,185	15,285	15,173	12,936	12,619	12,619	12,580
Balance Sheet								
Net Property	759,498	696,988	624,342	582,008	515,354	478,305	460,407	443,588
Total Assets	873,035	800,582	710,214	666,605	587,618	548,499	531,297	512,390
Long–Term Obligations	272,226	250,365	202,600	187,098	156,572	136,345	139,205	142,153
Net Stockholders' Equity	247,999	202,692	200,094	202,309	180,657	172,279	167,540	157,701
Shares Outstanding	16,932	15,182	15,182	15,146	12,936	12,619	12,619	12,620
Statistical Record								
Operating Profit Margin %	10.90	11.51	10.19	13.56	14.82	16.14	17.58	16.61
Net Inc./Net Property %	2.55	2.73	2.39	3.43	3.86	3.84	5.06	4.29
Net Inc./Tot. Capital %	3.47	3.93	3.46	4.81	5.55	5.46	7.00	5.89
Return on Equity %	7.82	9.40	7.47	9.86	11.02	10.67	13.91	12.09
Accum. Depr./Gross Prop. %	29.60	30.39	31.36	31.63	30.10	29.73	28.91	28.27
Price Range	30.97-23.65	26.69-21.60	28.60-23.38	30.94-21.69	31.88-22.94	32.75-21.00	29.53-18.81	21.88-16.25
P/E Ratio	25.60-19.55	21.35-17.28	29.48-24.10	23.62-16.56	20.83-14.99	22.59-14.48	16.14-10.28	14.58-10.83
Average Yield %	4.20	4.53	4.35	4.28	3.97	4.16	4.58	5.80

Address: 1720 North First Street, San Jose, CA 95112	**Officers:** Robert W. Foy – Chmn., Peter C. Nelson – Pres., C.E.O.	**Investor Contact:** (408) 367–8200
Telephone: (408) 367–8200	**Transfer Agents:**The First National Bank of Boston, Boston, MA	**Institutional Holding** **No of Institutions:** 63
Web Site: www.calwater.com		**Shares:** 2,548,306 **% Held:** 16.80%

CAMDEN PROPERTY TRUST

Exchange	Symbol	Price	52Wk Range	Yield	P/E
NYS	CPT	$44.95 (3/31/2004)	45.35–32.93	5.65	70.23

*7 Year Price Score 117.5   *NYSE Composite Index=100   *12 Month Price Score 103.4

Interim Earnings (Per Share)

Qtr.	Mar	Jun	Sep	Dec
2000	0.31	0.27	0.72	0.33
2001	0.41	0.40	0.43	0.18
2002	0.32	0.28	0.24	0.16
2003	0.20	0.14	0.14	0.23

Interim Dividends (Per Share)

Amt	Decl	Ex	Rec	Pay
0.635Q	6/13/2003	6/26/2003	6/30/2003	7/17/2003
0.635Q	9/17/2003	9/26/2003	9/30/2003	10/17/2003
0.635Q	12/8/2003	12/17/2003	12/19/2003	1/16/2004
0.635Q	3/15/2004	3/29/2004	3/31/2004	4/16/2004

Indicated Div: $2.54 (Div. Reinv. Plan)

Valuation Analysis

Forecast P/E	12.31	Trailing P/E	70.23
Market Cap	$1.8 Billion	Book Value	791.2 Million
Price/Book	1.91	Price/Sales	3.72

Dividend Achiever Status

Rank	14	10 Year Growth Rate	24.67%
Total Years of Dividend Growth	10	

Business Summary: Property, Real Estate &Development (MIC: 8.3 SIC: 6798 NAIC:525930)

Camden Property Trust is a self-administered and self-managed real estate investment trust. Co. is engaged in the ownership, development, construction, and management of multifamily apartment communities in ten states. As of Dec 31 2003, Co. owned interests in, operated or was developing 146 properties containing 52,346 apartment homes geographically dispersed in the Sunbelt and Midwestern markets, from Florida to California. At Dec 31 2003, Co. had two recently completed multifamily properties containing 786 apartment homes in lease-up. Two of Co.'s multifamily properties containing 1,002 apartment homes were under development at Dec 31 2003.

Recent Developments: For the year ended Dec 31 2003, net income dropped 30.4% to $29.4 million compared with income of $42.3 million, before a gain of $32.3 million from discontinued operations, in 2002. The decline in earnings reflected an oversupply of multifamily housing; low interest rates on mortgage debt, which continue to make home purchases attractive; and a slow economic recovery. Results for 2002 included losses of $234,000 related to early retirement of debt. Total revenues rose 1.4% to $416.5 million. Total property expenses grew 8.6% to $162.7 million, while total expenses advanced 6.5% to $377.9 million.

Prospects: Looking ahead, near-term results may continue to be negatively affected by the difficult economic environment. However, Co. has stated that it is well positioned for growth. For instance, Co.'s average borrowing costs should continue to decline as a result of the replacement of higher priced maturing debt. In addition, Co.'s operating results should be positively affected by the increase in the occupancy levels of its portfolio, and increases in contributions from its California and Houston development properties. Meanwhile, Co. will continue to focus on expense control in 2004.

Financial Data

(US$ in Thousands)	12/31/2003	12/31/2002	12/31/2001	12/31/2000	12/31/1999	12/31/1998	12/31/1997	12/31/1996
Earnings Per Share	0.71	1.00	1.42	1.63	1.23	1.12	1.41	0.58
Tang. Book Val. Per Share	15.67	17.05	18.88	25.54	26.00	26.40	22.23	17.88
Dividends Per Share	2.540	2.510	2.390	2.200	2.060	2.000	1.940	1.880
Dividend Payout %	357.74	251.50	168.48	135.42	167.88	178.57	137.94	324.13
Income Statement								
Rental Income	371,019	365,883	374,187	364,111	341,168	300,632	187,928	105,785
Total Income	416,540	410,983	428,215	403,539	371,296	323,839	199,789	111,606
Total Indirect Exp.	453,330	426,015	422,749	401,168	360,216	315,651	198,006	114,993
Depreciation	108,076	103,342	101,660	96,966	89,516	78,113	44,836	23,894
Interest Expense	150,828	142,998	139,682	138,072	115,712	100,934	57,074	34,672
Eqty Earns/Minority Int.	(11,784)	(14,313)	(15,999)	(15,306)	(10,292)	(1,322)	(1,655)	...
Income from Cont Ops	...	42,513	61,680	...	...	...	39,232	...
Net Income	29,430	74,612	61,292	74,424	61,623	57,333	38,438	8,713
Average Shs. Outstg.	41,354	44,216	41,603	41,388	44,291	44,183	28,356	14,940
Balance Sheet								
Cash & Cash Equivalents	10,012	4,621	8,782	9,411	10,229	9,933	10,516	4,789
Total Assets	2,625,561	2,609,899	2,449,665	2,430,881	2,487,922	2,347,982	1,323,620	603,510
Long-Term Obligations	1,509,700	1,427,000	1,207,047	1,140,067	1,168,496	1,006,144	486,779	271,884
Total Liabilities	1,840,699	1,770,430	1,531,414	1,456,698	1,471,257	1,177,594	613,056	308,082
Net Stockholders' Equity	784,885	839,453	918,251	974,183	1,016,675	1,170,388	710,564	295,428
Shares Outstanding	50,060	49,233	48,627	38,129	39,093	44,322	31,954	16,521
Statistical Record								
Net Inc.+Depr./Assets %	5.23	6.82	6.65	7.05	6.07	5.77	6.29	5.40
Return on Equity %	3.74	5.06	6.71	7.63	6.06	4.89	5.52	2.94
Return on Assets %	1.12	1.62	2.51	3.06	2.47	2.44	2.96	1.44
Price Range	44.30-30.70	41.54-29.74	39.32-31.07	33.81-25.88	28.19-24.13	31.00-24.88	33.00-26.63	28.63-21.75
P/E Ratio	62.39-43.24	41.54-29.74	27.69-21.88	20.74-15.87	22.92-19.61	27.68-22.21	23.40-18.88	49.35-37.50
Average Yield %	6.97	7.06	6.83	7.57	7.76	7.01	6.58	7.56

Address: 3 Greenway Plaza, Houston, TX 77046	Officers: Richard J. Campo – Chmn., C.E.O., D. Keith Oden – Pres., C.O.O.	Investor Contact: (713) 354-2500
Telephone: (713) 354-2500	Transfer Agents:American Stock Transfer and Trust	Institutional Holding
Web Site: www.camdenliving.com	Company, New York, NY	No of Institutions: 24
		Shares: 42,950,874 % Held: –

CARLISLE COMPANIES INC.

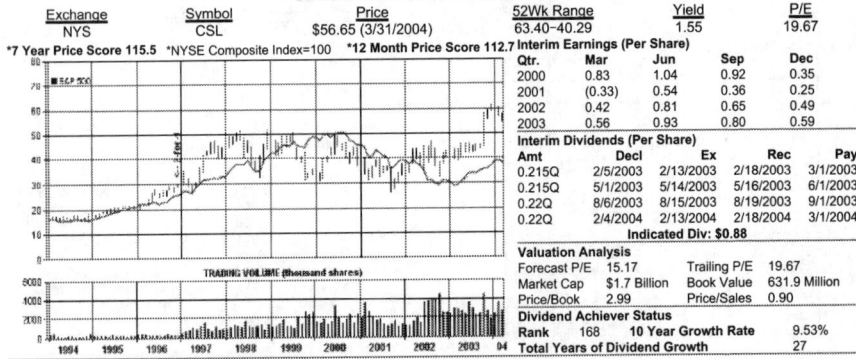

Exchange	Symbol	Price	52Wk Range	Yield	P/E
NYS	CSL	$56.65 (3/31/2004)	63.40–40.29	1.55	19.67

*7 Year Price Score 115.5 *NYSE Composite Index=100 *12 Month Price Score 112.7

Interim Earnings (Per Share)

Qtr.	Mar	Jun	Sep	Dec
2000	0.83	1.04	0.92	0.35
2001	(0.33)	0.54	0.36	0.25
2002	0.42	0.81	0.65	0.49
2003	0.56	0.93	0.80	0.59

Interim Dividends (Per Share)

Amt	Decl	Ex	Rec	Pay
0.215Q	2/13/2003	2/18/2003	2/18/2003	3/1/2003
0.215Q	5/1/2003	5/14/2003	5/16/2003	6/1/2003
0.22Q	8/6/2003	8/15/2003	8/19/2003	9/1/2003
0.22Q	2/4/2004	2/13/2004	2/18/2004	3/1/2004

Indicated Div: $0.88

Valuation Analysis

Forecast P/E	15.17	Trailing P/E	19.67
Market Cap	$1.7 Billion	Book Value	631.9 Million
Price/Book	2.99	Price/Sales	0.90

Dividend Achiever Status

Rank	168	10 Year Growth Rate	9.53%
Total Years of Dividend Growth		27

Business Summary: Rubber Products (MIC: 11.6 SIC: 3011 NAIC:326211)

Carlisle is a manufacturing company. The Industrial Components segment manufactures non–automotive tires, wheels, transmission belts and accessories. Co. produces rubber and plastic automotive components and roofing membranes and FleeceBACK™ sheeting for flat roofs in its Automotive Components and Construction Materials segments. The Specialty Products segment manufactures heavy–duty friction and braking systems for trucks and heavy equipment. The General Industry produces aerospace wire, electronic cable and cable assemblies and interconnects, plastic foodservice permanentware and refrigerated truck bodies. The Transportation Products segment produces high–payload trailers and dump bodies.

Recent Developments: For the year ended Dec 31 2003, net income advanced 22.9% to $88.9 million, versus income of $72.4 million, before an accounting change charge of $43.8 million, in the previous year. Net sales increased 6.9% to $2.11 billion from $1.97 billion a year earlier. Notably, Construction Materials segment sales grew 18.7% to $579.4 million, reflecting the acquisition of MiraDri and stronger commercial construction. General Industry segment sales climbed 14.0% to $438.1 million due to higher demand for cheese and powder equipment from Carlisle Process Systems. Automotive Components sales fell 11.3% to $209.1 million, due to lower customer production, customer design changes and price negotiations.

Prospects: Co. plans to continue its cost reduction efforts in the coming year and expects to incur additional expenses related to those efforts. Assuming modest growth in the markets served by Co., net earnings for 2004 are expected to be in the range of $3.25 to $3.40 per share, including plant closure and severance costs estimated at $0.10 to $0.20 per share. Meanwhile, Carlisle Process Systems (CPS) was recently awarded a $70.0 million project by the Southwest Cheese Company, USA for a new 300,000 square foot cheese and whey production facility in Clovis, NM. CPS will supply systems and equipment from its brands *Scherping, Damrow Downstream, Wincanton, Zimmer, Stork Friesland* and *Walker*.

Financial Data

(US$ in Thousands)	12/31/2003	12/31/2002	12/31/2001	12/31/2000	12/31/1999	12/31/1998	12/31/1997	12/31/1996
Earnings Per Share	2.88	2.37	0.82	3.14	3.13	2.77	2.28	1.80
Cash Flow Per Share	3.78	7.39	7.32	4.08	4.44	3.15	2.67	2.77
Tang. Book Val. Per Share	10.37	8.08	6.72	9.79	10.62	8.85	7.48	6.55
Dividends Per Share	0.870	0.850	0.820	0.760	0.680	0.600	0.520	0.460
Dividend Payout %	30.20	35.86	100.00	24.20	21.72	21.66	23.02	25.55
Income Statement								
Total Revenues	2,108,164	1,971,280	1,849,477	1,771,067	1,611,256	1,517,494	1,260,550	1,017,495
Total Indirect Exp.	224,603	231,917	252,385	186,055	175,568	176,544	159,070	140,576
Depreciation & Amort.	60,366	56,994	63,960	59,547	47,414	45,221	38,755	29,758
Operating Income	146,194	127,651	67,045	178,883	174,637	151,571	127,391	97,122
Net Interest Inc./(Exp.)	(14,461)	(17,151)	(29,120)	(28,018)	(19,154)	(22,715)	(16,502)	(9,062)
Income Taxes	42,813	26,050	13,084	54,685	59,689	55,403	46,118	36,360
Income from Cont Ops	...	72,378	...	...	...	...	...	...
Net Income	88,920	28,625	24,841	96,180	95,794	84,866	70,666	55,680
Average Shs. Outstg.	30,863	30,583	30,450	30,599	30,635	30,674	31,025	30,953
Balance Sheet								
Cash & Cash Equivalents	26,848	23,041	15,606	8,967	10,417	3,883	1,732	8,312
Total Current Assets	584,381	481,508	553,272	576,477	541,038	478,525	417,533	345,933
Total Assets	1,436,909	1,315,900	1,397,987	1,305,679	1,080,662	1,022,852	861,216	742,463
Total Current Liabilities	339,343	324,262	273,779	399,948	240,378	255,337	226,083	170,648
Long–Term Obligations	294,581	293,124	461,744	281,864	281,744	273,521	209,642	191,167
Net Stockholders' Equity	631,930	553,077	540,284	547,879	478,133	406,905	348,836	307,503
Net Working Capital	245,038	157,246	279,493	176,529	300,660	223,188	191,450	175,285
Shares Outstanding	30,991	30,597	30,263	30,251	30,127	30,178	30,351	30,351
Statistical Record								
Operating Profit Margin %	6.93	6.47	3.62	10.10	10.83	9.98	10.10	9.54
Return on Equity %	14.07	13.08	4.59	17.55	20.03	20.85	20.25	18.10
Return on Assets %	6.18	5.50	1.77	7.36	8.86	8.29	8.20	7.49
Debt/Total Assets %	20.50	22.27	33.02	21.58	26.07	26.74	24.34	25.74
Price Range	61.49–39.24	46.91–32.65	43.69–26.40	49.75–31.19	52.94–31.06	51.75–32.88	47.63–27.13	30.25–19.13
P/E Ratio	21.35–13.63	19.79–13.78	53.28–32.20	15.84–9.93	16.91–9.92	18.68–11.87	20.89–11.90	16.81–10.63
Average Yield %	1.87	2.12	2.33	1.86	1.60	1.34	1.41	1.83

Address: 13925 Ballantyne Corporate Place, Charlotte, NC 28277 **Telephone:** (704) 501–1100 **Web Site:** www.carlisle.com	**Officers:** Stephen P. Munn – Chmn., Richmond D. McKinnish – Pres., C.E.O. **Transfer Agents:** Computershare Investor Services, LLC., Chicago, IL	**Investor Contact:** 704–501–1100 **Institutional Holding** **No of Institutions:** 18 **Shares:** 1,176,098 **% Held:** –

48

CATERPILLAR INC.

Exchange	Symbol	Price	52Wk Range	Yield	P/E
NYS	CAT	$79.07 (3/31/2004)	85.01–49.65	1.87	25.26

*7 Year Price Score 123.6 ***NYSE Composite Index=100** ***12 Month Price Score 112.8**

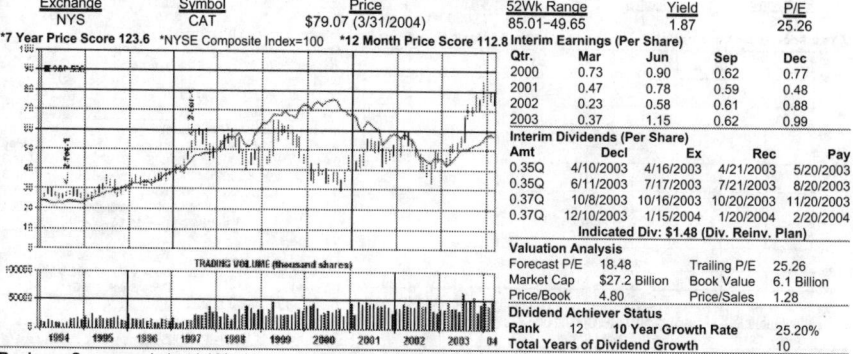

Interim Earnings (Per Share)

Qtr.	Mar	Jun	Sep	Dec
2000	0.73	0.90	0.62	0.77
2001	0.47	0.78	0.59	0.48
2002	0.23	0.58	0.61	0.88
2003	0.37	1.15	0.62	0.99

Interim Dividends (Per Share)

Amt	Decl	Ex	Rec	Pay
0.35Q	4/10/2003	4/16/2003	4/21/2003	5/20/2003
0.35Q	6/11/2003	7/17/2003	7/21/2003	8/20/2003
0.37Q	10/8/2003	10/16/2003	10/20/2003	11/20/2003
0.37Q	12/10/2003	1/15/2004	1/20/2004	2/20/2004

Indicated Div: $1.48 (Div. Reinv. Plan)

Valuation Analysis

Forecast P/E	18.48	Trailing P/E	25.26
Market Cap	$27.2 Billion	Book Value	6.1 Billion
Price/Book	4.80	Price/Sales	1.28

Dividend Achiever Status

Rank	12	10 Year Growth Rate	25.20%
Total Years of Dividend Growth		10

Business Summary: Industrial Machinery and Equipment (MIC: 11.5 SIC: 3531 NAIC:333120)

Caterpillar operates in three principal lines of business. The machinery division designs, manufactures and markets construction, mining, agricultural and forestry machinery. The engines division designs, manufactures and markets engines for Caterpillar machinery; electric power generation systems; on-highway trucks and locomotives; marine, petroleum, construction, industrial, agricultural, and other applications; and related parts. Engines range from 5 to over 22,000 horsepower, and turbines range from 1,600 to 19,500 horsepower. The financial products division consists primarily of Caterpillar Financial Services Corporation, Caterpillar Insurance Holdings, Inc. and their subsidiaries.

Recent Developments: For the year ended Dec 31 2003, net income increased 37.7% to $1.10 billion compared with $798.0 million a year earlier. Total sales and revenues advanced 13.0% to $22.76 billion from $20.15 billion in 2002, reflecting growth from across Co.'s operating businesses, as well as favorable currency effects due mainly to the stronger euro. Machinery sales rose 14.2% to $13.68 billion and engines sales improved to $7.37 billion, 10.4% higher than the year before. Financial products revenues increased 14.0% to $1.72 billion. Operating profit climbed 27.5% to $1.69 billion versus $1.32 billion the previous year.

Prospects: Near-term prospects appear reasonably positive, reflecting Co.'s ongoing cost-cutting efforts, expansion of its traditional business services, as well as positive top-line growth from across each of its four geographic regions. Accordingly, Co. now expects full-year 2004 sales and revenues to increase approximately 12.0% over 2003, and full-year profit to advance about 40.0%. Looking ahead, Co. appears well positioned to benefit from the resurgence in worldwide economic activity. Specifically, Co. views China, India and Russia as key emerging markets with favorable growth potential.

Financial Data

(US$ in Thousands)	12/31/2003	12/31/2002	12/31/2001	12/31/2000	12/31/1999	12/31/1998	12/31/1997	12/31/1996
Earnings Per Share	3.13	2.30	2.32	3.02	2.63	4.11	4.37	3.53
Cash Flow Per Share	5.87	6.82	5.72	5.90	7.15	4.82	5.50	4.61
Tang. Book Val. Per Share	12.91	11.00	11.47	11.91	11.08	10.89	12.09	10.21
Dividends Per Share	1.420	1.400	1.380	1.330	1.250	1.100	0.900	0.750
Dividend Payout %	45.36	60.86	59.48	44.03	47.52	26.76	20.59	21.25
Income Statement								
Total Revenues	22,763,000	20,152,000	20,450,000	20,175,000	19,702,000	20,977,000	18,925,000	16,522,000
Total Indirect Exp.	4,600,000	4,645,000	5,044,000	4,629,000	4,287,000	4,182,000	3,482,000	2,403,000
Depreciation & Amort.	1,347,000	1,220,000	1,169,000	1,022,000	945,000	865,000	738,000	696,000
Operating Income	1,688,000	1,319,000	1,311,000	1,737,000	1,494,000	2,253,000	2,430,000	2,287,000
Net Interest Inc./(Exp.)	(716,000)	(800,000)	(942,000)	(980,000)	(829,000)	(753,000)	(580,000)	(510,000)
Income Taxes	398,000	312,000	367,000	447,000	455,000	665,000	796,000	613,000
Eqty Earns/Minority Int.	20,000	(4,000)	3,000	(28,000)	(20,000)	4,000	48,000	33,000
Net Income	1,099,000	798,000	805,000	1,053,000	946,000	1,513,000	1,665,000	1,361,000
Average Shs. Outstg.	351,400	346,900	347,100	348,897	359,367	368,130	381,000	390,000
Balance Sheet								
Cash & Cash Equivalents	342,000	309,000	400,000	334,000	548,000	360,000	292,000	487,000
Total Current Assets	16,791,000	14,628,000	13,400,000	12,521,000	11,734,000	11,459,000	9,814,000	8,783,000
Total Assets	36,465,000	32,851,000	30,657,000	28,464,000	26,635,000	25,128,000	20,756,000	18,728,000
Total Current Liabilities	12,621,000	11,344,000	10,276,000	8,568,000	8,178,000	7,565,000	6,379,000	7,013,000
Long-Term Obligations	14,078,000	11,596,000	11,291,000	11,334,000	9,928,000	9,404,000	6,942,000	4,532,000
Net Stockholders' Equity	6,078,000	5,472,000	5,611,000	5,600,000	5,465,000	5,131,000	4,679,000	4,116,000
Net Working Capital	4,170,000	3,284,000	3,124,000	3,953,000	3,556,000	3,894,000	3,435,000	1,770,000
Shares Outstanding	343,762	344,255	343,376	343,396	353,748	357,198	368,000	380,000
Statistical Record								
Operating Profit Margin %	7.41	6.54	6.41	8.60	7.58	10.74	12.84	13.84
Return on Equity %	18.08	14.58	14.34	18.80	17.31	29.48	35.58	33.06
Return on Assets %	3.01	2.42	2.62	3.69	3.55	6.02	8.02	7.26
Debt/Total Assets %	38.60	35.29	36.83	39.81	37.27	37.42	33.44	24.19
Price Range	84.75-42.04	59.79-33.86	56.20-40.09	53.31-29.81	65.50-42.94	60.69-40.31	60.94-36.50	40.06-27.06
P/E Ratio	27.08-13.43	26.00-14.72	24.22-17.28	17.65-9.87	24.90-16.33	14.77-9.81	13.94-8.35	11.35-7.67
Average Yield %	2.34	2.91	2.84	3.44	2.31	2.18	1.84	2.17

Address: 100 NE Adams Street, Peoria, IL 61629-7310
Telephone: (309) 675-1000
Web Site: www.CAT.com

Officers: James W. Owens - Chmn., C.E.O., Ali M. Bahaj - V.P.
Transfer Agents: Mellon Investor Services of South Hackensack, NJ

Investor Contact: 309-675-4549
Institutional Holding
No of Institutions: 583
Shares: 249,420,375   **% Held:** 72.50%

CEDAR FAIR, L.P.

Exchange	Symbol	Price	52Wk Range	Yield	P/E
NYS	FUN	$34.97 (3/31/2004)	35.71–24.50	5.15	20.94

*7 Year Price Score 118.2 *NYSE Composite Index=100 *12 Month Price Score 99.1

Interim Earnings (Per Share)

Qtr.	Mar	Jun	Sep	Dec
2000	(0.51)	0.36	1.83	(0.18)
2001	(0.60)	0.13	2.10	(0.50)
2002	(0.63)	0.40	2.01	(0.39)
2003	(0.62)	0.33	2.16	(0.20)

Interim Dividends (Per Share)

Amt	Decl	Ex	Rec	Pay
0.44Q	6/23/2003	7/1/2003	7/3/2003	8/15/2003
0.44Q	9/26/2003	10/1/2003	10/3/2003	11/17/2003
0.44Q	12/12/2003	1/2/2004	1/6/2004	2/17/2004
0.45Q	3/8/2004	4/1/2004	4/5/2004	5/17/2004
		Indicated Div: $1.80		

Valuation Analysis

Forecast P/E	N/A	Trailing P/E	20.94
Market Cap	$1.8 Billion	Book Value	308.9 Million
Price/Book	5.06	Price/Sales	3.07

Dividend Achiever Status

Rank	228	10 Year Growth Rate	6.31%
Total Years of Dividend Growth		16

Business Summary: Sporting &Recreational (MIC: 13.5 SIC: 7996 NAIC:713110)

Cedar Fair is a limited partnership managed by Cedar Fair Management Company. Co. owns and operates six amusement parks: Cedar Point on Lake Erie in Sandusky, OH; Knott's Berry Farm, located in Buena Park, CA; Dorney Park & Wildwater Kingdom, near Allentown, PA; Valleyfair, near Minneapolis, MN; Worlds of Fun in Kansas City, MO; and Michigan's Adventure, located near Muskegon, MI. Co.'s five water parks are located near San Diego and Palm Springs, CA, and adjacent to Cedar Point, Knott's Berry Farm and Worlds of Fun. Co. owns and operates four hotel facilities. Co. also operates Knott's Camp Snoopy at the Mall of America in Bloomington, MN under a management contract.

Recent Developments: For the year ended Dec 31 2003, net income advanced 20.3% to $85.9 million compared with $71.4 million in 2002. Results for 2002 included provision for loss on retirement of assets of $3.2 million. Net revenues rose 1.4% to $510.0 million from $502.9 million a year earlier on a 1.0% increase in out–of–park revenues, including resort hotels, a 3.0% growth in average in–park guest per capita spending, and a 1.0% decrease in combined attendance. Operating income grew 3.3% to $125.1 million versus $121.2 million the year before. During 2003, Co.'s combined attendance at its eleven properties totaled 12.2 million guests, down 1.0% from 2002.

Prospects: For the 2004 season, Co. is investing $25.0 million investment in capital improvements at its 11 properties, including expansions to the Soak City water park and Lighthouse Point resort property at Cedar Point, and the addition of new intermediate–sized thrill rides at Knott's Berry Farm and Worlds of Fun. On Mar 10 2004, Co. announced that it has reached an agreement in principle for the acquisition of Six Flags Worlds of Adventure, located near Cleveland, OH from Six Flags. The transaction is valued at $145.0 million and involves the purchase of substantially all of the assets of the park, including the adjacent hotel and campground.

Financial Data

(US$ in Thousands)	12/31/2003	12/31/2002	12/31/2001	12/31/2000	12/31/1999	12/31/1998	12/31/1997	12/31/1996
Earnings Per Share	1.67	1.39	1.13	1.50	1.63	1.58	1.47	1.59
Cash Flow Per Share	2.62	2.85	2.44	2.20	2.36	2.45	2.08	2.04
Tang. Book Val. Per Share	...	N.M	N.M	N.M	N.M	N.M	N.M	N.M
Dividends Per Share	1.740	1.650	1.580	1.500	1.380	1.280	1.250	1.170
Dividend Payout %	104.19	118.70	139.82	100.16	85.12	81.32	85.54	73.58
Income Statement								
Total Revenues	509,976	502,851	477,256	472,920	438,001	419,500	264,137	250,523
Total Indirect Exp.	115,216	112,142	114,441	101,966	85,935	80,004	53,028	48,052
Depreciation & Amort.	44,693	41,682	42,486	39,572	35,082	32,065	21,528	19,072
Operating Income	125,149	121,192	98,557	115,516	116,725	112,608	76,303	81,121
Net Interest Inc./(Exp.)	(24,070)	(24,967)	(24,143)	(21,357)	(15,371)	(14,660)	(7,845)	(6,942)
Income Taxes	17,918	17,159	16,520	16,353	15,580	14,507	...	...
Income from Cont Ops	...	...	...	...	85,774	...	...	...
Net Income	85,888	71,417	57,894	77,806	85,804	83,441	68,458	74,179
Average Shs. Outstg.	51,334	51,263	51,113	51,679	52,390	52,414	46,265	46,116
Balance Sheet								
Cash & Cash Equivalents	2,194	2,171	2,280	2,392	638	1,137	2,520	1,279
Total Current Assets	29,777	29,237	26,868	25,378	24,184	20,967	21,954	11,730
Total Assets	819,341	822,257	810,231	764,143	708,961	631,325	599,619	304,104
Total Current Liabilities	111,694	106,338	96,700	114,024	86,559	77,231	62,426	39,241
Long–Term Obligations	348,647	365,150	373,000	300,000	261,200	200,350	189,750	87,600
Net Stockholders' Equity	308,891	305,320	308,250	330,589	349,986	341,991	285,381	169,994
Net Working Capital	(81,917)	(77,101)	(69,832)	(88,646)	(62,375)	(56,264)	(40,472)	(27,511)
Shares Outstanding	50,673	50,549	50,514	50,813	51,798	51,980	52,403	45,920
Statistical Record								
Operating Profit Margin %	24.54	24.10	20.65	24.42	26.64	26.84	28.88	32.38
Return on Equity %	27.80	23.39	18.78	23.53	24.50	24.39	23.98	43.63
Return on Assets %	10.48	8.68	7.14	10.18	12.09	13.21	11.41	24.39
Debt/Total Assets %	42.55	44.40	46.03	39.25	36.84	31.73	31.64	28.80
Price Range	31.03–22.74	24.79–20.30	24.98–18.03	20.75–17.56	26.00–18.50	29.50–22.00	28.19–17.88	19.50–16.94
P/E Ratio	18.58–13.61	17.83–14.60	22.11–15.96	13.83–11.71	15.95–11.35	18.67–13.92	19.18–12.16	12.26–10.65
Average Yield %	6.51	7.10	7.50	8.04	6.04	4.86	5.78	6.37

Address: One Cedar Point Drive, Sandusky, OH 44870–5259 **Telephone:** (419) 626–0830 **Web Site:** www.cedarfair.com	**Officers:** Richard L. Kinzel – Pres., C.E.O., Bruce A. Jackson – V.P., Fin., C.F.O. **Transfer Agents:** American Stock Transfer &Trust Company, New York, NY	**Investor Contact:** 419–627–2233 **Institutional Holding** **No of Institutions:** 3 **Shares:** 218,576 **% Held:** –

CENTURYTEL, INC.

Business Summary: Communications (MIC: 10.1 SIC: 4813 NAIC:517110)

CenturyTel is a regional telecommunications company that is primarily engaged in providing local exchange telephone services. Co. also provides long distance, Internet access, fiber transport, competitive local exchange carrier, security monitoring, and other communications and business information services in certain local and regional markets. As of Dec 31 2003, Co.'s local exchange telephone subsidiaries operated approximately 2.4 million telephone access lines, primarily in rural, suburban and small urban areas in 22 states, with over 70.0% of these lines located in Wisconsin, Missouri, Alabama, Arkansas and Washington.

Recent Developments: For the year ended Dec 31 2003, net income was $344.7 million compared with income from continuing operations of $193.5 million a year earlier. Results for 2002 included a net nonrecurring gain of $3.7 million. Total operating revenues rose 20.7% to $2.38 billion from $1.97 billion the previous year. Telephone revenue increased 19.5% to $2.07 billion, due in part to the properties acquired from Verizon in the third quarter of 2002. Other operations revenue grew 29.5% to $308.8 million, reflecting a 18.7% gain in long distance revenues to $173.9 million, and a 36.3% increase in Internet revenues to $79.9 million. Operating income was $750.4 million, 30.4% higher than the year before.

Prospects: Co.'s near–term outlook appears mixed. Co. anticipates a decline in 2004 telephone revenues primarily due to lower intrastate toll usage, lower cost study adjustments, lower universal service funding and access line declines. Given effect to these revenue declines, as well as the conversion and operating costs related to its new billing and customer care system, and an expected increase in its effective income tax rate to 38.5% primarily due to state income taxes, Co. sees full–year 2004 diluted earnings ranging between $2.05 and $2.20 per share. On the positive side, Co. expects that the development of integrated bundling during 2004 will stimulate further demand for its services.

Financial Data

(US$ in Thousands)	12/31/2003	12/31/2002	12/31/2001	12/31/2000	12/31/1999	12/31/1998	12/31/1997	12/31/1996
Earnings Per Share	2.38	1.33	2.41	1.63	1.70	1.64	1.86	0.95
Cash Flow Per Share	7.38	5.56	4.67	3.96	2.88	3.33	2.16	1.96
Tang. Book Val. Per Share	N.M	N.M	N.M	N.M	1.39	N.M	N.M	3.60
Dividends Per Share	0.220	0.210	0.200	0.190	0.180	0.170	0.164	0.160
Dividend Payout %	9.24	15.78	8.29	11.65	10.58	10.56	8.80	16.82
Income Statement								
Total Revenues	2,380,745	1,971,996	2,117,469	1,845,926	1,676,669	1,577,085	901,521	749,677
Total Indirect Exp.	1,630,349	1,396,590	1,559,550	1,320,513	1,168,600	1,097,274	633,751	526,381
Depreciation & Amort.	470,641	411,626	473,384	388,056	348,816	328,554	159,495	132,021
Operating Income	750,396	575,406	557,919	525,413	508,069	479,811	267,770	223,296
Net Interest Inc./(Exp.)	(226,751)	(221,845)	(225,523)	(183,302)	(150,557)	(167,552)	(56,474)	(44,662)
Income Taxes	187,252	103,537	210,025	154,711	189,503	158,701	152,363	74,565
Eqty Earns/Minority Int.	6,160	...	27,460	26,986	27,675	32,869	27,794	26,952
Income from Cont Ops	...	189,919	...	...	...	...	...	...
Net Income	344,707	801,624	343,031	231,474	239,769	228,757	255,978	129,077
Average Shs. Outstg.	144,700	142,879	142,307	141,864	141,432	140,105	137,412	136,485
Balance Sheet								
Cash & Cash Equivalents	203,181	3,661	13,362	19,039	56,640	5,742	26,017	8,402
Total Current Assets	462,939	295,902	300,273	376,504	286,073	226,238	283,480	109,234
Total Assets	7,895,852	7,770,048	6,318,684	6,393,290	4,705,407	4,935,455	4,709,201	2,028,505
Total Current Liabilities	471,383	388,104	1,293,956	743,370	309,177	304,844	322,078	144,144
Long-Term Obligations	3,109,302	3,578,132	2,087,500	3,050,292	2,078,311	2,558,000	2,609,541	625,930
Net Stockholders' Equity	3,478,516	3,088,004	2,337,380	2,032,079	1,847,992	1,531,482	1,300,272	1,028,153
Net Working Capital	(8,444)	(92,202)	(993,683)	(366,866)	(23,104)	(78,606)	(38,598)	(34,910)
Shares Outstanding	144,364	142,956	141,232	140,667	139,945	138,083	136,656	134,682
Statistical Record								
Operating Profit Margin %	31.51	29.17	26.34	28.46	30.30	30.42	29.70	29.78
Return on Equity %	9.90	6.15	14.67	11.39	12.97	14.93	19.68	12.55
Return on Assets %	4.36	2.44	5.42	3.62	5.09	4.63	5.43	6.36
Debt/Total Assets %	39.37	46.04	33.03	47.71	44.16	51.82	55.41	30.85
Price Range	36.63-25.51	35.20-22.18	39.00-26.18	47.38-24.50	48.88-36.44	45.00-21.75	22.36-12.78	15.67-12.83
P/E Ratio	15.39-10.72	26.47-16.68	16.18-10.86	29.06-15.03	28.75-21.43	27.44-13.26	12.02-6.87	16.49-13.51
Average Yield %	0.69	0.71	0.64	0.57	0.43	0.54	1.00	1.10

51

CHARTER ONE FINANCIAL, INC.

Exchange	Symbol	Price	52Wk Range	Yield	P/E
NYS	CF	$35.36 (3/31/2004)	37.24–27.32	2.94	12.91

*7 Year Price Score N/A *NYSE Composite Index=100 *12 Month Price Score 96.2

Interim Earnings (Per Share)

Qtr.	Mar	Jun	Sep	Dec
2000	0.45	0.43	0.46	0.47
2001	0.48	0.51	0.54	0.57
2002	0.59	0.60	0.61	0.65
2003	0.64	0.72	0.69	0.69

Interim Dividends (Per Share)

Amt	Decl	Ex	Rec	Pay
0.24Q	4/22/2003	5/2/2003	5/6/2003	5/20/2003
0.26Q	7/17/2003	8/4/2003	8/6/2003	8/20/2003
0.26Q	10/22/2003	11/4/2003	11/6/2003	11/20/2003
0.26Q	1/20/2004	2/4/2004	2/6/2004	2/20/2004

Indicated Div: $1.04

Valuation Analysis

Forecast P/E	10.73	Trailing P/E	12.91
Market Cap	$8.2 Billion	Book Value	3.3 Billion
Price/Book	2.35	Price/Sales	2.74

Dividend Achiever Status

Rank	28	10 Year Growth Rate	20.90%
Total Years of Dividend Growth		15

Business Summary: Other Depository Banking (MIC: 8.5 SIC: 6035 NAIC:522120)

Charter One Financial is a bank holding company whose principal line of business is consumer banking, which includes retail banking, mortgage banking and other related financial services. As of Dec 31 2003, Charter One Bank, with $42.63 billion in total assets, had 592 branch locations in Ohio, Michigan, Illinois, New York, Massachusetts, Vermont, Indiana, Connecticut and Pennsylvania, and operated 969 automated teller machines at various banking offices. Co. is a member of the Star Systems, which provides customers access to ATMs nationwide. As of Dec 31 2003, Charter One Mortgage, Co.'s mortgage banking subsidiary, operated 33 loan production offices nationwide.

Recent Developments: For the year ended Dec 31 2003, net income advanced 9.2% to $630.9 million compared with $577.7 million the year before. Earnings for 2003 and 2002 included pre-tax non-recurring net gains of $264.6 million and $205.0 million, respectively. Net interest income remained essentially the same at $1.17 billion versus the prior year. Provision for loan and lease losses fell 20.7% to $152.3 million. Total other income rose 27.6% to $698.5 million, while total administrative expenses increased 16.5% to $790.7 million. Net loans and leases grew 8.8% to $28.13 billion, and total deposits slid 1.2% to $27.20 billion.

Prospects: Co. is primarily focused on reducing single-family loan exposure and increasing noninterest-bearing deposits. During the fourth quarter of 2003, Co. reduced single-family loans and securities by $1.40 billion and replaced them with $719.0 million in non-single family loans and leases. Separately, Co. continues to implement its plans for aggressive de novo expansion. The 2004 goal is to open approximately 125 new banking centers, including 73 in-store locations. During the fourth quarter, Co. opened 26 banking centers, increasing its in-store franchise to 146 banking centers. Looking ahead, earnings per share are expected to range from $2.50 to $2.45 in 2004.

Financial Data

(US$ in Thousands)	12/31/2003	12/31/2002	12/31/2001	12/31/2000	12/31/1999	12/31/1998	12/31/1997	12/31/1996
Earnings Per Share	2.74	2.45	2.10	1.81	1.32	1.33	0.91	1.04
Tang. Book Val. Per Share	12.81	11.99	10.94	9.94	9.11	8.53	7.75	7.28
Dividends Per Share	0.980	0.820	0.710	0.610	0.510	0.430	0.370	0.320
Dividend Payout %	35.76	33.85	34.04	33.76	39.09	32.45	40.55	30.62
Income Statement								
Total Interest Income	2,112,029	2,286,461	2,378,246	2,247,088	2,128,455	1,760,371	1,377,687	1,004,478
Total Interest Expense	943,142	1,116,631	1,387,830	1,344,053	1,194,351	1,031,299	850,724	621,086
Net Interest Income	1,168,887	1,169,830	990,416	903,035	934,104	729,072	526,963	383,392
Provision for Loan Losses	152,272	192,000	100,766	54,205	35,237	29,465	40,861	4,001
Non-Interest Income	698,470	547,546	473,624	392,871	230,597	211,645	110,811	57,138
Non-Interest Expense	790,721	678,972	629,662	603,955	633,327	492,513	373,930	244,024
Income Before Taxes	924,364	846,401	733,612	637,746	496,137	418,739	222,983	192,505
Income from Cont Ops	...	...	...	...	335,530	277,019	151,136	...
Net Income	630,891	577,668	500,714	433,962	333,976	215,361	148,409	127,722
Average Shs. Outstg.	230,257	236,115	238,383	239,894	252,183	207,533	165,291	122,308
Balance Sheet								
Cash & Due from Banks	...	...	...	530,771	689,082	334,054	214,716	152,301
Securities Avail. for Sale	273,260	210,095	129,312	426,701	496,075	253,317	582,589	243,632
Net Loans & Leases	28,130,017	25,852,846	25,396,071	23,950,172	22,276,862	17,502,729	12,360,134	8,100,342
Total Assets	42,628,066	41,896,072	38,174,516	32,971,427	31,819,063	24,467,255	19,760,265	13,904,563
Total Deposits	27,203,319	27,527,843	25,123,309	19,605,671	19,073,975	15,165,064	10,219,200	7,841,197
Long-Term Obligations	10,545,046	9,746,778	8,961,648	9,921,085	9,458,427	6,316,454	5,600,301	3,405,513
Total Liabilities	39,352,197	38,812,247	35,246,016	30,515,223	29,421,363	22,592,143	18,383,376	12,975,870
Net Stockholders' Equity	3,275,869	3,083,825	2,928,500	2,456,204	2,397,700	1,875,112	1,376,889	928,693
Shares Outstanding	223,173	224,790	235,556	229,571	242,241	201,043	165,809	118,548
Statistical Record								
Return on Equity %	19.25	18.73	17.09	17.66	13.99	14.77	10.97	13.75
Return on Assets %	1.47	1.37	1.31	1.31	1.05	1.13	0.76	0.91
Equity/Assets %	7.68	7.36	7.67	7.44	7.53	7.66	6.96	6.67
Non-Int. Exp./Tot. Inc. %	28.13	23.95	22.07	22.87	26.84	24.97	25.12	22.98
Price Range	34.59–27.32	34.48–24.00	29.83–23.36	27.04–13.61	17.92–15.82	...	...	...
P/E Ratio	12.62–9.97	14.07–9.80	14.21–11.12	14.94–7.52	13.58–11.98	...	...	...
Average Yield %	3.20	2.70	2.69	3.20	3.10	N/A	N/A	N/A

Address: 1215 Superior Avenue, Cleveland, OH 44114
Telephone: (216) 566-5300
Web Site: www.charterone.com

Officers: Charles John Koch – Chmn., Pres., C.E.O., Herbert G. Chorbajian – Vice-Chmn.
Transfer Agents: EquiServe, Providence, RI

Investor Contact: 800-262-6301
Institutional Holding
No of Institutions: 16
Shares: 2,694,312 **% Held:** –

CHEMICAL FINANCIAL CORP.

Exchange	Symbol	Price	52Wk Range	Yield	P/E
NMS	CHFC	$35.81 (3/31/2004)	37.91-27.71	2.96	15.24

*7 Year Price Score 119.1 *NYSE Composite Index=100 *12 Month Price Score 102.8

Interim Earnings (Per Share)

Qtr.	Mar	Jun	Sep	Dec
2000	0.38	0.44	0.44	0.60
2001	0.15	0.48	0.55	0.62
2002	0.55	0.54	0.56	0.66
2003	0.59	0.58	0.61	0.57

Interim Dividends (Per Share)

Amt	Decl	Ex	Rec	Pay
0.25Q	4/21/2003	6/4/2003	6/6/2003	6/20/2003
0.25Q	7/21/2003	9/3/2003	9/5/2003	9/19/2003
0.25Q	10/20/2003	12/3/2003	12/5/2003	12/19/2003
0.265Q	12/8/2003	3/3/2004	3/5/2004	3/19/2004

Indicated Div: $1.06 (Div. Reinv. Plan)

Valuation Analysis

Forecast P/E	14.53	Trailing P/E	15.24
Market Cap	$807.5 Million	Book Value	448.6 Million
Price/Book	N/A	Price/Sales	N/A

Dividend Achiever Status

Rank	117	10 Year Growth Rate 12.13%
Total Years of Dividend Growth		28

Business Summary: Commercial Banking (MIC: 8.1 SIC: 6022 NAIC:522110)

Chemical Financial is a bank holding company headquartered in Midland, MI, with total assets of $3.71 billion as of Dec 31 2003. Co.'s four subsidiary banks, CB&T, Chemical Bank Shoreline, Chemical Bank West and State Bank of Caledonia, operate 133 branch offices and two loan production offices throughout 33 counties in the lower peninsula of Michigan. Non–bank subsidiaries include CFC Financial Services, an insurance company operating under the assumed names Chemical Financial Insurance Agency and CFC Investment Centers, and CFC Title Services, an issuer of title insurance to buyers and sellers of residential and commercial mortgage properties.

Recent Developments: For the year ended Dec 31 2003, net income rose 1.4% to $55.7 million from $54.9 million the year before. Net interest income slipped 4.1% to $139.8 million, due to a decrease in the yield on both loans and investment securities outpacing the decrease in the cost of funds. Provision for loan losses fell 24.7% to $2.8 million. Total non–interest income improved 13.2% to $39.1 million. Total non–interest expense slid 1.7% to $91.9 million. As of Dec 31 2003, total deposits were $2.97 billion versus $2.85 billion the year before. Total loans rose 19.6% to $2.48 billion, primarily due to growth in residential and commercial real estate loans.

Prospects: Co. continues to benefit from its acquisition of Caledonia Financial, which was completed on Dec 1 2003. As of that date, Caledonia had total assets of $211.0 million, total loans of $184.0 million, and total deposits of $171.0 million. Co. will continue to operate Caledonia's bank subsidiary, State Bank of Caledonia, as a separate subsidiary until mid–2004. At that time, Co. expects to restructure the State Bank of Caledonia into two of its three existing bank subsidiaries. The branches in Caledonia, Middleville and Dutton, MI are expected to become part of Chemical Bank West, and the Kalamazoo, MI branch is expected to become a part of Chemical Bank Shoreline.

Financial Data

(US$ in Thousands)	9 Mos	6 Mos	3 Mos	12/31/2002	12/31/2001	12/31/2000	12/31/1999	12/31/1998
Earnings Per Share	1.78	1.17	0.59	2.31	1.80	1.86	1.75	1.65
Tang. Book Val. Per Share	17.29	17.05	16.75	16.46	14.67	18.27	16.86	16.25
Dividends Per Share	0.970	0.950	0.930	0.910	0.870	0.790	0.720	0.660
Dividend Payout %	54.97	81.80	158.59	39.57	48.37	42.71	41.23	40.18
Income Statement								
Total Interest Income	140,180	94,943	48,246	211,044	219,250	131,085	121,917	121,633
Total Interest Expense	35,263	24,790	13,122	65,352	89,182	54,035	47,071	49,146
Net Interest Income	104,917	70,153	35,124	145,692	130,068	77,050	74,846	72,487
Provision for Loan Losses	2,107	1,567	295	3,765	2,004	487	483	964
Non–Interest Income	23,049	15,500	7,583	34,534	31,873	17,061	15,265	14,074
Non–Interest Expense	68,909	46,208	23,026	93,526	94,597	50,860	48,986	48,307
Income Before Taxes	63,575	41,778	21,117	82,935	65,340	43,067	41,380	38,826
Net Income	42,153	27,684	14,014	54,945	42,723	29,006	27,709	26,046
Average Shs. Outstg.	23,737	23,738	23,740	23,741	23,691	15,526	15,722	15,785
Balance Sheet								
Cash & Due from Banks	146,428	122,712	114,023	148,112	150,546	95,047	98,827	98,483
Securities Avail. for Sale	767,562	832,506	946,711	858,744	731,383	433,289	428,040	488,976
Net Loans & Leases	2,246,476	2,206,335	2,101,000	2,044,514	2,151,547	1,067,636	990,827	880,222
Total Assets	3,591,026	3,587,829	3,613,499	3,568,893	3,488,306	1,973,424	1,890,376	1,872,626
Total Deposits	2,869,814	2,877,426	2,904,102	2,847,272	2,789,524	1,606,217	1,561,702	1,554,271
Long–Term Obligations	148,573	148,573	153,591	157,393	167,893	185	200	8,000
Total Liabilities	448,644	443,140	3,176,459	3,138,554	3,098,850	1,704,695	1,640,795	1,630,787
Net Stockholders' Equity	23,685	23,665	437,040	430,339	389,456	268,729	249,581	241,839
Shares Outstanding	23,685	23,665	23,690	23,684	23,639	14,704	14,799	14,879
Statistical Record								
Return on Equity %	9.39	6.24	3.20	12.76	10.96	10.79	11.10	10.76
Return on Assets %	1.17	0.77	0.38	1.53	1.22	1.46	1.46	1.39
Equity/Assets %	12.49	12.35	12.09	12.05	11.16	13.61	13.20	12.91
Non–Int. Exp./Tot. Inc. %	42.21	41.83	41.24	38.08	37.66	34.33	35.70	35.59
Price Range	34.03–26.53	31.88–26.53	31.83–26.53	36.15–25.43	30.23–17.52	27.53–17.80	30.23–25.05	31.44–24.01
P/E Ratio	19.12–14.90	27.25–22.68	53.95–44.97	15.65–11.01	16.79–9.73	14.80–9.57	17.28–14.32	19.06–14.55
Average Yield %	3.25	3.29	3.29	3.13	3.64	3.55	2.61	2.31

Address: 333 East Main Street, Midland, MI 48640–0569 Telephone: (989) 839–5350 Web Site: www.chemicalbankmi.com	Officers: Aloysius J. Oliver – Chmn., David B. Ramaker – Pres., C.E.O.	Investor Contact: (989) 839–5350 Institutional Holding No of Institutions: 12 Shares: 174,928 % Held: –

CHEVRONTEXACO CORP.

Exchange	Symbol	Price	52Wk Range	Yield	P/E
NYS	CVX	$87.78 (3/31/2004)	90.70-62.81	3.33	12.29

*7 Year Price Score 88.2   *NYSE Composite Index=100   *12 Month Price Score 98.2

Interim Earnings (Per Share)

Qtr.	Mar	Jun	Sep	Dec
2000	1.59	1.71	2.35	2.32
2001	2.49	2.06	1.82	(2.67)
2002	0.68	0.39	(0.85)	0.85
2003	1.81	1.50	2.02	1.81

Interim Dividends (Per Share)

Amt	Decl	Ex	Rec	Pay
0.70Q	4/30/2003	5/15/2003	5/19/2003	6/10/2003
0.73Q	7/30/2003	8/15/2003	8/19/2003	9/10/2003
0.73Q	10/29/2003	11/14/2003	11/18/2003	12/10/2003
0.73Q	1/28/2004	2/13/2004	2/18/2004	3/10/2004

Indicated Div: $2.92 (Div. Reinv. Plan)

Valuation Analysis

Forecast P/E	15.22	Trailing P/E	12.29
Market Cap	$93.7 Billion	Book Value	36.3 Billion
Price/Book	2.53	Price/Sales	0.76

Dividend Achiever Status

Rank	254	10 Year Growth Rate	5.03%
Total Years of Dividend Growth	16		

Business Summary: Oil and Gas (MIC: 14.2 SIC: 2911 NAIC:324110)

ChevronTexaco is a global energy company engaged in fully integrated petroleum operations, chemicals operations and coal mining activities. Co. also holds investments in power generation and gasification businesses. Petroleum operations consist of exploring for, developing and producing crude oil and natural gas; refining crude oil into finished petroleum products; marketing crude oil, natural gas and the many products derived from petroleum; and transporting crude oil, natural gas and petroleum products. As of Dec 31 2003, net proved reserves of natural gas were 20,191 billion cubic feet and net proved reserves of crude oil, condensate and natural gas liquids totaled 8,599 million barrels.

Recent Developments: For the year ended Dec 31 2003, income was $7.43 billion, before an accounting change charge of $196.0 million, compared with net income of $1.13 billion a year earlier. Results for 2002 included a charge of $1.80 billion related to the write down of investments in Dynegy Inc. and merger–related expenses of $576.0 million. Total revenues and other income increased 23.1% to $121.76 billion and included a non–recurring gain of $365.0 million from the exchange of Dynegy preferred stock. Exploration and production income climbed 40.5% to $6.40 billion, while refining, marketing and transportation income totaled $1.17 billion versus a loss of $367.0 million the year before.

Prospects: The recent strength in crude oil and natural gas prices, coupled with significantly improved industry margins for refined products, reinforces Co.'s favorable near–term outlook. Meanwhile, in an effort to further its longer–term strategic objectives, Co. has formed two new business units. According to Co., the first business unit is focused on commercializing its significant international natural gas resource base, while the second business unit is dedicated solely to the identification and development of large–scale investment opportunities throughout the world.

Financial Data

(US$ in Millions)	12/31/2003	12/31/2002	12/31/2001	12/31/2000	12/31/1999	12/31/1998	12/31/1997	12/31/1996
Earnings Per Share	7.14	1.07	3.70	7.97	3.14	2.04	4.95	3.99
Cash Flow Per Share	11.57	9.34	10.77	13.30	6.79	5.67	6.96	8.87
Tang. Book Val. Per Share	33.94	29.58	31.81	31.08	27.04	25.80	26.63	23.81
Dividends Per Share	2.860	2.800	2.650	2.600	2.480	2.440	2.280	2.080
Dividend Payout %	40.05	261.68	71.62	32.62	78.98	119.60	46.06	52.13
Income Statement								
Total Revenues	121,761	99,049	106,245	52,129	36,586	30,557	41,950	43,893
Total Indirect Exp.	28,301	29,174	28,801	9,930	9,394	9,448	10,633	9,956
Depreciation & Amort.	5,384	5,231	7,059	2,848	2,866	2,320	2,300	2,216
Operating Income	12,295	4,667	8,101	8,980	3,594	2,011	5,126	4,337
Net Interest Inc./(Exp.)	(474)	(565)	(833)	(460)	(472)	(405)	(312)	(364)
Income Taxes	5,344	3,024	4,360	4,085	1,578	495	2,246	2,133
Eqty Earns/Minority Int.	1,029	111	1,144	750	526	228	688	767
Income from Cont Ops	7,426	...	3,931	...	...	...	...	...
Net Income	7,230	1,132	3,288	5,185	2,070	1,339	3,256	2,607
Average Shs. Outstg.	1,064	1,063	1,062	651	659	657	658	653
Balance Sheet								
Cash & Cash Equivalents	5,267	3,781	3,150	2,630	2,032	1,413	1,670	1,637
Total Current Assets	19,426	17,776	18,327	8,213	8,297	6,297	7,006	7,942
Total Assets	81,470	77,359	77,572	41,264	40,668	36,540	35,473	34,854
Total Current Liabilities	16,111	19,876	20,654	7,674	8,889	7,166	6,946	8,907
Long–Term Obligations	10,894	10,911	8,989	5,153	5,485	4,393	4,431	3,988
Net Stockholders' Equity	36,835	31,604	33,958	19,925	17,749	17,034	17,472	15,623
Net Working Capital	3,315	(2,100)	(2,327)	539	(592)	(869)	60	(965)
Shares Outstanding	1,069	1,068	1,067	641	656	660	655	656
Statistical Record								
Operating Profit Margin %	10.10	4.71	7.62	17.23	9.82	6.58	12.22	9.88
Return on Equity %	20.46	3.58	11.58	26.02	11.66	7.86	13.64	5.94
Return on Assets %	9.12	1.46	5.07	12.57	5.09	3.66	9.18	7.48
Debt/Total Assets %	13.37	14.10	11.58	12.48	13.48	12.02	12.49	11.44
Price Range	86.39-61.85	90.86-65.90	98.03-78.77	94.31-71.06	103.5-73.69	88.94-71.13	88.69-62.25	68.13-51.75
P/E Ratio	12.10-8.66	84.92-61.59	26.49-21.29	11.83-8.92	32.96-23.47	43.60-34.87	17.92-12.58	17.07-12.97
Average Yield %	4.04	3.51	2.98	3.07	2.76	3.00	3.06	3.49

Address: 6001 Bollinger Canyon Road, San Ramon, CA 94583-2324	**Officers:** David J. OReilly – Chmn., C.E.O., Peter J. Robertson – Vice–Chmn.	**Investor Contact:** 415–894–5690
Telephone: (415) 894–7700	**Transfer Agents:** Mellon Investor Services, Ridgefield Park, NJ	**Institutional Holding**
Web Site: www.chevrontexaco.com		**No of Institutions:** 30
		Shares: 278,790 **% Held:** –

54

CHITTENDEN CORP.

Exchange	Symbol	Price	52Wk Range	Yield	P/E
NYS	CHZ	$33.00 (3/31/2004)	34.40-25.87	2.42	15.94

*7 Year Price Score N/A *NYSE Composite Index=100 *12 Month Price Score 103.4

Interim Earnings (Per Share)

Qtr.	Mar	Jun	Sep	Dec
2000	0.40	0.42	0.44	0.46
2001	0.44	0.44	0.46	0.46
2002	0.46	0.47	0.48	0.55
2003	0.49	0.51	0.54	0.53

Interim Dividends (Per Share)

Amt	Decl	Ex	Rec	Pay
0.20Q	4/16/2003	4/30/2003	5/2/2003	5/16/2003
0.20Q	7/17/2003	7/30/2003	8/1/2003	8/15/2003
0.20Q	10/16/2003	10/29/2003	10/31/2003	11/14/2003
0.20Q	1/22/2004	1/28/2004	1/30/2004	2/13/2004

Indicated Div: $0.80 (Div. Reinv. Plan)

Valuation Analysis

Forecast P/E	13.92	Trailing P/E	15.94
Market Cap	$1.1 Billion	Book Value	580.0 Million
Price/Book	2.17	Price/Sales	3.41

Dividend Achiever Status

Rank	11	10 Year Growth Rate	25.35%
Total Years of Dividend Growth	11

Business Summary: Commercial Banking (MIC: 8.1 SIC: 6022 NAIC:522110)

Chittenden is a bank holding company with assets totaling $5.90 billion as of Dec 31 2003. Through its subsidiaries, Co. is engaged in providing financial services. Co. offers a variety of lending services, including commercial loans and residential real estate loans. In addition, Co. offers acceptance of demand, savings, money market, cash management and time deposits. Co. also provides personal trust services, including services as executor, trustee, administrator, custodian and guardian. Corporate trust services are also provided, including services as trustee for pension and profit sharing plans. Asset management services are provided for personal and corporate trust clients.

Recent Developments: For the year ended Dec 31 2003, net income advanced 17.5% to $74.8 million compared with $63.6 million in 2002. Total interest income grew 4.8% to $271.4 million. Total interest expense fell 20.5% to $53.4 million versus $66.4 million the year before. Net interest income advanced 13.2% to $218.1 million due to higher average earning assets. Provision for loan losses declined 13.9% to $7.2 million, reflecting Co.'s improved asset quality and stronger economic conditions throughout its primary market areas. Total noninterest income surged 49.1% to $97.0 million, while total noninterest expense increased 26.3% to $191.4 million.

Prospects: Near-term results are expected to benefit from a restructuring plan that Co. formulated and began implementing in the latter half of 2003. The initiative includes the consolidation or closure of certain branch locations, the majority of which are related to the anticipated merger of Granite Bank into Ocean National Bank in the second quarter of 200; the closure of certain offsite ATM locations, primarily in New Hampshire and southern Maine; a severance related to the branch consolidations and closures, and the centralization of back office functions planned as part of the information technology platform conversion in May 2004.

Financial Data

(US$ in Thousands)	12/31/2003	12/31/2002	12/31/2001	12/31/2000	12/31/1999	12/31/1998	12/31/1997	12/31/1996
Earnings Per Share	2.07	1.96	1.80	1.72	(0.07)	1.67	1.55	1.36
Tang. Book Val. Per Share	8.96	10.81	9.43	9.13	9.69	9.17	8.23	8.55
Dividends Per Share	0.800	0.790	0.760	0.750	0.680	0.620	1.030	0.460
Dividend Payout %	38.64	40.30	42.55	43.72	N.M.	37.32	66.39	33.64
Income Statement								
Total Interest Income	271,442	259,019	266,497	288,102	288,216	151,511	150,189	142,592
Total Interest Expense	53,379	66,404	96,192	121,030	113,235	60,508	59,545	58,599
Net Interest Income	218,063	192,615	170,305	167,072	174,981	91,003	90,644	83,993
Provision for Loan Losses	7,175	8,331	8,041	8,700	8,700	5,100	4,050	4,183
Non-Interest Income	97,031	65,060	63,733	54,810	64,226	32,402	28,210	24,920
Non-Interest Expense	191,371	151,544	135,760	126,462	203,929	71,767	70,072	64,557
Income Before Taxes	116,548	97,800	90,237	86,720	26,578	46,538	44,732	40,173
Net Income	74,799	63,645	58,501	58,687	(2,496)	30,665	29,406	26,721
Average Shs. Outstg.	36,120	32,495	32,547	34,100	35,795	18,353	18,958	19,481
Balance Sheet								
Securities Avail. for Sale	3,176,302	2,994,222	1,652,990	1,170,562	1,298,942	1,007,398	726,558	755,628
Net Loans & Leases	3,667,220	2,925,666	2,792,909	2,815,843	2,854,651	1,375,593	1,372,417	1,268,472
Total Assets	5,900,644	4,920,544	4,153,714	3,769,861	3,827,297	2,122,019	1,977,150	1,988,746
Total Deposits	4,969,891	4,126,092	3,669,846	3,292,407	3,204,098	1,890,754	1,757,545	1,761,579
Long-Term Obligations	162,434	173,654	44,409	93,757	197,072	23,369	2,239	2,540
Total Liabilities	5,320,693	4,501,752	3,783,060	3,427,795	3,464,837	1,946,872	1,791,627	1,790,353
Net Stockholders' Equity	579,951	418,792	370,654	342,066	362,460	175,147	162,273	174,401
Shares Outstanding	36,636	31,939	35,743	35,736	35,472	17,727	18,026	19,181
Statistical Record								
Return on Equity %	12.89	15.19	15.78	17.15	N.M.	17.50	18.12	15.32
Return on Assets %	1.26	1.29	1.40	1.55	N.M.	1.44	1.48	1.34
Equity/Assets %	9.82	8.51	8.92	9.07	9.47	8.25	8.20	8.76
Non-Int. Exp./Tot. Inc. %	51.93	46.76	41.11	36.87	57.86	39.02	39.27	38.53
Price Range	34.40-24.86	34.18-23.71	28.75-22.25	25.20-18.30	26.90-21.00	31.60-20.70	...	...
P/E Ratio	16.62-12.01	17.44-12.10	15.97-12.36	14.65-10.64	N/A	18.92-12.40	...	...
Average Yield %	2.78	2.76	3.01	3.49	2.92	2.28	N/A	N/A

Address: Two Burlington Square, Burlington, VT 05401 **Telephone:** (802) 658-4000 **Web Site:** www.chittendencorp.com	**Officers:** Paul A. Perrault - Chmn., Pres., C.E.O., Kirk W. Walters - Exec. V.P., C.F.O., Treas. **Transfer Agents:**BankBoston, N.A., Boston, MA	**Investor Contact:**802 660 1412 **Institutional Holding** **No of Institutions:** 2 **Shares:** 124,562 **% Held:** -

CHUBB CORP.

Exchange	Symbol	Price	52Wk Range	Yield	P/E
NYS	CB	$69.54 (3/31/2004)	73.66-44.81	2.24	15.59

*7 Year Price Score 91.9   ***NYSE Composite Index=100**   ***12 Month Price Score 98.0**

Interim Earnings (Per Share)

Qtr.	Mar	Jun	Sep	Dec
2000	0.87	1.02	1.17	0.95
2001	0.97	0.83	(1.40)	0.23
2002	1.15	1.20	(1.42)	0.36
2003	1.31	1.45	1.37	0.33

Interim Dividends (Per Share)

Amt	Decl	Ex	Rec	Pay
0.36Q	6/6/2003	6/18/2003	6/20/2003	7/8/2003
0.36Q	9/5/2003	9/17/2003	9/19/2003	10/7/2003
0.36Q	12/4/2003	12/16/2003	12/18/2003	1/6/2004
0.39Q	3/5/2004	3/17/2004	3/19/2004	4/6/2004

Indicated Div: $1.56 (Div. Reinv. Plan)

Valuation Analysis

Forecast P/E	10.96	Trailing P/E	15.59
Market Cap	$11.9 Billion	Book Value	8.5 Billion
Price/Book	1.50	Price/Sales	1.12

Dividend Achiever Status

Rank	241	10 Year Growth Rate	5.40%
Total Years of Dividend Growth		39

Business Summary: Insurance (MIC: 8.2 SIC: 6331 NAIC:524126)

Chubb is engaged in the property and casualty insurance business. Operations are divided into three strategic business units. Chubb Commercial Insurance specializes in commercial customer insurance products, including coverage for multiple peril, casualty, workers' compensation and property and marine. Chubb Specialty Insurance provides executive protection and professional liability products for privately and publicly owned companies. Chubb Specialty Insurance also includes Co.'s surety and accident businesses, as well as its reinsurance business. Chubb Personal Insurance offers products for individuals who require more coverage choices and higher limits than standard insurance policies.

Recent Developments: For the year ended Dec 31 2003, net income jumped to $808.8 million from $222.9 million the previous year. Results for 2003 included a charge of $250.0 million for asbestos loss reserves and a charge of $127.0 million from Chubb Financial Solutions (CFS), Co.'s non-insurance business. Results for 2002 included a charge of $741.0 million for the strengthening of asbestos and environmental reserves and a charge of $70.0 million from CFS. Total revenues increased 24.7% to $11.39 billion. Premiums earned climbed 25.9% to $10.18 billion, primarily due to higher premium rates particularly in the commercial and specialty classes. Co.'s combined ratio improved to 98.0% in 2003 versus 106.7% in 2002.

Prospects: Going forward, Co. expects the strong fundamentals in its property and casualty insurance business will form a solid foundation for growth in 2004. For the full-year, Co. expects net written premium growth of about 10.0% to 14.0%, including 8.0% to 11.0% growth in commercial insurance premiums, 14.0% to 17.0% growth in specialty premiums and 8.0% to 11.0% growth in personal insurance premiums. In addition, Co. expects its combined ratio to fall in a range of 94.0% to 96.0%, based on a combined ratio of 89.0% to 92.0% for commercial insurance, 97.0% to 100.0% for specialty insurance and 94.0% to 97.0% for personal insurance. Operating earnings should range from $5.90 to $6.30 per share.

Financial Data

(US$ in Thousands)	12/31/2003	12/31/2002	12/31/2001	12/31/2000	12/31/1999	12/31/1998	12/31/1997	12/31/1996
Earnings Per Share	4.46	1.29	0.63	4.01	3.66	4.19	4.39	2.75
Tang. Book Val. Per Share	42.85	37.33	35.61	37.12	32.84	34.78	32.10	31.24
Dividends Per Share	1.430	1.390	1.350	1.310	1.270	1.220	1.140	1.050
Dividend Payout %	32.06	107.75	214.28	32.66	34.76	29.11	25.96	38.18
Income Statement								
Total Premium Income	10,182,500	8,085,300	6,656,400	6,145,900	5,652,000	5,303,800	5,157,400	4,569,256
Other Income	1,211,500	1,055,000	1,097,600	1,105,600	1,077,600	1,046,000	1,506,600	1,111,276
Total Revenues	11,394,000	9,140,300	7,754,000	7,251,500	6,729,600	6,349,800	6,664,000	5,680,532
Total Indirect Exp.	2,709,100	2,187,100	1,855,000	1,722,600	1,588,400	1,537,700	1,415,400	1,264,584
Inc. Before Inc. Taxes	933,600	168,400	(66,000)	851,000	710,100	849,700	974,100	546,924
Income Taxes	124,800	(54,500)	(177,500)	136,400	89,000	142,700	204,600	60,731
Income from Cont Ops	...	...	...	...	...	...	...	486,193
Net Income	808,800	222,900	111,500	714,600	621,100	707,000	769,500	512,684
Average Shs. Outstg.	181,300	172,900	175,800	178,300	169,800	168,600	176,200	174,402
Balance Sheet								
Cash & Cash Equivalents	3,452,900	3,153,400	1,400,100	1,079,100	1,223,300	352,500	736,600	280,566
Premiums Due	2,474,800	2,287,500	1,940,500	1,656,600	1,477,600	1,420,300	1,348,200	1,180,252
Invst. Assets: Total	28,157,900	23,236,800	19,234,200	18,128,800	17,188,300	15,501,300	14,839,600	13,685,035
Total Assets	38,360,600	34,114,400	29,449,000	25,026,700	23,537,000	20,746,000	19,615,600	19,938,866
Long-Term Obligations	2,813,900	1,959,100	1,351,000	753,800	759,200	607,500	398,600	1,070,532
Net Stockholders' Equity	8,522,000	6,859,200	6,525,300	6,981,700	6,271,800	5,644,100	5,657,100	5,462,874
Shares Outstanding	187,963	171,201	170,071	174,919	175,489	162,267	176,200	174,861
Statistical Record								
Return on Revenues %	7.10	2.44	1.44	9.85	9.23	11.13	11.54	8.55
Return on Equity %	9.49	3.24	1.70	10.23	9.90	12.52	13.60	8.89
Return on Assets %	2.10	0.65	0.37	2.85	2.63	3.40	3.92	2.43
Price Range	69.24-42.45	78.20-52.20	83.44-58.59	90.00-44.75	75.94-45.50	88.25-57.00	78.13-51.25	55.50-41.38
P/E Ratio	15.52-9.52	60.62-40.47	132.4-93.00	22.44-11.16	20.75-12.43	21.06-13.60	17.80-11.67	20.18-15.05
Average Yield %	2.41	2.11	1.90	1.91	2.11	1.66	1.78	2.17

Address: 15 Mountain View Road, Warren, NJ 07061-1615
Telephone: (908) 903-2000
Web Site: www.chubb.com

Officers: John D. Finnegan – Chmn., Pres., C.E.O., Michael OReilly – Vice-Chmn., C.F.O., Chief Invest. Officer
Transfer Agents: EquiServe Trust Company, N.A., Jersey City, NJ

Investor Contact: (908) 903-3579
Institutional Holding
No of Institutions: 23
Shares: 498,213 **% Held:** –

CINCINNATI FINANCIAL CORP.

Exchange	Symbol	Price	52Wk Range	Yield	P/E
NMS	CINF	$43.45 (3/31/2004)	45.49–35.82	2.41	18.81

*7 Year Price Score 106.3 *NYSE Composite Index=100 *12 Month Price Score 95.0

Interim Earnings (Per Share)

Qtr.	Mar	Jun	Sep	Dec
2000	0.48	0.45	0.03	(0.23)
2001	0.44	0.30	0.22	0.23
2002	0.46	0.21	0.44	0.35
2003	0.35	0.52	0.64	0.80

Interim Dividends (Per Share)

Amt	Decl	Ex	Rec	Pay
0.25Q	8/15/2003	9/22/2003	9/24/2003	10/15/2003
0.25Q	11/14/2003	12/19/2003	12/23/2003	1/15/2004
0.275Q	1/31/2004	3/22/2004	3/24/2004	4/15/2004
5%	1/31/2004	4/28/2004	4/30/2004	6/15/2004

Indicated Div: $1.05 (Div. Reinv. Plan)

Valuation Analysis

Forecast P/E	16.12	Trailing P/E	18.81
Market Cap	$7.0 Billion	Book Value	6.2 Billion
Price/Book	1.08	Price/Sales	2.11

Dividend Achiever Status

Rank	135	10 Year Growth Rate	11.33%
Total Years of Dividend Growth		43

Business Summary: Insurance (MIC: 8.2 SIC: 6331 NAIC:524126)

Cincinnati Financial offers property and casualty insurance, its main business, through The Cincinnati Insurance Company, The Cincinnati Indemnity Company and The Cincinnati Casualty Company. The Cincinnati Life Insurance Company markets life and disability income insurance and annuities. CFC Investment Company supports the insurance subsidiaries and their independent agent representatives through commercial leasing and financing activities. CinFin Capital Management Company provides asset management services to institutions, corporations and high net worth individuals.

Recent Developments: For the year ended Dec 31 2003, net income climbed 57.1% to $374.0 million from $238.0 million the previous year. Results benefited from premium growth.Total revenues increased 11.9% to $3.18 billion. Revenues for 2003 and 2002 included realized investment losses of $41.0 million and $94.0 million, respectively. Property casualty premiums climbed 11.0% to $2.65 billion. Life insurance earned premiums grew 9.2% to $95.0 million. Net investment income rose 4.5% to $465.0 million. Insurance losses and policyholder benefits expenses increased 3.3% to $1.89 billion.

Prospects: Going forward, Co. believes further improvement in profitability can be achieved by sustaining or modestly improving commercial lines results. Meanwhile, Co. will continue to address homeowner results with a number of actions including re–underwriting programs with specific agencies, rate increases, deductible changes and modifications in policy terms and conditions. Co. believes these strategies will allow it to achieve full–year 2004 written premium growth in the high single digits and a combined ratio of about 95.0%.

Financial Data

(US$ in Thousands)	12/31/2003	12/31/2002	12/31/2001	12/31/2000	12/31/1999	12/31/1998	12/31/1997	12/31/1996
Earnings Per Share	2.31	1.46	1.19	0.73	1.52	1.41	1.77	1.30
Tang. Book Val. Per Share	38.77	34.55	37.02	37.26	33.46	33.72	28.35	18.94
Dividends Per Share	0.970	0.870	0.820	0.740	0.660	0.590	0.530	0.470
Dividend Payout %	42.09	60.10	68.90	101.36	43.63	42.31	30.13	36.15
Income Statement								
Total Premium Income	2,748,000	2,478,000	2,152,000	1,906,922	1,731,950	1,612,735	1,516,378	1,422,897
Other Income	433,000	365,000	409,000	424,072	396,273	441,554	426,006	385,852
Total Revenues	3,181,000	2,843,000	2,561,000	2,330,994	2,128,223	2,054,289	1,942,384	1,808,749
Total Indirect Exp.	686,000	628,000	559,000	539,104	445,649	416,810	382,417	350,290
Inc. Before Inc. Taxes	480,000	279,000	221,000	108,664	321,573	307,107	394,559	282,421
Income Taxes	106,000	41,000	28,000	(9,701)	66,851	65,540	95,184	58,661
Net Income	374,000	238,000	193,000	118,365	254,722	241,567	299,375	223,760
Average Shs. Outstg.	161,716	163,193	162,000	163,921	168,615	172,078	170,795	173,349
Balance Sheet								
Cash & Cash Equivalents	91,000	112,000	93,000	60,254	339,554	88,611	80,168	59,933
Premiums Due	1,729,000	1,563,000	1,302,000	912,880	383,429	358,945	322,976	327,739
Invst. Assets: Total	12,527,000	11,257,000	11,571,000	11,315,836	10,194,239	10,324,950	8,797,050	6,354,989
Total Assets	15,509,000	14,059,000	13,959,000	13,287,091	11,380,214	11,086,503	9,493,425	7,045,514
Long–Term Obligations	420,000	420,000	426,000	449,234	456,373	471,520	58,430	79,847
Net Stockholders' Equity	6,204,000	5,598,000	5,998,000	5,994,995	5,421,284	5,620,936	4,716,965	3,162,889
Shares Outstanding	160,000	162,000	162,000	160,891	162,021	166,681	166,356	166,908
Statistical Record								
Return on Revenues %	11.76	8.37	7.54	5.08	11.97	11.76	15.41	12.37
Return on Equity %	6.02	4.25	3.21	1.97	4.69	4.29	6.34	7.07
Return on Assets %	2.41	1.69	1.38	0.89	2.23	2.17	3.15	3.17
Price Range	41.80-33.65	47.04-32.69	42.70-35.31	42.88-26.75	42.25-30.13	46.92-30.75	46.92-20.67	21.73-18.00
P/E Ratio	18.10-14.57	32.22-22.39	35.88-29.67	58.73-36.64	27.80-19.82	33.27-21.81	26.51-11.68	16.71-13.85
Average Yield %	2.52	2.16	2.11	2.07	1.79	1.50	1.95	2.38

Address: 6200 S. Gilmore Road, Fairfield, OH 45014–5141 Telephone: (513) 870–2000 Web Site: www.cinfin.com	Officers: John J. Schiff – Chmn., Pres., C.E.O., James E. Benoski – Vice–Chmn., Chief Insurance Officer	Investor Contact:513–870–2639 Institutional Holding No of Institutions: 4 Shares: 26,364 % Held: –

CINTAS CORPORATION

Exchange	Symbol	Price	52Wk Range	Yield	P/E
NMS	CTAS	$43.49 (3/31/2004)	50.21–33.21	0.67	29.19

*7 Year Price Score 105.0 *NYSE Composite Index=100 *12 Month Price Score 105.2

Interim Earnings (Per Share)

Qtr.	Aug	Nov	Feb	May
2000–01	0.30	0.33	0.32	0.35
2001–02	0.33	0.34	0.32	0.37
2002–03	0.36	0.37	0.34	0.38
2003–04	0.37	0.40	...	...

Interim Dividends (Per Share)

Amt	Decl	Ex	Rec	Pay
0.22A	1/16/2001	1/31/2001	2/2/2001	3/26/2001
0.25A	1/31/2002	2/13/2002	2/15/2002	4/8/2002
0.27A	1/24/2003	2/5/2003	2/7/2003	3/14/2003
0.29A	1/27/2004	2/6/2004	2/10/2004	3/16/2004

Indicated Div: $0.29

Valuation Analysis

Forecast P/E	22.50	Trailing P/E	29.19
Market Cap	$7.4 Billion	Book Value	1.8 Billion
Price/Book	N/A	Price/Sales	N/A

Dividend Achiever Status

Rank	37	10 Year Growth Rate	19.19%
Total Years of Dividend Growth		21

Business Summary: Apparel (MIC: 4.4 SIC: 2326 NAIC:315225)

Cintas designs, manufactures, and implements corporate identity uniform programs, provides entrance mats, restroom supplies, promotional products, and first aid and safety products for over 500,000 businesses. Co. classifies its businesses into two operating segments: Rentals and Other Services. The Rentals operating segment designs and manufactures corporate identity uniforms which it rents, along with other items, to its customers. The Other Services operating segment involves the design, manufacture and direct sale of uniforms to its customers as well as the sale of ancillary services including sanitation supplies, first aid and safety products and services and cleanroom supplies.

Recent Developments: For the quarter ended Feb 29 2004, net income increased 12.6% to $66.5 million from $59.1 million in the prior–year quarter. Earnings benefited from higher organic revenue growth, cost containment initiatives and lower outstanding debt levels. Total revenue increased 5.0% to $696.9 million from $663.8 million the previous year. Rental revenue rose 4.6% to $547.5 million, while other services revenue grew 6.3% to $149.5 million. Cost of rentals increased 3.2% to $303.5 million. Cost of other services rose 2.5% to $97.8 million. Gross margins improved to 42.4% from 41.3% a year earlier. Interest expense dropped 19.9% to $6.0 million.

Prospects: Co.'s near–term growth prospects appear limited, reflecting continued weakness in employment growth at its existing customers. However, Co. continues to see positive demand for its other products and services including entrance mat services, restroom supply services and first aid and safety services. Also, Co. is pleased with its progress regarding Six Sigma, an analytical process that assists companies in improving quality and customer satisfaction while reducing cycle time and operating costs. Nevertheless, Co. narrowed its guidance for the remainder of fiscal 2004. For the full year, Co. expects revenue of about $2.78 billion to $2.82 billion and earnings per share of about $1.55 to $1.59.

Financial Data

(US$ in Thousands)	6 Mos	3 Mos	05/31/2003	05/31/2002	05/31/2001	05/31/2000	05/31/1999	05/31/1998
Earnings Per Share	1.49	1.46	1.45	1.36	1.30	1.14	0.82	0.79
Cash Flow Per Share	1.45	0.41	1.92	2.19	1.43	1.51	1.19	0.76
Tang. Book Val. Per Share	5.07	4.63	5.41	4.38	7.26	6.19	5.23	4.17
Dividends Per Share	0.270	0.270	0.270	0.250	0.220	0.180	0.140	0.120
Dividend Payout %	18.12	18.49	18.62	18.38	16.92	16.37	17.88	15.12
Income Statement								
Total Revenues	1,378,965	677,676	2,686,585	2,271,052	2,160,700	1,901,991	1,751,568	1,198,307
Total Indirect Exp.	357,427	180,473	695,437	580,740	528,354	455,794	403,580	287,155
Depreciation & Amort.	71,334	35,435	143,061	120,025	112,089	99,513	90,228	57,237
Operating Income	223,458	106,975	423,771	376,901	367,913	323,758	281,282	200,906
Net Interest Inc./(Exp.)	(12,375)	(6,467)	(28,012)	(5,316)	(10,750)	(11,165)	(11,771)	(4,356)
Income Taxes	78,099	37,181	146,506	137,334	134,003	118,372	85,055	56,577
Net Income	132,984	63,327	249,253	234,251	222,451	193,387	138,939	122,857
Average Shs. Outstg.	172,021	171,922	172,037	172,244	171,629	169,987	169,341	155,434
Balance Sheet								
Cash & Cash Equivalents	196,115	92,285	57,659	85,086	110,229	109,822	88,118	100,871
Total Current Assets	997,457	897,381	877,544	853,250	819,670	721,470	634,485	508,601
Total Assets	2,694,943	2,596,126	2,582,946	2,519,234	1,752,224	1,581,342	1,407,818	1,017,836
Total Current Liabilities	322,251	259,295	304,839	312,634	250,903	235,392	212,097	158,991
Long–Term Obligations	482,850	527,714	534,763	703,250	220,940	254,378	283,581	180,007
Net Stockholders' Equity	1,788,418	1,709,978	1,646,332	1,423,759	1,231,315	1,042,876	871,423	654,492
Net Working Capital	...	638,086	572,705	540,616	568,767	486,078	422,388	349,610
Shares Outstanding	170,890	170,731	170,599	169,930	169,370	168,281	166,423	156,916
Statistical Record								
Operating Profit Margin %	16.20	15.78	15.77	16.59	17.02	17.02	16.05	16.76
Return on Equity %	7.43	3.70	15.13	16.45	18.06	18.54	15.94	18.77
Return on Assets %	4.93	2.43	9.64	9.29	12.69	12.22	9.86	12.07
Debt/Total Assets %	17.91	20.32	20.70	27.91	12.60	16.08	20.14	17.68
Price Range	47.47–35.31	41.21–35.31	52.21–30.90	56.28–37.92	53.56–34.00	45.19–24.25	51.67–27.17	35.08–20.83
P/E Ratio	61.65–45.86	111.4–95.43	36.01–21.31	41.38–27.88	41.20–26.15	39.64–21.27	63.01–33.13	44.41–26.37
Average Yield %	0.67	0.71	0.64	0.53	0.50	0.49	0.36	0.45

Address: 6800 Cintas Boulevard, Cincinnati, OH 45262–5737 **Telephone:** (513) 459–1200 **Web Site:** www.cintas.com	**Officers:** Richard T. Farmer – Chmn., Robert J. Kohlhepp – Vice–Chmn.	**Investor Contact:** (513) 459–1200 **Institutional Holding** **No of Institutions:** 17 **Shares:** 11,895,379 **% Held:** –

CITIGROUP INC

Exchange	Symbol	Price	52Wk Range	Yield	P/E
NYS	C	$51.70 (3/31/2004)	51.94–35.60	3.09	19.36

*7 Year Price Score 114.5 *NYSE Composite Index=100 *12 Month Price Score 100.8

Interim Earnings (Per Share)

Qtr.	Mar	Jun	Sep	Dec
2000	0.78	0.65	0.67	0.52
2001	0.70	0.71	0.61	0.73
2002	0.94	0.78	0.72	0.15
2003	0.79	0.83	0.90	0.90

Interim Dividends (Per Share)

Amt	Decl	Ex	Rec	Pay
0.20Q	4/15/2003	5/1/2003	5/5/2003	5/23/2003
0.35Q	7/14/2003	7/31/2003	8/4/2003	8/22/2003
0.35Q	10/21/2003	10/30/2003	11/3/2003	11/26/2003
0.40Q	1/20/2004	1/29/2004	2/2/2004	2/27/2004

Indicated Div: $1.60

Valuation Analysis

Forecast P/E	12.89	Trailing P/E	19.36
Market Cap	$261.7 Billion	Book Value	94.1 Billion
Price/Book	2.49	Price/Sales	2.71

Dividend Achiever Status

Rank	6	10 Year Growth Rate 29.70%
Total Years of Dividend Growth		17

Business Summary: Commercial Banking (MIC: 8.1 SIC: 6021 NAIC:523930)

Citigroup is a bank holding company that provides financial services to consumers and corporations. Co.'s Global Consumer segment delivers banking, lending, insurance and investment services. Co.'s Global Corporate and Investment Bank segment provides corporations, governments, institutions and investors with financial products and services. Co.'s Private Client Services segment provides investment advice, financial planning and brokerage services. Co.'s Global Investment Management segment offers life insurance, annuity, asset management and personalized wealth management products and services. Proprietary Investment Activities include private equity investments and other investments.

Recent Developments: For the year ended Dec 31 2003, net income advanced 32.8% to $17.85 billion compared with income from continuing operations of $13.45 billion, before income of $1.88 billion from discontinued operations and a gain of $47.0 million from an accounting charge, in 2002. The improvement in earnings was primarily attributed to internal growth stemming from continued momentum with clients in an improved market environment, and acquisitions. Results for 2003 and 2002 included credits of $46.0 million and $15.0 million, respectively, from restructuring-related items. Total revenues grew 2.3% to $94.7 million from $92.6 million a year earlier.

Prospects: On Feb 22 2004, Co. and KorAm Bank announced that they, along with an investor consortium led by The Carlyle Group and JP Morgan Corsair II, have signed an agreement for the acquisition of KorAm by Co. The acquisition includes the consortium's 36.6% stake in KorAm and a tender offer for up to 100.0% of the remaining shares at a price of $2.73 billion. The tender offer will commence as soon as all required regulatory approvals are received, and the transaction is expected to close in the second quarter of 2004. KorAm has total assets of $36.80 billion. The combined businesses of Co. and KorAm will create the fifth largest financial business in Korea, in terms of revenues.

Financial Data

(US$ in Millions)	12/31/2003	12/31/2002	12/31/2001	12/31/2000	12/31/1999	12/31/1998	12/31/1997	12/31/1996
Earnings Per Share	3.42	2.59	2.75	2.62	2.14	1.21	1.27	1.15
Tang. Book Val. Per Share	10.74	9.69	15.57	12.83	10.63	8.94	6.98	4.95
Dividends Per Share	1.100	0.700	0.600	0.520	0.400	0.270	0.200	0.150
Dividend Payout %	32.16	27.02	21.81	19.84	18.88	22.83	15.74	13.04
Income Statement								
Total Premium Income	3,749	3,410	13,460	12,429	10,441	9,850	8,995	7,633
Net Investment Income	57,041	58,939	66,565	64,939	44,900	46,239	17,618	6,712
Other Income	33,917	30,207	31,997	34,458	26,664	20,342	10,996	7,000
Total Revenues	94,713	92,556	112,022	111,826	82,005	76,431	37,609	21,345
Total Indirect Exp.	39,168	37,298	39,601	38,559	29,781	28,551	36,049	12,977
Inc. Before Inc. Taxes	26,333	20,537	21,897	21,143	15,948	9,269	5,012	3,398
Income Taxes	8,195	6,998	7,526	7,525	5,703	3,234	1,696	1,051
Eqty Earns/Minority Int.	(285)	(91)	(87)	(99)	(251)	(228)	(212)	(47)
Income from Cont Ops	...	13,448	14,284	...	9,994	...	...	2,300
Net Income	17,853	15,276	14,126	13,519	9,867	5,807	3,104	2,331
Average Shs. Outstg.	5,193	5,166	5,147	5,122	4,591	4,630	2,359	1,916
Balance Sheet								
Cash & Cash Equivalents	276,245	188,916	182,635	163,298	136,742	145,325	143,765	58,331
Premiums Due	31,053	29,714	47,528	36,237	32,667	30,905	30,939	22,408
Invst. Assets: Total	418,211	324,721	305,741	252,635	222,281	223,517	201,566	63,488
Total Assets	1,264,032	1,097,190	1,051,450	902,210	716,937	668,641	386,555	151,067
Long–Term Obligations	162,702	126,927	121,631	111,778	47,092	48,671	28,352	11,327
Net Stockholders' Equity	98,014	86,718	81,200	61,286	44,766	38,248	18,233	11,056
Shares Outstanding	5,156	5,140	5,118	5,022	4,490	4,515	2,289	1,912
Statistical Record								
Return on Revenues %	18.84	14.52	12.75	12.08	12.18	7.59	8.25	10.77
Return on Equity %	18.21	15.50	17.58	20.41	20.11	13.59	14.85	17.57
Return on Assets %	1.41	1.22	1.35	1.49	1.39	0.86	0.80	1.52
Price Range	49.00–31.42	52.00–26.73	56.30–36.36	58.38–36.05	43.59–24.75	36.50–15.88	28.28–14.83	15.79–9.50
P/E Ratio	14.33–9.19	20.08–10.32	20.47–13.22	22.28–13.76	20.37–11.57	30.17–13.12	22.27–11.68	13.73–8.26
Average Yield %	2.63	1.75	1.23	1.08	1.17	0.99	0.95	1.29

Address: 399 Park Avenue, New York, NY 10043	**Officers:** Sanford I. Weill – Chmn., C.E.O., William R. Rhodes – Sr. Vice–Chmn.	**Investor Contact:** (212) 559–9446
Telephone: (212) 559–1000	**Transfer Agents:** Citibank Shareholder Services, Jersey City, NJ	**Institutional Holding**
Web Site: www.citigroup.com		**No of Institutions:** 8
		Shares: 5,710,204 **% Held:** –

CITIZENS BANKING CORP

Exchange	Symbol	Price	52Wk Range	Yield	P/E
NMS	CBCF	$32.63 (3/31/2004)	33.95-22.08	3.49	21.61

*7 Year Price Score 98.9   *NYSE Composite Index=100   *12 Month Price Score 105.8

Interim Earnings (Per Share)

Qtr.	Mar	Jun	Sep	Dec
2000	0.46	0.47	0.54	0.44
2001	0.51	0.58	0.60	0.56
2002	0.53	0.56	(1.03)	0.50
2003	0.34	0.30	0.45	0.42

Interim Dividends (Per Share)

Amt	Decl	Ex	Rec	Pay
0.285Q	4/15/2003	4/23/2003	4/25/2003	5/7/2003
0.285Q	7/17/2003	7/23/2003	7/25/2003	8/6/2003
0.285Q	10/16/2003	10/22/2003	10/24/2003	11/5/2003
0.285Q	1/15/2004	1/21/2004	1/23/2004	2/4/2004

Indicated Div: $1.14 (Div. Reinv. Plan)

Valuation Analysis

Forecast P/E	14.50	Trailing P/E 21.61
Market Cap	$1.4 Billion	Book Value 635.2 Million
Price/Book	2.31	Price/Sales 2.93

Dividend Achiever Status

Rank	183	10 Year Growth Rate 8.66%
Total Years of Dividend Growth	20	

Business Summary: Commercial Banking (MIC: 8.1 SIC: 6021 NAIC:522110)

Citizens Banking is a multibank holding company, which directly or indirectly owns four banking subsidiaries and four nonbanking subsidiaries, with total assets of $7.71 billion as of Dec 31 2003. Co.'s subsidiary banks are full–service commercial banks offering a variety of financial services to corporate, commercial, correspondent and individual bank customers. These services include commercial, mortgage and consumer lending, demand and time deposits, trust services, investment services, retirement, and other financial products and services. Citizens operated 176 branch, private banking, and financial center locations throughout Michigan, Wisconsin, Iowa, and Illinois as of Dec 31 2003.

Recent Developments: For the year ended Dec 31 2003, net income surged to $66.0 million from $25.0 million the year before. Results included a net gain of $691,000 in 2003 and a net charge of $10.9 million in 2002 related to various items. The increase in earnings was due to the restructuring of Co.'s three major lines of business. Net interest income slid 5.1% to $286.3 million. Provision for loan losses dropped 47.6% to $63.0 million, reflecting lower net charge–offs and improvement in nonperforming assets. Total non–interest income slid 6.8% to $94.8 million, primarily as a result of a special one–time gain in 2002. Total non–interest expense decreased 5.0% to $233.7 million.

Prospects: During 2004, Co. will continue to work toward computing its "Achieving the Vision" project. Market teams have been formed to focus on deposit and loan growth within each market, fee income growth, and improving teamwork across lines of business to create a more seamless approach to client service, while managing their interest margin and credit quality. Separately, Co. intends to make a capital investment of $35.0 to $40.0 million and to open as many as 10 to 14 new branches, including two hub offices over the next 24 months in Oakland County, MI.

Financial Data

(US$ in Thousands)	12/31/2003	12/31/2002	12/31/2001	12/31/2000	12/31/1999	12/31/1998	12/31/1997	12/31/1996
Earnings Per Share	1.51	0.56	2.25	1.91	1.28	1.98	1.11	1.27
Tang. Book Val. Per Share	13.03	13.17	13.70	12.66	11.28	13.75	12.47	8.72
Dividends Per Share	1.140	1.130	1.080	1.010	0.910	0.820	0.740	0.670
Dividend Payout %	75.49	201.78	48.22	53.14	71.48	41.41	66.96	52.81
Income Statement								
Total Interest Income	405,977	463,384	573,559	622,008	542,407	339,880	335,863	255,914
Total Interest Expense	119,719	161,602	265,578	307,134	231,917	142,034	144,015	109,798
Net Interest Income	286,258	301,782	307,981	314,874	310,490	197,846	191,848	146,116
Provision for Loan Losses	62,962	120,200	26,407	20,983	24,675	14,090	15,332	8,334
Non–Interest Income	94,819	101,776	117,481	90,344	81,144	56,252	46,694	40,530
Non–Interest Expense	233,679	245,981	251,183	242,221	236,778	158,291	153,427	125,986
Income Before Taxes	85,127	23,975	147,872	126,473	89,983	81,717	46,049	52,326
Net Income	65,951	25,038	104,657	90,660	61,994	56,785	31,508	37,421
Average Shs. Outstg.	43,609	45,076	46,589	47,542	48,617	28,743	28,420	29,394
Balance Sheet								
Cash & Due from Banks	182,545	171,864	224,416	318,115	250,745	140,543	168,351	137,867
Securities Avail. for Sale	1,965,201	1,457,281	1,297,696	1,384,108	1,397,347	613,529	575,382	580,171
Net Loans & Leases	5,122,157	5,323,094	5,842,107	6,342,736	5,841,086	3,538,062	3,495,708	2,584,734
Total Assets	7,711,070	7,522,034	7,678,875	8,405,091	7,899,357	4,501,409	4,439,271	3,483,850
Total Deposits	5,442,267	5,936,913	5,965,126	6,244,141	6,128,998	3,764,356	3,694,346	2,864,807
Long–Term Obligations	936,859	599,313	629,099	471,117	127,104	130,937	108,165	84,133
Total Liabilities	7,075,908	6,871,565	6,981,411	7,725,112	7,265,688	4,060,327	4,029,429	3,168,608
Net Stockholders' Equity	635,162	650,469	697,464	679,979	633,669	441,082	409,842	315,242
Shares Outstanding	43,241	43,702	45,097	46,510	47,567	28,100	28,048	28,680
Statistical Record								
Return on Equity %	10.38	3.84	15.00	13.33	9.78	12.87	7.68	11.87
Return on Assets %	0.85	0.33	1.36	1.07	0.78	1.26	0.70	1.07
Equity/Assets %	8.23	8.64	9.08	8.09	8.02	9.79	9.23	9.04
Non–Int. Exp./Tot. Inc. %	46.66	43.52	36.34	34.00	37.97	39.95	40.10	42.49
Price Range	33.95-22.08	33.78-21.61	33.92-23.94	29.06-15.50	39.75-21.38	37.13-28.56	34.75-20.00	21.50-18.17
P/E Ratio	22.48-14.62	60.32-38.59	15.08-10.64	15.22-8.12	31.05-16.70	18.75-14.43	31.31-18.02	16.93-14.30
Average Yield %	4.26	3.92	3.84	4.94	3.07	2.46	2.97	3.40

Address: 328 S. Saginaw Street, Flint, MI 48502-2401	Officers: Willaim R. Hartman – Chmn., Pres., C.E.O., Charles D. Christy – Exec. V.P., C.F.O.	Investor Contact: (810) 257-2489
Telephone: (810) 766-7500		Institutional Holding
Web Site: www.citizensonline.com		No of Institutions: 4
		Shares: 11,044 % Held: –

CLARCOR INC.

Exchange	Symbol	Price	52Wk Range	Yield	P/E
NYS	CLC	$44.15 (3/31/2004)	45.90–34.60	1.13	19.89

*7 Year Price Score 164.2 ***NYSE Composite Index=100** ***12 Month Price Score 100.5**

Interim Earnings (Per Share)

Qtr.	Feb	May	Aug	Nov
2000-01	0.40	0.36	0.41	0.51
2001-02	0.32	0.42	0.48	0.63
2002-03	0.38	0.51	0.56	0.70
2003-04	0.45	...	...	...

Interim Dividends (Per Share)

Amt	Decl	Ex	Rec	Pay
0.123Q	6/23/2003	7/9/2003	7/11/2003	7/25/2003
0.125Q	9/22/2003	10/15/2003	10/17/2003	10/31/2003
0.125Q	12/15/2003	1/14/2004	1/16/2004	1/30/2004
0.125Q	3/22/2004	4/14/2004	4/16/2004	4/30/2004

Indicated Div: $0.50 (Div. Reinv. Plan)

Valuation Analysis

Forecast P/E	18.12	Trailing P/E	19.89
Market Cap	$1.1 Billion	Book Value	381.9 Million
Price/Book	3.01	Price/Sales	1.54

Dividend Achiever Status

Rank	292	10 Year Growth Rate	1.93%
Total Years of Dividend Growth	23		

TRADING VOLUME (thousand shares)

Business Summary: Automotive (MIC: 15.1 SIC: 3714 NAIC:336399)

Clarcor manufactures filtration products and consumer and industrial packaging products. The Engine/Mobile Filtration segment includes filters for oil, air, fuel, coolants and hydraulic fluids for trucks, automobiles, construction, mining and industrial equipment, locomotives, marine and agricultural equipment. The Industrial/Environmental Filtration segment produces air and antimicrobial treated filters and high efficiency electronic air cleaners, specialty filters, industrial process liquid filters, pharmaceutical process and beverage filters, filtration systems, bilge separators and sand control filters. The Packaging segment includes a variety of containers and packaging items.

Recent Developments: For the year ended Nov 29 2003, net earnings advanced 17.0% to $54.6 million versus $46.6 million in the previous year. Net sales increased 3.6% to $741.4 million. On a segment basis, Engine/Mobile Filtration sales climbed 9.2% to $287.8 million, reflecting a 2002 acquisition, increased sales of heavy–duty filter products and price increases. Industrial/Environmental Filtration sales inched up 0.7% to $386.3 million, reflecting strong sales of specialty filters for industrial markets and sales of private label HVAC filters for retailers, partially offset by lower sales of filtration equipment and HVAC filters for automotive manufacturing plants. Packaging sales slipped 1.7% to $67.3 million.

Prospects: Looking ahead to 2004, Co. expects improved packaging sales as customer order rates strengthen primarily for its metal printing and coating business. Co. also sees improved sales from its filtration businesses with gains from non–automotive customers and expansion of its filter service business. For the full year, Co. anticipates earnings will range from $2.25 to $2.35 per diluted share. Capital expenditures should range from $25.0 million to $30.0 million as Co. focuses on the development of new products through an expansion of its air filtration technical center in Louisville, KY and its process liquid technical center in Greensboro, NC, and builds a new aviation fuel test facility.

Financial Data
(US$ in Thousands)

	3 Mos	11/30/2003	11/30/2002	11/30/2001	11/30/2000	11/27/1999	11/28/1998	11/29/1997
Earnings Per Share	0.45	2.15	1.85	1.68	1.64	1.46	1.30	1.09
Cash Flow Per Share	0.57	3.46	3.37	2.54	2.20	1.58	1.71	1.72
Tang. Book Val. Per Share	10.22	9.80	7.74	6.39	5.75	4.97	6.89	6.40
Dividends Per Share	0.495	0.493	0.483	0.473	0.463	0.453	0.443	0.435
Dividend Payout %	110.00	22.93	26.10	28.15	28.23	31.02	34.08	39.91
Income Statement								
Total Revenues	175,272	741,358	715,563	666,964	652,148	477,869	426,773	394,264
Total Indirect Exp.	33,671	134,629	129,515	119,677	122,358	92,510	83,573	76,138
Depreciation & Amort.	4,792	18,985	19,760	21,850	21,079	15,372	12,380	11,600
Operating Income	17,813	87,062	77,775	75,810	75,987	56,077	51,663	44,424
Net Interest Inc./(Exp.)	(67)	(1,532)	(5,612)	(9,616)	(10,836)	(2,282)	(1,053)	(2,759)
Income Taxes	6,703	31,371	24,773	23,804	23,201	20,137	19,262	17,164
Eqty Earns/Minority Int.	(34)	(136)	(76)	(37)	(49)	(66)	(6)	(110)
Net Income	11,661	54,552	46,601	41,893	40,237	35,412	32,079	26,918
Average Shs. Outstg.	25,813	25,372	25,171	24,892	24,506	24,313	24,648	24,603
Balance Sheet								
Cash & Cash Equivalents	18,150	8,348	13,747	7,418	10,864	14,745	33,121	30,324
Total Current Assets	266,484	257,402	259,746	244,350	230,479	227,670	168,173	160,527
Total Assets	548,365	538,237	546,119	530,617	501,930	472,991	305,766	282,519
Total Current Liabilities	106,978	111,373	174,255	94,931	97,826	97,475	61,183	54,237
Long–Term Obligations	18,414	16,913	22,648	135,203	141,486	145,981	36,419	37,656
Net Stockholders' Equity	381,859	370,392	315,461	274,261	242,093	210,718	186,807	171,162
Net Working Capital	159,506	146,029	85,491	149,419	132,653	130,195	106,990	106,290
Shares Outstanding	25,372	25,309	24,918	24,626	24,381	24,019	23,949	24,243
Statistical Record								
Operating Profit Margin %	10.16	11.74	10.86	11.36	11.65	11.73	12.10	11.26
Return on Equity %	3.05	14.72	14.77	15.27	16.62	16.80	17.17	15.72
Return on Assets %	2.12	10.13	8.53	7.89	8.01	7.48	10.49	9.52
Debt/Total Assets %	3.35	3.14	4.14	25.48	28.18	30.86	11.91	13.32
Price Range	45.59–41.75	45.90–31.05	34.00–25.64	27.60–17.13	21.38–16.69	21.25–15.31	24.35–14.50	20.14–13.92
P/E Ratio	101.3–92.78	21.35–14.44	18.38–13.86	16.43–10.19	13.03–10.18	14.55–10.49	18.73–11.15	18.47–12.77
Average Yield %	1.12	1.30	1.60	1.93	2.46	2.43	2.28	2.57

Address: 2323 Sixth St, Rockford, IL 61125	Officers: Norman E. Johnson – Chmn., Pres., C.E.O., William B. Walker – Vice-Chmn.	Institutional Holding
Telephone: (815) 962–8867	Transfer Agents: First Chicago Trust Company of New York, Jersey City, NJ	No of Institutions: 166
Web Site: www.clarcor.com		Shares: 18,754,210 % Held: 75%

CLECO CORP.

Exchange	Symbol	Price	52Wk Range	Yield	P/E
NYS	CNL	$19.03 (3/31/2004)	19.53–12.76	4.73	N.M.

*7 Year Price Score 91.4   *NYSE Composite Index=100   *12 Month Price Score 99.8

Interim Earnings (Per Share)

Qtr.	Mar	Jun	Sep	Dec
2000	0.43	0.35	0.63	0.04
2001	0.25	0.29	0.65	0.32
2002	0.29	0.36	0.74	0.08
2003	0.36	(1.42)	0.48	(0.21)

Interim Dividends (Per Share)

Amt	Decl	Ex	Rec	Pay
0.225Q	4/25/2003	5/1/2003	5/5/2003	5/15/2003
0.225Q	7/25/2003	7/31/2003	8/4/2003	8/15/2003
0.225Q	10/24/2003	10/30/2003	11/3/2003	11/15/2003
0.225Q	1/23/2004	1/29/2004	2/2/2004	2/15/2004

Indicated Div: $0.90 (Div. Reinv. Plan)

Valuation Analysis

Forecast P/E	14.51	Trailing P/E	N.M.
Market Cap	$895.0 Million	Book Value	482.8 Million
Price/Book	1.79	Price/Sales	0.99

Dividend Achiever Status

Rank	289	10 Year Growth Rate	2.47%
Total Years of Dividend Growth	22		

Business Summary: Electricity (MIC: 7.1 SIC: 4911 NAIC:221121)

Cleco, under an energy services holding structure, is the parent company of Cleco Power and Cleco Midstream Resources. Cleco Power is a regulated electric utility company that served approximately 264,000 customers in 104 communities in central and southeastern Louisiana as of Dec 31 2003. Cleco Midstream Resources is a nonregulated regional energy services group that develops and operates electric power generation facilities, invests in and develops natural gas pipelines and other gas-related assets, and provides energy services to organizations that operate electric utility systems. Co.'s other operations consists of a shared services subsidiary and an investment subsidiary.

Recent Developments: For the year ended Dec 31 2003, Co. reported a net loss of $34.9 million versus net income of $71.9 million in 2002. Results for 2003 and 2002 included impairment charges of $156.3 million and $3.6 million, respectively. Also, results for 2003 and 2002 included a restructuring credit of $757,000 and a charge of $10.2 million, respectively. Total revenue advanced 21.3% to $874.6 million. Revenue included a net loss of $855,000 in 2003 and a net gain of $1.7 million in 2002 from energy trading. Electric operations revenue climbed 19.0% to $676.0 million, while tolling operations revenue rose 9.4% to $98.7 million. Energy operations revenue surged 138.4% to $71.6 million.

Prospects: In early 2004, Co. reached an agreement to sell the Perryville facility to Entergy Louisiana, Inc. for $170.0 million. Co. will continue to work in 2004 to complete the sale of Perryville to Entergy as well as protect its claims against Mirant through the bankruptcy process. Separately, Co. will focus heavily on Cleco Power and its resource planning process. Meanwhile, for 2004, Co. expects earnings per share to range from $1.25 to $1.35 per share. Earnings contribution from Cleco Power should be between $1.00 and $1.10 per share, reflecting continuing expense pressures, largely higher administrative costs and escalating benefit cost, in particular post-retirement benefit plan costs.

Financial Data

(US$ in Thousands)	12/31/2003	12/31/2002	12/31/2001	12/31/2000	12/31/1999	12/31/1998	12/31/1997	12/31/1996
Earnings Per Share	(0.79)	1.47	1.51	1.45	1.18	1.12	1.09	1.08
Cash Flow Per Share	4.21	3.39	2.61	1.71	2.40	2.37	2.46	1.35
Tang. Book Val. Per Share	10.23	11.95	10.94	10.33	9.77	9.44	9.09	8.76
Dividends Per Share	0.900	0.890	0.870	0.840	0.830	0.810	0.79	0.77
Dividend Payout %	N.M.	60.88	57.61	58.07	69.70	72.30	72.50	68.80
Income Statement								
Total Revenues	874,637	721,224	1,058,619	820,015	768,200	515,175	456,245	435,416
Total Indirect Exp.	272,328	121,720	98,006	93,269	86,091	83,789	81,203	73,036
Costs & Expenses	893,277	564,228	909,079	672,820	655,659	408,210	349,706	330,841
Depreciation & Amort.	77,550	69,157	60,246	55,840	50,019	48,369	45,890	43,441
Operating Income	(18,640)	156,996	149,540	147,195	112,541	106,965	106,539	104,575
Net Interest Inc./(Exp.)	(69,063)	(59,033)	(40,002)	(42,677)	(27,915)	(26,988)	(28,159)	(27,753)
Income Taxes	(23,974)	42,243	38,356	34,961	27,224	26,666	27,729	26,154
Eqty Earns/Minority Int.	31,631	16,204	...	...	...	...	...	...
Income from Cont Ops	...	...	72,273	69,335	...	...	...	...
Net Income	(34,929)	71,875	70,238	64,982	56,766	53,801	52,519	52,135
Average Shs. Outstg.	46,820	48,771	47,763	47,654	47,697	47,734	47,728	47,718
Balance Sheet								
Net Property	1,417,066	1,566,155	1,224,659	1,232,758	1,211,617	1,089,798	1,025,562	952,898
Total Assets	2,159,426	2,344,606	1,768,125	1,845,704	1,704,650	1,429,000	1,361,044	1,321,771
Long-Term Obligations	907,058	868,684	626,777	659,135	579,595	343,042	365,897	340,859
Net Stockholders' Equity	501,468	579,978	507,954	480,015	452,545	431,806	413,967	396,551
Shares Outstanding	47,183	47,035	44,961	44,990	44,883	44,962	44,926	44,906
Statistical Record								
Operating Profit Margin %	N.M.	21.76	14.12	17.95	14.64	20.76	23.35	24.01
Net Inc./Net Property %	N.M.	4.58	5.73	5.27	4.68	4.93	5.12	5.47
Net Inc./Tot. Capital %	N.M.	4.11	5.22	4.48	3.91	4.68	4.58	4.80
Return on Equity %	N.M.	12.39	14.22	14.44	12.54	12.29	12.50	12.93
Accum. Depr./Gross Prop. %	35.47	31.31	34.87	32.88	31.44	33.60	33.58	33.27
Price Range	18.29–11.10	24.78–9.79	26.03–19.60	27.69–15.22	17.53–14.13	18.00–14.41	16.44–12.44	14.50–12.50
P/E Ratio	N/A	16.86–6.66	17.24–12.98	19.09–10.50	14.86–11.97	16.07–12.86	15.08–11.41	13.43–11.63
Average Yield %	5.79	4.79	3.94	4.35	2.58	5.00	5.47	5.69

Address: 2030 Donahue Ferry Road, Pineville, LA 71360–5226	**Officers:** David M. Eppler – Pres., C.E.O., R. ONeal Chadwick – Sr. V.P., Sec., Gen. Couns.	**Investor Contact:** (318) 484–7400
Telephone: (318) 484–7400	**Transfer Agents:** First Chicago Trust Company of New York, Jersey City, NJ	**Institutional Holding**
Web Site: www.cleco.com		**No of Institutions:** 1
		Shares: 97 **% Held:** –

CLOROX CO.

Exchange	Symbol	Price	52Wk Range	Yield	P/E
NYS	CLX	$48.91 (3/31/2004)	50.15-41.63	2.21	20.81

*7 Year Price Score 107.0   ***NYSE Composite Index=100**   ***12 Month Price Score 95.0**

TRADING VOLUME (thousand shares)

Interim Earnings (Per Share)

Qtr.	Sep	Dec	Mar	Jun
2000–01	0.42	0.27	0.33	0.34
2001–02	0.33	0.22	0.20	0.62
2002–03	0.71	0.39	0.51	0.72
2003–04	0.60	0.52	...	...

Interim Dividends (Per Share)

Amt	Decl	Ex	Rec	Pay
0.27Q	7/16/2003	7/29/2003	7/31/2003	8/15/2003
0.27Q	9/17/2003	10/28/2003	10/30/2003	11/14/2003
0.27Q	11/19/2003	1/27/2004	1/29/2004	2/13/2004
0.27Q	3/17/2004	4/26/2004	4/28/2004	5/14/2004

Indicated Div: $1.08 (Div. Reinv. Plan)

Valuation Analysis

Forecast P/E	16.69	Trailing P/E	20.81
Market Cap	$11.3 Billion	Book Value	1.2 Billion
Price/Book	8.66	Price/Sales	2.46

Dividend Achiever Status

Rank	196	10 Year Growth Rate	8.28%
Total Years of Dividend Growth	27	

Business Summary: Chemicals (MIC: 11.1 SIC: 2842 NAIC:325612)

Clorox is a manufacturer of household products and products for institutional markets. The Household Products North America segment includes products such as *Soft Scrub, Clorox, Tuffy, Formula 409, Liquid–Plumr, Pine– Sol, Tilex, and SOS*. The Specialty Products segment includes brand names such as *Armor All, STP, and Kingsford Charcoal, Hidden Valley and K C Masterpiece* dressings and sauces, *Glad, and GladWare* businesses and *Scoop Away, and Fresh Step* cat litters. The Household Products Latin America/Other segment includes Co.'s overseas operations, excluding the European automotive care business, which focuses on the laundry, household cleaning and insecticide categories.

Recent Developments: For the quarter ended Dec 31 2003, net income rose 22.5% to $109.0 million from $89.0 million in the prior year. Results included a loss from discontinued operations of $2.0 million in 2003 versus a gain of $2.0 million in 2002. Results for 2002 included restructuring and asset impairment charges of $30.0 million. Net sales grew 2.3% to $947.0 million. North American Household Product sales rose 0.7% to $549.0 million. Specialty product sales were flat at $265.0 million, while Latin America and other Household Product sales grew 14.7% to $133.0 million. Gross profit fell 4.2% to $412.0 million due to higher raw material costs and higher contract manufacturing costs for *Match Light* charcoal.

Prospects: For the third quarter, Co. expects low to mid single–digit volume growth and sales growth within its long–term target of 3.0% to 5.0%. Co. expects earnings per share in the range of $0.55 to $0.57. For the fourth quarter, Co. expects mid single–digit volume growth, with sales growing slightly faster than volume. Volume and sales are expected to benefit from new product introductions, including several food items and new scents of *Clorox*® liquid bleach. Co. expects earnings per share in the range of $0.82 to $0.85. Separately, Co. announced that the U.S. Internal Revenue Service has proposed tax adjustments related to an investment that could cost Co. an additional $200.0 million in taxes.

Financial Data

(US$ in Thousands)	6 Mos	3 Mos	06/30/2003	06/30/2002	06/30/2001	06/30/2000	06/30/1999	06/30/1998
Earnings Per Share	1.13	0.60	2.33	1.37	1.36	1.64	1.03	1.41
Cash Flow Per Share	1.53	0.65	3.63	3.73	3.11	2.74	2.44	1.47
Tang. Book Val. Per Share	N.M	N.M	N.M	0.23	1.37	1.09	0.31	N.M
Dividends Per Share	0.980	0.930	0.880	0.840	0.840	0.800	0.720	0.640
Dividend Payout %	86.72	155.00	37.76	61.31	61.76	48.78	69.90	45.39
Income Statement								
Total Revenues	1,995,000	1,048,000	4,144,000	4,061,000	3,903,000	4,083,000	4,003,000	2,741,270
Total Indirect Exp.	484,000	247,000	1,108,000	1,254,000	1,033,000	1,144,000	1,581,000	1,055,217
Depreciation & Amort.	95,000	47,000	22,000	24,000	120,000	110,000	122,000	89,124
Operating Income	385,000	210,000	822,000	511,000	611,000	744,000	551,000	538,081
Net Interest Inc./(Exp.)	(13,000)	(6,000)	(25,000)	(35,000)	(78,000)	(88,000)	(90,000)	(65,097)
Income Taxes	130,000	71,000	288,000	176,000	161,000	228,000	184,000	173,965
Eqty Earns/Minority Int.	...	...	(2,000)	4,000	(44,000)	(39,000)	(40,000)	(27,334)
Income from Cont Ops	241,000	130,000	514,000	...	326,000	...	...	...
Net Income	238,000	129,000	493,000	322,000	323,000	394,000	246,000	297,960
Average Shs. Outstg.	213,924	214,807	220,692	234,704	239,483	239,614	240,002	211,270
Balance Sheet								
Cash & Cash Equivalents	201,000	187,000	172,000	177,000	251,000	245,000	132,000	89,681
Total Current Assets	903,000	891,000	951,000	1,002,000	1,103,000	1,454,000	1,116,000	798,700
Total Assets	3,597,000	3,558,000	3,652,000	3,630,000	3,995,000	4,353,000	4,132,000	3,029,992
Total Current Liabilities	1,446,000	1,443,000	1,451,000	1,225,000	1,069,000	1,541,000	1,368,000	1,225,076
Long–Term Obligations	475,000	479,000	495,000	678,000	685,000	590,000	702,000	316,260
Net Stockholders' Equity	1,185,000	1,157,000	1,215,000	1,354,000	1,900,000	1,794,000	1,570,000	1,085,235
Net Working Capital	(543,000)	(552,000)	(500,000)	(223,000)	34,000	(87,000)	(252,000)	(426,376)
Shares Outstanding	210,151	211,027	213,676	223,009	236,691	235,361	235,311	207,370
Statistical Record								
Operating Profit Margin %	19.29	20.03	19.83	12.58	15.65	18.22	13.76	19.62
Return on Equity %	20.33	11.23	42.30	23.78	17.15	21.96	15.66	27.45
Return on Assets %	6.70	3.65	14.07	8.87	8.16	9.05	5.95	9.83
Debt/Total Assets %	13.20	13.46	13.55	18.67	17.14	13.55	16.98	10.43
Price Range	49.10-42.00	46.25-42.00	48.24-32.18	47.62-34.64	47.94-30.06	56.97-29.88	66.16-39.75	47.69-31.00
P/E Ratio	43.45-37.17	77.08-70.00	20.70-13.81	34.76-25.28	35.25-22.10	34.74-18.22	64.23-38.59	33.82-21.99
Average Yield %	2.16	2.11	2.07	2.07	2.28	1.83	1.33	1.66

Address: 1221 Broadway, Oakland, CA 94612-1888	Officers: G. Craig Sullivan – Chmn., C.E.O., Gerald E. Johnston – Pres., C.E.O.	Institutional Holding
Telephone: (510) 271–7000	Transfer Agents:EquiServe Trust Company, N.A., Providence, RI	No of Institutions: 7
Web Site: www.clorox.com		Shares: 61,600,469 % Held: –

COCA-COLA CO (THE)

Exchange	Symbol	Price	52Wk Range	Yield	P/E
NYS	KO	$50.30 (3/31/2004)	52.40–39.42	1.99	28.42

*7 Year Price Score 79.2   *NYSE Composite Index=100   *12 Month Price Score 96.9

TRADING VOLUME (thousand shares)

Interim Earnings (Per Share)

Qtr.	Mar	Jun	Sep	Dec
2000	(0.02)	0.37	0.43	0.10
2001	0.35	0.45	0.43	0.37
2002	0.32	0.52	0.47	0.29
2003	0.34	0.55	0.50	0.38

Interim Dividends (Per Share)

Amt	Decl	Ex	Rec	Pay
0.22Q	4/16/2003	6/11/2003	6/15/2003	7/1/2003
0.22Q	7/17/2003	9/11/2003	9/15/2003	10/1/2003
0.22Q	10/16/2003	11/26/2003	12/1/2003	12/15/2003
0.25Q	2/19/2004	3/11/2004	3/15/2004	4/1/2004

Indicated Div: $1.00 (Div. Reinv. Plan)

Valuation Analysis

Forecast P/E	21.17	Trailing P/E	28.42
Market Cap	$124.9 Billion	Book Value	14.1 Billion
Price/Book	8.79	Price/Sales	5.89

Dividend Achiever Status

Rank	157	10 Year Growth Rate	9.98%
Total Years of Dividend Growth	41		

Business Summary: Food (MIC: 4.1 SIC: 2086 NAIC:312111)

The Coca–Cola Company is engaged in the manufacturing, distributing and marketing of nonalcoholic beverage concentrates and syrups. Principal beverage products include: *Coca–Cola, Coca–Cola Classic, Diet Coke, Vanilla Coke, Cherry Coke, Fanta, Sprite, Mr. Pibb, Mello Yellow, Barq's, Powerade, Fresca, Dasani* plus other assorted diet and caffeine–free versions. Co. also produces, distributes and markets juice and juice–drink products. Brands include *Minute Maid, Simply Orange* orange juice, *Odwalla* super premium juices and drinks, *Five Alive, Bacardi* tropical fruit mixers (manufactured and marketed under a license from Bacardi & Company Limited) and *Hi–C* ready to serve fruit drinks.

Recent Developments: For the year ended Dec 31 2003, net income was $4.35 billion compared with income of $3.98 billion, before an accounting change charge of $926.0 million, the previous year. Results for 2003 included other operating charges of $573.0 million related primarily to streamlining initiatives. Net operating revenues advanced 7.6% to $21.04 billion from $19.56 billion in 2002. Worldwide unit case volume increased 4.0% to 19.4 billion cases, driven by 5.0% growth in international operations and 2.0% growth in North America. Operating income, which included the aforementioned streamlining charges, amounted to $5.22 billion versus $5.46 billion the year before.

Prospects: Positive unit case volume trends from across its worldwide operations strengthens Co.'s near–term outlook. Specifically, Co.'s North American results should be supported by its three–tiered water strategy that includes a focus on maintaining rational pricing and differentiating through a variety of brand, packaging and channel offerings The recent roll–out of *Sprite Remix, Simply Orange* and *Minute Maid Premium Heart Wise,* an orange juice product with plant sterols to help reduce cholesterol should also help. Meanwhile, Co. should continue to see positive growth in Asia, fueled by China and India, the latter of which is benefiting from its diverse portfolio of local and international brands.

Financial Data

(US$ in Millions)	12/31/2003	12/31/2002	12/31/2001	12/31/2000	12/31/1999	12/31/1998	12/31/1997	12/31/1996
Earnings Per Share	1.77	1.60	1.60	0.88	0.98	1.42	1.64	1.40
Cash Flow Per Share	2.21	1.90	1.65	1.44	1.56	1.37	1.60	1.38
Tang. Book Val. Per Share	4.13	3.33	3.53	2.97	3.05	3.18	2.66	2.17
Dividends Per Share	0.880	0.800	0.720	0.680	0.640	0.600	0.560	0.500
Dividend Payout %	49.71	50.00	45.00	77.27	65.30	42.25	34.14	35.71
Income Statement								
Total Revenues	21,044	19,564	20,092	20,458	19,805	18,813	18,868	18,546
Total Indirect Exp.	8,061	7,001	8,696	10,563	9,814	8,284	7,852	7,893
Depreciation & Amort.	850	806	803	773	792	645	626	479
Operating Income	5,221	5,458	5,352	3,691	3,982	4,967	5,001	3,915
Net Interest Inc./(Exp.)	(2)	10	36	(102)	(77)	(58)	(47)	(48)
Income Taxes	1,148	1,523	1,691	1,222	1,388	1,665	1,926	1,104
Eqty Earns/Minority Int.	406	384	152	(289)	(184)	32	155	211
Income from Cont Ops	...	3,976	3,979	...	...	...	...	...
Net Income	4,347	3,050	3,969	2,177	2,431	3,533	4,129	3,492
Average Shs. Outstg.	2,462	2,483	2,487	2,487	2,487	2,496	2,515	2,494
Balance Sheet								
Cash & Cash Equivalents	3,482	2,345	1,934	1,892	1,812	1,807	1,843	1,658
Total Current Assets	8,396	7,352	7,171	6,620	6,480	6,380	5,969	5,910
Total Assets	27,342	24,501	22,417	20,834	21,623	19,145	16,940	16,161
Total Current Liabilities	7,886	7,341	8,429	9,321	9,856	8,640	7,379	7,406
Long–Term Obligations	2,517	2,701	1,219	835	854	687	801	1,116
Net Stockholders' Equity	14,090	11,800	11,366	9,316	9,513	8,403	7,311	6,156
Net Working Capital	510	11	(1,258)	(2,701)	(3,376)	(2,260)	(1,410)	(1,496)
Shares Outstanding	2,441	2,470	2,486	2,484	2,471	2,466	2,471	2,481
Statistical Record								
Operating Profit Margin %	24.80	27.89	26.63	18.04	20.10	26.40	26.50	21.10
Return on Equity %	30.85	33.69	35.00	23.36	25.55	42.04	56.47	56.72
Return on Assets %	15.89	16.22	17.74	10.44	11.24	18.45	24.37	21.60
Debt/Total Assets %	9.20	11.02	5.43	4.00	3.94	3.58	4.72	6.90
Price Range	50.75-37.07	57.64-43.47	60.82-42.85	66.88-43.13	70.63-47.56	87.94-56.19	72.00-51.88	54.00-36.38
P/E Ratio	28.67-20.94	36.03-27.17	38.01-26.78	75.99-49.01	72.07-48.53	61.93-39.57	43.90-31.63	38.57-25.98
Average Yield %	2.00	1.61	1.48	1.23	1.03	0.83	0.90	1.09

Address: One Coca–Cola Plaza, Atlanta, GA 30313	Officers: Douglas N. Daft – Chmn., C.E.O., Steven J. Heyer – Pres., C.O.O.	Investor Contact: (404) 676–5766
Telephone: (404) 676–2121	Transfer Agents:EquiServe Trust Company, N.A., Providence, RI	Institutional Holding No of Institutions: 9
Web Site: www.coca-cola.com		Shares: 42,025 % Held: –

COLGATE-PALMOLIVE CO.

Exchange	Symbol	Price	52Wk Range	Yield	P/E
NYS	CL	$55.10 (3/31/2004)	60.88-49.13	1.74	22.40

*7 Year Price Score 112.9   ***NYSE Composite Index=100**   ***12 Month Price Score 84.8**

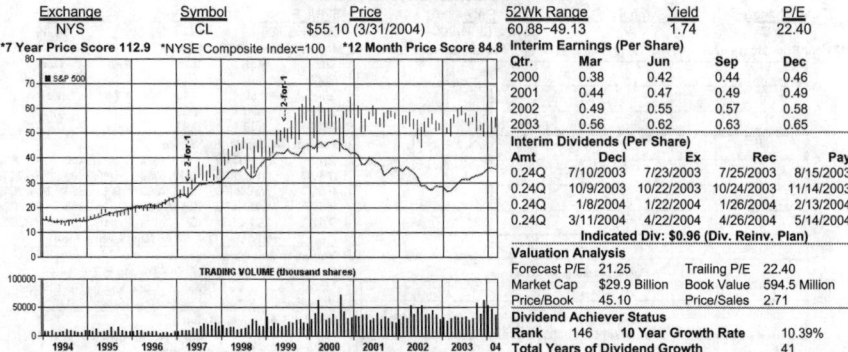

Interim Earnings (Per Share)

Qtr.	Mar	Jun	Sep	Dec
2000	0.38	0.42	0.44	0.46
2001	0.44	0.47	0.49	0.49
2002	0.49	0.55	0.57	0.58
2003	0.56	0.62	0.63	0.65

Interim Dividends (Per Share)

Amt	Decl	Ex	Rec	Pay
0.24Q	7/10/2003	7/23/2003	7/25/2003	8/15/2003
0.24Q	10/9/2003	10/22/2003	10/24/2003	11/14/2003
0.24Q	1/8/2004	1/22/2004	1/26/2004	2/13/2004
0.24Q	3/11/2004	4/22/2004	4/26/2004	5/14/2004

Indicated Div: $0.96 (Div. Reinv. Plan)

Valuation Analysis

Forecast P/E	21.25	Trailing P/E	22.40
Market Cap	$29.9 Billion	Book Value	594.5 Million
Price/Book	45.10	Price/Sales	2.71

Dividend Achiever Status

Rank	146	10 Year Growth Rate 10.39%
Total Years of Dividend Growth		41

Business Summary: Chemicals (MIC: 11.1 SIC: 2844 NAIC:325620)

Colgate-Palmolive is a consumer products company that markets its products in over 200 countries. Co. operates five segments. Oral, Personal, Fabric and Household Surface Care consists of tooth pastes, toothbrushes, soaps, shampoos, baby products, deodorants, detergents, cleaners, shave products and other similar items under brand names including *Colgate, Palmolive, Mennen, Softsoap, Irish Spring, Protex, Sorriso, Kolynos, Ajax, Axion, Soupline, Suavitel* and *Fab*. Pet Nutrition consists of pet food products manufactured and marketed by Hill's Pet Nutrition. Hill markets pet foods primarily under *Science Diet*, and *Prescription Diet* for dogs and cats with disease conditions.

Recent Developments: For the year ended Dec 31 2003, net income rose 10.3% to $1.42 billion from $1.29 billion the previous year. Net sales grew 6.6% to $9.90 billion. By segment, North American unit volume rose 0.5%, while sales and operating profit declined 1.0% and 5.0%, respectively. In Europe, unit volume increased 3.0%, sales grew 16.0% and operating profit rose 19.0%. Latin American unit volume grew 4.0%, while sales and operating profit declined 1.0% and 5.0%, respectively. In the Asia/Africa segment, unit volume grew 7.5%, sales increased 13.5% and operating profit climbed 21.0%. In the Hills Pet Nutrition business, unit volume was up 4.5%, while sales increased 11.0% and operating profit jumped 17.0%.

Prospects: On Dec 18 2003, Co. agreed to acquire GABA Holding AG, a privately-owned European oral care company, in an all-cash transaction of between $630.0 million and $830.0 million. The addition of GABA, which generates sales of almost $300.0 million in 15 European countries, is expected to provide Co. with a significant presence in the European pharmacy channel while also further strengthening its position in oral care. Co. expects GABA to have a dilutive effect of about 3.0% on earnings in 2004, a neutral effect in 2005 and a positive effect on earnings by 2006. Separately, Co. is optimistic that its accelerated new product activity will generate market share growth going forward.

Financial Data

(US$ in Thousands)	12/31/2003	12/31/2002	12/31/2001	12/31/2000	12/31/1999	12/31/1998	12/31/1997	12/31/1996
Earnings Per Share	2.46	2.19	1.89	1.70	1.47	1.30	1.13	0.97
Cash Flow Per Share	3.05	2.73	2.63	2.44	2.02	1.81	1.68	1.56
Dividends Per Share	0.900	0.720	0.670	0.630	0.590	0.550	0.530	0.470
Dividend Payout %	36.58	32.87	35.71	37.05	40.13	42.14	46.69	48.20
Income Statement								
Total Revenues	9,903,400	9,294,300	9,427,800	9,357,900	9,118,200	8,971,600	9,056,700	8,749,000
Total Indirect Exp.	3,149,500	3,026,200	3,342,500	3,299,500	3,295,600	3,209,700	3,266,200	3,239,700
Depreciation & Amort.	12,300	12,500	68,000	72,100	75,600	81,700	86,500	316,300
Operating Income	2,166,000	2,013,100	1,834,800	1,740,500	1,566,200	1,423,000	1,285,800	1,152,000
Net Interest Inc./(Exp.)	(124,100)	(142,800)	(166,100)	(173,300)	(171,600)	(172,900)	(183,500)	(197,400)
Income Taxes	620,600	582,000	522,100	503,400	457,300	401,500	361,900	319,600
Eqty Earns/Minority Int.	45,500	40,700	40,300	34,800	35,700	33,400	34,700	...
Net Income	1,421,300	1,288,300	1,146,600	1,063,800	937,300	848,600	740,400	635,000
Average Shs. Outstg.	578,800	589,100	607,700	627,300	638,800	648,400	650,200	586,400
Balance Sheet								
Cash & Cash Equivalents	265,300	167,900	172,700	212,500	235,200	194,500	205,300	307,800
Total Current Assets	2,496,500	2,228,100	2,203,400	2,347,200	2,354,800	2,244,900	2,196,500	2,372,300
Total Assets	7,478,800	7,087,200	6,984,800	7,252,300	7,423,100	7,685,200	7,538,700	7,901,500
Total Current Liabilities	2,445,400	2,148,700	2,123,500	2,244,100	2,273,500	2,114,400	1,959,500	1,904,300
Long-Term Obligations	2,684,900	3,210,800	2,812,000	2,536,900	2,243,300	2,300,600	2,340,300	2,786,800
Net Stockholders' Equity	887,100	350,300	846,400	1,468,100	1,833,700	2,085,600	2,178,600	2,034,100
Net Working Capital	51,100	79,400	79,900	103,100	81,300	130,500	237,000	468,000
Shares Outstanding	533,697	536,001	550,722	566,655	578,863	585,420	591,280	588,536
Statistical Record								
Operating Profit Margin %	21.87	21.65	19.46	18.59	17.17	15.86	14.19	13.16
Return on Equity %	160.21	367.77	135.46	72.46	51.11	40.68	33.98	31.21
Return on Assets %	19.00	18.17	16.41	14.66	12.62	11.04	9.82	8.03
Debt/Total Assets %	35.90	45.30	40.25	34.98	30.22	29.93	31.04	35.26
Price Range	60.88-49.10	58.73-44.36	62.50-51.00	65.00-42.75	65.00-37.47	48.47-32.78	38.56-22.72	23.88-17.22
P/E Ratio	24.75-19.96	26.82-20.26	33.07-26.98	38.24-25.15	44.22-25.49	37.28-25.22	34.13-20.11	24.61-17.75
Average Yield %	1.64	1.33	1.18	1.13	1.18	1.31	1.72	2.28

Address: 300 Park Avenue, New York, NY 10022-7499	**Officers:** Reuben Mark – Chmn., C.E.O., William S. Shanahan – Pres.	**Investor Contact:** (212) 310-3072
Telephone: (212) 310-2000	**Transfer Agents:** First Chicago Trust Company of New York, Jersey City, NJ	**Institutional Holding** **No of Institutions:** 9
Web Site: www.colgate.com		**Shares:** 260,874 **% Held:** –

COMERICA, INC.

Exchange	Symbol	Price	52Wk Range	Yield	P/E
NYS	CMA	$54.32 (3/31/2004)	58.25-37.86	3.83	14.49

*7 Year Price Score 87.8 *NYSE Composite Index=100 *12 Month Price Score 102.2

Interim Earnings (Per Share)

Qtr.	Mar	Jun	Sep	Dec
2000	1.10	1.15	1.18	1.20
2001	0.50	1.13	1.14	1.11
2002	1.20	1.03	0.14	1.03
2003	1.00	0.97	0.89	0.89

Interim Dividends (Per Share)

Amt	Decl	Ex	Rec	Pay
0.50Q	5/20/2003	6/11/2003	6/15/2003	7/1/2003
0.50Q	7/22/2003	9/11/2003	9/15/2003	10/1/2003
0.50Q	11/25/2003	12/11/2003	12/15/2003	1/1/2004
0.52Q	1/27/2004	3/11/2004	3/15/2004	4/1/2004
	Indicated Div: $2.08 (Div. Reinv. Plan)			

Valuation Analysis

Forecast P/E	11.79	Trailing P/E	14.49
Market Cap	$9.5 Billion	Book Value	5.1 Billion
Price/Book	1.93	Price/Sales	3.03

Dividend Achiever Status

Rank	137	10 Year Growth Rate	11.01%
Total Years of Dividend Growth		20

Business Summary: Commercial Banking (MIC: 8.1 SIC: 6021 NAIC:522110)

Comerica is a bank holding company with assets of $52.59 billion and total deposits of $41.46 billion as of Dec 31 2003. Co. operates banking subsidiaries in Michigan, Texas and California, banking operations in Florida, and businesses in several other states. Co. is a diversified financial services provider, offering a broad range of financial products and services for businesses and individuals. Through its subsidiaries, the Company has aligned its operations into three major lines of business: the Business Bank, the Individual Bank and the Investment Bank. Co. also has an investment services affiliate, Munder Capital Management, and operates banking subsidiaries in Canada and Mexico.

Recent Developments: For the year ended Dec 31 2003, net income climbed 10.0% to $661.0 million compared with $601.0 million the year before. Earnings for 2002 included goodwill impairment expenses of $86.0 million and a net gain on sales of businesses of $12.0 million. Net interest income slipped 9.7% to $1.93 billion. Net interest margin fell to 3.48% from 3.98% in 2002. Provision for loan losses dropped 40.6% to $377.0 million. Total non–interest income slipped 1.4% to $887.0 million, while total non–interest expense decreased 2.1% to $1.48 billion. Total loans slid 4.7% to $40.30 billion, while total deposits declined 0.7% to $41.46 billion.

Prospects: Average deposits continue to decrease, resulting from a slowdown in mortgage financing activity due to declines in title and escrow deposits. However, net charge–offs continue to decrease, reflecting an improving economy. Going forward, Co. will focus on increasing contributions from its Small Business & Personal Financial Services and Wealth & Institutional Management segments, building enhanced tools to more effectively manage risk throughout the company, and adding new branches in Texas, California and Michigan in order to grow market share.

Financial Data

(US$ in Thousands)	12/31/2003	12/31/2002	12/31/2001	12/31/2000	12/31/1999	12/31/1998	12/31/1997	12/31/1996
Earnings Per Share	3.75	3.40	3.88	4.63	4.14	3.72	3.19	2.36
Tang. Book Val. Per Share	29.19	28.30	27.14	23.94	20.60	17.94	16.01	14.76
Dividends Per Share	1.980	1.880	1.720	1.560	1.400	1.240	1.120	0.980
Dividend Payout %	52.80	55.29	44.32	33.69	33.81	33.51	35.10	41.80
Income Statement								
Total Interest Income	2,412,000	2,797,000	3,393,547	3,261,636	2,672,710	2,616,774	2,647,403	2,562,780
Total Interest Expense	486,000	665,000	1,291,209	1,602,785	1,125,569	1,155,503	1,204,627	1,150,502
Net Interest Income	1,926,000	2,132,000	2,102,338	1,658,851	1,547,141	1,461,271	1,442,776	1,412,278
Provision for Loan Losses	377,000	635,000	236,000	145,000	114,000	113,000	146,000	114,000
Non–Interest Income	887,000	900,000	803,332	825,890	716,888	603,148	527,952	506,954
Non–Interest Expense	1,483,000	1,515,000	1,559,033	1,188,370	1,116,957	1,020,044	1,007,986	1,159,026
Income Before Taxes	912,000	822,000	1,122,461	1,103,787	1,033,072	931,375	816,742	646,206
Eqty Earns/Minority Int.	6,000	8,000	(43,057)	...	...	...	...	...
Income from Cont Ops	620,000	541,000	721,402	701,742	...	...	...	...
Net Income	661,000	601,000	709,578	749,326	672,589	607,076	530,476	417,161
Average Shs. Outstg.	176,000	177,000	177,665	156,398	158,397	158,757	161,040	172,887
Balance Sheet								
Cash & Due from Banks	1,527,000	1,902,000	1,925,262	1,496,705	1,201,990	1,773,100	1,927,087	1,901,760
Securities Avail. for Sale	4,489,000	3,053,000	4,290,724	2,677,762	2,739,464	2,712,165	4,005,962	4,800,034
Net Loans & Leases	39,499,000	41,490,000	40,541,248	35,522,235	32,216,808	30,152,454	28,470,897	25,839,543
Total Assets	52,592,000	53,301,000	50,731,973	41,985,185	38,653,332	36,600,831	36,292,398	34,102,464
Total Deposits	41,463,000	41,775,000	37,570,379	27,168,012	23,291,403	24,313,133	22,586,317	22,367,173
Long–Term Obligations	4,801,000	5,216,000	5,502,511	8,088,661	8,579,857	5,282,259	7,286,387	4,241,769
Total Liabilities	47,482,000	48,354,000	45,924,509	37,977,919	33,743,054	33,083,050	30,930,581	28,496,851
Net Stockholders' Equity	5,110,000	4,947,000	4,807,464	4,007,266	3,474,644	3,046,613	2,761,776	2,615,569
Shares Outstanding	175,000	174,775	177,074	156,943	156,517	155,881	156,815	160,210
Statistical Record								
Return on Equity %	12.13	10.93	15.00	17.51	19.35	19.92	19.20	15.94
Return on Assets %	1.17	1.01	1.42	1.67	1.74	1.65	1.46	1.22
Equity/Assets %	9.71	9.28	9.47	9.54	8.98	8.32	7.60	7.66
Non–Int. Exp./Tot. Inc. %	44.95	40.97	37.14	29.07	32.95	31.67	31.74	37.75
Price Range	56.31-37.61	65.30-35.53	64.95-44.66	60.31-33.81	69.75-44.94	71.54-50.13	61.88-34.58	39.17-24.25
P/E Ratio	15.02-10.03	19.21-10.45	16.74-11.51	13.03-7.30	16.85-10.85	19.23-13.47	19.40-10.84	16.60-10.28
Average Yield %	4.29	3.40	3.04	3.21	2.38	1.93	2.42	3.19

Address: Comerica Tower at Detroit Center, Detroit, MI 48226–3509 **Telephone:** (313) 222–9743 **Web Site:** www.comerica.com	**Officers:** Ralph W. Babb – Chmn., Pres., C.E.O., Elizabeth S. Acton – Exec. V.P., C.F.O. **Transfer Agents:**Wells Fargo Shareowner Services, South St. Paul, MN	**Investor Contact:**313–222–2840 **Institutional Holding** **No of Institutions:** 23 **Shares:** 811,583 **% Held:** –

COMMERCE BANCORP, INC. (NJ)

Exchange	Symbol	Price	52Wk Range	Yield	P/E
NYS	CBH	$65.88 (3/31/2004)	65.88-36.37	1.15	25.24

*7 Year Price Score 155.5 *NYSE Composite Index=100 *12 Month Price Score 105.6

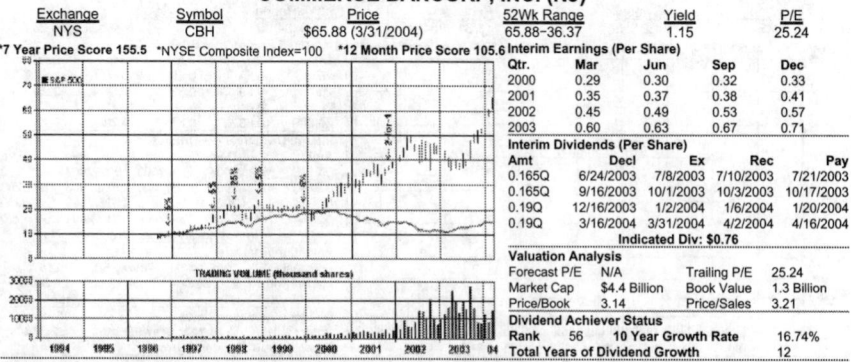

Interim Earnings (Per Share)

Qtr.	Mar	Jun	Sep	Dec
2000	0.29	0.30	0.32	0.33
2001	0.35	0.37	0.38	0.41
2002	0.45	0.49	0.53	0.57
2003	0.60	0.63	0.67	0.71

Interim Dividends (Per Share)

Amt	Decl	Ex	Rec	Pay
0.165Q	6/24/2003	7/8/2003	7/10/2003	7/21/2003
0.165Q	9/16/2003	10/1/2003	10/3/2003	10/17/2003
0.19Q	12/16/2003	1/2/2004	1/6/2004	1/20/2004
0.19Q	3/16/2004	3/31/2004	4/2/2004	4/16/2004

Indicated Div: $0.76

Valuation Analysis

Forecast P/E	N/A	Trailing P/E	25.24
Market Cap	$4.4 Billion	Book Value	1.3 Billion
Price/Book	3.14	Price/Sales	3.21

Dividend Achiever Status

Rank	56	10 Year Growth Rate 16.74%
Total Years of Dividend Growth		12

Business Summary: Commercial Banking (MIC: 8.1 SIC: 6021 NAIC:522110)

Commerce Bancorp, with assets of $22.71 billion as of Dec 31 2003, is a bank holding company primarily serving the Metropolitan Philadelphia, New Jersey, Delaware and New York markets. Co. operates five bank subsidiaries, including Commerce Bank, Commerce Bank/Pennsylvania, Commerce Bank/Shore, Commerce Bank/Delaware, and Commerce Bank/North. As of Dec 31 2003, these banks provided a full range of retail and commercial banking services through 270 retail branch offices. Co. also operates Commerce Capital Markets, which is engaged in securities, investment banking and brokerage activities, and Commerce National Insurance Services, which operates an insurance brokerage agency.

Recent Developments: For the year ended Dec 31 2003, net income increased 34.2% to $194.3 million from $144.8 million the year before. Earnings for 2003 included net investment securities gains of $3.9 million. Net interest income advanced 32.0% to $755.9 million, reflecting growth in deposits and earning assets. Net interest margin was 4.36% versus 4.69% in the previous year. Provision for loan losses declined 3.9% to $31.9 million. Total non-interest income improved 29.1% to $332.5 million, primarily as a result of increased deposit charges and service fees. Total non-interest expense grew 31.8% to $763.4 million.

Prospects: During the quarter, Co. opened 13 new offices, completing its goal of opening 46 new branches in 2003. For 2004, Co. plans to open 50 branches, including approximately 40 in Metro New York and 10 in Metro Philadelphia. This expansion is expected to create more than 1,800 positions in 2004. By 2009, Co. intends to nearly double its size to create a network of 700 stores along the eastern seaboard and hire approximately 10,000 new employees. Looking ahead, Co. expects earnings per share in 2004 to total $0.73 in the first quarter, $0.76 in the second quarter, $0.80 in the third quarter, $0.83 in the fourth quarter and $3.12 for the full year.

Financial Data

(US$ in Thousands)	12/31/2003	12/31/2002	12/31/2001	12/31/2000	12/31/1999	12/31/1998	12/31/1997	12/31/1996
Earnings Per Share	2.61	2.04	1.51	1.24	1.08	0.94	0.80	0.71
Tang. Book Val. Per Share	16.69	13.53	9.66	7.74	5.97	5.96	5.28	4.93
Dividends Per Share	0.660	0.600	0.550	0.480	0.410	0.430	0.270	0.220
Dividend Payout %	25.28	29.41	36.42	38.88	38.16	46.26	34.34	31.68
Income Statement								
Total Interest Income	915,631	755,371	604,367	505,300	386,448	289,280	244,177	179,364
Total Interest Expense	159,765	182,616	203,041	208,370	142,081	115,553	97,037	70,858
Net Interest Income	755,866	572,755	401,326	296,930	244,367	173,727	147,140	108,506
Provision for Loan Losses	31,850	33,150	26,384	13,931	9,175	5,867	4,668	2,997
Non-Interest Income	332,478	257,466	196,805	150,760	114,596	88,947	57,374	30,014
Non-Interest Expense	763,392	579,168	420,036	315,357	252,523	181,967	137,929	94,071
Income Before Taxes	293,102	217,903	151,711	118,402	97,265	74,840	61,917	41,452
Net Income	194,287	144,815	103,022	80,047	65,960	49,318	40,325	26,625
Average Shs. Outstg.	74,462	70,903	68,102	64,222	60,930	52,397	49,950	35,109
Balance Sheet								
Cash & Due from Banks	910,092	811,434	557,738	443,918	317,624	245,352	167,900	159,577
Securities Avail. for Sale	10,821,113	8,133,258	4,435,515	2,130,632	1,782,094	1,368,863	1,323,031	741,224
Net Loans & Leases	7,328,519	5,731,856	4,516,431	3,638,580	2,922,706	1,904,954	1,390,028	1,081,830
Total Assets	22,712,180	16,403,981	11,363,703	8,296,516	6,635,793	4,894,065	3,938,967	2,861,952
Total Deposits	20,701,400	14,548,841	10,185,594	7,387,594	5,608,920	4,435,115	3,369,404	2,573,405
Long-Term Obligations	200,000	200,000	80,500	80,500	80,500	80,500	80,500	23,000
Total Liabilities	21,434,892	15,485,971	10,727,133	7,804,292	6,279,037	4,593,349	3,688,207	2,680,599
Net Stockholders' Equity	1,277,288	918,010	636,570	492,224	356,756	300,716	250,760	181,353
Shares Outstanding	76,506	67,833	65,832	63,522	59,688	50,410	46,029	35,260
Statistical Record								
Return on Equity %	15.21	15.77	16.18	16.26	18.48	16.40	16.08	14.68
Return on Assets %	0.85	0.88	0.90	0.96	0.99	1.00	1.02	0.93
Equity/Assets %	5.62	5.59	5.60	5.93	5.37	6.14	6.36	6.33
Non-Int. Exp./Tot. Inc. %	61.16	57.18	52.42	48.06	50.39	48.11	45.73	44.92
Price Range	53.30-36.37	50.24-36.42	39.34-26.90	35.00-15.66	23.81-18.90	23.98-15.62	17.80-9.50	10.90-8.47
P/E Ratio	20.42-13.93	24.63-17.85	26.05-17.81	28.23-12.63	22.05-17.50	25.51-16.62	22.24-11.88	15.35-11.93
Average Yield %	1.53	1.35	1.60	2.04	1.99	2.23	2.18	2.39

Address: Commerce Atrium, Cherry Hill, NJ 08034-5400	**Officers:** Vernon W. Hill II - Chmn., Pres., C.E.O., Peter M. Musumeci - Exec. V.P., Sr. Credit Officer,	**Investor Contact:**888-751-9000	
Telephone: (856) 751-9000	**Transfer Agents:**Mellon Investor Services, LLP, New York, NY	**Institutional Holding** **No of Institutions:** 49	
Web Site: www.commerceonline.com		**Shares:** 5,842,619 **% Held:** -	

COMMERCE BANCSHARES, INC.

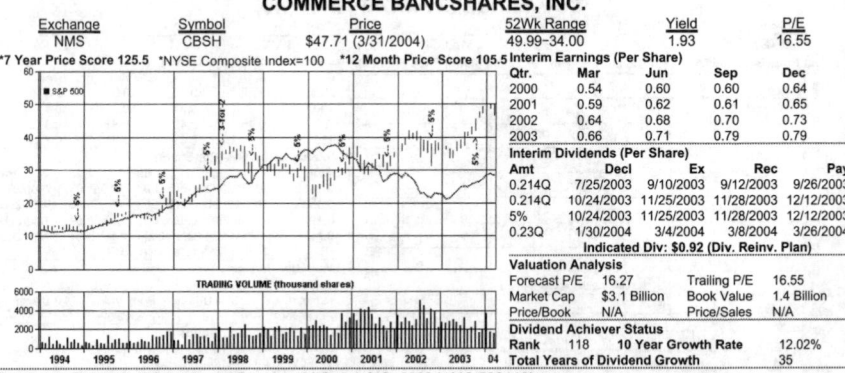

Business Summary: Commercial Banking (MIC: 8.1 SIC: 6022 NAIC:522110)

Commerce Bancshares, with assets of $14.29 billion as of Dec 31 2003, is a bank holding company that operates in approximately 330 banking locations. Co. presently owns all of the outstanding capital stock of four national banking associations, which are headquartered in Missouri, Illinois, Kansas, and Nebraska. The Nebraska bank is limited in its activities to the issuance of credit cards. The remaining three banking subsidiaries engage in general banking business, providing a broad range of retail, corporate, investment and private banking products and services to individuals and businesses. Co. also owns, directly or through its banking subsidiaries, various non-banking subsidiaries.

Recent Developments: For the year ended Dec 31 2003, net income rose 5.2% to $206.5 million from $196.3 million the year before. Net interest income improved slightly to $502.4 million from $500.0 million a year earlier, reflecting continued low short-term interest rates and weak commercial loan demand. Provision for loan losses grew 19.3% to $40.7 million from $34.1 million the previous year. Total non-interest income rose 7.5% to $301.7 million, primarily resulting from growth in deposit account fees and bank card fee income. Total non-interest expense increased 3.0% to $472.1 million from $458.2 million the year before, reflecting higher salary and occupancy costs.

Prospects: Despite the slowdown in the economy and the decline in short-term interest rates, net income remains solid, primarily due to increases in deposit account charges and other fees, bank card transaction fees, and trust fees, as well as continued tight expense management. Meanwhile, Co.'s asset quality remains strong with allowance for loan losses totaling more than $135.0 million, or 416.0% of non-performing loans as of Dec 31 2003. Moreover, net charge-offs for 2003 were 0.46% of average loans compared with 0.43% the year before. Loan loss reserve amounted to 1.66% of total loans at the end of 2003.

Financial Data

(US$ in Thousands)	12/31/2003	12/31/2002	12/31/2001	12/31/2000	12/31/1999	12/31/1998	12/31/1997	12/31/1996
Earnings Per Share	2.95	2.75	2.47	2.38	2.13	1.89	1.67	1.47
Tang. Book Val. Per Share	20.60	19.43	16.93	14.98	13.34	12.85	11.52	10.60
Dividends Per Share	0.740	0.580	0.550	0.510	0.470	0.430	0.380	0.340
Dividend Payout %	25.18	21.42	22.32	21.39	22.06	22.82	23.24	23.13
Income Statement								
Total Interest Income	617,410	652,553	750,962	812,168	750,626	728,471	682,876	647,603
Total Interest Expense	115,018	152,588	283,052	331,515	284,625	300,726	285,102	281,860
Net Interest Income	502,392	499,965	467,910	480,653	466,001	427,745	397,774	365,743
Provision for Loan Losses	40,676	34,108	36,423	35,159	35,335	36,874	31,354	24,522
Non-Interest Income	301,667	280,572	277,512	252,808	236,209	214,037	180,952	159,162
Non-Interest Expense	472,144	452,927	439,638	430,381	419,015	379,344	344,450	317,954
Income Before Taxes	291,239	293,502	269,361	267,921	247,860	225,564	202,062	182,429
Net Income	206,524	199,498	181,974	178,574	166,213	150,091	132,702	119,512
Average Shs. Outstg.	70,112	72,489	73,561	74,846	77,120	79,262	79,446	81,154
Balance Sheet								
Cash & Due from Banks	567,123	710,406	824,218	616,724	685,157	738,672	978,239	833,260
Securities Avail. for Sale	4,966,024	4,213,112	3,667,184	1,885,665	2,475,424	3,002,440	2,620,517	2,681,685
Net Loans & Leases	8,007,458	7,745,326	7,508,509	7,778,220	7,453,850	6,929,760	6,118,463	5,374,119
Total Assets	14,287,164	13,308,415	12,902,806	11,115,117	11,400,936	11,402,023	10,306,941	9,698,186
Total Deposits	10,206,208	9,913,311	10,031,966	9,081,738	9,164,213	9,530,197	8,700,578	8,166,429
Long-Term Obligations	400,977	338,457	392,586	224,684	25,735	27,130	7,207	14,120
Total Liabilities	12,836,210	11,892,078	11,630,323	9,971,362	10,321,104	10,321,238	9,326,157	8,773,915
Net Stockholders' Equity	1,450,954	1,416,337	1,272,483	1,143,755	1,079,832	1,080,785	980,784	924,271
Shares Outstanding	67,968	70,457	72,144	72,441	75,816	78,056	77,686	78,889
Statistical Record								
Return on Equity %	14.23	14.08	14.30	15.61	15.39	13.88	13.53	12.93
Return on Assets %	1.44	1.49	1.41	1.60	1.45	1.31	1.28	1.23
Equity/Assets %	10.15	10.64	9.86	10.29	9.47	9.47	9.51	9.53
Non-Int. Exp./Tot. Inc. %	51.37	48.53	42.74	40.41	42.46	40.24	39.91	39.41
Price Range	49.28-33.74	42.17-31.52	37.31-28.71	36.71-22.11	33.79-26.84	37.50-26.58	34.51-20.20	23.45-15.06
P/E Ratio	16.71-11.44	15.33-11.46	15.10-11.63	15.43-9.29	15.86-12.60	19.84-14.07	20.67-12.09	15.95-10.24
Average Yield %	1.84	1.53	1.68	1.83	1.53	1.53	1.25	1.54	1.98

COMMERCIAL NET LEASE REALTY, INC.

Exchange	Symbol	Price	52Wk Range	Yield	P/E
NYS	NNN	$19.75 (3/31/2004)	19.75–15.46	6.48	18.29

*7 Year Price Score 120.9   *NYSE Composite Index=100   *12 Month Price Score 94.9

Interim Earnings (Per Share)

Qtr.	Mar	Jun	Sep	Dec
2000	0.28	0.28	0.28	0.43
2001	0.38	0.34	...	0.19
2002	0.29	0.27	0.23	0.25
2003	0.21	0.28	0.30	0.29

Interim Dividends (Per Share)

Amt	Decl	Ex	Rec	Pay
0.32Q	4/15/2003	4/28/2003	4/30/2003	5/15/2003
0.32Q	7/15/2003	7/29/2003	7/31/2003	8/15/2003
0.32Q	10/15/2003	10/29/2003	10/31/2003	11/15/2003
0.32Q	1/16/2004	1/28/2004	1/30/2004	2/13/2004

Indicated Div: $1.28 (Div. Reinv. Plan)

Valuation Analysis

Forecast P/E	11.70	Trailing P/E	18.29
Market Cap	$797.1 Million	Book Value	661.2 Million
Price/Book	1.25	Price/Sales	8.05

Dividend Achiever Status

Rank	297	10 Year Growth Rate	1.53%
Total Years of Dividend Growth	14		

TRADING VOLUME (thousand shares)

Business Summary: Property, Real Estate &Development (MIC: 8.3 SIC: 6798 NAIC:525930)

Commercial Net Lease Realty is a fully integrated, self–administered real estate investment trust. Co. and its wholly–owned subsidiaries acquire, own, manage and indirectly, through investment interests, develop primarily single–tenant retail, office and industrial properties that are generally leased under long–term commercial net leases. As of Dec 31 2003, Co. owned 339 properties in 39 states that are generally leased to major retail businesses under long–term commercial net leases. These businesses include Academy, Barnes & Noble, Bennigan's, Best Buy, Borders, Eckerd, Jared Jewelers, OfficeMax, The Sports Authority and the United States of America.

Recent Developments: For the year ended Dec 31 2003, income was $51.3 million, before a gain of $2.2 million from discontinued operations, compared with income of $43.1 million, before a loss of $5.0 million from discontinued operations, the previous year. Results for 2003 included a pre–tax settlement charge of $2.4 million, while results for 2002 included a pre–tax provision of $2.3 million for a loss on the impairment of real estate. Total revenue increased 12.9% to $102.7 million from $90.9 million the year before. Rental and earned income jumped 16.3% to $95.8 million from $82.4 million, while interest and other income dropped 19.2% to $6.9 million from $8.5 million the prior year.

Prospects: Co. is looking to build upon its strong operating performance achieve in 2003. Notable highlights from the prior year include total net proceeds from the disposition of 14 properties of $25.0 million resulting in a net gain of $161,000. Also, Co. and its affiliated subsidiaries invested $325.3 million in additional properties, construction in progress and mezzanine loan investments on nine office properties in California. Occupancy growth for the year increased to 97.0% from 95.0%. Going forward, Co. will continue to focus on investing in additional properties and construction in progress to build up its portfolio.

Financial Data

(US$ in Thousands)	12/31/2003	12/31/2002	12/31/2001	12/31/2000	12/31/1999	12/31/1998	12/31/1997	12/31/1996
Earnings Per Share	1.08	1.04	0.91	1.27	1.16	1.10	1.25	1.18
Tang. Book Val. Per Share	13.22	12.48	12.67	12.93	12.93	13.00	12.95	15.03
Dividends Per Share	1.280	1.270	1.260	1.245	1.240	1.230	1.200	1.180
Dividend Payout %	118.51	122.11	138.46	98.03	106.89	111.81	96.00	100.00
Income Statement								
Rental Income	84,851	73,874	58,092	60,591	58,417	48,935	38,143	25,140
Interest Income	15,805	18,397	20,550	19,147	16,243	13,476	11,992	8,229
Total Income	102,658	93,827	80,526	80,891	76,543	64,773	50,135	33,369
Total Indirect Exp.	85,234	77,703	79,688	68,912	68,910	47,514	31,981	20,809
Depreciation	13,467	11,425	9,211	9,088	8,634	6,759	5,302	3,553
Interest Expense	55,462	53,440	49,904	53,056	43,840	26,920	22,956	14,412
Eqty Earns/Minority Int.	6,154	3,216	(1,475)	(3,980)	(966)	367	29,734	19,766
Income from Cont Ops	51,309	46,060	...	38,618	...	...	60,017	39,605
Net Income	53,473	48,058	28,963	38,251	35,311	32,441	30,385	19,839
Average Shs. Outstg.	43,896	40,588	31,717	30,407	30,408	29,397	24,220	16,798
Balance Sheet								
Cash & Cash Equivalents	4,364	1,737	6,974	2,190	3,329	1,442	2,160	1,410
Ttl Real Estate Inv.	887,124	703,465	706,280	514,962	546,193	519,948	400,977	269,031
Total Assets	1,208,310	954,108	1,006,628	761,611	749,789	685,595	537,014	370,953
Long–Term Obligations	437,338	345,689	327,933	258,681	242,271	154,807	56,736	116,956
Total Liabilities	477,556	404,967	441,988	367,710	358,427	301,705	174,870	118,379
Net Stockholders' Equity	730,754	549,141	564,640	393,901	391,362	383,890	362,144	252,574
Shares Outstanding	50,001	40,403	40,599	30,456	30,255	29,521	27,953	16,798
Statistical Record								
Net Inc.+Depr./Assets %	5.54	6.00	3.80	6.30	5.90	5.70	6.60	6.30
Return on Equity %	7.02	8.38	5.12	9.80	9.02	8.45	16.57	15.68
Return on Assets %	4.24	4.82	2.87	5.07	4.70	4.73	11.17	10.67
Price Range	18.30–14.37	16.34–13.00	14.25–10.25	11.31–9.69	13.88–9.50	18.00–12.63	18.06–14.13	16.00–12.88
P/E Ratio	16.94–13.31	15.71–12.50	15.66–11.26	8.91–7.63	11.96–8.19	16.36–11.48	14.45–11.30	13.56–10.91
Average Yield %	7.70	8.50	9.97	11.90	10.38	7.92	7.66	8.67

Address: 450 South Orange Avenue, Orlando, FL 32801 **Telephone:** (407) 265–7348 **Web Site:** www.cnlreit.com	**Officers:** James M. Seneff – Chmn., Robert A. Bourne – Vice–Chmn. **Transfer Agents:**First Union National Bank, Charlotte, NC	**Investor Contact:**407–265–7348 **Institutional Holding** **No of Institutions:** 98 **Shares:** 12,042,896 **% Held:** 30.10%

COMMUNITY BANK SYSTEM, INC.

Exchange	Symbol	Price	52Wk Range	Yield	P/E
NYS	CBU	$46.28 (3/31/2004)	50.50-31.61	2.77	15.48

*7 Year Price Score N/A   *NYSE Composite Index=100   *12 Month Price Score 109.3

Interim Earnings (Per Share)

Qtr.	Mar	Jun	Sep	Dec
2000	0.35	0.36	0.36	0.35
2001	0.28	0.09	0.27	0.17
2002	0.28	0.31	0.42	0.45
2003	0.37	0.37	0.43	0.32

Interim Dividends (Per Share)

Amt	Decl	Ex	Rec	Pay
0.32Q	8/21/2003	9/11/2003	9/15/2003	10/10/2003
0.32Q	11/21/2003	12/11/2003	12/15/2003	1/9/2004
100%	1/21/2004	4/13/2004	3/17/2004	4/12/2004
0.16Q	2/19/2004	3/11/2004	3/15/2004	4/9/2004

Indicated Div: $0.16 (Div. Reinv. Plan)

Valuation Analysis

Forecast P/E 14.36	Trailing P/E 15.48
Market Cap $599.8 Million	Book Value 404.8 Million
Price/Book 1.59	Price/Sales 2.84

Dividend Achiever Status

Rank 180	5 Year Growth Rate 8.84%
Total Years of Dividend Growth 12	

TRADING VOLUME (thousand shares)

Business Summary: Commercial Banking (MIC: 8.1 SIC: 6021 NAIC:522110)

Community Bank System is a bank holding company with $3.86 billion in assets and total deposits of $2.73 billion as of Dec 31 2003. As of Dec 31 2003, Co.'s wholly-owned community banking subsidiary, Community Bank, N.A., operated 126 customer facilities throughout 22 counties of Upstate New York and five counties of Northeastern Pennsylvania offering a range of commercial and retail banking services. Another Co. subsidiary, Benefit Plans Adminstrative Services, Inc., provides administration, consulting and actuarial services to sponsors of employee benefit plans.

Recent Developments: For the year ended Dec 31 2003, net income increased 4.8% to $40.4 million compared with $38.5 million a year earlier. Net interest income grew 3.1% to $131.8 million from $127.9 million the previous year. Loan loss provision amounted to $11.2 million versus $12.2 million in 2002. Total noninterest income advanced 10.0% to $35.0 million from $31.8 million last year, and included a loss of $2.7 million for 2003 and a gain of $1.7 million for 2002 on investment securities and debt extinguishment. Total noninterest income growth was driven by a particular new deposit services product in December 2002, as well as growth from Co.'s financial services businesses.

Prospects: On Jan 6 2004, Co. announced an agreement to acquire First Heritage Bank, a $275.0 million asset bank with three branches, in an all-stock transaction valued at about $74.0 million. Co. expects the transaction to be accretive to earnings within the first 12 months based on anticipated cost reductions, modest revenue enhancements, and opportunities to restructure the balance sheet. Looking ahead, Co. is hopeful that the acquisition of First Heritage, coupled with the 2003 acquisitions of Peoples Bancorp, Harbridge Consulting Group, and Grange National Bank, will lead to improved results in 2004. Accordingly, Co. estimates full-year 2004 diluted earnings of between $3.20 and $3.30 per share.

Financial Data
(US$ in Thousands)

	12/31/2003	12/31/2002	12/31/2001	12/31/2000	12/31/1999	12/31/1998	12/31/1997	12/31/1996
Earnings Per Share	1.49	1.46	0.81	1.42	1.21	1.02	1.01	0.91
Cash Flow Per Share	2.70	2.20	1.89	1.92	2.12	2.37	1.54	1.22
Tang. Book Val. Per Share	7.36	7.32	4.86	6.32	4.04	4.50	3.91	4.92
Dividends Per Share	1.190	1.100	1.080	1.020	0.940	0.830	0.740	0.670
Dividend Payout %	79.59	75.08	133.33	71.57	77.68	80.97	73.26	73.63
Income Statement								
Total Revenues	226,110	237,470	226,933	166,210	139,375	139,978	129,436	106,563
Total Indirect Exp.	102,461	95,824	89,039	55,989	52,733	51,876	45,799	37,450
Depreciation & Amort.	5,093	5,953	6,679	4,670	4,615	4,640	3,703	2,729
Operating Income	53,153	52,404	29,602	29,027	25,559	24,436	24,406	23,793
Income Taxes	12,773	13,887	8,891	8,708	7,923	8,902	8,844	9,660
Income from Cont Ops	...	...	20,711	...	...	15,534	...	...
Net Income	40,380	38,517	19,129	20,319	17,635	15,728	15,562	14,133
Average Shs. Outstg.	27,034	26,334	23,650	14,271	14,590	15,341	15,352	13,885
Balance Sheet								
Cash & Cash Equivalents	103,923	113,531	106,554	59,304	100,727	78,893	82,106	52,535
Total Current Assets	129,774	136,303	129,116	77,782	114,895	91,269	95,499	63,325
Total Assets	3,855,397	3,434,204	3,210,833	2,022,635	1,840,702	1,680,689	1,633,742	1,343,865
Total Current Liabilities	2,761,788	2,538,356	2,560,170	1,495,730	1,360,306	1,512,766	1,470,686	1,224,013
Long-Term Obligations	631,486	430,000	263,100	331,100	324,000	...	...	...
Net Stockholders' Equity	404,828	325,038	267,980	139,376	108,487	120,165	118,012	109,352
Net Working Capital	(2,632,014)	(2,402,053)	(2,431,054)	(1,417,947)	(1,245,411)	(1,421,497)	(1,375,187)	(1,160,688)
Shares Outstanding	28,330	25,957	25,805	13,986	14,592	14,592	15,173	14,948
Statistical Record								
Operating Profit Margin %	23.50	22.06	13.04	17.46	18.33	17.45	18.85	22.32
Return on Equity %	9.97	11.84	7.72	14.57	16.25	12.92	13.18	12.92
Return on Assets %	1.04	1.12	0.64	1.00	0.95	0.92	0.95	1.05
Debt/Total Assets %	16.37	12.52	8.19	16.36	17.60	...	...	...
Price Range	50.26-31.10	34.02-26.13	29.64-24.90	26.03-20.25	32.63-22.63	38.19-25.00	31.31-31.31	...
P/E Ratio	33.73-20.87	23.30-17.90	36.59-30.74	18.33-14.26	26.96-18.70	37.44-24.51	31.00-31.00	...
Average Yield %	2.99	3.60	3.95	4.46	3.65	2.64	2.36	N/A

Address: 5790 Widewaters Parkway, DeWitt, NY 13214-1883 **Telephone:** (315) 445-2282 **Web Site:** www.communitybankna.com	**Officers:** James A. Gabriel – Chmn., Sanford A. Belden – Pres., C.E.O. **Transfer Agents:**ChaseMellon Shareholder Services, L.L.C., Ridgefield Park, NJ	**Investor Contact:** (315) 445-2282 **Institutional Holding** **No of Institutions:** 87 **Shares:** 4,562,995 **% Held:** 35.10%

COMMUNITY FIRST BANKSHARES, INC.

Exchange	Symbol	Price	52Wk Range	Yield	P/E
NMS	CFBX	$32.14 (3/31/2004)	32.16–25.87	2.99	16.48

*7 Year Price Score 125.4 ***NYSE Composite Index=100** ***12 Month Price Score 93.1**

Interim Earnings (Per Share)

Qtr.	Mar	Jun	Sep	Dec
2000	0.37	0.38	0.40	0.39
2001	0.24	0.43	0.45	0.45
2002	0.47	0.49	0.51	0.50
2003	0.50	0.49	0.48	0.48

Interim Dividends (Per Share)

Amt	Decl	Ex	Rec	Pay
0.22Q	4/25/2003	5/28/2003	6/1/2003	6/15/2003
0.23Q	8/7/2003	8/27/2003	9/1/2003	9/15/2003
0.23Q	10/30/2003	11/26/2003	12/1/2003	12/15/2003
0.24Q	2/4/2004	2/26/2004	3/1/2004	3/15/2004

Indicated Div: $0.96 (Div. Reinv. Plan)

Valuation Analysis

Forecast P/E	12.66	Trailing P/E	16.48
Market Cap	$1.3 Billion	Book Value	366.1 Million
Price/Book	N/A	Price/Sales	N/A

Dividend Achiever Status

Rank	63	10 Year Growth Rate	16.23%
Total Years of Dividend Growth		12	

Business Summary: Commercial Banking (MIC: 8.1 SIC: 6022 NAIC:522110)

Community First Bankshares is a bank holding company that, as of Dec 31 2003 operated through one bank subsidiary with banking offices in 136 communities in Arizona, California, Colorado, Iowa, Minnesota, Nebraska, New Mexico, North Dakota, South Dakota, Utah, Wisconsin and Wyoming. The banks are community banks that offer a range of commercial and consumer banking services primarily to individuals and businesses in small and medium-sized communities and surrounding market areas. Co. provides its banking offices with the advantages of affiliation with a bank holding company, such as access to its lines of financial services. As of Dec 31 2003, Co. had total assets of $5.47 billion.

Recent Developments: For the year ended Dec 31 2003, net income declined 6.7% to $36.9 million compared with $39.5 million a year earlier. Net interest income decreased 6.0% to $238.7 million from $254.0 million the previous year. Provision for loan losses was $12.6 million versus $13.3 million the year before. Total non-interest income increased 8.9% to $92.7 million from $85.1 million in 2002. Total non-interest income for 2003 and 2002 included net gains on the sales of securities of $4.3 million and $373,000, and gains on the sales of loans of $4.1 million and $2.8 million, respectively. Non-interest income also benefited from a 10.1% increase in insurance commissions to $15.2 million.

Prospects: Co. continues to implement its 2003 market extension model strategy that includes opening additional offices in selected areas of its current geographic footprint that it believes are growth or emerging growth markets. Additional offices are expected to be within the 12-state area within which Co. currently operates. During 2003, Co. announced its initial five market extension locations in the metropolitan Minneapolis/St. Paul market, with the first two offices expected to open by June 30 2004. The additional offices, which Co. expects to open in late 2004, are pending regulatory approval. Co. has announced that it plans to open 30 new offices by 2007.

Financial Data

(US$ in Thousands)	12/31/2003	12/31/2002	12/31/2001	12/31/2000	12/31/1999	12/31/1998	12/31/1997	12/31/1996
Earnings Per Share	1.95	1.97	1.57	1.54	1.48	0.98	1.20	0.89
Tang. Book Val. Per Share	7.17	7.31	6.44	5.50	5.96	5.77	5.95	5.31
Dividends Per Share	0.900	0.800	0.680	0.600	0.560	0.440	0.350	0.290
Dividend Payout %	46.15	40.60	43.31	38.96	37.83	44.89	29.16	32.40
Income Statement								
Total Interest Income	309,242	358,183	434,016	477,558	465,206	449,244	278,597	229,426
Total Interest Expense	70,538	89,928	162,220	210,281	185,818	188,484	117,253	95,234
Net Interest Income	238,704	268,255	271,796	267,277	279,388	260,760	161,344	134,192
Provision for Loan Losses	12,602	13,262	17,520	15,781	20,184	22,509	5,352	6,757
Non-Interest Income	92,693	81,319	76,682	75,205	72,509	60,260	36,564	27,370
Non-Interest Expense	206,859	217,555	232,423	219,319	218,227	230,092	125,190	104,288
Income Before Taxes	111,936	118,757	98,535	107,382	113,486	68,419	67,366	50,517
Income from Cont Ops	...	...	...	...	...	46,971	45,850	...
Net Income	75,021	79,208	65,059	71,634	74,913	43,063	46,552	32,510
Average Shs. Outstg.	38,553	40,243	41,471	46,578	50,670	47,882	38,138	36,310
Balance Sheet								
Cash & Due from Banks	234,076	242,887	248,260	256,136	247,051	250,963	222,088	175,732
Securities Avail. for Sale	1,563,419	1,672,445	1,437,066	1,714,510	1,937,517	1,980,530	1,498,877	506,888
Net Loans & Leases	3,271,344	3,521,737	3,681,701	3,686,034	3,641,475	3,335,969	2,600,863	2,037,893
Total Assets	5,465,107	5,827,170	5,772,326	6,089,729	6,302,235	6,002,972	4,855,526	3,116,398
Total Deposits	4,389,210	4,669,746	4,750,813	5,019,891	4,909,863	4,884,672	3,619,334	2,537,440
Long-Term Obligations	222,211	127,500	136,841	123,957	75,622	93,472	116,476	46,750
Total Liabilities	5,103,307	5,328,721	5,295,621	5,624,298	5,774,966	5,477,726	4,396,232	2,871,827
Net Stockholders' Equity	361,800	378,449	356,705	345,431	407,269	405,246	339,294	244,571
Shares Outstanding	37,357	38,678	40,246	41,866	47,118	47,119	40,646	34,304
Statistical Record								
Return on Equity %	20.73	20.92	18.23	20.73	18.39	11.59	13.51	13.29
Return on Assets %	1.37	1.35	1.12	1.17	1.18	0.78	0.94	1.04
Equity/Assets %	6.62	6.49	6.17	5.67	6.46	6.75	6.98	7.84
Non-Int. Exp./Tot. Inc. %	51.46	49.50	45.51	39.67	40.58	45.15	39.72	40.61
Price Range	29.26-24.35	28.45-22.36	26.97-18.06	19.13-12.41	24.00-13.94	27.00-14.13	27.56-13.69	14.38-10.00
P/E Ratio	15.01-12.49	14.44-11.35	17.18-11.50	12.42-8.06	16.22-9.42	27.55-14.41	22.97-11.41	16.15-11.24
Average Yield %	3.32	3.04	3.03	3.75	2.85	1.92	1.83	2.47

Address: 520 Main Avenue, Fargo, ND 58124	Officers: Ronald K. Strand – Vice-Chmn., C.O.O., Mark A. Anderson – Pres., C.E.O.	Investor Contact: (888) 292–2378
Telephone: (701) 298–5600		Institutional Holding
Web Site: www.communityfirst.com		No of Institutions: 9
		Shares: 3,687,355 % Held: –

COMMUNITY TRUST BANCORP, INC.

Exchange	Symbol	Price	52Wk Range	Yield	P/E
NMS	CTBI P	$33.00 (3/31/2004)	33.30-23.31	2.79	15.64

*7 Year Price Score 141.5 *NYSE Composite Index=100 *12 Month Price Score 106.7

Interim Earnings (Per Share)

Qtr.	Mar	Jun	Sep	Dec
2000	0.34	0.39	0.39	0.42
2001	0.37	0.42	0.38	0.42
2002	0.45	0.45	0.57	0.52
2003	0.50	0.51	0.53	0.57

Interim Dividends (Per Share)

Amt	Decl	Ex	Rec	Pay
0.209Q	7/22/2003	9/11/2003	9/15/2003	10/1/2003
10%	10/29/2003	11/26/2003	12/1/2003	12/15/2003
0.23Q	10/29/2003	11/11/2003	12/15/2003	1/1/2004
0.23Q	1/27/2004	3/11/2004	3/15/2004	4/1/2004

Indicated Div: $0.92

Valuation Analysis

Forecast P/E	12.50	Trailing P/E	15.64
Market Cap	$374.3 Million	Book Value	N/A
Price/Book	N/A	Price/Sales	N/A

Dividend Achiever Status

Rank	177	10 Year Growth Rate	8.97%
Total Years of Dividend Growth		15

Business Summary: Commercial Banking (MIC: 8.1 SIC: 6021 NAIC:522110)

Community Trust Bancorp is a bank holding company with assets of $2.47 billion as of Dec 31 2003 that currently owns all the capital stock of one commercial bank and one trust company, serving small and mid-sized communities in eastern, northeast central, south central Kentucky, and southern West Virginia. The commercial bank is Community Trust Bank, Pikeville, KY. The trust company, Community Trust and Investment, Lexington, KY, has offices in Lexington, Pikeville, Ashland, Middlesboro and Versailles, KY. Co. operates 69 banking locations across Kentucky, and five banking locations in West Virginia.

Recent Developments: For the twelve months ended Dec 31 2003, net income climbed 4.7% to $28.9 million compared with $27.6 million in 2002. Results for 2003 and 2002 included securities gains of $3.0 million and $1.5 million, and gains on sales of loans of $5.7 million and $4.4 million, respectively. Net interest income declined 5.2% to $84.6 million from $89.3 million the year before. Provision for loan losses fell 7.5% to $9.3 million versus $10.1 million a year earlier. Non-interest income jumped 30.2% to $36.4 million due to increased deposit service charge income, gains on sales of securities, and other non-interest income. Non-interest expense grew 5.0% to $70.7 million from $67.3 million in 2002.

Prospects: Residential mortgage refinancing activity has slowed from the robust levels experienced in 2003 as interest rates have ticked upward in recent months. As a result, Co. will likely see a decrease in gains from the sales of loans. Also with the slow down, Co. expects an improvement in its non-interest income from the coming year, as charges to its valuation reserve for capitalized mortgage servicing rights should be less than in 2003. Meanwhile, the continuing low interest rate environment for deposit accounts has led Co. to move many of its customers into alternative investments through its full service brokerage operations.

Financial Data

(US$ in Thousands)	9 Mos	6 Mos	3 Mos	12/31/2002	12/31/2001	12/31/2000	12/31/1999	12/31/1998
Earnings Per Share	1.56	1.02	0.50	1.99	1.59	1.54	1.62	1.03
Tang. Book Val. Per Share	11.25	11.09	10.86	10.66	9.19	8.87	8.45	7.63
Dividends Per Share	0.740	0.720	0.710	0.690	0.660	0.610	0.580	0.540
Dividend Payout %	47.72	70.95	139.77	34.86	41.45	39.76	36.07	52.89
Income Statement								
Total Interest Income	96,775	65,355	32,667	146,550	176,835	175,749	163,516	160,570
Total Interest Expense	34,453	23,809	12,139	57,293	93,717	91,515	79,740	83,986
Net Interest Income	62,322	41,546	20,528	89,257	83,118	84,234	83,776	76,584
Provision for Loan Losses	7,217	5,132	1,547	10,086	9,185	9,217	9,105	16,008
Non-Interest Income	28,224	18,131	8,546	27,928	23,774	19,526	21,026	19,466
Non-Interest Expense	52,486	34,375	17,611	67,341	64,938	61,927	64,388	62,166
Income Before Taxes	30,843	20,170	9,916	39,758	32,769	32,616	31,309	17,876
Net Income	21,338	14,057	6,993	27,600	22,272	22,346	21,845	13,969
Average Shs. Outstg.	13,480	13,508	13,536	13,868	13,997	14,464	13,417	13,393
Balance Sheet								
Cash & Due from Banks	72,698	83,800	77,187	92,955	96,173	72,725	99,773	98,133
Securities Avail. for Sale	518,690	466,150	516,939	527,339	367,233	236,620	270,281	301,052
Net Loans & Leases	1,658,530	1,616,598	1,602,467	1,611,336	1,687,424	1,668,639	1,594,378	1,476,297
Total Assets	2,500,340	2,517,025	2,469,852	2,487,911	2,503,905	2,261,975	2,176,090	2,248,039
Total Deposits	2,107,619	2,130,071	2,109,865	2,127,716	2,155,772	1,943,916	1,877,334	1,921,141
Long-Term Obligations	3,634	5,208	5,826	6,721	22,969	61,386	70,598	105,207
Total Liabilities	2,285,039	2,293,967	2,258,794	2,278,492	2,312,299	2,080,071	2,003,671	2,083,244
Net Stockholders' Equity	215,301	213,058	211,058	209,419	191,606	181,904	172,419	164,795
Shares Outstanding	13,438	13,417	13,500	13,582	13,825	14,158	13,362	13,396
Statistical Record								
Return on Equity %	9.91	6.59	3.31	13.17	11.62	12.28	12.66	8.47
Return on Assets %	0.85	0.55	0.28	1.10	0.88	0.98	1.00	0.62
Equity/Assets %	8.61	8.46	8.54	8.41	7.65	8.04	7.92	7.33
Non-Int. Exp./Tot. Inc. %	41.98	41.17	42.73	38.59	32.37	31.71	34.89	34.52
Price Range	28.18-22.80	26.84-22.80	23.92-22.80	26.73-18.11	20.25-12.71	15.87-11.42	18.06-15.03	22.88-15.20
P/E Ratio	18.07-14.62	26.31-22.35	47.84-45.60	13.43-9.10	12.73-7.99	10.31-7.41	11.15-9.28	22.21-14.75
Average Yield %	2.98	3.01	3.05	3.18	3.90	4.62	3.51	2.79

Address: 346 North Mayo Trail, Pikeville, KY 41501-2947 Telephone: (606) 432-1414 Web Site: www.ctbi.com	Officers: Burlin Coleman - Chmn., Jean R. Hale - Vice-Chmn., Pres., C.E.O.	Investor Contact:606-432-1414 Institutional Holding No of Institutions: 14 Shares: 472,891 % Held: -

COMPASS BANCSHARES INC.

Exchange	Symbol	Price	52Wk Range	Yield	P/E
NMS	CBSS	$41.47 (3/31/2004)	42.86-31.72	3.01	15.42

*7 Year Price Score 132.2   *NYSE Composite Index=100   *12 Month Price Score 100.0

Interim Earnings (Per Share)

Qtr.	Mar	Jun	Sep	Dec
2000	0.48	0.50	0.52	0.50
2001	0.50	0.52	0.53	0.56
2002	0.59	0.60	0.61	0.62
2003	0.64	0.68	0.68	0.69

Interim Dividends (Per Share)

Amt	Decl	Ex	Rec	Pay
0.28Q	5/22/2003	6/11/2003	6/13/2003	7/1/2003
0.28Q	8/19/2003	9/11/2003	9/15/2003	10/1/2003
0.28Q	11/17/2003	12/11/2003	12/15/2003	1/2/2004
0.313Q	2/17/2004	3/11/2004	3/15/2004	4/1/2004

Indicated Div: $1.25 (Div. Reinv. Plan)

Valuation Analysis

Forecast P/E	12.74	Trailing P/E	15.42
Market Cap	$5.3 Billion	Book Value	1.9 Billion
Price/Book	2.57	Price/Sales	2.67

Dividend Achiever Status

Rank	108	10 Year Growth Rate	12.78%
Total Years of Dividend Growth			22

Business Summary: Commercial Banking (MIC: 8.1 SIC: 6021 NAIC:522110)

Compass Bancshares is a bank holding company headquartered in Birmingham, AL, with total assets of $26.96 billion as of Dec 31 2003. Co.'s principal subsidiary is Compass Bank, which operates 376 full-service bank offices, including 136 in Texas, 89 in Alabama, 71 in Arizona, 42 in Florida, 28 in Colorado, and 10 in New Mexico. In addition, Compass Bank operates loan production offices in Georgia and Maryland. Compass Bank provides general commercial banking and trust services such as receiving demand and time deposits, making personal and commercial loans and furnishing personal and commercial checking accounts.

Recent Developments: For the year ended Dec 31 2003, net income climbed 8.7% to $341.9 million from $314.4 million in the corresponding prior-year period. Results for 2003 and 2002 included merger and integration expenses of $1.9 million and $2.8 million, respectively. Net interest income slipped 1.7% to $909.5 million from $924.9 million a year earlier. Provision for loan losses declined 12.2% to $119.7 million from $136.3 million in 2002. Total non-interest income advanced 19.3% to $526.2 million from $441.1 million the year before, while total non-interest expense rose 6.0% to $797.9 million from $752.4 million in 2002. As of Dec 31 2003, total assets were up 12.7% year-over-year to $26.96 billion.

Prospects: Net interest margin continues to be pressured by low interest rates and the corresponding negative effect on investment opportunities. Meanwhile, Co. is enjoying solid loan and deposit growth, as well as stable credit quality. Earnings are benefiting from strong growth in most of Co.'s fee-based businesses, including service charges on deposit accounts and credit card service charges and fees. In addition, earnings are also being positively affected by Co.'s efforts to contain non-interest expense growth, following the addition of 30 new banking centers and the acquisition of three insurance agencies during 2003.

Financial Data

(US$ in Thousands)	12/31/2003	12/31/2002	12/31/2001	12/31/2000	12/31/1999	12/31/1998	12/31/1997	12/31/1996
Earnings Per Share	2.69	2.42	2.11	2.00	1.88	1.56	1.56	1.41
Tang. Book Val. Per Share	12.92	13.06	13.53	12.23	10.51	10.29	9.69	8.80
Dividends Per Share	1.090	0.980	0.910	0.860	0.770	0.680	0.610	0.550
Dividend Payout %	40.52	40.49	43.12	43.00	41.22	43.58	39.46	39.00
Income Statement								
Total Interest Income	1,277,287	1,386,923	1,517,721	1,432,844	1,247,571	1,134,544	949,034	820,370
Total Interest Expense	367,757	462,068	691,862	752,044	608,403	555,157	473,869	417,943
Net Interest Income	909,530	924,855	825,859	680,800	639,168	579,387	475,165	402,427
Provision for Loan Losses	119,681	136,331	106,241	53,539	31,122	38,445	22,412	17,630
Non-Interest Income	526,184	441,063	376,378	298,904	241,109	222,500	181,467	154,740
Non-Interest Expense	797,934	752,429	685,770	569,589	517,916	491,017	395,727	337,486
Income Before Taxes	518,150	477,158	410,226	356,576	331,239	272,425	238,493	202,051
Net Income	341,968	314,399	270,397	240,591	217,045	180,880	155,563	128,927
Average Shs. Outstg.	127,186	129,850	129,138	120,454	114,441	113,745	99,771	90,834
Balance Sheet								
Cash & Due from Banks	726,492	734,540	715,991	719,487	684,540	831,614	693,687	670,389
Securities Avail. for Sale	4,434,232	4,806,406	6,585,036	5,049,473	4,243,813	3,773,432	2,422,170	2,132,555
Net Loans & Leases	17,120,920	16,248,490	13,515,893	11,340,877	10,645,849	9,964,608	8,549,545	7,338,655
Total Assets	26,963,113	23,884,709	23,015,000	19,992,242	18,150,752	17,288,908	13,459,555	11,814,212
Total Deposits	15,687,823	15,135,387	13,735,245	14,033,244	12,808,918	12,013,446	9,632,545	9,220,599
Long-Term Obligations	4,827,814	4,900,132	3,837,450	2,529,264	2,564,532	2,045,980	1,387,121	701,470
Total Liabilities	25,091,230	21,953,207	21,299,359	18,511,780	16,954,548	16,092,767	12,499,547	11,011,150
Net Stockholders' Equity	1,871,883	1,931,502	1,715,641	1,480,462	1,196,204	1,196,141	960,008	803,062
Shares Outstanding	122,086	126,116	126,800	120,972	113,708	113,350	98,986	91,181
Statistical Record								
Return on Equity %	18.26	16.27	15.76	16.25	18.14	15.12	16.20	16.05
Return on Assets %	1.26	1.31	1.17	1.20	1.19	1.04	1.15	1.09
Equity/Assets %	6.94	8.08	7.45	7.40	6.59	6.91	7.13	6.79
Non-Int. Exp./Tot. Inc. %	44.24	41.16	36.20	32.89	34.79	36.18	35.00	34.61
Price Range	39.59-29.99	35.87-26.18	29.08-19.13	24.28-15.75	30.50-20.69	35.46-19.25	31.08-17.31	17.67-13.67
P/E Ratio	14.72-11.15	14.82-10.82	13.78-9.06	12.14-7.88	16.22-11.00	22.73-12.34	19.93-11.09	12.53-9.69
Average Yield %	3.14	3.10	3.69	4.54	2.95	2.41	2.65	3.64

Address: 15 South 20th Street, Birmingham, AL 35233 Telephone: (205) 297-3000 Web Site: www.compassweb.com	Officers: D. Paul Jones - Chmn., C.E.O., Charles E. McMahen - Vice-Chmn.	Investor Contact:205-297-3331 Institutional Holding No of Institutions: 9 Shares: 228,769 % Held: -

CONAGRA FOODS, INC.

Exchange	Symbol	Price	52Wk Range	Yield	P/E
NYS	CAG	$26.94 (3/31/2004)	27.76-20.26	3.86	17.49

*7 Year Price Score 93.2   *NYSE Composite Index=100   ***12 Month Price Score 95.2**

Interim Earnings (Per Share)

Qtr.	Aug	Nov	Feb	May
2000–01	0.30	0.58	0.19	0.26
2001–02	0.36	0.44	0.31	0.36
2002–03	0.42	0.45	0.30	0.41
2003–04	0.38	0.45	...	...

Interim Dividends (Per Share)

Amt	Decl	Ex	Rec	Pay
0.248Q	4/8/2003	4/30/2003	5/2/2003	6/1/2003
0.248Q	7/11/2003	7/30/2003	8/1/2003	9/1/2003
0.26Q	9/25/2003	10/29/2003	10/31/2003	12/1/2003
0.26Q	12/4/2003	1/28/2004	1/30/2004	3/1/2004

Indicated Div: $1.04 (Div. Reinv. Plan)

Valuation Analysis

Forecast P/E	12.97	Trailing P/E	17.49
Market Cap	$14.5 Billion	Book Value	4.9 Billion
Price/Book	2.33	Price/Sales	0.76

Dividend Achiever Status

Rank	119	10 Year Growth Rate 12.01%
Total Years of Dividend Growth		26

Business Summary: Food (MIC: 4.1 SIC: 2011 NAIC:311611)

ConAgra Foods operates through three business segments: Packaged Foods includes Co.'s shelf–stable, frozen and refrigerated foods, which are processed and packaged. Food Ingredients includes Co.'s basic ingredients, milled ingredients and specialty ingredients operations. Agricultural Products includes operations involved in the distribution of agricultural crop inputs. Co.'s major brands include: *Healthy Choice, Banquet, Chef Boyardee, Wesson, Hunt's, Orville Redenbacher's, Slim Jim, Peter Pan, Parkay, Van Camp's, PAM, Swiss Miss, Louis Kemp, Reddi–wip, Act II, La Choy, Butterball* and *Armour*, among numerous others.

Recent Developments: For the 13 weeks ended Feb 22 2004, income from continuing operations totaled $191.8 million, before a $1.4 million accounting change charge, compared with income from continuing operations of $200.3 million in the corresponding prior-year period. Net sales slipped 0.5% to $3.60 billion from $3.61 billion the year before. Packaged Foods segment sales slid 1.4% to $2.97 billion from $3.01 billion a year earlier, while Food Ingredients segment sales climbed 4.2% to $630.2 million from $605.0 million the previous year. Operating profit grew 1.0% to $450.5 million from $446.0 million the prior year.

Prospects: Results are being positively affected by Co.'s efforts to boost sales and increase profitability. In January 2004, Co. launched Life Choice, a new line of frozen meals that have fewer carbohydrates. Co. is pleased with the initial customer response to Life Choice and has expanded its availability throughout the U.S. Meanwhile, on Feb 17 2004, Co. introduced Golden Cuisine, a line of affordable and nutritional frozen meals targeting the growing market of Americans ages 55 and older. Co. has partnered with senior caregivers, including Meals On Wheels Association of America™ and Coordinated Care Solutions-CareGuide™, to deliver the Golden Cuisine meals to seniors at home.

Financial Data

(US$ in Thousands)	6 Mos	3 Mos	05/25/2003	05/26/2002	05/27/2001	05/28/2000	05/30/1999	05/31/1998
Earnings Per Share	0.76	0.38	1.58	1.47	1.33	0.86	0.75	1.36
Cash Flow Per Share	0.58	0.42	1.34	4.44	0.24	1.44	2.47	1.24
Tang. Book Val. Per Share	0.48	0.14	N.M	N.M	N.M	1.21	1.02	0.84
Dividends Per Share	0.990	0.970	0.960	0.920	0.850	0.760	0.660	0.580
Dividend Payout %	130.26	257.23	61.07	62.58	64.43	88.83	89.26	43.01
Income Statement								
Total Revenues	7,168,400	4,393,700	19,839,200	27,629,600	27,194,200	25,385,800	24,594,300	23,840,500
Total Indirect Exp.	903,500	550,800	2,308,400	2,423,400	2,355,100	3,210,400	3,039,200	2,357,700
Depreciation & Amort.	173,900	91,200	396,700	623,200	592,900	536,500	499,800	446,300
Operating Income	671,800	290,300	1,514,500	1,669,700	1,527,400	969,500	998,900	1,320,400
Net Interest Inc./(Exp.)	(133,900)	(65,700)	(276,300)	(401,500)	(423,300)	(303,400)	(316,600)	(299,300)
Income Taxes	129,400	20,900	436,000	483,200	421,600	253,100	323,900	393,100
Eqty Earns/Minority Int.	27,500	9,500	37,900	...	...	...	...	...
Income from Cont Ops	408,500	203,700	840,100	785,000	682,500	...	...	628,000
Net Income	465,000	194,900	774,800	783,000	638,600	413,000	358,400	613,200
Average Shs. Outstg.	531,700	531,500	530,700	528,000	514,300	478,600	476,700	461,300
Balance Sheet								
Cash & Cash Equivalents	26,700	680,700	628,600	157,900	198,100	157,600	62,800	95,200
Total Current Assets	5,772,400	6,573,700	6,059,600	6,433,900	7,362,600	5,966,500	5,656,100	5,487,400
Total Assets	14,532,700	15,539,200	15,071,400	15,496,200	16,480,800	12,295,800	12,146,100	11,702,800
Total Current Liabilities	3,532,200	4,368,900	3,803,400	4,313,400	6,935,600	5,489,200	5,386,400	5,070,200
Long–Term Obligations	4,965,900	5,284,300	5,395,200	5,743,700	4,109,500	2,566,800	2,543,100	2,487,400
Net Stockholders' Equity	4,898,300	4,743,600	4,621,700	4,308,200	3,983,200	2,964,100	2,908,800	2,778,900
Net Working Capital	2,240,200	2,204,800	2,256,200	2,120,500	427,000	477,300	269,700	417,200
Shares Outstanding	536,614	536,657	536,765	537,040	537,067	492,212	488,173	459,076
Statistical Record								
Operating Profit Margin %	9.37	6.60	7.63	6.04	5.61	3.81	4.06	5.53
Return on Equity %	8.33	4.29	18.17	18.22	17.13	13.93	12.32	22.59
Return on Assets %	2.81	1.31	5.57	5.06	4.14	3.35	2.95	5.36
Debt/Total Assets %	34.17	34.00	35.79	37.06	24.93	20.87	20.93	21.25
Price Range	25.41-21.15	25.41-21.71	27.65-19.65	25.64-19.02	26.13-17.99	28.06-15.50	34.19-23.31	38.19-28.00
P/E Ratio	33.43-27.83	66.87-57.13	17.50-12.44	17.44-12.94	19.64-13.53	32.63-18.02	45.58-31.08	28.08-20.59
Average Yield %	4.27	4.12	3.99	4.01	3.99	3.36	2.29	1.79

Address: One ConAgra Drive, Omaha, NE 68102–5001 Telephone: (402) 595–4000 Web Site: www.conagra.com	Officers: Bruce C. Rohde – Chmn., Pres., C.E.O., Dwight J. Goslee – Exec. V.P., Oper. Control & Devel. Transfer Agents: Wells Fargo Sharehowner Services, St. Paul, MN	Investor Contact: (800) 214–0349 Institutional Holding No of Institutions: 495 Shares: 328,005,141 % Held: 61.10%

CONNECTICUT WATER SERVICE, INC.

Exchange	Symbol	Price	52Wk Range	Yield	P/E
NMS	CTWS	$28.41 (3/31/2004)	30.40-25.02	2.92	24.70

*7 Year Price Score 131.9 *NYSE Composite Index=100 *12 Month Price Score 95.0

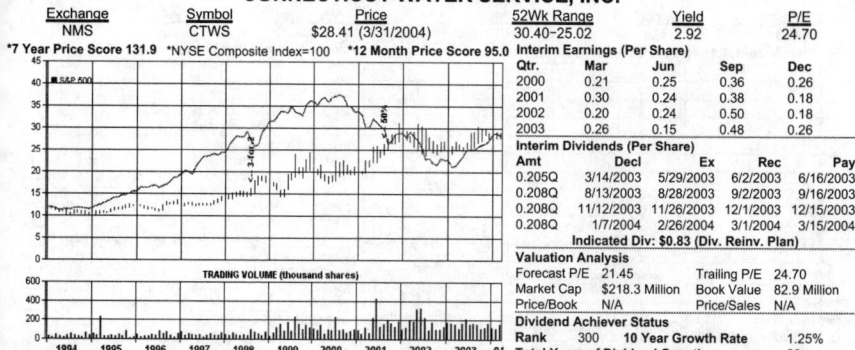

Interim Earnings (Per Share)

Qtr.	Mar	Jun	Sep	Dec
2000	0.21	0.25	0.36	0.26
2001	0.30	0.24	0.38	0.18
2002	0.20	0.24	0.50	0.18
2003	0.26	0.15	0.48	0.26

Interim Dividends (Per Share)

Amt	Decl	Ex	Rec	Pay
0.205Q	3/14/2003	5/29/2003	6/2/2003	6/16/2003
0.208Q	8/13/2003	8/28/2003	9/2/2003	9/16/2003
0.208Q	11/12/2003	11/26/2003	12/1/2003	12/15/2003
0.208Q	1/7/2004	2/26/2004	3/1/2004	3/15/2004

Indicated Div: $0.83 (Div. Reinv. Plan)

Valuation Analysis

Forecast P/E	21.45	Trailing P/E	24.70
Market Cap	$218.3 Million	Book Value	82.9 Million
Price/Book	N/A	Price/Sales	N/A

Dividend Achiever Status

Rank	300	10 Year Growth Rate	1.25%
Total Years of Dividend Growth			28

Business Summary: Water Utilities (MIC: 7.2 SIC: 4941 NAIC:221310)

Connecticut Water Service is a holding company of five regulated water utilities that supply water to 86,750 customers in 42 towns throughout Connecticut and Massachusetts as of Dec 31 2003. In addition, Co. owns six unregulated companies, including the real estate companies of Chester Realty, Inc. and BARLACO; New England Water Utility Services and Connecticut Water Emergency Services, which provide water-related services; Crystal Water Utilities, which owns The Crystal Water Company of Danielson and three rental properties; and Barnstable Holding Company, which owns Barnstable Water Co. and BARLACO.

Recent Developments: For the quarter ended Dec 31 2003, net income grew 4.9% to $9.2 million compared with $8.8 million in 2002. The improvement in earnings was attributed largely to higher profit margins from Co.'s service contract operations, increased customer participation in Co.'s Linebacker® service line maintenance program and higher revenues from the leasing of telecommunications antenna sites. Operating revenues climbed 2.8% to $47.1 million from $45.8 million a year earlier. Utility operating income fell 2.6% to $11.5 million versus $11.8 million a year earlier. Total other income leaped 56.4% to $2.3 million from $1.5 million in 2002.

Prospects: The continuing success of Co.'s non-water business services is helping to offset lower operating results from its core water operations, which have been largely affected by slower sales due to unusual weather patterns. Consequently, financial performance is expected to strengthen once water demand returns to more normal levels. Meanwhile, Co. will continue to maintain a tight control on operating costs. Additional factors that could affect the future profitability include the timeliness of rate relief, when necessary, industrial demand, financing costs, and energy and tax rates.

Financial Data

(US$ in Thousands)	12/31/2003	12/31/2002	12/31/2001	12/31/2000	12/31/1999	12/31/1998	12/31/1997	12/31/1996
Earnings Per Share	1.15	1.12	1.10	1.08	1.02	1.02	0.99	0.97
Cash Flow Per Share	1.68	1.77	1.93	2.04	1.93	1.71	2.06	1.56
Tang. Book Val. Per Share	10.00	9.61	9.25	8.91	8.61	8.51	8.25	8.02
Dividends Per Share	0.820	0.810	0.800	0.790	0.780	0.770	0.760	0.750
Dividend Payout %	71.73	72.71	73.13	73.20	76.61	76.25	77.23	77.32
Income Statement								
Total Revenues	47,115	45,830	45,392	41,512	42,624	37,924	38,501	38,592
Total Indirect Exp.	10,817	9,983	9,225	8,908	8,577	8,403	9,456	9,958
Costs & Expenses	35,584	33,996	34,078	30,353	31,397	27,620	28,167	28,464
Depreciation & Amort.	5,684	5,187	4,837	4,500	4,390	3,854	3,505	3,315
Operating Income	11,531	11,834	11,314	11,159	11,227	10,304	10,334	10,128
Net Interest Inc./(Exp.)	(4,635)	(4,534)	(4,632)	(4,541)	(4,391)	(4,177)	(4,182)	(3,788)
Income Taxes	2,008	4,482	4,777	4,417	5,065	3,641	3,876	3,899
Net Income	9,210	8,780	8,439	7,963	7,494	6,965	6,804	6,603
Average Shs. Outstg.	8,002	7,771	7,662	7,308	7,272	6,802	6,786	6,743
Balance Sheet								
Net Property	235,098	229,097	202,330	186,971	181,342	167,326	163,757	153,898
Total Assets	277,546	264,799	231,714	215,399	210,885	194,586	189,277	184,640
Long-Term Obligations	64,754	64,734	63,953	64,658	65,399	62,501	54,532	54,430
Net Stockholders' Equity	83,315	79,975	70,783	64,906	62,495	57,945	56,069	54,395
Shares Outstanding	7,967	7,939	7,649	7,279	7,258	6,804	6,790	6,777
Statistical Record								
Operating Profit Margin %	24.47	25.82	24.92	26.88	26.33	27.17	26.84	26.24
Net Inc./Net Property %	3.91	3.83	4.17	4.25	4.13	4.16	4.15	4.29
Net Inc./Tot. Capital %	5.00	5.01	5.21	5.10	4.89	4.84	5.13	5.05
Return on Equity %	11.05	10.97	11.92	12.26	11.99	12.02	12.13	12.13
Accum. Depr./Gross Prop. %	28.24	27.66	27.48	26.56	25.87	25.18	24.22	24.17
Price Range	30.40-24.15	31.00-23.79	31.25-19.50	22.58-17.37	24.50-14.50	19.00-13.67	14.44-12.22	13.56-11.00
P/E Ratio	26.43-21.00	27.68-21.24	28.41-17.73	20.91-16.09	24.02-14.22	18.63-13.40	14.59-12.35	13.97-11.34
Average Yield %	3.04	2.98	3.29	3.98	4.19	4.89	5.93	6.18

Address: 93 West Main Street, Clinton, CT 06413-1600	**Officers:** Marshall T. Chiaraluce – Chmn., Pres., C.E.O., David C. Benoit – V.P., Fin., C.F.O. Treas.	**Investor Contact:** (800) 428-3985 ex 3015 **Institutional Holding**
Telephone: (860) 669-8636		**No of Institutions:** 41
Web Site: www.ctwater.com		**Shares:** 1,155,804 **% Held:** 14%

CONSOLIDATED EDISON, INC.

Exchange	Symbol	Price	52Wk Range	Yield	P/E
NYS	ED	$44.10 (3/31/2004)	44.94-38.51	5.12	18.69

*7 Year Price Score 105.0   ***NYSE Composite Index=100**   ***12 Month Price Score 89.9**

Interim Earnings (Per Share)

Qtr.	Mar	Jun	Sep	Dec
2000	0.88	0.33	1.32	0.21
2001	0.84	0.48	1.30	0.59
2002	0.78	0.46	1.33	0.56
2003	0.72	0.29	1.16	0.19

Interim Dividends (Per Share)

Amt	Decl	Ex	Rec	Pay
0.56Q	4/17/2003	5/12/2003	5/14/2003	6/15/2003
0.56Q	7/17/2003	8/11/2003	8/13/2003	9/15/2003
0.56Q	10/16/2003	11/7/2003	11/12/2003	12/15/2003
0.565Q	1/22/2004	2/9/2004	2/11/2004	3/15/2004

Indicated Div: $2.26 (Div. Reinv. Plan)

Valuation Analysis

Forecast P/E	14.01	Trailing P/E	18.69
Market Cap	$9.4 Billion	Book Value	6.6 Billion
Price/Book	1.47	Price/Sales	0.99

Dividend Achiever Status

Rank	299	10 Year Growth Rate	1.45%
Total Years of Dividend Growth	29		

Business Summary: Electricity (MIC: 7.1 SIC: 4931 NAIC:221121)

Consolidated Edison provides a range of energy−related products and services through six subsidiaries. Consolidated Edison Company of New York is a regulated utility providing electric, gas and steam service to New York City and Westchester County, New York. Orange and Rockland Utilities is a regulated utility serving customers in southeastern New York state and adjacent sections of New Jersey and northeastern Pennsylvania. Con Edison Solutions is a retail energy services company and Con Edison Energy is a wholesale energy supply company. Con Edison Development is an infrastructure development company and Con Edison Communications is a telecommunications infrastructure company.

Recent Developments: For the twelve months ended Dec 31 2003, income declined 21.29% to $536.0 million compared with $680.6 million in 2002. Results were hampered by the recent economic slowdown and increased costs at Con Edison of New York. Results for 2003 included a one−time, after−tax goodwill impairment charge of $94.0 million related to telecommunications and other unregulated assets. Results excluded after−tax income of $3.0 million in 2003 and a loss of $22.0 million in 2002 from accounting change charges. Total operating revenues rose 15.6% to $9.83 billion from $8.50 billion in the prior year. Operating income decreased 11.9% to $934.0 million compared with $1.06 billion the year before.

Prospects: Co. expects earnings per share for full−year 2004 in the range of $2.60 to $2.80. This forecast reflects increased pension and other post−retirement benefit costs, insurance premiums and depreciation expense, partially offset by sales growth. Meanwhile, Con Edison of New York has filed gas and steam rate proposals that are scheduled to take effect in October 2004 and expects to file an electric rate proposal in the spring of 2004, which would take effect in April 2005. Separately, regulated utility construction expenditures for 2004 are estimated to be $1.10 billion versus $1.20 billion in 2003. Unregulated subsidiary construction expenditures are estimated to be $30.0 million in 2004.

Financial Data

(US$ in Thousands)	12/31/2003	12/31/2002	12/31/2001	12/31/2000	12/31/1999	12/31/1998	12/31/1997	12/31/1996
Earnings Per Share	2.36	3.13	3.21	2.74	3.13	3.04	2.95	2.93
Cash Flow Per Share	5.94	7.03	6.34	4.52	5.39	5.82	5.26	4.71
Tang. Book Val. Per Share	29.14	25.39	24.21	26.39	25.90	25.87	25.18	24.37
Dividends Per Share	2.240	2.220	2.200	2.180	2.140	2.120	2.100	2.080
Dividend Payout %	94.91	70.92	68.53	79.56	68.37	69.73	71.20	71.10
Income Statement								
Total Revenues	9,827,000	8,481,860	9,633,962	9,431,391	7,491,323	7,093,048	7,121,254	6,959,736
Total Indirect Exp.	2,236,000	1,913,362	2,129,915	2,026,040	2,105,694	2,134,255	2,066,770	2,059,771
Costs & Expenses	8,893,000	7,421,724	8,506,489	8,415,255	6,471,524	6,039,723	6,075,866	5,946,145
Depreciation & Amort.	529,000	494,553	526,235	586,407	526,182	518,514	502,779	496,412
Operating Income	934,000	1,060,136	1,127,473	1,016,136	1,019,799	1,053,325	1,045,388	1,013,591
Net Interest Inc./(Exp.)	(434,000)	(441,582)	(430,880)	(407,445)	(337,563)	(325,825)	(333,061)	(323,522)
Income Taxes	(117,000)	71,789	(21,922)	(10,622)	(26,891)	(2,229)	(3,190)	(970)
Income from Cont Ops	536,000	680,554	695,835	596,428	714,208	729,749	712,823	694,085
Net Income	528,000	646,036	682,242	582,835	700,615	712,742	694,479	688,169
Average Shs. Outstg.	221,800	214,049	212,919	212,186	223,442	234,308	235,082	234,977
Balance Sheet								
Net Property	15,225,000	13,329,175	12,248,375	11,893,419	11,353,845	11,406,543	11,267,102	11,067,310
Total Assets	20,966,000	18,820,310	16,996,111	16,767,245	15,531,476	14,381,403	14,722,518	14,057,185
Long−Term Obligations	6,769,000	6,206,917	5,542,305	5,446,913	4,559,148	4,087,403	4,228,785	4,281,283
Net Stockholders' Equity	6,423,000	5,921,079	5,629,218	5,435,339	5,374,957	5,988,555	5,845,529	5,643,018
Shares Outstanding	202,629	213,932	212,146	188,816	192,452	232,833	235,490	234,994
Statistical Record								
Operating Profit Margin %	9.50	12.49	11.70	10.77	13.61	14.85	14.67	14.56
Net Inc./Net Property %	3.46	4.84	5.57	4.90	6.17	6.24	6.16	6.21
Net Inc./Tot. Capital %	3.24	4.39	5.07	4.40	5.72	5.69	5.57	5.59
Return on Equity %	8.34	11.49	12.28	10.89	13.19	12.11	12.02	12.11
Accum. Depr./Gross Prop. %	21.08	25.94	26.75	30.75	29.57	29.47	28.23	28.10
Price Range	45.99-37.00	45.10-33.58	42.18-32.38	39.25-26.19	52.88-33.75	55.94-39.63	41.31-27.13	34.38-26.13
P/E Ratio	19.49-15.68	14.41-10.73	13.14-10.09	14.32-9.56	16.89-10.78	18.40-13.03	14.00-9.19	11.73-8.92
Average Yield %	5.53	5.35	5.72	6.65	4.89	4.57	6.14	6.87

Address: 4 Irving Place, New York, NY 10003	**Officers:** Eugene R. McGrath − Chmn., Pres., C.E.O., Joan S. Freilich − Exec. V.P., C.F.O.	**Investor Contact:** (212) 460−6611
Telephone: (212) 460−4600	**Transfer Agents:** The Bank of New York, New York, NY	**Institutional Holding** **No of Institutions:** 50
Web Site: www.conedison.com		**Shares:** 2,057,774 **% Held:** −

CORUS BANKSHARES, INC.

Exchange	Symbol	Price	52Wk Range	Yield	P/E
NMS	CORS	$40.29 (3/31/2004)	40.59-19.99	3.10	19.75

*7 Year Price Score 127.9 *NYSE Composite Index=100 ***12 Month Price Score 109.8**

Interim Earnings (Per Share)

Qtr.	Mar	Jun	Sep	Dec
2000	0.40	0.64	0.55	1.02
2001	0.49	0.51	0.41	0.48
2002	0.36	0.48	0.50	0.38
2003	0.44	0.44	0.56	0.60

Interim Dividends (Per Share)

Amt	Decl	Ex	Rec	Pay
0.25Q	8/8/2003	9/24/2003	9/27/2003	10/10/2003
2-for-1	11/19/2003	12/16/2003	12/1/2003	12/15/2003
0.25Q	11/19/2003	12/23/2003	12/27/2003	1/10/2004
0.313Q	2/6/2004	3/23/2004	3/25/2004	4/9/2004

Indicated Div: $1.25

Valuation Analysis

Forecast P/E	13.29	Trailing P/E	19.75
Market Cap	$570.5 Million	Book Value	518.4 Million
Price/Book	N/A	Price/Sales	N/A

Dividend Achiever Status

Rank	49	10 Year Growth Rate	17.42%
Total Years of Dividend Growth			17

Business Summary: Commercial Banking (MIC: 8.1 SIC: 6022 NAIC:522110)

Corus Bankshares is a bank holding company with total assets of $3.64 billion as of Dec 31 2003. Co. provides consumer and corporate banking products and services through its wholly-owned banking subsidiary, Corus Bank, N.A. The two main business activities for Co. are commercial real estate lending and deposit gathering. The third, and smaller, business is servicing the check cashing industry. The bank has eleven retail branches in the Chicago metropolitan area and offers general banking services such as checking, savings, money market and time deposit accounts, as well as safe deposit boxes and a variety of additional services.

Recent Developments: For the year ended Dec 31 2003, net income increased 18.4% to $58.4 million compared with $49.3 million a year earlier. Net interest income advanced 25.6% to $123.4 million from $98.3 million the previous year, primarily due to strong loan growth. Provision for loan losses amounted to nil in 2003 and 2002. Total noninterest income declined 26.7% to $16.9 million versus $23.1 million last year, reflecting lower net securities and other financial instrument gains of $2.4 million for 2003 compared with $7.3 million for 2002. Total nonperforming assets increased to $15.6 million, or 0.43% of total assets, versus $7.3 million, or 0.28% of total assets, the year before.

Prospects: Co.'s near-term outlook appears favorable, reflecting its successful commercial real estate lending growth strategy of concentrating a large portion of its assets in commercial real estate loans. It should be noted that Co. has taken steps to reduce its risk by diversifying its commercial real estate portfolio geographically and by property type, including 49.0% secured by condominiums, 19.0% by hotel, 15.0% by office, and 11.0% by residential apartment projects. The remaining 6.0% are secured by retail, industrial, vacant land and other types of property. Additionally, Co.'s business continues to be divided between construction lending and loans that are fully funded from the outset.

Financial Data

(US$ in Thousands)	12/31/2003	12/31/2002	12/31/2001	12/31/2000	12/31/1999	12/31/1998	12/31/1997	12/31/1996
Earnings Per Share	2.04	1.72	1.89	2.61	1.41	1.37	1.31	1.46
Tang. Book Val. Per Share	19.31	16.91	15.76	14.03	11.09	10.57	9.62	7.53
Dividends Per Share	0.660	0.310	0.300	0.290	0.280	0.270	0.260	0.220
Dividend Payout %	32.35	18.26	16.09	11.28	20.21	20.00	19.77	15.07
Income Statement								
Total Interest Income	170,239	152,878	188,630	223,676	196,580	187,525	183,932	190,950
Total Interest Expense	46,812	54,591	80,921	102,625	90,449	89,305	82,661	79,611
Net Interest Income	123,427	98,287	107,709	121,051	106,131	98,220	101,271	111,339
Provision for Loan Losses	...	...	...	...	...	10,000	16,000	16,000
Non-Interest Income	14,554	15,821	17,881	36,416	20,241	20,539	21,811	19,436
Non-Interest Expense	52,533	47,472	51,100	52,908	63,096	51,889	51,677	50,181
Income Before Taxes	87,814	73,894	82,325	113,657	61,983	61,997	60,507	67,910
Net Income	58,410	49,314	54,183	74,754	40,726	40,628	39,371	43,905
Average Shs. Outstg.	28,703	28,590	28,618	28,604	28,928	29,546	29,932	29,988
Balance Sheet								
Cash & Due from Banks	63,524	61,560	58,514	111,115	72,316	72,050	62,217	57,508
Securities Avail. for Sale	244,062	272,799						
Net Loans & Leases	2,397,323	1,705,340	1,434,788	1,512,279	1,695,267	1,515,814	1,515,315	1,590,477
Total Assets	3,643,630	2,617,050	2,659,322	2,598,467	2,388,198	2,589,415	2,251,927	2,218,528
Total Deposits	2,846,402	2,059,773	2,121,456	2,107,630	1,964,420	2,154,676	1,863,066	1,900,679
Long-Term Obligations	208,903	48,110	55,816	41,085	46,866	64,933	49,264	46,317
Total Liabilities	3,097,650	2,135,009	2,208,436	2,196,114	2,060,373	2,271,285	1,960,294	1,982,938
Net Stockholders' Equity	546,180	482,041	450,886	402,353	327,825	318,130	291,633	235,590
Shares Outstanding	28,036	28,238	28,319	28,286	28,738	29,102	29,362	29,640
Statistical Record								
Return on Equity %	10.69	10.23	12.01	18.57	12.42	12.77	13.50	18.63
Return on Assets %	1.60	1.88	2.03	2.87	1.70	1.56	1.74	1.97
Equity/Assets %	14.98	18.41	16.95	15.48	13.72	12.28	12.95	10.61
Non-Int. Exp./Tot. Inc. %	28.42	28.14	24.74	20.34	29.10	24.93	25.11	23.85
Price Range	32.09-19.73	26.69-19.49	30.58-20.26	24.94-10.22	17.94-11.50	23.44-14.31	19.88-11.75	16.50-12.50
P/E Ratio	15.73-9.67	15.52-11.33	16.18-10.72	9.55-3.92	12.72-8.16	17.11-10.45	15.17-8.97	11.30-8.56
Average Yield %	2.64	1.33	1.22	1.92	1.84	1.38	1.58	1.47

Address: 3959 N. Lincoln Avenue, Chicago, IL 60613-2431 **Telephone:** (773) 832-3088 **Web Site:** www.corusbank.com	**Officers:** Joseph C. Glickman – Chmn., Robert J. Glickman – Pres., C.E.O.	**Investor Contact:**773-832-3088 **Institutional Holding** **No of Institutions:** 2 **Shares:** 600 **% Held:** –

COURIER CORP.

Exchange	Symbol	Price	52Wk Range	Yield	P/E
NMS	CRRC	$44.89 (3/31/2004)	45.61–31.74	0.78	18.84

*7 Year Price Score 211.9 *NYSE Composite Index=100 *12 Month Price Score 99.6

TRADING VOLUME (thousand shares)

Interim Earnings (Per Share)

Qtr.	Dec	Mar	Jun	Sep
2000–01	0.38	0.27	0.37	0.67
2001–02	0.33	0.36	0.50	0.83
2002–03	0.46	0.46	0.58	0.87
2003–04	0.48	...	...	...

Interim Dividends (Per Share)

Amt	Decl	Ex	Rec	Pay
0.075Q	7/17/2003	8/6/2003	8/8/2003	8/29/2003
0.088Q	11/6/2003	11/13/2003	11/17/2003	12/5/2003
50%	11/6/2003	12/8/2003	11/17/2003	12/5/2003
0.088Q	1/15/2004	2/11/2004	2/13/2004	2/27/2004
		Indicated Div: $0.35		

Valuation Analysis

Forecast P/E	13.95	Trailing P/E	18.84
Market Cap	$232.5 Million	Book Value	119.1 Million
Price/Book	2.66	Price/Sales	1.58

Dividend Achiever Status

Rank	4	10 Year Growth Rate 35.65%
Total Years of Dividend Growth		10

Business Summary: Printing (MIC: 13.4 SIC: 2732 NAIC:323117)

Courier and its subsidiaries are engaged in book manufacturing and specialty publishing. Co. has two business segments. Co.'s book manufacturing segment produces hard and softcover books, as well as related services involved in managing the process of creating and distributing these products. Co.'s specialty publishing segment publishes over 30 specialty categories, including fine and commercial arts, children's books, crafts, musical scores, graphic design, mathematics, physics and other areas of science, puzzles, games, social science, stationery items, and classics of literature for both juvenile and adult markets, including the Dover Thrift Editions.

Recent Developments: For the three months ended Dec 27 2003, net income totaled $3.9 million, up 4.3% compared with income from continuing operations of $3.7 million in the corresponding prior–year period. Net sales slipped 4.0% to $46.8 million from $48.8 million the previous year. Gross profit climbed 1.6% to $15.6 million, or 33.4% of net sales, versus $15.4 million, or 31.5% of net sales, a year earlier. Selling and administrative expenses declined 0.6% to $9.6 million from $9.7 million the year before. Income before taxes was $6.0 million, up 6.6% compared with $5.6 million in 2002.

Prospects: Sales are being hampered by lower book manufacturing sales, reflecting reduced volume to the education and specialty trade publishing markets, partially offset by increased sales in Co.'s specialty book publishing segment. During the current fiscal year, book manufacturing sales are expected to benefit from the addition of significant new accounts from several religious trade publishers, as well as strong customer response to Co.'s expanding four–color capabilities. Looking ahead, Co. is targeting full fiscal–2004 sales of between $216.0 million and $221.0 million, and earnings per share in the range of $2.57 to $2.67.

Financial Data

(US$ in Thousands)	3 Mos	09/27/2003	09/28/2002	09/29/2001	09/30/2000	09/25/1999	09/26/1998	09/27/1997
Earnings Per Share	0.48	2.37	2.02	1.69	1.40	1.12	1.05	0.62
Cash Flow Per Share	0.57	3.83	3.62	3.60	2.96	1.92	1.72	2.03
Tang. Book Val. Per Share	11.87	11.42	9.00	7.15	5.54	6.43	5.37	4.44
Dividends Per Share	0.310	0.300	0.260	0.240	0.210	0.180	0.170	0.140
Dividend Payout %	65.10	12.65	13.15	14.17	15.23	16.66	16.24	22.69
Income Statement								
Total Revenues	46,819	202,002	202,184	211,943	188,320	163,991	151,591	131,433
Total Indirect Exp.	9,638	37,898	40,562	42,006	32,414	28,774	25,173	23,291
Depreciation & Amort.	2,590	9,798	10,687	1,466	8,062	8,282	8,541	7,237
Operating Income	5,991	29,526	24,111	20,034	15,886	12,557	11,755	6,004
Net Interest Inc./(Exp.)	27	(52)	(480)	(1,899)	(325)	(524)	(1,303)	(867)
Income Taxes	2,106	10,254	7,936	6,817	5,249	4,181	4,030	1,688
Income from Cont Ops	...	19,272	...	...	...	...	...	...
Net Income	3,912	20,120	16,115	13,217	10,637	8,376	7,725	4,316
Average Shs. Outstg.	8,189	8,120	7,992	7,797	7,589	7,467	7,321	6,900
Balance Sheet								
Cash & Cash Equivalents	22,838	23,824	5,630	173	562	3,460	722	27
Total Current Assets	76,196	77,673	61,722	59,709	71,353	49,266	42,096	38,063
Total Assets	152,091	151,101	131,658	133,615	142,241	91,512	87,630	89,643
Total Current Liabilities	23,424	26,813	27,755	31,029	38,006	27,351	25,569	23,975
Long–Term Obligations	573	593	674	16,501	31,327	1,193	6,781	18,593
Net Stockholders' Equity	119,102	115,420	95,919	80,325	67,771	57,559	49,790	41,748
Net Working Capital	52,772	50,860	33,967	28,680	33,347	21,915	16,527	14,088
Shares Outstanding	7,934	7,931	7,822	7,668	7,524	7,274	7,137	6,773
Statistical Record								
Operating Profit Margin %	12.79	14.61	11.92	9.45	8.43	7.65	7.75	4.56
Return on Equity %	3.28	16.69	16.86	16.45	15.69	14.55	15.51	10.33
Return on Assets %	2.57	12.75	12.28	9.89	7.47	9.15	8.81	4.81
Debt/Total Assets %	0.37	0.39	0.51	12.34	22.02	1.30	7.73	20.74
Price Range	39.51–33.94	37.33–23.61	29.67–14.00	19.10–12.00	13.67–9.50	13.78–8.00	13.33–6.15	6.44–3.85
P/E Ratio	82.32–70.71	15.75–9.96	14.69–6.93	11.30–7.10	9.76–6.79	12.30–7.14	12.70–5.86	10.39–6.21
Average Yield %	0.83	0.95	1.08	1.62	1.87	1.77	1.76	2.77

Address: 15 Wellman Avenue, North Chelmsford, MA 01863 Telephone: (978) 251–6000 Web Site: www.courier.com	Officers: James F. Conway III – Chmn., Pres., C.E.O., George Q. Nichols – Corp. Sr. V.P.	Investor Contact: (978) 251–6000 Institutional Holding No of Institutions: 52 Shares: 2,108,888 % Held: 42%

CULLEN/FROST BANKERS, INC.

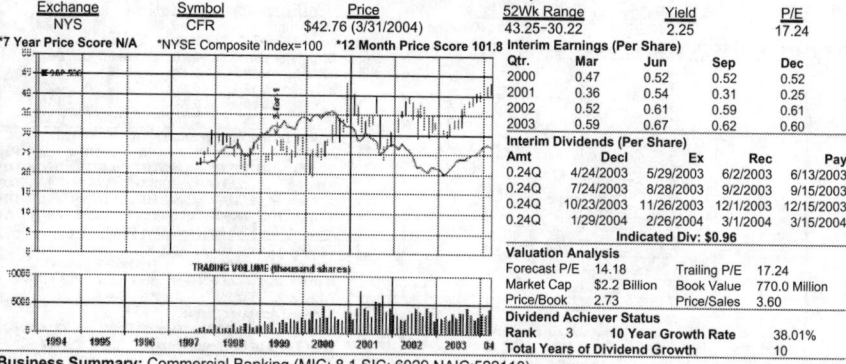

Exchange	Symbol	Price	52Wk Range	Yield	P/E
NYS	CFR	$42.76 (3/31/2004)	43.25-30.22	2.25	17.24

*7 Year Price Score N/A   *NYSE Composite Index=100   *12 Month Price Score 101.8

Interim Earnings (Per Share)

Qtr.	Mar	Jun	Sep	Dec
2000	0.47	0.52	0.52	0.52
2001	0.36	0.54	0.31	0.25
2002	0.52	0.61	0.59	0.61
2003	0.59	0.67	0.62	0.60

Interim Dividends (Per Share)

Amt	Decl	Ex	Rec	Pay
0.24Q	4/24/2003	5/29/2003	6/2/2003	6/13/2003
0.24Q	7/24/2003	8/28/2003	9/2/2003	9/15/2003
0.24Q	10/23/2003	11/26/2003	12/1/2003	12/15/2003
0.24Q	1/29/2004	2/26/2004	3/1/2004	3/15/2004

Indicated Div: $0.96

Valuation Analysis

Forecast P/E	14.18	Trailing P/E	17.24
Market Cap	$2.2 Billion	Book Value	770.0 Million
Price/Book	2.73	Price/Sales	3.60

Dividend Achiever Status

Rank	3	10 Year Growth Rate	38.01%
Total Years of Dividend Growth			10

Business Summary: Commercial Banking (MIC: 8.1 SIC: 6029 NAIC:522110)

Cullen/Frost Bankers is a financial holding company offering a broad range of banking and financial services to retail and commercial customers throughout Texas. As of Dec 31 2003, Co. operated 79 financial centers in Texas through its wholly-owned subsidiary, The Frost National Bank. In addition to general commercial banking, Co.'s other product and services include trust and investment management, investment banking, insurance brokerage, leasing, asset-based lending, treasury management and item processing. As of Dec 31 2003, Co. had consolidated total assets of $9.67 billion and total deposits of $8.07 billion.

Recent Developments: For the year ended Dec 31 2003, net income totaled $130.5 million, up 6.8% compared with income from continuing operations of $122.2 million in the corresponding period a year earlier. Net interest income was $313.8 million, essentially flat versus the previous year. Provision for possible loan losses fell 53.2% to $10.5 million from $22.5 million in 2002. Total non-interest income grew 7.2% to $215.4 million from $201.0 million the year before. Total non-interest expense increased 4.5% to $326.0 million from $312.1 million the prior year. Income before income taxes climbed 6.9% to $192.5 million from $180.1 million a year earlier.

Prospects: Earnings are being positively affected by continued growth of non-interest income. This growth is being fueled primarily by increases in overdraft fees on individual and commercial accounts, along with higher trust fees stemming from increased investment levels due to improved market conditions. Meanwhile, net interest income is being hampered by continued pressure from low interest rates, partially offset by strong deposit growth and an increase in average earning assets. Looking ahead, results may benefit from Co.'s efforts to control expenses.

Financial Data

(US$ in Thousands)	12/31/2003	12/31/2002	12/31/2001	12/31/2000	12/31/1999	12/31/1998	12/31/1997	12/31/1996
Earnings Per Share	2.48	2.33	1.46	2.03	1.78	1.38	1.37	1.19
Tang. Book Val. Per Share	12.65	11.39	11.58	11.14	9.64	9.60	9.17	8.42
Dividends Per Share	0.940	0.870	0.840	0.760	0.670	0.570	0.480	0.400
Dividend Payout %	37.90	37.55	57.53	37.43	37.92	41.51	34.90	33.68
Income Statement								
Total Interest Income	368,946	389,898	460,976	512,331	447,580	428,091	324,715	290,513
Total Interest Expense	55,188	75,865	144,759	189,568	150,602	160,118	127,471	111,431
Net Interest Income	313,758	314,033	316,217	322,763	296,978	267,973	197,244	179,082
Provision for Loan Losses	10,544	22,546	40,031	14,103	12,427	10,393	7,900	7,300
Non-Interest Income	215,361	200,709	192,891	170,865	157,085	138,666	109,332	94,535
Non-Interest Expense	326,035	312,142	352,606	313,280	293,015	278,506	199,956	180,580
Income Before Taxes	192,540	180,054	116,471	166,245	148,621	117,740	98,720	85,737
Income from Cont Ops	...	122,233	77,906	...	...	...	...	...
Net Income	130,501	116,986	80,916	108,817	97,642	75,645	63,485	54,978
Average Shs. Outstg.	52,658	52,423	53,348	53,657	54,746	54,678	46,130	46,034
Balance Sheet								
Cash & Due from Banks	1,067,888	1,331,136	994,622	820,459	760,612	684,941	604,227	872,028
Securities Avail. for Sale	2,946,327	2,422,121	2,105,365	1,597,331	1,544,866	1,980,264	1,342,759	1,299,285
Net Loans & Leases	4,507,245	4,436,329	4,445,727	4,471,380	4,108,383	3,592,987	2,601,676	2,215,842
Total Assets	9,672,114	9,552,318	8,369,584	7,660,372	6,996,680	6,869,605	5,230,588	4,888,384
Total Deposits	8,068,857	7,628,143	7,098,007	6,499,690	5,953,832	5,845,487	4,483,911	4,242,594
Long-Term Obligations	255,845	149,445	152,152	...	...	...	...	...
Total Liabilities	8,902,110	8,848,528	7,774,665	7,087,346	6,487,369	6,356,686	4,822,183	4,509,441
Net Stockholders' Equity	770,004	703,790	594,919	573,026	509,311	512,919	408,405	378,943
Shares Outstanding	51,776	51,295	51,355	51,430	52,823	53,426	44,530	44,964
Statistical Record								
Return on Equity %	16.94	17.36	13.09	18.98	19.17	14.74	15.54	14.50
Return on Assets %	1.34	1.27	0.93	1.42	1.39	1.10	1.21	1.12
Equity/Assets %	7.96	7.36	7.10	7.48	7.27	7.46	7.80	7.75
Non-Int. Exp./Tot. Inc. %	55.79	52.85	53.92	45.85	48.45	49.14	46.06	46.89
Price Range	41.00-29.40	40.04-29.40	41.19-23.84	43.19-19.63	29.94-23.00	30.47-20.78	31.09-22.13	...
P/E Ratio	16.53-11.85	17.18-12.62	28.21-16.33	21.27-9.67	16.82-12.92	22.08-15.06	22.70-16.15	...
Average Yield %	2.69	2.52	2.54	2.69	2.56	2.12	1.89	N/A

Address: 100 W. Houston Street, San Antonio, TX 78205 **Telephone:** (210) 220-4011 **Web Site:** www.frostbank.com	**Officers:** Tom C. Frost – Sr. Chmn., Richard W. Evans – Chmn., C.E.O. **Transfer Agents:** Bank of New York, New York, NY	**Institutional Holding** No of Institutions: 13 Shares: 794,060 % Held: –

CVB FINANCIAL CORP.

Exchange	Symbol	Price	52Wk Range	Yield	P/E
NMS	CVBF	$20.76 (3/31/2004)	21.30–16.69	2.31	19.22

*7 Year Price Score 167.4 *NYSE Composite Index=100 *12 Month Price Score 91.1

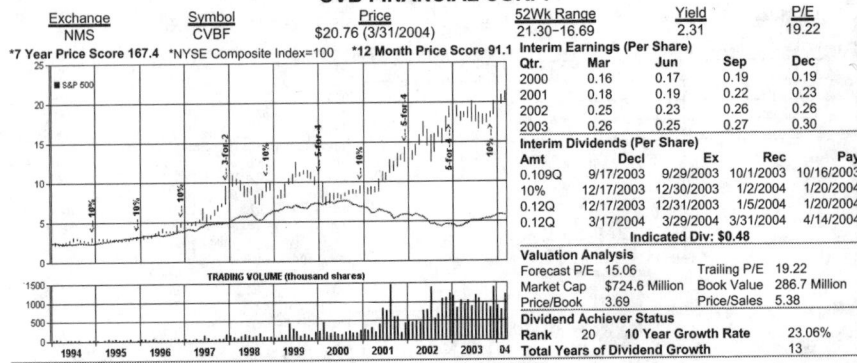

Interim Earnings (Per Share)

Qtr.	Mar	Jun	Sep	Dec
2000	0.16	0.17	0.19	0.19
2001	0.18	0.19	0.22	0.23
2002	0.25	0.23	0.26	0.26
2003	0.26	0.25	0.27	0.30

Interim Dividends (Per Share)

Amt	Decl	Ex	Rec	Pay
0.109Q	9/17/2003	9/29/2003	10/1/2003	10/16/2003
10%	12/17/2003	12/30/2003	1/2/2004	1/20/2004
0.12Q	12/17/2003	12/31/2003	1/5/2004	1/20/2004
0.12Q	3/17/2004	3/29/2004	3/31/2004	4/14/2004

Indicated Div: $0.48

Valuation Analysis

Forecast P/E	15.06	Trailing P/E	19.22
Market Cap	$724.6 Million	Book Value	286.7 Million
Price/Book	3.69	Price/Sales	5.38

Dividend Achiever Status

Rank	20	10 Year Growth Rate	23.06%
Total Years of Dividend Growth			13

Business Summary: Commercial Banking (MIC: 8.1 SIC: 6022 NAIC:522110)

CVB Financial is a bank holding company, with assets of $3.85 billion and deposits of $2.66 billion as of Dec 31 2003. Co.'s Citizens Business Bank, operates 37 business financial centers located in the Inland Empire, San Gabriel Valley, Orange County, Los Angeles County, Fresno County, Tulare County and Kern County. Co. provides a full complement of banking products and services to businesses and consumers, including asset management services. Golden West Enterprises, Inc. provides automobile and equipment leasing, and brokers mortgage loans. Community Trust Deed Services prepares and files notices of default and reconveyances and acts as a trustee under deeds of trust.

Recent Developments: For the year ended Dec 31 2003, net earnings increased 6.2% to $52.8 million compared with $49.7 million in the previous year. Net interest income advanced 13.5% to $129.3 million from $113.9 million a year earlier. There were no provisions for credit losses in either 2003 or 2002. Total interest income rose 7.8% to $166.3 million, reflecting an increase in average earning assets. Total interest expense declined 8.4% to $37.1 million. Non-interest income grew 3.3% to $30.0 million. Non-interest expense climbed 17.8% to $77.8 million. Return on average assets amounted to 1.54% versus 1.83% in 2002. Return on average equity decreased to 19.17% from 20.45% the year before.

Prospects: Co.'s recent acquisition of Kaweah National Bank is seen as an excellent complement to Co.'s existing business financial centers in Bakersfield and Fresno, CA. Looking ahead, Co. continues to strive to grow its business both internally and through strategic acquisitions. Co.'s long-term plans anticipates that assets will grow to $5.00 billion by the end of 2005 and $10.00 billion by the end of 2010. Separately, Co. and its principal subsidiary, Citizens Business Bank, expect to benefit from solid growth in the near term due to the recent stability of interest rates.

Financial Data

(US$ in Thousands)	12/31/2003	12/31/2002	12/31/2001	12/31/2000	12/31/1999	12/31/1998	12/31/1997	12/31/1996
Earnings Per Share	1.08	1.00	0.82	0.71	0.53	0.51	0.42	0.50
Tang. Book Val. Per Share	5.38	5.09	4.48	3.81	2.83	2.71	2.57	2.98
Dividends Per Share	0.430	0.400	0.320	0.250	0.200	0.150	0.100	0.070
Dividend Payout %	40.40	39.63	38.93	35.47	37.64	30.05	23.46	14.00
Income Statement								
Total Interest Income	166,346	154,323	155,877	150,867	128,478	96,840	84,656	74,894
Total Interest Expense	37,053	40,439	52,806	56,760	38,466	31,248	24,976	21,446
Net Interest Income	129,293	113,884	103,071	94,107	90,012	65,592	59,680	53,428
Provision for Loan Losses	...	...	1,750	2,800	2,700	2,500	2,670	2,888
Non-Interest Income	29,989	29,018	22,192	19,023	18,630	14,976	13,823	14,279
Non-Interest Expense	77,794	66,056	60,155	56,345	64,737	45,024	42,890	41,909
Income Before Taxes	81,488	76,846	63,358	53,985	41,205	33,043	27,943	22,910
Net Income	52,832	49,745	40,058	34,683	25,960	20,787	17,370	13,333
Average Shs. Outstg.	49,110	49,035	48,695	48,410	48,146	40,697	40,525	26,722
Balance Sheet								
Cash & Due from Banks	112,008	124,973	82,651	130,315	118,360	100,033	107,725	142,502
Securities Avail. for Sale	1,865,782	1,452,499	1,181,503	1,070,074	877,322	676,162	434,106	333,348
Net Loans & Leases	1,738,659	1,424,343	1,167,071	1,032,341	935,791	675,668	605,484	576,687
Total Assets	3,854,349	3,123,411	2,514,102	2,307,996	2,010,757	1,555,207	1,258,769	1,160,421
Total Deposits	2,660,510	2,309,964	1,876,959	1,595,030	1,501,073	1,215,305	1,075,695	990,597
Long-Term Obligations	467,310	286,888	334,999	11,234	16,951	95	7,922	12,610
Total Liabilities	3,567,628	2,863,590	2,293,354	2,119,366	1,869,987	1,439,500	1,156,684	1,071,334
Net Stockholders' Equity	286,721	259,821	220,748	188,630	140,770	115,707	102,085	89,087
Shares Outstanding	48,289	47,886	47,825	47,539	46,730	39,070	35,389	25,925
Statistical Record								
Return on Equity %	18.42	19.14	18.14	18.38	18.44	17.96	17.01	14.96
Return on Assets %	1.37	1.59	1.59	1.50	1.29	1.33	1.37	1.14
Equity/Assets %	7.43	8.31	8.78	8.17	7.00	7.43	8.10	7.67
Non-Int. Exp./Tot. Inc. %	39.62	36.02	33.78	33.16	44.00	40.26	43.55	46.99
Price Range	20.12-16.69	19.43-12.51	14.28-8.44	10.53-7.14	12.54-7.96	11.08-7.21	9.55-4.58	4.87-3.00
P/E Ratio	18.63-15.45	19.43-12.51	17.42-10.29	14.82-10.06	23.65-15.02	21.73-14.14	22.74-10.91	9.73-6.00
Average Yield %	2.33	2.57	2.97	2.94	2.00	1.65	1.69	1.90

Address: 701 North Haven Avenue, ON, CA 91764 **Telephone:** (909) 980-4030 **Web Site:** www.cvbcorp.com	**Officers:** George A. Borba - Chmn., D. Linn Wiley - Pres., C.E.O.	**Investor Contact:**909-980-4030 **Institutional Holding** **No of Institutions:** 13 **Shares:** 3,582,555 **% Held:** -

DANAHER CORP.

Exchange	Symbol	Price	52Wk Range	Yield	P/E
NYS	DHR	$93.37 (3/31/2004)	95.36-65.00	0.11	27.71

7 Year Price Score 141.1   *NYSE Composite Index=100   *12 Month Price Score 104.8

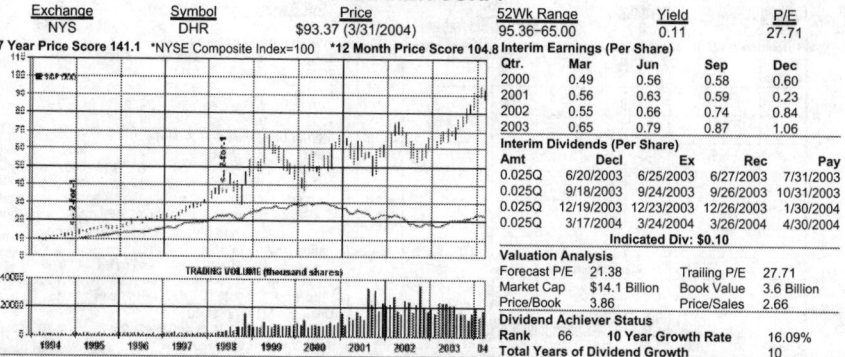

Interim Earnings (Per Share)

Qtr.	Mar	Jun	Sep	Dec
2000	0.49	0.56	0.58	0.60
2001	0.56	0.63	0.59	0.23
2002	0.55	0.66	0.74	0.84
2003	0.65	0.79	0.87	1.06

Interim Dividends (Per Share)

Amt	Decl	Ex	Rec	Pay
0.025Q	6/20/2003	6/25/2003	6/27/2003	7/31/2003
0.025Q	9/18/2003	9/24/2003	9/26/2003	10/31/2003
0.025Q	12/19/2003	12/23/2003	12/26/2003	1/30/2004
0.025Q	3/17/2004	3/24/2004	3/26/2004	4/30/2004

Indicated Div: $0.10

Valuation Analysis

Forecast P/E	21.38	Trailing P/E	27.71
Market Cap	$14.1 Billion	Book Value	3.6 Billion
Price/Book	3.86	Price/Sales	2.66

Dividend Achiever Status

Rank	66	10 Year Growth Rate	16.09%
Total Years of Dividend Growth			10

Business Summary: Metal Products (MIC: 11.4 SIC: 3429 NAIC:332510)

Danaher conducts its operations through two business segments: Process/Environmental Controls and Tools & Components. The Process/Environmental Controls segment encompasses five strategic platforms (Motion, Environmental, Electronic Test, Medical Technologies and Product Identification) and three focused niche businesses (Power Quality, Aerospace and Defense, and Industrial Controls). The Tools & Components segment encompasses one strategic platform, Mechanics'Hand Tools, and five focused niche businesses. Products are distributed by Co.'s sales personnel and independent representatives to distributors, end-users, and original equipment manufacturers.

Recent Developments: For the year ended Dec 31 2003, net income was $536.8 million compared with income of $434.1 million, before a tax credit of $30.0 million and an accounting change charge of $173.8 million, the previous year. Results for 2003 and 2002 included non-recurring gains of $23.3 million and $6.2 million, respectively. The 2002 results also included a pre-tax restructuring charge of $6.3 million. Net sales increased 15.7% to $5.29 billion from $4.58 billion the year before. The improvement in sales was largely due to the strong performance of Co.'s business segments. Operating income advanced 20.7% to $846.0 million versus $701.1 million the prior year.

Prospects: On Feb 27 2004, Co. announced that it completed the acquisition of the Gendex division of DENTSPLY International, Inc. for approximately $102.5 million in cash. Gendex is a manufacturer of dental imaging products, including intra-oral and panoramic x-ray machines, digital radiography systems, intra-oral cameras, and film processors. Meanwhile, Co. should continue to benefit from solid growth in its Process/Environmental Controls and Tools and Components segments. Looking ahead, Co. is optimistic about its ability to perform well in 2004 primarily due to increasing signs of economic recovery.

Financial Data

(US$ in Thousands)	12/31/2003	12/31/2002	12/31/2001	12/31/2000	12/31/1999	12/31/1998	12/31/1997	12/31/1996
Earnings Per Share	3.37	2.79	2.01	2.23	1.79	1.32	1.28	1.06
Cash Flow Per Share	5.33	4.48	4.00	3.52	2.86	2.38	2.30	1.81
Tang. Book Val. Per Share	1.98	0.01	N.M	0.55	2.92	0.49	0.60	0.06
Dividends Per Share	0.100	0.090	0.080	0.070	0.060	0.055	0.050	0.045
Dividend Payout %	2.96	3.23	3.98	3.14	3.35	4.17	3.89	4.25
Income Statement								
Total Revenues	5,293,876	4,577,232	3,782,444	3,777,777	3,197,238	2,910,038	2,050,968	1,811,878
Total Indirect Exp.	1,270,572	1,084,935	942,406	909,897	778,409	722,116	401,608	345,896
Depreciation & Amort.	133,436	129,565	178,390	149,721	126,419	108,651	76,116	68,626
Operating Income	845,995	701,122	502,011	552,149	458,007	366,838	266,885	226,136
Net Interest Inc./(Exp.)	(48,960)	(43,654)	(25,747)	(29,225)	(16,667)	(24,931)	(13,104)	(16,375)
Income Taxes	260,201	223,327	178,599	198,711	167,938	118,165	198,090	81,801
Income from Cont Ops	...	434,141	...	...	...	...	55,691	127,959
Net Income	536,834	290,391	297,665	324,213	261,624	182,946	154,806	207,770
Average Shs. Outstg.	161,570	158,482	151,848	145,499	146,089	138,885	120,512	119,910
Balance Sheet								
Cash & Cash Equivalents	1,230,156	810,463	706,559	176,924	260,281	41,923	33,317	26,444
Total Current Assets	2,942,151	2,387,266	1,874,615	1,474,306	1,202,117	886,904	618,339	546,741
Total Assets	6,890,050	6,029,145	4,820,483	4,031,679	3,047,071	2,738,715	1,879,717	1,765,074
Total Current Liabilities	1,380,003	1,265,312	1,017,294	1,018,540	708,786	688,705	524,235	474,573
Long-Term Obligations	1,284,498	1,197,422	1,119,333	713,557	341,037	412,918	162,720	219,570
Net Stockholders' Equity	3,646,709	3,009,599	2,228,586	1,942,333	1,708,754	1,351,831	916,881	800,261
Net Working Capital	1,562,148	1,121,954	857,321	455,766	493,331	198,199	94,104	72,168
Shares Outstanding	153,681	152,532	143,314	142,013	142,440	135,107	105,440	117,778
Statistical Record								
Operating Profit Margin %	15.98	15.31	13.27	14.61	14.32	12.60	13.01	12.48
Return on Equity %	14.72	14.42	13.35	16.69	15.31	13.53	6.07	15.98
Return on Assets %	7.79	7.20	6.17	8.04	8.58	6.67	2.96	7.24
Debt/Total Assets %	18.64	19.86	23.22	17.69	11.19	15.07	8.65	12.43
Price Range	91.95-60.45	75.33-53.24	67.69-45.53	68.69-37.13	68.56-43.13	54.31-29.38	31.88-19.81	23.31-14.75
P/E Ratio	27.28-17.94	27.00-19.08	33.68-22.65	30.80-16.65	38.30-24.09	41.15-22.25	24.90-15.48	21.99-13.92
Average Yield %	0.14	0.13	0.14	0.12	0.11	0.13	0.20	0.20

Address: 2099 Pennsylvania Ave. NW, Washington, DC 20006-1813	Officers: Steven M. Rales – Chmn., H. Lawrence Culp – Pres., C.E.O.	Investor Contact:202-828-0850
Telephone: (202) 828-0850	Transfer Agents:SunTrust Bank, Atlanta, GA	Institutional Holding No of Institutions: 440
Web Site: www.danaher.com		Shares: 111,017,252 % Held: 72.60%

DIEBOLD, INC.

Exchange	Symbol	Price	52Wk Range	Yield	P/E
NYS	DBD	$48.12 (3/31/2004)	57.43-34.27	1.54	20.05

*7 Year Price Score 127.1 *NYSE Composite Index=100 *12 Month Price Score 107.4

Interim Earnings (Per Share)

Qtr.	Mar	Jun	Sep	Dec
2000	0.44	0.50	0.49	0.49
2001	0.11	0.39	0.20	0.23
2002	0.37	0.55	0.61	0.30
2003	0.36	0.57	0.66	0.81

Interim Dividends (Per Share)

Amt	Decl	Ex	Rec	Pay
0.17Q	4/24/2003	5/14/2003	5/16/2003	6/6/2003
0.17Q	8/7/2003	8/13/2003	8/15/2003	9/5/2003
0.17Q	10/9/2003	11/12/2003	11/14/2003	12/5/2003
0.185Q	2/11/2004	2/17/2004	2/19/2004	3/11/2004

Indicated Div: $0.74 (Div. Reinv. Plan)

Valuation Analysis

Forecast P/E	20.07	Trailing P/E	20.05
Market Cap	$3.5 Billion	Book Value	1.1 Billion
Price/Book	3.40	Price/Sales	1.85

Dividend Achiever Status

Rank	220	10 Year Growth Rate	6.70%
Total Years of Dividend Growth			50

Business Summary: Office Equipment Supplies (MIC: 11.12 SIC: 3578 NAIC:333313)

Diebold develops, manufactures, sells and services self-service transaction systems, electronic and physical security systems, software and various products used to equip bank facilities to global financial and commercial markets and electronic voting terminals and solutions to the government. Co.'s primary customers include banks and financial institutions, as well as hospitals, colleges and universities, public libraries, government agencies, utilities and various retail outlets. Sales of systems and equipment are made directly to customers by Co.' sales personnel and by manufacturer's representatives and distributors.

Recent Developments: For the year ended Dec 31 2003, net income totaled $174.8 million, up 32.1% compared with income of $132.3 million, before a $33.1 million accounting change charge, in the prior year. Total net sales rose 8.7% to $2.11 billion from $1.94 billion a year earlier. Product net sales advanced 10.2% to $1.09 billion from $992.0 million the year before, while service net sales grew 7.2% to $1.02 billion from $948.2 million the previous year. Gross profit was $627.1 million, or 29.7% of net sales, versus $579.6 million, or 29.9% of net sales, in 2002. Operating profit climbed 9.0% to $262.8 million from $241.2 million the prior year.

Prospects: Results are being positively affected by strong sales of Co.'s security products, driven by market share gains and growth in the financial industry, government, and retail markets. Looking ahead, Co. anticipates first-quarter 2004 earnings of between $0.38 and $0.42 per share, and full-year 2004 earnings in the range of $2.58 to $2.70 per share. In addition, Co. is targeting first-quarter 2004 revenue growth of between 10.0% and 13.0%, driven by strong revenue increases for Co.'s financial self-service products and services, and full-year 2004 revenue growth of between 8.0% and 12.0%.

Financial Data

(US$ in Thousands)	12/31/2003	12/31/2002	12/31/2001	12/31/2000	12/31/1999	12/31/1998	12/31/1997	12/31/1996
Earnings Per Share	2.40	1.83	0.93	1.92	1.85	1.10	1.76	1.42
Cash Flow Per Share	2.87	2.26	2.15	2.04	2.71	2.55	1.60	1.36
Tang. Book Val. Per Share	11.24	9.32	8.79	8.94	9.62	9.86	9.68	8.36
Dividends Per Share	0.680	0.660	0.640	0.620	0.600	0.560	0.500	0.450
Dividend Payout %	28.33	36.06	68.81	32.29	32.43	50.90	28.40	31.69
Income Statement								
Total Revenues	2,109,673	1,940,163	1,760,297	1,743,608	1,259,177	1,185,707	1,226,936	1,030,191
Total Indirect Exp.	364,293	353,469	385,156	330,200	270,689	300,003	246,239	217,574
Depreciation & Amort.	64,301	61,296	45,453	35,901	34,709	25,649	18,701	20,984
Operating Income	262,848	241,169	138,909	228,955	186,123	106,247	183,861	140,364
Net Interest Inc./(Exp.)	(9,285)	(26,679)	(12,668)	(17,681)	...	...	...	...
Income Taxes	82,247	86,250	32,946	67,438	72,482	43,659	63,143	49,079
Income from Cont Ops	...	132,301	...	...	...	...	...	...
Net Income	174,776	99,154	66,893	136,919	128,856	76,148	122,516	97,425
Average Shs. Outstg.	72,924	72,297	71,783	71,479	69,562	69,310	69,490	68,796
Balance Sheet								
Cash & Cash Equivalents	176,101	163,355	125,669	126,512	84,647	79,973	56,769	65,134
Total Current Assets	1,105,159	924,888	952,426	804,363	647,936	543,548	549,837	479,592
Total Assets	1,900,502	1,625,081	1,651,913	1,585,427	1,298,831	1,004,188	991,050	859,101
Total Current Liabilities	618,653	564,962	658,018	566,792	382,407	235,533	242,080	228,220
Long-Term Obligations	...	...	20,800	20,800	20,800	20,800	20,800	...
Net Stockholders' Equity	1,148,238	940,823	903,110	936,066	844,395	699,123	668,581	575,570
Net Working Capital	486,506	359,926	294,408	237,571	265,529	308,015	307,757	251,372
Shares Outstanding	72,649	72,111	71,356	71,547	71,096	68,880	69,005	68,841
Statistical Record								
Operating Profit Margin %	12.45	12.43	7.89	13.13	14.78	8.96	14.98	13.62
Return on Equity %	15.22	14.06	7.40	14.62	15.26	10.89	18.32	16.92
Return on Assets %	9.19	8.14	4.04	8.63	9.92	7.58	12.36	11.34
Debt/Total Assets %	...	...	1.25	1.31	1.60	2.07	2.09	...
Price Range	57.43-33.94	42.41-31.00	41.00-25.96	34.56-21.63	39.88-20.50	54.63-20.13	50.63-31.38	41.92-22.50
P/E Ratio	23.93-14.14	23.17-16.94	44.09-27.91	18.00-11.26	21.55-11.08	49.66-18.30	28.76-17.83	29.52-15.85
Average Yield %	1.52	1.76	1.93	2.24	2.22	1.59	1.16	1.44

Address: 5995 Mayfair Road, North Canton, OH 44720-8077	**Officers:** Walden W. ODell – Chmn., C.E.O., Eric C. Evans – Pres., C.O.O.	**Investor Contact:** (800) 766-5859
Telephone: (330) 490-4000	**Transfer Agents:** The Bank of New York, New York, NY	**Institutional Holding**
Web Site: www.diebold.com		**No of Institutions:** 18
		Shares: 449,066 **% Held:** –

82

DONNELLEY (R.R.) & SONS CO.

Exchange	Symbol	Price	52Wk Range	Yield	P/E
NYS	DNY	$30.25 (3/31/2004)	32.21–18.30	3.44	27.75

*7 Year Price Score 80.3   *NYSE Composite Index=100   *12 Month Price Score 104.4

Interim Earnings (Per Share)

Qtr.	Mar	Jun	Sep	Dec
2000	0.38	0.46	0.75	0.58
2001	0.12	0.05	0.36	(0.32)
2002	0.20	0.22	0.42	0.40
2003	0.05	0.17	0.47	0.85

Interim Dividends (Per Share)

Amt	Decl	Ex	Rec	Pay
0.25Q	3/27/2003	5/7/2003	5/9/2003	5/31/2003
0.26Q	7/24/2003	8/6/2003	8/8/2003	8/30/2003
0.26Q	9/25/2003	11/5/2003	11/7/2003	11/29/2003
0.26Q	1/22/2004	2/2/2004	2/4/2004	2/28/2004

Indicated Div: $1.04 (Div. Reinv. Plan)

Valuation Analysis

Forecast P/E	N/A	Trailing P/E	27.75
Market Cap	$3.4 Billion	Book Value	890.4 Million
Price/Book	3.17	Price/Sales	0.59

Dividend Achiever Status

Rank	303	10 Year Growth Rate	0.82%
Total Years of Dividend Growth			34

Business Summary: Printing (MIC: 13.4 SIC: 2752 NAIC:323110)

Donnelley (R.R.) & Sons is engaged in preparing, producing and delivering integrated communications services designed to produce, manage and deliver its customers'content, regardless of the communications medium. Co.'s services include content creation, digital content management, production and distribution. Co. operates primarily in three business segments: print, logistics and financial. Co. serves the following end–markets: magazines, catalogs and retail, telecommunications, book publishing premedia, financial services, direct mail, international, and logistics.

Recent Developments: For the twelve months ended Dec 31 2003, net income rose 24.1% to $176.5 million versus $142.2 million in 2002. Results benefited from continued cost reduction and productivity efforts. Results for 2003 and 2002 included after–tax restructuring and impairment charges of $13.0 million and $54.0 million, respectively. Net sales climbed to $4.79 billion from $4.75 billion in the prior year. Net sales from Co.'s logistic services rose 16.5% to $913.2 million, while print solutions net sales declined 4.4% to $2.96 billion. Sales in the financial services segment slipped 0.3% to $426.2 million. Operating earnings increased 10.6% to $270.8 million versus $244.9 million the year before.

Prospects: On Feb 27 2004, Co. completed its acquisition of Moore Wallace Incorporated in a transaction valued at approximately $2.80 billion. The combined company will retain the R.R. Donnelley name and is now the largest printing company in North America. Under the terms of the agreement, all outstanding shares of Moore Wallace common stock will be exchanged for shares of Co. common stock based on a fixed exchange ratio of 0.63 of a Co. share for each Moore Wallace share. The transaction is expected to be accretive to Co.'s first full year of operations and generate cost savings of at least $100.0 million on an annualized basis.

Financial Data

(US$ in Thousands)	12/31/2003	12/31/2002	12/31/2001	12/31/2000	12/31/1999	12/31/1998	12/31/1997	12/31/1996
Earnings Per Share	1.54	1.24	0.21	2.17	2.40	2.08	1.40	(1.04)
Cash Flow Per Share	3.09	3.57	4.62	6.01	4.90	5.16	5.03	4.26
Tang. Book Val. Per Share	5.13	4.50	3.91	5.05	6.00	6.84	8.31	7.48
Dividends Per Share	1.020	0.980	0.940	0.900	· 0.860	0.820	0.780	0.740
Dividend Payout %	66.23	79.03	447.61	41.47	35.83	39.42	55.71	N.M.
Income Statement								
Total Revenues	4,787,162	4,754,937	5,297,760	5,764,335	5,183,408	5,018,436	4,850,033	6,598,958
Total Indirect Exp.	564,893	622,632	763,180	597,823	628,580	729,913	581,817	1,258,975
Depreciation & Amort.	329,359	352,372	378,723	390,402	374,382	367,803	370,445	389,148
Operating Income	270,793	244,937	147,271	501,040	530,427	408,351	368,788	(135,976)
Net Interest Inc./(Exp.)	(50,359)	(62,818)	(71,183)	(89,639)	(88,164)	(78,166)	(90,765)	(95,482)
Income Taxes	31,768	33,496	49,906	167,084	195,014	214,725	97,240	47,146
Income from Cont Ops	...	...	...	...	311,515	...	206,525	...
Net Income	176,509	142,237	24,988	266,900	308,314	294,580	130,631	(157,623)
Average Shs. Outstg.	114,302	114,372	118,498	123,093	129,566	141,865	147,508	151,800
Balance Sheet								
Cash & Cash Equivalents	60,837	60,543	48,615	60,873	41,873	66,226	47,814	31,142
Total Current Assets	999,510	866,439	940,194	1,206,449	1,229,850	1,144,993	1,146,571	1,752,857
Total Assets	3,188,950	3,151,772	3,400,017	3,914,202	3,853,464	3,787,819	4,134,166	4,849,004
Total Current Liabilities	883,582	954,730	984,290	1,190,561	1,203,463	898,300	812,622	1,147,547
Long–Term Obligations	752,497	752,870	881,318	739,190	748,498	998,978	1,153,226	1,430,671
Net Stockholders' Equity	983,152	914,594	888,407	1,232,548	1,138,258	1,300,878	1,591,497	1,631,281
Net Working Capital	115,928	(88,291)	(44,096)	15,888	26,387	246,693	333,949	605,310
Shares Outstanding	113,674	113,124	113,121	140,889	123,237	134,322	145,118	145,554
Statistical Record								
Operating Profit Margin %	5.65	5.15	2.77	8.69	10.23	8.13	7.60	N.M.
Return on Equity %	17.95	15.55	2.81	21.65	27.36	22.64	12.97	N.M.
Return on Assets %	5.53	4.51	0.73	6.81	8.08	7.77	4.99	N.M.
Debt/Total Assets %	23.59	23.88	25.92	18.88	19.42	26.37	27.89	29.50
Price Range	30.15–17.05	31.96–19.06	31.62–24.83	27.00–19.13	43.81–22.81	47.75–34.00	41.06–29.63	39.63–29.63
P/E Ratio	19.58–11.07	25.77–15.37	150.6–118.2	12.44–8.81	18.26–9.51	22.96–16.35	29.33–21.16	N/A
Average Yield %	4.29	3.70	3.33	3.88	2.65	1.98	2.22	2.16

Address: 77 West Wacker Drive, Chicago, IL 60601	Officers: William L. Davis – Pres., C.E.O., Gregory A. Stoklosa – Exec. V.P., C.F.O.	Investor Contact: (312) 326–8313
Telephone: (312) 326–8000	Transfer Agents:EquiServe Trust Company, N.A., Jersey City, NJ	Institutional Holding
Web Site: www.rrdonnelley.com		No of Institutions: 292
		Shares: 86,984,304 % Held: 76.80%

DORAL FINANCIAL CORP.

Exchange	Symbol	Price	52Wk Range	Yield	P/E
NYS	DRL	$35.20 (3/31/2004)	35.42-23.57	1.36	14.16

*7 Year Price Score 239.3 *NYSE Composite Index=100 *12 Month Price Score 107.1

Interim Earnings (Per Share)

Qtr.	Mar	Jun	Sep	Dec
2000	0.20	0.20	0.20	0.22
2001	0.26	0.28	0.32	0.39
2002	0.40	0.44	0.49	0.56
2003	0.60	0.64	0.70	0.78

Interim Dividends (Per Share)

Amt	Decl	Ex	Rec	Pay
0.093Q	8/8/2003	8/14/2003	8/18/2003	9/6/2003
0.12Q	10/15/2003	11/12/2003	11/14/2003	12/4/2003
50%	10/15/2003	12/12/2003	11/21/2003	12/11/2003
0.12Q	1/23/2004	2/11/2004	2/13/2004	3/5/2004
		Indicated Div: $0.48		

Valuation Analysis

Forecast P/E	N/A	Trailing P/E	14.16
Market Cap	$2.5 Billion	Book Value	980.0 Million
Price/Book	3.45	Price/Sales	4.13

Dividend Achiever Status

Rank	8	10 Year Growth Rate	28.21%
Total Years of Dividend Growth		14	

Business Summary: Finance Intermediaries &Services (MIC: 8.7 SIC: 6162 NAIC:522292)

Doral Financial is a diversified financial services company engaged in mortgage banking, commercial banking, institutional broker-dealer activities and insurance agency activities. Co.'s activities are principally conducted in Puerto Rico and in the New York City metropolitan area. As of Dec 31 2003, Doral Bank, Co.'s Puerto Rico banking subsidiary, operated 37 branches in Puerto Rico, concentrated in the greater San Juan metropolitan area and the Island's northeast region. As of Dec 31 2003, Co. had consolidated assets of $10.39 billion and deposits of $2.97 billion.

Recent Developments: For the year ended Dec 31 2003, net income advanced 45.4% to $321.3 million compared with $221.0 million a year earlier. Net interest income increased 19.1% to $181.5 million from $152.4 million the previous year. Provision for loan losses was $14.1 million versus $7.4 million in 2002. Total non-interest income climbed 61.2% to $411.8 million, driven by net gains on mortgage loans sales and fees the rose 76.8% to $411.8 million. Co. attributed this increase mainly due to a greater volume of loan securitizations and sales as a result of record mortgage loan production that was fueled by low interest rates and higher demand for housing.

Prospects: Co.'s near-term outlook appears reasonably positive. Co. noted that the main risk to its business in 2004 would be a sharp increase in interest rates, which appears unlikely at this time, that would adversely effect mortgage loan originations and the value of its fixed income loans and securities. Looking ahead, Co. expects fee income to make increasing contributions to consolidated revenues during 2004, especially from the insurance agency operation. Meanwhile, Co. remains on schedule to reach its goal of 50 branches in Puerto Rico by 2006. Also, Co.'s growth should be further enhanced by Doral Bank NY's plans to increase its number of branches from five to 10 branches during 2004.

Financial Data

(US$ in Thousands)	12/31/2003	12/31/2002	12/31/2001	12/31/2000	12/31/1999	12/31/1998	12/31/1997	12/31/1996
Earnings Per Share	2.72	1.89	1.25	0.82	0.66	0.56	0.37	0.31
Tang. Book Val. Per Share	9.44	7.57	5.92	3.89	4.10	2.90	2.18	1.75
Dividends Per Share	0.400	0.280	0.210	0.160	0.130	0.100	0.080	0.070
Dividend Payout %	14.70	14.78	16.84	20.54	19.99	18.25	22.64	23.23
Income Statement								
Total Interest Income	452,570	415,600	356,095	325,545	211,679	148,051	90,131	66,987
Total Interest Expense	271,090	263,178	271,668	283,241	161,795	114,786	61,438	...
Net Interest Income	181,480	152,422	84,427	42,304	49,884	33,265	28,693	66,987
Provision for Loan Losses	14,085	7,429	4,445	4,078	2,626	883	600	...
Non-Interest Income	411,772	255,393	191,132	164,585	126,911	88,340	45,286	40,846
Non-Interest Expense	185,802	139,410	112,854	106,659	97,556	60,883	35,582	122,997
Income Before Taxes	342,921	260,976	158,260	96,152	76,613	59,839	37,797	31,279
Income from Cont Ops	270,855	...	137,922	...	...	...	32,548	22,802
Net Income	321,299	220,968	143,851	84,656	67,926	52,832	20,231	27,041
Average Shs. Outstg.	110,434	109,438	102,381	94,710	95,448	94,338	87,139	87,131
Balance Sheet								
Cash & Due from Banks	84,713	156,137	45,970	28,999	25,793	31,945	17,390	...
Securities Avail. for Sale	2,850,598	862,090	928,179	182,374	66,325	408,888	240,876	12,007
Net Loans & Leases	1,410,849	1,022,342	644,113	398,191	231,184	166,987	133,055	128,766
Total Assets	10,393,996	8,421,689	6,694,283	5,463,386	4,537,343	2,918,113	1,857,789	1,101,955
Total Deposits	2,971,222	2,217,211	1,669,909	1,303,525	1,010,424	533,113	300,494	158,902
Long-Term Obligations	1,206,500	1,311,500	687,500	389,000	134,000	32,000	32,000	25,000
Total Liabilities	8,801,556	7,376,718	5,932,163	4,957,676	4,152,361	2,648,554	1,670,834	951,424
Net Stockholders' Equity	1,592,440	1,044,971	762,120	505,710	384,982	269,559	186,955	150,531
Shares Outstanding	107,903	107,761	107,573	95,384	90,965	90,965	82,788	81,999
Statistical Record								
Return on Equity %	17.00	21.14	18.09	16.74	17.64	19.59	17.40	15.14
Return on Assets %	2.60	2.62	2.06	1.54	1.49	1.81	1.75	2.06
Equity/Assets %	15.32	12.40	11.38	9.25	8.48	9.23	10.06	13.66
Non-Int. Exp./Tot. Inc. %	21.49	20.77	20.62	21.76	28.81	25.75	26.27	114.06
Price Range	34.67-18.73	19.94-13.68	17.50-9.97	11.36-3.89	9.83-4.72	10.08-4.67	5.67-2.72	3.12-1.98
P/E Ratio	12.75-6.89	10.55-7.24	14.00-7.98	13.85-4.74	14.90-7.15	18.01-8.33	15.32-7.36	10.08-6.38
Average Yield %	1.45	1.69	1.62	2.65	1.82	1.40	2.13	2.86

Address: 1451 Franklin D. Roosevelt Avenue, San Juan, PR 00920-2717, Puerto Rico Telephone: (787) 474-6700 Web Site: www.doralfinancial.com	Officers: Salomon Levis – Chmn., C.E.O., Zoila Levis – Pres., C.O.O. Transfer Agents:Mellon Investor Services, LLC, Ridgefield Park, NJ	Investor Contact:212-329-3729 Institutional Holding No of Institutions: 6 Shares: 1,623,032 % Held: –

DOVER CORP.

Exchange	Symbol	Price	52Wk Range	Yield	P/E
NYS	DOV	$38.77 (3/31/2004)	44.02–23.86	1.55	27.69

*7 Year Price Score 91.8   *NYSE Composite Index=100   *12 Month Price Score 106.4

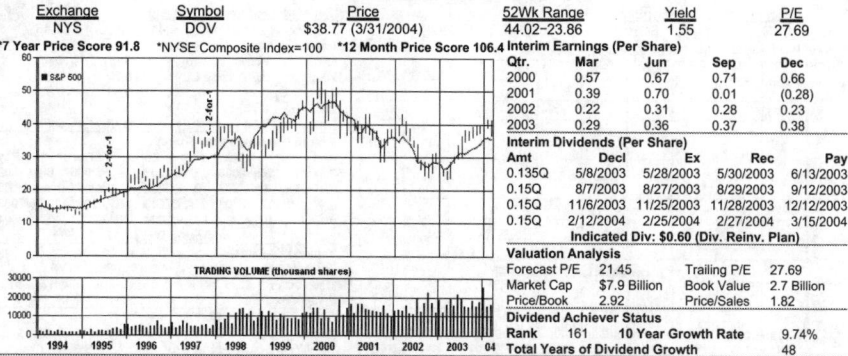

Interim Earnings (Per Share)

Qtr.	Mar	Jun	Sep	Dec
2000	0.57	0.67	0.71	0.66
2001	0.39	0.70	0.01	(0.28)
2002	0.22	0.31	0.28	0.23
2003	0.29	0.36	0.37	0.38

Interim Dividends (Per Share)

Amt	Decl	Ex	Rec	Pay
0.135Q	5/8/2003	5/28/2003	5/30/2003	6/13/2003
0.15Q	8/7/2003	8/27/2003	8/29/2003	9/12/2003
0.15Q	11/6/2003	11/25/2003	11/28/2003	12/12/2003
0.15Q	2/12/2004	2/25/2004	2/27/2004	3/15/2004

Indicated Div: $0.60 (Div. Reinv. Plan)

Valuation Analysis

Forecast P/E	21.45	Trailing P/E	27.69
Market Cap	$7.9 Billion	Book Value	2.7 Billion
Price/Book	2.92	Price/Sales	1.82

Dividend Achiever Status

Rank	161	10 Year Growth Rate	9.74%
Total Years of Dividend Growth		48	

Business Summary: Industrial Machinery and Equipment (MIC: 11.5 SIC: 3531 NAIC:333120)

Dover is a diversified industrial manufacturing corporation made up of 52 operating companies. Dover Diversified's products include packaging and printing machinery, heat transfer equipment, food refrigeration and display cases as well as products for use in the defense, aerospace and automotive industries. Dover Industries makes products for use in the waste handling, bulk transport, automotive service, commercial food service and packaging, welding, cash dispenser and construction industries. Dover Technologies' products include automated assembly and testing equipment, specialized electronic components and industrial printers. Dover Resources manufactures products for various industries.

Recent Developments: For the year ended Dec 31 2003, earnings from continuing operations were $285.2 million compared with earnings of $207.8 million a year earlier. Net sales advanced 8.9% to $4.41 billion from $4.05 billion the previous year, driven by increases of $194.8 million and $109.8 million from Co.'s Technology and Resources segments, respectively. Co. noted that Technologies' sales were aided by recovery in the electronics industry, while Resources' sales increased due to improved market conditions and the Oct 1 2003 acquisition of Warn Industries. Overall, acquisitions completed during 2003 contributed $67.7 million to sales. Gross profit margins amounted to 34.5% versus 32.8% the year before.

Prospects: Co.'s near–term outlook appears to be brightening, due in large part to improved bookings and rising backlogs across each of its operating segments. Specifically, Co. expects its Resources segment to benefit from the Oct 1 2003 acquisition of Warn Industries Inc. and further improvements in many of Resources' energy and fluids handling businesses. Also, Diversified and Industries stand to benefit from strong recent bookings, while an expanded line of marking and coding products from Technologies' Imaje business, coupled with planned new product introductions from Co.'s Circuit Board Assembly and Test equipment business, strengthen this segment's outlook going forward.

Financial Data

(US$ in Thousands)	12/31/2003	12/31/2002	12/31/2001	12/31/2000	12/31/1999	12/31/1998	12/31/1997	12/31/1996
Earnings Per Share	1.40	1.04	0.82	2.61	1.92	1.45	1.79	1.72
Cash Flow Per Share	2.91	1.94	3.32	2.70	2.18	2.17	2.03	1.81
Tang. Book Val. Per Share	2.70	2.65	1.97	1.78	1.06	2.10	2.66	2.29
Dividends Per Share	0.570	0.540	0.520	0.480	0.440	0.400	0.360	0.320
Dividend Payout %	40.71	51.92	63.41	18.39	22.91	27.58	20.11	18.60
Income Statement								
Total Revenues	4,413,296	4,183,664	4,459,695	5,400,717	4,446,420	3,977,666	4,547,656	4,076,284
Total Indirect Exp.	1,076,664	1,018,696	1,096,346	1,124,012	973,049	894,325	959,067	827,958
Depreciation & Amort.	151,309	161,003	219,963	203,384	183,244	167,687	170,663	125,084
Operating Income	443,758	341,620	299,023	843,210	635,411	531,960	612,669	538,674
Net Interest Inc./(Exp.)	(62,166)	(64,829)	(75,280)	(88,495)	(34,873)	(46,438)	(36,970)	(23,474)
Income Taxes	86,676	58,542	71,595	239,108	209,950	162,249	211,405	198,502
Income from Cont Ops	285,216	211,149	166,839	533,207	405,054	326,397	...	...
Net Income	292,927	(121,261)	248,537	519,612	928,992	378,845	405,431	390,223
Average Shs. Outstg.	203,614	203,346	204,013	204,677	210,679	224,386	226,815	226,524
Balance Sheet								
Cash & Cash Equivalents	370,379	294,959	176,862	186,740	138,038	96,774	146,709	217,795
Total Current Assets	1,849,640	1,658,001	1,654,928	1,974,849	1,611,562	1,304,524	1,591,345	1,489,813
Total Assets	5,133,752	4,437,385	4,602,202	4,892,116	4,131,940	3,627,276	3,277,524	2,993,379
Total Current Liabilities	910,801	696,938	819,171	1,604,640	1,334,865	989,747	1,196,573	1,139,105
Long–Term Obligations	1,003,915	1,030,299	1,033,243	631,846	608,025	610,090	262,630	252,955
Net Stockholders' Equity	2,742,671	2,394,623	2,519,539	2,441,575	2,038,756	1,910,884	1,703,584	1,489,703
Net Working Capital	938,839	961,063	835,757	370,209	276,697	314,777	394,772	350,708
Shares Outstanding	202,912	202,402	202,579	203,183	204,628	220,407	234,507	225,060
Statistical Record								
Operating Profit Margin %	10.05	8.16	6.70	15.61	14.29	13.37	13.47	13.21
Return on Equity %	10.39	8.81	6.62	21.83	19.86	17.08	23.79	26.19
Return on Assets %	5.55	4.75	3.62	10.89	9.80	8.99	12.37	13.03
Debt/Total Assets %	19.55	23.21	22.45	12.91	14.71	16.81	8.01	8.45
Price Range	40.08–23.35	43.31–23.91	43.32–28.77	53.81–36.00	47.25–29.50	39.81–25.94	36.31–24.38	27.44–18.44
P/E Ratio	28.63–16.68	41.64–22.99	52.83–35.09	20.62–13.79	24.61–15.36	27.46–17.89	20.29–13.62	15.95–10.72
Average Yield %	1.76	1.63	1.39	1.07	1.14	1.17	1.18	1.36

Address: 280 Park Avenue, New York, NY 10017	**Officers:** Thomas L. Reece – Chmn., C.E.O., Ronald L. Hoffman – Pres., C.O.O.	**Investor Contact:** (212) 922–1640
Telephone: (212) 922–1640	**Transfer Agents:** Mellon Investor Services, Ridgefield Park, NJ	**Institutional Holding**
Web Site: www.dovercorporation.com		**No of Institutions:** 11
		Shares: 1,880,755 **% Held:** –

EASTGROUP PROPERTIES, INC.

Exchange	Symbol	Price	52Wk Range	Yield	P/E
NYS	EGP	$35.50 (3/31/2004)	35.95–25.45	5.41	51.45

*7 Year Price Score 127.5 *NYSE Composite Index=100 *12 Month Price Score 101.9

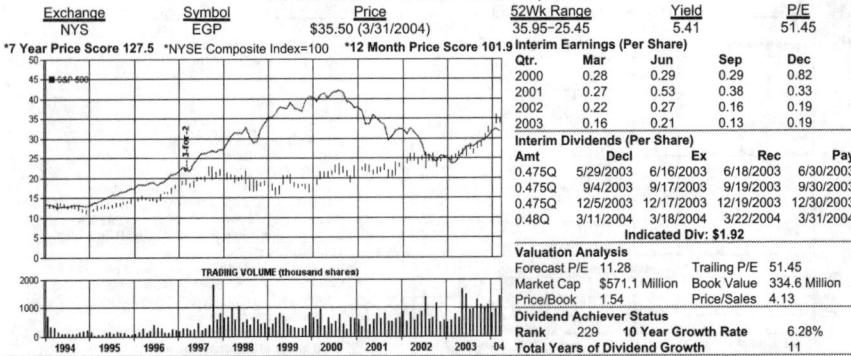

Interim Earnings (Per Share)

Qtr.	Mar	Jun	Sep	Dec
2000	0.28	0.29	0.29	0.82
2001	0.27	0.53	0.38	0.33
2002	0.22	0.27	0.16	0.19
2003	0.16	0.21	0.13	0.19

Interim Dividends (Per Share)

Amt	Decl	Ex	Rec	Pay
0.475Q	5/29/2003	6/16/2003	6/18/2003	6/30/2003
0.475Q	9/4/2003	9/17/2003	9/19/2003	9/30/2003
0.475Q	12/5/2003	12/17/2003	12/19/2003	12/30/2003
0.48Q	3/11/2004	3/18/2004	3/22/2004	3/31/2004

Indicated Div: $1.92

Valuation Analysis

Forecast P/E	11.28	Trailing P/E	51.45
Market Cap	$571.1 Million	Book Value	334.6 Million
Price/Book	1.54	Price/Sales	4.13

Dividend Achiever Status

Rank	229	10 Year Growth Rate	6.28%
Total Years of Dividend Growth	11		

Business Summary: Property, Real Estate &Development (MIC: 8.3 SIC: 6798 NAIC:525930)

Eastgroup Properties is a self–administered, equity real estate investment trust focused on the acquisition, operation and development of industrial properties in major sunbelt markets throughout the U.S. Co.'s strategy for growth is based on its property portfolio orientation toward premier distribution facilities located near major transportation centers. Co.'s portfolio includes 18.9 million square feet with an additional 510,000 square feet of properties under development as of Jul 21 2003.

Recent Developments: For the three months ended Sep 30 2003, income was $5.2 million, before a gain of $6,000 from discontinued operations, compared with income of $5.2 million, before a loss of $76,000 from discontinued operations, in the corresponding quarter of the previous year. Revenues grew 3.9% to $27.4 million from $26.4 million in 2002. Income from real estate operations climbed 5.4% to $27.3 million from $25.9 million in the year–earlier period. Property net operating income rose 5.5% to $19.2 million from $18.2 million the year before. Funds from operations declined 12.3% to $10.6 million from $12.1 million in the prior–year period.

Prospects: Going forward, Co. expects funds from operations to range from $2.35 to $2.38 per share and earnings per share to range from $0.70 to $0.73 for full–year 2003. Co. has been focused on strengthening its balance sheet, with capital transactions completed during the second and third quarters. As a result of these efforts, Co. should be well positioned to take advantage of future acquisition and development opportunities. At Sep 30 2003, Co. had seven development properties containing 543,000 square feet with a projected total cost approximately $30.0 million either in lease–up or under construction.

Financial Data

(US$ in Thousands)	12/31/2003	12/31/2002	12/31/2001	12/31/2000	12/31/1999	12/31/1998	12/31/1997	12/31/1996
Earnings Per Share	0.69	0.84	1.51	1.68	1.99	1.66	1.56	0.96
Tang. Book Val. Per Share	16.04	15.39	16.47	16.83	16.76	16.25	15.87	9.18
Dividends Per Share	1.900	1.880	1.800	1.580	1.480	1.400	1.330	1.280
Dividend Payout %	275.36	223.80	119.20	94.04	74.37	84.33	85.68	133.33
Income Statement								
Interest Income	22	45	560	136	244	164	558	74
Total Income	108,441	105,810	105,295	98,103	86,236	76,728	53,622	39,765
Total Indirect Exp.	75,462	69,661	67,610	66,196	60,134	54,292	13,844	28,264
Depreciation	32,050	30,333	27,041	23,449	20,178	16,574	10,409	7,759
Interest Expense	38,030	34,774	35,646	37,140	35,376	33,896	...	17,860
Eqty Earns/Minority Int.	416	375	350	...	...	...	512	289
Income from Cont Ops	20,335	23,705	...	...	38,773	...	...	...
Net Income	20,445	23,626	34,182	36,512	38,355	29,336	20,779	12,509
Average Shs. Outstg.	18,194	16,237	16,046	15,798	17,362	16,432	13,338	...
Balance Sheet								
Cash & Cash Equivalents	1,786	1,383	1,767	2,861	2,657	2,784	1,298	438
Ttl Real Estate Inv.	695,643	672,694	644,039	624,535	589,469	531,415	376,693	260,922
Total Assets	729,267	702,341	683,782	666,205	632,151	567,548	413,127	281,455
Long–Term Obligations	338,272	322,300	291,072	270,709	243,665	236,816	147,150	129,078
Total Liabilities	362,322	387,213	354,429	332,170	304,196	292,881	155,812	136,129
Net Stockholders' Equity	366,945	356,485	370,710	375,392	369,312	316,024	257,315	145,326
Shares Outstanding	20,853	16,104	15,912	15,849	15,555	16,307	16,205	15,823
Statistical Record								
Net Inc.+Depr./Assets %	7.20	7.70	9.00	9.00	9.30	8.10	7.50	7.20
Return on Equity %	5.54	6.64	9.22	9.72	10.49	9.28	8.07	8.60
Return on Assets %	2.78	3.37	4.99	5.48	6.13	5.16	5.02	4.44
Price Range	32.90–23.88	26.35–22.40	23.90–20.19	23.88–17.56	21.00–15.75	22.06–16.69	22.88–17.75	18.25–14.00
P/E Ratio	47.68–34.61	31.37–26.67	15.83–13.37	14.21–10.45	10.55–7.91	13.29–10.05	14.66–11.38	19.01–14.58
Average Yield %	6.93	7.61	8.10	7.55	8.09	7.14	6.68	8.32

Address: 300 One Jackson Place, Jackson, MS 39201-2195 **Telephone:** (601) 354–3555 **Web Site:** www.eastgroup.net	**Officers:** Leland R. Speed – Chmn., David H. Hoster II – Pres., C.E.O. **Transfer Agents:** First Chicago Trust Company of New York, Jersey City, NJ	**Institutional Holding** **No of Institutions:** 7 **Shares:** 1,448,160 **% Held:** –

EATON VANCE CORP

Exchange	Symbol	Price	52Wk Range	Yield	P/E
NYS	EV	$38.12 (3/31/2004)	39.74-27.12	1.26	24.13

*7 Year Price Score 147.9 *NYSE Composite Index=100 *12 Month Price Score 100.7

Interim Earnings (Per Share)

Qtr.	Jan	Apr	Jul	Oct
2000–01	0.44	0.29	0.44	0.43
2001–02	0.46	0.46	0.44	0.34
2002–03	0.37	0.36	0.38	0.40
2003–04	0.44	...	...	...

Interim Dividends (Per Share)

Amt	Decl	Ex	Rec	Pay
0.08Q	4/16/2003	4/28/2003	4/30/2003	5/12/2003
0.12Q	7/9/2003	7/29/2003	7/31/2003	8/11/2003
0.12Q	10/22/2003	10/29/2003	10/31/2003	11/10/2003
0.12Q	1/14/2004	1/28/2004	1/30/2004	2/9/2004
		Indicated Div: $0.48		

Valuation Analysis

Forecast P/E	17.75	Trailing P/E 24.13
Market Cap	$2.6 Billion	Book Value 423.7 Million
Price/Book	6.00	Price/Sales 4.58

Dividend Achiever Status

Rank	30	10 Year Growth Rate 20.64%
Total Years of Dividend Growth		22

Business Summary: Wealth Management (MIC: 8.8 SIC: 6282 NAIC:523930)

Eaton Vance is engaged in the provision of investment advisory and distribution services to mutual funds and other investment funds, and investment management services to individual high–net–worth investors, family offices and institutional clients. As of Oct 31 2003, Co. managed $75.0 billion in assets with investment objectives ranging from high current income to maximum long–term capital gain. Co. conducts its investment management business through its two wholly owned subsidiaries, Eaton Vance Management and Boston Management and Research, and its three majority–owned subsidiaries, Atlanta Capital, Fox Asset Management and Parametric.

Recent Developments: For the quarter ended Jan 31 2004, net income advanced 18.9% to $30.8 million compared with $25.9 million in the equivalent 2002 quarter. Net fund and separate account inflows surged to $5.60 billion compared with $1.30 billion in the first quarter a year ago. Total revenues grew 25.6% to $157.0 million from $124.9 million a year earlier. The improvement in revenues was primarily attributed to average assets under management growth of 25.7% to $157.0 million. Investment adviser and administration fees increased 35.7% to $93.8 million from $69.1 million a year earlier. Operating income climbed 30.5% to $50.1 million from $38.4 million in 2003.

Prospects: Co. is benefiting from recovering equity markets, successful closed-end fund offerings, and strong net sales of Co.'s open-end mutual funds. Also, recent results reflect a surge in net inflows largely due to the expansion of Co.'s product line as a result of the acquisitions of Atlanta Capital Management Company, LLC and Fox Asset Management LLC in September of 2001 and Parametric Portfolio Associates in September 2003, and an increase in the number of retail managed account programs in which Co. participates. Meanwhile, cash, cash equivalents and short-term investments were $262.6 million as of Jan 31 2004.

Financial Data

(US$ in Thousands)	3 Mos	10/31/2003	10/31/2002	10/31/2001	10/31/2000	10/31/1999	10/31/1998	10/31/1997
Earnings Per Share	1.58	1.51	1.70	1.60	1.58	0.70	0.40	0.52
Cash Flow Per Share	0.04	0.62	1.87	1.94	1.00	0.29	0.13	0.57
Tang. Book Val. Per Share	4.24	4.11	3.83	2.80	3.64	2.73	2.94	3.02
Dividends Per Share	0.400	0.360	0.290	0.240	0.190	0.150	0.120	0.100
Dividend Payout %	25.32	23.84	17.05	15.00	12.02	21.27	29.62	19.23
Income Statement								
Total Revenues	156,973	523,133	522,985	486,372	429,566	348,950	249,987	200,910
Total Indirect Exp.	106,870	359,989	339,062	295,479	246,902	271,046	201,335	137,005
Depreciation & Amort.	20,763	85,192	83,690	74,344	82,809	63,991	64,570	54,464
Operating Income	50,103	163,144	183,923	190,893	182,664	77,904	48,652	63,905
Net Interest Inc./(Exp.)	(863)	(913)	1,921	4,556	3,652	671	1,791	(380)
Income Taxes	19,131	57,700	65,184	62,469	71,128	33,505	19,515	27,236
Eqty Earns/Minority Int.	15	(772)	389	967	637	10	105	384
Income from Cont Ops	...	...	...	...	...	52,405	...	...
Net Income	30,813	106,123	121,057	116,020	116,051	15,798	30,523	40,234
Average Shs. Outstg.	70,336	70,375	71,412	72,300	73,222	74,494	75,514	78,392
Balance Sheet								
Cash & Cash Equivalents	262,632	242,812	187,964	210,709	102,479	77,395	96,435	140,520
Total Current Assets	316,942	272,317	213,567	237,480	120,242	90,488	130,433	164,168
Total Assets	695,205	658,702	616,619	675,301	432,989	358,229	380,260	387,375
Total Current Liabilities	58,769	82,795	68,270	83,844	61,793	48,890	48,957	39,968
Long–Term Obligations	119,180	118,736	124,118	215,488	21,429	28,571	35,714	50,964
Net Stockholders' Equity	423,690	416,277	372,302	301,126	254,950	194,268	211,809	226,280
Net Working Capital	257,723	189,522	145,297	153,636	58,449	41,598	81,476	124,200
Shares Outstanding	68,148	68,405	69,257	68,616	69,543	70,519	71,331	73,876
Statistical Record								
Operating Profit Margin %	31.91	31.18	35.16	39.24	42.52	22.32	19.46	31.80
Return on Equity %	7.27	25.49	32.51	38.52	45.51	26.97	14.41	17.78
Return on Assets %	4.43	16.11	19.63	17.18	26.80	14.62	8.02	10.38
Debt/Total Assets %	17.14	18.02	20.12	31.90	4.94	7.97	9.39	13.15
Price Range	38.63-34.31	35.60-23.40	40.71-23.95	38.20-22.31	27.38-16.94	19.44-9.50	12.38-8.09	9.28-5.23
P/E Ratio	87.80-77.98	23.58-15.50	23.95-14.09	23.88-13.95	17.33-10.72	27.77-13.57	30.94-20.23	17.85-10.07
Average Yield %	1.10	1.17	0.88	0.77	0.88	1.13	1.14	1.53

Address: 255 State Street, Boston, MA 02109	Officers: James B. Hawkes – Chmn., Pres., C.E.O., Thomas E. Faust – Exec. V.P., Chief Investment Officer	Investor Contact: (617) 482–8260
Telephone: (617) 482–8260		Institutional Holding
Web Site: www.eatonvance.com	Transfer Agents:EquiServe Trust Company, N.A., Providence, RI	No of Institutions: 5
		Shares: 36,197,532 % Held: –

ECOLAB, INC.

Exchange	Symbol	Price	52Wk Range	Yield	P/E
NYS	ECL	$28.53 (3/31/2004)	28.53–24.00	1.12	26.92

*7 Year Price Score 138.3   *NYSE Composite Index=100   *12 Month Price Score 93.1

Interim Earnings (Per Share)

Qtr.	Mar	Jun	Sep	Dec
2000	0.16	0.18	0.23	0.22
2001	0.17	0.18	0.22	0.15
2002	0.14	0.20	0.28	0.19
2003	0.21	0.25	0.33	0.27

Interim Dividends (Per Share)

Amt	Decl	Ex	Rec	Pay
100%	5/9/2003	6/9/2003	5/23/2003	6/6/2003
0.073Q	8/15/2003	9/12/2003	9/16/2003	10/15/2003
0.08Q	12/11/2003	12/19/2003	12/23/2003	1/15/2004
0.08Q	3/1/2004	3/12/2004	3/16/2004	4/15/2004

Indicated Div: $0.32 (Div. Reinv. Plan)

Valuation Analysis

Forecast P/E	23.75	Trailing P/E	26.92
Market Cap	$3.7 Billion	Book Value	1.3 Billion
Price/Book	5.43	Price/Sales	1.87

Dividend Achiever Status

Rank	124	10 Year Growth Rate	11.81%
Total Years of Dividend Growth		11	

Business Summary: Chemicals (MIC: 11.1 SIC: 2842 NAIC:325612)

Ecolab develops and markets cleaning, sanitizing, pest elimination, maintenance and repair products and services. The Cleaning and Sanitizing segment consists of seven business units and offers cleaners, sanitizers, detergents, lubricants, chemical cleaning, animal health, water treatment, infection control and janitorial products to customers in the U.S. Other U.S. Services consists of two business units focused on the elimination and prevention of pests, and the manufacturing of dishwashing and customized machines for the foodservice industry. The International segment serves customers in Europe, Asia Pacific, Canada, Latin America, the Middle East and Africa.

Recent Developments: For the year ended Dec 31 2003, net income grew 32.2% to $277.3 million from $209.8 million the prior year. Results for 2003 included a gain on the sale of an equity investment of $11.1 million. Results for 2002 included an accounting charge of $4.0 million and a gain from discontinued operations of $1.9 million. Also, results for 2003 and 2002 included special charges of $408,000 and $37.0 million, respectively. Net sales increased 10.5% to $3.76 billion, bolstered in part by favorable currency effects. U.S. cleaning and sanitizing sales rose 4.9% to $1.69 billion, while other U.S. sales improved 3.9% to $320.4 million. International cleaning and sanitizing sales grew 4.2% to $1.56 billion.

Prospects: Going forward, Co. will continue to aggressively pursue acquisitions and related strategic business development opportunities. In addition, Co will focus on developing its newer businesses. Meanwhile, Co. should benefit from improving trends in its key restaurant and lodging markets. For the first quarter of 2004, Co. expects sales for both domestic and international operations to increase over the prior-year quarter, with currency translation continuing to contribute positively to earnings. Diluted earnings per share are expected to range between $0.23 to $0.25. For the full year, Co. expects earnings from ongoing operations of about $1.03 to $1.06 per diluted share.

Financial Data

(US$ in Thousands)	12/31/2003	12/31/2002	12/31/2001	12/31/2000	12/31/1999	12/31/1998	12/31/1997	12/31/1996
Earnings Per Share	1.06	0.81	0.72	0.79	0.65	0.57	0.50	0.87
Cash Flow Per Share	2.01	1.61	1.40	1.19	1.09	0.87	0.87	1.97
Tang. Book Val. Per Share	1.14	0.82	0.40	1.76	1.97	1.75	1.29	4.01
Dividends Per Share	0.290	0.270	0.260	0.240	0.210	0.190	0.160	0.140
Dividend Payout %	27.35	33.33	35.86	30.37	32.06	33.04	32.00	16.09
Income Statement								
Total Revenues	3,761,819	3,403,585	2,354,723	2,264,313	2,080,012	1,888,226	1,640,352	1,490,009
Total Indirect Exp.	1,433,551	1,283,091	946,089	869,343	852,449	775,073	699,764	629,739
Depreciation & Amort.	229,656	223,428	162,990	148,436	134,530	121,971	100,879	89,523
Operating Income	482,658	395,866	318,179	343,139	289,951	261,980	218,504	185,317
Net Interest Inc./(Exp.)	(45,345)	(43,893)	(28,424)	(24,605)	(22,713)	(21,742)	(12,637)	(14,372)
Income Taxes	171,070	140,081	117,408	129,495	109,769	101,782	85,345	70,771
Eqty Earns/Minority Int.	...	...	15,833	19,516	18,317	16,050	13,433	13,011
Income from Cont Ops	...	211,890	...	208,555	...	154,506	...	...
Net Income	277,348	209,770	188,170	206,127	175,786	192,506	133,955	113,185
Average Shs. Outstg.	262,737	261,574	259,856	263,892	268,838	268,094	267,644	128,992
Balance Sheet								
Cash & Cash Equivalents	85,626	49,205	41,793	43,965	47,748	28,425	61,169	69,275
Total Current Assets	1,150,340	1,015,937	929,583	600,568	577,321	503,514	509,501	435,507
Total Assets	3,228,918	2,878,429	2,525,000	1,714,011	1,585,946	1,470,995	1,416,299	1,208,409
Total Current Liabilities	851,942	866,350	827,952	532,034	470,674	399,791	404,464	327,771
Long-Term Obligations	604,441	539,743	512,280	234,237	169,014	227,041	259,384	148,683
Net Stockholders' Equity	1,295,426	1,099,751	880,352	757,007	762,016	690,541	551,701	519,963
Net Working Capital	298,398	149,587	101,631	68,534	106,647	103,723	105,037	107,736
Shares Outstanding	257,416	259,880	255,800	254,322	258,832	258,958	258,254	129,600
Statistical Record								
Operating Profit Margin %	12.83	11.63	13.51	15.15	13.93	13.87	13.32	12.43
Return on Equity %	21.40	19.26	21.37	27.54	23.06	22.37	24.28	21.76
Return on Assets %	8.58	7.36	7.45	12.16	11.08	10.50	9.45	9.36
Debt/Total Assets %	18.71	18.75	20.28	13.67	10.65	15.43	18.31	12.30
Price Range	27.92-23.36	25.08-18.36	21.97-15.49	22.34-14.13	22.09-16.06	18.84-13.42	13.91-9.13	9.81-7.34
P/E Ratio	26.33-22.04	30.96-22.67	30.51-21.51	28.28-17.88	33.99-24.71	33.06-23.55	27.81-18.25	11.28-8.44
Average Yield %	1.13	1.20	1.32	1.29	1.09	1.26	1.44	1.71

Address: 370 Wabasha Street North, St. Paul, MN 55102-2233	Officers: Allan L. Schuman - Chmn., C.E.O., Douglas M. Baker - Pres., C.O.O.	Investor Contact: (612) 293-2809
Telephone: (651) 293-2233	Transfer Agents:EquiServe Trust Company, N.A., Canton, MA	Institutional Holding
Web Site: www.ecolab.com		No of Institutions: 8
		Shares: 352,379 % Held: –

EMERSON ELECTRIC CO.

Exchange	Symbol	Price	52Wk Range	Yield	P/E
NYS	EMR	$59.92 (3/31/2004)	68.46-46.15	2.67	24.26

*7 Year Price Score 93.0 *NYSE Composite Index=100 ***12 Month Price Score 103.6**

Interim Earnings (Per Share)

Qtr.	Dec	Mar	Jun	Sep
2000–01	0.83	0.83	0.77	(0.03)
2001–02	0.61	0.65	0.68	0.58
2002–03	0.52	0.56	0.66	0.67
2003–04	0.58	...	...	...

Interim Dividends (Per Share)

Amt	Decl	Ex	Rec	Pay
0.393Q	5/6/2003	5/14/2003	5/16/2003	6/10/2003
0.393Q	8/5/2003	8/13/2003	8/15/2003	9/10/2003
0.40Q	11/4/2003	11/12/2003	11/14/2003	12/10/2003
0.40Q	2/3/2004	2/11/2004	2/13/2004	3/10/2004

Indicated Div: $1.60 (Div. Reinv. Plan)

Valuation Analysis

Forecast P/E	20.70	Trailing P/E	24.26
Market Cap	$25.2 Billion	Book Value	6.7 Billion
Price/Book	4.05	Price/Sales	1.90

Dividend Achiever Status

Rank	202	10 Year Growth Rate	7.94%
Total Years of Dividend Growth		47	

Business Summary: Instruments and Related Products (MIC: 11.15 SIC: 3621 NAIC:335312)

Emerson Electric designs and manufactures electrical, electromechanical and electronic products, systems and services. The Process Control segment makes process management products. The Industrial automation (IA) segment provides industrial motors, drives, controls and equipment for IA markets. The Electronics and Telecommunications segment designs, manufactures, installs and maintains power products for network–dependent clients. The Heating, Ventilation and Air Conditioning segment engineers and manufactures climate control components and systems. The Appliance and Tools segment provides motors, controls and components for appliance, industrial and comfort control applications.

Recent Developments: For the quarter ended Dec 31 2003, net income increased 11.9% to $244.0 million versus income from continuing operations of $218.0 million in the corresponding prior–year quarter. Results for 2003 and 2002 included net rationalization and other charges of $33.0 million and $12.0 million, respectively. Net sales rose 11.6% to $3.60 billion. On a segment basis, Process Control sales grew 10.0% to $849.0 million, while Industrial automation sales climbed 11.6% to $695.0 million. Electronics and Telecommunications sales were up 15.5% to $657.0 million, and Heating, Ventilation, and Air Conditioning sales jumped 16.4% to $596.0 million. Appliance and Tools sales rose 5.8% to $901.0 million.

Prospects: Co. is experiencing a solid pace of customer orders and business activity, which should drive growth through the remainder of fiscal 2004. The competitive strength of Co.'s business platforms combined with the significant restructuring efforts over the past couple of years is driving both revenues and earnings. All five of Co.'s business segments had growth in underlying sales driven by strong growth in the Heating, Ventilation, and Air Conditioning business and the electronics and telecommunications business. Meanwhile, Co. remains focused on improving capital efficiency as sales growth expands. Looking ahead, Co. expects fiscal 2004 earnings to range from $2.65 to $2.75 per share.

Financial Data

(US$ in Thousands)	3 Mos	09/30/2003	09/30/2002	09/30/2001	09/30/2000	09/30/1999	09/30/1998	09/30/1997
Earnings Per Share	0.58	2.41	2.52	2.40	3.30	3.00	2.77	2.50
Cash Flow Per Share	0.67	4.11	4.31	3.97	4.26	4.12	3.71	3.36
Tang. Book Val. Per Share	4.06	3.60	1.97	2.22	2.53	4.42	4.79	5.22
Dividends Per Share	1.570	1.570	1.550	1.530	1.430	1.300	1.180	1.080
Dividend Payout %	271.98	65.14	61.50	63.75	43.33	43.33	42.59	43.20
Income Statement								
Total Revenues	3,600,000	13,958,000	13,824,000	15,479,600	15,544,800	14,269,500	13,447,200	12,298,600
Total Indirect Exp.	796,000	3,229,000	2,795,000	3,468,200	3,062,900	2,865,100	2,776,400	2,528,500
Depreciation & Amort.	12,000	17,000	28,000	708,500	678,500	637,500	562,500	511,600
Operating Income	492,000	1,645,000	1,798,000	1,892,900	2,465,900	2,210,600	2,075,200	1,904,500
Net Interest Inc./(Exp.)	(57,000)	(231,000)	(233,000)	(304,300)	(287,600)	(189,700)	(151,700)	(120,900)
Income Taxes	113,000	401,000	505,000	556,800	755,900	707,300	694,900	661,700
Eqty Earns/Minority Int.	(6,000)	...	...	...	...	...	...	...
Income from Cont Ops	...	1,013,000	1,060,000	...	...	...	...	...
Net Income	244,000	1,089,000	122,000	1,031,800	1,422,400	1,313,600	1,228,600	1,121,900
Average Shs. Outstg.	422,200	420,900	420,900	429,500	431,400	438,400	444,100	449,500
Balance Sheet								
Cash & Cash Equivalents	1,009,000	696,000	381,000	355,700	280,800	266,100	209,700	221,100
Total Current Assets	5,980,000	5,500,000	4,961,000	5,320,100	5,482,700	5,124,400	5,001,300	4,716,800
Total Assets	15,707,000	15,194,000	14,545,000	15,046,400	15,164,300	13,623,500	12,659,800	11,463,300
Total Current Liabilities	3,643,000	3,417,000	4,400,000	5,379,100	5,218,800	4,590,400	4,021,700	3,842,400
Long–Term Obligations	3,733,000	3,733,000	2,990,000	2,255,600	2,247,100	1,317,100	1,056,600	570,700
Net Stockholders' Equity	6,726,000	6,460,000	5,741,000	6,114,000	6,402,800	6,180,500	5,803,300	5,420,700
Net Working Capital	2,337,000	2,083,000	561,000	(59,000)	263,900	534,000	979,600	874,400
Shares Outstanding	421,567	421,154	420,709	419,625	427,476	433,044	438,224	440,804
Statistical Record								
Operating Profit Margin %	13.66	11.78	13.00	12.22	15.86	15.49	15.43	15.48
Return on Equity %	3.62	15.68	18.46	16.87	22.21	21.25	21.17	20.69
Return on Assets %	1.55	6.66	7.28	6.85	9.37	9.64	9.70	9.78
Debt/Total Assets %	23.76	24.56	20.55	14.99	14.82	9.66	8.34	4.97
Price Range	64.95–52.65	56.79–42.42	65.51–43.20	78.81–45.80	70.19–41.13	70.94–51.81	67.13–51.56	59.81–44.13
P/E Ratio	112.00–90.78	23.56–17.60	26.00–17.14	32.84–19.08	21.27–12.46	23.65–17.27	24.23–18.61	23.93–17.65
Average Yield %	2.65	3.11	2.88	2.34	2.47	2.09	1.96	2.10

Address: 8000 West Florissant Avenue, St. Louis, MO 63136	**Officers:** Charles F. Knight – Chmn., J. G. Berges – Pres.	**Institutional Holding** No of Institutions: 2
Telephone: (314) 553–2000 **Web Site:** www.gotoemerson.com	**Transfer Agents:** Mellon Investor Services, LLC, South Hackensack, NJ	Shares: 140,486 % Held: –

ENERGEN CORP.

Exchange	Symbol	Price	52Wk Range	Yield	P/E
NYS	EGN	$41.25 (3/31/2004)	44.70-31.70	1.79	13.35

*7 Year Price Score 146.6   *NYSE Composite Index=100   *12 Month Price Score 102.2

Interim Earnings (Per Share)

Qtr.	Dec	Jun	Sep	Dec
2001	0.12	...	...	...
Qtr.	Mar	Jun	Sep	Dec
2002	1.24	0.01	0.01	0.83
2003	1.52	0.69	0.32	0.56

Interim Dividends (Per Share)

Amt	Decl	Ex	Rec	Pay
0.18Q	4/23/2003	5/13/2003	5/15/2003	6/2/2003
0.185Q	7/23/2003	8/13/2003	8/15/2003	9/2/2003
0.185Q	10/29/2003	11/12/2003	11/14/2003	12/1/2003
0.185Q	1/28/2004	2/11/2004	2/13/2004	3/1/2004

Indicated Div: $0.74

Valuation Analysis

Forecast P/E	13.56	Trailing P/E	13.35
Market Cap	$1.4 Billion	Book Value	699.0 Million
Price/Book	2.17	Price/Sales	1.80

Dividend Achiever Status

Rank	280	10 Year Growth Rate	3.25%
Total Years of Dividend Growth		21	

Business Summary: Gas Utilities (MIC: 7.4 SIC: 4924 NAIC:221210)

Energen is a diversified energy holding company engaged primarily in the acquisition, development, exploration and production of oil, natural gas and natural gas liquids in the continental U.S. and in the purchase, distribution, and sale of natural gas, principally in central and north Alabama. Alagasco, Co.'s principal subsidiary, is the largest natural gas distribution utility in Alabama, and services a territory that includes approximately 185 cities and communities in 28 countries. The oil and gas exploration and production arm of Co. is Energen Resources, which conducts its activities onshore in North America.

Recent Developments: For the year ended Dec 31 2003, income was $110.3 million compared with income of $70.4 million the previous year. Results for 2003 and 2002 excluded gains of $389,000 and $463,000, respectively, from discontinued operations. The 2002 results also excluded an accounting change charge of $2.2 million. Total operating revenues jumped 26.0% to $842.2 million from $668.6 million the year before. Operating income advanced 61.9% to $219.8 million versus $135.8 million the prior year. The earnings and revenue improvements were primarily attributable to higher prices for natural gas, oil and natural gas liquids production at Energen Resources Corporation.

Prospects: Co. is benefiting from solid growth in its production levels, largely due to contributions from the 2002 acquisition of the Permian Basin properties, a new gas project in the Permian Basin, and the San Juan Basin acquisitions. Co. is also benefiting from its ability to hedge a significant portion of its flowing production at higher prices. Energen Resources' total natural gas hedge position for 2004 is approximately 44.60 billion cubic feet, or about 80.0% of its estimated 2004 natural gas production. Energen Resources' 2004 oil hedge position now stands at about 2.9 million barrels, or some 87.0% of total production for the year.

Financial Data

(US$ in Thousands)	12/31/2003	12/31/2002	12/31/2001	09/30/2001	09/30/2000	09/30/1999	09/30/1998	09/30/1997
Earnings Per Share	3.09	2.09	1.12	2.18	1.75	1.38	1.23	1.15
Cash Flow Per Share	6.80	6.30	0.68	5.03	3.45	4.36	4.19	2.65
Tang. Book Val. Per Share	19.29	16.77	15.17	15.60	13.20	12.08	11.22	13.48
Dividends Per Share	0.730	0.710	0.690	0.680	0.660	0.640	0.620	0.600
Dividend Payout %	23.62	33.97	61.60	31.42	38.00	46.73	50.81	52.17
Income Statement								
Total Revenues	842,221	677,175	146,164	784,973	555,595	497,517	502,627	448,230
Total Indirect Exp.	182,291	155,325	35,383	149,183	133,957	125,881	118,715	92,732
Costs & Expenses	624,333	541,089	135,304	660,964	459,794	420,134	441,142	396,244
Depreciation & Amort.	116,858	105,087	24,502	86,975	87,073	88,615	80,999	59,688
Operating Income	217,888	136,086	10,860	124,009	95,801	77,383	61,485	51,986
Net Interest Inc./(Exp.)	(42,262)	(43,713)	(10,634)	(42,070)	(37,769)	(37,173)	(30,001)	(22,906)
Income Taxes	64,128	20,509	(3,384)	15,976	6,789	135	(2,221)	3,097
Income from Cont Ops	110,265	70,586	3,579	...	...	...	...	...
Net Income	110,654	68,639	3,658	67,896	53,018	41,410	36,249	28,997
Average Shs. Outstg.	35,716	33,838	31,277	31,083	30,359	29,920	29,437	25,126
Balance Sheet								
Net Property	1,433,451	1,256,803	1,005,679	998,334	907,829	861,107	756,344	667,003
Total Assets	1,781,432	1,530,891	1,240,356	1,223,879	1,203,041	1,184,895	993,455	919,797
Long-Term Obligations	552,842	512,954	544,133	544,110	353,932	371,824	372,782	279,602
Net Stockholders' Equity	699,032	582,810	474,205	480,767	400,860	361,504	329,249	301,143
Shares Outstanding	36,223	34,745	31,248	30,799	30,350	29,903	29,326	22,326
Statistical Record								
Operating Profit Margin %	25.87	20.09	7.43	15.79	17.24	15.55	12.23	11.59
Net Inc./Net Property %	7.71	5.46	0.36	6.80	5.84	4.80	4.79	4.34
Net Inc./Tot. Capital %	8.61	6.26	0.35	6.62	7.02	5.64	5.16	4.99
Return on Equity %	15.77	12.11	0.75	14.12	13.22	11.45	11.00	9.62
Accum. Depr./Gross Prop. %	31.34	35.13	37.99	37.16	36.50	34.86	34.47	36.16
Price Range	41.96-28.23	29.80-21.86	25.20-22.00	39.71-22.21	30.06-14.75	20.25-13.63	22.31-15.56	18.75-11.94
P/E Ratio	13.58-9.14	14.26-10.46	22.50-19.64	18.22-10.19	17.18-8.43	14.67-9.87	18.14-12.65	16.30-10.38
Average Yield %	2.14	2.76	2.91	2.25	3.33	3.59	3.22	3.86

Address: 605 Richard Arrington Jr. Boulevard North, Birmingham, AL 35203-2707 **Telephone:** (205) 326-2700 **Web Site:** www.energen.com	**Officers:** William Michael Warren - Chmn., Pres., C.E.O., Geoffrey C. Ketcham - Exec. V.P., C.F.O., Treas. **Transfer Agents:** EquiServe Trust Company, N.A., Providence, RI	**Investor Contact:** **Institutional Holding** **No of Institutions:** 12 **Shares:** 191,272 **% Held:** –

ENERGYSOUTH, INC.

Exchange	Symbol	Price	52Wk Range	Yield	P/E
NMS	ENSI	$34.91 (3/31/2004)	37.14-25.99	3.27	15.24

*7 Year Price Score 124.2   *NYSE Composite Index=100   *12 Month Price Score 100.9

Interim Earnings (Per Share)

Qtr.	Dec	Mar	Jun	Sep
2000–01	0.55	0.73	0.10	0.14
2001–02	0.75	0.93	0.18	0.17
2002–03	0.66	1.09	0.19	0.23
2003–04	0.78	...	...	...

Interim Dividends (Per Share)

Amt	Decl	Ex	Rec	Pay
0.285Q	4/25/2003	6/12/2003	6/16/2003	7/1/2003
0.285Q	7/25/2003	9/11/2003	9/15/2003	10/1/2003
0.285Q	10/25/2003	12/8/2003	12/10/2003	1/1/2004
0.285Q	1/30/2004	3/11/2004	3/15/2004	4/1/2004

Indicated Div: $1.14 (Div. Reinv. Plan)

Valuation Analysis

Forecast P/E	N/A	Trailing P/E	15.24
Market Cap	$175.1 Million	Book Value	87.5 Million
Price/Book	N/A	Price/Sales	N/A

Dividend Achiever Status

Rank	298	10 Year Growth Rate	1.46%
Total Years of Dividend Growth	26		

Business Summary: Gas Utilities (MIC: 7.4 SIC: 4924 NAIC:221210)

EnergySouth is a holding company for a family of energy businesses. Co.'s operations are classified into three business segments. The Natural Gas Distribution segment is engaged in the distribution and transportation of natural gas to about 100,000 residential, commercial and industrial customers in Southwest Alabama, including the City of Mobile, through Mobile Gas and Southern Gas Transmission Company. The Natural Gas Storage segment provides for the underground storage of natural gas and transportation services through the operations of Bay Gas and Storage. Co.'s Other business segment includes marketing, merchandising, and other energy–related services.

Recent Developments: For the quarter ended Dec 31 2003, net income advanced 20.6% to $4.1 million from $3.4 million in the prior–year quarter. The increase in earnings was attributed to improved results from the natural gas distribution operations at Co.'s Mobile Gas subsidiary and continued growth in the storage operations of the Co.'s Bay Gas subsidiary. Total operating revenues grew 27.2% to $32.7 million from $25.7 million the previous year. Gas revenues climbed 29.1% to $31.3 million, while merchandise sales declined 1.9% to $1.1 million. Total operating expenses increased 29.0% to $24.0 million. Operating income was $8.7 million, up 22.6% from $7.1 million a year earlier.

Prospects: Co.'s Mobile Gas' distribution business is benefiting from an increase in gas margins, reflecting the impact of rate adjustments and seasonally higher gas demand. This increase is being partially offset by a 2.8% increase in operating and maintenance expenses and an increase in depreciation expense due to additional plant placed in service. Meanwhile, Co.'s Bay Gas operations are being positively affected by additional storage revenues associated with the commencement of operations of a second storage cavern in April 2003 and a new storage agreement, which was entered into during the first quarter of fiscal 2004.

Financial Data

(US$ in Thousands)	3 Mos	09/30/2003	09/30/2002	09/30/2001	09/30/2000	09/30/1999	09/30/1998
Earnings Per Share	2.29	2.17	2.03	1.52	1.78	1.75	1.71
Cash Flow Per Share	0.0006	3.35	4.38	3.36	2.75	3.74	2.95
Tang. Book Val. Per Share	16.99	16.49	15.30	14.20	13.95	13.10	12.29
Dividends Per Share	1.110	1.090	1.050	1.010	0.950	0.890	0.420
Dividend Payout %	48.47	50.46	51.72	66.44	53.65	51.14	24.56
Income Statement							
Total Revenues	32,716	99,615	86,419	107,759	74,097	68,060	74,022
Total Indirect Exp.	4,687	16,200	14,720	14,861	12,557	11,829	11,870
Costs & Expenses	23,979	73,957	63,675	90,160	54,843	49,072	55,872
Depreciation & Amort.	4,868	8,923	8,172	7,312	6,735	6,467	6,278
Operating Income	8,737	25,658	22,744	17,599	19,254	18,988	18,150
Net Interest Inc./(Exp.)	(2,015)	(7,067)	(5,791)	(4,783)	(4,424)	(4,850)	(4,240)
Income Taxes	2,458	6,702	5,983	4,604	5,270	5,003	4,967
Income from Cont Ops	...	...	...	7,561	...	8,624	...
Net Income	4,068	11,135	10,231	6,138	8,792	8,275	8,417
Average Shs. Outstg.	5,200	5,124	5,046	4,987	4,944	4,933	4,926
Balance Sheet							
Net Property	194,434	194,367	187,823	170,592	134,351	129,676	127,128
Total Assets	233,367	225,686	221,474	218,852	167,380	173,635	166,541
Long-Term Obligations	88,488	92,640	98,645	90,592	55,222	58,017	58,979
Net Stockholders' Equity	87,458	84,655	77,283	70,124	68,544	64,154	59,895
Shares Outstanding	5,145	5,133	5,048	4,937	4,912	4,894	4,872
Statistical Record							
Operating Profit Margin %	26.70	25.75	26.31	16.33	25.98	27.89	24.51
Net Inc./Net Property %	2.09	5.72	5.44	3.59	6.54	6.38	6.62
Net Inc./Tot. Capital %	2.08	5.68	5.35	3.51	6.45	6.18	6.48
Return on Equity %	4.65	13.15	13.23	10.78	12.82	13.44	14.05
Accum. Depr./Gross Prop. %	28.12	27.54	26.26	26.29	28.97	27.76	26.08
Price Range	37.14-31.34	33.96-24.28	32.04-21.10	23.30-19.75	22.00-17.00	23.00-18.94	40.25-18.94
P/E Ratio	47.62-40.18	15.65-11.19	15.78-10.39	15.33-12.99	12.36-9.55	13.14-10.82	23.54-11.07
Average Yield %	3.25	3.83	4.00	4.72	4.96	4.32	1.54

Address: 2828 Dauphin Street, Mobile, AL 36606 Telephone: (251) 450-4774 Web Site: www.energysouth.com	Officers: John C. Hope III – Chmn., Walter L. Hovell – Vice–Chmn.	Institutional Holding No of Institutions: 23 Shares: 331,614 % Held: –

EXXON MOBIL CORP.

Exchange	Symbol	Price	52Wk Range	Yield	P/E
NYS	XOM	$41.59 (3/31/2004)	42.78-34.33	2.40	13.20

*7 Year Price Score 99.3 *NYSE Composite Index=100 *12 Month Price Score 92.1

Interim Earnings (Per Share)

Qtr.	Mar	Jun	Sep	Dec
2000	0.43	0.56	0.58	0.70
2001	0.71	0.63	0.46	0.38
2002	0.30	0.38	0.39	0.54
2003	0.97	0.62	0.55	1.01

Interim Dividends (Per Share)

Amt	Decl	Ex	Rec	Pay
0.25Q	4/30/2003	5/9/2003	5/13/2003	6/10/2003
0.25Q	7/30/2003	8/11/2003	8/13/2003	9/10/2003
0.25Q	10/29/2003	11/7/2003	11/12/2003	12/10/2003
0.25Q	1/28/2004	2/9/2004	2/11/2004	3/10/2004

Indicated Div: $1.00 (Div. Reinv. Plan)

Valuation Analysis

Forecast P/E	18.17	Trailing P/E	N/A
Market Cap	$279.9 Billion	Book Value	N/A
Price/Book	N/A	Price/Sales	N/A

Dividend Achiever Status

Rank	282	10 Year Growth Rate	3.13%
Total Years of Dividend Growth	21	

Business Summary: Oil and Gas (MIC: 14.2 SIC: 2911 NAIC:324110)

Exxon Mobil's principal business is energy, involving exploration for, and production of, crude oil and natural gas, manufacturing of petroleum products and transportation and sale of crude oil, natural gas and petroleum products. Co. is a major manufacturer and marketer of basic petrochemicals, including olefins, aromatics, polyethylene and polypropylene plastics and a wide variety of specialty products. Co. also has interests in electric power generation facilities. As of Dec 31 2003, worldwide proved developed and undeveloped reserves were: crude oil and natural gas liquids, 12,075 million barrels; and natural gas, 54,769 billion cubic feet.

Recent Developments: For the twelve months ended Dec 31 2003, income from continuing operations was $20.96 billion compared with income of $11.01 billion a year earlier. Results for 2003 included a non-recurring special gain of $2.23 billion related to the positive settlement of a U.S. tax dispute and a $1.70 billion gain on the transfer of shares in Ruhrgas AG, a German gas transmission company. Results for 2002 included a non-recurring charge of $215.0 million related to the deferred income tax effect of the 10.0% supplementary U.K. tax on North Sea operations and merger expenses of $275.0 million. Total revenue advanced 20.7% to $246.74 billion from $204.51 billion the previous year.

Prospects: Co.'s near-term outlook appears solid, reflecting favorable crude oil and natural gas prices and significantly improved chemicals results. Meanwhile, Co. has indicated that its plans for long-term capacity increases remain on track as evidenced by liquids volumes growth of 3.9% to 2.6 million daily barrels for the three months ended Dec 31 2003, primarily due to production from new projects in West Africa and Norway. Additionally, during the quarter ended Dec 31 2003, capital and exploration expenditures climbed 8.3% to $4.36 billion from $4.03 billion in the year-ago period, reflecting a continuation of Co.'s active investment program.

Financial Data

(US$ in Millions)	12/31/2003	12/31/2002	12/31/2001	12/31/2000	12/31/1999	12/31/1998	12/31/1997	12/31/1996
Earnings Per Share	3.15	1.61	2.18	2.27	1.12	1.30	1.68	1.50
Cash Flow Per Share	4.27	3.12	3.29	3.26	2.17	2.27	2.92	2.64
Tang. Book Val. Per Share	13.68	11.13	10.74	10.21	9.11	8.98	8.84	8.70
Dividends Per Share	0.980	0.920	0.910	0.880	0.830	0.820	0.810	0.780
Dividend Payout %	31.11	57.14	41.74	38.68	74.22	62.83	48.21	...
Income Statement								
Total Revenues	246,738	204,506	213,488	232,748	185,527	117,772	137,242	134,249
Total Indirect Exp.	106,213	95,439	96,221	95,715	96,526	63,411	65,652	65,079
Depreciation & Amort.	9,047	8,310	7,944	8,130	8,304	5,340	5,474	5,329
Operating Income	28,494	18,117	24,981	28,082	11,990	9,341	13,619	12,764
Net Interest Inc./(Exp.)	(207)	(398)	(293)	(589)	(695)	(100)	(415)	(464)
Income Taxes	11,006	6,499	9,014	11,091	3,240	2,616	4,338	4,406
Eqty Earns/Minority Int.	4,373	...	...	...	...	...	...	...
Income from Cont Ops	20,960	11,011	15,105	15,990	...	6,440	...	...
Net Income	21,510	11,460	15,320	17,720	7,910	6,370	8,460	7,510
Average Shs. Outstg.	6,662	6,803	6,941	7,034	6,906	4,856	5,010	4,968
Balance Sheet								
Net Property	104,965	94,940	89,602	89,829	94,043	65,199	66,414	66,607
Total Assets	174,278	152,644	143,174	149,000	144,521	92,630	96,064	95,527
Long-Term Obligations	4,756	6,655	7,099	7,280	8,402	4,530	7,050	7,236
Net Stockholders' Equity	89,915	74,597	73,161	70,757	63,466	43,750	43,660	43,542
Shares Outstanding	6,568	6,700	6,809	6,930	6,959	4,856	4,914	4,968
Statistical Record								
Operating Profit Margin %	11.55	8.85	11.70	12.06	6.46	7.93	9.92	9.50
Net Inc./Net Property %	20.49	12.07	17.09	19.72	8.41	9.77	12.73	11.27
Net Inc./Tot. Capital %	18.20	11.40	15.40	18.13	8.61	10.07	12.71	11.35
Return on Equity %	23.31	14.76	20.64	22.59	12.46	14.72	19.37	17.24
Accum. Depr./Gross Prop. %	54.22	53.67	52.96	52.15	50.29	49.16	48.02	47.29
Price Range	41.00-31.82	44.38-30.27	45.78-35.83	47.16-35.50	43.22-32.41	38.34-29.06	33.41-24.50	25.13-19.50
P/E Ratio	13.02-10.10	27.57-18.80	21.00-16.44	20.77-15.64	38.59-28.93	29.50-22.36	19.88-14.58	16.75-13.00
Average Yield %	2.71	2.44	2.20	2.13	2.16	2.37	2.76	3.65

Address: 5959 Las Colinas Blvd., Irving, TX 75039-2298	Officers: Lee R. Raymond - Chmn., C.E.O., Harry J. Longwell - Exec. V.P.	Investor Contact:212-444-1900
Telephone: (972) 444-1000	Transfer Agents:ExxonMobil Shareholder Services c/o EquiServe Trust Company, NA, Boston, MA	Institutional Holding
Web Site: www.exxon.mobil.com		No of Institutions: 74
		Shares: 30,807,999 % Held: -

F.N.B. CORP

Exchange	Symbol	Price	52Wk Range	Yield	P/E
NYS	FNB	$22.10 (3/31/2004)	35.45-19.30	4.16	17.68

*7 Year Price Score 131.9   *NYSE Composite Index=100   *12 Month Price Score 98.8

Interim Earnings (Per Share)

Qtr.	Mar	Jun	Sep	Dec
2000	0.38	0.39	0.41	0.44
2001	0.21	0.37	0.46	0.48
2002	(0.19)	0.50	0.51	0.52
2003	0.50	0.53	0.01	0.21

Interim Dividends (Per Share)

Amt	Decl	Ex	Rec	Pay
0.24Q	4/23/2003	5/29/2003	6/2/2003	6/15/2003
0.24Q	8/15/2003	8/27/2003	9/1/2003	9/15/2003
0.24Q	11/18/2003	11/26/2003	12/1/2003	12/15/2003
0.23Q	2/19/2004	2/26/2004	3/1/2004	3/15/2004

Indicated Div: $0.92 (Div. Reinv. Plan)

Valuation Analysis

Forecast P/E	N/A	Trailing P/E	17.68
Market Cap	$967.7 Million	Book Value	606.9 Million
Price/Book	2.68	Price/Sales	2.94

Dividend Achiever Status

Rank	50	10 Year Growth Rate	17.38%
Total Years of Dividend Growth		19

Business Summary: Commercial Banking (MIC: 8.1 SIC: 6021 NAIC:522110)

F.N.B., with assets of $8.31 billion as of Dec 31 2003, is a financial holding company that provides a full range of financial services to consumers and small- to medium-size businesses in its market areas. Co.'s bank subsidiaries offer traditional full-service commercial banking services, including commercial and individual demand and time deposit accounts and commercial, mortgage and individual installment loans. In addition, Co.'s bank subsidiaries offer various alternative investment products, including mutual funds and annuities. The consumer finance subsidiary offers personal installment loans to individuals and purchase installment sales finance contracts from retail merchants.

Recent Developments: For the year ended Dec 31 2003, net income slipped 7.2% to $58.8 million compared with $63.3 million in 2002. Results for 2003 and 2002 included gains on the sale of securities of $2.4 million and $1.9 million, gains on the sale of mortgage loans of $8.5 million and $6.5 million, and merger expenses of $1.2 million and $2.4 million, respectively. Net interest income grew 4.4% to $293.5 million versus $281.1 million a year earlier. Provision for loan losses rose 27.5% to $24.3 million from $19.1 million the year before. Total non-interest income grew 8.0% to $130.6 million from $120.9 million, while total non-interest expense increased 8.9% to $315.3 million from $289.4 million.

Prospects: Co. is optimistic about its ability to achieve its financial goals in 2004. Based on a stable net interest margin and an efficiency ratio of 55.0%, Co. projects diluted earnings per share for full-year 2004 in the range of $1.26 to $1.32. Moreover, Co. expects its dividend payout ratio to be in the range of 65.0% to 75.0% for the year. Also, Co. expects diluted earnings per share for the first quarter of 2004 to range from $0.28 to $0.30. Separately, on Jan 2 2004, Co. completed the spin-off of First National Bankshares of Florida. As a result of the spin off, the combined cash dividend for the companies is expected to increase by about 25.0% to 30.0% for 2004.

Financial Data

(US$ in Thousands)	12/31/2003	12/31/2002	12/31/2001	12/31/2000	12/31/1999	12/31/1998	12/31/1997	12/31/1996
Earnings Per Share	1.25	1.34	1.52	1.62	1.48	1.31	1.62	1.30
Tang. Book Val. Per Share	8.73	11.07	13.02	12.51	11.35	11.76	11.61	11.68
Dividends Per Share	0.920	0.800	0.690	0.650	0.620	0.580	0.500	0.480
Dividend Payout %	74.36	60.31	45.40	40.10	41.90	43.90	30.70	35.00
Income Statement								
Total Interest Income	423,313	426,784	296,693	290,936	254,916	235,985	195,508	138,986
Total Interest Expense	129,836	145,671	125,667	135,308	106,467	103,385	84,478	58,242
Net Interest Income	293,477	281,113	171,026	155,628	148,449	132,600	111,030	80,744
Provision for Loan Losses	24,339	19,094	12,915	10,877	9,240	7,255	10,585	6,137
Non-Interest Income	130,571	120,873	82,799	55,645	46,928	31,745	23,113	15,318
Non-Interest Expense	315,323	289,444	174,830	137,501	129,679	109,174	88,208	62,826
Income Before Taxes	84,386	93,448	66,080	62,895	56,458	47,916	35,350	27,099
Income from Cont Ops	...	...	...	...	...	...	24,314	...
Net Income	58,789	63,335	44,572	42,776	39,295	31,872	33,123	18,433
Average Shs. Outstg.	46,972	47,073	29,311	25,484	26,468	24,265	20,322	12,787
Balance Sheet								
Cash & Due from Banks	204,824	246,802	155,946	141,844	171,183	128,868	87,869	70,338
Securities Avail. for Sale	1,641,972	1,026,191	413,793	436,441	408,731	447,005	432,327	152,776
Net Loans & Leases	5,634,336	5,152,098	3,161,659	2,923,336	2,767,463	2,298,834	1,858,214	1,281,383
Total Assets	8,308,310	7,090,232	4,129,087	3,886,548	3,706,184	3,250,695	2,649,494	1,726,748
Total Deposits	6,159,449	5,426,157	3,292,360	3,102,937	2,909,434	2,708,572	2,192,713	1,429,708
Long-Term Obligations	855,808	450,647	103,013	116,140	117,634	69,492	67,246	34,179
Total Liabilities	7,701,401	6,491,636	3,759,890	3,565,304	3,415,869	2,978,537	2,418,858	1,571,995
Net Stockholders' Equity	606,909	598,596	369,197	321,244	290,315	272,158	230,636	154,753
Shares Outstanding	46,313	46,055	28,346	25,541	25,385	22,928	19,612	12,946
Statistical Record								
Return on Equity %	9.68	10.58	12.07	13.31	13.53	11.71	10.54	11.91
Return on Assets %	0.70	0.89	1.07	1.10	1.06	0.98	0.91	1.06
Equity/Assets %	7.30	8.44	8.94	8.26	7.83	8.37	8.70	8.96
Non-Int. Exp./Tot. Inc. %	56.92	52.85	46.06	39.67	42.96	40.77	40.34	40.71
Price Range	35.45-25.61	30.23-23.36	25.49-18.57	19.65-15.01	23.04-17.24	29.97-19.20	28.92-16.35	17.77-13.71
P/E Ratio	28.36-20.49	22.56-17.43	16.77-12.22	12.13-9.27	15.56-11.65	22.88-14.65	17.85-10.09	13.67-10.54
Average Yield %	3.02	2.94	2.34	3.75	3.08	2.36	2.21	3.05

Address: 2150 Goodlette Road North, Naples, FL 34102 Telephone: (239) 262-7600 Web Site: www.fnbcorporation.com	Officers: Peter Mortensen - Chmn., Stephen J. Gurgovits - Pres., C.E.O.	Investor Contact: (239) 659-9894 Institutional Holding No of Institutions: 20 Shares: 1,023,816 % Held: -

FAMILY DOLLAR STORES, INC.

Exchange	Symbol	Price	52Wk Range	Yield	P/E
NYS	FDO	$35.95 (3/31/2004)	43.61-31.09	0.95	24.46

*7 Year Price Score 158.0 *NYSE Composite Index=100 *12 Month Price Score 95.1

Interim Earnings (Per Share)

Qtr.	Nov	Feb	May	Aug
2000-01	0.24	0.35	0.31	0.20
2001-02	0.29	0.37	0.35	0.24
2002-03	0.33	0.42	0.40	0.28
2003-04	0.37	...	...	...

Interim Dividends (Per Share)

Amt	Decl	Ex	Rec	Pay
0.075Q	5/15/2003	6/12/2003	6/16/2003	7/15/2003
0.075Q	8/21/2003	9/11/2003	9/15/2003	10/15/2003
0.075Q	11/5/2003	12/11/2003	12/15/2003	1/15/2004
0.085Q	1/15/2004	3/11/2004	3/15/2004	4/15/2004
		Indicated Div: $0.34		

Valuation Analysis

Forecast P/E	25.13	Trailing P/E	24.46
Market Cap	$6.2 Billion	Book Value	1.4 Billion
Price/Book	5.01	Price/Sales	1.40

Dividend Achiever Status

Rank	131	10 Year Growth Rate	11.61%
Total Years of Dividend Growth			27

Business Summary: Retail – General (MIC: 5.2 SIC: 5331 NAIC:452990)

Family Dollar Stores is engaged in the operation of a chain of self–service retail discount stores. The stores offer a variety of hardlines and softlines merchandise. Hardlines merchandise includes primarily household chemical and paper products, candy, snack and other food, health and beauty aids, electronics, housewares and giftware, pet food and supplies, toys, stationery and school supplies, seasonal goods, hardware and automotive supplies. Softlines merchandise includes men's, women's, boys', girls' and infants' clothing, shoes, and domestic items such as blankets, sheets and towels. As of Nov 1 2003, Co. operated 5,066 stores in 43 states and the District of Columbia.

Recent Developments: For the quarter ended Feb 28 2004, net income climbed 12.0% to $81.4 million from $72.7 million in the corresponding prior-year period. Net sales totaled $1.40 billion, up 11.7% compared with $1.26 billion the previous year. Results for the recent period benefited from a 2.2% increase in existing-store sales and sales from new stores opened as part of Co.'s store expansion program. During the quarter, Co. opened 95 new stores and closed 22 existing locations. Gross margin advanced 13.5% to $473.8 million, or 33.8% net sales, from $417.5 million, or 33.2% of net sales, the year before.

Prospects: Results are benefiting from higher initial margins on merchandise reflecting improved sourcing, lower levels of markdowns, and improved inventory management. Looking ahead, Co. anticipates earnings per share growth of between 14.0% and 16.0% during the second half of fiscal 2004. This guidance is based on the expectation that sales in existing stores will increase by 3.0% to 5.0% in the second half of the current fiscal year. Separately, Co. plans to open between 525 and 565 new stores during the current fiscal year. Co. is focusing on opening stores in urban locations, however, Co. is targeting certain small and mid-sized towns, where new stores can typically be opened more quickly.

Financial Data

(US$ in Thousands)	3 Mos	08/30/2003	08/31/2002	09/01/2001	08/26/2000	08/28/1999	08/29/1998	08/31/1997
Earnings Per Share	0.37	1.43	1.25	1.10	1.00	0.81	0.60	0.44
Cash Flow Per Share	0.42	1.70	2.31	0.96	1.06	0.64	1.22	0.71
Tang. Book Val. Per Share	7.93	7.61	6.66	5.57	4.66	3.99	3.35	2.74
Dividends Per Share	0.290	0.280	0.250	0.230	0.210	0.190	0.170	0.150
Dividend Payout %	78.37	19.58	20.00	20.90	21.00	23.45	28.33	34.84
Income Statement								
Total Revenues	1,244,683	4,750,171	4,162,652	3,665,362	3,132,639	2,751,181	2,361,930	1,994,973
Total Indirect Exp.	329,826	1,214,658	1,054,298	927,679	784,812	695,060	607,287	523,339
Depreciation & Amort.	24,009	88,315	77,015	67,685	54,509	43,788	34,843	29,117
Operating Income	101,499	389,725	341,621	298,422	270,911	222,679	165,988	121,477
Income Taxes	37,047	142,250	124,692	108,917	98,894	82,600	62,700	46,800
Net Income	64,452	247,475	216,929	189,505	172,017	140,079	103,288	74,677
Average Shs. Outstg.	173,641	173,354	174,049	172,774	172,648	172,511	173,223	171,187
Balance Sheet								
Cash & Cash Equivalents	247,809	206,731	220,265	21,753	43,558	95,301	134,221	42,468
Total Current Assets	1,203,433	1,156,492	1,055,859	807,265	750,673	719,955	646,630	544,703
Total Assets	2,035,940	1,985,695	1,754,619	1,399,745	1,243,714	1,095,252	942,180	780,294
Total Current Liabilities	582,527	595,331	530,780	390,294	412,017	378,546	343,275	261,227
Net Stockholders' Equity	1,369,187	1,310,969	1,154,948	959,015	797,964	690,651	578,151	500,198
Net Working Capital	620,906	561,161	525,079	416,971	338,656	341,408	303,354	283,476
Shares Outstanding	172,446	172,208	173,329	172,035	171,131	172,750	172,203	182,062
Statistical Record								
Operating Profit Margin %	8.15	8.20	8.20	8.14	8.64	8.09	7.02	6.08
Return on Equity %	4.70	18.87	18.78	19.76	21.55	20.28	17.86	14.92
Return on Assets %	3.16	12.46	12.36	13.53	13.83	12.78	10.96	9.57
Price Range	43.61-38.41	40.25-24.16	36.86-24.56	30.09-16.88	23.25-14.38	25.56-12.69	21.50-10.91	11.69-5.50
P/E Ratio	117.9-103.8	28.15-16.90	29.49-19.65	27.35-15.34	23.25-14.38	31.56-15.66	35.83-18.18	26.56-12.50
Average Yield %	0.71	0.87	0.80	0.96	1.13	0.92	1.07	1.94

Address: 10401 Old Monroe Road, Charlotte, NC 28205
Telephone: (704) 847–6961
Web Site: www.familydollar.com

Officers: Howard R. Levine – Chmn., C.E.O., R. James Kelly – Vice–Chmn., C.F.O., Admin. Officer
Transfer Agents: Mellon Investor Services LLC, Ridgefield Park, NJ

Investor Contact: (704) 847–6961
Institutional Holding
No of Institutions: 70
Shares: 46,633,515 **% Held:** –

FANNIE MAE

Exchange	Symbol	Price	52Wk Range	Yield	P/E
NYS	FNM	$74.35 (3/31/2004)	79.88-60.40	2.80	9.63

*7 Year Price Score 105.6 *NYSE Composite Index=100 *12 Month Price Score 92.8

Interim Earnings (Per Share)

Qtr.	Mar	Jun	Sep	Dec
2000	1.02	1.02	1.09	1.13
2001	1.25	1.36	1.33	1.95
2002	1.17	1.44	0.98	0.94
2003	1.93	1.09	2.50	2.20

Interim Dividends (Per Share)

Amt	Decl	Ex	Rec	Pay
0.39Q	4/15/2003	4/28/2003	4/30/2003	5/25/2003
0.45Q	7/14/2003	7/29/2003	7/31/2003	8/25/2003
0.45Q	10/21/2003	10/29/2003	10/31/2003	11/25/2003
0.52Q	1/23/2004	1/28/2004	1/31/2004	2/25/2004

Indicated Div: $2.08 (Div. Reinv. Plan)

Valuation Analysis

Forecast P/E	16.64	Trailing P/E	9.63
Market Cap	$74.4 Billion	Book Value	18.3 Billion
Price/Book	3.99	Price/Sales	1.35

Dividend Achiever Status

Rank	96	10 Year Growth Rate	13.83%
Total Years of Dividend Growth		18	

Business Summary: Credit &Lending (MIC: 8.6 SIC: 6111 NAIC:522292)

Fannie Mae facilitates the flow of low–cost mortgage capital in order to increase the availability and affordability of homeownership for low–, moderate– and middle–income Americans. Co. is the nation's largest source of funds for mortgage lenders and investors, providing resources for customers to make additional mortgage loans or investments in mortgage–related securities. Co. operates exclusively in the secondary mortgage market by purchasing mortgages and mortgage–related securities from primary market institutions, such as commercial banks, savings and loan associations, mortgage companies, securities dealers and other investors.

Recent Developments: For the year ended Dec 31 2003, income was $7.72 billion, before an accounting gain of $185.0 million, versus net income of $4.62 billion in the prior year. Earnings benefited from strong growth in net interest income and a decline in unrealized market–to–market losses on purchased options. This increase was partially offset by a significant increase in losses on the extinguishment of debt, which jumped to $2.26 billion in 2003 from $710.0 million in 2002. Purchased options expense for 2003 and 2002 totaled $2.17 billion and $4.55 billion, respectively. Net interest income climbed 28.4% to $13.57 billion.

Prospects: With the decline in its net interest margin during the second half of 2003 and the current period of very low commitments to purchase mortgages, growth in Co.'s core business earnings per share in the first half of 2004 should be well below trend. However, Co. does expect mortgage spreads to move back to more normal levels as the year progresses. This spread widening could be amplified if banks slow their purchases or become net mortgage sellers. Given these considerations, and its expectations for a continued strong purchase market, Co. anticipates being able to achieve double–digit portfolio growth for 2004. Co. is targeting earnings per share of about $8.01 for the full year.

Financial Data

(US$ in Thousands)	12/31/2003	12/31/2002	12/31/2001	12/31/2000	12/31/1999	12/31/1998	12/31/1997	12/31/1996
Earnings Per Share	7.72	4.53	5.89	4.26	3.73	3.26	2.84	2.50
Tang. Book Val. Per Share	18.82	13.76	15.86	18.57	16.02	13.95	12.33	11.09
Dividends Per Share	1.680	1.320	1.200	1.120	1.080	0.960	0.840	0.760
Dividend Payout %	21.76	29.13	20.37	26.29	28.95	29.44	29.57	30.40
Income Statement								
Total Interest Income	50,920,000	50,853,000	49,170,000	42,781,000	35,495,000	29,995,000	26,378,000	23,772,000
Total Interest Expense	37,351,000	40,287,000	41,080,000	37,107,000	30,601,000	25,885,000	22,429,000	20,180,000
Net Interest Income	13,569,000	10,566,000	8,090,000	5,674,000	4,894,000	4,110,000	3,949,000	3,592,000
Provision for Loan Losses	100,000	128,000	(115,000)	(120,000)	(120,000)	(50,000)	100,000	195,000
Non–Interest Income	2,848,000	2,048,000	1,633,000	1,307,000	1,473,000	1,504,000	1,399,000	1,282,000
Non–Interest Expense	3,631,000	5,764,000	1,354,000	905,000	800,000	708,000	636,000	560,000
Income Before Taxes	10,413,000	6,048,000	8,291,000	5,982,000	5,440,000	4,645,000	4,337,000	3,905,000
Income from Cont Ops	7,720,000	...	6,067,000	4,416,000	3,921,000	3,444,000	3,068,000	2,754,000
Net Income	7,905,000	4,619,000	5,894,000	4,448,000	3,912,000	3,418,000	3,056,000	2,725,000
Average Shs. Outstg.	981,000	997,000	1,006,000	1,009,000	1,031,000	1,037,000	1,056,000	1,083,000
Balance Sheet								
Securities Avail. for Sale	527,823,000	474,726,000	35,883,000	21,136,000	18,091,000	16,216,000	5,906,000	3,500,000
Net Loans & Leases	240,582,000	186,055,000	705,167,000	607,399,000	522,780,000	415,223,000	316,016,000	...
Total Assets	1,009,569,000	887,515,000	799,791,000	675,072,000	575,167,000	485,014,000	391,373,000	64,782,000
Long–Term Obligations	478,539,000	468,570,000	419,975,000	362,360,000	321,037,000	254,878,000	194,374,000	171,370,000
Total Liabilities	987,196,000	871,227,000	781,673,000	654,234,000	557,538,000	469,561,000	377,880,000	338,268,000
Net Stockholders' Equity	22,373,000	16,288,000	18,118,000	20,838,000	17,629,000	15,453,000	13,793,000	12,773,000
Shares Outstanding	970,000	989,000	997,000	999,000	1,019,000	1,025,000	1,037,000	1,061,000
Statistical Record								
Return on Equity %	34.50	28.35	33.48	21.19	22.24	22.28	22.24	21.56
Return on Assets %	0.76	0.52	0.75	0.65	0.68	0.71	0.78	4.25
Equity/Assets %	2.21	1.83	2.26	3.08	3.06	3.18	3.52	19.71
Non–Int. Exp./Tot. Inc. %	6.75	10.89	2.66	2.05	2.16	2.24	2.28	2.23
Price Range	75.37–58.93	83.15–59.54	87.49–72.95	87.81–48.19	75.31–58.88	75.94–56.31	57.06–36.13	41.25–28.00
P/E Ratio	9.76–7.63	18.36–13.14	14.85–12.39	20.61–11.31	20.19–15.78	23.29–17.27	20.09–12.72	16.50–11.20
Average Yield %	2.45	1.78	1.50	1.78	1.60	1.51	1.88	2.26

Address: 3900 Wisconsin Avenue, NW, Washington, DC 20016-2892	Officers: Franklin D. Raines – Chmn., C.E.O., J. Timothy Howard – Vice–Chmn., Exec. V.P., C.F.O.	Investor Contact: (202) 752-7115
Telephone: (202) 752-7000	Transfer Agents:First Chicago Trust Company of New York, Jersey City, NJ	Institutional Holding
Web Site: www.fanniemae.com		No of Institutions: 12
		Shares: 688,038 % Held: –

FARMER BROS. CO.

Exchange	Symbol	Price	52Wk Range	Yield	P/E
NMS	FARM	$360.00 (3/31/2004)	360.0-302.0	1.06	37.42

*7 Year Price Score 145.4 *NYSE Composite Index=100 *12 Month Price Score 87.8

Interim Earnings (Per Share)

Qtr.	Sep	Dec	Mar	Jun
2000–01	0.43	0.64	0.53	0.37
2001–02	0.42	0.52	0.34	0.37
2002–03	0.30	0.32	0.35	0.33
2003–04	0.14	0.14	...	...

Interim Dividends (Per Share)

Amt	Decl	Ex	Rec	Pay
0.95Q	8/19/2003	10/22/2003	10/24/2003	11/10/2003
0.95Q	1/7/2004	1/21/2004	1/23/2004	2/9/2004
0.95Q	3/5/2004	4/21/2004	4/23/2004	5/10/2004
900%	3/5/2004	5/11/2004	4/23/2004	5/10/2004

Indicated Div: $3.80

Valuation Analysis

Forecast P/E	N/A	Trailing P/E	37.42
Market Cap	$693.5 Million	Book Value	261.1 Million
Price/Book	N/A	Price/Sales	N/A

Dividend Achiever Status

Rank	211	10 Year Growth Rate	7.33%
Total Years of Dividend Growth		15	

TRADING VOLUME (thousand shares)

1994 1995 1996 1997 1998 1999 2000 2001 2002 2003 04

Business Summary: Food (MIC: 4.1 SIC: 2095 NAIC:311920)

Farmer Bros. manufactures and distributes a product line that includes roasted coffee, coffee related products (coffee filters, stir sticks, sugar and creamers), teas, cocoa, spices, and soup and beverage bases to restaurants and other institutional establishments that prepare food, including hotels, hospitals, convenience stores and fast food outlets. As of June 30 2003, Co.'s product line included over 300 items. Co.'s products are sold directly from its delivery trucks by sales representatives who solicit, sell, and otherwise maintain its customer's accounts.

Recent Developments: For the three months ended Dec 31 2003, net income dropped 56.5% to $2.6 million compared with $5.9 million in the corresponding quarter of 2002. Results were hampered by higher costs related to legal and other services associated with litigation and proxy matters, increased employee related costs and the implementation of a new information system. Net sales slipped 4.8% to $51.5 million from $54.1 million a year earlier, primarily due to weak economic conditions. Gross profit declined 7.3% to $32.6 million versus $35.2 million the previous year. Income from operations plunged 62.4% to $3.1 million compared with $8.3 million the year before.

Prospects: The recent decline in earnings was primarily due to increased competition and weak economic conditions. However, Co. continues to benefit from a strong base of 50,000 customers and efforts to strengthen its sales force and push ahead with information systems upgrades. Estimated future costs to complete the information systems project exceed $7.0 million, and the project is expected to continue until December of 2004. These initiatives are designed to reduce costs, lower inventory levels, and improve customer service and operating efficiencies.

Financial Data

(US$ in Thousands)	6 Mos	3 Mos	06/30/2003	06/30/2002	06/30/2001	06/30/2000	06/30/1999	06/30/1998
Earnings Per Share	0.28	0.14	1.30	1.65	1.97	2.02	1.51	1.73
Tang. Book Val. Per Share	17.61	19.26	19.16	19.36	18.01	16.25	15.37	14.27
Dividends Per Share	3.650	3.600	3.550	3.350	3.150	2.950	2.750	2.500
Dividend Payout %	N.M.	N.M.	273.08	203.3	159.90	146.04	182.12	144.51
Income Statement								
Total Revenues	97,176	45,665	201,558	205,857	215,431	218,688	221,571	240,092
Total Indirect Exp.	58,024	28,575	107,008	99,883	99,285	92,754	94,967	91,169
Depreciation & Amort.	3,508	1,745	5,776	5,493	5,527	5,628	5,202	4,980
Operating Income	4,181	1,057	23,888	38,210	42,115	48,965	36,770	40,955
Net Interest Inc./(Exp.)	1,221	651	3,974	7,261	12,308	10,080	8,870	8,055
Income Taxes	3,178	1,571	13,942	18,791	23,028	23,643	19,650	19,437
Income from Cont Ops	...	...	...	...	36,488	...	...	...
Net Income	5,076	2,511	23,629	30,569	36,178	37,576	28,865	33,400
Average Shs. Outstg.	17,670	17,829	18,145	18,483	18,433	18,580	19,030	19,260
Balance Sheet								
Cash & Cash Equivalents	187,060	299,349	294,405	292,587	263,180	129,850	126,606	134,804
Total Current Assets	239,656	348,703	346,617	348,434	318,879	188,560	181,549	194,828
Total Assets	308,490	417,997	416,415	417,524	390,395	353,467	324,836	307,012
Total Current Liabilities	15,574	15,665	16,659	16,259	17,655	16,966	15,918	16,159
Net Stockholders' Equity	261,138	371,174	369,145	373,053	347,048	313,113	287,711	274,912
Net Working Capital	224,082	333,038	329,958	332,175	301,224	171,594	165,631	178,669
Shares Outstanding	14,825	19,264	19,264	19,264	19,264	19,264	18,710	19,260
Statistical Record								
Operating Profit Margin %	4.30	2.31	11.85	18.56	19.54	22.39	16.59	17.05
Return on Equity %	1.94	0.67	6.40	8.19	10.51	12.00	10.03	12.14
Return on Assets %	1.64	0.60	5.67	7.32	9.34	10.63	8.88	10.87
Price Range	352.0-312.3	352.0-320.0	348.0-304.0	362.8-202.0	249.0-165.3	207.0-151.0	239.0-174.3	239.0-127.0
P/E Ratio	122.6-108.8	249.6-227.0	267.7-233.8	219.9-122.4	126.4-83.88	102.5-74.75	158.3-115.4	138.2-73.41
Average Yield %	1.10	1.06	1.11	1.23	1.57	1.71	1.34	1.46

Address: 20333 South Normandie Avenue, Torrance, CA 90502	Officers: Roy F. Farmer – Chmn., Roy E. Farmer – Pres.	Institutional Holding
Telephone: (310) 787-5200		No of Institutions: 6
Web Site: N/A		Shares: 451,406 % Held: –

FEDERAL REALTY INVESTMENT TRUST

Exchange	Symbol	Price	52Wk Range	Yield	P/E
NYS	FRT	$46.20 (3/31/2004)	46.20–30.78	4.24	40.17

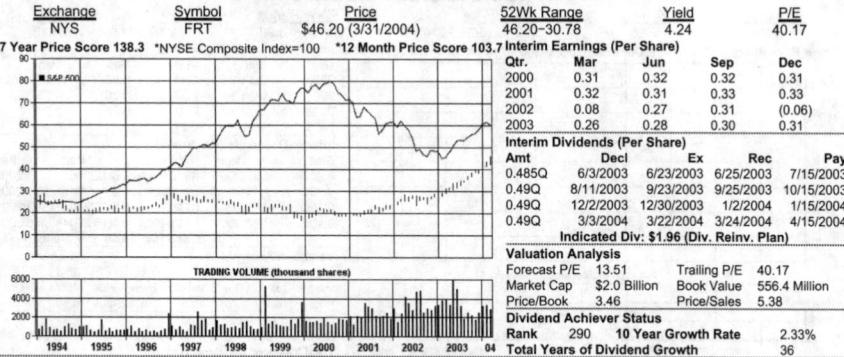

*7 Year Price Score 138.3 *NYSE Composite Index=100 *12 Month Price Score 103.7

Interim Earnings (Per Share)

Qtr.	Mar	Jun	Sep	Dec
2000	0.31	0.32	0.32	0.31
2001	0.32	0.31	0.33	0.33
2002	0.08	0.27	0.31	(0.06)
2003	0.26	0.28	0.30	0.31

Interim Dividends (Per Share)

Amt	Decl	Ex	Rec	Pay
0.485Q	6/3/2003	6/23/2003	6/25/2003	7/15/2003
0.49Q	8/11/2003	9/23/2003	9/25/2003	10/15/2003
0.49Q	12/2/2003	12/30/2003	1/2/2004	1/15/2004
0.49Q	3/3/2004	3/22/2004	3/24/2004	4/15/2004

Indicated Div: $1.96 (Div. Reinv. Plan)

Valuation Analysis

Forecast P/E	13.51	Trailing P/E	40.17
Market Cap	$2.0 Billion	Book Value	556.4 Million
Price/Book	3.46	Price/Sales	5.38

Dividend Achiever Status

Rank	290	10 Year Growth Rate	2.33%
Total Years of Dividend Growth			36

Business Summary: Property, Real Estate &Development (MIC: 8.3 SIC: 6798 NAIC:525930)
Federal Realty Investment Trust specializes in the ownership, management, development and redevelopment of high quality retail and mixed-use properties. As of Dec 31 2003, Co. owned or had an interest in 62 community and neighborhood shopping centers comprising about 13.5 million square feet, primarily located in densely populated and affluent communities throughout the Northeast and Mid-Atlantic U.S. In addition, Co. owned 49 urban and retail mixed-use properties comprising over 2.7 million square feet and one apartment complex, primarily located in strategic metropolitan markets in the Northeast and Mid-Atlantic regions and California. As of Dec 31 2003, Co.'s properties were 93.1% leased.

Recent Developments: For the year ended Dec 31 2003, income was $73.0 million versus income of $44.6 million in the prior year. Results for 2003 and 2002 excluded income from discontinued operations of $21.5 million and $12.3 million, respectively. Results for 2002 included restructuring charge of $22.3 million. Revenue advanced 13.4% to $357.9 million, reflecting increased rental rates at redeveloped, expanded and retenanted centers, partially offset by higher vacancy levels. Rental income increased 13.5% to $334.7 million. Funds from operations were $131.3 million, up 45.0% from $90.5 million a year earlier. Overall, Co.'s portfolio was 93.1% leased as of Dec 31 2003 compared with 94.7% on Dec 31 2002.

Prospects: Looking ahead, the fundamentals of Co.'s business and core markets should remain sound. For instance, Co.'s core redevelopment plan is thriving with grocers expanding and new anchor tenants doing business in many of its shopping centers. However, with its focus on redevelopment, Co. expects to have periods where portfolio vacancy is temporarily above normal. Nevertheless, Co. expects much of this increased vacancy to be the source of long–term growth. Separately, Co. announced it has settled an insurance claim stemming from the August 2002 fire at Santana Row. Accordingly, Co. raised its full–year 2004 outlook for funds from operations to a range of $2.78 to $2.82 per share.

Financial Data

(US$ in Thousands)	12/31/2003	12/31/2002	12/31/2001	12/31/2000	12/31/1999	12/31/1998	12/31/1997	12/31/1996
Earnings Per Share	1.15	0.60	1.29	1.26	1.19	0.94	0.98	0.86
Tang. Book Val. Per Share	11.30	9.40	8.91	9.31	9.99	10.72	11.59	10.83
Dividends Per Share	1.940	1.920	1.890	1.820	1.770	1.750	1.690	1.650
Dividend Payout %	169.13	320.83	146.51	144.44	148.74	186.17	172.45	191.86
Income Statement								
Rental Income	334,697	298,085	279,935	260,684	245,833	222,186	188,529	164,887
Total Income	357,876	318,834	300,502	279,281	264,713	238,478	204,271	179,055
Total Indirect Exp.	86,909	100,310	74,195	66,577	65,131	62,508	53,143	47,254
Depreciation	75,089	64,251	59,914	53,259	50,011	46,047	41,399	38,154
Interest Expense	75,232	65,054	69,313	66,418	61,492	55,125	47,288	45,555
Eqty Earns/Minority Int.	(4,670)	(4,112)	(5,170)	(6,544)	(3,899)	(3,124)	(1,342)	(394)
Income from Cont Ops	73,022	44,581	59,571	56,842	55,493	...	40,129	28,754
Net Income	94,497	55,287	68,756	60,523	48,443	44,960	46,504	28,742
Average Shs. Outstg.	48,619	42,882	40,266	39,910	40,638	40,080	38,988	33,573
Balance Sheet								
Cash & Cash Equivalents	34,968	23,123	17,563	11,357	11,738	17,230	17,043	11,041
Ttl Real Estate Inv.	1,955,972	1,856,129	1,708,537	1,503,655	1,403,538	1,356,083	1,206,142	924,312
Total Assets	2,143,435	1,999,378	1,837,978	1,621,079	1,534,048	1,484,317	1,316,573	1,035,306
Long–Term Obligations	949,357	1,003,212	935,625	809,200	757,862	583,769	551,862	519,478
Total Liabilities	1,452,061	1,355,091	1,245,590	1,153,425	1,032,221	954,370	762,763	646,421
Net Stockholders' Equity	691,374	644,287	592,388	467,654	501,827	529,947	553,810	388,885
Shares Outstanding	49,200	43,535	40,071	39,469	40,201	40,080	39,148	35,886
Statistical Record								
Net Inc.+Depr./Assets %	6.91	5.44	6.50	6.79	6.88	6.13	6.19	6.46
Return on Equity %	10.56	6.91	10.05	12.15	11.05	8.48	7.24	7.39
Return on Assets %	3.40	2.22	3.24	3.50	3.61	3.02	3.04	2.77
Price Range	39.80–26.75	28.75–22.93	23.71–18.98	22.31–17.88	24.50–16.63	25.94–19.56	28.75–24.63	28.13–20.38
P/E Ratio	34.61–23.26	47.92–38.22	18.38–14.71	17.71–14.19	20.59–13.97	27.59–20.81	29.34–25.13	32.70–23.69
Average Yield %	5.78	7.28	8.98	9.03	2.10	7.69	6.33	6.81

Address: 1626 East Jefferson Street, Rockville, MD 20852–4041	**Officers:** Mark Ordan – Chmn., Donald C. Wood – Pres., C.E.O., C.O.O.	**Institutional Holding**	
Telephone: (301) 998–8100	**Transfer Agents:** American Stock Transfer &Trust Company, New York, NY	No of Institutions: 4	
Web Site: www.federalrealty.com		Shares: 74,400 % Held: –	

FEDERAL SIGNAL CORP.

Exchange	Symbol	Price	52Wk Range	Yield	P/E
NYS	FSS	$19.85 (3/31/2004)	20.70-13.90	2.02	28.13

*7 Year Price Score 80.5   *NYSE Composite Index=100   ***12 Month Price Score 83.8**

Interim Earnings (Per Share)

Qtr.	Mar	Jun	Sep	Dec
2000	0.33	0.35	0.35	0.24
2001	0.26	0.37	0.20	0.20
2002	0.22	0.24	0.28	0.27
2003	0.14	0.21	0.21	0.23

Interim Dividends (Per Share)

Amt	Decl	Ex	Rec	Pay
0.20Q	4/17/2003	6/10/2003	6/12/2003	7/1/2003
0.20Q	7/17/2003	9/9/2003	9/11/2003	10/1/2003
0.10Q	10/17/2003	12/10/2003	12/12/2003	1/2/2004
0.10Q	2/13/2004	3/11/2004	3/15/2004	4/5/2004

Indicated Div: $0.40 (Div. Reinv. Plan)

Valuation Analysis

Forecast P/E	15.91	Trailing P/E	28.13
Market Cap	$899.3 Million	Book Value	408.4 Million
Price/Book	1.75	Price/Sales	0.60

Dividend Achiever Status

Rank	184	10 Year Growth Rate	8.66%
Total Years of Dividend Growth	16		

Business Summary: Automotive (MIC: 15.1 SIC: 3711 NAIC:336120)

Federal Signal is a manufacturer and supplier of street cleaning, vacuum loader and refuse collection vehicles; fire rescue vehicles; safety, signaling and communication equipment and tooling products. The Environmental Products Group manufactures and markets a full range of street cleaning, vacuum loader and refuse collection vehicles as well as high–performance water blasting equipment. The Fire Rescue Group manufactures a broad range of fire rescue vehicles. The Safety Products Group manufactures warning, signaling and communication products. The Tool Group manufactures a broad range of consumable carbide and superhard insert tooling.

Recent Developments: For the year ended Dec 31 2003, income from continuing operations was $37.7 million compared with income of $46.2 million in the previous year. Earnings were hampered by a less favorable sales mix and higher costs due to manufacturing facility shutdowns. Results for 2003 excluded a loss of $369,000 from discontinued operations, while results for 2002 excluded an accounting change charge of $8.0 million. Sales advanced 14.2% to $1.21 billion. Environmental Products Group sales jumped 19.1% to $352.9 million, while Fire Rescue Group sales improved 24.4% to $415.8 million. Safety Products Group sales rose 3.0% to $278.4 million, while Tool Group sales grew 2.2% to $159.7 million.

Prospects: Co. is benefiting from strong sales growth, largely due to the refuse truck body business acquisitions, and solid deliveries of fire rescue equipment in North America. However, Co. is experiencing a decline in earnings and operating margins, reflecting a less favorable sales mix in several groups and costs and expenses incurred from shutdowns of manufacturing facilities. Looking ahead, Co. expects continuing growth in North America fire rescue orders and an uptick in its tooling and other short lead–time industrial–based businesses. Nevertheless, refuse truck orders may remain soft and Co. is predicting mixed results in its other global municipal and industrial markets.

Financial Data
(US$ in Thousands)

	12/31/2003	12/31/2002	12/31/2001	12/31/2000	12/31/1999	12/31/1998	12/31/1997	12/31/1996
Earnings Per Share	0.79	1.01	1.03	1.27	1.25	1.30	1.29	1.35
Cash Flow Per Share	1.57	1.92	2.09	1.41	1.25	1.64	1.40	1.33
Tang. Book Val. Per Share	1.17	1.04	1.74	1.82	1.66	1.97	2.45	2.35
Dividends Per Share	0.800	0.790	0.770	0.750	0.730	0.700	0.640	0.560
Dividend Payout %	101.26	78.71	75.24	59.44	58.60	53.84	50.19	41.48
Income Statement								
Total Revenues	1,206,798	1,057,201	1,072,175	1,106,127	1,061,896	1,002,787	924,912	896,357
Total Indirect Exp.	249,097	217,053	220,257	220,690	214,856	206,378	191,170	173,514
Depreciation & Amort.	24,435	23,995	30,258	29,057	27,237	23,586	20,545	18,410
Operating Income	65,978	81,943	92,004	116,654	106,505	101,750	99,674	102,892
Net Interest Inc./(Exp.)	(19,750)	(20,075)	(26,368)	(31,401)	(23,339)	(19,336)	(17,163)	(15,359)
Income Taxes	8,345	14,923	17,864	26,759	26,859	26,838	25,878	31,382
Income from Cont Ops	37,672	46,179	46,590	57,655	...	...	...	...
Net Income	37,303	38,195	47,573	57,537	57,537	59,396	58,969	62,033
Average Shs. Outstg.	47,984	45,939	45,443	45,521	45,958	45,846	45,840	45,952
Balance Sheet								
Cash & Cash Equivalents	10,119	9,782	16,882	13,556	8,764	15,316	10,686	12,431
Total Current Assets	403,552	394,817	342,325	348,936	346,137	311,207	268,622	267,006
Total Assets	1,186,409	1,168,410	1,015,614	991,118	960,961	835,999	727,905	703,901
Total Current Liabilities	284,370	221,884	179,430	288,920	269,463	195,193	227,029	374,618
Long–Term Obligations	395,477	481,566	446,595	316,932	307,020	288,812	177,523	34,311
Net Stockholders' Equity	422,509	398,065	359,436	357,431	354,033	321,782	299,772	272,789
Net Working Capital	119,182	172,933	162,895	60,016	76,674	116,014	41,593	(107,612)
Shares Outstanding	47,918	47,660	45,129	45,304	46,114	45,329	45,606	45,318
Statistical Record								
Operating Profit Margin %	5.46	7.75	8.58	10.54	10.02	10.14	10.77	11.47
Return on Equity %	8.91	11.60	12.96	16.13	16.25	18.45	19.67	22.74
Return on Assets %	3.17	3.95	4.58	5.81	5.98	7.10	8.10	8.81
Debt/Total Assets %	33.33	41.21	43.97	31.97	31.94	34.54	24.38	4.87
Price Range	20.70-13.67	26.75-16.16	24.50-17.25	23.88-14.88	27.38-15.13	27.38-20.25	27.25-20.19	27.88-21.13
P/E Ratio	26.20-17.30	26.49-16.00	23.79-16.75	18.80-11.71	21.90-12.10	21.06-15.58	21.12-15.65	20.65-15.65
Average Yield %	4.73	3.64	3.59	3.89	3.41	3.06	2.57	2.24

Address: 1415 West 22nd Street, Oak Brook, IL 60523–2004	**Officers:** Robert D. Welding – Pres., C.E.O., John A. DeLeonardis – V.P., Taxes	**Investor Contact:** (630) 954–2000
Telephone: (630) 954–2000	**Transfer Agents:** National City Bank, Cleveland, OH	**Institutional Holding**
Web Site: www.federalsignal.com		**No of Institutions:** 5
		Shares: 21,819 **% Held:** –

FIDELITY NATIONAL FINANCIAL, INC.

Exchange	Symbol	Price	52Wk Range	Yield	P/E
NYS	FNF	$39.60 (3/31/2004)	39.62-25.02	1.82	7.03

*7 Year Price Score 170.5   *NYSE Composite Index=100   *12 Month Price Score 104.3

Interim Earnings (Per Share)

Qtr.	Mar	Jun	Sep	Dec
2000	0.03	0.27	0.32	0.45
2001	0.34	0.67	0.62	0.71
2002	0.74	0.82	1.05	1.30
2003	1.05	1.61	1.80	1.17

Interim Dividends (Per Share)

Amt	Decl	Ex	Rec	Pay
0.164Q	7/23/2003	8/15/2003	8/19/2003	9/3/2003
0.164Q	10/22/2003	11/17/2003	11/19/2003	12/4/2003
0.18Q	1/28/2004	3/5/2004	3/9/2004	3/23/2004
10%	1/28/2004	2/10/2004	2/12/2004	2/26/2004

Indicated Div: $0.72

Valuation Analysis

Forecast P/E	8.56	Trailing P/E	7.03
Market Cap	$3.8 Billion	Book Value	3.9 Billion
Price/Book	1.48	Price/Sales	0.75

Dividend Achiever Status

Rank	23	10 Year Growth Rate	22.29%
Total Years of Dividend Growth		16

Business Summary: Insurance (MIC: 8.2 SIC: 6361 NAIC:524127)

Fidelity National Financial, through its principal subsidiaries, is a major U.S. title insurance and diversified real estate–related services company. As of Dec 31 2003, Co. provided title insurance in 49 states, the District of Columbia, Guam, Mexico, Puerto Rico, the U.S. Virgin Islands and in Canada and Mexico. Co. also provides information–based technology applications and processing services to financial institutions and the mortgage and financial services industries. Co.'s reporting segments include title insurance; financial institution processing and outsourcing; real estate information services; specialty insurance; and corporate and other.

Recent Developments: For the year ended Dec 31 2003, net earnings rose 62.1% to $861.8 million compared with $531.7 million a year earlier. Total revenues advanced 51.8% to $7.72 billion from $5.08 billion the previous year. Co. attributed the increase in total revenues to higher real estate and refinance activity as a result of decreasing interest rates. In addition, Co. noted that revenues benefited from the acquisitions of financial institution processing and outsourcing service companies, real estate information service companies and specialty insurance companies and the integration of these operations into its core businesses in 2003 and increased realized gains on investments.

Prospects: Co.'s overall prospects look promising, reflecting progress in its ongoing strategy of diversifying into financial institution processing and outsourcing, thus increasing its recurring revenue and earnings streams and providing a more balanced financial profile going forward. For instance, Co. noted that nearly 25.0% of its revenue for the three months ended Dec 31 2003 came from non-title related operations or investment activity. Co. stated that it is striving to increase this amount to 50.0% of revenues over the next three years. Meanwhile, Co.'s near-term outlook appears acceptable, despite a drop in monthly direct title and escrow orders from the refinancing peak of the summer of 2003.

Financial Data

(US$ in Thousands)	12/31/2003	12/31/2002	12/31/2001	12/31/2000	12/31/1999	12/31/1998	12/31/1997	12/31/1996
Earnings Per Share	5.63	3.91	2.34	1.07	1.36	1.94	1.13	0.73
Tang. Book Val. Per Share	6.83	9.55	12.64	10.52	9.56	8.25	5.95	3.93
Dividends Per Share	0.630	0.290	0.240	0.240	0.160	0.150	0.130	0.120
Dividend Payout %	11.23	7.46	10.52	22.44	12.33	7.88	12.23	17.31
Income Statement								
Total Premium Income	4,873,482	3,547,729	2,694,479	1,946,159	939,452	910,278	533,220	475,961
Other Income	2,628,963	1,510,873	1,179,628	795,835	412,752	378,187	213,492	160,952
Total Revenues	7,502,445	5,058,602	3,874,107	2,741,994	1,352,204	1,288,465	746,712	636,913
Total Indirect Exp.	4,172,538	2,498,323	2,075,845	1,506,660	742,362	651,364	401,423	365,711
Inc. Before Inc. Taxes	1,314,254	839,281	518,641	194,140	117,828	175,134	73,430	40,553
Income Taxes	539,843	306,468	207,456	85,825	46,975	69,442	31,959	16,216
Eqty Earns/Minority Int.	(18,976)	(13,115)	...	...	...	...	...	...
Income from Cont Ops	755,435	519,698	311,185	...	...	...	41,471	...
Net Income	861,820	531,717	305,476	108,315	70,853	105,692	39,771	24,337
Average Shs. Outstg.	153,171	135,870	133,189	101,382	52,135	55,692	39,316	37,609
Balance Sheet								
Cash & Cash Equivalents	1,370,205	1,371,463	1,034,159	672,272	112,801	136,614	71,798	64,844
Premiums Due	446,102	233,205	992,694	936,417	79,088	86,701	61,548	65,672
Invst. Assets: Total	2,689,817	2,565,608	1,803,821	1,685,331	506,916	510,515	326,277	227,674
Total Assets	7,295,339	5,245,744	4,415,998	3,833,985	1,029,173	969,470	600,559	509,296
Long–Term Obligations	659,186	493,458	565,690	791,430	226,359	214,624	123,023	148,922
Net Stockholders' Equity	3,873,359	2,253,936	1,638,870	1,106,737	432,494	396,740	196,319	110,251
Shares Outstanding	164,840	131,594	129,592	105,117	45,234	48,074	32,967	28,024
Statistical Record								
Return on Equity %	19.50	23.05	18.98	9.78	16.38	26.64	21.12	22.07
Return on Assets %	10.35	9.90	7.04	2.82	6.88	10.90	6.90	4.77
Price Range	35.25-22.36	24.44-15.78	22.20-12.08	23.67-7.10	18.33-8.26	23.53-13.28	17.08-5.71	8.02-5.64
P/E Ratio	6.26-3.97	6.25-4.04	9.49-5.16	22.12-6.64	13.48-6.08	12.13-6.85	15.11-5.06	10.98-7.73
Average Yield %	2.33	1.42	1.46	2.11	1.49	0.82	1.47	1.74

Address: 17911 Von Karman Avenue, Irvine, CA 92614 Telephone: (949) 622–4333 Web Site: www.fnf.com	Officers: William P. Foley II – Chmn., C.E.O., Frank P. Willey – Vice–Chmn. Transfer Agents:Continental Stock Transfer and Trust Co., New York, NY	Investor Contact:949–622–4333 Institutional Holding No of Institutions: 19 Shares: 228,483 % Held: –

FIFTH THIRD BANCORP

Exchange	Symbol	Price	52Wk Range	Yield	P/E
NMS	FITB	$55.37 (3/31/2004)	60.18-47.73	2.31	18.64

*7 Year Price Score 119.0 *NYSE Composite Index=100 *12 Month Price Score 93.1

Interim Earnings (Per Share)

Qtr.	Mar	Jun	Sep	Dec
2000	0.44	0.41	0.48	0.50
2001	0.51	0.22	0.47	0.66
2002	0.66	0.68	0.70	0.72
2003	0.72	0.75	0.76	0.74

Interim Dividends (Per Share)

Amt	Decl	Ex	Rec	Pay
0.29Q	6/17/2003	6/26/2003	6/30/2003	7/15/2003
0.29Q	9/16/2003	9/26/2003	9/30/2003	10/14/2003
0.29Q	12/16/2003	12/29/2003	12/31/2003	1/15/2004
0.32Q	3/16/2004	3/29/2004	3/31/2004	4/15/2004
Indicated Div: $1.28 (Div. Reinv. Plan)				

Valuation Analysis

Forecast P/E	17.31	Trailing P/E	18.64
Market Cap	$32.1 Billion	Book Value	8.5 Billion
Price/Book	3.92	Price/Sales	5.15

Dividend Achiever Status

Rank	38	10 Year Growth Rate 18.85%
Total Years of Dividend Growth		31

Business Summary: Commercial Banking (MIC: 8.1 SIC: 6022 NAIC:522110)

Fifth Third Bancorp is a bank holding company headquartered in Cincinnati, OH. As of Dec 31 2003, Co. had $91.14 billion in assets and operated 17 affiliates with 960 full-service banking centers, including 133 Bank Mart® locations open seven days a week inside select grocery stores and 1,905 Jeanie® ATMs in Ohio, Kentucky, Indiana, Florida, Michigan, Illinois, Tennessee and West Virginia. Co. operates four main businesses: Retail, Commercial, Investment Advisors and Fifth Third Processing Solutions. Through its subsidiaries, Co. engages primarily in commercial, retail and trust banking, investment services and leasing activities.

Recent Developments: For the year ended Dec 31 2003, income from continuing operations was $1.72 billion, before an accounting charge of $11.0 million, versus income of $1.63 billion in 2002. Earnings for 2003 and 2002 included net securities gains of $84.0 million and $147.0 million, and excluded net gains from discontinued operations of $44.0 million and $4.0 million, respectively. Earnings benefited from strong loan and deposit sales results and strength from its service businesses. Net interest income rose 7.6% to $2.91 billion. Provision for credit losses grew 62.0% to $399.4 million. Total other operating income climbed 13.7% to $2.48 billion. Total other operating expenses grew 10.5% to $2.44 billion.

Prospects: Despite the negative impact of low interest rates and the sluggish economy, Co. continues to produce solid earnings growth, growth, supported by improved loan and deposit sales and continued growth from its services businesses. Co. also continues to add new banking center locations and increase automation of processes. Separately, on Dec 29 2003, Co. completed the sale of its corporate trust business to the Bank of New York. The transaction involved the sale of approximately 5,000 bond trustee and agency appointments representing $45.00 billion of principal debt outstanding for nearly 4,000 clients. The sale should allow Co. to refine its focus and reinvest in its core businesses.

Financial Data

(US$ in Thousands)	12/31/2003	12/31/2002	12/31/2001	12/31/2000	12/31/1999	12/31/1998	12/31/1997	12/31/1996
Earnings Per Share	2.97	2.76	1.86	1.83	1.43	1.17	1.12	0.95
Tang. Book Val. Per Share	12.92	12.64	13.09	10.50	8.79	7.93	6.52	5.99
Dividends Per Share	1.100	0.950	0.780	0.680	0.550	0.430	0.360	0.310
Dividend Payout %	37.03	34.42	41.93	37.15	39.07	37.31	32.54	32.63
Income Statement								
Total Interest Income	3,991,000	4,129,000	4,709,000	3,263,000	2,738,000	2,018,677	1,478,388	1,385,113
Total Interest Expense	1,086,000	1,429,000	2,276,000	1,793,000	1,333,000	1,015,853	733,426	695,869
Net Interest Income	2,905,000	2,700,000	2,433,000	1,470,000	1,405,000	1,002,824	744,962	689,244
Provision for Loan Losses	399,000	246,000	236,000	89,000	134,000	109,171	80,342	64,014
Non-Interest Income	2,483,000	2,194,000	1,797,000	1,013,000	877,000	636,106	445,461	368,415
Non-Interest Expense	2,442,000	2,216,000	2,341,000	1,119,000	1,122,000	803,577	506,158	493,330
Income Before Taxes	2,547,000	2,432,000	1,653,000	1,275,000	1,026,000	726,270	603,923	500,315
Eqty Earns/Minority Int.	(20,000)	(38,000)	(2,000)	...	...	...	...	...
Income from Cont Ops	1,722,000	1,634,700	1,101,000	...	...	...	...	...
Net Income	1,755,000	1,635,000	1,094,000	863,000	668,000	476,128	401,237	335,059
Average Shs. Outstg.	580,000	592,020	591,316	475,978	471,855	398,007	354,789	350,979
Balance Sheet								
Cash & Due from Banks	2,359,000	1,891,000	2,301,000	985,000	1,213,000	819,862	720,133	808,926
Securities Avail. for Sale	29,054,000	25,464,000	20,507,000	15,602,000	12,688,000	8,334,625	6,397,077	6,223,881
Net Loans & Leases	51,538,000	45,245,000	40,924,000	25,569,000	24,597,000	17,512,163	13,237,786	12,327,514
Total Assets	91,143,000	80,894,000	71,296,000	45,857,000	41,589,000	28,921,782	21,375,054	20,548,998
Total Deposits	57,095,000	52,208,000	45,854,000	30,948,000	26,083,000	18,780,355	14,914,132	14,374,656
Long-Term Obligations	9,063,000	8,178,700	7,029,900	4,034,000	1,977,000	2,288,151	457,878	277,661
Total Liabilities	82,618,000	72,418,700	63,386,900	40,966,000	37,512,000	25,743,260	19,097,643	18,404,873
Net Stockholders' Equity	8,525,000	8,475,000	7,639,000	4,891,000	4,077,000	3,178,522	2,277,411	2,144,125
Shares Outstanding	566,685	574,355	582,674	465,651	463,329	400,377	349,256	357,388
Statistical Record								
Return on Equity %	20.19	19.28	14.41	17.64	16.38	14.97	17.61	15.62
Return on Assets %	1.88	2.02	1.54	1.88	1.60	1.64	1.87	1.63
Equity/Assets %	9.35	10.47	10.71	10.66	9.80	10.99	10.65	10.43
Non-Int. Exp./Tot. Inc. %	37.72	35.04	35.98	26.16	31.03	30.26	26.30	28.13
Price Range	61.81-47.73	69.40-55.86	64.43-47.19	60.50-30.00	50.29-39.42	48.92-32.33	36.72-18.37	21.85-12.96
P/E Ratio	20.81-16.07	25.14-20.24	34.64-25.37	33.06-16.39	35.17-27.56	41.81-27.64	32.79-16.40	23.00-13.65
Average Yield %	1.98	1.49	1.35	1.50	1.22	1.10	1.37	1.88

Address: 38 Fountain Square Plaza, Cincinnati, OH 45263 Telephone: (513) 534-5300 Web Site: www.53.com	Officers: George A. Schaefer - Pres., C.E.O., Neal E. Arnold - Exec. V.P., C.F.O.	Investor Contact: (513) 579-4356 Institutional Holding No of Institutions: 4 Shares: 294,606 % Held: -

FIRST CHARTER CORP.

Exchange	Symbol	Price	52Wk Range	Yield	P/E
NMS	FCTR	$21.14 (3/31/2004)	21.68–16.69	3.50	24.58

*7 Year Price Score 102.5   *NYSE Composite Index=100   *12 Month Price Score 95.3

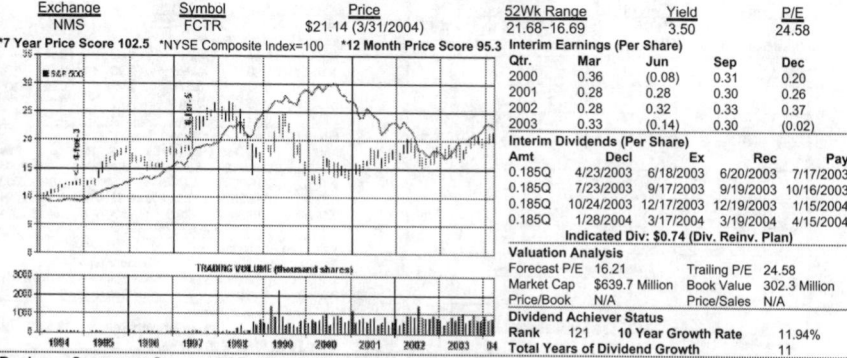

Interim Earnings (Per Share)

Qtr.	Mar	Jun	Sep	Dec
2000	0.36	(0.08)	0.31	0.20
2001	0.28	0.28	0.30	0.26
2002	0.28	0.32	0.33	0.37
2003	0.33	(0.14)	0.30	(0.02)

Interim Dividends (Per Share)

Amt	Decl	Ex	Rec	Pay
0.185Q	4/23/2003	6/18/2003	6/20/2003	7/17/2003
0.185Q	7/23/2003	9/17/2003	9/19/2003	10/16/2003
0.185Q	10/24/2003	12/17/2003	12/19/2003	1/15/2004
0.185Q	1/28/2004	3/17/2004	3/19/2004	4/15/2004

Indicated Div: $0.74 (Div. Reinv. Plan)

Valuation Analysis

Forecast P/E	16.21	Trailing P/E	24.58
Market Cap	$639.7 Million	Book Value	302.3 Million
Price/Book	N/A	Price/Sales	N/A

Dividend Achiever Status

Rank	121	10 Year Growth Rate	11.94%
Total Years of Dividend Growth			11

Business Summary: Commercial Banking (MIC: 8.1 SIC: 6021 NAIC:522110)

First Charter is a regional financial services company with assets of $4.21 billion as of Dec 31 2003. Co. is the holding company for First Charter Bank, which operates 54 financial centers, five insurance offices and 93 ATMs located in 17 counties throughout the piedmont and western half of North Carolina. Co. also operates one mortgage origination office in Virginia. Co. provides businesses and individuals with a broad range of financial services, including banking, financial planning, funds management, investments, insurance, mortgages and employee benefit programs.

Recent Developments: For the twelve months ended Dec 31 2003, net income totaled $14.1 million, down 64.5% compared with $39.8 million in the corresponding prior-year period. Total interest income was down 9.2% to $178.3 million, while interest expense declined 15.3% to $70.5 million. Net interest income slipped 4.7% to $107.8 million from $113.2 million the previous year. Provision for loan losses was $27.5 million versus $8.3 million a year earlier. Non-interest income advanced 34.7% to $64.2 million from $47.6 million the year before. Non-interest expense climbed 29.9% to $127.0 million from $97.8 million in 2002.

Prospects: Earnings are being negatively affected by significantly lower interest rates, which are pressuring net interest margin. In addition, results are being hurt by costs stemming from the prepayment of certain borrowings and an increase in the provision for loan losses, primarily due to loan portfolio growth. Separately, yields on Co.'s mortgage-backed securities portfolio are being hampered by increased prepayments on the underlying mortgages. Meanwhile, results should benefit from increased revenue from brokerage services, insurance services, financial management and service charges.

Financial Data

(US$ in Thousands)	12/31/2003	12/31/2002	12/31/2001	12/31/2000	12/31/1999	12/31/1998	12/31/1997	12/31/1996
Earnings Per Share	0.47	1.30	1.12	0.79	1.45	0.50	0.90	1.16
Tang. Book Val. Per Share	10.07	10.79	10.06	9.78	12.95	13.33	8.39	7.85
Dividends Per Share	0.740	0.730	0.720	0.690	0.680	0.580	0.510	0.480
Dividend Payout %	157.44	56.15	64.28	87.34	46.89	116.00	57.22	41.42
Income Statement								
Total Interest Income	178,292	196,388	215,276	216,244	136,717	136,509	55,954	40,569
Total Interest Expense	70,490	83,227	109,912	108,314	67,269	70,623	24,751	17,256
Net Interest Income	107,802	113,161	105,364	107,930	69,448	65,886	31,203	23,313
Provision for Loan Losses	27,518	8,270	4,465	7,615	3,350	2,376	2,702	920
Non-Interest Income	64,180	47,631	38,773	30,565	18,213	13,650	9,452	6,271
Non-Interest Expense	127,032	97,772	87,579	92,727	45,869	59,166	25,642	16,074
Income Before Taxes	17,432	54,750	52,093	38,153	38,442	17,994	12,311	12,590
Net Income	14,146	39,803	35,325	24,841	26,092	9,236	8,401	8,853
Average Shs. Outstg.	30,007	30,702	31,660	31,580	18,053	18,572	9,339	7,601
Balance Sheet								
Cash & Due from Banks	88,564	162,087	134,084	71,196	59,967	41,884	33,077	31,300
Securities Avail. for Sale	1,601,900	1,129,212	1,077,365	441,031	342,136	331,799	...	...
Net Loans & Leases	2,227,030	2,045,266	1,929,052	2,128,960	1,408,953	1,406,967	515,799	355,353
Total Assets	4,206,693	3,745,949	3,332,737	2,932,199	1,894,317	2,196,156	938,725	678,978
Total Deposits	2,427,897	2,322,647	2,162,945	1,998,234	1,149,512	1,123,035	621,354	455,215
Long-Term Obligations	1,432,200	1,042,440	808,512	570,024	491,976	469,944	53,279	27,261
Total Liabilities	3,907,254	3,421,263	3,023,396	2,622,912	1,666,605	1,618,385	683,890	487,447
Net Stockholders' Equity	299,439	324,686	309,341	309,287	227,712	245,972	77,804	59,409
Shares Outstanding	29,720	30,069	30,742	31,601	17,571	18,442	9,268	7,561
Statistical Record								
Return on Equity %	4.72	12.25	11.41	8.03	11.45	3.75	10.79	14.90
Return on Assets %	0.33	1.06	1.05	0.84	1.37	0.42	0.89	1.30
Equity/Assets %	7.11	8.66	9.28	10.54	12.02	11.20	8.28	8.74
Non-Int. Exp./Tot. Inc. %	52.39	40.06	34.47	37.57	29.60	39.40	39.20	34.31
Price Range	21.20–16.69	20.57–15.33	18.75–13.44	17.50–12.50	24.88–14.00	27.00–14.00	26.75–17.71	18.75–14.79
P/E Ratio	45.11–35.51	15.82–11.79	16.74–12.00	22.15–15.82	17.16–9.66	54.00–28.00	29.72–19.68	16.16–12.75
Average Yield %	3.92	4.06	4.37	4.71	3.46	2.64	2.34	2.89

Address: 10200 David Taylor Drive, Charlotte, NC 28262-2373	Officers: J. Roy Davis – Chmn., Michael R. Coltrane – Vice-Chmn.	Investor Contact:800-422-4650
Telephone: (704) 688-4300		Institutional Holding
Web Site: www.firstcharter.com		No of Institutions: 71
		Shares: 4,869,666 % Held: 16.2

101

FIRST COMMONWEALTH FINANCIAL CORP.

Exchange	Symbol	Price	52Wk Range	Yield	P/E
NYS	FCF	$14.78 (3/31/2004)	14.98-11.69	4.33	16.42

*7 Year Price Score 111.2   *NYSE Composite Index=100   *12 Month Price Score 99.0

Interim Earnings (Per Share)

Qtr.	Mar	Jun	Sep	Dec
2000	0.20	0.23	0.20	0.19
2001	0.21	0.21	0.22	0.22
2002	0.13	0.19	0.21	0.21
2003	0.23	0.23	0.23	0.21

Interim Dividends (Per Share)

Amt	Decl	Ex	Rec	Pay
0.155Q	6/10/2003	6/26/2003	6/30/2003	7/15/2003
0.155Q	9/16/2003	9/26/2003	9/30/2003	10/15/2003
0.16Q	12/16/2003	12/29/2003	12/31/2003	1/16/2004
0.16Q	3/16/2004	3/29/2004	3/31/2004	4/15/2004

Indicated Div: $0.64

Valuation Analysis

Forecast P/E	N/A	Trailing P/E	16.42
Market Cap	$869.6 Million	Book Value	430.9 Million
Price/Book	2.01	Price/Sales	3.03

Dividend Achiever Status

Rank	169	10 Year Growth Rate	9.51%
Total Years of Dividend Growth			16

Business Summary: Commercial Banking (MIC: 8.1 SIC: 6021 NAIC:522110)
First Commonwealth Financial is a financial services holding company with $5.19 billion in assets, as of Dec 31 2003. Co. operates 91 community banking offices in Pennsylvania through First Commonwealth Bank, a Pennsylvania chartered bank. Financial services and insurance products are also provided by First Commonwealth Trust, First Commonwealth Financial Advisors, and First Commonwealth Insurance Agency. Co. also operates First Commonwealth Systems, a data processing subsidiary, First Commonwealth Professional Resources, a support services subsidiary, and jointly owns Commonwealth Trust Credit Life Insurance, a credit life reinsurance company.

Recent Developments: For the twelve months ended Dec 31 2003, net income rose 22.5% to $53.3 million compared with $43.5 million in 2002. Results for 2003 and 2002 included securities gains of $5.9 million and $642,000, and a litigation settlement credit of $610,000 and a charge of $8.0 million, respectively. Results for 2003 also included a gain on the sale of branches of $3.0 million, while results for 2002 included restructuring charges of $6.1 million. Net interest income slipped 6.1% to $143.5 million from $152.9 million the year before. Provision for credit losses grew 4.5% to $12.8 million. Total other income jumped 30.2% to $48.4 million, while total other expenses were $112.7 million.

Prospects: On Dec 12 2003, Co. agreed to acquire GA Financial and Great American Federal and merge the operations into its own and First Commonwealth Bank, respectively. Under the terms of the agreement, shareholders of GA Financial can elect to receive $35.00 in cash or an equivalent value of Co.'s common stock for each share held. The transaction is subject to regulatory and shareholder approvals and is expected to be completed in mid-2004. Separately, on Dec 5 2003, Co. completed the acquisition of Pittsburgh Financial. Both the pending acquisition of GA Financial and the completed acquisition of Pittsburgh Financial should further strengthen Co.'s presence in the Pittsburgh, PA market

Financial Data

(US$ in Thousands)	12/31/2003	12/31/2002	12/31/2001	12/31/2000	12/31/1999	12/31/1998	12/31/1997	12/31/1996
Earnings Per Share	0.90	0.74	0.86	0.82	0.88	0.55	0.69	0.63
Tang. Book Val. Per Share	6.55	6.66	6.33	5.74	4.93	5.74	6.16	5.88
Dividends Per Share	0.620	0.600	0.580	0.560	0.490	0.440	0.400	0.360
Dividend Payout %	68.88	81.08	67.44	68.29	55.68	80.00	57.55	57.14
Income Statement								
Total Interest Income	243,773	275,568	308,891	311,882	297,507	283,421	199,811	182,329
Total Interest Expense	100,241	122,673	167,170	174,539	152,653	148,282	102,753	88,325
Net Interest Income	143,532	152,895	141,721	137,343	144,854	135,139	97,058	94,004
Provision for Loan Losses	12,770	12,223	11,495	10,030	9,450	15,049	6,929	4,501
Non–Interest Income	48,444	37,206	40,224	33,683	30,853	26,338	19,843	13,741
Non–Interest Expense	112,655	125,441	105,007	99,461	93,615	100,201	65,909	63,589
Income Before Taxes	60,700	51,795	62,114	59,790	72,077	44,770	37,337	38,252
Income from Cont Ops	47,449	42,884	46,860	45,501	52,465	32,541	23,848	26,180
Net Income	53,300	43,526	50,189	47,246	53,030	33,374	30,534	27,583
Average Shs. Outstg.	59,387	58,742	58,118	57,618	60,569	61,666	43,932	43,908
Balance Sheet								
Cash & Due from Banks	82,510	81,114	98,130	90,723	92,673	96,615	60,109	69,406
Securities Avail. for Sale	1,969,176	1,482,771	1,469,118	1,238,230	1,144,042	1,042,636	396,631	244,415
Net Loans & Leases	2,787,497	2,574,138	2,533,777	2,457,226	2,466,520	2,342,546	1,901,137	1,728,011
Total Assets	5,189,195	4,524,743	4,583,504	4,372,312	4,340,846	4,096,789	2,929,315	2,584,638
Total Deposits	3,288,275	3,044,124	3,093,150	3,064,146	2,948,829	2,931,131	2,242,478	2,104,783
Long–Term Obligations	793,972	579,934	664,220	656,855	638,355	630,850	193,054	40,880
Total Liabilities	4,758,249	4,123,353	4,213,464	4,038,156	4,054,163	3,741,384	2,657,481	2,323,280
Net Stockholders' Equity	430,946	401,390	370,066	334,156	286,683	355,405	271,834	261,358
Shares Outstanding	60,712	58,962	58,451	58,195	58,142	61,876	44,092	44,388
Statistical Record								
Return on Equity %	11.01	10.68	12.66	13.61	18.30	9.15	8.77	10.01
Return on Assets %	0.91	0.94	1.02	1.04	1.20	0.79	0.81	1.01
Equity/Assets %	8.30	8.87	8.07	7.64	6.62	8.67	9.27	10.11
Non–Int. Exp./Tot. Inc. %	38.55	40.10	30.07	28.78	28.50	32.34	30.00	32.43
Price Range	14.98-11.50	14.12-10.84	15.00-9.50	12.00-8.63	14.31-10.16	17.53-11.50	17.53-8.63	9.88-8.38
P/E Ratio	16.64-12.78	19.08-14.65	17.44-11.05	14.63-10.52	16.26-11.54	31.87-20.91	25.41-12.50	15.67-13.29
Average Yield %	4.78	4.83	4.99	5.67	4.13	3.26	3.78	3.89

Address: Old Courthouse Square, Indiana, PA 15701 **Telephone:** (724) 349-7220 **Web Site:** www.fcbanking.com	**Officers:** E. James Trimarchi – Chmn., Johnston A. Glass – Vice-Chmn. **Transfer Agents:** The Bank of New York, New York, NY	**Investor Contact:** 800-331-4107 **Institutional Holding** **No of Institutions:** 12 **Shares:** 905,058 **% Held:** –

FIRST FEDERAL CAPITAL CORP. (LA CROSSE, WI)

Exchange	Symbol	Price	52Wk Range	Yield	P/E
NMS	FTFC	$21.32 (3/31/2004)	24.00–18.50	2.63	12.61

*7 Year Price Score 136.2   *NYSE Composite Index=100   *12 Month Price Score 99.4

Interim Earnings (Per Share)

Qtr.	Mar	Jun	Sep	Dec
2000	0.29	0.30	0.32	0.34
2001	0.32	0.34	0.36	0.49
2002	0.38	0.40	0.45	0.50
2003	0.40	0.44	0.51	0.34

Interim Dividends (Per Share)

Amt	Decl	Ex	Rec	Pay
0.14Q	4/23/2003	5/13/2003	5/15/2003	6/5/2003
0.14Q	7/24/2003	8/12/2003	8/14/2003	9/4/2003
0.14Q	10/30/2003	11/18/2003	11/20/2003	12/11/2003
0.14Q	1/29/2004	2/17/2004	2/19/2004	3/11/2004
		Indicated Div: $0.56 (Div. Reinv. Plan)		

Valuation Analysis

Forecast P/E	N/A	Trailing P/E	12.61
Market Cap	$420.6 Million	Book Value	225.7 Million
Price/Book	N/A	Price/Sales	N/A

Dividend Achiever Status

Rank	44	10 Year Growth Rate	17.72%
Total Years of Dividend Growth			12

Business Summary: Other Depository Banking (MIC: 8.5 SIC: 6035 NAIC:522120)

First Federal Capital, through its First Federal Capital Bank subsidiary, is a savings bank with assets of $3.31 billion, as of Dec 31 2003. Co.'s primary business is community banking, which includes attracting deposits from and making loans to the general public, private businesses, as well as governmental and non-profit entities. Co.'s primary market areas consist of communities located in the southern two-thirds of Wisconsin, northern Illinois, and southeastern Minnesota. As of Dec 31 2003, Co. maintained 95 banking offices in its market areas.

Recent Developments: For the year ended Dec 31 2003, net income was $34.7 million compared with $34.9 million the previous year. Results for 2003 included a Federal Home Loan Bank prepayment penalty of $7.4 million. Net interest income rose slightly to $81.8 million from $81.5 million a year earlier. Provision for loan losses amounted to $1.5 million versus $3.5 million in 2002. Total non-interest income climbed 36.0% to $86.5 million from $63.6 million the year before, mainly due to significantly higher mortgage banking revenue of $44.0 million compared with $27.5 million last year. Non-interest income was also aided by a 18.2% increase in community banking revenue to $39.7 million versus $33.6 million in 2002.

Prospects: Co.'s near-term outlook is mixed. On one hand, the improving economy should lead to increased loan demand as 2004 unfolds, which could result in Co. attaining its long-term asset and earnings growth goals of 10.0%. Also, Co. indicated that it believes that it will be able to maintain its interest rate spread at or near current levels in a modestly rising interest rate environment. However, Co. expects mortgage banking revenue in 2004 to be significantly lower than it was in 2003, due to a higher interest rate environment. Additionally, Co. noted that its revenue mix in mortgage banking is expected to shift from gains on sales of loans to loan servicing fees.

Financial Data (US$ in Thousands)	12/31/2003	12/31/2002	12/31/2001	12/31/2000	12/31/1999	12/31/1998	12/31/1997	12/31/1996
Earnings Per Share	1.69	1.73	1.51	1.25	1.17	0.98	0.88	0.50
Tang. Book Val. Per Share	6.64	6.67	6.80	6.09	5.05	4.79	4.74	4.26
Dividends Per Share	0.550	0.510	0.470	0.420	0.340	0.270	0.230	0.200
Dividend Payout %	32.54	29.47	31.12	33.60	29.05	27.55	26.36	41.33
Income Statement								
Total Interest Income	147,918	161,250	171,533	161,436	130,071	118,668	114,976	103,977
Total Interest Expense	66,125	79,726	108,330	101,896	75,953	71,457	70,265	63,684
Net Interest Income	81,793	81,525	63,202	59,540	54,117	47,211	44,711	40,293
Provision for Loan Losses	1,456	3,468	1,763	1,009	387	293	539	...
Non–Interest Income	86,546	63,635	49,527	35,633	35,178	31,360	24,294	19,831
Non–Interest Expense	111,717	87,378	67,119	58,250	54,299	47,597	40,197	44,245
Income Before Taxes	55,166	54,313	43,847	35,914	34,609	30,681	28,269	15,880
Income from Cont Ops	34,727	34,916	...	23,144	...	19,424	...	...
Net Income	34,727	34,916	28,448	23,144	22,441	19,424	17,390	10,074
Average Shs. Outstg.	20,597	20,163	18,870	18,472	19,137	19,864	19,690	20,125
Balance Sheet								
Cash & Due from Banks	94,536	84,483	70,757	25,446	65,566	43,643	29,939	24,644
Securities Avail. for Sale	...	...	35,462	817	873	...	21,377	74,029
Net Loans & Leases	2,518,683	2,100,642	1,851,316	1,772,477	1,538,595	1,177,526	1,193,893	1,106,040
Total Assets	3,308,324	3,025,624	2,717,710	2,352,726	2,084,554	1,786,504	1,544,294	1,515,413
Total Deposits	2,552,837	2,355,148	2,029,254	1,699,252	1,471,259	1,460,136	381,994	1,024,093
Long–Term Obligations	416,699	417,613	467,447	370,846	469,580	189,778	275,779	383,593
Total Liabilities	3,031,735	2,820,172	2,525,312	2,206,176	1,957,279	1,663,819	670,393	1,419,999
Net Stockholders' Equity	276,589	205,452	192,398	146,549	127,275	122,685	109,361	95,414
Shares Outstanding	22,394	19,704	20,200	18,345	18,403	18,360	18,381	18,381
Statistical Record								
Return on Equity %	12.55	16.99	14.78	15.79	17.63	15.83	15.90	10.55
Return on Assets %	1.04	1.15	1.04	0.98	1.07	1.08	1.12	0.66
Equity/Assets %	8.36	6.79	7.07	6.22	6.10	6.86	7.08	6.29
Non–Int. Exp./Tot. Inc. %	47.64	38.85	30.36	29.55	32.85	31.72	28.86	35.73
Price Range	24.00–18.50	22.47–14.68	16.63–12.75	14.88–10.13	18.00–11.75	18.38–12.00	17.00–7.83	8.08–6.17
P/E Ratio	14.20–10.95	12.99–8.49	11.01–8.44	11.90–8.10	15.38–10.04	18.75–12.24	19.32–8.90	16.17–12.33
Average Yield %	2.66	2.71	3.17	3.62	2.29	1.70	2.03	2.82

Address: 605 State Street, La Crosse, WI 54601-1868 Telephone: (608) 784-8000 Web Site: www.firstfed.com	Officers: Thomas W. Schini – Chmn. Dale A. Nordeen – Vice-Chmn.	Investor Contact: (608) 784-8000 Institutional Holding No of Institutions: 13 Shares: 2,288,882 % Held: –

FIRST FINANCIAL CORP.

Exchange	Symbol	Price	52Wk Range	Yield	P/E
NMS	THFF	$29.31 (3/31/2004)	32.25–23.56	2.46	15.03

*7 Year Price Score 130.0   *NYSE Composite Index=100   *12 Month Price Score 97.6

Interim Earnings (Per Share)

Qtr.	Mar	Jun	Sep	Dec
2000	0.40	0.45	0.44	0.43
2001	0.44	0.42	0.46	0.46
2002	0.49	0.48	0.45	0.68
2003	0.52	0.45	0.47	0.51

Interim Dividends (Per Share)

Amt	Decl	Ex	Rec	Pay
0.31S	11/20/2002	12/4/2002	12/6/2002	1/2/2003
0.34S	5/22/2003	6/9/2003	6/11/2003	7/1/2003
2-for-1	9/10/2003	10/16/2003	9/30/2003	10/15/2003
0.36S	11/19/2003	12/3/2003	12/5/2003	1/2/2004

Indicated Div: $0.72

Valuation Analysis

Forecast P/E	N/A	Trailing P/E	15.03
Market Cap	$200.1 Million	Book Value	255.3 Million
Price/Book	1.68	Price/Sales	2.79

Dividend Achiever Status

Rank	127	10 Year Growth Rate	11.65%
Total Years of Dividend Growth			11

Business Summary: Commercial Banking (MIC: 8.1 SIC: 6022 NAIC:522110)

First Financial is a multi-bank holding company with $2.22 billion in assets as of Dec 31 2003. Co. offers a wide variety of financial services, including commercial, mortgage and consumer lending, lease financing, trust account services, and depositor services through 46 branch offices of its ten wholly-owned subsidiaries located in Indiana and Illinois. First Financial Bank, N.A. of Vigo County, IN, a wholly-owned subsidiary, operates 14 full-service banking branches and two investment subsidiaries, which hold and manage $230.9 million of securities.

Recent Developments: For the twelve months ended Dec 31 2003, net income slipped 7.5% to $26.5 million from $28.6 million in the corresponding period a year earlier. Net interest income declined 4.8% to $74.4 million from $78.2 million the previous year. Provision for loan losses totaled $7.5 million, down 21.3% compared with $9.5 million the prior year. Non-interest income rose 1.2% to $30.8 million from $30.5 million the year before. Non-interest expense decreased 1.4% to $62.5 million from $63.3 million in 2002. Net interest margin declined to 4.0% compared with 4.1% a year earlier.

Prospects: Co. is focusing on implementing initiatives to help boost non-interest income growth in an effort to offset the decline in net interest income, which is being negatively affected by significantly lower long-term interest rates. Meanwhile, results are being positively affected by increased loan and deposit fees, insurance commissions, and trust and financial services fees. Results are also benefiting from increased income from capitalized mortgage servicing rights, higher loan servicing and origination fees, and net cash gains on sales of low fixed-rate mortgage loans in the secondary market.

Financial Data

(US$ in Thousands)	12/31/2003	12/31/2002	12/31/2001	12/31/2000	12/31/1999	12/31/1998	12/31/1997	12/31/1996
Earnings Per Share	1.95	2.10	1.78	1.72	1.55	1.29	1.29	1.14
Tang. Book Val. Per Share	18.00	16.93	15.09	14.28	12.32	12.76	11.79	10.71
Dividends Per Share	0.650	0.600	0.560	0.510	0.440	0.390	0.330	0.260
Dividend Payout %	33.33	28.57	31.46	29.56	28.38	30.23	25.58	22.81
Income Statement								
Total Interest Income	122,661	136,262	144,673	146,417	133,576	129,137	122,372	115,836
Total Interest Expense	48,225	58,086	74,125	80,583	66,815	66,430	62,072	57,810
Net Interest Income	74,436	78,176	70,548	65,834	66,761	62,707	60,300	58,026
Provision for Loan Losses	7,455	9,478	6,615	4,392	4,725	5,396	5,382	4,461
Non-Interest Income	30,819	30,468	21,468	13,610	12,012	10,611	8,957	7,849
Non-Interest Expense	62,461	63,317	53,329	42,703	43,543	42,567	39,629	39,280
Income Before Taxes	35,339	35,849	32,072	32,349	30,505	25,355	24,246	22,134
Net Income	26,493	28,640	24,196	23,213	21,622	18,558	18,100	15,971
Average Shs. Outstg.	13,588	13,652	13,600	13,460	13,928	14,412	14,032	14,025
Balance Sheet								
Cash & Due from Banks	94,198	96,043	68,205	68,755	58,075	54,877	53,815	66,658
Securities Avail. for Sale	567,733	511,548	463,509	568,405	594,319	633,365	527,993	582,744
Net Loans & Leases	1,408,286	1,411,315	1,330,148	1,278,934	1,173,949	1,095,336	992,296	908,011
Total Assets	2,223,057	2,169,748	2,041,905	2,043,267	1,905,201	1,849,752	1,634,936	1,619,642
Total Deposits	1,479,347	1,434,654	1,313,656	1,322,559	1,256,115	1,260,365	1,194,524	1,175,228
Long-Term Obligations	383,223	423,290	426,078	489,063	382,322	89,519	30,596	63,924
Total Liabilities	1,967,778	1,927,777	1,824,394	1,852,044	1,736,519	1,660,950	1,462,815	1,462,628
Net Stockholders' Equity	255,279	241,971	217,511	191,223	168,682	182,183	165,480	150,377
Shares Outstanding	13,578	13,618	13,688	13,388	13,690	14,268	14,032	14,025
Statistical Record								
Return on Equity %	10.37	11.83	11.12	12.13	12.81	10.18	10.93	10.62
Return on Assets %	1.19	1.31	1.18	1.13	1.13	1.00	1.10	0.98
Equity/Assets %	11.48	11.15	10.65	9.35	8.85	9.84	10.12	9.28
Non-Int. Exp./Tot. Inc. %	40.69	37.97	32.09	26.68	29.90	30.45	30.17	31.75
Price Range	32.25–23.36	26.84–21.35	24.07–15.25	20.75–13.75	25.75–17.25	28.81–19.44	28.81–15.71	17.62–13.72
P/E Ratio	16.54–11.98	12.78–10.17	13.52–8.57	12.06–7.99	16.61–11.13	22.33–15.07	22.33–12.18	15.46–12.03
Average Yield %	2.38	2.52	2.88	3.18	2.19	1.61	1.77	1.71

Address: One First Financial Plaza, Terre Haute, IN 47807 Telephone: (812) 238-6000 Web Site: www.first-online.com	Officers: Donald E. Smith – Pres., C.E.O., Michael A. Carty – C.F.O., Treas., Principal Acctg. Officer	Investor Contact:812-238-6264 Institutional Holding No of Institutions: 8 Shares: 240,100 % Held: –

FIRST FINANCIAL HOLDINGS, INC.

Exchange	Symbol	Price	52Wk Range	Yield	P/E
NMS	FFCH	$29.95 (3/31/2004)	33.10–24.10	2.94	14.68

*7 Year Price Score 134.1 *NYSE Composite Index=100 ***12 Month Price Score 99.7**

Interim Earnings (Per Share)

Qtr.	Dec	Mar	Jun	Sep
2000–01	0.36	0.42	0.43	0.43
2001–02	0.49	0.54	0.51	0.50
2002–03	0.50	0.54	0.50	0.53
2003–04	0.41	...	...	...

Interim Dividends (Per Share)

Amt	Decl	Ex	Rec	Pay
0.19Q	4/25/2003	5/7/2003	5/9/2003	5/23/2003
0.19Q	7/25/2003	8/6/2003	8/8/2003	8/22/2003
0.22Q	10/24/2003	11/5/2003	11/7/2003	11/21/2003
0.22Q	2/2/2004	2/11/2004	2/13/2004	2/27/2004

Indicated Div: $0.88 (Div. Reinv. Plan)

Valuation Analysis

Forecast P/E	13.46	Trailing P/E	14.68
Market Cap	$400.3 Million	Book Value	162.0 Million
Price/Book	N/A	Price/Sales	N/A

Dividend Achiever Status

Rank	77	10 Year Growth Rate	15.02%
Total Years of Dividend Growth			11

Business Summary: Other Depository Banking (MIC: 8.5 SIC: 6035 NAIC:522120)

First Financial Holdings, with assets of $2.30 billion as of Sep 30 2003, is a savings and loan holding company. Through its subsidiary, First Federal Savings and Loan Association of Charleston, Co. offers a complete line of banking and related financial services to consumer and commercial customers through its 45 branch sales offices. Co. also engages in full-service brokerage activities, property, casualty, life and health insurance, third-party administrative services, trust and fiduciary services, reinsurance of private mortgage insurance and certain passive investment activities.

Recent Developments: For the three months ended Dec 31 2003, net income declined 21.7% to $5.3 million compared with $6.7 million in the equivalent quarter of 2002. Results for 2003 and 2002 included net gains on the sale of loans of $210,000 and $2.0 million, and net gains on the sale of investments and mortgage-backed securities of $436,000 and $326,000, respectively. Net interest income declined 6.1% to $19.1 million from $20.4 million the year before. Provision for loan losses slipped 4.0% to $1.4 million versus $1.5 million a year earlier. Non-interest income decreased 8.0% to $8.5 million, while non-interest expense climbed 1.9% to $18.0 million.

Prospects: In recent weeks, Co. has seen a significant decline in demand for new commitments to residential lending, and it may take several quarters for activity to regain momentum. As a result, Co. has taken steps to reduce the number of mortgage processing units and personnel in light of slower originations. Separately, on Feb 2 2004, Co. completed the acquisitions of The Kimbrell Company, Preferred Markets and Atlantic Acceptance in a combined sale. Kimbrell is a managing general agency that provides excess and surplus lines insurance products. Preferred Markets offers standard lines insurance products, and Atlantic Acceptance is a finance company.

Financial Data

(US$ in Thousands)	3 Mos	09/30/2003	09/30/2002	09/30/2001	09/30/2000	09/30/1999	09/30/1998	09/30/1997
Earnings Per Share	1.98	2.07	2.04	1.64	1.47	1.40	1.20	1.11
Tang. Book Val. Per Share	11.81	13.01	12.55	11.71	10.35	9.42	9.16	8.21
Dividends Per Share	0.790	0.760	0.680	0.620	0.560	0.480	0.420	0.360
Dividend Payout %	39.90	36.71	33.33	37.80	38.09	34.28	35.00	32.43
Income Statement								
Total Interest Income	31,760	134,381	154,026	173,277	161,642	140,832	136,345	121,762
Total Interest Expense	12,621	55,921	71,342	102,908	98,888	80,394	81,689	72,909
Net Interest Income	19,139	78,460	82,684	70,369	62,754	60,438	54,656	48,853
Provision for Loan Losses	1,425	6,235	5,888	4,975	2,745	2,765	2,405	2,375
Non-Interest Income	8,465	40,965	30,959	24,918	18,310	15,314	13,357	12,252
Non-Interest Expense	18,005	70,781	63,944	55,143	47,884	43,280	40,158	36,372
Income Before Taxes	8,174	42,409	43,811	35,169	30,435	29,707	25,450	22,358
Income from Cont Ops	...	...	...	...	...	...	16,879	...
Net Income	5,254	27,211	28,152	22,559	19,928	19,307	16,539	14,116
Average Shs. Outstg.	12,949	13,173	13,832	13,733	13,559	13,786	14,101	12,678
Balance Sheet								
Securities Avail. for Sale	24,626	13,787	7,285	6,259	5,918	7,569	11,264	40,826
Net Loans & Leases	1,789,790	1,781,681	1,924,828	1,905,333	1,838,497	1,742,150	1,565,040	1,405,494
Total Assets	2,434,081	2,322,882	2,264,674	2,325,664	2,256,511	2,070,752	1,839,708	1,712,931
Total Deposits	1,428,440	1,481,651	1,440,271	1,395,785	1,241,295	1,219,848	1,164,440	1,069,253
Long-Term Obligations	664,000	598,000	577,000	625,000	766,500	594,500	471,500	439,340
Total Liabilities	2,269,271	2,159,876	2,099,026	2,168,771	2,118,660	1,944,871	1,714,545	1,608,146
Net Stockholders' Equity	164,810	163,006	165,648	156,893	137,851	125,881	125,163	104,785
Shares Outstanding	12,574	12,522	13,195	13,395	13,317	13,353	13,659	12,756
Statistical Record								
Return on Equity %	3.18	16.69	16.99	14.37	14.45	15.33	13.48	13.47
Return on Assets %	0.21	1.17	1.24	0.97	0.88	0.93	0.91	0.82
Equity/Assets %	6.77	7.01	7.31	6.74	6.10	6.07	6.80	6.11
Non-Int. Exp./Tot. Inc. %	44.76	40.36	34.56	27.82	26.60	27.71	26.82	27.14
Price Range	33.10–29.41	30.96–23.70	32.74–22.04	26.00–15.13	19.06–12.75	20.88–14.50	27.00–17.00	19.63–9.75
P/E Ratio	80.73–71.73	14.96–11.45	16.05–10.80	15.85–9.22	12.97–8.67	14.91–10.36	22.50–14.17	17.68–8.78
Average Yield %	2.54	2.84	2.51	3.07	3.75	2.58	1.85	2.71

Address: 34 Broad Street, Charleston, SC 29401 **Telephone:** (843) 529 5933 **Web Site:** www.firstfinancialholdings.com	**Officers:** A. Thomas Hood – Pres., C.E.O., John L. Ott – Sr. V.P.	**Investor Contact:** (843) 529–5933 **Institutional Holding** No of Institutions: 2 Shares: 28,656 % Held: –

FIRST INDIANA CORP.

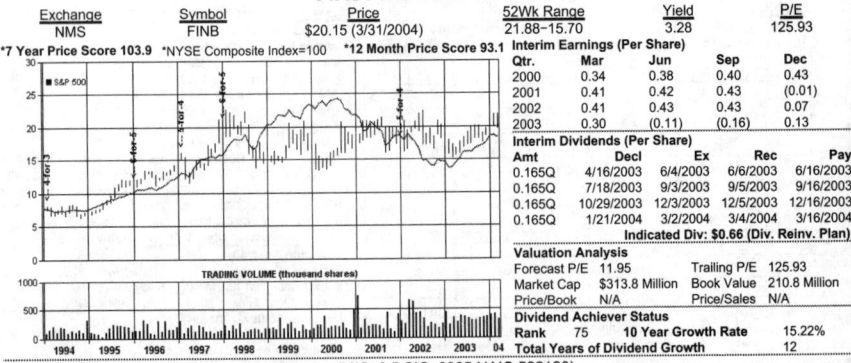

Exchange	Symbol	Price	52Wk Range	Yield	P/E
NMS	FINB	$20.15 (3/31/2004)	21.88-15.70	3.28	125.93

*7 Year Price Score 103.9   ***NYSE Composite Index=100**   ***12 Month Price Score 93.1**

Interim Earnings (Per Share)

Qtr.	Mar	Jun	Sep	Dec
2000	0.34	0.38	0.40	0.43
2001	0.41	0.42	0.43	(0.01)
2002	0.41	0.43	0.43	0.07
2003	0.30	(0.11)	(0.16)	0.13

Interim Dividends (Per Share)

Amt	Decl	Ex	Rec	Pay
0.165Q	4/16/2003	6/4/2003	6/6/2003	6/16/2003
0.165Q	7/18/2003	9/3/2003	9/5/2003	9/16/2003
0.165Q	10/29/2003	12/3/2003	12/5/2003	12/16/2003
0.165Q	1/21/2004	3/2/2004	3/4/2004	3/16/2004

Indicated Div: $0.66 (Div. Reinv. Plan)

Valuation Analysis

Forecast P/E	11.95	Trailing P/E	125.93
Market Cap	$313.8 Million	Book Value	210.8 Million
Price/Book	N/A	Price/Sales	N/A

Dividend Achiever Status

Rank	75	10 Year Growth Rate	15.22%
Total Years of Dividend Growth			12

Business Summary: Other Depository Banking (MIC: 8.5 SIC: 6035 NAIC:522120)

First Indiana Corporation is a full-service financial services company offering comprehensive financial solutions to businesses and individuals. Co. is the holding company for First Indiana Bank, N.A., a national bank headquartered in Indianapolis, and Somerset Financial Services, an accounting and consulting firm. As of Dec 31 2003, First Indiana Bank has $2.19 billion in assets and owned 33 offices in Central Indiana, plus construction and consumer loan offices in Indiana, Arizona, Florida, Illinois, North Carolina, and Ohio. Co. also originates consumer loans in 47 states through a national independent agent network.

Recent Developments: For the year ended Dec 31 2003, net income plummeted 88.1% to $2.5 million compared with $21.2 million the previous year. Total interest income decreased 9.2% to $114.3 million from $125.9 million the year before. Total interest expense fell 28.4% to $37.4 million from $52.1 million in 2002. Net interest income rose 4.2% to $76.9 million from $73.8 million the prior year. Provision for loan losses leapt 87.8% to $39.0 million from $20.8 million a year earlier. Total non-interest income climbed 6.0% to $49.6 million from $46.8 million, while total non-interest expense jumped 25.8% to $83.6 million from $66.5 million the previous year.

Prospects: Co.'s results continue to be negatively affected by higher provision for loan losses and net charge-offs. Also, average loans outstanding are down due to lower demand for single-family construction loans, rapid prepayments on consumer and residential loans and increased sales of consumer loan production. Meanwhile, low interest rates continue to compress net interest margin and net interest income. As a result, deposit rates have been unable to fully absorb reductions in market interest rates over the last several years. Separately, Co.'s demand deposits continue to grow with an average of $447.4 million in the fourth quarter of 2003, an increase of 19.0% over the same quarter of 2002.

Financial Data

(US$ in Thousands)	12/31/2003	12/31/2002	12/31/2001	12/31/2000	12/31/1999	12/31/1998	12/31/1997	12/31/1996
Earnings Per Share	0.16	1.34	1.25	1.55	1.41	1.15	1.08	0.84
Tang. Book Val. Per Share	10.37	13.39	12.69	11.87	11.31	10.45	9.66	8.42
Dividends Per Share	0.660	0.640	0.510	0.440	0.410	0.380	0.320	0.290
Dividend Payout %	412.50	47.76	40.96	28.86	29.37	33.33	29.41	35.27
Income Statement								
Total Interest Income	114,330	125,923	157,128	172,810	146,015	135,834	127,330	125,468
Total Interest Expense	37,430	52,143	83,079	95,042	75,575	73,080	64,351	63,785
Net Interest Income	76,900	73,780	74,049	77,768	70,440	62,754	62,979	61,683
Provision for Loan Losses	38,974	20,756	15,228	9,756	9,410	9,780	10,700	10,794
Non-Interest Income	49,563	46,765	43,963	25,638	26,958	23,773	18,005	17,848
Non-Interest Expense	83,637	66,502	70,501	53,728	52,346	45,756	41,104	47,253
Income Before Taxes	3,852	33,287	32,283	39,922	35,642	30,991	29,180	21,484
Income from Cont Ops	...	...	...	...	22,322	...	...	...
Net Income	2,529	21,180	20,009	24,817	22,733	19,147	17,744	13,704
Average Shs. Outstg.	15,720	15,809	15,998	15,997	16,049	16,571	16,313	16,201
Balance Sheet								
Securities Avail. for Sale	430,906	276,914	295,726	317,568	206,338	226,582	212,190	202,714
Net Loans & Leases	1,761,794	1,793,164	1,719,351	1,750,848	1,673,422	1,518,543	1,348,529	1,215,550
Total Assets	2,193,137	2,125,214	2,046,657	2,085,948	2,012,341	1,908,388	1,670,923	1,519,644
Total Deposits	1,489,972	1,339,204	1,379,478	1,399,983	1,312,115	1,227,918	1,107,555	1,095,480
Long-Term Obligations	312,022	346,532	296,647	336,754	366,854	327,247	257,458	215,46
Total Liabilities	1,984,243	1,904,003	1,837,626	1,887,136	1,802,671	1,626,230	1,460,369	1,357,76
Net Stockholders' Equity	208,894	221,211	209,031	198,812	177,103	165,970	153,036	138,65
Shares Outstanding	15,546	15,540	15,443	15,574	15,653	15,878	15,835	16,45
Statistical Record								
Return on Equity %	1.21	9.57	9.57	12.48	12.60	11.53	11.59	9.8
Return on Assets %	0.11	0.99	0.97	1.18	1.10	1.00	1.06	0.9
Equity/Assets %	9.52	10.40	10.21	9.53	8.80	8.69	9.15	9.1
Non-Int. Exp./Tot. Inc. %	51.03	38.50	35.05	27.07	30.26	28.66	28.28	32.9
Price Range	20.39-15.30	22.46-16.25	21.48-16.12	20.85-13.45	20.90-14.40	22.67-13.90	21.17-11.58	14.27-10.5
P/E Ratio	127.4-95.63	16.76-12.13	17.18-12.90	13.45-8.68	14.82-10.21	19.71-12.09	19.60-10.73	16.98-12.5
Average Yield %	3.67	3.39	2.63	2.73	2.44	2.02	2.11	2.3

Address: 135 North Pennsylvania Street, Indianapolis, IN 46204 **Telephone:** (317) 269-1200 **Web Site:** www.firstindiana.com	**Officers:** Robert H. McKinney - Chmn., Marni M. McKinney - Vice-Chmn., C.E.O.	**Investor Contact:**317-472-2184 **Institutional Holding** **No of Institutions:** 8 **Shares:** 338,909 **% Held:** -

FIRST MERCHANTS CORP.

Exchange	Symbol	Price	52Wk Range	Yield	P/E
NMS	FRME	$24.05 (3/31/2004)	27.25-22.02	3.83	15.30

7 Year Price Score 115.7 *NYSE Composite Index=100 *12 Month Price Score 95.4

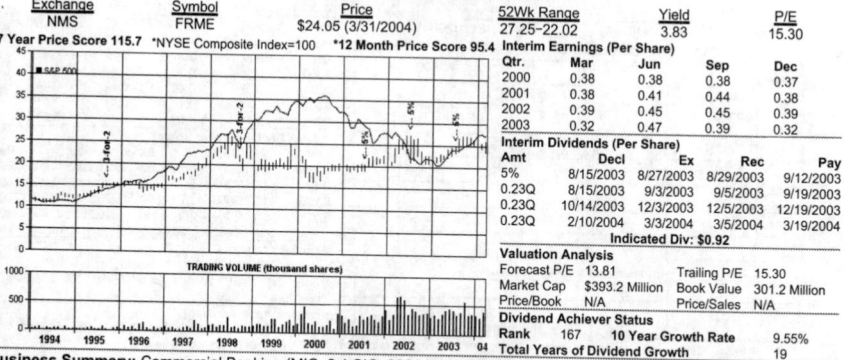

Interim Earnings (Per Share)

Qtr.	Mar	Jun	Sep	Dec
2000	0.38	0.38	0.38	0.37
2001	0.38	0.41	0.44	0.38
2002	0.39	0.45	0.45	0.39
2003	0.32	0.47	0.39	0.32

Interim Dividends (Per Share)

Amt	Decl	Ex	Rec	Pay
5%	8/15/2003	8/27/2003	8/29/2003	9/12/2003
0.23Q	8/15/2003	9/3/2003	9/5/2003	9/19/2003
0.23Q	10/14/2003	12/3/2003	12/5/2003	12/19/2003
0.23Q	2/10/2004	3/3/2004	3/5/2004	3/19/2004

Indicated Div: $0.92

Valuation Analysis

Forecast P/E	13.81	Trailing P/E	15.30
Market Cap	$393.2 Million	Book Value	301.2 Million
Price/Book	N/A	Price/Sales	N/A

Dividend Achiever Status

Rank	167	10 Year Growth Rate 9.55%
Total Years of Dividend Growth		19

TRADING VOLUME (thousand shares)

Business Summary: Commercial Banking (MIC: 8.1 SIC: 6021 NAIC:522110)

Co. is a bank holding company. Through its bank subsidiaries, Co. offers a range of financial services, including: accepting time, savings and demand deposits; making consumer, commercial, agri-business and real estate mortgage loans; renting safe deposit facilities; providing personal and corporate trust services; providing full service brokerage; and providing other corporate services. Through various nonbank subsidiaries, Co. also offers personal and commercial lines of insurance and engages in the title agency business and the reinsurance of credit life, accident, and health insurance. As of Dec 31 2003, Co. had total assets of $3.08 billion and deposits of $2.36 billion.

Recent Developments: For the year ended Dec 31 2003, net income totaled $27.6 million, down 1.0% compared with $27.8 million in the corresponding period a year earlier. Net interest income rose 11.0% to $103.1 million from $92.9 million in 2002. Provision for loan losses increased 32.1% to $9.5 million from $7.2 million the year before. Total other income climbed 32.6% to $35.9 million from $27.1 million the prior year. Total other expenses increased 28.5% to $91.3 million from $71.0 million the previous year. As of Dec 31 2003, total assets were $3.08 billion, up 14.9% versus $2.68 billion on Dec 31 2002.

Prospects: Earnings are being hampered by significantly lower interest rates, increased provision for loan losses, and higher salary, benefits, occupancy and equipment expenses related to acquisitions completed in 2003. Meanwhile, results are benefiting from Co.'s focus on boosting non-interest income through a range of fee-based services, increased mortgage refinancing and higher service charge income on deposit accounts. Separately, on Jan 1 2004, Co. completed the conversion of all of its state chartered banks to national charters. Results should benefit from increased efficiencies and consistency to the regulatory process.

Financial Data

(US$ in Thousands)	12/31/2003	12/31/2002	12/31/2001	12/31/2000	12/31/1999	12/31/1998	12/31/1997	12/31/1996
Earnings Per Share	1.50	1.68	1.61	1.51	1.36	1.30	1.23	1.15
Tang. Book Val. Per Share	8.70	8.98	10.51	10.52	9.74	10.99	10.39	9.67
Dividends Per Share	0.890	0.850	0.810	0.770	0.720	0.660	0.590	0.500
Dividend Payout %	59.87	50.74	50.45	51.42	53.16	51.21	48.59	43.47
Income Statement								
Total Interest Income	155,530	146,682	120,435	116,528	100,463	79,728	75,475	69,496
Total Interest Expense	52,388	53,759	56,074	60,546	46,898	38,050	35,725	32,349
Net Interest Income	103,142	92,923	64,361	55,982	53,565	41,678	39,750	37,147
Provision for Loan Losses	9,477	7,174	3,576	2,625	2,241	1,984	1,297	1,253
Non-Interest Income	35,902	27,077	18,543	16,634	14,573	11,725	9,229	8,342
Non-Interest Expense	91,279	71,009	45,195	40,083	36,710	27,895	25,748	24,135
Income Before Taxes	38,288	41,817	34,133	29,908	29,187	23,524	21,934	20,101
Net Income	27,571	27,836	22,209	19,940	19,088	15,399	14,373	13,142
Average Shs. Outstg.	18,371	16,502	13,769	13,442	14,026	11,808	11,675	11,427
Balance Sheet								
Cash & Due from Banks	77,112	87,638	68,743	52,563	58,893	33,908	33,127	33,882
Securities Avail. for Sale	348,860	332,925	231,668	295,730	329,668	308,507	212,040	228,379
Net Loans & Leases	2,328,010	1,981,960	1,344,445	1,163,132	988,767	735,560	696,535	626,158
Total Assets	3,076,812	2,678,687	1,787,035	1,621,063	1,474,048	1,177,172	1,020,136	968,322
Total Deposits	2,362,101	2,036,687	1,421,251	1,288,299	1,147,203	926,844	843,812	794,451
Long-Term Obligations	383,170	356,927	174,404	163,581	189,862	111,400	47,529	54,187
Total Liabilities	2,772,847	2,417,558	1,607,907	1,465,000	1,347,752	1,045,675	898,167	855,306
Net Stockholders' Equity	303,965	261,129	179,128	156,063	126,296	131,497	121,969	112,687
Shares Outstanding	18,512	17,138	13,969	12,823	12,660	11,675	11,572	11,466
Statistical Record								
Return on Equity %	9.07	10.65	12.39	12.77	15.11	11.71	11.78	11.66
Return on Assets %	0.89	1.03	1.24	1.23	1.29	1.30	1.40	1.35
Equity/Assets %	9.87	9.74	10.02	9.62	8.56	11.17	11.95	11.63
Non-Int. Exp./Tot. Inc. %	47.68	40.86	32.51	30.10	31.91	30.50	30.39	31.00
Price Range	27.25-21.29	27.21-19.95	22.66-18.09	23.00-16.20	25.05-18.57	26.92-18.72	21.45-14.54	15.84-13.39
P/E Ratio	18.17-14.19	16.20-11.88	14.07-11.23	15.23-10.73	18.42-13.66	20.71-14.40	17.44-11.82	13.77-11.64
Average Yield %	3.69	3.68	3.99	4.00	3.52	2.87	3.31	3.36

Address: 200 East Jackson Street, Muncie, IN 47305-2814	**Officers:** Michael L. Cox – Pres., C.E.O., Roger M. Arwood – Exec. V.P., C.O.O.	**Investor Contact:** 4261 Ext7282
Telephone: (765) 747-1500		**Institutional Holding**
Web Site: www.firstmerchants.com		**No of Institutions:** 20
		Shares: 899,990 **% Held:** –

FIRST MIDWEST BANCORP, INC.

Exchange	Symbol	Price	52Wk Range	Yield	P/E
NMS	FMBI	$34.22 (3/31/2004)	34.24–26.09	2.57	17.37

*7 Year Price Score 126.5 *NYSE Composite Index=100 *12 Month Price Score 97.5

Interim Earnings (Per Share)

Qtr.	Mar	Jun	Sep	Dec
2000	0.35	0.36	0.37	0.38
2001	0.37	0.40	0.42	0.44
2002	0.45	0.47	0.47	0.47
2003	0.48	0.53	0.45	0.51

Interim Dividends (Per Share)

Amt	Decl	Ex	Rec	Pay
0.19Q	5/21/2003	6/25/2003	6/27/2003	7/22/2003
0.19Q	8/21/2003	9/24/2003	9/26/2003	10/21/2003
0.22Q	11/20/2003	12/23/2003	12/26/2003	1/20/2004
0.22Q	2/24/2004	3/24/2004	3/26/2004	4/20/2004

Indicated Div: $0.88 (Div. Reinv. Plan)

Valuation Analysis

Forecast P/E	14.42	Trailing P/E	17.37
Market Cap	$1.5 Billion	Book Value	522.5 Million
Price/Book	2.89	Price/Sales	4.14

Dividend Achiever Status

Rank	123	10 Year Growth Rate	11.87%
Total Years of Dividend Growth			11

Business Summary: Commercial Banking (MIC: 8.1 SIC: 6021 NAIC:522110)

First Midwest Bancorp is a bank holding company with assets of approximately $6.91 billion as of Dec 31 2003. Co. operates two wholly-owned subsidiaries, First Midwest Bank and First Midwest Insurance Company. First Midwest Bank is engaged in commercial and retail banking and offers a range of lending, depository, and related financial services. As of Dec 31 2003, First Midwest Bank operated 66 banking offices that are located in various communities throughout Northern Illinois. First Midwest Insurance Company operates as a reinsurer of credit life, accident, and health insurance sold through First Midwest Bank, primarily in conjunction with the consumer lending operations.

Recent Developments: For the year ended Dec 31 2003, net income rose 2.9% to $92.8 million compared with $90.2 million a year earlier. Net interest income slid 4.1% to $209.8 million from $218.8 million the previous year, reflecting low interest rates that pressured net interest margins. Provision for loan losses amounted to $10.8 million versus $15.4 million in 2002. Total noninterest income advanced 10.7% to $74.2 million from $67.0 million in 2002, and included net security gains of $3.0 million and $460,000, respectively. Total noninterest income for 2003 also included losses of $6.0 million on the early extinguishment of debt. Excluding these items, noninterest income grew 9.1%.

Prospects: Co.'s results going forward should benefit from its Dec 31 2003 acquisition of CoVest Bancshares, Inc., a bank holding company with three full-service offices located in the northwest Chicago suburbs of Des Plaines, Arlington Heights and Schaumburg. Co. has indicated that it expects to use these three new branches as additional selling platforms to sell its full range of banking and trust services. Separately, service charges on deposit accounts, commissions earned from the sale of third-party investment products and trust income are all trending higher. Accordingly, Co. expects full-year 2004 diluted earnings to range between $2.15 and $2.20 per share.

Financial Data (US$ in Thousands)	12/31/2003	12/31/2002	12/31/2001	12/31/2000	12/31/1999	12/31/1998	12/31/1997	12/31/1996
Earnings Per Share	1.97	1.86	1.63	1.46	1.33	0.98	1.02	1.05
Tang. Book Val. Per Share	9.08	10.07	9.17	8.74	7.18	8.31	8.96	8.20
Dividends Per Share	0.760	0.680	0.640	0.570	0.510	0.480	0.420	0.340
Dividend Payout %	38.57	36.55	39.26	39.34	38.32	48.90	41.66	32.38
Income Statement								
Total Interest Income	291,067	329,664	385,218	421,517	361,279	364,597	270,506	237,171
Total Interest Expense	81,313	110,910	180,838	231,906	168,615	177,016	125,782	114,422
Net Interest Income	209,754	218,754	204,380	189,611	192,664	187,581	144,724	122,749
Provision for Loan Losses	10,805	15,410	19,084	9,094	5,760	5,542	8,765	7,464
Non-Interest Income	74,170	66,991	68,866	63,198	58,334	55,462	37,222	31,433
Non-Interest Expense	149,452	148,052	145,356	144,416	149,809	158,802	113,810	94,321
Income Before Taxes	123,667	122,283	108,806	99,299	95,429	78,699	59,371	52,386
Net Income	92,778	90,152	82,138	75,540	70,909	54,704	38,815	33,714
Average Shs. Outstg.	46,982	48,415	50,401	51,603	53,071	55,880	37,946	32,036
Balance Sheet								
Cash & Due from Banks	186,900	195,153	155,822	166,423	155,407	156,524	117,974	107,590
Securities Avail. for Sale	2,229,650	1,986,186	1,771,607	2,130,148	2,033,247	1,979,115	974,467	770,254
Net Loans & Leases	4,003,378	3,358,917	3,324,561	3,188,103	2,919,842	2,621,127	2,295,908	2,055,121
Total Assets	6,906,658	5,980,533	5,667,919	5,906,484	5,511,588	5,192,887	3,614,173	3,119,238
Total Deposits	4,815,108	4,172,964	4,193,921	4,252,205	4,001,183	4,050,451	2,795,975	2,260,668
Long-Term Obligations	1,500,388	1,237,408	971,851	1,145,872	1,077,732	623,899	438,032	493,140
Total Liabilities	6,384,118	5,488,580	5,220,652	5,459,761	5,142,327	4,739,989	3,276,661	2,857,094
Net Stockholders' Equity	522,540	491,953	447,267	446,723	369,261	452,898	337,512	262,144
Shares Outstanding	46,581	47,206	48,725	51,082	51,391	54,435	37,635	31,700
Statistical Record								
Return on Equity %	17.75	18.32	18.36	16.90	19.20	12.07	11.50	12.86
Return on Assets %	1.34	1.50	1.44	1.27	1.28	1.05	1.07	1.08
Equity/Assets %	7.56	8.22	7.89	7.56	6.69	8.72	9.33	8.40
Non-Int. Exp./Tot. Inc. %	40.91	37.32	32.01	29.79	35.70	37.80	36.98	35.15
Price Range	32.57–25.08	31.85–24.02	29.19–20.95	23.20–17.00	23.37–18.43	27.67–18.90	23.47–15.67	17.40–11.43
P/E Ratio	16.53–12.73	17.12–12.91	17.91–12.85	15.89–11.64	17.57–13.86	28.23–19.29	23.01–15.36	16.57–10.88
Average Yield %	2.63	2.41	2.60	2.91	2.44	2.15	2.31	2.64

Address: 300 Park Blvd., Itasca, IL 60143–9768	Officers: Robert P. OMeara – Chmn., John M. OMeara – Pres., C.E.O., C.O.O.	Investor Contact:630–875–7345
Telephone: (630) 875–7450		Institutional Holding
Web Site: www.firstmidwest.com		No of Institutions: 4
		Shares: 593,189 % Held: –

FIRSTMERIT CORP

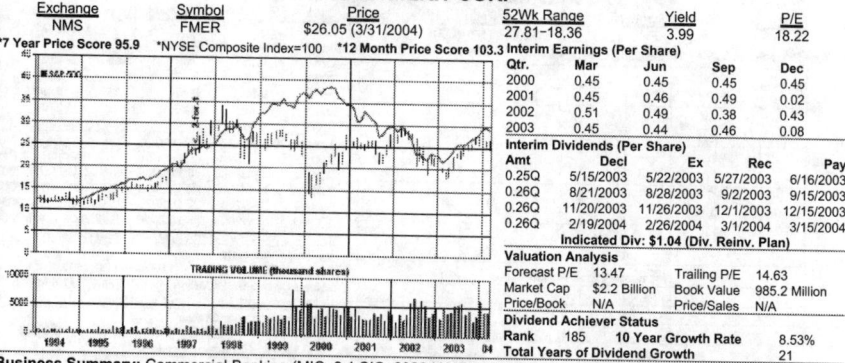

Exchange	Symbol	Price	52Wk Range	Yield	P/E
NMS	FMER	$26.05 (3/31/2004)	27.81–18.36	3.99	18.22

*7 Year Price Score 95.9   *NYSE Composite Index=100   *12 Month Price Score 103.3

Interim Earnings (Per Share)

Qtr.	Mar	Jun	Sep	Dec
2000	0.45	0.45	0.45	0.45
2001	0.45	0.46	0.49	0.02
2002	0.51	0.49	0.38	0.43
2003	0.45	0.44	0.46	0.08

Interim Dividends (Per Share)

Amt	Decl	Ex	Rec	Pay
0.25Q	5/15/2003	5/22/2003	5/27/2003	6/16/2003
0.26Q	8/21/2003	8/28/2003	9/2/2003	9/15/2003
0.26Q	11/20/2003	11/26/2003	12/1/2003	12/15/2003
0.26Q	2/19/2004	2/26/2004	3/1/2004	3/15/2004

Indicated Div: $1.04 (Div. Reinv. Plan)

Valuation Analysis

Forecast P/E	13.47	Trailing P/E	14.63
Market Cap	$2.2 Billion	Book Value	985.2 Million
Price/Book	N/A	Price/Sales	N/A

Dividend Achiever Status

Rank	185	10 Year Growth Rate	8.53%
		Total Years of Dividend Growth	21

TRADING VOLUME (thousand shares)

Business Summary: Commercial Banking (MIC: 8.1 SIC: 6022 NAIC:522110)

FirstMerit is a multi-bank holding company with $10.47 billion in assets as of Dec 31 2003. Co., through its affiliates, operates principally as a regional banking organization, providing banking, fiduciary, financial, insurance and investment services to corporate, institutional and individual customers throughout northeastern and Central Ohio and Western Pennsylvania counties. FirstMerit Bank, Co.'s largest subsidiary, is the parent company of 16 wholly-owned subsidiaries. At Dec 31 2003, FirstMerit Bank operated 158 full-service banking offices in 24 Ohio and western Pennsylvania counties.

Recent Developments: For the year ended Dec 31 2003, Co. reported income of $121.7 million, before an accounting change charge of $688,000, versus net income of $154.4 million the year before. Net interest income slipped 6.6% to $393.6 million from $421.6 million a year earlier, reflecting continued weakness in margins, partially offset by an increase in average earning assets. Net interest margin was 4.02% compared with 4.39% in 2002. Provision for loan losses grew 3.6% to $102.2 million. Non-interest income rose 12.7% to $210.1 million, driven by significant growth in loan sales and servicing income. Non-interest expenses increased 13.9% to $327.0 million, reflecting an increase in salary and benefits expense.

Prospects: The slowdown of the economy has negatively affected Co.'s performance. However, during the fourth quarter of 2003, Co. completed several initiatives that reduced risk and strengthened its balance sheet. These initiatives included the sale of Co.s $621.0 million portfolio of manufactured housing loans and prepayment of $221.0 million in Federal Home Loan Bank borrowings, as part of Co.'s strategy to remove high-risk, non-core businesses. Additionally, Co. sold $22.6 million of commercial loans, which improved its asset quality. These actions should position Co. well once economic conditions recover.

Financial Data

(US$ in Thousands)	12/31/2003	12/31/2002	12/31/2001	12/31/2000	12/31/1999	12/31/1998	12/31/1997	12/31/1996
Earnings Per Share	1.43	1.81	1.42	1.80	1.31	1.34	1.36	1.09
Tang. Book Val. Per Share	9.94	9.67	9.06	10.48	9.38	10.38	8.55	8.19
Dividends Per Share	1.020	0.980	0.930	0.860	0.760	0.660	0.610	0.550
Dividend Payout %	71.32	54.14	65.49	47.77	58.01	49.25	44.85	50.46
Income Statement								
Total Interest Income	567,269	648,013	726,899	791,495	684,851	503,097	407,825	411,745
Total Interest Expense	173,656	226,417	335,443	415,251	300,865	197,651	152,369	160,773
Net Interest Income	393,613	421,596	391,456	376,244	383,986	305,446	255,456	250,972
Provision for Loan Losses	102,211	98,628	61,807	32,708	37,430	28,383	21,593	17,751
Non-Interest Income	210,146	186,402	176,780	163,891	154,710	110,480	83,578	82,496
Non-Interest Expense	326,952	287,030	328,597	275,192	316,506	242,723	191,080	209,702
Income Before Taxes	174,596	222,340	177,832	232,235	184,760	144,820	126,361	106,015
Income from Cont Ops	121,657	...	116,965	...	125,717	...	...	...
Net Income	120,969	154,366	116,305	159,787	119,870	97,478	86,363	70,940
Average Shs. Outstg.	84,929	85,317	86,288	88,861	91,523	72,703	63,537	65,216
Balance Sheet								
Cash & Due from Banks	199,049	233,568	190,020	235,918	215,071	245,950	166,742	222,164
Securities Avail. for Sale	3,061,497	...	...	...	...	...	...	...
Net Loans & Leases	6,454,046	7,091,515	7,262,085	7,128,800	6,909,284	4,918,447	3,781,101	3,606,662
Total Assets	10,473,635	10,688,206	10,193,374	10,215,203	10,115,477	7,127,365	5,307,461	5,227,980
Total Deposits	7,502,758	7,711,259	7,539,400	7,614,932	6,860,147	5,461,563	4,255,211	4,204,875
Long-Term Obligations	311,038	1,821,120	1,588,279	1,563,404	2,281,243	807,433	441,755	423,701
Total Liabilities	9,486,460	9,723,549	9,282,567	9,300,314	9,260,452	6,358,729	4,777,125	4,704,273
Net Stockholders' Equity	987,175	964,657	910,807	914,889	812,125	768,636	530,336	523,707
Shares Outstanding	84,724	84,505	84,991	87,032	88,375	74,009	61,967	63,912
Statistical Record								
Return on Equity %	12.32	16.00	12.84	17.46	15.08	12.68	16.28	13.54
Return on Assets %	1.16	1.44	1.14	1.56	1.24	1.36	1.62	1.35
Equity/Assets %	9.42	9.02	8.93	8.95	8.24	10.78	9.99	10.01
Non-Int. Exp./Tot. Inc. %	42.05	34.39	36.13	28.80	37.69	39.55	38.88	42.42
Price Range	27.81-18.16	29.49-18.89	27.94-21.10	27.63-13.50	28.78-22.94	34.00-21.00	30.38-17.50	17.81-14.00
P/E Ratio	19.45-12.70	16.29-10.44	19.68-14.86	15.35-7.50	21.97-17.51	25.37-15.67	22.33-12.87	16.34-12.84
Average Yield %	4.42	3.87	3.71	4.24	2.87	2.37	2.62	3.56

Address: III Cascade Plaza, Akron, OH 4308-1103	Officers: John R. Cochran – Chmn., C.E.O., Sid A. Bostic – Pres., C.O.O.	Investor Contact:330-996-6300
Telephone: (330) 996-6300		Institutional Holding
Web Site: www.firstmerit.com		No of Institutions: 2
		Shares: 30,358 % Held: –

FLORIDA PUBLIC UTILITIES CO.

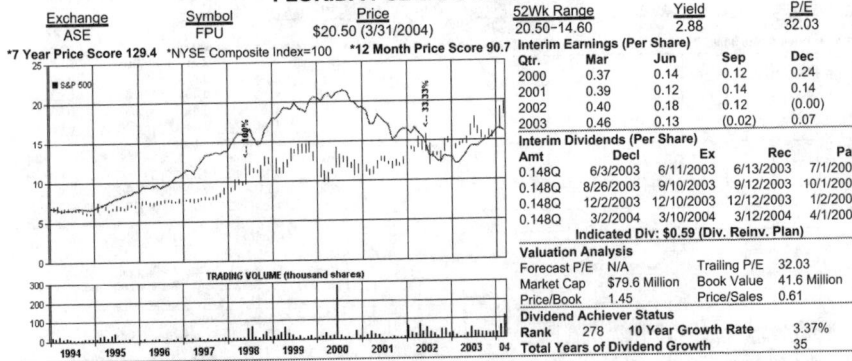

Exchange	Symbol	Price	52Wk Range	Yield	P/E
ASE	FPU	$20.50 (3/31/2004)	20.50–14.60	2.88	32.03

*7 Year Price Score 129.4 *NYSE Composite Index=100 *12 Month Price Score 90.7

Interim Earnings (Per Share)

Qtr.	Mar	Jun	Sep	Dec
2000	0.37	0.14	0.12	0.24
2001	0.39	0.12	0.14	0.14
2002	0.40	0.18	0.12	(0.00)
2003	0.46	0.13	(0.02)	0.07

Interim Dividends (Per Share)

Amt	Decl	Ex	Rec	Pay
0.148Q	6/3/2003	6/11/2003	6/13/2003	7/1/2003
0.148Q	8/26/2003	9/10/2003	9/12/2003	10/1/2003
0.148Q	12/2/2003	12/10/2003	12/12/2003	1/2/2004
0.148Q	3/2/2004	3/10/2004	3/12/2004	4/1/2004

Indicated Div: $0.59 (Div. Reinv. Plan)

Valuation Analysis

Forecast P/E	N/A	Trailing P/E	32.03
Market Cap	$79.6 Million	Book Value	41.6 Million
Price/Book	1.45	Price/Sales	0.61

Dividend Achiever Status

Rank	278	10 Year Growth Rate	3.37%
Total Years of Dividend Growth			35

Business Summary: Electricity (MIC: 7.1 SIC: 4931 NAIC:221121)

Florida Public Utilities is regulated by the Florida Public Service Commission (except for propane gas service) and provides natural gas, electricity and propane gas services to retail and commercial customers in Florida. As of Dec 31 2003, Co.'s regulated segment sold natural gas and electricity to 74,582 customers in Central, Northeast, Northwest and Southern Florida. Co.'s unregulated segment operates through its wholly owned subsidiary, Flo-Gas Corporation, and sells propane gas to 12,413 customers throughout the State of Florida.

Recent Developments: For the year ended Dec 31 2003, income was $2.5 million, before income from discontinued operations of $9.9 million, versus income of $2.8 million, before income from discontinued operations of $602,000, the year before. Results were hurt by higher operating expenses for pension, casualty and property insurance, employee medical benefits, auditing and underground gas line detection. Total revenues increased 16.1% to $102.7 million, primarily due to higher natural gas costs, which are recovered through revenue. Revenues also benefited from higher propane revenues, reflecting the Nature Coast acquisition, late fees and the new assessment of regulatory compliance fees for propane customers.

Prospects: On Aug 14 2003, Co. filed a request for rate relief with the Florida Public Service Commission (FPSC) for the electric segment. Co. had a hearing before the FPSC on February 18 2004, at which time the FPSC approved a $1.8 million increase in annual revenue. The effective date for the increase has not been set but is anticipated to occur in the second quarter of 2004, resulting in less than a full year of the annual increase for 2004. Going forward, Co. should continue to benefit from the strong fundamentals of its natural gas and propane operations. However, higher insurance and employee benefit expenses may continue to drive operating expenses higher and contribute to reduced earnings.

Financial Data

(US$ in Thousands)	12/31/2003	12/31/2002	12/31/2001	12/31/2000	12/31/1999	12/31/1998	12/31/1997	12/31/1996
Earnings Per Share	0.64	0.70	0.79	0.87	0.87	0.76	0.79	0.69
Cash Flow Per Share	1.78	1.88	2.00	1.81	1.88	...	...	1.89
Tang. Book Val. Per Share	9.00	6.36	6.08	7.29	6.92	6.90	6.59	6.23
Dividends Per Share	0.580	0.560	0.540	0.520	0.490	0.460	0.450	0.440
Dividend Payout %	90.62	80.35	68.86	60.34	56.41	60.53	56.96	63.77
Income Statement								
Total Revenues	102,723	88,461	92,143	84,759	74,098	76,192	78,134	78,810
Total Indirect Exp.	8,144	7,338	8,626	8,463	8,396	8,033	7,366	7,016
Costs & Expenses	95,030	80,692	85,876	78,231	67,928	70,296	72,616	73,182
Depreciation & Amort.	5,492	5,026	4,839	4,698	4,557	4,269	4,029	3,876
Operating Income	7,693	7,769	6,267	6,528	6,170	5,896	5,518	5,628
Net Interest Inc./(Exp.)	(4,488)	(4,513)	(3,591)	(3,487)	(2,968)	(2,840)	(2,895)	(2,858)
Income Taxes	1,167	1,402	...	...	...	...	...	...
Income from Cont Ops	2,522	2,761	...	...	...	...	...	...
Net Income	12,423	3,363	3,052	3,288	3,529	3,068	3,191	2,75
Average Shs. Outstg.	3,905	3,871	3,801	3,759	3,994	3,990	3,957	3,91
Balance Sheet								
Net Property	108,342	97,955	97,329	84,200	78,272	75,227	72,724	69,876
Total Assets	162,990	144,823	139,989	108,588	96,807	92,406	88,622	90,99
Long–Term Obligations	52,500	52,500	52,500	23,500	23,500	23,500	23,500	23,500
Net Stockholders' Equity	41,463	30,883	29,329	27,510	25,866	27,622	26,189	24,51
Shares Outstanding	3,916	3,881	3,848	3,770	3,736	3,999	3,970	3,93
Statistical Record								
Operating Profit Margin %	7.48	8.78	6.80	7.70	8.32	7.73	7.06	7.1
Net Inc./Net Property %	11.46	3.43	3.13	3.90	4.50	4.07	4.38	3.9
Net Inc./Tot. Capital %	11.29	3.70	3.42	5.62	6.27	5.36	5.74	5.4
Return on Equity %	6.08	8.94	10.40	11.95	13.64	11.10	12.18	11.2
Accum. Depr./Gross Prop. %	32.55	35.93	35.82	36.64	36.82	36.06	35.27	34.5
Price Range	17.90–13.90	15.82–11.85	13.02–10.69	14.25–9.84	15.00–10.97	13.13–8.67	9.23–7.36	7.88–6.9
P/E Ratio	27.97–21.72	22.60–16.93	16.48–13.53	16.38–11.31	17.24–12.61	17.27–11.41	11.69–9.32	11.41–10.0
Average Yield %	3.75	4.01	4.55	4.45	3.77	4.27	5.66	5.9

Address: 401 South Dixie Highway, West Palm Beach, FL 33401 **Telephone:** (561) 832–2461 **Web Site:** www.fpuc.com	**Officers:** John T. English – Pres., C.E.O. Charles L. Stein – Sr. V.P., C.O.O.	**Investor Contact:** (561) 838–1729 **Institutional Holding** **No of Institutions:** 19 **Shares:** 1,095,891 **% Held:** 27%

110

FRANKLIN ELECTRIC CO., INC.

Exchange	Symbol	Price	52Wk Range	Yield	P/E
NMS	FELE	$63.68 (3/31/2004)	65.00-46.27	0.88	20.88

*7 Year Price Score 150.8 *NYSE Composite Index=100 *12 Month Price Score 97.5

Interim Earnings (Per Share)

Qtr.	Mar	Jun	Sep	Dec
2000	0.34	0.69	0.30	0.62
2001	0.26	0.58	0.72	0.83
2002	0.32	0.79	0.85	0.87
2003	0.36	0.83	0.93	0.93

Interim Dividends (Per Share)

Amt	Decl	Ex	Rec	Pay
0.14Q	4/25/2003	5/6/2003	5/8/2003	5/22/2003
0.14Q	7/18/2003	8/5/2003	8/7/2003	8/21/2003
0.14Q	10/24/2003	11/4/2003	11/6/2003	11/20/2003
0.14Q	2/6/2004	2/10/2004	2/12/2004	2/26/2004

Indicated Div: $0.56

Valuation Analysis

Forecast P/E	18.15	Trailing P/E	20.88
Market Cap	$689.5 Million	Book Value	192.9 Million
Price/Book	3.44	Price/Sales	1.85

Dividend Achiever Status

Rank	25	10 Year Growth Rate	22.05%
Total Years of Dividend Growth		10	

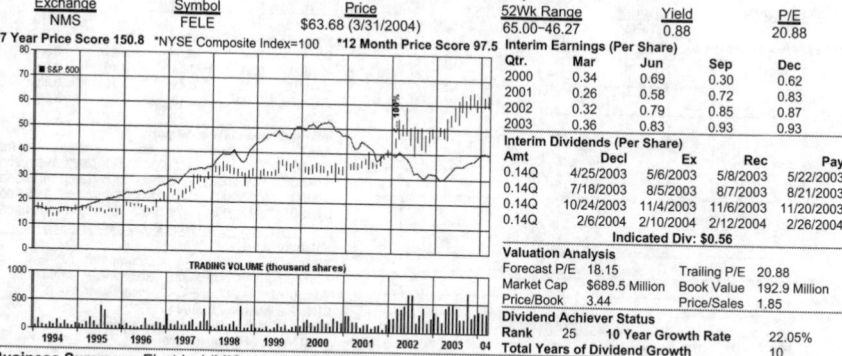

Business Summary: Electrical (MIC: 11.14 SIC: 3621 NAIC:335312)

Franklin Electric is a manufacturer of submersible water and fueling systems motors, underground fueling systems hardware and flexible piping systems and engineered industrial motor products. Co.'s motors are used principally in submersible motor applications for pumping fresh water, fuel, wastewater and other liquids in a variety of applications including residential, industrial, agriculture, fueling, off-shore drilling, and mining. Co. also manufactures other industrial electric motors, which are used in a wide variety of applications, and manufactures electronic controls for the motors that control functionality and

Recent Developments: For the year ended Jan 3 2004, net income climbed 7.1% to $34.5 million compared with $32.2 million the previous year. Net sales inched up 1.3% to $359.5 million from $354.9 million the year before, primarily due to strong foreign currency exchange rates, particularly the Euro. Sales growth was also attributed to the inclusion of the sales of Intelligent Controls, Inc., acquired in Jul 2002. Europe motor sales were down due to negative impact of the war in the Middle East during the second half of the year. Gross profit grew 5.8% to $111.0 million from $104.9 million the prior year. Operating income rose 3.2% to $51.9 million.

Prospects: On Jan 13 2003, Co.announced plans to consolidate the submersible turbine pump operations of FE Petro, Inc. in the in the Madison, WI area, and the service station hardware and flexible piping operations of EBW, Inc. and Advanced Polymer Technology, Inc. in Muskegon, MI into a new leased facility in Madison, WI. The cost of the consolidation is included in the estimate for the multi-year global manufacturing re-alignment totaling $10.0 million. Co. expects the consolidation will improve customer service levels, increase efficiencies, enhance product development, and reduce overhead costs.

Financial Data

US$ in Thousands	01/03/2004	12/28/2002	12/29/2001	12/30/2000	01/01/2000	01/02/1999	01/03/1998	12/28/1996
Earnings Per Share	3.05	2.83	2.39	1.95	2.30	2.01	2.00	1.61
Cash Flow Per Share	4.15	5.09	3.51	1.64	3.09	2.51	1.72	2.31
Tang. Book Val. Per Share	12.52	10.56	10.19	9.12	8.89	8.21	7.93	7.83
Dividends Per Share	0.550	0.510	0.470	0.430	0.380	0.330	0.280	0.230
Dividend Payout %	18.03	18.02	19.66	21.99	16.73	16.41	14.21	14.29
Income Statement								
Total Revenues	359,502	354,872	322,908	325,731	293,236	272,533	303,298	300,689
Total Indirect Exp.	59,106	54,637	47,522	44,967	41,898	42,027	49,194	45,854
Depreciation & Amort.	13,748	12,878	12,660	10,839	7,460	6,687	7,628	8,389
Operating Income	51,890	50,298	45,349	40,219	42,273	37,928	36,339	33,199
Net Interest Inc./(Exp.)	(1,107)	(1,317)	(1,193)	(1,111)	(1,317)	(1,364)	(1,435)	(1,308)
Income Taxes	16,847	18,273	16,235	13,683	15,591	15,237	15,004	11,827
Net Income	34,480	32,204	27,150	22,226	26,805	24,784	25,505	21,510
Average Shs. Outstg.	11,313	11,366	11,370	11,368	11,646	12,340	12,732	13,352
Balance Sheet								
Cash & Cash Equivalents	29,962	20,133	23,749	9,631	36,812	44,955	71,688	54,592
Total Current Assets	128,041	113,009	109,583	101,961	104,243	106,283	128,500	131,516
Total Assets	281,971	258,583	195,643	197,179	176,101	167,590	163,110	173,459
Total Current Liabilities	45,401	50,247	40,425	47,064	47,357	44,405	40,527	43,292
Long-Term Obligations	14,960	25,946	14,465	15,874	17,057	18,089	19,163	20,276
Net Stockholders' Equity	192,938	153,138	123,269	115,998	96,293	91,597	92,841	99,823
Net Working Capital	82,640	62,762	69,158	54,897	56,886	61,878	87,973	88,224
Shares Outstanding	10,914	10,824	10,668	11,008	10,826	11,148	11,694	12,742
Statistical Record								
Operating Profit Margin %	14.43	14.17	14.04	12.34	14.41	13.91	11.98	11.04
Return on Equity %	17.87	21.02	22.02	19.16	27.83	27.05	27.47	21.54
Return on Assets %	12.22	12.45	13.87	11.27	15.22	14.78	15.63	12.40
Debt/Total Assets %	5.30	10.03	7.39	8.05	9.68	10.79	11.74	11.68
Price Range	65.00-46.27	59.00-39.96	42.05-32.00	36.38-28.72	37.44-29.50	36.25-26.75	32.13-20.63	22.63-15.38
P/E Ratio	21.31-15.17	20.85-14.12	17.59-13.39	18.65-14.73	16.28-12.83	18.03-13.31	16.06-10.31	14.05-9.55
Average Yield %	0.98	1.08	1.30	1.28	1.13	1.02	1.10	1.28

Address: 400 East Spring Street, Huffton, IN 46714-3798 **Telephone:** (260) 824-2900 **Web Site:** www.franklin-electric.com	**Officers:** R. Scott Trumbull – Chmn., C.E.O., Gregg C. Sengstack – Sr. V.P., C.F.O., Sec.	**Investor Contact:** (219) 824-2900 **Institutional Holding** **No of Institutions:** 6 **Shares:** 72,000 **% Held:** –

FRANKLIN RESOURCES, INC.

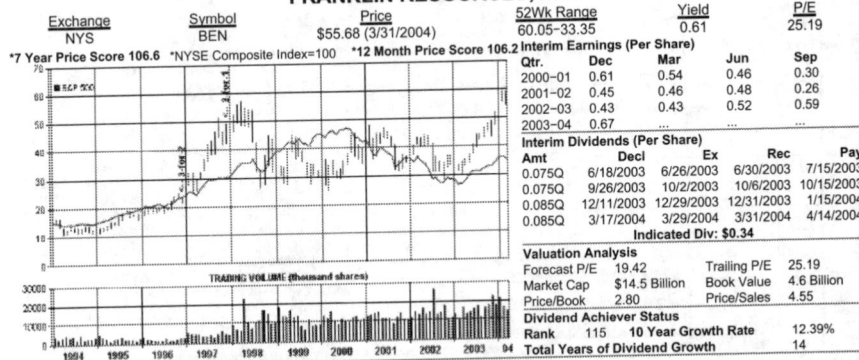

Exchange	Symbol	Price	52Wk Range	Yield	P/E
NYS	BEN	$55.68 (3/31/2004)	60.05–33.35	0.61	25.19

*7 Year Price Score 106.6   ***NYSE Composite Index=100**   ***12 Month Price Score 106.2**

Interim Earnings (Per Share)

Qtr.	Dec	Mar	Jun	Sep
2000–01	0.61	0.54	0.46	0.30
2001–02	0.45	0.46	0.48	0.26
2002–03	0.43	0.43	0.52	0.59
2003–04	0.67	...	...	...

Interim Dividends (Per Share)

Amt	Decl	Ex	Rec	Pay
0.075Q	6/18/2003	6/26/2003	6/30/2003	7/15/2003
0.075Q	9/26/2003	10/2/2003	10/6/2003	10/15/2003
0.085Q	12/11/2003	12/29/2003	12/31/2003	1/15/2004
0.085Q	3/17/2004	3/29/2004	3/31/2004	4/14/2004

Indicated Div: $0.34

Valuation Analysis

Forecast P/E	19.42	Trailing P/E	25.19
Market Cap	$14.5 Billion	Book Value	4.6 Billion
Price/Book	2.80	Price/Sales	4.55

Dividend Achiever Status

Rank	115	10 Year Growth Rate	12.39%
Total Years of Dividend Growth			14

Business Summary: Wealth Management (MIC: 8.8 SIC: 6282 NAIC:523930)

Franklin Resources, operating as Franklin Templeton Investments, is engaged in providing investment management, marketing, distribution, transfer agency and other administrative services to the open–end investment companies of the Franklin Templeton Group, and to U.S. and international managed and institutional accounts. Co. also provides investment management and related services to a number of closed–end investment companies. In addition, Co. provides investment management, marketing and distribution services to certain sponsored investment companies organized in the Grand Duchy of Luxembourg. As of Sep 30 2003, Co.'s subsidiaries had $301.90 billion in assets under management.

Recent Developments: For the quarter ended Dec 31 2003, Co. reported income of $167.5 million, before an accounting change credit of $4.8 million, compared with net income of $109.8 million the year before. Results for 2003 included net investment product gains of $4.0 million. Total operating revenues grew 33.2% to $806.2 million from $605.5 million a year earlier. Investment management fees increased 29.3% to $454.5 million from $351.4 million the prior year. Underwriting and distribution fees advanced 46.7% to $272.8 million, while shareholder servicing fees increased 27.7% to $61.3 million. Operating income climbed 59.8% to $222.9 million.

Prospects: Co. continues to benefit from significant growth in assets under management, both domestically and globally. For instance, during the first quarter of 2004, Franklin Templeton's assets under management in Italy, Hong Kong and India totaled more than $1.00 billion, $2.00 billion and $3.00 billion, respectively. Additionally, Bisset assets under management have increased approximately 90.0% to more than $7.00 billion since its acquisition in Oct 2000. Meanwhile, as of Dec 31 2003, equity assets comprised 54.0% of total assets under management, while fixed–income assets comprised 29.0%.

Financial Data
(US$ in Thousands)

	3 Mos	09/30/2003	09/30/2002	09/30/2001	09/30/2000	09/30/1999	09/30/1998	09/30/1997
Earnings Per Share	2.21	1.97	1.65	1.91	2.28	1.69	1.98	1.71
Cash Flow Per Share	0.41	2.15	2.81	2.18	2.84	2.31	2.74	1.69
Tang. Book Val. Per Share	10.20	9.31	8.69	7.62	7.36	5.79	4.07	2.56
Dividends Per Share	0.300	0.290	0.270	0.250	0.230	0.210	0.190	0.168
Dividend Payout %	13.57	14.97	16.66	13.35	10.30	12.72	9.84	9.42
Income Statement								
Total Revenues	806,169	2,624,448	2,518,532	2,354,843	2,340,140	2,262,497	2,577,272	2,163,275
Total Indirect Exp.	583,309	1,976,372	1,933,030	1,842,848	1,676,697	1,723,389	1,935,176	1,571,815
Depreciation & Amort.	26,850	90,462	84,715	125,567	120,790	133,168	142,262	93,762
Operating Income	222,860	648,076	585,502	511,995	663,443	539,108	642,096	591,466
Net Interest Inc./(Exp.)	(7,111)	(19,910)	(12,302)	(10,556)	(13,960)	(20,958)	(22,535)	(25,333)
Income Taxes	68,423	197,373	145,552	153,069	177,502	147,373	175,834	181,656
Income from Cont Ops	167,517	...	...	...	...	...	...	...
Net Income	172,296	502,830	432,723	484,721	562,089	426,711	500,450	434,067
Average Shs. Outstg.	250,234	254,681	262,054	253,663	246,624	252,757	252,941	253,464
Balance Sheet								
Cash & Cash Equivalents	3,266,479	2,934,015	2,533,696	2,081,232	1,408,675	1,231,750	1,047,955	656,643
Total Current Assets	3,729,237	3,887,252	3,414,031	3,159,520	1,955,856	1,703,667	1,470,756	1,210,474
Total Assets	7,417,402	6,970,749	6,422,738	6,265,650	4,042,443	3,666,790	3,480,049	2,878,113
Total Current Liabilities	649,846	1,290,506	1,338,955	1,528,094	728,513	662,896	655,474	709,905
Long–Term Obligations	1,158,846	1,108,881	595,148	566,013	294,090	294,262	494,459	493,243
Net Stockholders' Equity	4,598,629	4,310,108	4,266,946	3,977,896	2,965,493	2,656,994	2,280,767	1,854,223
Net Working Capital	3,079,391	2,596,746	2,075,076	1,631,426	1,227,343	1,040,771	815,282	500,571
Shares Outstanding	248,761	245,931	258,555	260,797	243,730	251,006	251,742	252,064
Statistical Record								
Operating Profit Margin %	27.64	24.69	23.24	21.74	28.35	23.82	24.91	27.34
Return on Equity %	3.64	11.66	10.14	12.18	18.95	16.05	21.94	23.41
Return on Assets %	2.25	7.21	6.73	7.73	13.90	11.63	14.38	15.08
Debt/Total Assets %	15.62	15.90	9.26	9.03	7.27	8.02	14.20	17.13
Price Range	52.06–43.56	46.80–28.18	44.13–30.97	47.83–31.90	44.75–25.19	45.00–27.25	57.31–26.38	46.75–21.50
P/E Ratio	77.70–65.01	23.76–14.30	26.75–18.77	25.04–16.70	19.63–11.05	26.63–16.12	28.95–13.32	27.34–12.62
Average Yield %	0.63	0.79	0.72	0.60	0.70	0.58	0.41	0.50

Address: One Franklin Parkway, San Mateo, CA 94403 **Telephone:** (650) 312–2000 **Web Site:** www.frk.com	**Officers:** Charles B. Johnson – Chmn., Co–C.E.O., Harmon E. Burns – Vice–Chmn. **Transfer Agents:**Bank of New York, New York, NY	**Investor Contact:**650–525–8900 **Institutional Holding** **No of Institutions:** 68 **Shares:** 167,571,600 **% Held:** –

FREDDIE MAC

Exchange	Symbol	Price	52Wk Range	Yield	P/E
NYS	FRE	$59.06 (3/31/2004)	65.00–47.35	2.03	7.56

*7 Year Price Score 106.3 *NYSE Composite Index=100 *12 Month Price Score 89.7

Interim Earnings (Per Share)

Qtr.	Mar	Jun	Sep	Dec
1999	0.69	0.74	0.74	0.79
2000	0.81	0.83	0.86	0.89
2001	1.12	1.24	1.49	2.11
2002	2.07	1.50	2.13	...

Interim Dividends (Per Share)

Amt	Decl	Ex	Rec	Pay
0.26Q	6/6/2003	6/12/2003	6/16/2003	6/30/2003
0.26Q	9/5/2003	9/11/2003	9/15/2003	9/30/2003
0.26Q	12/5/2003	12/11/2003	12/15/2003	12/31/2003
0.30Q	3/5/2004	3/11/2004	3/15/2004	3/31/2004

Indicated Div: $1.20 (Div. Reinv. Plan)

Valuation Analysis

Forecast P/E	11.00	Trailing P/E	7.56
Market Cap	$41.1 Billion	Book Value	22.6 Billion
Price/Book	1.72	Price/Sales	1.02

Dividend Achiever Status

Rank	54	10 Year Growth Rate	16.80%
Total Years of Dividend Growth		13	

Business Summary: Credit &Lending (MIC: 8.6 SIC: 6111 NAIC:522292)

Freddie Mac purchases conventional residential mortgages from mortgage lending institutions and finances most of its purchases with sales of guaranteed mortgage securities called Mortgage Participation Certificates for which Co. ultimately assumes the risk of borrower default. Co. also maintains an investment portfolio that consists principally of federal funds sold, reverse repurchase agreements and tax–advantaged and other short–term investments. Co.'s financial performance is driven primarily by the growth of its total servicing portfolio, the mix of sold versus retained portfolios, the spreads earned on the sold and retained portfolios and mortgage default costs.

Recent Developments: Spurred by low interest rates and record home sales, home prices took off in the fourth quarter of 2003, jumping at an annualized rate of 17.8% nationwide. This represents a marked increase from the third quarter of 2003, when the annualized growth rate was revised upward to 5.9%. The largest annual home price gains were in the Pacific states, where prices rose 13.1%, followed by Middle Atlantic states, with an 11.9% growth rate. In the West South Central states, values rose 3.9%. Co. noted that these figures are subject to revision as Co. does not yet have all of the data on originations in the fourth quarter.

Prospects: Looking ahead to 2004, housing construction and home sales are expected to slow from the strong fourth quarter pace. Likewise, house-price appreciation is anticipated to moderate, but remain at a healthy 6.5%. Co. expects the refinance share to gradually decline from about 55.0% of applications during the first quarter of 2004 to 35.0% in the fourth quarter, and average 42% for the year. In addition, because of lesser refinance volume, single-family originations are expected to drop by about one-third to $2.40 trillion. Separately, Co. expects to provide its 2002 annual report in the first quarter 2004 and release quarterly and full-year 2003 results by June 30 2004.

Financial Data

(US$ in Millions)	9 Mos	6 Mos	3 Mos	12/31/2001	12/31/2000	12/31/1999	12/31/1998	12/31/1997
Earnings Per Share	5.57	...	2.07	5.96	3.39	2.96	2.31	1.88
Tang. Book Val. Per Share	32.53	25.77	22.79	15.49	16.80	11.98	11.54	8.73
Dividends Per Share	0.640	0.840	0.820	0.800	0.680	0.570	0.460	0.380
Dividend Payout %	11.49	...	39.61	13.42	20.06	19.25	19.91	20.61
Income Statement								
Total Interest Income	27,431	...	9,176	34,288	28,350	22,753	16,638	13,001
Total Interest Expense	22,337	...	7,453	28,808	25,512	20,213	14,711	11,370
Net Interest Income	5,094	...	1,723	5,480	2,838	2,540	1,927	1,631
Provision for Loan Losses	(17)	...	15	45	40	60	190	310
Non–Interest Income	1,286	...	765	1,639	1,489	1,405	1,307	1,298
Non–Interest Expense	640	...	228	1,020	883	834	791	755
Income Before Taxes	5,881	...	2,194	6,300	3,534	3,161	2,356	1,964
Income from Cont Ops	...	...	1,505	4,373	2,539	2,218	...	...
Net Income	4,061	...	1,413	4,147	2,547	2,223	1,700	1,395
Average Shs. Outstg.	969	...	697	696	696	700	684	692
Balance Sheet								
Net Loans & Leases	542,415	524,904	527,640	494,259	385,117	322,569	255,348	164,250
Total Assets	681,980	644,013	646,397	617,340	459,297	386,684	321,421	194,597
Long–Term Obligations	623,267	601,363	603,446	314,733	243,323	185,186	93,525	87,714
Total Liabilities	659,414	626,079	630,532	601,967	444,460	375,159	310,586	187,076
Net Stockholders' Equity	22,566	17,934	15,865	15,373	14,837	11,525	10,835	7,521
Shares Outstanding	693	...	695	695	692	695	695	679
Statistical Record								
Return on Equity %	17.99	...	9.48	28.44	17.11	19.24	15.68	18.54
Return on Assets %	0.59	...	0.23	0.70	0.55	0.57	0.52	0.71
Equity/Assets %	3.30	2.78	2.45	2.49	3.23	2.98	3.37	3.86
Non–Int. Exp./Tot. Inc. %	2.22	...	2.29	2.83	2.95	3.45	4.40	5.28
Price Range	68.60-54.67	68.60-60.42	68.60-61.00	70.79-60.00	69.00-37.69	64.63-45.75	65.13-39.50	43.38-27.00
P/E Ratio	12.32-9.82	N/A	33.14-29.47	11.88-10.07	20.35-11.12	21.83-15.46	28.19-17.10	23.07-14.36
Average Yield %	1.01	1.29	1.26	0.92	1.72	1.03	0.94	1.12

Address: 8200 Jones Branch Drive, McLean, VA 22102–3110 Telephone: (703) 903–2000 Web Site: www.freddiemac.com	Officers: Richard F. Syron – Chmn., C.E.O., Martin F. Baumann – Exec. V.P., Fin., C.F.O. Transfer Agents: Equiserve Trust Company, N.A., Jersey City, NJ	Institutional Holding No of Institutions: 1 Shares: 20,000 % Held: –

FRISCH'S RESTAURANTS, INC.

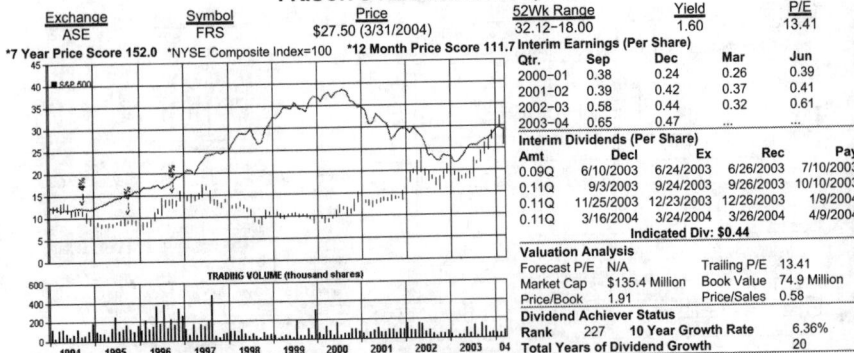

Exchange	Symbol	Price	52Wk Range	Yield	P/E
ASE	FRS	$27.50 (3/31/2004)	32.12–18.00	1.60	13.41

*7 Year Price Score 152.0   *NYSE Composite Index=100   *12 Month Price Score 111.7

Interim Earnings (Per Share)

Qtr.	Sep	Dec	Mar	Jun
2000–01	0.38	0.24	0.26	0.39
2001–02	0.39	0.42	0.37	0.41
2002–03	0.58	0.44	0.32	0.61
2003–04	0.65	0.47	...	...

Interim Dividends (Per Share)

Amt	Decl	Ex	Rec	Pay
0.09Q	6/10/2003	6/24/2003	6/26/2003	7/10/2003
0.11Q	9/3/2003	9/24/2003	9/26/2003	10/10/2003
0.11Q	11/25/2003	12/23/2003	12/26/2003	1/9/2004
0.11Q	3/16/2004	3/24/2004	3/26/2004	4/9/2004

Indicated Div: $0.44

Valuation Analysis

Forecast P/E	N/A	Trailing P/E	13.41
Market Cap	$135.4 Million	Book Value	74.9 Million
Price/Book	1.91	Price/Sales	0.58

Dividend Achiever Status

Rank	227	10 Year Growth Rate	6.36%
Total Years of Dividend Growth			20

Business Summary: Hospitality &Tourism (MIC: 5.1 SIC: 5812 NAIC:722310)

Frisch's Restaurants is a regional company that operates and licenses others to operate full service family–style restaurants under the name "Frisch's Big Boy," and operates grill buffet style restaurants under the name "Golden Corral" under certain licensing agreements. As of June 1 2003, Co. operated 88 family–style restaurants using the "Big Boy" trade name and 20 "Golden Corral" grill–buffet style family restaurants. Additionally, Co. had licensed 32 "Big Boy" restaurants to other operators. All of these restaurants are located in various markets of Ohio, Kentucky and Indiana.

Recent Developments: For the twelve weeks ended Dec 14 2003, net earnings rose 9.1% to $2.4 million compared with $2.2 million in the corresponding quarter of 2002. Total revenue climbed 10.2% to $60.4 million from $54.8 million a year earlier. Sales grew 10.2% to $60.1 million from $54.5 million, while other revenues slipped 0.3% to $292,000 from $293,000 the year before. Same–store sales at Co.'s Big Boy restaurants increased 5.1% year over year, while same–store sales at Co.'s Golden Corral restaurants decreased 2.4% year over year, but were up year to date by 2.6%.

Prospects: Co.'s development schedule for its Golden Corral restaurants is on track with a total of 24 restaurants opened in four markets. Two Golden Corrals are under construction and will open before the end of the fiscal year. Three more Golden Corrals are scheduled to open in the latter part of 2004. Meanwhile, higher commodity costs, particularly beef, dairy and pork, are driving the food and paper cost percentages higher for both Big Boy and Golden Corral. Nevertheless, Co. plans to implement menu price increases at both Golden Corral and Big Boy restaurants, which should enhance comparable–store sales growth.

Financial Data
(US$ in Thousands)

	6 Mos	3 Mos	06/01/2003	06/02/2002	06/03/2001	05/28/2000	05/30/1999	05/31/1998
Earnings Per Share	1.12	0.65	1.95	1.59	1.27	1.08	1.36	0.73
Cash Flow Per Share	2.76	1.41	4.48	4.00	3.13	2.74	2.16	1.99
Tang. Book Val. Per Share	14.55	14.18	13.72	12.11	11.11	9.99	9.24	6.67
Dividends Per Share	0.380	0.360	0.360	0.350	0.320	0.310	0.280	0.260
Dividend Payout %	33.92	55.38	18.46	22.01	25.19	28.70	20.58	35.61
Income Statement								
Total Revenues	137,787	77,403	234,911	211,758	190,030	167,200	159,551	152,222
Total Indirect Exp.	9,547	5,426	11,311	11,061	11,834	9,225	10,421	8,262
Depreciation & Amort.	5,736	3,328	10,973	9,551	8,599	9,621	9,937	9,256
Operating Income	8,836	5,059	17,501	14,654	12,599	11,837	9,394	9,889
Net Interest Inc./(Exp.)	(1,316)	(734)	(2,800)	(2,420)	(2,607)	(2,410)	(2,437)	(3,076)
Income Taxes	3,137	1,771	4,924	4,262	3,435	3,351	2,539	2,268
Income from Cont Ops	...	...	...	...	6,557	6,075	4,418	...
Net Income	5,699	3,288	9,778	7,971	7,686	6,146	8,130	4,545
Average Shs. Outstg.	5,096	5,067	5,023	5,012	5,144	5,658	5,966	6,237
Balance Sheet								
Cash & Cash Equivalents	1,424	2,691	1,133	671	280	565	200	84
Total Current Assets	9,293	12,269	9,809	7,487	6,965	20,778	6,924	6,508
Total Assets	147,235	142,980	138,636	129,335	108,310	107,779	103,426	106,724
Total Current Liabilities	28,013	26,010	23,746	22,351	17,932	17,722	16,534	14,958
Long–Term Obligations	37,700	37,875	37,990	40,151	28,183	30,842	26,395	35,512
Net Stockholders' Equity	74,907	72,597	69,766	61,230	56,446	54,167	55,288	49,910
Net Working Capital	...	(13,741)	(13,937)	(14,864)	(10,967)	3,056	(9,610)	(8,450)
Shares Outstanding	5,015	4,986	4,951	4,910	5,011	5,345	5,901	7,36
Statistical Record								
Operating Profit Margin %	6.41	6.53	7.45	6.92	6.62	7.07	5.88	6.4
Return on Equity %	7.60	4.52	14.01	13.01	11.61	11.21	7.99	9.11
Return on Assets %	3.87	2.29	7.05	6.16	6.05	5.63	4.27	4.2
Debt/Total Assets %	25.60	26.48	27.40	31.04	26.02	28.61	25.52	33.2
Price Range	27.90–18.00	24.48–18.00	21.35–15.51	24.75–12.90	15.13–9.63	10.75–8.50	12.00–8.25	17.38–11.9
P/E Ratio	24.91–16.07	37.66–27.69	10.95–7.95	15.57–8.11	11.91–7.58	9.95–7.87	8.82–6.07	23.80–16.3
Average Yield %	1.66	1.72	1.92	2.14	2.61	3.19	2.71	1.8

Address: 2800 Gilbert Avenue, Cincinnati, OH 45206–1206 **Telephone:** (513) 961–2660 **Web Site:** www.frischs.com	**Officers:** Jack C. Maier – Chmn., Craig F. Maier – Pres., C.E.O.	**Investor Contact:**513–961–2660 **Institutional Holding** **No of Institutions:** 19 **Shares:** 73,132 **% Held:** –

FULLER (H.B.) COMPANY

Exchange	Symbol	Price	52Wk Range	Yield	P/E
NYS	FUL	$28.44 (3/31/2004)	30.19–21.74	1.58	21.07

*7 Year Price Score 97.9 *NYSE Composite Index=100 *12 Month Price Score 99.1

Interim Earnings (Per Share)

Qtr.	Feb	May	Aug	Nov
1999	0.34	0.63	0.26	0.51
2001	0.19	0.42	0.51	0.47
2002	0.02	0.28	0.32	0.36
2003	0.11	0.34	0.43	0.47

Interim Dividends (Per Share)

Amt	Decl	Ex	Rec	Pay
0.113Q	4/18/2003	4/30/2003	5/2/2003	5/16/2003
0.113Q	7/11/2003	8/1/2003	8/5/2003	8/15/2003
0.113Q	10/3/2003	10/15/2003	10/17/2003	10/31/2003
0.113Q	1/29/2004	2/10/2004	2/12/2004	2/26/2004

Indicated Div: $0.45 (Div. Reinv. Plan)

Valuation Analysis

Forecast P/E	14.34	Trailing P/E	21.07
Market Cap	$806.4 Million	Book Value	509.3 Million
Price/Book	1.35	Price/Sales	0.54

Dividend Achiever Status

Rank	247	10 Year Growth Rate	5.18%
Total Years of Dividend Growth		36	

Business Summary: Chemicals (MIC: 11.1 SIC: 2891 NAIC:325520)

H.B. Fuller and its subsidiaries manufacture and market adhesives and specialty chemical products globally, with sales operations in 33 countries in North America, Europe, Latin America and the Asia/Pacific region. Co.'s products, in thousands of formulations, are sold to customers in a wide range of industries. Also, Co. is a producer and supplier of specialty chemical products for a variety of applications such as ceramic tile installation, HVAC insulation installation, powder coatings applied to metal surfaces such as office furniture, appliances and lawn and garden equipment, specialty hot melt adhesives for packaging applications, and liquid paint sold through retail outlets.

Recent Developments: For the 52 weeks ended Nov 29 2003, net income advanced 37.1% to $38.6 million compared with $28.2 million the year before. Earnings for 2003 and 2002 included net charges related to Co.'s restructuring initiative of $4.9 million and $19.1 million, respectively. Net sales grew 2.5% to $1.29 billion from $1.26 billion a year earlier, reflecting improved volumes and positive currency effects. Gross profit improved 4.2% to $352.2 million from $338.0 million, while gross profit as a percentage of sales rose to 27.4% from 26.9% the year before. Interest expense decreased 16.2% to $14.5 million.

Prospects: The combined effects of intensive price competition in many of Co.'s principal markets and increased raw material costs decreased profit margins in 2003. However, continued sales growth in Latin America and the Asia/Pacific, coupled with the improving economic environment in North America should position Co. well for the coming year. Meanwhile, Co. has streamlined cost structures over the past two years through restructuring initiatives. In 2004, the trend of higher costs related to pension and other postretirement benefit plans is expected to reverse as expenses associated with these plans are projected to decrease approximately $2.5 million from 2003.

Financial Data

(US$ in Thousands)	11/29/2003	11/30/2002	12/01/2001	12/02/2000	11/27/1999	11/28/1998	11/29/1997	11/30/1996
Earnings Per Share	1.35	0.98	1.59	1.74	1.57	0.57	1.43	1.61
Cash Flow Per Share	2.07	2.87	3.16	2.76	4.06	1.87	2.43	2.87
Tang. Book Val. Per Share	14.52	12.59	12.37	11.07	9.87	8.50	10.51	10.06
Dividends Per Share	0.440	0.430	0.420	0.410	0.400	0.390	0.360	0.320
Dividend Payout %	33.14	44.64	26.88	23.99	25.87	68.26	25.17	19.88
Income Statement								
Total Revenues	1,287,331	1,256,210	1,274,059	1,352,562	1,364,458	1,347,241	1,306,789	1,275,716
Total Indirect Exp.	286,324	283,978	257,446	311,010	322,171	333,912	325,702	323,461
Depreciation & Amort.	4,164	4,836	54,401	52,165	50,776	49,541	46,773	46,992
Operating Income	67,954	56,422	88,107	102,501	103,747	61,212	87,252	80,754
Net Interest Inc./(Exp.)	(13,741)	(16,613)	(21,247)	(23,814)	(26,823)	(26,989)	(19,836)	(18,881)
Income Taxes	14,307	12,973	19,833	28,455	31,807	18,826	26,661	31,233
Eqty Earns/Minority Int.	36	(1,581)	1,303	713	1,492	2,030	1,639	112
Income from Cont Ops	...	...	44,900	...	44,111	...	40,308	...
Net Income	38,619	28,176	44,439	49,163	43,370	15,990	36,940	45,430
Average Shs. Outstg.	28,694	28,601	28,330	28,206	27,956	27,688	28,200	28,228
Balance Sheet								
Cash & Cash Equivalents	3,260	3,666	11,454	10,489	5,821	4,605	2,710	3,515
Total Current Assets	448,492	408,874	403,873	435,064	440,143	457,900	409,156	388,198
Total Assets	1,007,588	961,439	966,173	1,010,361	1,025,615	1,046,169	917,646	869,275
Total Current Liabilities	200,026	214,846	204,163	226,725	265,920	285,160	237,549	246,581
Long–Term Obligations	161,047	161,763	203,001	250,464	263,715	300,074	229,996	172,779
Net Stockholders' Equity	509,338	448,330	434,026	404,710	376,380	341,404	339,114	334,740
Net Working Capital	248,466	194,028	199,710	208,339	174,223	172,740	171,607	141,617
Shares Outstanding	28,435	28,362	28,280	28,240	28,080	27,965	27,682	28,132
Statistical Record								
Operating Profit Margin %	5.27	4.49	6.91	7.57	7.60	4.54	6.67	6.33
Return on Equity %	7.58	6.28	10.35	12.14	11.71	4.68	11.88	13.57
Return on Assets %	3.83	2.93	4.63	4.86	4.30	1.52	4.39	5.22
Debt/Total Assets %	15.98	16.82	21.01	24.78	25.71	28.68	25.06	19.87
Price Range	29.50–20.00	32.50–24.54	30.95–16.59	34.25–14.34	36.09–19.19	34.41–17.25	30.00–22.88	23.63–14.88
P/E Ratio	21.85–14.81	33.16–25.04	19.47–10.44	19.68–8.24	22.99–12.22	56.85–30.26	20.98–16.00	14.67–9.24
Average Yield %	1.80	1.51	1.82	1.88	1.40	1.50	1.41	1.80

Address: 1200 Willow Lake Boulevard, Vadnais Heights, MN 55110–5101	**Officers:** Albert P. L. Stroucken – Chmn., Pres., C.E.O., John A. Feenan – Sr. V.P., C.F.O.	**Investor Contact:** (651) 236–5150
Telephone: (651) 236–5900	**Transfer Agents:** Wells Fargo Shareowner Services, Minnesota, MN	**Institutional Holding**
Web Site: www.hbfuller.com		**No of Institutions:** 2
		Shares: 10,000 **% Held:** –

115

FULTON FINANCIAL CORP. (PA)

Exchange	Symbol	Price	52Wk Range	Yield	P/E
NMS	FULT	$22.27 (3/31/2004)	22.71–18.05	2.87	17.40

*7 Year Price Score 127.6   *NYSE Composite Index=100   *12 Month Price Score 97.0

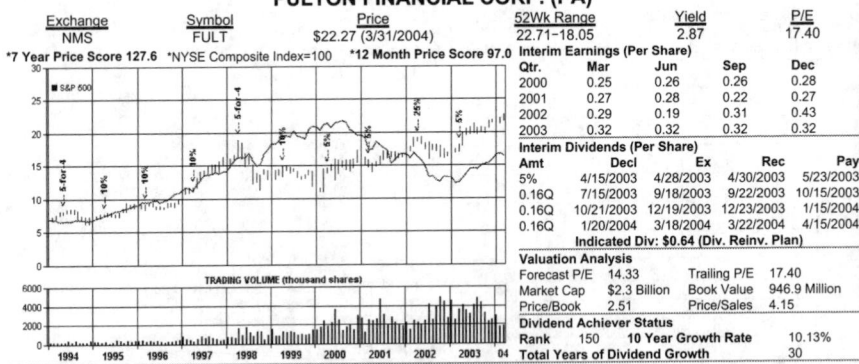

Interim Earnings (Per Share)

Qtr.	Mar	Jun	Sep	Dec
2000	0.25	0.26	0.26	0.28
2001	0.27	0.28	0.22	0.27
2002	0.29	0.19	0.31	0.43
2003	0.32	0.32	0.32	0.32

Interim Dividends (Per Share)

Amt	Decl	Ex	Rec	Pay
5%	4/15/2003	4/28/2003	4/30/2003	5/23/2003
0.16Q	7/15/2003	9/18/2003	9/22/2003	10/15/2003
0.16Q	10/21/2003	12/19/2003	12/23/2003	1/15/2004
0.16Q	1/20/2004	3/18/2004	3/22/2004	4/15/2004
		Indicated Div: $0.64 (Div. Reinv. Plan)		

Valuation Analysis

Forecast P/E	14.33	Trailing P/E	17.40
Market Cap	$2.3 Billion	Book Value	946.9 Million
Price/Book	2.51	Price/Sales	4.15

Dividend Achiever Status

Rank	150	10 Year Growth Rate	10.13%
Total Years of Dividend Growth		30

Business Summary: Commercial Banking (MIC: 8.1 SIC: 6021 NAIC:522110)

Fulton Financial, with $9.77 billion in assets at Dec 31 2003, is a financial holding company. As of Dec 31 2003, Co. operated 200 banking offices in Delaware, Maryland, New Jersey and Pennsylvania through the following affiliates: Fulton Bank, Lebanon Valley Farmers Bank, Swineford National Bank, Lafayette Ambassador Bank, FNB Bank, Hagerstown Trust, Delaware National Bank, The Bank, The Peoples Bank of Elkton, Skylands Community Bank and Premier Bank. Co.'s financial services affiliates include Fulton Financial Advisors, Fulton Insurance Services Group, and Dearden, Maguire, Weaver and Barrett. Residential mortgage lending is offered by all banks through Fulton Mortgage.

Recent Developments: For the year ended Dec 31 2003, net income climbed 3.9% to $138.2 million compared with $132.9 million in 2002. Results for 2003 and 2002 included investment securities gains of $19.9 million and $9.0 million, respectively. Net interest income slipped 2.1% to $304.4 million from $311.1 million in the prior year. Net interest income benefited from balance sheet growth and the addition of Premier Bank. Provision for loan losses declined 18.4% to $9.7 million. Non–interest income rose 18.3% to $137.0 million from $115.8 million a year earlier. Non–interest expense grew 3.8% to $234.2 million from $225.5 million the year before.

Prospects: On Feb 26 2004, shareholders of Resource Bankshares approved the acquisition of Resource Bank by Co. Resource Bank operates six community banking offices in Virginia and 14 loan production and residential mortgage offices in Virginia, North Carolina, Maryland and Florida. All regulatory approvals have been received. Resource Bank will become Co.'s 12th banking affiliate and continue to operate as Resource Bank. Separately, on Dec 19 2003, Fulton Bank purchased a portfolio of agricultural and agri–business loans in Pennsylvania and Delaware from Wachovia. These loans total about $170.0 million.

Financial Data

(US$ in Thousands)	12/31/2003	12/31/2002	12/31/2001	12/31/2000	12/31/1999	12/31/1998	12/31/1997	12/31/1996
Earnings Per Share	1.28	1.22	1.04	1.05	0.96	0.87	0.73	0.72
Tang. Book Val. Per Share	7.56	7.45	6.80	6.85	6.20	6.06	5.34	5.33
Dividends Per Share	0.600	0.540	0.490	0.430	0.390	0.350	0.320	0.290
Dividend Payout %	47.32	44.34	47.06	41.77	40.91	40.85	44.62	40.28
Income Statement								
Total Interest Income	435,531	469,288	518,178	462,581	418,914	409,292	319,628	268,657
Total Interest Expense	131,094	158,219	227,962	210,481	174,827	177,805	137,018	113,802
Net Interest Income	304,437	311,069	290,216	252,100	244,087	231,487	182,610	154,855
Provision for Loan Losses	9,705	11,900	14,585	8,645	8,216	5,582	7,742	4,192
Non–Interest Income	136,987	115,783	100,994	69,611	62,822	60,641	41,055	32,803
Non–Interest Expense	234,176	225,536	216,669	165,022	160,988	158,203	122,293	110,151
Income Before Taxes	197,543	189,416	159,956	148,044	137,705	128,343	93,630	73,315
Net Income	138,180	132,948	113,589	103,804	97,226	88,511	65,199	52,018
Average Shs. Outstg.	107,748	108,474	109,135	98,748	100,367	100,546	89,449	72,124
Balance Sheet								
Cash & Due from Banks	300,966	314,857	356,539	267,178	245,572	247,558	172,392	164,975
Securities Avail. for Sale	2,904,157	2,383,607	1,687,787	1,140,646	1,137,846	1,206,121	597,448	317,100
Net Loans & Leases	6,082,294	5,245,148	5,301,148	4,806,498	4,364,776	3,972,976	3,260,606	2,735,418
Total Assets	9,767,288	8,387,778	7,770,711	6,571,155	6,070,019	5,838,663	4,460,823	3,769,385
Total Deposits	6,751,783	6,245,528	5,986,804	4,934,405	4,546,813	4,592,969	3,621,569	3,054,174
Long–Term Obligations	568,730	535,555	456,802	441,973	328,250	296,018	47,695	49,160
Total Liabilities	8,820,352	7,524,036	6,959,257	5,891,819	5,455,725	5,230,329	3,985,529	3,383,707
Net Stockholders' Equity	946,936	863,742	811,454	679,336	614,294	608,334	475,294	385,678
Shares Outstanding	108,400	106,155	108,412	99,087	99,048	100,256	88,862	72,275
Statistical Record								
Return on Equity %	14.59	15.39	13.99	15.28	15.82	14.54	13.71	13.48
Return on Assets %	1.41	1.58	1.46	1.57	1.60	1.51	1.46	1.38
Equity/Assets %	9.69	10.29	10.44	10.33	10.12	10.41	10.65	10.23
Non–Int. Exp./Tot. Inc. %	40.90	38.54	34.99	31.00	33.41	33.66	33.90	36.53
Price Range	21.90-16.82	19.32-16.05	17.37-13.97	17.32-11.01	14.94-11.88	18.89-11.31	16.33-9.37	9.82-8.41
P/E Ratio	17.11-13.14	15.84-13.15	16.70-13.43	16.50-10.49	15.57-12.37	21.71-13.00	22.38-12.83	13.64-11.68
Average Yield %	3.05	3.05	3.05	3.02	2.83	2.30	2.44	3.21

Address: One Penn Square, Lancaster, PA 17604	Officers: Rufus A. Fulton – Chmn., C.E.O., R. Scott Smith – Pres., C.O.O.	Investor Contact: (717) 291–2739
Telephone: (717) 291–2411		Institutional Holding
Web Site: www.fult.com		No of Institutions: 20
		Shares: 9,356,088 % Held: –

116

GALLAGHER (ARTHUR J.) & CO.

Exchange	Symbol	Price	52Wk Range	Yield	P/E
NYS	AJG	$32.57 (3/31/2004)	33.86-24.08	3.07	20.75

7 Year Price Score 137.8   *NYSE Composite Index=100   *12 Month Price Score 102.5

TRADING VOLUME (thousand shares)

Interim Earnings (Per Share)

Qtr.	Mar	Jun	Sep	Dec
2000	0.19	0.18	0.36	0.32
2001	0.27	0.26	0.47	0.39
2002	0.37	0.37	0.26	0.41
2003	0.13	0.39	0.52	0.53

Interim Dividends (Per Share)

Amt	Decl	Ex	Rec	Pay
0.18Q	5/21/2003	6/26/2003	6/30/2003	7/15/2003
0.18Q	9/15/2003	9/26/2003	9/30/2003	10/15/2003
0.18Q	11/20/2003	12/29/2003	12/31/2003	1/15/2004
0.25Q	1/22/2004	3/29/2004	3/31/2004	4/15/2004

Indicated Div: $1.00

Valuation Analysis

Forecast P/E	13.36	Trailing P/E	20.75
Market Cap	$2.9 Billion	Book Value	588.2 Million
Price/Book	4.95	Price/Sales	2.38

Dividend Achiever Status

Rank	82	10 Year Growth Rate	14.70%
Total Years of Dividend Growth		19	

Business Summary: Insurance (MIC: 8.2 SIC: 6411 NAIC:524210)

Arthur J. Gallagher & Co. is engaged in providing insurance brokerage, risk management and related services to clients in the U.S. and abroad. Co.'s principal activity is the negotiation and placement of insurance for its clients. Co. also specializes in furnishing risk management services. Risk management involves assisting clients in analyzing risks and determining whether proper protection is best obtained through the purchase of insurance or through retention of all or a portion of those risks and the adoption of corporate risk management policies and cost−effective loss control and prevention programs. Co. also has a financial services group that manages its investment portfolio.

Recent Developments: For the year ended Dec 31 2003, net income grew 12.5% to $146.2 million from $129.9 million the prior year. Earnings benefited from new business production, renewal rate increases and favorable retention rates on existing business across all lines of insurance. Revenues rose 19.2% to $1.26 billion. By segment, revenues from the brokerage group advanced 14.6% to $848.5 million and earnings increased 25.1% to $130.2 million. Revenues from the risk management group rose 14.4% to $321.7 million and earnings climbed 46.4% to $32.5 million. Revenues from the financial services group jumped 140.6% to $93.6 million, while net loss was $16.5 million versus net income of $3.6 million a year earlier.

Prospects: Going forward, Co. should be well positioned for continued growth due to the current favorable rate environment and its acquisition pipeline. Moreover, solid retention levels for existing business, coupled with continued attention to operating efficiency should enable Co. to maintain the positive trend experienced in 2003. Separately, on Feb 12 2003, Co. acquired R. P. O'Brien & Co., Inc., a provider of risk management, property, casualty and employee benefit insurance services in the Northeast. On Feb 19 2003, Co. acquired The Romine Group, Inc., a Texas−based employee benefits brokerage and consulting services provider to both self−funded and fully insured markets.

Financial Data

(US$ in Thousands)	12/31/2003	12/31/2002	12/31/2001	12/31/2000	12/31/1999	12/31/1998	12/31/1997	12/31/1996
Earnings Per Share	1.57	1.41	1.39	1.05	0.88	0.77	0.78	0.65
Tang. Book Val. Per Share	4.40	4.43	3.59	3.75	3.14	2.69	2.31	1.89
Dividends Per Share	0.690	0.580	0.500	0.440	0.380	0.340	0.300	0.280
Dividend Payout %	43.94	41.13	36.33	42.38	44.03	43.87	38.97	43.07
Income Statement								
Net Investment Income	8,500	3,438	...	...	...	...	...	...
Other Income	1,173,900	1,097,784	910,043	740,596	605,836	540,655	488,028	456,679
Total Revenues	1,182,400	1,101,222	910,043	740,596	605,836	540,655	488,028	456,679
Total Indirect Exp.	964,700	915,880	747,111	615,202	501,601	456,126	407,246	387,280
Inc. Before Inc. Taxes	152,600	185,342	141,853	125,394	104,235	84,529	80,782	69,399
Income Taxes	47,100	55,603	16,597	37,618	36,482	28,028	27,466	23,596
Eqty Earns/Minority Int.	(41,100)	(44,278)	...	...	...	...	...	...
Income from Cont Ops	105,500	...	...	...	...	...	...	...
Net Income	146,200	129,739	125,256	87,776	67,753	56,501	53,316	45,803
Average Shs. Outstg.	93,300	91,861	90,127	83,924	77,132	72,824	68,152	71,100
Balance Sheet								
Cash & Cash Equivalents	663,100	479,415	359,431	318,077	233,812	205,508	211,019	197,623
Premiums Due	1,286,400	1,183,737	555,276	405,164	364,854	288,276	217,555	237,640
Invst. Assets: Total	152,900	70,556	70,878	83,251	84,131	77,457	101,884	90,290
Total Assets	2,901,600	2,463,574	1,471,823	1,062,298	884,146	746,010	641,752	590,424
Long−Term Obligations	153,000	128,349	...	...	...	...	...	...
Net Stockholders' Equity	619,100	528,155	371,613	314,372	242,467	202,468	163,907	134,530
Shares Outstanding	90,000	88,548	85,111	79,497	73,680	70,580	66,364	65,172
Statistical Record								
Return on Equity %	17.04	24.56	33.70	27.92	27.94	27.90	32.52	34.04
Return on Assets %	3.63	5.26	8.51	8.26	7.66	7.57	8.30	7.75
Price Range	32.65−23.45	36.86−22.10	38.30−22.00	33.66−11.75	16.19−10.59	11.59−8.44	9.56−7.47	9.81−7.31
P/E Ratio	20.80−14.94	26.14−15.67	27.55−15.83	32.05−11.19	18.39−12.04	15.06−10.96	12.26−9.58	15.10−11.25
Average Yield %	2.52	1.87	1.71	2.04	3.01	3.26	3.54	3.34

Address: Two Pierce Place, Itasca, IL 60143−3141	Officers: Robert E. Gallagher − Chmn., J. Patrick Gallagher − Pres., C.E.O.	Institutional Holding
Telephone: (630) 773−3800	Transfer Agents:Computershare Investor Services, Chicago, IL	No of Institutions: 17
Web Site: www.ajg.com		Shares: 1,338,088 % Held: −

GANNETT CO., INC.

Exchange	Symbol	Price	52Wk Range	Yield	P/E
NYS	GCI	$88.14 (3/31/2004)	90.01-70.82	1.13	19.76

*7 Year Price Score 120.3 *NYSE Composite Index=100 *12 Month Price Score 99.4

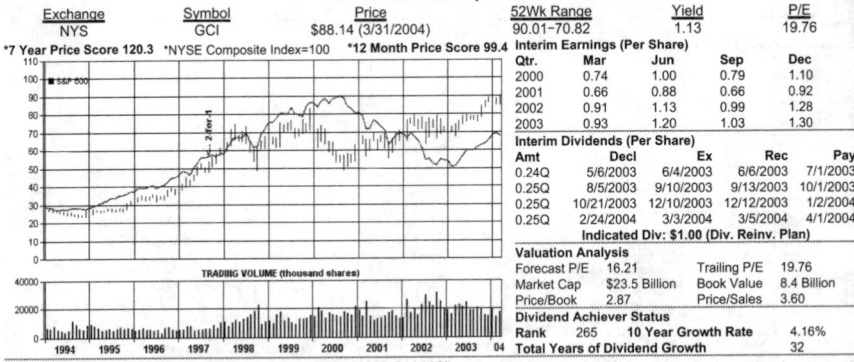

Interim Earnings (Per Share)

Qtr.	Mar	Jun	Sep	Dec
2000	0.74	1.00	0.79	1.10
2001	0.66	0.88	0.66	0.92
2002	0.91	1.13	0.99	1.28
2003	0.93	1.20	1.03	1.30

Interim Dividends (Per Share)

Amt	Decl	Ex	Rec	Pay
0.24Q	5/6/2003	6/4/2003	6/6/2003	7/1/2003
0.25Q	8/5/2003	9/10/2003	9/13/2003	10/1/2003
0.25Q	10/21/2003	12/10/2003	12/12/2003	1/2/2004
0.25Q	2/24/2004	3/3/2004	3/5/2004	4/1/2004
	Indicated Div: $1.00 (Div. Reinv. Plan)			

Valuation Analysis

Forecast P/E	16.21	Trailing P/E	19.76
Market Cap	$23.5 Billion	Book Value	8.4 Billion
Price/Book	2.87	Price/Sales	3.60

Dividend Achiever Status

Rank	265	10 Year Growth Rate	4.16%
Total Years of Dividend Growth			32

Business Summary: Media (MIC: 13.1 SIC: 2711 NAIC:511110)

Gannett is a news and information company that publishes newspapers and operates broadcasting stations. Co. is also engaged in marketing, commercial printing, a newswire service, data services, and news programming. Co. has operations in 43 states, the District of Columbia, Guam, the U.K., and in certain European and Asian markets. Co. is the largest U.S. newspaper group in terms of circulation, with 100 daily newspapers, including *USA Today*, more than 500 non–daily publications and *USA Weekend*, a weekly newspaper magazine. In the U.K., Co.'s subsidiary Newsquest publishes nearly 300 titles, including 17 daily newspapers. Co. owns and operates 22 television stations in major markets.

Recent Developments: For the year ended Dec 28 2003, net income climbed 4.4% to $1.21 billion compared with $1.16 billion in 2002. Results benefited from the solid performance of Newsquest in the U.K. due to strong advertising revenue gains and solid results from the newspaper segment despite continued subdued advertising demand in the U.S. Results also benefited from a favorable foreign exchange rate and a decrease in interest expense. Total operating revenues were $6.71 billion, up 4.5% from $6.42 billion in the previous year. Operating income increased 2.8% to $1.98 billion compared with $1.93 billion the year before.

Prospects: Looking ahead to 2004, Co. anticipates modest advertising revenue and volume growth in most categories and in most newspaper markets. New products are being developed throughout the newspaper segment and added resources are planned for sales and marketing efforts. Revenue for 2004 will be affected by the general economic performance in the U.S. and the U.K., consumer confidence, the strength of the job market, the weakening or strengthening of the British pound compared to the U.S. dollar exchange rate and the geopolitical environment. For 2004, television revenues and earnings are expected to improve with higher advertising spending from political campaigns and the Summer Olympics.

Financial Data

(US$ in Thousands)	12/28/2003	12/29/2002	12/30/2001	12/31/2000	12/26/1999	12/27/1998	12/28/1997	12/31/1996
Earnings Per Share	4.46	4.31	3.12	3.63	3.26	3.50	2.50	2.21
Cash Flow Per Share	5.44	3.83	4.94	1.87	4.07	3.39	3.08	2.15
Tang. Book Val. Per Share	N.M	N.M	N.M	N.M	N.M	0.66	N.M	N.M
Dividends Per Share	0.970	0.930	0.890	0.850	0.810	0.770	0.730	0.700
Dividend Payout %	21.74	21.57	28.52	23.41	24.84	22.00	29.20	31.67
Income Statement								
Total Revenues	6,711,115	6,422,249	6,344,245	6,222,318	5,260,190	5,121,291	4,729,491	4,421,107
Total Indirect Exp.	1,276,328	1,241,937	1,434,249	1,347,810	1,088,620	1,083,807	1,044,651	986,854
Depreciation & Amort.	231,532	222,444	443,777	375,915	280,091	310,206	301,073	287,370
Operating Income	1,981,018	1,926,309	1,589,835	1,817,256	1,563,101	1,443,502	1,316,268	1,066,405
Net Interest Inc./(Exp.)	(134,064)	(142,911)	(217,178)	(192,019)	(88,880)	(60,094)	(91,725)	(128,836)
Income Taxes	629,100	604,400	539,400	636,900	607,800	669,500	496,300	462,700
Income from Cont Ops	...	...	...	971,940	919,387	...	...	623,967
Net Income	1,211,213	1,160,128	831,197	1,719,077	957,928	999,913	712,679	943,087
Average Shs. Outstg.	271,872	269,286	266,833	268,118	281,608	285,711	285,610	281,782
Balance Sheet								
Cash & Cash Equivalents	67,188	90,374	140,629	193,196	46,160	66,187	52,778	31,202
Total Current Assets	1,223,261	1,133,079	1,178,198	1,302,336	1,075,222	906,385	884,634	766,605
Total Assets	14,706,239	13,733,014	13,096,101	12,980,411	9,006,446	6,979,480	6,890,351	6,349,597
Total Current Liabilities	961,837	958,625	1,127,737	1,174,001	883,778	727,967	767,501	718,996
Long–Term Obligations	3,834,511	4,547,265	5,080,025	5,747,856	2,463,250	1,306,859	1,740,534	1,880,293
Net Stockholders' Equity	8,422,981	6,911,795	5,735,922	5,103,410	4,629,646	3,979,824	3,479,736	2,930,818
Net Working Capital	261,424	174,454	50,461	128,335	191,444	178,418	117,133	47,609
Shares Outstanding	272,417	267,909	265,797	264,271	277,926	279,001	283,874	282,636
Statistical Record								
Operating Profit Margin %	29.51	29.99	25.05	29.20	29.71	28.18	27.83	24.12
Return on Equity %	14.37	16.78	14.49	19.04	19.85	25.12	20.48	21.28
Return on Assets %	8.23	8.44	6.34	7.48	10.20	14.32	10.34	9.82
Debt/Total Assets %	26.07	33.11	38.79	44.28	27.34	18.72	25.26	29.61
Price Range	88.93-67.68	79.87-63.39	71.10-55.55	83.25-48.69	79.31-61.81	74.69-48.94	61.00-35.81	39.25-29.63
P/E Ratio	19.94-15.17	18.53-14.71	22.79-17.80	22.93-13.41	24.33-18.96	21.34-13.98	24.40-14.33	17.76-13.40
Average Yield %	1.25	1.27	1.38	1.39	1.15	1.21	1.52	2.03

Address: 7950 Jones Branch Drive, McLean, VA 22107–0910	Officers: Douglas H. McCorkindale – Chmn., Pres., C.E.O., Larry F. Miller – Exec. V.P., Oper.	Investor Contact: (703) 854–6918
Telephone: (703) 854-6000	Transfer Agents: Wells Fargo Bank Minnesota, N.A., St. Paul, MN	Institutional Holding
Web Site: www.gannett.com		No of Institutions: 42
		Shares: 1,733,994 % Held: –

GENERAL DYNAMICS CORP.

Exchange	Symbol	Price	52Wk Range	Yield	P/E
NYS	GD	$89.33 (3/31/2004)	96.88–53.90	1.61	17.87

7 Year Price Score 116.7 *NYSE Composite Index=100 *12 Month Price Score 102.5

Interim Earnings (Per Share)

Qtr.	Mar	Jun	Sep	Dec
2000	0.91	1.01	1.47	1.09
2001	1.19	1.12	1.13	1.21
2002	1.13	1.29	1.32	1.44
2003	1.11	1.22	1.28	1.39

Interim Dividends (Per Share)

Amt	Decl	Ex	Rec	Pay
0.32Q	6/4/2003	7/2/2003	7/7/2003	8/8/2003
0.32Q	8/6/2003	10/8/2003	10/10/2003	11/14/2003
0.32Q	12/3/2003	1/14/2004	1/16/2004	2/6/2004
0.36Q	3/3/2004	4/6/2004	4/8/2004	5/7/2004
		Indicated Div: $1.44		

Valuation Analysis

Forecast P/E	14.64	Trailing P/E	17.87
Market Cap	$18.0 Billion	Book Value	5.9 Billion
Price/Book	3.01	Price/Sales	1.07

Dividend Achiever Status

Rank	173	10 Year Growth Rate	10.84%
Total Years of Dividend Growth		12	

Business Summary: Shipping (MIC: 15.3 SIC: 3731 NAIC:336611)

General Dynamics is a major defense contractor operating in four business segments. Information Systems and Technology provides defense and commercial customers with infrastructure and systems integration skills required to process, communicate and manage information. Marine Systems provides the U.S. Navy with combat vessels. Aerospace designs and develops technologically advanced business jet aircraft. Combat Systems provides systems integration, design, and production for armored vehicles, armaments, munitions and components. Other businesses consist of a coal mining operation, an aggregates operation and a leasing operation for liquefied natural gas tankers.

Recent Developments: For the year ended Dec 31 2003, Co. reported income from continuing operations of $997.0 million compared with income of $1.05 billion the year before. Earnings excluded a net gain of $7.0 million in 2003 and a net loss of $134.0 million in 2002 from discontinued operations. Net sales rose 20.2% to $16.62 billion. Information Systems and Technology segment sales improved 5.2% to $4.98 billion, while Combat Systems segment sales advanced 42.5% to $4.17 billion. Marine Systems segment sales increased 7.0% to $4.27 billion. However, Aerospace segment sales fell 10.4% to $2.95 billion. Co. ended the quarter with a total backlog of 41.08 billion.

Prospects: Co.'s new contract wins include a $2.00 billion contract from the U.S. Army for the engineering development and demonstration of a family of manned ground vehicles for its future combat systems program. Looking ahead in 2004, Co. anticipates continued solid performance from Combat Systems and Information Systems and Technology as well as margin improvement in Marine Systems. Co.'s business aviation group, which signed 34 new orders during the quarter, should also continue to perform well. Revenue growth is expected to be over $19.00 billion, while earnings are anticipated to be at the high end of the guidance range of $5.40 to $5.50 per share.

Financial Data

(US$ in Millions)	12/31/2003	12/31/2002	12/31/2001	12/31/2000	12/31/1999	12/31/1998	12/31/1997	12/31/1996
Earnings Per Share	5.00	5.18	4.65	4.48	4.36	2.86	2.50	2.13
Cash Flow Per Share	8.65	5.54	5.43	5.32	5.02	2.91	4.38	8.22
Tang. Book Val. Per Share	N.M	5.61	3.83	6.42	3.27	5.46	5.64	13.60
Dividends Per Share	1.260	1.180	1.100	1.020	0.940	0.860	0.820	0.800
Dividend Payout %	25.20	22.77	23.65	22.76	21.55	30.24	32.80	37.56
Income Statement								
Total Revenues	16,617	13,829	12,163	10,356	8,959	4,970	4,062	3,581
Total Indirect Exp.	15,150	12,247	10,678	9,027	7,756	4,428	3,616	3,228
Depreciation & Amort.	277	213	271	226	200	126	91	67
Operating Income	1,467	1,582	1,485	1,329	1,203	542	446	353
Net Interest Inc./(Exp.)	(98)	(45)	(56)	(60)	(34)	4	36	55
Income Taxes	375	533	481	361	246	185	163	139
Income from Cont Ops	997	1,051	...	...	...	...	...	...
Net Income	1,004	917	943	901	880	364	316	270
Average Shs. Outstg.	199	202	202	201	202	127	127	126
Balance Sheet								
Cash & Cash Equivalents	860	328	442	177	270	220	441	894
Total Current Assets	6,316	5,098	4,893	3,551	3,491	1,873	1,689	1,858
Total Assets	16,183	11,731	11,069	7,987	7,774	4,572	4,091	3,299
Total Current Liabilities	5,616	4,582	4,579	2,901	3,453	1,461	1,291	833
Long-Term Obligations	3,296	718	724	162	169	249	257	156
Net Stockholders' Equity	5,921	5,199	4,528	3,820	3,171	2,219	1,915	1,714
Net Working Capital	778	516	314	650	38	412	398	1,025
Shares Outstanding	197	200	200	200	201	127	126	126
Statistical Record								
Operating Profit Margin %	8.82	11.43	12.20	12.83	13.42	10.90	10.97	9.85
Return on Equity %	16.83	20.21	20.82	23.58	27.75	16.40	16.50	15.75
Return on Assets %	6.16	8.95	8.51	11.28	11.31	7.96	7.72	8.18
Debt/Total Assets %	20.36	6.12	6.54	2.02	2.17	5.44	6.28	4.72
Price Range	90.39–52.37	110.6–74.57	94.99–61.00	78.00–37.00	74.81–46.94	61.25–40.38	44.97–31.63	37.50–28.81
P/E Ratio	18.08–10.47	21.35–14.40	20.43–13.12	17.41–8.26	17.16–10.77	21.42–14.12	17.99–12.65	17.61–13.53
Average Yield %	1.72	1.34	1.43	1.76	1.53	1.79	2.12	2.49

Address: 3190 Fairview Park Drive, Falls Church, VA 22042–4523	**Officers:** Nicholas D. Chabraja – Chmn., C.E.O., Michael W. Toner – Exec. V.P., Group Exec., Marine Systems	**Investor Contact:** 703–876–3195 **Institutional Holding**
Telephone: (703) 876–3000	**Transfer Agents:** EquiServe Trust Company, N.A., Jersey City, NJ	**No of Institutions:** 4
Web Site: www.generaldynamics.com		**Shares:** 272,865 **% Held:** –

GENERAL ELECTRIC CO.

Exchange	Symbol	Price	52Wk Range	Yield	P/E
NYS	GE	$30.52 (3/31/2004)	34.19-26.13	2.62	19.69

*7 Year Price Score 82.4 *NYSE Composite Index=100 *12 Month Price Score 93.5

Interim Earnings (Per Share)

Qtr.	Mar	Jun	Sep	Dec
2000	0.26	0.34	0.32	0.35
2001	0.30	0.39	0.33	0.39
2002	0.35	0.44	0.41	0.31
2003	0.32	0.38	0.40	0.45

Interim Dividends (Per Share)

Amt	Decl	Ex	Rec	Pay
0.19Q	6/13/2003	6/26/2003	6/30/2003	7/25/2003
0.19Q	9/12/2003	9/25/2003	9/29/2003	10/27/2003
0.20Q	12/12/2003	12/29/2003	12/31/2003	1/26/2004
0.20Q	2/13/2004	2/26/2004	3/1/2004	4/26/2004
		Indicated Div: $0.80 (Div. Reinv. Plan)		

Valuation Analysis

Forecast P/E	17.45	Trailing P/E	19.69
Market Cap	$303.7 Billion	Book Value	79.2 Billion
Price/Book	3.90	Price/Sales	2.31

Dividend Achiever Status

Rank	98	10 Year Growth Rate 13.73%
Total Years of Dividend Growth	28	

Business Summary: Electrical (MIC: 11.14 SIC: 3641 NAIC:335110)

General Electric is engaged in developing, manufacturing and marketing a wide variety of products for the generation, transmission, distribution, control and utilization of electricity. Co.'s operating segments include: Commercial Finance, Consumer Finance, Energy, Healthcare, Infrastructure, Transportation, NBC, Advanced Materials, Consumer and Industrial, Equipment Services and Insurance. Co. products include major appliances; lighting products; industrial automation products; medical diagnostic imaging equipment; motors; electrical distribution and control equipment; locomotives; power generation and delivery products; nuclear power support services and fuel assemblies.

Recent Developments: For the year ended Dec 31 2003, income was $15.59 billion, before an accounting change charge of $587.0 million, compared with income of $15.13 billion, before an accounting change charge of $1.02 billion, the previous year. Results for 2003 and 2002 included pre-tax provisions of $3.75 billion and $3.08 billion, respectively, for losses on financing receivables. Total revenues rose 1.5% to $134.19 billion from $132.21 billion the year before. Revenue growth was largely due to higher sales in the consumer finance and insurance segment, partially offset by lower power system sales. Total costs and expenses grew to $114.28 billion from $113.32 billion the prior year.

Prospects: Co. reorganized its thirteen businesses into eleven as of Jan 1 2004 in an effort to focus on markets and customers. Co. expects to generate double-digit earnings growth in nine of its eleven businesses in 2004, with cash flow growing at a double-digit rate. Co. will work through the final year of Power Systems' down cycle, lowering non-cash pension earnings, and the impact of its major transactions. Co. expects to enter 2005 positioned for double-digit earnings growth. Separately, Co. announced that pre-conditions to the completion of its acquisition of Amersham plc for $9.50 billion have been satisfied.

Financial Data

(US$ in Millions)	12/31/2003	12/31/2002	12/31/2001	12/31/2000	12/31/1999	12/31/1998	12/31/1997	12/31/1996
Earnings Per Share	1.55	1.51	1.41	1.27	1.07	0.93	0.82	0.73
Cash Flow Per Share	3.00	2.94	3.20	2.25	2.46	1.93	1.41	1.79
Tang. Book Val. Per Share	2.40	1.75	2.33	2.32	1.67	1.55	1.56	1.53
Dividends Per Share	0.760	0.720	0.640	0.540	0.460	0.400	0.340	0.300
Dividend Payout %	49.03	47.68	45.39	43.04	43.49	42.85	42.27	41.10
Income Statement								
Total Revenues	134,187	131,698	125,913	129,853	111,630	100,469	90,840	79,179
Depreciation & Amort.	6,956	5,998	7,089	7,736	6,691	5,860	5,269	3,785
Operating Income	82,286	78,842	76,816	78,030	65,672	58,189	50,752	46,308
Net Interest Inc./(Exp.)	(10,432)	(10,216)	(11,062)	(11,720)	(10,013)	(9,753)	(8,384)	(7,904)
Income Taxes	4,315	3,758	5,573	5,711	4,860	4,181	2,976	3,526
Eqty Earns/Minority Int.	695	...	...	...	...	...	...	...
Income from Cont Ops	15,589	15,133	14,128	...	...	...	...	...
Net Income	15,002	14,118	13,684	12,735	10,717	9,296	8,203	7,280
Average Shs. Outstg.	10,075	10,028	10,052	10,057	9,996	9,990	10,035	9,924
Balance Sheet								
Cash & Cash Equivalents	12,664	8,910	9,082	8,195	8,554	4,317	5,861	4,191
Total Current Assets	32,148	28,838	27,237	25,509	24,092	18,590	20,680	17,368
Total Assets	647,483	575,244	495,023	437,006	405,200	355,935	304,012	272,402
Total Current Liabilities	176,530	181,827	198,904	156,112	161,216	141,579	120,668	100,507
Long-Term Obligations	170,004	140,632	79,806	82,132	71,427	59,663	46,603	49,246
Net Stockholders' Equity	79,180	63,706	54,824	50,492	42,557	38,880	34,438	31,125
Net Working Capital	(144,382)	(152,989)	(171,667)	(130,603)	(137,124)	(122,989)	(99,988)	(83,139)
Shares Outstanding	10,063	9,969	9,925	9,932	9,854	9,813	9,795	9,870
Statistical Record								
Operating Profit Margin %	61.32	59.86	61.00	60.09	58.83	57.91	55.86	58.48
Return on Equity %	19.69	23.75	25.76	25.22	25.18	23.90	23.81	23.38
Return on Assets %	2.41	2.63	2.85	2.91	2.64	2.61	2.69	2.67
Debt/Total Assets %	26.25	24.44	16.12	18.79	17.62	16.76	15.32	18.07
Price Range	32.11-22.17	41.55-22.00	53.40-30.37	60.00-41.71	53.17-31.98	34.35-23.85	25.15-16.25	17.48-11.71
P/E Ratio	20.72-14.30	27.52-14.57	37.87-21.54	47.24-32.84	49.69-29.89	36.94-25.65	30.67-19.82	23.94-16.04
Average Yield %	2.71	2.31	1.47	1.04	1.20	1.42	1.64	2.11

Address: 3135 Easton Turnpike, Fairfield, CT 06828-0001	**Officers:** Jeffrey R. Immelt - Chmn., C.E.O., Dennis D. Dammerman - Vice-Chmn.	**Investor Contact:** (203) 373-2816
Telephone: (203) 373-2211	**Transfer Agents:** GE Share Owner Services, c/o The	**Institutional Holding**
Web Site: www.ge.com	Bank of New York, New York, NY.	**No of Institutions:** 41
		Shares: 7,407,325 **% Held:** –

120

GENERAL GROWTH PROPERTIES, INC. (DE)

Exchange	Symbol	Price	52Wk Range	Yield	P/E
NYS	GGP	$35.15 (3/31/2004)	35.15–18.00	3.41	30.48

*7 Year Price Score 161.5 *NYSE Composite Index=100 *12 Month Price Score 111.8

Interim Earnings (Per Share)
Qtr.	Mar	Jun	Sep	Dec
2000	0.14	0.14	0.16	0.28
2001	0.13	(0.15)	0.18	0.37
2002	0.17	0.18	0.23	0.41
2003	0.24	0.23	0.28	0.45

Interim Dividends (Per Share)
Amt	Decl	Ex	Rec	Pay
0.24Q	6/9/2003	7/2/2003	7/7/2003	7/31/2003
0.30Q	10/1/2003	10/10/2003	10/15/2003	10/31/2003
3–for–1	10/1/2003	12/8/2003	11/20/2003	12/5/2003
0.30Q	1/5/2004	1/13/2004	1/15/2004	1/30/2004

Indicated Div: $1.20 (Div. Reinv. Plan)

Valuation Analysis
Forecast P/E	N/A	Trailing P/E	30.48
Market Cap	$2.2 Billion	Book Value	1.6 Billion
Price/Book	3.21	Price/Sales	4.29

Dividend Achiever Status
Rank	63	10 Year Growth Rate	16.23%
Total Years of Dividend Growth			10

Business Summary: Property, Real Estate &Development (MIC: 8.3 SIC: 6798 NAIC:525930)

General Growth Properties is primarily engaged in the ownership, operation, management, leasing, acquisition, development and expansion of regional mall and community shopping centers in the United States. As of December 31, 2003 Co. Portfolio is comprised primarily of 162 operating retail properties (regional malls or community centers). Co. also has certain office space associated with Co.'s retail properties and approximately 1.4 million square feet of commercial/industrial space at 6 former JP Realty properties. The 162 operating retail properties are shopping centers with a variety of smaller Mall Stores.

Recent Developments: For the twelve months ended Dec 31 2003, income was $259.5 million, before income from discontinued operations of $3.9 million, versus income of $208.2 million, before income from discontinued operations of $1.1 million, in the prior year. Total revenues climbed 30.1% to $1.27 billion. Minimum rent revenues increased 33.8% to $781.7 million, while tenant recoveries advanced 30.6% to $333.7 million. Mall shop occupancy increased to 91.3%, up slightly from 91.0% in 2002. Average rent per square foot for new or renewed leases for the year was $33.29 versus $36.00 a year earlier. Funds from operations were $480.0 million, up 30.0% from $369.1 million the year before.

Prospects: On Jan 16 2004, Co. acquired 50.0% of Burlington Town Center in Burlington, VT. The center, which has about 414,000 On Jan 16 2004, Co. acquired 50.0% of Burlington Town Center in Burlington, VT. The center, which has about 414,000 square feet and also includes an office tower with about 55,000 square feet, is expected to become the premier upscale shopping destination in the State of Vermont. Retailers include J.Crew, Pottery Barn, Williams-Sonoma and Ann Taylor Loft. Co. also announced the acquisition of 100.0% of Redlands Mall in Redlands, CA. The mall is located in a downtown area and is currently anchored by Harris-Gottschalks and Sav-on Drugs. For 2004, Co. is targeting funds from operations per diluted share in the range of $2.56 to $2.66.

Financial Data
(US$ in Thousands)	12/31/2003	12/31/2002	12/31/2001	12/31/2000	12/31/1999	12/31/1998	12/31/1997	12/31/1996
Earnings Per Share	1.20	0.99	0.53	0.72	0.65	0.53	0.92	0.73
Tang. Book Val. Per Share	7.68	6.39	6.37	5.98	5.98	5.00	5.39	3.57
Dividends Per Share	1.020	0.890	0.740	0.680	0.640	0.620	0.590	0.570
Dividend Payout %	85.00	89.89	139.12	93.57	98.98	116.98	64.49	78.08
Income Statement								
Rental Income	816,603	615,307	491,466	468,607	414,558	285,202	183,806	145,880
Total Income	1,270,728	980,466	803,709	698,767	612,342	426,576	291,147	217,405
Total Indirect Exp.	563,610	254,821	272,960	188,951	175,340	120,025	79,011	64,297
Depreciation	231,172	180,028	145,352	126,689	112,874	75,227	48,509	39,809
Interest Expense	278,543	218,935	214,277	218,075	185,984	125,851	78,775	70,272
Eqty Earns/Minority Int.	(17,631)	(4,885)	22,774	(2,273)	(8,957)	(18,531)	27,994	26,830
Income from Cont Ops	259,466	210,576	109,666	...	114,921	71,194	90,703	62,033
Net Income	263,411	209,258	92,310	137,948	101,125	66,445	89,551	59,742
Average Shs. Outstg.	215,079	212,553	158,721	156,288	138,093	109,146	98,520	84,435
Balance Sheet								
Cash & Cash Equivalents	10,677	54,116	315,858	27,229	25,593	19,630	25,898	15,947
Ttl Real Estate Inv.	8,573,613	6,159,565	4,460,905	4,203,070	3,949,473	3,375,007	1,630,190	1,366,324
Total Assets	9,582,897	7,280,822	5,646,807	5,284,104	4,954,895	4,027,474	2,097,719	1,757,717
Long–Term Obligations	6,649,490	4,592,311	3,398,207	3,244,126	3,119,534	2,648,776	1,275,785	1,168,522
Total Liabilities	7,912,488	5,746,797	4,125,921	4,008,186	3,689,637	3,104,267	1,599,214	1,427,450
Net Stockholders' Equity	1,670,409	1,196,525	1,183,386	938,418	927,758	585,507	498,505	330,267
Shares Outstanding	217,293	187,191	185,771	156,843	155,092	117,003	92,367	92,367
Statistical Record								
Net Inc.+Depr./Asscts %	5.16	5.40	4.50	5.00	4.60	3.60	6.60	5.80
Return on Equity %	15.53	17.59	9.26	14.70	12.38	12.15	18.19	18.78
Return on Assets %	2.70	2.89	1.94	2.61	2.31	1.76	4.32	3.52
Price Range	27.89–16.09	17.33–12.91	13.39–11.00	12.06–8.94	12.85–8.35	12.90–10.96	12.67–10.17	10.87–7.00
P/E Ratio	23.24–13.41	17.51–13.04	25.27–20.75	16.75–12.41	19.78–12.85	24.33–20.68	13.77–11.05	14.90–9.59
Average Yield %	4.78	5.71	6.04	6.47	5.79	5.14	5.29	6.97

Address: 110 North Wacker Drive, Chicago, IL 60606	Officers: Matthew Bucksbaum – Chmn., Robert Michaels – Pres., C.O.O.	Institutional Holding
Telephone: (312) 960–5000	Transfer Agents:Mellon Investor Services, LLC, South Hackensack, NJ	No of Institutions: 5
Web Site: www.generalgrowth.com		Shares: 7,721,143 % Held: –

GENUINE PARTS CO.

Exchange	Symbol	Price	52Wk Range	Yield	P/E
NYS	GPC	$32.72 (3/31/2004)	34.95-30.03	3.67	16.12

*7 Year Price Score 105.2 *NYSE Composite Index=100 *12 Month Price Score 90.6

Interim Earnings (Per Share)

Qtr.	Mar	Jun	Sep	Dec
2000	0.52	0.55	0.53	0.60
2001	0.52	0.55	0.51	0.13
2002	0.50	0.55	0.54	0.51
2003	0.51	0.52	0.51	0.49

Interim Dividends (Per Share)

Amt	Decl	Ex	Rec	Pay
0.295Q	4/17/2003	6/4/2003	6/6/2003	7/1/2003
0.295Q	8/18/2003	9/3/2003	9/5/2003	10/1/2003
0.295Q	11/17/2003	12/3/2003	12/5/2003	1/2/2004
0.30Q	2/16/2004	3/3/2004	3/5/2004	4/1/2004

Indicated Div: $1.20 (Div. Reinv. Plan)

Valuation Analysis

Forecast P/E	14.85	Trailing P/E	16.12
Market Cap	$5.7 Billion	Book Value	N/A
Price/Book	N/A	Price/Sales	N/A

Dividend Achiever Status

Rank	243	10 Year Growth Rate	5.37%
Total Years of Dividend Growth			47

Business Summary: Retail – Automotive (MIC: 5.7 SIC: 5013 NAIC:423120)

Genuine Parts is a service distribution and sales organization. Co.'s Automotive Parts group distributes automotive replacement parts and accessory items to independent and company-owned NAPA auto parts stores. The Industrial Parts group's Motion Industries distributes industrial bearings and power transmission replacement parts, including hydraulic and pneumatic products, material handling equipment and agricultural and irrigation equipment. The Office Products group's S. P. Richards Company distributes a line of office and business-related products. The Electrical and Electronic Materials Group's EIS distributes a range of materials and products for electrical and electronic apparatus.

Recent Developments: For the year ended Dec 31 2003, income declined 3.8% to $353.6 million compared with $367.5 million in the previous year. Earnings for 2003 and 2002 excluded accounting change charges of $19.5 million and $395.1 million, respectively. Net sales increased 2.3% to $8.45 billion from $8.26 billion a year earlier. On a segment basis, Automotive sales rose 3.3% to $4.48 billion, while Industrial sales inched up 0.3% to $2.25 billion. Office product sales climbed 4.3% to $1.46 billion, while Electrical/Electronic Material sales fell 5.8% to $297.6 million. Gross profit advanced 2.7% to $2.62 billion from $2.55 billion the year before.

Prospects: Co. is benefiting from sales growth in both its Automotive and Office Product segments, as well as sales improvement in its Industrial and Electrical/Electronic Materials segments as the manufacturing economy gains momentum. Also, previously implemented sales initiatives are driving sales higher across all of Co.'s businesses.Co. is optimistic that stronger sales trends experienced in the fourth quarter of 2003 will carry over into 2004. Looking ahead, Co. has plans to accelerate its level of growth and increase its market leadership in all of its businesses.

Financial Data

(US$ in Thousands)	12/31/2003	12/31/2002	12/31/2001	12/31/2000	12/31/1999	12/31/1998	12/31/1997	12/31/1996
Earnings Per Share	2.03	2.10	1.71	2.20	2.11	1.98	1.90	1.82
Cash Flow Per Share	2.30	1.55	1.91	1.79	2.04	1.57	1.39	1.80
Tang. Book Val. Per Share	12.95	11.87	10.97	10.49	9.79	9.51	10.39	9.61
Dividends Per Share	1.170	1.150	1.130	1.080	1.030	0.990	0.940	0.870
Dividend Payout %	57.88	55.00	66.08	49.31	48.81	50.00	49.64	47.80
Income Statement								
Total Revenues	8,449,300	8,258,927	8,220,668	8,369,857	7,981,687	6,614,032	6,005,245	5,720,474
Total Indirect Exp.	2,050,873	1,948,442	1,951,559	1,958,747	1,766,063	1,413,390	1,261,003	1,172,270
Depreciation & Amort.	69,013	70,151	85,793	92,303	89,967	69,305	58,867	50,445
Operating Income	571,743	605,736	496,013	646,750	628,067	589,011	565,600	545,233
Income Taxes	218,101	238,236	198,866	261,427	250,445	233,323	223,203	215,157
Income from Cont Ops	353,642	367,500	...	...	...	...	...	...
Net Income	334,101	(27,590)	297,147	385,323	377,622	355,794	342,397	330,076
Average Shs. Outstg.	174,480	175,104	173,633	175,327	179,238	180,081	180,165	181,567
Balance Sheet								
Cash & Cash Equivalents	15,393	19,995	85,770	27,738	45,735	84,972	72,823	67,373
Total Current Assets	3,417,626	3,335,775	3,146,212	3,019,481	2,895,203	2,683,357	2,093,551	1,937,642
Total Assets	4,116,497	4,019,843	4,206,646	4,142,114	3,929,672	3,600,380	2,754,363	2,521,631
Total Current Liabilities	1,016,931	1,069,718	919,181	988,313	916,012	818,409	556,938	568,379
Long–Term Obligations	625,120	674,796	835,580	770,581	702,417	588,640	209,490	110,241
Net Stockholders' Equity	2,312,283	2,130,009	2,345,123	2,260,806	2,177,517	2,053,332	1,859,468	1,732,054
Net Working Capital	2,400,695	2,266,057	2,227,031	2,031,168	1,979,191	1,864,948	1,536,613	1,369,263
Shares Outstanding	174,045	174,380	173,473	172,389	177,275	179,505	178,948	180,048
Statistical Record								
Operating Profit Margin %	6.76	7.33	6.03	7.72	7.86	8.90	9.41	9.53
Return on Equity %	15.29	17.25	12.67	17.04	17.34	17.32	18.41	19.05
Return on Assets %	8.59	9.14	7.06	9.30	9.60	9.88	12.43	13.08
Debt/Total Assets %	15.18	16.78	19.86	18.60	17.87	16.34	7.60	4.37
Price Range	33.66-27.43	38.08-27.64	37.44-24.26	26.44-18.63	35.75-23.13	38.13-29.38	35.63-28.92	31.17-26.63
P/E Ratio	16.58-13.51	18.13-13.16	21.89-14.19	12.02-8.47	16.94-10.96	19.26-14.84	18.75-15.22	17.12-14.74
Average Yield %	3.70	3.45	3.74	4.89	3.46	2.92	2.93	2.96

Address: 2999 Circle 75 Parkway, Atlanta, GA 30339	Officers: Larry L. Prince – Chmn., C.E.O., Thomas C. Gallagher – Pres., C.O.O.	Investor Contact: (770) 953-1700
Telephone: (770) 953-1700	Transfer Agents:Sun Trust Bank, Atlanta, GA	Institutional Holding
Web Site: www.genpt.com		No of Institutions: 8
		Shares: 45,035 % Held: –

GLACIER BANCORP, INC.

Exchange	Symbol	Price	52Wk Range	Yield	P/E
NMS	GBCI	$32.25 (3/31/2004)	33.43–23.14	2.60	16.62

*7 Year Price Score 157.0 *NYSE Composite Index=100 *12 Month Price Score 105.2

Interim Earnings (Per Share)

Qtr.	Mar	Jun	Sep	Dec
2000	0.28	0.25	0.30	0.27
2001	0.26	0.30	0.30	0.35
2002	0.35	0.41	0.44	0.49
2003	0.50	0.51	0.49	0.44

Interim Dividends (Per Share)

Amt	Decl	Ex	Rec	Pay
0.19Q	6/25/2003	7/3/2003	7/8/2003	7/17/2003
0.20Q	9/24/2003	10/3/2003	10/7/2003	10/16/2003
0.20Q	12/29/2003	1/9/2004	1/13/2004	1/22/2004
0.21Q	3/10/2004	4/8/2004	4/13/2004	4/22/2004

Indicated Div: $0.84 (Div. Reinv. Plan)

Valuation Analysis

Forecast P/E	14.06	Trailing P/E	16.62
Market Cap	$555.0 Million	Book Value	228.1 Million
Price/Book	N/A	Price/Sales	N/A

Dividend Achiever Status

Rank	80	10 Year Growth Rate	14.76%
Total Years of Dividend Growth	12	

Business Summary: Other Depository Banking (MIC: 8.5 SIC: 6035 NAIC:522120)

Glacier Bancorp is the parent holding company of its eight wholly-owned subsidiaries, Glacier Bank, First Security Bank of Missoula, Western Security Bank, Mountain West Bank in Idaho, Big Sky Western Bank, Valley Bank of Helena, Glacier Bank of Whitefish and Glacier Capital Trust I. Co. provides commercial banking services from 54 banking offices throughout Montana, Idaho and Utah. Co. offers a range of banking products and services, including transaction and savings deposits, commercial, consumer and real estate loans, mortgage origination services, and retail brokerage services. As of Dec 31 2003, Co. had total assets of $2.74 billion and total deposits of $1.60 billion.

Recent Developments: For the year ended Dec 31 2003, net earnings advanced 17.3% to $38.0 million versus $32.4 million in 2002. Results for 2003 included merger expense of $56,000. Earnings for 2003 included results from the acquisition of Pend Oreille Bank as of Jul 15 2003. Net interest income increased 6.8% to $92.4 million from $86.5 million a year earlier. Total interest income decreased 2.4% to $130.8 million, while total interest expense fell 19.0% to $38.5 million. Provision for loan losses dropped 33.7% to $3.8 million. Total non-interest income jumped 29.5% to $33.6 million, primarily due to an increased number of loan and deposit accounts, and increased home purchase and loan refinancings.

Prospects: Looking ahead, Co. is planning to reincorporate to Montana from Delaware through a merger with a newly formed unit, Glacier Bancorp of Montana Inc. Montana has adopted a version of the revised model business corporation act, which modernizes the state's corporate statutes. As a result, Co. will no longer have to pay corporate franchise fees of about $150,000 per year to the state of Delaware. With the continuing change in loan mix from residential real estate to commercial and consumer loans, which historically have greater credit risk, Co. is continuing to increase the balance in the allowance for loan losses, which amounted to $24.0 million, or 1.65% of loan losses as of Dec 31 2003.

Financial Data

(US$ in Thousands)	12/31/2003	12/31/2002	12/31/2001	12/31/2000	12/31/1999	12/31/1998	12/31/1997	12/31/1996
Earnings Per Share	1.94	1.69	1.21	1.10	1.04	0.96	0.90	0.75
Tang. Book Val. Per Share	10.07	9.05	7.28	7.27	6.21	6.49	5.80	5.06
Dividends Per Share	0.710	0.582	0.545	0.562	0.510	0.380	0.300	0.270
Dividend Payout %	36.97	34.44	45.04	51.09	49.39	39.98	34.34	36.00
Income Statement								
Total Interest Income	130,830	133,989	137,920	78,837	58,921	51,081	44,004	41,148
Total Interest Expense	38,478	47,522	65,546	37,357	25,592	22,204	19,878	18,556
Net Interest Income	92,352	86,467	72,374	41,480	33,329	28,877	24,126	22,592
Provision for Loan Losses	3,809	5,745	4,525	1,864	1,506	1,490	747	880
Non–Interest Income	33,562	25,917	23,251	13,294	11,064	11,259	8,339	8,339
Non–Interest Expense	65,944	57,813	57,385	31,327	24,077	21,606	17,219	17,536
Income Before Taxes	56,161	48,826	33,715	21,583	18,810	17,040	14,499	12,515
Eqty Earns/Minority Int.	...	...	35	61	51	145	68	64
Net Income	38,008	32,402	21,689	14,003	12,179	10,744	9,180	7,425
Average Shs. Outstg.	19,620	19,188	17,755	12,698	11,630	11,167	9,936	9,904
Balance Sheet								
Cash & Due from Banks	77,093	74,624	73,456	41,456	46,277	31,509	26,463	24,666
Securities Avail. for Sale	1,050,311	739,961	508,578	211,888	191,385	90,735	93,254	85,050
Net Loans & Leases	1,413,392	1,248,666	1,294,924	726,503	586,952	494,249	421,048	386,641
Total Assets	2,739,633	2,281,344	2,085,747	1,056,712	884,117	666,651	580,398	545,992
Total Deposits	1,597,625	1,459,923	1,446,064	720,570	576,282	444,459	346,784	321,739
Long–Term Obligations	812,294	483,660	367,295	196,791	194,650	120,586	139,257	143,289
Total Liabilities	2,501,794	2,069,095	1,908,764	958,599	805,304	591,714	520,789	494,044
Net Stockholders' Equity	237,839	212,249	176,983	98,113	78,813	74,937	59,609	51,948
Shares Outstanding	19,362	19,014	18,561	12,591	11,556	11,144	10,024	9,946
Statistical Record								
Return on Equity %	15.98	15.26	12.25	14.27	15.45	14.33	15.40	14.29
Return on Assets %	1.38	1.42	1.03	1.32	1.37	1.61	1.58	1.35
Equity/Assets %	8.68	9.30	8.48	9.28	8.91	11.24	10.27	9.51
Non–Int. Exp./Tot. Inc. %	40.11	36.15	35.60	34.00	34.40	34.65	32.89	35.43
Price Range	32.98–21.42	22.50–17.38	19.09–11.42	13.33–10.00	19.83–12.76	20.15–14.27	17.08–10.47	11.50–8.07
P/E Ratio	17.00–11.04	13.31–10.29	15.78–9.44	12.11–9.09	19.07–12.27	20.99–14.87	18.97–11.64	15.33–10.76
Average Yield %	2.70	2.87	3.52	4.90	3.23	2.16	2.41	2.74

Address: 49 Commons Loop, Kalispell, MT 59901	Officers: John S. MacMillan – Chmn., Michael J. Blodnick – Pres., C.E.O.	Institutional Holding
Telephone: (406) 756–4200		No of Institutions: 17
Web Site: www.glacierbank.com		Shares: 1,694,935 % Held: –

GOLDEN WEST FINANCIAL CORP.

Exchange	Symbol	Price	52Wk Range	Yield	P/E
NYS	GDW	$111.95 (3/31/2004)	116.8-72.07	0.36	15.68

*7 Year Price Score 175.0   *NYSE Composite Index=100   *12 Month Price Score 107.1

Interim Earnings (Per Share)

Qtr.	Mar	Jun	Sep	Dec
2000	0.78	0.84	0.86	0.93
2001	1.10	1.30	1.28	1.43
2002	1.51	1.44	1.56	1.61
2003	1.67	1.76	1.83	1.88

Interim Dividends (Per Share)

Amt	Decl	Ex	Rec	Pay
0.085Q	4/29/2003	5/13/2003	5/15/2003	6/10/2003
0.085Q	7/31/2003	8/13/2003	8/15/2003	9/10/2003
0.10Q	10/28/2003	11/12/2003	11/15/2003	12/10/2003
0.10Q	1/28/2004	2/11/2004	2/15/2004	3/10/2004

Indicated Div: $0.40

Valuation Analysis

Forecast P/E	13.13	Trailing P/E	15.68
Market Cap	$17.3 Billion	Book Value	5.9 Billion
Price/Book	2.64	Price/Sales	4.09

Dividend Achiever Status

Rank	81	10 Year Growth Rate 14.71%
Total Years of Dividend Growth		20

Business Summary: Other Depository Banking (MIC: 8.5 SIC: 6035 NAIC:522120)

Golden West Financial, with assets of $82.55 billion as of Dec 31 2003, is the holding company of World Savings Bank, FSB, a federally chartered savings and lending institution. As of Dec 31 2003, Co. operated 479 savings and lending offices in 38 states under the World name. Also, Co. has two other subsidiaries, Atlas Advisers and Atlas Securities, which provide services to Atlas Assets, a registered open-end management investment company sponsored by Co. Atlas Advisers is a registered investment adviser and the investment manager of Atlas Assets' portfolios. Atlas Securities is a registered broker-dealer and the sole distributor of Atlas Fund shares.

Recent Developments: For the year ended Dec 31 2003, net income increased 15.4% to $1.11 billion from $958.3 million the year before. Results for 2003 and 2002 included gains on the sale of securities, mortgage-backed securities and loans of $72.3 million and $45.1 million, and pre-tax gains from changes in the fair value of derivatives of $10.9 million and $7.6 million, respectively. Net interest income advanced 14.4% to $2.21 billion. Provision for loan losses dropped 44.0% to $11.9 million. Total non-interest income advanced 26.9% to $313.3 million, while total non-interest expense rose 19.8% to $720.5 million.

Prospects: Earnings continue to benefit from the expansion of Co.'s mortgage portfolio. In 2003, Co.'s mortgage originations amounted to $36.00 billion of loans, driven by low interest rates on new home loans. Additionally, earnings continue to improve due to higher noninterest income, resulting from gains received from the sale of fixed-rate mortgages. Meanwhile, with regard to lending activity, Co.'s primary product is an adjustable rate mortgage (ARM). In 2003, ARMs comprised 98.0% of Co.'s new volumes during the fourth quarter and 94.0% of all new lending for the year, which should help limit Co.'s earnings exposure once market interest rates rise.

Financial Data

(US$ in Thousands)	12/31/2003	12/31/2002	12/31/2001	12/31/2000	12/31/1999	12/31/1998	12/31/1997	12/31/1996
Earnings Per Share	7.14	6.12	5.11	3.41	2.87	2.58	2.04	2.11
Tang. Book Val. Per Share	39.09	32.73	27.54	23.27	19.79	18.31	15.75	13.66
Dividends Per Share	0.350	0.300	0.260	0.220	0.190	0.170	0.150	0.130
Dividend Payout %	4.97	4.94	5.08	6.45	6.70	6.65	7.42	61.6
Income Statement								
Total Interest Income	3,528,344	3,497,034	4,209,612	3,796,540	2,825,845	2,962,553	2,832,497	2,581,561
Total Interest Expense	1,319,960	1,566,740	2,578,280	2,645,372	1,822,360	1,995,231	1,942,002	1,750,601
Net Interest Income	2,208,384	1,930,294	1,631,332	1,151,168	1,003,485	967,322	890,495	830,960
Provision for Loan Losses	11,864	21,170	22,265	9,195	(2,089)	11,260	57,609	84,256
Non-Interest Income	313,330	247,000	236,739	160,820	143,302	137,613	81,268	74,899
Non-Interest Expense	720,511	601,494	513,802	424,847	386,147	354,507	326,959	453,422
Income Before Taxes	1,789,335	1,554,630	1,332,004	877,946	762,729	739,168	587,195	368,181
Income from Cont Ops	...	...	818,823	...	...	447,091	...	369,913
Net Income	1,106,099	958,279	812,805	545,791	479,979	434,580	354,138	164,671
Average Shs. Outstg.	154,987	156,682	160,358	160,277	166,951	173,461	173,319	173,967
Balance Sheet								
Securities Avail. for Sale	3,803,028	1,913,440	1,712,146	925,602	796,906	981,180	1,531,742	2,017,582
Net Loans & Leases	74,205,578	58,268,899	41,065,375	33,762,643	27,919,817	25,721,288	33,260,709	30,113,421
Total Assets	82,549,890	68,405,828	58,586,271	55,703,969	42,142,205	38,468,729	39,421,342	37,730,598
Total Deposits	46,726,965	41,038,797	34,472,585	30,047,919	27,714,910	26,219,095	24,109,717	22,099,934
Long-Term Obligations	22,991,491	19,824,656	18,835,235	20,330,588	9,728,168	7,075,225	9,737,085	10,712,274
Total Liabilities	76,602,622	63,380,578	54,302,081	52,016,682	38,947,351	35,344,411	36,892,240	35,380,121
Net Stockholders' Equity	5,947,268	5,025,250	4,284,190	3,687,287	3,194,854	3,124,318	2,698,031	2,350,477
Shares Outstanding	152,119	153,521	155,531	158,410	161,357	170,583	171,207	172,026
Statistical Record								
Return on Equity %	18.59	19.06	19.11	14.80	15.02	14.31	13.12	15.73
Return on Assets %	1.33	1.40	1.39	0.97	1.13	1.16	0.89	0.98
Equity/Assets %	7.20	7.34	7.31	6.61	7.58	8.12	6.84	6.22
Non-Int. Exp./Tot. Inc. %	18.75	16.06	11.55	10.73	13.00	11.43	11.22	17.06
Price Range	103.5-69.67	72.98-57.91	70.00-47.15	69.44-27.19	38.02-29.27	38.08-24.12	32.60-19.96	22.50-16.50
P/E Ratio	14.49-9.76	11.92-9.46	13.70-9.23	20.36-7.97	13.25-10.20	14.76-9.35	15.98-9.78	10.66-7.82
Average Yield %	0.42	0.45	0.45	0.52	0.58	0.55	0.59	0.69

Address: 1901 Harrison Street, Oakland, CA 94612	Officers: Herbert M. Sandler – Co-Chmn., Co-C.E.O., Marion O. Sandler – Co-Chmn., Co-C.E.O.	Investor Contact: (510) 446-3614
Telephone: (510) 446-3420		Institutional Holding
Web Site: www.gdw.com	Transfer Agents:Mellon Investor Services, LLC, San Francisco, CA	No of Institutions: 20
		Shares: 28,991,892 % Held: –

GORMAN-RUPP CO.

Exchange	Symbol	Price	52Wk Range	Yield	P/E
ASE	GRC	$25.90 (3/31/2004)	27.17-19.69	2.63	22.52

*7 Year Price Score 116.1   *NYSE Composite Index=100   *12 Month Price Score 95.4

Interim Earnings (Per Share)

Qtr.	Mar	Jun	Sep	Dec
2000	0.48	0.42	0.37	0.34
2001	0.42	0.47	0.42	0.39
2002	0.25	0.38	0.23	0.19
2003	0.14	0.30	0.30	0.41

Interim Dividends (Per Share)

Amt	Decl	Ex	Rec	Pay
0.17Q	4/24/2003	5/13/2003	5/15/2003	6/10/2003
0.17Q	7/24/2003	8/13/2003	8/15/2003	9/10/2003
0.17Q	10/23/2003	11/12/2003	11/14/2003	12/10/2003
0.17Q	1/26/2004	2/11/2004	2/13/2004	3/10/2004

Indicated Div: $0.68 (Div. Reinv. Plan)

Valuation Analysis

Forecast P/E	21.17	Trailing P/E	22.52
Market Cap	$221.1 Million	Book Value	116.5 Million
Price/Book	1.98	Price/Sales	1.18

Dividend Achiever Status

Rank 273	10 Year Growth Rate 3.54%
Total Years of Dividend Growth	31

Business Summary: Industrial Machinery and Equipment (MIC: 11.5 SIC: 3561 NAIC:333911)

Gorman-Rupp designs, manufactures and sells pumps and related equipment for use in water, wastewater, construction, industrial, petroleum, original equipment, agricultural, fire protection, heating, ventilating and air conditioning, military and other liquid-handling applications. The types of pumps Co. produces include self-priming, standard and magnetic drive centrifugal, axial and mixed flow, rotary gear, diaphragm, bellows and oscillating. Co.'s larger pumps are sold for use in the construction, industrial, sewage and waste handling fields; for boosting low residential water pressure; for pumping refined petroleum products, for agricultural applications; and for fire fighting.

Recent Developments: For the twelve months ended Dec 31 2003, net income rose 9.5% to $9.8 million compared with $8.9 million in 2002. Net sales were $195.8 million, up 0.4% from $195.1 million in the prior year. Increased sales of pumps and related products were partially offset by a decrease in sales to the power generation business, which resulted in a slight increase in net sales for the year. Gross profit grew 1.3% to $42.0 million, or 21.4% of net sales, from $41.5 million, or 21.2% of net sales, the previous year. Operating profit increased 3.6% to $14.0 million compared with $13.5 million the year before.

Prospects: Co. is encouraged that certain indicators are starting to show an increase in overall economic activity and is cautiously optimistic that domestic capital spending will increase during 2004. However, Co. expects the economic environment for industrial manufacturers that serve the capital goods sector to continue to remain stagnant in the near term. Meanwhile, Co. should be well-positioned for the future, given its favorable cash flow position, ongoing profitability of all of its subsidiaries and divisions, and no bank debt. Also, Co. should benefit from the favorable effect of cost containment programs and productivity improvements.

Financial Data (US$ in Thousands)	12/31/2003	12/31/2002	12/31/2001	12/31/2000	12/31/1999	12/31/1998	12/31/1997	12/31/1996
Earnings Per Share	1.15	1.05	1.70	1.61	1.52	1.37	1.23	1.15
Cash Flow Per Share	1.64	2.50	3.07	1.90	2.03	2.54	1.37	2.07
Tang. Book Val. Per Share	12.79	12.21	12.63	11.67	10.74	9.75	9.06	8.44
Dividends Per Share	0.680	0.650	0.640	0.620	0.600	0.580	0.560	0.530
Dividend Payout %	59.13	61.90	37.64	38.50	39.47	42.33	45.52	46.09
Income Statement								
Total Revenues	195,826	194,075	203,813	191,484	180,165	172,246	165,568	155,678
Total Indirect Exp.	27,974	27,921	25,959	27,574	25,687	25,562	24,718	23,955
Depreciation & Amort.	7,117	7,035	7,128	6,863	6,489	6,330	5,959	5,675
Operating Income	14,020	13,530	23,035	22,196	21,541	19,152	16,952	15,663
Income Taxes	4,613	5,267	8,450	8,400	8,460	7,400	6,340	5,735
Net Income	9,787	8,936	14,585	13,796	13,081	11,752	10,612	9,928
Average Shs. Outstg.	8,542	8,539	8,555	8,583	8,585	8,600	8,609	8,617
Balance Sheet								
Cash & Cash Equivalents	17,446	13,086	20,583	7,630	7,339	8,665	7,737	4,284
Total Current Assets	94,262	83,859	89,119	82,289	78,185	78,556	81,695	71,926
Total Assets	160,939	152,846	148,113	145,881	136,875	127,477	127,865	117,650
Total Current Liabilities	21,908	19,282	18,103	19,079	17,439	17,431	17,036	15,199
Long-Term Obligations	...	291	...	3,413	3,107	783	6,689	3,796
Net Stockholders' Equity	116,462	111,456	107,910	99,999	92,295	83,706	78,060	72,737
Net Working Capital	72,354	64,577	71,016	63,210	60,746	61,125	64,659	56,727
Shares Outstanding	8,543	8,540	8,537	8,565	8,592	8,581	8,609	8,618
Statistical Record								
Operating Profit Margin %	7.15	6.97	11.30	11.59	11.95	11.11	10.23	10.06
Return on Equity %	8.40	8.01	13.51	13.79	14.17	14.03	13.59	13.64
Return on Assets %	6.08	5.84	9.84	9.45	9.55	9.21	8.29	8.43
Debt/Total Assets %	...	0.19	...	2.33	2.26	0.61	5.23	3.22
Price Range	26.98-18.50	31.50-20.51	27.15-17.50	19.00-14.50	18.00-14.44	21.13-13.75	22.00-13.38	16.38-12.00
P/E Ratio	23.46-16.09	30.00-19.53	15.97-10.29	11.80-9.01	11.84-9.50	15.42-10.04	17.89-10.87	14.24-10.43
Average Yield %	2.97	2.53	2.91	3.71	3.73	3.19	3.17	3.78

Address: 305 Bowman St., Mansfield, OH 44903	Officers: James C. Gorman - Chmn., Jeffrey S. Gorman - Pres., C.E.O., Gen. Man., Mansfield Div.	Investor Contact:419-755-1294
Telephone: (419) 755-1011		Institutional Holding
Web Site: www.gormanrupp.com		No of Institutions: 43
		Shares: 3,813,871 % Held: 44.70%

GRAINGER (W.W.) INC.

Exchange	Symbol	Price	52Wk Range	Yield	P/E
NYS	GWW	$48.00 (3/31/2004)	52.25–43.12	1.54	19.51

*7 Year Price Score 107.1 *NYSE Composite Index=100   *12 Month Price Score 87.9

Interim Earnings (Per Share)

Qtr.	Mar	Jun	Sep	Dec
2000	0.44	0.59	0.51	0.51
2001	0.45	0.15	0.59	0.65
2002	0.61	0.57	0.64	0.68
2003	0.57	0.60	0.62	0.67

Interim Dividends (Per Share)

Amt	Decl	Ex	Rec	Pay
0.185Q	4/30/2003	5/8/2003	5/12/2003	6/1/2003
0.185Q	7/30/2003	8/7/2003	8/11/2003	9/1/2003
0.185Q	10/29/2003	11/6/2003	11/10/2003	12/1/2003
0.185Q	1/29/2004	2/5/2004	2/9/2004	3/1/2004
		Indicated Div: $0.74		

Valuation Analysis

Forecast P/E	17.14	Trailing P/E	N/A
Market Cap	$4.5 Billion	Book Value	N/A
Price/Book	N/A	Price/Sales	N/A

Dividend Achiever Status

Rank	209	10 Year Growth Rate	7.62%
Total Years of Dividend Growth			32

TRADING VOLUME (thousand shares)

Business Summary: Engineering Services (MIC: 12.1 SIC: 5063 NAIC:423610)

W.W. Grainger is primarily a supplier of facilities maintenance products in North America through its Branch-based Distribution segment, which includes a network of 575 branches in the U.S., Canada, and Mexico, 17 distribution facilities, and multiple Web sites. Co.'s Lab Safety segment is a direct marketer of safety and other industrial products to U.S. and Canadian businesses. Co.'s Integrated Supply segment offers customers on-site outsourcing services, including business process reengineering, inventory and tool crib management, purchasing management and information management.

Recent Developments: For the twelve months ended Dec 31 2003, net earnings totaled $227.0 million, down 3.6% compared with earnings of $235.5 million, before a $23.9 million accounting change charge, in the corresponding period the year before. Results included pre-tax gains of $1.2 million and $7.3 million from the sale of investment securities, partially offset by restructuring charges of $564,000 and $1.9 million in 2003 and 2002, respectively. Results for 2003 also included a $1.9 million charge for investment write-downs. Net sales grew 0.5% to $4.67 billion from $4.64 billion a year earlier. Gross profit was $1.64 billion, or 35.1% of net sales, versus $1.60 billion, or 34.4% of net sales, in 2002.

Prospects: Results are being negatively affected by declining employment levels in the manufacturing industry, reflecting increased productivity and production moving overseas. Co. is taking steps to offset these trends, which are expected to continue over the near term, including reaching new customer groups such as governments and healthcare institutions. Co. plans to enter these new markets through a multi-year branch expansion program, as well as implementing initiatives focused on improving its sales force and increasing the availability of its products. Looking ahead, Co. anticipates full-year 2004 earnings of between $2.45 and $2.70 per share.

Financial Data

(US$ in Thousands)	12/31/2003	12/31/2002	12/31/2001	12/31/2000	12/31/1999	12/31/1998	12/31/1997	12/31/1996
Earnings Per Share	2.46	2.50	1.84	2.05	1.92	2.44	2.27	2.02
Cash Flow Per Share	4.26	3.21	5.39	2.94	0.31	3.41	4.16	2.62
Tang. Book Val. Per Share	18.20	16.58	15.08	14.07	13.46	11.38	11.13	11.64
Dividends Per Share	0.730	0.710	0.690	0.670	0.630	0.580	0.530	0.490
Dividend Payout %	29.87	28.60	37.77	32.68	32.81	23.97	23.34	24.26
Income Statement								
Total Revenues	4,667,014	4,643,898	4,754,317	4,977,044	4,533,853	4,341,269	4,136,560	3,537,207
Total Indirect Exp.	1,250,816	1,205,057	1,250,714	1,250,217	1,335,406	1,189,689	1,101,193	921,685
Depreciation & Amort.	90,253	93,488	103,209	106,893	98,227	78,865	79,651	74,261
Operating Income	387,261	393,155	338,573	335,120	317,228	407,982	393,159	345,529
Net Interest Inc./(Exp.)	(2,668)	(1,590)	(7,847)	(22,512)	(13,990)	(5,092)	(2,565)	3,326
Income Taxes	154,119	162,349	122,750	138,692	123,019	162,343	157,803	140,362
Eqty Earns/Minority Int.	(2,288)	(3,025)	(27,328)	(10,855)	...	...	...	...
Income from Cont Ops	...	235,488	...	...	...	...	...	...
Net Income	226,971	211,567	174,530	192,903	180,731	238,504	231,833	208,526
Average Shs. Outstg.	92,394	94,303	94,727	94,223	94,315	97,846	102,178	103,272
Balance Sheet								
Cash & Cash Equivalents	402,824	208,528	168,846	63,384	62,683	43,107	46,929	126,935
Total Current Assets	1,633,413	1,484,947	1,392,611	1,483,002	1,471,145	1,206,365	1,182,988	1,320,243
Total Assets	2,624,678	2,437,448	2,331,246	2,459,601	2,564,826	2,103,902	1,997,821	2,119,021
Total Current Liabilities	706,640	586,266	553,811	747,324	870,534	664,493	533,881	616,068
Long-Term Obligations	4,895	119,693	118,219	125,258	124,928	122,883	131,201	6,152
Net Stockholders' Equity	1,845,135	1,667,698	1,603,189	1,537,386	1,480,529	1,278,741	1,294,661	1,462,662
Net Working Capital	926,773	898,681	838,800	735,678	600,611	541,872	649,107	704,175
Shares Outstanding	91,020	91,568	93,344	93,932	93,381	93,505	97,722	105,856
Statistical Record								
Operating Profit Margin %	8.29	8.46	7.12	6.73	6.99	9.39	9.50	9.76
Return on Equity %	12.30	14.12	10.88	12.54	12.20	18.65	17.90	14.25
Return on Assets %	8.64	9.66	7.48	7.84	7.04	11.33	11.60	9.84
Debt/Total Assets %	0.18	4.91	5.07	5.09	4.87	5.84	6.56	0.29
Price Range	53.11–41.93	59.27–39.82	48.52–30.23	56.00–24.63	58.06–37.13	54.47–37.63	49.00–36.06	40.56–31.44
P/E Ratio	21.59–17.04	23.71–15.93	26.37–16.43	27.32–12.01	30.24–19.34	22.32–15.42	21.59–15.89	20.08–15.56
Average Yield %	1.55	1.41	1.75	1.71	1.34	1.23	1.23	1.39

Address: 100 Grainger Parkway, Lake Forest, IL 60045–5201 Telephone: (847) 535–1000 Web Site: www.grainger.com	Officers: Richard L. Keyser – Chmn., C.E.O., Wesley M. Clark – Pres., C.O.O. Transfer Agents:BankBoston, N.A. c/o EquiServe, Boston, MA	Investor Contact:847–535–0881 Institutional Holding No of Institutions: 354 Shares: 61,231,668 % Held: 66.60%

HARLEY-DAVIDSON, INC.

Exchange	Symbol	Price	52Wk Range	Yield	P/E
NYS	HDI	$53.34 (3/31/2004)	54.09–37.42	0.60	21.34

*7 Year Price Score 131.5 *NYSE Composite Index=100 *12 Month Price Score 93.9

Interim Earnings (Per Share)

Qtr.	Mar	Jun	Sep	Dec
2000	0.26	0.29	0.27	0.31
2001	0.30	0.38	0.36	0.39
2002	0.39	0.47	0.54	0.50
2003	0.61	0.66	0.62	0.61

Interim Dividends (Per Share)

Amt	Decl	Ex	Rec	Pay
0.04Q	5/7/2003	6/6/2003	6/10/2003	6/20/2003
0.04Q	8/5/2003	9/15/2003	9/17/2003	9/30/2003
0.08Q	12/5/2003	12/11/2003	12/15/2003	12/29/2003
0.08Q	2/10/2004	3/9/2004	3/11/2004	3/25/2004

Indicated Div: $0.32

Valuation Analysis

Forecast P/E	18.92	Trailing P/E	21.34
Market Cap	$16.1 Billion	Book Value	3.0 Billion
Price/Book	4.89	Price/Sales	2.95

Dividend Achiever Status

Rank	7	10 Year Growth Rate	29.24%
Total Years of Dividend Growth		10	

Business Summary: Automotive (MIC: 15.1 SIC: 3751 NAIC:336991)

Harley–Davidson operates in two business segments. Co.'s Motorcycles and Related Products segment consists primarily of the wholly–owned subsidiaries: H–D Michigan, Inc., Harley–Davidson Motor Company and Buell Motorcycle Company LLC. The Motorcycles segment designs, manufactures and sells primarily heavyweight touring, custom and performance motorcycles and a range of related products, which include motorcycle parts and accessories and general merchandise, such as clothing and collectibles. The Financial Services segment, which is comprised of Harley–Davidson Financial Services, Inc., provides retail and wholesale financing and insurance for Co.'s dealers and customers.

Recent Developments: For the year ended Dec 31 2003, net income advanced 31.1% to $760.9 million compared with $580.2 million in the previous year. Earnings benefited from increased motorcycle sales as well as higher sales of parts and accessories and merchandise, particularly items related to Co.'s 100th anniversary. Total revenue increased 14.0% to $4.90 billion. Net product revenue rose 13.0% to $4.62 billion from $4.09 billion, while financial service revenue climbed 32.1% to $279.5 million from $211.5 million a year earlier. Total Harley–Davidson motorcycle shipments grew 10.4% to 291,147 units. Operating income increased 30.2% to $1.15 billion from $882.7 million the year before.

Prospects: In 2004, Co. expects to grow its business further with a continuing stream of new motorcycles, as well as related products and services. Looking ahead, Co. has set a goal of being able to satisfy a yearly demand of 400,000 Harley–Davidson motorcycles by 2007. The increased production may align supply more closely with demand and reduce the gap between the excess prices dealers charge customers and Co.'s suggested retail prices. Separately, Co. has made new agreements with suppliers, employees and unions, which, along with the ramp up of production at the recently opened York, PA plant, should improve margins and productivity. For 2004, Co. expects to ship 317,000 motorcycles.

Financial Data

(US$ in Thousands)	12/31/2003	12/31/2002	12/31/2001	12/31/2000	12/31/1999	12/31/1998	12/31/1997	12/31/1996
Earnings Per Share	2.50	1.90	1.43	1.13	0.86	0.69	0.56	0.47
Cash Flow Per Share	3.07	2.55	2.47	1.83	1.34	1.02	1.17	0.75
Tang. Book Val. Per Share	9.63	7.21	5.63	4.47	3.65	3.19	2.58	2.05
Dividends Per Share	0.195	0.135	0.115	0.098	0.088	0.078	0.068	0.055
Dividend Payout %	7.80	7.11	8.04	8.67	10.23	11.30	12.14	11.70
Income Statement								
Total Revenues	4,903,733	4,302,470	3,544,959	2,943,543	2,480,624	2,084,167	1,774,924	1,539,028
Total Indirect Exp.	684,175	639,366	578,777	513,024	447,512	377,265	328,569	269,449
Depreciation & Amort.	196,918	175,778	153,061	133,348	113,822	87,422	70,178	55,282
Operating Income	1,149,264	882,702	662,501	514,972	415,859	333,616	270,003	228,446
Net Interest Inc./(Exp.)	23,088	16,541	17,478	17,583	8,014	3,828	7,871	3,309
Income Taxes	405,107	305,610	235,709	200,843	153,592	122,729	102,232	84,213
Income from Cont Ops	...	...	...	...	...	...	...	143,409
Net Income	760,928	580,217	437,746	347,713	267,201	213,500	174,070	166,028
Average Shs. Outstg.	304,470	305,158	306,248	307,470	309,714	309,406	307,896	302,000
Balance Sheet								
Cash & Cash Equivalents	1,322,660	795,728	635,449	419,736	183,415	165,170	147,462	142,479
Total Current Assets	2,729,127	2,066,586	1,665,264	1,297,264	948,994	844,963	704,021	429,321
Total Assets	4,923,088	3,861,217	3,118,495	2,436,404	2,112,077	1,920,209	1,598,901	1,319,985
Total Current Liabilities	955,773	990,052	716,110	497,743	518,154	468,515	361,688	263,594
Long–Term Obligations	670,000	380,000	380,000	355,000	280,000	280,000	280,000	258,065
Net Stockholders' Equity	2,957,692	2,232,915	1,756,283	1,405,655	1,161,080	1,029,911	826,668	662,720
Net Working Capital	1,773,354	1,076,534	949,154	799,521	430,840	376,448	342,333	165,727
Shares Outstanding	301,510	302,662	302,789	302,070	302,722	305,862	304,650	302,676
Statistical Record								
Operating Profit Margin %	23.43	20.51	18.68	17.49	16.76	16.00	15.21	14.84
Return on Equity %	25.72	25.98	24.92	24.73	23.01	20.72	21.05	21.63
Return on Assets %	15.45	15.02	14.03	14.27	12.65	11.11	10.88	10.86
Debt/Total Assets %	13.60	9.84	12.18	14.57	13.25	14.58	17.51	19.55
Price Range	52.45–35.95	57.00–42.83	55.66–35.19	50.00–29.63	32.03–23.22	23.69–12.56	15.41–8.47	12.28–6.66
P/E Ratio	20.98–14.38	30.00–22.54	38.92–24.61	44.25–26.22	37.25–27.00	34.33–18.21	27.51–15.12	26.13–14.16
Average Yield %	0.52	0.20	0.24	0.22	0.28	0.52	0.42	0.49

Address: 3700 West Juneau Avenue, Milwaukee, WI 53208 Telephone: (414) 342–4680 Web Site: www.harley–davidson.com	Officers: Jeffrey L. Bleustein – Chmn., C.E.O., James M. Brostowitz – V.P., Treas., Contr. Transfer Agents:ComputerShare Investor Services, Chicago, IL	Investor Contact: (877) 437–8625 Institutional Holding No of Institutions: 3 Shares: 837,804 % Held: –

HARLEYSVILLE GROUP, INC. (PA)

Exchange	Symbol	Price	52Wk Range	Yield	P/E
NMS	HGIC	$18.71 (3/31/2004)	26.15–17.84	3.63	N.M.

*7 Year Price Score 108.2 *NYSE Composite Index=100 *12 Month Price Score 77.5

Interim Earnings (Per Share)

Qtr.	Mar	Jun	Sep	Dec
2000	0.25	0.37	0.45	0.60
2001	0.33	0.37	0.26	0.50
2002	0.44	0.01	0.50	0.58
2003	(0.11)	0.33	(1.16)	(0.65)

Interim Dividends (Per Share)

Amt	Decl	Ex	Rec	Pay
0.165Q	5/20/2003	6/12/2003	6/16/2003	6/30/2003
0.17Q	8/5/2003	9/11/2003	9/15/2003	9/30/2003
0.17Q	11/4/2003	12/11/2003	12/15/2003	12/30/2003
0.17Q	2/25/2004	3/11/2004	3/15/2004	3/30/2004

Indicated Div: $0.68 (Div. Reinv. Plan)

Valuation Analysis

Forecast P/E	10.98	Trailing P/E	N.M.
Market Cap	$559.5 Million	Book Value	572.7 Million
Price/Book	1.07	Price/Sales	0.67

Dividend Achiever Status

Rank	193	10 Year Growth Rate 8.37%
Total Years of Dividend Growth		17

TRADING VOLUME (thousand shares)

Business Summary: Insurance (MIC: 8.2 SIC: 6331 NAIC:524126)

Harleysville Group is a regional insurance holding company engages, through its subsidiaries, in the property and casualty insurance business on a regional basis. Harleysville Group and Harleysville Mutual Insurance Company, which owned 57.0% of Co.'s outstanding shares as of Dec 31 2003, operate together as a network of regional insurance companies that underwrite a broad line of personal and commercial coverages, including automobile, homeowners, commercial multi-peril and workers compensation. These insurance overages are marketed primarily in the Eastern and Midwestern U.S. through approximately 1,700 insurance agencies.

Recent Developments: For the year ended Dec 31 2003, net loss was $47.6 million versus net income of $46.3 million the previous year. Results were hampered by loss and loss reserve increases in several business lines for prior accident years.Total revenues increased 9.1% to $925.0 million from $847.7 million in the prior year. Revenues for 2003 and 2002 included a realized investment loss of $920,000 and $18.4 million, respectively. Premiums earned increased 7.7% to $823.4 million. Net investment income rose 0.4% to $86.6 million. Losses and loss settlement expenses climbed 39.5% to $727.9 million. Co.'s combined ratio was 123.2% versus 101.9% the year before

Prospects: For 2004, Co. will focus on improving four areas: underwriting, claims handling, service to agents and policyholders, and productivity. To do this, Co. has strengthened its management in key areas, including claims, and conducted thorough claims and actuarial reviews, using internal and external resources, in order to address the issues that led to additions to loss reserves in 2003. Nevertheless, further adjustments to prior accident years may continue. Moreover, with pricing increases moderating and increased competition, Co.'s retention level may weaken as it is forced to increase rates higher than its competitors.

Financial Data

(US$ in Thousands)	12/31/2003	12/31/2002	12/31/2001	12/31/2000	12/31/1999	12/31/1998	12/31/1997	12/31/1996
Earnings Per Share	(1.59)	1.53	1.46	1.67	1.45	2.15	1.86	1.03
Tang. Book Val. Per Share	19.15	21.12	20.04	19.53	18.28	18.16	15.49	13.09
Dividends Per Share	0.670	0.630	0.580	0.550	0.520	0.480	0.440	0.400
Dividend Payout %	N.M.	41.18	39.73	32.93	35.86	22.32	23.65	38.83
Income Statement								
Total Premium Income	823,407	764,636	729,889	688,330	707,200	664,604	624,905	615,197
Net Investment Income	86,597	86,265	85,518	86,791	85,894	86,025	81,783	78,008
Other Income	14,961	(3,165)	12,344	27,450	31,662	28,682	17,491	14,220
Total Revenues	924,965	847,736	827,751	802,571	824,756	779,311	724,179	707,425
Total Indirect Exp.	207,762	189,834	185,655	184,537	187,386	173,766	160,705	157,047
Inc. Before Inc. Taxes	(89,450)	56,482	51,800	57,705	47,752	80,441	67,281	31,375
Income Taxes	(41,821)	10,227	8,307	9,013	4,935	17,028	13,209	2,695
Income from Cont Ops	...	...	...	...	42,817	...	...	...
Net Income	(47,629)	46,255	43,493	48,692	39,913	63,413	54,072	28,680
Average Shs. Outstg.	29,985	30,295	29,818	29,136	29,565	29,519	29,032	27,844
Balance Sheet								
Cash & Cash Equivalents	13,430	2,944	1,839	28,395	20,273	3,799	1,460	2,120
Premiums Due	328,601	235,945	226,010	201,668	196,293	197,569	183,951	173,653
Invst. Assets: Total	1,823,222	1,617,208	1,574,449	1,575,244	1,544,799	1,564,544	1,423,240	1,256,104
Total Assets	2,680,389	2,311,524	2,045,290	2,021,862	2,020,056	1,934,491	1,801,195	1,622,612
Long–Term Obligations	120,145	95,620	96,055	96,450	96,801	97,140	97,440	97,715
Net Stockholders' Equity	572,747	632,112	590,298	566,581	526,894	529,658	446,515	370,245
Shares Outstanding	29,900	29,917	29,444	29,001	28,812	29,150	28,821	28,278
Statistical Record								
Return on Equity %	N.M.	7.31	7.36	8.59	8.12	11.97	12.10	7.74
Return on Assets %	N.M.	2.00	2.12	2.40	2.11	3.27	3.00	1.76
Price Range	27.50–18.99	31.44–19.90	30.00–20.40	29.81–11.81	25.81–13.13	28.22–18.88	27.13–14.50	16.38–12.38
P/E Ratio	N/A	20.55–13.01	20.55–13.97	17.85–7.07	17.80–9.05	13.13–8.78	14.58–7.80	15.90–12.01
Average Yield %	2.86	3.01	1.69	3.09	2.79	2.06	2.30	2.90

Address: 355 Maple Avenue, Harleysville, PA 19438–2297 Telephone: (215) 256–5000 Web Site: www.harleysvillegroup.com	Officers: M. Lee Patkus – Pres., C.O.O., Michael L. Browne – C.E.O.	Investor Contact:215–256–5020 Institutional Holding No of Institutions: 11 Shares: 185,306,015 % Held: –

HARLEYSVILLE NATIONAL CORP.

Exchange	Symbol	Price	52Wk Range	Yield	P/E
NMS	HNBC	$27.83 (3/31/2004)	32.47-19.99	2.44	19.32

*7 Year Price Score 158.1 *NYSE Composite Index=100 *12 Month Price Score 116.2

Interim Earnings (Per Share)

Qtr.	Mar	Jun	Sep	Dec
2000	0.26	0.27	0.27	0.25
2001	0.26	0.28	0.32	0.31
2002	0.32	0.33	0.35	0.33
2003	0.34	0.36	0.37	0.37

Interim Dividends (Per Share)

Amt	Decl	Ex	Rec	Pay
25%	8/18/2003	9/16/2003	9/2/2003	9/15/2003
0.16Q	11/13/2003	11/25/2003	11/28/2003	12/15/2003
0.03Q	11/13/2003	11/25/2003	11/28/2003	12/15/2003
0.17Q	2/17/2004	2/25/2004	2/27/2004	3/15/2004

Indicated Div: $0.68 (Div. Reinv. Plan)

Valuation Analysis

Forecast P/E	N/A	Trailing P/E	19.32
Market Cap	$532.8 Million	Book Value	218.9 Million
Price/Book	N/A	Price/Sales	N/A

Dividend Achiever Status

Rank	73	10 Year Growth Rate	15.58%
Total Years of Dividend Growth			17

Business Summary: Commercial Banking (MIC: 8.1 SIC: 6021 NAIC:522110)

Harleysville National Corporation, is the parent bank holding company of Harleysville National Bank and Trust Company, Citizen's National Bank and Security National Bank. Through its banking subsidiaries, Co. is engaged in the full−service commercial banking and trust business, including accepting time and demand deposits, making secured and unsecured commercial and consumer loans, financing commercial transactions, making construction and mortgage loans and performing corporate pension and personal investment and trust services. Co. operates 40 branch offices located in ten counties throughout Eastern Pennsylvania. As of Dec 31 2003, Co. had total assets of $2.51 billion.

Recent Developments: For the year ended Dec 31 2003, net income climbed 7.3% to $35.3 million compared with $32.9 million the previous year. Interest income decreased 10.1% to $119.2 million from $132.6 million the year before. Interest expense fell 23.8% to $40.1 million from $52.6 million a year earlier. Net interest income slipped 1.1% to $79.1 million from $80.0 million in 2002. Total non−interest income jumped 22.7% to $27.6 million from $22.5 million the prior year due to an increase in earning asset volumes and a rise in the net interest margin. Total non−interest expense grew 5.9% to $59.6 million from $56.3 million the previous year.

Prospects: Prospects appear favorable as Co. feels that it is well positioned to benefit from an expected improvement in economic conditions in the coming year. Meanwhile, Co is benefiting from stronger returns and improved loan quality. Co.'s loan balance at Dec 31 2003 was $1.41 billion, up 5.6% from $1.33 billion at Dec 31 2002, driven by increases in commercial related and home equity loans. In addition, Co. continues to experience improvement in its asset quality. Looking ahead, Co. plans to continue its efforts to grow funding through its core deposits.

Financial Data

(US$ in Thousands)	12/31/2003	12/31/2002	12/31/2001	12/31/2000	12/31/1999	12/31/1998	12/31/1997	12/31/1996
Earnings Per Share	1.44	1.33	1.17	1.05	1.02	0.92	0.82	0.71
Tang. Book Val. Per Share	9.52	8.66	7.83	7.06	5.85	5.93	5.31	4.74
Dividends Per Share	0.650	0.564	0.495	0.430	0.360	0.340	0.300	0.190
Dividend Payout %	45.41	42.41	42.31	40.95	35.79	37.07	37.27	27.35
Income Statement								
Total Interest Income	119,200	132,630	138,679	131,811	106,117	87,597	80,202	73,718
Total Interest Expense	40,079	52,610	64,937	65,774	46,873	37,809	33,851	30,876
Net Interest Income	79,121	80,020	73,742	66,037	59,244	49,788	46,351	42,842
Provision for Loan Losses	3,200	4,370	3,930	2,312	1,907	2,140	2,500	2,082
Non−Interest Income	27,638	22,523	22,225	12,206	10,092	9,810	7,391	5,115
Non−Interest Expense	59,629	56,297	55,043	44,677	38,438	32,573	28,529	25,874
Income Before Taxes	43,930	41,876	36,994	31,254	28,991	24,885	22,713	20,001
Net Income	35,333	32,927	28,820	25,604	22,347	18,776	16,662	14,408
Average Shs. Outstg.	24,624	24,625	24,623	24,358	21,844	20,353	20,293	20,241
Balance Sheet								
Cash & Due from Banks	56,306	62,177	62,974	52,018	42,154	37,763	38,471	39,407
Securities Avail. for Sale	904,870	949,056	706,371	570,619	450,959	389,344	257,068	209,795
Net Loans & Leases	1,391,638	1,316,102	1,301,051	1,196,845	1,047,768	829,937	727,528	670,700
Total Assets	2,510,939	2,490,864	2,208,971	1,935,213	1,635,679	1,332,389	1,116,254	1,026,128
Total Deposits	1,979,081	1,979,822	1,746,862	1,489,050	1,231,265	1,033,968	919,071	847,649
Long−Term Obligations	177,750	167,750	132,750	110,750	130,250	93,500	17,000	35,000
Total Liabilities	2,283,886	2,284,658	2,019,622	1,761,677	1,506,019	1,209,578	1,006,462	928,497
Net Stockholders' Equity	227,053	206,206	189,349	173,536	129,660	122,811	109,792	97,631
Shares Outstanding	23,845	23,785	23,997	24,305	21,816	20,368	20,316	20,229
Statistical Record								
Return on Equity %	15.56	15.96	15.22	14.75	17.23	15.28	15.17	14.75
Return on Assets %	1.40	1.32	1.30	1.32	1.36	1.40	1.49	1.40
Equity/Assets %	9.04	8.27	8.57	8.96	7.92	9.21	9.83	9.51
Non−Int. Exp./Tot. Inc. %	40.60	36.28	34.20	31.02	33.07	33.44	32.56	32.82
Price Range	32.47-19.46	21.52-16.82	19.76-13.05	13.21-8.62	13.82-11.43	15.03-11.23	14.51-7.98	9.01-7.73
P/E Ratio	22.55-13.52	16.18-12.65	16.89-11.15	12.59-8.21	13.55-11.20	16.34-12.21	17.70-9.73	12.69-10.89
Average Yield %	2.76	2.93	3.07	5.00	2.96	2.48	2.76	2.28

Address: 483 Main Street, Harleysville, PA 19438
Telephone: (215) 256−8851
Web Site: www.hncbank.com

Officers: Walter E. Daller − Chmn., Pres., C.E.O., Gregg J. Wagner − Exec. V.P., C.O.O., Treas.

Investor Contact: (800) 423−3955
Institutional Holding
No of Institutions: 53
Shares: 4,027,434 **% Held:** 17

HAVERTY FURNITURE COS., INC.

Exchange	Symbol	Price	52Wk Range	Yield	P/E
NYS	HVT	$21.28 (3/31/2004)	24.35-10.50	1.17	19.70

*7 Year Price Score N/A   *NYSE Composite Index=100   *12 Month Price Score 121.0

Interim Earnings (Per Share)

Qtr.	Mar	Jun	Sep	Dec
2000	0.30	0.28	0.35	0.38
2001	0.20	0.12	0.26	0.48
2002	0.30	0.17	0.27	0.36
2003	0.22	0.10	0.33	0.43

Interim Dividends (Per Share)

Amt	Decl	Ex	Rec	Pay
0.058Q	4/25/2003	5/7/2003	5/9/2003	5/23/2003
0.058Q	7/21/2003	8/6/2003	8/8/2003	8/22/2003
0.063Q	10/30/2003	11/7/2003	11/12/2003	11/26/2003
0.063Q	2/6/2004	2/11/2004	2/16/2004	2/27/2004
	Indicated Div: $0.25			

Valuation Analysis

Forecast P/E	15.86	Trailing P/E	19.70
Market Cap	$364.7 Million	Book Value	252.7 Million
Price/Book	1.42	Price/Sales	0.48

Dividend Achiever Status

Rank	236	10 Year Growth Rate	5.90%
Total Years of Dividend Growth			33

Business Summary: Retail – Furniture &Home Furnishings (MIC: 5.9 SIC: 5712 NAIC:442110)

Haverty Furniture Companies is a full-service home furnishings retailer with 113 stores in 15 southern and central states as of Dec 31 2003. Co.'s stores, primarily targeted at middle and upper-middle income families, offer a wide selection of well-known brand names of furniture, such as Broyhill, Lane, Bernhardt, La-Z-Boy, Sealy and Serta. Co. also carries merchandise that bears the Havertys brand. Co. offers a revolving charge credit plan with credit limits determined through its on-line credit approval system and an additional credit program outsourced to a third-party finance company

Recent Developments: For the year ended Dec 31 2003, income was unchanged at $24.3 million, before an accounting change gain of $1.1 million, compared with net income the year before. Net sales advanced 5.8% to $744.6 million from $704.0 million a year earlier. The improvement in sales was primarily attributed to increased demand for Co.'s merchandise offerings. Gross profit rose to $365.7 million, or 49.1% as a percentage of sales, versus $339.4 million, or 48.2% as a percentage of sales, a year earlier. Comparable-store sales in 2003 increased 1.0% year over year. During 2003, Co. paid down $30.1 million of debt.

Prospects: Going forward, Co. expects to achieve significant savings from its new distribution methods. Co.'s quick delivery capabilities are a competitive strength and better efficiencies are expected to be achieved as Co. refines the process for optimal frequency of deliveries to local markets and the most economical routing of home deliveries. Co. began construction of its new Florida Distribution Center in Lakeland in February and expects to open the new hub in October 2004. Moreover, Co. intends to use this additional infrastructure to more efficiently serve its customers in Florida. In addition, Co. plans to continue to expand in existing markets in 2004.

Financial Data
(US$ in Thousands)

	12/31/2003	12/31/2002	12/31/2001	12/31/2000	12/31/1999	12/31/1998	12/31/1997	12/31/1996
Earnings Per Share	1.08	1.10	1.06	1.31	1.19	0.72	0.57	0.52
Cash Flow Per Share	3.65	3.84	1.39	0.78	3.04	2.36	1.06	(0.13)
Tang. Book Val. Per Share	11.02	10.30	9.45	8.63	7.81	7.07	6.79	6.41
Dividends Per Share	0.235	0.220	0.210	0.203	0.190	0.165	0.160	0.153
Dividend Payout %	21.76	20.00	19.81	15.50	15.96	22.92	28.07	29.42
Income Statement								
Total Revenues	751,027	713,010	689,178	693,575	633,721	557,258	506,118	470,250
Total Indirect Exp.	331,600	307,196	288,088	280,753	253,921	231,407	211,887	196,861
Depreciation & Amort.	17,199	15,903	16,239	15,738	14,844	14,272	13,792	12,644
Operating Income	40,442	41,287	46,602	55,324	54,008	40,102	35,028	33,413
Net Interest Inc./(Exp.)	(3,872)	(6,561)	(10,581)	(11,707)	(11,402)	(13,183)	(14,330)	(14,463)
Income Taxes	14,444	14,588	13,630	16,010	15,470	9,460	7,400	6,885
Income from Cont Ops	24,281	...	...	27,851	...	...	...	...
Net Income	25,331	24,315	22,710	24,495	27,400	16,835	13,387	12,247
Average Shs. Outstg.	22,437	22,145	21,502	21,203	22,982	23,404	23,340	23,388
Balance Sheet								
Cash & Cash Equivalents	31,591	3,764	727	3,256	1,762	1,874	390	414
Total Current Assets	256,485	263,825	305,755	295,992	271,678	278,177	289,629	283,130
Total Assets	433,202	404,839	460,905	448,163	404,648	392,901	406,514	399,875
Total Current Liabilities	104,196	101,520	123,903	95,520	98,434	70,467	132,908	125,440
Long−Term Obligations	65,402	69,821	131,599	170,369	134,687	161,778	111,489	120,434
Net Stockholders' Equity	252,736	224,881	201,398	179,375	168,793	158,058	159,554	150,916
Net Working Capital	152,289	162,305	181,852	200,472	173,244	207,710	156,721	157,690
Shares Outstanding	22,931	21,832	21,302	20,773	21,610	22,330	23,482	23,510
Statistical Record								
Operating Profit Margin %	5.38	5.79	6.76	7.97	8.52	7.19	6.92	7.10
Return on Equity %	9.60	10.81	11.27	15.52	16.23	10.65	8.39	8.11
Return on Assets %	5.60	6.00	4.92	6.21	6.77	4.28	3.29	3.06
Debt/Total Assets %	15.09	17.24	28.55	38.01	33.28	41.17	27.42	30.11
Price Range	24.35−9.38	20.96−9.57	16.55−9.32	13.38−8.19	18.97−9.16	11.22−8.84	...	...
P/E Ratio	22.55−8.69	19.05−8.70	15.61−8.79	10.21−6.25	15.94−7.69	15.58−12.28	...	...
Average Yield %	1.44	1.41	1.57	1.84	1.39	1.64	N/A	N/A

Address: 780 Johnson Ferry Road, Atlanta, GA 30342 **Telephone:** (404) 443−2900 **Web Site:** www.havertys.com	**Officers:** Clarence H. Ridley − Chmn., Clarence H. Smith − Pres., C.E.O. **Transfer Agents:**SunTrust Bank, Atlanta, GA	**Investor Contact:** (404) 443−2900 **Institutional Holding** **No of Institutions:** 22 **Shares:** 2,576,185 **% Held:** −

HEALTH CARE PROPERTY INVESTORS, INC.

Exchange	Symbol	Price	52Wk Range	Yield	P/E
NYS	HCP	$28.30 (3/31/2004)	29.09–16.76	5.87	30.11

*7 Year Price Score 121.0 *NYSE Composite Index=100 *12 Month Price Score 102.5

Interim Earnings (Per Share)

Qtr.	Mar	Jun	Sep	Dec
2000	0.26	0.27	0.23	0.30
2001	0.19	0.27	0.16	0.27
2002	0.21	0.29	0.26	0.20
2003	0.18	0.18	0.26	0.32

Interim Dividends (Per Share)

Amt	Decl	Ex	Rec	Pay
0.415Q	7/24/2003	7/31/2003	8/4/2003	8/20/2003
0.415Q	10/23/2003	10/31/2003	11/4/2003	11/20/2003
0.418Q	1/22/2004	2/2/2004	2/4/2004	2/19/2004
100%	1/22/2004	3/2/2004	2/4/2004	3/1/2004
		Indicated Div: $1.66		

Valuation Analysis

Forecast P/E	13.19	Trailing P/E	30.11
Market Cap	$1.6 Billion	Book Value	1.2 Billion
Price/Book	2.87	Price/Sales	8.36

Dividend Achiever Status

Rank	233	10 Year Growth Rate	6.05%
Total Years of Dividend Growth		18	

Business Summary: Property, Real Estate &Development (MIC: 8.3 SIC: 6798 NAIC:525930)

Health Care Property Investors is a real estate investment trust that invests in healthcare–related facilities throughout the United States, including long–term care facilities, congregate care and assisted living facilities, acute care and rehabilitation hospitals, medical office buildings and physician group practice clinics. Co.'s investment portfolio as of Dec 31 2003 included 554 facilities in 44 states. Co.'s investments included 173 long–term care facilities, 124 retirement and assisted living facilities, 196 medical office buildings, 31 hospitals and 30 other health care facilities.

Recent Developments: For the year ended Dec 31 2003, income from continuing operations increased 11.0% to $155.1 million from $139.8 million a year earlier. Results for 2003 included an impairment loss on real estate of $2.1 million. Earnings excluded income of $3.5 million in 2003 and a loss of $2.4 million in 2002 from discontinued operations. Total revenue climbed 14.6% to $400.2 million from $349.1 million a year earlier. Notably, rental income rose 6.7% to $248.8 million, and medical office building rental income grew 12.2% to $99.9 million. Income from operations advanced 11.3% to $164.8 million. Funds from operations rose 3.5% to $206.2 million.

Prospects: As of Dec 31 2003, Co. had contractual commitments to acquire or construct $116.0 million of health care real estate and capital projects including the remaining $29.0 million of construction related to the MedCap Properties, LLC acquisition. Co. expects the acquisitions and construction will be substantially completed by the end of 2004. On Jan 22 2004, Co. declared a 100.0% stock dividend to effect a 2–for–1 split. Looking ahead to 2004, Co. expects earnings to range from $2.27 to $2.42 per diluted share on a pre–split basis. Co. projects diluted funds from operations for 2004 to range between $3.52 and $3.62 per share on a pre–split basis.

Financial Data

(US$ in Thousands)	12/31/2003	12/31/2002	12/31/2001	12/31/2000	12/31/1999	12/31/1998	12/31/1997	12/31/1996
Earnings Per Share	0.94	0.96	0.89	1.06	1.12	1.27	1.09	1.05
Tang. Book Val. Per Share	8.81	8.46	8.62	8.55	8.99	6.57	6.36	5.87
Dividends Per Share	1.660	1.630	1.550	1.470	1.390	1.310	1.230	1.150
Dividend Payout %	176.59	168.91	174.15	138.02	123.55	103.14	112.32	109.52
Income Statement								
Rental Income	248,773	331,737	310,602	306,830	199,570	138,439	113,920	104,627
Total Income	394,405	359,576	332,460	329,807	224,793	161,549	128,503	120,393
Total Indirect Exp.	105,916	103,330	97,337	87,856	75,694	46,142	33,232	29,975
Depreciation	79,095	75,722	84,098	72,590	47,860	32,523	25,656	23,149
Eqty Earns/Minority Int.	2,889	...	...	...	...	...	...	...
Income from Cont Ops	155,073	137,178	...	133,493	...	...	...	...
Net Income	158,585	137,380	121,166	133,767	96,225	87,167	64,789	60,641
Average Shs. Outstg.	126,130	116,294	107,950	102,200	69,722	67,328	57,988	57,652
Balance Sheet								
Cash & Cash Equivalents	17,768	8,495	8,408	58,623	7,696	4,504	4,084	2,811
Ttl Real Estate Inv.	2,505,845	2,371,411	2,194,556	2,100,509	2,192,988	1,131,119	786,502	623,734
Total Assets	3,035,957	2,748,417	2,431,153	2,398,703	2,469,390	1,356,612	940,964	753,653
Long–Term Obligations	1,407,284	1,333,848	1,057,752	1,158,928	1,179,507	709,045	452,858	379,504
Total Liabilities	1,595,340	1,467,528	1,184,429	1,254,148	1,269,133	761,193	498,695	416,847
Net Stockholders' Equity	1,440,617	1,280,889	1,246,724	1,144,555	1,200,257	595,419	442,269	336,806
Shares Outstanding	131,039	118,939	112,773	101,747	102,842	61,974	60,432	57,356
Statistical Record								
Net Inc.+Depr./Assets %	7.82	7.70	8.40	8.60	5.80	8.80	9.60	11.10
Return on Equity %	10.56	10.70	9.71	11.66	8.01	14.63	14.64	18.00
Return on Assets %	5.01	4.99	4.98	5.56	3.89	6.42	6.88	8.04
Price Range	25.63-16.68	22.43-18.11	19.51-14.78	14.97-11.84	16.47-10.97	19.63-14.44	20.16-16.00	18.75-15.50
P/E Ratio	27.27-17.74	23.36-18.86	21.92-16.61	14.12-11.17	14.70-9.79	15.45-11.37	18.49-14.68	17.86-14.76
Average Yield %	8.01	8.00	8.87	10.77	10.09	7.57	6.83	6.81

Address: 4675 MacArthur Court, Newport Beach, CA 92660	**Officers:** Kenneth B. Roath – Chmn., James F. Flaherty III – Pres., C.E.O.	**Investor Contact:** (949) 221–0600
Telephone: (949) 221–0600	**Transfer Agents:**The Bank of New York, New York, NY	**Institutional Holding**
Web Site: www.hcpi.com		**No of Institutions:** 20
		Shares: 1,759,046 **% Held:** –

HEALTHCARE REALTY TRUST, INC.

Exchange	Symbol	Price	52Wk Range	Yield	P/E
NYS	HR	$42.70 (3/31/2004)	42.83-24.70	5.90	29.25

*7 Year Price Score 122.0 *NYSE Composite Index=100 *12 Month Price Score 101.7

Interim Earnings (Per Share)

Qtr.	Mar	Jun	Sep	Dec
2000	0.47	0.49	0.46	0.40
2001	0.47	0.44	0.45	0.45
2002	0.44	0.50	0.44	0.17
2003	0.45	0.42	0.42	0.37

Interim Dividends (Per Share)

Amt	Decl	Ex	Rec	Pay
0.615Q	4/22/2003	5/13/2003	5/15/2003	6/5/2003
0.62Q	7/22/2003	8/13/2003	8/15/2003	9/4/2003
0.625Q	10/28/2003	11/12/2003	11/14/2003	12/4/2003
0.63Q	1/27/2004	2/11/2004	2/13/2004	3/4/2004

Indicated Div: $2.52 (Div. Reinv. Plan)

Valuation Analysis

Forecast P/E	11.88	Trailing P/E	29.25
Market Cap	$1.8 Billion	Book Value	911.1 Million
Price/Book	1.48	Price/Sales	7.02

Dividend Achiever Status

Rank	65	10 Year Growth Rate	16.19%
Total Years of Dividend Growth	10		

Business Summary: Property, Real Estate &Development (MIC: 8.3 SIC: 6798 NAIC:525930)

Healthcare Realty Trust is a self-managed and self-administered real estate investment trust (REIT) that integrates owning, acquiring, managing and developing real estate properties and mortgages associated with the delivery of healthcare services throughout the U.S. Co. focuses predominantly on outpatient healthcare facilities, which are designed to provide medical services outside of traditional inpatient hospital or nursing home settings. As of Dec 31 2003, Co. had investments of $1.70 billion in 218 properties and mortgages located in 30 states, and affiliated with 61 healthcare-related entities.

Recent Developments: For the year ended Dec 31 2003, Co. reported income from continuing operations of $69.2 million compared with income of $61.1 million the year before. Results for 2003 and 2002 excluded net gains of $1.3 million and $9.0 million, respectively, from discontinued operations. Revenues rose 3.4% to $192.0 million from $185.7 million the year before. Property operating income grew 15.4% to $86.0 million. However, mortgage interest income fee decreased 21.5% to $10.4 million, due mainly to the repayment of 24 mortgage loans. Master lease rental income declined 3.3% to $89.0 million from $92.0 million a year earlier.

Prospects: On Jan 8 2004, Co. announced it has reached agreements in principle to acquire 18 medical office facilities from various healthcare companies in Tennessee, Arizona, Michigan, Maryland, Washington, D.C. and Illinois. These acquisitions, which are expected to be completed in the first quarter of 2004, are valued at approximately $166.0 million. Separately, Co. invested approximately $13.2 million in two developments in progress, which have a total remaining funded commitment of about $30.1 million. Co. also began construction of another medical office building that should have a total funding commitment of approximately $21.8 million.

Financial Data

(US$ in Thousands)	12/31/2003	12/31/2002	12/31/2001	12/31/2000	12/31/1999	12/31/1998	12/31/1997	12/31/1996
Earnings Per Share	1.66	1.55	1.81	1.82	1.99	1.63	1.68	1.49
Tang. Book Val. Per Share	21.06	21.71	24.40	25.00	25.44	25.57	19.52	17.69
Dividends Per Share	2.470	2.390	2.310	2.230	2.150	2.070	1.990	1.910
Dividend Payout %	148.79	154.19	127.62	122.52	108.04	126.99	118.45	128.18
Income Statement								
Rental Income	91,516	101,210	105,711	105,065	98,955	48,777	40,298	35,329
Interest Income	10,441	13,308	17,254	22,755	26,254	...	...	...
Total Income	191,997	194,527	194,538	195,338	187,257	93,104	59,796	38,574
Total Indirect Exp.	88,193	93,629	77,751	72,874	67,403	39,568	20,615	11,498
Depreciation	42,195	41,598	41,126	39,507	39,039	16,464	11,800	8,996
Interest Expense	34,601	34,195	38,110	42,995	38,603	13,057	7,969	7,344
Income from Cont Ops	69,203	...	...	...	...	...	...	...
Net Income	70,507	70,091	79,887	79,801	86,027	40,479	31,212	19,732
Average Shs. Outstg.	41,780	41,606	40,463	40,301	39,810	24,524	18,572	13,254
Balance Sheet								
Cash & Cash Equivalents	3,840	402	2,930	2,365	4,386	14,411	5,325	1,354
Ttl Real Estate Inv.	1,340,009	1,292,646	1,349,664	1,358,826	1,315,150	1,337,439	470,981	416,034
Total Assets	1,525,710	1,489,546	1,555,910	1,587,076	1,607,964	1,615,423	488,514	427,505
Long−Term Obligations	590,281	545,063	505,222	536,781	563,884	559,924	101,300	168,618
Total Liabilities	623,432	581,347	543,823	579,039	590,061	597,719	112,042	181,541
Net Stockholders' Equity	902,278	908,199	1,012,087	1,008,037	1,017,903	1,017,704	376,472	245,964
Shares Outstanding	42,823	41,823	41,465	40,314	40,004	39,792	19,286	13,898
Statistical Record								
Net Inc.+Depr./Assets %	7.38	7.50	7.78	7.52	7.78	3.52	8.80	6.33
Return on Equity %	7.66	7.71	7.89	7.91	8.45	3.97	8.29	8.02
Return on Assets %	4.53	4.70	5.13	5.02	5.35	2.50	6.38	4.61
Price Range	36.45−24.42	32.15−27.28	28.25−21.38	21.44−15.63	22.81−14.69	29.94−21.25	29.88−25.50	26.88−20.88
P/E Ratio	21.96−14.71	20.74−17.60	15.61−11.81	11.78−8.59	11.46−7.38	18.37−13.04	17.78−15.18	18.04−14.01
Average Yield %	8.06	7.94	9.14	12.25	10.90	7.86	7.17	8.33

Address: 3310 West End Avenue, Nashville, TN 37203 Telephone: (615) 269−8175 Web Site: www.healthcarerealty.com	Officers: David R. Emery − Chmn., C.E.O., Roger O. West − Exec. V.P., Gen. Couns. Transfer Agents:BankBoston, Boston, MA	Investor Contact: (781) 575−3400 Institutional Holding No of Institutions: 4 Shares: 268,149 % Held: −

HEINZ (H.J.) CO.

Exchange	Symbol	Price	52Wk Range	Yield	P/E
NYS	HNZ	$37.29 (3/31/2004)	38.95–29.05	2.90	21.43

*7 Year Price Score 78.1 *NYSE Composite Index=100 *12 Month Price Score 96.9

Interim Earnings (Per Share)

Qtr.	Jul	Oct	Jan	Apr
2000–01	0.57	0.54	0.77	(0.47)
2001–02	0.57	0.59	0.57	0.63
2002–03	0.50	0.60	0.37	0.10
2003–05	0.53	0.54	0.57	...

Interim Dividends (Per Share)

Amt	Decl	Ex	Rec	Pay
0.27Q	6/11/2003	6/20/2003	6/24/2003	7/10/2003
0.27Q	9/12/2003	9/19/2003	9/23/2003	10/10/2003
0.27Q	11/12/2003	12/19/2003	12/23/2003	1/10/2004
0.27Q	3/10/2004	3/22/2004	3/24/2004	4/10/2004

Indicated Div: $1.08 (Div. Reinv. Plan)

Valuation Analysis

Forecast P/E	14.79	Trailing P/E	21.43
Market Cap	$13.1 Billion	Book Value	1.8 Billion
Price/Book	7.13	Price/Sales	1.72

Dividend Achiever Status

Rank	112	10 Year Growth Rate	12.44%
Total Years of Dividend Growth		40	

Business Summary: Food (MIC: 4.1 SIC: 2099 NAIC:311941)

H.J. Heinz manufactures and markets an extensive line of processed food products throughout the world, including ketchup and other sauces/condiments, frozen dinners, pet food, baby food, frozen potato products and canned soups, vegetables and fruits. Major U.S. brands include *Heinz, Ore–Ida, Boston Market* and *Smart Ones*. Overseas, well–known brands include *Plasmon, Pudliszki, Orlando, Wattie's, Olivine, Farley's, ABC,* and *Juran.*

Recent Developments: For the three months ended Jan 28 2004, net income totaled $202.2 million, up 55.7% versus income from continuing operations of $129.8 million in the corresponding period the year before. Results for the prior year included one–time pre–tax charges of $61.6 million. Sales slipped 0.4% to $2.10 billion from $2.11 billion a year earlier. Sales gains from favorable foreign currency exchange rates were more than offset by the reduction in sales stemming from divestitures. Gross profit was $779.2 million, or 37.2% of sales, compared with $762.0 million, or 36.2% of sales, the previous year. Operating income climbed 10.5% to $355.4 million from $321.6 million in 2002.

Prospects: Co. anticipates full fiscal–2004 earnings per share in the range of $2.19 to $2.21 per share, along with net sales growth of between 1.0% and 2.0%. Results are being positively affected by improved marketing and new product introductions. Co. is enjoying strong customer response to its new *Ore–Ida®* Extra Crispy frozen french fries, which were launched in January 2004, and its new *Smart Ones®* "Truth About Carbs" line of frozen entrees. Meanwhile, Co. is taking aggressive steps to reduce costs in an effort to improve profitability. Co. is targeting capital expenditures of about 2.5% of net sales in fiscal 2004, and between 2.5% and 3.0% of net sales in fiscal 2005.

Financial Data

(US$ in Thousands)	9 Mos	6 Mos	3 Mos	04/30/2003	05/01/2002	05/02/2001	05/03/2000	04/28/1999
Earnings Per Share	1.64	1.07	0.53	1.57	2.36	1.41	2.47	1.29
Cash Flow Per Share	2.30	1.39	0.75	2.55	2.52	1.44	1.50	2.47
Dividends Per Share	1.080	1.210	1.350	1.480	1.600	1.540	1.440	1.340
Dividend Payout %	65.85	113.55	254.71	94.58	68.11	109.57	58.50	104.06
Income Statement								
Total Revenues	6,083,166	3,985,985	1,895,524	8,236,836	9,431,000	9,430,422	9,407,949	9,299,610
Total Indirect Exp.	1,214,063	790,183	358,000	1,758,658	1,746,702	2,564,450	1,421,708	2,245,431
Depreciation & Amort.	169,780	112,061	56,232	214,762	301,697	299,166	306,483	302,212
Operating Income	1,053,478	698,111	349,076	1,173,816	1,590,451	982,354	1,733,099	1,109,312
Net Interest Inc./(Exp.)	(144,353)	(96,216)	(46,472)	(192,449)	(266,824)	(310,265)	(244,418)	(233,731)
Income Taxes	293,557	193,659	98,800	313,372	444,701	178,140	573,123	360,790
Income from Cont Ops	580,549	378,312	186,825	555,359	...	494,918	...	...
Net Income	607,749	405,512	214,025	566,285	833,889	478,012	890,553	474,341
Average Shs. Outstg.	354,254	354,258	354,522	354,144	352,871	351,041	360,095	367,830
Balance Sheet								
Cash & Cash Equivalents	1,016,166	848,696	804,734	801,732	206,921	144,220	154,129	123,121
Total Current Assets	3,609,028	3,456,619	3,224,421	3,284,320	3,373,566	3,116,814	3,169,949	2,886,778
Total Assets	9,909,977	9,410,200	9,060,814	9,224,751	10,278,354	9,035,150	8,850,657	8,053,634
Total Current Liabilities	2,340,734	1,871,450	1,760,988	1,926,134	2,509,169	3,655,097	2,126,070	2,786,322
Long–Term Obligations	4,717,385	4,971,816	4,608,272	4,776,143	4,642,968	3,014,853	3,935,826	2,472,206
Net Stockholders' Equity	1,797,678	1,541,908	1,358,297	1,199,157	1,718,616	1,373,727	1,595,856	1,803,004
Net Working Capital	1,268,294	1,585,169	1,463,433	1,358,186	864,397	(538,283)	1,043,879	100,456
Shares Outstanding	352,096	351,868	351,675	351,448	350,904	348,948	347,443	359,127
Statistical Record								
Operating Profit Margin %	17.31	17.51	18.41	14.25	16.86	10.41	18.42	11.92
Return on Equity %	32.29	24.53	13.75	46.31	48.52	36.02	55.80	26.30
Return on Assets %	5.85	4.02	2.06	6.02	8.11	5.47	10.06	5.88
Debt/Total Assets %	47.60	52.83	50.85	51.77	45.17	33.36	44.46	30.69
Price Range	36.62–29.71	35.67–29.71	34.40–29.71	43.19–29.05	46.96–38.12	47.63–35.44	53.88–31.06	61.25–44.56
P/E Ratio	22.33–18.12	33.34–27.77	64.91–56.06	27.51–18.50	19.90–16.15	33.78–25.13	21.81–12.58	47.48–34.54
Average Yield %	3.16	3.62	4.13	4.24	3.83	3.76	3.39	2.46

Address: 600 Grant Street, Pittsburgh, PA 15219 Telephone: (412) 456–5700 Web Site: www.heinz.com	Officers: William R. Johnson – Chmn., Pres., C.E.O., Arthur Winkleblack – Exec. V.P., C.F.O. Transfer Agents:ChaseMellon Shareholder Services, L.L.C., Ridgefield Park, NJ	Investor Contact:412–456–6034 Institutional Holding No of Institutions: 548 Shares: 221,630,503 % Held: 63.10%

HELMERICH & PAYNE, INC.

Exchange	Symbol	Price	52Wk Range	Yield	P/E
NYS	HP	$28.65 (3/31/2004)	32.34–23.77	1.12	63.67

*7 Year Price Score 92.6   *NYSE Composite Index=100   *12 Month Price Score 84.4

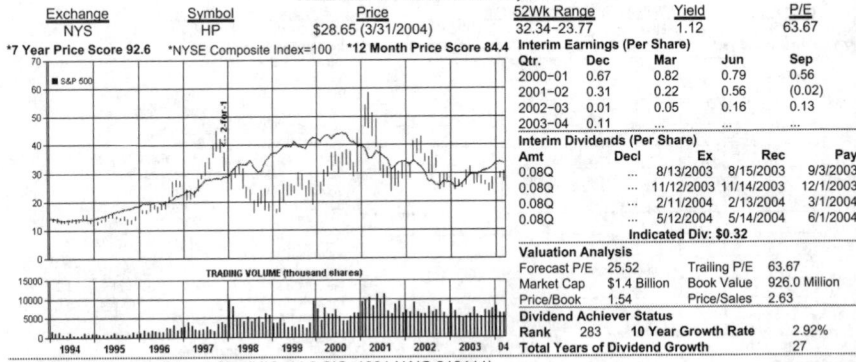

Interim Earnings (Per Share)
Qtr.	Dec	Mar	Jun	Sep
2000–01	0.67	0.82	0.79	0.56
2001–02	0.31	0.22	0.56	(0.02)
2002–03	0.01	0.05	0.16	0.13
2003–04	0.11	...	...	...

Interim Dividends (Per Share)
Amt	Decl	Ex	Rec	Pay
0.08Q	...	8/13/2003	8/15/2003	9/3/2003
0.08Q	...	11/12/2003	11/14/2003	12/1/2003
0.08Q	...	2/11/2004	2/13/2004	3/1/2004
0.08Q	...	5/12/2004	5/14/2004	6/1/2004
		Indicated Div: $0.32		

Valuation Analysis
Forecast P/E	25.52	Trailing P/E	63.67
Market Cap	$1.4 Billion	Book Value	926.0 Million
Price/Book	1.54	Price/Sales	2.63

Dividend Achiever Status
Rank	283	10 Year Growth Rate	2.92%
Total Years of Dividend Growth			27

Business Summary: Oil and Gas (MIC: 14.2 SIC: 1381 NAIC:213111)

Helmerich & Payne is engaged in contract drilling of oil and gas wells for others. Co. is also engaged in the ownership, development, and operation of commercial real estate. Co.'s contract drilling business is composed of three business segments: domestic land drilling, domestic offshore platform drilling and international drilling. Co.'s domestic contract drilling is conducted primarily in Oklahoma, Texas, Wyoming, and Louisiana, and offshore from platforms in the Gulf of Mexico and California. Co. also operates in Venezuela, Ecuador, Colombia, Argentina, Bolivia, Equatorial Guinea, and Hungary. As of Dec 31 2003, Co.'s total rig fleet was comprised of 127 drilling rigs.

Recent Developments: For the three months ended Dec 31 2003, net income increased to $5.6 million compared with $607,000 in the corresponding year–earlier period. Total revenues advanced 22.6% to $138.9 million from $113.3 million the previous year and included income from investments of $4.0 million and $809,000, respectively. Co. attributed the operating improvement to sharply higher profits from its U.S. land and international segments, partially offset by lower U.S. offshore platform rig results. The latter unit was negatively affected by one rig being stacked and two rigs going from full dayrate to standby status.

Prospects: Co.'s near–term outlook has turned somewhat positive, reflecting the recent strength in commodity prices that should lead to additional U.S. land rig opportunities and an improving international outlook. Also, Co. noted that it has reached an agreement for H&P platform Rig 100 to work in the Gulf of Mexico beginning in March of 2004, which should aid in improving the performance of Co.'s U.S. offshore platform rig unit. Separately, Co. stated that it intends to suspend construction activities of its FlexRig3 project following the completion of the final two rigs in March of 2004 and review future possibilities and plans for the FlexRig project.

Financial Data
(US$ in Thousands)	3 Mos	09/30/2003	09/30/2002	09/30/2001	09/30/2000	09/30/1999	09/30/1998	09/30/1997
Earnings Per Share	0.11	0.35	1.07	2.84	1.64	0.86	2.00	1.69
Cash Flow Per Share	0.50	1.90	3.00	5.49	4.03	3.18	2.24	3.32
Tang. Book Val. Per Share	18.44	18.29	17.89	20.59	19.12	17.09	16.06	15.60
Dividends Per Share	0.320	0.320	0.305	0.300	0.285	0.280	0.270	0.260
Dividend Payout %	290.90	91.42	28.50	10.56	17.37	32.55	13.75	15.38
Income Statement								
Total Revenues	138,894	515,284	510,928	826,854	631,095	564,319	636,640	517,859
Total Indirect Exp.	131,341	123,516	81,838	178,406	174,323	160,570	137,412	110,138
Depreciation & Amort.	22,268	82,513	61,447	87,309	110,851	109,167	88,350	71,691
Operating Income	10,775	46,231	92,200	235,070	139,839	71,419	153,162	131,627
Net Interest Inc./(Exp.)	(3,222)	(12,289)	(980)	32	(3,076)	(6,481)	(942)	(4,212)
Income Taxes	4,526	14,649	40,573	93,027	57,684	25,706	56,677	45,511
Eqty Earns/Minority Int.	(620)	(1,420)	3,059	2,179	3,221	3,556	5,611	2,282
Income from Cont Ops	...	...	53,706	...	...	...	...	...
Net Income	5,629	17,873	63,517	144,254	82,300	42,788	101,154	84,186
Average Shs. Outstg.	50,667	50,596	50,345	50,772	50,035	49,817	50,565	49,779
Balance Sheet								
Cash & Cash Equivalents	35,497	38,189	46,883	122,962	108,087	21,758	24,476	27,963
Total Current Assets	205,335	197,531	178,751	331,412	265,144	160,624	184,345	158,004
Total Assets	1,440,075	1,415,835	1,227,313	1,364,507	1,259,492	1,109,699	1,090,430	1,033,595
Total Current Liabilities	88,471	88,618	72,899	121,221	78,894	71,904	125,484	95,167
Long–Term Obligations	200,000	200,000	100,000	50,000	50,000	50,000	50,000	...
Net Stockholders' Equity	926,047	917,251	895,170	1,026,477	955,703	848,109	793,148	780,580
Net Working Capital	116,864	108,913	105,852	210,191	186,250	88,720	58,861	62,837
Shares Outstanding	50,204	50,140	50,010	49,852	49,980	49,625	49,383	50,028
Statistical Record								
Operating Profit Margin %	7.75	8.97	18.04	28.42	22.15	12.65	24.05	25.41
Return on Equity %	0.60	1.94	5.99	14.05	8.61	5.04	12.75	10.78
Return on Assets %	0.39	1.26	4.37	10.57	6.53	3.85	9.27	8.14
Debt/Total Assets %	13.88	14.12	8.14	3.66	3.96	4.50	4.58	
Price Range	28.37–23.77	34.23–23.57	42.91–25.13	58.51–23.74	38.31–19.13	30.19–16.06	44.97–16.25	40.00–21.00
P/E Ratio	257.9–216.1	97.80–67.34	40.10–23.49	20.60–8.36	23.36–11.66	35.10–18.68	22.48–8.13	23.67–12.43
Average Yield %	1.22	1.17	0.89	0.77	0.96	1.24	0.93	0.94

Address: Utica at Twenty–First Street, Tulsa, OK 74114	Officers: W. H. Helmerich III – Chmn., Hans C. Helmerich – Pres., C.E.O.	Investor Contact:918–742–5531
Telephone: (918) 742–5531	Transfer Agents:UMB Bank, Kansas City, MO	Institutional Holding
Web Site: www.hpinc.com		No of Institutions: 5
		Shares: 3,726,949 % Held: –

HERSHEY FOODS CORP.

Exchange	Symbol	Price	52Wk Range	Yield	P/E
NYS	HSY	$82.85 (3/31/2004)	85.45-62.82	1.91	23.54

*7 Year Price Score 117.2 *NYSE Composite Index=100 *12 Month Price Score 97.9

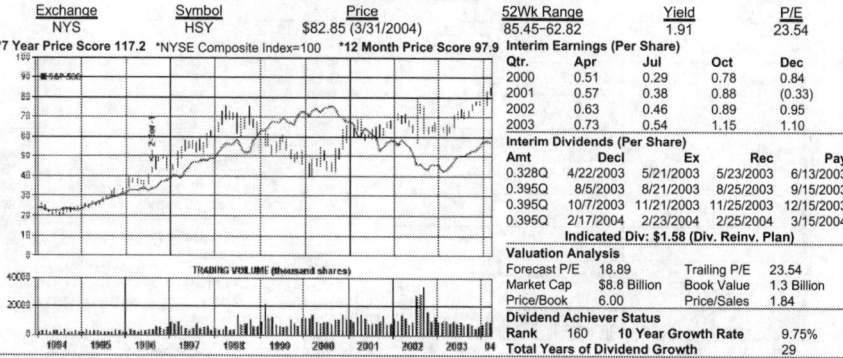

Interim Earnings (Per Share)

Qtr.	Apr	Jul	Oct	Dec
2000	0.51	0.29	0.78	0.84
2001	0.57	0.38	0.88	(0.33)
2002	0.63	0.46	0.89	0.95
2003	0.73	0.54	1.15	1.10

Interim Dividends (Per Share)

Amt	Decl	Ex	Rec	Pay
0.328Q	4/22/2003	5/21/2003	5/23/2003	6/13/2003
0.395Q	8/5/2003	8/21/2003	8/25/2003	9/15/2003
0.395Q	10/7/2003	11/21/2003	11/25/2003	12/15/2003
0.395Q	2/17/2004	2/23/2004	2/25/2004	3/15/2004

Indicated Div: $1.58 (Div. Reinv. Plan)

Valuation Analysis

Forecast P/E	18.89	Trailing P/E	23.54
Market Cap	$8.8 Billion	Book Value	1.3 Billion
Price/Book	6.00	Price/Sales	1.84

Dividend Achiever Status

Rank	160	10 Year Growth Rate	9.75%
Total Years of Dividend Growth		29

Business Summary: Food (MIC: 4.1 SIC: 2066 NAIC:311320)

Hershey Foods and its subsidiaries is engaged in the manufacture, distribution and sale of consumer food products including: chocolate and non-chocolate confectionery products sold in the form of bar goods, bagged items and boxed items; and grocery products sold in the form of baking ingredients, chocolate drink mixes, peanut butter, dessert toppings and beverages. Co.'s products are marketed in over 90 countries worldwide under more than 50 brands. Principal confectionery brands include: *Hershey's®, Reese's®, Mr. Goodbar®, Jolly Rancher®, Kit Kat®, Milk Duds®, Whoppers®, York®, Twizzlers®, Super Bubble®, Ice Breakers®, Breath Savers®and Care*free®*.

Recent Developments: For the year ended Dec 31 2003, income advanced 15.2% to $465.0 million, before an accounting change charge of $7.4 million, compared with net income of $403.6 million in the previous year. Results for 2003 and 2002 included net business realignment charges of $23.4 million and $27.6 million, respectively. Results for 2003 also included a gain on the sale of business of $8.3 million. Earnings for 2003 benefited from a more profitable sales mix, continued supply chain efficiency, and solid expense controls across the organization. Net sales increased 1.3% to $4.17 billion from $4.12 billion a year earlier. Gross profit as a percentage of sales improved to 39.0% from 37.8% in 2002.

Prospects: Looking ahead, Co. expects to leverage its core brands and advantaged business systems to build sales, market share, and profitability while managing higher costs for raw materials. Co.'s plans for 2004 include accelerating new product efforts and introducing exciting on-trend, higher-margin items to the category. In 2004, Co. plans to invest in new growth platforms both within its core confectionery market, as well as in the broader snack market. For full-year 2004, Co. expects net sales to grow from 3.0% to 4.0% and diluted earnings per share to grow between 9.0% and 11.0%.

Financial Data

(US$ in Thousands)	12/31/2003	12/31/2002	12/31/2001	12/31/2000	12/31/1999	12/31/1998	12/31/1997	12/31/1996
Earnings Per Share	3.52	2.93	1.50	2.42	3.26	2.34	2.23	1.77
Cash Flow Per Share	4.48	4.54	5.13	2.97	2.31	2.67	3.15	3.01
Tang. Book Val. Per Share	6.58	7.10	4.32	5.14	4.68	3.57	2.10	3.89
Dividends Per Share	1.440	1.260	1.160	1.080	1.000	0.920	0.840	0.760
Dividend Payout %	41.05	43.00	77.66	44.62	30.67	39.31	37.66	42.94
Income Statement								
Total Revenues	4,172,551	4,120,317	4,557,241	4,220,976	3,970,924	4,435,615	4,302,236	3,989,308
Total Indirect Exp.	823,139	860,978	1,459,804	1,127,175	570,270	1,167,895	1,183,130	1,194,791
Depreciation & Amort.	180,567	177,908	190,494	175,964	163,308	158,161	152,750	133,476
Operating Income	796,356	698,287	412,634	622,650	802,145	642,663	630,210	527,780
Net Interest Inc./(Exp.)	(63,529)	(60,722)	(69,093)	(76,011)	(74,271)	(85,657)	(76,255)	(48,043)
Income Taxes	267,875	233,987	136,385	212,096	267,564	216,118	217,704	206,551
Income from Cont Ops	464,952	...	...	...	...	...	...	...
Net Income	457,584	403,578	207,156	334,543	460,310	340,888	336,251	273,186
Average Shs. Outstg.	132,266	137,714	137,696	138,365	141,300	145,563	151,016	153,995
Balance Sheet								
Cash & Cash Equivalents	114,793	297,743	134,147	31,969	118,078	39,024	54,237	61,422
Total Current Assets	1,131,569	1,263,618	1,167,541	1,295,348	1,279,980	1,133,966	1,034,814	986,229
Total Assets	3,582,540	3,480,551	3,247,430	3,447,764	3,346,652	3,404,098	3,291,236	3,184,796
Total Current Liabilities	585,810	546,846	606,444	766,901	712,829	814,824	795,715	817,274
Long-Term Obligations	968,499	851,800	876,972	877,654	878,213	879,103	1,029,136	655,289
Net Stockholders' Equity	1,279,866	1,371,703	1,147,204	1,175,036	1,098,627	1,042,301	852,806	1,161,021
Net Working Capital	545,759	716,772	561,097	528,447	567,151	319,142	239,099	168,955
Shares Outstanding	129,529	134,220	166,072	136,281	138,459	143,147	142,932	152,942
Statistical Record								
Operating Profit Margin %	19.08	16.94	9.05	14.75	20.20	14.48	14.64	13.22
Return on Equity %	36.32	29.42	18.05	28.47	41.89	32.70	39.42	23.52
Return on Assets %	12.97	11.59	6.37	9.70	13.75	10.01	10.21	8.57
Debt/Total Assets %	27.03	24.47	27.00	25.45	26.24	25.82	31.26	20.57
Price Range	78.51-61.30	79.49-57.36	69.32-57.00	65.63-37.75	64.00-46.31	76.06-59.81	63.31-42.25	51.25-32.31
P/E Ratio	22.30-17.41	27.13-19.58	46.21-38.00	27.12-15.60	19.63-14.21	32.51-25.56	28.39-18.95	28.95-18.26
Average Yield %	2.05	1.86	1.84	2.20	1.82	1.36	1.57	1.86

Address: 100 Crystal A Drive, Hershey, PA 17033 Telephone: (717) 534-6799 Web Site: www.hersheys.com	Officers: Richard H. Lenny - Chmn., Pres., C.E.O., Frank Cerminara - Sr. V.P., C.F.O. Transfer Agents:Mellon Investor Services, LLC, Ridgefield Park, NJ	Investor Contact: (800) 539-0291 Institutional Holding No of Institutions: 8 Shares: 2,809 % Held: -

HIBERNIA CORP.

Exchange	Symbol	Price	52Wk Range	Yield	P/E
NYS	HIB	$23.49 (3/31/2004)	24.04−16.82	3.07	14.32

*7 Year Price Score 124.1 *NYSE Composite Index=100 *12 Month Price Score 103.8

Interim Earnings (Per Share)

Qtr.	Mar	Jun	Sep	Dec
2000	0.31	0.31	0.33	0.09
2001	0.31	0.34	0.35	0.35
2002	0.37	0.39	0.40	0.40
2003	0.36	0.39	0.44	0.45

Interim Dividends (Per Share)

Amt	Decl	Ex	Rec	Pay
0.15Q	4/23/2003	5/1/2003	5/5/2003	5/20/2003
0.15Q	7/15/2003	7/23/2003	7/25/2003	8/20/2003
0.18Q	10/22/2003	10/30/2003	11/3/2003	11/20/2003
0.18Q	1/27/2004	2/4/2004	2/6/2004	2/20/2004

Indicated Div: $0.72

Valuation Analysis

Forecast P/E	11.62	Trailing P/E	14.32
Market Cap	$3.7 Billion	Book Value	1.8 Billion
Price/Book	2.07	Price/Sales	2.92

Dividend Achiever Status

Rank	5	10 Year Growth Rate	35.59%
Total Years of Dividend Growth			10

Business Summary: Commercial Banking (MIC: 8.1 SIC: 6021 NAIC:522110)

Hibernia is a bank holding company headquartered in Louisiana. As of Dec 31 2003, Co. had assets of $18.60 billion and deposits of $14.20 billion with 259 locations in 34 Louisiana parishes, 18 Texas counties and two Mississippi counties. Co. conducts its business through its sole depository institution subsidiary, Hibernia National Bank. In addition, Co. offers financial products and services, including retail, small business, commercial, international, mortgage and private banking; leasing; investment banking; corporate finance; treasury management; and insurance.

Recent Developments: For the year ended Dec 31 2003, net income grew 3.4% to $258.3 million from $249.9 million the year before. Results for 2003 and 2002 included net foreclosed property expenses of $9.9 million and $1.1 million, and net securities losses of $6.8 million and $13.4 million, respectively. Net interest income declined 4.8% to $670.8 million from $704.2 million a year earlier. Provision for loan losses decreased 25.5% to $60.1 million from $80.6 million in the previous year. Non-interest income advanced 16.3% to $350.1 million due to double-digit growth in service charges on deposits, card-related fees and insurance. Non-interest expense rose 4.2% to $564.4 million.

Prospects: In Dec 2003, the Company signed a definitive agreement to acquire Coastal Bancorp, based in Houston, TX, for about $230.0 million in cash. The acquisition would expand Co.'s presence in Houston and give it entry into markets from Austin to Houston to the Rio Grande Valley. The transaction, which is expected to be completed in May 2004, would increase Co.'s total assets to over $20.00 billion and nearly double its Texas branches. Separately, Co. continues to focus on its Texas expansion program. During the remainder of 2004, approximately 16 additional de novo branches are scheduled to open in Texas. For full-year 2004, diluted earnings per share are expected to range from $1.77 to $1.80.

Financial Data (US$ in Thousands)	12/31/2003	12/31/2002	12/31/2001	12/31/2000	12/31/1999	12/31/1998	12/31/1997	12/31/1996
Earnings Per Share	1.64	1.56	1.35	1.04	1.06	1.10	0.98	0.85
Tang. Book Val. Per Share	9.25	8.51	9.80	8.82	7.95	7.78	7.14	6.49
Dividends Per Share	0.630	0.570	0.530	0.490	0.430	0.370	0.330	0.290
Dividend Payout %	38.41	36.53	39.25	47.11	41.03	34.09	33.67	34.12
Income Statement								
Total Interest Income	910,305	987,094	1,159,400	1,217,319	1,055,325	953,722	750,082	625,628
Total Interest Expense	239,552	282,857	494,729	606,760	470,520	423,188	322,325	259,411
Net Interest Income	670,753	704,237	664,671	610,559	584,805	530,534	427,757	366,217
Provision for Loan Losses	60,050	80,625	97,250	120,650	87,800	26,000	620	(12,625)
Non-Interest Income	350,083	352,905	318,124	248,685	214,703	184,935	145,431	110,359
Non-Interest Expense	564,383	593,697	548,295	476,078	440,921	416,584	361,944	319,733
Income Before Taxes	396,403	382,820	337,250	262,516	270,787	272,885	210,624	169,468
Net Income	258,336	249,857	218,798	170,633	175,103	178,629	137,389	109,950
Average Shs. Outstg.	157,600	160,057	159,236	158,020	158,902	156,165	133,325	126,766
Balance Sheet								
Cash & Due from Banks	699,060	...	...	...	...	555,756	529,724	558,440
Securities Avail. for Sale	3,866,470	3,519,714	3,259,355	2,686,988	2,660,322	3,026,443	2,541,320	2,336,967
Net Loans & Leases	12,669,711	11,279,447	11,045,216	11,946,425	10,700,604	9,878,206	7,472,711	5,915,260
Total Assets	18,560,442	17,392,661	16,618,176	16,698,046	15,314,179	14,011,531	11,023,038	9,306,796
Total Deposits	14,159,519	13,481,022	12,953,112	12,692,732	11,855,903	10,603,006	8,633,329	7,821,803
Long−Term Obligations	1,101,812	1,102,241	1,042,983	1,043,996	844,959	805,689	506,548	51,349
Total Liabilities	16,782,957	15,711,799	15,058,397	15,218,395	13,938,664	12,693,430	9,972,724	8,370,441
Net Stockholders' Equity	1,777,485	1,680,862	1,559,779	1,479,651	1,375,515	1,318,101	1,050,314	936,385
Shares Outstanding	155,261	157,412	159,066	157,729	160,324	156,400	133,001	128,755
Statistical Record								
Return on Equity %	14.53	14.86	14.02	11.53	12.72	13.55	13.08	11.74
Return on Assets %	1.39	1.43	1.31	1.02	1.14	1.27	1.24	1.18
Equity/Assets %	9.57	9.66	9.38	8.86	8.98	9.40	9.52	10.06
Non−Int. Exp./Tot. Inc. %	44.77	44.30	37.10	32.47	34.71	36.58	40.41	43.44
Price Range	23.69−16.47	21.60−16.80	19.23−11.88	13.75−8.75	17.38−10.38	21.94−13.06	19.38−12.38	13.50−10.00
P/E Ratio	14.45−10.04	13.85−10.77	14.24−8.80	13.22−8.41	16.39−9.79	19.94−11.87	19.77−12.63	15.88−11.76
Average Yield %	3.18	2.95	3.34	4.33	3.09	2.02	2.18	2.63

Address: 313 Carondelet Street, New Orleans, LA 70130	Officers: E. R. "Bo" Campbell − Vice−Chmn., Paul J. Bonitatibus − Pres., Consumer & Buss. Banking	Investor Contact: (504) 533−2180
Telephone: (504) 533−2831	Transfer Agents: Mellon Investor Services, Ridgefield Park, NJ	Institutional Holding No of Institutions: 12
Web Site: www.hibernia.com		Shares: 424,049 % Held: −

HILB, ROGAL AND HAMILTON CO.

Exchange	Symbol	Price	52Wk Range	Yield	P/E
NYS	HRH	$38.10 (3/31/2004)	38.10–28.34	0.97	18.50

*7 Year Price Score 169.3 *NYSE Composite Index=100 *12 Month Price Score 81.2

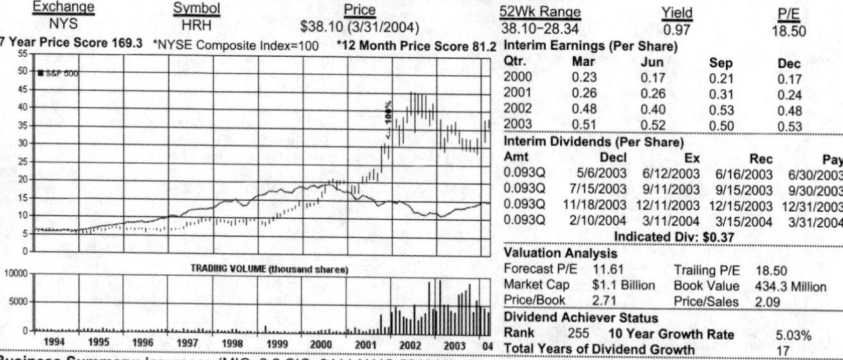

Interim Earnings (Per Share)

Qtr.	Mar	Jun	Sep	Dec
2000	0.23	0.17	0.21	0.17
2001	0.26	0.26	0.31	0.24
2002	0.48	0.40	0.53	0.48
2003	0.51	0.52	0.50	0.53

Interim Dividends (Per Share)

Amt	Decl	Ex	Rec	Pay
0.093Q	5/6/2003	6/12/2003	6/16/2003	6/30/2003
0.093Q	7/15/2003	9/11/2003	9/15/2003	9/30/2003
0.093Q	11/18/2003	12/11/2003	12/15/2003	12/31/2003
0.093Q	2/10/2004	3/11/2004	3/15/2004	3/31/2004

Indicated Div: $0.37

Valuation Analysis

Forecast P/E	11.61	Trailing P/E	18.50
Market Cap	$1.1 Billion	Book Value	434.3 Million
Price/Book	2.71	Price/Sales	2.09

Dividend Achiever Status

Rank	255	10 Year Growth Rate	5.03%
Total Years of Dividend Growth			17

Business Summary: Insurance (MIC: 8.2 SIC: 6411 NAIC:524210)

Hilb, Rogal & Hamilton serves as an intermediary between its clients and insurance companies that underwrite client risks. Co. assists clients in managing their risks in areas such as property and casualty, executive and employee benefits and other areas of specialized exposure. Co. has offices located throughout the U.S. and London, England. Co.'s client base ranges from personal to large national accounts and is primarily comprised of middle-market and top-tier commercial and industrial accounts. Co. also advises clients on risk management and employee benefits and provides claims administration and loss control consulting services to clients.

Recent Developments: For the year ended Dec 31 2003, net income rose 22.5% to $75.0 million compared with income of $61.2 million, before an accounting change charge of $3.9 million, in 2002. Results for 2003 included integration costs of $4.1 million and a retirement benefit charge of $5.2 million. Total revenues were $563.6 million, up 24.5% from $452.7 million the previous year. Commissions and fees increased 24.4% to $555.7 million from $446.7 million the year before, reflecting acquisitions and organic growth. Operating margin improved to 27.4% from 26.3% a year earlier.

Prospects: Acquisitions in 2003 have accelerated Co.'s entry into the excess and surplus lines and reinsurance brokerage markets, strengthening its agency presence in selected markets and giving Co. the ability to directly place business that has been outsourced in the past. Co. expects 2004 to be another active year for acquisitions, although it will maintain a more selective and disciplined approach. Looking ahead, Co.'s business pipeline is expected to continue to be robust and should attract new partners in 2004, despite increased competition. As a result, Co. expects to generate annualized revenues of between $30.0 million and $60.0 million in 2004.

Financial Data

(US$ in Thousands)	12/31/2003	12/31/2002	12/31/2001	12/31/2000	12/31/1999	12/31/1998	12/31/1997	12/31/1996
Earnings Per Share	2.06	1.89	1.07	0.78	0.72	0.59	0.48	0.42
Tang. Book Val. Per Share	N.M	N.M	N.M	N.M	N.M	N.M	1.73	1.94
Dividends Per Share	0.368	0.358	0.348	0.338	0.328	0.318	0.310	0.303
Dividend Payout %	17.86	18.94	32.52	43.33	45.56	53.90	63.91	72.14
Income Statement								
Net Investment Income	3,151	2,439	2,585	2,626	2,046	1,579	...	...
Other Income	560,496	450,287	327,683	259,493	225,180	173,785	173,709	158,243
Total Revenues	563,647	452,726	330,267	262,119	227,226	175,364	173,709	158,243
Total Indirect Exp.	418,765	338,804	264,476	214,202	185,768	147,683	149,827	137,954
Inc. Before Inc. Taxes	124,901	103,257	56,730	39,737	33,069	25,364	21,845	19,045
Income Taxes	49,947	42,082	24,381	17,610	13,583	10,418	9,055	7,638
Income from Cont Ops	...	61,175	...	22,127	...	...	...	...
Net Income	74,954	65,119	32,349	21,802	19,486	14,945	12,790	11,406
Average Shs. Outstg.	36,304	29,240	27,411	29,783	28,014	25,417	26,430	26,986
Balance Sheet								
Cash & Cash Equivalents	126,464	134,692	51,580	28,881	22,337	19,395	22,315	19,774
Premiums Due	255,251	201,364	133,892	94,001	75,271	51,571	47,013	47,576
Invst. Assets: Total	...	1,260	1,336	1,654	1,761	3,068	5,030	6,186
Total Assets	1,049,227	833,024	499,301	353,371	317,981	188,066	106,413	105,073
Long-Term Obligations	174,012	177,151	114,443	103,113	111,826	43,658	32,458	27,196
Net Stockholders' Equity	434,267	310,648	142,801	88,222	71,176	45,710	51,339	55,298
Shares Outstanding	35,446	33,484	28,310	26,560	26,117	24,234	25,626	26,641
Statistical Record								
Return on Equity %	17.25	19.69	22.65	25.08	27.37	32.69	24.91	20.62
Return on Assets %	7.14	7.34	6.47	6.12	6.26	7.94	12.01	10.85
Price Range	43.85–28.34	45.40–27.75	31.08–16.97	20.97–12.91	14.56–7.78	9.94–7.75	9.69–6.31	7.00–5.81
P/E Ratio	21.29–13.76	24.02–14.68	29.05–15.86	26.88–16.55	20.23–10.81	16.84–13.14	20.18–13.15	16.67–13.84
Average Yield %	1.09	0.67	1.53	2.46	2.95	3.43	3.92	3.31

Address: 4951 Lake Brook Drive, Glen Allen, VA 23060	Officers: Martin L. Vaughan III – Chmn., C.E.O., Robert B. Lockhart – Pres., C.O.O.	Investor Contact: (804) 747–6500
Telephone: (804) 747–6500	Transfer Agents:Mellon Investor Services, LLC, Ridgefield Park, NJ	Institutional Holding
Web Site: www.hrh.com		No of Institutions: 18
		Shares: 781,645 % Held: –

HILLENBRAND INDUSTRIES, INC.

Exchange	Symbol	Price	52Wk Range	Yield	P/E
NYS	HB	$67.89 (3/31/2004)	70.01-48.16	1.59	18.35

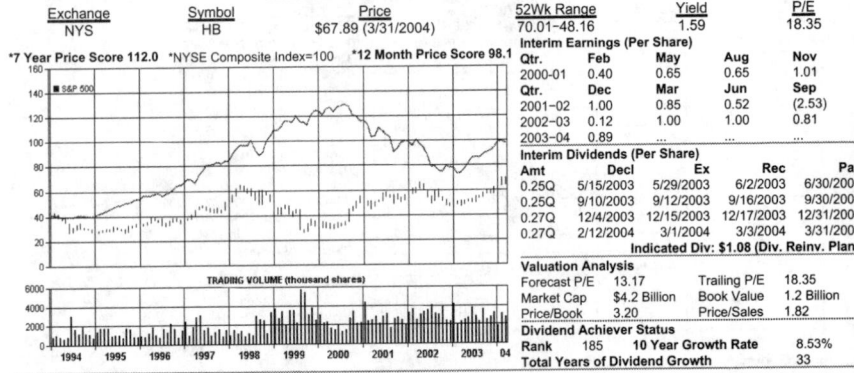

*7 Year Price Score 112.0 *NYSE Composite Index=100 *12 Month Price Score 98.1

Interim Earnings (Per Share)

Qtr.	Feb	May	Aug	Nov
2000-01	0.40	0.65	0.65	1.01
Qtr.	Dec	Mar	Jun	Sep
2001-02	1.00	0.85	0.52	(2.53)
2002-03	0.12	1.00	1.00	0.81
2003-04	0.89	...	...	...

Interim Dividends (Per Share)

Amt	Decl	Ex	Rec	Pay
0.25Q	5/15/2003	5/29/2003	6/2/2003	6/30/2003
0.25Q	9/10/2003	9/12/2003	9/16/2003	9/30/2003
0.27Q	12/4/2003	12/15/2003	12/17/2003	12/31/2003
0.27Q	2/12/2004	3/1/2004	3/3/2004	3/31/2004

Indicated Div: $1.08 (Div. Reinv. Plan)

Valuation Analysis

Forecast P/E	13.17	Trailing P/E	18.35
Market Cap	$4.2 Billion	Book Value	1.2 Billion
Price/Book	3.20	Price/Sales	1.82

Dividend Achiever Status

Rank	185	10 Year Growth Rate	8.53%
Total Years of Dividend Growth			33

Business Summary: Chemicals (MIC: 11.1 SIC: 2599 NAIC:339995)

Hillenbrand is a diversified, holding company and the owner of 100% of the capital stock of its three major operating companies serving the health care and funeral services industries in the United States and abroad. Hill-Rom Company is a manufacturer of equipment for the health care industry and a provider of associated systems for wound, pulmonary and circulatory care. Batesville Casket Company, Inc. and Forethought Financial Services both serve the funeral services industry. Batesville Casket is a manufacturer of caskets and cremation-related products while Forethought is a provider of financial products and services designed to help people prefund anticipated funeral and cemetery costs.

Recent Developments: For the first quarter ended Dec 31 2003, income from continuing operations surged 700.0% to $56.0 million from $7.0 million in the previous year. Total revenues increased 17.6% to $528.0 million. Health care therapy rental revenue climbed 14.8% to $93.0 million, primarily due to the acquisition of Advanced Respiratory, Inc. Funeral services revenue rose 7.9% to $164.0 million, reflecting increased burial casket volume and favorable pricing. Funeral insurance revenue jumped 140.9% to $106.0 million, due to a net capital gain versus a net capital loss in 2002. Health care sales decreased 4.1% to $165.0 million, primarily due to volume declines, partially offset by foreign currency translation.

Prospects: On Feb 13 2004, Co. announced an agreement to sell its wholly-owned subsidiary, Forethought Financial Services, Inc. and its subsidiaries to FFS Holdings, Inc. for total consideration of approximately $280.0 million, including certain Forethought assets retained by Co. The transaction should allow Co. to focus its resources on future growth opportunities in the health care marketplace, and maintain its commitment to Batesville Casket Company. Separately, Batesville's strategy to improve profitability will require it to differentiate its products, while at the same time continuing to control costs through manufacturing efficiencies, strategic sourcing and other cost reduction efforts.

Financial Data

(US$ in Thousands)	3 Mos	09/30/2003	09/30/2002	12/01/2001	12/02/2000	11/27/1999	11/28/1998	11/29/1997
Earnings Per Share	0.89	2.93	(0.16)	2.71	2.44	1.87	2.73	2.28
Cash Flow Per Share	(0.20)	6.04	5.21	7.08	4.70	2.26	2.56	3.57
Tang. Book Val. Per Share	14.94	15.78	12.72	13.23	10.41	10.16	11.29	11.09
Dividends Per Share	1.020	1.000	0.767	0.840	0.800	0.780	0.720	0.660
Dividend Payout %	114.61	34.13	N.M.	30.99	32.78	41.71	26.37	28.95
Income Statement								
Total Revenues	528,000	2,042,000	1,757,000	2,107,000	2,096,000	2,047,000	2,001,000	1,776,000
Total Indirect Exp.	153,000	582,000	780,000	618,000	582,000	565,000	606,000	481,000
Operating Income	90,000	319,000	(32,000)	236,000	244,000	211,000	228,000	264,000
Net Interest Inc./(Exp.)	(3,000)	(19,000)	(14,000)	(23,000)	(27,000)	(27,000)	(27,000)	(21,000)
Income Taxes	30,000	100,000	(25,000)	53,000	86,000	71,000	109,000	102,000
Income from Cont Ops	56,000	182,000	...	...	...	...	...	...
Net Income	57,000	138,000	(10,000)	170,000	154,000	124,000	184,000	157,000
Average Shs. Outstg.	62,432	62,184	62,921	62,814	62,913	66,295	67,577	68,796
Balance Sheet								
Cash & Cash Equivalents	70,000	180,000	296,000	284,000	132,000	170,000	297,000	364,000
Total Current Assets	627,000	708,000	958,000	868,000	724,000	782,000	858,000	821,000
Total Assets	5,401,000	5,412,000	5,442,000	5,049,000	4,597,000	4,433,000	4,280,000	3,828,000
Total Current Liabilities	266,000	367,000	551,000	320,000	282,000	371,000	375,000	359,000
Long-Term Obligations	154,000	155,000	322,000	305,000	302,000	302,000	303,000	203,000
Net Stockholders' Equity	1,190,000	1,159,000	999,000	1,026,000	831,000	838,000	952,000	886,000
Net Working Capital	361,000	341,000	407,000	548,000	442,000	411,000	483,000	462,000
Shares Outstanding	61,903	61,814	61,702	62,466	62,404	63,546	66,759	68,511
Statistical Record								
Operating Profit Margin %	17.04	15.62	N.M.	11.20	11.64	10.30	11.39	14.86
Return on Equity %	4.70	15.70	N.M.	16.56	18.53	14.79	19.32	17.72
Return on Assets %	1.03	3.36	N.M.	3.36	3.35	2.79	4.29	4.10
Debt/Total Assets %	2.85	2.86	5.91	6.04	6.56	6.81	7.07	5.30
Price Range	62.06-56.42	57.64-46.91	65.99-48.75	58.10-43.88	51.00-29.06	56.88-26.38	64.38-44.69	48.25-34.13
P/E Ratio	69.73-63.39	19.67-16.01	N/A	21.44-16.19	20.90-11.91	30.41-14.10	23.58-16.37	21.16-14.97
Average Yield %	1.72	1.91	1.28	1.62	2.28	2.33	1.54	1.89

Address: 700 State Route 46 East, Batesville, IN 47006-8835	**Officers:** Ray J. Hillenbrand - Chmn., Rolf A. Classon - Vice-Chmn.	**Investor Contact:** 812-934-8400	
Telephone: (812) 934-7000	**Transfer Agents:** Computershare Investor Services, Chicago, IL	**Institutional Holding** **No of Institutions:** 215	
Web Site: www.hillenbrand.com		**Shares:** 29,055,573 **% Held:** 46.90%	

HOLLY CORP.

Exchange	Symbol	Price	52Wk Range	Yield	P/E
ASE	HOC	$31.86 (3/31/2004)	31.86-24.30	1.63	11.06

7 Year Price Score 187.3 *NYSE Composite Index=100 **12 Month Price Score 90.7**

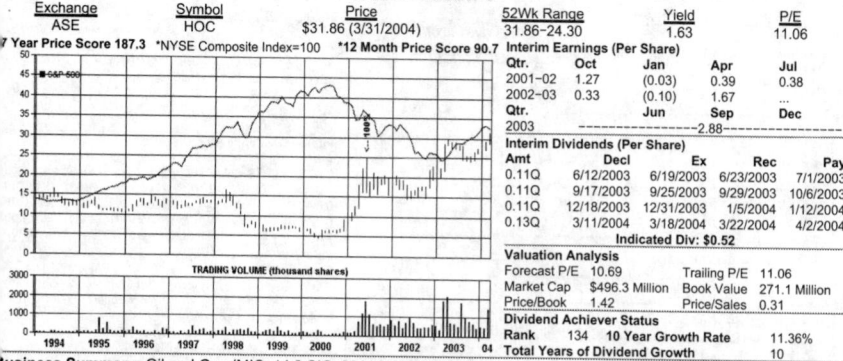

Interim Earnings (Per Share)

Qtr.	Oct	Jan	Apr	Jul
2001–02	1.27	(0.03)	0.39	0.38
2002–03	0.33	(0.10)	1.67	...
Qtr.	Jun	Sep	Dec	
2003	----------2.88----------			

Interim Dividends (Per Share)

Amt	Decl	Ex	Rec	Pay
0.11Q	6/12/2003	6/19/2003	6/23/2003	7/1/2003
0.11Q	9/17/2003	9/25/2003	9/29/2003	10/6/2003
0.11Q	12/18/2003	12/31/2003	1/5/2004	1/12/2004
0.13Q	3/11/2004	3/18/2004	3/22/2004	4/2/2004

Indicated Div: $0.52

Valuation Analysis

Forecast P/E	10.69	Trailing P/E	11.06
Market Cap	$496.3 Million	Book Value	271.1 Million
Price/Book	1.42	Price/Sales	0.31

Dividend Achiever Status

Rank	134	10 Year Growth Rate	11.36%
Total Years of Dividend Growth		10	

Business Summary: Oil and Gas (MIC: 14.2 SIC: 2911 NAIC:324110)

Holly is an indepedent petroleum refiner. The Refining segment refines crude oil and markets wholesale refined products, such as gasoline, diesel fuel and jet fuel, and includes refineries in New Mexico, Utah, and Montana. Co. also owns and operates or owns interests in thirteen refined products storage terminals in New Mexico, Texas, Utah, Montana, Washington, Idaho and Arizona. Also, Co. owns or leases about 1,000 miles of pipeline located principally in west Texas and New Mexico. The Pipeline Transportation segment uses 500 miles of the pipeline and owns a 70.0% interest in Rio Grande Pipeline Company, which transports liquid petroleum gases to Mexico.

Recent Developments: For the year ended Dec 31 2003, net income surged 144.6% to $46.1 million from $18.8 million in the previous year. Earnings benefited from high refined product margins and from the contribution to earnings from the Woods Cross, Utah refinery, which was acquired from ConocoPhillips on June 1 2003. Results for 2003 included a gain on the sale of assets of $15.8 million and income from a reparations payment received of $15.3 million. Sales and other revenues advanced 44.1% to $1.40 billion from $973.7 million a year earlier. Sales for the Refining segment climbed 44.1% to $1.37 billion, while Pipeline Transportation segments sales increased 10.2% to $21.0 million.

Prospects: Co.'s capital budget for 2004 totals approximately $45.0 million, comprised of $7.0 million for refining and pipeline transportation improvement projects for the Navajo Refinery, $19.5 million for projects at the Woods Cross Refinery, $500,000 for projects at the Montana Refinery, $300,000 for oil and gas exploration and production, $700,000 for information technology, and $17.0 million to pursue new high-return pipeline transportation and terminal opportunities relating to the distribution network of the Navajo refinery. Co. is finalizing its clean fuels strategy for the Woods Cross Refinery, which will be required to address mandated lower sulfur in on-road diesel fuel on June 1 2006.

Financial Data

(US$ in Thousands)	12/31/2003	07/31/2002	07/31/2001	07/31/2000	07/31/1999	07/31/1998	07/31/1997	07/31/1996
Earnings Per Share	2.88	2.01	4.77	0.71	1.21	0.92	0.79	1.16
Cash Flow Per Share	4.41	2.64	6.86	2.90	2.88	2.31	0.33	2.69
Tang. Book Val. Per Share	16.63	14.68	13.03	8.58	7.80	6.92	6.36	5.83
Dividends Per Share	0.440	0.410	0.370	0.340	0.320	0.300	0.250	0.210
Dividend Payout %	15.27	20.39	7.75	47.88	26.44	32.60	32.07	18.02
Income Statement								
Total Revenues	1,403,244	888,906	1,142,130	965,946	597,986	590,299	721,346	676,290
Total Indirect Exp.	187,319	147,615	152,902	145,282	130,541	117,492	37,233	37,414
Depreciation & Amort.	36,275	27,699	27,327	27,496	26,358	24,379	20,153	19,315
Operating Income	60,067	43,046	117,907	20,001	38,973	32,765	27,500	38,398
Net Interest Inc./(Exp.)	(1,678)	(1,425)	(2,467)	(5,153)	(7,779)	(7,725)	(6,095)	(6,610)
Income Taxes	28,306	18,867	48,445	7,189	13,222	9,699	8,732	12,554
Equity Earns/Minority Int.	1,398	7,753	5,302	1,586	1,965	1,766	414	...
Net Income	46,053	32,029	73,450	11,445	19,937	15,167	13,087	19,234
Average Shs. Outstg.	16,016	15,971	15,387	16,130	16,508	16,508	16,508	16,508
Balance Sheet								
Cash & Cash Equivalents	11,690	71,630	65,840	3,628	4,194	2,602	20,042	63,959
Total Current Assets	336,406	278,844	284,130	267,104	194,778	154,387	194,728	217,026
Total Assets	708,892	502,306	490,429	464,362	390,982	349,857	349,803	351,271
Total Current Liabilities	364,667	218,971	226,399	266,741	180,927	139,594	149,487	150,377
Long-Term Obligations	8,571	25,714	34,286	42,857	56,595	70,341	75,516	86,290
Net Stockholders' Equity	268,600	228,556	201,734	129,581	128,880	114,349	105,121	96,243
Net Working Capital	(28,261)	59,873	57,731	363	13,851	14,793	45,241	66,649
Shares Outstanding	15,514	15,561	15,480	15,101	16,508	16,508	16,508	16,508
Statistical Record								
Operating Profit Margin %	4.28	4.84	10.32	2.07	6.51	5.55	3.81	5.67
Return on Equity %	17.14	14.01	36.40	8.83	15.46	13.26	12.44	19.98
Return on Assets %	6.49	6.37	14.97	2.46	5.09	4.33	3.74	5.47
Debt/Total Assets %	1.20	5.11	6.99	9.22	14.47	20.10	21.58	24.56
Price Range	29.98-15.00	21.15-14.66	24.98-6.00	7.63-4.69	13.00-6.22	16.44-12.06	14.81-11.63	14.06-10.69
P/E Ratio	10.41-5.21	10.52-7.29	5.24-1.26	10.74-6.60	10.74-5.14	17.87-13.11	18.75-14.72	12.12-9.21
Average Yield %	1.88	2.27	3.29	5.24	4.18	2.20	1.91	1.77

Address: 100 Crescent Court, Dallas, TX 75201-6927 Telephone: (214) 871-3555 Web Site: www.hollycorp.com	Officers: Lamar Norsworthy – Chmn., C.E.O., Matthew P. Clifton – Pres.	Institutional Holding No of Institutions: 82 Shares: 11,423,372 % Held: 71.4

HOME DEPOT, INC.

Exchange	Symbol	Price	52Wk Range	Yield	P/E
NYS	HD	$37.36 (3/31/2004)	37.52–24.79	0.75	19.98

*7 Year Price Score 85.5   *NYSE Composite Index=100   *12 Month Price Score 104.8

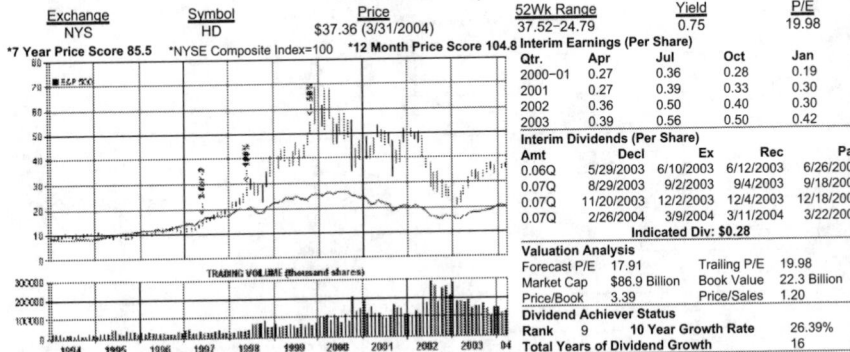

Interim Earnings (Per Share)

Qtr.	Apr	Jul	Oct	Jan
2000–01	0.27	0.36	0.28	0.19
2001	0.27	0.39	0.33	0.30
2002	0.36	0.50	0.40	0.30
2003	0.39	0.56	0.50	0.42

Interim Dividends (Per Share)

Amt	Decl	Ex	Rec	Pa
0.06Q	5/29/2003	6/10/2003	6/12/2003	6/26/200
0.07Q	8/29/2003	9/2/2003	9/4/2003	9/18/200
0.07Q	11/20/2003	12/2/2003	12/4/2003	12/18/200
0.07Q	2/26/2004	3/9/2004	3/11/2004	3/22/200

Indicated Div: $0.28

Valuation Analysis

Forecast P/E	17.91	Trailing P/E	19.98
Market Cap	$86.9 Billion	Book Value	22.3 Billion
Price/Book	3.39	Price/Sales	1.20

Dividend Achiever Status

Rank	9	10 Year Growth Rate 26.39%
Total Years of Dividend Growth		16

Business Summary: Retail – Hardware (MIC: 5.6 SIC: 5211 NAIC:444110)

The Home Depot operated 1,607 retail warehouse stores as of Aug 3 2003 in the United States, Canada and Mexico that offer a wid assortment of building materials and home improvement products. The average Home Depot store has about 108,000 square feet o interior floor space and is stocked with approximately 40,000 to 50,000 separate items. Most stores have about 22,000 square feet o additional outdoor selling area for landscaping supplies. Co. also operates 53 EXPO Design Center stores that sell products and service primarily for home decorating and remodeling projects, five Home Depot Supply stores, nine Home Depot Landscape Supply stores an one Home Depot Floor Store outlet.

Recent Developments: For the year ended Feb 1 2004, net earnings advanced 17.5% to $4.30 billion from $3.66 billion in the prio year. Net sales increased 11.3% to $64.82 billion from $58.25 billion a year earlier. Comparable–store sales were up 3.8% year over yea while the average sale per customer transaction rose to $51.15 from $49.43 in fiscal 2002. Gross profit totaled $20.58 billion, or 31.8% o net sales, compared with $18.11 billion, or 31.1% of net sales, the year before. Operating income climbed 17.4% to $6.85 billion from $5.83 billion the previous year. During the fourth quarter of fiscal 2003, Co. opened 64 new stores.

Prospects: Results are benefiting from Co.'s aggressive efforts to remodel existing stores, improve customer service, and offer new merchandise. Profitability is also being positively affected by increased revenue from services, such as installation of countertops an flooring, and a reduction in inventory shrink, or lost or stolen goods. Co. plans to spend approximately $1.50 billion in fiscal 2004 t remodel stores and introduce new technology, such as self–checkout systems, wireless scanners and touch–screen registers. Lookin ahead, Co. is projecting sales growth of between 9.0% and 12.0% and earnings per share growth of 7.0% to 11.0% during the curren fiscal year.

Financial Data

(US$ in Thousands)	9 Mos	6 Mos	3 Mos	02/02/2003	02/03/2002	01/28/2001	01/30/2000	01/31/199
Earnings Per Share	1.76	1.66	1.59	1.56	1.29	1.10	1.00	0.7
Cash Flow Per Share	2.67	2.00	1.20	2.04	2.53	1.18	1.04	0.8
Tang. Book Val. Per Share	9.51	9.02	8.75	8.38	7.52	6.32	5.22	3.8
Dividends Per Share	0.250	0.230	0.220	0.210	0.170	0.160	0.110	0.07
Dividend Payout %	14.20	13.86	13.84	13.46	13.17	14.54	11.33	10.7
Income Statement								
Total Revenues	49,691,000	33,093,000	15,104,000	58,247,000	53,553,000	45,738,000	38,434,000	30,219,0
Total Indirect Exp.	10,290,000	6,920,000	3,381,000	12,278,000	11,215,000	9,490,000	7,616,000	5,944,0
Depreciation & Amort.	786,000	505,000	248,000	903,000	764,000	601,000	463,000	373,0
Operating Income	5,337,000	3,514,000	1,448,000	5,830,000	4,932,000	4,191,000	3,795,000	2,661,0
Net Interest Inc./(Exp.)	(7,000)	(7,000)	(6,000)	42,000	25,000	26,000	9,000	(7,00
Income Taxes	1,977,000	1,301,000	535,000	2,208,000	1,913,000	1,636,000	1,484,000	1,040,0
Net Income	3,353,000	2,206,000	907,000	3,664,000	3,044,000	2,581,000	2,320,000	1,614,0
Average Shs. Outstg.	2,295,000	2,300,000	2,297,000	2,344,000	2,353,000	2,352,000	2,342,000	2,320,0
Balance Sheet								
Cash & Cash Equivalents	4,966,000	5,254,000	4,340,000	2,253,000	2,546,000	177,000	170,000	62,0
Total Current Assets	15,697,000	15,567,000	15,309,000	11,917,000	10,361,000	7,777,000	6,390,000	4,933,0
Total Assets	35,374,000	34,612,000	33,747,000	30,011,000	26,394,000	21,385,000	17,081,000	13,465,0
Total Current Liabilities	10,972,000	10,389,000	10,925,000	8,035,000	6,501,000	4,385,000	3,656,000	2,857,0
Long–Term Obligations	847,000	1,327,000	1,321,000	1,321,000	1,250,000	1,545,000	750,000	1,566,0
Net Stockholders' Equity	22,261,000	21,933,000	20,678,000	19,802,000	18,082,000	15,004,000	12,341,000	8,740,0
Net Working Capital	4,725,000	5,178,000	4,384,000	3,882,000	3,860,000	3,392,000	2,734,000	2,076,0
Shares Outstanding	2,273,000	2,365,000	2,294,000	2,293,000	2,345,888	2,323,747	2,304,317	2,213,1
Statistical Record								
Operating Profit Margin %	10.74	10.61	9.58	10.00	9.20	9.16	9.87	8.8
Return on Equity %	15.06	10.05	4.38	18.50	16.83	17.20	18.79	18.4
Return on Assets %	9.47	6.37	2.68	12.20	11.53	12.06	13.58	11.9
Debt/Total Assets %	2.39	3.83	3.91	4.40	4.73	7.22	4.39	11.6
Price Range	37.50–20.70	34.55–20.70	28.51–20.70	52.07–20.53	53.45–32.80	68.00–34.88	68.56–36.29	41.04–20.6
P/E Ratio	25.68–14.18	35.99–21.56	73.10–53.08	33.38–13.16	41.43–25.43	61.82–31.70	68.56–36.29	57.81–29.
Average Yield %	0.83	0.82	0.91	0.60	0.37	0.31	0.24	0.

Address: 2455 Paces Ferry Road N.W., Atlanta, GA 30339–4024 **Telephone:** (770) 433–8211 **Web Site:** www.homedepot.com	**Officers:** Robert L. Nardelli – Chmn. Pres., C.E.O., Francis S. Blake – Exec. V.P., **Transfer Agents:** EquiServe Trust Company, N.A., Providence, RI	**Investor Contact:** 770–384–4388 **Institutional Holding** **No of Institutions:** 10 **Shares:** 5,387,488 **% Held:** –

HON INDUSTRIES INC.

Exchange	Symbol	Price	52Wk Range	Yield	P/E
NYS	HNI	$37.16 (3/31/2004)	45.71-27.45	1.51	22.12

*7 Year Price Score N/A   *NYSE Composite Index=100   *12 Month Price Score 114.6

Interim Earnings (Per Share)

Qtr.	Mar	Jun	Sep	Dec
2000	0.41	0.39	0.57	0.40
2001	0.31	0.07	0.48	0.40
2002	0.27	0.34	0.46	0.48
2003	0.27	0.35	0.59	0.47

Interim Dividends (Per Share)

Amt	Decl	Ex	Rec	Pay
0.13Q	5/6/2003	5/13/2003	5/15/2003	5/30/2003
0.13Q	8/4/2003	8/12/2003	8/14/2003	8/29/2003
0.13Q	11/7/2003	11/13/2003	11/17/2003	12/1/2003
0.14Q	2/11/2004	2/18/2004	2/20/2004	3/1/2004

Indicated Div: $0.56

Valuation Analysis

Forecast P/E	20.03	Trailing P/E	22.12
Market Cap	$2.2 Billion	Book Value	709.9 Million
Price/Book	3.54	Price/Sales	1.43

Dividend Achiever Status

Rank	155	10 Year Growth Rate	10.03%
Total Years of Dividend Growth		15

Business Summary: Chemicals (MIC: 11.1 SIC: 2522 NAIC:337214)

Hon Industries manufactures and markets office furniture and hearth products. Co.'s office furniture products are in four categories: storage, seating, office systems, and desks and related products. The office products are sold to dealers, wholesalers, warehouse clubs, retail superstores, end–user customers, and federal and state governments. Co.'s hearth products include wood–burning, pellet–burning, gas–burning and electric factory–built fireplaces, fireplace inserts, stoves, gas logs, and accessories. The hearth products are sold through a national system of dealers, wholesalers, large regional contractors and Co.–owned retail outlets. Co. has locations in the U.S., Canada and Mexico.

Recent Developments: For the year ended Jan 3 2004, net income advanced 7.4% to $98.1 million compared with $91.4 million in 2002. Results for 2003 and 2002 included restructuring and impairment charges of $8.5 million and $3.0 million, respectively. Net sales grew 3.7% to $1.76 billion from $1.69 billion a year earlier. Gross profit rose 6.6% to $639.2 million. Co.'s office furniture products segment sales grew 2.0% to $1.30 billion. Co.'s hearth products segment sales increased 9.2% to $451.7 million, reflecting strong housing starts, growth in market share in both the new construction and retail channels, strengthening alliances with key distributors and dealers, as well as focused new product introductions.

Prospects: Looking ahead, Co. is encouraged by indications that the economy is recovering and is cautiously optimistic that the office furniture industry will begin to rebound in the second half of 2004. Meanwhile, Co.'s hearth segment may experience weaker conditions in the housing market, but should remain healthy due to its strong brand recognition, new product introductions and strengthened distribution channels. On Jan 5 2004, Co. acquired Paoli, a provider of wood case goods and seating. Co. plans to build on Paoli's strong position in the market and selling capabilities while leveraging its lean enterprise practices to achieve greater cost efficiencies and improved customer performance.

Financial Data

(US$ in Thousands)	01/03/2004	12/28/2002	12/29/2001	12/30/2000	01/01/2000	01/02/1999	01/03/1998	12/28/1996
Earnings Per Share	1.68	1.55	1.26	1.77	1.44	1.72	1.45	1.13
Cash Flow Per Share	2.41	3.42	3.85	3.40	2.53	2.38	2.37	1.54
Tang. Book Val. Per Share	8.89	7.78	6.44	5.96	6.45	5.76	4.58	3.38
Dividends Per Share	0.520	0.500	0.480	0.440	0.380	0.320	0.280	0.250
Dividend Payout %	30.95	32.25	38.09	24.85	26.39	18.60	19.31	22.12
Income Statement								
Total Revenues	1,755,728	1,692,622	1,792,438	2,046,286	1,789,281	1,696,433	1,362,713	998,135
Total Indirect Exp.	489,254	457,189	488,206	487,848	406,226	344,259	284,397	209,246
Depreciation & Amort.	4,625	4,317	12,646	10,679	5,362	4,789	2,943	25,252
Operating Income	149,961	142,690	123,092	178,034	146,443	179,177	145,159	106,193
Net Interest Inc./(Exp.)	970	(2,136)	(6,831)	(12,007)	(8,868)	(9,068)	(6,031)	(926)
Income Taxes	52,826	49,194	41,854	59,747	50,215	63,796	52,173	37,173
Net Income	98,105	91,360	74,407	106,217	87,360	106,313	86,955	68,094
Average Shs. Outstg.	58,545	59,040	59,087	60,140	60,855	61,650	59,780	60,228
Balance Sheet								
Cash & Cash Equivalents	204,190	155,543	78,838	3,181	22,168	17,669	46,340	32,698
Total Current Assets	462,122	405,054	319,657	330,141	316,556	290,329	295,150	205,527
Total Assets	1,021,826	1,020,552	961,891	1,022,470	906,723	864,469	754,673	513,514
Total Current Liabilities	245,816	298,680	230,443	264,868	225,123	217,438	200,759	152,553
Long–Term Obligations	4,126	9,837	80,830	128,285	124,173	135,563	134,511	97,788
Net Stockholders' Equity	709,889	646,893	592,680	573,342	501,271	462,022	381,662	252,397
Net Working Capital	216,306	106,374	89,214	65,273	91,433	72,891	94,391	52,974
Shares Outstanding	58,239	58,373	58,672	59,796	60,171	61,290	61,659	59,426
Statistical Record								
Operating Profit Margin %	8.54	8.43	6.86	8.70	8.18	10.56	10.65	10.63
Return on Equity %	13.81	14.12	12.55	18.52	17.42	23.01	22.78	26.97
Return on Assets %	9.60	8.95	7.73	10.38	9.63	12.29	11.52	13.26
Debt/Total Assets %	0.40	0.96	8.40	12.54	13.69	15.68	17.82	19.04
Price Range	43.87-24.67	30.64-23.37	28.82-19.96	27.81-16.00	29.88-18.88	32.38-20.31	...	...
P/E Ratio	26.11-14.68	19.77-15.08	22.87-15.84	15.71-9.04	20.75-13.11	18.82-11.81	...	...
Average Yield %	1.57	1.83	1.95	1.87	1.63	1.29	N/A	N/A

Address: 414 East Third Street, Muscatine, IA 52761–0071	**Officers:** Jack D. Michaels – Chmn., Pres., C.E.O., Stanley A. Askren – Pres.,, Chief, Oper. Officer	**Investor Contact:**563–264–7400
Telephone: (563) 264–7400	**Transfer Agents:**Computershare Investor Services, LLC, Chicago, IL	**Institutional Holding** **No of Institutions:** 24
Web Site: www.honi.com		**Shares:** 951,268 **% Held:** –

141

HORMEL FOODS CORP.

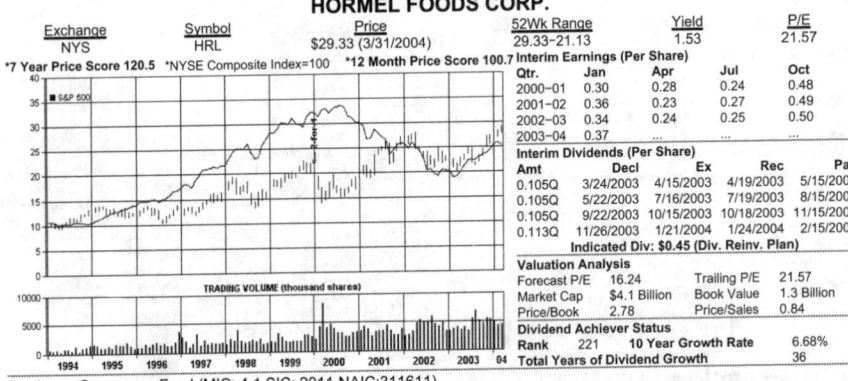

Exchange	Symbol	Price	52Wk Range	Yield	P/E
NYS	HRL	$29.33 (3/31/2004)	29.33–21.13	1.53	21.57

*7 Year Price Score 120.5 *NYSE Composite Index=100 *12 Month Price Score 100.7

Interim Earnings (Per Share)

Qtr.	Jan	Apr	Jul	Oct
2000–01	0.30	0.28	0.24	0.48
2001–02	0.36	0.23	0.27	0.49
2002–03	0.34	0.24	0.25	0.50
2003–04	0.37	...	...	...

Interim Dividends (Per Share)

Amt	Decl	Ex	Rec	Pay
0.105Q	3/24/2003	4/15/2003	4/19/2003	5/15/2003
0.105Q	5/22/2003	7/16/2003	7/19/2003	8/15/2003
0.105Q	9/22/2003	10/15/2003	10/18/2003	11/15/2003
0.113Q	11/26/2003	1/21/2004	1/24/2004	2/15/2004

Indicated Div: $0.45 (Div. Reinv. Plan)

Valuation Analysis

Forecast P/E	16.24	Trailing P/E	21.57
Market Cap	$4.1 Billion	Book Value	1.3 Billion
Price/Book	2.78	Price/Sales	0.84

Dividend Achiever Status

Rank	221	10 Year Growth Rate	6.68%
Total Years of Dividend Growth	36		

Business Summary: Food (MIC: 4.1 SIC: 2011 NAIC:311611)

Hormel Foods is primarily engaged in the production of a variety of meat and food products and the marketing of those products throughout the United States. Although pork and turkey remain the major raw materials for Co. products, Co. has emphasized for several years the manufacture and distribution of branded, consumer packaged items rather than the commodity fresh meat business. Co.'s business is reported in five segments: Grocery Products, Refrigerated Foods, Jennie–O Turkey Store, Specialty Foods, and All Other. Co.'s products primarily consist of meat and other food products. The meat products are sold fresh, frozen, cured, smoked, cooked and canned.

Recent Developments: For the three months ended Jan 24 2004, net earnings were $51.8 million, up 10.4% from $46.9 million in the prior year. Net sales improved 11.5% to $1.14 billion from $1.02 billion the year before. This increase was driven primarily by a 128.8% increase to $112.2 million in Specialty Foods sales, which benefited from the acquisitions of Diamond Crystal Brands and Century Foods International. Gross profit was $271.8 million, or 23.9% of net sales, versus $252.2 million, or 24.8% of net sales, the year before. Operating income advanced 10.6% to $85.2 million from $77.1 million a year earlier.

Prospects: Results are being positively affected by increased demand for Co.'s pork and turkey products, such as fully–cooked entrees sold under the *Hormel* and *Jennie–O Turkey Store* brands. Strong sales growth in Co.'s foodservice segment is being driven by several products including *Always Tender* boneless pork, *Bread Ready* meats, and *Austin Blues* BBQ, while higher margins from Co.'s international operations are being fueled by strong sales of *Stagg* chili and *Spam* products. Meanwhile, Grocery Products segment sales and volume are being hampered by increased pork and beef raw material costs. Looking ahead, Co. is targeting full fiscal–2004 earnings of between $1.46 and $1.60 per share.

Financial Data

(US$ in Thousands)	3 Mos	10/25/2003	10/26/2002	10/27/2001	10/28/2000	10/30/1999	10/31/1998	10/25/1997
Earnings Per Share	0.37	1.33	1.35	1.30	1.20	1.11	0.92	0.71
Cash Flow Per Share	0.22	1.81	2.32	2.28	1.06	1.62	1.52	1.06
Tang. Book Val. Per Share	5.68	5.35	5.41	4.45	5.63	5.20	4.81	4.55
Dividends Per Share	0.420	0.410	0.380	0.360	0.340	0.320	0.310	0.300
Dividend Payout %	113.51	31.01	28.51	28.07	28.75	29.50	34.32	43.00
Income Statement								
Total Revenues	1,135,533	4,200,328	3,910,314	4,124,112	3,675,132	3,357,757	3,261,045	3,256,551
Total Indirect Exp.	184,846	696,857	636,862	834,469	737,651	737,125	620,449	585,543
Depreciation & Amort.	23,025	88,020	83,238	90,193	65,886	64,656	60,273	52,925
Operating Income	85,224	310,410	318,250	300,306	262,607	240,907	211,884	173,346
Net Interest Inc./(Exp.)	(6,810)	(31,864)	(31,425)	(27,953)	(14,906)	(13,746)	(13,692)	(15,043)
Income Taxes	29,790	103,552	104,648	102,573	94,164	88,035	78,045	61,369
Eqty Earns/Minority Int.	1,706	5,886	7,741	2,866	476	6,995	4,323	3,402
Net Income	51,826	185,779	189,322	182,441	170,217	163,438	139,291	109,492
Average Shs. Outstg.	140,102	139,710	140,292	140,125	141,523	147,010	150,406	153,458
Balance Sheet								
Cash & Cash Equivalents	85,188	97,976	309,563	186,276	106,610	248,562	238,032	152,386
Total Current Assets	827,212	823,974	962,170	883,281	711,109	800,143	717,365	671,352
Total Assets	2,416,384	2,393,121	2,220,196	2,162,698	1,641,940	1,685,585	1,555,892	1,528,535
Total Current Liabilities	419,654	441,990	410,111	420,203	342,625	385,407	267,651	260,578
Long–Term Obligations	395,256	395,273	409,648	462,407	145,928	184,723	204,874	198,232
Net Stockholders' Equity	1,299,179	1,252,735	1,115,255	995,881	873,877	841,142	813,315	802,202
Net Working Capital	407,558	381,984	552,059	463,078	368,484	414,736	449,714	410,774
Shares Outstanding	138,421	138,596	138,411	138,663	138,569	142,724	146,992	151,552
Statistical Record								
Operating Profit Margin %	7.50	7.39	8.13	7.28	7.14	7.17	6.49	5.32
Return on Equity %	3.98	14.82	16.97	18.31	19.47	19.43	17.12	13.64
Return on Assets %	2.14	7.76	8.52	8.43	10.36	9.69	8.95	7.16
Debt/Total Assets %	16.35	16.51	18.45	21.38	8.88	10.95	13.16	12.96
Price Range	27.45–23.80	24.98–20.18	28.03–20.50	26.39–16.75	22.28–14.13	22.63–14.78	19.44–13.09	16.25–11.75
P/E Ratio	74.19–64.32	18.78–15.17	20.76–15.19	20.30–12.88	18.57–11.77	20.38–13.32	21.13–14.23	22.89–16.55
Average Yield %	1.62	1.81	1.54	1.68	1.94	1.72	1.91	2.23

Address: 1 Hormel Place, Austin, MN 55912–3680	Officers: Joel W. Johnson – Chmn., Pres., C.E.O., Michael J. McCoy – Exec. V.P., C.F.O.	Investor Contact: (507) 437–5007
Telephone: (507) 437–5611	Transfer Agents: Wells Fargo Bank Minnesota, N.A., South St. Paul, MN	Institutional Holding
Web Site: www.hormel.com		No of Institutions: 11
		Shares: 16,330 % Held: –

HUDSON UNITED BANCORP

Exchange	Symbol	Price	52Wk Range	Yield	P/E
NYS	HU	$38.05 (3/31/2004)	40.39-30.83	3.47	15.22

*7 Year Price Score N/A *NYSE Composite Index=100 *12 Month Price Score 94.4

Interim Earnings (Per Share)

Qtr.	Mar	Jun	Sep	Dec
2000	0.52	(0.22)	0.40	0.22
2001	0.46	0.49	0.51	0.54
2002	0.93	0.56	0.60	0.63
2003	0.63	0.65	0.68	0.54

Interim Dividends (Per Share)

Amt	Decl	Ex	Rec	Pay
0.30Q	4/16/2003	5/14/2003	5/16/2003	6/2/2003
0.30Q	6/18/2003	8/13/2003	8/15/2003	9/2/2003
0.30Q	10/23/2003	11/12/2003	11/14/2003	12/1/2003
0.33Q	1/27/2004	2/11/2004	2/13/2004	3/1/2004

Indicated Div: $1.32

Valuation Analysis

Forecast P/E	12.37	Trailing P/E	15.22
Market Cap	$1.7 Billion	Book Value	458.2 Million
Price/Book	3.67	Price/Sales	3.19

Dividend Achiever Status

Rank	59	10 Year Growth Rate	16.64%
Total Years of Dividend Growth		13	

Business Summary: Commercial Banking (MIC: 8.1 SIC: 6022 NAIC:522110)

Hudson United Bancorp is a bank holding company. Co. directly owns Hudson United Bank, a full-service commercial bank that operated 205 offices, as of Dec 31 2003, throughout the state of New Jersey; in the Hudson Valley area of New York State; in New York City; in southern Connecticut; and in Philadelphia and surrounding areas in Pennsylvania. Co. also directly owns six additional subsidiaries, which are HUBCO Capital Trust I, HUBCO Capital Trust II, JBI Capital Trust I, Hudson United Capital Trust I, Hudson United Capital Trust II and Jefferson Delaware Inc. As of Dec 31 2003, Co., through its subsidiaries, had total deposits of $6.24 billion and total assets of $8.10 billion.

Recent Developments: For the year ended Dec 31 2003, net income was $112.3 million compared with $123.2 million a year earlier. Results for 2002 included a $77.0 million gain related to the Dime merger termination payment, partially offset by $8.3 million in termination-related expenses. Net interest income slipped to $299.3 million from $300.8 million the previous year. Provision for loan and lease losses was $26.0 million versus $51.3 million in 2002, the latter of which included $21.3 million related to non-performing loans held for accelerated disposition or sale. Non-interest income declined to $133.0 million from $185.1 million last year, reflecting the aforementioned Dime merger termination payment.

Prospects: Co.'s near-term outlook appears satisfactory, reflecting its increasing focus on the high growth, high profit areas of its business such as commercial lending and its third party credit card business. Accordingly, Co. estimates that full-year 2004 earnings would range between $2.85 and $2.90 per share. Co. also indicated that during 2004 and subsequent years, it expects to continue to focus on the internal growth of its businesses as well as supplementing internal growth through acquisitions. However, Co. noted that acquisitions will be considered only if they add customer relationships, product capabilities and can be accretive to earnings per share.

Financial Data

(US$ in Thousands)	12/31/2003	12/31/2002	12/31/2001	12/31/2000	12/31/1999	12/31/1998	12/31/1997	12/31/1996
Earnings Per Share	2.50	2.72	2.00	0.92	1.18	0.49	1.79	0.77
Tang. Book Val. Per Share	7.91	7.38	6.49	5.58	7.06	8.25	6.32	6.51
Dividends Per Share	1.180	1.100	1.010	0.930	0.880	0.770	0.640	0.570
Dividend Payout %	47.20	40.44	50.50	101.28	74.68	157.32	35.87	73.67
Income Statement								
Total Interest Income	394,129	430,003	470,363	608,309	644,576	468,547	218,041	204,182
Total Interest Expense	94,871	129,246	184,997	288,583	301,510	214,353	77,797	72,828
Net Interest Income	299,258	300,757	285,366	319,726	343,066	254,194	140,244	131,354
Provision for Loan Losses	26,000	51,333	34,147	24,000	52,200	14,374	7,327	12,295
Non-Interest Income	133,045	185,122	109,425	31,095	88,698	33,299	41,107	30,276
Non-Interest Expense	256,295	247,126	227,240	250,031	271,287	232,096	93,593	116,239
Income Before Taxes	150,008	187,420	133,404	76,790	108,277	41,023	80,431	33,096
Net Income	112,321	123,206	94,461	49,821	69,338	23,151	49,314	21,497
Average Shs. Outstg.	44,892	45,349	47,160	54,186	58,566	47,241	27,357	27,916
Balance Sheet								
Cash & Due from Banks	272,636	275,580	231,641	276,784	277,558	217,954	167,096	128,868
Securities Avail. for Sale	2,706,185	2,616,452	1,302,397	422,727	2,804,302	2,260,625	550,505	655,492
Net Loans & Leases	4,591,909	4,267,546	4,374,556	5,182,343	5,571,759	3,333,311	1,736,598	1,849,202
Total Assets	8,100,658	7,651,261	6,999,535	6,817,226	9,686,286	6,778,661	3,046,505	3,115,687
Total Deposits	6,243,539	6,199,701	5,983,545	5,813,267	6,455,345	5,051,369	2,314,399	2,592,092
Long-Term Obligations	1,160,992	751,939	123,000	123,000	132,000	100,000	461,319	287,979
Total Liabilities	7,642,468	7,218,735	6,615,631	6,448,753	9,167,120	6,321,846	2,860,365	2,909,354
Net Stockholders' Equity	458,190	432,526	383,904	368,473	519,166	456,815	186,140	206,333
Shares Outstanding	44,798	45,023	45,814	47,964	57,085	45,786	25,571	26,584
Statistical Record								
Return on Equity %	24.51	28.48	24.60	13.52	13.35	5.06	26.49	10.41
Return on Assets %	1.38	1.61	1.34	0.73	0.71	0.34	1.61	0.68
Equity/Assets %	5.65	5.65	5.48	5.40	5.35	6.73	6.10	6.62
Non-Int. Exp./Tot. Inc. %	48.61	40.17	39.19	39.10	36.99	46.24	36.11	49.57
Price Range	40.39-29.80	32.85-23.30	29.33-20.00	25.11-16.42	31.77-22.73	...	...	...
P/E Ratio	16.16-11.92	12.08-8.57	14.67-10.00	27.30-17.85	26.93-19.26	...	...	...
Average Yield %	3.43	3.71	4.06	4.53	3.17	N/A	N/A	N/A

Address: 1000 Macarthur Boulevard, Mahwah, NJ 07430 Telephone: (201) 236-2600 Web Site: www.hudsonunitedbank.com	Officers: Kenneth T. Neilson - Chmn., Pres., C.E.O., James Mayo - Exec. V.P., Transfer Agents:American Stock Transfer Company, New York, NY	Investor Contact:201-236-2803 Institutional Holding No of Institutions: 182 Shares: 21,597,254 % Held: 48%

ILLINOIS TOOL WORKS, INC.

Exchange	Symbol	Price	52Wk Range	Yield	P/E
NYS	ITW	$79.23 (3/31/2004)	84.78-58.63	1.21	23.51

*7 Year Price Score 110.2 *NYSE Composite Index=100 *12 Month Price Score 104.2

Interim Earnings (Per Share)

Qtr.	Mar	Jun	Sep	Dec
2000	0.72	0.90	0.87	0.66
2001	0.60	0.76	0.65	0.61
2002	0.63	0.86	0.79	0.74
2003	0.65	0.92	0.87	0.93

Interim Dividends (Per Share)

Amt	Decl	Ex	Rec	Pay
0.23Q	5/9/2003	6/26/2003	6/30/2003	7/21/2003
0.24Q	8/8/2003	9/26/2003	9/30/2003	10/20/2003
0.24Q	10/31/2003	12/29/2003	12/31/2003	1/26/2004
0.24Q	2/11/2004	3/29/2004	3/31/2004	4/19/2004

Indicated Div: $0.96 (Div. Reinv. Plan)

Valuation Analysis

Forecast P/E	19.82	Trailing P/E	23.51
Market Cap	$24.3 Billion	Book Value	7.9 Billion
Price/Book	3.28	Price/Sales	2.57

Dividend Achiever Status

Rank	88	10 Year Growth Rate	14.27%
Total Years of Dividend Growth			41

Business Summary: Plastics (MIC: 11.7 SIC: 3089 NAIC:326199)

Illinois Tool Works is a global manufacturer of engineered products and specialty systems, and has 625 operations in 44 countries that are organized into five segments. Engineered Products – North America segment and Engineered Products – International segment manufacture short lead–time plastic and metal components and fasteners, and specialty products. Specialty Systems – North America segment and Specialty Systems – International segment design and manufacture longer lead–time machinery and related consumables and specialty equipment. Leasing and Investments segment invests in mortgage entities, and leases telecommunications, aircraft, air traffic control and other equipment.

Recent Developments: For the twelve months ended Dec 31 2003, income from continuing operations climbed 11.6% to $1.04 billion compared with income of $931.8 million, before an accounting change charge of $221.9 million, in 2002. Results benefited from improved operating performance in Co.'s international and North American businesses, currency translation, and a lower effective tax rate. Results for 2003 and 2002 excluded a loss of $16.5 million and a gain of $2.7 million, respectively, from discontinued operations. Operating revenues grew 6.0% to $10.04 billion from $9.47 billion in the prior year. Operating income increased 8.5% to $1.63 billion compared with $1.51 billion the year before.

Prospects: Looking ahead, Co. is cautiously optimistic about prospects for gradual improvement in its North American end markets. Based on actual results in the first quarter of 2004, Co. changed its diluted earnings per share from continuing operations to range from $0.80 to $0.84, up from $0.73 to $0.81. For full–year 2004, Co. revised its diluted earnings per share from continuing operations range upward to $3.70 to $4.00 versus $3.66 to $3.96. The improvement in Co.'s forecast is based on improving end market activity in North America and the related effect on base revenues. In addition, translation continues to be a strong contributor to income growth.

Financial Data (US$ in Thousands)	12/31/2003	12/31/2002	12/31/2001	12/31/2000	12/31/1999	12/31/1998	12/31/1997	12/31/1996
Earnings Per Share	3.37	3.02	2.62	3.15	2.76	2.67	2.33	1.96
Cash Flow Per Share	4.43	4.18	4.41	3.68	3.40	2.85	2.62	2.54
Tang. Book Val. Per Share	16.44	13.12	10.82	9.55	9.26	8.59	8.14	6.79
Dividends Per Share	0.930	0.890	0.820	0.740	0.630	0.510	0.430	0.350
Dividend Payout %	27.59	29.47	31.29	23.49	22.82	19.10	18.45	17.86
Income Statement								
Total Revenues	10,035,623	9,467,740	9,292,791	9,983,577	9,333,185	5,647,889	5,220,433	4,996,681
Total Indirect Exp.	1,874,473	1,748,178	1,795,435	1,934,911	1,885,273	942,480	914,416	914,561
Depreciation & Amort.	24,276	27,933	104,585	121,456	74,222	51,899	44,148	39,179
Operating Income	1,633,458	1,505,771	1,306,103	1,563,437	1,405,364	1,079,286	927,223	800,586
Net Interest Inc./(Exp.)	(44,501)	(50,881)	(51,875)	(56,528)	(49,950)	(4,487)	(4,791)	(27,834)
Income Taxes	535,900	501,750	428,400	520,200	511,600	386,800	337,400	284,000
Income from Cont Ops	1,040,214	931,810	802,449	...	...	...	...	...
Net Income	1,023,680	712,592	805,659	957,980	841,112	672,784	586,951	486,313
Average Shs. Outstg.	308,750	308,045	306,306	304,414	304,649	252,443	251,760	247,556
Balance Sheet								
Cash & Cash Equivalents	1,684,483	1,057,687	282,224	151,295	232,953	93,485	185,856	137,694
Total Current Assets	4,783,202	3,878,809	3,163,244	3,329,061	3,272,931	1,834,473	1,858,642	1,701,092
Total Assets	11,193,321	10,623,101	9,822,349	9,603,456	9,060,259	5,997,379	5,291,830	4,806,161
Total Current Liabilities	1,488,903	1,567,162	1,518,158	1,817,610	2,045,361	1,222,000	1,157,880	1,219,321
Long–Term Obligations	920,360	1,460,381	1,267,141	1,549,038	1,360,746	947,008	854,328	818,941
Net Stockholders' Equity	7,874,286	6,649,071	6,040,738	5,400,987	4,815,423	3,338,035	2,806,454	2,396,021
Net Working Capital	3,294,299	2,311,647	1,645,086	1,511,451	1,227,570	612,464	700,762	481,769
Shares Outstanding	308,636	306,582	304,926	305,448	300,568	250,128	249,598	247,774
Statistical Record								
Operating Profit Margin %	16.27	15.90	14.05	15.66	15.05	19.10	17.76	16.02
Return on Equity %	13.21	14.01	13.28	17.73	17.46	20.15	20.91	20.29
Return on Assets %	9.29	8.77	8.16	9.97	9.28	11.21	11.09	10.11
Debt/Total Assets %	8.22	13.74	12.90	16.13	15.01	15.79	16.14	17.03
Price Range	84.15-55.15	77.38-55.73	71.20-49.15	68.31-51.06	82.00-58.00	81.81-45.44	60.13-38.38	43.13-26.13
P/E Ratio	24.97-16.36	25.62-18.45	27.18-18.76	21.69-16.21	29.71-21.01	26.90-17.02	25.80-16.47	22.00-13.31
Average Yield %	1.37	1.32	1.31	1.27	0.88	0.84	0.89	1.01

Address: 3600 West Lake Avenue, Glenview, IL 60025–5811 Telephone: (847) 724–7500 Web Site: www.itw.com	Officers: W. James Farrell – Chmn., C.E.O., Frank S. Ptak – Vice–Chmn. Transfer Agents:Computershare Investor Service, L.L.C., Chicago, IL	Institutional Holding No of Institutions: 25 Shares: 49,367,852 % Held: –

INDEPENDENT BANK CORPORATION

Exchange	Symbol	Price	52Wk Range	Yield	P/E
NMS	IBCP	$27.86 (3/31/2004)	30.50–17.97	2.30	14.90

7 Year Price Score 181.9 *NYSE Composite Index=100 *12 Month Price Score 109.9

Interim Earnings (Per Share)

Qtr.	Mar	Jun	Sep	Dec
2000	0.20	0.21	0.25	0.26
2001	0.24	0.29	0.29	0.33
2002	0.34	0.35	0.34	0.40
2003	0.44	0.45	0.51	0.47

Interim Dividends (Per Share)

Amt	Decl	Ex	Rec	Pay
10%	9/19/2003	10/2/2003	10/6/2003	10/31/2003
0.16Q	9/19/2003	10/2/2003	10/6/2003	10/31/2003
0.16Q	12/4/2003	12/31/2003	1/5/2004	1/30/2004
0.16Q	3/19/2004	4/1/2004	4/5/2004	4/30/2004

Indicated Div: $0.64 (Div. Reinv. Plan)

Valuation Analysis

Forecast P/E	N/A
Market Cap	$333.6 Million
Price/Book	N/A

Trailing P/E	14.90
Book Value	154.6 Million
Price/Sales	N/A

Dividend Achiever Status

Rank	42	10 Year Growth Rate 18.14%
Total Years of Dividend Growth		15

TRADING VOLUME (thousand shares)

1994 1995 1996 1997 1998 1999 2000 2001 2002 2003 04

Business Summary: Commercial Banking (MIC: 8.1 SIC: 6022 NAIC:522110)

Independent Bank is a bank holding company. Through its subsidiaries, Co. covers all phases of commercial banking, including checking and savings accounts, commercial lending, direct and indirect consumer financing, mortgage lending and safe deposit box services. Co. also offers title insurance services. Co.'s principal markets are the rural and suburban communities across lower Michigan, in which it serves through four main offices and a total of 77 branches, four drive–thru facilities and 12 loan production offices. As of Dec 31 2003, total assets were $2.36 billion and deposits amounted to $1.70 billion.

Recent Developments: For the year ended Dec 31 2003, net income advanced 27.6% to $37.6 million from $29.5 million the year before. The increase was due to higher net interest income, fee income on deposits, and gains on the sale of real estate mortgage loans. Results for 2003 and 2002 included a net gain of $15.5 million and $8.2 million, respectively, on asset sales. Net interest income grew 5.4% to $95.3 million. Provision for loan losses increased 13.2% to $4.0 million. Total non–interest income improved 37.8% to $42.6 million, while total non–interest expense climbed 20.8% to $82.5 million.

Prospects: Co. continues to expand through strategic acquisitions. For instance, on Feb 5 2004, Co. announced a definitive agreement to acquire Midwest Guaranty Bancorp, a $235.0 million bank that operates six full–service branches in southeastern Michigan. Also, on Mar 5 2004, Co. announced a definitive agreement to acquire North Bancorp, a $173.0 million bank that operates three branches in the northern Lower Peninsula of Michigan. Co. expects both transactions, which are scheduled to close by Jul 31 2004, to be accretive to earnings per share in their first full year of operation. Looking ahead, Co. expects earnings growth to be relatively flat in 2004 compared with earnings levels in 2003.

Financial Data

(US$ in Thousands)	9 Mos	6 Mos	3 Mos	12/31/2002	12/31/2001	12/31/2000	12/31/1999	12/31/1998
Earnings Per Share	1.41	0.89	0.44	1.43	1.15	0.92	0.39	0.68
Tang. Book Val. Per Share	6.67	6.54	7.37	7.04	6.41	6.38	5.30	4.70
Dividends Per Share	0.500	0.460	0.430	0.410	0.340	0.300	0.270	0.240
Dividend Payout %	35.73	51.89	98.53	28.93	30.00	33.24	69.83	35.42
Income Statement								
Total Interest Income	103,049	67,078	31,620	129,815	141,359	138,415	125,510	86,073
Total Interest Expense	33,516	22,804	10,813	48,008	62,460	67,865	58,730	36,840
Net Interest Income	69,533	44,274	20,807	81,807	78,899	70,550	66,780	49,233
Provision for Loan Losses	2,279	1,710	1,000	3,562	3,737	3,287	2,661	3,043
Non–Interest Income	32,640	20,826	10,415	30,911	27,085	18,961	17,323	13,845
Non–Interest Expense	60,996	38,702	18,055	68,293	68,526	58,949	69,480	45,688
Income Before Taxes	38,898	24,688	12,167	40,863	33,721	27,275	11,962	14,347
Income from Cont Ops	...	...	...	...	24,433	...	...	...
Net Income	28,268	17,948	8,817	29,467	24,398	20,009	8,669	10,221
Average Shs. Outstg.	20,072	20,072	19,990	20,516	21,174	21,525	21,985	14,893
Balance Sheet								
Cash & Due from Banks	54,633	73,114	59,798	60,731	50,525	58,149	58,646	42,846
Securities Avail. for Sale	875,374	859,212	772,582	371,246	290,303	217,447	195,300	99,515
Net Loans & Leases	1,597,717	1,516,531	1,372,763	1,364,737	1,368,517	1,365,682	1,277,656	812,890
Total Assets	2,315,762	2,300,281	2,061,493	2,057,562	1,888,457	1,783,791	1,725,205	1,085,258
Total Deposits	1,639,358	1,635,396	1,560,345	1,535,603	1,387,367	1,389,900	1,310,810	830,514
Long–Term Obligations	50,600	50,600	67,850	310,413	288,010	196,032	224,570	130,964
Total Liabilities	2,161,113	2,146,773	1,916,100	1,919,515	1,756,554	1,655,455	1,611,459	1,015,553
Net Stockholders' Equity	154,649	153,508	145,393	138,047	131,903	128,336	113,746	69,705
Shares Outstanding	19,525	19,668	19,714	19,604	20,555	20,113	21,459	14,806
Statistical Record								
Return on Equity %	18.27	11.69	6.06	21.34	18.52	15.59	7.62	14.66
Return on Assets %	1.22	0.78	0.42	1.43	1.29	1.12	0.50	0.94
Equity/Assets %	6.67	6.67	7.05	6.70	6.98	7.19	6.59	6.42
Non–Int. Exp./Tot. Inc. %	44.95	44.02	42.95	42.49	40.68	37.45	48.64	45.72
Price Range	27.82–17.74	24.38–17.74	19.36–17.74	20.32–15.02	16.74–10.24	10.86–5.66	10.47–6.94	15.04–9.47
P/E Ratio	19.73–12.58	27.40–19.93	44.01–40.31	14.21–10.51	14.56–8.90	11.80–6.15	26.85–17.79	22.11–13.93
Average Yield %	2.29	2.30	2.33	2.29	2.53	3.82	3.15	2.00

Address: 230 West Main Street, Ionia, MI 48846 **Telephone:** (616) 527–9450 **Web Site:** www.ibcp.com	**Officers:** Terry L. Haske – Chmn., Charles C. Van Loan – Pres., C.E.O.	**Investor Contact:** (616) 527–9450 **Institutional Holding** **No of Institutions:** 21 **Shares:** 723,878 **% Held:** –

145

IRWIN FINANCIAL CORP. (COLUMBUS, IN)

Exchange	Symbol	Price	52Wk Range	Yield	P/E
NYS	IFC	$26.98 (3/31/2004)	35.95–19.42	1.19	11.01

*7 Year Price Score N/A *NYSE Composite Index=100 *12 Month Price Score 114.3

TRADING VOLUME (thousand shares)

Interim Earnings (Per Share)

Qtr.	Mar	Jun	Sep	Dec
2000	0.40	0.41	0.43	0.43
2001	0.41	0.56	0.50	0.52
2002	0.37	0.28	0.29	0.93
2003	0.41	0.45	1.03	0.56

Interim Dividends (Per Share)

Amt	Decl	Ex	Rec	Pa
0.07Q	4/24/2003	6/11/2003	6/13/2003	6/27/200
0.07Q	8/27/2003	9/10/2003	9/12/2003	9/26/200
0.07Q	12/1/2003	12/10/2003	12/12/2003	12/26/200
0.08Q	2/20/2004	3/10/2004	3/12/2004	3/26/200

Indicated Div: $0.32 (Div. Reinv. Plan)

Valuation Analysis

Forecast P/E	10.68	Trailing P/E	11.01
Market Cap	$748.3 Million	Book Value	432.3 Million
Price/Book	2.08	Price/Sales	1.47

Dividend Achiever Status

Rank	91	10 Year Growth Rate 14.08%
Total Years of Dividend Growth		14

Business Summary: Commercial Banking (MIC: 8.1 SIC: 6022 NAIC:522110)

Irwin Financial is a diversified financial services company with $4.99 billion in assets at Dec 31 2003. Co.'s major lines of business are mortgage banking, commercial banking, home equity lending, commercial finance and venture capital. Direct and indirect major subsidiaries include Irwin Union Bank and Trust, a commercial bank, which together with Irwin Union Bank, F.S.B., a federal savings bank, conduct Co.'s commercial banking activities; Irwin Mortgage Corporation, a mortgage banking company; Irwin Home Equity Corporation, a consumer home equity lending company; Irwin Commercial Finance Corporation, a commercial finance subsidiary; and IrwinVentures LLC, a venture capital company.

Recent Developments: For the year ended Dec 31 2003, net income was $72.8 million compared with income of $52.8 million before an accounting change gain of $495,000, the previous year. Net income was driven by significantly higher earnings from Co.'s mortgage banking operations, which climbed 75.3% to $78.1 million from $44.5 million last year. Net interest income rose 27.3% to $271.9 million. Provision for loan and lease losses amounted to $47.6 million versus $44.0 million in 2002. Noninterest income jumped 40.1% to $329.3 million, primarily due to a $127.0 million or 53.0% increase in gain from sale of loans as a result of increased production and increased secondary market deliveries.

Prospects: Despite a decline in mortgage originations due to rising interest rates, Co.'s near–term outlook appears reasonably positive. Co. noted that it expects a higher proportion of earnings in 2004 to come from its commercial banking, home equity and commercial finance lines of business, rather than from mortgage banking, which has benefited significantly from heavy mortgage refinancing volumes from late 2002 through the third quarter of 2003. In addition, Co. indicated that it is experiencing improving credit quality and that its expenses for credit reserves should decline in 2004.

Financial Data

(US$ in Thousands)	12/31/2003	12/31/2002	12/31/2001	12/31/2000	12/31/1999	12/31/1998	12/31/1997	12/31/1996
Earnings Per Share	2.45	1.87	1.99	1.67	1.51	1.38	1.07	0.9
Tang. Book Val. Per Share	15.36	12.98	10.83	8.96	7.54	6.70	5.81	2.2
Dividends Per Share	0.280	0.270	0.260	0.240	0.200	0.160	0.140	0.12
Dividend Payout %	11.42	14.43	13.06	14.37	13.24	11.59	13.02	
Income Statement								
Total Interest Income	370,984	311,442	268,233	184,530	126,613	122,386	99,441	89,44
Total Interest Expense	99,099	97,795	121,084	93,534	54,794	59,202	44,582	41,62
Net Interest Income	271,885	213,647	147,149	90,996	71,819	63,184	54,859	47,82
Provision for Loan Losses	47,583	43,996	17,505	5,403	4,443	5,995	6,238	4,45
Non–Interest Income	329,299	257,433	271,391	211,711	204,069	243,729	174,564	153,64
Non–Interest Expense	435,199	340,853	327,420	237,962	214,111	245,436	176,534	159,73
Income Before Taxes	27,399	(122,330)	23,481	19,813	41,632	55,482	46,652	37,28
Eqty Earns/Minority Int.	...	...	...	350	...	...	...	...
Income from Cont Ops	(18,186)	(155,728)	(4,793)	...	22,151	...	...	...
Net Income	72,811	53,328	45,516	...	37,853	35,128	28,918	22,42
Average Shs. Outstg.	30,850	29,675	24,173	21,593	21,886	22,139	22,722	23,21
Balance Sheet								
Securities Avail. for Sale	67,569	62,599	...	...	...	...	...	...
Net Loans & Leases	3,096,769	2,764,340	2,115,464	1,221,793	724,869	547,103	602,281	522,45
Total Assets	4,988,359	4,884,722	3,439,795	2,422,429	1,680,847	1,946,179	1,496,794	1,303,88
Total Deposits	2,899,662	2,694,344	2,309,018	1,443,330	870,318	1,009,211	719,596	640,15
Long–Term Obligations	860,315	421,495	29,654	29,608	29,784	2,839	7,096	17,64
Total Liabilities	4,556,099	4,524,167	3,207,472	2,232,504	1,521,551	1,800,946	1,368,811	1,184,98
Net Stockholders' Equity	432,260	360,555	232,323	189,925	159,296	145,233	127,983	118,90
Shares Outstanding	28,134	27,771	21,305	21,025	21,104	21,672	22,000	22,73
Statistical Record								
Return on Equity %	N.M	N.M	N.M	N.M.	13.90	24.18	22.59	18.8
Return on Assets %	N.M.	N.M.	N.M.	N.M.	1.31	1.80	1.93	1.7
Equity/Assets %	8.66	7.38	6.75	7.84	9.47	7.46	8.55	9.1
Non–Int. Exp./Tot. Inc. %	62.14	59.91	60.67	60.05	64.74	67.03	64.42	65.7
Price Range	31.99–16.10	20.36–13.90	21.74–14.51	...	...	...	...	...
P/E Ratio	13.06–6.57	10.89–7.43	10.92–7.29	...	...	...	...	...
Average Yield %	1.20	1.58	1.48	N/A	N/A	N/A	N/A	N/

Address: 500 Washington Street, Columbus, IN 47201	Officers: William I. Miller – Chmn., C.E.O., Thomas D. Washburn – Exec. V.P.	Investor Contact:812–376–1020
Telephone: (812) 376–1909	Transfer Agents:National City Bank	Institutional Holding No of Institutions: 30
Web Site: www.irwinfinancial.com		Shares: 104,437 % Held: –

JACK HENRY & ASSOCIATES, INC.

Exchange	Symbol	Price	52Wk Range	Yield	P/E
NMS	JKHY	$19.13 (3/31/2004)	21.97-10.75	0.84	31.88

7 Year Price Score 108.9 *NYSE Composite Index=100 *12 Month Price Score 114.7

Interim Earnings (Per Share)

Qtr.	Sep	Dec	Mar	Jun
2000–01	0.13	0.14	0.17	0.17
2001–02	0.16	0.14	0.15	0.17
2002–03	0.13	0.13	0.14	0.15
2003–04	0.15	0.16	...	

Interim Dividends (Per Share)

Amt	Decl	Ex	Rec	Pay
0.035Q	4/25/2003	4/29/2003	5/1/2003	5/16/2003
0.035Q	8/27/2003	9/3/2003	9/5/2003	9/19/2003
0.035Q	10/29/2003	11/14/2003	11/18/2003	12/2/2003
0.04Q	1/26/2004	2/9/2004	2/11/2004	2/26/2004

Indicated Div: $0.16 (Div. Reinv. Plan)

Valuation Analysis

Forecast P/E	N/A	Trailing P/E	31.88
Market Cap	$1.7 Billion	Book Value	406.8 Million
Price/Book	4.57	Price/Sales	4.32

Dividend Achiever Status

Rank	46	10 Year Growth Rate	17.67%
Total Years of Dividend Growth			12

Business Summary: IT &Technology (MIC: 10.2 SIC: 7373 NAIC:541512)

Jack Henry & Associates offers a suite of integrated computer systems that provide data processing and management information to banks, credit unions and other financial institutions in the U.S. Co.'s core proprietary applications include: Silverlake System®, typically for banks with total assets up to $30,000,000,000; CIF 20/20®, used primarily by banks with total assets up to $300,000,000; and Core Director®, which is used by banks employing client–server technology. Also, Co. offers Episys™, used primarily by credit unions with total assets greater than $25,000,000 and Cruise™, which is mainly used by credit unions with total assets under $25,000,000.

Recent Developments: For the three months ended Dec 31 2003, net income rose 24.4% to $14.5 million compared with $11.7 million in the equivalent quarter of 2002. Total revenues increased 9.9% to $112.7 million from $102.6 million a year earlier. Gross profit climbed 21.3% to $44.7 million, or 39.7% of total revenues, from $36.9 million, or 35.9% of total revenues, in the previous year. The increase in gross margin was primarily due to sales mix of hardware, and an increase over 2002 in incentives and rebates received on specific hardware sold. Operating income grew 23.9% to $22.6 million compared with $18.2 million the year before.

Prospects: The gradual recovery of new core sales and Co.'s outsourcing efforts are expected to continue to contribute to stronger results. Also, ATM and debit card processing and sales of complementary products and services are expected to continue to drive revenue growth. Even though Co. has a number of bank core system proposals, including several with large institutions, sales in this part of Co.'s business are returning slowly. Meanwhile, geographic expansion for item processing sites continues to drive growth in Co.'s outsourcing business. Co. anticipates opening three new item processing sites each year to support growth opportunities.

Financial Data
(US$ in Thousands)

	6 Mos	3 Mos	06/30/2003	06/30/2002	06/30/2001	06/30/2000	06/30/1999	06/30/1998
Earnings Per Share	0.60	0.57	0.55	0.62	0.61	0.40	0.38	0.28
Cash Flow Per Share	1.00	0.93	1.10	0.97	0.79	0.57	0.44	0.32
Tang. Book Val. Per Share	3.22	2.99	2.78	2.54	2.19	0.47	1.07	0.73
Dividends Per Share	0.140	0.140	0.140	0.130	0.110	0.090	0.070	0.060
Dividend Payout %	45.16	93.33	25.45	20.96	18.03	22.22	18.83	21.23
Income Statement								
Total Revenues	221,670	108,940	404,627	396,657	345,468	225,300	184,497	113,423
Total Indirect Exp.	43,212	21,096	76,065	74,574	65,857	47,106	35,636	24,017
Depreciation & Amort.	16,526	7,958	30,194	27,470	21,888	15,473	7,858	5,105
Operating Income	44,154	21,561	77,271	86,646	85,740	51,010	49,406	33,776
Net Interest Inc./(Exp.)	539	261	520	1,827	466	(1,047)	1,571	1,221
Income Taxes	16,313	7,965	28,394	31,408	31,292	17,415	18,821	13,127
Income from Cont Ops	...	...	...	...	...	34,350	32,526	22,237
Net Income	28,380	13,857	49,397	57,065	55,631	34,018	31,768	21,569
Average Shs. Outstg.	91,534	91,069	89,270	92,367	91,344	85,278	84,448	79,044
Balance Sheet								
Cash & Cash Equivalents	108,536	103,032	32,014	17,765	18,589	5,186	3,185	23,306
Total Current Assets	210,592	201,898	217,262	179,977	172,050	104,000	79,842	69,138
Total Assets	548,375	543,252	548,575	486,142	433,121	321,082	174,721	115,286
Total Current Liabilities	102,419	120,290	146,780	112,656	107,018	151,140	57,666	39,260
Long–Term Obligations	...	...	...	...	228	320	...	...
Net Stockholders' Equity	406,802	385,479	365,223	340,739	302,504	154,545	114,459	73,500
Net Working Capital	108,173	81,608	70,482	67,321	65,032	(47,140)	22,176	29,878
Shares Outstanding	89,558	88,856	88,156	88,950	88,846	82,715	80,400	75,740
Statistical Record								
Operating Profit Margin %	19.91	19.79	19.09	21.84	24.81	22.64	26.77	29.77
Return on Equity %	6.97	3.59	13.52	16.74	18.39	22.22	28.41	30.25
Return on Assets %	5.17	2.55	9.00	11.73	12.84	10.69	18.61	19.28
Debt/Total Assets %	...	...	...	...	0.05	0.09	...	...
Price Range	21.97-16.53	19.31-16.53	17.79-8.31	31.51-16.09	31.47-18.88	25.97-8.13	13.50-6.63	9.50-5.75
P/E Ratio	70.87-53.32	128.7-110.2	32.35-15.11	50.82-25.95	51.59-30.94	64.92-20.31	35.53-17.43	33.93-20.54
Average Yield %	0.73	0.77	1.07	0.56	0.43	0.64	0.69	0.81

Address: 663 Highway 60, Monett, MO 65708	**Officers:** Michael E. Henry – Chmn., C.E.O., John W. Henry – Vice–Chmn., Sr. V.P.	**Investor Contact:** 417–235–6652
Telephone: (417) 235 6652		**Institutional Holding**
Web Site: www.jackhenry.com		**No of Institutions:** 15
		Shares: 49,826,088 **% Held:** –

JEFFERSON-PILOT CORP.

Exchange	Symbol	Price	52Wk Range	Yield	P/E
NYS	JP	$55.01 (3/31/2004)	55.01-38.79	2.76	15.99

*7 Year Price Score 104.7 *NYSE Composite Index=100 *12 Month Price Score 101.1

Interim Earnings (Per Share)

Qtr.	Mar	Jun	Sep	Dec
2000	0.89	0.83	0.82	0.74
2001	0.71	0.87	0.87	0.89
2002	0.78	0.83	0.81	0.62
2003	0.76	0.98	0.88	0.82

Interim Dividends (Per Share)

Amt	Decl	Ex	Rec	Pay
0.33Q	5/5/2003	8/20/2003	8/22/2003	9/5/200:
0.33Q	8/4/2003	11/19/2003	11/21/2003	12/5/200:
0.33Q	11/3/2003	2/18/2004	2/20/2004	3/5/200
0.38Q	2/9/2004	5/19/2004	5/21/2004	6/5/200

Indicated Div: $1.52 (Div. Reinv. Plan)

Valuation Analysis

Forecast P/E	11.78	Trailing P/E	15.99
Market Cap	$8.1 Billion	Book Value	3.8 Billion
Price/Book	1.65	Price/Sales	1.76

Dividend Achiever Status

Rank	136	10 Year Growth Rate	11.19%
Total Years of Dividend Growth			36

Business Summary: Insurance (MIC: 8.2 SIC: 6311 NAIC:524110)

Jefferson-Pilot is a holding company that conducts insurance, investment, broadcasting and other business through its subsidiaries Jefferson-Pilot Life Insurance Company, Jefferson Pilot Financial Insurance Company, and Jefferson Pilot LifeAmerica Insurance Company, together known as Jefferson Pilot Financial, offer full lines of individual and group life insurance products as well as annuity and investment products. As of Dec 31 2003, Jefferson-Pilot Communications Company owned and operated three network television stations and 17 radio stations, and produced and syndicated sports programming.

Recent Developments: For the year ended Dec 31 2003, net income increased 9.3% to $492.0 million from $450.0 million in the prior year. Total revenue grew 4.9% to $3.57 billion from $3.41 billion the previous year. Revenue included realized investment losses c $47.0 million and $22.0 million, respectively. Premiums and other considerations advanced 13.1% to $951.0 million. Universal life and investment product charges improved 8.3% to $691.0 million. Net investment income rose 1.4% to $1.66 billion from $1.63 billion a year earlier. Communication sales increased 2.9% to $216.0 million. Insurance and annuity benefits expenses increased 4.8% to $2.01 billion.

Prospects: Co.'s prospects are encouraging. For instance, Premier Partnering continues as the cornerstone of its individual lif insurance business and remains a powerful platform for growth as Co. builds its key distribution channels. In addition, both the Annuit and Investment Products and Co.'s Benefit Partners' business continue to show strong and healthy progress. Separately, in March 2004 Co. acquired the U.S. group life, disability and dental business of The Canada Life Assurance Company, an indirect subsidiary o Great-West Lifeco Inc. Co. noted that it will invest about $200.0 million in the business.

Financial Data

(US$ in Millions)	12/31/2003	12/31/2002	12/31/2001	12/31/2000	12/31/1999	12/31/1998	12/31/1997	12/31/1996
Earnings Per Share	3.44	3.04	3.34	3.28	2.94	2.60	2.31	1.8
Tang. Book Val. Per Share	24.84	22.60	20.52	18.37	15.80	17.77	15.72	13.8
Dividends Per Share	1.290	1.180	1.070	0.960	0.850	0.760	0.690	0.62
Dividend Payout %	37.57	38.89	32.08	29.20	29.07	29.45	30.00	34.2:
Income Statement								
Total Premium Income	951	1,564	1,424	1,365	903	1,049	1,135	99
Net Investment Income	1,657	1,623	1,533	1,430	1,272	1,202	1,103	89.
Other Income	965	293	373	443	386	359	340	23
Total Revenues	3,573	3,480	3,330	3,238	2,561	2,610	2,578	2,12
Total Indirect Exp.	523	485	497	503	402	745	697	52
Inc. Before Inc. Taxes	738	710	800	814	751	670	591	44
Income Taxes	246	235	263	277	256	226	195	14
Net Income	492	475	538	537	495	444	396	29
Average Shs. Outstg.	142	148	153	155	159	160	160	15
Balance Sheet								
Cash & Cash Equivalents	72	67	139	26	62	21	9	10.
Premiums Due	1,340	1,375	1,433	1,450	1,576	1,342	1,526	1,26
Invst. Assets: Total	21,411	20,076	18,130	16,805	16,087	15,570	14,956	11,60
Total Assets	32,696	30,609	28,996	27,321	26,446	24,338	23,131	17,56.
Long-Term Obligations	309	300	450	439	590	627	631	14
Net Stockholders' Equity	3,806	3,540	3,391	3,159	2,753	3,049	2,679	2,24
Shares Outstanding	140	142	150	154	155	158	159	15
Statistical Record								
Return on Revenues %	13.77	13.65	16.16	16.58	19.33	17.01	15.36	13.8
Return on Equity %	12.92	13.41	15.83	16.99	17.98	14.54	14.49	12.7
Return on Assets %	1.50	1.55	1.85	1.96	1.87	1.82	1.71	1.6
Price Range	50.65-36.20	52.60-36.53	48.95-39.60	50.29-33.63	52.92-41.21	52.21-32.89	38.47-23.11	26.11-20.2
P/E Ratio	14.72-10.52	17.30-12.02	14.66-11.86	15.33-10.25	18.00-14.02	20.08-12.65	16.65-10.00	14.43-11.2
Average Yield %	3.02	2.64	2.37	2.28	1.84	1.92	2.31	2.6

Address: 100 North Greene Street, Greensboro, NC 27401
Telephone: (336) 691-3000
Web Site: www.jpfinancial.com

Officers: David A. Stonecipher - Chmn., Dennis R. Glass - Pres., C.E.O., C.O.O.
Transfer Agents: Wachovia Bank, Charlotte, NC

Investor Contact: (336) 691-3379
Institutional Holding
No of Institutions: 21
Shares: 1,730,156 **% Held:** -

JOHNSON & JOHNSON

Exchange	Symbol	Price	52Wk Range	Yield	P/E
NYS	JNJ	$50.72 (3/31/2004)	58.42–48.73	1.89	21.13

7 Year Price Score 116.4 *NYSE Composite Index=100* ***12 Month Price Score 85.4**

Interim Earnings (Per Share)

Qtr.	Apr	Jul	Oct	Dec
2000	0.46	0.47	0.44	0.33
2001	0.53	0.48	0.49	0.34
2002	0.59	0.54	0.57	0.46
2003	0.69	0.40	0.69	0.62

Interim Dividends (Per Share)

Amt	Decl	Ex	Rec	Pay
0.24Q	4/24/2003	5/16/2003	5/20/2003	6/10/2003
0.24Q	7/22/2003	8/15/2003	8/19/2003	9/9/2003
0.24Q	10/16/2003	11/14/2003	11/18/2003	12/9/2003
0.24Q	1/5/2004	2/12/2004	2/17/2004	3/9/2004

Indicated Div: $0.96 (Div. Reinv. Plan)

Valuation Analysis

Forecast P/E	16.69	Trailing P/E	21.13
Market Cap	$150.7 Billion	Book Value	26.9 Billion
Price/Book	5.67	Price/Sales	3.64

Dividend Achiever Status

Rank	94	10 Year Growth Rate	13.86%
Total Years of Dividend Growth			41

Business Summary: Pharmaceuticals (MIC: 9.1 SIC: 2834 NAIC:325412)

Johnson & Johnson is engaged in the manufacture and sale of a broad range of products in the health care field. The Pharmaceutical segment consists of prescription drugs in the antifungal, anti–infective, cardiovascular, dermatology, gastrointestinal, hematology, immunology, neurology, oncology, pain management, psychotropic and urology fields. The Medical Devices and Diagnostics segment includes products used by or under the direction of health care professionals. The Consumer segment manufactures and markets products used in the baby and child care, skin care, oral and wound care and women's health care fields, as well as nutritional and over–the–counter pharmaceutical products.

Recent Developments: For the year ended Dec 28 2003, net earnings climbed 9.1% to $7.20 billion compared with $6.60 billion the previous year. Results for 2003 and 2002 included pre–tax in–process research and development charges of $918.0 million and $189.0 million, respectively. Sales advanced 15.3% to $41.86 billion from $36.30 billion the year before. Consumer segment sales increased 13.2% to $7.43 billion from $6.56 billion, while Pharmaceutical segment sales jumped 13.8% to $19.52 billion from $17.15 billion the prior year. Sales in the Medical Device and Diagnostics segment improved 18.5% to $14.91 billion from $12.58 billion a year earlier.

Prospects: Sales growth for Co.'s Medical Devices and Diagnostics segment is being driven by *Cypher* sirolimus–eluting coronary stent, a treatment for coronary artery disease. The Pharmaceutical segment should continue to generate favorable results due to the strong performance of *Topamax, Aciphex/Pariet, Remicade, Duragesic* and *Risperdal*. Results for the Consumer segment should continue to benefit from McNeil Nutritional's *Splenda* sweetner, *Neutrogena* and *Aveeno* skin care lines, and Wound Care products. Separately, Co. and Merck & Co., Inc signed a definitive agreement for Co. to acquire Merck's 50.0% interest in their European non–prescription pharmaceuticals joint venture.

Financial Data

(US$ in Millions)	12/28/2003	12/29/2002	12/30/2001	12/31/2000	01/02/2000	01/03/1999	12/28/1997	12/29/1996
Earnings Per Share	2.40	2.16	1.84	1.70	1.47	1.11	1.20	1.08
Cash Flow Per Share	3.52	2.67	2.86	2.31	2.00	1.78	1.58	1.45
Tang. Book Val. Per Share	5.16	4.53	4.97	4.15	3.10	2.37	3.38	2.90
Dividends Per Share	0.920	0.790	0.700	0.620	0.540	0.480	0.420	0.360
Dividend Payout %	38.54	36.80	38.04	36.47	37.07	43.49	35.26	33.33
Income Statement								
Total Revenues	41,862	36,298	33,004	29,139	27,471	23,657	22,629	21,620
Total Indirect Exp.	19,733	16,362	15,688	13,822	13,103	11,893	10,855	10,299
Depreciation & Amort.	1,869	1,662	1,605	1,515	1,444	1,246	1,067	1,009
Operating Income	9,953	9,489	7,780	6,456	5,926	4,268	4,622	4,303
Net Interest Inc./(Exp.)	(30)	96	303	233	49	152	83	14
Income Taxes	3,111	2,694	2,230	1,822	1,586	1,210	1,273	569
Income from Cont Ops	...	...	...	...	...	...	...	3,464
Net Income	7,197	6,597	5,668	4,800	4,167	3,059	3,303	2,887
Average Shs. Outstg.	3,008	3,054	3,099	2,834	2,836	2,743	2,739	2,666
Balance Sheet								
Cash & Cash Equivalents	9,523	7,475	7,972	5,744	3,879	2,578	2,899	2,136
Total Current Assets	22,995	19,266	18,473	15,450	13,200	11,132	10,563	9,370
Total Assets	48,263	40,556	38,488	31,321	29,163	26,211	21,453	20,010
Total Current Liabilities	13,448	11,449	8,044	7,161	7,448	8,115	5,283	5,184
Long–Term Obligations	2,955	2,022	2,217	2,037	2,450	1,269	1,126	1,410
Net Stockholders' Equity	26,869	22,697	24,233	18,808	16,213	13,590	12,359	10,836
Net Working Capital	9,547	7,817	10,429	8,289	5,752	3,017	5,280	4,186
Shares Outstanding	2,967	2,968	3,047	2,781	2,779	2,688	2,690	2,664
Statistical Record								
Operating Profit Margin %	23.77	26.14	23.57	22.15	21.57	18.04	20.42	19.90
Return on Equity %	26.78	29.06	23.38	25.52	25.70	22.50	26.72	31.96
Return on Assets %	14.91	16.26	14.72	15.32	14.28	11.67	15.39	17.31
Debt/Total Assets %	6.12	4.98	5.76	6.50	8.40	4.84	5.24	7.04
Price Range	58.67–48.73	65.49–41.85	60.97–41.63	52.53–33.50	53.06–39.03	44.44–32.00	33.47–24.81	26.88–20.94
P/E Ratio	24.45–20.30	30.32–19.38	33.14–22.62	30.90–19.71	36.10–26.55	40.03–28.83	27.89–20.68	24.88–19.39
Average Yield %	1.75	1.37	1.35	1.39	1.15	1.28	1.41	1.48

Address: One Johnson &Johnson Plaza, NB, NJ 08933 **Telephone:** (732) 524–0400 **Web Site:** www.jnj.com	**Officers:** William C. Weldon – Chmn., C.E.O., Robert J. Darretta – Vice–Chmn., C.F.O. **Transfer Agents:** EquiServe Trust Company, N.A., Providence, RI	**Investor Contact:** (800) 950–5089 **Institutional Holding** **No of Institutions:** 18 **Shares:** 1,225,161 **% Held:** –

JOHNSON CONTROLS INC

Exchange	Symbol	Price	52Wk Range	Yield	P/E
NYS	JCI	$59.15 (3/31/2004)	60.90-36.66	1.52	15.90

*7 Year Price Score 140.1   *NYSE Composite Index=100   *12 Month Price Score 107.7

Interim Earnings (Per Share)

Qtr.	Dec	Mar	Jun	Sep
2000-01	0.55	0.44	0.72	0.84
2001-02	0.63	0.60	0.92	1.02
2002-03	0.74	0.70	1.00	1.16
2003-04	0.86	...	...	...

Interim Dividends (Per Share)

Amt	Decl	Ex	Rec	Pay
0.18Q	7/23/2003	9/10/2003	9/12/2003	9/30/200
0.225Q	11/19/2003	12/10/2003	12/12/2003	1/2/200
2-for-1	11/19/2003	1/5/2004	12/12/2003	1/2/200
0.225Q	1/28/2004	3/10/2004	3/12/2004	3/31/200

Indicated Div: $0.90 (Div. Reinv. Plan)

Valuation Analysis

Forecast P/E	12.89	Trailing P/E	15.90
Market Cap	$5.3 Billion	Book Value	4.6 Billion
Price/Book	2.27	Price/Sales	0.44

Dividend Achiever Status

Rank 205	10 Year Growth Rate	7.79%
Total Years of Dividend Growth	28

Business Summary: Chemicals (MIC: 11.1 SIC: 2531 NAIC:561790)

Johnson Controls conducts its business in two operating segments: the Controls Group and the Automotive Group. The Controls Grou provides installed building control systems and technical and facility management services, including comfort, energy and securit management for the non-residential buildings market. The Automotive Group designs and manufactures products and systems fo passenger cars and light trucks, including vans and SUVs. The segment produces automotive interior systems for original equipmen manufacturers and automotive batteries for the replacement and original equipment markets.

Recent Developments: For the three months ended Dec 31 2003, net income rose 17.2% to $164.5 million compared with $140.(million in the corresponding quarter of 2002. Net sales were $6.38 billion, up 23.2% from $5.18 billion in the prior-year period. Sales in the Automotive Group grew 26.3% to $4.98 billion from $3.94 billion due to higher shipments of interior systems and batteries in Nort America and Europe. Sales in the Controls Group rose 13.3% to $1.41 billion from $1.24 billion due to strong revenue growth in Nort America. Operating income climbed 5.6% to $261.8 million compared with $247.9 million a year earlier.

Prospects: For the remainder of the year, Co. anticipates vehicle production levels in its major geographic markets to be flat to slightl higher. The environment for controls is mixed, with overall weak new building construction remaining weak, while certain sector continue to provide opportunities. Nevertheless, Co.'s backlog and market share should lead to strong growth. Consolidated sales fo full-year 2004 are expected to increase in a range of 13.0% to 15.0%. Growth for the Automotive Group is expected to be betweer 13.0% and 18.0%, while growth for the Controls Group is expected at the high end of the 5.0% to 10.0% range.

Financial Data
(US$ in Thousands)

	3 Mos	09/30/2003	09/30/2002	09/30/2001	09/30/2000	09/30/1999	09/30/1998	09/30/1997
Earnings Per Share	0.86	3.60	3.17	2.55	2.54	2.24	1.81	1.18
Cash Flow Per Share	1.29	4.06	5.25	5.23	4.05	5.49	3.04	3.59
Tang. Book Val. Per Share	5.12	3.79	2.23	3.51	1.82	0.22	N.M	N.M
Dividends Per Share	0.765	0.720	0.660	0.620	0.560	0.500	0.460	0.430
Dividend Payout %	88.95	20	20.82	24.31	22.05	22.32	25.41	36.44
Income Statement								
Total Revenues	6,384,100	22,646,000	20,103,400	18,427,200	17,154,600	16,139,400	12,586,800	11,145,40(
Total Indirect Exp.	599,500	2,058,600	1,724,900	1,642,900	1,629,500	1,469,000	1,146,600	1,132,70(
Depreciation & Amort.	148,600	558,000	516,800	515,900	461,600	445,600	384,200	354,90(
Operating Income	261,800	1,161,600	1,122,000	961,100	965,000	854,900	664,000	527,10(
Net Interest Inc./(Exp.)	(25,300)	(103,500)	(110,400)	(110,000)	(111,500)	(136,000)	(118,700)	(112,800
Income Taxes	49,700	327,800	347,600	335,500	338,900	311,700	256,000	180,90(
Eqty Earns/Minority Int.	2,300	8,100	(20,000)	(21,500)	(44,400)	(38,600)	(23,100)	(24,100
Income from Cont Ops	...	...	...	...	...	...	...	220,60(
Net Income	164,500	682,900	600,500	478,300	472,400	419,600	337,700	288,50(
Average Shs. Outstg.	191,800	189,200	188,200	186,000	183,800	184,200	183,200	181,80(
Balance Sheet								
Cash & Cash Equivalents	302,600	136,100	262,000	374,600	275,600	276,200	134,000	111,80(
Total Current Assets	5,750,100	5,620,300	4,946,200	4,544,000	4,277,200	3,848,500	3,404,200	2,529,30(
Total Assets	13,670,900	13,127,300	11,165,300	9,911,500	9,428,000	8,614,200	7,942,100	6,048,60(
Total Current Liabilities	5,731,500	5,584,100	4,806,200	4,579,700	4,510,000	4,266,600	4,288,400	2,972,70(
Long-Term Obligations	1,830,600	1,776,600	1,826,600	1,394,800	1,315,300	1,283,300	997,500	806,40(
Net Stockholders' Equity	4,581,600	4,261,300	3,499,700	2,985,400	2,576,100	2,270,000	1,941,400	1,687,90(
Net Working Capital	18,600	36,200	140,000	(35,700)	(232,800)	(418,100)	(884,200)	(443,400
Shares Outstanding	188,551	180,310	177,760	174,997	171,978	170,790	169,400	168,20(
Statistical Record								
Operating Profit Margin %	4.10	5.12	5.58	5.21	5.62	5.29	5.27	4.7;
Return on Equity %	3.59	16.02	17.15	16.02	18.33	18.48	17.39	13.0(
Return on Assets %	1.20	5.20	5.37	4.82	5.01	4.87	4.25	3.6<
Debt/Total Assets %	13.39	13.53	16.35	14.07	13.95	14.89	12.55	13.3:
Price Range	58.06-47.30	50.35-35.26	46.53-32.75	40.78-23.84	35.19-23.50	37.56-20.97	30.50-21.38	24.78-18.0(
P/E Ratio	67.51-55.00	13.98-9.79	14.68-10.33	15.99-9.35	13.85-9.25	16.77-9.36	16.85-11.81	21.00-15.3:
Average Yield %	1.34	1.66	1.19	1.88	2.41	1.55	1.73	2.0(

Address: 5757 N. Green Bay Avenue, Milwaukee, WI 53201	Officers: John M. Barth - Chmn., Pres., C.E.O., Giovanni Fiori - Exec. V.P.	Investor Contact: (414) 524-2363
Telephone: (414) 524-1200	Transfer Agents:Firstar Trust Company,	Institutional Holding No of Institutions: 9
Web Site: www.johnsoncontrols.com	Milwaukee, WI	Shares: 124,664 % Held: -

KEYCORP (NEW)

Exchange	Symbol	Price	52Wk Range	Yield	P/E
NYS	KEY	$30.29 (3/31/2004)	32.94–22.93	4.09	14.29

7 Year Price Score 96.9 *NYSE Composite Index=100* **12 Month Price Score 97.8**

Interim Earnings (Per Share)

Qtr.	Mar	Jun	Sep	Dec
2000	0.83	0.57	0.28	0.62
2001	0.51	(0.38)	0.58	(0.34)
2002	0.56	0.57	0.57	0.57
2003	0.51	0.53	0.53	0.55

Interim Dividends (Per Share)

Amt	Decl	Ex	Rec	Pay
0.305Q	5/23/2003	6/2/2003	6/4/2003	6/16/2003
0.305Q	7/17/2003	8/28/2003	9/2/2003	9/15/2003
0.305Q	11/21/2003	11/28/2003	12/2/2003	12/12/2003
0.31Q	1/16/2004	2/27/2004	3/2/2004	3/15/2004

Indicated Div: $1.24 (Div. Reinv. Plan)

Valuation Analysis

Forecast P/E	11.39	Trailing P/E	14.29
Market Cap	$12.9 Billion	Book Value	7.0 Billion
Price/Book	1.76	Price/Sales	2.14

Dividend Achiever Status

Rank	199	10 Year Growth Rate	8.10%
Total Years of Dividend Growth	24		

Business Summary: Commercial Banking (MIC: 8.1 SIC: 6021 NAIC:522110)

KeyCorp is a multi-line financial services company, with assets of $84.49 billion as of Dec 31 2003. Co. provides investment management, retail and commercial banking, consumer finance, and investment banking products and services to individuals and companies throughout the United States and, for certain businesses, internationally. As of Dec 31 2003, Co. operates nationwide through 906 KeyCenters and offices, a network of 2,167 ATMs, telephone banking centers, and a Web site named Key.com that provides account access and financial products 24 hours a day.

Recent Developments: For the year ended Dec 31 2003, net income declined 7.5% to $903.0 million compared with $976.0 million the year before. Results for 2003 and 2003 included net gains from loan securitizations and sales of $90.0 million and $56.0 million, respectively. Net interest income slipped 0.9% to $2.73 billion from $2.75 billion in the previous year. Provision for loan losses decreased 9.4% to $501.0 million. Total non-interest income slid 0.5% to $1.76 billion from $1.77 billion in the prior year. Total non-interest expense grew 3.4% to $2.74 billion from $2.65 billion a year earlier, primarily as a result of higher pension costs, stock-based compensation and severance expense.

Prospects: Co. continues to focus on improving net interest margin, growing core deposits, and managing expenses effectively. Co.'s commercial lease financing and home equity lending businesses continue to grow at a steady pace. In addition, Co.'s asset quality trends remain positive. Nonperforming loans fell by $101.0 million during the fourth quarter of 2003, primarily due to reductions in the middle market, large corporate, structured finance and commercial real estate portfolios. Nonperforming loans represented 1.11% of loans outstanding at Dec 31 2003, down from 1.51% the year before. Looking ahead, Co. expects earnings per share to range from $2.25 to $2.35 for 2004.

Financial Data

(US$ in Thousands)	12/31/2003	12/31/2002	12/31/2001	12/31/2000	12/31/1999	12/31/1998	12/31/1997	12/31/1996
Earnings Per Share	2.12	2.27	0.37	2.30	2.45	2.23	2.07	1.65
Tang. Book Val. Per Share	13.88	13.34	11.84	12.41	11.14	10.29	9.14	7.96
Dividends Per Share	1.220	1.200	1.180	1.120	1.040	0.940	0.840	0.760
Dividend Payout %	57.54	52.86	318.91	48.69	42.44	42.15	40.57	46.06
Income Statement								
Total Interest Income	3,970,000	4,366,000	5,627,000	6,277,000	5,695,000	5,525,000	5,262,000	4,951,000
Total Interest Expense	1,245,000	1,617,000	2,802,000	3,547,000	2,908,000	2,841,000	2,468,000	2,234,000
Net Interest Income	2,725,000	2,749,000	2,825,000	2,730,000	2,787,000	2,684,000	2,794,000	2,717,000
Provision for Loan Losses	501,000	553,000	1,350,000	490,000	348,000	297,000	320,000	197,000
Non-Interest Income	1,760,000	1,769,000	1,725,000	1,862,000	2,133,000	1,525,000	1,306,000	1,087,000
Non-Interest Expense	2,742,000	2,653,000	2,941,000	2,917,000	3,049,000	2,483,000	2,435,000	2,464,000
Income Before Taxes	1,242,000	1,312,000	259,000	1,185,000	1,523,000	1,429,000	1,345,000	1,143,000
Income from Cont Ops	...	...	157,000	670,000	946,000	946,000	...	...
Net Income	903,000	976,000	132,000	1,002,000	1,107,000	996,000	919,000	783,000
Average Shs. Outstg.	426,157	430,703	429,573	435,573	452,363	447,437	444,544	469,816
Balance Sheet								
Cash & Due from Banks	2,712,000	3,364,000	2,891,000	3,189,000	2,816,000	3,296,000	3,651,000	3,444,000
Securities Avail. for Sale	7,638,000	8,507,000	5,346,000	7,329,000	6,665,000	5,278,000	7,708,000	7,728,000
Net Loans & Leases	61,305,000	61,005,000	61,632,000	65,904,000	56,894,000	54,103,000	52,480,000	48,365,000
Total Assets	84,487,000	85,202,000	80,938,000	87,270,000	76,997,000	73,011,000	73,699,000	67,621,000
Total Deposits	50,858,000	49,346,000	44,795,000	48,649,000	43,233,000	42,583,000	45,073,000	45,317,000
Long-Term Obligations	15,294,000	15,605,000	14,554,000	14,161,000	15,881,000	12,967,000	7,446,000	4,213,000
Total Liabilities	77,518,000	78,367,000	74,783,000	80,647,000	77,006,000	73,853,000	67,768,000	62,240,000
Net Stockholders' Equity	6,969,000	6,835,000	6,155,000	6,623,000	6,389,000	6,167,000	4,431,000	4,381,000
Shares Outstanding	416,494	423,943	424,005	423,254	443,427	452,452	438,064	491,888
Statistical Record								
Return on Equity %	12.95	14.27	2.55	10.11	14.80	15.33	17.73	16.04
Return on Assets %	1.06	1.14	0.19	0.76	1.22	1.29	1.24	1.15
Equity/Assets %	8.24	8.02	7.60	7.58	8.29	8.44	7.02	7.21
Non-Int. Exp./Tot. Inc. %	47.85	43.24	40.00	34.43	38.16	34.97	37.07	40.80
Price Range	29.32–22.52	29.00–21.30	28.44–20.75	28.25–15.69	36.94–21.19	42.94–24.94	36.44–24.19	26.56–16.81
P/E Ratio	13.83–10.62	12.78–9.38	76.86–56.08	12.28–6.82	15.08–8.65	19.25–11.18	17.60–11.68	16.10–10.19
Average Yield %	4.71	4.66	4.75	5.36	3.48	2.77	2.88	3.71

Address: 127 Public Square, Cleveland, OH 44114–1306	**Officers:** Henry L. Meyer III – Chmn., Pres., C.E.O., Thomas C. Stevens – Vice-Chmn., Chief Admin.	**Investor Contact:** 416-689–4520
Telephone: (216) 689–6300	**Transfer Agents:** Computershare Investor Services, Chicago, IL	**Institutional Holding**
Web Site: www.key.com		**No of Institutions:** 437
		Shares: 222,276,452 **% Held:** 52.50%

KIMBERLY-CLARK CORP.

Exchange	Symbol	Price	52Wk Range	Yield	P/E
NYS	KMB	$63.10 (3/31/2004)	65.03–45.55	2.54	18.95

*7 Year Price Score 92.4 *NYSE Composite Index=100 ***12 Month Price Score 98.3**

Interim Earnings (Per Share)

Qtr.	Mar	Jun	Sep	Dec
2000	0.86	0.79	0.81	0.85
2001	0.81	0.78	0.79	0.64
2002	0.86	0.81	0.85	0.72
2003	0.78	0.82	0.83	0.90

Interim Dividends (Per Share)

Amt	Decl	Ex	Rec	Pay
0.34Q	5/1/2003	6/4/2003	6/6/2003	7/2/2003
0.34Q	8/1/2003	9/3/2003	9/5/2003	10/2/2003
0.34Q	11/12/2003	12/3/2003	12/5/2003	1/5/2004
0.40Q	2/24/2004	3/3/2004	3/5/2004	4/2/2004

Indicated Div: $1.60 (Div. Reinv. Plan)

Valuation Analysis

Forecast P/E	14.55	Trailing P/E	18.95
Market Cap	$32.6 Billion	Book Value	7.3 Billion
Price/Book	4.05	Price/Sales	2.07

Dividend Achiever Status

Rank	262	10 Year Growth Rate	4.50%
Total Years of Dividend Growth			29

TRADING VOLUME (thousand shares)

Business Summary: Paper Products (MIC: 11.11 SIC: 2621 NAIC:322121)

Kimberly-Clark is engaged in the manufacturing and marketing of health and hygiene products. The Personal Care segment manufactures disposable diapers, training and youth pants and swimpants and feminine and incontinence care products. The Consumer Tissue segment manufactures facial and bathroom tissue, paper towels and napkins for household use and wet wipes. The Business-to-Business segment manufactures facial and bathroom tissue, paper towels, wipers and napkins for away-from-home use; health care products; and printing papers. Brands include *Huggies, Pull-Ups, Little Swimmers, GoodNites, Kotex, Lightdays, Depend, Kleenex, Scott, Cottonelle, Viva, Scottex, Kimberly-Clark and Kimwipes.*

Recent Developments: For the year ended Dec 31 2003, income was essentially unchanged at $1.69 billion compared with 2002 Results for 2002 excluded an accounting change charge of $11.4 million. Net sales rose 5.8% to $14.35 billion due to higher sales volumes in all three of Co.'s global businesses and favorable currency exchange rates. Operating income fell 2.1% to $2.41 billion. Overall results were hampered by competitive pricing and package sizing pressures in the diaper and pants categories in North America and Europe, and lower net selling prices and higher materials input costs in the consumer tissue business.

Prospects: In 2004, Co. plans to reduce costs by $150.0 million. These cost savings should more than offset inflationary cost increases in fiber, energy and health care in 2004, along with a modest increase in pension expense. Meanwhile, Co. is anticipating improved results at K-C de Mexico in 2004, building on strong momentum in its consumer businesses in the second half of 2003. Accordingly, Co. expects that its bottom-line results in 2004 will be in the range of $3.55 to $3.65 per share. Capital spending for 2004 should be approximately $750.0 million.

Financial Data

(US$ in Thousands)	12/31/2003	12/31/2002	12/31/2001	12/31/2000	12/31/1999	12/31/1998	12/31/1997	12/31/1996
Earnings Per Share	3.33	3.24	3.02	3.31	3.09	2.13	1.58	2.49
Cash Flow Per Share	5.13	4.66	4.22	3.92	3.95	3.60	2.51	2.96
Tang. Book Val. Per Share	8.20	6.64	7.09	7.04	7.11	6.12	6.34	7.95
Dividends Per Share	1.320	1.180	1.110	1.070	1.030	0.990	0.950	0.910
Dividend Payout %	39.63	36.41	36.75	32.32	33.33	46.47	60.12	36.55
Income Statement								
Total Revenues	14,348,000	13,566,300	14,524,400	13,982,000	13,006,800	12,297,800	12,546,600	13,149,100
Total Indirect Exp.	2,487,500	2,351,800	3,570,700	3,119,700	2,889,800	3,023,900	3,270,800	2,854,000
Depreciation & Amort.	745,800	706,600	89,400	81,700	41,800	33,300	16,800	561,000
Operating Income	2,412,400	2,463,800	2,338,200	2,633,800	2,435,400	1,676,100	1,303,200	2,053,700
Net Interest Inc./(Exp.)	(149,900)	(166,400)	(173,800)	(197,800)	(183,700)	(174,400)	(133,400)	(158,600)
Income Taxes	514,200	666,600	645,700	758,500	730,200	561,900	433,100	700,600
Eqty Earns/Minority Int.	51,400	55,200	91,200	123,100	146,600	112,800	129,600	102,300
Income from Cont Ops	...	1,686,000	...	...	...	1,177,000	884,000	...
Net Income	1,694,000	1,674,600	1,609,900	1,800,000	1,668,100	1,165,800	901,500	1,403,800
Average Shs. Outstg.	508,600	520,000	533,200	543,800	540,100	553,100	559,300	564,000
Balance Sheet								
Cash & Cash Equivalents	290,600	494,500	405,200	206,500	322,800	144,000	90,800	83,200
Total Current Assets	4,438,100	4,273,900	3,922,200	3,789,900	3,561,800	3,366,900	3,489,000	3,539,200
Total Assets	16,779,900	15,585,800	15,007,600	14,479,800	12,815,500	11,510,300	11,266,000	11,845,700
Total Current Liabilities	3,918,600	4,038,100	4,168,300	4,573,900	3,845,800	3,790,700	3,706,300	3,686,900
Long-Term Obligations	2,733,700	2,844,000	2,424,000	2,000,600	1,926,600	2,068,200	1,803,900	1,738,600
Net Stockholders' Equity	6,766,300	5,650,300	5,646,900	5,767,300	5,093,100	3,887,200	4,125,300	4,483,100
Net Working Capital	519,400	235,600	(246,100)	(784,000)	(284,000)	(423,800)	(217,300)	(147,700)
Shares Outstanding	501,589	510,800	521,000	533,400	540,600	538,300	556,300	563,400
Statistical Record								
Operating Profit Margin %	16.81	18.16	16.09	18.83	18.72	13.62	10.38	15.61
Return on Equity %	25.03	29.83	28.50	31.22	32.75	30.27	21.42	31.31
Return on Assets %	10.09	10.81	10.72	12.43	13.01	10.22	7.84	11.85
Debt/Total Assets %	16.29	18.24	16.15	13.81	15.03	17.96	16.01	14.67
Price Range	59.09–43.39	66.50–46.05	71.79–52.24	71.80–45.19	68.06–45.75	58.94–37.38	56.25–44.75	49.50–34.94
P/E Ratio	17.74–13.03	20.52–14.21	23.77–17.30	21.69–13.65	22.03–14.81	27.67–17.55	35.60–28.32	19.88–14.03
Average Yield %	2.63	2.01	1.81	1.80	1.82	2.04	1.88	2.24

Address: P.O. Box 619100, Dallas, TX 75261-9100	**Officers:** Thomas J. Falk - Chmn., Pres., C.E.O., Mark A. Buthman - Sr. V.P., C.F.O.	**Investor Contact:** (800) 639-1352 **Institutional Holding**
Telephone: (972) 281-1200 **Web Site:** www.kimberly-clark.com	**Transfer Agents:** EquiServe Trust Company, N.A., Providence, RI	**No of Institutions:** 834 **Shares:** 360,807,114 **% Held:** 70.90%

KIMCO REALTY CORP.

Exchange	Symbol	Price	52Wk Range	Yield	P/E
NYS	KIM	$50.98 (3/31/2004)	50.98-34.91	4.47	22.86

7 Year Price Score 138.0 *NYSE Composite Index=100   *12 Month Price Score 101.6

Interim Earnings (Per Share)

Qtr.	Mar	Jun	Sep	Dec
2000	0.46	0.48	0.47	0.49
2001	0.51	0.54	0.54	0.57
2002	0.53	0.53	0.54	0.59
2003	0.63	0.47	0.54	0.43

Interim Dividends (Per Share)

Amt	Decl	Ex	Rec	Pay
0.54Q	6/16/2003	7/1/2003	7/3/2003	7/15/2003
0.54Q	9/15/2003	10/1/2003	10/3/2003	10/15/2003
0.57Q	10/23/2003	12/30/2003	1/2/2004	1/15/2004
0.57Q	3/15/2004	4/1/2004	4/5/2004	4/15/2004

Indicated Div: $2.28

Valuation Analysis

Forecast P/E	11.96	Trailing P/E	22.86
Market Cap	$5.3 Billion	Book Value	2.1 Billion
Price/Book	2.09	Price/Sales	9.34

Dividend Achiever Status

Rank	158	10 Year Growth Rate	9.96%
Total Years of Dividend Growth		11

Business Summary: Property, Real Estate &Development (MIC: 8.3 SIC: 6798 NAIC:525930)

Kimco Realty is an owner and operator of neighborhood and community shopping centers. As of Feb 5 2004, Co. had interests in 699 properties totaling approximately 102.6 million square feet of leaseable space located in 41 states, Canada and Mexico. Co.'s portfolio includes properties relating to the Kimco Income REIT, a joint venture arrangement with institutional investors established for the purpose of investing in retail properties financed primarily with individual non-recourse mortgages debt. Co.'s ownership interests also include the RioCan Venture and Kimco Retail Opportunity Portfolio and other properties or portfolios where Co. also retains management.

Recent Developments: For the year ended Dec 31 2003, income from continuing operations slipped to $233.8 million compared with $234.2 million in 2002. Results for 2003 and 2002 included gains on the early extinguishment of debt of $2.9 million and $19.0 million, respectively. Results for 2003 and 2002 excluded gains from discontinued operations of $60.4 million and $1.9 million, and gains on the sale of development properties of $13.7 million and $9.5 million, respectively. Revenues from rental properties increased 10.8% to $479.7 million versus $432.8 million in the prior year. Funds from operations rose 14.3% to $353.1 million from $308.9 million in 2002.

Prospects: Co. continues to acquire additional properties to build upon its portfolio. For instance, during the fourth quarter of 2003, Co. acquired interests in seven shopping centers in the U.S. totaling $71.2 million in addition to the 52 properties Co. acquired of the $700.0 million Mid-Atlantic transaction. During 2003, Co. completed approximately $1.50 billion in shopping center acquisitions totaling 12.4 million square feet. Subsequent to year end, Co. acquired interests in three additional shopping centers and a parcel of land for an additional $91.7 million. Looking ahead, Co. increased its guidance for funds from operations per share for full-year 2004 to between $3.41 and $3.46.

Financial Data

(US$ in Thousands)	12/31/2003	12/31/2002	12/31/2001	12/31/2000	12/31/1999	12/31/1998	12/31/1997	12/31/1996
Earnings Per Share	2.07	2.19	2.16	1.90	1.64	1.34	1.18	1.07
Tang. Book Val. Per Share	19.30	18.22	18.27	17.98	17.59	17.55	12.25	11.12
Dividends Per Share	2.160	2.080	1.920	1.770	1.580	1.310	1.140	1.040
Dividend Payout %	104.34	94.97	88.88	93.00	96.34	97.52	96.62	97.19
Income Statement								
Rental Income	479,664	450,829	468,616	459,407	433,880	338,798	198,929	168,144
Total Income	479,664	450,829	468,616	459,407	433,880	338,798	198,929	168,144
Total Indirect Exp.	240,149	147,624	93,437	160,209	161,165	136,306	81,330	70,443
Depreciation	86,237	74,223	148,418	142,258	134,832	102,695	60,105	54,133
Interest Expense	102,709	86,896	...	...	...	...	...	...
Income Taxes	1,516	12,904	19,376	...	...	...	...	...
Eqty Earns/Minority Int.	34,408	37,999	56,451	16,624	12,000	4,382	1,581	1,291
Income from Cont Ops	233,781	248,570	...	...	...	127,166	...	...
Net Income	307,879	245,668	236,538	205,025	176,778	122,266	85,836	73,827
Average Shs. Outstg.	108,770	105,969	101,163	93,653	91,466	75,960	56,775	53,859
Balance Sheet								
Cash & Cash Equivalents	93,965	102,954	176,844	19,097	28,076	43,921	30,978	37,425
Rtl Real Estate Inv.	4,168,988	3,394,627	3,027,539	2,935,116	2,822,791	2,847,387	1,222,520	925,641
Total Assets	4,603,925	3,756,878	3,384,779	3,171,348	3,007,476	3,051,178	1,343,890	1,022,566
Long-Term Obligations	468,698	274,732	292,829	245,413	212,321	434,311	121,364	54,405
Total Liabilities	2,468,079	1,849,550	1,494,695	1,467,009	1,402,041	1,466,160	600,571	417,262
Net Stockholders' Equity	2,135,846	1,907,328	1,890,084	1,704,339	1,605,435	1,585,019	743,319	605,305
Shares Outstanding	110,623	104,601	103,352	94,717	91,193	90,200	60,592	54,322
Statistical Record								
Net Inc.+Depr./Assets %	8.56	8.60	7.00	6.50	5.90	4.20	6.40	7.20
Return on Equity %	10.94	13.03	12.51	12.02	11.01	8.02	11.54	12.19
Return on Assets %	5.07	6.61	6.98	6.46	5.87	4.16	6.38	7.21
Price Range	45.86-30.50	33.61-28.01	34.00-27.27	29.75-22.04	26.92-20.83	27.37-22.42	23.83-20.33	23.25-17.00
P/E Ratio	22.15-14.73	15.35-12.79	15.74-12.62	15.66-11.60	16.41-12.70	20.43-16.73	20.20-17.23	21.73-15.89
Average Yield %	5.62	6.62	6.29	6.73	6.41	5.28	5.16	5.55

Address: 3333 New Hyde Park Road, New Hyde Park, NY 11042-0020	Officers: Milton Cooper – Chmn., C.E.O., Michael J. Flynn – Vice-Chmn., Pres., C.O.O.	Investor Contact:516-869-9000
Telephone: (516) 869-9000	Transfer Agents:The Bank of New York, New York, N.Y	Institutional Holding No of Institutions: 31
Web Site: www.kimcorealty.com		Shares: 46,703,074 % Held: –

LANCASTER COLONY CORP.

Exchange	Symbol	Price	52Wk Range	Yield	P/E
NMS	LANC	$40.40 (3/31/2004)	46.11-37.55	2.28	16.76

*7 Year Price Score 120.8 *NYSE Composite Index=100 *12 Month Price Score 94.6

Interim Earnings (Per Share)

Qtr.	Sep	Dec	Mar	Jun
2000–01	0.57	0.78	0.52	0.53
2001–02	0.55	0.47	0.78	0.69
2002–03	0.56	1.43	0.50	0.62
2003–04	0.55	0.74	...	...

Interim Dividends (Per Share)

Amt	Decl	Ex	Rec	Pay
0.20Q	5/28/2003	6/6/2003	6/10/2003	6/30/2003
0.20Q	8/27/2003	9/8/2003	9/10/2003	9/30/2003
0.23Q	11/17/2003	12/8/2003	12/10/2003	12/31/2003
0.23Q	2/25/2004	3/8/2004	3/10/2004	3/31/2004

Indicated Div: $0.92 (Div. Reinv. Plan)

Valuation Analysis

Forecast P/E	14.17	Trailing P/E	16.76
Market Cap	$1.5 Billion	Book Value	576.4 Million
Price/Book	2.80	Price/Sales	1.49

Dividend Achiever Status

Rank	122	10 Year Growth Rate	11.94%
Total Years of Dividend Growth		34

Business Summary: Food (MIC: 4.1 SIC: 2038 NAIC:311412)

Lancaster Colony operates in three business segments. The Specialty Foods segment manufactures and sells salad dressings and sauces, frozen unbaked pies, frozen breads, refrigerated chip and produce dips, dairy snacks and desserts, premium dry egg noodles, frozen noodles, pastas and specialty items, croutons, and caviar. The Glassware and Candles segment produces machine–pressed and machine–blown consumer glassware, technical glass products, and candles and other home fragrances of all sizes, forms and fragrance. The Automotive segment manufactures and sells rubber, vinyl and carpeted car mats, pickup truck bed mats, running boards, bed liners, tool boxes, and other accessories.

Recent Developments: For the three months ended Dec 31 2003, net income totaled $26.7 million, down 48.7% versus $52.0 million in the previous year. Results for 2002 included a $4.9 million pre–tax restructuring and impairment charge. Net sales slipped 5.4% to $291.2 million from $307.7 million a year earlier. Specialty foods segment net sales declined 0.3% to $16.9 million from $164.3 million in 2002. Net sales in the glassware and candles segment slid 11.1% to $72.7 million, while net sales in the automotive segment fell 11.4% to $54.6 million. Gross profit was $65.1 million, or 22.3% of net sales, versus $74.2 million, or 24.1% of net sales, the year before. Operating income was down 6.7% to $40.1 million.

Prospects: Sales and earnings are being negatively affected by lackluster consumer demand and increased competitive pressures. Meanwhile, operating profitability is being hurt by sharply higher costs for soybean oil and certain dairy products. Looking ahead, Co. anticipates challenging market conditions to persist over the near term. In an effort to boost operating profitability, Co. is taking aggressive steps expected to help lower production costs and improve plant efficiencies. In addition, long–term results may benefit from upcoming new product introductions including *Marzetti* one–carb pourable salad dressings and *New York* six–carb Texas Garlic Toast.

Financial Data

(US$ in Thousands)	6 Mos	3 Mos	06/30/2003	06/30/2002	06/30/2001	06/30/2000	06/30/1999	06/30/1998
Earnings Per Share	1.29	0.55	3.11	2.49	2.40	2.51	2.28	2.22
Cash Flow Per Share	1.65	0.47	4.30	4.34	3.35	3.24	3.02	2.76
Tang. Book Val. Per Share	13.91	13.54	13.19	11.71	10.37	10.03	9.34	8.73
Dividends Per Share	0.830	0.800	0.780	0.710	0.670	0.630	0.590	0.500
Dividend Payout %	63.56	145.45	25.08	28.51	27.92	25.10	25.88	22.52
Income Statement								
Total Revenues	557,848	266,652	1,106,800	1,129,687	1,098,464	1,104,258	1,045,702	1,008,752
Total Indirect Exp.	49,072	24,169	103,917	119,196	113,858	173,449	166,228	168,526
Depreciation & Amort.	15,322	7,432	31,669	35,287	35,528	34,340	35,569	32,571
Operating Income	71,786	31,638	139,943	134,369	147,674	161,949	155,688	155,871
Net Interest Inc./(Exp.)	...	...	...	(54)	(1,239)	(1,588)	(2,718)	(2,626)
Income Taxes	28,262	12,284	68,255	57,402	55,649	60,925	58,333	59,243
Income from Cont Ops	...	...	...	...	90,236	...	...	...
Net Income	46,350	19,700	112,546	91,940	89,238	99,264	95,129	96,130
Average Shs. Outstg.	35,815	35,831	36,243	36,910	37,636	39,554	41,799	43,364
Balance Sheet								
Cash & Cash Equivalents	152,505	145,633	142,847	83,378	4,873	2,656	18,860	23,224
Total Current Assets	436,247	444,574	414,385	366,100	317,605	315,895	328,379	311,548
Total Assets	705,014	697,639	667,716	616,707	571,937	531,844	550,014	529,367
Total Current Liabilities	91,585	101,617	84,923	89,304	92,294	96,475	116,217	76,517
Long–Term Obligations	...	...	...	...	1,095	3,040	3,575	29,095
Net Stockholders' Equity	576,385	559,807	547,665	501,277	459,901	415,483	414,855	410,543
Net Working Capital	344,662	342,957	329,462	276,796	225,311	219,420	212,162	235,031
Shares Outstanding	35,364	35,757	35,770	36,598	37,253	37,962	40,547	42,753
Statistical Record								
Operating Profit Margin %	12.86	11.86	12.64	11.89	13.44	14.66	14.88	15.45
Return on Equity %	8.04	3.51	20.55	18.34	19.62	23.89	22.93	23.41
Return on Assets %	6.57	2.82	16.85	14.86	15.77	18.66	17.29	18.15
Debt/Total Assets %	...	...	...	...	0.19	0.57	0.64	5.49
Price Range	45.18-38.68	42.00-38.68	46.74-32.68	40.16-26.10	33.46-19.50	36.25-19.50	39.44-25.50	45.00-32.17
P/E Ratio	35.02-29.98	76.36-70.33	15.03-10.51	16.13-10.48	13.94-8.13	14.44-7.77	17.30-11.18	20.27-14.49
Average Yield %	1.96	1.94	1.49	2.06	3.05	2.03	1.88	1.38

Address: 37 West Broad Street, Columbus, OH 43215
Telephone: (614) 224–7141
Web Site: www.lancastercolony.com

Officers: John B. Gerlach – Chmn., Pres., C.E.O., John L. Boylan – V.P., C.F.O., Treas., Asst. Sec.

Institutional Holding
No of Institutions: 179
Shares:16,854,671 % Held: 46.8%

154

LA-Z-BOY INC.

Exchange	Symbol	Price	52Wk Range	Yield	P/E
NYS	LZB	$21.76 (3/31/2004)	24.12-16.96	1.84	19.43

*7 Year Price Score 114.5   *NYSE Composite Index=100   *12 Month Price Score 86.5

Interim Earnings (Per Share)

Qtr.	Jul	Oct	Jan	Apr
2000-01	0.21	0.48	0.27	0.17
2001-02	0.05	0.20	0.35	0.41
2002-03	0.32	0.50	0.41	0.44
2003-04	0.11	0.28	0.29	...

Interim Dividends (Per Share)

Amt	Decl	Ex	Rec	Pay
0.10Q	5/6/2003	5/21/2003	5/23/2003	6/10/2003
0.10Q	8/12/2003	8/27/2003	8/29/2003	9/10/2003
0.10Q	11/10/2003	11/25/2003	11/28/2003	12/10/2003
0.10Q	2/10/2004	2/25/2004	2/27/2004	3/10/2004

Indicated Div: $0.40 (Div. Reinv. Plan)

Valuation Analysis

Forecast P/E	11.19	Trailing P/E	19.43
Market Cap	$1.3 Billion	Book Value	583.4 Million
Price/Book	1.91	Price/Sales	0.56

Dividend Achiever Status

Rank	217	10 Year Growth Rate 6.83%
Total Years of Dividend Growth		22

Business Summary: Chemicals (MIC: 11.1 SIC: 2511 NAIC:337121)

La-Z-Boy is a furniture manufacturer in the United States. Co. is comprised of two business groups: upholstery and casegoods. The upholstery segment includes recliners, sofas, occasional chairs, reclining sofas and office and health care seating. The casegoods segment includes dining room tables and chairs, bed frames and bed boards, dressers, coffee tables and end tables manufactured using hardwood or hardwood veneer, as well as hospitality and assisted-living furniture. Brand names include *La-Z-Boy, England, Sam Moore, Bauhaus, Centurion, Pennsylvania House, Clayton Marcus, Kincaid, Hammary, Alexvale, American Drew, La-Z-Boy Contract Furniture, American of Martinsville,* and *Lea.*

Recent Developments: For the third quarter ended Jan 24 2003, net income plunged 34.0% to $15.3 million compared with $23.2 million in the equivalent 2003 quarter. Earnings were hampered by a change in product mix and increased selling, general and administrative expenses and higher rent and advertising costs in the upholstery segment, as well as weakness in the lodging market initiated by 9-11, which is hurting Co.'s hospitality business in the casegoods segment. Sales dropped 3.6% to $492.2 million from $510.5 million a year earlier. Gross profit fell 8.7% to $108.1 million versus $118.3 million in 2002. Operating income decreased 34.2% to $26.0 million.

Prospects: Co. expects fourth quarter results to be lifted by the recent pickup in its incoming order rate. Accordingly, Co. anticipates April 2004 fourth quarter sales to be up in the low single-digit range, with earnings in the range of $0.40 to $0.45 per diluted share. Meanwhile, Co. is forecasting full-year fiscal 2004 earnings per diluted share to be between $1.07 and $1.12, including $0.11 of restructuring charges. Going forward, Co. plans to aggressively expand its furniture Galleries® stores. Co.'s plans include opening as many as 20 or more new stores per year and relocating or remodeling an equal number of stores annually for the next four to five years.

Financial Data

(US$ in Thousands)	9 Mos	6 Mos	3 Mos	04/26/2003	04/27/2002	04/28/2001	04/29/2000	04/24/1999
Earnings Per Share	0.67	0.38	0.11	1.67	1.01	1.13	1.60	1.24
Cash Flow Per Share	2.12	1.31	0.30	2.17	2.17	1.91	1.06	1.54
Tang. Book Val. Per Share	8.24	8.19	8.29	8.35	8.14	7.40	6.70	7.02
Dividends Per Share	0.400	0.400	0.400	0.400	0.360	0.350	0.320	0.310
Dividend Payout %	59.70	105.26	363.63	23.95	35.64	30.97	20.00	25.00
Income Statement								
Total Revenues	1,454,657	962,490	451,472	2,111,830	2,153,952	2,256,197	1,717,420	1,287,645
Total Indirect Exp.	251,164	169,146	81,419	331,695	421,607	382,403	288,962	234,075
Depreciation & Amort.	21,830	14,637	7,311	30,695	43,988	45,697	30,342	22,081
Operating Income	64,397	38,357	11,299	162,874	96,700	120,794	144,300	106,839
Net Interest Inc./(Exp.)	(8,936)	(6,239)	(3,213)	(10,510)	(8,701)	(16,181)	(7,679)	(2,259)
Income Taxes	22,223	12,858	3,555	58,899	27,185	43,708	52,699	41,096
Income from Cont Ops	...	...	...	96,098				
Net Income	36,259	20,980	5,803	36,316	61,751	68,336	87,614	66,142
Average Shs. Outstg.	54,066	54,627	54,916	57,435	61,125	60,692	54,860	53,148
Balance Sheet								
Cash & Cash Equivalents	25,774	24,587	28,422	28,817	26,771	23,565	14,353	33,550
Total Current Assets	602,653	639,237	622,772	679,494	671,692	708,776	692,369	425,588
Total Assets	1,043,500	1,078,265	1,058,170	1,123,066	1,160,776	1,222,503	1,218,297	629,792
Total Current Liabilities	198,385	218,405	156,027	214,587	226,893	249,915	237,006	132,428
Long-Term Obligations	185,903	196,174	222,762	222,371	139,386	199,419	236,094	62,688
Net Stockholders' Equity	583,417	587,746	603,231	609,939	713,522	695,146	663,092	414,915
Net Working Capital	404,268	420,832	466,745	464,907	444,799	458,861	455,363	293,160
Shares Outstanding	52,584	53,408	54,645	55,027	59,953	60,501	61,328	52,340
Statistical Record								
Operating Profit Margin %	4.42	3.98	2.50	7.71	4.48	5.35	8.40	8.29
Return on Equity %	6.21	3.56	0.96	15.75	8.65	9.83	13.21	15.94
Return on Assets %	3.47	1.94	0.54	8.55	5.31	5.58	7.19	10.50
Debt/Total Assets %	17.81	18.19	21.05	19.80	12.00	16.31	19.37	9.95
Price Range	24.12-18.90	24.12-18.90	23.86-18.90	30.04-16.45	30.88-15.16	18.50-13.44	24.44-13.69	22.50-15.25
P/E Ratio	36.00-28.21	63.47-49.74	216.9-171.8	17.99-9.85	30.57-15.01	16.37-11.89	15.27-8.55	18.15-12.30
Average Yield %	1.88	1.85	1.85	1.74	1.71	2.21	1.67	1.71

Address: 1284 North Telegraph Road, Monroe, MI 48162	Officers: Patrick H. Norton - Chmn., Kurt L. Darrow - Pres., C.E.O.	Investor Contact: (734) 241-4414
Telephone: (734) 241-1444	Transfer Agents: American Stock Transfer & Trust Company, New York, NY	Institutional Holding
Web Site: www.la-z-boy.com		No of Institutions: 157
		Shares: 34,290,439 % Held: 58.80%

LEGG MASON, INC.

Exchange	Symbol	Price	52Wk Range	Yield	P/E
NYS	LM	$92.78 (3/31/2004)	94.83–49.09	0.65	26.97

*7 Year Price Score 157.5   *NYSE Composite Index=100   *12 Month Price Score 108.6

TRADING VOLUME (thousand shares)

Interim Earnings (Per Share)

Qtr.	Jun	Sep	Dec	Mar
2000–01	0.60	0.55	0.61	0.54
2001–02	0.52	0.45	0.60	0.67
2002–03	0.71	0.66	0.70	0.71
2003–04	0.83	0.83	1.07	...

Interim Dividends (Per Share)

Amt	Decl	Ex	Rec	Pay
0.11Q	4/22/2003	6/6/2003	6/10/2003	7/7/2003
0.15Q	7/22/2003	9/30/2003	10/2/2003	10/20/2003
0.15Q	10/22/2003	12/8/2003	12/10/2003	1/5/2004
0.15Q	1/24/2004	3/2/2004	3/4/2004	4/5/2004
		Indicated Div: $0.60		

Valuation Analysis

Forecast P/E	18.56	Trailing P/E	26.97
Market Cap	$6.0 Billion	Book Value	1.4 Billion
Price/Book	3.40	Price/Sales	2.77

Dividend Achiever Status

Rank	90	10 Year Growth Rate 14.18%
Total Years of Dividend Growth		20

Business Summary: Finance Intermediaries &Services (MIC: 8.7 SIC: 6211 NAIC:523120)

Legg Mason, through its subsidiaries, is engaged in providing asset management, securities brokerage, investment advisory, corporate and public finance, and mortgage banking services to individuals, institutions, corporations, governments and government agencies. As an investment advisor, Co. managed about $264.90 billion in assets as of December 31 2003. Co.'s mortgage–banking subsidiaries have direct and master servicing responsibility for commercial mortgages. Co. provides financial services through four business segments: Asset Management, Private Client, Capital Markets and Other.

Recent Developments: For the quarter ended Dec 31 2003, Co. reported net earnings of $80.8 million compared with earnings from continuing operations of $46.9 million in the equivalent prior–year period. Results for 2003 excluded a net gain of $966.0 million from discontinued operations. Total revenues rose 33.0% to $521.2 million from $392.0 million a year earlier. Investment advisory and related fees improved 51.2% to $326.5 million, reflecting substantial increases in Co.'s institutional, mutual funds and wealth managers divisions, reflecting strong investment performance and net cash flows. Commissions revenues rose 7.0% to $85.3 million.

Prospects: Assets under management are benefiting from the strength in the equity markets, as well as strong investment performance and net cash flows. As of Dec 31 2003, Co.'s institutional asset management division contributed 66.0% to total assets under management, while Co.'s mutual funds management division contributed 22.0% and Co.'s wealth management division, 12.0%. As of Dec 31 2003, equity assets increased to 39.0% of the total managed assets from 33.0% the previous year, reflecting the improved equity markets. Separately, on Jan 2 2004, Co. acquired the business of Singapore-based Rothschild Asset Management, which manages about $1.00 billion of fixed income and equity assets.

Financial Data

(US$ in Thousands)	6 Mos	3 Mos	03/31/2003	03/31/2002	03/31/2001	03/31/2000	03/31/1999	03/31/1998
Earnings Per Share	3.07	2.90	2.78	2.24	2.30	2.33	1.55	1.31
Cash Flow Per Share	(3.53)	(2.58)	4.44	1.26	3.29	2.70	(1.02)	1.69
Tang. Book Val. Per Share	7.28	6.07	4.98	2.28	12.38	10.60	8.83	7.97
Dividends Per Share	0.440	0.430	0.420	0.380	0.340	0.290	0.240	0.200
Dividend Payout %	14.33	14.83	15.10	16.96	14.78	12.44	15.48	15.77
Income Statement								
Total Revenues	906,618	440,150	1,615,382	1,578,612	1,536,253	1,370,804	1,046,006	889,060
Total Indirect Exp.	683,113	328,281	1,079,655	1,063,376	966,919	886,737	703,759	616,343
Depreciation & Amort.	10,858	5,992	24,915	18,808	36,495	29,320	21,566	21,986
Operating Income	191,958	95,058	448,591	387,965	393,945	349,745	342,247	272,717
Net Interest Inc./(Exp.)	...	...	...	...	...	...	(94,910)	(73,706)
Income Taxes	74,108	36,692	117,412	100,313	109,590	96,616	59,441	52,258
Income from Cont Ops	117,850	...	...	...	...	...	...	...
Net Income	125,006	58,366	190,909	152,936	156,230	142,525	89,334	76,121
Average Shs. Outstg.	70,914	70,125	68,760	68,262	67,916	60,787	57,657	58,006
Balance Sheet								
Cash & Cash Equivalents	3,686,587	3,432,235	3,351,708	3,094,990	2,627,534	2,058,106	1,740,643	1,334,327
Total Current Assets	4,983,642	4,742,257	4,669,691	4,458,426	4,087,802	3,813,436	2,805,908	2,129,175
Total Assets	6,511,202	6,209,081	6,067,450	5,939,614	4,687,626	4,785,053	3,473,687	2,832,329
Total Current Liabilities	4,092,777	3,874,179	3,866,288	3,808,048	3,397,852	3,532,642	2,718,386	2,147,235
Long–Term Obligations	790,471	788,603	786,753	877,122	218,970	338,991	99,676	99,628
Net Stockholders' Equity	1,395,367	1,324,802	1,247,957	1,084,548	927,720	751,929	554,177	500,095
Net Working Capital	890,865	868,078	803,403	650,378	689,950	280,794	87,522	(18,060)
Shares Outstanding	66,200	65,731	64,827	64,443	62,849	58,599	56,376	55,050
Statistical Record								
Operating Profit Margin %	21.17	21.59	27.76	24.57	25.64	25.51	32.71	30.67
Return on Equity %	8.44	4.40	15.29	14.10	16.84	18.95	16.12	15.22
Return on Assets %	1.80	0.94	3.14	2.57	3.33	2.97	2.57	2.68
Debt/Total Assets %	12.14	12.70	12.96	14.76	4.67	7.08	2.86	3.51
Price Range	76.70-48.74	66.38-48.74	56.97-38.16	56.80-35.75	59.94-35.94	49.00-31.25	35.69-18.50	31.72-15.84
P/E Ratio	46.20-29.36	79.98-58.72	20.49-13.73	25.36-15.96	26.06-15.63	21.03-13.41	23.02-11.94	24.21-12.09
Average Yield %	0.68	0.73	0.87	0.80	0.68	0.79	0.84	0.85

Address: 100 Light Street, Baltimore, MD 21202	Officers: Raymond A. Mason – Chmn., Pres., C.E.O., James W. Brinkley – Sr. Exec. V.P.	Investor Contact:410–539–0000
Telephone: (410) 539–0000	Transfer Agents:Wachovia Bank, N.A., Charlotte,	Institutional Holding No of Institutions: 42
Web Site: www.leggmason.com	North Carolina	Shares: 20,100,609 % Held: –

LEGGETT & PLATT, INC.

Exchange	Symbol	Price	52Wk Range	Yield	P/E
NYS	LEG	$23.71 (3/31/2004)	25.45-18.44	2.36	22.58

*7 Year Price Score 99.1 *NYSE Composite Index=100 *12 Month Price Score 88.1

Interim Earnings (Per Share)

Qtr.	Mar	Jun	Sep	Dec
2000	0.37	0.38	0.34	0.23
2001	0.23	0.25	0.28	0.18
2002	0.28	0.35	0.29	0.25
2003	0.25	0.24	0.26	0.30

Interim Dividends (Per Share)

Amt	Decl	Ex	Rec	Pay
0.13Q	5/14/2003	6/11/2003	6/13/2003	7/15/2003
0.14Q	8/6/2003	9/11/2003	9/15/2003	10/15/2003
0.14Q	11/11/2003	12/11/2003	12/15/2003	1/15/2004
0.14Q	2/11/2004	3/11/2004	3/15/2004	4/15/2004

Indicated Div: $0.56

Valuation Analysis

Forecast P/E	17.06	Trailing P/E	22.58
Market Cap	$4.6 Billion	Book Value	2.1 Billion
Price/Book	1.95	Price/Sales	0.94

Dividend Achiever Status

Rank	83	10 Year Growth Rate	14.66%
Total Years of Dividend Growth			32

Business Summary: Chemicals (MIC: 11.1 SIC: 2515 NAIC:337121)

Leggett & Platt is primarily engaged in the manufacture of engineered components and products that are used in homes, offices, retail stores, and automobiles. Products include: retail store fixtures and point of purchase displays; components for residential furniture and bedding; components for office furniture; non-automotive aluminum die castings; drawn steel wire; automotive seat support and lumbar systems; and bedding industry machinery for wire forming, sewing and quilting. Operations consists of 29 business units, which are organized into 11 groups that make up five business segments.

Recent Developments: For the year ended Dec 31 2003, net income decreased 11.7% to $205.9 million compared with $233.1 million in 2002. The decline in earnings reflected sharply higher energy and steel costs, a weaker U.S. dollar, and inventory write-downs, partially offset by higher sales and lower restructuring costs. Net sales grew 2.7% to $4.39 billion from $4.27 billion a year earlier. The improvement in sales was primarily attributed to internal growth and acquisitions. Gross profit fell 6.1% to $771.7 million from $821.7 million the year before. Selling and administrative expenses as a percentage of net sales was 9.3% in 2003 and 9.2% in 2002.

Prospects: Prospects appear promising as the economy and Co.'s markets are improving, consumer sentiment is growing, interest rates and inflation remain low, and manufacturing activity is strengthening. Internally, Co. has implemented price increases to mitigate the sharp incline in scrap steel prices, and has initiated a vigorous plan to improve its fixture and display operations. In addition, Co. acquired seven firms during the fourth quarter that will add approximately $65.0 million to annual sales. Based on these components, Co. expects first quarter earnings in the range of $0.26 to $0.31 per share. For full-year 2004, Co. anticipates earnings of between $1.15 and $1.35 per share.

Financial Data

(US$ in Thousands)	12/31/2003	12/31/2002	12/31/2001	12/31/2000	12/31/1999	12/31/1998	12/31/1997	12/31/1996
Earnings Per Share	1.05	1.17	0.94	1.32	1.45	1.24	1.08	0.83
Cash Flow Per Share	2.00	2.28	2.66	2.19	1.84	1.76	1.49	1.29
Tang. Book Val. Per Share	5.62	5.35	4.80	4.58	4.50	4.59	3.88	3.36
Dividends Per Share	0.530	0.490	0.470	0.400	0.350	0.300	0.260	0.220
Dividend Payout %	50.47	41.88	50.00	30.30	24.13	24.59	24.07	26.51
Income Statement								
Total Revenues	4,388,200	4,271,800	4,113,800	4,276,300	3,779,000	3,370,400	2,909,200	2,466,200
Total Indirect Exp.	416,400	437,800	651,400	612,800	515,600	440,200	369,300	341,100
Depreciation & Amort.	8,400	10,200	39,900	34,100	28,800	21,800	17,300	16,400
Operating Income	355,300	400,600	351,200	480,800	502,500	429,100	365,100	279,700
Net Interest Inc./(Exp.)	(40,200)	(37,100)	(53,900)	(62,200)	(39,900)	(33,500)	(31,800)	(30,000)
Income Taxes	109,200	130,400	109,700	154,500	172,100	147,600	125,000	96,700
Income from Cont Ops	...	...	...	...	...	...	...	153,000
Net Income	205,900	233,100	187,600	264,100	290,500	248,000	208,300	140,500
Average Shs. Outstg.	196,953	199,795	200,434	200,388	200,938	200,669	193,190	183,600
Balance Sheet								
Cash & Cash Equivalents	443,900	225,000	187,200	37,300	20,600	83,500	7,700	3,700
Total Current Assets	1,819,400	1,488,000	1,421,900	1,405,300	1,256,200	1,137,100	944,600	763,300
Total Assets	3,889,700	3,501,100	3,412,900	3,373,200	2,977,500	2,535,300	2,106,300	1,712,900
Total Current Liabilities	625,900	598,000	457,000	476,600	431,500	401,400	372,500	292,800
Long-Term Obligations	1,012,200	808,600	977,600	988,400	787,400	574,100	466,200	388,500
Net Stockholders' Equity	2,114,000	1,976,900	1,866,600	1,793,800	1,646,200	1,436,800	1,174,000	941,100
Net Working Capital	1,193,500	890,000	964,900	928,700	824,700	735,700	572,100	470,500
Shares Outstanding	192,102	194,498	196,298	196,097	196,880	197,683	192,754	184,216
Statistical Record								
Operating Profit Margin %	8.09	9.37	8.53	11.24	13.29	12.73	12.54	11.34
Return on Equity %	9.73	11.79	10.05	14.72	17.64	17.26	17.74	16.25
Return on Assets %	5.29	6.65	5.49	7.82	9.75	9.78	9.88	8.93
Debt/Total Assets %	26.02	23.09	28.64	29.30	26.44	22.64	22.13	22.68
Price Range	23.57-17.40	27.16-18.90	24.23-17.00	22.38-14.44	27.88-18.81	28.44-17.13	23.53-15.81	17.31-10.31
P/E Ratio	22.45-16.57	23.21-16.15	25.78-18.09	16.95-10.94	19.22-12.97	22.93-13.81	21.79-14.64	20.86-12.42
Average Yield %	2.53	2.08	2.22	2.23	1.53	1.24	1.31	1.63

Address: No. 1 Leggett Road, Carthage, MO 64836 Telephone: (417) 358-8131 Web Site: www.leggett.com	Officers: Felix E. Wright – Chmn., C.E.O., David S. Haffner – Pres., C.O.O. Transfer Agents: U.M.B. Bank, Kansas City, MO	Institutional Holding No of Institutions: 277 Shares: 117,648,191 % Held: 61%

LILLY (ELI) & CO.

Exchange	Symbol	Price	52Wk Range	Yield	P/E
NYS	LLY	$66.90 (3/31/2004)	74.70-57.73	2.12	28.23

*7 Year Price Score 92.7   *NYSE Composite Index=100   ***12 Month Price Score 98.1**

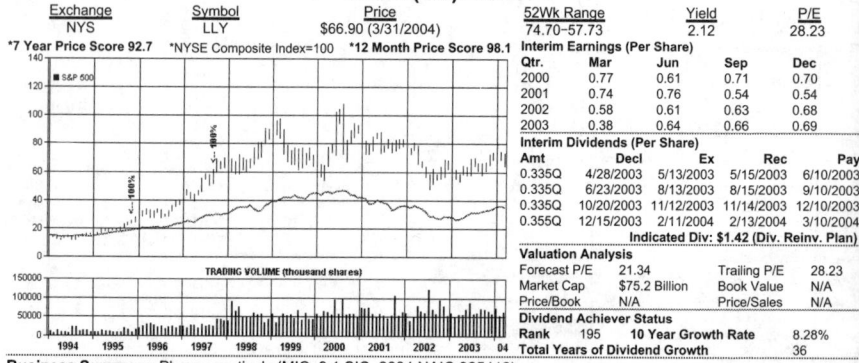

Interim Earnings (Per Share)

Qtr.	Mar	Jun	Sep	Dec
2000	0.77	0.61	0.71	0.70
2001	0.74	0.76	0.54	0.54
2002	0.58	0.61	0.63	0.68
2003	0.38	0.64	0.66	0.69

Interim Dividends (Per Share)

Amt	Decl	Ex	Rec	Pay
0.335Q	4/28/2003	5/13/2003	5/15/2003	6/10/2003
0.335Q	6/23/2003	8/13/2003	8/15/2003	9/10/2003
0.335Q	10/20/2003	11/12/2003	11/14/2003	12/10/2003
0.355Q	12/15/2003	2/11/2004	2/13/2004	3/10/2004

Indicated Div: $1.42 (Div. Reinv. Plan)

Valuation Analysis

Forecast P/E	21.34	Trailing P/E	28.23
Market Cap	$75.2 Billion	Book Value	N/A
Price/Book	N/A	Price/Sales	N/A

Dividend Achiever Status

Rank	195	10 Year Growth Rate	8.28%
Total Years of Dividend Growth			36

Business Summary: Pharmaceuticals (MIC: 9.1 SIC: 2834 NAIC:325412)

Eli Lilly discovers, develops, manufactures, and sells pharmaceuticals and animal health products. Neuroscience products include *Prozac®, Zyprexa®, Strattera™Darvon®, Permax®, Symbyax®*and *Sarafem™*. Endocrine products include *Humulin®, Humalog®, Humalog Mix 75/25®, Actos®, Evista®, Forteo®*and *Humatrope®*. Oncology products include *Gemzar®*and *Alimta®*. Animal Health products include *Tylan®, Rumensin®, Coban®, Monteban®, Maxiban®, Apralan®, Micotil®, Pulmotil®, Surmax®, Optaflexx®*and *Paylean®*. Cardiovascular products, consist primarily of *ReoPro®, Dobutrex®, Xigris®*and *Cynt®*. Anti-infective products include *Ceclor®, Keflex®, Keftab®, Lorabid®*, and *Vancocin®*, and other products.

Recent Developments: For the year ended Dec 31 2003, net income declined 5.4% to $2.56 billion compared with $2.71 billion the previous year. Results for 2003 included pre-tax asset impairments, restructuring and other special charges of $382.2 million, while results for 2002 included a pre-tax charge of $84.0 million from acquired in-process technology. Net sales increased 13.6% to $12.58 billion from $11.08 billion the year before. Sales growth was largely attributed to double-digit results of Zyprexa®, Gemzar®, Humalog®, and Evista®, as well as sales from the recent launches of Strattera®, Cialis®, and Forteo®. Operating income slipped 3.8% to $3.12 billion from $3.24 billion the prior year.

Prospects: Prospects appear promising as revenues continue to benefit from higher sales of *Zyprexa®, Humalog®, Genzar®*and *Evista®*, as well as sales from new product launches. In addition, Co. has several potential new indications and formulations to boost its current growth products, no major patent expirations for the remainder of the decade and strong pipeline of new products. Co. will continue to invest in research and development to develop these new products, which should enhance long-term growth. Meanwhile, Co. expects low double-digit sales growth and earnings to range from $2.80 to $2.85 per share. The range reflects *Zyprexa®*'s ongoing domestic competitive pressures.

Financial Data

(US$ in Thousands)	12/31/2003	12/31/2002	12/31/2001	12/31/2000	12/31/1999	12/31/1998	12/31/1997	12/31/1996
Earnings Per Share	2.37	2.50	2.58	2.79	2.30	1.87	(0.35)	1.39
Cash Flow Per Share	3.36	1.90	3.35	3.39	2.36	2.34	2.18	1.82
Tang. Book Val. Per Share	8.68	7.37	6.32	5.37	4.48	2.85	2.78	1.87
Dividends Per Share	1.340	1.240	1.120	1.040	0.920	0.800	0.740	0.680
Dividend Payout %	56.54	49.60	43.41	37.27	40.00	42.78	N.M.	48.92
Income Statement								
Total Revenues	12,582,500	11,077,500	11,542,500	10,862,200	10,002,900	9,236,800	8,517,600	7,346,600
Total Indirect Exp.	6,405,600	5,657,300	5,843,000	5,246,800	4,541,200	4,524,700	3,696,400	3,181,400
Depreciation & Amort.	548,500	493,000	454,900	435,800	439,700	490,400	509,800	543,500
Operating Income	3,119,600	3,243,700	3,539,300	3,559,700	3,363,700	2,697,000	2,458,300	2,046,800
Net Interest Inc./(Exp.)	(61,000)	(79,700)	(146,500)	(182,300)	(183,800)	(181,300)	(234,100)	(288,800)
Income Taxes	700,900	749,800	742,700	800,900	698,700	568,700	895,300	507,800
Income from Cont Ops	...	...	2,809,400	...	2,546,700	2,096,300	...	...
Net Income	2,560,800	2,707,900	2,780,000	3,057,800	2,721,000	2,097,900	(385,100)	1,523,500
Average Shs. Outstg.	1,082,230	1,085,088	1,090,793	1,097,525	1,106,055	1,121,486	1,101,099	1,093,654
Balance Sheet								
Cash & Cash Equivalents	2,756,300	1,945,900	2,702,300	4,114,900	3,700,400	1,495,700	1,947,500	813,700
Total Current Assets	8,758,700	7,804,100	6,938,900	7,943,000	7,055,500	5,406,800	5,320,700	3,891,300
Total Assets	21,678,100	19,042,000	16,434,100	14,690,800	12,825,200	12,595,500	12,577,400	14,307,200
Total Current Liabilities	5,550,600	5,063,500	5,203,000	4,960,700	3,935,400	4,607,200	4,191,600	4,222,200
Long-Term Obligations	4,687,800	4,358,200	3,132,100	2,633,700	2,811,900	2,185,500	2,326,100	2,516,500
Net Stockholders' Equity	9,764,800	8,273,600	7,104,000	6,046,900	5,013,000	4,429,600	4,645,600	6,100,100
Net Working Capital	3,208,100	2,740,600	1,735,900	2,982,300	3,120,100	799,600	1,129,100	(330,900)
Shares Outstanding	1,123,725	1,122,443	1,123,348	1,125,560	1,090,238	1,019,090	1,110,522	1,105,646
Statistical Record								
Operating Profit Margin %	24.79	29.28	30.66	32.77	33.62	29.19	28.86	27.86
Return on Equity %	26.22	32.72	39.54	50.56	50.80	47.32	N.M.	24.97
Return on Assets %	11.81	14.22	17.09	20.81	19.85	16.64	N.M.	10.64
Debt/Total Assets %	21.62	22.88	19.05	17.92	21.92	17.35	18.49	17.58
Price Range	73.89-53.70	80.69-48.15	91.50-72.59	108.6-54.38	97.44-61.50	90.88-58.19	69.94-36.25	39.50-24.75
P/E Ratio	31.18-22.66	32.28-19.26	35.47-28.14	38.91-19.49	42.36-26.74	48.60-31.12	N/A	28.42-17.81
Average Yield %	2.11	1.91	1.40	1.32	1.21	1.12	1.41	2.15

Address: Lilly Corporate Center, Indianapolis, IN 46285 Telephone: (317) 276-2000 Web Site: www.lilly.com	Officers: Sidney Taurel – Chmn., Pres., C.E.O., Charles E. Golden – Exec. V.P., C.F.O. Transfer Agents:Norwest Shareowner Services, South St. Paul, MN	Investor Contact: (317) 276-2506 Institutional Holding No of Institutions: 31 Shares: 1,725,606,124 % Held: –

LINCOLN NATIONAL CORP. (ID)

Exchange	Symbol	Price	52Wk Range	Yield	P/E
NYS	LNC	$47.32 (3/31/2004)	48.72-28.57	2.96	11.08

*7 Year Price Score 87.2   *NYSE Composite Index=100   *12 Month Price Score 101.1

Interim Earnings (Per Share)

Qtr.	Mar	Jun	Sep	Dec
2000	0.87	0.84	0.71	0.77
2001	0.83	0.74	0.61	0.87
2002	0.49	0.81	(0.68)	(0.13)
2003	0.23	0.80	0.74	2.50

Interim Dividends (Per Share)

Amt	Decl	Ex	Rec	Pay
0.335Q	5/9/2003	7/8/2003	7/10/2003	8/1/2003
0.335Q	9/11/2003	10/8/2003	10/10/2003	11/1/2003
0.35Q	11/13/2003	1/7/2004	1/9/2004	2/1/2004
0.35Q	3/11/2004	4/6/2004	4/9/2004	5/1/2004

Indicated Div: $1.40 (Div. Reinv. Plan)

Valuation Analysis

Forecast P/E	10.84	Trailing P/E	11.08
Market Cap	$8.7 Billion	Book Value	5.8 Billion
Price/Book	1.23	Price/Sales	1.33

Dividend Achiever Status

Rank	237	10 Year Growth Rate	5.83%
Total Years of Dividend Growth		20

Business Summary: Insurance (MIC: 8.2 SIC: 6311 NAIC:524113)

Lincoln National operates multiple insurance and investment management businesses, divided into four business segments. The Lincoln Retirement segment provides fixed and variable annuities products to the individual annuities and employer-sponsored markets. The Life Insurance segment provides life insurance products designed specifically for the high net-worth and affluent markets. The Investment Management segment provides investment products and services to both individual and institutional investors. The Lincoln UK segment provides life insurance products in the United Kingdom.

Recent Developments: For the year ended Dec 31 2003, income totaled $767.2 million, before a $255.2 million accounting change charge, compared with net income of $48.8 million in the prior year. Total revenue climbed 14.0% to $5.28 billion from $4.64 billion the previous year. Revenue for 2003 included a $371.5 million gain on transfer of securities from available-for-sale to trading and a $4.1 million gain on reinsurance embedded derivative/trading securities. Net investment income grew 0.3% to $2.64 billion from $2.63 billion the year before. Income before taxes was $1.05 billion versus a loss before taxes of $53.8 million a year earlier.

Prospects: Co. continues to implement initiatives focused on combining its retirement and life insurance businesses into a single operating unit focused on providing wealth accumulation and protection, income distribution and wealth transfer products. Earnings should benefit from significantly reduced operating expenses stemming from these realignment activities, which are anticipated to be completed by the first quarter of 2006. Meanwhile, Co. is enjoying strong sales in its life insurance segment driven by increased retail sales of universal life, term and whole life insurance products. In addition, results are benefiting improved conditions in the equity markets.

Financial Data

(US$ in Thousands)	12/31/2003	12/31/2002	12/31/2001	12/31/2000	12/31/1999	12/31/1998	12/31/1997	12/31/1996
Earnings Per Share	4.27	0.49	3.05	3.19	2.30	2.51	0.10	2.45
Tang. Book Val. Per Share	18.77	15.62	14.11	11.06	5.59	10.16	19.38	15.96
Dividends Per Share	1.340	1.280	1.220	1.160	1.100	1.040	0.980	0.920
Dividend Payout %	31.38	261.22	40.00	36.36	47.82	41.43	933.33	37.55
Income Statement								
Total Premium Income	280,951	315,943	1,704,002	1,813,111	1,881,515	1,620,629	1,328,735	3,181,999
Total Revenues	5,283,881	4,635,462	6,380,638	6,851,507	6,803,700	6,087,063	4,898,479	6,721,270
Total Indirect Exp.	(75,842)	(74,381)	...	...	...	...	...	...
Inc. Before Inc. Taxes	1,123,405	76,652	758,467	836,670	564,167	694,062	34,881	710,837
Income Taxes	280,400	(90,000)	158,362	214,898	109,610	187,623	12,651	179,152
Eqty Earns/Minority Int.	...	(647)	5,672	(379)	5,797	3,336	...	(18,127)
Income from Cont Ops	767,155	...	605,777	...	...	...	...	...
Net Income	511,936	91,596	590,211	621,393	460,354	509,775	933,988	513,558
Average Shs. Outstg.	179,441	185,596	193,303	194,920	200,417	203,262	207,992	209,122
Balance Sheet								
Cash & Cash Equivalents	4,831,323	1,690,534	3,095,480	1,927,393	1,895,883	2,433,350	3,794,706	1,231,724
Premiums Due	8,759,932	8,296,179	7,009,051	4,798,380	5,092,168	4,105,871	2,971,283	3,678,049
Invst. Assets: Total	36,658,220	33,848,755	29,645,979	28,751,167	28,976,420	31,715,232	25,788,561	30,035,041
Total Assets	106,744,868	93,133,422	98,001,304	99,844,059	103,095,733	93,836,260	77,174,708	71,713,405
Long-Term Obligations	1,458,835	1,511,858	1,336,410	1,457,231	711,963	712,171	511,037	626,311
Net Stockholders' Equity	5,811,625	5,296,267	5,263,484	4,954,084	4,263,868	5,387,941	4,982,915	4,154,956
Shares Outstanding	178,212	177,307	186,943	190,748	195,494	202,112	201,718	207,318
Statistical Record								
Return on Equity %	13.20	1.73	11.51	12.54	10.80	9.46	18.74	12.36
Return on Assets %	0.72	0.10	0.62	0.62	0.44	0.53	1.21	0.71
Price Range	41.32-25.17	53.50-25.17	52.55-39.10	56.13-23.19	57.31-36.50	48.78-34.38	39.06-24.69	28.13-21.00
P/E Ratio	9.68-5.89	109.2-51.37	17.23-12.82	17.59-7.27	24.92-15.87	19.43-13.70	390.6-246.9	11.48-8.57
Average Yield %	3.87	3.13	2.63	2.87	2.38	2.44	3.07	3.78

Address: 1500 Market Street, Philadelphia, PA 19102-2112 Telephone: (215) 448-1400 Web Site: www.lfg.com	Officers: Jon A. Boscia – Chmn., C.E.O., Richard C. Vaughan – Exec. V.P., C.F.O. Transfer Agents:First Chicago Trust Company of New York, Jersey City, NJ	Investor Contact:215-448-1422 Institutional Holding No of Institutions: 5 Shares: 69,197 % Held: –

LINEAR TECHNOLOGY CORP.

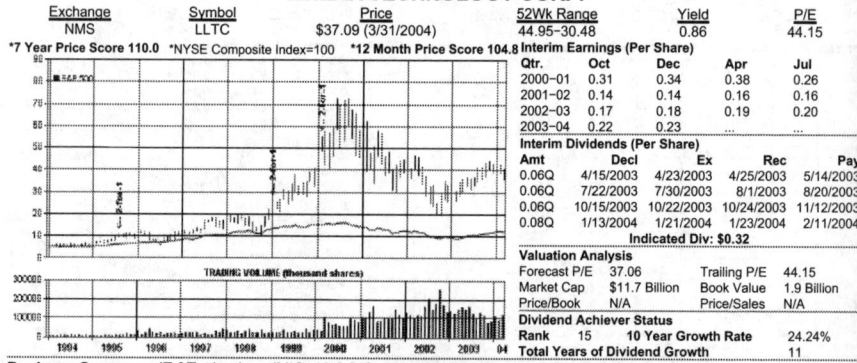

Exchange	Symbol	Price	52Wk Range	Yield	P/E
NMS	LLTC	$37.09 (3/31/2004)	44.95–30.48	0.86	44.15

*7 Year Price Score 110.0   *NYSE Composite Index=100   *12 Month Price Score 104.8

Interim Earnings (Per Share)

Qtr.	Oct	Dec	Apr	Jul
2000–01	0.31	0.34	0.38	0.26
2001–02	0.14	0.14	0.16	0.16
2002–03	0.17	0.18	0.19	0.20
2003–04	0.22	0.23	...	...

Interim Dividends (Per Share)

Amt	Decl	Ex	Rec	Pay
0.06Q	4/15/2003	4/23/2003	4/25/2003	5/14/2003
0.06Q	7/22/2003	7/30/2003	8/1/2003	8/20/2003
0.06Q	10/15/2003	10/22/2003	10/24/2003	11/12/2003
0.08Q	1/13/2004	1/21/2004	1/23/2004	2/11/2004

Indicated Div: $0.32

Valuation Analysis

Forecast P/E	37.06	Trailing P/E	44.15
Market Cap	$11.7 Billion	Book Value	1.9 Billion
Price/Book	N/A	Price/Sales	N/A

Dividend Achiever Status

Rank	15	10 Year Growth Rate	24.24%
Total Years of Dividend Growth			11

Business Summary: IT &Technology (MIC: 10.2 SIC: 3674 NAIC:334413)

Linear Technology designs, manufactures and markets a broad line of standard high performance linear integrated circuits. Applications for Co.'s products include telecommunications, cellular telephones, networking products, notebook and desktop computers, computer peripherals, video/multimedia, industrial instrumentation, security monitoring devices, high–end consumer products such as digital cameras and MP3 players, complex medical devices, automotive electronics, factory automation, process control, and military and space systems. Co. focuses its product development and marketing efforts on high–performance applications where it can compete effectively.

Recent Developments: For the second quarter ended Dec 28 2003, net income advanced 32.4% to $74.3 million compared with $56.2 million a year earlier. Net sales climbed 28.3% to $186.0 million from $145.0 million a year earlier. Sales benefited from strong demand for Co.'s products, which increased in each end–market, led by industrial and communications. Gross profit increased 33.7% to $142.2 million from $106.4 million the year before. As a percentage of sales, gross profit rose to 76.5% from 73.4% in the previous year. Operating income jumped 42.9% to $98.0 million from $68.6 million in 2002.

Prospects: Co. is experiencing particularly strong demand across each of its end markets. This broad cross section of strength crosses all regions and is widely disbursed over many customers. Co. continues to be both strongly profitable and strongly cash flow positive from operations. Looking ahead, Co. sees continuing strength in its marketplace. As a result, Co. expects to grow both sales and profits in the high single–digit range sequentially in the third quarter of fiscal 2004. Meanwhile, Co. recently increased its quarterly dividend 33.3% to $0.08 from $0.06 per share.

Financial Data

(US$ in Thousands)	6 Mos	3 Mos	06/29/2003	06/30/2002	07/01/2001	07/02/2000	06/27/1999	06/28/1998
Earnings Per Share	0.84	0.79	0.74	0.60	1.29	0.88	0.61	0.58
Cash Flow Per Share	0.58	0.23	0.88	0.78	1.68	1.34	0.88	0.83
Tang. Book Val. Per Share	6.03	6.03	5.80	5.63	5.58	4.19	2.94	2.45
Dividends Per Share	0.230	0.220	0.210	0.170	0.130	0.090	0.070	0.060
Dividend Payout %	27.38	27.85	28.37	28.33	10.07	10.22	11.88	10.34
Income Statement								
Total Revenues	360,098	174,077	606,573	512,282	972,625	705,917	506,669	484,799
Total Indirect Exp.	86,138	41,906	156,996	142,464	195,218	152,572	108,922	99,473
Depreciation & Amort.	24,512	12,234	45,903	46,261	35,788	24,958	21,972	20,122
Operating Income	188,774	90,762	294,511	225,099	546,285	374,396	257,926	247,547
Net Interest Inc./(Exp.)	13,769	7,085	38,715	53,251	64,366	42,858	27,801	23,710
Income Taxes	58,737	28,376	96,635	80,721	183,195	129,348	91,434	90,355
Net Income	143,806	69,471	236,591	197,629	427,456	287,906	194,293	180,902
Average Shs. Outstg.	323,167	322,894	321,375	328,538	332,527	328,002	317,888	319,876
Balance Sheet								
Cash & Cash Equivalents	1,686,773	1,667,116	1,593,567	1,552,030	1,549,002	1,175,558	786,707	637,893
Total Current Assets	1,881,009	1,865,573	1,776,000	1,727,581	1,727,848	1,310,103	905,112	768,176
Total Assets	2,142,498	2,135,390	2,056,879	1,988,433	2,017,074	1,507,256	1,046,914	892,822
Total Current Liabilities	176,641	160,793	162,029	168,997	202,224	168,677	125,275	123,026
Net Stockholders' Equity	1,889,907	1,896,639	1,814,929	1,781,454	1,781,957	1,322,197	906,794	755,913
Net Working Capital	1,704,368	1,704,780	1,613,971	1,558,584	1,525,624	1,141,426	779,837	645,150
Shares Outstanding	313,134	314,244	312,706	316,150	318,908	315,167	307,462	307,292
Statistical Record								
Operating Profit Margin %	52.42	52.13	48.55	43.94	56.16	53.03	50.90	51.06
Return on Equity %	7.60	3.66	13.03	11.09	23.98	21.77	21.42	23.93
Return on Assets %	6.71	3.25	11.50	9.93	21.19	19.10	18.55	20.26
Price Range	44.33–32.38	41.94–32.38	36.77–19.61	48.24–28.58	72.94–33.95	72.31–27.89	32.84–10.25	20.13–12.94
P/E Ratio	100.8–73.59	190.6–147.2	49.69–26.50	80.40–47.63	56.54–26.32	82.17–31.69	53.84–16.80	34.70–22.31
Average Yield %	0.59	0.59	0.71	0.42	0.24	0.21	0.33	0.36

Address: 1630 McCarthy Blvd., Milpitas, CA 95035–7417 Telephone: (408) 432–1900 Web Site: www.linear.com	Officers: Robert H. Swanson – Chmn., C.E.O., David B. Bell – Pres.	Investor Contact:408–432–1900 Institutional Holding No of Institutions: 35 Shares: 2,667,159 % Held: –

LOWE'S COS., INC.

Exchange	Symbol	Price	52Wk Range	Yield	P/E
NYS	LOW	$56.13 (3/31/2004)	60.05-39.00	0.21	25.17

7 Year Price Score 166.0   *NYSE Composite Index=100   *12 Month Price Score 108.8

Interim Earnings (Per Share)

Qtr.	Apr	Jul	Oct	Feb
2000–01	0.24	0.36	0.26	0.19
2001–02	0.29	0.42	0.32	0.27
2002–03	0.44	0.59	0.43	0.39
2003–04	0.53	0.75	0.56	...

Interim Dividends (Per Share)

Amt	Decl	Ex	Rec	Pay
0.025Q	4/4/2003	4/15/2003	4/17/2003	5/2/2003
0.025Q	5/30/2003	7/16/2003	7/18/2003	8/1/2003
0.03Q	9/16/2003	10/15/2003	10/17/2003	10/31/2003
0.03Q	12/8/2003	1/14/2004	1/16/2004	1/30/2004

Indicated Div: $0.12 (Div. Reinv. Plan)

Valuation Analysis

Forecast P/E	21.72	Trailing P/E	25.17
Market Cap	$43.7 Billion	Book Value	9.9 Billion
Price/Book	4.14	Price/Sales	1.36

Dividend Achiever Status

Rank	151	10 Year Growth Rate	10.13%
Total Years of Dividend Growth		42

Business Summary: Retail – Hardware (MIC: 5.6 SIC: 5211 NAIC:444110)

Lowe's Companies is a major worldwide retailer of home improvement products, with a specific emphasis on retail do–it–yourself and commercial business customers. Co. specializes in offering products and services for home improvement, home decor, home maintenance, home repair and remodeling and maintenance of commercial buildings. As of Aug 1 2003, Co. operated 896 stores in 45 states representing 99.7 million square feet of selling space. Each store is stocked with more than 40,000 separate items, while Co.'s special order program features more than 400,000 additional items.

Recent Developments: For the quarter ended Oct 31 2003, net earnings advanced 33.3% to $452.0 million from $339.0 million in the corresponding period of the previous year. Earnings for 2003 and 2002 included store opening costs of $37.0 million and $28.0 million, respectively. Net sales climbed 23.5% to $7.92 billion from $6.42 billion the previous year, reflecting strength in every product category and in every region of the country. Comparable–store sales increased 12.4% year over year. Gross margin totaled $2.46 billion, or 31.1% of net sales, compared with $1.97 billion, or 30.6% of net sales, a year earlier. During the quarter, Co. opened 38 new stores.

Prospects: On Nov 21 2003, Co. entered into an agreement with The Strober Organization, based in Brooklyn, NY, to sell 26 commodity–focused locations operating under The Contractor Yard banner. The sale will finalize Co.'s transformation to a national store home improvement chain from a commodity–focused lumber and building materials retailer. Separately, Co. expects to open 130 stores in fiscal 2003, reflecting square footage growth of approximately 15.0%, and resulting in store opening costs of about $132.0 million. In fiscal 2003, Co. expects total sales growth of about 18.0%; comparable–store sales to increase between 6.0% and 7.0%; and diluted earnings per share of $2.32 to $2.33.

Financial Data

(US$ in Thousands)	9 Mos	6 Mos	3 Mos	01/31/2003	02/01/2002	02/02/2001	01/28/2000	01/29/1999
Earnings Per Share	1.84	1.27	0.53	1.85	1.30	1.05	0.87	0.68
Cash Flow Per Share	2.53	2.09	1.30	3.37	2.03	1.46	1.52	0.98
Tang. Book Val. Per Share	12.54	11.94	11.15	10.61	8.60	7.16	6.14	4.44
Dividends Per Share	0.105	0.095	0.090	0.085	0.078	0.070	0.063	0.059
Dividend Payout %	5.71	7.48	16.98	4.59	7.43	6.67	7.24	8.68
Income Statement								
Total Revenues	23,909,000	15,984,000	7,211,000	26,491,000	22,111,108	18,778,559	15,905,595	12,244,882
Total Indirect Exp.	4,769,000	3,110,000	1,494,000	5,485,000	4,570,053	3,888,503	3,232,613	2,461,569
Depreciation & Amort.	557,000	364,000	180,000	626,000	516,828	408,618	337,359	271,769
Operating Income	2,498,000	1,728,000	725,000	2,541,000	1,797,788	1,402,265	1,147,969	833,157
Net Interest Inc./(Exp.)	(136,000)	(93,000)	(48,000)	(182,000)	(173,537)	(120,825)	(84,852)	(74,735)
Income Taxes	893,000	618,000	256,000	888,000	600,989	471,569	390,322	276,000
Net Income	1,469,000	1,017,000	421,000	1,471,000	1,023,262	809,871	672,795	482,422
Average Shs. Outstg.	805,000	803,000	802,000	800,000	794,597	768,950	767,708	707,590
Balance Sheet								
Cash & Cash Equivalents	1,196,000	1,550,000	1,600,000	853,000	798,839	455,658	491,122	222,709
Total Current Assets	6,902,000	6,831,000	7,053,000	5,568,000	4,920,392	4,175,013	3,709,541	2,585,683
Total Assets	18,675,000	18,074,000	17,900,000	16,109,000	13,736,219	11,375,754	9,012,323	6,344,651
Total Current Liabilities	4,523,000	4,473,000	4,915,000	3,578,000	3,016,830	2,928,585	2,385,954	1,765,344
Long–Term Obligations	3,681,000	3,684,000	3,733,000	3,736,000	3,734,011	2,697,669	1,726,579	1,283,092
Net Stockholders' Equity	9,862,000	9,373,000	8,735,000	8,302,000	6,674,442	5,494,885	4,695,471	3,135,952
Net Working Capital	2,379,000	2,358,000	2,138,000	1,990,000	1,903,562	1,246,428	1,323,587	820,339
Shares Outstanding	786,000	785,000	783,000	781,900	775,714	766,484	764,718	705,286
Statistical Record								
Operating Profit Margin %	10.44	10.81	10.05	9.59	8.13	7.46	7.21	6.80
Return on Equity %	14.89	10.85	4.81	17.71	15.33	14.73	14.32	15.38
Return on Assets %	7.86	5.62	2.35	9.13	7.44	7.11	7.46	7.60
Debt/Total Assets %	19.71	20.38	20.85	23.19	27.18	23.71	19.15	20.22
Price Range	59.95-34.01	48.34-34.01	45.70-34.01	48.10-33.50	47.50-25.00	31.75-18.72	32.56-21.50	29.16-12.47
P/E Ratio	32.58-18.48	38.06-26.78	86.23-64.17	26.00-18.11	36.54-19.23	30.24-17.83	37.43-24.71	42.88-18.34
Average Yield %	0.20	0.21	0.20	0.19	0.20	0.22	0.22	0.26

Address: 1605 Curtis Bridge Road, Wilkesboro, NC 28697 **Telephone:** (336) 658-4000 **Web Site:** www.lowes.com	**Officers:** Robert L. Tillman – Chmn., C.E.O., Robert A. Niblock – Pres. **Transfer Agents:** EquiServe Trust Company, NA, Boston, MA	**Investor Contact:** 336–658–4385 **Institutional Holding** **No of Institutions:** 2 **Shares:** 14,180 **% Held:** –

M & T BANK CORP

Exchange	Symbol	Price	52Wk Range	Yield	P/E
NYS	MTB	$89.85 (3/31/2004)	98.55–80.57	1.78	18.15

*7 Year Price Score 146.5   *NYSE Composite Index=100   *12 Month Price Score 98.4

TRADING VOLUME (thousand shares)

Interim Earnings (Per Share)

Qtr.	Mar	Jun	Sep	Dec
2000	0.86	0.91	0.94	0.73
2001	0.85	0.94	0.98	1.05
2002	1.25	1.26	1.23	1.33
2003	1.23	1.10	1.28	1.34

Interim Dividends (Per Share)

Amt	Decl	Ex	Rec	Pay
0.30Q	5/20/2003	5/29/2003	6/2/2003	6/30/2003
0.30Q	7/15/2003	8/28/2003	9/2/2003	9/30/2003
0.30Q	10/21/2003	11/26/2003	12/1/2003	12/31/2003
0.40Q	2/17/2004	2/25/2004	2/27/2004	3/31/2004

Indicated Div: $1.60 (Div. Reinv. Plan)

Valuation Analysis

Forecast P/E	15.11	Trailing P/E	18.15
Market Cap	$8.3 Billion	Book Value	5.7 Billion
Price/Book	2.07	Price/Sales	4.00

Dividend Achiever Status

Rank	33	10 Year Growth Rate	20.24%
Total Years of Dividend Growth		23

Business Summary: Commercial Banking (MIC: 8.1 SIC: 6022 NAIC:522110)

M&T Bank, with assets of $49.83 billion as of Dec 31 2003, is a bank holding company with two wholly-owned bank subsidiaries, Manufacturers and Traders Trust and M&T Bank, National Association. The banks collectively offer commercial banking, trust and investment services to their customers. Through its subsidiaries, Co. provides individuals, corporations and institutions with operations in the following six segments: Commercial Banking, Commercial Real Estate, Discretionary Portfolio, Residential Mortgage Banking, Retail Banking, and All Other.

Recent Developments: For the year ended Dec 31 2003, net income increased 25.7% to $573.9 million from $456.8 million the year before. Earnings for 2003 and 2002 included charges for impairment of capitalized residential mortgage servicing rights of $2.0 million and $32.0 million, respectively. Earnings for 2003 also included after-tax merger-related expenses of $39.0 million. Net interest income advanced 28.1% to $1.60 billion. Provision for credit losses rose 7.4% to $131.0 million. Total other income surged 62.3% to $831.1 million, primarily reflecting revenues related to operations in market areas associated with Allfirst Financial. Total other expense increased 50.6% to $1.45 billion.

Prospects: Co. is benefiting from its acquisition of Allfirst Financial, which was completed on Apr 1 2003. For instance, average loans outstanding as of Dec 31 2003 were $34.00 billion, up 33.3% year over year, reflecting the positive impact of the $10.30 billion of loans obtained through the Allfirst acquisition. Additionally, although Co. incurred merger-related expenses of $60.4 million during 2003, it does not expect to report any additional significant expenses. Meanwhile, higher mortgage banking revenues and service charges on deposit accounts are contributing to growth in non-interest income. Looking ahead, diluted earnings per share for 2004 are expected to range from $5.90 to $6.10.

Financial Data

(US$ in Thousands)	12/31/2003	12/31/2002	12/31/2001	12/31/2000	12/31/1999	12/31/1998	12/31/1997	12/31/1996
Earnings Per Share	4.95	5.07	3.82	3.44	3.28	2.61	2.52	2.09
Tang. Book Val. Per Share	21.41	21.35	17.84	16.09	14.87	13.72	15.58	13.54
Dividends Per Share	1.200	1.050	1.000	0.625	0.450	0.380	0.320	0.280
Dividend Payout %	24.24	20.71	26.18	18.17	13.72	14.56	12.70	13.40
Income Statement								
Total Interest Income	2,126,565	1,842,099	2,101,885	1,772,784	1,478,631	1,351,794	1,064,961	997,432
Total Interest Expense	527,810	594,514	943,597	918,597	719,234	687,503	508,093	466,408
Net Interest Income	1,598,755	1,247,585	1,158,288	854,187	759,397	664,291	556,868	531,024
Provision for Loan Losses	131,000	122,000	103,500	38,000	44,500	43,200	46,000	43,325
Non-Interest Income	831,095	511,931	477,426	324,672	282,375	270,595	193,067	170,248
Non-Interest Expense	1,448,180	921,032	948,318	694,453	578,958	566,123	421,776	408,978
Income Before Taxes	850,670	716,484	583,896	446,406	418,314	325,563	282,159	248,969
Net Income	573,942	485,092	378,075	286,156	265,626	207,974	176,241	151,103
Average Shs. Outstg.	115,932	95,663	99,024	83,171	80,900	79,500	69,770	72,060
Balance Sheet								
Cash & Due from Banks	1,877,494	963,772	965,664	750,259	592,755	493,792	333,805	324,659
Securities Avail. for Sale	7,077,770	3,650,763	2,702,113	3,071,735	2,321,874	2,756,862	1,640,564	1,433,989
Net Loans & Leases	35,158,377	25,291,312	24,762,752	22,368,111	17,090,606	15,485,183	11,221,912	10,451,657
Total Assets	49,826,081	33,174,525	31,450,196	28,949,456	22,409,115	20,583,891	14,002,935	12,943,915
Total Deposits	33,114,944	21,664,923	21,580,400	20,232,673	15,373,620	14,737,152	11,163,158	10,514,489
Long-Term Obligations	5,535,425	4,497,374	3,461,769	3,414,516	1,775,133	1,567,543	427,819	178,002
Total Liabilities	44,108,871	29,992,702	28,510,745	26,248,971	20,612,069	18,981,525	12,972,669	12,038,256
Net Stockholders' Equity	5,717,210	3,181,823	2,939,451	2,700,485	1,797,046	1,602,366	1,030,266	905,659
Shares Outstanding	120,106	92,028	93,683	93,244	77,238	76,980	66,100	66,860
Statistical Record								
Return on Equity %	10.03	15.24	12.86	10.59	14.78	12.97	17.10	16.68
Return on Assets %	1.15	1.46	1.20	0.98	1.18	1.01	1.25	1.16
Equity/Assets %	11.47	9.59	9.34	9.32	8.01	7.78	7.35	6.99
Non-Int. Exp./Tot. Inc. %	48.96	39.12	36.76	32.87	34.89	33.52	35.02	
Price Range	98.55-75.69	89.94-68.00	81.23-61.09	68.00-36.40	56.66-41.00	57.53-41.00	46.50-28.10	28.96-20.91
P/E Ratio	19.91-15.29	17.74-13.41	21.26-15.99	19.77-10.58	17.27-12.50	22.04-15.71	18.45-11.15	13.86-10.01
Average Yield %	1.39	1.24	1.05	1.33	0.91	0.94	0.87	0.85

Address: One MTPlaza, Buffalo, NY 14203	Officers: Robert G. Wilmers – Chmn., Pres., CEO, Carl L. Campbell – Vice–Chmn.	Investor Contact: (716) 842–5445
Telephone: (716) 842–5445	Transfer Agents:BankBoston, N.A. c/o Equiserve, Boston, MA	Institutional Holding
Web Site: www.mandtbank.com		No of Institutions: 26
		Shares: 15,630,683 % Held: –

MARSH & MCLENNAN COS., INC.

Exchange	Symbol	Price	52Wk Range	Yield	P/E
NYS	MMC	$46.30 (3/31/2004)	54.74-42.75	2.68	16.48

*7 Year Price Score 115.9 *NYSE Composite Index=100 *12 Month Price Score 86.1

Interim Earnings (Per Share)

Qtr.	Mar	Jun	Sep	Dec
2000	0.59	0.48	0.48	0.50
2001	0.63	0.51	0.29	0.26
2002	0.73	0.60	0.55	0.57
2003	0.81	0.66	0.65	0.69

Interim Dividends (Per Share)

Amt	Decl	Ex	Rec	Pay
0.31Q	5/15/2003	7/7/2003	7/9/2003	8/15/2003
0.31Q	9/18/2003	10/10/2003	10/15/2003	11/14/2003
0.31Q	11/20/2003	12/31/2003	1/5/2004	2/13/2004
0.31Q	3/18/2004	4/6/2004	4/8/2004	5/14/2004

Indicated Div: $1.24 (Div. Reinv. Plan)

Valuation Analysis

Forecast P/E	14.92	Trailing P/E	16.48
Market Cap	$24.8 Billion	Book Value	N/A
Price/Book	N/A	Price/Sales	N/A

Dividend Achiever Status

Rank	152	10 Year Growth Rate 10.12%
Total Years of Dividend Growth		42

Business Summary: Insurance (MIC: 8.2 SIC: 6411 NAIC:524210)

Marsh & McLennan Companies is engaged in the worldwide business of providing retail and wholesale insurance services, principally as a broker or consultant for insurers, insurance underwriters and other brokers. Co.'s subsidiaries include Marsh, a risk and insurance services firm; Putman Investments, one of the largest investment management companies in the U.S.; and Mercer Consulting Group, a major global provider of consulting services. Other subsidiaries render advisory services in the area of employee benefits and compensation consulting, management consulting, economic consulting and environmental consulting.

Recent Developments: For the year ended Dec 31 2003, net income increased 13.0% to $1.54 billion from $1.37 billion the previous year. Results were driven by the strong performance of Co.'s largest business, risk and insurance services. Total revenue increased 11.0% to $11.59 billion. By segment, revenue from risk and insurance services grew 16.2% to $6.87 billion, and operating income advanced 17.5% to $1.75 billion. Revenue from investment management services fell 7.6% to $2.00 billion, and operating income dropped 11.3% to $503.0 million. Consulting revenue rose 15.0% to $2.72 billion, and operating income grew 11.3% to $363.0 million.

Prospects: Co.'s consulting business should continue to grow revenues despite the difficult operating environment. In addition, the recent acquisition of Oliver Wyman should add important capabilities to Co.'s risk and strategy consulting services. Co. has acquired other businesses in an effort to broaden its global retirement and benefits consulting business. For instance, the recently completed acquisition of Synhrgy HR Technologies brings Co. a new platform for employee benefits outsourcing in the U.S. Meanwhile, Putnam's business may continue to be adversely affected by the fraud allegations that led to administrative proceedings by the SEC and state securities regulators.

Financial Data

(US$ in Thousands)	12/31/2003	12/31/2002	12/31/2001	12/31/2000	12/31/1999	12/31/1998	12/31/1997	12/31/1996
Earnings Per Share	2.81	2.45	1.69	2.05	1.31	1.49	0.79	1.05
Tang. Book Val. Per Share	N.M	N.M	N.M	N.M	N.M	N.M	1.53	3.09
Dividends Per Share	1.180	1.090	1.030	0.950	0.850	0.730	0.630	0.540
Dividend Payout %	41.99	44.48	60.76	46.34	64.88	49.21	79.49	51.43
Income Statement								
Total Revenues	11,588,000	10,440,000	9,943,000	10,157,000	9,157,000	7,190,000	6,008,600	4,149,000
Total Indirect Exp.	9,092,000	8,166,000	8,180,000	7,978,000	7,698,000	5,770,000	5,263,800	3,433,700
Inc. Before Inc. Taxes	2,335,000	2,133,000	1,590,000	1,955,000	1,247,000	1,305,000	662,400	668,000
Income Taxes	770,000	747,000	599,000	753,000	521,000	509,000	263,000	208,700
Eqty Earns/Minority Int.	(25,000)	(21,000)	(17,000)	(21,000)	...	...	...	...
Net Income	1,540,000	1,365,000	974,000	1,181,000	726,000	796,000	399,400	459,300
Average Shs. Outstg.	548,000	557,000	572,000	568,000	544,000	528,000	501,600	434,400
Balance Sheet								
Cash & Cash Equivalents	665,000	546,000	537,000	240,000	428,000	610,000	424,300	299,600
Premiums Due	2,703,000	2,478,000	2,692,000	2,812,000	2,323,000	1,909,000	1,498,200	1,085,800
Invst. Assets: Total	648,000	578,000	826,000	976,000	687,000	828,000	720,200	573,300
Total Assets	15,053,000	13,855,000	13,293,000	13,769,000	13,021,000	11,871,000	7,914,200	4,545,200
Long–Term Obligations	2,910,000	2,891,000	2,334,000	2,347,000	2,357,000	1,590,000	1,239,800	458,200
Net Stockholders' Equity	5,451,000	5,018,000	5,173,000	5,228,000	4,170,000	3,659,000	3,198,800	1,888,600
Shares Outstanding	526,736	538,199	548,654	552,052	534,051	514,000	509,850	433,914
Statistical Record								
Return on Equity %	28.71	27.62	19.15	22.99	17.41	21.75	12.48	24.31
Return on Assets %	10.39	10.00	7.45	8.72	5.57	6.70	5.04	10.10
Price Range	54.74–38.52	56.85–35.53	58.56–40.25	67.44–36.50	48.16–28.72	32.00–22.25	26.58–17.23	19.04–14.04
P/E Ratio	19.48–13.71	23.20–14.50	34.65–23.82	32.90–17.80	36.76–21.92	21.48–14.93	33.65–21.81	18.13–13.37
Average Yield %	2.51	2.23	2.04	1.75	2.30	2.59	2.81	3.36

Address: 1166 Avenue Of The Americas, New York, NY 10036
Telephone: (212) 345–5000
Web Site: www.mmc.com

Officers: Jeffrey W. Greenberg – Chmn., C.E.O., Mathis Cabiallavetta – Vice–Chmn.
Transfer Agents: The Bank of New York, New York, NY

Investor Contact: (212) 345–5475
Institutional Holding
No of Institutions: 1
Shares: 22,000 % Held: –

MARSHALL & ILSLEY CORP.

Exchange	Symbol	Price	52Wk Range	Yield	P/E
NYS	MI	$37.81 (3/31/2004)	40.39-25.79	1.90	15.89

*7 Year Price Score N/A   ***NYSE Composite Index=100**   ***12 Month Price Score 106.9**

Interim Earnings (Per Share)

Qtr.	Mar	Jun	Sep	Dec
2000	0.41	0.41	0.24	0.39
2001	0.40	0.27	0.37	0.50
2002	0.52	0.54	0.54	0.56
2003	0.56	0.59	0.61	0.62

Interim Dividends (Per Share)

Amt	Decl	Ex	Rec	Pay
0.18Q	4/22/2003	5/28/2003	5/30/2003	6/13/2003
0.18Q	8/21/2003	8/27/2003	9/1/2003	9/12/2003
0.18Q	10/16/2003	11/26/2003	12/1/2003	12/12/2003
0.18Q	2/19/2004	2/26/2004	3/1/2004	3/12/2004

Indicated Div: $0.72 (Div. Reinv. Plan)

Valuation Analysis

Forecast P/E	13.27	Trailing P/E	15.89
Market Cap	$8.3 Billion	Book Value	3.3 Billion
Price/Book	2.61	Price/Sales	3.23

Dividend Achiever Status

Rank	159	10 Year Growth Rate	9.93%
Total Years of Dividend Growth	31		

Business Summary: Commercial Banking (MIC: 8.1 SIC: 6021 NAIC:522110)

Marshall & Ilsley, a multibank holding company with assets of $34.40 billion as of Dec 31 2003, is headquartered in Milwaukee, WI. Co. has 199 banking offices in Wisconsin, 28 locations throughout Arizona, 11 offices in Minnesota, six offices in Missouri, two offices in Florida, one office in Nevada and one office in Illinois, as well as on the Internet. Co. also provides trust services, residential mortgage banking, capital markets, brokerage and insurance, commercial leasing and commercial mortgage banking. Co.'s principal subsidiary is Metavante Corporation, a provider of integrated financial transaction processing, outsourcing services, software, and consulting services.

Recent Developments: For the twelve months ended Dec 31 2003, net income rose 13.3% to $544.1 million compared with $480.3 million in 2002. Results for 2003 and 2002 included a net gain of $21.6 million and a net loss of $6.3 million, respectively, from investment securities. Net interest income grew 5.1% to $1.06 billion from $1.0 billion the year before. Provision for loan and lease losses declined to $63.0 million versus $74.4 million a year earlier. Total non-interest revenues increased 12.3% to $1.22 billion from $1.08 billion in the previous year. Total non-interest expense rose 12.4% to $1.45 billion versus $1.29 billion the year before.

Prospects: Looking ahead, Co. expects that commercial loan growth in 2004 for the banking segment will be in the high single digits and personal loan growth will be in the mid-to-high single digits. Non-interest bearing deposit growth is expected to be lower in 2004 versus 2003. Based on the general improvement in various segments of the loan portfolio, non-performing loans and leases as a percentage of total loans and leases outstanding are expected to be in the 70.0 to 85.0 basis point range and net charge-offs as a percentage of average loans and leases are expected to be in the 15.0 to 20.0 basis point range. Metavante's 2004 revenue growth is expected to be in the mid-to-high single digits.

Financial Data

(US$ in Thousands)	12/31/2003	12/31/2002	12/31/2001	12/31/2000	12/31/1999	12/31/1998	12/31/1997	12/31/1996
Earnings Per Share	2.38	2.16	1.54	1.45	1.57	1.30	1.21	1.01
Tang. Book Val. Per Share	9.96	8.60	9.16	9.22	8.26	8.98	9.45	7.11
Dividends Per Share	0.700	0.620	0.560	0.510	0.470	0.430	0.390	0.360
Dividend Payout %	29.41	28.93	36.73	35.56	29.93	32.95	32.43	35.64
Income Statement								
Total Interest Income	1,529,920	1,567,336	1,709,107	1,747,982	1,496,584	1,434,044	1,143,670	971,436
Total Interest Expense	472,634	561,038	866,328	1,074,976	791,303	757,974	579,623	465,717
Net Interest Income	1,057,286	1,006,298	842,779	673,006	705,281	676,070	564,047	505,719
Provision for Loan Losses	62,993	74,416	54,115	30,352	25,419	27,090	17,253	15,194
Non-Interest Income	1,215,801	1,082,688	1,002,812	928,352	845,774	756,333	598,858	503,320
Non-Interest Expense	1,451,707	1,295,978	1,290,431	1,100,656	997,697	940,028	775,401	680,704
Income Before Taxes	704,244	718,592	501,045	470,350	527,939	465,285	370,251	313,141
Income from Cont Ops	489,962	...	337,620	317,402	...	...	...	...
Net Income	544,105	480,327	337,485	315,123	354,511	301,323	245,144	203,430
Average Shs. Outstg.	228,285	222,048	218,264	217,766	226,010	230,480	203,020	202,394
Balance Sheet								
Cash & Due from Banks	810,088	1,012,090	617,183	760,103	705,293	760,405	800,120	780,562
Securities Avail. for Sale	4,843,908	4,370,697	4,210,653	4,785,869	4,429,837	4,161,318	4,101,500	3,128,530
Net Loans & Leases	24,800,756	23,570,437	19,027,174	17,351,972	16,109,199	13,770,114	12,339,463	9,145,989
Total Assets	34,372,643	32,874,642	27,253,734	26,077,739	24,369,723	21,566,293	19,477,452	14,763,313
Total Deposits	22,270,105	20,393,706	16,493,047	19,248,621	16,435,182	15,919,919	14,355,998	10,952,358
Long-Term Obligations	2,734,623	2,283,781	1,560,177	921,276	665,024	794,482	791,176	336,096
Total Liabilities	31,043,950	29,837,974	24,760,766	23,835,502	22,252,797	19,322,514	17,557,381	13,502,103
Net Stockholders' Equity	3,328,693	3,036,668	2,492,968	2,242,189	2,116,926	2,243,779	1,920,071	1,261,210
Shares Outstanding	223,226	226,232	207,897	205,693	211,632	212,206	203,074	177,168
Statistical Record								
Return on Equity %	14.71	15.81	13.55	14.15	16.74	13.42	12.76	16.12
Return on Assets %	1.42	1.46	1.23	1.21	1.45	1.39	1.25	1.37
Equity/Assets %	9.68	9.23	9.14	8.59	8.68	10.40	9.85	8.54
Non-Int. Exp./Tot. Inc. %	52.87	48.90	47.58	41.12	42.59	42.91	44.49	46.15
Price Range	38.40-25.07	31.96-23.25	32.06-24.02	31.41-19.31	34.66-30.00	...	...	...
P/E Ratio	16.13-10.53	14.79-10.76	20.82-15.60	21.66-13.32	22.07-19.11	...	...	...
Average Yield %	2.26	2.09	2.03	2.13	1.46	N/A	N/A	N/A

Address: 770 North Water Street, Milwaukee, WI 53202	Officers: James B. Wigdale – Chmn., Dennis J. Kuester – Pres., C.E.O.	Investor Contact:414-765-7801
Telephone: (414) 765-7801	Transfer Agents:Continental Stock Transfer &Trust Company, New York, NY	Institutional Holding
Web Site: www.micorp.com		No of Institutions: 24
		Shares: 2,729,615 % Held: –

MASCO CORP.

Exchange	Symbol	Price	52Wk Range	Yield	P/E
NYS	MAS	$30.44 (3/31/2004)	30.62-18.95	2.10	20.16

*7 Year Price Score 98.0   *NYSE Composite Index=100   *12 Month Price Score 105.7

Interim Earnings (Per Share)

Qtr.	Mar	Jun	Sep	Dec
2000	0.39	0.41	0.41	0.10
2001	0.25	0.30	(0.39)	0.26
2002	0.31	0.43	0.24	0.35
2003	0.32	0.46	0.53	0.20

Interim Dividends (Per Share)

Amt	Decl	Ex	Rec	Pay
0.14Q	6/26/2003	7/9/2003	7/11/2003	8/11/2003
0.16Q	9/17/2003	10/8/2003	10/10/2003	11/10/2003
0.16Q	12/10/2003	1/7/2004	1/9/2004	2/9/2004
0.16Q	3/18/2004	4/6/2004	4/9/2004	5/10/2004

Indicated Div: $0.64 (Div. Reinv. Plan)

Valuation Analysis

Forecast P/E	13.26	Trailing P/E 20.16
Market Cap	$14.7 Billion	Book Value 5.5 Billion
Price/Book	2.32	Price/Sales 1.16

Dividend Achiever Status

Rank	234
10 Year Growth Rate	5.96%
Total Years of Dividend Growth	45

Business Summary: Metal Products (MIC: 11.4 SIC: 3432 NAIC:337122)

Masco is engaged in the manufacture and sale of cabinets and related products, plumbing products, architectural coatings and other specialty home improvement and building products. These products are sold to the home improvement and home construction markets through mass merchandisers, hardware stores, home centers, builders, distributors and other outlets for consumers and builders. Co.'s brand names and tradenames include the following: *Kraftmaid®, Merillat®, Mill's Pride®, Quality Cabinets®, Delta®, Peerless®, Newport Brass®, Behr®, Premium Plus®, Masterchem®, Franklin Brass®, Ginger®, Bath Unlimited®, Milgard®, Griffin*™, and *Cambrian*™.

Recent Developments: For the year ended Dec 31 2003, income increased 11.4% to $740.0 million compared with income of $664.0 million in 2003. Results for 2003 and 2002 excluded gains of $66.0 million and $18.0 million, respectively, from discontinued operations. Results for 2002 also excluded a loss of $92.0 million from an accounting change charge. Results included a gain of $72.0 million in 2003 and a charge of $147.0 million in 2002 related to a litigation settlement. Results for 2002 included a gain of $16.0 million from the planned disposition of a business. Net sales advanced 19.5% to $10.94 billion mostly due to higher unit sales volume of certain products.

Prospects: Co. has initiated a plan of disposition for several of its European businesses that are not core to its long-term growth strategy. The dispositions should be completed within the next twelve months, and Co. expects to recognize a loss from the disposal of all of these businesses. Looking ahead, Co. is projecting full-year 2004 earnings from continuing operations in a range of $1.80 to $1.90, including a reduction of approximately $0.05 per common share resulting from the absence of earnings related to the European businesses to be divested. This outlook is based on favorable sales performance in early 2004 and existing business trends.

Financial Data

(US$ in Thousands)	12/31/2003	12/31/2002	12/31/2001	12/31/2000	12/31/1999	12/31/1998	12/31/1997	12/31/1996
Earnings Per Share	1.51	1.33	0.42	1.31	1.28	1.39	1.15	0.92
Cash Flow Per Share	2.89	2.38	2.03	1.62	1.09	1.21	1.19	1.05
Tang. Book Val. Per Share	1.35	1.31	1.30	2.77	3.14	4.98	4.52	4.29
Dividends Per Share	0.580	0.540	0.520	0.490	0.450	0.430	0.400	0.380
Dividend Payout %	38.41	40.97	125.00	37.40	35.15	30.93	35.21	41.30
Income Statement								
Total Revenues	10,936,000	9,419,400	8,358,000	7,243,000	6,307,000	4,345,000	3,760,000	3,237,000
Total Indirect Exp.	1,926,000	1,653,340	1,511,400	1,288,140	1,400,070	870,510	794,650	708,430
Depreciation & Amort.	244,000	220,300	93,200	66,200	45,430	28,510	18,720	12,140
Operating Income	1,424,000	1,331,100	1,039,800	966,700	911,400	680,500	587,100	480,500
Net Interest Inc./(Exp.)	(254,000)	(230,840)	(203,660)	(130,930)	(67,890)	(38,920)	(32,300)	(74,680)
Income Taxes	463,000	348,900	102,200	301,700	334,500	279,000	248,500	207,500
Eqty Earns/Minority Int.	(13,000)	14,230	6,160	19,470	23,930	29,200	24,140	20,090
Income from Cont Ops	740,000	682,100	...	...	...	...	...	...
Net Income	806,000	589,700	198,500	591,700	569,600	476,000	382,400	295,200
Average Shs. Outstg.	491,000	514,100	474,900	451,800	446,200	343,700	337,600	321,200
Balance Sheet								
Cash & Cash Equivalents	795,000	1,066,570	311,990	169,430	230,780	541,740	441,330	473,730
Total Current Assets	3,804,000	3,949,770	2,626,920	2,308,160	2,109,780	1,862,620	1,626,720	1,429,770
Total Assets	12,149,000	12,050,430	9,183,330	7,744,000	6,634,920	5,167,350	4,333,760	3,701,650
Total Current Liabilities	2,099,000	1,932,450	1,236,560	1,078,050	846,430	846,580	620,000	518,440
Long-Term Obligations	3,848,000	4,316,470	3,627,630	3,018,240	2,431,270	1,391,420	1,321,470	1,236,320
Net Stockholders' Equity	5,456,000	5,293,840	4,119,830	3,426,060	3,136,500	2,728,580	2,229,020	1,839,810
Net Working Capital	1,705,000	2,017,320	1,390,360	1,230,110	1,263,350	1,016,040	1,006,720	911,330
Shares Outstanding	458,380	488,890	459,050	444,750	443,510	339,330	331,140	321,740
Statistical Record								
Operating Profit Margin %	13.02	14.13	12.44	13.34	14.45	15.66	15.61	14.84
Return on Equity %	13.56	12.88	4.81	17.27	18.16	17.44	17.15	16.04
Return on Assets %	6.09	5.66	2.16	7.64	8.58	9.21	8.82	7.97
Debt/Total Assets %	31.67	35.82	39.50	38.97	36.64	26.92	30.49	33.39
Price Range	28.31-16.82	29.08-17.68	26.49-18.00	25.69-14.81	33.50-23.00	32.50-21.13	26.53-17.06	18.31-13.44
P/E Ratio	18.75-11.14	21.86-13.29	63.07-42.86	19.61-11.31	26.17-17.97	23.38-15.20	23.07-14.84	19.90-14.61
Average Yield %	2.50	2.22	2.44	2.46	1.55	1.54	1.92	2.50

Address: 21001 Van Born Road, Taylor, MI 48180	Officers: Richard A. Manoogian – Chmn., C.E.O., Alan Barry – Pres., C.O.O.	Investor Contact:313-274-7400
Telephone: (313) 274-7400	Transfer Agents:Bank of New York, New York, NY	Institutional Holding
Web Site: www.masco.com		No of Institutions: 4
		Shares: 1,029,779 % Held: –

MAY DEPARTMENT STORES CO. (THE)

Exchange	Symbol	Price	52Wk Range	Yield	P/E
NYS	MAY	$34.58 (3/31/2004)	36.31–19.77	2.81	24.52

*7 Year Price Score 74.5   *NYSE Composite Index=100   *12 Month Price Score 106.9

Interim Earnings (Per Share)

Qtr.	Apr	Jul	Oct	Feb
2000–01	0.35	0.41	0.27	1.59
2001–02	0.34	0.35	0.17	1.36
2002–03	0.23	0.22	0.05	1.26
2003–04	0.23	(0.39)	0.15	1.42

Interim Dividends (Per Share)

Amt	Decl	Ex	Rec	Pay
0.24Q	3/21/2003	5/28/2003	6/1/2003	6/15/2003
0.24Q	11/14/2003	11/26/2003	12/1/2003	12/15/2003
0.243Q	2/12/2004	2/26/2004	3/1/2004	3/15/2004
0.243Q	3/19/2004	5/27/2004	6/1/2004	6/15/2004

Indicated Div: $0.97 (Div. Reinv. Plan)

Valuation Analysis

Forecast P/E	12.78	Trailing P/E	24.52
Market Cap	$10.0 Billion	Book Value	3.7 Billion
Price/Book	1.90	Price/Sales	0.55

Dividend Achiever Status

Rank	257	10 Year Growth Rate	4.84%
Total Years of Dividend Growth		28	

Business Summary: Retail – General (MIC: 5.2 SIC: 5311 NAIC:452111)

The May Department Stores Company operated 447 department stores in 45 states, the District of Columbia and Puerto Rico as of Aug 2 2003 under the following names: Lord & Taylor, Hecht's, Strawbridge's, Foley's, Robinsons–May, Filene's, Kaufmann's, Famous–Barr, L.S. Ayers, The Jones Store and Meier & Frank. In addition, Co. operated 191 David's Bridal stores, 259 After Hours Formalwear stores and ten Priscilla of Boston stores.

Recent Developments: For the 52 weeks ended Jan 31 2004, net earnings totaled $434.0 million, down 19.9% compared with $542.0 million in the corresponding prior–year period. Results included pre–tax restructuring charges of $328.0 million and $114.0 million in fiscal 2003 and fiscal 2002, respectively. Net sales slipped 1.1% to $13.34 billion from $13.49 billion the year before. Comparable–store sales declined 2.8% year–over–year. Cost of sales, excluding one–time restructuring charges, totaled $9.37 billion, or 70.3% of net sales, versus $9.44 billion, or 70.0% of net sales, a year earlier. Earnings before income taxes was $639.0 million compared with $820.0 million the previous year.

Prospects: Results are benefiting from strong sales of fragrances, skin–care products, handbags, and designer dress shirts. In addition, customers are responding favorably to an expanded selection of non–apparel products, including Apple iPods, DVD players, and home decor items. Meanwhile, Co. continues to aggressively expand its store base. In fiscal 2004, Co. plans to open nine new department stores, 30 David's Bridal stores, 20 After Hours stores, and two Priscilla of Boston stores. Separately, as of the end of fiscal 2003, Co. had completed the closure of nine of the 34 department stores scheduled to be divested as part of a cost–reduction plan announced in July 2003.

Financial Data

(US$ in Millions)	01/31/2004	02/01/2003	02/02/2002	02/03/2001	01/29/2000	01/30/1999	01/31/1998	02/01/1997
Earnings Per Share	1.41	1.76	2.22	2.62	2.60	2.30	2.07	1.88
Cash Flow Per Share	5.45	4.74	5.17	4.10	4.30	4.09	4.08	3.43
Tang. Book Val. Per Share	8.72	8.38	7.76	8.52	9.51	8.67	8.82	8.08
Dividends Per Share	0.960	0.950	0.940	0.930	0.890	0.840	0.800	0.760
Dividend Payout %	68.08	53.97	42.34	35.49	34.23	36.81	38.64	40.95
Income Statement								
Total Revenues	13,343	13,491	14,175	14,511	13,866	13,413	12,685	12,000
Total Indirect Exp.	3,008	2,863	2,912	2,835	2,686	2,516	2,375	2,265
Depreciation & Amort.	564	557	559	511	469	439	412	373
Operating Income	957	1,165	1,493	1,747	1,810	1,673	1,578	1,509
Net Interest Inc./(Exp.)	(318)	(345)	(349)	(345)	(287)	(278)	(299)	(277)
Income Taxes	205	278	438	544	596	546	500	483
Income from Cont Ops	...	...	706	...	...	...	779	749
Net Income	434	542	703	858	927	849	775	755
Average Shs. Outstg.	307	307	317	327	355	367	373	396
Balance Sheet								
Cash & Cash Equivalents	564	55	52	156	41	112	199	102
Total Current Assets	5,143	4,722	4,925	5,270	5,115	4,987	4,878	5,035
Total Assets	12,097	11,936	11,920	11,574	10,935	10,533	9,913	10,059
Total Current Liabilities	2,685	2,666	2,538	2,214	2,415	2,059	1,828	1,923
Long–Term Obligations	3,797	4,035	4,403	4,534	3,560	3,825	3,512	3,849
Net Stockholders' Equity	4,191	4,035	3,841	3,855	4,077	3,836	3,809	3,650
Net Working Capital	2,458	2,056	2,387	3,056	2,700	2,928	3,050	3,112
Shares Outstanding	288	288	287	298	325	334	346	355
Statistical Record								
Operating Profit Margin %	7.17	8.63	10.53	12.03	13.05	12.47	12.43	12.57
Return on Equity %	10.35	13.43	18.38	22.25	22.73	22.13	20.45	20.52
Return on Assets %	3.58	4.54	5.92	7.41	8.47	8.06	7.85	7.44
Debt/Total Assets %	31.38	33.80	36.93	39.17	32.55	36.31	35.42	38.26
Price Range	33.61–18.01	37.60–20.43	41.25–27.98	38.95–19.63	45.00–29.56	47.08–33.50	37.96–29.33	34.17–27.42
P/E Ratio	23.84–12.77	21.36–11.61	18.58–12.60	14.87–7.49	17.31–11.37	20.47–14.57	18.34–14.17	18.17–14.58
Average Yield %	3.91	3.22	2.71	3.41	2.34	2.04	2.35	2.43

Address: 611 Olive Street, St. Louis, MO 63101-1799	**Officers:** Eugene S. Kahn – Chmn., C.E.O., William P. McNamara – Vice–Chmn.	**Investor Contact:**314–342–6413
Telephone: (314) 342–6300	**Transfer Agents:**The Bank of New York, New York, NY	**Institutional Holding** **No of Institutions:** 7
Web Site: www.maycompany.com		**Shares:** 756,476 **% Held:** –

MBIA INC.

Exchange	Symbol	Price	52Wk Range	Yield	P/E
NYS	MBI	$62.70 (3/31/2004)	67.13-39.27	1.53	11.18

*7 Year Price Score 113.9 *NYSE Composite Index=100 *12 Month Price Score 105.0

Interim Earnings (Per Share)

Qtr.	Mar	Jun	Sep	Dec
2000	0.88	0.87	0.88	0.92
2001	0.78	0.96	1.03	1.05
2002	1.03	0.97	1.11	0.87
2003	1.54	1.51	1.31	1.25

Interim Dividends (Per Share)

Amt	Decl	Ex	Rec	Pay
0.20Q	6/13/2003	6/23/2003	6/25/2003	7/15/2003
0.20Q	9/15/2003	9/23/2003	9/25/2003	10/15/2003
0.20Q	12/8/2003	12/17/2003	12/19/2003	1/15/2004
0.24Q	3/11/2004	3/24/2004	3/26/2004	4/15/2004

Indicated Div: $0.96

Valuation Analysis

Forecast P/E	11.67	Trailing P/E	11.18
Market Cap	$9.2 Billion	Book Value	6.3 Billion
Price/Book	1.36	Price/Sales	5.03

Dividend Achiever Status

Rank	156	10 Year Growth Rate	10.01%
Total Years of Dividend Growth		16

Business Summary: Insurance (MIC: 8.2 SIC: 6351 NAIC:524130)

MBIA is engaged in providing financial guarantee insurance, investment management services and municipal and other services to public finance clients and structured finance clients on a global basis. Financial guarantee insurance provides an unconditional and irrevocable guarantee of the payment of the principal of, and interest or other amounts owing on, insured obligations when due. Co. conducts its financial guarantee business through its wholly-owned subsidiary, MBIA Insurance Corporation. Co. also owns MBIA Assurance S.A., a French insurance company, which writes financial guarantee insurance in the member countries of the European Union.

Recent Developments: For the year ended Dec 31 2003, net income rose 40.5% to $813.6 million compared with $579.1 million a year earlier. Consolidated revenues advanced 27.9% to $1.86 billion from $1.45 billion in 2002. Consolidated revenues included a net gain of $99.7 million for 2003 and net losses of $81.9 million for 2002 on derivative instruments and foreign exchange. Results for 2003 and 2002 also included net realized gains of $80.7 million and $15.4 million, respectively. Co. attributed the top-line growth primarily to a higher insurance premium and fee revenues, as well as the aforementioned net gains on insured credit derivative instruments and net realized gains on Co.'s investment portfolio.

Prospects: Co. has indicated that its long-term growth target for new business production is in the 12.0% to 15.0% range over any three to five year period. Following three consecutive years of very strong adjusted direct premium (ADP) growth averaging 25.0%, Co. expects that 2004 ADP will increase only slightly over 2003 before returning to more historic levels. Also, the strong new business production over the last three years should lead to scheduled earned premium growth of 15.0% to 20.0% in the 2004 to 2006 timeframe. Accordingly, operating earnings per share is expected to fall within Co.'s long-term target range of 12.0% to 15.0% for years 2004 through 2006 driven by earned premium growth.

Financial Data

(US$ in Thousands)	12/31/2003	12/31/2002	12/31/2001	12/31/2000	12/31/1999	12/31/1998	12/31/1997	12/31/1996
Earnings Per Share	5.61	3.98	3.82	3.55	2.12	2.88	2.81	2.47
Tang. Book Val. Per Share	42.87	37.32	31.56	27.86	22.78	24.58	21.81	18.28
Dividends Per Share	0.770	0.660	0.580	0.540	0.530	0.520	0.510	0.470
Dividend Payout %	13.72	16.58	15.35	15.38	25.07	18.17	18.12	19.02
Income Statement								
Total Premium Income	732,997	588,509	523,870	446,353	442,796	424,550	297,377	251,712
Net Investment Income	437,696	432,949	412,763	393,985	359,456	331,802	281,459	247,561
Other Income	518,188	195,900	199,152	184,232	162,169	164,695	75,146	46,264
Total Revenues	1,688,881	1,217,358	1,135,785	1,024,570	964,421	921,047	653,982	545,537
Total Indirect Exp.	14,874	17,259	20,874	19,494	126,075	85,904	40,470	17,297
Inc. Before Inc. Taxes	1,148,640	792,581	790,984	714,857	387,883	565,038	479,569	408,130
Income Taxes	335,055	205,763	207,826	186,220	67,353	132,310	105,393	85,967
Income from Cont Ops	...	586,818	583,158	...	...	...	...	...
Net Income	813,585	579,087	570,091	528,637	320,530	432,728	374,176	322,163
Average Shs. Outstg.	144,980	147,574	149,282	148,668	150,603	150,244	133,120	130,044
Balance Sheet								
Cash & Cash Equivalents	778,783	8,184,687	6,781,021	5,405,194	4,844,281	4,237,267	3,837,538	3,517,654
Premiums Due	81,461	135,595	192,954	45,186	55,741	49,497	13,435	980
Invst. Assets: Total	26,373,625	16,195,119	14,087,004	12,051,359	10,534,701	10,100,563	8,681,611	7,659,998
Total Assets	30,267,734	18,852,101	16,199,685	13,894,338	12,263,899	11,796,564	9,810,762	8,562,015
Long-Term Obligations	1,021,795	1,033,070	805,062	795,102	689,204	688,996	473,878	374,010
Net Stockholders' Equity	6,259,015	5,493,351	4,782,634	4,223,413	3,513,101	3,792,217	3,048,253	2,479,697
Shares Outstanding	143,875	144,773	148,434	147,845	149,328	149,322	134,191	129,882
Statistical Record								
Return on Equity %	12.99	10.68	12.19	12.51	9.12	11.41	12.27	12.99
Return on Assets %	2.68	3.11	3.59	3.80	2.61	3.66	3.81	3.76
Price Range	60.08-34.64	59.65-35.32	57.25-39.21	49.96-24.42	47.71-30.37	53.46-31.71	44.83-30.58	34.71-23.50
P/E Ratio	10.71-6.17	14.99-8.87	14.99-10.26	14.07-6.88	22.50-14.33	18.56-11.01	15.95-10.88	14.05-9.51
Average Yield %	1.55	1.33	1.14	1.42	1.36	1.15	1.37	1.74

Address: 113 King Street, Armonk, NY 10504	**Officers:** Joseph W. Brown – Chmn., C.E.O., Gary C. Dunton – Pres., C.O.O.	**Investor Contact:**914-765-3014
Telephone: (914) 273-4545	**Transfer Agents:**Mellon Investor Services, LLC, Ridgefield Park, NJ	**Institutional Holding**
Web Site: www.mbia.com		**No of Institutions:** 6
		Shares: 877,908 **% Held:** –

MBNA CORP.

Exchange	Symbol	Price	52Wk Range	Yield	P/E
NYS	KRB	$27.63 (3/31/2004)	28.78-15.23	1.74	16.54

*7 Year Price Score 115.1 *NYSE Composite Index=100 *12 Month Price Score 105.9

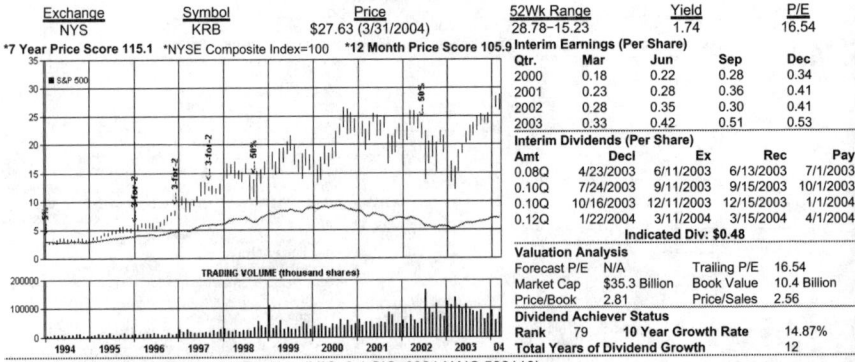

Interim Earnings (Per Share)

Qtr.	Mar	Jun	Sep	Dec
2000	0.18	0.22	0.28	0.34
2001	0.23	0.28	0.36	0.41
2002	0.28	0.35	0.30	0.41
2003	0.33	0.42	0.51	0.53

Interim Dividends (Per Share)

Amt	Decl	Ex	Rec	Pay
0.08Q	4/23/2003	6/11/2003	6/13/2003	7/1/2003
0.10Q	7/24/2003	9/11/2003	9/15/2003	10/1/2003
0.10Q	10/16/2003	12/11/2003	12/15/2003	1/1/2004
0.12Q	1/22/2004	3/11/2004	3/15/2004	4/1/2004

Indicated Div: $0.48

Valuation Analysis

Forecast P/E	N/A	Trailing P/E	16.54
Market Cap	$35.3 Billion	Book Value	10.4 Billion
Price/Book	2.81	Price/Sales	2.56

Dividend Achiever Status

Rank	79	10 Year Growth Rate	14.87%
Total Years of Dividend Growth		12

Business Summary: Commercial Banking (MIC: 8.1 SIC: 6021 NAIC:522110)

MBNA is a registered bank holding company, with assets of $59.13 billion as of Dec 31 2003. Co. is the parent of MBNA America Bank, N.A., which has two wholly-owned foreign bank subsidiaries, MBNA Europe Bank and MBNA Canada Bank. MBNA.com, provides credit card, consumer loan, retail deposit, travel and shopping services. Co. is an independent credit card lender and an issuer of affinity credit cards, marketed primarily to members of associations and customers of financial institutions. Co. offers credit cards in the U.S., the U.K., Ireland, Canada and Spain. In addition to its credit card lending, Co. also makes other consumer loans and offers insurance and deposit products.

Recent Developments: For the year ended Dec 31 2003, net income advanced 32.4% to $2.34 billion compared with $1.77 billion in the previous year. Net interest income climbed 13.3% to $2.35 billion from $2.07 billion a year earlier. Provision for possible credit losses increased 3.9% to $1.39 billion from $1.34 billion the year before. Non-interest income jumped 15.9% to $7.83 billion, while non-interest expense rose 9.0% to $5.12 billion. During the year, Co. added 10.7 million new accounts, including 2.7 million added in the fourth quarter of 2003. In addition, Co. acquired 384 new endorsements from organizations in 2003, including Merrill Lynch, Arizona State University, eBay and Royal Caribbean International.

Prospects: Co. recently announced that it plans to issue its own American Express-branded credit cards in the U.S. In addition, Co. also has plans to issue American Express-branded credit cards in Canada, Spain and the U.K. The cards will carry the American Express logo and will be accepted on the American Express global merchant network. Co. will own the loans and manage and service the accounts on its own systems. Separately, Co.'s Europe Bank Ltd. unit has agreed to acquire Premium Credit Ltd. of the U.K. for an undisclosed amount. Premium Credit provides loans to about 2.0 million business customers for the purpose of paying insurance premiums.

Financial Data

(US$ in Thousands)	12/31/2003	12/31/2002	12/31/2001	12/31/2000	12/31/1999	12/31/1998	12/31/1997	12/31/1996
Earnings Per Share	1.79	1.34	1.28	1.02	0.80	0.64	0.51	0.39
Tang. Book Val. Per Share	6.20	4.62	4.08	3.03	3.49	2.12	1.74	1.51
Dividends Per Share	0.330	0.260	0.230	0.200	0.180	0.150	0.130	0.120
Dividend Payout %	18.43	19.65	18.22	20.26	22.31	24.05	27.05	30.76
Income Statement								
Total Interest Income	3,858,884	3,678,070	3,205,102	2,775,679	2,262,271	1,966,172	1,711,013	1,383,267
Total Interest Expense	1,508,511	1,603,495	1,814,065	1,691,727	1,328,506	1,223,833	1,018,623	742,790
Net Interest Income	2,350,373	2,074,575	1,391,037	1,083,952	933,765	742,339	692,390	640,477
Provision for Loan Losses	1,392,701	1,340,157	1,140,615	409,017	408,914	310,039	260,040	178,224
Non-Interest Income	7,825,480	6,752,923	6,939,619	5,093,174	4,207,821	3,228,969	2,812,879	1,895,923
Non-Interest Expense	5,124,147	4,701,925	4,474,831	3,647,702	3,077,708	2,407,204	2,223,121	1,626,882
Income Before Taxes	3,659,005	2,785,416	2,715,210	2,120,407	1,654,964	1,254,065	1,022,108	731,294
Net Income	2,338,104	1,765,954	1,694,291	1,312,532	1,024,423	776,266	622,500	474,495
Average Shs. Outstg.	1,295,142	1,277,787	1,314,229	1,269,796	1,255,557	1,184,131	1,184,701	1,167,709
Balance Sheet								
Cash & Due from Banks	660,022	721,972	962,118	971,469	488,386	382,882	263,064	225,063
Securities Avail. for Sale	4,363,087	3,655,808	3,106,884	2,666,196	2,752,663	1,663,704	2,162,464	1,719,730
Net Loans & Leases	19,323,656	16,585,582	13,870,193	11,296,336	7,615,134	11,559,188	8,099,400	7,540,651
Total Assets	59,113,355	52,856,746	45,447,945	38,678,096	30,859,132	25,806,260	21,305,513	17,035,342
Total Deposits	31,836,081	30,616,216	27,094,745	24,343,595	18,714,753	15,407,040	12,913,213	10,151,686
Long-Term Obligations	12,145,628	9,538,173	6,867,033	5,735,635	5,708,880	5,939,025	5,478,917	3,950,358
Total Liabilities	48,000,315	43,755,427	37,649,227	32,050,818	26,659,689	23,415,225	19,335,463	15,331,034
Net Stockholders' Equity	11,113,040	9,101,319	7,798,718	6,627,278	4,199,443	2,391,035	1,970,050	1,704,308
Shares Outstanding	1,277,597	1,277,671	1,277,671	1,277,705	1,202,671	1,127,693	1,127,673	1,127,671
Statistical Record								
Return on Equity %	21.03	19.40	21.72	19.80	24.39	32.46	31.59	27.84
Return on Assets %	3.95	3.34	3.72	3.39	3.31	3.00	2.92	2.78
Equity/Assets %	18.79	17.21	17.15	17.13	13.60	9.26	9.24	10.00
Non-Int. Exp./Tot. Inc. %	43.85	45.07	44.10	46.35	47.56	46.33	49.14	49.61
Price Range	25.45-12.15	25.97-13.80	26.04-16.70	26.54-13.33	21.67-13.96	19.42-9.46	13.39-8.07	8.44-4.49
P/E Ratio	14.22-6.79	19.38-10.30	20.34-13.05	26.02-13.07	27.08-17.45	26.43-14.78	26.25-15.83	21.65-11.52
Average Yield %	1.59	1.20	1.02	0.99	1.03	1.04	1.18	1.93

Address: 1100 North King Street, Wilmington, DE 19884-0141 **Telephone:** (302) 456-8588 **Web Site:** www.mbna.com	**Officers:** Randolph D. Lerner Esq. – Chmn., John R. Cochran III – Vice–Chmn. **Transfer Agents:** National City Bank, Cleveland, OH	**Investor Contact:** (800) 362–6255 **Institutional Holding** **No of Institutions:** 37 **Shares:** 55,454,894 **% Held:** –

MCCORMICK & CO., INC.

Exchange	Symbol	Price	52Wk Range	Yield	P/E
NYS	MKC	$33.10 (3/31/2004)	33.10-23.89	1.69	23.64

*7 Year Price Score 142.6 *NYSE Composite Index=100 *12 Month Price Score 99.3

Interim Earnings (Per Share)

Qtr.	Feb	May	Aug	Nov
1999-00	0.17	0.17	0.22	0.43
2000-01	0.19	0.19	0.24	0.42
2001-02	0.24	0.24	0.25	0.53
2002-03	0.25	0.28	0.28	0.59

Interim Dividends (Per Share)

Amt	Decl	Ex	Rec	Pay
0.12Q	6/24/2003	7/2/2003	7/7/2003	7/18/2003
0.12Q	9/23/2003	10/1/2003	10/3/2003	10/17/2003
0.14Q	11/25/2003	12/29/2003	12/31/2003	1/21/2004
0.14Q	3/24/2004	4/1/2004	4/5/2004	4/16/2004

Indicated Div: $0.56 (Div. Reinv. Plan)

Valuation Analysis

Forecast P/E	N/A	Trailing P/E 23.64
Market Cap	$4.1 Billion	Book Value 755.2 Million
Price/Book	0.57	Price/Sales 0.19

Dividend Achiever Status

Rank	208	10 Year Growth Rate 7.65%
Total Years of Dividend Growth		17

Business Summary: Food (MIC: 4.1 SIC: 2099 NAIC:311942)

McCormick & Co. is engaged in the manufacture, marketing and distribution of spices, herbs, seasonings and other flavors to the entire food industry. Co. operates in two business segments: consumer and industrial. The consumer segment sells spices, herbs, extracts, seasoning blends, sauces, marinades and specialty foods to the consumer food market under a variety of brands, including *McCormick*, *Zatarain's* in the US, *Ducros* in continental Europe, *Club House* in Canada and *Schwartz* in the U.K. The industrial segment sells spices, blended seasonings, condiments, coatings and compound flavors to food processors, restaurants, distributors, warehouse clubs and institutional operations.

Recent Developments: For the twelve months ended Nov 30 2003, income from continuing operations totaled $199.1 million, before a $2.1 million accounting change charge, up 14.5% compared with income from continuing operations of $173.9 million in the corresponding period a year earlier. Results included one-time pre-tax special charges of $5.5 million and $7.5 million in fiscal 2003 and fiscal 2002, respectively. Net sales climbed 11.0% to $2.27 billion from $2.04 billion the year before, driven primarily by acquisitions and favorable foreign currency exchange rates. Gross profit was $898.6 million, or 39.6% of net sales, versus $799.5 million, or 39.1% of net sales, the prior year.

Prospects: Results are being positively affected by the 2003 acquisitions of Zatarain's and Uniqsauces, favorable foreign currency exchange rates, and Co.'s aggressive cost-control efforts. Co. expects to complete a series of cost-reduction initiatives for its U.S. industrial operations during 2004, and will implement these improvements in its Canadian and European businesses in 2005. Meanwhile, recently-introduced products should help boost sales and operating profitability in Co.'s industrial business during the first half of 2004. Looking ahead, Co. is targeting full-year 2004 sales growth of between 7.0% and 9.0%, and earnings of $1.51 to $1.54 per share.

Financial Data
(US$ in Thousands)

	11/30/2003	11/30/2002	11/30/2001	11/30/2000	11/30/1999	11/30/1998	11/30/1997	11/30/1996
Earnings Per Share	1.40	1.26	1.04	0.99	0.71	0.70	0.64	0.27
Cash Flow Per Share	1.37	1.57	1.45	1.45	1.59	0.97	1.19	1.25
Tang. Book Val. Per Share	0.27	0.61	N.M	N.M	1.70	1.56	1.58	1.82
Dividends Per Share	0.460	0.420	0.400	0.380	0.340	0.320	0.300	0.280
Dividend Payout %	32.85	33.33	38.27	38.38	47.55	45.39	46.51	103.70
Income Statement								
Total Revenues	2,269,600	2,320,000	2,218,500	2,123,500	2,006,900	1,881,100	1,800,966	1,732,506
Total Indirect Exp.	597,600	570,900	546,100	578,700	522,300	463,800	461,022	453,088
Depreciation & Amort.	65,300	66,800	73,000	61,300	57,400	54,800	49,344	63,788
Operating Income	295,500	277,700	240,600	225,000	176,900	182,800	170,843	93,291
Net Interest Inc./(Exp.)	(38,600)	(43,600)	(52,300)	(39,700)	(32,400)	(36,900)	(36,332)	(33,811)
Income Taxes	83,400	74,300	62,900	66,600	60,100	54,900	52,653	23,871
Eqty Earns/Minority Int.	12,600	19,300	19,100	18,100	13,400	6,200	7,762	5,612
Income from Cont Ops	199,200	...	...	...	...	...	97,415	43,475
Net Income	210,800	179,800	146,600	137,500	103,300	103,800	98,428	41,918
Average Shs. Outstg.	142,600	142,300	140,200	139,200	144,000	147,600	151,800	161,400
Balance Sheet								
Cash & Cash Equivalents	25,100	47,300	31,300	23,900	12,000	17,700	13,500	22,418
Total Current Assets	762,100	724,600	635,800	620,000	490,600	503,800	506,518	534,412
Total Assets	2,148,200	1,930,800	1,772,000	1,659,900	1,188,800	1,259,100	1,256,232	1,326,609
Total Current Liabilities	712,700	673,400	713,700	1,027,200	470,500	518,000	498,249	499,302
Long-Term Obligations	448,600	453,900	454,100	160,200	241,400	250,400	276,489	291,194
Net Stockholders' Equity	755,200	592,300	463,100	359,300	382,400	388,100	393,110	450,043
Net Working Capital	49,400	51,200	(77,900)	(407,200)	20,000	(14,200)	8,269	35,110
Shares Outstanding	137,200	140,000	138,400	136,600	140,800	145,000	148,048	156,410
Statistical Record								
Operating Profit Margin %	13.01	11.96	10.84	10.59	8.81	9.71	9.48	5.38
Return on Equity %	26.37	30.35	31.65	38.26	27.01	26.74	24.78	9.66
Return on Assets %	9.27	9.31	8.27	8.28	8.68	8.24	7.75	3.27
Debt/Total Assets %	20.88	23.50	25.62	9.65	20.30	19.88	22.00	21.95
Price Range	30.15-22.10	26.90-20.35	23.03-17.00	18.25-12.13	17.32-13.18	18.00-13.00	13.63-11.31	12.44-9.46
P/E Ratio	21.54-15.79	21.35-16.15	22.14-16.35	18.43-12.25	24.39-18.84	25.71-18.57	21.29-17.67	46.06-35.02
Average Yield %	1.79	1.78	1.95	2.49	2.16	2.05	2.43	2.50

Address: 18 Loveton Circle, Sparks, MD 21152	**Officers:** Robert J. Lawless – Chmn., Pres., C.E.O., Francis A. Contino – Exec. V.P., Supply Chain, CFO	**Investor Contact:** 410-771-7244
Telephone: (410) 771-7301	**Transfer Agents:** Wells Fargo Shareowner Services, St. Paul, MN	**Institutional Holding** No of Institutions: 7
Web Site: www.mccormick.com		**Shares:** 7,016 **% Held:** –

MCDONALD'S CORP

Exchange	Symbol	Price	52Wk Range	Yield	P/E
NYS	MCD	$28.57 (3/31/2004)	29.85-14.05	1.40	24.21

*7 Year Price Score 70.2 ***NYSE Composite Index=100** ***12 Month Price Score 112.8**

Interim Earnings (Per Share)

Qtr.	Mar	Jun	Sep	Dec
2000	0.33	0.39	0.41	0.33
2001	0.29	0.34	0.42	0.20
2002	0.27	0.39	0.38	(0.27)
2003	0.29	0.37	0.43	0.09

Interim Dividends (Per Share)

Amt	Decl	Ex	Rec	Pay
0.215A	9/12/2000	11/13/2000	11/15/2000	12/1/2000
0.225A	10/29/2001	11/13/2001	11/15/2001	12/3/2001
0.235A	10/22/2002	11/13/2002	11/15/2002	12/2/2002
0.40A	9/24/2003	11/12/2003	11/14/2003	12/1/2003

Indicated Div: $0.40 (Div. Reinv. Plan)

Valuation Analysis

Forecast P/E	16.41	Trailing P/E	24.21
Market Cap	$36.3 Billion	Book Value	N/A
Price/Book	N/A	Price/Sales	N/A

Dividend Achiever Status

Rank	89	10 Year Growth Rate	14.24%

Total Years of Dividend Growth 27

Business Summary: Hospitality &Tourism (MIC: 5.1 SIC: 5812 NAIC:722211)

McDonald's develops, licenses, leases and services a worldwide system of restaurants in more than 100 countries. Co.'s menu includes hamburgers, cheeseburgers, the Big Mac, Quarter Pounder with Cheese, Big N'Tasty, Filet–O–Fish, Chicken McNuggets, several chicken sandwiches, french fries, salads, milk shakes, McFlurry desserts, ice cream sundaes and cones, pies, cookies and beverages. As of Dec 31 2003, there were approximately18,000 units operated by franchisees, more than 8,000 units operated by Co., and about 4,000 units operated by affiliates. The Company also operates Boston Market and Chipotle Mexican Grill in the U.S. and has a minority ownership interest in U.K.–based Pret A Manger.

Recent Developments: For the year ended Dec 31 2003, Co. reported income of $1.51 billion compared with income of $992.1 million the year before. Results for 2003 and 2002 excluded accounting change charges of $36.8 million and $98.6 million, respectively. Systemwide sales improved 11.0%. Total revenues increased 11.3% to $17.14 billion from $15.41 billion a year earlier, reflecting healthy sales and margins in the U.S. Sales by Company–operated restaurants climbed 11.3% to $12.80 billion, while revenues from franchised and affiliated restaurants rose 11.2% to $4.35 billion.

Prospects: In Dec 2003, Co. sold its Donatos Pizzeria business as part of its revitalization plan, which includes reallocating resources to McDonald's restaurants, and concentrating its efforts primarily on Chipotle and Boston Market in the U.S. Additionally, Co. is expanding in markets where good returns are expected, such as China. Meanwhile, capital expenditures for 2004 are expected to range from $1.50 billion to $1.60 billion. Co. also intends to pay down $400.0 million to $700.0 million in debt. Looking ahead to 2005 and beyond, Co. anticipates annual Systemwide sales and revenue growth of 3.0% to 5.0% and annual operating income growth of 6.0% to 7.0%.

Financial Data

(US$ in Thousands)	12/31/2003	12/31/2002	12/31/2001	12/31/2000	12/31/1999	12/31/1998	12/31/1997	12/31/1996
Earnings Per Share	1.18	0.77	1.25	1.46	1.39	1.10	1.14	1.10
Cash Flow Per Share	2.56	2.25	2.05	2.02	2.14	1.96	1.73	1.76
Tang. Book Val. Per Share	8.17	6.87	6.30	5.94	6.20	6.26	4.83	5.48
Dividends Per Share	0.400	0.230	0.220	0.210	0.190	0.170	0.160	0.140
Dividend Payout %	33.89	30.51	18.00	14.72	14.02	16.02	14.08	12.73
Income Statement								
Total Revenues	17,140,500	15,405,700	14,870,000	14,243,000	13,259,300	12,421,400	11,408,800	10,686,500
Total Indirect Exp.	9,902,100	9,237,700	8,093,100	7,160,600	6,611,200	6,441,900	5,714,400	5,317,500
Depreciation & Amort.	1,148,200	1,050,800	1,086,300	1,010,700	956,300	881,100	793,800	742,900
Operating Income	2,832,200	2,112,900	2,697,000	3,329,300	3,319,500	2,761,900	2,808,300	2,632,600
Net Interest Inc./(Exp.)	(388,000)	(374,100)	(452,400)	(429,900)	(396,300)	(413,800)	(364,400)	(342,500)
Income Taxes	838,200	670,000	693,100	905,000	936,200	757,300	764,800	678,400
Eqty Earns/Minority Int.	36,900	24,100	61,500	121,000	138,000	88,700	72,800	76,800
Income from Cont Ops	1,508,200	992,100	...	1,976,900	1,947,800	...	...	...
Net Income	1,471,400	893,500	1,636,600	1,977,300	1,947,900	1,550,100	1,642,500	1,572,600
Average Shs. Outstg.	1,276,500	1,281,500	1,309,300	1,356,500	1,404,200	1,405,700	1,410,200	1,396,400
Balance Sheet								
Cash & Cash Equivalents	492,800	330,400	418,100	421,700	419,500	299,200	341,400	329,900
Total Current Assets	1,885,400	1,715,400	1,819,300	1,662,400	1,572,300	1,309,400	1,142,300	1,102,500
Total Assets	25,525,100	23,970,500	22,534,500	21,683,500	20,983,200	19,784,400	18,241,500	17,386,000
Total Current Liabilities	2,485,800	2,422,300	2,248,300	2,360,900	3,274,300	2,497,100	2,984,500	2,135,300
Long–Term Obligations	9,342,500	9,703,600	8,555,500	7,843,900	5,632,400	6,188,600	4,834,100	4,830,100
Net Stockholders' Equity	11,981,900	10,280,900	9,488,400	9,204,400	9,639,100	9,464,700	8,851,600	8,718,200
Net Working Capital	(600,400)	(706,900)	(429,000)	(698,500)	(1,702,000)	(1,187,700)	(1,842,200)	(1,032,800)
Shares Outstanding	1,261,900	1,268,200	1,280,700	1,304,900	1,350,800	1,356,200	1,660,600	1,389,200
Statistical Record								
Operating Profit Margin %	16.52	13.71	18.13	23.37	25.03	22.23	24.61	24.63
Return on Equity %	12.58	9.64	17.24	21.47	20.20	16.37	18.55	18.03
Return on Assets %	5.90	4.13	7.26	9.11	9.28	7.83	9.00	9.04
Debt/Total Assets %	36.60	40.48	37.96	36.17	26.84	31.28	26.50	27.78
Price Range	26.56-12.38	30.65-15.48	34.69-25.00	42.81-26.81	48.38-37.66	39.16-22.69	27.34-21.63	27.06-21.38
P/E Ratio	22.51-10.49	39.81-20.10	27.75-20.00	29.32-18.36	34.80-27.09	35.60-20.63	23.99-18.97	24.60-19.43
Average Yield %	1.98	0.95	0.77	0.63	0.45	0.55	0.67	0.59

Address: McDonald's Plaza, Oak Brook, IL 60523 Telephone: (630) 623-3000 Web Site: www.mcdonalds.com	Officers: James R. Cantalupo – Chmn., C.E.O., James A. Skinner – Vice–Chmn. Transfer Agents:First Chicago Trust Company, Jersey City, NJ	Investor Contact:630–623–7428 Institutional Holding No of Institutions: 36 Shares: 1,068,717 % Held: –

MCGRATH RENTCORP

Exchange	Symbol	Price	52Wk Range	Yield	P/E
NMS	MGRC	$30.49 (3/31/2004)	30.90–22.57	2.89	16.48

*7 Year Price Score 122.7 *NYSE Composite Index=100 *12 Month Price Score 95.2

Interim Earnings (Per Share)

Qtr.	Mar	Jun	Sep	Dec
2000	(0.13)	0.52	0.73	1.07
2001	0.54	0.62	0.58	0.40
2002	(0.19)	(0.10)	0.68	0.61
2003	0.40	0.39	0.50	0.56

Interim Dividends (Per Share)

Amt	Decl	Ex	Rec	Pay
0.20Q	5/28/2003	7/11/2003	7/15/2003	7/31/2003
0.20Q	8/28/2003	10/10/2003	10/15/2003	10/31/2003
0.20Q	11/21/2003	1/13/2004	1/15/2004	1/30/2004
0.22Q	3/9/2004	4/13/2004	4/15/2004	4/30/2004

Indicated Div: $0.88

Valuation Analysis

Forecast P/E	N/A		
Market Cap	$380.6 Million	Trailing P/E	16.48
Price/Book	2.29	Book Value	144.0 Million
		Price/Sales	2.52

Dividend Achiever Status

Rank	78	10 Year Growth Rate 14.87%
Total Years of Dividend Growth		13

Business Summary: General Construction Supplies &Services (MIC: 3.3 SIC: 7359 NAIC:532490)

McGrath RentCorp is comprised of three business segments: Mobile Modular Management Corporation (MMMC), its modular building rental division; RenTelco, its electronic test equipment rental division; and Enviroplex, its 81.0%–owned portable classroom manufacturing business. MMMC rents and sells modular buildings and accessories to fulfill customers' temporary and permanent space needs in California and Texas. RenTelco rents and sells electronic test equipment nationally from its two locations in Plano, TX and Livermore, CA. Enviroplex sells its portable classrooms directly to the California public school districts.

Recent Developments: For the twelve months ended Dec 31 2003, net income soared 79.6% to $22.7 million compared with $12.6 million in 2002. Results for 2002 included an impairment of rental equipment of $24.1 million. Total revenues decreased 9.7% to $131.0 million from $145.1 million a year earlier. Rental revenues were down 6.5% to $76.7 million from $82.0 million due to unexpected project delays by customers. Sales decreased 15.0% to $131.0 million from $145.1 million the year before. Income from operations was $40.7 million, up 61.3% from $25.2 million in 2002.

Prospects: Looking ahead, Co. is encouraged by increased momentum in order activity for RenTelco, especially in product areas that have been relatively dormant for several years. Meanwhile, as the communication industry continues to recover, Co. anticipates increased business levels. As a result, this segment has potential for favorable income growth in the near future. Additionally, Co. expects its modular rental business to continue its strong performance in 2004. Mobile Modular has produced favorable results despite uncertain economic conditions. Based on continuing favorable overall results, Co. expects diluted earnings per share for full–year 2004 in the range of $2.00 to $2.10.

Financial Data
(US$ in Thousands)

	12/31/2003	12/31/2002	12/31/2001	12/31/2000	12/31/1999	12/31/1998	12/31/1997	12/31/1996
Earnings Per Share	1.85	1.00	2.14	2.19	1.78	1.67	1.58	1.01
Cash Flow Per Share	3.91	4.14	4.71	4.02	3.97	3.88	3.89	1.44
Tang. Book Val. Per Share	11.87	11.13	10.66	8.98	7.60	7.54	6.79	5.99
Dividends Per Share	0.780	0.680	0.620	0.540	0.460	0.380	0.310	0.270
Dividend Payout %	42.16	68.00	28.97	24.65	25.84	22.75	19.62	26.73
Income Statement								
Total Revenues	130,971	145,086	159,394	164,158	129,962	135,428	134,976	89,005
Total Indirect Exp.	35,371	37,891	52,225	43,832	36,883	33,082	30,315	26,097
Depreciation & Amort.	25,490	31,584	54,540	47,700	39,560	33,724	28,717	24,912
Operating Income	40,708	25,235	52,045	56,516	45,564	47,236	45,450	28,159
Net Interest Inc./(Exp.)	(2,668)	(3,982)	(7,078)	(8,840)	(6,606)	(6,326)	(4,070)	(2,887)
Income Taxes	15,178	8,459	17,807	19,762	14,874	16,010	16,323	9,750
Eqty Earns/Minority Int.	(170)	(161)	(482)	(670)	(251)	(1,005)	(1,011)	...
Income from Cont Ops	...	...	...	...	23,833	...	...	...
Net Income	22,692	12,633	26,678	27,244	22,466	23,895	24,045	15,522
Average Shs. Outstg.	12,259	12,619	12,495	12,428	13,383	14,349	15,181	15,305
Balance Sheet								
Cash & Cash Equivalents	4	4	4	643	490	857	538	686
Total Current Assets	32,203	33,253	36,900	46,330	25,585	22,668	22,332	20,606
Total Assets	323,858	313,134	354,884	357,246	297,722	278,676	252,392	200,035
Total Current Liabilities	28,695	29,889	30,745	37,012	24,811	22,964	27,047	15,281
Long–Term Obligations	47,266	55,523	...	...	...	...	...	...
Net Stockholders' Equity	143,978	139,019	131,595	108,958	95,403	105,394	98,646	88,808
Net Working Capital	3,508	3,364	6,155	9,318	774	(296)	(4,715)	5,326
Shares Outstanding	12,122	12,490	12,335	12,125	12,546	13,970	14,521	14,820
Statistical Record								
Operating Profit Margin %	31.08	17.39	32.65	34.42	35.05	34.87	33.67	31.63
Return on Equity %	15.76	9.08	20.27	25.00	24.98	22.67	24.37	17.47
Return on Assets %	7.00	4.03	7.51	7.62	8.00	8.57	9.52	7.75
Debt/Total Assets %	14.59	17.73	...	...	...	...	...	...
Price Range	29.76–21.81	37.64–18.80	37.53–18.13	19.88–14.00	22.50–16.75	24.50–16.75	27.25–12.38	13.38–8.38
P/E Ratio	16.09–11.79	37.64–18.80	17.54–8.47	9.08–6.39	12.64–9.06	14.67–10.03	17.25–7.83	13.24–8.29
Average Yield %	3.01	2.65	2.60	3.24	2.47	1.86	1.63	2.45

Address: 5700 Las Positas Road, Livermore, CA 94550
Telephone: (925) 606–9200
Web Site: www.mgrc.com

Officers: Robert P. McGrath – Chmn., C.E.O., Dennis C. Kakures – Pres., C.O.O.

Investor Contact: 925–606–9200
Institutional Holding
No of Institutions: 10
Shares: 10,108,508 % Held: –

MCGRAW–HILL COS., INC. (THE)

Exchange	Symbol	Price	52Wk Range	Yield	P/E
NYS	MHP	$76.14 (3/31/2004)	80.12-56.51	1.58	21.27

*7 Year Price Score 119.8 ***NYSE Composite Index=100** ***12 Month Price Score 98.1**

Interim Earnings (Per Share)

Qtr.	Mar	Jun	Sep	Dec
2000	0.29	0.55	1.11	0.46
2001	0.10	0.61	1.22	(0.01)
2002	0.15	0.70	1.42	0.69
2003	0.20	0.74	1.51	1.13

Interim Dividends (Per Share)

Amt	Decl	Ex	Rec	Pay
0.27Q	4/30/2003	5/23/2003	5/28/2003	6/11/2003
0.27Q	7/30/2003	8/22/2003	8/26/2003	9/10/2003
0.27Q	10/29/2003	11/21/2003	11/25/2003	12/10/2003
0.30Q	1/28/2004	2/23/2004	2/25/2004	3/10/2004

Indicated Div: $1.20 (Div. Reinv. Plan)

Valuation Analysis

Forecast P/E	18.27	Trailing P/E	21.27
Market Cap	$14.8 Billion	Book Value	2.6 Billion
Price/Book	5.24	Price/Sales	2.77

Dividend Achiever Status

Rank	224	10 Year Growth Rate	6.60%
Total Years of Dividend Growth	30

TRADING VOLUME (thousand shares)

Business Summary: Non–Media Publishing (MIC: 13.3 SIC: 2731 NAIC:511130)

McGraw-Hill, a multimedia publishing and information services company, serves worldwide markets in education, finance and business information. As of Dec 31 2003, Co. operated more than 322 offices in 33 countries. Co. provides information in print through books, newsletters, and magazines, including Business Week; on-line over electronic networks; over the air by television, satellite and FM sideband; and on software, videotape, facsimile and compact disks. Among Co.'s business units are Standard & Poor's Financial Information Services and Standard & Poor's Ratings Services divisions.

Recent Developments: For the year ended Dec 31 2003, Co. reported income from continuing operations of $687.8 million versus income of $572.0 million the year before. Earnings excluded a loss of $161,000 in 2003 and a gain of $4.8 million in 2002 from discontinued operations. Operating revenue rose 4.0% to $4.83 billion. On a segment basis, revenue from McGraw-Hill Education climbed 0.5% to $2.29 billion, while revenue from Financial Services grew 13.7% to $1.77 billion. However, revenue from Information and Media Services slipped 4.6% to $772.6 million. Overall results reflected continued gains in higher education markets, strict cost containment, and favorable foreign exchange rates.

Prospects: On Dec 29 2003, Co. sold its 45.0% interest in Rock-McGraw, which owns Co.'s Rockefeller Center headquarters building in New York, in a transaction valued at $450.0 million. Co. will continue to lease space from Rock-McGraw for the next 17 years. The sale is part of Co.'s strategy of directing its resources toward opportunities to develop and expand its financial services, education and business information franchises. As a result of this transaction, 2004 earnings per share will be diluted by $0.01 to $0.02. Separately, despite an anticipated decline in the elementary-high school marketplace, Co. expects income from continuing operations to increase in the mid-to-high single digits in 2004.

Financial Data
(US$ in Thousands)

	12/31/2003	12/31/2002	12/31/2001	12/31/2000	12/31/1999	12/31/1998	12/31/1997	12/31/1996
Earnings Per Share	3.58	2.96	1.92	2.41	2.14	1.71	1.45	2.48
Cash Flow Per Share	7.19	5.87	5.46	3.59	3.56	3.79	1.87	2.30
Tang. Book Val. Per Share	4.48	1.87	0.18	0.32	2.24	1.48	0.63	0.27
Dividends Per Share	1.080	1.020	0.980	0.940	0.860	0.780	0.720	0.660
Dividend Payout %	30.16	34.45	51.04	39.00	40.18	45.76	49.48	26.61
Income Statement								
Total Revenues	4,827,857	4,787,668	4,645,535	4,280,968	3,991,997	3,729,145	3,534,095	3,074,697
Total Indirect Exp.	1,512,493	1,781,775	1,850,753	1,643,541	1,449,936	1,402,368	1,332,087	327,751
Depreciation & Amort.	115,860	128,378	420,598	362,325	308,355	299,240	293,518	238,558
Operating Income	1,137,374	927,582	670,128	820,183	739,987	608,383	523,808	862,463
Net Interest Inc./(Exp.)	(7,097)	(22,517)	(55,070)	(52,841)	(42,013)	(47,961)	(52,542)	(47,656)
Income Taxes	442,500	328,300	238,100	295,400	272,200	218,600	180,600	319,100
Income from Cont Ops	687,771	576,765	376,958	471,942	425,774	341,822	290,666	495,707
Net Income	687,650	576,760	377,031	403,794	425,764	333,141	290,675	495,733
Average Shs. Outstg.	192,005	194,573	195,873	196,072	198,557	199,104	199,504	199,994
Balance Sheet								
Cash & Cash Equivalents	695,591	58,186	53,535	3,171	6,489	10,451	4,768	3,430
Total Current Assets	2,256,152	1,674,307	1,812,947	1,801,690	1,553,725	1,428,761	1,464,421	1,349,583
Total Assets	5,394,068	5,032,182	5,161,191	4,931,444	4,088,797	3,788,144	3,724,474	3,642,239
Total Current Liabilities	1,993,734	1,775,291	1,876,393	1,780,785	1,525,453	1,291,451	1,206,242	1,218,663
Long–Term Obligations	389	458,900	833,600	817,500	354,800	452,100	607,030	556,850
Net Stockholders' Equity	2,557,051	2,165,822	1,853,885	1,761,044	1,691,493	1,551,808	1,434,651	1,361,118
Net Working Capital	262,418	(100,984)	(63,446)	20,905	28,272	137,310	258,179	130,920
Shares Outstanding	190,396	191,832	193,218	194,285	195,708	197,111	198,204	199,062
Statistical Record								
Operating Profit Margin %	23.55	19.37	14.42	19.15	18.53	16.31	14.82	28.05
Return on Equity %	26.89	26.63	20.33	26.79	25.17	22.02	20.26	36.41
Return on Assets %	12.75	11.46	7.30	9.57	10.41	9.02	7.80	13.60
Debt/Total Assets %	0.01	9.11	16.15	16.57	8.67	11.93	16.29	15.28
Price Range	69.92-52.50	68.89-51.15	70.45-49.30	67.13-42.75	62.25-47.63	51.53-34.72	37.31-22.69	24.19-19.31
P/E Ratio	19.53-14.66	23.27-17.28	36.69-25.68	27.85-17.74	29.09-22.25	30.14-20.30	25.73-15.65	9.75-7.79
Average Yield %	1.76	1.63	1.62	1.69	1.58	1.93	2.42	2.93

Address: 1221 Avenue Of The Americas, New York, NY 10020	Officers: Harold McGraw III – Chmn., Pres., C.E.O., Robert J. Bahash – Exec. V.P., C.F.O.	Investor Contact: (212) 512–4321
Telephone: (212) 512–2000	Transfer Agents: Mellon Investor Services, South Hackensack, NJ	Institutional Holding No of Institutions: 3
Web Site: www.mcgraw-hill.com		Shares: 399,735 % Held: –

MDU RESOURCES GROUP INC.

Exchange	Symbol	Price	52Wk Range	Yield	P/E
NYS	MDU	$23.49 (3/31/2004)	24.26-18.66	2.89	14.50

7 Year Price Score 127.3   *NYSE Composite Index=100   *12 Month Price Score 99.3

Interim Earnings (Per Share)
Qtr.	Mar	Jun	Sep	Dec
2000	0.15	0.23	0.42	0.40
2001	0.32	0.42	0.49	0.29
2002	0.22	0.23	0.50	0.43
2003	0.24	0.38	0.58	0.42

Interim Dividends (Per Share)
Amt	Decl	Ex	Rec	Pay
0.17Q	8/14/2003	9/9/2003	9/11/2003	10/1/2003
50%	8/14/2003	10/30/2003	10/10/2003	10/29/2003
0.17Q	11/13/2003	12/9/2003	12/11/2003	1/1/2004
0.17Q	2/12/2004	3/9/2004	3/11/2004	4/1/2004

Indicated Div: $0.68

Valuation Analysis
Forecast P/E	14.48	Trailing P/E	14.50
Market Cap	$1.7 Billion	Book Value	N/A
Price/Book	N/A	Price/Sales	N/A

Dividend Achiever Status
Rank	269	10 Year Growth Rate	3.87%
Total Years of Dividend Growth		13

Business Summary: Construction - Public Infrastructure (MIC: 3.1 SIC: 1611 NAIC:237310)

MDU Resources Group is a diversified natural resource company generates, transmits and distributes electricity and distributes natural gas in the northern Great Plains. Great Plains Natural Gas Co., another public utility division of Co., distributes natural gas in southeastern North Dakota and western Minnesota. Co. also owns WBI Holdings, Inc., a provider of pipeline and energy services and a natural gas and oil producer; Knife River Corporation, a producer of construction materials; Utility Services, Inc., a utility infrastructure company; and Centennial Resources, which owns United States electric generating facilities.

Recent Developments: For the year ended Dec 31 2003, income was $182.9 million, before an accounting charge of $7.6 million, versus net income of $148.4 million the previous year. Operating revenues climbed 15.8% to $2.35 billion. By segment, electric earnings rose 7.0% to $16.9 million. Natural gas distribution earnings grew 8.3% to $3.9 million, while utility earnings slipped 3.1% to $6.2 million. Pipeline and energy earnings declined 4.7% to $18.2 million. Natural gas and oil production earnings climbed 18.4% to $63.0 million. Construction materials and mining earnings grew 11.7% to $54.4 million, while independent power production and other earnings jumped to $12.0 million from $900,000 in 2002.

Prospects: Going forward, Co. expects a combined total natural gas production increase of about 10.0% over 2003 levels, largely due to the recently completed natural gas pipeline construction project, the largest in its history, which will allow Co. to access broader markets. Co. expects revenues in the construction materials and mining segment to increase by about 5.0% to 10.0%. As of Dec 31 2003, this segment had $332.0 million in work backlog. Separately, due to the continued strength of natural gas and oil commodity prices, Co. has increased its 2004 earnings per share guidance. Co. is now targeting earnings per share in the range $1.55 to $1.68 for full-year 2004.

Financial Data
(US$ in Thousands)	12/31/2003	12/31/2002	12/31/2001	12/31/2000	12/31/1999	12/31/1998	12/31/1997	12/31/1996
Earnings Per Share	1.62	1.38	1.52	1.20	1.01	0.44	0.82	0.69
Cash Flow Per Share	3.72	3.05	3.42	2.24	1.88	1.81	2.12	1.65
Tang. Book Val. Per Share	9.19	8.25	10.60	9.03	7.82	6.92	5.89	5.47
Dividends Per Share	0.650	0.610	0.590	0.560	0.530	0.510	0.490	0.480
Dividend Payout %	40.12	44.92	38.86	47.22	53.29	117.42	60.21	69.57
Income Statement								
Total Revenues	2,352,189	2,031,537	2,223,632	1,873,671	1,279,809	896,627	607,674	514,701
Total Indirect Exp.	268,587	223,854	195,344	146,765	110,937	171,221	89,533	84,625
Depreciation & Amort.	188,337	157,961	139,917	110,888	81,818	77,786	65,767	62,651
Operating Income	312,072	266,117	273,268	216,987	159,751	70,943	111,561	111,525
Net Interest Inc./(Exp.)	(52,794)	(45,015)	(45,899)	(48,033)	(36,006)	(30,273)	(30,209)	(28,832)
Income Taxes	99,168	86,814	98,341	69,650	49,310	17,485	30,743	16,087
Income from Cont Ops	182,913	...	...	...	...	...	...	...
Net Income	175,324	148,444	155,849	111,028	84,080	34,107	54,617	45,470
Average Shs. Outstg.	112,460	106,863	101,803	92,085	82,305	76,255	65,217	64,073
Balance Sheet								
Cash & Cash Equivalents	86,341	67,556	41,811	36,512	77,504	39,216	28,174	47,799
Total Current Assets	613,540	537,548	481,492	480,286	351,696	240,649	179,916	191,658
Total Assets	3,380,592	2,937,249	2,623,071	2,312,959	1,766,303	1,452,775	1,113,892	1,089,173
Total Current Liabilities	314,061	299,645	245,327	284,473	187,327	169,469	149,014	165,104
Long-Term Obligations	939,450	819,558	783,709	728,166	563,545	413,264	298,561	280,666
Net Stockholders' Equity	1,450,636	1,298,645	1,124,671	895,960	684,433	565,742	401,196	365,574
Net Working Capital	299,479	237,903	236,165	195,813	164,369	71,180	30,902	26,554
Shares Outstanding	113,357	111,063	104,665	97,542	85,557	79,549	65,572	64,073
Statistical Record								
Operating Profit Margin %	13.26	13.09	12.28	11.58	12.48	7.91	18.35	21.66
Return on Equity %	12.61	11.43	13.85	12.39	12.28	6.02	13.61	12.43
Return on Assets %	5.41	5.05	5.94	4.80	4.76	2.34	4.90	4.17
Debt/Total Assets %	27.78	27.90	29.87	31.48	31.90	28.44	26.80	25.76
Price Range	24.25-16.69	22.23-12.47	26.82-15.20	22.00-12.00	17.96-12.83	18.83-12.67	14.86-9.44	10.33-9.00
P/E Ratio	14.97-10.30	16.11-9.03	17.64-10.00	18.33-10.00	17.78-12.71	42.80-28.79	18.12-11.52	14.98-13.04
Average Yield %	3.10	3.45	2.92	3.52	3.46	3.20	4.43	4.96

Address: Schuchart Building, Bismarck, ND 58506-5650	Officers: Martin A. White - Chmn., Pres., C.E.O.	Investor Contact:
Telephone: (701) 222-7900	Warren L. Robinson - Exec. V.P., Treas., C.F.O.	Institutional Holding
Web Site: www.mdu.com	Transfer Agents: Wells Fargo Bank Minnesota, N.A.Shareowner Services, St. Paul, MN	No of Institutions: 6 Shares: 9,708 % Held: -

MEDTRONIC, INC.

Exchange	Symbol	Price	52Wk Range	Yield	P/E
NYS	MDT	$47.75 (3/31/2004)	52.65-43.36	0.61	31.21

*7 Year Price Score 122.3 *NYSE Composite Index=100 *12 Month Price Score 87.0

Interim Earnings (Per Share)

Qtr.	Jul	Oct	Jan	Apr
2000-01	0.24	0.26	0.25	0.10
2001-02	0.25	0.05	0.26	0.24
2002-03	0.31	0.25	0.35	0.39
2003-05	0.37	0.39	0.38	...

Interim Dividends (Per Share)

Amt	Decl	Ex	Rec	Pay
0.073Q	6/26/2003	7/1/2003	7/3/2003	7/25/2003
0.073Q	8/28/2003	10/1/2003	10/3/2003	10/24/2003
0.073Q	10/23/2003	12/30/2003	1/2/2004	1/23/2004
0.073Q	2/27/2004	3/31/2004	4/2/2004	4/30/2004

Indicated Div: $0.29 (Div. Reinv. Plan)

Valuation Analysis

Forecast P/E	23.63	Trailing P/E	31.21
Market Cap	$58.0 Billion	Book Value	8.7 Billion
Price/Book	6.82	Price/Sales	6.92

Dividend Achiever Status

Rank	27	10 Year Growth Rate	21.43%
Total Years of Dividend Growth	26

Business Summary: Medical Instruments &Equipment (MIC: 9.6 SIC: 3845 NAIC:334510)

Medtronic is a medical technology company operating in five operating segments that manufacture and sell device-based medical therapies. Cardiac Rhythm Management offers physicians and their patients a product line to treat bradycardia. Cardiac Surgery offers a broad range of products for use by cardiac surgeons in the operating room. The Vascular segment offers minimally invasive products for the treatment of coronary vascular disease. The Neurological and Diabetes segment offers products for the treatment of neurological disorders. The Spinal and Ear, Nose & Throat segment offers a range of products and therapies to treat a variety of disorders of the cranium, spine, ear, nose and throat.

Recent Developments: For the three months ended Jan 23 2004, net earnings climbed 8.6% to $464.4 million compared with $427.7 million in the corresponding quarter of the previous year. Results for 2003 included a pre-tax purchased in-process research and development charge of $22.0 million. Net sales advanced 14.8% to $2.19 billion from $1.91 billion in 2003. Revenues for the Cardiac Rhythm Management segment increased 11.0% to $1.00 billion, while revenues for the Spinal and Ear, Nose & Throat segment improved 26.0% to $433.9 million. Neurological and Diabetes segment revenues jumped 15.0% to $395.3 million, while revenues for the Vascular segment rose 16.0% to $211.7 million.

Prospects: Results continue to benefit from strong sales growth in Co.'s spinal, implantable defibrillators, diabetes and vascular product lines. Conversely, revenue growth for pacemakers, external defibrillators and several neurological devices are not meeting expectations. Nevertheless, Co. remains well-positioned in a number of attractive, under-penetrated markets. In order to expand patient access and to further improve market share, Co. will continue to invest in research and development, clinical trials, technical support and other market development activities.

Financial Data (US$ in Thousands)	9 Mos	6 Mos	3 Mos	04/25/2003	04/26/2002	04/27/2001	04/30/2000	04/30/1999
Earnings Per Share	1.53	1.50	1.36	1.30	0.80	0.85	0.90	0.39
Cash Flow Per Share	1.52	0.89	0.47	1.69	1.29	1.49	0.85	0.38
Tang. Book Val. Per Share	2.81	2.50	2.43	2.20	1.09	3.53	2.61	1.98
Dividends Per Share	0.280	0.270	0.260	0.250	0.230	0.200	0.160	0.130
Dividend Payout %	18.30	18.00	19.12	19.23	28.75	23.53	17.78	33.33
Income Statement								
Total Revenues	6,421,800	4,228,000	2,064,200	7,665,200	6,410,800	5,551,800	5,014,600	4,134,100
Total Indirect Exp.	2,627,800	1,719,400	841,800	3,238,000	3,192,900	2,601,600	2,081,400	2,231,500
Depreciation & Amort.	332,600	216,800	99,700	408,100	329,800	297,300	243,300	213,100
Operating Income	2,210,400	1,463,400	708,400	2,536,900	1,565,200	1,539,600	1,613,600	799,800
Net Interest Inc./(Exp.)	1,100	(2,500)	(1,400)	(7,200)	(6,600)	74,200	15,400	22,200
Income Taxes	592,300	398,400	193,000	741,500	540,200	503,400	530,500	353,600
Net Income	1,390,400	926,500	450,400	1,599,800	984,000	1,046,000	1,098,500	468,400
Average Shs. Outstg.	1,226,400	1,228,700	1,229,900	1,227,900	1,224,400	1,226,000	1,220,800	1,185,800
Balance Sheet								
Cash & Cash Equivalents	1,443,900	1,190,300	1,279,500	1,492,800	533,700	1,231,700	558,100	375,900
Total Current Assets	4,636,200	4,393,000	4,367,600	4,605,500	3,488,000	3,756,800	3,013,400	2,395,200
Total Assets	13,437,700	12,901,100	12,626,600	12,320,800	10,904,500	7,038,900	5,669,400	4,870,300
Total Current Liabilities	4,074,400	3,947,000	1,813,200	1,813,300	3,984,900	1,359,200	991,500	990,300
Long-Term Obligations	2,100	2,100	1,979,600	1,980,300	9,500	13,300	14,100	17,600
Net Stockholders' Equity	8,687,500	8,301,900	8,176,700	7,906,400	6,431,100	5,509,500	4,491,500	3,654,600
Net Working Capital	561,800	446,000	2,554,400	2,792,200	(496,900)	2,397,500	2,021,900	1,404,900
Shares Outstanding	1,212,202	1,212,066	1,216,705	1,218,128	1,215,208	1,209,514	1,197,698	1,170,453
Statistical Record								
Operating Profit Margin %	34.42	34.61	34.31	33.09	24.41	27.73	32.17	19.3
Return on Equity %	16.00	11.16	5.50	20.23	15.30	18.98	24.45	12.8
Return on Assets %	10.34	7.18	3.56	12.98	9.02	14.86	19.37	9.6
Debt/Total Assets %	0.01	0.01	15.67	16.07	0.08	0.18	0.24	0.3
Price Range	52.65-43.36	52.65-44.27	50.64-46.45	48.95-33.74	51.24-38.99	61.00-40.71	57.19-31.19	44.06-24.4
P/E Ratio	46.59-38.37	70.20-59.03	136.9-125.5	37.65-25.95	64.05-48.74	71.76-47.89	63.54-34.65	113.0-62.6
Average Yield %	0.56	0.53	0.51	0.54	0.48	0.37	0.47	0.3

Address: 710 Medtronic Parkway, Minneapolis, MN 55432 **Telephone:** (763) 514-4000 **Web Site:** www.medtronic.com	**Officers:** Arthur D. Collins - Chmn., C.E.O., Robert L. Ryan - Sr. V.P., C.F.O. **Transfer Agents:** Wells Fargo Bank Minnesota N.A., St. Paul, MN	**Investor Contact:** (612) 514-3035 **Institutional Holding** **No of Institutions:** 10 **Shares:** 2,060,498 **% Held:** -

MERCANTILE BANKSHARES CORP.

Exchange	Symbol	Price	52Wk Range	Yield	P/E
NMS	MRBK	$42.93 (3/31/2004)	45.69–34.02	3.07	16.02

*7 Year Price Score 113.2 *NYSE Composite Index=100 *12 Month Price Score 99.3

Interim Earnings (Per Share)

Qtr.	Mar	Jun	Sep	Dec
2000	0.60	0.62	0.64	0.65
2001	0.65	0.62	0.65	0.63
2002	0.66	0.67	0.69	0.70
2003	0.71	0.72	0.63	0.62

Interim Dividends (Per Share)

Amt	Decl	Ex	Rec	Pay
0.30Q	3/11/2003	3/20/2003	3/24/2003	3/31/2003
0.33Q	6/10/2003	6/19/2003	6/23/2003	6/30/2003
0.33Q	9/9/2003	9/19/2003	9/23/2003	9/30/2003
0.33Q	3/9/2004	3/22/2004	3/24/2004	3/31/2004

Indicated Div: $1.32 (Div. Reinv. Plan)

Valuation Analysis

Forecast P/E	N/A	Trailing P/E	16.02
Market Cap	$3.0 Billion	Book Value	1.8 Billion
Price/Book	1.97	Price/Sales	4.69

Dividend Achiever Status

Rank	126	10 Year Growth Rate	11.70%
Total Years of Dividend Growth		27

Business Summary: Commercial Banking (MIC: 8.1 SIC: 6022 NAIC:522110)

Mercantile Bankshares, with assets of $13.70 billion as of Dec 31 2003, is a bank holding company that owns substantially all of the outstanding shares of capital stock of Mercantile–Safe Deposit and Trust (MSD&T) and 19 community banks and a mortgage banking company. Sixteen banks are located in Maryland, three are in Virginia and one is in southern Delaware. MSD&T is Co.'s largest bank and operates 24 offices in Maryland, one office in Washington, D.C., and one commercial office in Pennsylvania. The banks are engaged in the general commercial and retail banking business, including acceptance of demand, savings and time deposits and the making of various types of loans.

Recent Developments: For the twelve months ended Dec 31 2003, net income climbed 3.5% to $196.8 million compared with $190.2 million in 2002. Results for 2003 and 2002 included investment securities gains of $7.1 million and $846,000, respectively. Net interest income grew 8.5% to $479.3 million from $441.8 million the year before. The growth in net interest income was attributed to 14.0% growth in average loans and 20.0% growth in average securities. Provision for loan losses declined 26.1% to $12.1 million. Total non–interest income rose 22.8% to $176.6 million, while total non–interest expenses jumped 23.8% to $337.4 million.

Prospects: Co. expects to incur additional merger–related expenses in 2004 related to the acquisition of F&M Bancorp, which was acquired on Aug 12 2003. These expenses are not expected to amount to more than $0.01 per share after–tax. In addition, Co. expects to complete any remaining groundwork for realizing substantially all of the projected $26.5 million in annual cost savings related to the acquisition and integration of F&M by the end of the first quarter of 2004. Meanwhile, signs of improving loan growth, stable credit quality and improving investment and wealth management business conditions bode well for 2004.

Financial Data

(US$ in Thousands)	12/31/2003	12/31/2002	12/31/2001	12/31/2000	12/31/1999	12/31/1998	12/31/1997	12/31/1996
Earnings Per Share	2.68	2.72	2.55	2.51	2.25	2.04	1.84	1.64
Tang. Book Val. Per Share	15.83	17.63	16.02	15.02	13.51	13.36	12.50	11.35
Dividends Per Share	1.290	1.180	1.100	1.260	1.020	0.860	0.773	0.653
Dividend Payout %	48.13	43.38	43.14	40.64	41.78	42.16	42.01	39.82
Income Statement								
Total Interest Income	596,575	586,386	649,766	646,495	559,168	555,392	533,970	498,139
Total Interest Expense	117,245	144,582	231,525	237,110	190,082	202,027	197,921	187,558
Net Interest Income	479,330	441,804	418,241	409,385	369,086	353,365	336,049	310,581
Provision for Loan Losses	12,105	16,378	13,434	17,231	12,056	11,489	13,703	14,666
Non–Interest Income	176,591	143,750	145,490	125,541	121,991	108,693	98,653	89,428
Non–Interest Expense	337,447	272,608	263,959	243,505	230,420	219,005	213,404	198,415
Income Before Taxes	306,369	296,568	286,338	274,190	248,601	231,564	207,595	186,928
Net Income	196,814	190,238	181,295	175,230	157,737	147,128	132,043	117,400
Average Shs. Outstg.	73,421	70,067	71,199	69,719	70,020	72,237	71,904	71,476
Balance Sheet								
Cash & Due from Banks	321,882	281,130	290,177	244,913	219,420	254,994	337,234	257,337
Securities Avail. for Sale	3,123,514	2,511,192	2,288,694	1,676,554	1,743,942	1,880,462	1,607,313	1,596,687
Net Loans & Leases	9,116,823	7,173,426	6,764,783	6,554,682	5,600,945	5,108,467	4,872,425	4,484,994
Total Assets	13,695,472	10,790,376	9,928,786	8,938,030	7,895,024	7,609,563	7,170,669	6,642,681
Total Deposits	10,262,553	8,260,940	7,447,372	6,796,541	5,925,083	5,958,346	5,693,911	5,339,655
Long–Term Obligations	647,252	287,214	269,437	92,547	82,683	40,934	50,016	49,395
Total Liabilities	11,854,031	9,466,018	8,698,580	7,764,729	6,920,984	6,610,204	6,235,665	5,806,645
Net Stockholders' Equity	1,841,441	1,324,358	1,230,206	1,173,301	974,040	999,359	935,004	836,036
Shares Outstanding	79,772	68,836	69,775	71,098	68,646	71,027	71,874	71,152
Statistical Record								
Return on Equity %	10.68	14.36	14.73	14.93	16.19	14.72	14.12	14.04
Return on Assets %	1.43	1.76	1.82	1.96	1.99	1.93	1.84	1.76
Equity/Assets %	13.44	12.27	12.39	13.12	12.33	13.13	13.03	12.58
Price Range	43.64	37.33	33.19	31.54	33.82	32.97	33.73	33.76
	45.59–32.75	45.20–32.65	43.74–34.06	44.69–23.84	39.88–30.38	39.94–26.38	40.00–21.21	22.42–16.50
P/E Ratio	17.01–12.22	16.62–12.00	17.15–13.36	17.80–9.50	17.72–13.50	19.58–12.93	21.74–11.53	13.67–10.06
Average Yield %	3.16	2.86	2.07	3.88	2.63	2.44	1.99	3.53

Address: 2 Hopkins Plaza, Baltimore, MD 21201
Telephone: (410) 237–5900
Web Site: www.mrbk.com

Officers: Edward J. Kelly III – Chmn., Pres., C.E.O., Alexander T. Mason – Vice-Chmn.

Investor Contact:410–347–8039
Institutional Holding
No of Institutions: 204
Shares: 30,099,393 % Held: –

MERCK & CO., INC

Exchange	Symbol	Price	52Wk Range	Yield	P/E
NYS	MRK	$44.19 (3/31/2004)	63.24-40.60	3.35	15.13

*7 Year Price Score 86.3 ***NYSE Composite Index=100** ***12 Month Price Score 73.7**

Interim Earnings (Per Share)

Qtr.	Mar	Jun	Sep	Dec
2000	0.63	0.73	0.78	0.76
2001	0.71	0.78	0.84	0.81
2002	0.71	0.77	0.83	0.83
2003	0.76	0.83	0.83	0.50

Interim Dividends (Per Share)

Amt	Decl	Ex	Rec	Pay
0.36Q	5/27/2003	6/4/2003	6/6/2003	7/1/2003
0.37Q	7/22/2003	9/3/2003	9/5/2003	10/1/2003
0.37Q	11/25/2003	12/3/2003	12/5/2003	1/2/2004
0.37Q	2/24/2004	3/3/2004	3/5/2004	4/1/2004

Indicated Div: $1.48 (Div. Reinv. Plan)

Valuation Analysis

Forecast P/E	14.14	Trailing P/E	15.13
Market Cap	$99.4 Billion	Book Value	15.6 Billion
Price/Book	6.50	Price/Sales	4.50

Dividend Achiever Status

Rank	139	10 Year Growth Rate	10.91%
Total Years of Dividend Growth	20		

Business Summary: Pharmaceuticals (MIC: 9.1 SIC: 2834 NAIC:325412)

Merck & Co. is a research-driven pharmaceutical company that discovers, develops, manufactures and markets human and animal health products, directly and through its joint ventures. Co.'s products include therapeutic and preventive agents, generally sold by prescription, for the treatment of human disorders. Among these products are Zocor, a cholesterol-lowering medicine, Fosamax, a treatment for osteoporosis, Vioxx, a prescription arthritis medicine, Singulair, for the treatment of chronic asthma, and Cozaar and Hyzaar for the treatment of high blood pressure.

Recent Developments: For the year ended Dec 31 2003, income was $6.59 billion, before a gain of $241.3 million from discontinued operations, compared with income of $6.79 billion, before a gain of $354.7 million from discontinued operations, the previous year. Results for 2003 included a pre-tax acquired research charge of $101.8 million. Sales rose 4.8% to $22.49 billion from $21.45 billion the year before. The improvement in sales is largely due to strong sales growth of Zocor, Fosamax, Cozaar, Hyzaar, Singulair and Vioxx. Research and development expenses jumped 18.7% to $3.18 billion from $2.68 billion a year earlier, reflecting Co.'s focus on internal development and external collaborations.

Prospects: Going forward, Co. remains committed to its strategy of discovering and developing novel medicines and vaccines to help drive long-term growth. In addition, Co. will continue to invest in research and development, despite recent setbacks. Moreover, Co. plans to aggressively pursue external alliances, lower its cost structure and build its in-line franchises. In 2004, Co. expects earnings to range from $3.11 to $3.17 per share. Separately in December 2003, Co. submitted a new drug application for Arcoxia, a once-daily pain medication, to the U.S. Food and Drug Administration.

Financial Data

(US$ in Thousands)	12/31/2003	12/31/2002	12/31/2001	12/31/2000	12/31/1999	12/31/1998	12/31/1997	12/31/1996
Earnings Per Share	2.92	3.14	3.14	2.90	2.45	2.15	1.87	1.60
Cash Flow Per Share	3.73	4.18	3.90	3.26	2.54	2.18	2.55	2.23
Tang. Book Val. Per Share	6.13	4.88	3.77	3.23	2.42	1.91	2.44	N.M
Dividends Per Share	1.450	1.410	1.370	1.210	1.100	0.940	0.840	0.710
Dividend Payout %	49.65	44.90	43.63	41.72	44.89	43.95	45.18	44.38
Income Statement								
Total Revenues	22,485,900	51,790,300	47,715,700	40,363,200	32,714,000	26,898,200	23,636,900	19,828,700
Total Indirect Exp.	8,867,200	7,779,500	7,639,100	7,300,800	6,112,700	1,572,300	4,297,500	4,127,200
Depreciation & Amort.	281,600	409,800	660,200	638,200	634,800	528,600	394,400	730,900
Operating Income	8,970,000	10,517,400	10,744,300	10,173,100	8,622,500	8,632,800	6,805,000	5,781,600
Net Interest Inc./(Exp.)	(42,200)	28,500	25,400	(13,800)	47,800	102,100	91,900	
Income Taxes	2,462,000	3,064,100	3,120,800	3,002,400	2,729,000	2,884,900	1,848,200	1,659,500
Eqty Earns/Minority Int.	333,400	439,800	355,800	445,800	444,600	620,000	530,700	600,700
Income from Cont Ops	6,589,600	...	...	...	...	...	...	4,122,100
Net Income	6,830,900	7,149,500	7,281,800	6,821,700	5,890,500	5,248,200	4,614,100	3,881,300
Average Shs. Outstg.	2,253,100	2,277,000	2,322,300	2,353,200	2,404,600	2,441,100	2,469,400	2,427,200
Balance Sheet								
Cash & Cash Equivalents	4,173,000	4,971,200	3,286,600	4,254,600	3,202,400	3,355,700	2,309,300	2,181,600
Total Current Assets	11,527,200	14,833,900	12,961,600	13,353,400	11,259,200	10,228,500	8,213,000	7,726,600
Total Assets	40,587,500	47,561,200	44,006,700	39,910,400	35,634,900	31,853,400	25,811,900	31,029,700
Total Current Liabilities	9,569,600	12,375,200	11,544,200	9,709,600	8,758,800	6,068,800	5,568,600	4,829,200
Long–Term Obligations	5,096,000	4,879,000	4,798,600	3,600,700	3,143,900	3,220,800	1,346,500	1,155,900
Net Stockholders' Equity	15,576,400	18,200,500	16,050,100	14,832,400	13,241,600	12,801,800	12,613,500	11,970,500
Net Working Capital	1,957,600	2,458,700	1,417,400	3,643,800	2,500,400	4,159,700	2,644,400	2,897,400
Shares Outstanding	2,221,763	2,244,983	2,272,729	2,307,599	2,329,077	2,360,452	2,387,296	2,413,204
Statistical Record								
Operating Profit Margin %	39.89	20.30	22.51	25.20	26.35	32.09	28.78	29.15
Return on Equity %	42.30	39.28	45.36	45.99	44.48	40.99	36.58	34.43
Return on Assets %	16.23	15.03	16.54	17.09	16.53	16.47	17.87	13.28
Debt/Total Assets %	12.55	10.25	10.90	9.02	8.82	10.11	5.21	3.72
Price Range	63.24-40.60	64.37-39.05	93.00-57.17	94.88-53.94	86.38-60.94	79.41-51.56	53.66-39.63	42.13-28.50
P/E Ratio	21.66-13.90	20.50-12.44	29.62-18.21	32.72-18.60	35.26-24.87	36.93-23.98	28.69-21.19	26.33-17.81
Average Yield %	2.72	2.61	1.92	1.50	1.50	1.46	1.78	2.08

Address: One Merck Drive, Whitehouse Station, NJ 08889–0100	Officers: Raymond V. Gilmartin – Chmn., Pres., C.E.O., Judy C. Lewent – Exec. V.P., C.F.O.	Investor Contact:908–423–5881
Telephone: (908) 423–1000	Transfer Agents:Wells Fargo Bank Minnesota, N.A., South St. Paul, MN	Institutional Holding No of Institutions: 17
Web Site: www.merck.com		Shares: 388,274 % Held: –

MERCURY GENERAL CORP.

Exchange	Symbol	Price	52Wk Range	Yield	P/E
NYS	MCY	$49.93 (3/31/2004)	52.36-38.27	2.96	17.83

*7 Year Price Score 111.7 *NYSE Composite Index=100 *12 Month Price Score 97.2

Interim Earnings (Per Share)

Qtr.	Mar	Jun	Sep	Dec
2000	0.55	0.48	0.51	0.48
2001	0.45	0.49	0.59	0.41
2002	0.53	0.02	0.34	0.32
2003	0.77	0.80	0.91	0.90

Interim Dividends (Per Share)

Amt	Decl	Ex	Rec	Pay
0.33Q	1/31/2003	3/13/2003	3/17/2003	3/27/2003
0.33Q	4/28/2003	6/11/2003	6/15/2003	6/30/2003
0.33Q	7/28/2003	9/10/2003	9/12/2003	9/25/2003
0.37Q	2/2/2004	3/11/2004	3/15/2004	3/31/2004

Indicated Div: $1.48

Valuation Analysis

Forecast P/E	13.12	Trailing P/E	17.83
Market Cap	$2.7 Billion	Book Value	1.2 Billion
Price/Book	2.01	Price/Sales	1.13

Dividend Achiever Status

Rank	69	10 Year Growth Rate	15.97%
Total Years of Dividend Growth	17		

Business Summary: Insurance (MIC: 8.2 SIC: 6331 NAIC:524126)

Mercury General, through its subsidiaries, engages primarily in writing all risk classifications of automobile insurance in a number of states, principally in California. Co. offers automobile policyholders the following types of coverage: bodily injury liability, underinsured and uninsured motorist, personal injury protection, property damage liability, comprehensive, collision and other hazards specified in the policy. Co. sells its policies through independent agents in California, Florida, Georgia, Illinois, New York, Texas, Oklahoma, New Jersey and Virginia. In addition, Co. writes other lines of insurance in various states, including mechanical breakdown and homeowners insurance.

Recent Developments: For the year ended Dec 31 2003, net income jumped 178.8% to $184.3 million from $66.1 million in the prior prior year. Total revenues climbed 26.8% to $2.27 billion from $1.79 billion the previous year. Revenues included a net realized investment gain of $11.2 million in 2003 and a net realized investment loss of $70.4 million in 2002. Net premiums written increased 21.6% to $2.27 billion, primarily due to increased policy sales and rate increases in the California, Florida and Texas automobile lines and the California homeowner's insurance lines of business. Earned premiums grew 23.2% to $2.15 billion from $1.74 billion a year earlier. Co.'s combined ratio improved to 94.0% from 98.8% in 2002.

Prospects: Many of the Co.'s major competitors have announced better operating results in 2003, which typically signals a softening in the market. Consequently, Co. expects that its policies in force will be difficult to grow in 2004, particularly in California. Nevertheless, Co. is optimistic about its ability to demonstrate continuing improvement as 2004 unfolds by expanding its business into additional states. Co. expects to begin writing business in Arizona and possibly other states by the end of 2004, with the long-term objective for non-California premiums to eventually account for as much as half of its total premiums.

Financial Data

(US$ in Thousands)	12/31/2003	12/31/2002	12/31/2001	12/31/2000	12/31/1999	12/31/1998	12/31/1997	12/31/1996
Earnings Per Share	3.38	1.21	1.94	2.02	2.44	3.21	2.82	1.93
Tang. Book Val. Per Share	23.06	20.21	19.70	19.05	16.71	16.77	14.50	11.65
Dividends Per Share	1.320	1.200	1.060	0.960	0.840	0.700	0.580	0.480
Dividend Payout %	39.05	99.17	54.63	47.52	34.42	21.80	20.56	24.87
Income Statement								
Total Premium Income	2,145,047	1,741,527	1,380,561	1,249,259	1,188,307	1,121,584	1,031,280	754,724
Net Investment Income	104,520	113,083	114,511	106,466	99,374	96,169	86,812	70,180
Other Income	15,950	(68,339)	11,908	10,293	(7,005)	4,370	9,854	60
Total Revenues	2,265,517	1,786,271	1,506,980	1,366,018	1,280,676	1,222,123	1,127,946	824,964
Total Indirect Exp.	91,295	74,875	62,335	59,733	50,675	44,941	33,579	24,493
Inc. Before Inc. Taxes	245,801	60,668	124,809	128,555	168,539	235,280	209,779	136,590
Income Taxes	61,480	(5,437)	19,470	19,189	34,830	57,754	53,473	30,826
Net Income	184,321	66,105	105,339	109,366	133,709	177,526	156,306	105,764
Average Shs. Outstg.	54,547	54,502	54,382	54,258	54,815	55,354	55,383	54,794
Balance Sheet								
Cash & Cash Equivalents	36,964	13,191	3,851	5,935	8,052	1,887	3,011	3,605
Premiums Due	299,094	259,445	218,376	199,392	172,079	168,929	166,149	144,208
Invst. Assets: Total	2,209,702	1,863,852	1,864,220	1,761,984	1,531,897	1,544,653	1,388,508	1,102,220
Total Assets	3,119,766	2,645,296	2,316,540	2,142,263	1,906,367	1,877,025	1,725,532	1,419,927
Long-Term Obligations	124,714	128,859	129,513	107,889	92,000	78,000	75,000	75,000
Net Stockholders' Equity	1,255,503	1,098,786	1,069,711	1,032,905	909,591	917,375	799,592	641,222
Shares Outstanding	54,424	54,361	54,276	54,193	54,425	54,684	55,125	55,014
Statistical Record								
Return on Equity %	14.68	6.01	9.84	10.58	14.69	19.35	19.54	16.49
Return on Assets %	5.90	2.49	4.54	5.10	7.01	9.45	9.05	7.44
Price Range	48.58-34.74	50.63-37.37	43.85-32.21	43.88-21.25	45.50-21.06	69.44-33.25	55.25-26.19	29.00-24.38
P/E Ratio	14.37-10.28	41.84-30.88	22.60-16.60	21.72-10.52	18.65-8.63	21.63-10.36	19.59-9.29	15.03-12.63
Average Yield %	3.07	2.74	2.83	3.44	2.59	1.36	1.52	1.80

Address: 4484 Wilshire Boulevard, Los Angeles, CA 90010	Officers: George Joseph – Chmn., C.E.O., Gabriel Tirador – Pres., C.O.O.	Investor Contact: (800) 900–6729
Telephone: (323) 937–1060	Transfer Agents: The Bank of New York, New York, NY	Institutional Holding
Web Site: www.mercuryinsurance.com		No of Institutions: 7
		Shares: 109,840 % Held: –

MEREDITH CORP.

Exchange	Symbol	Price	52Wk Range	Yield	P/E
NYS	MDP	$50.56 (3/31/2004)	52.90–38.46	0.95	27.18

*7 Year Price Score 124.7   *NYSE Composite Index=100   *12 Month Price Score 97.2

Interim Earnings (Per Share)

Qtr.	Sep	Dec	Mar	Jun
2000–01	0.32	0.47	0.37	0.23
2001–02	0.17	0.17	0.35	1.10
2002–03	0.32	0.38	0.50	0.58
2003–04	0.39	0.39	...	...

Interim Dividends (Per Share)

Amt	Decl	Ex	Rec	Pay
0.095Q	5/14/2003	5/28/2003	5/30/2003	6/13/2003
0.095Q	8/13/2003	8/27/2003	8/29/2003	9/15/2003
0.095Q	11/10/2003	11/24/2003	11/26/2003	12/15/2003
0.12Q	2/1/2004	2/25/2004	2/27/2004	3/15/2004

Indicated Div: $0.48 (Div. Reinv. Plan)

Valuation Analysis

Forecast P/E	19.67	Trailing P/E	27.18
Market Cap	$2.0 Billion	Book Value	525.8 Million
Price/Book	3.73	Price/Sales	1.73

Dividend Achiever Status

Rank	176	10 Year Growth Rate	9.04%
Total Years of Dividend Growth			10

Business Summary: Media (MIC: 13.1 SIC: 2721 NAIC:511120)

Meredith is engaged in magazine and book publishing, television broadcasting, integrated marketing, and interactive media. The publishing segment consists of 17 magazine brands, including *Better Homes and Gardens, Ladies' Home Journal*, and *American Baby*, as well as 170 special interest publications; book publishing with nearly 300 books in print; integrated marketing relationships; a consumer database; an Internet presence, including 24 web sites and strategic alliances with Internet destinations; brand licensing relationships; and other related operations. The broadcasting segment includes the operations of 11 network–affiliated television stations located across the continental U.S.

Recent Developments: For the quarter ended Dec 31 2003, net income improved 4.5% to $20.2 million compared with $19.3 million in the corresponding period of the prior year. Total revenues increased 11.4% to $280.4 million from $251.7 million the year before. Publishing segment revenues grew 21.1% to $206.9 million, driven primarily by strong advertising revenue growth, market share gains and the acquisition of the American Baby Group in Dec 2002. Broadcasting segment revenues declined 9.0% to $73.5 million. Income from operations rose 0.8% to $38.6 million from $38.3 million the previous year.

Prospects: Co. continues to benefit from the acquisition of the American Baby Group, which appeals to younger readers and the rapidly growing Hispanic market. Additionally, Co.'s titles, Better Homes and Gardens and Ladies' Home Journal, continue to produce strong advertising growth. Separately, on Mar 19 2004, Co. agreed to acquire AM radio station WKNX 1250, which serves the mid-Michigan market, from J&K Media. The transaction is expected to close in late May 2004. Looking ahead, Co. expects earnings per share of $0.61 for the third quarter of fiscal 2004 and $2.07 for the full year. Also, publishing advertising revenues are anticipated to grow in the low- to mid-single digits for the third quarter.

Financial Data

(US$ in Thousands)	6 Mos	3 Mos	06/30/2003	06/30/2002	06/30/2001	06/30/2000	06/30/1999	06/30/1998
Earnings Per Share	0.78	0.39	1.78	1.79	1.39	1.35	1.67	1.4
Cash Flow Per Share	1.20	0.38	3.37	2.75	2.66	2.80	2.50	2.8
Dividends Per Share	0.380	0.375	0.370	0.350	0.330	0.310	0.290	0.27
Dividend Payout %	48.71	96.15	20.78	19.55	23.74	22.96	17.36	18.4
Income Statement								
Total Revenues	553,049	272,670	1,080,104	987,829	1,053,213	1,097,165	1,036,122	1,009,92
Total Indirect Exp.	231,563	111,517	438,021	436,335	438,840	459,048	437,479	448,86
Depreciation & Amort.	15,104	7,479	31,443	53,640	51,172	52,349	44,083	36,84
Operating Income	76,716	38,102	177,319	117,849	126,624	161,337	171,087	152,50
Net Interest Inc./(Exp.)	(11,477)	(5,799)	(27,209)	(32,589)	(31,901)	(33,751)	(21,287)	(13,38)
Income Taxes	25,251	12,502	57,491	57,691	44,928	56,556	62,518	59,25
Income from Cont Ops	...	...	91,068	...	...	...	...	...
Net Income	39,988	19,801	5,319	91,381	71,272	71,030	89,657	79,85
Average Shs. Outstg.	51,583	51,557	51,093	50,921	51,354	52,774	53,761	54,60
Balance Sheet								
Cash & Cash Equivalents	9,693	9,403	22,294	28,225	36,254	22,861	11,029	4,95
Total Current Assets	275,199	290,208	268,429	272,211	291,082	288,799	256,175	246,80
Total Assets	1,443,118	1,456,821	1,436,721	1,460,264	1,437,747	1,439,773	1,423,396	1,066,56
Total Current Liabilities	306,799	311,774	297,199	307,406	371,406	358,701	344,115	346,86
Long–Term Obligations	349,232	380,135	375,000	385,000	400,000	455,000	485,000	175,00
Net Stockholders' Equity	525,798	515,743	500,765	507,717	447,908	379,844	360,158	349,73
Net Working Capital	31.600	(21,566)	(28,770)	(35,195)	(80,324)	(69,902)	(87,940)	(100,06)
Shares Outstanding	50,083	50,184	50,149	49,575	49,791	49,209	50,284	52,27
Statistical Record								
Operating Profit Margin %	13.87	13.97	16.41	11.93	12.02	14.70	16.51	15.
Return on Equity %	7.60	3.83	18.18	17.99	15.91	18.69	24.89	22.8
Return on Assets %	2.77	1.35	6.33	6.25	4.95	4.93	6.29	7.4
Debt/Total Assets %	24.19	26.09	26.10	26.36	27.82	31.60	34.07	16.4
Price Range	50.28-44.00	48.12-44.00	47.58-34.09	44.75-27.20	38.52-27.19	41.94-22.44	48.25-27.19	46.94-27.2
P/E Ratio	64.46-56.41	123.4-112.8	26.73-19.15	25.00-15.20	27.71-19.56	31.06-16.62	28.89-16.28	32.15-18.6
Average Yield %	0.80	0.79	0.94	0.89	0.94	1.00	0.92	0.7

Address: 1716 Locust Street, Des Moines, IA 50309-3023	Officers: William T. Kerr – Chmn., C.E.O., Suku V. Radia – V.P., C.F.O.	Investor Contact: (800) 284–4236
Telephone: (515) 284-3000	Transfer Agents:Boston EquiServe, Boston, MA	Institutional Holding
Web Site: www.meredith.com		No of Institutions: 4
		Shares: 10,678 % Held: –

MERIDIAN BIOSCIENCE INC.

Exchange	Symbol	Price	52Wk Range	Yield	P/E
NMS	VIVO	$8.28 (3/31/2004)	10.25–7.10	4.83	16.90

7 Year Price Score N/A   *NYSE Composite Index=100   *12 Month Price Score 95.1

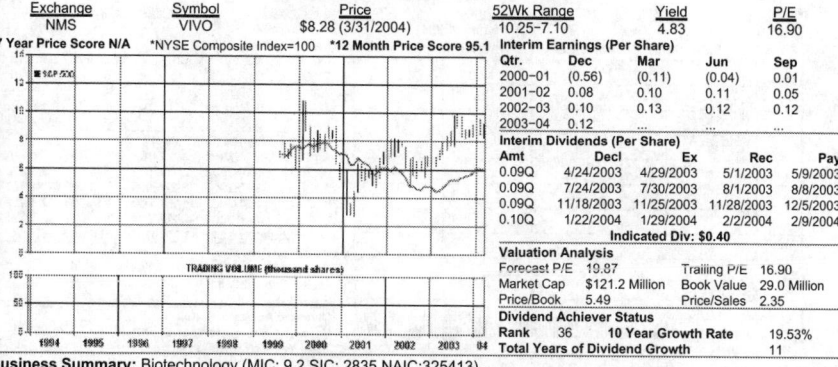

TRADING VOLUME (thousand shares)

Interim Earnings (Per Share)

Qtr.	Dec	Mar	Jun	Sep
2000–01	(0.56)	(0.11)	(0.04)	0.01
2001–02	0.08	0.10	0.11	0.05
2002–03	0.10	0.13	0.12	0.12
2003–04	0.12	...	...	...

Interim Dividends (Per Share)

Amt	Decl	Ex	Rec	Pay
0.09Q	4/24/2003	4/29/2003	5/1/2003	5/9/2003
0.09Q	7/24/2003	7/30/2003	8/1/2003	8/8/2003
0.09Q	11/18/2003	11/25/2003	11/28/2003	12/5/2003
0.10Q	1/22/2004	1/29/2004	2/2/2004	2/9/2004

Indicated Div: $0.40

Valuation Analysis

Forecast P/E	19.87	Trailing P/E	16.90
Market Cap	$121.2 Million	Book Value	29.0 Million
Price/Book	5.49	Price/Sales	2.35

Dividend Achiever Status

Rank	36	10 Year Growth Rate	19.53%
Total Years of Dividend Growth		11	

Business Summary: Biotechnology (MIC: 9.2 SIC: 2835 NAIC:325413)

Meridian Bioscience is an integrated life sciences company whose principal businesses include the development, manufacture, sale and distribution of diagnostic test kits, primarily for certain respiratory, gastrointestinal, viral and parasitic infectious diseases; the manufacture and distribution of bulk antigens and reagents used by researchers and other diagnostic manufacturers; and the contract manufacture of proteins and other biologicals for use by biopharmaceutical and biotechnology companies engaged in research for new drugs and vaccines.

Recent Developments: For the quarter ended Dec 31 2003, net earnings increased 26.1% to $1.8 million compared with $1.4 million in the corresponding year–earlier period. Net sales advanced 12.8% to $18.2 million. US Diagnostics segment sales climbed 25.2% to $13.3 million, primarily due to volume growth in respiratory products. European Diagnostics sales rose 3.6% to $3.2 million; however, sales in local currency, the Euro, fell 12.0%. Life Science segment sales slid 29.3% to $1.7 million, due primarily to orders for make–to–order bulk antigen products with one customer, which are expected to resume in the second quarter of fiscal 2004. Operating income was $3.1 million, 14.0% higher than last year.

Prospects: Co.'s near–term prospects appear promising, reflecting diagnostic product revenue growth and several pending new product introductions. Co. noted that these include the launch of new products that will enable the rapid detection of stomach ulcers and antibiotic associated colitis. Accordingly, Co. has reaffirmed its guidance for full–year fiscal 2004 of net sales ranging from $71.0 million to $75.0 million and earnings of between $0.47 and $0.53 per share. Co. stated that these sales and earnings figures do not include the effect of any acquisitions it might complete during fiscal 2004.

Financial Data

(US$ in Thousands)	3 Mos	09/30/2003	09/30/2002	09/30/2001	09/30/2000	09/30/1999	09/30/1998	09/30/1997
Earnings Per Share	0.49	0.47	0.34	(0.70)	0.49	0.16	0.34	0.42
Cash Flow Per Share	0.24	0.82	0.77	0.59	0.35	0.61	0.46	0.44
Tang. Book Val. Per Share	0.95	0.83	0.57	0.49	0.83	0.66	1.87	1.65
Dividends Per Share	0.360	0.340	0.275	0.255	0.230	0.200	0.218	0.188
Dividend Payout %	73.47	72.34	80.88	N.M.	46.93	125.00	64.12	44.64
Income Statement								
Total Revenues	18,166	65,864	59,104	56,527	57,096	54,351	33,169	35,229
Total Indirect Exp.	6,969	25,499	24,604	39,213	26,092	27,842	14,168	13,021
Depreciation & Amort.	984	3,780	3,719	4,746	4,811	5,673	2,884	3,017
Operating Income	3,148	12,789	9,994	(12,507)	9,354	7,036	8,351	9,910
Net Interest Inc./(Exp.)	(358)	(1,676)	(1,936)	(2,380)	(1,742)	(1,638)	(284)	(159)
Income Taxes	1,029	4,573	3,212	(4,631)	(173)	2,935	3,097	3,729
Net Income	1,795	7,018	5,031	(10,275)	7,111	2,386	4,958	5,982
Average Shs. Outstg.	15,170	14,950	14,760	14,589	14,652	14,580	14,703	14,341
Balance Sheet								
Cash & Cash Equivalents	3,714	2,683	3,060	4,677	4,779	7,231	23,769	21,736
Total Current Assets	33,690	33,161	30,375	32,502	40,166	31,972	39,763	37,841
Total Assets	66,931	66,420	65,095	65,982	84,769	72,389	59,147	57,491
Total Current Liabilities	14,980	15,330	15,249	16,368	17,303	13,517	3,869	4,271
Long–Term Obligations	20,879	21,505	23,626	24,349	27,105	21,366	20,595	20,581
Net Stockholders' Equity	29,018	27,484	24,381	22,944	36,611	33,904	34,683	32,639
Net Working Capital	18,710	17,831	15,126	16,134	22,863	18,455	35,895	33,570
Shares Outstanding	14,823	14,720	14,624	14,590	14,587	14,429	14,382	14,365
Statistical Record								
Operating Profit Margin %	17.32	19.41	16.90	N.M.	16.38	12.94	25.17	28.13
Return on Equity %	6.18	25.53	20.63	N.M.	19.42	7.03	14.29	18.32
Return on Assets %	2.68	10.56	7.72	N.M.	8.38	3.29	8.38	10.40
Debt/Total Assets %	31.19	32.37	36.29	36.90	31.97	29.51	34.82	35.79
Price Range	9.24–8.30	10.00–5.50	8.20–4.80	9.10–2.70	10.90–6.00	8.00–6.80	...	...
P/E Ratio	77.00–69.17	21.28–11.70	24.12–14.12	N/A	22.24–12.24	50.00–42.50	...	...
Average Yield %	4.16	4.47	4.02	4.45	2.93	2.74	N/A	N/A

Address: 3471 River Hills Drive, Cincinnati, OH 45244	Officers: William J. Motto – Chmn., C.E.O., John A. Kraeutler – Pres., C.O.O.	Investor Contact:513–271–3700
Telephone: (513) 271–3700		Institutional Holding
Web Site: www.meridianbioscience.com		No of Institutions: 3
		Shares: 7,166,604 % Held: –

MGE ENERGY INC

Exchange	Symbol	Price	52Wk Range	Yield	P/E
NMS	MGEE	$30.85 (3/31/2004)	34.45-26.89	4.39	19.16

*7 Year Price Score 129.8 *NYSE Composite Index=100 *12 Month Price Score 94.4

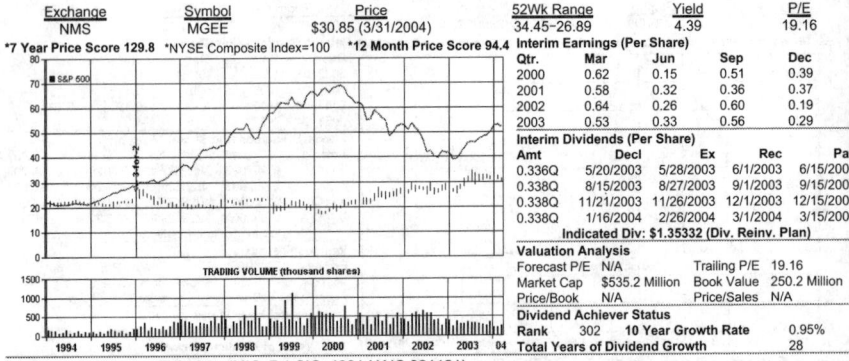

Interim Earnings (Per Share)

Qtr.	Mar	Jun	Sep	Dec
2000	0.62	0.15	0.51	0.39
2001	0.58	0.32	0.36	0.37
2002	0.64	0.26	0.60	0.19
2003	0.53	0.33	0.56	0.29

Interim Dividends (Per Share)

Amt	Decl	Ex	Rec	Pa'
0.336Q	5/20/2003	5/28/2003	6/1/2003	6/15/200
0.338Q	8/15/2003	8/27/2003	9/1/2003	9/15/200
0.338Q	11/21/2003	11/26/2003	12/1/2003	12/15/200
0.338Q	1/16/2004	2/26/2004	3/1/2004	3/15/200

Indicated Div: $1.35332 (Div. Reinv. Plan)

Valuation Analysis

Forecast P/E	N/A	Trailing P/E	19.16
Market Cap	$535.2 Million	Book Value	250.2 Million
Price/Book	N/A	Price/Sales	N/A

Dividend Achiever Status

Rank	302	10 Year Growth Rate	0.95%
Total Years of Dividend Growth			28

Business Summary: Electricity (MIC: 7.1 SIC: 4931 NAIC:221121)

MGE Energy is the holding company for Madison Gas & Electric, which is a public utility that generates and distributes electricity to nearly 132,000 customers in Dane County, WI as of Dec 31 2003. Co. also purchases, transports and distributes natural gas to more than 129,000 customers in the Wisconsin cities of Elroy, Fitchburg, Lodi, Madison, Middleton, Monona, Prairie du Chien, Verona, and Viroqua; 24 villages and 46 townships. Co. has a 22.0% ownership interest in two, 512-megawatt coal-burning units at the Columbia Energy Center in Columbia, WI. The units burn low-sulfur coal obtained from the Powder River Basin coal fields located in Wyoming and Montana.

Recent Developments: For the year ended Dec 31 2003, net income climbed 5.0% to $30.6 million compared with $29.2 million in 2002. Total operating revenues rose 15.7% to $401.5 million from $347.1 million a year earlier. Electric revenues rose 7.4% to $241.7 million, reflecting an increase in electric rates, partially offset by a slight decrease in electric sales and customer fuel credit. Gas revenues jumped 30.9% to $159.8 million, primarily due to a 6.4% increase in natural gas deliveries and significantly higher gas commodity costs. Operating expenses increased 17.6% to $360.4 million. Operating income increased 2.9% to $59.8 million compared with $58.1 million the year before.

Prospects: Co.'s liquidity and capital position remains strong, although its overall debt is higher due in part to the natural gas-fired cogeneration facility that MGE Power West Campus is constructing on the University of Wisconsin - Madison campus. The facility will have capacity to produce 20,000 tons of chilled water, 500,000 pounds per hour of steam, and about 150 megawatts of electricity. Co. anticipates relying on short- and long-term borrowing to support construction and the related capital expenditures. The cost to construct the cogeneration facility is approximately $180.0 million and is expected to be completed in the spring of 2005.

Financial Data

(US$ in Thousands)	12/31/2003	12/31/2002	12/31/2001	12/31/2000	12/31/1999	12/31/1998	12/31/1997	12/31/1996
Earnings Per Share	1.71	1.69	1.63	1.67	1.48	1.38	1.40	0.4
Cash Flow Per Share	3.83	3.27	4.44	2.91	3.74	4.38	2.53	3.0
Tang. Book Val. Per Share	14.34	12.93	12.66	12.05	11.48	11.33	11.25	11.1
Dividends Per Share	1.340	1.330	1.320	1.310	1.300	1.290	1.280	1.27
Dividend Payout %	78.84	79.18	81.48	78.93	88.37	94.07	91.90	317.5
Income Statement								
Total Revenues	401,547	347,096	333,711	324,108	274,034	249,752	264,648	253,29
Total Indirect Exp.	34,936	40,223	60,359	60,677	56,728	53,171	49,054	46,79
Costs & Expenses	341,716	288,966	299,040	284,007	241,484	219,940	233,658	221,77
Depreciation & Amort.	23,344	29,362	35,669	35,081	35,154	33,185	28,317	25,51
Operating Income	59,831	58,130	34,671	40,101	32,550	29,812	30,990	31,51
Net Interest Inc./(Exp.)	(11,776)	(12,545)	(13,572)	(14,129)	(12,039)	(10,855)	(10,724)	(10,891
Income Taxes	19,901	18,727	2,105	...	...	...	...	.
Eqty Earns/Minority Int.	...	...	3,345	...	...	...	...	.
Income from Cont Ops	...	...	27,362	...	...	...	...	.
Net Income	30,640	29,193	27,245	27,355	23,746	22,230	22,523	6,42
Average Shs. Outstg.	17,894	17,311	16,819	16,382	16,084	16,080	16,080	16,08
Balance Sheet								
Net Property	537,511	460,328	401,249	441,654	394,825	367,302	363,093	365,19
Total Assets	721,687	628,895	541,451	571,469	495,510	466,265	471,790	484,16
Long-Term Obligations	202,204	192,149	157,600	183,437	148,599	159,761	129,923	128,88
Net Stockholders' Equity	263,070	227,370	216,292	200,312	185,686	182,275	180,923	179,08
Shares Outstanding	18,343	17,574	17,071	16,618	16,161	16,080	16,080	16,08
Statistical Record								
Operating Profit Margin %	14.90	16.74	10.38	12.37	11.87	11.93	11.70	12.4
Net Inc./Net Property %	5.70	6.34	6.79	6.19	6.01	6.05	6.20	1.7
Net Inc./Tot. Capital %	5.66	6.05	6.33	6.40	6.29	5.75	6.31	1.8
Return on Equity %	11.64	12.83	12.65	13.65	12.78	12.19	12.44	3.5
Accum. Depr./Gross Prop. %	...	44.24	45.91	53.60	55.09	54.89	52.88	50.6
Price Range	34.45-25.20	29.84-25.01	27.80-21.06	22.75-17.00	23.38-17.25	23.56-20.88	23.00-19.25	27.50-20.0
P/E Ratio	20.15-14.74	17.66-14.80	17.06-12.92	13.62-10.18	15.79-11.66	17.07-15.13	16.43-13.75	68.75-50.0
Average Yield %	4.47	4.94	5.50	6.66	6.25	5.75	6.30	5.5

Address: 133 South Blair Street, Madison, WI 53701-1231 Telephone: (608) 252-7000 Web Site: www.mge.com	Officers: Gary J. Wolter – Chmn., Pres., C.E.O., David C. Mebane – Vice-Chmn.	Investor Contact: (608) 252-7907 Institutional Holding No of Institutions: 69 Shares: 3,834,206 % Held: -

MIDDLESEX WATER CO.

Exchange	Symbol	Price	52Wk Range	Yield	P/E
NMS	MSEX	$20.70 (3/31/2004)	21.01-16.42	3.19	33.93

Year Price Score 130.5 *NYSE Composite Index=100 *12 Month Price Score 96.7

Interim Earnings (Per Share)

Qtr.	Mar	Jun	Sep	Dec
2000	0.08	0.13	0.14	0.15
2001	0.08	0.18	0.22	0.18
2002	0.12	0.18	0.24	0.18
2003	0.11	0.16	0.22	0.12

Interim Dividends (Per Share)

Amt	Decl	Ex	Rec	Pay
0.161Q	7/24/2003	8/13/2003	8/15/2003	9/2/2003
4-for-3	8/28/2003	11/17/2003	11/1/2003	11/14/2003
0.165Q	10/30/2003	11/12/2003	11/14/2003	12/1/2003
0.165Q	1/29/2004	2/12/2004	2/17/2004	3/1/2004

Indicated Div: $0.66 (Div. Reinv. Plan)

Valuation Analysis

Forecast P/E	21.63	Trailing P/E	33.93
Market Cap	$160.0 Million	Book Value	79.7 Million
Price/Book	N/A	Price/Sales	N/A

Dividend Achiever Status

Rank	288	10 Year Growth Rate	2.51%
Total Years of Dividend Growth			31

Business Summary: Water Utilities (MIC: 7.2 SIC: 4941 NAIC:221310)

Middlesex Water is a water utility company that owns and operates water utility systems in central and southern New Jersey and in Delaware as well as a wastewater utility in southern New Jersey. Operations are divided into two segments. Co.'s regulated segment collects, treats and distributes water on a retail and wholesale basis to residential, commercial, industrial and fire protection customers in parts of New Jersey and Delaware. Co. also operates a regulated wastewater system in New Jersey. Co.'s non-regulated contract services segment operates and maintains municipal and private water and wastewater systems in New Jersey and Delaware.

Recent Developments: For the year ended Dec 31 2003, net income decreased 14.6% to $6.6 million compared with $7.8 million in 2002. Operating revenues rose 3.5% to $64.1 million from $61.9 million a year earlier. The improvement in sales was primarily attributed to customer growth of 10.9% in Delaware, higher base rates in Co.'s Delaware services territories, and increased revenues from Co.'s operations and maintenance contracts due to scheduled increases in fixed fees under the City of Perth Amboy contract. Operating income fell 7.8% to $11.5 million versus $12.5 million the year before. Total other income dropped 19.1% to $357,487 versus $441,878 in 2002.

Prospects: Looking ahead, Co. is optimistic that its revenues should continue to increase in 2004 based on continued customer growth in Delaware and Co.'s pursuit of non-regulated opportunities in Delaware and elsewhere. However, the level of revenues and earnings will be affected by the ultimate outcome of the New Jersey base rate cases currently under review by the Board of Public Utilities and the anticipated base rate filing in Delaware for Co.'s Tidewater System. In addition, Co.'s results could also be influenced by weather. Changes in these factors as well as Co.'s projected capital program are the primary factors that will determine the need for future rate increase filings.

Financial Data

(US$ in Thousands)	12/31/2003	12/31/2002	12/31/2001	12/31/2000	12/31/1999	12/31/1998	12/31/1997	12/31/1996
Earnings Per Share	0.61	0.72	0.66	0.50	0.76	0.70	0.66	0.60
Cash Flow Per Share	1.31	1.04	1.17	0.96	0.97	1.13	1.44	1.23
Tang. Book Val. Per Share	7.53	7.38	7.10	6.99	7.04	6.81	5.99	5.85
Dividends Per Share	0.640	0.630	0.620	0.610	0.590	0.570	0.560	0.550
Dividend Payout %	106.35	87.11	94.31	121.28	78.28	81.56	84.58	91.67
Income Statement								
Total Revenues	64,111	61,933	59,638	54,477	53,497	43,058	40,294	38,025
Total Indirect Exp.	13,581	12,822	12,692	11,633	10,756	9,386	8,852	8,498
Costs & Expenses	52,611	49,466	48,145	44,538	42,832	33,909	31,501	29,802
Depreciation & Amort.	10,725	9,927	10,103	9,402	7,769	6,569	6,142	5,858
Operating Income	11,500	12,467	11,493	9,938	10,665	9,149	8,793	8,222
Net Interest Inc./(Exp.)	(5,227)	(5,143)	(5,042)	(4,997)	(4,695)	(4,424)	(3,337)	(3,280)
Income Taxes	2,835	3,878	3,714	2,637	3,189	2,999	3,135	2,526
Income from Cont Ops	6,631	...	...	...	...	...	...	...
Net Income	6,631	7,765	6,953	5,305	7,881	6,521	5,861	5,167
Average Shs. Outstg.	10,818	10,623	10,474	10,387	10,296	9,160	8,764	8,338
Balance Sheet								
Net Property	230,932	211,368	199,060	191,196	181,809	162,827	137,109	123,019
Total Assets	263,192	244,604	236,374	219,400	215,036	203,501	159,761	148,660
Long-Term Obligations	97,377	87,483	88,140	82,109	82,330	78,032	52,918	52,961
Net Stockholders' Equity	83,706	80,564	76,353	74,698	74,552	71,725	56,221	51,882
Shares Outstanding	10,566	10,356	10,168	10,097	10,001	9,794	8,538	8,409
Statistical Record								
Operating Profit Margin %	17.93	20.12	19.27	18.24	19.93	21.24	21.82	21.62
Net Inc./Net Property %	2.87	3.67	3.49	2.77	4.33	4.00	4.27	4.20
Net Inc./Tot. Capital %	3.39	4.28	3.92	3.13	4.66	4.02	4.83	4.41
Return on Equity %	7.92	9.63	9.10	7.10	10.57	9.09	10.42	9.96
Accum. Depr./Gross Prop. %	17.32	18.72	18.21	17.10	16.36	16.90	18.29	19.01
Price Range	20.82-15.73	20.04-14.92	17.92-14.94	16.87-12.87	19.75-10.69	12.81-9.69	11.25-8.19	9.62-8.00
P/E Ratio	34.13-25.78	27.83-20.72	27.16-22.63	33.75-25.75	25.99-14.06	18.30-13.84	17.05-12.41	16.04-13.33
Average Yield %	3.51	3.67	3.81	4.20	4.42	5.31	6.30	6.35

Address: 1500 Ronson Road, Iselin, NJ 8830-3020	Officers: J. Richard Tompkins – Chmn., Dennis G. Sullivan – Pres., C.E.O.	Investor Contact: (732) 634-1500
Telephone: (732) 634-1500		Institutional Holding
Web Site: www.middlesexwater.com		No of Institutions: 24
		Shares: 81,570 % Held: –

181

MIDLAND CO.

Exchange	Symbol	Price	52Wk Range	Yield	P/E
NMS	MLAN	$24.95 (3/31/2004)	25.45–17.57	0.82	19.34

*7 Year Price Score 140.4 *NYSE Composite Index=100 *12 Month Price Score 93.8

Interim Earnings (Per Share)

Qtr.	Mar	Jun	Sep	Dec
2000	0.48	0.39	0.41	0.61
2001	0.53	0.34	0.10	0.54
2002	0.52	0.33	(0.15)	0.44
2003	0.56	(0.06)	0.23	0.56

Interim Dividends (Per Share)

Amt	Decl	Ex	Rec	Pa
0.048Q	6/18/2003	6/20/2003	6/20/2003	7/3/200
0.048Q	7/31/2003	9/17/2003	9/19/2003	10/2/200
0.048Q	10/30/2003	12/19/2003	12/23/2003	1/6/200
0.051Q	1/29/2004	3/17/2004	3/19/2004	4/1/200

Indicated Div: $0.205 (Div. Reinv. Plan)

Valuation Analysis

Forecast P/E	18.26	Trailing P/E	19.34
Market Cap	$437.3 Million	Book Value	333.9 Million
Price/Book	N/A	Price/Sales	N/A

Dividend Achiever Status

Rank	206	10 Year Growth Rate	7.75%
Total Years of Dividend Growth			17

Business Summary: Insurance (MIC: 8.2 SIC: 6399 NAIC:524128)

Midland is a provider of specialty insurance products and services through two wholly owned subsidiaries. American Modern specialize in writing physical damage insurance and related coverages on manufactured housing, as well as other areas of insurance, including coverage for site–built homes, motorcycles, watercraft, snowmobiles, recreational vehicles, physical damage on long–haul trucks extended service contracts, credit life and related products as well as collateral protection and mortgage fire products sold to financia institutions and their customers. Co.'s other subsidiary, M/G Transport, charters barges and brokers freight for the movement c commodities on the inland waterways.

Recent Developments: For the year ended Dec 31 2003, Co. reported net income of $23.3 million compared with income of $20. million, before an accounting change charge of $1.5 million, the previous year. Total revenues increased 11.6% to $718.2 million fror $643.7 million a year earlier. Revenues included a net realized investment gain of $4.6 million in 2003 and a net realized investment los of $6.9 million in 2002. Premiums earned grew 10.5% to $638.0 million. Transportation revenues advanced 21.3% to $28.2 million. Ne investment income dropped 7.0% to $33.0 million. Losses and loss adjustment expenses grew 15.0% to $392.2 million. Co.'s combine ratio was 103.1% compared with 101.9% the year before.

Prospects: Co. is encouraged by the underwriting results developing from its manufactured housing segment. Meanwhile, rat increases averaging more than 21.0% in the motorcycle line have already been approved and are in place for the 2004 season. Thes increases, along with additional rate increases and underwriting and product modifications should drive double–digit premium an combined ratio improvement in this line of business in 2004. For the full year 2004, Co. expects near double–digit top–line growth, with a combined ratio in the range of 97.0% to 99.0%. Co. expects net income, excluding capital gains and losses, in the range of $2.00 t $2.20 per share.

Financial Data
(US$ in Thousands)

	9 Mos	6 Mos	3 Mos	12/31/2002	12/31/2001	12/31/2000	12/31/1999	12/31/1998
Earnings Per Share	1.17	0.79	1.18	1.14	1.51	1.89	1.65	1.4.
Tang. Book Val. Per Share	18.94	18.93	17.96	17.58	16.52	15.73	13.55	13.3
Dividends Per Share	0.186	0.183	0.179	0.175	0.160	0.150	0.135	0.12
Dividend Payout %	15.90	23.16	15.17	15.35	10.60	7.94	8.18	8.7
Income Statement								
Total Premium Income	512,209	334,966	161,488	577,668	508,233	456,120	400,991	375,47
Other Income	19,943	12,964	5,907	59,022	78,310	78,302	68,135	66,88
Total Revenues	532,152	347,930	167,395	636,690	586,543	534,422	469,126	442,36
Total Indirect Exp.	...	541	325	508	1,286	2,305	6,973	4,06
Inc. Before Inc. Taxes	16,381	11,163	14,104	25,741	36,704	50,669	43,713	37,52
Income Taxes	3,060	2,131	4,055	5,437	9,482	15,206	12,534	10,59
Income from Cont Ops	...	...	...	20,304	...	...	...	...
Net Income	13,321	9,032	10,049	18,841	27,222	35,463	31,179	26,93
Average Shs. Outstg.	17,919	17,883	17,829	17,789	17,990	18,758	18,926	18,82
Balance Sheet								
Cash & Cash Equivalents	798,975	782,325	730,592	745,733	715,295	701,048	620,957	593,85
Premiums Due	...	...	87,361	91,633	88,108	70,396	60,426	(753
Invst. Assets: Total	792,667	770,011	723,013	739,758	704,009	692,657	610,859	590,17(
Total Assets	1,149,396	1,123,901	1,059,855	1,090,674	1,053,942	993,850	888,057	777,12(
Long–Term Obligations	55,447	46,413	46,787	47,163	48,619	40,025	44,288	54,56.
Net Stockholders' Equity	333,937	333,984	316,404	308,908	291,876	283,177	258,002	248,83.
Shares Outstanding	17,626	17,636	17,609	17,566	17,660	18,000	19,032	18,70.
Statistical Record								
Return on Revenues %	0.62	2.60	6.00	2.96	4.64	6.64	6.64	6.0
Return on Equity %	3.98	2.70	3.17	6.57	9.32	12.52	12.08	10.8
Return on Assets %	1.15	0.80	0.94	1.86	2.58	3.56	3.51	3.4(
Price Range	24.29–16.32	23.20–16.32	20.15–16.32	25.24–16.44	23.60–13.25	14.75–9.25	14.38–9.63	15.83–9.7
P/E Ratio	32.82–22.05	45.49–32.00	35.98–29.14	22.14–14.42	15.63–8.77	7.80–4.89	8.71–5.83	11.07–6.7
Average Yield %	0.88	0.87	0.93	0.82	0.81	1.13	1.07	0.9

Address: 7000 Midland Blvd., Amelia, OH 45102–2607	**Officers:** John P. Hayden III – Chmn., C.O.O., John W. Hayden – Pres., C.E.O.	**Investor Contact:**513–943–7100 **Institutional Holding** **No of Institutions:** 4
Telephone: (513) 943–7100		
Web Site: www.midlandcompany.com		**Shares:** 4,474,168 **% Held:** –

MINE SAFETY APPLIANCES CO

Exchange	Symbol	Price	52Wk Range	Yield	P/E
ASE	MSA	$28.36 (3/31/2004)	31.77-11.98	0.99	21.65

*Year Price Score N/A *NYSE Composite Index=100 *12 Month Price Score 131.1

TRADING VOLUME (thousand shares)

Interim Earnings (Per Share)

Qtr.	Mar	Jun	Sep	Dec
2000	0.57	0.07	0.11	(0.13)
2001	0.22	0.19	0.21	0.25
2002	0.21	0.25	0.15	0.23
2003	0.28	0.33	0.29	0.41

Interim Dividends (Per Share)

Amt	Decl	Ex	Rec	Pay
1.46E	11/4/2003	11/12/2003	11/14/2003	11/24/2003
0.067Q	11/4/2003	11/13/2003	11/17/2003	12/10/2003
3-for-1	12/10/2003	1/29/2004	1/16/2004	1/28/2004
0.07Q	1/20/2004	2/18/2004	2/20/2004	3/10/2004

Indicated Div: $0.28

Valuation Analysis

Forecast P/E	N/A	Trailing P/E	21.65
Market Cap	$345.7 Million	Book Value	N/A
Price/Book	N/A	Price/Sales	N/A

Dividend Achiever Status

Rank	165	10 Year Growth Rate	9.64%
Total Years of Dividend Growth			33

Business Summary: Apparel (MIC: 4.4 SIC: 2326 NAIC:423840)

Mine Safety Appliances manufactures and sells products designed to protect the safety and health of people throughout the world. Co.'s principal products include respiratory protective equipment; instruments that monitor and analyze workplace environments and control industrial processes; thermal imaging cameras; and personal protective products including head, eye and face, hearing protectors and fall protection equipment. Many of these products have wide applications, including manufacturing, municipal and volunteer fire departments, public utilities, mining, chemicals, petroleum, construction, transportation, the military and hazardous materials clean-up.

Recent Developments: For the year ended Dec 31 2003, income was $48.9 million versus income of $31.2 million in the prior year. Results for 2003 and 2002 excluded income from discontinued operations of $16.3 million and $3.9 million, respectively. Net sales increased 23.4% to $696.5 million. The most significant growth was in North America, where shipments of gas masks and protective helmets to homeland security and military markets were strong all year. Sales also grew in Europe, particularly in the MSA Gallet line of protective helmets for fire service and military markets. In addition, Co.'s other international markets benefited from higher activity in the Asia Pacific and Latin American regions.

Prospects: Going forward, Co. should continue to benefit from strong demand for respiratory protection products in the U.S. fire service, military and homeland security markets, and in international markets. Since November 2003, Co. has secured three contracts with the U.S. Army totaling more than $78.0 million and covering production of more than 230,000 helmets. With the overall increase in helmet production, Co. plans to expand employment at manufacturing sights in Murrysville, PA. Separately, on Mar 12 2004, Federal regulators approved Co.'s *Millennium®CBRN Gas Mask*, the first gas mask intended to protect civilian emergency personnel from chemical, biological, radiological and nuclear agents.

Financial Data

(US$ in Thousands)	12/31/2003	12/31/2002	12/31/2001	12/31/2000	12/31/1999	12/31/1998	12/31/1997	12/31/1995
Earnings Per Share	1.31	0.84	0.87	0.62	0.41	0.45	0.53	0.36
Cash Flow Per Share	1.08	1.33	0.85	1.41	1.01	0.53	0.75	0.69
Tang. Book Val. Per Share	7.02	6.62	5.95	6.28	6.18	6.07	5.93	5.35
Dividends Per Share	1.717	0.217	0.180	0.158	0.151	0.148	0.138	0.110
Dividend Payout %	131.07	25.83	20.68	25.48	36.83	32.89	26.04	30.56
Income Statement								
Total Revenues	698,197	566,697	545,666	502,833	498,051	497,207	499,409	491,859
Total Indirect Exp.	217,427	171,605	174,376	159,562	163,952	160,900	163,766	164,845
Depreciation & Amort.	23,208	21,525	26,471	24,557	23,356	22,398	21,516	20,002
Operating Income	73,759	48,083	52,886	34,050	23,185	28,208	36,239	33,132
Net Interest Inc./(Exp.)	(4,564)	(4,769)	(6,061)	(4,502)	(4,273)	(3,258)	(2,781)	(1,730)
Income Taxes	24,835	16,870	21,255	10,811	6,859	9,933	14,385	14,220
Income from Cont Ops	48,924	31,213	...	...	16,326	...	...	...
Net Income	65,267	35,077	31,631	23,239	15,134	18,275	21,854	18,912
Average Shs. Outstg.	37,264	36,885	36,237	37,068	39,015	40,023	40,941	51,129
Balance Sheet								
Cash & Cash Equivalents	73,244	36,477	26,992	26,541	17,108	24,020	19,921	31,950
Total Current Assets	323,242	282,944	217,686	201,153	203,090	229,209	219,613	228,625
Total Assets	643,885	579,765	520,698	489,683	451,741	456,716	406,404	406,600
Total Current Liabilities	114,715	99,700	82,500	86,978	80,005	110,006	103,240	71,984
Long-Term Obligations	59,915	64,530	67,381	71,806	36,550	11,919	12,270	14,746
Net Stockholders' Equity	307,858	289,062	253,504	226,465	242,457	242,846	241,449	253,540
Net Working Capital	208,527	183,244	135,186	114,175	123,085	119,203	116,373	156,641
Shares Outstanding	36,927	36,621	36,302	35,482	38,625	39,411	40,104	46,647
Statistical Record								
Operating Profit Margin %	10.56	8.48	9.69	6.77	4.65	5.67	7.25	6.73
Return on Equity %	15.89	10.79	12.47	10.26	6.73	7.52	9.05	7.45
Return on Assets %	7.59	5.38	6.07	4.74	3.61	4.00	5.37	4.65
Debt/Total Assets %	9.30	11.09	12.94	14.66	8.09	2.60	3.01	3.62
Price Range	28.21-10.23	16.83-9.17	16.98-7.58	8.67-6.33	...	...	...	...
P/E Ratio	21.53-7.81	20.04-10.91	19.52-8.72	13.98-10.21	...	...	...	...
Average Yield %	10.87	1.65	1.69	2.01	N/A	N/A	N/A	N/A

Address: 121 Gamma Drive, Pittsburgh, PA 15238	Officers: John T. Ryan III – Chmn., C.E.O., J. H. Baillie – V.P.	Investor Contact:412-967-3000
Telephone: (412) 967-3000		Institutional Holding
Web Site: www.msanet.com		No of Institutions: 23
		Shares: 264,664 % Held: –

MYERS INDUSTRIES INC.

Exchange	Symbol	Price	52Wk Range	Yield	P/E
NYS	MYE	$12.30 (3/31/2004)	13.26–9.40	1.63	22.78

*7 Year Price Score 98.9 *NYSE Composite Index=100 *12 Month Price Score 104.4

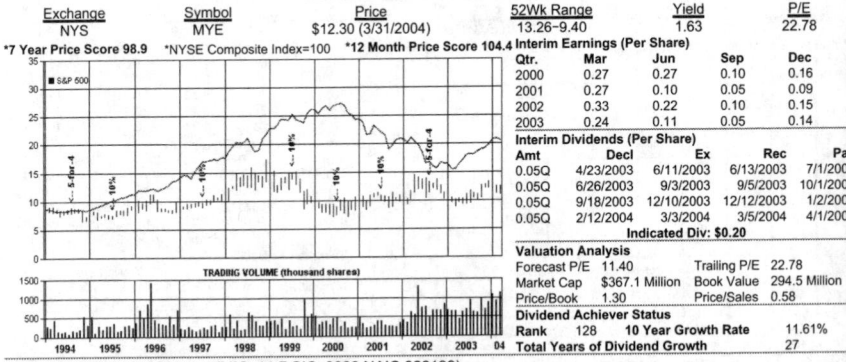

Interim Earnings (Per Share)

Qtr.	Mar	Jun	Sep	Dec
2000	0.27	0.27	0.10	0.16
2001	0.27	0.10	0.05	0.09
2002	0.33	0.22	0.10	0.15
2003	0.24	0.11	0.05	0.14

Interim Dividends (Per Share)

Amt	Decl	Ex	Rec	Pa
0.05Q	4/23/2003	6/11/2003	6/13/2003	7/1/200
0.05Q	6/26/2003	9/3/2003	9/5/2003	10/1/200
0.05Q	9/18/2003	12/10/2003	12/12/2003	1/2/200
0.05Q	2/12/2004	3/3/2004	3/5/2004	4/1/200

Indicated Div: $0.20

Valuation Analysis

Forecast P/E	11.40	Trailing P/E	22.78
Market Cap	$367.1 Million	Book Value	294.5 Million
Price/Book	1.30	Price/Sales	0.58

Dividend Achiever Status

Rank	128	10 Year Growth Rate	11.61%
Total Years of Dividend Growth			27

Business Summary: Plastics (MIC: 11.7 SIC: 3089 NAIC:326199)

Myers Industries designs, manufactures and markets plastic and rubber products, including plastic material handling containers and storage boxes to rubber OEM parts and tire repair materials. These products are made through a variety of molding processes in 2 facilities throughout North America and Europe. Co. also distributes tools, equipment, and supplies used for tire and wheel service and automotive underbody repair. Co.'s distribution operations are conducted through 40 branches located in major cities throughout the U.S and in foreign countries through export and businesses in which Co. holds an equity interest.

Recent Developments: For the year ended Dec 31 2003, net income dropped 31.9% to $16.3 million compared with $24.0 million in 2002. The decline in earnings was primarily attributed to higher raw material costs and competitive pricing pressures. Net sales climbed 8.7% to $661.1 million from $608.0 million a year earlier. Sales in the distribution segment grew 3.0% from a year ago, reflecting higher unit volumes for both supplies and capital equipment. Sales in the manufacturing segment increased 10.0% year over year. Gross profit slid 0.6% to $200.3 million versus $201.4 million the year before. Operating income decreased 33.4% to $34.7 million from $52.. million in 2002.

Prospects: Looking ahead, manufacturing sales should continue to benefit from favorable foreign currency translation and higher un sales growth to both existing and new customers in the automotive, industrial, horticulture, and heavy–truck markets. Meanwhile, Co plans to help mitigate higher raw material costs by increasing productivity, volume purchasing of raw materials, and streamlining manufacturing operations. In the distribution segment, earnings may be pressured by lower operating margins due to increased competition. Co. plans to pursue new opportunities that are arising in the service niche of the automotive dealer market.

Financial Data

(US$ in Thousands)	12/31/2003	12/31/2002	12/31/2001	12/31/2000	12/31/1999	12/31/1998	12/31/1997	12/31/1996
Earnings Per Share	0.54	0.80	0.51	0.80	1.02	0.94	0.72	0.6
Cash Flow Per Share	1.69	2.18	2.58	2.25	1.88	1.38	1.17	1.1
Tang. Book Val. Per Share	2.24	1.62	0.89	0.56	0.27	5.34	5.05	4.7
Dividends Per Share	0.200	0.190	0.170	0.160	0.140	0.120	0.110	0.090
Dividend Payout %	37.03	24.25	34.94	20.14	14.42	13.37	15.40	13.4
Income Statement								
Total Revenues	661,092	607,991	607,950	652,660	580,761	392,020	339,626	320,94
Total Indirect Exp.	165,567	149,248	159,000	154,308	143,618	86,141	68,936	65,89
Depreciation & Amort.	36,555	35,714	43,905	42,828	37,542	17,518	13,214	11,31
Operating Income	34,721	52,171	45,939	63,270	69,507	49,373	38,313	35,90
Net Interest Inc./(Exp.)	(10,074)	(11,810)	(18,959)	(22,360)	(15,206)	(888)	(248)	(285
Income Taxes	8,321	16,401	12,049	16,909	23,125	19,806	15,727	14,61
Net Income	16,326	23,960	15,191	24,001	31,176	28,679	22,339	21,00
Average Shs. Outstg.	30,125	29,971	29,752	29,828	30,502	30,454	30,731	30,97
Balance Sheet								
Cash & Cash Equivalents	5,667	1,702	7,075	2,178	1,094	34,832	6,298	5,60
Total Current Assets	207,933	201,140	196,619	219,307	206,991	153,650	107,427	106,31
Total Assets	621,627	602,482	582,166	624,797	600,410	306,708	224,078	207,12
Total Current Liabilities	94,175	117,369	104,899	115,583	102,244	51,234	39,644	36,85
Long–Term Obligations	211,003	212,223	247,145	284,273	280,104	48,832	4,261	14,46
Net Stockholders' Equity	294,524	255,690	217,526	213,903	207,747	202,689	176,677	162,44
Net Working Capital	113,758	83,771	91,719	103,724	104,747	102,417	67,783	69,45
Shares Outstanding	30,183	30,071	29,809	29,686	30,231	30,509	30,411	30,84
Statistical Record								
Operating Profit Margin %	5.25	8.58	7.55	9.69	11.96	12.59	11.28	11.18
Return on Equity %	5.54	9.37	6.98	11.22	15.00	14.14	12.64	12.9
Return on Assets %	2.62	3.97	2.60	3.84	5.19	9.35	9.96	10.1
Debt/Total Assets %	33.94	35.22	42.45	45.49	46.65	15.92	1.90	2.2
Price Range	13.26–8.80	14.48–9.36	11.45–8.36	10.55–7.09	18.03–8.60	17.24–9.99	11.27–8.47	11.27–7.9
P/E Ratio	24.56–16.30	18.10–11.70	22.46–16.40	13.18–8.86	17.68–8.43	18.34–10.63	15.65–11.76	16.82–11.8
Average Yield %	1.87	1.61	1.68	1.79	1.09	0.91	1.14	0.9

Address: 1293 South Main Street, Akron, OH 44301 **Telephone:** (330) 253–5592 **Web Site:** www.myersind.com	**Officers:** Stephen E. Myers – Chmn., C.E.O., Milton I. Wiskind – Vice–Chmn., Sec. **Transfer Agents:**National City Bank, Cleveland, Ohio	**Investor Contact:**330–253–5592 **Institutional Holding** **No of Institutions:** 6 **Shares:** 1,255,496 **% Held:** –

NACCO INDUSTRIES INC.

Exchange	Symbol	Price	52Wk Range	Yield	P/E
NYS	NC	$82.40 (3/31/2004)	95.00–48.02	1.84	13.57

7 Year Price Score 91.2   *NYSE Composite Index=100*   **12 Month Price Score 117.6**

Interim Earnings (Per Share)

Qtr.	Mar	Jun	Sep	Dec
2000	1.13	1.67	1.09	0.74
2001	1.76	0.74	(3.36)	(3.38)
2002	0.77	0.34	0.98	3.96
2003	0.35	1.17	1.43	3.12

Interim Dividends (Per Share)

Amt	Decl	Ex	Rec	Pay
0.255Q	5/14/2003	5/29/2003	6/2/2003	6/16/2003
0.38Q	8/13/2003	8/28/2003	9/2/2003	9/15/2003
0.38Q	11/12/2003	11/26/2003	12/1/2003	12/15/2003
0.38Q	2/11/2004	2/26/2004	3/1/2004	3/15/2004

Indicated Div: $1.52

Valuation Analysis

Forecast P/E	N/A	Trailing P/E	13.57
Market Cap	$541.8 Million	Book Value	598.7 Million
Price/Book	0.79	Price/Sales	0.18

Dividend Achiever Status

Rank	218	10 Year Growth Rate	6.76%
Total Years of Dividend Growth			20

Business Summary: Industrial Machinery and Equipment (MIC: 11.5 SIC: 3537 NAIC:333924)

NACCO Industries is a holding company with three principal businesses. NACCO Materials Handling Group (NMHG) designs, engineers, manufactures, sells, services and leases a full line of lift trucks and replacement parts marketed worldwide under the Hyster™and Yale™brand names. NACCO Housewares Group consists of Hamilton Beach/Procter–Silex, Inc., a manufacturer and marketer of small household appliances and commercial products for restaurants, bars and hotels, and The Kitchen Collection, Inc., a national specialty retailer of brand–name kitchenware and electrical appliances. The North American Coal Corporation mines and markets lignite coal primarily as fuel for power generators.

Recent Developments: For the year ended Dec 31 2003, income was $49.8 million, before an accounting change gain of $1.2 million and extraordinary gain of $1.8 million, versus income of $49.6 million, before an extraordinary loss of $2.2 million, the previous year. Results included a credit of $1.2 million in 2003 and a charge of $12.3 million in 2002 for restructuring. Results also included a loss on sales of dealers of $1.2 million in both 2003 and 2002. Total revenues advanced 8.2% to $2.47 billion. Material Handling group revenue climbed 12.0% to $1.78 billion, while North American Coal Corp. revenue increased 9.2% to $94.1 million. Housewares group revenue decreased 1.9% to $598.7 million.

Prospects: Looking ahead to 2004, Co.'s Material Handling group expects modest strengthening of global lift truck markets. High product development and introduction costs are expected to continue, while manufacturing restructuring costs should decline. Co.'s Housewares group expects to focus on reducing operating costs and enhancing manufacturing efficiencies. Hamilton Beach*Proctor–Silex is planning a range of new product introductions to improve revenues in 2004. Meanwhile, North American Coal Corp. anticipates increased lignite coal deliveries in 2004, primarily from the Mississippi Lignite Mining Company, as well as higher royalty income.

Financial Data
(US$ in Thousands)

	12/31/2003	12/31/2002	12/31/2001	12/31/2000	12/31/1999	12/31/1998	12/31/1997	12/31/1996
Earnings Per Share	6.07	6.05	(4.24)	4.63	6.66	12.53	7.55	5.66
Cash Flow Per Share	15.02	18.19	16.60	16.28	15.83	17.67	25.53	27.02
Tang. Book Val. Per Share	14.67	5.73	1.97	9.43	11.50	9.51	N.M	N.M
Dividends Per Share	1.260	0.970	0.930	0.890	0.850	0.810	0.770	0.740
Dividend Payout %	20.75	16.03	N.M.	19.22	12.76	6.46	10.23	13.11
Income Statement								
Total Revenues	2,472,600	2,285,000	2,637,900	2,871,300	2,602,800	2,536,200	2,246,900	2,273,200
Total Indirect Exp.	350,700	340,500	439,200	398,300	353,400	317,400	289,000	297,800
Depreciation & Amort.	68,400	70,200	15,900	15,700	15,200	14,700	15,800	15,400
Operating Income	117,200	115,500	5,700	117,900	131,300	198,100	132,000	131,200
Net Interest Inc./(Exp.)	(51,000)	(52,900)	(56,900)	(47,100)	(43,300)	(34,600)	(36,600)	(45,900)
Income Taxes	15,800	11,300	(9,900)	22,300	31,700	60,700	26,400	34,300
Eqty Earns/Minority Int.	4,200	1,700	800	100	(600)	(3,000)	(900)	(1,400)
Income from Cont Ops	49,800	49,600	(34,700)	37,800	54,300	...	...	...
Net Income	52,800	42,400	(36,000)	67,700	53,100	102,500	61,800	50,600
Average Shs. Outstg.	8,204	8,198	8,190	8,167	8,154	8,166	8,189	8,931
Balance Sheet								
Cash & Cash Equivalents	68,900	57,800	71,900	33,700	36,200	34,700	24,100	47,800
Total Current Assets	812,900	739,500	770,000	815,700	772,200	703,200	599,600	591,800
Total Assets	1,839,800	1,780,800	2,161,900	2,193,900	2,013,000	1,898,300	1,729,100	1,708,100
Total Current Liabilities	589,800	545,500	874,300	650,200	583,100	548,600	506,500	416,000
Long–Term Obligations	363,200	416,100	519,400	732,700	615,500	569,600	558,200	674,800
Net Stockholders' Equity	637,000	559,400	529,300	606,400	562,200	518,300	425,100	379,300
Net Working Capital	223,100	194,000	(104,300)	165,500	189,100	154,600	93,100	175,800
Shares Outstanding	8,206	8,201	8,195	8,171	9,804	8,120	8,154	8,186
Statistical Record								
Operating Profit Margin %	4.73	5.05	0.21	4.10	5.04	7.81	5.87	5.77
Return on Equity %	7.81	8.86	N.M	6.23	9.65	19.73	14.53	13.34
Return on Assets %	2.70	2.78	N.M.	1.72	2.69	5.38	3.57	2.96
Debt/Total Assets %	19.74	23.36	24.02	33.39	30.57	30.00	32.28	39.50
Price Range	93.77–37.99	75.25–36.65	81.47–42.63	55.56–45.13	96.25–45.13	172.5–78.94	125.9–44.63	63.50–43.25
P/E Ratio	15.45–6.26	12.44–6.06	N/A	12.00–7.29	14.45–6.78	13.77–6.30	16.67–5.91	11.22–7.64
Average Yield %	2.01	1.79	1.47	2.09	1.17	0.69	1.05	1.39

Address: 5875 Landerbrook Drive, Mayfield Heights, OH 44124–4017 **Telephone:** (440) 449–9600 **Web Site:** www.naccoind.com	**Officers:** Alfred M. Rankin – Chmn., Pres., C.E.O., J. C. Butler – V.P., Corp. Devel., Treas. **Transfer Agents:** National City Bank, Cleveland, OH	**Investor Contact:** 40 449–9676) **Institutional Holding** **No of Institutions:** 21 **Shares:** 1,819,161 **% Held:** –

NATIONAL CITY CORP

Exchange	Symbol	Price	52Wk Range	Yield	P/E
NYS	NCC	$35.58 (3/31/2004)	36.89–28.42	3.60	10.37

*7 Year Price Score 109.2   *NYSE Composite Index=100   *12 Month Price Score 95.2

Interim Earnings (Per Share)

Qtr.	Mar	Jun	Sep	Dec
2000	0.53	0.56	0.54	0.50
2001	0.55	0.57	0.58	0.57
2002	0.73	0.63	0.61	0.62
2003	0.81	0.99	0.62	1.01

Interim Dividends (Per Share)

Amt	Decl	Ex	Rec	Pa
0.305Q	4/1/2003	4/9/2003	4/11/2003	5/1/200
0.32Q	7/1/2003	7/9/2003	7/11/2003	8/1/200
0.32Q	10/1/2003	10/8/2003	10/13/2003	11/1/200
0.32Q	1/2/2004	1/8/2004	1/12/2004	2/1/200

Indicated Div: $1.28 (Div. Reinv. Plan)

Valuation Analysis

Forecast P/E	N/A	Trailing P/E	10.37
Market Cap	$21.7 Billion	Book Value	9.3 Billion
Price/Book	2.20	Price/Sales	2.14

Dividend Achiever Status

Rank	178	10 Year Growth Rate	8.96%
Total Years of Dividend Growth		11	

Business Summary: Commercial Banking (MIC: 8.1 SIC: 6021 NAIC:522110)

National City is a financial holding company with total assets of $113.93 billion and total deposits of $63.93 billion as of Dec 3 2003. Co. operates through a distribution network in Ohio, Michigan, Pennsylvania, Indiana, Kentucky, and Illinois and conducts selecte consumer lending businesses and other financial services nationwide. Co.'s businesses include commercial and retail banking, consume finance, asset management, mortgage financing and servicing, and payment processing. Operations are primarily conducted through mor than 1,100 branch banking offices located within Co.'s six–state footprint and over 330 retail mortgage offices located throughout th United States.

Recent Developments: For the year ended Dec 31 2003, net income increased 46.3% to $2.12 billion from $1.45 billion the yea before. Net interest income rose 8.2% to $4.40 billion from $4.37 billion a year earlier. Total fees and other income grew 42.3% to $3.5 billion, driven by higher mortgage banking revenue due to strong sales of mortgage loans and successful hedging strategies designed t protect the value of mortgage servicing assets. The increase in total fees and other income also reflected strong deposit service charge and payment processing revenue. Total non–interest expense increased 9.6% to $4.09 billion from $3.73 billion a year earlier Comparisons were made with restated 2002 figures.

Prospects: Earnings continue to benefit from growth in Co.'s mortgage and consumer lending businesses. Co. also continues efforts t strengthen its balance sheet and improve its credit quality. As a result, Co. expects to perform well in 2004, specifically in its cor middle–market, small business and consumer banking franchises. Separately, on Feb 17 2004, Co. signed a definitive agreement t acquire Provident Financial Group, a bank holding company that operates through 65 branches in Southwestern Ohio and Norther Kentucky. Meanwhile, on Jan 7 2004, Co. announced a $30.0 million initiative that will replace or upgrade all of its six–state network c about 1,580 ATM's over the next 30 months.

Financial Data

(US$ in Thousands)	12/31/2003	12/31/2002	12/31/2001	12/31/2000	12/31/1999	12/31/1998	12/31/1997	12/31/1996
Earnings Per Share	3.43	2.59	2.27	2.13	2.22	1.61	1.83	1.6
Tang. Book Val. Per Share	13.47	11.70	12.15	11.06	9.38	10.68	10.14	9.9
Dividends Per Share	1.250	1.200	1.160	1.140	1.060	0.940	0.830	0.73
Dividend Payout %	36.44	46.33	51.10	53.52	47.74	58.38	45.62	44.9
Income Statement								
Total Interest Income	5,997,822	5,915,920	6,414,752	6,566,583	5,912,609	5,756,677	3,776,140	3,655,33
Total Interest Expense	1,629,816	1,910,541	2,975,903	3,608,221	2,912,587	2,845,029	1,833,312	1,712,75
Net Interest Income	4,368,006	4,005,379	3,438,849	2,958,362	3,000,022	2,911,648	1,942,828	1,942,57
Provision for Loan Losses	638,418	681,918	605,295	286,795	249,674	201,400	139,660	146,48
Non–Interest Income	3,596,001	2,811,999	2,677,823	2,484,234	2,380,769	2,314,142	1,375,936	1,273,02
Non–Interest Expense	4,088,123	3,729,634	3,344,876	3,183,909	2,982,504	3,377,113	2,010,577	2,010,68
Income Before Taxes	3,237,466	2,405,826	2,166,501	1,971,892	2,148,613	1,647,277	1,168,527	1,058,44
Net Income	2,117,064	1,593,598	1,388,108	1,302,377	1,405,485	1,070,681	807,433	736,63
Average Shs. Outstg.	616,410	616,174	611,936	612,625	632,452	665,720	441,380	451,00
Balance Sheet								
Cash & Due from Banks	3,595,706	3,756,426	4,403,962	3,535,186	3,480,756	4,783,491	2,967,181	2,935,28
Securities Avail. for Sale	13,731,232	18,422,536	19,717,736	19,809,066	29,808,686	32,238,740	17,745,186	18,097,13
Net Loans & Leases	78,153,524	71,035,824	67,043,315	64,675,857	59,233,441	57,040,923	37,743,821	34,789,43
Total Assets	113,933,460	118,258,415	105,816,700	88,534,609	87,121,499	88,245,632	54,683,521	50,855,83
Total Deposits	63,930,020	65,118,768	63,129,932	55,256,422	50,066,310	58,246,909	36,861,136	35,999,74
Long–Term Obligations	23,666,292	22,550,295	17,136,232	17,964,800	14,858,014	9,009,448	4,810,417	2,994,41
Total Liabilities	104,604,789	109,950,403	98,435,477	81,764,788	81,393,766	81,232,724	50,402,170	46,423,77
Net Stockholders' Equity	9,328,671	8,308,012	7,381,223	6,769,821	5,727,733	7,012,908	4,281,351	4,432,06
Shares Outstanding	605,996	611,491	607,354	609,188	607,058	652,654	422,196	446,39
Statistical Record								
Return on Equity %	22.69	19.18	18.80	19.23	24.53	15.26	18.85	16.6
Return on Assets %	1.85	1.34	1.31	1.47	1.61	1.21	1.47	1.4
Equity/Assets %	8.18	7.02	6.97	7.64	6.57	7.94	7.82	8.7
Non–Int. Exp./Tot. Inc. %	42.61	42.73	36.78	35.17	35.96	41.84	39.02	40.7
Price Range	34.58–26.75	33.69–24.68	32.51–24.50	29.38–16.00	37.81–22.13	38.75–28.72	33.50–21.88	23.44–15.3
P/E Ratio	10.08–7.80	13.01–9.53	14.32–10.79	13.79–7.51	17.03–9.97	24.07–17.84	18.31–11.95	14.38–9.4
Average Yield %	4.03	4.06	4.06	5.53	3.40	2.79	3.03	3.8

Address: 1900 East Ninth Street, Cleveland, OH 44114–3484 Telephone: (216) 222–2000 Web Site: www.nationalcity.com	Officers: David A. Daberko – Chmn., C.E.O., William E. MacDonald III – Vice–Chmn. Transfer Agents:National City Bank Corporate Trust Operations, Cleveland, OH	Investor Contact: (800) 622–4204 Institutional Holding No of Institutions: 38 Shares: 1,107,727 % Held: –

NATIONAL COMMERCE FINANCIAL CORP.

Exchange	Symbol	Price	52Wk Range	Yield	P/E
NYS	NCF	$28.61 (3/31/2004)	29.25-19.33	2.80	20.58

7 Year Price Score N/A *NYSE Composite Index=100 **12 Month Price Score 101.1

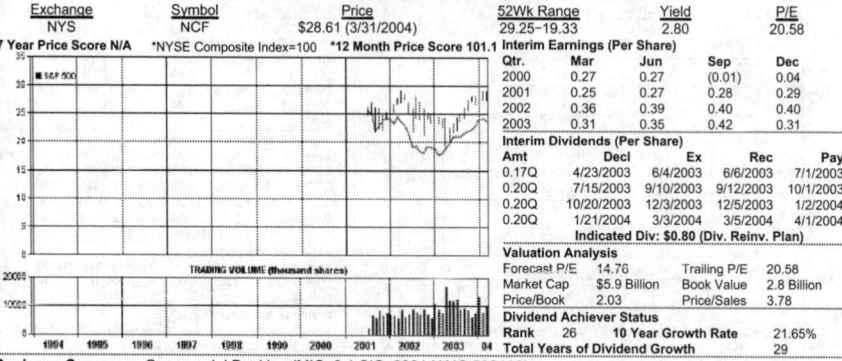

Interim Earnings (Per Share)

Qtr.	Mar	Jun	Sep	Dec
2000	0.27	0.27	(0.01)	0.04
2001	0.25	0.27	0.28	0.29
2002	0.36	0.39	0.40	0.40
2003	0.31	0.35	0.42	0.31

Interim Dividends (Per Share)

Amt	Decl	Ex	Rec	Pay
0.17Q	4/23/2003	6/4/2003	6/6/2003	7/1/2003
0.20Q	7/15/2003	9/10/2003	9/12/2003	10/1/2003
0.20Q	10/20/2003	12/3/2003	12/5/2003	1/2/2004
0.20Q	1/21/2004	3/3/2004	3/5/2004	4/1/2004

Indicated Div: $0.80 (Div. Reinv. Plan)

Valuation Analysis

Forecast P/E	14.76	Trailing P/E	20.58
Market Cap	$5.9 Billion	Book Value	2.8 Billion
Price/Book	2.03	Price/Sales	3.78

Dividend Achiever Status

Rank	26	10 Year Growth Rate	21.65%
Total Years of Dividend Growth		29

Business Summary: Commercial Banking (MIC: 8.1 SIC: 6021 NAIC:522110)

National Commerce Financial is a bank holding company with assets of $23.02 billion as of Dec 31 2003. Co.'s primary banking subsidiary, National Bank of Commerce (NBC), provides commercial and retail banking, savings and trust services through 258 Central Carolina Bank offices located in North Carolina and South Carolina, 16 Wal-Mart Money Centers in Georgia and Tennessee, and 175 NBC offices located in Tennessee, Mississippi, Arkansas, Georgia, Virginia and West Virginia. Co. also owns a 49.0% interest in First Market Bank, FSB, which operates 30 offices in the Richmond, VA area. In addition to its banking subsidiaries, Co. operates several other non-banking financial businesses.

Recent Developments: For the year ended Dec 31 2003, income from continuing operations was $286.8 million, down 11.4% compared with net income of $323.6 million a year earlier. Results for 2003 and 2002 included one-time gains of $51.4 million and $11.5 million, as well as one-time charges of $72.7 million and $4.9 million, respectively. Net interest income rose 0.8% to $739.5 million from $733.6 million the previous year. Provision for loan losses was $48.4 million versus $32.3 million in 2002. Total non-interest income climbed 19.5% to $454.7 million from $380.5 million the year before. Total non-interest expense increased 19.2% to $724.4 million from $607.8 million the prior year.

Prospects: Results are being positively affected by Co.'s efforts to spur loan and deposit growth, along with lowering its sensitivity to interest rate fluctuations and improving operational efficiencies. Meanwhile, Co. continues to focus on de novo expansion opportunities to help boost profitability. In 2003, Co. and First Market opened 32 new branches, including 20 in Atlanta, GA. This expansion was funded by the sale or consolidation of 30 existing branches during the year. During 2004, Co. plans to continue its expansion by adding 38 new branches, primarily in Atlanta or Wal-Mart Money Centers.

Financial Data

(US$ in Thousands)	12/31/2003	12/31/2002	12/31/2001	12/31/2000	12/31/1999	12/31/1998	12/31/1997	12/31/1996
Earnings Per Share	1.39	1.55	1.09	0.57	0.99	0.83	0.69	0.57
Tang. Book Val. Per Share	7.42	6.66	6.13	6.22	5.15	4.02	3.60	3.21
Dividends Per Share	0.710	0.620	0.540	0.440	0.360	0.290	0.220	0.190
Dividend Payout %	51.07	40.00	49.54	78.07	36.36	34.93	31.88	33.33
Income Statement								
Total Interest Income	1,054,136	1,130,497	1,222,865	1,250,478	468,028	383,587	336,993	286,567
Total Interest Expense	314,626	396,891	571,752	664,737	231,490	190,969	174,172	151,101
Net Interest Income	739,510	733,606	651,113	585,741	236,538	192,618	162,821	135,466
Provision for Loan Losses	48,414	32,344	29,199	20,892	15,206	9,599	17,013	14,134
Non-Interest Income	454,722	390,988	324,888	247,545	92,514	84,871	82,405	70,929
Non-Interest Expense	724,439	618,228	588,118	627,897	155,258	140,304	123,460	105,169
Income Before Taxes	407,739	470,575	358,684	184,497	158,588	127,586	104,753	87,092
Eqty Earns/Minority Int.	4,530	3,447	...	...	...	...	...	...
Income from Cont Ops	286,765	...	...	...	...	...	...	...
Net Income	311,764	323,610	225,296	117,474	107,234	85,141	69,780	57,513
Average Shs. Outstg.	206,368	208,144	207,484	207,496	108,823	102,884	101,368	100,196
Balance Sheet								
Cash & Due from Banks	558,313	517,295	561,429	446,712	179,082	224,875	206,191	164,894
Securities Avail. for Sale	5,238,429	4,777,009	3,611,706	2,401,526	553,928	721,268	408,083	700,775
Net Loans & Leases	13,079,628	12,760,516	11,818,364	10,889,477	3,926,192	3,148,551	2,565,670	2,312,459
Total Assets	23,016,916	21,472,116	19,273,713	16,553,514	6,806,173	5,811,054	4,692,011	4,200,409
Total Deposits	15,549,587	14,494,734	12,619,479	11,982,283	4,495,900	3,947,275	3,251,242	2,976,430
Long-Term Obligations	2,579,187	2,403,181	2,588,572	1,696,472	720,707	737,982	546,136	552,174
Total Liabilities	20,235,730	18,789,684	16,818,382	15,225,038	6,198,886	5,352,609	4,289,979	3,887,080
Net Stockholders' Equity	2,781,186	2,682,432	2,455,331	1,278,554	557,378	408,549	352,148	313,329
Shares Outstanding	205,136	205,408	205,058	205,246	108,223	101,443	97,703	97,540
Statistical Record								
Return on Equity %	10.31	8.29	9.17	9.18	19.23	20.83	19.81	18.35
Return on Assets %	1.25	1.51	1.16	0.70	1.57	1.46	1.48	1.36
Equity/Assets %	12.08	12.49	12.73	7.72	8.18	7.03	7.50	7.45
Non-Int. Exp./Tot. Inc. %	48.01	40.63	37.99	41.91	27.69	29.95	29.43	29.41
Price Range	28.25-19.33	29.25-21.38	27.05-22.00	...	...	...	...	...
P/E Ratio	20.32-13.91	18.87-13.79	24.82-20.18	...	...	...	...	...
Average Yield %	2.94	2.39	2.19	N/A	N/A	N/A	N/A	N/A

Address: One Commerce Square, Memphis, TN 38150	Officers: Eugene J. nald – Chmn., William R. Reed – Pres., C.E.O.	Institutional Holding
Telephone: (901) 523-3434	Transfer Agents:Bank of New York, New York, NY	No of Institutions: 30
Web Site: www.ncbccorp.com		Shares: 1,665,555 % Held: –

187

NATIONAL FUEL GAS CO.

Exchange	Symbol	Price	52Wk Range	Yield	P/E
NYS	NFG	$24.60 (3/31/2004)	27.17–21.86	4.39	10.56

*7 Year Price Score 100.9   *NYSE Composite Index=100   *12 Month Price Score 90.6

Interim Earnings (Per Share)

Qtr.	Dec	Mar	Jun	Sep
2000–01	0.66	0.93	0.45	(1.22)
2001–02	0.41	0.77	0.22	0.06
2002–03	0.58	0.99	0.03	0.71
2003–04	0.60	...	...	...

Interim Dividends (Per Share)

Amt	Decl	Ex	Rec	Pa
0.27Q	6/5/2003	6/26/2003	6/30/2003	7/15/200
0.27Q	9/11/2003	9/26/2003	9/30/2003	10/15/200
0.27Q	12/11/2003	12/29/2003	12/31/2003	1/15/200
0.27Q	3/11/2004	3/29/2004	3/31/2004	4/15/200

Indicated Div: $1.08

Valuation Analysis

Forecast P/E	13.74	Trailing P/E	10.56
Market Cap	$2.0 Billion	Book Value	1.2 Billion
Price/Book	1.71	Price/Sales	0.97

Dividend Achiever Status

Rank	167	10 Year Growth Rate	3.38%
Total Years of Dividend Growth			32

Business Summary: Gas Utilities (MIC: 7.4 SIC: 4924 NAIC:221210)

National Fuel Gas is a diversified energy holding company. Through its subsidiaries, Co. ioperates in six business segments. The Utility segment operations are carried out by National Fuel Gas Distribution Corporation, sells natural gas to approximately 733,000 customers ir western New York and northwestern Pennsylvania. Other business segments include the Exploration and Production segment, the Energy Marketing segment, the International segment, the Pipeline and Storage segment, and the Timber segment. As of Sept. 30, 2003, prover developed reserves for crude oil and natural gas were 45,142,000 barrels and 223,545,000 billions cubic feet, respectively.

Recent Developments: For the three months ended Dec 31 2003, net income was $49.2 million compared with income of $46.9 million, before an accounting change charge of $8.9 million, the previous year. Results for 2003 included a non-recurring $5.2 millio benefit to deferred income tax expense. Co. attributed the decrease in earnings to a number factors, including warmer weather and highe operating costs in the Utility segment, and lower harvesting activity in the Timber segment. These factors more than offset increase earnings in the Exploration and Production segment, due to higher commodity prices and lower interest expense. Operating revenues ros 11.0% to $532.5 million from $479.7 million the year before.

Prospects: On Feb 17 2004, Co. announced plans to expand its natural gas pipeline operations to serve new markets in New York and the Northeast by extending the Empire State Pipeline. The pipeline extension will be designed to move at least 250.0 million cubic feet o natural gas per day and will provide customers on Empire with access to a number of underground storage facilities and local distributio companies' pipeline systems in New York State. The targeted in-service date for this pipeline expansion, which will cost an estimate $140.0 million, is late 2006. Meanwhile, Co. has reaffirmed its full-year fiscal 2004 earnings guidance of $1.65 to $1.75 per share excluding non-recurring items.

Financial Data

(US$ in Thousands)	3 Mos	09/30/2003	09/30/2002	09/30/2001	09/30/2000	09/30/1999	09/30/1998	09/30/1997
Earnings Per Share	2.33	2.31	1.46	0.82	1.60	1.47	0.42	1.49
Cash Flow Per Share	1.22	4.01	4.29	5.15	3.00	3.48	3.26	3.8
Tang. Book Val. Per Share	13.76	13.28	12.44	12.62	12.55	12.09	11.38	12.02
Dividends Per Share	1.060	1.050	1.010	0.970	0.930	0.900	0.870	0.84
Dividend Payout %	45.49	45.45	69.69	118.59	58.41	61.52	208.92	56.8
Income Statement								
Total Revenues	532,513	2,035,471	1,464,496	2,100,352	1,425,277	1,263,274	1,248,000	1,265,812
Total Indirect Exp.	64,680	99,874	252,823	439,425	221,048	220,836	340,693	212,199
Depreciation & Amort.	46,458	195,226	180,668	174,914	142,170	129,690	118,880	111,650
Operating Income	95,817	414,416	231,990	158,730	218,268	192,008	83,931	168,303
Net Interest Inc./(Exp.)	(25,333)	(104,521)	(120,595)	(107,145)	(100,085)	(87,698)	(85,284)	(56,811
Income Taxes	21,567	128,161	72,034	37,106	77,068	64,829	24,024	68,674
Eqty Earns/Minority Int.	(1,734)	(785)	(730)	(1,342)	(1,384)	(1,616)	(2,213)	..
Income from Cont Ops	...	187,836	...	...	...	...	32,304	..
Net Income	49,214	178,944	117,682	65,499	127,207	115,037	23,188	114,688
Average Shs. Outstg.	82,307	81,357	80,534	80,361	79,166	78,084	77,406	76,880
Balance Sheet								
Net Property	3,020,513	2,999,087	2,844,745	2,780,713	2,683,391	2,353,894	2,248,137	1,819,360
Total Assets	3,840,027	3,727,915	3,401,309	3,445,566	3,236,888	2,842,586	2,684,459	2,267,331
Long–Term Obligations	1,144,094	1,147,779	1,145,341	1,046,694	953,622	822,743	692,669	581,640
Net Stockholders' Equity	1,178,564	1,137,390	1,006,858	1,002,655	987,437	939,293	875,555	917,874
Shares Outstanding	81,652	81,438	80,264	79,406	78,659	77,674	76,938	76,332
Statistical Record								
Operating Profit Margin %	17.99	20.35	15.84	7.55	15.31	15.19	6.72	13.29
Net Inc./Net Property %	1.62	5.96	4.13	2.35	4.74	4.88	1.03	6.30
Net Inc./Tot. Capital %	1.76	6.52	4.63	2.71	5.55	5.57	1.25	6.4
Return on Equity %	4.17	16.51	11.68	6.53	12.88	12.24	3.68	12.49
Accum. Depr./Gross Prop. %	36.27	35.60	36.96	34.93	29.93	30.43	29.45	31.82
Price Range	24.72–21.86	27.17–18.33	25.37–15.97	32.06–22.12	28.97–19.84	24.94–18.94	24.41–19.97	22.53–18.38
P/E Ratio	41.20–36.43	11.76–7.94	17.38–10.94	39.10–26.98	18.11–12.40	16.96–12.88	58.11–47.54	15.12–12.33
Average Yield %	4.55	4.68	4.48	3.62	3.86	3.94	3.87	4.00

Address: 6363 Main Street, Williamsville, NY 14221
Telephone: (716) 857–7000
Web Site: www.nationalfuelgas.com

Officers: Philip C. Ackerman – Chmn., Pres., C.E.O., Joseph P. Pawlowski – Treas.
Transfer Agents: Computershare Investor Services, LLC Chicago, IL

Investor Contact: (716) 857–6987
Institutional Holding
No of Institutions: 201
Shares: 36,489,525   **% Held:** 45%

NATIONAL PENN BANCSHARES, INC.

Exchange	Symbol	Price	52Wk Range	Yield	P/E
NMS	NPBC	$31.53 (3/31/2004)	34.28–25.76	3.04	17.71

7 Year Price Score 136.2 *NYSE Composite Index=100 *12 Month Price Score 104.5

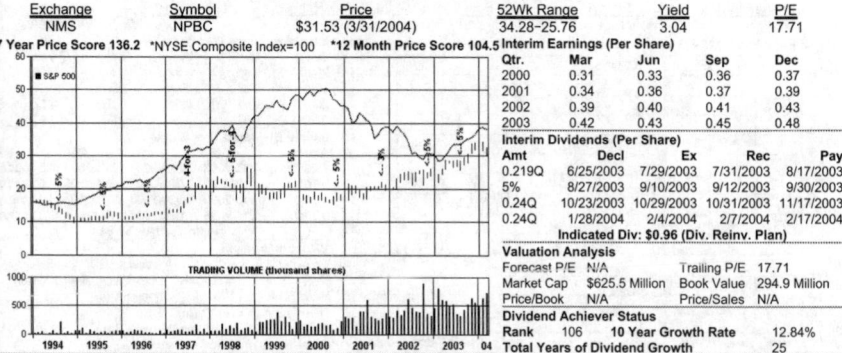

Interim Earnings (Per Share)

Qtr.	Mar	Jun	Sep	Dec
2000	0.31	0.33	0.36	0.37
2001	0.34	0.36	0.37	0.39
2002	0.39	0.40	0.41	0.43
2003	0.42	0.43	0.45	0.48

Interim Dividends (Per Share)

Amt	Decl	Ex	Rec	Pay
0.219Q	6/25/2003	7/29/2003	7/31/2003	8/17/2003
5%	8/27/2003	9/10/2003	9/12/2003	9/30/2003
0.24Q	10/23/2003	10/29/2003	10/31/2003	11/17/2003
0.24Q	1/28/2004	2/4/2004	2/7/2004	2/17/2004

Indicated Div: $0.96 (Div. Reinv. Plan)

Valuation Analysis

Forecast P/E	N/A	Trailing P/E	17.71
Market Cap	$625.5 Million	Book Value	294.9 Million
Price/Book	N/A	Price/Sales	N/A

Dividend Achiever Status

Rank	106	10 Year Growth Rate	12.84%
Total Years of Dividend Growth			25

Business Summary: Commercial Banking (MIC: 8.1 SIC: 6021 NAIC:522110)

National Penn Bancshares, with total assets of $3.51 billion as of Dec 31 2003, is a bank holding company. As of Dec 31 2003, Co. operated 96 community offices throughout nine counties in southeastern Pennsylvania through National Penn Bank. Trust and investment management services are provided through Investors Trust Company; brokerage services are provided through Penn Securities, Inc.; mortgage banking activities are provided through Penn 1st Financial Services, Inc.; leasing products are offered through National Penn Leasing Company; and insurance products are provided through FirstService Insurance Agency, Inc.

Recent Developments: For the year ended Dec 31 2003, income from continuing operations amounted to $34.7 million compared with income of $34.2 million a year earlier. Results for 2003 included a Federal Home Loan Bank prepayment fee of $7.0 million. Net interest income advanced 12.2% to $114.5 million from $102.1 million the previous year. Provision for loan losses amounted to $9.4 million versus $13.6 million in 2002. Total noninterest income rose 13.0% to $41.3 million, reflecting higher insurance commissions and fees associated with the February 2003 acquisition of FirstService Insurance, increased service charges on deposit accounts, and higher other service charges and fees.

Prospects: Co.'s outlook is enhanced by its December 2003 acquisition of HomeTowne Heritage Bank, as well as its pending agreement to acquire Peoples First, Inc., parent company of The Peoples Bank of Oxford. The latter transaction, which is expected to close in the second quarter of 2004, will expand Co.'s presence in southern Chester County and represent its first entry into Maryland. Meanwhile, Co.'s interest rate margin fell slightly to 4.30% in 2003 from 4.46% in 2002 due to the low interest rate environment. Co. noted that the pricing of liabilities is near a floor; however, assets continue to reprice at these low interest rate levels.

Financial Data

(US$ in Thousands)	12/31/2003	12/31/2002	12/31/2001	12/31/2000	12/31/1999	12/31/1998	12/31/1997	12/31/1996
Earnings Per Share	1.78	1.63	1.46	1.37	1.26	1.21	1.09	1.01
Tang. Book Val. Per Share	8.50	10.23	8.90	8.35	7.33	7.91	7.40	6.88
Dividends Per Share	0.890	0.800	0.740	0.670	0.630	0.570	0.490	0.420
Dividend Payout %	50.40	49.28	50.94	49.44	49.75	47.63	45.54	41.58
Income Statement								
Total Interest Income	165,648	173,010	188,497	184,652	164,270	131,910	119,027	106,558
Total Interest Expense	51,099	63,446	92,512	99,702	82,753	67,002	54,620	46,018
Net Interest Income	114,549	109,564	95,985	84,950	81,517	64,908	64,407	60,540
Provision for Loan Losses	9,371	14,000	9,000	5,600	5,960	5,100	4,575	3,900
Non–Interest Income	41,019	39,579	34,332	27,047	23,160	16,668	11,660	8,684
Non–Interest Expense	103,033	89,831	80,723	70,777	65,724	51,283	46,147	41,258
Income Before Taxes	43,164	45,312	40,594	35,620	32,993	25,193	25,345	24,066
Eqty Earns/Minority Int.	266	268	170	117	178	329	422	404
Income from Cont Ops	34,467	35,966	32,564	29,120	27,231	20,154	18,194	16,518
Net Income	43,354	36,234	32,734	29,237	27,409	20,483	18,616	16,922
Average Shs. Outstg.	24,411	22,102	22,295	21,334	21,551	16,895	17,061	16,638
Balance Sheet								
Cash & Due from Banks	96,164	83,831	101,796	80,859	62,953	46,574	40,009	40,194
Securities Avail. for Sale	934,375	733,774	658,581	593,316	516,027	421,738	321,760	236,814
Net Loans & Leases	2,192,092	1,842,987	1,814,162	1,683,198	1,536,404	1,220,673	1,097,662	1,028,334
Total Assets	3,512,576	2,858,262	2,727,482	2,512,508	2,242,432	1,811,594	1,534,378	1,358,013
Total Deposits	2,435,296	2,112,640	2,076,795	1,814,253	1,593,254	1,208,061	1,115,600	980,808
Long–Term Obligations	164,037	169,703	139,974	146,432	223,077	248,478	155,460	76,110
Total Liabilities	3,194,761	2,635,902	2,531,800	2,335,080	2,094,736	1,681,138	1,411,190	1,243,292
Net Stockholders' Equity	317,813	222,360	195,682	177,428	147,696	130,456	123,188	114,721
Shares Outstanding	24,284	21,734	21,969	21,224	20,141	16,485	16,631	16,657
Statistical Record								
Return on Equity %	10.84	16.17	16.64	16.41	18.43	15.44	14.76	14.39
Return on Assets %	0.98	1.25	1.19	1.15	1.21	1.11	1.18	1.21
Equity/Assets %	9.04	7.77	7.17	7.06	6.58	7.20	8.02	8.44
Non–Int. Exp./Tot. Inc. %	49.79	42.20	36.19	33.41	35.03	34.43	35.19	35.67
Price Range	34.20-22.13	26.01-19.95	22.02-16.62	21.07-15.52	22.43-16.97	26.76-16.22	21.97-12.52	13.18-10.84
P/E Ratio	19.21-12.43	15.96-12.24	15.08-11.38	15.38-11.33	17.81-13.47	22.11-13.41	20.15-11.49	13.05-10.73
Average Yield %	3.19	3.43	3.78	3.84	3.23	2.69	3.00	3.52

Address: Philadelphia and Reading Avenues, Boyertown, PA 19512 **Telephone:** (610) 367–6001 **Web Site:** www.nationalpennbancshares.com	**Officers:** Wayne R. Weidner – Chmn., C.E.O., Glenn E. Moyer – Pres.	**Investor Contact:** (610) 369–6291 **Institutional Holding** **No of Institutions:** 29 **Shares:** 1,603,181 **% Held:** –

NATIONAL SECURITY GROUP, INC

Exchange	Symbol	Price	52Wk Range	Yield	P/E
NMS	NSEC	23.10	26.00-12.57	N/A	13.92

*7 Year Price Score 120.0   *NYSE Composite Index=100   *12 Month Price Score 111.8

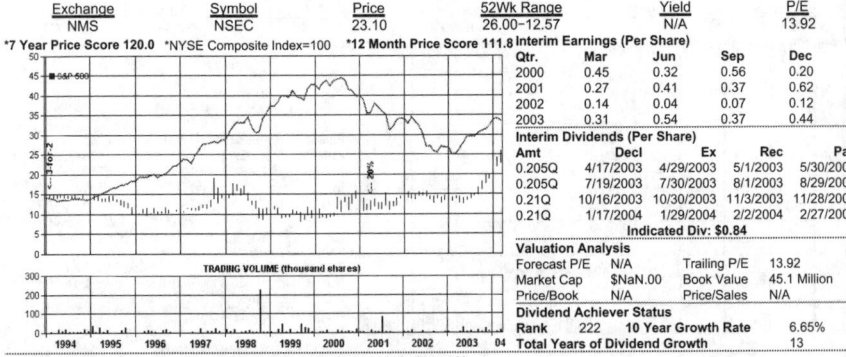

Interim Earnings (Per Share)

Qtr.	Mar	Jun	Sep	Dec
2000	0.45	0.32	0.56	0.20
2001	0.27	0.41	0.37	0.62
2002	0.14	0.04	0.07	0.12
2003	0.31	0.54	0.37	0.44

Interim Dividends (Per Share)

Amt	Decl	Ex	Rec	Pay
0.205Q	4/17/2003	4/29/2003	5/1/2003	5/30/2003
0.205Q	7/19/2003	7/30/2003	8/1/2003	8/29/2003
0.21Q	10/16/2003	10/30/2003	11/3/2003	11/28/2003
0.21Q	1/17/2004	1/29/2004	2/2/2004	2/27/2004

Indicated Div: $0.84

Valuation Analysis

Forecast P/E	N/A	Trailing P/E	13.92
Market Cap	$NaN.00	Book Value	45.1 Million
Price/Book	N/A	Price/Sales	N/A

Dividend Achiever Status

Rank	222	10 Year Growth Rate 6.65%
Total Years of Dividend Growth		13

Business Summary: Insurance (MIC: 8.2 SIC: 6311 NAIC:524113)

National Security Group is an insurance holding company that, through its subsidiaries, writes primarily dwelling fire and windstorm homeowners, mobile homeowners, and personal non-standard automobile lines of insurance. Co., through its life insurance subsidiary offers a basic line of life, and health and accident insurance products. Property-casualty insurance is Co.'s most significant segment. Co.'s property-casualty insurance is conducted through National Security Fire & Casualty Company, a wholly-owned subsidiary of Co., and Omega One Insurance Company, a wholly-owned subsidiary of National Security Fire & Casualty Company.

Recent Developments: For the year ended Dec 31 2003, net income surged to $4.1 million compared with $908,000 a year earlier. Total revenues advanced 38.7% to $54.7 million from $39.4 million the previous year, lead by a 45.7% gain in insurance premium earned to $47.5 million. Results for 2003 and 2002 included investment income of $4.4 million, and realized investment gains of $1.4 million and $1.2 million, respectively. For the three months ended Dec 31 2003, net income climbed to $1.1 million compared with $292,000 in the corresponding prior-year period. Total revenues climbed 35.3% to $15.3 million from $11.3 million the year before.

Prospects: Co.'s results are benefiting from its sharp focus on rates on several insurance programs in several states. For instance, in an effort to improve underwriting results, Co. increased homeowners rates by an average of 18.0% in Alabama, 15.0% in Georgia, and 14.0% in Mississippi in the first nine months of 2003. In addition, Co. has increased mobile homeowners rates 13.0% in Alabama, and 8.7% in Mississippi during the third quarter of 2003. Furthermore, Co. noted that it has filed rate adjustments in Alabama and Mississippi private passenger auto programs with rate adjustments slated to take effect during the fourth quarter of 2003 and first quarter of 2004.

Financial Data

(US$ in Thousands)	9 Mos	6 Mos	3 Mos	12/31/2002	12/31/2001	12/31/2000	12/31/1999	12/31/1998
Earnings Per Share	1.34	1.04	0.74	0.37	1.67	1.53	1.52	0.35
Tang. Book Val. Per Share	18.28	18.16	17.22	17.09	18.19	17.74	16.97	17.05
Dividends Per Share	0.820	0.815	0.810	0.805	0.750	0.700	0.670	0.640
Dividend Payout %	61.19	78.37	109.46	217.57	44.91	45.75	44.08	182.86
Income Statement								
Total Premium Income	34,349	21,952	9,927	32,631	25,357	22,921	25,936	28,451
Other Income	5,068	3,569	1,458	6,454	7,426	6,754	6,690	8,853
Total Revenues	39,417	25,521	11,385	39,085	32,783	29,675	32,626	37,304
Total Indirect Exp.	1,531	1,014	444	8,939	7,331	5,282	5,752	6,814
Inc. Before Inc. Taxes	4,730	3,103	1,182	1,194	5,470	4,844	4,516	1,106
Income Taxes	1,711	990	400	422	1,392	1,068	760	176
Eqty Earns/Minority Int.	(11)	(17)	(12)	136	52	...	...	...
Income from Cont Ops	3,019	2,113	782	...	...	...	...	...
Net Income	3,008	2,096	770	908	4,130	3,776	3,756	930
Average Shs. Outstg.	2,466	2,466	2,466	2,466	2,466	2,466	2,466	2,674
Balance Sheet								
Cash & Cash Equivalents	3,668	5,930	2,881	65,497	61,039	54,277	53,124	55,308
Premiums Due	...	...	2,492	4,597	3,824	3,677	4,687	7,223
Invst. Assets: Total	94,140	95,114	85,940	86,567	84,195	83,767	84,209	86,961
Total Assets	110,914	111,011	101,238	101,602	99,484	97,563	98,105	103,973
Long-Term Obligations	...	...	...	3,380	2,108	2,401	2,672	3,004
Net Stockholders' Equity	45,110	44,816	42,493	42,159	44,884	43,780	41,888	41,968
Shares Outstanding	2,466	2,466	2,466	2,466	2,466	2,466	2,466	2,461
Statistical Record								
Return on Revenues %	7.65	8.27	6.86	...	...	...	...	...
Return on Equity %	6.69	4.71	1.84	2.15	9.20	8.62	8.96	2.21
Return on Assets %	2.72	1.90	0.77	0.89	4.15	3.87	3.82	0.89
Price Range	16.59-12.57	14.50-12.57	14.50-13.35	15.80-13.00	15.62-10.89	15.83-9.17	12.08-8.12	17.71-8.75
P/E Ratio	13.60-10.30	17.06-14.79	46.77-43.06	42.70-35.14	9.36-6.52	10.35-5.99	7.95-5.35	50.60-25.00
Average Yield %	5.78	5.92	5.80	5.51	6.03	5.95	6.49	4.70

Address: 661 East Davis Street, Elba, AL 36323
Telephone: (334) 897-2273
Web Site: www.nationalsecuritygroup.com

Officers: W. L. Brunson - Pres., C.E.O., Brian R. McLeod - C.F.O., Treas.

Investor Contact: (334) 897-2273
Institutional Holding
No of Institutions: 4
Shares: 86,508   **% Held:** -

NICOR INC.

Exchange	Symbol	Price	52Wk Range	Yield	P/E
NYS	GAS	$35.23 (3/31/2004)	39.10–27.64	5.28	14.21

7 Year Price Score 91.7   *NYSE Composite Index=100   *12 Month Price Score 89.7

Interim Earnings (Per Share)

Qtr.	Mar	Jun	Sep	Dec
2000	0.83	0.66	(1.37)	0.88
2001	0.85	0.59	0.73	1.00
2002	0.90	0.46	0.68	0.84
2003	1.14	0.54	0.01	0.79

Interim Dividends (Per Share)

Amt	Decl	Ex	Rec	Pay
0.465Q	4/30/2003	6/26/2003	6/30/2003	8/1/2003
0.465Q	7/17/2003	9/26/2003	9/30/2003	11/1/2003
0.465Q	11/20/2003	12/29/2003	12/31/2003	2/1/2004
0.465Q	3/18/2004	3/29/2004	3/31/2004	5/1/2004
		Indicated Div: $1.86		

Valuation Analysis

Forecast P/E	14.46	Trailing P/E	14.21
Market Cap	$1.6 Billion	Book Value	754.6 Million
Price/Book	1.99	Price/Sales	0.56

Dividend Achiever Status

Rank	264	10 Year Growth Rate	4.37%
Total Years of Dividend Growth		16	

Business Summary: Gas Utilities (MIC: 7.4 SIC: 4924 NAIC:221210)

NICOR is engaged in the purchase, storage, distribution, transportation, sale, and gathering of natural gas. Co.'s natural gas unit, Northern Illinois Gas, is the largest gas distribution company in Illinois and one of the biggest in the nation. As of Dec 31 2003, Northern Illinois served more than 2.0 million customers in the northern third of the state, generally outside of Chicago. Co. also owns Tropical Shipping Co., a transporter of containerized freight in the Bahamas and Caribbean. Co.'s shipments consist primarily of southbound cargo such as food, building materials and other necessities for developers, manufacturers and residents, as well as tourist–related shipments.

Recent Developments: For the year ended Dec 31 2003, income was $109.8 million, before an accounting change charge of $4.5 million, compared with net income of $128.0 million the previous year. Results for 2003 and 2002 included pre–tax mercury–related recoveries of $17.8 million and $29.0 million, respectively. Results also included pre–tax property sale gains of $400,000 and $4.1 million in 2003 and 2002, respectively. The decreased in earnings was largely due to lower results in Co.'s gas distribution segment, partially offset by higher equity investment income and improved results in its shipping segment. Operating revenues soared 40.3% to $2.66 billion from $1.90 billion the year before.

Prospects: Results are being adversely affected by higher operating costs at Co.'s utility business, including the negative impact of high natural gas costs. Many of these unfavorable pressures are expected to continue to affect the performance of Co.'s gas distribution results in 2004. However, Co. should be able to offset these lower results with improved performance in its shipping segment and other energy–related businesses. Looking ahead, Co. expects earnings to range from $2.10 to $2.30 per diluted share, assuming normal weather. The estimate is based on lower operating results in Co.'s gas distribution segment and modest improvement in the shipping segment.

Financial Data

(US$ in Thousands)	12/31/2003	12/31/2002	12/31/2001	12/31/2000	12/31/1999	12/31/1998	12/31/1997	12/31/1996
Earnings Per Share	2.48	2.88	3.17	1.00	2.62	2.42	2.61	2.42
Cash Flow Per Share	(0.28)	6.05	10.86	4.97	4.33	7.65	4.29	2.55
Tang. Book Val. Per Share	17.13	16.55	16.38	15.55	16.79	15.97	15.43	14.74
Dividends Per Share	1.850	1.820	1.730	1.630	1.540	1.460	1.370	1.310
Dividend Payout %	74.79	63.19	54.73	163.50	58.77	60.33	52.49	54.13
Income Statement								
Total Revenues	2,662,700	1,897,400	2,544,100	2,298,100	1,615,200	1,465,100	1,992,600	1,850,700
Total Indirect Exp.	577,900	526,100	266,100	413,300	244,900	235,800	258,300	246,200
Depreciation & Amort.	143,500	137,600	148,800	144,300	140,300	136,500	131,200	125,300
Operating Income	189,400	226,500	243,500	94,100	212,000	208,600	229,800	233,100
Net Interest Inc./(Exp.)	(35,400)	(38,500)	(44,900)	(48,600)	(45,100)	(46,600)	(46,200)	(46,200)
Income Taxes	59,600	57,600	73,400	14,400	65,700	61,100	69,000	67,700
Eqty Earns/Minority Int.	15,300	(5,800)	...	...	...	...	...	...
Income from Cont Ops	109,800	...	...	...	...	...	...	121,200
Net Income	105,300	128,000	143,700	46,700	124,400	116,400	127,900	136,200
Average Shs. Outstg.	44,200	44,300	45,200	46,300	47,400	48,100	48,900	50,000
Balance Sheet								
Net Property	2,484,200	1,796,800	1,768,600	1,729,600	1,735,200	1,731,800	1,735,800	1,771,900
Total Assets	3,797,200	2,899,400	2,574,800	2,885,400	2,451,800	2,364,600	2,394,600	2,438,600
Long–Term Obligations	495,100	396,200	446,400	347,100	436,100	557,300	550,200	518,000
Net Stockholders' Equity	754,600	728,400	727,600	707,800	787,700	759,000	744,100	729,700
Shares Outstanding	44,040	44,011	44,397	45,491	46,890	47,514	48,217	49,492
Statistical Record								
Operating Profit Margin %	7.11	11.93	9.57	4.09	13.12	14.23	11.53	12.59
Net Inc./Net Property %	4.23	7.12	8.12	2.70	7.16	6.72	7.36	7.68
Net Inc./Tot. Capital %	5.65	8.11	9.12	3.26	7.91	7.09	8.00	8.78
Return on Equity %	14.55	17.57	19.74	6.59	15.79	15.33	17.18	16.60
Accum. Depr./Gross Prop. %	37.88	53.60	52.62	51.64	50.18	48.76	46.88	44.50
Price Range	39.10–23.85	48.96–22.75	41.66–34.12	43.56–29.81	42.88–31.31	44.00–37.25	42.56–31.25	36.88–26.00
P/E Ratio	15.77–9.62	17.00–7.90	13.14–10.76	43.56–29.81	16.36–11.95	18.18–15.39	16.31–11.97	15.24–10.74
Average Yield %	5.55	4.84	4.51	4.66	4.11	3.59	3.79	4.33

Address: 1844 Ferry Road, Naperville, IL 60563–9600	Officers: Thomas L. Fisher – Chmn., C.E.O., Russ M. Strobel – Pres.	Institutional Holding No of Institutions: 7
Telephone: (630) 305–9500	Transfer Agents:ComputerShare Investor Services., Chicago, IL	Shares: 71,790 % Held: –
Web Site: www.nicor.com		

NORDSON CORP.

Exchange	Symbol	Price	52Wk Range	Yield	P/E
NMS	NDSN	$37.46 (3/31/2004)	38.25–22.69	1.66	32.29

*7 Year Price Score 101.2 *NYSE Composite Index=100 *12 Month Price Score 111.3

Interim Earnings (Per Share)

Qtr.	Jan	Apr	Jul	Oct
2000–01	0.23	0.27	0.17	0.07
2001–02	0.17	0.23	0.21	0.05
2002–03	0.15	0.24	0.26	0.39
2003–04	0.27	...	...	...

Interim Dividends (Per Share)

Amt	Decl	Ex	Rec	Pa
0.15Q	5/21/2003	6/4/2003	6/6/2003	6/24/200
0.155Q	8/6/2003	8/27/2003	8/29/2003	9/16/200
0.155Q	11/5/2003	12/11/2003	12/15/2003	1/6/200
0.155Q	2/4/2004	2/18/2004	2/20/2004	3/9/200

Indicated Div: $0.62 (Div. Reinv. Plan)

Valuation Analysis

Forecast P/E	21.96	Trailing P/E	32.29
Market Cap	$1.3 Billion	Book Value	339.8 Million
Price/Book	N/A	Price/Sales	N/A

Dividend Achiever Status

Rank	164	10 Year Growth Rate	9.69%
Total Years of Dividend Growth	23		

TRADING VOLUME (thousand shares)

Business Summary: Industrial Machinery and Equipment (MIC: 11.5 SIC: 3569 NAIC:333999)

Nordson designs, manufactures and markets precision dispensing systems that apply adhesives, sealants and coatings to a range c consumer and industrial products during manufacturing operations, helping customers meet quality, productivity and environmenta targets. Co. also manufactures technology–based systems for curing and surface treatment processes. Co. products are used in a divers range of industries, including appliance, automotive, bookbinding, container, converting, electronics, food and beverage, furniture medical, metal finishing, nonwovens, packaging, semiconductor and other diverse industries.

Recent Developments: For the quarter ended Feb 1 2004, net income surged 93.7% to $9.7 million from $5.0 million in th corresponding period of the prior year. Net sales rose 17.4% to $170.6 million, reflecting volume gains and favorable currency effects du to the weaker U.S. dollar. On a segment basis, adhesive dispensing and nonwoven fiber systems sales grew 20.7% to $106.1 million Advanced technology systems sales advanced 24.1% to $35.3 million, driven by the early stages of economic recovery in North Americ coupled with strong growth in Asia. On a geographic basis, North America sales improved 7.1% to $62.3 million, while sales in Europ climbed 25.4% to $65.9 million.

Prospects: Co.'s new product and business development programs, which are being aided by a rebound in the global manufacturing sector and favorable currency effects due to the weakening dollar, should further enhance sales and earnings in fiscal 2005. Meanwhile, Cc continues to benefit from an increase in new orders. Backlog at the end of the first quarter of fiscal 2005, amounted to $81.0 million, a increase of approximately $20.0 million since the beginning of the year. Additionally, Co. expects demand for capital equipment to remain strong.

Financial Data

(US$ in Thousands)	3 Mos	11/02/2003	11/03/2002	10/28/2001	10/29/2000	10/31/1999	11/01/1998	11/02/1997
Earnings Per Share	1.16	1.04	0.66	0.74	1.67	1.42	0.62	1.4
Cash Flow Per Share	0.66	2.58	3.87	2.22	2.59	2.46	2.10	1.5
Tang. Book Val. Per Share	N.M	N.M	N.M	N.M	4.72	2.44	3.89	4.7
Dividends Per Share	0.610	0.600	0.570	0.560	0.520	0.480	0.440	0.40
Dividend Payout %	52.59	58.17	86.36	75.67	31.13	33.80	70.40	28.0
Income Statement								
Total Revenues	170,640	667,347	647,756	731,416	740,568	700,465	660,900	636,71
Total Indirect Exp.	74,733	297,185	284,195	334,750	316,519	305,250	312,158	286,22
Depreciation & Amort.	7,060	29,240	29,487	16,052	30,325	29,300	25,003	25,30
Operating Income	18,140	68,596	53,019	59,537	91,452	76,985	45,071	74,05
Net Interest Inc./(Exp.)	(3,989)	(18,063)	(21,713)	(29,489)	(11,665)	(10,244)	(9,647)	(7,76)
Income Taxes	4,760	17,317	10,872	13,106	28,776	23,932	18,102	21,77
Net Income	9,664	35,160	22,072	24,610	54,632	47,506	20,825	49,96
Average Shs. Outstg.	35,632	33,899	33,690	33,050	32,767	33,048	33,322	35,10
Balance Sheet								
Cash & Cash Equivalents	16,924	6,972	5,897	7,943	815	16,060	6,850	1,71
Total Current Assets	284,066	277,370	274,573	362,177	369,238	341,316	328,476	318,81
Total Assets	771,050	766,806	764,472	862,453	610,040	591,790	538,944	502,99
Total Current Liabilities	173,126	211,662	252,647	355,653	253,008	251,940	207,082	179,66
Long–Term Obligations	172,683	176,725	174,895	191,773	60,800	65,975	70,444	66,50
Net Stockholders' Equity	339,797	300,109	268,890	263,726	247,223	221,398	214,775	220,54
Net Working Capital	110,940	65,708	21,926	6,524	116,230	89,376	121,394	139,15
Shares Outstanding	35,231	34,035	33,613	33,137	32,449	49,012	33,480	33,67
Statistical Record								
Operating Profit Margin %	10.63	10.27	8.18	8.13	12.34	10.99	6.81	11.6
Return on Equity %	2.84	11.71	8.20	9.33	22.09	21.45	9.69	22.6
Return on Assets %	1.25	4.58	2.88	2.85	8.95	8.02	3.86	9.9
Debt/Total Assets %	22.39	23.04	22.87	22.23	9.96	11.14	13.07	13.2
Price Range	37.73–28.23	28.11–20.72	33.32–21.45	31.75–21.14	32.56–18.09	32.38–22.13	26.75–21.31	32.13–23.7
P/E Ratio	139.7–104.6	27.03–19.92	50.48–32.50	42.91–28.57	19.50–10.83	22.80–15.58	43.15–34.38	22.62–16.7
Average Yield %	1.80	2.40	2.17	2.10	2.10	1.77	1.83	1.4

Address: 28601 Clemens Road, Westlake, OH 44145–4551 Telephone: (440) 892–1580 Web Site: www.nordson.com	Officers: Edward P. Campbell – Chmn., C.E.O., Peter S. Hellman – Pres., C.F.O., Chief Admin. Officer	Investor Contact: (440) 414–5344 Institutional Holding No of Institutions: 12 Shares: 487,942 % Held: –

NORTHERN TRUST CORP.

Exchange	Symbol	Price	52Wk Range	Yield	P/E
NMS	NTRS	$46.59 (3/31/2004)	50.76-30.83	1.63	24.65

7 Year Price Score 85.8   *NYSE Composite Index=100   *12 Month Price Score 102.7

Interim Earnings (Per Share)

Qtr.	Mar	Jun	Sep	Dec
2000	0.49	0.53	0.53	0.53
2001	0.49	0.57	0.55	0.50
2002	0.56	0.56	0.43	0.42
2003	0.42	0.36	0.51	0.60

Interim Dividends (Per Share)

Amt	Decl	Ex	Rec	Pay
0.17Q	4/16/2003	6/6/2003	6/10/2003	7/1/2003
0.17Q	7/15/2003	9/8/2003	9/10/2003	10/1/2003
0.19Q	11/18/2003	12/8/2003	12/10/2003	1/2/2004
0.19Q	2/17/2004	3/8/2004	3/10/2004	4/1/2004

Indicated Div: $0.76

Valuation Analysis

Forecast P/E	21.28	Trailing P/E	24.65
Market Cap	$10.3 Billion	Book Value	3.1 Billion
Price/Book	3.29	Price/Sales	3.89

Dividend Achiever Status

Rank	99	10 Year Growth Rate	13.71%
Total Years of Dividend Growth			18

Business Summary: Commercial Banking (MIC: 8.1 SIC: 6022 NAIC:522110)

Northern Trust is a multibank holding company. Co.'s principal subsidiary is The Northern Trust Company, an Illinois banking corporation. Co. also owns national bank subsidiaries in Arizona, California, Colorado, Florida and Texas; a federal savings bank with offices in ten states; trust companies in New York and Connecticut; and various other nonbank subsidiaries. Co. offers financial services including fiduciary, banking, investment and financial consulting services for individuals as well as credit operating, trust and investment management services for corporations. Total assets for Co. were $41.45 billion as of Dec 31 2003.

Recent Developments: For the year ended Dec 31 2003, Co. reported income from continuing operations of $423.3 million versus net income of $447.1 million the year before. Results for 2003 excluded a loss of $18.5 million from discontinued operations. Net interest income declined 8.9% to $548.2 million. Net interest margin decreased to 1.73% from 1.93%, primarily due to a decline in the yield on the residential mortgage loan portfolio from refinancing activity. Provision for credit losses dropped to $2.5 million from $37.5 million in 2002. Total non-interest income grew 5.3% to $1.54 billion. Total non-interest expense rose 7.1% to $1.46 billion.

Prospects: Recent earnings are being driven by growth in trust fees, resulting from significant increases in assets under administration and assets under management. Also, earnings continue to benefit from the improved credit quality of Co.'s loan portfolio, reflecting a reduction in reserve for credit losses, combined with continued effective expense control. Meanwhile, strategic steps taken in 2003 aimed at reducing operating costs and positioning Co. for improved profitability, coupled with stronger economic and equity market conditions, should provide a solid foundation for continued growth in the coming year.

Financial Data

(US$ in Thousands)	12/31/2003	12/31/2002	12/31/2001	12/31/2000	12/31/1999	12/31/1998	12/31/1997	12/31/1996
Earnings Per Share	1.89	1.97	2.11	2.08	1.74	1.52	1.33	1.10
Tang. Book Val. Per Share	13.88	13.04	11.97	10.53	9.24	8.18	7.26	6.40
Dividends Per Share	7.000	0.680	0.635	0.560	0.495	0.435	0.375	0.323
Dividend Payout %	37.03	34.51	30.09	26.92	28.48	28.62	28.20	29.36
Income Statement								
Total Interest Income	1,055,700	1,238,300	1,681,500	2,011,100	1,568,600	1,503,100	1,332,800	1,151,500
Total Interest Expense	507,500	636,500	1,086,200	1,442,500	1,049,800	1,025,900	894,600	763,200
Net Interest Income	548,200	601,800	595,300	568,600	518,800	477,200	438,200	388,300
Provision for Loan Losses	2,500	37,500	66,500	24,000	12,500	9,000	9,000	12,000
Non-Interest Income	1,542,200	1,536,800	1,580,000	1,537,000	1,235,000	1,071,600	934,500	777,900
Non-Interest Expense	1,456,800	1,432,100	1,376,900	1,351,500	1,125,000	997,100	891,800	766,800
Income Before Taxes	613,300	669,000	731,900	730,100	616,500	542,700	471,900	387,400
Income from Cont Ops	423,300	...	...	...	...	...	...	...
Net Income	404,800	447,100	487,500	485,100	405,000	353,900	309,400	258,800
Average Shs. Outstg.	224,067	225,834	228,971	230,613	229,874	229,734	229,322	230,934
Balance Sheet								
Cash & Due from Banks	1,595,900	2,672,200	2,592,300	2,287,800	1,977,900	2,366,000	1,738,900	1,292,500
Securities Avail. for Sale	8,422,400	5,681,200	5,648,600	6,477,800	5,480,000	5,375,200	3,733,000	4,311,700
Net Loans & Leases	17,664,600	17,902,600	17,818,300	17,981,700	15,223,600	13,500,100	12,440,600	10,789,100
Total Assets	41,450,200	39,478,200	39,664,500	36,022,300	28,708,200	27,870,000	25,315,100	21,608,300
Total Deposits	26,270,000	26,062,100	25,019,300	22,827,900	21,371,000	18,202,700	16,360,000	13,796,200
Long-Term Obligations	1,490,900	1,483,600	1,484,500	1,405,700	1,426,900	1,425,600	1,491,900	732,800
Total Liabilities	38,394,900	36,478,400	36,891,000	33,560,100	26,533,500	25,929,700	23,576,400	20,064,200
Net Stockholders' Equity	3,055,300	2,999,800	2,773,500	2,462,200	2,174,700	1,940,300	1,739,000	1,544,100
Shares Outstanding	220,118	220,800	221,647	222,232	222,161	222,430	222,734	222,496
Statistical Record								
Return on Equity %	13.27	14.90	17.57	19.70	18.62	18.23	17.79	16.76
Return on Assets %	0.97	1.13	1.22	1.34	1.41	1.26	1.22	1.19
Equity/Assets %	7.37	7.59	6.99	6.83	7.57	6.96	6.86	7.14
Non-Int. Exp./Tot. Inc. %	56.07	51.60	42.21	38.09	40.12	38.72	39.33	39.74
Price Range	48.02-28.27	62.02-30.74	81.30-45.25	90.19-47.19	53.83-40.44	43.81-27.88	35.19-17.38	18.75-12.41
P/E Ratio	25.41-14.96	31.48-15.60	38.53-21.45	43.36-22.69	30.94-23.24	28.82-18.34	26.46-13.06	17.05-11.28
Average Yield %	1.72	1.47	0.99	0.76	1.06	1.15	1.41	2.06

Address: 50 South La Salle Street, Chicago, IL 60675 **Telephone:** (312) 630-6000 **Web Site:** www.northerntrust.com	Officers: William A. Osborn - Chmn., C.E.O., Pres., Perry R. Pero - Vice-Chmn., Corp. Risk Management	Investor Contact: (312) 444-7811 **Institutional Holding** **No of Institutions:** 10 **Shares:** 1,138,485 **% Held:** -

NUCOR CORP.

Exchange	Symbol	Price	52Wk Range	Yield	P/E
NYS	NUE	$61.48 (3/31/2004)	65.48-38.21	1.37	76.85

*7 Year Price Score 98.8   *NYSE Composite Index=100   *12 Month Price Score 103.8

Interim Earnings (Per Share)

Qtr.	Apr	Jul	Sep	Dec
2000	0.94	0.98	0.85	1.03
2001	0.42	1.92	0.26	(1.15)
2002	0.26	0.76	0.50	0.55
2003	0.23	0.11	0.20	0.26

Interim Dividends (Per Share)

Amt	Decl	Ex	Rec	Pay
0.20Q	6/3/2003	6/26/2003	6/30/2003	8/11/2003
0.20Q	9/3/2003	9/26/2003	9/30/2003	11/11/2003
0.20Q	12/3/2003	12/29/2003	12/31/2003	2/11/2004
0.21Q	2/25/2004	3/29/2004	3/31/2004	5/11/2004

Indicated Div: $0.84

Valuation Analysis

Forecast P/E	19.29	Trailing P/E	76.85
Market Cap	$4.8 Billion	Book Value	2.3 Billion
Price/Book	1.87	Price/Sales	0.70

Dividend Achiever Status

Rank	45	10 Year Growth Rate	17.69%
Total Years of Dividend Growth	31		

Business Summary: Metal Works (MIC: 11.3 SIC: 3312 NAIC:331111)

Nucor is engaged in the manufacture and sale of steel and steel products. Co.'s principal products from the steel mills segment are hot- and cold-rolled steel, while the steel products segment produces steel joists and joist girders, steel deck, cold finished steel, steel fasteners, metal building systems and light gauge steel framing. Steel joists and hoist girders, and steel deck are sold to general contractors and fabricators domestically. Cold finished steel and steel fasteners are sold primarily to distributors and manufacturers, and hot-rolled steel and cold-rolled steel are sold primarily to steel services centers, fabricators and manufacturers in the U.S.

Recent Developments: For the year ended Dec 31 2003, net income dropped 61.3% to $62.8 million compared with $162.1 million in 2002. The decline in earnings was primarily attributed to the substantial rise in the prices of scrap steel and other raw materials. Co.'s average scrap cost per ton purchased increased $65.00 year-over-year. Net sales advanced 30.5% to $6.27 billion from $4.80 billion a year earlier due to growth in total shipments to outside customers, reflecting the additional production capacity obtained from the acquisitions of the assets of Trico and Birmingham Steel in 2002. Average sales price per ton increased less than 1.0% to $359.00.

Prospects: In the near term, Co. expects high scrap costs will adversely affect results, but higher average selling prices should provide increased margins. Co. expects earnings for the first quarter of 2004 to range from $0.40 to $0.60 per share. Longer term, Co. anticipates improved profitability as 2004 progresses, provided economic conditions continue to recover. Also, Co. expects to obtain additional capacity through expansions at its existing steel mills and future acquisitions. Capital expenditures are projected to increase 7.0% to approximately $230.0 million in 2004 from a year earlier.

Financial Data

(US$ in Thousands)	12/31/2003	12/31/2002	12/31/2001	12/31/2000	12/31/1999	12/31/1998	12/31/1997	12/31/1996
Earnings Per Share	0.80	2.07	1.45	3.80	2.80	3.00	3.35	2.82
Cash Flow Per Share	6.30	6.35	6.36	10.01	6.92	7.30	6.56	5.13
Tang. Book Val. Per Share	29.80	29.71	28.32	27.46	25.92	23.72	21.32	18.32
Dividends Per Share	0.790	0.740	0.660	0.580	0.510	0.460	0.380	0.310
Dividend Payout %	98.75	35.74	45.51	15.26	18.21	15.33	11.34	10.99
Income Statement								
Total Revenues	6,265,823	4,801,777	4,139,249	4,586,146	4,009,346	4,151,232	4,184,498	3,647,030
Total Indirect Exp.	165,369	175,588	138,559	183,176	154,774	147,973	145,410	120,387
Depreciation & Amort.	364,112	307,101	289,063	259,365	256,637	253,119	218,764	182,233
Operating Income	103,907	293,911	180,386	477,492	374,094	411,476	460,147	387,485
Net Interest Inc./(Exp.)	(24,627)	(14,286)	(6,525)	816	5,095	3,832	35	284
Income Taxes	4,096	67,973	60,900	167,400	134,600	151,600	165,700	139,600
Net Income	62,781	162,080	112,961	310,908	244,589	263,709	294,482	248,169
Average Shs. Outstg.	78,416	78,249	77,783	81,777	87,287	87,878	87,922	87,686
Balance Sheet								
Cash & Cash Equivalents	350,332	219,005	462,349	490,576	572,185	308,696	283,381	104,401
Total Current Assets	1,620,635	1,424,139	1,373,666	1,381,447	1,538,509	1,129,467	1,125,508	828,381
Total Assets	4,492,353	4,381,001	3,759,348	3,721,788	3,729,848	3,226,546	2,984,383	2,619,535
Total Current Liabilities	629,595	591,536	484,159	558,068	531,031	486,897	524,454	465,653
Long-Term Obligations	903,550	878,550	460,450	460,450	390,450	215,450	167,950	152,600
Net Stockholders' Equity	2,342,078	2,322,989	2,201,460	2,130,952	2,262,248	2,072,552	1,876,426	1,609,290
Net Working Capital	990,965	832,603	889,507	823,378	1,007,478	642,570	601,055	362,728
Shares Outstanding	78,590	78,180	77,707	77,582	87,247	87,352	87,996	87,796
Statistical Record								
Operating Profit Margin %	1.65	6.12	4.35	10.41	9.33	9.91	10.99	10.62
Return on Equity %	2.68	6.97	5.13	14.59	10.81	12.72	15.69	15.42
Return on Assets %	1.39	3.69	3.00	8.35	6.55	8.17	9.86	9.47
Debt/Total Assets %	20.11	20.05	12.24	12.37	10.46	6.67	5.62	5.82
Price Range	57.90-35.98	69.15-37.90	56.00-34.50	55.94-30.00	60.69-41.81	60.06-35.94	62.31-45.25	62.50-45.13
P/E Ratio	72.38-44.97	33.41-18.31	38.62-23.79	14.72-7.89	21.67-14.93	20.02-11.98	18.60-13.51	22.16-16.00
Average Yield %	1.68	1.37	1.43	1.43	1.04	0.98	0.71	0.59

Address: 2100 Rexford Road, Charlotte, NC 28211	**Officers:** Peter C. Browning – Chmn., Daniel R. DiMicco – Vice-Chmn., Pres., C.E.O.	**Investor Contact:** (704) 366-7000
Telephone: (704) 366-7000	**Transfer Agents:** American Stock Transfer & Trust Company, New York, NY	**Institutional Holding**
Web Site: www.nucor.com		**No of Institutions:** 27
		Shares: 216,632 **% Held:** –

NUVEEN INVESTMENTS INC

Exchange	Symbol	Price	52Wk Range	Yield	P/E
NYS	JNC	$27.86 (3/31/2004)	30.30–22.38	2.15	18.57

*7 Year Price Score 149.8   *NYSE Composite Index=100   *12 Month Price Score 92.4

Interim Earnings (Per Share)

Qtr.	Mar	Jun	Sep	Dec
2000	0.26	0.26	0.26	0.26
2001	0.27	0.28	0.28	0.30
2002	0.30	0.31	0.33	0.35
2003	0.34	0.36	0.39	0.41

Interim Dividends (Per Share)

Amt	Decl	Ex	Rec	Pay
0.13Q	5/16/2003	5/29/2003	6/2/2003	6/16/2003
0.15Q	8/7/2003	8/28/2003	9/2/2003	9/15/2003
0.15Q	11/7/2003	11/26/2003	12/1/2003	12/15/2003
0.15Q	2/5/2004	2/26/2004	3/1/2004	3/15/2004

Indicated Div: $0.60

Valuation Analysis

Forecast P/E	N/A	Trailing P/E	18.57
Market Cap	$2.6 Billion	Book Value	464.0 Million
Price/Book	1.10	Price/Sales	1.13

Dividend Achiever Status

Rank	130	10 Year Growth Rate	11.61%
Total Years of Dividend Growth			11

Business Summary: Finance Intermediaries &Services (MIC: 8.7 SIC: 6211 NAIC:523110)

Nuveen Investments is engaged in asset management and related research, as well as the development, marketing and distribution of investment products and services primarily targeted at affluent, high net–worth individuals and institutional markets. As of Dec 31 2003, total assets under management was approximately $95.36 billion. Co. distributes closed–end exchange–traded funds, mutual funds and defined portfolios through unaffiliated intermediary firms, including broker/dealers, commercial banks, affiliates of insurance providers, financial planners, accountants, consultants and investment advisors. The St. Paul Companies, Inc. owned about 79.0% of Co.'s common stock as of Mar 15 2004.

Recent Developments: For the year ended Dec 31 2003, net income rose 14.1% to $144.0 million compared with $126.2 million a year earlier. Total operating revenues advanced 14.0% to $452.0 million from $396.4 million the previous year. Investment advisory fees from assets under management rose 13.9% to $404.8 million, while performance fees/other revenue climbed 31.5% to $38.0 million. Product distribution revenues slid 23.8% to $9.2 million. Operating income grew 13.5% to $240.5 million from $211.9 million before. As of Dec 31 2003, total assets under management were $95.36 billion, up 19.6% versus $79.72 billion at Dec 31 2002.

Prospects: Results are being positively affected by the recent strength in the equity markets. Co. is enjoying strong sales of both equity and fixed income products and positive net flows into its managed accounts, closed–end exchange–traded funds, and mutual funds. Demand continues to be strong for municipal as well as high–quality taxable income–oriented investments. Meanwhile, Co. continues to broaden its asset base beyond its traditional municipal bond offerings and into equity–based investments that can help provide higher long–term returns through improved portfolio diversification.

Financial Data

US$ in Thousands)	12/31/2003	12/31/2002	12/31/2001	12/31/2000	12/31/1999	12/31/1998	12/31/1997	12/31/1996
Earnings Per Share	1.50	1.29	1.13	1.04	0.95	0.81	0.71	0.65
Cash Flow Per Share	2.18	2.24	2.04	1.16	1.27	1.25	1.55	1.58
Tang. Book Val. Per Share	N.M	N.M	0.0083	2.40	1.58	1.07	0.66	2.73
Dividends Per Share	0.560	0.500	0.460	0.400	0.370	0.320	0.290	0.260
Dividend Payout %	37.33	38.75	41.29	38.85	39.64	40.32	41.31	39.59
Income Statement								
Total Revenues	452,028	396,447	371,103	358,393	338,760	307,535	268,927	232,452
Total Indirect Exp.	211,569	184,602	182,348	190,275	188,689	172,395	150,443	117,275
Depreciation & Amort.	5,208	3,803	9,409	8,005	14,298	14,093	10,865	6,708
Operating Income	240,459	211,845	188,755	168,118	150,071	137,737	122,170	117,502
Net Interest Inc./(Exp.)	(7,435)	(4,892)	(3,798)	(3,025)	(2,994)	...	...	...
Income Taxes	91,292	80,675	74,856	70,700	63,701	54,092	47,990	44,973
Net Income	143,996	126,185	114,698	106,666	97,310	83,645	74,180	72,529
Average Shs. Outstg.	95,944	98,042	101,688	101,979	102,429	103,281	104,706	110,667
Balance Sheet								
Cash & Cash Equivalents	161,584	70,480	83,659	72,351	27,422	77,898	106,476	178,183
Total Current Assets	226,659	138,375	149,999	199,778	150,772	124,731	147,193	213,745
Total Assets	954,393	841,042	696,611	576,039	540,965	467,961	492,232	355,251
Total Current Liabilities	33,242	...	739	4,172	296	17,413	84,500	...
Long–Term Obligations	302,113	305,000	183,000	...	...	...	...	...
Net Stockholders' Equity	463,953	385,763	400,640	388,828	301,062	259,108	228,120	271,894
Net Working Capital	193,417	138,375	149,260	195,606	150,476	107,318	62,693	213,745
Shares Outstanding	92,506	92,726	95,142	93,941	93,189	94,068	95,347	99,357
Statistical Record								
Operating Profit Margin %	53.19	53.43	50.86	46.90	44.30	44.78	45.42	50.54
Return on Equity %	31.03	32.71	28.23	24.58	28.11	27.50	27.16	26.67
Return on Assets %	15.08	15.00	16.46	18.51	17.98	17.87	15.07	20.41
Debt/Total Assets %	31.65	36.26	26.27	...	...	...	...	...
Price Range	30.30–19.99	30.79–20.18	26.87–16.83	19.17–11.19	14.46–11.50	13.83–10.52	12.58–8.79	9.50–7.96
P/E Ratio	20.20–13.33	23.86–15.64	23.77–14.90	18.43–10.76	15.22–12.11	17.08–12.99	17.72–12.38	14.62–12.24
Average Yield %	2.18	1.93	2.23	2.82	2.83	2.65	2.76	3.04

Address: 333 West Wacker Drive, Chicago, IL 60606 **Telephone:** (312) 917-7700 **Web Site:** www.nuveen.com	**Officers:** Timothy R. Schwertfeger – Chmn., C.E.O., John P. Amboian – Pres. **Transfer Agents:**The Bank of New York, New York, NY	**Institutional Holding** **No of Institutions:** 97 **Shares:** 13,046,264 **% Held:** 14

OLD NATIONAL BANCORP

Exchange	Symbol	Price	52Wk Range	Yield	P/E
NYS	ONB	$22.60 (3/31/2004)	22.88-20.52	3.36	21.52

*7 Year Price Score N/A *NYSE Composite Index=100 *12 Month Price Score 86.9

Interim Earnings (Per Share)

Qtr.	Mar	Jun	Sep	Dec
2000	0.13	0.34	0.19	0.22
2001	0.31	0.28	0.38	0.38
2002	0.41	0.41	0.51	0.42
2003	0.39	0.40	0.17	0.09

Interim Dividends (Per Share)

Amt	Decl	Ex	Rec	Pay
0.181Q	7/24/2003	8/28/2003	9/2/2003	9/16/200
0.181Q	10/23/2003	11/26/2003	12/1/2003	12/15/200
5%	12/5/2003	1/2/2004	1/6/2004	1/27/2004
0.19Q	1/22/2004	2/26/2004	3/1/2004	3/15/2004

Indicated Div: $0.76 (Div. Reinv. Plan)

Valuation Analysis

Forecast P/E	N/A	Trailing P/E	21.52
Market Cap	$1.4 Billion	Book Value	715.5 Million
Price/Book	2.03	Price/Sales	2.19

Dividend Achiever Status

Rank	197	10 Year Growth Rate	8.26%
Total Years of Dividend Growth		20	

Business Summary: Commercial Banking (MIC: 8.1 SIC: 6021 NAIC:522110)

Old National Bancorp, with total assets of $9.35 billion as of Dec 31 2003, is a financial holding company headquartered in Evansville, IN with banking activity in Indiana, Illinois, Kentucky, Tennessee, and Ohio. As of Dec 31 2003, Co. operated over 120 banking office serving customers in both urban and rural markets. Co.'s banking centers provide a wide range of financial services, such as commercial real estate, and consumer loans; lease financing; checking, savings, time deposits; and letters of credit. Co.'s non-bank affiliates provide additional financial or support services incidental to its operations, including issuance and reinsurance of credit life services.

Recent Developments: For the year ended Dec 31 2003, net income declined 40.3% to $70.4 million from $117.9 million the year before. Results for 2003 and 2002 included net securities gains of $23.6 million and $12.4 million, respectively. Results for 2002 also included an after-tax gain on branch sales of $8.3 million. Net interest income slipped 6.0% to $272.0 million. Net interest margin fell to 3.37% from 3.65% in 2002 due to a shift from loans into lower-yielding securities and lower levels of interest rates. Provision for loan losses advanced to $85.0 million from $33.5 million in 2002. Total non-interest income climbed 24.4% to $192.1 million, while total non-interest expense rose 16.2% to $299.7 million.

Prospects: Commercial loan demand continues to be weak in Co.'s core markets. Although the national economy has shown recent signs of recovery, the heavy manufacturing and industrial based economy in Co.'s market has been slower to respond. As a result, Co. is refocusing its commercial lending activities toward a greater emphasis on small business lending and on the newer markets of Indianapolis, Louisville and St. Louis. Separately, Co. expects improved credit quality in the near future as it has completely redesigned its processes and controls and have implemented significant changes in its overall credit risk management structure.

Financial Data

(US$ in Thousands)	12/31/2003	12/31/2002	12/31/2001	12/31/2000	12/31/1999	12/31/1998	12/31/1997	12/31/1996
Earnings Per Share	1.05	1.75	1.35	0.88	1.37	1.25	1.05	1.01
Tang. Book Val. Per Share	7.95	8.82	9.47	8.97	8.57	9.00	9.07	8.11
Dividends Per Share	0.720	0.650	0.580	0.550	0.510	0.450	0.430	0.410
Dividend Payout %	68.93	37.26	43.46	62.87	37.82	36.35	41.32	40.94
Income Statement								
Total Interest Income	469,748	547,383	629,707	638,275	488,923	437,909	429,446	394,413
Total Interest Expense	197,741	257,954	338,408	368,404	250,536	223,059	210,208	190,631
Net Interest Income	272,007	289,429	291,299	269,871	238,387	214,850	219,238	203,782
Provision for Loan Losses	85,000	33,500	28,700	29,803	11,489	11,420	26,965	11,012
Non-Interest Income	192,149	154,497	112,967	101,713	67,508	54,557	47,090	44,801
Non-Interest Expense	299,716	257,845	254,812	265,537	185,564	158,125	154,364	152,320
Income Before Taxes	79,440	152,581	120,754	76,244	108,842	99,862	84,999	85,251
Income from Cont Ops	...	118,638	...	...	82,694	71,718	...	...
Net Income	70,413	117,932	93,044	61,696	86,795	61,864	60,660	60,175
Average Shs. Outstg.	66,832	67,308	68,607	69,689	60,623	57,838	58,879	60,883
Balance Sheet								
Cash & Due from Banks	222,385	223,007	224,663	202,600	169,184	150,884	147,337	180,405
Securities Avail. for Sale	2,720,844	3,091,017	2,320,888	1,825,112	1,678,651	1,596,882	1,566,976	1,514,649
Net Loans & Leases	5,465,546	5,681,893	6,058,613	6,274,480	4,780,888	4,112,804	3,683,969	3,479,247
Total Assets	9,353,896	9,612,556	9,080,473	8,767,748	6,982,932	6,165,968	5,688,215	5,366,591
Total Deposits	6,493,092	6,439,280	6,616,440	6,583,906	5,071,294	4,443,472	4,298,730	4,268,024
Long-Term Obligations	1,624,092	1,247,857	1,000,046	863,165	662,973	629,868	388,832	74,564
Total Liabilities	8,638,406	8,871,846	8,441,238	8,141,407	6,490,188	5,671,388	5,211,012	4,908,065
Net Stockholders' Equity	715,490	740,710	639,235	626,341	492,744	494,580	477,203	458,526
Shares Outstanding	66,575	67,048	67,444	69,817	57,480	54,917	52,564	56,519
Statistical Record								
Return on Equity %	9.84	16.01	14.55	9.85	16.78	14.50	12.71	13.12
Return on Assets %	0.75	1.23	1.02	0.70	1.18	1.16	1.06	1.12
Equity/Assets %	7.64	7.70	7.03	7.14	7.05	8.02	8.38	8.54
Non-Int. Exp./Tot. Inc. %	45.28	36.73	34.31	35.88	33.34	32.10	32.39	34.68
Price Range	22.82-20.18	24.04-20.69	...	...	...	...	...	...
P/E Ratio	21.73-19.22	13.74-11.82	...	...	...	...	...	...
Average Yield %	3.33	2.91	N/A	N/A	N/A	N/A	N/A	N/A

Address: 420 Main Street, Evansville, IN 47708	Officers: James A. Risinger - Chmn., C.E.O., Michael R. Hinton - Pres., C.O.O.	Investor Contact: 812-464-1366
Telephone: (812) 464-1200	Transfer Agents: Old National Bancorp, Evansville, IN	Institutional Holding No of Institutions: 32
Web Site: www.oldnational.com		Shares: 1,181,632 % Held: -

OLD REPUBLIC INTERNATIONAL CORP.

Exchange	Symbol	Price	52Wk Range	Yield	P/E
NYS	ORI	$24.56 (3/31/2004)	27.19-18.31	1.84	9.78

*7 Year Price Score 132.8 *NYSE Composite Index=100 *12 Month Price Score 102.4

Interim Earnings (Per Share)

Qtr.	Mar	Jun	Sep	Dec
2000	0.30	0.38	0.44	0.52
2001	0.46	0.50	0.46	0.50
2002	0.52	0.58	0.52	0.53
2003	0.57	0.66	0.65	0.63

Interim Dividends (Per Share)

Amt	Decl	Ex	Rec	Pay
0.113Q	5/15/2003	6/4/2003	6/6/2003	6/16/2003
0.667Q	12/4/2003	12/11/2003	12/15/2003	12/26/2003
50%	12/4/2003	12/15/2003	12/15/2003	12/30/2003
0.113Q	...	3/3/2004	3/5/2004	3/15/2004

Indicated Div: $0.452

Valuation Analysis

Forecast P/E	8.64
Market Cap	$3.0 Billion
Price/Book	1.92

Trailing P/E	9.78
Book Value	3.6 Billion
Price/Sales	2.08

Dividend Achiever Status

Rank	103	10 Year Growth Rate 13.19%
Total Years of Dividend Growth		22

Business Summary: Insurance (MIC: 8.2 SIC: 6351 NAIC:524130)

Old Republic International is an insurance holding company. Through its general insurance group, Co. assumes risks and provides related risk management and marketing services pertaining to a large variety of property and liability commercial insurance coverages. Through its mortgage guaranty group, Co. protects mortgage lenders and investors from default related losses on residential mortgage loans. Through its title insurance group, Co. issues policies to real estate purchasers and investors. Co.'s life insurance group markets and writes consumer credit life and disability insurance primarily through automobile dealers.

Recent Developments: For the year ended Dec 31 2003, net income increased 17.0% to $459.8 million from $392.9 million the prior year. Co. attributed this increase to greater underwriting and service income in Co.'s three largest segments. Total revenues grew 19.2% to $3.29 billion. Revenues for 2003 and 2002 included realized investment gains of $19.3 million and $13.9 million, respectively. By segment, operating income for the general insurance group grew 42.2% to $259.0 million. Operating income for the mortgage guaranty group rose 3.2% to $276.4 million, while operating income for the title group climbed 32.8% to $129.8 million. Operating income for the life and health group slid 32.9% to $4.3 million.

Prospects: Going forward, Co.'s property and liability insurance business, representing about 48.0% of total revenues in 2003, should continue to contribute to growth through new and existing business. Also, underwriting continues to be Co.'s strong suit, and its ongoing emphasis to conservative underwriting practices should enable Co. to keep its loss development down. Meanwhile, mortgage guaranty operations should benefit from relatively low interest rates and reasonably stable operating costs. However, should interest rates begin to rise, refinancing activity could subside and profits from Co.'s title insurance business will likely trend lower.

Financial Data

(US$ in Millions)	12/31/2003	12/31/2002	12/31/2001	12/31/2000	12/31/1999	12/31/1998	12/31/1997	12/31/1996
Earnings Per Share	2.51	2.15	1.92	1.64	1.16	1.55	1.40	1.08
Tang. Book Val. Per Share	19.26	16.99	15.18	13.38	9.35	11.51	10.39	9.71
Dividends Per Share	1.110	0.420	0.390	0.360	0.320	0.250	0.220	0.180
Dividend Payout %	44.35	19.50	20.48	22.26	27.99	16.59	15.87	17.07
Income Statement								
Total Premium Income	2,582	2,135	1,787	1,550	1,567	1,568	1,465	1,360
Net Investment Income	279	273	275	274	263	273	271	261
Other Income	424	348	312	246	272	330	227	183
Total Revenues	3,286	2,756	2,373	2,070	2,102	2,172	1,963	1,804
Inc. Before Inc. Taxes	680	561	504	426	317	467	426	342
Income Taxes	220	168	160	131	93	146	129	109
Eqty Earns/Minority Int.	0	0	3	2	3	3	1	1
Income from Cont Ops	460	393	...	297	...	324	298	235
Net Income	460	393	347	298	227	324	298	230
Average Shs. Outstg.	183	182	180	180	194	208	212	213
Balance Sheet								
Cash & Cash Equivalents	451	291	337	411	294	401	355	301
Premiums Due	2,249	2,005	1,835	1,660	1,626	1,572	1,634	1,678
Invst. Assets: Total	6,720	6,051	5,473	5,039	4,739	4,854	4,720	4,414
Total Assets	9,712	8,715	7,920	7,281	6,938	7,019	6,923	6,656
Long–Term Obligations	138	142	159	238	208	145	143	154
Net Stockholders' Equity	3,554	3,156	2,784	2,439	2,199	2,305	2,153	1,882
Shares Outstanding	184	185	183	182	235	200	207	195
Statistical Record								
Return on Equity %	12.94	12.45	12.46	12.19	10.31	14.04	13.82	12.34
Return on Assets %	4.73	4.50	4.38	4.08	3.26	4.61	4.29	3.52
Price Range	25.79-16.53	23.15-16.85	20.04-15.10	21.33-7.17	15.04-8.25	21.25-12.00	17.75-10.94	12.28-9.04
P/E Ratio	10.27-6.58	10.77-7.84	10.44-7.86	13.01-4.37	12.97-7.11	13.71-7.74	12.68-7.82	11.37-8.37
Average Yield %	5.15	2.06	2.14	2.81	2.82	1.45	1.55	1.74

Address: 307 North Michigan Avenue, Chicago, IL 60601 Telephone: (312) 346–8100 Web Site: www.oldrepublic.com	Officers: Aldo C. Zucaro – Chmn., Pres., C.E.O., John S. Adams – Sr. V.P., C.F.O. Transfer Agents:EquiServe, First Chicago Trust Division, Jersey City, NJ	Institutional Holding No of Institutions: 10 Shares: 539,906 % Held: –

197

OTTER TAIL CORP.

Exchange	Symbol	Price	52Wk Range	Yield	P/E
NMS	OTTR	$26.42 (3/31/2004)	28.49-25.88	4.16	16.11

*7 Year Price Score 119.1 *NYSE Composite Index=100 *12 Month Price Score 89.3

Interim Earnings (Per Share)

Qtr.	Mar	Jun	Sep	Dec
2000	0.42	0.36	0.42	0.40
2001	0.45	0.34	0.43	0.46
2002	0.40	0.41	0.50	0.48
2003	0.38	0.32	0.46	0.35

Interim Dividends (Per Share)

Amt	Decl	Ex	Rec	Pay
0.27Q	4/14/2003	5/13/2003	5/15/2003	6/10/2003
0.27Q	7/28/2003	8/13/2003	8/15/2003	9/10/2003
0.27Q	11/3/2003	11/12/2003	11/14/2003	12/10/2003
0.275Q	2/2/2004	2/11/2004	2/13/2004	3/10/2004

Indicated Div: $1.10 (Div. Reinv. Plan)

Valuation Analysis

Forecast P/E	16.13	Trailing P/E	16.11
Market Cap	$676.1 Million	Book Value	323.4 Million
Price/Book	N/A	Price/Sales	N/A

Dividend Achiever Status

Rank	286	10 Year Growth Rate	2.54%
Total Years of Dividend Growth	28		

Business Summary: Electricity (MIC: 7.1 SIC: 4911 NAIC:221121)

Otter Tail is an operating electric utility engaged in the production, transmission and distribution and sale of electric energy in 48 states and 6 Canadian provinces. The Electric segment includes the production, transmission, distribution and sale of electric energy in Minnesota, North Dakota and South Dakota. The Manufacturing segment includes the production of waterfront equipment, wind towers, custom plastic pallets, and material and handling trays. The Health Services segment consists of the sale of diagnostic medical and patient monitoring equipment. The Plastics segment produces polyvinyl chloride pipe and polyethylene pipe.

Recent Developments: For the twelve months ended Dec 31 2003, net income declined 14.0% to $39.7 million compared with $46.1 million in 2002. The decline in earnings was attributed to continued weakness in plastics, manufacturing and other business operations resulting mostly from soft economic conditions and pricing pressures. Operating revenues rose 16.5% to $753.2 million from $646.3 million the year before. Electric revenues benefited from the recovery of increased fuel and purchased power costs, and increases in steam sales and transmission charges. Operating income decreased 13.6% to $71.2 million compared with $82.3 million a year earlier.

Prospects: Co. anticipates diluted earnings per share for full-year 2004 in the range of $1.55 to $1.70. Co. expects the electric segment to have a strong year with earnings returning to historical levels. The increase in projected earnings for 2004 is expected to stem from the non-electric operations through internal growth and acquisitions. However, the uncertainty of economic conditions, the production tax credit in the wind energy business, the effect of steel pricing and a potential rise in interest rates may negatively affect Co.'s earnings guidance for 2004. Meanwhile, Co. anticipates investing about $41.0 million in capital expenditures during 2004 in addition to future acquisitions.

Financial Data

(US$ in Thousands)	12/31/2003	12/31/2002	12/31/2001	12/31/2000	12/31/1999	12/31/1998	12/31/1997	12/31/1996
Earnings Per Share	1.51	1.79	1.68	1.60	1.79	1.20	1.29	1.23
Cash Flow Per Share	2.97	3.02	3.12	2.51	3.28	2.71	2.98	3.00
Tang. Book Val. Per Share	9.88	9.50	9.30	9.05	9.32	8.58	8.06	7.63
Dividends Per Share	1.080	1.060	1.040	1.020	0.990	0.960	0.930	0.900
Dividend Payout %	71.52	59.21	61.90	63.75	55.30	79.66	72.09	73.17
Income Statement								
Total Revenues	753,239	710,116	654,132	559,445	464,577	431,078	394,279	361,739
Total Indirect Exp.	55,560	52,036	51,564	38,624	35,598	36,537	36,401	34,429
Depreciation & Amort.	45,962	42,613	42,100	28,648	25,420	25,813	335,246	22,904
Operating Income	71,160	81,982	77,484	72,490	67,366	57,230	59,033	58,226
Net Interest Inc./(Exp.)	(17,866)	(17,850)	(15,991)	(16,583)	(14,771)	(15,566)	(18,519)	(16,601)
Income Taxes	14,930	20,061	20,083	17,515	23,915	15,140	14,308	14,040
Income from Cont Ops	...	...	...	...	...	30,701	...	...
Net Income	39,656	46,128	43,603	40,224	44,977	34,520	32,346	29,955
Average Shs. Outstg.	25,826	25,397	24,832	23,928	23,831	23,596	23,278	22,364
Balance Sheet								
Net Property	633,325	587,886	542,977	515,929	502,956	500,186	509,766	519,838
Total Assets	986,423	878,736	782,541	722,115	680,788	655,612	655,441	662,287
Long-Term Obligations	265,193	258,229	227,360	191,493	176,437	181,046	189,973	160,492
Net Stockholders' Equity	349,382	328,965	294,808	292,879	279,193	245,907	230,987	214,057
Shares Outstanding	25,723	25,592	24,653	23,852	23,849	23,760	23,462	22,438
Statistical Record								
Operating Profit Margin %	9.44	11.54	11.84	12.95	14.50	13.27	14.97	16.09
Net Inc./Net Property %	6.26	7.84	8.03	7.79	8.94	6.90	6.34	5.76
Net Inc./Tot. Capital %	5.53	6.77	7.17	7.05	8.27	6.44	6.02	6.10
Return on Equity %	11.35	14.02	14.79	13.73	16.10	12.48	14.00	13.99
Accum. Depr./Gross Prop. %	41.74	44.31	44.86	44.29	43.46	42.53	40.75	38.60
Price Range	28.50-24.00	34.12-23.80	30.69-23.88	29.00-17.81	22.63-17.00	20.78-15.63	18.94-15.13	19.25-16.00
P/E Ratio	18.87-15.89	19.06-13.30	18.27-14.21	18.13-11.13	12.64-9.50	17.32-13.02	14.68-11.72	15.65-13.0
Average Yield %	4.02	3.70	3.76	4.72	4.91	5.16	5.63	5.2

Address: 215 South Cascade Street, Fergus Falls, MN 56538-0496 **Telephone:** (218) 739-8479 **Web Site:** www.ottertail.com	**Officers:** John C. MacFarlane - Chmn., John C. MacFarlane - Pres., C.E.O.	**Investor Contact:** (800) 664 1259 **Institutional Holding** **No of Institutions:** 68 **Shares:** 5,508,010 **% Held:** 21%

PACIFIC CAPITAL BANCORP

Exchange	Symbol	Price	52Wk Range	Yield	P/E
NMS	PCBC	$39.67 (3/31/2004)	40.25-30.28	2.22	17.38

7 Year Price Score 148.8 *NYSE Composite Index=100 **12 Month Price Score 100.6

Interim Earnings (Per Share)

Qtr.	Mar	Jun	Sep	Dec
2000	0.60	0.35	0.18	0.31
2001	0.64	0.32	0.31	0.31
2002	0.75	0.43	0.50	0.46
2003	1.05	0.39	0.39	0.36

Interim Dividends (Per Share)

Amt	Decl	Ex	Rec	Pay
0.20Q	4/2/2003	4/17/2003	4/22/2003	5/15/2003
0.21Q	7/1/2003	7/18/2003	7/22/2003	8/12/2003
0.21Q	10/1/2003	10/17/2003	10/21/2003	11/12/2003
0.22Q	1/5/2004	1/15/2004	1/20/2004	2/10/2004

Indicated Div: $0.88

Valuation Analysis

Forecast P/E	N/A	Trailing P/E	17.38
Market Cap	$1.4 Billion	Book Value	389.9 Million
Price/Book	N/A	Price/Sales	N/A

Dividend Achiever Status

Rank	55	10 Year Growth Rate	16.75%
Total Years of Dividend Growth			34

Business Summary: Commercial Banking (MIC: 8.1 SIC: 6022 NAIC:522110)

Pacific Capital Bancorp is the parent of Pacific Capital Bank, N.A., a nationally chartered bank with four brands: Santa Barbara Bank and Trust, First National Bank of Central California, South Valley National Bank and San Benito Bank. The banks provide commercial banking services to households, professionals, and small-to medium-sized businesses. Co. also offers products related to income tax returns filed electronically. As of Dec 31 2003, Co. had assets of $4.86 billion and deposits of $3.85 billion. Pacific Capital Bank, N.A. is a 41-branch community bank network serving the California central coast counties of Monterey, Santa Cruz, San Benito, Santa Barbara, Ventura and Santa Clara.

Recent Developments: For the year ended Dec 31 2003, net income increased 1.2% to $75.7 million compared with $74.9 million in the previous year. Earnings for 2003 benefited from new deposit accounts and a 30.0% decline in non-performing loans. Net interest income rose 7.0% to $218.3 million from $203.9 million a year earlier. Total interest income grew 2.0% to $272.2 million, while total interest expense fell 14.1% to $53.9 million. Provision for credit losses decreased 7.3% to $18.3 million. Total non-interest income advanced 10.8% to $81.7 million from $73.8 million the year before. Total non-interest expense climbed 14.2% to $163.7 million. Return on average equity amounted to 19.44% versus 21.46% in 2002.

Prospects: Economic conditions are strengthening in Co.'s markets, and its efforts to capitalize on the growing number of quality lending opportunities is driving solid growth in its residential real estate and commercial lending portfolios. In addition, Co.'s new no-fee checking account is being well-received and is generating growth in new account openings. Looking ahead to 2004, Co. expects earnings to range from $2.39 to $2.51 per diluted share, before acquisitions. In March 2004, Co. acquired Pacific Crest Capital, Inc. for $136.1 million in cash. The acquisition is expected to add $0.10 per share to earnings in 2004, before acquisition costs, and between $0.14 and $0.17 per share in 2005.

Financial Data

(US$ in Thousands)	12/31/2003	12/31/2002	12/31/2001	12/31/2000	12/31/1999	12/31/1998	12/31/1997	12/31/1996
Earnings Per Share	2.19	2.14	1.58	1.44	1.34	0.90	0.96	0.76
Tang. Book Val. Per Share	10.77	9.74	9.32	8.39	7.16	6.62	5.81	5.31
Dividends Per Share	0.800	0.690	0.660	0.600	0.540	0.450	0.340	0.240
Dividend Payout %	36.52	32.24	41.70	41.45	40.22	50.41	35.65	32.03
Income Statement								
Total Interest Income	272,189	266,746	291,108	290,916	211,643	193,516	114,935	89,578
Total Interest Expense	53,933	62,799	97,226	110,526	6,556	3,343	43,205	35,049
Net Interest Income	218,256	203,947	193,882	180,390	205,087	190,173	71,730	54,529
Provision for Loan Losses	18,286	19,727	26,671	14,440	6,375	9,123	6,980	4,264
Non-Interest Income	81,745	73,784	65,726	49,388	41,618	35,972	25,144	18,942
Non-Interest Expense	163,702	143,288	143,150	131,957	110,389	103,710	60,105	46,589
Income Before Taxes	118,013	114,716	89,787	83,381	129,941	113,312	29,789	22,618
Income from Cont Ops	...	...	...	...	105,574	94,337	...	...
Net Income	75,671	74,851	56,111	51,456	44,274	29,567	20,136	15,665
Average Shs. Outstg.	34,562	34,990	35,518	35,478	33,053	32,595	20,778	20,359
Balance Sheet								
Cash & Due from Banks	150,010	151,540	136,457	176,274	121,500	114,206	67,799	51,181
Securities Avail. for Sale	1,317,962	803,429	699,076	669,631	528,426	596,996	286,998	141,679
Net Loans & Leases	3,131,329	2,965,999	2,750,220	2,481,979	1,953,193	1,553,485	860,440	667,595
Total Assets	4,859,630	4,219,213	3,960,929	3,677,625	2,879,282	2,649,418	1,592,386	1,301,320
Total Deposits	3,854,717	3,516,017	3,365,575	3,102,819	2,440,181	2,329,676	1,404,155	1,113,083
Long-Term Obligations	499,548	264,969	188,331	129,658	98,801	44,953	39,000	39,000
Total Liabilities	4,460,582	3,848,138	3,635,053	3,381,364	2,644,709	2,435,418	1,474,220	1,193,727
Net Stockholders' Equity	399,048	371,075	325,876	296,261	234,573	214,000	118,166	107,593
Shares Outstanding	33,963	34,550	34,942	35,307	32,738	32,278	20,322	20,234
Statistical Record								
Return on Equity %	18.96	20.17	17.21	17.36	45.00	44.08	17.04	14.55
Return on Assets %	1.55	1.77	1.41	1.39	3.66	3.56	1.26	1.20
Equity/Assets %	8.21	8.79	8.22	8.05	8.14	8.07	7.42	8.26
Non-Int. Exp./Tot. Inc. %	46.25	42.07	40.11	38.77	43.58	45.19	42.90	42.93
Price Range	38.22-25.37	29.00-20.50	23.10-19.08	23.06-17.58	25.92-15.47	24.75-16.59	18.19-10.36	10.78-7.41
P/E Ratio	17.45-11.58	13.55-9.58	14.62-12.07	16.02-12.21	19.34-11.54	27.50-18.44	18.95-10.79	14.19-9.75
Average Yield %	2.47	2.81	3.11	2.96	2.52	2.29	2.32	2.48

Address: 1021 Anacapa Street, Santa Barbara, CA 93101 **Telephone:** (805) 564-6300 **Web Site:** www.pcbancorp.com	**Officers:** David W. Spainhour – Chmn., D. Vernon Horton – Vice-Chmn.	**Investor Contact:**05 564-6298) **Institutional Holding** **No of Institutions:** 9 **Shares:** 336,050 **% Held:** –

PARK NATIONAL CORP. (NEWARK, OH)

Exchange	Symbol	Price	52Wk Range	Yield	P/E
ASE	PRK	$113.30 (3/31/2004)	120.0–95.55	3.11	18.07

*7 Year Price Score 120.9 *NYSE Composite Index=100 *12 Month Price Score 93.2

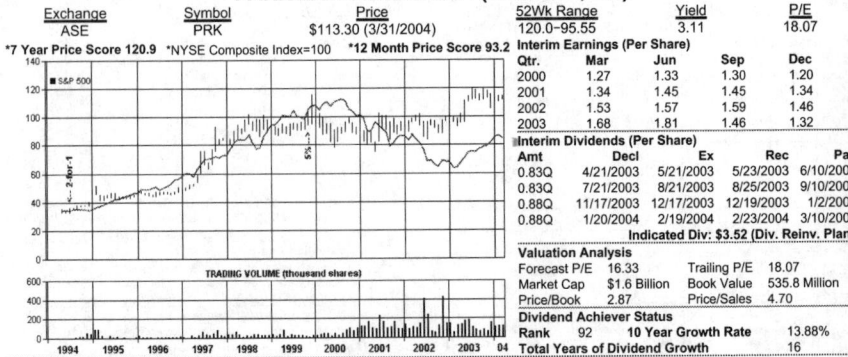

Interim Earnings (Per Share)

Qtr.	Mar	Jun	Sep	Dec
2000	1.27	1.33	1.30	1.20
2001	1.34	1.45	1.45	1.34
2002	1.53	1.57	1.59	1.46
2003	1.68	1.81	1.46	1.32

Interim Dividends (Per Share)

Amt	Decl	Ex	Rec	Pay
0.83Q	4/21/2003	5/21/2003	5/23/2003	6/10/200:
0.83Q	7/21/2003	8/21/2003	8/25/2003	9/10/200:
0.88Q	11/17/2003	12/17/2003	12/19/2003	1/2/2004
0.88Q	1/20/2004	2/19/2004	2/23/2004	3/10/2004

Indicated Div: $3.52 (Div. Reinv. Plan)

Valuation Analysis

Forecast P/E	16.33	Trailing P/E	18.07
Market Cap	$1.6 Billion	Book Value	535.8 Million
Price/Book	2.87	Price/Sales	4.70

Dividend Achiever Status

Rank	92	10 Year Growth Rate	13.88%
Total Years of Dividend Growth			16

Business Summary: Commercial Banking (MIC: 8.1 SIC: 6021 NAIC:522110)

Park National is a bank holding company with $5.03 billion in total assets at Dec 31 2003. Through its subsidiaries, Co. engages in general commercial banking and trust business in small and medium population Ohio communities. Co.'s subsidiaries provide th following services: the acceptance and servicing of demand, savings and time deposit accounts; commercial, industrial, consumer and rea estate lending, including installment loans, credit cards, home equity lines of credit and commercial and auto leasing; trust services; cash management; safe deposit operations; electronic funds transfers; and online Internet banking with bill pay service.

Recent Developments: For the year ended Dec 31 2003, net income rose 1.5% to $86.9 million compared with $85.6 million a year earlier. Net interest income declined 1.3% to $202.6 million from $205.3 million the previous year. Co. attributed the drop in net interes income to a decrease in the net interest spread, or the difference between rates received for interest earning assets and the rates paid fo interest bearing liabilities. Provision for loan losses amounted to $12.6 million versus $15.0 million in 2002. Total non–interest incom increased 9.2% to $55.5 million, mainly due to higher fee income earned from the origination and sale of fixed rate mortgage loans.

Prospects: Co.'s near term prospects are mixed. For instance, Co.'s results may be restrained by the expected significant decline in fixe rate mortgage loan volume in 2004 due to higher long–term interest rates. Additionally, Co. anticipates that its salaries and employe benefit expense will increase by about 4.0% in 2004, while the net yield on interest earnings assets is expected to decrease to about 4.5% from 4.6% for 2003. On the positive side, Co. expects that net interest income will increase during 2004, due to the anticipated growth i interest earning assets. Further, Co. expects an increase in service charges on deposit accounts in 2004 due to pricing increases, whic should aid results.

Financial Data

(US$ in Thousands)	12/31/2003	12/31/2002	12/31/2001	12/31/2000	12/31/1999	12/31/1998	12/31/1997	12/31/1996
Earnings Per Share	6.27	6.15	5.58	5.10	4.67	4.21	3.80	3.4
Tang. Book Val. Per Share	39.44	36.92	33.59	29.66	24.59	23.49	22.52	19.8
Dividends Per Share	3.320	3.040	2.840	2.600	2.280	1.820	1.520	1.33
Dividend Payout %	52.95	49.43	50.89	50.98	48.94	43.34	40.00	38.85
Income Statement								
Total Interest Income	264,629	287,920	320,348	249,332	191,920	185,946	180,511	122,29
Total Interest Expense	61,992	82,588	127,404	110,437	76,063	78,295	77,033	49,33
Net Interest Income	202,637	205,332	192,944	138,895	115,857	107,651	103,478	72,95
Provision for Loan Losses	12,595	15,043	13,059	8,729	6,969	6,798	6,999	4,52
Non–Interest Income	55,523	50,850	45,238	29,691	23,088	23,969	20,479	13,14
Non–Interest Expense	122,376	119,964	114,207	82,919	67,540	64,309	62,408	43,23
Income Before Taxes	123,189	121,175	110,916	76,938	64,436	60,513	54,550	38,34
Net Income	86,878	85,579	78,362	55,405	45,747	41,572	37,693	25,66
Average Shs. Outstg.	13,858	13,909	14,051	10,876	9,810	9,855	9,907	7,49
Balance Sheet								
Cash & Due from Banks	169,782	157,088	169,143	109,870	104,222	100,291	93,585	61,45
Securities Avail. for Sale	1,928,697	1,030,264	1,436,661	740,924	619,009	646,403	532,922	386,18
Net Loans & Leases	2,667,661	2,630,159	2,735,849	2,229,259	1,792,682	1,603,523	1,556,332	1,084,80
Total Assets	5,034,956	4,446,625	4,569,515	3,211,068	2,634,337	2,460,779	2,288,383	1,614,76
Total Deposits	3,414,249	3,495,135	3,314,203	2,415,575	2,015,147	1,939,778	1,854,964	1,336,61
Long–Term Obligations	485,977	187,226	392,540	181,578	76	8,430	30,868	
Total Liabilities	4,491,915	3,937,333	4,101,169	2,891,316	2,394,757	2,225,089	2,066,266	1,465,78
Net Stockholders' Equity	543,041	509,292	468,346	319,752	239,580	235,690	222,117	148,98
Shares Outstanding	13,766	13,791	13,940	10,778	9,739	10,030	9,861	7,48
Statistical Record								
Return on Equity %	15.99	16.80	16.73	17.32	19.09	17.63	16.96	17.2
Return on Assets %	1.72	1.92	1.71	1.72	1.73	1.68	1.64	1.5
Equity/Assets %	10.78	11.45	10.24	9.95	9.09	9.57	9.70	9.2
Non–Int. Exp./Tot. Inc. %	38.22	35.41	31.23	29.71	31.41	30.63	31.05	31.9
Price Range	120.0–93.30	102.1–84.01	102.5–75.10	103.9–78.50	116.0–87.32	102.1–80.95	93.33–48.69	50.48–44.1
P/E Ratio	19.14–14.88	16.60–13.66	18.37–13.46	20.37–15.39	24.84–18.70	24.26–19.23	24.56–12.81	14.76–12.9
Average Yield %	3.07	3.21	3.18	2.82	2.43	1.98	2.28	2.8

Address: 50 North Third Street, Newark, OH 43055	Officers: William T. McConnell – Chmn., Harry O. Egger – Vice Chmn.	Investor Contact: (740) 349–3708
Telephone: (740) 349–8451		Institutional Holding
Web Site: www.parknationalcorp.com		No of Institutions: 3
		Shares: 21,589 % Held: –

PARKER HANNIFIN CORP.

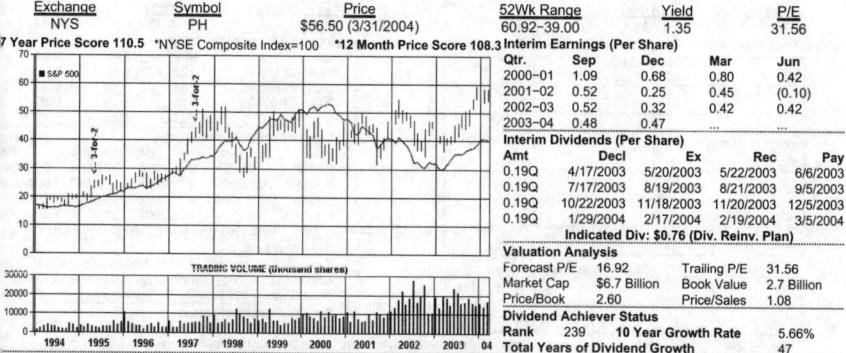

Exchange	Symbol	Price	52Wk Range	Yield	P/E
NYS	PH	$56.50 (3/31/2004)	60.92-39.00	1.35	31.56

7 Year Price Score 110.5   *NYSE Composite Index=100   *12 Month Price Score 108.3

Interim Earnings (Per Share)

Qtr.	Sep	Dec	Mar	Jun
2000–01	1.09	0.68	0.80	0.42
2001–02	0.52	0.25	0.45	(0.10)
2002–03	0.52	0.32	0.42	0.42
2003–04	0.48	0.47	...	...

Interim Dividends (Per Share)

Amt	Decl	Ex	Rec	Pay
0.19Q	4/17/2003	5/20/2003	5/22/2003	6/6/2003
0.19Q	7/17/2003	8/19/2003	8/21/2003	9/5/2003
0.19Q	10/22/2003	11/18/2003	11/20/2003	12/5/2003
0.19Q	1/29/2004	2/17/2004	2/19/2004	3/5/2004

Indicated Div: $0.76 (Div. Reinv. Plan)

Valuation Analysis

Forecast P/E	16.92	Trailing P/E	31.56
Market Cap	$6.7 Billion	Book Value	2.7 Billion
Price/Book	2.60	Price/Sales	1.08

Dividend Achiever Status

Rank	239	10 Year Growth Rate	5.66%
Total Years of Dividend Growth			47

Business Summary: Metal Products (MIC: 11.4 SIC: 3491 NAIC:332911)

Parker–Hannifin is a manufacturer of motion–control products, including fluid power systems, electromechanical controls and related components. Co. operates in two main business segments: The Industrial segment includes several business units that manufacture motion–control and fluid power system components for builders and users of various types of manufacturing, packaging, processing, transportation, agricultural, construction, and military vehicles and equipment. The Aerospace segment produces hydraulic, fuel and pneumatic systems and components for domestic commercial, military and general aviation aircraft, and naval vessels, land–based weapons systems, satellites and space vehicles.

Recent Developments: For the quarter ended Dec 31 2003, net income increased 48.5% to $55.8 million compared with $37.6 million in the same period a year earlier. Net sales advanced 6.8% to $1.62 billion from $1.52 billion in 2002. Co.'s results were driven by its North American Industrial segment, which posted a 5.0% increase in sales to $703.1 million and 92.8% jump in operating profit to $52.9 million. Specifically, Co. noted improved strength in construction, heavy–duty truck and semiconductor markets. Each of Co.'s remaining segments also reported improved top–line and operating profit with the exception of the Aerospace segment, which posted a 1.2% drop in sales and 27.7% decline in operating profit.

Prospects: For the second half of fiscal–year 2004, Co. expects sales in its Industrial and Other segments to rise modestly, with continued profitability improvements. Co. foresees sales and margins declining slightly in the Climate & Industrial Controls segment. In Aerospace, Co. indicated that sales should stabilize, but said that it did not expect near–term margins to improve without a corresponding improvement in aftermarket volume. Separately, in February 2004, Co. completed its acquisition of Denison International plc. Denison, with annual revenues of about $180.0 million, is an industrial manufacturer and service provider for highly engineered hydraulic fluid power systems and components.

Financial Data

($S in Thousands)	6 Mos	3 Mos	06/30/2003	06/30/2002	06/30/2001	06/30/2000	06/30/1999	06/30/1998
Earnings Per Share	0.95	0.48	1.68	1.12	2.99	3.31	2.83	2.88
Cash Flow Per Share	3.19	1.22	4.76	5.43	4.62	4.83	4.18	2.86
Tang. Book Val. Per Share	12.60	11.94	11.44	12.27	13.42	14.93	12.62	11.74
Dividends Per Share	0.760	0.750	0.740	0.720	0.700	0.680	0.640	0.600
Dividend Payout %	80.00	156.25	44.04	64.28	23.41	20.54	22.61	20.83
Income Statement								
Total Revenues	3,207,939	1,586,918	6,410,610	6,149,122	5,979,644	5,355,337	4,958,800	4,633,023
Total Indirect Exp.	370,294	180,204	721,065	726,001	679,963	575,906	550,681	532,134
Depreciation & Amort.	127,664	63,379	259,178	281,598	264,527	206,408	202,046	182,679
Operating Income	207,225	107,938	379,770	306,551	571,485	622,862	538,749	549,897
Net Interest Inc./(Exp.)	(39,122)	(21,780)	(81,561)	(82,484)	(90,362)	(59,183)	(63,697)	(52,787)
Income Taxes	53,522	27,922	101,110	87,886	189,426	193,955	167,193	180,762
Income from Cont Ops	...	...	...	...	344,170	...	...	323,226
Net Income	112,462	56,691	196,272	130,150	340,792	368,232	310,501	319,551
Average Shs. Outstg.	118,386	117,769	116,894	116,060	115,064	111,224	109,679	111,959
Balance Sheet								
Cash & Cash Equivalents	138,047	205,409	245,850	46,384	23,565	68,460	33,277	30,488
Total Current Assets	2,206,928	2,305,955	2,396,807	2,235,618	2,196,362	2,153,113	1,774,684	1,780,075
Total Assets	5,799,495	5,882,592	5,985,633	5,752,583	5,337,661	4,646,299	3,705,888	3,524,821
Total Current Liabilities	1,015,965	1,256,363	1,423,727	1,359,837	1,413,129	1,186,303	754,513	988,770
Long–Term Obligations	975,235	956,356	966,332	1,088,883	857,078	701,762	724,757	512,943
Net Stockholders' Equity	2,704,273	2,587,861	2,520,911	2,583,516	2,528,915	2,309,458	1,853,862	1,683,450
Net Working Capital	...	1,049,592	973,080	875,781	783,233	966,810	1,020,171	791,305
Shares Outstanding	119,239	118,572	118,165	118,024	117,309	116,387	111,901	109,308
Statistical Record								
Operating Profit Margin %	6.45	6.80	5.92	4.98	9.55	11.63	10.86	11.86
Return on Equity %	4.15	2.19	7.78	5.03	13.60	15.94	16.74	19.20
Return on Assets %	1.93	0.96	3.27	2.26	6.44	7.92	8.37	9.16
Debt/Total Assets %	16.81	16.25	16.14	18.92	16.05	15.10	19.55	14.55
Price Range	59.50–41.71	50.65–41.71	48.80–34.65	54.63–31.65	50.03–31.94	52.13–33.94	50.44–27.19	52.00–37.56
P/E Ratio	62.63–43.91	105.5–86.90	29.05–20.63	48.78–28.26	16.73–10.68	15.75–10.25	17.82–9.61	18.06–13.04
Average Yield %	1.53	1.63	1.77	1.59	1.72	1.55	1.77	1.34

Address: 6035 Parkland Blvd., Cleveland, OH 44124–4141 Telephone: (216) 896–3000 Web Site: www.parker.com	Officers: Duane E. Collins – Chmn., Donald E. Washkewicz – Pres., C.E.O. Transfer Agents: National City Bank, Cleveland, OH	Investor Contact: (216) 896–2240 Institutional Holding No of Institutions: 19 Shares: 343,242 % Held: –

201

PAYCHEX INC

Exchange	Symbol	Price	52Wk Range	Yield	P/E
NMS	PAYX	$35.60 (3/31/2004)	40.14–27.97	1.35	43.41

*7 Year Price Score 118.3   *NYSE Composite Index=100   ***12 Month Price Score 107.0**

TRADING VOLUME (thousand shares)

Years on chart: 1994 1995 1996 1997 1998 1999 2000 2001 2002 2003 04

Interim Earnings (Per Share)

Qtr.	Aug	Nov	Feb	May
2000–01	0.16	0.16	0.18	0.18
2001–02	0.19	0.18	0.18	0.18
2002–03	0.20	0.20	0.19	0.19
2003–04	0.21	0.21	0.21	...

Interim Dividends (Per Share)

Amt	Decl	Ex	Rec	Pa
0.11Q	4/10/2003	4/29/2003	5/1/2003	5/15/200
0.11Q	7/10/2003	7/30/2003	8/1/2003	8/15/200
0.12Q	10/2/2003	10/30/2003	11/3/2003	11/17/200
0.12Q	1/9/2004	1/29/2004	2/2/2004	2/16/200

Indicated Div: $0.48 (Div. Reinv. Plan)

Valuation Analysis

Forecast P/E	37.76	Trailing P/E	43.41
Market Cap	$13.4 Billion	Book Value	1.2 Billion
Price/Book	11.64	Price/Sales	11.10

Dividend Achiever Status

Rank	2	10 Year Growth Rate	39.78%
Total Years of Dividend Growth			15

Business Summary: Accounting &Management Consulting Services (MIC: 12.2 SIC: 8721 NAIC:541214)

Paychex operates in two business segments: Payroll and Human Resource Services–Professional Employer Organizatic (HRS–PEO). The Payroll segment is engaged in the preparation of payroll checks, internal accounting records, all federal, state and loc payroll tax returns, and collection and remittance of payroll obligations for small– to medium–sized businesses. The HRS–PEO segme specializes in providing small– and medium–sized businesses with outsourcing services for their employee benefits. HRS–PEO produc include 401(k) plan recordkeeping services, group benefits and workers' compensation insurance services, section 125 plans, employe handbooks and management services.

Recent Developments: For the third quarter ended Feb 29 2004, net income advanced 12.6% to $80.5 million compared with $71 million in the equivalent period of the previous year. Revenues improved 19.0% to $342.6 million from $287.8 million in the year–earli quarter, largely due to recent acquisitions. Services revenues increased 19.6% to $328.1 million from $274.3 million in the prior–ye period, primarily due to client base growth, increased utilization of ancillary services and price increases. Interest on funds held for clien rose 7.7% to $14.5 million from $13.5 million in 2002, due to increased net realized gains on the sale of securities. and higher avera portfolio balances.

Prospects: Co. is pleased with its operating results and remains optimistic that the signs of improving small business conditions w continue. Meanwhile, Co.'s payroll service should continue to benefit from the integration of the Advantage and InterPay acquisitions a strong growth in the client base. Co.'s human resource and benefits service should also benefit from client growth. However, operati income growth may continue to be hampered by lower average interest rates earned funds held for clients. Nevertheless, for fiscal 200 Co. expects total revenue growth to range from 16.0% to 18.0%, and net income growth to range from 8.0% to 10.0%.

Financial Data
(US$ in Thousands)

	9 Mos	6 Mos	3 Mos	05/31/2003	05/31/2002	05/31/2001	05/31/2000	05/31/199
Earnings Per Share	0.82	0.80	0.79	0.78	0.73	0.68	0.51	0.
Cash Flow Per Share	0.85	0.48	0.29	0.98	0.80	0.80	0.66	0.
Tang. Book Val. Per Share	1.88	1.76	1.64	1.55	2.43	2.00	1.50	1.
Dividends Per Share	0.460	0.450	0.440	0.440	0.420	0.330	0.220	0.1
Dividend Payout %	56.10	56.25	55.70	56.41	57.53	48.52	43.13	39.
Income Statement								
Total Revenues	963,958	621,352	309,253	1,099,079	954,910	869,857	728,119	597,2
Total Indirect Exp.	392,247	245,353	122,504	440,389	370,519	332,803	295,745	257,7
Depreciation & Amort.	61,116	40,154	19,796	64,555	47,392	39,139	36,484	32,9
Operating Income	346,366	229,893	115,078	401,041	363,694	336,702	258,893	187,5
Net Interest Inc./(Exp.)				30,503	31,315	27,279	16,479	12,5
Income Taxes	117,007	77,886	38,684	138,092	120,478	109,112	85,365	61,0
Net Income	241,545	161,027	80,343	293,452	274,531	254,869	190,007	139,0
Average Shs. Outstg.	379,410	379,234	378,815	378,083	378,002	377,510	375,081	373,1
Balance Sheet								
Cash & Cash Equivalents	537,195	449,743	438,072	5,377,281	4,613,387	4,696,091	4,013,429	3,066,2
Total Current Assets	3,616,734	2,998,451	2,956,641	3,032,642	2,814,574	2,791,273	2,362,575	1,793,1
Total Assets	4,275,062	3,660,508	3,612,336	3,690,783	2,953,075	2,907,196	2,455,577	1,873,1
Total Current Liabilities	3,052,708	2,477,506	2,476,089	2,587,525	2,023,406	2,143,842	1,886,945	1,432,3
Net Stockholders' Equity	1,195,512	1,154,600	1,109,227	1,077,371	923,981	757,842	563,432	435,8
Net Working Capital	564,026	520,945	480,552	445,117	791,168	647,431	475,630	360,7
Shares Outstanding	377,663	377,526	377,036	376,698	375,859	373,647	371,769	369,4
Statistical Record								
Operating Profit Margin %	35.93	36.99	37.21	36.48	38.08	38.70	35.55	31.
Return on Equity %	20.20	13.94	7.24	27.23	29.71	33.63	33.72	31.
Return on Assets %	5.65	4.39	2.22	7.95	9.29	8.76	7.73	7.
Price Range	40.14–28.84	40.14–28.84	36.53–28.84	35.00–20.55	42.00–29.28	59.69–31.44	36.88–16.58	24.06–16.
P/E Ratio	62.72–45.06	95.57–68.67	174.0–137.3	44.87–26.35	57.53–40.11	87.78–46.24	72.30–32.52	65.02–44.
Average Yield %	1.32	1.31	1.39	1.61	1.14	0.75	0.84	0.

Address: 911 Panorama Trail South, Rochester, NY 14625–2396
Telephone: (585) 385–6666
Web Site: www.paychex.com

Officers: B. Thomas Golisano – Chmn., Pres., C.E.O., Martin Mucci – Sr. V.P., Oper.

Investor Contact: (585) 383–3406
Institutional Holding
No of Institutions: 26
Shares: 159,676,830   **% Held:** –

PENNICHUCK CORP.

Exchange	Symbol	Price	52Wk Range	Yield	P/E
NMS	PNNW	$28.70 (3/31/2004)	28.99–21.75	3.00	55.19

7 Year Price Score 132.6 *NYSE Composite Index=100 **12 Month Price Score 97.1**

Interim Earnings (Per Share)

Qtr.	Mar	Jun	Sep	Dec
2000	0.19	0.25	0.48	0.63
2001	0.17	0.40	0.42	0.51
2002	0.26	(0.30)	0.57	0.44
2003	0.06	0.16	0.43	(0.13)

Interim Dividends (Per Share)

Amt	Decl	Ex	Rec	Pay
0.215Q	3/10/2003	5/13/2003	5/15/2003	6/2/2003
0.215Q	8/5/2003	8/13/2003	8/15/2003	9/2/2003
0.215Q	10/3/2003	11/12/2003	11/14/2003	12/1/2003
0.215Q	1/26/2004	2/11/2004	2/13/2004	3/1/2004

Indicated Div: $0.86 (Div. Reinv. Plan)

Valuation Analysis

Forecast P/E	N/A	Trailing P/E	55.19
Market Cap	$68.6 Million	Book Value	30.6 Million
Price/Book	N/A	Price/Sales	N/A

Dividend Achiever Status

Rank	153	10 Year Growth Rate	10.10%
Total Years of Dividend Growth		10

Business Summary: Water Utilities (MIC: 7.2 SIC: 4941 NAIC:221310)

Pennichuck is a holding company. Through its subsidiaries, Co. is engaged primarily in the collection, storage, treatment, distribution and sale of potable water throughout southern and central New Hampshire. Pennichuck Water Works, Pennichuck East Utility and Pittsfield Aquaduct Company each operate as regulated public utilities. As of Dec 31 2003, Co. served approximately 29,400 residential and commercial and industrial customers. Co. is also involved in the development of commercial and residential real estate through its Southwood real estate subsidiary, and additional non–regulated, water–related management services and contract operations through Pennichuck Water Service Corporation.

Recent Developments: For the year ended Dec 31 2003, net income dropped 46.7% to $1.2 million compared with $2.3 million in the previous year. Earnings were adversely affected by the damper–than–normal weather conditions experienced during the summer of 2003. In addition, earnings were pressured by increased operating costs as a result of aggressive distribution system maintenance programs conducted in the second and third quarters of 2003. Total revenues advanced 8.7% to $21.4 million from $23.4 million a year earlier. Water utility revenue slipped 0.8% to $18.7 million, while revenues from real estate activities fell 69.3% to $949,000. Contract operations revenue advanced 17.3% to $1.8 million.

Prospects: In Jan 2004, Co. announced the signing of purchase and sales agreements to acquire community water systems in Bow and Windham, NH. White Rock Senior Living Community in Bow serves about 400 people in a residential setting, while Lamplighter Village in Windham serves about 200 customers. Co. will assume complete ownership of the two water systems upon completion of the water system construction. Separately, Co. continues to secure new water service contracts in southern New Hampshire with a total of 68 contract customers being serviced as of Jan 12 2004.

Financial Data

(US$ in Thousands)	12/31/2003	12/31/2002	12/31/2001	12/31/2000	12/31/1999	12/31/1998	12/31/1997	12/31/1996
Earnings Per Share	0.52	0.97	1.50	1.55	1.12	1.19	0.85	0.84
Cash Flow Per Share	1.77	1.65	3.02	3.25	2.09	1.56	2.10	1.55
Tang. Book Val. Per Share	12.59	12.72	12.81	12.19	11.30	10.91	9.16	8.87
Dividends Per Share	0.840	0.810	0.750	0.720	0.690	0.590	0.530	0.510
Dividend Payout %	161.53	83.81	50.62	46.85	61.74	49.47	61.99	60.71
Income Statement								
Total Revenues	21,388	23,422	22,754	23,671	17,809	17,395	11,841	12,203
Costs & Expenses	16,193	15,774	14,202	14,456	11,733	11,676	8,031	8,589
Operating Income	5,195	7,647	8,552	9,216	6,076	5,719	3,810	3,614
Net Interest Inc./(Exp.)	(1,969)	(1,978)	(1,981)	(1,991)	(2,025)	(2,264)	(1,774)	(1,631)
Income Taxes	888	1,450	2,657	2,870	1,625	1,342	791	752
Equity Earns/Minority Int.	(33)	2	(523)	(855)	19	(41)	...	...
Net Income	1,247	2,341	3,612	3,683	2,616	2,106	1,290	1,238
Average Shs. Outstg.	2,398	2,411	2,400	2,363	2,335	1,765	1,506	1,469
Balance Sheet								
Net Property	85,727	79,672	73,960	68,438	63,005	58,389	47,094	43,338
Total Assets	97,210	90,982	87,841	82,880	75,581	70,838	55,090	50,070
Long–Term Obligations	26,879	26,860	27,072	26,918	27,223	28,002	25,436	20,995
Net Stockholders' Equity	30,172	30,434	30,595	28,596	26,257	24,811	13,833	13,196
Shares Outstanding	2,396	2,391	2,387	2,343	2,323	2,274	1,508	1,487
Statistical Record								
Operating Profit Margin %	24.28	32.65	37.58	38.93	34.11	32.87	32.17	29.61
Net Inc./Net Property %	1.45	2.93	4.88	5.38	4.15	3.60	2.73	2.85
Net Inc./Tot. Capital %	1.90	3.66	5.65	5.94	4.49	3.72	3.07	3.39
Return on Equity %	4.13	7.69	11.80	12.87	9.96	8.48	9.32	9.38
Accum. Depr./Gross Prop. %	25.76	25.50	25.22	24.70	24.15	23.82	25.56	25.58
Price Range	28.94–21.01	32.01–24.00	27.00–19.50	24.75–15.66	25.50–14.48	19.97–9.00	10.13–7.75	11.00–7.75
P/E Ratio	55.65–40.40	33.00–24.74	18.00–13.00	15.97–10.10	22.77–12.93	16.78–7.56	11.91–9.12	13.10–9.23
Average Yield %	3.36	2.94	3.39	3.66	3.95	4.37	5.81	5.54

Address: Four Water Street, Nashua, NH 03061	Officers: Maurice L. Arel – Pres., C.E.O., Stephen J. Densberger – Exec. V.P.	Investor Contact: (603)–882–5191
Telephone: (603) 882–5191		Institutional Holding
Web Site: www.pennichuck.com		No of Institutions: 12
		Shares: 255,297 % Held: 12.8%

203

PENTAIR, INC.

Exchange	Symbol	Price	52Wk Range	Yield	P/E
NYS	PNR	$59.00 (3/31/2004)	59.00–35.77	1.42	20.34

*7 Year Price Score 108.5 *NYSE Composite Index=100 *12 Month Price Score 100.0

Interim Earnings (Per Share)

Qtr.	Apr	Jul	Sep	Dec
2000	0.70	0.75	0.26	(0.03)
2001	0.42	0.58	0.50	(0.33)
2002	0.43	0.86	0.75	0.57
2003	0.56	0.88	0.77	0.69

Interim Dividends (Per Share)

Amt	Decl	Ex	Rec	Pay
0.21Q	2/26/2003	4/23/2003	4/25/2003	5/9/200
0.21Q	...	7/23/2003	7/25/2003	8/8/200
0.21Q	...	10/22/2003	10/24/2003	11/7/200
0.21Q	1/15/2004	1/28/2004	1/30/2004	2/13/200
		Indicated Div: $0.84		

Valuation Analysis

Forecast P/E	12.05	Trailing P/E	20.34
Market Cap	$2.9 Billion	Book Value	1.3 Billion
Price/Book	1.80	Price/Sales	0.83

Dividend Achiever Status

Rank	175	10 Year Growth Rate	9.20%
Total Years of Dividend Growth			27

Business Summary: Industrial Machinery and Equipment (MIC: 11.5 SIC: 3553 NAIC:333210)

Pentair is a diversified industrial manufacturer operating in three segments. The Water segment manufactures and markets products an systems used in the movement, treatment, storage and use of water. The Enclosures segment designs, manufactures, and market standard, modified and custom enclosures that protect sensitive controls and components. The Tools segment designs, manufactures an markets a range of power tools under such trade names as PorterCable™, Delta®, Delta Shopmaster™, Delta Industrial™ Biesemeyer®, FLEX™, Ex–Cell™, Air America®, Charge Air Pro®, 2 x 4™, Oldham®, Contractor SuperDuty™, Viper®, Hickor Woodworking®, and The Woodworker's Choice®.

Recent Developments: For the year ended Dec 31 2003, income from continuing operations was $144.3 million compared with ne income of $129.9 million a year earlier. Net sales advanced 5.6% to $2.72 billion from $2.58 billion the previous year. Co.'s results wer fueled by a 13.7% increase in sales to $1.06 billion and 13.8% growth in operating profit to $144.0 million from its Water segmen Additionally, Co.'s Enclosures segment reported a 4.9% sales increase to $583.4 million, while operating profit climbed 70.6% to $51. million. Gross profit improved to $679.0 million, or 24.9% of net sales, versus 23.9% of net sales, the year before.

Prospects: On Feb 4 2004, Co. announced that it has entered into an agreement to acquire WICOR Industries in an $850.0 million cas transaction. WICOR, which manufactures water system, filtration, and pool equipment products, is expected to generate sales of abou $750.0 million in 2003. Co. also announced that it is exploring strategic alternatives for its Tool segment businesses. Meanwhile, Co. ha raised its full–year 2004 earnings guidance to between $3.25 and $3.35 per share versus its previous estimate of $3.15 to $3.30 per share Co. attributed the improved outlook to its expectations of continued organic growth and improved profit contributions from each of i three groups.

Financial Data

(US$ in Thousands)	12/31/2003	12/31/2002	12/31/2001	12/31/2000	12/31/1999	12/31/1998	12/31/1997	12/31/199
Earnings Per Share	2.90	2.61	1.17	1.68	2.33	2.46	2.11	1.7
Cash Flow Per Share	5.27	5.44	4.71	3.80	3.29	3.13	2.73	2.6
Tang. Book Val. Per Share	N.M	N.M	N.M	N.M	N.M	4.70	3.70	5.3
Dividends Per Share	0.820	0.740	0.700	0.660	0.640	0.600	0.540	0.50
Dividend Payout %	28.27	28.35	59.82	39.28	27.46	24.39	25.59	28.9
Income Statement								
Total Revenues	2,724,365	2,580,783	2,615,944	2,748,013	2,367,753	1,937,578	1,839,056	1,567,06
Total Indirect Exp.	419,484	379,715	490,238	494,468	520,699	414,076	378,456	326,08
Depreciation & Amort.	65,643	64,702	104,349	99,028	88,645	68,388	67,836	59,52
Operating Income	259,554	235,992	157,761	202,030	214,331	193,192	169,802	142,91
Net Interest Inc./(Exp.)	(40,936)	(43,545)	(61,488)	(74,899)	(47,802)	(22,248)	(21,733)	(18,31
Income Taxes	74,330	62,545	35,772	45,263	63,220	64,104	66,782	50,09
Income from Cont Ops	144,288	...	57,516	81,868	...	...	...	
Net Income	141,352	129,902	32,869	55,887	103,309	106,840	91,600	74,50
Average Shs. Outstg.	49,810	49,744	49,297	48,645	44,287	43,149	43,067	42,75
Balance Sheet								
Cash & Cash Equivalents	47,989	39,648	39,844	34,944	66,228	32,039	34,340	22,97
Total Current Assets	829,451	810,808	835,603	1,091,802	1,150,478	748,569	705,370	614,25
Total Assets	2,780,677	2,514,450	2,372,198	2,644,025	2,802,966	1,554,666	1,472,862	1,289,01
Total Current Liabilities	497,451	476,200	428,433	648,792	760,947	394,793	392,177	301,63
Long–Term Obligations	732,862	673,911	714,977	781,834	857,296	288,026	294,549	279,88
Net Stockholders' Equity	1,261,478	1,105,724	1,015,002	1,010,591	993,205	709,365	630,562	563,85
Net Working Capital	332,000	334,608	407,170	443,010	389,531	353,776	313,193	312,61
Shares Outstanding	49,502	49,222	49,110	48,711	48,317	38,503	38,185	37,71
Statistical Record								
Operating Profit Margin %	9.52	9.14	6.03	7.35	9.05	9.97	9.23	9.1
Return on Equity %	11.43	11.74	5.66	8.10	10.40	15.06	14.52	13.2
Return on Assets %	5.18	5.16	2.42	3.09	3.68	6.87	6.21	5.7
Debt/Total Assets %	26.35	26.80	30.13	29.56	30.58	18.52	19.99	21.7
Price Range	46.57-32.80	49.61-29.34	39.28-22.50	44.00-21.00	48.88-30.94	45.75-27.88	39.63-27.50	32.25-24.6
P/E Ratio	16.06-11.31	19.01-11.24	33.57-19.23	26.19-12.50	20.98-13.28	18.60-11.33	18.78-13.03	18.64-14.2
Average Yield %	2.09	1.85	2.19	2.00	1.57	1.55	1.59	1.8

Address: 1500 Country Road B2 West, St. Paul, MN 55113	Officers: Randall J. Hogan – Chmn., Pres., C.E.O., David D. Harrison – Exec. V.P., C.F.O., Chief Acctg. Officer	Investor Contact: (651) 639–5278 Institutional Holding
Telephone: (651) 636–7920		No of Institutions: 19
Web Site: www.pentair.com	Transfer Agents:Wells Fargo Bank Minnesota, N.A.	Shares: 272,559 % Held: –

PEOPLE'S BANK

Exchange	Symbol	Price	52Wk Range	Yield	P/E
NMS	PBCT	$46.49 (3/31/2004)	46.49–25.38	3.36	45.14

*7 Year Price Score 111.1 *NYSE Composite Index=100 *12 Month Price Score 102.0

Interim Earnings (Per Share)

Qtr.	Mar	Jun	Sep	Dec
2001	0.22	0.69	0.34	0.12
2002	0.18	0.20	0.24	0.28
2003	0.26	0.25	...	...

Interim Dividends (Per Share)

Amt	Decl	Ex	Rec	Pay
0.39Q	4/24/2003	4/29/2003	5/1/2003	5/15/2003
0.39Q	7/17/2003	7/30/2003	8/1/2003	8/15/2003
0.39Q	10/16/2003	10/29/2003	11/1/2003	11/15/2003
0.39Q	1/15/2004	1/28/2004	2/1/2004	2/15/2004

Indicated Div: $1.56 (Div. Reinv. Plan)

Valuation Analysis

Forecast P/E	29.12	Trailing P/E	45.14
Market Cap	$239.3 Million	Book Value	N/A
Price/Book	N/A	Price/Sales	N/A

Dividend Achiever Status

Rank	1	10 Year Growth Rate	43.97%
Total Years of Dividend Growth			10

Business Summary: Commercial Banking (MIC: 8.1 SIC: 6022 NAIC:522110)

People's Bank had assets of $11.67 billion as of Dec 31 2003. Co. is a diversified financial services company providing commercial, consumer, insurance and investment services. In addition, Co. is an international credit card issuer, ranking 19th nationally as a provider of MasterCard and Visa. As of Dec 31 2003, Co. served the entire Connecticut market through a network of 154 branches, with 64 located in Super Stop and Shop stores. Co.'s subsidiaries offer brokerage services through People's Securities, asset management through Olson, Mobeck and Associates, equipment financing and leasing through People's Capital and Leasing, and insurance services through R.C. Knox and Company.

Recent Developments: For the year ended Dec 31 2003, net income advanced 15.2% to $63.8 million compared with $55.4 million the year before. Results for 2003 and 2002 included net gains on the sales of residential mortgage loans of $14.9 million and $8.4 million, and net security losses of $600,000 and $3.3 million, respectively. Net interest income declined 8.8% to $320.4 million from $351.2 million year earlier. Provision for loan losses fell 37.5% to $48.5 million. Total non-interest income improved 0.9% to $250.9 million, while total non-interest expense decreased 1.3% to $435.9 million.

Prospects: Co. continues to generate strong growth across its lending businesses, particularly its residential mortgage business, and in core deposits, and is steadily progressing in its credit card services business. On Mar 5 2004, Co. completed the sale of its credit card business to The Royal Bank of Scotland Group. Co. obtained a 15.5% premium on the credit card portfolio sold in the transaction. The strategic decision to exit the credit card business better enables Co. to focus on its core retail and commercial banking businesses. Proceeds from the transaction will be used in part to restructure Co.'s balance sheet, expand its Connecticut businesses, and grow its franchise.

Financial Data

(US$ in Thousands)	12/31/2003	12/31/2002	12/31/2001	12/31/2000	12/31/1999	12/31/1998	12/31/1997	12/31/1996
Earnings Per Share	1.03	0.90	1.40	1.77	1.81	1.44	1.51	1.30
Tang. Book Val. Per Share	14.33	13.39	13.32	12.35	10.60	11.23	11.60	10.15
Dividends Per Share	1.530	1.420	1.340	1.200	1.030	0.840	0.670	0.530
Dividend Payout %	148.54	157.77	95.71	67.79	56.90	58.33	44.59	40.81
Income Statement								
Total Interest Income	514,700	614,200	727,100	766,800	666,800	593,100	524,800	480,000
Total Interest Expense	194,300	263,000	373,100	381,700	328,900	305,900	271,800	245,500
Net Interest Income	320,400	351,200	354,000	385,100	337,900	287,200	253,000	234,500
Provision for Loan Losses	48,600	77,700	101,100	59,900	54,500	45,800	39,900	51,100
Non–Interest Income	251,000	247,900	320,500	293,000	300,800	310,500	250,000	176,700
Non–Interest Expense	435,900	441,000	440,500	452,700	413,800	378,500	319,000	259,000
Income Before Taxes	86,900	80,400	132,900	165,500	170,400	173,400	144,100	101,100
Income from Cont Ops	...	...	86,700	...	...	...	...	...
Net Income	63,800	55,400	75,800	108,400	112,000	91,700	92,400	80,100
Average Shs. Outstg.	61,900	61,700	61,600	61,400	62,000	63,870	61,400	61,410
Balance Sheet								
Cash & Due from Banks	343,000	451,900	802,400	373,900	328,800	288,700	241,500	196,200
Securities Avail. for Sale	2,554,600	3,334,600	2,895,900	2,437,400	2,197,300	2,052,600	1,446,600	1,230,400
Net Loans & Leases	8,121,800	7,336,200	6,931,000	7,344,700	6,969,600	6,481,100	5,389,600	5,189,400
Total Assets	11,671,500	12,260,600	11,890,600	11,570,900	10,738,100	9,918,700	8,184,000	7,645,200
Total Deposits	8,714,000	8,426,100	7,983,400	7,761,300	7,191,100	6,937,500	5,818,400	5,245,200
Long–Term Obligations	1,217,200	1,848,400	1,576,500	2,039,600	1,613,600	1,267,000	925,500	984,800
Total Liabilities	10,669,500	11,321,000	10,955,600	10,689,100	9,956,400	9,066,400	7,474,400	7,027,200
Net Stockholders' Equity	1,002,000	939,600	935,000	881,800	781,700	852,300	709,900	618,000
Shares Outstanding	62,000	61,700	61,500	61,300	61,100	63,716	61,160	60,829
Statistical Record								
Return on Equity %	6.36	5.89	9.27	12.29	14.32	10.75	13.01	12.96
Return on Assets %	0.54	0.45	0.72	0.93	1.04	0.92	1.12	1.04
Equity/Assets %	8.58	7.66	7.86	7.62	7.27	8.59	8.67	8.08
Non–Int. Exp./Tot. Inc. %	56.92	51.15	42.04	42.71	42.76	41.88	41.17	39.43
Price Range	33.89–24.49	27.90–20.75	28.25–21.01	26.81–17.00	31.94–20.00	41.13–19.13	38.00–18.96	20.00–12.42
P/E Ratio	32.90–23.78	31.00–23.06	20.18–15.01	15.15–9.60	17.65–11.05	28.56–13.28	25.17–12.56	15.38–9.55
Average Yield %	5.34	5.83	5.61	5.86	3.80	2.59	2.48	3.54

Address: 850 Main Street, Bridgeport, CT 06604	Officers: John A. Klein – Chmn., Pres., C.E.O., Jacinta A. Coleman – Exec. V.P., Chief Info. Off.	Investor Contact: (203) 338–4114
Telephone: (203) 338–7171		Institutional Holding
Web Site: www.peoples.com		No of Institutions: –
		Shares: – % Held: –

PEOPLES ENERGY CORP.

Exchange	Symbol	Price	52Wk Range	Yield	P/E
NYS	PGL	$44.65 (3/31/2004)	45.91-35.85	4.84	15.67

*7 Year Price Score 110.4 *NYSE Composite Index=100 *12 Month Price Score 90.1

Interim Earnings (Per Share)

Qtr.	Dec	Mar	Jun	Sep
2000-01	1.03	1.76	0.33	(0.38)
2001-02	0.87	1.55	0.04	0.05
2002-03	0.87	1.77	0.22	0.01
2003-04	0.85	...	...	...

Interim Dividends (Per Share)

Amt	Decl	Ex	Rec	Pa
0.53Q	6/4/2003	6/18/2003	6/20/2003	7/15/200
0.53Q	8/6/2003	9/18/2003	9/22/2003	10/15/200
0.53Q	12/5/2003	12/18/2003	12/22/2003	1/15/200
0.54Q	2/4/2004	3/18/2004	3/22/2004	4/15/200
		Indicated Div: $2.16		

Valuation Analysis

Forecast P/E	14.69	Trailing P/E	15.67
Market Cap	$1.6 Billion	Book Value	862.6 Million
Price/Book	1.79	Price/Sales	0.70

Dividend Achiever Status

Rank	293	10 Year Growth Rate	1.74%
Total Years of Dividend Growth		20	

Business Summary: Gas Utilities (MIC: 7.4 SIC: 4924 NAIC:221210)

Peoples Energy is a holding company. Income is derived principally from Co.'s subsidiaries, The Peoples Gas Light and Coke Compan and North Shore Gas Company. Co. also derives income from its other subsidiaries, Peoples Energy Resources Company, LLC, Peopl Energy Services Corporation, Peoples Energy Production Company, Peoples District Energy Corporation, Peoples Energy Ventures, LL and Peoples NGV Corp. Through its subsidiary, Co. operates six business segments: Gas Distribution, Power Generation, Midstrea Services, Retail Energy Services, Oil and Gas Production and Other. As of Sep 30 2003, Co. has approximately 1,000,000 elect customers and approximately 150,000 gas customers.

Recent Developments: For the three months ended Dec 31 2003, net income inched up 1.1% to $31.4 million compared with $31 million in the corresponding quarter of the previous year. Results for 2003 and 2002 included pre-tax equity investment losses o $245,000 and $253,000, respectively. Total revenues increased 10.2% to $604.9 million from $549.1 million in the year-earlier perio Results benefited from continued strong growth in Co.'s diversified energy businesses, partially offset by the negative effect of weathe that was 10.0% warmer than the same period of 2003 in its Gas Distribution business.

Prospects: Co. continues to benefit from solid growth in its diversified energy businesses, largely due to increased results from i wholesale marketing and asset management activities, and customer growth and higher margins in retail energy services. Looking ahea Co. will continue to focus on controlling operating costs in its core Gas Distribution business. Also, Co.'s Oil and Gas Productio business should benefit from higher production volumes and natural gas and oil prices versus a year ago. Meanwhile, Co. expec earnings to range from $2.70 to $2.85 for full-year 2004.

Financial Data

(US$ in Thousands)	3 Mos	09/30/2003	09/30/2002	09/30/2001	09/30/2000	09/30/1999	09/30/1998	09/30/199
Earnings Per Share	2.85	2.87	2.51	2.74	2.44	2.61	2.25	2.8
Cash Flow Per Share	(1.61)	5.68	9.24	4.78	1.44	5.17	4.49	4.7
Tang. Book Val. Per Share	23.32	23.11	22.73	22.66	21.86	21.66	20.94	20.4
Dividends Per Share	2.110	2.100	2.060	2.020	1.980	1.940	1.900	1.8
Dividend Payout %	74.04	73.17	82.07	73.72	81.14	74.32	84.44	66.1
Income Statement								
Total Revenues	604,884	2,138,394	1,482,534	2,270,218	1,417,533	1,194,381	1,138,057	1,274,37
Total Indirect Exp.	77,107	243,690	234,809	287,894	242,457	214,043	207,293	221,59
Costs & Expenses	544,732	1,928,880	1,311,185	2,108,201	1,258,350	1,038,367	1,024,248	1,140,82
Depreciation & Amort.	28,921	111,825	98,852	95,046	100,935	83,531	77,195	74,07
Operating Income	60,152	209,514	171,349	162,017	159,183	156,014	113,809	133,54
Net Interest Inc./(Exp.)	(12,281)	(49,441)	(60,930)	(72,051)	(52,919)	(39,511)	(35,468)	(33,06
Income Taxes	17,125	59,182	46,321	51,417	43,346	52,581	45,124	56,43
Eqty Earns/Minority Int.	(245)	...	...	...	...	...	...	
Income from Cont Ops	...	...	...	97,054	...	...	...	
Net Income	31,351	103,934	89,071	97,200	86,415	92,636	79,423	98,4
Average Shs. Outstg.	36,976	36,193	35,492	35,439	35,413	35,490	35,276	35,00
Balance Sheet								
Net Property	1,888,216	1,838,173	1,773,901	1,753,912	1,645,340	1,519,836	1,446,661	1,402,2
Total Assets	3,184,729	2,928,538	2,723,647	2,994,054	2,501,918	2,100,164	1,904,500	1,820,80
Long-Term Obligations	846,330	744,345	554,014	644,308	419,663	521,734	516,604	527,00
Net Stockholders' Equity	862,584	847,999	806,324	805,517	777,082	768,730	741,361	716,49
Shares Outstanding	36,985	36,689	35,459	35,544	35,544	35,489	35,402	35,07
Statistical Record								
Operating Profit Margin %	9.94	9.79	11.55	7.13	11.22	13.06	10.00	10.4
Net Inc./Net Property %	1.66	5.65	5.02	5.53	5.25	6.09	5.49	7.0
Net Inc./Tot. Capital %	1.48	5.19	5.12	5.43	5.61	5.82	5.19	6.5
Return on Equity %	3.63	12.25	11.04	12.04	11.12	12.05	10.71	13.7
Accum. Depr./Gross Prop. %	37.82	37.94	36.52	35.12	34.63	34.79	34.53	33.7
Price Range	42.65-38.92	45.12-31.68	42.62-29.83	46.56-31.81	39.44-26.81	40.00-32.31	39.63-33.13	39.63-31.7
P/E Ratio	50.18-45.79	15.72-11.04	16.98-11.88	16.99-11.61	16.16-10.99	15.33-12.38	17.61-14.72	14.10-11.3
Average Yield %	5.16	5.43	5.53	5.20	6.03	5.25	5.22	5.2

Address: 130 East Randolph Drive, Chicago, IL 60601-6207	**Officers:** Thomas M. Patrick – Chmn., Pres., C.E.O., William E. Morrow – Exec. V.P.	**Investor Contact:** (312) 240-7534
Telephone: (312) 240-4000	**Transfer Agents:** Computershare Investor Services, Chicago, IL	**Institutional Holding**
Web Site: www.peoplesenergy.com		**No of Institutions:** 3
		Shares: 45,906 **% Held:** –

PEPSICO INC.

Exchange	Symbol	Price	52Wk Range	Yield	P/E
NYS	PEP	$53.85 (3/31/2004)	53.85–38.17	1.19	26.27

*7 Year Price Score 109.1 *NYSE Composite Index=100 *12 Month Price Score 96.3

Interim Earnings (Per Share)

Qtr.	Mar	Jun	Sep	Dec
2000	0.29	0.38	0.40	0.41
2001	0.34	0.44	0.34	0.35
2002	0.36	0.49	0.54	0.46
2003	0.45	0.58	0.62	0.40

Interim Dividends (Per Share)

Amt	Decl	Ex	Rec	Pay
0.16Q	5/7/2003	6/11/2003	6/13/2003	6/30/2003
0.16Q	7/24/2003	9/10/2003	9/12/2003	9/30/2003
0.16Q	11/21/2003	12/10/2003	12/12/2003	1/2/2004
0.16Q	1/29/2004	3/10/2004	3/12/2004	3/31/2004

Indicated Div: $0.64

Valuation Analysis

Forecast P/E	12.68	Trailing P/E	26.27
Market Cap	$95.4 Billion	Book Value	11.9 Billion
Price/Book	6.73	Price/Sales	2.97

Dividend Achiever Status

Rank	203	10 Year Growth Rate	7.89%
Total Years of Dividend Growth		32

Business Summary: Food (MIC: 4.1 SIC: 2086 NAIC:312111)

PepsiCo is a global snack and beverage company. Co. manufactures, markets and sells a variety of salty, convenient, sweet and grain-based snacks, carbonated and non-carbonated beverages and foods. Co.'s Frito-Lay North America division's brands include *Lay's* potato chips, *Fritos* corn chips, *Quaker Chewy* granola bars and *Rold Gold* pretzels. PepsiCo Beverages North America brands include *Pepsi*, *Mountain Dew*, *Sierra Mist*, *Mug*, *SoBe*, *Gatorade*, *Tropicana Pure Premium* and *Propel*. PepsiCo International brands include *Sabritas* in Mexico, *Walkers* in the UK, and *Smith's* in Australia. Quaker Foods North America's products include *Quaker* oatmeal and *Cap'n Crunch* and *Life* ready-to-eat cereals.

Recent Developments: For the year ended Dec 27 2003, net income amounted to $3.57 billion compared with $3.00 billion a year earlier. Results for 2003 and 2002 included merger-related costs of $59.0 million and $224.0 million, respectively. Results for 2003 also included impairment and restructuring charges of $147.0 million. Net revenue advanced 7.4% to $26.97 billion from $25.11 billion the previous year. Co.'s results were driven by increased revenues and improved operating profit from across each of its four operating divisions. Operating profit was $4.78 billion, 11.3% higher than the year before.

Prospects: Co.'s near-term prospects appear favorable, reflecting solid growth trends from across each of its four operating divisions. Results in 2004 should also be aided by the introduction of a number of new products. For instance, Co. expects to roll out new beverage products at Tropicana, including new *Light 'n Healthy*, with 1/3 fewer calories and *Healthy Heart*, with vitamins, potassium and folate. New snack products for 2004 include low-carb *Doritos* and *Tostitos* offerings, *Doritos Rollitos*, a new *Muchies* kid mix, new multi-serve options and *Frito-Lay Natural* line-extensions. Accordingly, Co. is targeting full-year 2004 earnings in the $2.24 to $2.28 per share range.

Financial Data

($S in Thousands)	12/27/2003	12/28/2002	12/29/2001	12/30/2000	12/25/1999	12/26/1998	12/27/1997	12/28/1996
Earnings Per Share	2.05	1.85	1.47	1.48	1.37	1.31	0.95	0.72
Cash Flow Per Share	2.48	2.58	2.32	2.65	2.02	2.11	2.17	2.61
Tang. Book Val. Per Share	3.81	2.36	2.16	1.91	1.47	N.M	0.71	N.M
Dividends Per Share	0.620	0.590	0.570	0.550	0.530	0.510	0.480	0.430
Dividend Payout %	30.24	31.89	38.77	37.16	38.68	38.93	50.52	59.72
Income Statement								
Total Revenues	26,971,000	25,112,000	26,935,000	20,438,000	20,367,000	22,348,000	20,917,000	31,645,000
Total Indirect Exp.	9,811,000	8,885,000	12,160,000	9,270,000	9,351,000	10,434,000	9,730,000	13,716,000
Depreciation & Amort.	145,000	138,000	165,000	138,000	183,000	222,000	199,000	301,000
Operating Income	4,781,000	4,730,000	4,021,000	3,225,000	2,818,000	2,584,000	2,662,000	2,546,000
Net Interest Inc./(Exp.)	(112,000)	(142,000)	(152,000)	(145,000)	(245,000)	(321,000)	(353,000)	(499,000)
Income Taxes	1,424,000	1,555,000	1,367,000	1,027,000	1,606,000	270,000	818,000	898,000
Equity Earns/Minority Int.	323,000	280,000	160,000	130,000	83,000	...	...	...
Income from Cont Ops	...	...	...	...	...	...	1,491,000	...
Net Income	3,568,000	3,313,000	2,662,000	2,183,000	2,050,000	1,993,000	2,142,000	1,149,000
Average Shs. Outstg.	1,739,000	1,789,000	1,807,000	1,475,000	1,496,000	1,519,000	1,570,000	1,606,000
Balance Sheet								
Cash & Cash Equivalents	2,001,000	1,845,000	1,649,000	1,330,000	1,056,000	394,000	2,883,000	786,000
Total Current Assets	6,930,000	6,413,000	5,853,000	4,604,000	4,173,000	4,362,000	6,251,000	5,139,000
Total Assets	25,327,000	23,474,000	21,695,000	18,339,000	17,551,000	22,660,000	20,101,000	24,512,000
Total Current Liabilities	6,415,000	6,052,000	4,998,000	3,935,000	3,788,000	7,914,000	4,257,000	5,139,000
Long-Term Obligations	1,702,000	2,187,000	2,651,000	2,346,000	2,812,000	4,028,000	4,946,000	8,439,000
Net Stockholders' Equity	11,896,000	9,298,000	8,648,000	7,249,000	6,881,000	6,401,000	6,936,000	6,623,000
Net Working Capital	515,000	361,000	855,000	669,000	385,000	(3,552,000)	1,994,000	...
Shares Outstanding	1,705,000	1,722,000	1,756,000	1,446,000	1,455,000	1,471,000	1,502,000	1,545,000
Statistical Record								
Operating Profit Margin %	17.72	18.83	14.92	15.77	13.83	11.56	12.72	8.04
Return on Equity %	29.99	35.63	30.78	30.11	29.79	31.13	21.49	17.34
Return on Assets %	14.08	14.11	12.27	11.90	11.68	8.79	7.41	4.68
Debt/Total Assets %	6.72	9.31	12.21	12.79	16.02	17.77	24.60	34.42
Price Range	48.71–37.30	53.12–35.50	50.28–41.26	49.75–30.63	41.81–30.25	44.69–27.69	41.06–29.13	35.63–27.50
P/E Ratio	23.76–18.20	28.71–19.19	34.20–28.07	33.61–20.69	30.52–22.08	34.11–21.14	43.22–30.66	49.48–38.19
Average Yield %	1.41	1.28	1.24	1.34	1.44	1.31	1.35	1.39

Address: 700 Anderson Hill Road, Purchase, NY 10577-1444	**Officers:** Steven S. Reinemund – Chmn., C.E.O., Indra K. Nooyi – Pres., C.F.O.	**Investor Contact:** (914) 253-3691
Telephone: (914) 253-2000	**Transfer Agents:** The Bank of New York, Newark, NJ	**Institutional Holding**
Web Site: www.pepsico.com		**No of Institutions:** 44
		Shares: 1,317,724 **% Held:** –

PFIZER INC

Exchange	Symbol	Price	52Wk Range	Yield	P/E
NYS	PFE	$35.05 (3/31/2004)	38.85-29.55	1.94	159.32

*7 Year Price Score 94.1   *NYSE Composite Index=100   *12 Month Price Score 94.3

Interim Earnings (Per Share)

Qtr.	Apr	Jul	Oct	Dec
2000	0.31	0.18	0.21	(0.11)
2001	0.30	0.29	0.33	0.30
2002	0.37	0.32	0.38	0.40
2003	0.40	(0.49)	0.29	0.02

Interim Dividends (Per Share)

Amt	Decl	Ex	Rec	Pa
0.15Q	4/24/2003	5/14/2003	5/16/2003	6/5/200
0.15Q	6/26/2003	8/13/2003	8/15/2003	9/4/200
0.15Q	10/23/2003	11/12/2003	11/14/2003	12/4/200
0.17Q	12/15/2003	2/11/2004	2/13/2004	3/5/200

Indicated Div: $0.68 (Div. Reinv. Plan)

Valuation Analysis

Forecast P/E	14.59	Trailing P/E	159.32
Market Cap	$216.0 Billion	Book Value	65.2 Billion
Price/Book	4.11	Price/Sales	5.92

Dividend Achiever Status

Rank	72	10 Year Growth Rate	15.67%
Total Years of Dividend Growth			36

TRADING VOLUME (thousand shares)

Business Summary: Pharmaceuticals (MIC: 9.1 SIC: 2834 NAIC:325412)

Pfizer is a research-based, global pharmaceutical company that discovers, develops, manufactures and markets medicines for humans an animals as well as consumer healthcare products. The products include *Norvasc*, for the treatment of hypertension and angina, *Zyrtec*, a anti-allergy medicine, *Viagra*, an oral medication for the treatment of erectile dysfunction, *Zoloft*, a selective serotonin re-uptak inhibitor for the treatment of depression. The animal health segment includes anti-parasitic, anti-infective and anti-inflammator medicines, and vaccines. The consumer healthcare segment includes *Nicorette*, for tobacco dependence, *Benadryl* antihistamine fc allergies

Recent Developments: For the year ended Dec 31 2003, income was $1.64 billion, before a gain of $2.30 billion from discontinue operations and an accounting change charge of $30.0 million, compared with income of $9.18 billion, before a gain of $355.0 millio from discontinued operations and an accounting change charge of $410.0 million, the previous year. Results for 2003 and 2002 include pre-tax merger-related costs of $1.06 billion and $630.0 million, respectively. The 2003 results also included a pre-tax merger-relate in-process research and development charge of $5.05 billion. Revenues jumped 39.6% to $45.19 billion from $32.37 billion the yea before, reflecting Co.'s strong product portfolio.

Prospects: Co. should continue to benefit from the integration of Pharmacia, the success of key products compared with ne* competition, new product launches, and continued advances of product candidates in its research and development pipeline. Also, Cc should benefit from ongoing development of its business through strategic acquisitions, licensing agreements, and divestitures Meanwhile, Co. expects revenues to be approximately $54.00 billion and diluted earnings per share to be $1.68 for full-year 200 Separately, Co. completed the cash offer to acquire Esperion Therapeutics, Inc., a biopharmaceutical company, for approximately $1.3 billion.

Financial Data

(US$ in Thousands)	12/31/2003	12/31/2002	12/31/2001	12/31/2000	12/31/1999	12/31/1998	12/31/1997	12/31/199●
Earnings Per Share	0.22	1.47	1.22	0.59	0.82	0.49	0.56	0.4●
Cash Flow Per Share	1.60	1.58	1.46	0.97	0.79	0.74	0.41	0.5●
Tang. Book Val. Per Share	0.85	3.04	2.63	2.26	2.11	2.05	1.71	1.4●
Dividends Per Share	0.600	0.520	0.440	0.360	0.300	0.250	0.220	0.20●
Dividend Payout %	272.72	35.37	36.06	61.01	37.39	51.70	39.99	40.1●
Income Statement								
Total Revenues	45,188,000	32,373,000	32,259,000	29,574,000	16,204,000	13,544,000	12,504,000	11,306,0●
Total Indirect Exp.	35,703,000	16,680,000	17,088,000	19,254,000	9,170,000	7,892,000	6,952,000	6,602,0●
Depreciation & Amort.	4,078,000	56,000	206,000	240,000	86,000	90,000	136,000	430,0●
Operating Income	3,263,000	11,676,000	10,240,000	5,533,000	4,549,000	3,603,000	3,346,000	2,804,0●
Net Interest Inc./(Exp.)	...	131,000	273,000	172,000	78,000	49,000	9,000	
Income Taxes	1,621,000	2,609,000	2,561,000	2,049,000	1,244,000	642,000	865,000	869,0●
Eqty Earns/Minority Int.	(3,000)	(34,000)	(119,000)	(134,000)	(48,000)	(47,000)	(78,000)	(6,00●
Income from Cont Ops	1,639,000	9,181,000	7,752,000	3,718,000	3,199,000	1,950,000	...	
Net Income	3,910,000	9,126,000	7,788,000	3,726,000	3,179,000	3,351,000	2,213,000	1,929,0●
Average Shs. Outstg.	7,286,000	6,241,000	6,361,000	6,368,000	3,884,000	3,945,000	3,909,000	3,870,0●
Balance Sheet								
Cash & Cash Equivalents	11,952,000	12,551,000	8,615,000	6,863,000	4,442,000	3,929,000	1,589,000	1,637,0●
Total Current Assets	29,741,000	24,781,000	18,450,000	17,187,000	11,191,000	9,931,000	6,820,000	6,468,0●
Total Assets	116,775,000	46,356,000	39,153,000	33,510,000	20,574,000	18,302,000	15,336,000	14,667,0●
Total Current Liabilities	23,657,000	18,555,000	13,640,000	11,981,000	9,185,000	7,192,000	5,305,000	5,640,0●
Long-Term Obligations	5,755,000	3,140,000	2,609,000	1,123,000	525,000	527,000	729,000	687,0●
Net Stockholders' Equity	65,377,000	19,950,000	18,293,000	16,076,000	8,887,000	8,810,000	7,933,000	6,954,0●
Net Working Capital	6,084,000	6,226,000	4,810,000	5,206,000	2,006,000	2,739,000	1,515,000	828,0●
Shares Outstanding	7,629,000	6,162,000	6,277,000	6,314,000	3,847,000	3,883,000	3,882,000	3,870,0●
Statistical Record								
Operating Profit Margin %	7.22	36.06	31.74	18.70	28.07	26.60	26.75	24.8●
Return on Equity %	2.50	46.02	42.37	23.12	35.99	22.13	27.89	27.7●
Return on Assets %	1.40	19.80	19.79	11.09	15.54	10.65	14.43	13.1●
Debt/Total Assets %	4.92	6.77	6.66	3.35	2.55	2.87	4.75	4.6●
Price Range	36.18-28.56	42.15-25.92	46.13-35.67	48.94-30.44	50.00-31.71	41.98-24.65	25.94-13.62	15.08-10.●
P/E Ratio	164.5-129.8	28.67-17.63	37.81-29.24	82.94-51.59	60.98-38.67	85.67-50.30	46.32-24.33	30.78-20.●
Average Yield %	1.88	1.49	1.06	0.87	0.78	0.74	1.18	1.●

Address: 235 East 42nd Street, New York, NY 10017-5755 Telephone: (212) 573-2323 Web Site: www.pfizer.com	Officers: Henry A. McKinnell – Chmn., Pres., C.E.O., David L. Shedlarz – Exec. V.P., C.F.O. Transfer Agents:EquiServe Trust Company, N.A., Jersey City, NJ	Institutional Holding No of Institutions: 13 Shares: 9,641,163 % Held: –

PIEDMONT NATURAL GAS CO., INC.

Exchange	Symbol	Price	52Wk Range	Yield	P/E
NYS	PNY	$42.22 (3/31/2004)	43.46–35.52	4.07	15.87

Year Price Score 119.2 *NYSE Composite Index=100 *12 Month Price Score 96.5

Interim Earnings (Per Share)

Qtr.	Jan	Apr	Jul	Oct
2000–01	1.56	1.23	(0.52)	(0.25)
2001–02	1.26	1.27	(0.27)	(0.37)
2002–03	1.74	0.93	(0.29)	(0.16)
2003–04	2.18	...	...	...

Interim Dividends (Per Share)

Amt	Decl	Ex	Rec	Pay
0.415Q	5/30/2003	6/20/2003	6/24/2003	7/15/2003
0.415Q	...	9/22/2003	9/24/2003	10/15/2003
0.415Q	12/12/2003	12/19/2003	12/23/2003	1/15/2004
0.43Q	2/27/2004	3/23/2004	3/25/2004	4/15/2004

Indicated Div: $1.72

Valuation Analysis

Forecast P/E	17.06	Trailing P/E	15.87
Market Cap	$1.4 Billion	Book Value	871.4 Million
Price/Book	1.67	Price/Sales	1.08

Dividend Achiever Status

Rank	240	10 Year Growth Rate	5.48%
Total Years of Dividend Growth		24	

Business Summary: Gas Utilities (MIC: 7.4 SIC: 4924 NAIC:221210)

Piedmont Natural Gas Co. is an energy services company primarily engaged in the distribution of natural gas to 940,000 residential, commercial and industrial customers in North Carolina, South Carolina and Tennessee, including 60,000 customers served by municipalities who are our wholesale customers. Co.'s subsidiaries are invested in joint venture, energy-related businesses, including unregulated retail natural gas and propane marketing, interstate natural gas storage, intrastate natural gas transportation and regulated natural gas distribution. Co. also sells residential and commercial gas appliances in Tennessee.

Recent Developments: For the three months ended Jan 31 2004, net income advanced 28.7% to $74.6 million compared with $58.0 million in the corresponding quarter of the previous year. Earnings growth was primarily attributable to the acquisition of North Carolina Natural Gas on Sep 30 2003. Operating revenues improved 25.4% to $618.8 million from $493.5 million in the year-earlier period. Margin (revenues less the cost of gas) increased 21.5% to $196.5 million from $161.7 million the year before. Operating income jumped 17.8% to $77.3 million versus $65.7 million in the prior-year quarter. System throughput climbed 15.6% to 73,492 dekatherms from 63,589 dekatherms in 2003.

Prospects: Co. is benefiting from strong revenue growth, reflecting the acquisition of North Carolina Natural Gas (NCNG) and internal customer expansion. Accordingly, Co. increased its earnings guidance to range from $2.35 to $2.45 per share, up from its previous guidance of $2.25 to $2.40 per diluted share. This revision includes earnings accretion related to the NCNG acquisition, recent rate case approvals for NCNG and Nashville Gas divisions and the expected negative impact of higher wholesale natural gas prices. Separately, on Jan 20 2004, Co. announced that it and three other utility partners have completed the sale of their interests in Heritage

Financial Data

(US$ in Thousands)	3 Mos	10/31/2003	10/31/2002	10/31/2001	10/31/2000	10/31/1999	10/31/1998	10/31/1997
Earnings Per Share	2.66	2.22	1.89	2.02	2.01	1.86	1.96	1.79
Cash Flow Per Share	1.68	2.97	3.30	4.94	1.71	1.01	4.01	4.66
Tang. Book Val. Per Share	21.54	17.21	17.81	17.26	16.52	15.71	14.90	13.90
Dividends Per Share	1.660	1.640	1.580	1.520	1.440	1.360	1.280	1.200
Dividend Payout %	62.41	74.09	83.86	75.24	71.64	73.11	65.30	67.31
Income Statement								
Total Revenues	618,785	1,220,822	832,028	1,107,856	830,377	686,470	765,277	775,517
Total Indirect Exp.	26,455	127,667	112,240	110,587	101,630	111,961	112,057	104,017
Costs & Expenses	541,436	1,117,716	741,901	1,013,887	740,677	594,748	674,120	691,531
Depreciation & Amort.	20,453	63,164	57,593	52,060	48,894	44,131	42,175	39,187
Operating Income	77,349	103,106	90,127	93,969	89,700	91,722	91,157	83,986
Net Interest Inc./(Exp.)	(11,211)	(40,197)	(40,604)	(39,414)	(40,272)	(32,371)	(33,187)	(33,996)
Income Taxes	48,595	8,524	9,010	7,300	...	...	...	...
Equity Earns/Minority Int.	(11)	...	...	...	...	...	...	...
Net Income	74,622	74,362	62,217	65,485	64,031	58,207	60,313	54,074
Average Shs. Outstg.	34,222	33,503	32,937	32,420	31,779	31,242	30,717	30,229
Balance Sheet								
Net Property	1,816,349	1,813,414	1,159,601	1,115,862	1,071,983	1,046,975	990,640	941,736
Total Assets	2,443,841	2,296,406	1,445,088	1,393,658	1,445,003	1,288,657	1,162,844	1,098,156
Long-Term Obligations	660,000	460,000	462,000	509,000	451,000	423,000	371,000	381,000
Net Stockholders' Equity	871,448	630,195	589,596	560,379	527,372	491,747	458,268	419,826
Shares Outstanding	38,042	33,655	33,090	32,463	31,914	31,294	30,738	30,193
Statistical Record								
Operating Profit Margin %	12.50	8.44	10.83	8.48	10.80	13.36	11.91	10.82
Inc./Net Property %	4.11	4.10	5.36	5.86	5.97	5.55	6.08	5.74
Inc./Tot. Capital %	4.31	5.81	5.14	5.40	5.69	5.64	6.41	5.96
Return on Equity %	8.56	11.79	10.55	11.68	12.14	11.83	13.16	12.88
Accum. Depr./Gross Prop. %	24.55	24.14	23.07	31.45	30.18	29.14	28.35	27.24
Price Range	43.46–39.54	40.75–32.90	37.95–28.36	39.38–29.44	33.00–23.75	36.13–28.88	36.44–27.19	30.19–22.38
P/E Ratio	19.94–18.14	18.36–14.82	20.08–15.01	19.49–14.57	16.42–11.82	19.42–15.52	18.59–13.87	16.86–12.50
Average Yield %	3.99	4.43	4.55	4.51	5.01	4.14	4.00	4.78

Address: 1915 Rexford Road, Charlotte, NC 28211
Telephone: (704) 364–3120
Web Site: www.piedmontng.com

Officers: Thomas E. Skains – Chmn., Pres., C.E.O., David J. Dzuricky – Sr. V.P., C.F.O.
Transfer Agents: Wachovia Bank of North Carolina, NA, Boston, MA

Investor Contact: 704-731-4438
Institutional Holding
No of Institutions: 16
Shares: 115,224   % Held: –

PIER 1 IMPORTS INC.

Exchange	Symbol	Price	52Wk Range	Yield	P/E
NYS	PIR	$23.70 (3/31/2004)	26.19-15.09	1.69	17.82

*7 Year Price Score 148.5   ***NYSE Composite Index=100**   ***12 Month Price Score 109.7**

Interim Earnings (Per Share)

Qtr.	May	Aug	Nov	Feb
2000-01	0.17	0.18	0.24	0.38
2001-02	0.13	0.14	0.26	0.51
2002-03	0.23	0.23	0.33	0.57
2003-04	0.21	0.20	0.35	...

Interim Dividends (Per Share)

Amt	Decl	Ex	Rec	Pa
0.08Q	6/26/2003	8/4/2003	8/6/2003	8/20/20
0.08Q	9/25/2003	11/3/2003	11/5/2003	11/19/200
0.08Q	12/4/2003	2/2/2004	2/4/2004	2/18/200
0.10Q	3/25/2004	5/3/2004	5/5/2004	5/19/200

Indicated Div: $0.40 (Div. Reinv. Plan)

Valuation Analysis

Forecast P/E	14.12	Trailing P/E	17.82
Market Cap	$2.2 Billion	Book Value	663.4 Million
Price/Book	2.60	Price/Sales	0.94

Dividend Achiever Status

Rank	24 10 Year Growth Rate 22.08%
Total Years of Dividend Growth	12

Business Summary: Retail – Furniture &Home Furnishings (MIC: 5.9 SIC: 5712 NAIC:442110)

Pier 1 Imports is a retailer of decorative home furnishings, furniture, dining and kitchen goods, bath and bedding accessories and oth specialty items for the home imported from over 40 countries. As of May 31 2003, Co. operated *Pier 1 Imports®* stores in 50 state Canada, Puerto Rico, and Mexico; *The Pier®* stores in the U.K.; and *Cargokids®* in six states. Also, Co. supplies merchandise a licenses the Pier 1 Imports name to Sears Mexico and Sears Puerto Rico, which sell Pier 1 merchandise in a "store–within–a–stor format in 17 Sears Mexico stores and in seven Sears Puerto Rico stores.

Recent Developments: For the quarter ended Nov 29 2003, net income improved 3.5% to $32.2 million compared with $31.1 millie in the corresponding period of the previous year. Net sales totaled $482.4 million, up 10.0% compared with $438.5 million the prior ye Comparable–store sales were up 1.6% year over year. Cost of sales, including buying and store occupancy costs, increased 11.2% $274.3 million from $246.7 million in the previous year. Selling, general and administrative expenses increased 10.6% to $144.0 millic Operating income grew 3.4% to $51.0 million. During the quarter, Co. opened 55 new *Pier 1* stores, and relocated or closed 13 store and opened 9 net new *Cargokids* stores.

Prospects: Co. continues to improve its balance sheet by managing working capital and increasing operating cash flow, wh accelerating store openings and buying back its common stock. Looking ahead, Co. has a number of new programs planned. Six maj merchandise introductions will rollout during fiscal 2005 compared to four traditionally. Additionally, Co. is working on seven operational initiatives to increase sales and profitability for fiscal 2005, including new product introductions and new national televisie commercials. Meanwhile, increased furniture sales and early indications of the March Dining Event should favorably affect sales in t first quarter of fiscal 2005.

Financial Data

(US$ in Thousands)	9 Mos	6 Mos	3 Mos	03/01/2003	03/02/2002	03/03/2001	02/26/2000	02/27/199
Earnings Per Share	0.76	0.41	0.21	1.36	1.04	0.97	0.75	0.7
Cash Flow Per Share	0.67	0.19	(0.02)	1.84	2.54	1.12	1.15	0.8
Tang. Book Val. Per Share	7.43	7.14	7.15	7.09	6.26	5.53	4.69	4.
Dividends Per Share	0.280	0.250	0.220	0.210	0.160	0.150	0.120	0.1
Dividend Payout %	36.84	60.97	104.76	15.44	15.38	15.46	16.00	15.
Income Statement								
Total Revenues	1,312,987	830,543	402,712	1,754,867	1,548,556	1,411,498	1,231,095	1,138,5
Total Indirect Exp.	435,064	277,927	137,939	548,751	490,948	442,939	389,367	365,7
Depreciation & Amort.	37,564	24,424	12,161	46,432	42,821	43,184	39,973	31,1
Operating Income	110,343	59,382	30,258	204,654	158,813	151,516	123,181	134,6
Net Interest Inc./(Exp.)	(1,344)	(1,022)	(637)	(2,327)	(2,300)	(3,130)	(6,918)	(7,91
Income Taxes	40,930	22,023	11,196	75,988	58,788	55,590	43,887	49,2
Net Income	69,692	37,498	19,062	129,386	100,209	94,650	74,725	80,3
Average Shs. Outstg.	91,803	91,910	90,145	95,305	96,185	97,952	103,297	108,8
Balance Sheet								
Cash & Cash Equivalents	178,731	185,888	219,679	282,652	280,229	122,244	104,196	41,9
Total Current Assets	692,521	652,027	655,620	663,601	605,153	477,066	415,280	381,9
Total Assets	1,013,093	947,518	935,988	967,487	862,672	735,710	670,710	653,9
Total Current Liabilities	270,173	233,089	217,351	243,589	208,396	144,110	175,966	129,8
Long–Term Obligations	19,000	19,000	19,000	25,000	25,356	25,000	25,000	96,0
Net Stockholders' Equity	663,402	635,295	642,593	643,936	585,656	531,879	440,663	403,8
Net Working Capital	...	...	438,269	420,012	396,757	332,956	239,314	252,1
Shares Outstanding	89,220	88,973	89,824	90,734	93,417	96,160	93,830	97,6
Statistical Record								
Operating Profit Margin %	8.40	7.14	7.51	11.66	10.25	10.73	10.00	11.
Return on Equity %	10.50	5.90	2.96	20.09	17.11	17.79	16.95	19.
Return on Assets %	6.87	3.95	2.03	13.37	11.61	12.86	11.14	12.
Debt/Total Assets %	1.87	2.00	2.02	2.58	2.93	3.39	3.72	14.
Price Range	26.15-14.85	21.80-14.85	20.76-14.85	23.95-15.20	20.24-8.13	14.00-7.88	12.25-5.38	20.63-6.
P/E Ratio	34.41-19.54	53.17-36.22	98.86-70.71	17.61-11.18	19.46-7.82	14.43-8.12	16.33-7.17	26.79-8.
Average Yield %	1.40	1.32	1.25	1.08	1.20	1.36	1.52	0

Address: 301 Commerce Street, Fort Worth, TX 76102
Telephone: (817) 252–8000
Web Site: www.pier1.com

Officers: Marvin J. Girouard – Chmn., C.E.O., Charles H. Turner – Exec. V.P., Fin., C.F.O., Treas.
Transfer Agents: Mellon Investor Services, Ridgefield Park, NJ

Investor Contact: (817) 252–7835
Institutional Holding
No of Institutions: 23
Shares: 669,559   **% Held:** –

PINNACLE WEST CAPITAL CORP.

Exchange	Symbol	Price	52Wk Range	Yield	P/E
NYS	PNW	$39.35 (3/31/2004)	40.29–32.23	4.57	20.60

7 Year Price Score 93.6   *NYSE Composite Index=100   *12 Month Price Score 97.9

Interim Earnings (Per Share)
Qtr.	Mar	Jun	Sep	Dec
2000	0.64	1.06	1.37	0.49
2001	0.70	0.79	1.77	0.59
2002	0.63	0.89	1.19	(0.18)
2003	0.28	0.61	1.20	0.43

Interim Dividends (Per Share)
Amt	Decl	Ex	Rec	Pay
0.425Q	7/17/2003	7/30/2003	8/1/2003	9/1/2003
0.45Q	10/22/2003	10/30/2003	11/3/2003	12/1/2003
0.45Q	1/21/2004	1/29/2004	2/2/2004	3/1/2004
0.45Q	3/17/2004	3/29/2004	5/3/2004	6/1/2004

Indicated Div: $1.80

Valuation Analysis
Forecast P/E	12.24	Trailing P/E	20.60
Market Cap	$3.3 Billion	Book Value	2.8 Billion
Price/Book	1.16	Price/Sales	1.18

Dividend Achiever Status
Rank	17	10 Year Growth Rate	24.04%
Total Years of Dividend Growth			10

Business Summary: Electricity (MIC: 7.1 SIC: 4911 NAIC:221121)

Pinnacle West Capital is a holding company whose principal asset is Arizona Public Service (APS), the state's largest utility with more than 902,000 customers as of Dec 30 2002. APS provides wholesale and retail electric service to substantially all of Arizona, with the major exceptions of the Tucson metropolitan area and about one–half of the Phoenix metropolitan area. Co.'s other major subsidiaries are Pinnacle West Energy, which conducts competitive electricity generation operations; APS Energy Services, which provides competitive commodity–related energy services; SunCor Development, a real estate developer; and El Dorado Investment, which holds miscellaneous small investments.

Recent Developments: For the year ended Dec 31 2003, net income increased 61.0% to $240.6 million from $149.4 million the previous year. Results for 2003 and 2002 included income from discontinued operations of $10.0 million and $9.0 million, respectively. Results for 2003 included a gain for equity funds used during construction of $14.2 million and income tax credits related to prior years of $17.2 million. Results for 2002 included an accounting change charge of $65.7 million and non–recurring charges of $87.0 million. Total operating revenues climbed 15.5% to $2.82 billion, due in large part to strong increases in regulated electricity revenues related to customer growth and higher average usage.

Prospects: On Feb 3 2003, Co.'s subsidiary, APS Energy Services, received an unfavorable recommendation by the Staff of the Arizona Corporation Commission (ACC) concerning APS' rate request. The ACC Staff recommended that APS rates should be cut by an average of about 8.0%. APS had sought an increase of nearly 10.0%. The staff also stated that several power plants built by Co. should not be included in the rate base. APS believes that its rate request is necessary to ensure APS' continued ability to reliably serve its customers. An Administrative Law Judge is due to hear the case in late April 2003 and will make another recommendation to the ACC's commissioners, who will ultimately decide the case.

Financial Data
(US$ in Thousands)	12/31/2003	12/31/2002	12/31/2001	12/31/2000	12/31/1999	12/31/1998	12/31/1997	12/31/1996
Earnings Per Share	2.52	2.53	3.85	3.56	3.17	2.85	2.74	2.41
Cash Flow Per Share	9.86	10.24	6.72	8.23	7.47	7.09	7.41	6.54
Tang. Book Val. Per Share	30.99	29.43	29.46	28.08	26.00	25.50	23.90	22.51
Dividends Per Share	1.720	1.620	1.520	1.420	1.320	1.220	1.120	1.020
Dividend Payout %	68.45	64.22	39.61	40.02	41.79	42.98	41.05	42.32
Income Statement								
Total Revenues	2,817,852	2,637,279	4,551,373	3,690,175	2,423,353	2,130,586	1,995,026	1,817,760
Total Indirect Exp.	548,413	532,838	528,971	494,190	482,174	496,585	489,831	421,584
Costs & Expenses	2,335,799	2,121,232	3,876,746	3,014,204	1,844,576	1,563,458	1,437,520	1,273,901
Depreciation & Amort.	438,143	424,886	427,903	394,410	385,568	379,679	368,285	299,507
Operating Income	482,053	516,047	674,627	675,971	578,777	567,128	557,506	543,859
Net Interest Inc./(Exp.)	(160,906)	(144,243)	(127,960)	(149,601)	(150,717)	(150,549)	(163,135)	(185,713)
Income Taxes	105,560	138,100	213,535	223,852	168,065	164,593	150,281	128,456
Income from Cont Ops	230,576	215,153	327,367	...	269,772	...	...	211,059
Net Income	240,579	149,408	312,166	302,332	167,887	242,892	235,856	181,180
Average Shs. Outstg.	91,405	84,964	84,930	84,935	85,008	85,345	86,023	87,442
Balance Sheet								
Net Property	7,480,090	6,479,398	5,907,315	5,133,193	4,778,515	4,730,563	4,677,568	4,655,140
Total Assets	9,536,378	8,425,806	7,981,748	7,149,151	6,608,506	6,824,546	6,850,417	6,989,289
Long–Term Obligations	2,897,725	2,881,695	2,673,078	1,955,083	2,206,052	2,048,961	2,244,248	2,372,113
Net Stockholders' Equity	2,829,779	2,686,153	2,499,323	2,382,714	2,205,733	2,163,351	2,027,436	1,970,323
Shares Outstanding	91,287	91,255	84,824	84,824	84,824	84,824	84,825	87,516
Statistical Record								
Operating Profit Margin %	17.10	19.56	14.82	18.31	23.88	26.61	27.94	29.91
Net Inc./Net Property %	3.21	2.30	5.28	5.88	3.51	5.13	5.04	3.89
Net Inc./Tot. Capital %	3.40	2.20	5.00	5.51	3.00	4.29	4.06	3.06
Return on Equity %	8.14	8.00	13.09	12.68	12.23	11.22	11.63	10.71
Accum. Depr./Gross Prop. %	29.70	34.90	36.38	38.31	38.77	37.30	35.90	34.26
Price Range	40.24-29.07	46.16-22.49	50.37-38.10	51.88-25.94	42.88-30.44	48.88-39.75	42.50-27.88	32.25-26.38
P/E Ratio	15.97-11.54	18.25-8.89	13.08-9.90	14.57-7.29	13.53-9.60	17.15-13.95	15.51-10.17	13.38-10.94
Average Yield %	4.89	4.44	3.44	3.76	3.48	2.81	3.45	3.51

Address: 400 North Fifth Street, Phoenix, AZ 85072-3999	Officers: William J. Post – Chmn., C.E.O., Jack E. Davis – Pres., C.O.O	Investor Contact:602–250–5668
Telephone: (602) 250–1000	Transfer Agents:Pinnacle West Capital Corporation, Phoenix, AZ	Institutional Holding No of Institutions: 5
Web Site: www.pinnaclewest.com		Shares: 335,939 % Held: –

PITNEY BOWES, INC.

Exchange	Symbol	Price	52Wk Range	Yield	P/E
NYS	PBI	$42.61 (3/31/2004)	43.27–32.06	2.86	20.29

*7 Year Price Score 87.3   *NYSE Composite Index=100   *12 Month Price Score 96.7

Interim Earnings (Per Share)

Qtr.	Mar	Jun	Sep	Dec
2000	0.57	0.64	0.63	0.34
2001	0.42	0.76	0.49	0.41
2002	0.53	0.59	0.61	0.08
2003	0.48	0.50	0.50	0.62

Interim Dividends (Per Share)

Amt	Decl	Ex	Rec	Pa
0.30Q	4/14/2003	5/21/2003	5/23/2003	6/12/200
0.30Q	7/14/2003	8/20/2003	8/22/2003	9/12/200
0.30Q	11/10/2003	11/19/2003	11/21/2003	12/12/200
0.305Q	2/2/2004	2/18/2004	2/20/2004	3/12/200

Indicated Div: $1.22

Valuation Analysis

Forecast P/E	15.79	Trailing P/E	20.29
Market Cap	$10.2 Billion	Book Value	N/A
Price/Book	N/A	Price/Sales	N/A

Dividend Achiever Status

Rank	148	10 Year Growth Rate	10.31%
Total Years of Dividend Growth			20

Business Summary: Office Equipment Supplies (MIC: 11.12 SIC: 3579 NAIC:423420)

Pitney Bowes provides integrated mail and document management solutions for organizations of all sizes. Global Mailstream Solution includes the sale, rental, and financing of postage meters, mailing machines, address hygiene software, manifest systems, letter and parce scales, mail openers, mailroom furniture, folders, table–top inserters, and postal payment solutions. Global Enterprise Solutions include facilities management, through Pitney Bowes Management Services, and sales, service and financing of high–speed, software–enable production mail systems, through Document Messaging Technologies. Capital Services provides large–ticket financing programs for broad range of products.

Recent Developments: For the year ended Dec 31 2003, income advanced 13.1% to $494.8 million compared with income of $437. million in 2002. Results excluded gains from discontinued operations of $3.3 million for 2003 and $38.0 million for 2002. Result included restructuring charges of $116.7 million for 2003 and included capital services charges of $213.2 million for 2002. Tota revenues climbed 3.8% to $4.58 billion. Revenues in the Global Mailstream segment rose 4.8% to $3.16 billion. Revenues in the Globa Enterprise segment increased 4.2% to $1.27 billion. Revenues in the Capital Services segment fell 16.4% to $150.5 million as Co reduced its exposure to long–term, non–core financing.

Prospects: Looking ahead, Co. expects revenue growth in the range of 3.0% to 5.0% for the first quarter and full year 2004. During th year, Co. intends to continue its restructuring initiatives related to realigned infrastructure requirements and reduced manufacturing need for digital equipment. Consequently, Co. is still finalizing its plans for the first quarter and for the remainder of 2004, and as a resul earnings guidance will exclude the impact of these charges and the impact of any new accounting standards. Adjusted diluted earning per share are expected in the range of $0.55 to $0.57 for the first quarter and in the range of $2.44 to $2.51 for the full year 2004.

Financial Data

(US$ in Thousands)	12/31/2003	12/31/2002	12/31/2001	12/31/2000	12/31/1999	12/31/1998	12/31/1997	12/31/1996
Earnings Per Share	2.10	1.81	2.08	2.18	2.42	2.03	1.80	1.5
Cash Flow Per Share	3.60	2.08	4.18	3.37	3.60	2.74	2.40	2.1
Tang. Book Val. Per Share	N.M	0.10	1.04	4.33	5.27	5.26	5.96	6.8
Dividends Per Share	1.200	1.180	1.160	1.140	1.020	0.900	0.800	0.69
Dividend Payout %	57.14	65.19	55.76	52.29	42.14	44.33	44.44	44.2
Income Statement								
Total Revenues	4,576,853	4,409,758	4,122,474	3,880,868	4,432,608	4,220,517	4,100,464	3,858,57
Total Indirect Exp.	1,483,848	1,837,931	1,619,399	1,438,234	1,628,249	1,543,536	1,457,325	1,422,00
Depreciation & Amort.	288,808	264,250	317,449	321,157	412,104	361,333	300,086	278,16
Operating Income	885,915	798,599	612,460	995,225	1,114,323	1,013,410	1,003,833	881,58
Net Interest Inc./(Exp.)	(164,941)	(179,154)	(184,173)	(192,377)	(179,325)	(149,233)	(200,735)	(197,204
Income Taxes	226,244	181,739	252,064	239,723	325,413	296,236	277,071	214,97
Income from Cont Ops	494,847	437,706	514,320	563,125	659,159	567,941	...	
Net Income	498,117	475,750	488,343	622,546	636,212	576,394	526,027	469,41
Average Shs. Outstg.	236,165	241,483	247,615	258,602	272,006	279,656	292,517	298,23
Balance Sheet								
Cash & Cash Equivalents	293,812	315,156	231,588	198,255	254,270	125,684	137,073	135,27
Total Current Assets	2,513,175	2,552,625	2,556,608	2,626,708	3,342,574	2,508,963	2,463,515	2,222,06
Total Assets	8,891,388	8,732,314	8,318,471	7,901,266	8,222,672	7,661,039	7,893,389	8,155,72
Total Current Liabilities	2,646,969	3,350,309	3,083,042	2,881,577	2,872,764	2,721,812	3,373,233	3,305,28
Long–Term Obligations	2,840,943	2,316,844	2,419,150	1,881,947	1,997,856	1,712,937	1,068,395	1,300,43
Net Stockholders' Equity	1,087,362	853,327	891,355	1,284,975	1,625,610	1,648,002	1,872,577	2,239,04
Net Working Capital	(133,794)	(797,684)	(526,434)	(254,869)	469,810	(212,849)	(909,718)	(1,083,22
Shares Outstanding	232,288	235,373	242,028	248,800	264,694	270,378	279,674	295,96
Statistical Record								
Operating Profit Margin %	19.35	18.10	14.85	25.64	25.13	24.01	24.48	22.8
Return on Equity %	45.50	51.29	57.70	43.82	40.54	34.46	28.09	20.9
Return on Assets %	5.56	5.01	6.18	7.12	8.01	7.41	6.66	5.7
Debt/Total Assets %	31.95	26.53	29.08	23.81	24.29	22.35	13.53	15.9
Price Range	42.44–29.90	43.92–28.80	44.40–32.56	53.75–25.50	71.13–41.75	66.06–43.00	45.22–27.19	30.25–21.6
P/E Ratio	20.21–14.24	24.27–15.91	21.35–15.66	24.66–11.70	29.39–17.25	32.54–21.18	25.12–15.10	19.39–13.9
Average Yield %	3.26	3.11	3.02	2.94	1.68	1.75	2.23	2.7

Address: One Elmcroft Road, Stamford, CT 06926–0700	**Officers:** Michael J. Critelli – Chmn., C.E.O., Karen M. Garrison – Exec. V.P.	**Investor Contact:** (203) 351–6349
Telephone: (203) 356–5000	**Transfer Agents:**EquiServe Trust Company, N.A., Providence, RI	**Institutional Holding**
Web Site: www.pb.com		**No of Institutions:** 2
		Shares: 5,800 **% Held:** –

POPULAR INC.

Exchange	Symbol	Price	52Wk Range	Yield	P/E
NMS	BPOP	$43.10 (3/31/2004)	48.10-34.16	2.51	13.06

Year Price Score 134.2 *NYSE Composite Index=100 *12 Month Price Score 106.6

Interim Earnings (Per Share)

Qtr.	Mar	Jun	Sep	Dec
2000	0.46	0.46	0.51	0.54
2001	0.53	0.55	0.55	0.54
2002	0.63	0.72	0.65	0.61
2003	0.74	0.99	0.96	0.78

Interim Dividends (Per Share)

Amt	Decl	Ex	Rec	Pay
0.27Q	4/30/2003	6/11/2003	6/13/2003	7/1/2003
0.27Q	8/13/2003	9/10/2003	9/12/2003	10/1/2003
0.27Q	11/12/2003	12/10/2003	12/12/2003	1/2/2004
0.27Q	2/11/2004	3/10/2004	3/12/2004	4/1/2004

Indicated Div: $1.08 (Div. Reinv. Plan)

Valuation Analysis

Forecast P/E	11.95	Trailing P/E	13.06
Market Cap	$5.7 Billion	Book Value	2.6 Billion
Price/Book	N/A	Price/Sales	N/A

Dividend Achiever Status

Rank	67	10 Year Growth Rate	16.03%
Total Years of Dividend Growth			11

Business Summary: Commercial Banking (MIC: 8.1 SIC: 6022 NAIC:522110)

Popular is a diversified, holding company incorporated under the laws of the Commonwealth of Puerto Rico. As of Dec 31 2003, Co. had total assets of $36.43 billion. Co.'s principal subsidiary, Banco Popular de Puerto Rico, is a consumer-oriented bank operating 193 branches and over 550 automated teller machines in Puerto Rico. The bank also operates seven branches in the U.S. Virgin Islands, one branch in the British Islands and one branch in New York. Co. has three other principal subsidiaries; Popular Securities, Inc., Popular International Bank, Inc. and GM Group, Inc. Another wholly owned subsidiary, Levitt Mortgage Corporation, is a mortgage loan company with operations in Puerto Rico.

Recent Developments: For the year ended Dec 31 2003, net income increased 33.8% to $470.9 million compared with $351.9 million a year earlier. Net interest income rose 10.7% to $1.28 billion from $1.16 billion the previous year. Provision for loan losses was $195.9 million versus $205.6 million in 2002. Total non-interest income advanced 15.1% to $626.0 million from $543.8 million the year before. Non-interest income included a gain of $71.1 million for 2003 and a loss of $3.3 million for 2002 on the sale of investment securities, mainly marketable equity securities.

Prospects: On Mar 19 2004, Co. and Quaker City Bancorp, Inc. jointly announced the signing of a definitive agreement pursuant to which Co. will acquire all of the common stock of Quaker City at the price of $55.00 cash per share. The acquisition, which will greatly expand Co.'s California banking presence, is expected to be completed by Sep 30 2004. Quaker City is a savings and loan holding company for Quaker City Bank, based in Whittier, CA. Quaker City Bank operates 27 retail full service branches in Southern California, including one inside Wal-Mart stores. At Dec 31, 2003, Quaker City reported total assets of $1.80 billion and total deposits of $1.10 billion.

Financial Data

(US$ in Thousands)	12/31/2003	12/31/2002	12/31/2001	12/31/2000	12/31/1999	12/31/1998	12/31/1997	12/31/1996
Earnings Per Share	3.47	2.61	2.17	1.97	1.84	1.65	1.50	1.34
Tang. Book Val. Per Share	17.67	16.56	14.03	11.85	9.26	9.84	8.64	7.80
Dividends Per Share	0.940	0.800	0.720	0.640	0.580	0.470	0.380	0.330
Dividend Payout %	27.08	30.65	33.17	32.48	31.52	28.48	25.33	24.62
Income Statement								
Total Interest Income	2,034,238	2,023,797	2,095,862	2,150,157	1,851,670	1,651,703	1,491,303	1,272,853
Total Interest Expense	749,550	843,468	1,018,877	1,167,396	897,932	778,691	707,348	591,540
Net Interest Income	1,284,688	1,180,329	1,076,985	982,761	953,738	873,012	783,955	681,313
Provision for Loan Losses	195,939	205,570	213,250	194,640	148,948	137,213	110,607	88,839
Non-Interest Income	626,010	523,678	465,516	465,098	372,916	291,246	247,598	205,472
Non-Interest Expense	1,113,083	1,029,002	920,137	877,471	837,482	720,354	636,920	541,919
Income Before Taxes	601,676	469,435	409,114	375,748	340,224	306,691	284,026	256,027
Equity Earns/Minority Int.	(435)	(248)	18	1,152	2,454	328	...	...
Income from Cont Ops	...	...	303,852	...	...	...	...	...
Net Income	470,901	351,932	304,538	276,103	257,558	232,348	209,565	185,150
Average Shs. Outstg.	132,797	133,915	136,238	135,907	135,585	135,532	134,036	132,044
Balance Sheet								
Cash & Due from Banks	688,090	652,556	606,142	726,051	663,696	667,707	463,151	492,368
Securities Avail. for Sale	20,708,277	21,574,152	18,838,988	17,562,029	14,886,510	14,359,519	10,700,313	7,124,018
Net Loans & Leases	21,922,058	18,116,395	16,892,431	14,942,531	13,996,446	12,167,387	10,899,752	9,338,325
Total Assets	36,434,715	33,660,352	30,744,676	28,057,051	25,460,539	23,160,357	19,300,507	16,764,103
Total Deposits	18,097,828	17,614,740	16,370,042	14,804,907	14,173,715	13,672,214	11,749,586	10,763,275
Long-Term Obligations	7,117,025	4,567,853	4,009,211	1,451,912	2,127,599	1,582,160	1,678,696	1,141,713
Total Liabilities	33,867,173	31,249,473	28,571,858	26,163,407	23,899,553	21,551,244	17,897,415	15,601,571
Net Stockholders' Equity	2,754,417	2,410,879	2,272,818	1,993,644	1,660,986	1,709,113	1,503,092	1,262,532
Shares Outstanding	132,891	132,439	136,362	135,998	135,585	135,532	135,366	132,178
Statistical Record								
Return on Equity %	17.09	14.59	13.36	13.84	15.50	13.59	13.94	14.66
Return on Assets %	1.29	1.04	0.98	0.98	1.01	1.00	1.08	1.10
Equity/Assets %	7.55	7.16	7.39	7.10	6.52	7.37	7.78	7.53
Non-Int. Exp./Tot. Inc. %	41.84	40.39	35.92	33.55	37.64	37.07	36.62	36.65
Price Range	47.57-31.95	35.85-27.50	36.26-25.25	27.94-18.63	37.88-25.44	36.75-23.03	27.94-16.53	17.50-9.69
P/E Ratio	13.71-9.21	13.74-10.54	16.71-11.64	14.18-9.45	20.58-13.82	22.27-13.96	18.63-11.02	13.06-7.23
Average Yield %	2.43	2.55	2.41	2.79	1.91	1.53	1.83	2.67

Address: Popular Center Building, San Juan, PR 00918	**Officers:** Richard L. Carrion – Chmn., Pres., C.E.O., Antonion Luis Ferre – Vice-Chmn.	**Investor Contact:** (787) 754-1685
Telephone: (787) 765-9800		**Institutional Holding**
Web Site: www.popularinc.com		**No of Institutions:** 10
		Shares: 10,440,374 **% Held:** –

PPG INDUSTRIES, INC.

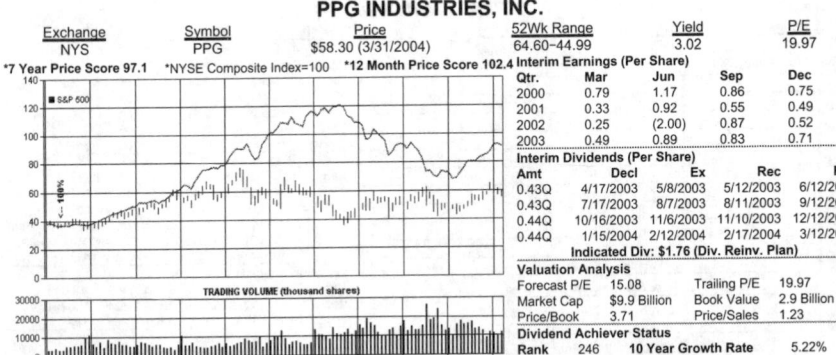

Exchange	Symbol	Price	52Wk Range	Yield	P/E
NYS	PPG	$58.30 (3/31/2004)	64.60–44.99	3.02	19.97

*7 Year Price Score 97.1   *NYSE Composite Index=100   *12 Month Price Score 102.4

Interim Earnings (Per Share)

Qtr.	Mar	Jun	Sep	Dec
2000	0.79	1.17	0.86	0.75
2001	0.33	0.92	0.55	0.49
2002	0.25	(2.00)	0.87	0.52
2003	0.49	0.89	0.83	0.71

Interim Dividends (Per Share)

Amt	Decl	Ex	Rec	Pa
0.43Q	4/17/2003	5/8/2003	5/12/2003	6/12/200
0.43Q	7/17/2003	8/7/2003	8/11/2003	9/12/200
0.44Q	10/16/2003	11/6/2003	11/10/2003	12/12/200
0.44Q	1/15/2004	2/12/2004	2/17/2004	3/12/200

Indicated Div: $1.76 (Div. Reinv. Plan)

Valuation Analysis

Forecast P/E	15.08	Trailing P/E	19.97
Market Cap	$9.9 Billion	Book Value	2.9 Billion
Price/Book	3.71	Price/Sales	1.23

Dividend Achiever Status

Rank	246	10 Year Growth Rate	5.22%
Total Years of Dividend Growth		32

Business Summary: Chemicals (MIC: 11.1 SIC: 2851 NAIC:325510)

PPG Industries is a supplier of products for manufacturing, construction, automotive, chemical processing and numerous other worl industries. Co. is comprised of three basic business segments: coatings, glass and chemicals. Co. is focused on industrial, aerospace packaging, architectural, automotive original and refinish coatings, flat glass, automotive original and replacement glass, an continuous–strand fiber glass, and chlor–alkali and specialty chemicals. Co. operates manufacturing facilities in countries includin Canada, China, England, France, Germany, Ireland, Italy, Mexico, the Netherlands, Portugal, Spain, Taiwan, Argentina, Australi Malaysia, Thailand, Turkey and the U.S.

Recent Developments: For the year ended Dec 31 2003, income jumped to $500.0 million, before an accounting change charge $6.0 million, versus a loss of $60.0 million, before an accounting change charge of $9.0 million, in 2002. Results benefited from improved cost performance, increased volumes across all of Co.'s businesses, stronger pricing, the growth of Co.'s optical product business and favorable currency translation. Results for 2003 and 2002 included an asbestos settlement charge of $38.0 million an $755.0 million, and business realignment charges of $4.0 million and $77.0 million, respectively. Net sales climbed 8.5% to $8.76 billio from $8.07 billion the year before.

Prospects: Co. is optimistic about future business levels due to the continued growth of the global economy, particularly in Nort America and Asia, where Co. is well positioned. Also, there are positive signs of some economic improvement in Europe; however, tha improvement could be negatively affected by a stronger euro. Meanwhile, Co. will continue to focus on cost–reduction efforts, whic should lead to even better results once economic conditions recover. Also, Co. will continue to develop new products and pursue strategi growth opportunities. Separately, Co. and Kansai Paint entered negotiations for the creation of an alliance focused on products fo automotive original equipment manufacturers.

Financial Data

(US$ in Thousands)	12/31/2003	12/31/2002	12/31/2001	12/31/2000	12/31/1999	12/31/1998	12/31/1997	12/31/1996
Earnings Per Share	2.92	(0.36)	2.29	3.57	3.23	4.48	3.94	3.9
Cash Flow Per Share	6.57	5.13	6.29	5.04	5.13	5.27	5.54	5.3
Tang. Book Val. Per Share	7.36	3.47	9.11	8.61	8.29	13.16	21.29	13.5
Dividends Per Share	1.730	1.700	1.680	1.600	1.520	1.420	1.330	1.26
Dividend Payout %	59.24	N.M.	73.36	44.81	47.05	31.69	33.75	32.0
Income Statement								
Total Revenues	8,756,000	8,067,000	8,169,000	8,629,000	7,995,000	7,510,000	7,379,000	7,218,10
Total Indirect Exp.	2,396,000	3,062,000	2,437,000	2,317,000	2,074,000	1,614,000	1,750,000	1,610,60
Depreciation & Amort.	394,000	398,000	447,000	447,000	415,000	381,000	348,000	340,20
Operating Income	843,000	(28,000)	666,000	1,017,000	973,000	1,294,000	1,175,000	1,239,60
Net Interest Inc./(Exp.)	(97,000)	(119,000)	(154,000)	(165,000)	(125,000)	(98,000)	(97,000)	(95,60
Income Taxes	293,000	(7,000)	247,000	369,000	377,000	466,000	435,000	471,00
Eqty Earns/Minority Int.	(54,000)	(40,000)	(17,000)	11,000	...	3,000	(16,000)	(24,60
Income from Cont Ops	500,000	(60,000)	...	...	...	...	...	...
Net Income	494,000	(69,000)	387,000	620,000	568,000	801,000	714,000	744,00
Average Shs. Outstg.	170,900	169,900	168,300	172,300	175,500	178,700	181,500	189,50
Balance Sheet								
Cash & Cash Equivalents	499,000	117,000	108,000	111,000	158,000	128,000	129,000	69,60
Total Current Assets	3,537,000	2,945,000	2,703,000	3,093,000	3,062,000	2,660,000	2,584,000	2,296,40
Total Assets	8,424,000	7,863,000	8,452,000	9,125,000	8,914,000	7,387,000	6,868,000	6,441,40
Total Current Liabilities	2,139,000	1,920,000	1,955,000	2,543,000	2,384,000	1,912,000	1,662,000	1,768,90
Long–Term Obligations	1,339,000	1,699,000	1,699,000	1,810,000	1,836,000	1,081,000	1,257,000	833,90
Net Stockholders' Equity	2,911,000	2,150,000	3,080,000	3,097,000	3,106,000	2,880,000	2,509,000	2,482,60
Net Working Capital	1,398,000	1,025,000	748,000	550,000	678,000	748,000	922,000	527,50
Shares Outstanding	170,926	169,442	168,713	168,222	173,988	175,000	117,826	183,21
Statistical Record								
Operating Profit Margin %	9.62	N.M.	8.15	11.78	12.17	17.23	15.92	17.1
Return on Equity %	17.17	N.M	12.56	20.01	18.28	27.81	28.45	29.9
Return on Assets %	5.93	N.M.	4.57	6.79	6.37	10.84	10.39	11.5
Debt/Total Assets %	15.89	21.60	20.10	19.83	20.59	14.63	18.30	12.9
Price Range	64.42–42.64	62.44–41.41	59.54–40.71	64.38–36.13	69.69–48.06	76.31–50.50	67.19–49.00	61.75–43.7
P/E Ratio	22.06–14.60	N/A	26.00–17.78	18.03–10.12	21.58–14.88	17.03–11.27	17.05–12.44	15.71–11.1
Average Yield %	3.31	3.24	3.27	3.39	2.57	2.27	2.29	2.4

Address: One PPG Place, Pittsburgh, PA 15272	Officers: Raymond W. LeBoeuf – Chmn., C.E.O., Charles E. Bunch – Pres., C.O.O.	Investor Contact: (412) 434–2120
Telephone: (412) 434–3131	Transfer Agents: Mellon Investor Services LLC, Ridgefield Park, NJ	Institutional Holding No of Institutions: 14
Web Site: www.ppg.com		Shares: 193,580 % Held: –

PRAXAIR, INC.

Exchange	Symbol	Price	52Wk Range	Yield	P/E
NYS	PX	$37.12 (3/31/2004)	38.76–28.15	1.62	10.73

Year Price Score 128.7   *NYSE Composite Index=100   *12 Month Price Score 104.1

Interim Earnings (Per Share)

Qtr.	Mar	Jun	Sep	Dec
2000	0.35	0.38	0.38	0.01
2001	0.38	0.38	0.19	0.37
2002	0.38	0.45	0.40	0.43
2003	0.39	0.45	0.45	0.48

Interim Dividends (Per Share)

Amt	Decl	Ex	Rec	Pay
0.108Q	7/22/2003	9/3/2003	9/5/2003	9/15/2003
0.135Q	10/29/2003	12/3/2003	12/5/2003	12/15/2003
100%	10/29/2003	12/16/2003	12/5/2003	12/18/2003
0.15Q	1/27/2004	3/3/2004	3/5/2004	3/15/2004

Indicated Div: $0.60 (Div. Reinv. Plan)

Valuation Analysis

Forecast P/E	17.07	Trailing P/E	10.73
Market Cap	$6.0 Billion	Book Value	2.9 Billion
Price/Book	3.51	Price/Sales	1.85

Dividend Achiever Status

Rank	95	10 Year Growth Rate 13.85%
Total Years of Dividend Growth		11

Business Summary: Chemicals (MIC: 11.1 SIC: 2813 NAIC:325120)

Praxair is one of the largest global suppliers of industrial gases, particularly in North and South America, and has a growing business in Asia and southern Europe. Co.'s primary products are atmospheric gases (oxygen, nitrogen, argon, and rare gases) and process gases (carbon dioxide, helium, hydrogen, electronics gases, and acetylene). Co. also designs, engineers, and builds equipment that produces industrial gases for internal use and external sales. Co.'s surface technology segment supplies wear-resistant and high-temperature corrosion-resistant metallic and ceramic coatings and powders. Co. serves approximately 25 diverse industries.

Recent Developments: For the year ended Dec 31 2003, net income rose 6.8% to $585.0 million compared with income of $548.0 million, before an accounting change charge of $139.0 million, in 2002. Results benefited from new global business gains and productivity improvements. Results for 2003 and 2002 included a loss of $9.0 million and a gain of $17.0 million, respectively, from currency hedges. Results for 2002 included a litigation settlement gain of $7.0 million. Sales grew 9.5% to $5.61 billion from $5.13 billion in the prior year. Operating profit slipped 0.1% to $922.0 million compared with $923.0 million the year before.

Prospects: Looking ahead, Co. is cautiously optimistic about its outlook. Business conditions have improved from 2003, particularly in the U.S. However, Co. is uncertain whether the level of economic stimulus will be adequate to maintain the U.S. economy. Nonetheless, Co. will continue to focus on productivity improvements in its base business and monitor capital investments. Meanwhile, Co. expects sales growth for full-year 2004 in the range of 6.0% to 10.0% and operating profit growth of 8.0% to 14.0% from 2003 levels. Earnings per share for full-year 2004 are expected in the range of $1.90 to $2.05, which reflects growth of 8.0% to 15.0% and assumes a higher effective tax rate of 25.0%.

Financial Data

(US$ in Thousands)	12/31/2003	12/31/2002	12/31/2001	12/31/2000	12/31/1999	12/31/1998	12/31/1997	12/31/1996
Earnings Per Share	1.77	1.66	1.32	1.12	1.36	1.30	1.26	0.88
Cash Flow Per Share	3.43	3.03	3.11	2.79	2.93	2.86	2.29	1.90
Tang. Book Val. Per Share	6.00	4.02	3.99	3.95	3.70	3.36	2.88	6.09
Dividends Per Share	0.450	0.380	0.340	0.310	0.280	0.250	0.220	0.190
Dividend Payout %	25.84	22.82	25.75	27.55	20.58	19.23	17.39	21.59
Income Statement								
Total Revenues	5,613,000	5,128,000	5,158,000	5,043,000	4,639,000	4,833,000	4,735,000	4,449,000
Total Indirect Exp.	1,368,000	1,223,000	1,211,000	1,100,000	999,000	1,128,000	1,071,000	1,319,000
Depreciation & Amort.	517,000	483,000	499,000	471,000	445,000	467,000	444,000	420,000
Operating Income	922,000	923,000	800,000	707,000	831,000	856,000	838,000	593,000
Net Interest Inc./(Exp.)	(151,000)	(206,000)	(224,000)	(224,000)	(204,000)	(260,000)	(216,000)	(195,000)
Income Taxes	174,000	158,000	135,000	103,000	152,000	127,000	151,000	110,000
Eqty Earns/Minority Int.	(12,000)	(11,000)	(9,000)	(17,000)	(34,000)	(44,000)	(55,000)	(60,000)
Income from Cont Ops	...	548,000	432,000	...	441,000	...	416,000	228,000
Net Income	585,000	409,000	430,000	363,000	431,000	425,000	405,000	282,000
Average Shs. Outstg.	330,991	329,490	327,014	322,184	324,444	326,712	328,106	318,076
Balance Sheet								
Cash & Cash Equivalents	50,000	39,000	39,000	31,000	76,000	34,000	43,000	63,000
Total Current Assets	1,449,000	1,286,000	1,276,000	1,361,000	1,335,000	1,394,000	1,497,000	1,666,000
Total Assets	8,305,000	7,401,000	7,715,000	7,762,000	7,722,000	8,096,000	7,810,000	7,538,000
Total Current Liabilities	1,117,000	1,100,000	1,194,000	1,439,000	1,725,000	1,289,000	1,366,000	2,550,000
Long-Term Obligations	2,661,000	2,510,000	2,725,000	2,641,000	2,111,000	2,895,000	2,874,000	1,703,000
Net Stockholders' Equity	3,088,000	2,340,000	2,477,000	2,357,000	2,290,000	2,332,000	2,122,000	1,924,000
Net Working Capital	332,000	186,000	82,000	(78,000)	(390,000)	105,000	131,000	(884,000)
Shares Outstanding	326,085	324,536	324,285	318,758	318,095	315,142	314,746	315,498
Statistical Record								
Operating Profit Margin %	16.42	17.99	15.50	14.01	17.91	17.71	17.69	13.32
Return on Equity %	18.94	23.41	17.44	15.40	19.25	18.22	19.60	11.85
Return on Assets %	7.04	7.40	5.59	4.67	5.71	5.24	5.32	3.02
Debt/Total Assets %	32.04	33.91	35.32	34.02	27.33	35.75	36.79	22.59
Price Range	38.20-25.33	30.30-22.81	27.64-18.65	27.25-15.84	29.06-16.16	26.78-15.69	28.78-20.44	24.69-15.84
P/E Ratio	21.58-14.31	18.25-13.74	20.94-14.13	24.33-14.15	21.37-11.88	20.60-12.07	22.84-16.22	28.05-18.04
Average Yield %	1.46	1.37	1.44	1.54	1.26	1.15	0.89	0.94

Address: 39 Old Ridgebury Rd., Danbury, CT 06810-5113	Officers: Dennis H. Reilley – Chmn., Pres., C.E.O., Stephen F. Angel – Exec. V.P.	Investor Contact: (203) 837-2210
Telephone: (203) 837-2000	Transfer Agents: Registrar and Transfer Company, Cranford, NJ	Institutional Holding No of Institutions: 12
Web Site: www.praxair.com		Shares: 32,526 % Held: –

PROCTER & GAMBLE CO.

Exchange	Symbol	Price	52Wk Range	Yield	P/E
NYS	PG	$104.88 (3/31/2004)	106.0–86.70	1.91	25.27

*7 Year Price Score 113.3 *NYSE Composite Index=100 *12 Month Price Score 95.9

Interim Earnings (Per Share)

Qtr.	Sep	Dec	Mar	Jun
2000–01	0.82	0.84	0.63	(0.22)
2001–02	0.79	0.93	0.74	0.63
2002–03	1.04	1.06	0.91	0.68
2003–04	1.26	1.30	...	...

Interim Dividends (Per Share)

Amt	Decl	Ex	Rec	Pa
0.455Q	10/14/2003	10/22/2003	10/24/2003	11/14/200
0.455Q	1/13/2004	1/21/2004	1/23/2004	2/17/200
0.50Q	3/9/2004	4/21/2004	4/23/2004	5/14/200
100%	3/9/2004	6/21/2004	5/21/2004	6/18/200

Indicated Div: $2.00 (Div. Reinv. Plan)

Valuation Analysis

Forecast P/E	19.25	Trailing P/E	25.27
Market Cap	$136.3 Billion	Book Value	17.0 Billion
Price/Book	7.59	Price/Sales	2.75

Dividend Achiever Status

Rank	132	10 Year Growth Rate	11.45%
Total Years of Dividend Growth			50

Business Summary: Chemicals (MIC: 11.1 SIC: 2841 NAIC:325611)

Procter & Gamble manufactures and markets consumer products. Co. is comprised of five product units. Fabric and Home Care includes laundry detergents, dish care, fabric enhancers and surface cleaners. Beauty Care includes hair care, skin care, cosmetics, fine fragrance deodorants, tampons, pads and pantiliners. Baby and Family Care includes diapers, wipes, tissue and towels. Health Care includes or care, personal health care, pharmaceuticals and pet health and nutrition. Snacks and Beverages includes coffee, snacks, commerci services and juice. Co.'s brands include *Always, Ariel, Bounty, Charmin, Crest, Downy, Folgers, Iams, Olay, Pampers, Pantene, Pringle* and *Tide*.

Recent Developments: For the quarter ended Dec 31 2003, net earnings grew 21.7% to $1.82 billion from $1.49 billion in th prior–year quarter. Results were driven by unit volume growth and manufacturing cost savings, which enabled marketing investments sustain top line growth. Product initiatives, such as *Prilosec OTC®, Olay Regenerist®* and *Crest®* tooth whitening products, an developing markets contributed to the growth in volume. Net sales increased 20.1% to $13.22 billion, with much of this growth comin from the September 2003 acquisition of Wella AG. Gross profit climbed 25.1% to $6.90 billion. Operating income grew 22.0% to $2.7 billion.

Prospects: Going forward, the combination of base business growth, strong new product initiatives and the expansion of developin market businesses should continue to allow Co. to generate consistent operating earnings and cash flow. For the third quarter of 200 sales are expected to rise 14.0% to 18.0%, with a 2.0% to 3.0% boost from the continued strength of the Euro, Canadian dollar and Britis pound and a 7.0% to 9.0% increase from acquisitions, primarily Wella. Volume is expected to rise in the high single–digits, excludin acquisitions and divestitures. For the second half of the fiscal year, earnings per share are expected to increase about 25.0%.

Financial Data

(US$ in Millions)	6 Mos	3 Mos	06/30/2003	06/30/2002	06/30/2001	06/30/2000	06/30/1999	06/30/199
Earnings Per Share	2.56	1.26	3.69	3.09	2.07	2.47	2.59	2.5
Cash Flow Per Share	2.83	1.14	6.20	5.51	4.12	3.27	3.83	3.3
Tang. Book Val. Per Share	N.M	N.M	0.84	N.M	1.55	1.35	2.61	2.5
Dividends Per Share	1.730	1.680	1.640	1.520	1.400	1.280	1.140	1.0
Dividend Payout %	67.57	133.73	44.44	49.19	67.63	51.82	44.01	39.4
Income Statement								
Total Revenues	25,416	12,195	43,377	40,238	39,244	39,951	38,125	37,1
Total Indirect Exp.	7,828	3,673	13,383	12,571	12,406	12,483	10,666	10,0
Depreciation & Amort.	857	407	1,703	1,693	2,271	2,191	2,148	1,59
Operating Income	5,385	2,643	7,853	6,678	4,736	5,954	6,253	6,05
Net Interest Inc./(Exp.)	(290)	(141)	(561)	(603)	(794)	(722)	(650)	(54
Income Taxes	1,585	781	2,344	2,031	1,694	1,994	2,075	1,92
Net Income	3,579	1,761	5,186	4,352	2,922	3,542	3,763	3,78
Average Shs. Outstg.	1,399	1,398	1,401	1,404	1,405	1,427	1,446	1,46
Balance Sheet								
Cash & Cash Equivalents	5,294	4,379	6,212	3,623	2,518	1,600	2,800	2,40
Total Current Assets	17,165	15,673	15,220	12,166	10,889	10,069	11,358	10,57
Total Assets	53,862	50,496	43,706	40,776	34,387	34,194	32,113	30,96
Total Current Liabilities	17,607	16,812	12,358	12,704	9,846	10,065	10,761	9,25
Long–Term Obligations	12,636	11,993	11,475	11,201	9,792	8,916	6,231	5,76
Net Stockholders' Equity	18,572	17,371	16,186	13,706	12,010	12,287	12,058	12,23
Net Working Capital	(442)	(1,139)	2,862	(538)	1,043	4	597	1,32
Shares Outstanding	1,292	1,296	1,297	1,300	1,295	1,305	1,319	1,33
Statistical Record								
Operating Profit Margin %	21.18	21.67	18.10	16.59	12.06	14.90	16.40	16.2
Return on Equity %	19.27	10.13	32.04	31.75	24.32	28.82	31.20	30.8
Return on Assets %	6.64	3.48	11.86	10.67	8.49	10.35	11.71	12.2
Debt/Total Assets %	23.45	23.75	26.25	27.46	28.47	26.07	19.40	18.6
Price Range	99.88–86.70	93.25–86.70	93.00–74.46	94.40–64.47	78.50–54.56	117.8–53.06	102.9–67.00	92.25–64.6
P/E Ratio	39.02–33.87	74.01–68.81	25.20–20.18	30.55–20.86	37.92–26.34	47.67–21.48	39.74–25.87	36.04–25.2
Average Yield %	1.86	1.88	1.87	1.89	2.10	1.47	1.30	1.2

Address: One Procter &Gamble Plaza, Cincinnati, OH 45202 Telephone: (513) 983–1100 Web Site: www.pg.com	Officers: Alan G. Lafley – Chmn., Pres., C.E.O., Bruce L. Byrnes – Vice–Chmn., Pres., Global Beauty Care & Health Care Transfer Agents:The Procter and Gamble Company, Cincinnati, OH	Institutional Holding No of Institutions: 32 Shares: 1,529,927 % Held: –

PROGRESS ENERGY, INC.

Exchange	Symbol	Price	52Wk Range	Yield	P/E
NYS	PGN	$47.08 (3/31/2004)	88.75–47.08	4.89	13.85

Year Price Score 102.2 *NYSE Composite Index=100 *12 Month Price Score 92.9

TRADING VOLUME (thousand shares)

Interim Earnings (Per Share)

Qtr.	Mar	Jun	Sep	Dec
2000	0.56	0.70	1.93	(0.16)
2001	0.77	0.56	1.77	(0.46)
2002	0.62	0.56	0.70	0.65
2003	0.84	0.63	1.42	0.51

Interim Dividends (Per Share)

Amt	Decl	Ex	Rec	Pay
0.56Q	5/14/2003	7/8/2003	7/10/2003	8/1/2003
0.56Q	9/19/2003	10/8/2003	10/10/2003	11/1/2003
0.575Q	12/10/2003	1/8/2004	1/12/2004	2/2/2004
0.575Q	3/17/2004	4/7/2004	4/12/2004	5/1/2004

Indicated Div: $2.30 (Div. Reinv. Plan)

Valuation Analysis

Forecast P/E	11.50	Trailing P/E	13.85
Market Cap	$10.4 Billion	Book Value	7.4 Billion
Price/Book	1.49	Price/Sales	1.27

Dividend Achiever Status

Rank	281	10 Year Growth Rate	3.17%
Total Years of Dividend Growth			15

Business Summary: Electricity (MIC: 7.1 SIC: 4911 NAIC:221121)

Progress Energy is a utility holding company with over 24,000 megawatts of generating capacity as of Dec 31 2003. Co.'s utility segment includes two major electric utilities, Progress Energy Carolinas and Progress Energy Florida. At Dec 31 2003, Co.'s electric utilities served more than 2.8 million customers in North Carolina, South Carolina and Florida. Co.'s Competitive Commercial Operations segment provides non-regulated electricity generation. The Fuels segment is involved in natural gas drilling and production, coal mining and terminal services and fuel delivery. The Rail Services segment engages in rail and railcar services. Other activities include Co.'s telecommunication services.

Recent Developments: For the year ended Dec 31 2003, income from continuing operations advanced 46.9% to $811.0 million, before an accounting change charge of $21.0 million, compared with $552.0 million in the previous year. Results for 2003 and 2002 included impairment charges of $38.0 million and $389.0 million, respectively. Earnings for 2003 and 2002 excluded losses from discontinued operations of $8.0 million and $24.0 million. Total revenues rose 8.1% to $8.73 billion from $8.08 billion a year earlier. Utility revenues increased 2.1% to $6.74 billion, while revenues from diversified businesses climbed 35.1% to $1.99 billion. Operating income grew 35.1% to $1.36 billion.

Prospects: In 2004, Co. will continue to focus on financial discipline, including generating free cash flow, striving to reduce its leverage to approximately 57.0%, securing new electricity sales contracts with wholesale customers, and maintaining tight control of capital spending. Co. expects to produce full-year 2004 earnings of between $845.0 million and $880.0 million representing an earnings range of $3.50 to $3.65 per share. Earnings from regulated utilities are projected to improve on a year-over-year basis, provided normal weather, the elimination of a revenue sharing adjustment in Florida, growth in customers and usage and the investment recovery of the Hines 2 facility in Florida.

Financial Data

(US$ in Thousands)	12/31/2003	12/31/2002	12/31/2001	12/31/2000	12/31/1999	12/31/1998	12/31/1997	12/31/1996
Earnings Per Share	3.40	2.53	2.64	3.03	2.55	2.75	2.66	2.66
Cash Flow Per Share	7.54	7.32	7.05	5.47	5.60	6.39	5.69	6.70
Tang. Book Val. Per Share	13.78	12.42	10.57	8.59	19.57	19.48	18.62	17.76
Dividends Per Share	2.240	2.180	2.120	2.060	2.000	1.940	1.880	1.820
Dividend Payout %	65.88	86.16	80.30	67.99	78.43	70.55	70.68	68.42
Income Statement								
Total Revenues	8,743,000	7,945,120	8,461,459	4,118,873	3,357,615	3,130,045	3,024,089	2,995,715
Total Indirect Exp.	3,405,000	3,102,174	3,299,322	1,273,133	820,435	636,090	645,424	554,121
Costs & Expenses	7,381,000	6,940,637	7,217,684	3,399,315	2,517,072	1,661,115	1,947,234	1,966,578
Depreciation & Amort.	1,040,000	820,279	1,090,178	740,470	495,670	487,097	481,650	386,927
Operating Income	1,362,000	1,004,483	1,243,775	719,558	840,543	1,468,930	1,076,855	1,029,137
Net Interest Inc./(Exp.)	(614,000)	(618,915)	(662,607)	(235,301)	(169,128)	(164,710)	(139,621)	(167,460)
Income Taxes	(109,000)	(157,808)	(151,643)	202,774	258,421	257,494	253,048	269,763
Income from Cont Ops	811,000	552,169	...	...	...	...	...	...
Net Income	782,000	528,386	541,640	478,361	382,255	970,657	922,585	906,327
Average Shs. Outstg.	237,000	218,166	204,683	157,169	148,344	399,238	388,317	391,277
Balance Sheet								
Net Property	14,434,000	10,656,234	10,914,915	10,436,698	6,764,813	6,299,540	6,293,176	6,399,877
Total Assets	26,202,000	21,352,704	20,739,791	20,091,012	9,494,019	8,347,406	8,220,394	8,369,159
Long-Term Obligations	9,934,000	9,747,293	9,483,745	5,890,099	3,028,561	2,614,414	2,415,656	2,525,607
Net Stockholders' Equity	7,537,000	6,769,840	6,096,364	5,517,032	3,472,023	3,008,681	2,878,183	2,834,255
Shares Outstanding	246,000	237,992	218,725	206,089	159,599	151,338	151,340	151,416
Statistical Record								
Operating Profit Margin %	15.57	12.64	14.69	17.46	25.03	46.92	35.60	34.35
Net Inc./Net Property %	5.41	4.95	4.96	4.58	5.65	6.33	6.17	6.11
Net Inc./Tot. Capital %	4.29	3.02	3.18	3.62	4.69	5.46	5.53	5.44
Return on Equity %	10.76	8.15	8.88	8.67	11.00	32.26	32.05	31.97
Accum. Depr./Gross Prop. %	35.99	49.58	48.05	47.25	42.37	41.65	39.91	37.23
Price Range	84.25–63.00	79.25–68.00	80.00–65.00	80.00–60.00	93.00–68.00	92.50–76.00	81.25–70.13	79.75–65.75
P/E Ratio	24.78–18.53	31.32–26.88	30.30–24.62	26.40–19.80	36.47–26.67	33.64–27.64	30.55–26.36	29.98–24.72
Average Yield %	2.94	3.01	3.01	1.55	2.48	2.30	2.48	2.50

Address: 410 South Wilmington Street, Raleigh, NC 27601-1748	**Officers:** William Cavanaugh III – Chmn., Robert B. McGehee – Pres., C.E.O., C.O.O.	**Investor Contact:** (919) 546-7474
Telephone: (919) 546-6111	**Transfer Agents:** EquiServe Trust Company, N.A., Providence, RI	**Institutional Holding** No of Institutions: 11
Web Site: www.progress-energy.com		Shares: 306,332 % Held: –

217

PROGRESSIVE CORP.

Exchange	Symbol	Price	52Wk Range	Yield	P/E
NYS	PGR	$87.60 (3/31/2004)	88.00–61.61	0.11	15.40

*7 Year Price Score 159.1   *NYSE Composite Index=100   *12 Month Price Score 105.3

Interim Earnings (Per Share)

Qtr.	Mar	Jun	Sep	Dec
2000	(0.21)	(0.06)	0.26	0.21
2001	0.38	0.46	0.43	0.55
2002	0.78	0.71	0.80	0.70
2003	1.32	1.29	1.45	1.63

Interim Dividends (Per Share)

Amt	Decl	Ex	Rec	Pa
0.025Q	4/18/2003	6/11/2003	6/13/2003	6/30/200
0.025Q	8/22/2003	9/10/2003	9/12/2003	9/30/200
0.025Q	10/3/2003	12/10/2003	12/12/2003	12/31/200
0.025Q	2/2/2004	3/10/2004	3/12/2004	3/31/200

Indicated Div: $0.10

Valuation Analysis

Forecast P/E	15.12	Trailing P/E	15.40
Market Cap	$19.1 Billion	Book Value	5.0 Billion
Price/Book	3.57	Price/Sales	1.51

Dividend Achiever Status

Rank	267	10 Year Growth Rate	4.14%
Total Years of Dividend Growth			34

Business Summary: Insurance (MIC: 8.2 SIC: 6331 NAIC:524126)

Progressive, through its subsidiaries and affiliates, provides personal automobile insurance and other specialty property–casualt insurance and related services throughout the U.S. Co.'s personal lines business units write insurance for private passenger automobile and recreation vehicles. Co.'s commercial auto business unit writes insurance for automobiles and trucks owned by small businesse Co.'s other businesses include writing lenders' collateral protection and directors' and officers' liability insurance and providir insurance–related services, primarily processing business for Commercial Auto Insurance Procedures, which are state supervised plas serving the involuntary market.

Recent Developments: For the year ended Dec 31 2003, net income climbed 88.1% to $1.26 billion from $667.3 million the previou year. Total revenues increased 27.9% to $11.89 billion from $9.29 billion in the prior year. Net written premiums grew 26.0% to $11.9 billion. Net premiums earned advanced 27.9% to $11.34 billion from $8.88 billion a year earlier, as good rate adequacy, improve customer retention and new business drove premium growth. Net investment income rose 2.2% to $465.3 million. The combined rati combined ratio improved 5.1 percentage points to 87.3% from 92.4% in the same period the year before.

Prospects: Co. continues to reap the benefits of the profitable growth phase of this insurance cycle. However, beginning late in 200 and into 2004, Co. saw many of its competitors in the independent agency channel being more aggressive with their advertisin Moreover, it appears as if some competitors have increased their on–line presence at a faster pace. As a result, the year–over–yea percentage growth will likely decline in 2004. Nevertheless, Co. is confident that its market position and ongoing efforts to cultiva competitive advantages in prices, claims handling and brand development will allow it to build sustainable margin advantages over mar of its competitors.

Financial Data

(US$ in Thousands)	12/31/2003	12/31/2002	12/31/2001	12/31/2000	12/31/1999	12/31/1998	12/31/1997	12/31/199
Earnings Per Share	5.69	2.99	1.82	0.20	1.32	2.03	1.77	1.3
Tang. Book Val. Per Share	23.24	17.28	14.76	13.01	12.55	11.75	9.84	7.8
Dividends Per Share	0.100	0.097	0.093	0.090	0.087	0.083	0.080	0.07
Dividend Payout %	1.75	3.24	5.10	45.00	6.59	4.09	4.51	5.6
Income Statement								
Total Premium Income	11,341,000	8,883,500	7,161,800	6,348,400	5,683,600	4,948,000	4,189,500	3,199,3(
Other Income	551,000	410,900	326,400	422,600	440,600	344,400	418,700	279,1(
Total Revenues	11,892,000	9,294,400	7,488,200	6,771,000	6,124,200	5,292,400	4,608,200	3,478,4(
Inc. Before Inc. Taxes	1,859,700	981,400	587,600	31,800	412,200	661,100	578,500	441,7(
Income Taxes	604,300	314,100	176,200	(14,300)	117,000	204,400	178,500	128,0(
Net Income	1,255,600	667,300	411,400	46,100	295,200	456,700	400,000	313,7(
Average Shs. Outstg.	220,500	223,200	225,299	222,900	223,800	224,100	225,900	224,4(
Balance Sheet								
Cash & Cash Equivalents	660,100	584,700	238,600	195,700	243,200	460,500	432,700	175,1(
Premiums Due	2,448,300	2,036,400	1,773,800	1,868,900	2,069,500	1,790,300	1,522,600	1,177,7(
Invst. Assets: Total	12,532,300	10,284,300	8,226,300	6,983,300	6,427,700	5,674,300	5,270,400	4,450,6(
Total Assets	16,281,500	13,564,400	11,122,400	10,051,600	9,704,700	8,463,100	7,559,600	6,183,9(
Long–Term Obligations	1,489,800	1,489,400	1,095,700	748,800	1,048,600	776,600	775,900	775,7(
Net Stockholders' Equity	5,030,600	3,768,000	3,250,700	2,869,800	2,752,800	2,557,100	2,135,900	1,676,9(
Shares Outstanding	216,400	218,000	220,200	220,500	219,300	217,500	216,900	214,5(
Statistical Record								
Return on Equity %	24.95	17.70	12.65	1.60	10.72	17.86	18.72	18.7
Return on Assets %	7.71	4.91	3.69	0.45	3.04	5.39	5.29	5.0
Price Range	83.59–46.55	59.49–46.15	50.28–28.00	36.67–16.40	56.92–23.69	56.69–31.98	39.96–20.67	23.92–13.ʃ
P/E Ratio	14.69–8.18	19.90–15.43	27.63–15.38	183.3–81.98	43.12–17.95	27.92–15.75	22.58–11.68	17.46–9.8
Average Yield %	0.15	0.17	0.22	0.31	0.20	0.19	0.27	0.4

Address: 6300 Wilson Mills Road, Mayfield Village, OH 44143 Telephone: (440) 461–5000 Web Site: www.progressive.com	Officers: Peter B. Lewis – Chmn., Glenn M. Renwick – Pres., C.E.O. Transfer Agents:Corporate Trust Customer Service, National City Bank, Cleveland, OH	Investor Contact: (440) 446–7165 Institutional Holding No of Institutions: 13 Shares: 44,567,540 % Held: –

PROTECTIVE LIFE CORP.

Exchange	Symbol	Price	52Wk Range	Yield	P/E
NYS	PL	$37.45 (3/31/2004)	38.25-25.99	1.71	12.20

*7 Year Price Score 98.2   *NYSE Composite Index=100   *12 Month Price Score 100.2

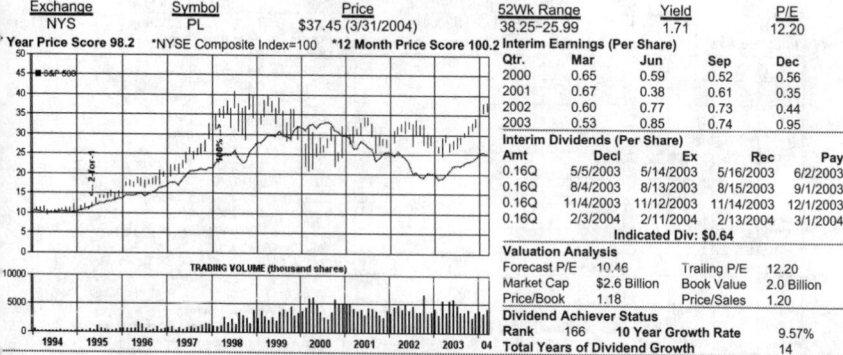

Interim Earnings (Per Share)

Qtr.	Mar	Jun	Sep	Dec
2000	0.65	0.59	0.52	0.56
2001	0.67	0.38	0.61	0.35
2002	0.60	0.77	0.73	0.44
2003	0.53	0.85	0.74	0.95

Interim Dividends (Per Share)

Amt	Decl	Ex	Rec	Pay
0.16Q	5/5/2003	5/14/2003	5/16/2003	6/2/2003
0.16Q	8/4/2003	8/13/2003	8/15/2003	9/1/2003
0.16Q	11/4/2003	11/12/2003	11/14/2003	12/1/2003
0.16Q	2/3/2004	2/11/2004	2/13/2004	3/1/2004

Indicated Div: $0.64

Valuation Analysis

Forecast P/E	10.46	Trailing P/E	12.20
Market Cap	$2.6 Billion	Book Value	2.0 Billion
Price/Book	1.18	Price/Sales	1.20

Dividend Achiever Status

Rank	166	10 Year Growth Rate 9.57%
Total Years of Dividend Growth		14

Business Summary: Insurance (MIC: 8.2 SIC: 6311 NAIC:524113)

Protective Life is a holding company that provides financial services through the production, distribution and administration of insurance and investment products. The Life Marketing segment markets level premium term and term-like insurance, universal life, variable universal life and "bank-owned life insurance" products. The Acquisitions segment focuses on acquiring, converting, and servicing policies acquired from other companies. The Annuities segment manufactures, sells, and supports fixed and variable annuity products. The Stable Value Products segment markets guaranteed investment contracts and other qualified retirement savings plans. The Asset Protection segment markets extended service contracts and credit life and disability insurance.

Recent Developments: For the year ended Dec 31 2003, net income increased 22.4% to $217.1 million compared with $177.4 million the previous year. Earnings growth was primarily attributed to lower benefits and expenses, partially offset by slightly lower premium and policy fees and reserve adjustments in Co.'s asset protection segment. Total revenues were essentially unchanged at $1.96 billion versus the year before. Net premium and policy fees decreased 9.2% to $735.9 million from $810.3 million a year earlier. Net investment income rose to $1.03 billion from $1.02 billion the prior year.

Prospects: Results continue to benefit from strong life insurance sales and expense management. Specifically, earnings from Co.'s acquisitions segment reflect the integration of the Conseco block and favorable mortality. Co. is optimistic that the launch of a registered funding agreement-backed note program during the fourth quarter will boost earnings growth in the Stable Value segment. Meanwhile, Co. is showing improvements in the Annuities segment, despite challenging conditions for the sale of fixed annuities. Also, Co.'s core lines of business in the Asset Protection segment continues to see positive trends. Meanwhile, Co. believes the life insurance industry will continue to be affected by low interest rates.

Financial Data

(US$ in Thousands)	12/31/2003	12/31/2002	12/31/2001	12/31/2000	12/31/1999	12/31/1998	12/31/1997	12/31/1996
Earnings Per Share	3.07	2.54	2.01	2.32	2.32	2.04	1.78	1.47
Tang. Book Val. Per Share	28.33	24.36	19.72	13.37	10.02	11.50	12.30	9.98
Dividends Per Share	0.630	0.590	0.550	0.510	0.470	0.430	0.390	0.350
Dividend Payout %	20.52	23.22	27.36	21.98	20.25	21.07	21.91	23.81
Income Statement								
Total Premium Income	735,877	783,132	618,669	833,658	761,284	662,795	522,335	494,153
Net Investment Income	1,030,752	1,031,204	884,041	737,284	676,401	636,396	591,376	517,483
Other Income	190,896	106,342	111,507	163,025	96,197	67,224	33,614	26,367
Total Revenues	1,957,525	1,920,678	1,614,217	1,733,967	1,533,882	1,366,415	1,147,325	1,038,003
Total Indirect Exp.	480,539	491,244	431,997	490,607	413,525	359,926	284,844	253,222
Inc. Before Inc. Taxes	325,412	267,203	209,596	253,795	255,775	220,724	179,373	139,741
Income Taxes	108,362	88,444	68,538	90,858	92,079	77,845	60,987	47,512
Eqty Earns/Minority Int.	...	...	...	(9,461)	(10,606)	(12,098)	(6,393)	(3,217)
Income from Cont Ops	...	178,759	141,058	...	153,000	...	...	...
Net Income	217,050	177,355	102,943	153,476	151,327	130,781	111,993	89,012
Average Shs. Outstg.	70,644	70,462	69,950	66,281	66,161	64,088	62,850	61,608
Balance Sheet								
Cash & Cash Equivalents	656,117	550,352	363,713	244,655	165,299	225,735	123,588	235,309
Premiums Due	2,408,550	2,477,916	2,239,179	1,185,354	940,252	797,164	639,397	379,985
Invst. Assets: Total	17,426,151	15,481,501	13,317,678	10,241,409	8,722,009	8,606,610	8,049,420	6,552,175
Total Assets	24,573,991	21,953,004	19,718,824	15,145,633	12,994,164	11,989,495	10,511,635	8,263,205
Long-Term Obligations	461,329	406,110	376,211	306,125	181,023	152,286	120,000	168,200
Net Stockholders' Equity	2,002,144	1,720,702	1,400,144	1,039,058	790,223	814,194	628,197	560,316
Shares Outstanding	68,991	68,675	68,555	64,557	64,502	64,435	61,642	61,608
Statistical Record								
Return on Equity %	10.84	10.38	10.07	13.77	17.69	13.85	14.77	14.46
Return on Assets %	0.88	0.81	0.71	1.01	1.17	1.09	1.06	1.07
Price Range	34.22-24.71	33.75-27.20	34.51-25.55	32.25-20.81	40.00-28.50	40.88-28.63	32.63-18.81	20.81-15.25
P/E Ratio	11.15-8.05	13.29-10.71	17.17-12.71	13.90-8.97	17.24-12.28	20.04-14.03	18.33-10.57	14.16-10.37
Average Yield %	2.16	1.93	1.82	1.90	1.35	1.23	1.61	1.96

Address: 2801 Highway 280 South, Birmingham, AL 35223 **Telephone:** (205) 268-1000 **Web Site:** www.protective.com	**Officers:** John D. Johns - Chmn., Pres., C.E.O., Allen W. Ritchie - Exec. V.P., C.F.O. **Transfer Agents:** The Bank of New York	**Investor Contact:** (205) 268-1000 **Institutional Holding** **No of Institutions:** 2 **Shares:** 54,496 **% Held:** –

QUAKER CHEMICAL CORP.

Exchange	Symbol	Price	52Wk Range	Yield	P/E
NYS	KWR	$25.40 (3/31/2004)	30.75-20.50	3.39	16.71

*7 Year Price Score 128.1   *NYSE Composite Index=100   *12 Month Price Score 101.6

Interim Earnings (Per Share)

Qtr.	Mar	Jun	Sep	Dec
2000	0.49	0.53	0.53	0.38
2001	0.45	0.45	0.12	(0.18)
2002	0.26	0.35	0.45	0.45
2003	0.33	0.36	0.42	0.41

Interim Dividends (Per Share)

Amt	Decl	Ex	Rec	Pa
0.21Q	5/14/2003	7/15/2003	7/17/2003	7/31/200
0.21Q	9/24/2003	10/15/2003	10/17/2003	10/31/200
0.21Q	11/19/2003	1/14/2004	1/16/2004	1/30/200
0.215Q	3/10/2004	4/14/2004	4/16/2004	4/30/200

Indicated Div: $0.86 (Div. Reinv. Plan)

Valuation Analysis

Forecast P/E	N/A	Trailing P/E	16.71
Market Cap	$236.5 Million	Book Value	112.4 Million
Price/Book	2.57	Price/Sales	0.85

Dividend Achiever Status

Rank	276	10 Year Growth Rate	3.42%
Total Years of Dividend Growth			32

Business Summary: Petroleum and Coal Products (MIC: 11.8 SIC: 2992 NAIC:324191)

Quaker Chemical develops, produces, and markets a wide range of formulated chemical specialty products for various heavy industria and manufacturing applications and, in addition, offers and markets chemical management services. Co. operates in three segment: metalworking process chemicals, coatings, and other chemical products. Co.'s principal product lines include rolling lubricants, corrosio preventives, hydraulic fluids, machining and grinding compounds, forming compounds, chemical milling maskants, metal finishin compounds, technology for the removal of hydrogen sulfides, construction products and programs to provide chemical managemer services.

Recent Developments: For the twelve months ended Dec 31 2003, net income climbed 3.7% to $14.8 million compared with $14 million in 2002. Results for 2003 included a restructuring charge of $57,000. Net sales were $340.2 million, up 23.9% from $274 million in the prior year. Sales growth benefited from acquisitions and new chemical management services revenues. Gross margin as percentage of sales fell to 35.7% versus 40.6% a year earlier. Operating income increased 0.6% to $24.1 million compared with $24. million in the previous year. Co.'s bottom line was hampered by softness in a number of its core steel markets, and higher pension an insurance costs.

Prospects: For 2004, Co. anticipates stronger revenue growth in all of its businesses and regions due to selling initiatives and improve economic conditions. Operating costs are also expected to be higher due to increased expenses related to administrative areas, includir pension, insurance and compliances. However, Co. does expect some improvement in the costs of key raw materials, such as cruc oil-based materials, animal fats, and vegetable oils as the year progresses. Consequently, Co. expects earnings for the first quarter « 2004 will be similar to results from the first quarter of 2003.

Financial Data

(US$ in Thousands)	12/31/2003	12/31/2002	12/31/2001	12/31/2000	12/31/1999	12/31/1998	12/31/1997	12/31/199
Earnings Per Share	1.52	1.51	0.84	1.93	1.74	1.20	1.45	(0.8£
Cash Flow Per Share	0.85	2.57	2.48	2.40	1.58	1.41	1.74	3.2
Tang. Book Val. Per Share	7.22	6.46	7.05	7.63	7.29	7.01	7.01	6.C
Dividends Per Share	0.840	0.830	0.820	0.790	0.760	0.730	0.700	0.68
Dividend Payout %	55.26	55.29	97.61	40.93	43.96	60.83	48.62	N.M
Income Statement								
Total Revenues	340,192	274,521	251,074	267,570	258,461	257,100	241,534	240,25
Total Indirect Exp.	97,259	87,604	86,838	86,892	89,595	98,371	82,822	106,08
Depreciation & Amort.	7,637	6,237	6,380	6,812	6,956	7,111	7,264	8,70
Operating Income	24,115	23,973	14,191	25,148	27,281	17,270	21,148	(4,03
Net Interest Inc./(Exp.)	(761)	(790)	(850)	(1,096)	(1,992)	(1,589)	(1,218)	(1,47«
Income Taxes	7,488	7,782	4,473	8,211	10,860	6,719	7,893	4€
Eqty Earns/Minority Int.	(1,797)	(2,239)	(2,292)	(1,112)	(640)	572	769	(3,13«
Net Income	14,833	14,297	7,665	17,163	15,651	10,650	12,611	(7,59«
Average Shs. Outstg.	9,761	9,474	9,114	8,896	8,975	8,860	8,707	8,6:
Balance Sheet								
Cash & Cash Equivalents	21,915	13,857	20,549	16,552	8,677	10,213	18,416	8,52
Total Current Assets	143,524	103,673	92,087	103,181	96,241	96,068	98,126	86,5!
Total Assets	287,347	213,858	178,823	188,161	182,213	189,903	170,640	165,6(
Total Current Liabilities	105,805	66,144	44,663	50,200	44,657	50,432	47,759	64,0:
Long-Term Obligations	15,827	16,590	19,380	22,295	25,122	25,344	25,203	5,18
Net Stockholders' Equity	112,352	88,055	80,899	84,907	81,199	83,735	75,642	74,2!
Net Working Capital	37,719	37,529	47,424	52,981	51,584	45,636	50,367	22,5
Shares Outstanding	9,609	9,321	9,137	8,851	8,934	8,894	8,720	9,6(
Statistical Record								
Operating Profit Margin %	7.08	8.73	5.65	9.39	10.55	6.71	8.75	N.M
Return on Equity %	13.20	16.23	9.47	20.21	19.27	12.71	16.67	N.M
Return on Assets %	5.16	6.68	4.28	9.12	8.58	5.60	7.39	N.M
Debt/Total Assets %	5.50	7.75	10.83	11.84	13.78	13.34	14.76	3.1
Price Range	30.75-18.79	25.30-18.35	22.21-16.15	18.81-13.63	18.13-13.56	21.00-13.06	19.63-15.13	16.88-14.0
P/E Ratio	20.23-12.36	16.75-12.15	26.44-19.23	9.75-7.06	10.42-7.79	17.50-10.89	13.53-10.43	N/
Average Yield %	3.54	3.78	4.32	4.82	4.82	4.08	4.09	4.4

Address: One Quaker Park,	Officers: Ronald J. Naples — Chmn., C.E.O., Joseph	Investor Contact: (610) 832-8500
Conshohocken, PA 19428-0809	W. Bauer — Pres., C.O.O.	Institutional Holding
Telephone: (610) 832-4000	Transfer Agents:American Stock Transfer &Trust	No of Institutions: 47
Web Site: www.quakerchem.com	Company, New	Shares: 353,764 % Held: —

QUESTAR CORP.

Exchange	Symbol	Price	52Wk Range	Yield	P/E
NYS	STR	$36.44 (3/31/2004)	36.85-29.71	2.25	17.11

*7 Year Price Score 138.4 *NYSE Composite Index=100 *12 Month Price Score 96.5

Interim Earnings (Per Share)

Qtr.	Mar	Jun	Sep	Dec
2000	0.62	0.33	0.34	0.65
2001	0.80	0.33	0.27	0.54
2002	0.61	0.36	0.28	0.82
2003	0.84	0.24	0.34	0.71

Interim Dividends (Per Share)

Amt	Decl	Ex	Rec	Pay
0.185Q	5/20/2003	5/28/2003	5/30/2003	6/16/2003
0.205Q	8/12/2003	8/20/2003	8/22/2003	9/15/2003
0.205Q	10/23/2003	11/19/2003	11/21/2003	12/15/2003
0.205Q	2/10/2004	2/18/2004	2/20/2004	3/15/2004

Indicated Div: $0.82

Valuation Analysis

Forecast P/E	13.80	Trailing P/E	17.11
Market Cap	$3.0 Billion	Book Value	1.3 Billion
Price/Book	2.32	Price/Sales	2.00

Dividend Achiever Status

Rank	270	10 Year Growth Rate	3.65%
Total Years of Dividend Growth		24

Business Summary: Gas Utilities (MIC: 7.4 SIC: 4923 NAIC:221210)

Questar is a natural gas-focused energy company that is involved in a range of natural gas activities through its Market Resources and Regulated Services groups. Market Resources is engaged in gas and oil development and production; cost-of-service gas development; gas gathering and processing; and wholesale gas and hydrocarbon liquids marketing, risk management, and gas storage. Regulated services, through its two primary subsidiaries, Questar Pipeline Company and Questar Gas Company, conducts interstate gas transmission and storage activities and retail gas distribution services.

Recent Developments: For the year ended Dec 31 2003, income was $179.2 million compared with income of $170.9 million a year earlier. Results for 2003 included a $24.9 million charge related to a distribution rate-refund obligation. Results for 2003 and 2002 excluded accounting change charges of $5.6 million and $15.3 million, respectively. Total revenues advanced 21.9% to $1.46 billion from $1.20 billion the year before. Co.'s top-line growth was fueled by 43.8% jump in revenues to $751.5 million from Co.'s Market Resources business, which benefited from average realized sales prices for natural gas that were 40.3% higher than the previous year.

Prospects: Co.'s near-term outlook appears moderately positive, reflecting the recent strength in crude oil, solid natural gas prices and Co.'s hedging program, which protects against price declines. Accordingly, Co. now believes that 2004 full-year earnings could range from $2.30 to $2.45 per diluted share versus its previous 2004 guidance of between $2.25 and $2.40 per diluted share. Meanwhile, Co.'s Questar Gas unit has announced an expansion of its southern system in central Utah. This expansion, which is scheduled to be in service before the 2005-2006 heating season, is fully supported by long-term contracts. Also, Questar Pipeline is evaluating customer support for two additional projects.

Financial Data

(US$ in Thousands)	12/31/2003	12/31/2002	12/31/2001	12/31/2000	12/31/1999	12/31/1998	12/31/1997	12/31/1996
Earnings Per Share	2.13	2.07	1.94	1.94	1.20	0.93	1.26	1.19
Cash Flow Per Share	5.30	5.62	4.56	3.21	2.60	3.43	2.45	2.24
Tang. Book Val. Per Share	14.12	12.80	12.14	12.00	11.37	10.62	10.29	9.40
Dividends Per Share	0.780	0.720	0.700	0.680	0.670	0.650	0.620	0.590
Dividend Payout %	36.61	35.02	36.34	35.30	55.83	70.16	49.20	49.57
Income Statement								
Total Revenues	1,463,188	1,200,667	1,439,350	1,266,153	924,219	906,256	933,274	817,981
Total Indirect Exp.	296,651	246,413	219,877	192,595	220,168	195,949	158,344	135,698
Costs & Expenses	1,123,358	926,472	1,165,243	1,006,243	794,001	773,475	763,119	646,358
Depreciation & Amort.	192,382	184,952	151,735	141,941	137,744	125,157	124,037	105,209
Operating Income	339,830	274,195	274,107	259,910	130,218	132,781	170,155	171,623
Income Taxes	102,563	91,126	88,270	85,367	47,788	29,030	45,602	45,362
Eqty Earns/Minority Int.	5,008	11,777	159	3,996	(4,356)	2,917	...	...
Income from Cont Ops	179,196	170,893	...	...	...	...	...	...
Net Income	173,616	155,596	158,186	156,711	98,830	76,899	104,795	98,145
Average Shs. Outstg.	84,190	82,573	81,658	80,915	82,676	82,817	82,668	81,656
Balance Sheet								
Net Property	2,768,529	2,617,798	2,565,098	1,953,993	1,786,914	1,747,641	1,531,220	1,477,336
Total Assets	3,309,055	3,067,850	3,235,711	2,539,045	2,237,997	2,161,281	1,945,017	1,816,225
Long-Term Obligations	950,189	1,145,180	997,423	714,537	735,043	615,770	541,986	555,509
Net Stockholders' Equity	1,261,265	1,138,761	1,080,781	991,066	925,845	877,958	845,778	772,085
Shares Outstanding	83,233	82,053	81,523	80,818	81,418	82,632	82,142	82,050
Statistical Record								
Operating Profit Margin %	23.22	22.83	19.04	20.52	14.08	14.65	18.23	20.98
Net Inc./Net Property %	6.27	5.94	6.16	8.02	5.53	4.40	6.84	6.64
Net Inc./Tot. Capital %	6.52	5.82	6.53	7.97	5.27	4.54	6.53	6.41
Return on Equity %	14.20	15.00	14.63	15.81	10.67	8.75	12.39	12.71
Accum. Depr./Gross Prop. %	38.51	37.84	37.27	44.86	45.16	43.70	44.15	42.62
Price Range	35.35-26.66	29.27-19.40	33.51-18.70	31.50-13.81	19.88-14.94	22.31-16.25	22.31-17.25	20.31-15.50
P/E Ratio	16.60-12.52	14.14-9.37	17.27-9.64	16.24-7.12	16.56-12.45	23.99-17.47	17.71-13.69	17.07-13.03
Average Yield %	2.49	2.89	2.71	3.21	3.72	3.31	3.15	3.44

Address: 180 East 100 South Street, Salt Lake City, UT 84145-0433 Telephone: (801) 324-5000 Web Site: www.questar.com	Officers: Keith O. Rattie – Chmn., Pres., C.E.O., Stephen E. Parks – Sr. V.P., C.F.O. Transfer Agents:Questar Corp., Salt Lake City, UT	Investor Contact:801-324-5497 Institutional Holding No of Institutions: 16 Shares: 1,199,651 % Held: -

QUIXOTE CORP.

Exchange	Symbol	Price	52Wk Range	Yield	P/E
NMS	QUIX	$21.00 (3/31/2004)	28.18-16.05	1.62	17.21

*7 Year Price Score 139.6 ***NYSE Composite Index=100** ***12 Month Price Score 100.1**

Interim Earnings (Per Share)

Qtr.	Sep	Dec	Mar	Jun
2000–01	0.29	0.17	0.23	0.66
2001–02	0.16	0.05	0.07	0.45
2002–03	0.22	0.19	0.20	0.56
2003–04	0.27	0.05	...	

Interim Dividends (Per Share)

Amt	Decl	Ex	Rec	Pa
0.16S	4/25/2002	6/3/2002	6/5/2002	7/3/200
0.16S	11/18/2002	12/4/2002	12/6/2002	1/3/200
0.17S	5/9/2003	5/30/2003	6/3/2003	7/3/200
0.17S	11/13/2003	12/3/2003	12/5/2003	1/6/20▪

Indicated Div: $0.34

Valuation Analysis

Forecast P/E	13.71	Trailing P/E	17.21
Market Cap	$163.1 Million	Book Value	78.6 Million
Price/Book	N/A	Price/Sales	N/A

Dividend Achiever Status

Rank	251	10 Year Growth Rate	5.14%
Total Years of Dividend Growth			10

Business Summary: Construction – Public Infrastructure (MIC: 3.1 SIC: 1611 NAIC:237310)

Quixote and its subsidiaries develop, manufacture and market highway and transportation safety products to protect, direct and infor motorists and highway workers in both domestic and international markets. These products include energy–absorbing highway cra cushions, flexible post delineators, electronic wireless measuring and sensing devices, weather information systems and forecasti services, variable message signs, highway advisory radios, intelligent intersection control devices and other highway and transportatic safety devices. Co.'s two reportable segments, the Protect and Direct segment and Inform segment, are within the highway ar transportation safety industry.

Recent Developments: For the three months ended Dec 31 2003, net income totaled $466,000, down 70.0% compared with $1 million in the corresponding prior–year quarter. Net sales jumped 38.4% to $35.5 million from $25.6 million a year earlier, drive primarily by the acquisitions of U.S. Traffic Corporation and Peek Traffic Corporation in 2003. Gross profit rose 12.8% to $11.1 milli from $9.8 million the year before, However, as a percentage of net sales gross profit slipped to 31.2% from 38.3% due to lower gro margins generated by U.S. Traffic and Peek Traffic. Operating profit slid 51.5% to $1.2 million from $2.5 million the previous ye reflecting higher selling and administrative expenses.

Prospects: Over the near–term, top–line results are expected to be negatively affected by state budgetary constraints and transportatic funding uncertainties stemming from the delay in the passage of a new federal highway funding bill. Going forward, Co. is focusing integrating the operations of U.S. Traffic and Peek Traffic, and is taking steps to boost profitability through increased marketing and t implementation of cost–reduction initiatives. Co. is targeting third–quarter 2004 earnings in the range of $0.05 to $0.10 per share. addition, Co. anticipates that gross profit margins for the current fiscal year will be lower than its previous estimate of between 38.0% a 40.0%.

Financial Data
(US$ in Thousands)

	6 Mos	3 Mos	06/30/2003	06/30/2002	06/30/2001	06/30/2000	06/30/1999	06/30/199
Earnings Per Share	0.32	0.27	1.17	0.73	1.35	1.10	0.92	0.?
Cash Flow Per Share	0.10	(0.32)	2.00	1.56	1.34	1.03	1.57	(0.5
Tang. Book Val. Per Share	1.50	2.62	2.23	3.17	3.36	2.77	2.71	3.?
Dividends Per Share	0.330	0.330	0.320	0.310	0.300	0.280	0.270	0.2◆
Dividend Payout %	103.12	122.22	27.35	42.46	22.22	25.45	29.34	34.?
Income Statement								
Total Revenues	74,678	39,184	114,310	89,694	93,554	83,770	71,987	55,98
Total Indirect Exp.	18,510	8,667	31,086	26,443	25,051	25,822	21,150	16,9◆
Depreciation & Amort.	2,985	1,417	3,978	3,539	3,916	3,834	3,425	2,3?
Operating Income	5,336	4,109	15,154	9,489	18,887	15,289	12,483	8,5◆
Net Interest Inc./(Exp.)	(982)	(483)	(802)	(1,106)	(1,411)	(901)	(938)	1◆
Income Taxes	1,567	1,305	4,880	3,316	6,645	5,466	4,256	2,6◆
Income from Cont Ops	...	...	...	5,897	...	...	7,562	6,1◆
Net Income	2,787	2,321	9,472	6,824	10,843	8,919	7,802	
Average Shs. Outstg.	8,710	8,679	8,062	8,121	8,049	8,124	8,228	8,0?
Balance Sheet								
Cash & Cash Equivalents	1,354	1,169	3,753	1,798	4,118	1,524	2,153	3,9?
Total Current Assets	65,159	62,869	67,088	43,094	44,578	34,319	30,797	26,8?
Total Assets	164,095	145,608	150,825	100,044	88,029	73,264	71,774	59,0◆
Total Current Liabilities	26,967	21,039	30,999	12,171	13,542	12,192	12,218	11,7◆
Long–Term Obligations	50,325	41,493	39,789	24,772	21,526	15,596	11,901	7,6◆
Net Stockholders' Equity	82,516	78,649	75,555	59,226	50,606	43,116	45,982	38,8◆
Net Working Capital	...	41,830	36,089	30,923	31,036	22,127	18,579	15,1◆
Shares Outstanding	8,577	8,377	8,305	7,776	7,517	7,388	8,072	7,8◆
Statistical Record								
Operating Profit Margin %	7.14	10.48	13.25	10.57	20.18	18.25	17.34	15.?
Return on Equity %	3.37	2.95	12.53	9.95	21.42	20.68	16.44	15.8
Return on Assets %	1.69	1.59	6.28	5.89	12.31	12.17	10.53	10.?
Debt/Total Assets %	30.66	28.49	26.38	24.76	24.45	21.28	16.58	12.◆
Price Range	28.00-22.55	28.00-22.55	26.05-14.75	27.83-15.82	28.61-13.00	16.13-11.06	15.50-11.31	13.00-7.◆
P/E Ratio	87.50-70.47	103.7-83.52	22.26-12.61	38.12-21.67	21.19-9.63	14.66-10.06	16.85-12.30	17.11-10.◆
Average Yield %	1.33	1.33	1.72	1.48	1.51	2.00	2.10	2.?

Address: 35 East Wacker Drive, Chicago, IL 60601 **Telephone:** (312) 467–6755 **Web Site:** www.quixotecorp.com	**Officers:** Leslie J. Jezuit – Chmn., Pres., C.E.O., Daniel P. Gorey – V.P., C.F.O., Treas.	**Investor Contact:** (312) 467–6755 **Institutional Holding** **No of Institutions:** 2 **Shares:** 170,847 **% Held:** –

RAVEN INDUSTRIES, INC.

Exchange	Symbol	Price	52Wk Range	Yield	P/E
NMS	RAVN	$30.56 (3/31/2004)	32.31-15.74	1.44	20.37

7 Year Price Score 228.9   *NYSE Composite Index=100   *12 Month Price Score 113.8

Interim Earnings (Per Share)

Qtr.	Apr	Jul	Oct	Jan
2000-01	0.14	0.11	0.16	0.21
2001-02	0.23	0.21	0.26	0.23
2002-03	0.36	0.24	0.34	0.26
2003-04	0.45	0.34	0.42	0.29

Interim Dividends (Per Share)

Amt	Decl	Ex	Rec	Pay
0.09Q	8/19/2003	9/23/2003	9/25/2003	10/15/2003
0.09Q	11/24/2003	12/22/2003	12/24/2003	1/15/2004
0.11Q	3/9/2004	3/24/2004	3/26/2004	4/15/2004
1.25Q	3/9/2004	4/29/2004	5/3/2004	5/20/2004

Indicated Div: $0.44 (Div. Reinv. Plan)

Valuation Analysis

Forecast P/E	N/A	Trailing P/E	20.37
Market Cap	$139.8 Million	Book Value	65.3 Million
Price/Book	N/A	Price/Sales	N/A

Dividend Achiever Status

Rank	116	10 Year Growth Rate	12.33%
Total Years of Dividend Growth		16	

Business Summary: Apparel (MIC: 4.4 SIC: 2399 NAIC:315999)

Raven Industries is a manufacturing company that operates through four core divisions. The Engineered Films division produces rugged reinforced plastic sheeting and high-altitude research balloons for public and commercial research. The Electronics Systems unit provides electronic manufacturing services. The Flow Controls division develops global positioning systems–based control systems, computerized control hardware and software for precision farming, and systems for the precision application of insecticides, fertilizer and road de-icers. Aerostar International Inc. produces custom-shaped advertising inflatables.

Recent Developments: For the year ended Jan 31 2004, net income advanced 23.7% to $13.8 million compared with $11.2 million in 2002. Results included a loss of $173,000 in 2004 and a gain of $179,000 in 2003 on the sale of businesses and assets. Net sales climbed 18.1% to $142.7 million from $120.9 million a year earlier, reflecting solid sales growth across each of Co.'s four business units, which was driven by new product introductions and market share growth. Gross profit rose 22.7% to $33.8 million versus $27.5 million the year before. Operating income grew 26.7% to $21.6 million from $17.1 million in 2003.

Prospects: Although sales for 2004 are expected to show double-digit growth, Co. remains cautious in its planning due to the absence of $6.0 million in sales of special Flow Controls division chemical injection systems, which occurred in 2003. Also, profit pressures are continuing due to volatile raw material prices in Co.'s Engineered Films division. Meanwhile, Co.'s Electronic Systems Division should see better margins, which have been previously constricted by start-up costs with new customers. Lastly, Co.'s Aerostar business is focusing on three new business platforms in 2004, including military cargo parachutes, specialty uniforms for government agencies and large inflatables.

Financial Data
(US$ in Thousands)

	01/31/2004	01/31/2003	01/31/2002	01/31/2001	01/31/2000	01/31/1999	01/31/1998	01/31/1997
Earnings Per Share	1.50	1.20	0.93	0.62	0.51	0.43	0.55	0.53
Cash Flow Per Share	2.13	1.36	1.94	0.91	0.79	0.74	0.78	0.83
Tang. Book Val. Per Share	6.50	5.66	5.64	5.06	3.87	4.42	4.25	3.78
Dividends Per Share	0.340	0.280	0.250	0.230	0.220	0.200	0.180	0.160
Dividend Payout %	22.66	23.33	27.41	37.63	42.58	47.69	33.93	30.19
Income Statement								
Total Revenues	142,727	120,903	118,515	132,858	147,906	152,798	149,619	139,441
Total Indirect Exp.	12,306	10,271	10,309	6,867	12,761	15,142	14,367	13,316
Depreciation & Amort.	4,145	3,966	3,145	3,667	4,884	5,133	5,137	4,566
Operating Income	21,626	17,065	13,175	10,748	10,577	9,673	10,562	11,971
Net Interest Inc./(Exp.)	(70)	(63)	(129)	(258)	(418)	(474)	(323)	(310)
Income Taxes	7,880	6,069	4,718	4,513	3,741	3,467	4,478	4,227
Net Income	13,836	11,185	8,847	6,411	6,762	6,182	8,062	7,688
Average Shs. Outstg.	9,244	9,347	9,491	10,337	13,116	14,271	14,673	14,265
Balance Sheet								
Cash & Cash Equivalents	18,442	9,217	7,478	10,673	5,707	5,335	2,850	3,439
Total Current Assets	55,710	49,351	45,308	52,236	55,371	60,861	57,831	56,696
Total Assets	79,508	72,816	67,836	65,656	74,047	83,674	82,590	80,662
Total Current Liabilities	11,895	13,167	13,810	13,935	14,702	16,792	19,375	20,016
Long-Term Obligations	57	151	280	2,013	3,024	4,572	1,128	3,181
Net Stockholders' Equity	66,471	58,236	52,032	47,989	54,519	62,293	61,563	56,729
Net Working Capital	43,815	36,184	31,498	38,301	40,669	44,069	38,456	36,680
Shares Outstanding	9,020	9,066	9,211	9,478	14,082	14,082	14,472	14,508
Statistical Record								
Operating Profit Margin %	15.15	14.11	11.11	8.08	7.15	6.33	7.05	8.58
Return on Equity %	20.81	19.20	17.00	13.35	12.40	9.92	13.09	13.55
Return on Assets %	17.40	15.36	13.04	9.76	9.13	7.38	9.76	9.53
Debt/Total Assets %	0.07	0.20	0.41	3.06	4.08	5.46	1.36	3.94
Price Range	30.14-15.68	18.00-9.78	11.75-6.04	6.08-3.71	6.00-4.50	7.50-5.17	8.58-6.54	7.83-5.33
P/E Ratio	20.09-10.45	15.00-8.15	12.63-6.50	9.81-5.98	11.76-8.82	17.44-12.02	15.61-11.89	14.78-10.06
Average Yield %	1.52	2.08	2.94	4.62	4.32	3.20	2.33	2.42

Address: 205 East 6th Street, Sioux Falls, SD 57117-5107 **Telephone:** (605) 336-2750 **Web Site:** www.ravenind.com	**Officers:** Ronald M. Moquist – Pres., C.E.O., Thomas Iacarella – V.P., C.F.O., Treas., Sec.	**Investor Contact:** (605) 336-2750 **Institutional Holding** **No of Institutions:** 42 **Shares:** 3,102,548 **% Held:** 35%

223

REGIONS FINANCIAL CORP.

Exchange	Symbol	Price	52Wk Range	Yield	P/E
NYS	RF	$36.52 (3/31/2004)	39.75–31.57	3.61	12.59

*7 Year Price Score N/A   *NYSE Composite Index=100   *12 Month Price Score 95.1

Interim Earnings (Per Share)

Qtr.	Mar	Jun	Sep	Dec
2000	0.66	0.57	0.58	0.57
2001	0.57	0.49	0.59	0.59
2002	0.66	0.67	0.70	0.69
2003	0.71	0.73	0.73	0.73

Interim Dividends (Per Share)

Amt	Decl	Ex	Rec	Pa
0.32Q	7/16/2003	9/11/2003	9/15/2003	10/1/200
0.32Q	10/16/2003	12/17/2003	12/19/2003	1/2/200
0.33Q	1/21/2004	3/16/2004	3/18/2004	4/1/200
0.082Q	1/21/2004	3/16/2004	3/18/2004	4/1/200

Indicated Div: $1.32 (Div. Reinv. Plan)

Valuation Analysis

Forecast P/E	11.84	Trailing P/E	12.59
Market Cap	$8.1 Billion	Book Value	4.5 Billion
Price/Book	1.85	Price/Sales	2.37

Dividend Achiever Status

Rank	171	10 Year Growth Rate	9.42%
Total Years of Dividend Growth			32

Business Summary: Commercial Banking (MIC: 8.1 SIC: 6021 NAIC:522110)

Regions Financial is a regional financial holding company with assets of $48.60 billion as of Dec 31 2003. Co. provides traditiona commercial and retail banking services, brokerage and investment services, mortgage banking, insurance brokerage, credit life insuranc commercial accounts receivable factoring and specialty financing. Co.'s banking affiliate, Regions Bank, offers banking services fron 681 full-service banking offices in Alabama, Arkansas, Florida, Georgia, Louisiana, North Carolina, South Carolina, Tennessee an Texas. Co. also provides investment and brokerage services, asset management, mutual funds and financial planning from 142 offices c Morgan Keegan & Company, Inc.

Recent Developments: For the year ended Dec 31 2003, net income increased 5.2% to $651.8 million from $619.9 million in the prio year. Net interest income slipped 1.5% to $1.47 billion from $1.50 billion the year before. Provision for loan losses totaled $121. million, down 4.7% compared with $127.5 million the previous year. Total non-interest income advanced 11.1% to $1.40 billion from $1.26 billion a year earlier. Total non-interest expense grew 4.6% to $1.84 billion from $1.76 billion in 2002. Income before incom taxes climbed 4.9% to $911.6 million from $869.2 million the prior year. At Dec 31 2003, total assets were $48.60 billion, up 1.4% compared with $47.94 billion at Dec 31 2002.

Prospects: On Jan 23 2004, Co. announced that its has signed a definitive merger agreement with Union Planters Corp., a Memphi Tennessee-based bank holding company with total assets of $31.90 billion as of Dec 31 2003. The transaction is expected to b completed in mid 2004, subject to customary regulatory and shareholder approvals. Upon completion, the transaction is anticipated to b accretive to earnings beginning in 2005, with the integration of the two companies being completed in 2006. The combined compan expects to realize pre-tax annual cost savings of approximately $200.0 million.

Financial Data

(US$ in Thousands)	12/31/2003	12/31/2002	12/31/2001	12/31/2000	12/31/1999	12/31/1998	12/31/1997	12/31/1996
Earnings Per Share	2.90	2.72	2.24	2.38	2.35	1.88	2.15	1.8
Tang. Book Val. Per Share	20.05	18.87	17.54	15.73	13.89	13.61	13.99	12.7
Dividends Per Share	1.210	1.150	1.110	1.060	0.980	0.890	0.770	0.69
Dividend Payout %	41.72	42.27	49.55	44.53	41.70	47.34	36.04	37.3
Income Statement								
Total Interest Income	2,219,130	2,536,989	3,055,637	3,234,243	2,854,686	2,597,786	1,653,084	1,386,12
Total Interest Expense	744,532	1,039,401	1,630,144	1,845,446	1,428,831	1,272,968	824,203	685,65
Net Interest Income	1,474,598	1,497,588	1,425,493	1,388,797	1,425,855	1,324,818	828,881	700,46
Provision for Loan Losses	121,500	127,500	165,402	127,099	113,658	60,505	41,773	29,04
Non-Interest Income	1,398,757	1,258,878	981,885	601,210	537,141	474,697	258,553	220,73
Non-Interest Expense	1,840,283	1,759,726	1,524,025	1,121,182	1,064,312	1,103,708	600,341	553,80
Income Before Taxes	911,572	869,240	717,951	741,726	785,026	635,302	445,320	338,36
Net Income	651,841	619,902	508,934	527,523	525,386	421,712	299,692	229,68
Average Shs. Outstg.	225,118	227,639	227,063	221,989	223,967	223,781	139,421	124,27
Balance Sheet								
Cash & Due from Banks	1,255,853	1,577,536	1,239,598	1,210,872	1,393,418	1,619,006	726,059	774,84
Securities Avail. for Sale	9,872,935	9,747,683	8,555,005	5,468,406	6,873,308	4,893,410	1,576,648	1,797,49
Net Loans & Leases	31,730,266	30,548,610	30,466,181	30,999,955	27,806,300	24,050,175	16,200,599	13,135,62
Total Assets	48,597,996	47,938,840	45,382,712	43,688,293	42,714,395	36,831,940	23,034,228	18,930,17
Total Deposits	32,732,535	32,926,201	31,548,323	32,022,491	29,989,094	28,350,066	17,750,926	15,048,33
Long-Term Obligations	5,711,752	5,386,109	4,747,674	4,478,027	1,750,861	571,040	400,199	447,26
Total Liabilities	44,145,881	43,760,418	41,346,947	40,230,349	39,649,283	33,831,539	21,121,373	17,331,44
Net Stockholders' Equity	4,452,115	4,178,422	4,035,765	3,457,944	3,065,112	3,000,401	1,912,855	1,598,72
Shares Outstanding	221,967	221,336	230,081	219,769	220,635	220,454	136,696	125,31
Statistical Record								
Return on Equity %	11.43	14.83	12.61	15.25	17.14	14.05	15.66	14.3
Return on Assets %	1.04	1.29	1.12	1.20	1.22	1.14	1.30	1.2
Equity/Assets %	9.16	8.71	8.89	7.91	7.17	8.14	8.30	8.4
Non-Int. Exp./Tot. Inc. %	31.57	39.79	37.74	29.23	31.37	35.92	31.40	34.4
Price Range	37.85-30.49	36.13-27.10	...	...	...	...	...	...
P/E Ratio	13.05-10.51	13.28-9.96	...	...	...	...	...	...
Average Yield %	3.49	3.38	N/A	N/A	N/A	N/A	N/A	N/

Address: 417 North 20th Street, Birmingham, AL 35203 **Telephone:** (205) 944-1300 **Web Site:** www.regionsbank.com	**Officers:** Carl E. Jones - Chmn., Pres., C.E.O., Richard D. Horsley - Vice-Chmn., C.O.O. **Transfer Agents:**EquiServe, Jersey City, NJ	**Investor Contact:** (205) 326-7090 **Institutional Holding** **No of Institutions:** 268 **Shares:** 65,887,146 **% Held:** 29.80%

REPUBLIC BANCORP, INC.

Exchange	Symbol	Price	52Wk Range	Yield	P/E
NMS	RBNC	$14.05 (3/31/2004)	14.10-10.55	2.70	14.78

7 Year Price Score 134.5 *NYSE Composite Index=100 ***12 Month Price Score 99.6**

Interim Earnings (Per Share)

Qtr.	Mar	Jun	Sep	Dec
2000	0.17	0.18	0.17	0.17
2001	0.01	0.32	0.21	0.17
2002	0.21	0.22	0.24	0.20
2003	0.23	0.23	0.27	0.22

Interim Dividends (Per Share)

Amt	Decl	Ex	Rec	Pay
0.086Q	7/17/2003	9/10/2003	9/12/2003	10/6/2003
10%	10/17/2003	11/5/2003	11/7/2003	12/1/2003
0.095Q	11/20/2003	12/10/2003	12/12/2003	1/5/2004
0.095Q	2/20/2004	3/10/2004	3/12/2004	4/5/2004

Indicated Div: $0.38 (Div. Reinv. Plan)

Valuation Analysis

Forecast P/E	29.79	Trailing P/E	14.78
Market Cap	$737.1 Million	Book Value	355.3 Million
Price/Book	N/A	Price/Sales	N/A

Dividend Achiever Status

Rank	57	10 Year Growth Rate	16.71%
Total Years of Dividend Growth		11

Business Summary: Commercial Banking (MIC: 8.1 SIC: 6021 NAIC:522110)

Republic Bancorp, with $5.35 billion in assets as of Dec 31 2003, is the third largest bank holding company headquartered in Michigan and the 82nd largest bank holding company nationwide. Co. provides retail, commercial and mortgage banking products and services through its wholly-owned banking subsidiary, Republic Bank, a state-chartered banking corporation. As of Dec 31 2003, Republic Bank served customers in Michigan, Ohio and Indiana with 93 retail, commercial and mortgage banking offices and 93 ATMs. In addition, Co. performs residential mortgage loan servicing for the benefit of others, including collecting and remitting loan payments and supervising foreclosure proceedings.

Recent Developments: For the year ended Dec 31 2003, net income rose 7.1% to $60.7 million compared with $56.7 million in the prior year. Total interest income slid 6.7% to $265.7 million, while interest expense fell 13.8% to $123.2 million. Net interest income rose 0.5% to $142.5 million from $141.9 million the year before, primarily due to higher interest earning assets. Provision for loan losses fell 25.0% to $12.0 million. Total non-interest income grew 8.5% to $60.8 million, primarily due to higher levels of service charges, mortgage banking income, and income from bank-owned life insurance. Non-interest expense rose 4.1% to $104.7 million from $100.5 million the previous year.

Prospects: Results continue to reflect strong performances in Co.'s commercial loan portfolio, mortgage banking, and retail banking. During 2003, Co. originated $4.00 billion in single-family residential mortgages. Additionally, the residential mortgage portfolio grew $421.0 million, or 26.0% compared with 2002. At Dec 31 2003, Co.'s mortgage loan pipeline of applications in process amounted to $312.0 million. Meanwhile, Co.'s asset quality remains steady as total non-performing assets were unchanged at Dec 31 2003 compared with the prior year. Separately, during the fourth quarter of 2003, Co. completed the sale of its Menominee, MI branch office.

Financial Data

(US$ in Thousands)	12/31/2003	12/31/2002	12/31/2001	12/31/2000	12/31/1999	12/31/1998	12/31/1997	12/31/1996
Earnings Per Share	0.95	0.87	0.71	0.69	0.22	0.59	0.49	0.36
Tang. Book Val. Per Share	5.81	5.26	4.70	3.69	3.00	2.39	1.97	2.17
Dividends Per Share	0.310	0.280	0.250	0.230	0.210	0.190	0.180	0.160
Dividend Payout %	33.49	32.19	35.52	33.59	96.41	33.33	36.82	43.78
Income Statement								
Total Interest Income	265,680	284,704	333,376	348,328	299,662	146,005	118,852	99,147
Total Interest Expense	123,183	137,024	189,767	213,680	171,396	86,364	71,912	62,427
Net Interest Income	142,497	147,680	143,609	134,648	128,266	59,641	46,940	36,720
Provision for Loan Losses	12,000	16,000	8,700	6,500	11,650	4,000	3,031	290
Non-Interest Income	60,779	56,027	59,384	70,838	137,731	137,441	102,515	90,846
Non-Interest Expense	104,654	100,515	132,213	127,641	225,968	157,466	117,742	104,492
Income Before Taxes	86,622	87,192	62,080	71,345	28,379	35,616	28,682	22,784
Income from Cont Ops	...	...	39,565	...	...	...	...	15,066
Net Income	60,726	62,505	51,565	48,400	17,634	22,890	18,789	14,678
Average Shs. Outstg.	64,171	64,927	66,574	66,416	66,996	38,481	38,389	39,946
Balance Sheet								
Cash & Due from Banks	63,749	75,540	75,270	76,558	74,423	17,627	27,458	33,590
Securities Avail. for Sale	607,450	248,931	364,648	211,860	206,459	47,269	119,881	228,621
Net Loans & Leases	4,117,243	3,620,466	3,429,224	3,743,226	3,346,297	1,201,979	1,088,410	779,919
Total Assets	5,353,688	4,778,195	4,740,605	4,610,641	4,301,615	2,195,612	1,872,893	1,490,365
Total Deposits	2,815,269	2,788,272	2,753,468	2,728,526	2,613,050	1,378,691	1,177,293	1,013,707
Long-Term Obligations	1,616,726	1,321,443	1,314,218	1,431,013	1,219,711	504,068	414,132	183,389
Total Liabilities	4,984,268	4,395,467	4,356,969	4,287,058	4,006,455	2,045,195	1,741,805	1,253,394
Net Stockholders' Equity	369,420	332,728	304,917	294,864	266,441	150,891	132,684	126,711
Shares Outstanding	63,527	63,185	64,330	65,783	66,302	38,254	37,602	37,931
Statistical Record								
Return on Equity %	16.43	18.78	12.97	16.41	6.61	15.16	14.16	11.89
Return on Assets %	1.13	1.30	0.83	1.04	0.40	1.04	1.00	1.01
Equity/Assets %	6.90	6.96	6.43	6.39	6.19	6.87	7.08	8.50
Non-Int. Exp./Tot. Inc. %	32.05	29.49	32.66	30.45	51.66	55.55	53.18	54.99
Price Range	13.98-10.55	12.69-9.29	12.00-8.08	8.64-5.17	9.43-7.06	10.63-7.45	10.62-5.25	5.59-4.36
P/E Ratio	14.72-11.10	14.58-10.68	16.90-11.38	12.52-7.49	42.86-32.10	18.02-12.63	21.67-10.71	15.54-12.12
Average Yield %	2.55	2.53	2.44	3.60	2.57	2.03	2.63	3.30

Address: 1070 East Main Street, Owosso, MI 48867	**Officers:** Jerry D. Campbell – Chmn., George J. Butvilas – Vice-Chmn.	**Investor Contact:** (989) 725-7337
Telephone: (989) 725-7337		**Institutional Holding**
Web Site: www.republicbancorp.com		**No of Institutions:** 22
		Shares: 3,456,166 **% Held:** –

225

RLI CORP.

*7 Year Price Score 151.5 *NYSE Composite Index=100 *12 Month Price Score 102.8

Interim Earnings (Per Share)

Qtr.	Mar	Jun	Sep	Dec
2000	0.33	0.35	0.35	0.32
2001	0.31	0.35	0.34	0.37
2002	0.39	0.45	0.28	0.63
2003	0.56	0.60	0.98	0.62

Interim Dividends (Per Share)

Amt	Decl	Ex	Rec	Pay
0.10Q	5/2/2003	6/26/2003	6/30/2003	7/15/200
0.10Q	9/2/2003	9/26/2003	9/30/2003	10/15/200
0.11Q	11/24/2003	12/29/2003	12/31/2003	1/15/200
0.11Q	2/9/2004	3/29/2004	3/31/2004	4/15/2004

Indicated Div: $0.44 (Div. Reinv. Plan)

Valuation Analysis

Forecast P/E	13.42	Trailing P/E	13.94
Market Cap	$767.2 Million	Book Value	526.7 Million
Price/Book	1.57	Price/Sales	1.67

Dividend Achiever Status

Rank	191	10 Year Growth Rate 8.40%
Total Years of Dividend Growth	27	

Business Summary: Insurance (MIC: 8.2 SIC: 6331 NAIC:524126)

RLI is a holding company primarily of three main insurance companies. RLI Insurance Company, the principal subsidiary writes multiple lines insurance on an admitted basis in all 50 states, the District of Columbia and Puerto Rico. Mt. Hawley Insurance Company, a subsidiary of RLI Insurance Company, writes surplus lines insurance in all 50 states, the District of Columbia, Puerto Rico the Virgin Islands and Guam. RLI Indemnity Company, a subsidiary of Mt. Hawley, has authority to write multiple lines insurance on a admitted basis in 48 states and the District of Colombia.

Recent Developments: For the year ended Dec 31 2003, net income advanced 98.8% to $71.3 million compared with $35.9 millio the previous year. The improvement in earnings was largely attributed to continued premium growth Total revenues jumped 36.0% to $519.9 million from $382.2 million the year before. Net premiums earned improved 33.2% to $463.6 million from $348.1 million, while net investment income increased 17.3% to $44.2 million from $37.6 million the prior year. Revenues included a net realized gain of $12. million and a net realized loss of $3.6 million in 2003 and 2002, respectively.

Prospects: Co. is well-positioned to benefit from favorable opportunities for profitable writings in property lines and growth potentia in casualty writings. Co.'s property segment should continue to deliver solid results. Casualty results are benefiting from the strong rate environment that is likely to persist well into the current year. Meanwhile, Co.'s surety results have improved slightly due to the favorabl performance of bonds written recently; however, business written prior to 2003 continues to hinder the segment's results.As of Dec 3 2003, Co.'s investment portfolio contained $149.5 million of cumulative unrealized gains, of which $131.5 million were related to th equity portfolio.

Financial Data

(US$ in Thousands)	12/31/2003	12/31/2002	12/31/2001	12/31/2000	12/31/1999	12/31/1998	12/31/1997	12/31/1996
Earnings Per Share	2.76	1.75	1.37	1.35	1.39	1.27	1.56	1.14
Tang. Book Val. Per Share	20.97	17.36	15.36	14.99	13.11	14.12	15.43	10.22
Dividends Per Share	0.380	0.330	0.310	0.290	0.270	0.250	0.230	0.21
Dividend Payout %	13.76	19.14	22.54	21.48	19.35	19.68	14.87	18.94
Income Statement								
Total Premium Income	463,597	348,065	273,008	231,603	195,274	142,324	141,884	130,656
Net Investment Income	44,151	37,640	32,178	29,046	26,015	23,937	24,558	23,68
Other Income	47,711	34,088	36,344	31,893	30,482	25,790	27,540	24,698
Total Revenues	519,886	382,153	309,354	263,496	225,756	168,114	169,424	155,354
Total Indirect Exp.	3,886	3,505	2,636	3,388	2,091	3,915	4,172	3,278
Inc. Before Inc. Taxes	94,278	48,728	41,018	38,293	43,035	37,721	41,522	35,240
Income Taxes	22,987	12,876	10,771	9,600	11,584	9,482	11,351	9,544
Eqty Earns/Minority Int.	5,548	4,397	2,845	2,979	1,613	1,337	951	231
Income from Cont Ops	...	...	30,247	...	...	...	...	..
Net Income	71,291	35,852	31,047	28,693	31,451	28,239	30,171	25,696
Average Shs. Outstg.	25,846	20,512	20,004	19,890	20,444	21,276	18,742	24,164
Balance Sheet								
Cash & Cash Equivalents	33,004	47,889	53,648	48,095	64,092	51,917	18,697	40,824
Premiums Due	639,571	568,004	456,919	406,761	368,794	281,165	248,454	261,725
Invst. Assets: Total	1,364,043	1,025,288	814,435	774,159	706,314	690,751	617,472	546,917
Total Assets	2,134,354	1,719,327	1,390,970	1,281,323	1,170,363	1,012,685	911,741	845,474
Long-Term Obligations	100,000	...	...	...	...	...	...	46,000
Net Stockholders' Equity	554,134	456,555	335,432	326,654	293,069	293,959	266,552	200,039
Shares Outstanding	25,165	24,681	19,825	19,607	19,746	20,811	17,268	19,554
Statistical Record								
Return on Equity %	12.86	7.85	9.01	8.78	10.73	9.60	11.31	12.84
Return on Assets %	3.34	2.08	2.17	2.23	2.68	2.78	3.30	3.03
Price Range	38.10-25.40	29.60-22.25	23.00-19.40	22.34-13.25	19.38-13.97	22.65-15.41	20.05-12.20	13.40-9.00
P/E Ratio	13.80-9.20	16.91-12.71	16.79-14.16	16.55-9.81	13.94-10.05	17.83-12.13	12.85-7.82	11.75-7.89
Average Yield %	1.21	1.27	1.48	1.63	1.61	1.28	1.53	2.04

Address: 9025 North Lindbergh Drive, Peoria, IL 61615-1499 Telephone: (309) 692-1000 Web Site: www.rlicorp.com	Officers: Jonathan E. Michael - Pres., C.E.O., Joseph E. Dondanville - Sr. V.P., C.F.O.	Investor Contact: (309) 693-5880 Institutional Holding No of Institutions: 8 Shares: 123,312 % Held: -

ROHM & HAAS CO.

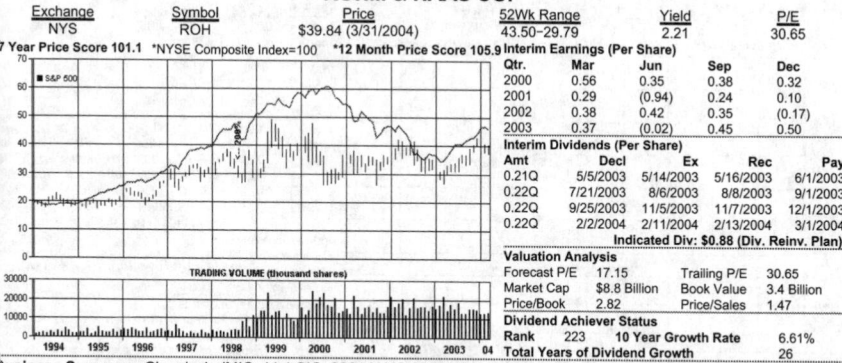

Exchange	Symbol	Price	52Wk Range	Yield	P/E
NYS	ROH	$39.84 (3/3/2004)	43.50-29.79	2.21	30.65

7 Year Price Score 101.1 *NYSE Composite Index=100 *12 Month Price Score 105.9

Interim Earnings (Per Share)

Qtr.	Mar	Jun	Sep	Dec
2000	0.56	0.35	0.38	0.32
2001	0.29	(0.94)	0.24	0.10
2002	0.38	0.42	0.35	(0.17)
2003	0.37	(0.02)	0.45	0.50

Interim Dividends (Per Share)

Amt	Decl	Ex	Rec	Pay
0.21Q	5/5/2003	5/14/2003	5/16/2003	6/1/2003
0.22Q	7/21/2003	8/6/2003	8/8/2003	9/1/2003
0.22Q	9/25/2003	11/5/2003	11/7/2003	12/1/2003
0.22Q	2/2/2004	2/11/2004	2/13/2004	3/1/2004

Indicated Div: $0.88 (Div. Reinv. Plan)

Valuation Analysis

Forecast P/E	17.15	Trailing P/E	30.65
Market Cap	$8.8 Billion	Book Value	3.4 Billion
Price/Book	2.82	Price/Sales	1.47

Dividend Achiever Status

Rank	223	10 Year Growth Rate	6.61%
Total Years of Dividend Growth	26		

Business Summary: Chemicals (MIC: 11.1 SIC: 2821 NAIC:325211)

Rohm & Haas is a global specialty materials company that operates through six reportable segments: coatings, adhesives and sealants, electronic materials, performance chemicals, salt and monomers. Coatings is Co.'s largest segment in terms of sales, and is comprised of three businesses including architectural functional coatings, powder coatings and automotive coatings. Co. operates over 100 manufacturing and 30 research facilities in 27 countries, and serves several industries, including construction and building, electronics, household products and personal care, packaging, food and retail, and automotive.

Recent Developments: For the twelve months ended Dec 31 2003, earnings jumped 37.1% to $288.0 million, before an accounting change charge of $8.0 million, versus earnings of $210.0 million, before an accounting change charge of $773.0 million, in 2002. Earnings benefited from strong organic growth and favorable currency exchange rates. Results for 2003 and 2002 included provisions for restructuring and asset impairments of $196.0 million and $177.0 million, and losses on the early extinguishment of debt of $4.0 million and $12.0 million, respectively. Results for 2002 excluded an after-tax loss of $7.0 million from discontinued operations. Net sales rose 12.1% to $6.42 billion from $5.73 billion the year before.

Prospects: Co. plans to continue growth and productivity improvements in 2004. These initiatives, coupled with improvements in the global economy and a strong recovery in the electronics market, should well-position Co. for improved performance. Global economic growth, which is estimated at about 3.0%, should result in sales growth for Co. in the range of 6.0% to 8.0%. Quarterly sales are expected to be in the range of $1.65 billion to $1.75 billion. Full-year 2004 gross profit margin should be in the 30.0% range, while first quarter margin should be below average due to higher raw material and energy costs. Meanwhile, Co. expects full-year 2004 earnings per share in the range of $1.90 to $2.10.

Financial Data

(US$ in Thousands)	12/31/2003	12/31/2002	12/31/2001	12/31/2000	12/31/1999	12/31/1998	12/31/1997	12/31/1996
Earnings Per Share	1.30	0.98	(0.31)	1.61	1.27	2.52	2.13	1.81
Cash Flow Per Share	4.49	4.39	3.17	3.49	3.72	3.79	4.11	3.59
Tang. Book Val. Per Share	0.13	N.M.	N.M.	N.M.	N.M.	9.06	8.51	8.43
Dividends Per Share	0.860	0.820	0.800	0.780	0.740	0.690	0.630	0.570
Dividend Payout %	66.15	83.67	N.M.	48.44	58.26	27.51	29.73	31.49
Income Statement								
Total Revenues	6,421,000	5,727,000	5,666,000	6,879,000	5,339,000	3,720,000	3,999,000	3,982,000
Total Indirect Exp.	1,400,000	1,385,000	1,567,000	1,490,000	1,337,000	847,000	844,000	828,000
Depreciation & Amort.	67,000	69,000	156,000	159,000	83,000	10,000	12,000	10,000
Operating Income	519,000	432,000	91,000	756,000	628,000	622,000	617,000	567,000
Net Interest Inc./(Exp.)	(121,000)	(126,000)	(174,000)	(234,000)	(146,000)	(21,000)	(33,000)	(32,000)
Income Taxes	127,000	102,000	6,000	227,000	215,000	247,000	201,000	167,000
Eqty Earns/Minority Int.	15,000	15,000	12,000	19,000	7,000	(3,000)	5,000	(12,000)
Income from Cont Ops	288,000	218,000	(70,000)	...	...	453,000	...	...
Net Income	280,000	(570,000)	395,000	354,000	249,000	440,000	410,000	363,000
Average Shs. Outstg.	222,400	221,900	220,200	220,500	218,981	179,700	192,300	196,200
Balance Sheet								
Cash & Cash Equivalents	196,000	295,000	92,000	92,000	57,000	16,000	40,000	11,000
Total Current Assets	2,527,000	2,543,000	2,421,000	2,781,000	2,497,000	1,287,000	1,397,000	1,456,000
Total Assets	9,445,000	9,706,000	10,350,000	11,267,000	11,256,000	3,648,000	3,900,000	3,933,000
Total Current Liabilities	1,797,000	1,621,000	1,624,000	2,194,000	2,510,000	875,000	850,000	886,000
Long-Term Obligations	2,468,000	2,872,000	2,720,000	3,225,000	3,122,000	409,000	509,000	562,000
Net Stockholders' Equity	3,357,000	3,119,000	3,815,000	3,653,000	3,475,000	1,561,000	1,797,000	1,728,000
Net Working Capital	730,000	922,000	797,000	587,000	(13,000)	412,000	547,000	570,000
Shares Outstanding	222,453	221,131	220,427	219,937	218,981	154,000	182,700	189,300
Statistical Record								
Operating Profit Margin %	8.08	7.54	1.60	10.98	11.76	16.72	15.42	14.23
Return on Equity %	8.57	6.98	N.M	9.69	7.16	29.01	22.81	21.00
Return on Assets %	3.04	2.24	N.M.	3.14	2.21	12.41	10.51	9.22
Debt/Total Assets %	26.13	29.58	26.28	28.62	27.73	11.21	13.05	14.28
Price Range	42.92-26.67	44.27-30.55	38.27-26.12	47.88-26.00	49.13-28.75	38.54-26.75	33.23-23.83	27.21-18.62
P/E Ratio	33.02-20.52	43.13-31.17	N/A	29.74-16.15	38.68-22.64	15.29-10.62	15.60-11.19	15.03-10.29
Average Yield %	2.53	2.25	2.35	2.26	1.96	2.09	2.14	2.51

Address: 100 Independence Mall West, Philadelphia, PA 19106 **Telephone:** (215) 592-3000 **Web Site:** www.rohmhaas.com	**Officers:** Rajiv L. Gupta – Chmn., C.E.O., J. Michael Fitzpatrick – Pres., C.O.O. **Transfer Agents:** EquiServe, LP, Boston, MA	**Investor Contact:** (215) 592-3052 **Institutional Holding** No of Institutions: 14 Shares: 162,154,220 % Held: –

ROPER INDUSTRIES, INC

Exchange	Symbol	Price	52Wk Range	Yield	P/E
NYS	ROP	$48.25 (3/31/2004)	52.88-29.00	0.80	28.89

*7 Year Price Score 120.1 *NYSE Composite Index=100 *12 Month Price Score 114.0

Interim Earnings (Per Share)

Qtr.	Jan	Apr	Jul	Oct
2001-02	0.46	0.55	0.46	0.61
2002-03	0.26	0.46	0.53	...
Qtr.	Mar	Jun	Sep	Dec
2003	...	...	0.62	0.06

Interim Dividends (Per Share)

Amt	Decl	Ex	Rec	Pa
0.088Q	5/28/2003	7/15/2003	7/17/2003	7/31/200
0.088Q	8/20/2003	10/15/2003	10/17/2003	10/31/200
0.096Q	11/21/2003	1/14/2004	1/16/2004	1/30/200
0.096Q	2/27/2004	4/14/2004	4/16/2004	4/30/200

Indicated Div: $0.385

Valuation Analysis

Forecast P/E	19.22	Trailing P/E	28.89
Market Cap	$1.5 Billion	Book Value	442.3 Million
Price/Book	3.12	Price/Sales	2.15

Dividend Achiever Status

Rank	21	10 Year Growth Rate 22.77%
Total Years of Dividend Growth		11

Business Summary: Industrial Machinery and Equipment (MIC: 11.5 SIC: 3561 NAIC:333911)

Roper Industries is a diversified industrial company. The Instrumentation segment provides equipment and consumables for material analysis, fluid properties testing and industrial leak testing. The industrial technology segment produces industrial pumps, flow measurement and metering equipment, and water meter and automatic meter reading products and systems. The Energy Systems and Controls segment produces control systems, machinery vibration and other non-destructive inspection and measurement products. The Scientific and Industrial Imaging segment produces high-performance digital imaging products and software and handheld computers and software.

Recent Developments: For the twelve months ended Dec 31 2003, income from continuing operations declined 27.7% to $48.1 million versus $66.4 million, before goodwill impairment of $26.0 million, in the twelve months ended Oct 31 2002. Results included a debt extinguishment loss of $25.1 million in 2003 and a Euro debt currency exchange loss of $4.1 million in 2002. Net sales increased 6.5% to $657.4 million, primarily due to acquisitions. On a segment basis, Instrumentation sales rose 3.3% to $181.3 million, while Industrial Technology sales grew 3.8% to $170.3 million. Energy Systems and Controls sales advanced 9.7% to $139.0 million, and Scientific and Industrial Imaging sales rose 10.3% to $166.7 million.

Prospects: In 2004, Co. plans to build on its 2003 success by capturing the opportunities available from the Neptune Technology Grou Holdings Inc. acquisition, continuing its initiatives to drive organic growth, making strategic acquisitions, driving down net working capital and increasing organizational capabilities. Co. expects these activities to contribute to record 2004 results. Co. is forecasting full-year 2004 net sales of $875.0 million to $925.0 million, earnings in the range of $2.45 to $2.70 per diluted share, and cash flow from operating activities between $140.0 million and $160.0 million.

Financial Data
(US$ in Thousands)

	12/31/2003	12/31/2002	10/31/2002	10/31/2001	10/31/2000	10/31/1999	10/31/1998	10/31/1997
Earnings Per Share	1.50	0.04	2.08	1.77	1.58	1.53	1.24	1.1
Cash Flow Per Share	2.22	0.23	2.73	3.25	2.16	1.70	2.40	1.1
Tang. Book Val. Per Share	N.M	N.M	N.M	N.M	N.M	0.55	N.M	0.7
Dividends Per Share	0.350	0.330	0.320	0.290	0.210	0.260	0.300	0.18
Dividend Payout %	23.33	825.00	15.50	16.66	13.29	16.99	24.19	15.5
Income Statement								
Total Revenues	657,356	83,885	627,030	586,506	503,813	407,256	389,170	298,23
Total Indirect Exp.	238,038	36,997	221,490	210,542	170,628	132,548	124,861	92,51
Depreciation & Amort.	16,378	2,620	15,176	27,455	22,298	15,966	14,434	11,40
Operating Income	108,100	4,568	114,829	98,428	88,196	77,955	66,092	60,87
Net Interest Inc./(Exp.)	(16,384)	(2,978)	(18,506)	(15,917)	(13,483)	(7,254)	(7,856)	(6,048
Income Taxes	18,229	529	29,663	30,600	26,653	24,938	20,300	18,75
Income from Cont Ops	48,061	1,240	66,023	...	...	...	...	...
Net Income	45,239	853	40,053	55,839	49,278	47,346	39,316	36,35
Average Shs. Outstg.	31,992	31,854	31,815	31,493	31,182	30,992	31,717	31,45
Balance Sheet								
Cash & Cash Equivalents	70,234	15,270	12,362	16,190	11,372	13,490	9,350	64
Total Current Assets	381,192	247,565	247,622	233,053	213,955	161,819	139,852	131,89
Total Assets	1,514,995	824,966	828,973	762,122	596,902	420,163	381,533	329,32
Total Current Liabilities	161,497	121,079	130,237	103,880	84,492	72,243	57,578	44,93
Long–Term Obligations	630,186	308,684	311,590	323,830	234,603	109,659	120,307	99,63
Net Stockholders' Equity	655,781	380,981	376,012	323,506	270,191	231,968	197,033	177,86
Net Working Capital	219,695	126,486	117,385	129,173	129,463	89,576	82,274	86,95
Shares Outstanding	36,042	31,370	31,363	30,879	30,599	30,282	30,343	30,92
Statistical Record								
Operating Profit Margin %	16.44	5.44	18.31	16.78	17.50	19.14	16.98	20.4
Return on Equity %	7.32	0.32	17.55	17.26	18.23	20.41	19.95	20.4
Return on Assets %	3.17	0.15	7.96	7.32	8.25	11.26	10.30	11.0
Debt/Total Assets %	41.59	37.41	37.58	42.49	39.30	26.09	31.53	30.2
Price Range	51.58-26.75	43.15-36.46	51.80-27.36	45.50-30.06	38.31-25.00	38.38-15.94	33.88-13.88	33.88-18.6
P/E Ratio	34.39-17.83	N.M.	24.90-13.15	25.71-16.98	24.25-15.82	25.08-10.42	27.32-11.19	29.20-16.0
Average Yield %	0.89	0.84	0.77	0.77	0.65	0.93	1.16	0.7

Address: 2160 Satellite Boulevard, Duluth, GA 30097 **Telephone:** (770) 495-5100 **Web Site:** www.roperind.com	**Officers:** Brian D. Jellison – Chmn., Pres., C.E.O., Martin S. Headley – V.P., C.F.O. **Transfer Agents:**Wachovia Bank, N.A., Charlotte, NC	**Institutional Holding** **No of Institutions:** 167 **Shares:** 28,922,445 **% Held:** 57.60%

228

ROUSE CO.

Exchange	Symbol	Price	52Wk Range	Yield	P/E
NYS	RSE	$53.60 (3/31/2004)	53.60–34.33	3.51	38.29

7 Year Price Score 134.5   *NYSE Composite Index=100   *12 Month Price Score 105.6

Interim Earnings (Per Share)

Qtr.	Mar	Jun	Sep	Dec
2000	0.40	0.45	0.91	0.45
2001	0.41	0.34	0.37	0.30
2002	0.18	0.76	0.33	(0.12)
2003	0.19	0.41	0.37	0.43

Interim Dividends (Per Share)

Amt	Decl	Ex	Rec	Pay
0.42Q	5/8/2003	6/12/2003	6/16/2003	6/30/2003
0.42Q	5/8/2003	9/12/2003	9/16/2003	9/30/2003
0.42Q	12/4/2003	12/10/2003	12/12/2003	12/23/2003
0.47Q	1/15/2004	3/15/2004	3/17/2004	3/31/2004

Indicated Div: $1.88 (Div. Reinv. Plan)

Valuation Analysis

Forecast P/E	10.31	Trailing P/E	38.29
Market Cap	$4.7 Billion	Book Value	1.3 Billion
Price/Book	3.23	Price/Sales	3.87

Dividend Achiever Status

Rank	145	10 Year Growth Rate	10.48%
Total Years of Dividend Growth			11

Business Summary: Property, Real Estate &Development (MIC: 8.3 SIC: 6512 NAIC:531210)

Rouse operates more than 150 properties encompassing retail, office, research and development, and industrial space in 22 states. Co. owns and/or operates 32 regional retail centers and four community centers, with more than 37.7 million square feet. Co. also owns and/or operates six mixed–use projects with 2.2 million square feet of office/industrial space, and 104 office and industrial buildings with 3.8 million square feet located in and around Las Vegas, NV, Columbia, MD and the Baltimore–Washington corridor. Co., through its affiliates, is the developer of the cities of Columbia, MD and Summerlin, NV.

Recent Developments: For the twelve months ended Dec 31 2003, earnings from continuing operations climbed 3.1% to $139.5 million compared with $135.3 million in 2002. Results for 2003 and 2002 included net gains on dispositions of interests in operating properties of $26.6 million and $48.9 million, respectively. Results for 2003 also included impairment losses on operating properties of $7.9 million partially related to the sale of two industrial buildings. Results for 2003 and 2002 excluded gains from discontinued operations of $121.1 million and $4.6 million, respectively. Total revenues rose 16.4% to $1.10 billion from $949.2 million the year before. Funds from operations jumped 52.3% to $369.8 million.

Prospects: Looking ahead, prospects for Co.'s nationwide portfolio of retail centers for continued strong growth, with comparable center retail net operating income projected to grow between 2.5% to 3.0%. Even though demand for office space is still weak, which will hamper results for 2004, Co.'s community development activities are well–positioned for a strong year. As a result, Co. expects funds from operations for full–year 2004 in the range of $4.10 to $4.20 and diluted earnings per share in the range of $2.84 to $2.94. Separately, on Feb 3 2004, Co. announced a contract to purchase Providence Place, a 1.3 million square foot regional shopping center in Providence, RI, for $522.0 million.

Financial Data

(US$ in Thousands)	12/31/2003	12/31/2002	12/31/2001	12/31/2000	12/31/1999	12/31/1998	12/31/1997	12/31/1996
Earnings Per Share	1.40	1.15	1.42	2.21	1.77	1.34	2.59	0.14
Cash Flow Per Share	4.25	4.42	4.17	3.64	2.78	3.84	2.44	3.02
Tang. Book Val. Per Share	14.43	12.79	9.44	9.28	9.03	8.70	6.95	2.65
Dividends Per Share	1.680	1.560	1.420	1.320	1.200	1.120	1.00	0.880
Dividend Payout %	120.00	135.65	100.00	59.72	67.79	83.58	38.61	628.57
Income Statement								
Total Revenues	1,104,866	1,104,734	966,337	633,738	715,657	692,571	916,771	831,917
Total Indirect Exp.	173,280	161,333	125,504	90,307	100,329	84,068	82,944	79,990
Depreciation & Amort.	173,280	161,333	125,504	90,307	100,329	84,068	82,944	79,990
Operating Income	377,810	385,884	337,089	242,708	276,941	250,121	297,985	279,873
Net Interest Inc./(Exp.)	(222,766)	(245,321)	(228,765)	(236,744)	(244,515)	(209,564)	(207,490)	(220,381)
Income Taxes	42,500	(36,543)	(36,727)	(258,858)	284	(24)	(116,066)	25,719
Eqty Earns/Minority Int.	58,053	40,082	32,374	162,706	76,468	75,769	6,815	...
Income from Cont Ops	139,523	112,829	111,813	168,285	141,176	105,176	189,892	17,886
Net Income	260,589	139,851	110,706	170,485	135,297	104,902	167,336	16,433
Average Shs. Outstg.	88,453	84,954	69,694	69,475	71,705	67,874	76,005	55,572
Balance Sheet								
Cash & Cash Equivalents	139,543	73,736	54,280	37,588	49,211	41,950	90,686	47,362
Total Current Assets	193,237	130,663	142,033	82,155	110,435	117,867	204,986	139,731
Total Assets	6,639,244	6,386,168	4,880,443	4,175,538	4,427,216	5,154,643	3,589,768	3,643,452
Total Current Liabilities	179,530	...	...	...	...	...	...	...
Long–Term Obligations	4,444,492	4,441,477	3,488,820	3,045,769	3,334,419	4,068,459	2,684,140	2,895,447
Net Stockholders' Equity	1,324,964	1,112,084	655,360	630,468	638,580	628,926	465,515	177,149
Net Working Capital	13,707	130,663	142,033	82,155	110,435	117,867	204,986	139,731
Shares Outstanding	91,759	86,909	69,354	67,880	70,693	72,225	66,911	66,743
Statistical Record								
Operating Profit Margin %	34.19	34.93	34.88	38.29	38.69	36.11	32.50	33.64
Return on Equity %	10.53	10.14	17.06	26.69	22.10	16.72	40.79	10.09
Return on Assets %	2.10	1.76	2.29	4.03	3.18	2.04	5.28	0.49
Debt/Total Assets %	66.94	69.54	71.48	72.94	75.31	78.92	74.77	79.46
Price Range	47.22–30.45	33.35–27.50	30.16–23.82	27.13–20.31	27.50–19.88	35.69–23.44	32.88–25.75	31.75–18.25
P/E Ratio	33.73–21.75	29.00–23.91	21.24–16.77	12.27–9.19	15.54–11.23	26.63–17.49	12.69–9.94	226.8–130.4
Average Yield %	4.37	5.06	5.22	5.49	5.07	3.76	3.38	3.67

Address: 10275 Little Patuxent Parkway, Columbia, MD 21044–3456 Telephone: (410) 992–6000 Web Site: www.therousecompany.com	Officers: Anthony W. Deering – Chmn., Pres., C.E.O., Thomas J. DeRosa – Vice–Chmn., C.F.O. Transfer Agents:The Bank of New York, New York, NY	Investor Contact: (410) 992–6546 Institutional Holding No of Institutions: 21 Shares: 3,496,001 % Held: –

RPM INTERNATIONAL INC

Exchange	Symbol	Price	52Wk Range	Yield	P/E
NYS	RPM	$16.54 (3/31/2004)	17.10-10.75	3.39	44.70

*7 Year Price Score N/A   *NYSE Composite Index=100   *12 Month Price Score 105.3

Interim Earnings (Per Share)

Qtr.	Aug	Nov	Feb	May
2000-01	0.28	0.17	(0.07)	0.24
2001-02	0.36	0.24	0.03	0.34
2002-03	0.38	0.26	0.04	(0.38)
2003-04	0.41	0.30	...	...

Interim Dividends (Per Share)

Amt	Decl	Ex	Rec	Pay
0.13Q	4/4/2003	4/10/2003	4/14/2003	4/30/2003
0.13Q	7/1/2003	7/10/2003	7/14/2003	7/31/2003
0.14Q	10/10/2003	10/16/2003	10/20/2003	10/31/2003
0.14Q	1/2/2004	1/8/2004	1/12/2004	1/30/2004

Indicated Div: $0.56 (Div. Reinv. Plan)

Valuation Analysis

Forecast P/E	11.19	Trailing P/E	44.70
Market Cap	$1.9 Billion	Book Value	945.3 Million
Price/Book	1.60	Price/Sales	0.69

Dividend Achiever Status

Rank	242	10 Year Growth Rate	5.39%
Total Years of Dividend Growth			30

Business Summary: Chemicals (MIC: 11.1 SIC: 2851 NAIC:325510)

RPM International manufactures and markets specialty paints, protective coatings and roofing systems, sealants and adhesives, focusing on the maintenance and improvement needs of both the industrial and consumer markets. Co.'s family of products includes those marketed under the following brands: Carboline, DAP, Day-Glo, Flecto, Rust-Oleum, Stonhard, Tremco and Zinsser. Co. markets its products in approximately 130 countries and operates manufacturing facilities in locations in the US, Argentina, Belgium, Brazil, Canada, China, Colombia, Germany, Italy, Mexico, New Zealand, The Netherlands, Poland, South Africa, the United Arab Emirates and the UK.

Recent Developments: For the quarter ended Nov 30 2003, net income climbed 18.8% to $35.2 million compared with $29.6 million in the equivalent 2002 quarter. Net sales grew 13.9% to $589.8 million from $518.0 million a year earlier. The improvement in sales was primarily attributed to strong contributions from Co.'s businesses, as well as net favorable foreign exchange differences and the contribution of product line acquisitions. Industrial segment net sales grew 15.0% year-over-year, while consumer segment net sales climbed 12.0% from a year earlier. Gross profit advanced 14.2% to $265.9 million versus $232.8 million the year before.

Prospects: The months from December to February are Co.'s seasonally slowest period; however, its performance through the first half of fiscal 2004 supports Co.'s confidence for improved operating results for the full year. Accordingly, Co. anticipates high single-digit revenue growth, with earnings per share in between 10.0% and 20.0% growth for full-year 2004. Meanwhile, Co.'s operating segments should continue to benefit from internal and external growth, including acquisitions. Gross profit margin productivity gains and volume leverage may be partially offset by a number of higher raw material costs.

Financial Data

(US$ in Thousands)	6 Mos	3 Mos	05/31/2003	05/31/2002	05/31/2001	05/31/2000	05/31/1999	05/31/1998
Earnings Per Share	0.37	0.33	0.30	0.97	0.62	0.38	0.86	0.84
Cash Flow Per Share	0.56	0.22	1.38	1.82	0.72	0.95	1.05	0.96
Tang. Book Val. Per Share	0.16	N.M	N.M	0.01	N.M	N.M	0.77	N.M
Dividends Per Share	0.530	0.520	0.510	0.500	0.490	0.480	0.460	0.446
Dividend Payout %	143.24	157.58	171.66	51.54	80.24	127.63	54.01	52.38
Income Statement								
Total Revenues	1,179,925	590,091	2,083,489	1,986,126	2,007,762	1,954,131	1,712,154	1,615,274
Total Indirect Exp.	400,466	195,918	879,987	717,628	713,285	678,970	592,666	537,156
Depreciation & Amort.	30,925	15,127	58,674	56,859	81,494	79,150	62,135	57,000
Operating Income	141,513	80,193	74,565	194,588	166,690	175,524	192,378	186,256
Net Interest Inc./(Exp.)	(12,994)	(6,283)	(26,712)	(40,464)	(65,203)	(51,793)	(32,781)	(36,700)
Income Taxes	45,624	26,238	12,526	52,570	38,526	30,769	65,051	61,710
Net Income	82,895	47,672	35,327	101,554	62,961	40,992	94,546	87,834
Average Shs. Outstg.	116,335	116,233	115,986	105,131	102,212	107,384	111,376	111,662
Balance Sheet								
Cash & Cash Equivalents	48,498	47,512	50,725	42,172	23,926	31,340	19,729	40,782
Total Current Assets	930,473	918,742	928,094	801,314	819,420	785,092	705,419	672,475
Total Assets	2,261,234	2,234,278	2,247,211	2,036,403	2,078,490	2,099,203	1,737,236	1,683,275
Total Current Liabilities	391,600	389,029	427,650	364,714	375,768	376,202	302,549	285,764
Long-Term Obligations	721,620	728,367	724,846	707,921	955,399	959,330	582,109	715,688
Net Stockholders' Equity	945,340	901,604	877,008	858,106	639,710	645,724	742,876	567,055
Net Working Capital	...	529,713	500,444	436,600	443,652	408,890	402,870	386,708
Shares Outstanding	115,702	115,624	115,496	114,696	102,211	103,134	109,443	100,258
Statistical Record								
Operating Profit Margin %	11.99	13.58	3.57	9.79	8.30	8.98	11.23	11.53
Return on Equity %	8.76	5.28	4.02	11.83	9.84	6.34	12.72	15.48
Return on Assets %	3.66	2.13	1.57	4.98	3.02	1.95	5.44	5.21
Debt/Total Assets %	31.91	32.59	32.25	34.76	45.96	45.69	33.50	42.51
Price Range	15.24-12.55	14.13-12.55	16.06-9.20	17.61-8.05	10.63-7.75	15.00-9.56	17.50-12.81	
P/E Ratio	21.46-17.68	34.46-30.61	53.53-30.67	18.15-8.30	17.14-12.50	39.47-25.16	20.35-14.90	
Average Yield %	3.85	3.87	3.84	3.84	5.28	4.09	3.09	N/A

Address: P.O. Box 777, Medina, OH 44258	Officers: Thomas C. Sullivan – Chmn., Frank C. Sullivan – Pres., C.E.O.	Investor Contact: (330) 273-8820
Telephone: (330) 273-5090		Institutional Holding
Web Site: www.rpminc.com		No of Institutions: 257
		Shares: 73,050,845 % Held: 63.60%

S & T BANCORP, INC.

Exchange	Symbol	Price	52Wk Range	Yield	P/E
NMS	STBA	$30.06 (3/31/2004)	31.42–26.11	3.46	15.49

*7 Year Price Score 121.2   *NYSE Composite Index=100   ***12 Month Price Score 96.0**

Interim Earnings (Per Share)

Qtr.	Mar	Jun	Sep	Dec
2000	0.40	0.41	0.42	0.43
2001	0.43	0.44	0.51	0.44
2002	0.43	0.44	0.46	0.48
2003	0.47	0.48	0.50	0.49

Interim Dividends (Per Share)

Amt	Decl	Ex	Rec	Pay
0.25Q	6/16/2003	6/27/2003	7/1/2003	7/25/2003
0.26Q	9/15/2003	9/29/2003	10/1/2003	10/24/2003
0.26Q	12/16/2003	12/29/2003	12/31/2003	1/23/2004
0.26Q	3/15/2004	3/29/2004	3/31/2004	4/23/2004

Indicated Div: $1.04 (Div. Reinv. Plan)

Valuation Analysis

Forecast P/E	15.63	Trailing P/E	15.49
Market Cap	$797.4 Million	Book Value	320.9 Million
Price/Book	N/A	Price/Sales	N/A

Dividend Achiever Status

Rank	71	10 Year Growth Rate	15.70%
Total Years of Dividend Growth			14

Business Summary: Commercial Banking (MIC: 8.1 SIC: 6022 NAIC:522110)

S&T Bancorp is a bank holding company with assets of $2.90 billion as of Dec 31 2003. Co. has two wholly-owned subsidiaries, S&T Bank and S&T Investment, and owns one-half interest in Commonwealth Trust Credit Life Insurance. S&T Bank offers a variety of services including time and demand deposit accounts, secured and unsecured commercial and consumer loans, letters of credit, discount brokerage services, personal finance planning and credit card services. S&T Investment is an investment holding company, which manages investments previously owned by the bank. Co. operates through a branch network of 49 offices in 10 Pennsylvania counties.

Recent Developments: For the year ended Dec 31 2003, net income climbed 6.5% to $51.8 million compared with $48.6 million in 2002. Results benefited from strong commercial loan and core deposit growth, and increased revenue streams from the acquisitions of the Peoples Financial and Evergreen Insurance. Results for 2003 and 2002 included security gains of $8.1 million and $7.1 million, respectively. Net interest income rose 10.5% to $108.1 million from $97.8 million in the previous year. Provision for loan losses decreased 6.4% to $7.3 million from $7.8 million the year before. Total non-interest income grew 9.9% to $28.1 million, while total non-interest expense rose 17.2% to $60.7 million.

Prospects: Co. is maintaining a cautious outlook in regard to 2004 due to a number of factors that could influence its results in a positive or negative tone. Since the majority of Co.'s revenue comes from the net interest margin, internally generated loan and deposit growth and the mix of that growth are major factors. As a result, Co. has focused much of its effort in planning for 2004 and improve the generation and retention of low-cost core deposits. Meanwhile, a slowing economy could cause deterioration in the asset quality measurements. Co. recognizes that the shift to a greater dependence on commercial loans exposes it to larger credit risks and more non-performing loans and charge-offs.

Financial Data

(US$ in Thousands)	9 Mos	6 Mos	3 Mos	12/31/2002	12/31/2001	12/31/2000	12/31/1999	12/31/1998
Earnings Per Share	1.45	0.95	0.47	1.81	1.82	1.66	1.51	1.35
Tang. Book Val. Per Share	...	...	9.49	9.47	11.00	10.28	8.87	9.38
Dividends Per Share	0.990	0.980	0.970	0.960	0.900	0.820	0.740	0.630
Dividend Payout %	68.27	103.15	206.38	53.03	49.45	49.39	49.00	46.66
Income Statement								
Total Interest Income	114,949	78,040	39,318	151,160	166,702	176,184	156,727	151,438
Total Interest Expense	36,743	25,304	12,924	56,300	76,713	86,141	69,942	69,156
Net Interest Income	78,206	52,736	26,394	94,860	89,989	90,043	86,785	82,282
Provision for Loan Losses	5,800	4,300	2,400	7,800	5,000	4,000	4,000	10,550
Non–Interest Income	24,535	15,278	7,713	32,680	31,230	22,154	20,100	24,418
Non–Interest Expense	42,869	28,170	14,182	51,766	46,972	45,658	43,490	41,988
Income Before Taxes	54,072	35,544	17,525	67,974	69,247	62,539	59,395	54,162
Income from Cont Ops	...	...	...	...	49,185	...	...	...
Net Income	38,591	25,314	12,538	48,604	47,298	44,973	41,418	37,963
Average Shs. Outstg.	26,682	26,668	26,722	26,784	27,051	27,073	27,366	28,055
Balance Sheet								
Cash & Due from Banks	...	...	58,407	50,258	52,783	43,665	38,663	48,736
Securities Avail. for Sale	...	...	640,855	640,783	578,450	567,400	557,994	565,141
Net Loans & Leases	...	...	1,994,390	1,968,755	1,615,842	1,577,629	1,469,143	1,339,232
Total Assets	...	...	2,855,658	2,823,867	2,357,874	2,310,290	2,194,073	2,069,611
Total Deposits	...	...	1,947,249	1,926,119	1,611,317	1,525,332	1,435,065	1,380,063
Long–Term Obligations	...	...	242,191	211,656	251,226	377,997	364,062	240,068
Total Liabilities	...	...	2,551,346	2,517,753	2,064,547	2,033,193	1,954,373	1,809,974
Net Stockholders' Equity	...	...	304,312	306,114	293,327	277,097	239,700	259,637
Shares Outstanding	26,483	26,383	26,323	26,584	26,646	26,947	26,998	27,676
Statistical Record								
Return on Equity %	...	...	4.12	15.87	16.16	16.23	17.27	14.62
Return on Assets %	...	...	0.43	1.72	2.08	1.94	1.88	1.83
Equity/Assets %	...	...	10.65	10.84	12.44	11.99	10.92	12.54
Non–Int. Exp./Tot. Inc. %	30.73	30.18	30.15	28.15	23.73	23.02	24.59	23.87
Price Range	29.84–25.20	28.86–25.20	26.67–25.20	28.30–23.30	25.70–20.31	23.44–16.75	29.00–19.13	29.00–21.19
P/E Ratio	20.58–17.38	30.38–26.53	56.74–53.62	15.64–12.87	14.12–11.16	14.12–10.09	19.21–12.67	21.48–15.69
Average Yield %	3.62	3.68	3.77	3.76	3.90	4.32	3.01	2.39

Address: 43 South Ninth Street, Indiana, PA 15701 **Telephone:** (724) 465-1466 **Web Site:** www.stbank.com	**Officers:** Robert D. Duggan – Chmn., James C. Miller – Pres., C.E.O.	**Investor Contact:** 724–465–1466 **Institutional Holding** **No of Institutions:** 30 **Shares:** 301,628 **% Held:** –

SARA LEE CORP.

Exchange	Symbol	Price	52Wk Range	Yield	P/E
NYS	SLE	$21.86 (3/31/2004)	22.62–16.50	3.43	15.84

*7 Year Price Score 89.0   *NYSE Composite Index=100   *12 Month Price Score 94.4

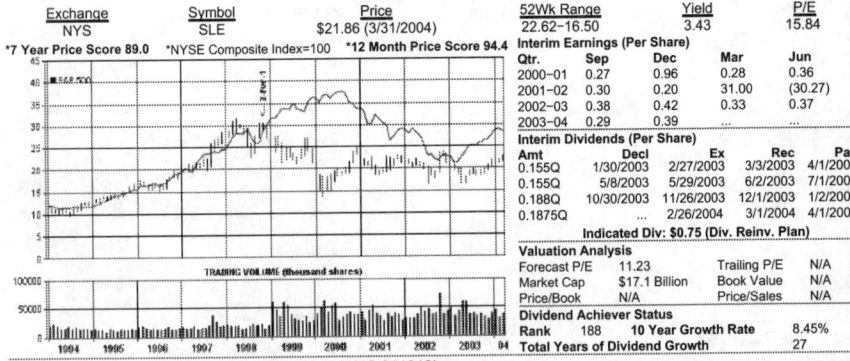

Interim Earnings (Per Share)

Qtr.	Sep	Dec	Mar	Jun
2000–01	0.27	0.96	0.28	0.36
2001–02	0.30	0.20	31.00	(30.27)
2002–03	0.38	0.42	0.33	0.37
2003–04	0.29	0.39	...	...

Interim Dividends (Per Share)

Amt	Decl	Ex	Rec	Pay
0.155Q	1/30/2003	2/27/2003	3/3/2003	4/1/2003
0.155Q	5/8/2003	5/29/2003	6/2/2003	7/1/2003
0.188Q	10/30/2003	11/26/2003	12/1/2003	1/2/2004
0.1875Q	...	2/26/2004	3/1/2004	4/1/2004

Indicated Div: $0.75 (Div. Reinv. Plan)

Valuation Analysis

Forecast P/E	11.23	Trailing P/E	N/A
Market Cap	$17.1 Billion	Book Value	N/A
Price/Book	N/A	Price/Sales	N/A

Dividend Achiever Status

Rank	188	10 Year Growth Rate	8.45%
Total Years of Dividend Growth		27

Business Summary: Food (MIC: 4.1 SIC: 2013 NAIC:311613)

Sara Lee is a global manufacturer and marketer of brand–name products for consumers throughout the world. Co. has five reportable segmentsSara Lee Meats, Sara Lee Bakery, Beverage, Household Products, and Intimates and Underwear. Co.'s products and services include fresh and frozen baked goods, processed meats, coffee and tea, beverage systems, intimate apparel, underwear, sportswear legwear and other apparel, and personal, household and shoe care products. Prominent brands include *Ball Park, Hillshire Farm, Jimmy Dean, Sara Lee, Bryan, Kahn's, Hanes, Hanes Her Way, Playtex, L'eggs, Just My Size, Wonderbra, Lovable, Sanex, Duschdas, Badedas Radox and Monsavon, Kiwi, Vapona* and *Ridsect*.

Recent Developments: For the 13 weeks ended Dec 27 2003, net income slid 10.3% to $312.0 million from $348.0 million in the corresponding prior–year period due primarily to higher costs for raw materials, pricing pressures, and weak foodservice market conditions. Results included a pre–tax charge of $1.0 million and a pre–tax gain of $3.0 million in 2003 and 2002, respectively, primarily related to restructuring and business dispositions. Net sales grew 5.0% to $5.02 billion from $4.78 billion the year before. Cost of sale totaled $3.07 billion, or 61.2% of net sales, up 4.2% versus $2.87 billion, or 60.2% of net sales, a year earlier. Operating income decline 10.2% to $423.0 million.

Prospects: Near–term results are expected to be negatively affected by continued challenging market conditions, including higher raw material costs, competitive pricing in printables and weak foodservice markets. Looking ahead, Co. is targeting full–year fiscal 200 earnings of between $1.51 and $1.61 per share, driven by improved profitability stemming from new product launches, select pric increases to help offset higher raw material costs, improved economic conditions, and favorable foreign currency exchange rates Separately, Co. announced that it will introduce its new Senseo single–serve coffee system in March 2003. Co. expects Senseo te generate worldwide sales of $500.0 million by fiscal 2007.

Financial Data
(US$ in Thousands)

	6 Mos	3 Mos	06/28/2003	06/29/2002	06/30/2001	07/01/2000	07/03/1999	06/27/1998
Earnings Per Share	0.68	0.29	1.50	1.23	1.87	1.27	1.26	(0.57)
Cash Flow Per Share	1.26	0.39	2.24	2.12	1.75	1.68	1.69	2.0
Tang. Book Val. Per Share	N.M	N.M	N.M	N.M	N.M	N.M	N.M	N.M
Dividends Per Share	0.650	0.610	0.610	0.590	0.560	0.520	0.490	0.44
Dividend Payout %	95.95	212.06	40.66	47.96	29.94	40.94	38.88	N.M
Income Statement								
Total Revenues	9,683,000	4,666,000	18,291,000	17,628,000	17,747,000	17,511,000	20,012,000	20,011,000
Total Indirect Exp.	2,988,000	1,465,000	5,568,000	5,356,000	5,865,000	5,668,000	6,053,000	5,907,000
Depreciation & Amort.	343,000	170,000	674,000	582,000	599,000	602,000	553,000	618,000
Operating Income	757,000	333,000	1,671,000	1,570,000	1,592,000	1,743,000	1,751,000	1,773,000
Net Interest Inc./(Exp.)	(92,000)	(49,000)	(198,000)	(208,000)	(180,000)	(176,000)	(141,000)	(176,000)
Income Taxes	118,000	50,000	263,000	175,000	248,000	409,000	480,000	80,00
Income from Cont Ops	...	...	...	...	1,603,000	1,158,000	...	.
Net Income	542,000	230,000	1,221,000	1,010,000	2,266,000	1,222,000	1,191,000	(523,000)
Average Shs. Outstg.	802,000	804,000	812,000	818,000	854,000	912,000	944,000	939,000
Balance Sheet								
Cash & Cash Equivalents	591,000	121,000	942,000	298,000	548,000	314,000	279,000	273,000
Total Current Assets	5,781,000	5,231,000	5,953,000	4,986,000	5,083,000	5,974,000	4,987,000	5,220,000
Total Assets	14,908,000	14,224,000	15,084,000	13,753,000	10,167,000	11,611,000	10,521,000	10,989,000
Total Current Liabilities	5,528,000	5,306,000	5,199,000	5,463,000	4,958,000	6,759,000	5,953,000	5,733,000
Long–Term Obligations	4,608,000	4,544,000	5,157,000	4,326,000	2,640,000	2,248,000	1,892,000	2,270,000
Net Stockholders' Equity	2,321,000	1,958,000	1,870,000	1,534,000	899,000	1,007,000	1,034,000	1,561,000
Net Working Capital	253,000	(75,000)	754,000	(477,000)	125,000	(785,000)	(966,000)	(513,000)
Shares Outstanding	791,179	790,306	777,347	784,720	781,964	846,331	883,783	921,32
Statistical Record								
Operating Profit Margin %	7.81	7.13	9.13	8.90	8.97	9.95	8.74	8.8
Return on Equity %	23.35	11.74	65.29	65.84	178.30	114.99	115.18	N.M
Return on Assets %	3.63	1.61	8.09	7.34	15.76	9.97	11.32	N.M
Debt/Total Assets %	30.90	31.94	34.18	31.45	25.96	19.36	17.98	20.6
Price Range	21.24–18.36	19.90–18.42	23.75–16.50	23.04–19.04	25.19–18.44	27.06–13.63	30.69–21.50	31.59–19.7
P/E Ratio	31.24–27.00	68.62–63.52	15.83–11.00	18.73–15.48	13.47–9.86	21.31–10.73	24.36–17.06	N/
Average Yield %	3.33	3.19	3.05	2.79	2.70	2.54	1.86	1.6

Address: Three First National Plaza, Chicago, IL 60602–4260 Telephone: (312) 726–2600 Web Site: www.saralee.com	Officers: C. Steven McMillan – Chmn., Pres., C.E.O., Lee A. Chaden – Exec. V.P., Global Marketing & Sales Transfer Agents:Sara Lee Corporation, Chicago, IL	Investor Contact:312–558–8651 Institutional Holding No of Institutions: 7 Shares: 734,213 % Held: –

SBC COMMUNICATIONS, INC.

Exchange	Symbol	Price	52Wk Range	Yield	P/E
NYS	SBC	$24.54 (3/31/2004)	27.59-19.98	5.09	13.63

*7 Year Price Score 63.1   *NYSE Composite Index=100   *12 Month Price Score 90.2

Interim Earnings (Per Share)

Qtr.	Mar	Jun	Sep	Dec
2000	0.53	0.54	0.88	0.37
2001	0.55	0.61	0.61	0.37
2002	0.51	0.55	0.53	0.64
2003	0.74	0.42	0.37	0.27

Interim Dividends (Per Share)

Amt	Decl	Ex	Rec	Pay
0.283Q	9/26/2003	10/8/2003	10/10/2003	11/3/2003
0.10Q	9/26/2003	10/8/2003	10/10/2003	11/3/2003
0.313Q	12/12/2003	1/7/2004	1/10/2004	2/2/2004
0.313Q	3/26/2004	4/6/2004	4/10/2004	5/3/2004

Indicated Div: $1.25 (Div. Reinv. Plan)

Valuation Analysis

Forecast P/E	N/A	Trailing P/E	13.63
Market Cap	$81.5 Billion	Book Value	38.2 Billion
Price/Book	2.26	Price/Sales	2.11

Dividend Achiever Status

Rank	231 10 Year Growth Rate	6.21%
Total Years of Dividend Growth		19

Business Summary: Communications (MIC: 10.1 SIC: 4813 NAIC:551112)

SBC Communications is a global provider of telecommunications services. Co.'s products and services include local exchange services, wireless communications, long–distance services, internet services, telecommunications equipment, and directory advertising and publishing. Co.'s principal wireline subsidiaries provide telecommunications services in thirteen states: Arkansas, California, Connecticut, Illinois, Indiana, Kansas, Michigan, Missouri, Nevada, Ohio, Oklahoma, Texas, and Wisconsin. As of Dec 31 2003, Co. had 54.7 million network access lines in service and maintained a 60.0% equity interest in Cingular Wireless, which serves more than 24.0 million wireless customers.

Recent Developments: For the year ended Dec 31 2003, income amounted to $5.97 billion versus income of $7.47 billion a year earlier. Total revenues fell 5.3% to $40.84 billion from $43.14 billion in 2002. Co. attributed the decreased results primarily to lower voice revenues of 10.6% to $22.13 billion resulting from the continued loss of retail access lines to the unbundled network element – platform rules. Co. also cited additional factors contributing to lower revenues such as the uncertain U.S. economy and heightened competition, including customers using wireless technology and cable instead of phone lines for voice and data. Operating income was $6.47 billion, a decrease of 25.0% from the year before.

Prospects: On Feb 17 2004, Cingular Wireless LLC, a joint venture between Co. and BellSouth Corp., announced an agreement to acquire AT&T Wireless for approximately $41.00 billion. Co.'s and BellSouth's proportionate equity stake in Cingular will remain unchanged following the transaction, with Co. holding 60.0% and BellSouth 40.0% of the equity. Meanwhile, Co.'s near–term outlook appears mixed. Co. noted that although retail access line losses are continuing, the trend has recently slowed, reflecting its ability to now offer retail interLATA, or traditional, long–distance in all of its regions as well as the introduction of offerings combining multiple services for one fixed price.

Financial Data
(US$ in Thousands)

	12/31/2003	12/31/2002	12/31/2001	12/31/2000	12/31/1999	12/31/1998	12/31/1997	12/31/1996
Earnings Per Share	1.80	2.23	2.14	2.32	1.90	2.05	0.80	1.73
Cash Flow Per Share	4.06	4.54	4.35	4.16	4.79	4.22	3.77	3.97
Tang. Book Val. Per Share	11.08	9.51	8.62	7.37	5.86	4.94	3.60	3.62
Dividends Per Share	1.360	1.060	1.020	1.000	0.960	0.920	0.880	0.850
Dividend Payout %	75.97	47.81	47.78	43.31	50.78	45.12	110.78	49.13
Income Statement								
Total Revenues	40,843,000	43,138,000	45,908,000	51,476,000	49,489,000	28,777,000	24,856,000	13,898,000
Total Indirect Exp.	17,721,000	8,578,000	9,077,000	9,748,000	8,553,000	5,177,000	12,198,000	6,207,000
Depreciation & Amort.	7,870,000	8,578,000	9,077,000	9,748,000	8,553,000	5,177,000	4,922,000	2,240,000
Operating Income	6,469,000	8,623,000	10,888,000	10,743,000	11,598,000	6,886,000	3,170,000	3,556,000
Net Interest Inc./(Exp.)	(638,000)	(821,000)	(917,000)	(1,313,000)	(1,430,000)	(993,000)	(947,000)	(472,000)
Income Taxes	2,930,000	2,984,000	4,097,000	4,921,000	4,280,000	2,306,000	863,000	1,166,000
Eqty Earns/Minority Int.	1,253,000	1,921,000	1,595,000	897,000	912,000	236,000	201,000	244,000
Income from Cont Ops	5,971,000	7,473,000	7,260,000	...	6,573,000	4,068,000	...	...
Net Income	8,505,000	5,653,000	7,242,000	7,967,000	8,159,000	4,023,000	1,474,000	2,101,000
Average Shs. Outstg.	3,329,000	3,348,000	3,396,000	3,433,000	3,458,000	1,984,000	1,844,000	1,214,000
Balance Sheet								
Cash & Cash Equivalents	5,184,000	3,567,000	703,000	643,000	495,000	466,000	718,000	755,000
Total Current Assets	13,968,000	14,089,000	12,580,000	23,216,000	11,930,000	7,538,000	7,062,000	3,912,000
Total Assets	100,166,000	95,057,000	96,322,000	98,651,000	83,215,000	45,066,000	42,132,000	23,449,000
Total Current Liabilities	14,260,000	14,683,000	23,948,000	30,357,000	19,313,000	9,989,000	10,252,000	5,820,000
Long–Term Obligations	16,060,000	18,536,000	17,133,000	15,492,000	17,475,000	11,612,000	12,019,000	5,505,000
Net Stockholders' Equity	38,248,000	33,199,000	32,491,000	30,463,000	26,726,000	12,780,000	9,892,000	6,835,000
Net Working Capital	(292,000)	(594,000)	(11,368,000)	(7,141,000)	(7,383,000)	(2,451,000)	(3,190,000)	(1,908,000)
Shares Outstanding	3,305,235	3,318,000	3,354,215	3,386,708	3,395,272	1,959,000	1,837,000	1,200,000
Statistical Record								
Operating Profit Margin %	15.83	19.98	23.71	20.86	23.43	23.92	12.75	25.58
Return on Equity %	15.61	22.50	22.34	26.15	24.59	31.83	14.90	30.73
Return on Assets %	5.96	7.86	7.53	8.07	7.89	9.02	3.49	8.95
Debt/Total Assets %	16.03	19.49	17.78	15.70	20.99	25.76	28.52	23.47
Price Range	31.19-19.34	40.17-20.10	52.38-37.38	58.50-35.00	59.19-44.38	54.13-35.78	38.00-25.00	30.06-23.06
P/E Ratio	17.33-10.74	18.01-9.01	24.47-17.47	25.22-15.09	31.15-23.36	26.40-17.45	47.50-31.25	17.38-13.33
Average Yield %	5.74	3.46	2.37	2.18	1.83	2.19	2.97	3.34

Address: 175 E. Houston, San Antonio, TX 78205-2233	Officers: Edward E. Whitacre – Chmn., C.E.O., William M. Daley – Pres.	Investor Contact: (210) –351–3990
Telephone: (210) 821-4105	Transfer Agents:EquiServe Trust Company, N.A., Jersey City, NJ	Institutional Holding
Web Site: www.sbc.com		No of Institutions: 9
		Shares: 18,597,556 % Held: –

233

SECOND BANCORP, INC.

Exchange	Symbol	Price	52Wk Range	Yield	P/E
NMS	SECD	$32.44 (3/31/2004)	34.42-21.64	2.34	13.46

*7 Year Price Score 115.1 *NYSE Composite Index=100 *12 Month Price Score 95.0

Interim Earnings (Per Share)

Qtr.	Mar	Jun	Sep	Dec
2000	0.38	0.36	(0.55)	0.41
2001	0.42	0.42	0.43	0.43
2002	0.47	0.43	0.55	0.34
2003	0.89	0.57	0.51	0.44

Interim Dividends (Per Share)

Amt	Decl	Ex	Rec	Pay
0.19Q	2/20/2003	4/11/2003	4/15/2003	4/30/2003
0.19Q	6/10/2003	7/11/2003	7/15/2003	7/31/2003
0.19Q	12/9/2003	1/13/2004	1/15/2004	1/30/2004
0.19Q	3/9/2004	4/13/2004	4/15/2004	4/30/2004

Indicated Div: $0.76 (Div. Reinv. Plan)

Valuation Analysis

Forecast P/E	12.99	Trailing P/E	13.46
Market Cap	$319.9 Million	Book Value	135.8 Million
Price/Book	N/A	Price/Sales	N/A

Dividend Achiever Status

Rank	154	10 Year Growth Rate 10.10%
Total Years of Dividend Growth	16	

TRADING VOLUME (thousand shares)

1994 1995 1996 1997 1998 1999 2000 2001 2002 2003 04

Business Summary: Commercial Banking (MIC: 8.1 SIC: 6021 NAIC:522110)

Second Bancorp is a one-bank financial holding company with its most significant subsidiary being The Second National Bank of Warren, a Warren, OH based commercial bank. Operating through 33 retail banking centers and five loan production offices as of Dec 31 2003, Second National offers a range of commercial and consumer banking and trust services primarily to business and individual customers in various communities in a nine county area in northeast and east-central Ohio. A second operating subsidiary is Stouffer-Herzog Insurance Agency, which sells a range of property, casualty, life and health insurance products in northeast Ohio. At Dec 31 2003, Co. had total assets of $2.12 billion.

Recent Developments: For the year ended Dec 31 2003, net income rose 28.6% to $23.2 million compared with $18.0 million in 2002. Results for 2003 and 2002 included security gains of $4.6 million and $592,000, respectively. Results for 2003 also included a gain on the sale of banking centers of $5.6 million, while results for 2002 included non-recurring charges totaling $2.2 million. Net interest income slipped 1.0% to $55.9 million from $56.5 million a year earlier. Provision for loan losses grew 23.6% to $7.6 million. Total non-interest income jumped 64.6% to $38.6 million from $23.4 million in 2002. Total non-interest expense climbed 10.6% $54.8 million from $49.5 million the previous year.

Prospects: Operating performance has been slowed by a narrowing net interest margin and reduced earnings from mortgage lending as refinancing activity has abated. Separately, on Jan 8 2004, Co. announced a definitive agreement to be acquired by Sky Financial Group in a transaction valued at $321.0 million. Under the terms of the agreement, shareholders of Co. will receive 1.26 shares of Sky Financial common stock for each share held. The acquisition is subject to shareholder and regulatory approvals and is expected to be completed by the end of the second quarter of 2004.

Financial Data

(US$ in Thousands)	9 Mos	6 Mos	3 Mos	12/31/2002	12/31/2001	12/31/2000	12/31/1999	12/31/1998
Earnings Per Share	1.97	1.46	0.89	1.79	1.70	0.60	1.51	0.52
Tang. Book Val. Per Share	...	...	12.21	11.87	10.22	11.05	10.55	11.0
Dividends Per Share	0.740	0.730	0.720	0.710	0.670	0.620	0.550	0.510
Dividend Payout %	37.56	50.00	80.89	39.66	39.41	103.33	36.42	98.0
Income Statement								
Total Interest Income	76,518	51,289	25,901	107,272	112,557	116,298	104,582	106,99
Total Interest Expense	34,828	23,416	11,818	50,812	62,367	66,921	55,310	55,88
Net Interest Income	41,690	27,873	14,083	56,460	50,190	49,377	49,272	51,10
Provision for Loan Losses	6,124	5,028	2,173	6,159	4,718	7,129	3,195	10,57
Non-Interest Income	32,019	24,962	14,262	23,425	19,528	8,275	14,792	12,75
Non-Interest Expense	40,765	27,689	13,673	49,496	41,939	44,213	39,330	46,24
Income Before Taxes	26,820	20,118	12,499	24,230	23,061	6,310	21,539	7,03
Income from Cont Ops	...	...	...	...	17,181	...	...	...
Net Income	19,006	14,099	8,661	18,000	17,080	6,134	16,178	5,63
Average Shs. Outstg.	9,632	9,645	9,715	10,040	10,271	10,271	10,698	10,74
Balance Sheet								
Cash & Due from Banks	...	...	43,334	60,822	40,837	35,272	35,238	45,47
Securities Avail. for Sale	...	...	539,309	523,669	417,496	382,098	367,587	354,41
Net Loans & Leases	...	...	1,197,725	1,150,196	1,105,197	1,054,872	1,060,493	960,11
Total Assets	...	...	1,909,027	1,894,775	1,680,356	1,546,290	1,537,278	1,430,23
Total Deposits	...	...	1,121,866	1,195,112	1,123,131	1,036,135	1,097,589	1,102,59
Long-Term Obligations	...	...	379,971	372,844	275,152	252,733	204,276	72,78
Total Liabilities	...	...	1,772,658	1,758,441	1,552,057	1,429,093	1,420,931	1,306,96
Net Stockholders' Equity	...	...	136,369	136,334	128,299	117,197	116,347	123,27
Shares Outstanding	9,470	9,468	9,498	9,762	9,949	10,057	10,458	10,66
Statistical Record								
Return on Equity %	...	...	6.35	13.20	13.39	5.23	13.90	4.5
Return on Assets %	...	...	0.45	0.94	1.02	0.39	1.05	0.3
Equity/Assets %	...	...	7.14	7.19	7.63	7.57	7.56	8.6
Non-Int. Exp./Tot. Inc. %	37.55	36.31	34.04	37.87	31.75	35.49	32.94	38.6
Price Range	28.50-21.64	26.50-21.64	26.50-22.15	28.32-20.56	22.90-13.75	22.38-12.25	29.88-19.25	37.25-19.7
P/E Ratio	14.47-10.98	18.15-14.82	29.78-24.89	15.82-11.49	13.47-8.09	37.29-20.42	19.78-12.75	71.63-37.9
Average Yield %	2.92	3.00	2.94	2.77	3.52	3.85	2.28	1.8

Address: 108 Main Ave. S.W., Warren, OH 44482-1311	**Officers:** Rick L. Blossom - Chmn., Pres., C.E.O., Christopher Stanitz - Exec. V.P., Sec.	**Investor Contact:**330-841-0234
Telephone: (330) 841-0123		**Institutional Holding** No of Institutions: 12
Web Site:www.secondnationalbank.com		**Shares:** 171,092 **% Held:** —

234

SEI INVESTMENTS CO.

Exchange	Symbol	Price	52Wk Range	Yield	P/E
NMS	SEIC	$33.00 (3/31/2004)	36.09-25.79	0.55	25.00

*7 Year Price Score 129.4 *NYSE Composite Index=100 *12 Month Price Score 87.5

Interim Earnings (Per Share)

Qtr.	Mar	Jun	Sep	Dec
2001	0.25	0.27	0.28	0.29
2002	0.30	0.31	0.93	(0.29)
2003	0.32	0.32	0.50	0.18

Interim Dividends (Per Share)

Amt	Decl	Ex	Rec	Pay
0.06S	5/14/2002	5/23/2002	5/28/2002	6/21/2002
0.06S	12/10/2002	12/31/2002	1/3/2003	1/21/2003
0.07S	5/28/2003	6/5/2003	6/9/2003	6/25/2003
0.09S	12/16/2003	1/2/2004	1/6/2004	1/22/2004

Indicated Div: $0.18

Valuation Analysis

Forecast P/E	22.48	Trailing P/E	25.78
Market Cap	$3.5 Billion	Book Value	314.3 Million
Price/Book	N/A	Price/Sales	N/A

Dividend Achiever Status

Rank	18	10 Year Growth Rate	23.11%
Total Years of Dividend Growth		12	

Business Summary: Finance Intermediaries &Services (MIC: 8.7 SIC: 6211 NAIC:523120)

SEI Investments is a provider of asset management and investment technology services with operations in five business segments: Private Banking & Trust, which provides investment processing services and investment management programs; Investment Advisors, which provides investment management programs and investment processing services to investors; Enterprises, which provides retirement and treasury business services for corporations; Money Managers, which provides business services to U.S. investment managers and alternative investment managers worldwide; and Investments in New Businesses, which includes Co.'s global businesses. As of Dec 31 2003, Co. operated 22 offices in 11 countries.

Recent Developments: For the year ended Dec 31 2003, net income rose 1.8% to $143.0 million from $140.5 million the year before. Results for 2003 and 2002 included net losses on investments of $6.9 million and $2.4 million, respectively. Total revenues improved 1.1% to $636.2 million from $629.6 million a year earlier. On a segment basis, Private Banking and Trust revenue slipped 6.5% to $311.5 million, reflecting lower investment processing, fund processing and investment management fees. However, Investment Advisors revenue climbed 4.6% to $156.1 million, while Enterprises revenue advanced 11.1% to $62.1 million, driven by new relationships and the rising capital markets.

Prospects: Revenues and net income are gradually improving as Co. continues to invest in new products and services to help build long-term sustainable growth. Additionally, Co. remains encouraged by the growing market acceptance of its new strategies. Moreover, business activity appears to be picking up in selected areas of Co.'s operations. However, the outlook for the capital markets is still uncertain, which could lead to further devaluation in the assets Co. manages or administers, continued redemption rates, and prolonged buying decisions among its clients.

Financial Data

(US$ in Thousands)	12/31/2003	12/31/2002	12/31/2001	12/31/2000	12/31/1999	12/31/1998	12/31/1997	12/31/1996
Earnings Per Share	1.32	1.25	1.09	0.87	0.59	0.37	0.23	0.20
Cash Flow Per Share	1.64	1.55	1.51	1.30	0.81	0.87	0.43	0.28
Tang. Book Val. Per Share	3.26	2.54	2.37	1.70	0.59	0.39	0.26	0.36
Dividends Per Share	0.130	0.110	0.090	0.070	0.060	0.050	0.040	0.030
Dividend Payout %	9.84	8.80	8.25	8.42	10.16	13.33	18.56	15.00
Income Statement								
Total Revenues	636,233	620,819	658,013	598,806	456,192	366,119	292,749	247,817
Total Indirect Exp.	146,428	146,968	176,099	171,823	138,482	117,297	98,701	81,954
Depreciation & Amort.	16,788	18,060	19,650	17,305	15,793	15,688	14,068	10,039
Operating Income	206,181	209,819	183,186	147,959	102,494	67,885	45,512	36,087
Net Interest Inc./(Exp.)	2,060	2,937	4,796	4,126	(90)	(1,017)	(1,505)	760
Income Taxes	81,303	82,528	73,380	60,655	42,030	26,904	17,163	14,798
Eqty Earns/Minority Int.	22,461	12,652	10,342	7,533	6,765	3,015	...	...
Income from Cont Ops	...	...	...	...	67,139	42,979	...	23,146
Net Income	142,981	140,520	124,944	98,963	68,431	43,689	26,844	6,811
Average Shs. Outstg.	108,137	112,803	114,810	113,820	113,743	114,756	115,416	116,088
Balance Sheet								
Cash & Cash Equivalents	253,434	175,724	173,685	159,576	73,206	52,980	16,891	13,167
Total Current Assets	352,413	261,435	266,142	249,031	146,992	113,509	83,995	64,956
Total Assets	592,629	464,147	460,916	375,582	253,779	208,772	168,884	141,041
Total Current Liabilities	193,474	134,247	144,343	146,453	138,918	110,794	81,676	79,957
Long-Term Obligations	23,944	33,500	43,055	27,000	29,000	31,000	33,000	...
Net Stockholders' Equity	363,773	290,007	270,593	197,421	79,002	59,685	46,410	56,108
Net Working Capital	158,939	127,188	121,799	102,578	8,074	2,715	2,319	(15,001)
Shares Outstanding	104,869	109,180	109,180	108,560	106,152	107,166	106,602	110,988
Statistical Record								
Operating Profit Margin %	32.40	33.79	27.83	24.70	22.46	18.54	15.54	14.56
Return on Equity %	39.30	48.45	46.17	50.12	84.98	72.00	57.84	41.25
Return on Assets %	24.12	30.27	27.10	26.34	26.45	20.58	15.89	16.41
Debt/Total Assets %	4.04	7.21	9.34	7.18	11.42	14.84	19.54	...
Price Range	35.92-22.90	45.75-19.30	51.31-27.90	61.72-14.89	21.50-13.23	16.67-6.37	7.37-3.19	4.17-3.06
P/E Ratio	27.21-17.35	36.60-15.44	47.07-25.60	70.94-17.11	36.44-22.42	45.05-17.23	32.07-13.86	20.83-15.31
Average Yield %	0.44	0.34	0.23	0.25	0.37	0.43	0.84	0.82

Address: 1 Freedom Valley Drive, Oaks, PA 19456-1100 **Telephone:** (610) 676-1000 **Web Site:** www.seic.com	**Officers:** Alfred P. West – Chmn., C.E.O., Carmen V. Romeo – Exec. V.P.	**Investor Contact:** 610-676-1000 **Institutional Holding** **No of Institutions:** 202 **Shares:** 58,699,578 **% Held:** 55.9

235

SERVICEMASTER CO. (THE)

Exchange	Symbol	Price	52Wk Range	Yield	P/E
NYS	SVM	$12.01 (3/31/2004)	12.01-9.05	3.50	N.M.

*7 Year Price Score 75.4   *NYSE Composite Index=100   *12 Month Price Score 97.1

Interim Earnings (Per Share)

Qtr.	Mar	Jun	Sep	Dec
2000	0.13	0.22	0.16	0.10
2001	0.08	0.17	0.12	(0.91)
2002	0.10	0.20	0.19	0.07
2003	0.02	0.22	(1.08)	0.09

Interim Dividends (Per Share)

Amt	Decl	Ex	Rec	Pay
0.105Q	5/21/2003	7/9/2003	7/11/2003	7/31/2003
0.105Q	7/18/2003	10/8/2003	10/10/2003	10/31/2003
0.105Q	10/28/2003	1/7/2004	1/9/2004	1/30/2004
0.105Q	3/8/2004	4/6/2004	4/9/2004	4/30/2004

Indicated Div: $0.42 (Div. Reinv.Plan)

Valuation Analysis

Forecast P/E	19.83	Trailing P/E	N.M.
Market Cap	$3.6 Billion	Book Value	843.7 Million
Price/Book	3.59	Price/Sales	0.84

Dividend Achiever Status

Rank	259	10 Year Growth Rate	4.76%
Total Years of Dividend Growth			33

TRADING VOLUME (thousand shares)

Business Summary: Accounting &Management Consulting Services (MIC: 12.2 SIC: 8741 NAIC:561110)

The ServiceMaster Company provides outsourcing services to residential and commercial customers. The TruGreen segment include lawn care operations performed under the and landscaping services. The Terminix segment includes domestic termite and pest contro services. The American Residential Services and American Mechanical Services (ARS/AMS) segment provides heating, ventilation, ai conditioning and plumbing services. The American Home Shield segment offers warranty contracts on home systems and appliances ane home inspection services. The Other Operations segment includes ServiceMaster Clean, Merry Maids and Furniture Medic franchise operations.

Recent Developments: For the year ended Dec 31 2003, Co. reported a loss from continuing operations of $222.0 million compare with income of $157.3 million in 2002. Results included a charge of $480.7 million in 2003 and a credit of $2.0 million in 2002 fo impaired assets and other items.Total revenue increased 1.9% to $3.57 billion from $3.50 billion a year earlier. On a segment basis TruGreen revenue rose 4.9% to $1.35 billion, while Terminix revenue grew 2.3% to $945.3 million. American Home Shield revenu climbed 6.3% to $450.3 million, while American Residential Services/American Mechanical services revenue fell 6.3% to $673.6 million. Other revenue increased 1.9% to $152.1 million.

Prospects: In 2004, Co. plans to focus on top–line sales, increased retention, pricing discipline, and improving margins in TruGree LandCare and the American Mechanical Services segment.Growth in 2004 is expected to be partiall offset by higher insurance costs and a return to a more normal level of variable compensation. These factors, combined with the curren economic and employment outlook, lead Co. to expect revenue growth in the mid–single digits in 2004 and earnings per share growt somewhat higher than revenues. In addition, Co. expects cash from operations to increase with earnings and to continue to substantiall exceed net income.

Financial Data
(US$ in Thousands)

	9 Mos	6 Mos	3 Mos	12/31/2002	12/31/2001	12/31/2000	12/31/1999	12/31/1998
Earnings Per Share	(0.83)	0.24	0.02	0.56	(0.54)	0.61	0.55	0.6
Cash Flow Per Share	0.56	0.19	(0.12)	1.21	1.16	1.31	0.81	1.3
Tang. Book Val. Per Share	...	...	N.M	N.M	N.M	N.M	N.M	N.M
Dividends Per Share	0.420	0.420	0.410	0.410	0.400	0.380	0.360	0.330
Dividends Payout %	N.M.	175.00	N.M.	73.21	N.M.	62.29	65.45	51.56
Income Statement								
Total Revenues	2,762,076	1,786,294	733,665	3,589,089	3,601,429	5,970,615	5,703,535	4,724,119
Total Indirect Exp.	641,850	419,693	170,885	766,527	1,142,667	857,249	861,326	648,08
Depreciation & Amort.	4,488	3,362	1,640	7,442	126,937	157,691	138,444	104,60
Operating Income	(205,002)	149,441	24,861	341,336	(87,445)	416,899	383,174	396,42
Net Interest Inc./(Exp.)	(49,223)	(32,938)	(16,283)	(77,519)	(125,057)	(136,831)	(108,955)	(92,945)
Income Taxes	(8,774)	45,867	3,050	93,468	(29,594)	133,319	122,630	128,78
Income from Cont Ops	(245,354)	70,862	...	170,098	(171,779)	184,988	...	...
Net Income	(247,741)	70,225	4,675	156,994	155,033	173,827	173,563	189,99
Average Shs. Outstg.	296,233	301,188	301,635	314,112	311,408	305,518	314,406	298,82
Balance Sheet								
Cash & Cash Equivalents	261,281	197,446	196,794	302,603	483,111	100,917	114,210	120,42
Total Current Assets	927,873	917,949	887,508	919,174	1,150,658	984,759	959,238	670,20
Total Assets	2,975,073	3,436,612	3,397,337	3,414,938	3,674,739	3,967,668	3,870,215	2,914,85
Total Current Liabilities	798,626	845,888	849,325	839,064	814,401	833,414	845,804	753,69
Long–Term Obligations	795,964	796,627	796,888	804,340	1,105,518	1,756,757	1,697,582	1,076,16
Net Stockholders' Equity	843,676	1,194,102	1,195,751	1,218,700	1,220,961	1,161,588	1,205,716	956,48
Net Working Capital	129,247	72,061	38,183	80,110	336,257	151,345	113,434	(83,495)
Shares Outstanding	295,172	295,035	316,049	311,039	300,531	298,474	307,530	298,03
Statistical Record								
Operating Profit Margin %	N.M.	8.36	3.38	9.51	N.M.	6.98	6.71	8.3
Return on Equity %	N.M.	5.93	0.39	13.95	N.M	15.92	14.39	19.8
Return on Assets %	N.M.	2.06	0.13	4.98	N.M.	4.66	4.48	6.5
Debt/Total Assets %	26.75	23.18	23.45	23.55	30.08	44.27	43.86	36.9
Price Range	11.12-9.05	11.12-9.05	11.12-9.15	15.49-9.11	14.10-10.05	14.69-8.75	22.06-10.13	25.38-17.3
P/E Ratio	N/A	46.33-37.71	556.0-457.5	27.66-16.27	N/A	24.08-14.34	40.11-18.41	39.65-27.0
Average Yield %	4.16	4.13	4.01	3.29	3.46	3.43	2.14	1.6

Address: 3250 Lacey Road, Downers Grove, IL 60515–1700	Officers: Johnathan P. Ward – Chmn. , C.E.O., Ernest J. zek – Pres., C.O.O.	Investor Contact: (630) 271–1300
Telephone: (630) 663–2000	Transfer Agents:Computershare Investor Services, Chicago, IL	Institutional Holding
Web Site: www. servicemaster.com		No of Institutions: 3
		Shares: 852,473 % Held: –

SHERWIN-WILLIAMS CO.

Exchange	Symbol	Price	52Wk Range	Yield	P/E
NYS	SHW	$38.43 (3/31/2004)	38.43-26.60	1.77	17.00

7 Year Price Score 110.6   *NYSE Composite Index=100   *12 Month Price Score 101.5

Interim Earnings (Per Share)

Qtr.	Mar	Jun	Sep	Dec
2000	0.25	0.71	0.66	(1.52)
2001	0.23	0.58	0.58	0.29
2002	0.23	0.70	0.73	0.38
2003	0.21	0.75	0.82	0.48

Interim Dividends (Per Share)

Amt	Decl	Ex	Rec	Pay
0.155Q	4/23/2003	5/21/2003	5/23/2003	6/6/2003
0.155Q	7/23/2003	8/20/2003	8/22/2003	9/5/2003
0.155Q	10/24/2003	11/12/2003	11/14/2003	11/28/2003
0.17Q	2/4/2004	2/19/2004	2/23/2004	3/15/2004

Indicated Div: $0.68 (Div. Reinv. Plan)

Valuation Analysis

Forecast P/E	13.49	Trailing P/E	17.00
Market Cap	$5.8 Billion	Book Value	1.2 Billion
Price/Book	4.25	Price/Sales	0.92

Dividend Achiever Status

Rank	169	10 Year Growth Rate	9.51%
Total Years of Dividend Growth			24

Business Summary: Chemicals (MIC: 11.1 SIC: 2851 NAIC:325510)

Sherwin–Williams manufactures, distributes and sells coatings and related products. The Paint Stores' division consists of Co.–operated specialty paint stores in the U.S., Canada, the Virgin Islands, Puerto Rico and Mexico. The Consumer segment manufactures and distributes a variety of paints, coatings and related products to third party customers and the Paint stores segment. Automotive Finishes manufactures and distributes motor vehicle finish products in North and South America, the Caribbean Islands and Europe. International coatings licenses, and distributes a variety of paints, coatings and related products worldwide. Co.'s brands include Sherwin–Williams®, Dutch Boy®, and Krylon®.

Recent Developments: For the year ended Dec 31 2003, net income advanced 7.1% to $332.1 million compared with income of $310.7 million, before an accounting change charge of $183.1 million, in 2002. Net sales rose 4.3% to $5.41 billion from $5.18 billion a year earlier. The improvement in sales was primarily attributed to solid U.S. architectural paint sales and a favorable do–it–yourself market that gained momentum throughout the year. This growth was partially offset by weakness in domestic commercial architectural, industrial maintenance and product finishes markets, which struggled through the first three quarters of the year.

Prospects: Co. anticipates sales in the first quarter of 2004 will increase in the single digits with diluted earnings per share in the range of $0.26 to $0.30. Co. expects sales for full–year 2004 to be in the mid–single digits with diluted earnings per share in the range of $2.45 to $2.55. Co.'s cost containment efforts implemented over the past few years in its Consumer, Automotive Finishes and International coatings segments should continue to boost operating profit. In addition, results for Co.'s Paint Stores and Consumer segments should strengthen in the near term as the domestic economic recovery appears to be gaining steam.

Financial Data

(US$ in Thousands)	12/31/2003	12/31/2002	12/31/2001	12/31/2000	12/31/1999	12/31/1998	12/31/1997	12/31/1996
Earnings Per Share	2.26	2.04	1.68	0.10	1.80	1.57	1.50	1.33
Cash Flow Per Share	3.80	3.66	3.57	2.83	2.87	2.75	2.52	1.94
Tang. Book Val. Per Share	2.95	3.77	2.59	3.17	2.31	1.76	0.69	4.97
Dividends Per Share	0.620	0.600	0.580	0.540	0.480	0.450	0.400	0.350
Dividend Payout %	27.43	29.41	34.52	540.00	26.66	28.66	26.83	26.31
Income Statement								
Total Revenues	5,407,764	5,184,788	5,066,005	5,211,624	5,003,837	4,934,430	4,881,103	4,132,879
Total Indirect Exp.	1,881,664	1,784,527	1,729,855	2,092,407	1,673,449	1,598,333	1,573,510	1,309,086
Depreciation & Amort.	116,564	115,648	148,098	160,030	155,744	147,888	139,246	103,623
Operating Income	573,631	554,060	489,774	215,204	575,065	531,638	523,201	418,615
Net Interest Inc./(Exp.)	(38,742)	(40,475)	(54,627)	(62,026)	(61,168)	(71,971)	(80,837)	(24,537)
Income Taxes	190,868	186,463	161,291	127,380	186,258	167,239	166,663	146,220
Income from Cont Ops	...	310,701	...	...	...	...	...	224,923
Net Income	332,058	127,565	263,158	16,026	303,860	272,864	260,614	229,157
Average Shs. Outstg.	147,005	152,435	156,893	162,695	169,026	173,536	174,032	172,826
Balance Sheet								
Cash & Cash Equivalents	302,813	164,012	118,814	2,896	18,623	19,133	3,530	1,880
Total Current Assets	1,715,144	1,505,993	1,506,945	1,551,539	1,597,377	1,547,290	1,532,253	1,416,187
Total Assets	3,682,608	3,432,312	3,627,925	3,750,670	4,052,090	4,065,462	4,035,801	2,994,590
Total Current Liabilities	1,154,170	1,083,496	1,141,353	1,115,243	1,189,862	1,111,973	1,115,663	1,051,007
Long–Term Obligations	502,992	506,682	503,517	623,587	624,365	730,283	843,919	142,679
Net Stockholders' Equity	1,458,857	1,341,890	1,487,764	1,471,864	1,698,532	1,715,940	1,592,180	1,401,232
Net Working Capital	560,974	422,497	365,592	436,296	407,515	435,317	416,590	365,180
Shares Outstanding	143,406	148,910	153,978	159,558	165,664	171,033	172,907	171,831
Statistical Record								
Operating Profit Margin %	10.60	10.68	9.66	4.12	11.49	10.77	10.71	10.12
Return on Equity %	22.76	23.15	17.68	1.08	17.88	15.90	16.36	16.05
Return on Assets %	9.01	9.05	7.25	0.42	7.49	6.71	6.45	7.51
Debt/Total Assets %	13.65	14.76	13.87	16.62	15.40	17.96	20.91	4.76
Price Range	34.74-24.82	33.00-22.06	28.02-20.31	27.00-17.44	32.44-19.00	37.50-20.06	32.69-24.88	28.63-19.56
P/E Ratio	15.37-10.98	16.18-10.81	16.68-12.09	270.0-174.4	18.02-10.56	23.89-12.78	21.79-16.58	21.52-14.71
Average Yield %	2.12	2.14	2.42	2.45	1.87	1.51	1.38	1.51

Address: 101 Prospect Avenue, N.W., Cleveland, OH 44115-1075	**Officers:** Christopher M. Connor – Chmn., C.E.O., Joseph M. Scaminace – Pres., C.O.O.	**Investor Contact:** (216) 566-2000	
Telephone: (216) 566-2000	**Transfer Agents:** The Bank of New York, New York, NY	**Institutional Holding** **No of Institutions:** 4	
Web Site: www.sherwin.com		**Shares:** 308,392 **% Held:** –	

SIGMA–ALDRICH CORP.

Exchange	Symbol	Price	52Wk Range	Yield	P/E
NMS	SIAL	$55.38 (3/31/2004)	58.93–43.00	1.23	20.66

*7 Year Price Score 134.4 *NYSE Composite Index=100 *12 Month Price Score 94.6

Interim Earnings (Per Share)

Qtr.	Mar	Jun	Sep	Dec
2000	0.45	0.45	0.35	0.41
2001	0.48	0.49	0.45	0.45
2002	0.54	0.58	0.55	0.87
2003	0.68	0.67	0.66	0.67

Interim Dividends (Per Share)

Amt	Decl	Ex	Rec	Pay
0.09Q	5/6/2003	5/28/2003	5/30/2003	6/13/2003
0.16Q	8/12/2003	8/28/2003	9/2/2003	9/15/2003
0.16Q	11/11/2003	11/26/2003	12/1/2003	12/15/2003
0.17Q	2/10/2004	2/26/2004	3/1/2004	3/15/2004

Indicated Div: $0.68

Valuation Analysis

Forecast P/E	19.05	Trailing P/E	20.66
Market Cap	$4.1 Billion	Book Value	N/A
Price/Book	N/A	Price/Sales	N/A

Dividend Achiever Status

Rank	76	10 Year Growth Rate	15.07%
Total Years of Dividend Growth			22

Business Summary: (MIC: null SIC: 5169 NAIC:424690)
Sigma-Aldrich develops, manufactures and distributes a broad range of biochemicals and organic chemicals. These chemical products and kits are used in scientific and genomic research, biotechnology, pharmaceutical development, the diagnosis of disease, and chemical manufacturing. Co. consists of three business units: Scientific Research, Biotechnology and Fine Chemicals. The Scientific Research unit sells biochemicals, organic chemicals, and reagents. The Biotechnology unit supplies immunochemical, cell culture, molecular biology, cell signaling and neuroscience biochemicals. The Fine Chemicals unit supplies organic chemicals and biochemicals.

Recent Developments: For the twelve months ended Dec 31 2003, income from continuing operations rose 2.0% to $190.4 million compared with $186.7 million in 2002. Results for 2002 included a gain on the sale of Milwaukee, WI facility of $29.3 million. Results for 2003 and 2002 excluded a gain of $2.6 million and a loss of $56.0 million, respectively, from discontinued operations. Net sales climbed 7.6% to $1.30 million from $1.21 billion in the previous year. Sales benefited from year-over-year growth in Co.'s Scientific Research, Biotechnology and Fine Chemicals businesses. Gross profit grew 9.1% to $670.7 million from $614.5 million the year before.

Prospects: Looking ahead, Co. expects gradual improvement in the overall currency adjusted sale growth rate as the benefit of new sales and marketing initiatives launched in 2003 is expected to continue to drive sales. Although modest growth in U.S. sales during the fourth quarter of 2003 is encouraging, Co. anticipates global market softness will continue at least through the first half of 2004. Short-term growth should benefit from sales force additions and marketing efforts, while long-term growth will depend on Co.'s marketing efforts and the addition of new products. As a result, Co. expects diluted earnings per share from continuing operations for full-year 2004 in the range of $3.10 to $3.15.

Financial Data

(US$ in Thousands)	12/31/2003	12/31/2002	12/31/2001	12/31/2000	12/31/1999	12/31/1998	12/31/1997	12/31/1996
Earnings Per Share	2.68	2.54	1.87	1.66	1.47	1.64	1.62	1.48
Cash Flow Per Share	4.34	4.78	2.11	1.37	2.28	1.60	1.28	1.5
Tang. Book Val. Per Share	12.82	10.89	9.34	9.72	11.88	10.95	9.73	9.4
Dividends Per Share	0.500	0.345	0.333	0.315	0.295	0.283	0.258	0.22
Dividend Payout %	18.66	13.58	17.81	18.98	20.07	17.26	15.93	15.4
Income Statement								
Total Revenues	1,298,146	1,206,982	1,179,447	1,096,270	1,037,945	1,194,290	1,127,084	1,034,562
Total Indirect Exp.	387,760	299,217	348,230	322,430	354,822	393,836	355,619	328,76
Depreciation & Amort.	69,267	66,326	71,373	67,563	66,919	61,827	48,053	45,21
Operating Income	282,949	285,976	218,175	209,480	203,717	242,590	252,754	229,68
Net Interest Inc./(Exp.)	(10,126)	(13,837)	(16,542)	(6,571)	...	...	...	...
Income Taxes	82,393	85,404	60,928	63,859	55,112	76,243	86,695	81,824
Income from Cont Ops	190,430	186,735	...	139,050	148,605	...	...	...
Net Income	193,102	130,714	140,705	320,198	172,270	166,347	166,059	147,856
Average Shs. Outstg.	71,126	73,412	75,175	83,585	100,984	101,188	102,804	99,936
Balance Sheet								
Cash & Cash Equivalents	127,628	52,382	37,637	31,058	43,847	24,345	46,228	103,68
Total Current Assets	815,030	694,887	727,311	713,625	774,571	772,681	706,674	666,63
Total Assets	1,548,242	1,389,656	1,439,802	1,347,707	1,432,001	1,432,835	1,243,822	1,099,95
Total Current Liabilities	257,248	265,653	397,563	335,280	105,612	142,372	119,479	110,31
Long-Term Obligations	176,259	176,805	177,700	100,846	205	415	552	3,78
Net Stockholders' Equity	999,261	882,174	809,715	859,275	1,259,351	1,216,316	1,060,334	942,27
Net Working Capital	557,652	429,234	329,748	378,345	668,959	630,309	587,195	556,32
Shares Outstanding	69,101	71,253	73,014	76,216	98,292	100,623	100,377	100,10
Statistical Record								
Operating Profit Margin %	21.79	23.69	18.49	19.10	19.62	20.31	22.42	22.2
Return on Equity %	19.05	21.16	17.37	16.18	11.80	13.67	15.66	15.6
Return on Assets %	12.29	13.43	9.77	10.31	10.37	11.60	13.35	13.4
Debt/Total Assets %	11.38	12.72	12.34	7.48	0.01	0.02	0.04	0.3
Price Range	57.46–41.17	52.51–39.41	51.21–37.10	40.25–20.75	35.13–25.75	42.75–26.38	39.75–27.50	32.00–24.3
P/E Ratio	21.44–15.36	20.67–15.52	27.39–19.84	24.25–12.50	23.89–17.52	26.07–16.08	24.54–16.98	21.62–16.4
Average Yield %	1.15	0.72	0.76	1.00	0.94	0.81	0.76	0.7

Address: 3050 Spruce Street, St. Louis, MO 63103	Officers: David R. Harvey – Chmn., Pres., C.E.O., Larry S. Blazevich – V.P., Info. Systems	Investor Contact:314–286–8004
Telephone: (314) 771–5765		Institutional Holding
Web Site: www.sigma–aldrich.com		No of Institutions: 25
		Shares: 776,807 % Held: –

SIMMONS FIRST NATIONAL CORP.

Exchange	Symbol	Price	52Wk Range	Yield	P/E
NMS	SFNC	$27.55 (3/31/2004)	30.00–18.19	2.03	16.70

*7 Year Price Score 129.6 *NYSE Composite Index=100 *12 Month Price Score 109.6

Interim Earnings (Per Share)

Qtr.	Mar	Jun	Sep	Dec
2000	0.29	0.31	0.33	0.36
2001	0.32	0.31	0.24	0.28
2002	0.34	0.40	0.40	0.39
2003	0.37	0.45	0.46	0.37

Interim Dividends (Per Share)

Amt	Decl	Ex	Rec	Pay
0.13Q	6/3/2003	6/12/2003	6/16/2003	7/1/2003
0.13Q	8/29/2003	9/11/2003	9/15/2003	10/1/2003
0.14Q	11/24/2003	12/11/2003	12/15/2003	1/2/2004
0.14Q	2/27/2004	3/11/2004	3/15/2004	4/1/2004

Indicated Div: $0.56

Valuation Analysis

Forecast P/E 13.79		Trailing P/E 16.70
Market Cap $194.6 Million		Book Value 210.0 Million
Price/Book 1.94		Price/Sales 2.78

Dividend Achiever Status

Rank 86	10 Year Growth Rate	14.36%
Total Years of Dividend Growth		12

Business Summary: Commercial Banking (MIC: 8.1 SIC: 6021 NAIC:522110)

Simmons First National is a bank holding company. Co. owns seven community banks in Arkansas and conducts its operations through offices. Co.'s subsidiaries provide banking services to individuals and businesses throughout the market areas it serves. Services include consumer (credit card, student and other consumer), real estate (construction, single family residential and other commercial) and commercial (commercial, agriculture and financial institutions) loans, checking, time deposits, trust and investment management services, and securities and investment services. As of Dec 31 2003, Co. had total assets of $1.20 billion and deposits of $1865.0 million.

Recent Developments: For the year ended Dec 31 2003, net income climbed 7.8% to $23.8 million compared with $22.1 million in 2002. Earnings benefited from the increased volume of Co.'s mortgage banking operation, growth in the loan portfolio and a lower provision for loan losses. Results for 2003 included a gain on the sale of mortgage servicing of $771,000. Net interest income increased 9% to $77.9 million from $75.7 million a year earlier. Provision for loan losses declined 14.1% to $8.8 million from $10.2 million in the previous year. Total non-interest income climbed 9.7% to $38.7 million from $35.3 million, while total non-interest expense grew 9% to $73.1 million from $69.0 million in 2002.

Prospects: On Mar 23 2004, Co. completed the acquisition of Alliance Bancorporation and its subsidiary, Alliance Bank of Hot Springs. As a part of the transaction, Alliance Bank will remain as a separate bank and continue its banking operations as a subsidiary of Co. Alliance Bank will change its name to Simmons First Bank of Hot Springs. Separately, on Jan 8 2004, Co. announced an agreement in which Cross County Bank will sell its Weiner, AR location to Simmons First Bank of Jonesboro, a subsidiary of Co. The acquisition involves about $6.0 million in total deposits and the fixed assets used in the branch operation. Both acquisitions will further expand Co.'s presence in Arkansas.

Financial Data

(US$ in Thousands)	12/31/2003	12/31/2002	12/31/2001	12/31/2000	12/31/1999	12/31/1998	12/31/1997	12/31/1996
Earnings Per Share	1.65	1.53	1.15	1.29	1.16	1.13	1.03	0.90
Tang. Book Val. Per Share	11.31	11.60	10.59	9.61	9.03	8.34	6.50	7.95
Dividends Per Share	0.510	0.470	0.430	0.390	0.350	0.310	0.270	0.220
Dividend Payout %	30.90	30.61	37.22	30.23	30.04	27.31	26.08	24.44
Income Statement								
Total Interest Income	107,607	116,142	135,868	136,754	121,490	105,966	78,406	61,367
Total Interest Expense	29,737	40,434	68,463	69,693	56,759	53,732	37,991	27,562
Net Interest Income	77,870	75,708	67,405	67,061	64,731	52,234	40,415	33,805
Provision for Loan Losses	8,786	10,223	9,958	7,531	6,551	7,749	4,013	2,341
Non-Interest Income	38,717	35,303	33,569	30,355	28,277	31,664	27,545	25,116
Non-Interest Expense	73,101	69,013	68,130	62,556	61,929	56,235	46,934	41,956
Income Before Taxes	34,684	31,775	22,886	27,329	24,528	19,914	17,013	14,624
Net Income	23,790	22,078	16,528	18,869	17,168	14,331	11,989	10,301
Average Shs. Outstg.	14,415	14,376	14,324	14,638	14,748	12,632	11,608	11,422
Balance Sheet								
Cash & Due from Banks	78,205	76,452	81,785	77,495	60,324	47,170	58,327	41,989
Securities Avail. for Sale	...	...	...	...	...	...	160,475	109,515
Net Loans & Leases	1,392,967	1,235,357	1,238,288	1,273,553	1,096,550	898,519	781,555	502,447
Total Assets	2,235,758	1,977,579	2,016,918	1,912,493	1,697,430	1,464,362	1,326,145	881,332
Total Deposits	1,803,468	1,619,196	1,686,404	1,605,586	1,410,633	1,187,913	1,104,501	736,367
Long-Term Obligations	100,916	54,282	42,150	41,681	46,219	49,340	50,281	1,067
Total Liabilities	2,025,783	1,779,974	1,834,555	1,739,150	1,538,059	1,332,182	1,214,063	778,507
Net Stockholders' Equity	209,995	197,605	182,363	173,343	159,371	132,180	112,082	102,825
Shares Outstanding	14,101	14,142	14,174	14,361	14,631	12,418	11,452	11,410
Statistical Record								
Return on Equity %	11.32	11.17	9.06	10.88	10.77	10.84	10.69	10.01
Return on Assets %	1.06	1.11	0.81	0.98	1.01	0.97	0.90	1.16
Equity/Assets %	9.39	9.99	9.04	9.06	9.38	9.02	8.45	11.66
Non-Int. Exp./Tot. Inc. %	49.96	45.56	40.20	37.43	41.35	40.85	44.29	48.51
Price Range	28.90–17.06	21.30–15.64	18.90–11.13	13.75–9.06	20.25–11.50	26.63–16.81	21.00–12.75	13.75–10.17
P/E Ratio	17.52–10.34	13.92–10.22	16.43–9.67	10.66–7.03	17.46–9.91	23.56–14.88	20.39–12.38	15.28–11.30
Average Yield %	2.34	2.65	2.87	3.60	2.18	1.41	1.72	1.93

Address: 501 Main Street, Pine Bluff, AR 71601

Telephone: (870) 541–1000

Web Site: www.simmonsfirst.com

Officers: J. Thomas May – Chmn., Pres., C.E.O., Barry L. Crow – Exec. V.P., C.F.O.

Institutional Holding
No of Institutions: 38
Shares: 1,527,264 % Held: 21.60%

SJW CORP.

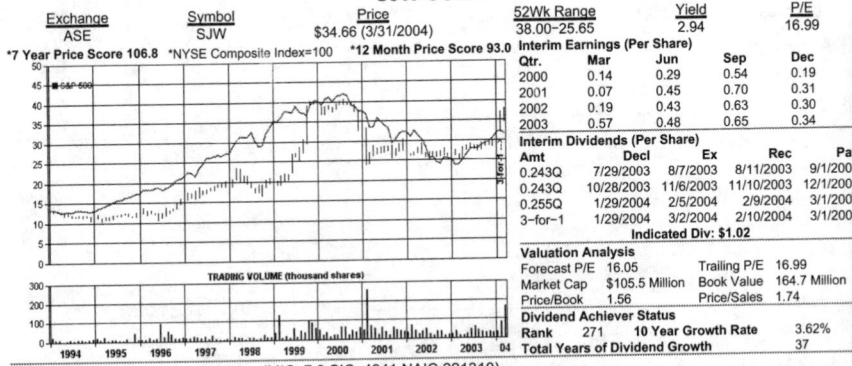

Exchange	Symbol	Price	52Wk Range	Yield	P/E
ASE	SJW	$34.66 (3/31/2004)	38.00-25.65	2.94	16.99

*7 Year Price Score 106.8 *NYSE Composite Index=100 *12 Month Price Score 93.0

Interim Earnings (Per Share)

Qtr.	Mar	Jun	Sep	Dec
2000	0.14	0.29	0.54	0.19
2001	0.07	0.45	0.70	0.31
2002	0.19	0.43	0.63	0.30
2003	0.57	0.48	0.65	0.34

Interim Dividends (Per Share)

Amt	Decl	Ex	Rec	Pa
0.243Q	7/29/2003	8/7/2003	8/11/2003	9/1/2003
0.243Q	10/28/2003	11/6/2003	11/10/2003	12/1/200
0.255Q	1/29/2004	2/5/2004	2/9/2004	3/1/200
3-for-1	1/29/2004	3/2/2004	2/10/2004	3/1/200

Indicated Div: $1.02

Valuation Analysis

Forecast P/E	16.05	Trailing P/E	16.99
Market Cap	$105.5 Million	Book Value	164.7 Million
Price/Book	1.56	Price/Sales	1.74

Dividend Achiever Status

Rank	271	10 Year Growth Rate	3.62%
Total Years of Dividend Growth			37

Business Summary: Water Utilities (MIC: 7.2 SIC: 4941 NAIC:221310)

SJW is a holding company with three subsidiaries. San Jose Water Company is a public utility in the business of providing water servic to a population of about 1.0 million people, as of Dec 31 2003, in an area comprising about 138 square miles in the metropolitan San Jos area. SJW Land Company owns and operates parking facilities, which are adjacent to San Jose Water Company's headquarters and th HP Pavilion in San Jose, CA. SJW Land Company also owns commercial buildings and other undeveloped land primarily in the San Jos Metropolitan area. Crystal Choice Water Service LLC is engaged in the sale and rental of water conditioning and purification equipment.

Recent Developments: For the year ended Dec 31 2003, net income was $18.7 million compared with $14.2 million a year earlie Results for 2003 included a net gain of $3.0 million on the sale of nonutility property. Operating revenue increased 2.8% to $149. million from $145.7 million the previous year, due mainly to an increase in revenue from San Jose Water Company. Co. attributed th increase primarily to cumulative rate increases from January through July 2003. SJW Land Company and Crystal Choice Water Servic LLC also posted higher revenues. Operating income advanced 11.7% to $23.0 million versus $20.6 million the year before.

Prospects: Co. has budgeted capital expenditures for 2004, exclusive of capital expenditures financed by customer contributions an advances, at $31.2 million. Looking ahead, Co. expects to incur about $176.0 million in capital expenditures, which includes replacemen of pipes and mains, and maintaining water systems, exclusive of customer contributions and advances, over the next five years. Co. note that a substantial portion of San Jose Water Company's distribution system was constructed during the period from 1945 to 1980 Expenditure levels for renewal and modernization of this part of the system will grow at an increasing rate as these components reach th end of their useful lives.

Financial Data

(US$ in Thousands)	12/31/2003	12/31/2002	12/31/2001	12/31/2000	12/31/1999	12/31/1998	12/31/1997	12/31/199
Earnings Per Share	2.04	1.55	1.53	1.16	1.73	1.68	1.60	1.9
Cash Flow Per Share	4.58	...	...	...	...	...	...	1.9
Tang. Book Val. Per Share	17.83	16.22	15.75	15.19	15.11	14.42	13.40	11.9
Dividends Per Share	0.970	0.920	0.850	0.820	0.800	0.780	0.760	0.74
Dividend Payout %	47.54	59.35	55.55	70.68	46.24	46.42	47.80	38.7
Income Statement								
Total Revenues	149,732	145,652	136,083	123,157	117,001	106,010	110,084	102,59
Total Indirect Exp.	26,614	23,351	21,064	23,343	22,948	22,800	22,301	20,90
Costs & Expenses	126,778	125,094	116,256	105,232	97,262	87,163	90,770	84,98
Depreciation & Amort.	15,225	14,013	13,240	11,847	10,235	9,594	8,847	8,67
Operating Income	22,954	20,558	19,827	17,925	19,739	18,847	19,314	17,60
Net Interest Inc./(Exp.)	(8,471)	(7,803)	(6,737)	(6,434)	(6,552)	(5,629)	(5,695)	(5,89
Income Taxes	4,199	4,740	3,946	...	...	...	...	...
Net Income	18,677	14,232	14,017	10,665	15,884	16,018	15,216	18,56
Average Shs. Outstg.	9,148	9,135	9,135	9,135	9,164	9,509	9,510	9,68
Balance Sheet								
Net Property	436,353	390,830	367,815	333,475	312,567	291,778	263,650	242,07
Total Assets	511,717	453,223	431,017	391,930	372,427	359,380	323,223	296,53
Long-Term Obligations	139,614	110,000	110,000	90,000	90,000	90,000	75,000	75,00
Net Stockholders' Equity	166,368	153,499	149,354	144,325	143,894	143,149	133,553	120,02
Shares Outstanding	9,135	9,135	9,135	9,135	9,135	9,502	9,510	9,5
Statistical Record								
Operating Profit Margin %	15.33	14.11	14.56	14.55	16.87	17.77	17.54	17.1
Net Inc./Net Property %	4.28	3.64	3.81	3.19	5.08	5.48	5.77	7.6
Net Inc./Tot. Capital %	5.45	4.88	4.93	4.15	6.11	6.19	6.60	8.7
Return on Equity %	11.22	9.27	9.38	7.38	11.03	11.18	11.39	15.4
Accum. Depr./Gross Prop. %	29.97	29.81	29.51	30.11	30.03	30.45	30.94	31.4
Price Range	29.90-25.13	29.67-25.42	35.50-23.97	40.58-32.67	40.19-19.08	23.46-16.42	20.17-15.33	16.04-10.1
P/E Ratio	14.66-12.32	19.14-16.40	23.20-15.66	34.99-28.16	23.23-11.03	13.96-9.77	12.60-9.58	8.40-5.6
Average Yield %	3.46	3.42	3.01	2.13	2.97	3.95	4.28	5.

Address: 374 West Santa Clara Street, San Jose, CA 95196 **Telephone:** (408) 279-7800 **Web Site:** www.sjwater.com	**Officers:** Drew Gibson – Chmn., W. Richard Roth – Pres., C.E.O.	**Institutional Holding** No of Institutions: 8 Shares: 13,000 % Held: –

240

SLM CORP.

*7 Year Price Score 181.2 *NYSE Composite Index=100   *12 Month Price Score 88.0

Interim Earnings (Per Share)

Qtr.	Mar	Jun	Sep	Dec
2000	0.31	0.24	0.18	0.19
2001	0.05	0.56	(0.41)	0.56
2002	0.87	0.26	(0.14)	0.65
2003	0.88	0.80	0.76	0.57

Interim Dividends (Per Share)

Amt	Decl	Ex	Rec	Pay
200%	5/15/2003	6/23/2003	6/6/2003	6/20/2003
0.17Q	7/25/2003	9/3/2003	9/5/2003	9/19/2003
0.17Q	11/14/2003	12/3/2003	12/5/2003	12/19/2003
0.17Q	1/29/2004	3/3/2004	3/5/2004	3/19/2004

Indicated Div: $0.68 (Div. Reinv. Plan)

Valuation Analysis

Forecast P/E	N/A	Trailing P/E	13.90
Market Cap	$6.4 Billion	Book Value	2.5 Billion
Price/Book	7.11	Price/Sales	4.26

Dividend Achiever Status

Rank	48	10 Year Growth Rate	17.42%
Total Years of Dividend Growth		23

Business Summary: Credit &Lending (MIC: 8.6 SIC: 6141 NAIC:522291)

SLM is a provider of education funding, managing nearly $89.00 billion in student loans for more than seven million borrowers. Co. primarily provides federally guaranteed student loans originated under the Federal Family Education Loan Program, and offers comprehensive information and resources to help guide students, parents and guidance professionals through the financial aid process. Through its subsidiaries and divisions, Co. also provides an array of consumer credit loans, including those for lifelong learning and K-12 education, and business and technical outsourcing services for colleges and universities.

Recent Developments: For the year ended Dec 31 2003, Co. reported income of $1.40 billion, before an accounting change credit of $30.0 million, versus net income of $792.0 million the year before. Earnings were fueled by a 23.0% gain in preferred-channel loan originations. Results for 2003 and 2002 included losses from derivative market value adjustments of $237.8 million and $1.08 billion, and gains on student loan securitizations of $744.3 million and $337.9 million, respectively. Net interest income slid 6.9% to $1.33 billion. Provision for loan losses grew 26.5% to $147.5 million. Total non-interest income nearly tripled to $1.81 billion. Total operating expenses grew 17.1% to $807.9 million.

Prospects: Looking ahead, Co. should continue to benefit significantly in 2004 from high demand for education loans. During the fourth quarter of 2003, Co.'s preferred-channel loans, loans created by Co.'s owned or affiliated brands and an indicator of future loan acquisition volume, grew 23.0% to a record $15.20 billion year over year. Separately, on Jan 26 2004, Co. signed a definitive agreement to sell its campus-based loan servicing business to JPT Partners. The operation services primarily Perkins and other institution-based loans. The divestiture was undertaken to comply with federal regulations that prevent schools from contracting with a single entity for servicing Perkins loans.

Financial Data

(US$ in Thousands)	12/31/2003	12/31/2002	12/31/2001	12/31/2000	12/31/1999	12/31/1998	12/31/1997	12/31/1996
Earnings Per Share	3.01	1.64	0.76	0.92	1.02	0.98	0.93	0.70
Tang. Book Val. Per Share	5.50	4.00	3.23	2.53	1.42	1.32	1.22	1.20
Dividends Per Share	0.590	0.280	0.240	0.220	0.200	0.190	0.17	0.16
Dividend Payout %	19.71	17.24	31.79	23.91	19.61	19.39	18.28	22.86
Income Statement								
Total Interest Income	2,348,275	2,211,761	2,997,531	3,478,659	2,808,575	2,587,649	3,283,834	3,449,321
Total Interest Expense	1,021,906	1,202,620	2,124,115	2,836,871	2,114,875	1,924,997	2,526,156	2,582,885
Net Interest Income	1,326,369	1,009,141	873,416	641,788	693,790	662,652	757,678	866,436
Provision for Loan Losses	147,480	116,624	65,991	32,119	34,358	28,619	...	...
Non-Interest Income	1,811,951	1,020,654	517,617	687,632	450,790	476,967	500,872	146,916
Non-Interest Expense	807,871	689,772	707,654	585,710	358,570	360,869	493,767	405,652
Income Before Taxes	2,182,969	1,223,399	617,388	711,591	751,652	750,131	764,783	607,700
Equity Earns/Minority Int.	...	...	(10,070)	(10,694)	(10,694)	(10,694)	(10,694)	(10,694)
Income from Cont Ops	1,403,589	...	...	...	...	...	511,168	413,508
Net Income	1,533,560	791,996	383,996	465,017	500,831	501,464	507,895	408,716
Average Shs. Outstg.	463,335	474,519	490,200	493,065	489,474	510,198	548,823	586,017
Balance Sheet								
Securities Avail. for Sale	4,573,497	3,537,117	4,053,719	4,244,762	4,396,776	3,306,972	4,549,977	6,833,695
Net Loans & Leases	51,078,136	43,541,720	42,769,017	39,485,817	35,879,327	31,005,649	32,764,280	38,016,342
Total Assets	64,610,651	53,175,005	52,873,959	48,791,788	44,024,784	37,210,009	39,908,797	47,629,890
Long-Term Obligations	39,808,174	22,242,115	17,285,350	14,910,939	4,496,267	8,810,597	14,541,316	22,606,226
Total Liabilities	61,980,605	51,177,055	51,201,497	47,376,452	43,183,870	36,556,383	39,234,225	46,795,943
Net Stockholders' Equity	2,630,046	1,997,950	1,672,462	1,415,336	840,914	653,626	674,572	833,947
Shares Outstanding	447,678	457,740	466,485	492,434	472,729	492,381	550,899	689,802
Statistical Record								
Return on Equity %	53.36	39.64	22.95	32.85	59.55	76.72	75.77	49.58
Return on Assets %	2.17	1.48	0.72	0.95	1.13	1.34	1.28	0.86
Equity/Assets %	4.07	3.75	3.16	2.90	1.91	1.75	1.69	1.75
Net Int. Exp./Tot. Inc. %	19.41	21.33	20.13	14.05	11.00	11.77	13.04	11.27
Price Range	42.64-33.85	35.63-26.38	29.13-19.37	22.67-9.44	17.87-13.37	17.00-9.33	15.60-8.56	9.31-6.07
P/E Ratio	14.16-11.24	21.73-16.09	38.33-25.49	24.64-10.26	17.52-13.11	17.35-9.52	16.77-9.20	13.30-8.67
Average Yield %	1.54	0.89	0.95	1.37	1.28	1.44	1.41	2.08

Address: 11600 Sallie Mae Drive, Reston, VA 20193 **Telephone:** (703) 810-3000 **Web Site:** www.salliemae.com	**Officers:** Edward A. Fox - Chmn., Albert L. Lord - Vice-Chmn., C.E.O. **Transfer Agents:** The Bank of New York, New York, NY	**Investor Contact:** 703-810-7751 **Institutional Holding** **No of Institutions:** 25 **Shares:** 2,585,516 **% Held:** -

241

SMITH (A.O.) CORP

Exchange	Symbol	Price	52Wk Range	Yield	P/E
NYS	AOS	$28.95 (3/31/2004)	36.50–26.95	2.07	16.45

*7 Year Price Score 127.4 ***NYSE Composite Index=100** ***12 Month Price Score 101.3**

Interim Earnings (Per Share)

Qtr.	Mar	Jun	Sep	Dec
2000	0.60	0.74	0.31	0.11
2001	0.36	0.45	0.02	(0.22)
2002	0.50	0.66	0.34	0.36
2003	0.46	0.67	0.20	0.43

Interim Dividends (Per Share)

Amt	Decl	Ex	Rec	Pa
0.14Q	4/8/2003	4/28/2003	4/30/2003	5/15/200
0.15Q	7/8/2003	7/29/2003	7/31/2003	8/15/200
0.15Q	10/7/2003	10/29/2003	10/31/2003	11/17/200
0.15Q	1/15/2004	1/28/2004	1/30/2004	2/17/200

Indicated Div: $0.60 (Div. Reinv. Plan)

Valuation Analysis

Forecast P/E	12.96	Trailing P/E	16.45
Market Cap	$579.1 Million	Book Value	576.2 Million
Price/Book	1.05	Price/Sales	0.38

Dividend Achiever Status

Rank	285	10 Year Growth Rate	2.65%
Total Years of Dividend Growth			11

Business Summary: Electrical (MIC: 11.14 SIC: 3621 NAIC:335312)

A.O. Smith is a manufacturer of electric motors and water heating equipment serving residential, commercial and industrial end market primarily in the United States. The Electric Products segment manufactures hermetic motors, fractional horsepower alternating current an direct current motors, and integral horsepower motors. The Water Systems segment manufactures and markets a line of residential gas an electric water heaters, standard and specialty commercial water heating equipment, high-efficiency copper-tube boilers, and water system tanks. Co. operates manufacturing facilities in the United States, Canada, Mexico, England, Ireland, Hungary, the Netherlands and China

Recent Developments: For the year ended Dec 31 2003, net earnings increased 1.8% to $52.2 million from $51.3 million in th previous year. Net sales advanced 4.2% to $1.53 billion from $1.47 billion a year earlier. Electrical products segment sales climbed 4.3% to $824.6 million, primarily due to the prior-year acquisitions of Athens and the Jiangsu Changheng Motor Group Co. Ltd. Water System segment sales grew 4.0% to $706.1 million, driven by a January 2003 price increase to cover higher steel costs, a 44.0% increase i Chinese operations and the introduction of new flammable vapor ignition resistant products, partially offset by lower unit sales o commercial and residential retail products.

Prospects: Looking ahead to 2004, Co. anticipates earnings in the range of $2.20 to $2.40 per share, despite raw material cost pressure and the loss of a sales contract with a major motor customer. In the motors business, Co.'s transition to Mexico and ramp-up in China shou improve pre-tax earnings by $15.0 million. In the water heater business, a full year's sales of flammable vapor ignition resistant product, a well as the introduction high-efficiency products should improve pre-tax earnings by $15.0 million. Meanwhile, the focusing commercial water heater production in Co.'s McBee, SC plant, with residential product relocated to Ashland City, TN should provide $5 million in pre-tax impact.

Financial Data
(US$ in Thousands)

	12/31/2003	12/31/2002	12/31/2001	12/31/2000	12/31/1999	12/31/1998	12/31/1997	12/31/199
Earnings Per Share	1.76	1.86	0.61	1.76	2.11	1.84	1.33	0.
Cash Flow Per Share	0.85	4.05	2.08	3.23	2.00	3.20	2.84	2.
Tang. Book Val. Per Share	9.07	6.95	6.30	8.64	7.69	10.93	10.68	13.
Dividends Per Share	0.580	0.540	0.520	0.500	0.480	0.460	0.450	0.4
Dividend Payout %	32.95	29.03	85.24	28.40	22.74	25.36	34.00	53.
Income Statement								
Total Revenues	1,530,700	1,469,100	1,151,156	1,247,945	1,039,281	917,569	832,937	781,1
Total Indirect Exp.	206,400	206,451	162,066	160,627	110,613	106,622	106,999	107,3
Depreciation & Amort.	200	282	6,956	6,932	37,315	31,173	26,286	22,5
Operating Income	92,300	93,309	40,275	87,497	96,299	80,404	63,711	59,6
Net Interest Inc./(Exp.)	(12,200)	(13,926)	(16,418)	(22,102)	(11,429)	(3,059)	1,273	(8,1
Income Taxes	26,800	27,045	7,984	23,432	26,822	25,283	21,359	17,0
Eqty Earns/Minority Int.	...	...	...	...	...	(3,189)	(2,744)	(3,89
Income from Cont Ops	...	...	...	41,656	50,270	...	37,553	25,2
Net Income	52,200	51,345	14,502	29,753	42,422	44,491	153,830	65,4
Average Shs. Outstg.	29,710	27,649	23,914	23,691	23,787	24,184	28,191	31,7
Balance Sheet								
Cash & Cash Equivalents	18,700	32,847	20,759	15,287	14,761	37,666	145,896	6,4
Total Current Assets	547,700	488,251	477,574	406,099	388,627	287,389	365,728	239,2
Total Assets	1,279,900	1,224,857	1,293,923	1,059,176	1,063,986	767,432	716,516	884,9
Total Current Liabilities	338,600	261,679	255,950	170,431	168,440	132,157	127,882	138,3
Long–Term Obligations	170,100	239,084	390,385	316,372	351,251	131,203	100,972	238,4
Net Stockholders' Equity	576,200	511,552	451,878	448,395	431,084	401,093	399,705	424,6
Net Working Capital	209,100	226,572	221,624	235,668	220,187	155,232	237,846	100,8
Shares Outstanding	29,246	29,039	23,786	23,549	23,394	23,252	32,550	31,4
Statistical Record								
Operating Profit Margin %	6.02	6.35	3.49	7.01	9.26	8.76	7.64	7
Return on Equity %	9.05	10.04	3.20	9.29	11.66	11.09	9.39	5
Return on Assets %	4.07	4.19	1.12	3.93	4.72	5.79	5.24	2
Debt/Total Assets %	13.29	19.51	30.17	29.86	33.01	17.09	14.09	26
Price Range	36.50–23.80	32.10–19.15	20.00–14.68	22.63–11.75	31.94–19.00	35.88–15.94	28.58–19.33	21.25–14
P/E Ratio	20.74–13.52	17.26–10.30	32.79–24.07	12.86–6.68	15.14–9.00	19.50–8.66	21.49–14.54	26.56–17
Average Yield %	1.91	2.02	2.96	2.83	1.95	1.68	1.84	2

Address: P.O. Box 245008, Milwaukee, WI 53224–9508
Telephone: (414) 359–4000
Web Site: www.aosmith.com

Officers: Robert J. OToole – Chmn., C.E.O., Paul W. Jones – Pres., C.O.O.
Transfer Agents: Wells Fargo Bank Minnesota, N.A., St. Paul, MN

Investor Contact: (414) 359–4009
Institutional Holding
No of Institutions: 137
Shares: 17,692,136 **% Held:** 61%

SONOCO PRODUCTS CO.

Exchange	Symbol	Price	52Wk Range	Yield	P/E
NYS	SON	$24.28 (3/31/2004)	25.10-20.64	3.46	16.98

Year Price Score 89.5 *NYSE Composite Index=100 *12 Month Price Score 89.2

Interim Earnings (Per Share)

Qtr.	Apr	Jul	Oct	Dec
2000	0.45	0.47	0.39	0.35
2001	0.05	0.18	0.45	0.28
2002	0.35	0.39	0.30	0.35
2003	0.30	0.24	0.14	0.75

Interim Dividends (Per Share)

Amt	Decl	Ex	Rec	Pay
0.21Q	4/16/2003	5/14/2003	5/16/2003	6/10/2003
0.21Q	7/16/2003	8/13/2003	8/15/2003	9/10/2003
0.21Q	10/14/2003	11/19/2003	11/21/2003	12/10/2003
0.21Q	2/4/2004	2/18/2004	2/20/2004	3/10/2004

Indicated Div: $0.84 (Div. Reinv. Plan)

Valuation Analysis

Forecast P/E	15.01	Trailing P/E	16.98
Market Cap	$2.3 Billion	Book Value	1.0 Billion
Price/Book	2.37	Price/Sales	0.87

Dividend Achiever Status

Rank	230	10 Year Growth Rate	6.23%
Total Years of Dividend Growth	20	

Business Summary: Paper Products (MIC: 11.11 SIC: 2631 NAIC:322130)

Sonoco Products is a manufacturer of industrial and consumer packaging products and provider of packaging services, with 295 locations in 32 countries as of Dec 31 2003. Each of Co.'s operating units has its own sales staff and maintains direct sales relationships with its customers. The industrial packaging segment includes engineered carriers, paper, molded & extruded plastics, wire & cable reels, and protective packaging. The consumer packaging segment includes rigid packaging, closures, printed flexible packaging, packaging services & folding cartons, glass covers & coasters, and artwork management.

Recent Developments: For the year ended Dec 31 2003, income from continuing operations decreased 37.7% to $78.2 million, before income from discontinued operations of $60.8 million, compared with income of $125.5 million, before income from discontinued operations of $9.8 million, in 2002. The decline in earnings was primarily attributed to higher raw material costs, additional pension and postretirement expenses, continued pricing pressure and increased energy and healthcare expenses. Results for 2003 and 2002 included restructuring charges of $50.1 million and $10.4 million, respectively. Sales advanced 2.1% to $2.76 billion from $2.70 billion a year earlier.

Prospects: In 2004, Co. expects to benefit from cost reductions and continued productivity improvements, but does not anticipate a significant increase in pension and postretirement expenses. These positive factors are, however, likely to be partially offset by continued price/cost pressures, the loss of earnings from the High Density Film business and higher benefit costs. In addition, Co. does not expect significant volume improvements in its industrial packaging segment at least through the first quarter of 2004. Co. expects earnings for the first quarter of 2004 in the range of $0.31 to $0.35 per diluted share, excluding any restructuring charges.

Financial Data

(US $ in Thousands)	12/31/2003	12/31/2002	12/31/2001	12/31/2000	12/31/1999	12/31/1998	12/31/1997	12/31/1996
Earnings Per Share	1.43	1.39	0.96	1.66	1.83	1.84	0.00	1.58
Cash Flow Per Share	3.41	2.79	3.80	3.62	2.33	2.18	3.07	2.93
Tang. Book Val. Per Share	6.48	5.25	4.64	5.94	6.37	6.40	7.35	3.49
Dividends Per Share	0.840	0.830	0.800	0.790	0.750	0.700	0.640	0.580
Dividend Payout %	58.74	59.71	83.33	47.59	40.98	38.24	...	37.11
Income Statement								
Total Revenues	2,758,326	2,812,150	2,606,276	2,711,493	2,546,734	2,557,917	2,847,831	2,788,075
Total Indirect Exp.	339,895	301,320	320,232	277,693	252,917	100,902	750,155	310,605
Depreciation & Amort.	163,234	159,256	158,574	150,816	145,846	145,669	153,524	142,927
Operating Income	158,544	251,040	224,198	326,405	336,712	388,461	115,942	329,365
Net Interest Inc./(Exp.)	(50,211)	(52,547)	(48,417)	(55,810)	(47,152)	(48,863)	(52,223)	(49,290)
Income Taxes	57,797	70,614	82,958	111,999	108,585	153,989	60,111	107,433
Equity Earns/Minority Int.	7,543	7,437	(1,214)	7,702	6,830	6,387	(991)	(1,771)
Income from Cont Ops	78,178	...	...	...	...	191,996	...	...
Net Income	138,949	135,316	91,609	166,298	187,805	180,243	2,617	170,871
Average Shs. Outstg.	97,129	97,178	95,807	99,900	102,780	104,275	97,591	108,517
Balance Sheet								
Cash & Cash Equivalents	84,854	31,405	36,130	35,219	36,515	57,249	53,600	71,260
Total Current Assets	755,265	663,267	665,169	695,793	723,081	661,416	873,040	737,649
Total Assets	2,520,633	2,390,094	2,352,197	2,212,611	2,297,020	2,082,983	2,176,865	2,387,540
Total Current Liabilities	679,594	600,027	460,270	437,080	416,631	436,069	434,144	475,116
Long-Term Obligations	473,220	699,346	885,961	812,085	819,540	686,826	696,669	791,026
Net Stockholders' Equity	1,014,160	867,425	804,122	801,471	901,220	821,592	848,819	920,613
Net Working Capital	75,671	63,240	204,899	258,713	306,450	225,347	438,896	262,533
Shares Outstanding	97,217	96,640	95,713	95,000	101,448	101,683	95,834	98,850
Statistical Record								
Operating Profit Margin %	5.74	8.92	8.60	12.03	13.22	15.18	4.07	11.81
Return on Equity %	7.71	15.59	11.39	20.74	20.83	23.36	0.30	18.56
Return on Assets %	3.10	5.66	3.89	7.51	8.17	9.21	0.12	7.15
Debt/Total Assets %	18.77	29.26	37.66	36.70	35.67	32.97	32.00	33.13
Price Range	24.73-19.47	29.70-19.81	26.58-19.69	23.50-16.88	29.94-21.06	38.92-22.44	32.16-22.61	28.07-23.52
P/E Ratio	17.29-13.62	21.37-14.25	27.69-20.51	14.16-10.17	16.36-11.51	21.15-12.19	N/A	17.76-14.89
Average Yield %	3.78	3.25	3.36	3.97	2.95	2.24	2.31	2.30

Address: One North Second Street, Hartsville, SC 29551-0160	**Officers:** Charles W. Coker – Chmn., Harris E. DeLoach – Pres., C.E.O.	**Investor Contact:**843-383-7524
Telephone: (843) 383-7000	**Transfer Agents:**EquiServe Trust Company, NA Providence, RI	**Institutional Holding**
Web Site: www.sonoco.com		**No of Institutions:** 211
		Shares: 47,928,315 **% Held:** 49.40%

243

SOUTHTRUST CORP.

Exchange	Symbol	Price	52Wk Range	Yield	P/E
NMS	SOTR	$33.17 (3/31/2004)	34.57-25.49	2.89	16.10

*7 Year Price Score 140.3 *NYSE Composite Index=100 *12 Month Price Score 100.6

Interim Earnings (Per Share)

Qtr.	Mar	Jun	Sep	Dec
2000	0.35	0.35	0.36	0.37
2001	0.38	0.40	0.41	0.42
2002	0.44	0.45	0.47	0.49
2003	0.49	0.51	0.53	0.53

Interim Dividends (Per Share)

Amt	Decl	Ex	Rec	Pa
0.21Q	4/16/2003	5/21/2003	5/23/2003	7/1/200
0.21Q	7/16/2003	8/20/2003	8/22/2003	10/1/200
0.21Q	10/15/2003	11/19/2003	11/21/2003	1/2/200
0.24Q	1/21/2004	2/18/2004	2/20/2004	4/1/200

Indicated Div: $0.96 (Div. Reinv. Plan)

Valuation Analysis

Forecast P/E	13.71	Trailing P/E	16.10
Market Cap	$11.5 Billion	Book Value	4.4 Billion
Price/Book	2.49	Price/Sales	3.56

Dividend Achiever Status

Rank	74	10 Year Growth Rate	15.33%
Total Years of Dividend Growth		33

Business Summary: Commercial Banking (MIC: 8.1 SIC: 6021 NAIC:522110)

SouthTrust is a financial holding company. Co. is engaged, through its subsidiary bank, SouthTrust Bank, and its non-bankin subsidiaries, in a full range of banking services from 717 banking locations in Alabama, Florida, Georgia, Mississippi, North Carolina South Carolina, Tennessee, Texas and Virginia. Co. generates revenues from retail and commercial lending, depository services, cas management, and international and commercial leasing services. In addition, Co. provides trust, brokerage, investment, and insuranc services. Consolidated total assets as of Dec 31 2003 amounted to $51.92 billion.

Recent Developments: For the year ended Dec 31 2003, net income increased 8.5% to $705.2 million from $649.9 million in the pric year. Net interest income slipped 3.1% to $1.66 billion from $1.72 billion the year before. Provision for loan losses declined 1.7% $124.6 million from $126.7 million the previous year. Non-interest income climbed 10.3% to $679.7 million from $616.5 million a ye earlier. Non-interest expense was down 4.3% to $1.18 billion from $1.23 billion in 2002. Total deposits amounted to $34.75 billior up 5.5% compared with $32.95 billion the prior year.

Prospects: On Feb 5 2004, Co. announced that it has signed a definitive agreement to acquire FloridaFirst Bancorp, Inc. and i subsidiary, FloridaFirst Bank, for approximately $146.1 million. FloridaFirst operates 38 branches in Florida and reported assets $821.0 million at Dec 31 2003. The transaction is expected to be completed during the second quarter of 2004, subject to shareholder an regulatory approval. Separately, earnings are benefiting from non-interest income growth, which is being fueled by increases mortgage-banking income, investment fees, debit card fees, and service charges.

Financial Data

(US$ in Thousands)	12/31/2003	12/31/2002	12/31/2001	12/31/2000	12/31/1999	12/31/1998	12/31/1997	12/31/1996
Earnings Per Share	2.06	1.85	1.61	1.43	1.31	1.12	1.01	0.8
Tang. Book Val. Per Share	10.78	11.03	9.19	8.19	6.74	6.36	7.14	6.0
Dividends Per Share	0.800	0.650	0.540	0.480	0.420	0.360	0.320	0.28
Dividend Payout %	38.83	35.13	33.85	33.91	32.31	32.74	31.85	31.5
Income Statement								
Total Interest Income	2,367,085	2,665,411	3,170,760	3,394,088	2,906,447	2,557,462	2,232,252	1,804,22
Total Interest Expense	713,776	960,327	1,642,658	2,008,351	1,539,538	1,386,256	1,186,079	938,19
Net Interest Income	1,653,309	1,705,084	1,528,102	1,385,737	1,366,909	1,171,206	1,046,173	866,02
Provision for Loan Losses	124,550	126,732	118,293	92,827	141,249	94,796	90,613	90,02
Non-Interest Income	679,712	660,996	571,029	505,683	443,557	386,094	270,507	254,80
Non-interest Expense	1,179,849	1,276,651	1,153,368	1,087,196	1,010,501	914,443	748,216	643,29
Income Before Taxes	1,028,622	962,497	827,470	711,397	658,716	548,061	477,851	387,51
Income from Cont Ops	...	...	...	...	...	368,862	...	...
Net Income	705,186	649,871	554,648	482,330	443,173	368,610	306,708	254,70
Average Shs. Outstg.	342,498	350,937	345,294	337,812	337,556	328,296	302,016	284,30
Balance Sheet								
Cash & Due from Banks	1,061,502	1,005,327	1,159,236	959,750	874,999	970,778	877,885	903,13
Securities Avail. for Sale	11,493,045	10,700,990	10,062,158	7,049,966	5,130,509	3,875,933	2,975,830	2,859,01
Net Loans & Leases	34,778,985	33,739,078	32,939,475	30,945,808	31,255,498	26,939,981	22,159,314	19,061,26
Total Assets	51,924,888	50,570,856	48,754,548	45,146,531	43,262,512	38,133,774	30,906,445	26,223,19
Total Deposits	34,746,597	32,945,406	32,634,111	30,702,539	27,739,345	24,839,892	19,586,584	17,305,49
Long-Term Obligations	6,087,721	6,652,838	5,484,485	4,178,092	4,655,801	3,935,277	3,888,798	2,727,40
Total Liabilities	47,565,050	45,943,275	44,792,173	41,794,071	40,335,083	35,395,508	28,711,804	24,488,30
Net Stockholders' Equity	4,359,838	4,627,581	3,962,375	3,352,460	2,927,429	2,738,266	2,194,641	1,734,89
Shares Outstanding	330,242	346,924	346,272	338,106	335,810	334,422	307,328	288,35
Statistical Record								
Return on Equity %	16.17	14.04	13.99	14.38	15.13	13.47	13.97	14.6
Return on Assets %	1.35	1.28	1.13	1.06	1.02	0.96	0.99	0.9
Equity/Assets %	8.39	9.15	8.12	7.42	6.76	7.18	7.10	6.6
Non-Int. Exp./Tot. Inc. %	38.72	38.38	30.82	27.87	30.16	31.06	29.89	31.2
Price Range	32.75-24.70	27.50-20.84	26.90-19.56	20.34-10.50	21.31-16.47	22.47-14.19	21.15-11.50	12.04-8.4
P/E Ratio	15.90-11.99	14.86-11.26	16.71-12.15	14.23-7.34	16.27-12.57	20.06-12.67	20.94-11.39	13.53-9.4
Average Yield %	2.80	2.57	2.29	3.39	2.22	1.85	2.18	2.8

Address: 420 North 20th Street, Birmingham, AL 35203 **Telephone:** (205) 254-5000 **Web Site:** www.southtrust.com	**Officers:** Wallace D. Malone – Chmn., C.E.O., Thomas H. Coley – Vice-Chmn.	**Investor Contact:** 205-254-5187 **Institutional Holding** **No of Institutions:** 45 **Shares:** 2,741,676 **% Held:** –

ST. PAUL TRAVELERS COMPANIES, INC.

Exchange	Symbol	Price	52Wk Range	Yield	P/E
NYS	STA	$40.01 (3/31/2004)	43.35-32.32	2.90	13.89

Year Price Score 93.9 *NYSE Composite Index=100 *12 Month Price Score 95.5

Interim Earnings (Per Share)

Qtr.	Mar	Jun	Sep	Dec
2000	1.53	0.95	0.98	0.86
2001	0.90	0.41	(2.86)	(3.29)
2002	0.67	(1.07)	0.29	1.17
2003	0.75	0.89	0.98	0.26

Interim Dividends (Per Share)

Amt	Decl	Ex	Rec	Pay
0.29Q	8/5/2003	9/26/2003	9/30/2003	10/17/2003
0.29Q	11/4/2003	12/29/2003	12/31/2003	1/16/2004
0.29Q	2/3/2004	3/29/2004	3/31/2004	4/16/2004
0.21Q	3/19/2004	4/2/2004.	3/26/2004	5/14/2004

Indicated Div: $0.84 (Div. Reinv. Plan)

Valuation Analysis

Forecast P/E	8.62	Trailing P/E	13.89
Market Cap	$9.1 Billion	Book Value	6.2 Billion
Price/Book	1.47	Price/Sales	1.02

Dividend Achiever Status

Rank	244	10 Year Growth Rate	5.26%
Total Years of Dividend Growth		17	

Business Summary: Insurance (MIC: 8.2 SIC: 6331 NAIC:524130)

St. Paul Travelers is a management company principally engaged in two industry segments: commercial property–liability insurance and nonlife reinsurance products and services. Co. also has a presence in the asset management industry through its 77.0% majority ownership of Nuveen Investments, Inc. As a management company, Co. oversees the operations of its subsidiaries and provides those subsidiaries with capital, management and administrative services. The primary business of Co. is underwriting, which produced 95.4% of consolidated revenues in 2002.

Recent Developments: For the year ended Dec 31 2003, income was $699.0 million versus income of $249.0 million the prior year. Results for 2003 and 2002 excluded an accounting charge of $21.0 million and $6.0 million, and a loss from discontinued operations of $7.0 million and $25.0 million, respectively. Total revenues declined 1.9% to $8.85 billion. Premiums earned fell 6.2% to $7.04 billion, reflecting Co.'s decision to withdraw from several lines of business. Net investment dropped 4.2% to $1.12 billion. Insurance losses and loss adjustment expenses fell 13.5% to $5.19 billion.

Prospects: Co.'s ongoing businesses should continue to produce strong and improving results due to Co.'s focus on profitable growth, disciplined underwriting and expense control. In addition, Nuveen Investments should benefit from continued growth in earnings. Separately, Co. acquired Travelers Property Casualty Corp. on April 2, 2004 The combined company, named The St. Paul Travelers, is the second largest commercial insurer and eighth largest personal life insurer in the U.S.

Financial Data

(US$ in Thousands)	12/31/2003	12/31/2002	12/31/2001	12/31/2000	12/31/1999	12/31/1998	12/31/1997	12/31/1996
Earnings Per Share	2.88	1.06	(4.84)	4.32	3.19	0.32	4.19	3.05
Tang. Book Val. Per Share	22.26	20.58	21.02	30.54	26.41	25.79	25.08	22.87
Dividends Per Share	1.160	1.150	1.110	1.070	1.030	0.980	0.920	0.860
Dividend Payout %	40.27	108.49	N.M.	24.76	32.28	307.81	22.05	28.19
Income Statement								
Total Premium Income	7,039,000	7,390,000	7,296,000	5,898,000	5,290,000	6,944,575	4,616,456	4,448,248
Net Investment Income	1,120,000	1,169,000	1,217,000	1,616,000	1,557,000	1,584,982	886,213	807,305
Other Income	695,000	359,000	430,000	1,094,000	722,000	578,844	716,604	478,603
Total Revenues	8,854,000	8,918,000	8,943,000	8,608,000	7,569,000	9,108,401	6,219,273	5,734,156
Total Indirect Exp.	1,266,000	1,184,000	1,306,000	1,306,000	1,140,000	1,624,758	833,749	741,263
Inc. Before Inc. Taxes	836,000	176,000	(1,431,000)	1,453,000	1,017,000	(46,287)	1,018,733	699,136
Income Taxes	137,000	(73,000)	(422,000)	440,000	238,000	(135,635)	245,510	141,278
Income from Cont Ops	699,000	249,000	(1,009,000)	1,013,000	779,000	...	773,223	557,858
Net Income	661,000	218,000	(1,088,000)	993,000	834,000	89,348	705,473	450,099
Average Shs. Outstg.	240,000	227,000	212,000	233,000	246,000	238,682	184,522	184,080
Balance Sheet								
Cash & Cash Equivalents	150,000	315,000	151,000	83,000	210,000	226,668	152,863	180,808
Premiums Due	9,792,000	11,127,000	10,569,000	8,661,000	7,185,000	6,404,548	3,544,672	3,622,629
Invest. Assets: Total	20,471,000	20,581,000	20,025,000	25,835,000	24,879,000	26,240,231	14,766,281	14,219,417
Total Assets	39,563,000	39,920,000	38,321,000	41,075,000	38,873,000	38,322,708	21,500,657	20,680,976
Long–Term Obligations	3,750,000	2,713,000	2,130,000	1,647,000	1,466,000	1,260,392	782,825	689,141
Net Stockholders' Equity	6,225,000	4,857,000	4,221,000	6,890,000	6,047,000	6,133,687	4,419,710	3,796,820
Shares Outstanding	228,393	226,798	207,624	218,308	224,830	233,750	167,456	167,032
Statistical Record								
Return on Revenues %	7.65	2.72	N.M.	11.76	9.89	0.98	12.43	9.72
Return on Equity %	11.22	4.33	N.M	14.01	12.03	1.34	16.71	13.93
Return on Assets %	1.76	0.62	N.M.	2.46	2.00	0.23	3.59	2.69
Price Range	39.65-29.33	50.12-24.20	52.12-35.50	56.38-21.63	36.75-25.56	47.06-29.00	42.66-28.94	30.00-25.31
P/E Ratio	13.77-10.18	47.28-22.83	N/A	13.05-5.01	11.52-8.01	147.1-90.63	10.18-6.91	9.84-8.30
Average Yield %	3.30	2.99	2.41	2.71	3.23	2.49	2.48	3.13

Address: 385 Washington Street, Saint Paul, MN 55102	**Officers:** Jay S. Fishman – Chmn., Pres., C.E.O., John A. MacColl – Vice–Chmn., Gen. Couns.	**Institutional Holding** No of Institutions: 405
Telephone: (651) 310–7911	**Transfer Agents:** Wells Fargo Bank, Minnesota, N.A., St. Paul, MN	Shares: 206,910,671 % Held: 90.80%
Web Site: www.stpaul.com		

STANLEY WORKS

Exchange	Symbol	Price	52Wk Range	Yield	P/E
NYS	SWK	$42.68 (3/31/2004)	43.53–21.00	2.44	37.44

*7 Year Price Score 84.2   *NYSE Composite Index=100   *12 Month Price Score 105.2

Interim Earnings (Per Share)

Qtr.	Mar	Jun	Sep	Dec
2000	0.54	0.58	0.56	0.54
2001	0.54	0.58	0.62	0.07
2002	0.56	0.72	0.62	0.20
2003	0.22	0.14	0.51	0.27

Interim Dividends (Per Share)

Amt	Decl	Ex	Rec	P
0.255Q	4/22/2003	5/29/2003	6/2/2003	6/27/20
0.26Q	7/15/2003	8/28/2003	9/2/2003	9/23/20
0.26Q	10/15/2003	11/19/2003	11/21/2003	12/31/20
0.26Q	1/23/2004	3/4/2004	3/8/2004	3/30/20

Indicated Div: $1.04 (Div. Reinv. Plan)

Valuation Analysis

Forecast P/E	12.51	Trailing P/E	37.44
Market Cap	$3.7 Billion	Book Value	858.6 Million
Price/Book	3.56	Price/Sales	1.14

Dividend Achiever Status

Rank	263	10 Year Growth Rate	4.39%
Total Years of Dividend Growth			36

Business Summary: Metal Products (MIC: 11.4 SIC: 3423 NAIC:332212)

Stanley Works is a worldwide producer of tools and door products for professional, industrial and consumer use. The Tools segme manufactures and markets carpenters', mechanics', pneumatic and hydraulic tools as well as tool sets. The Doors segment manufactu and markets automatic doors as well as closet doors and systems, home decor, door locking systems, commercial and consumer hardwa security access control systems and patient monitoring devices. A substantial portion of Co.'s products are sold through home centers a mass merchant distribution channels in the U.S.

Recent Developments: For the year ended Jan 3 2004, earnings from continuing operations dropped 43.2% to $96.7 million compar with $170.3 million in 2002. Results for 2003 included restructuring charges and asset impairments of $53.2 million. Results for 2003 a 2002 excluded earnings of $11.2 million and $14.7 million, respectively, from the discontinued operations of the residential entry dc business. Net sales rose 12.4% to $2.68 billion from $2.38 billion in the previous year due to double–digit percentage sales growth hand tools, access technologies, assembly technologies, consumer hardware and ZAG®storage. Sales in Europe and Asia continued benefit from the weaker U.S. dollar.

Prospects: Sales from continuing operations in January and February 2004 increased more than 20.0% over the same months of 200 Accordingly, Co. expects organic sales for the first quarter of 2004 to increase by a low to mid–teens percentage. As a result, Co. expe diluted earnings per share for the first quarter of 2004 to be in the range of $0.63 to $0.67, up from its previous estimate of $0.49 to $0.5 Estimates for the first quarter are from continuing operations and exclude the pre–tax gain of about $100.0 million from the sale of Cc residential entry door business to Masonite on Mar 2 2004. Meanwhile, Co. expects full–year 2004 earnings per share in the range $2.50 to $2.60.

Financial Data

(US$ in Thousands)	01/03/2004	12/28/2002	12/29/2001	12/30/2000	01/01/2000	01/02/1999	01/03/1998	12/28/199
Earnings Per Share	1.14	2.10	1.81	2.22	1.67	1.53	(0.47)	1.0
Cash Flow Per Share	5.47	3.23	2.53	2.69	2.47	0.62	2.69	2.0
Tang. Book Val. Per Share	2.64	5.05	9.59	8.46	8.07	7.31	6.56	8.
Dividends Per Share	1.030	0.990	0.940	0.900	0.870	0.830	0.770	0.9
Dividend Payout %	90.35	47.14	51.93	40.54	52.09	54.24	N.M.	83.
Income Statement								
Total Revenues	2,678,100	2,593,000	2,624,400	2,748,900	2,751,800	2,729,100	2,669,500	2,670,8
Total Indirect Exp.	691,000	547,200	666,100	656,600	681,700	684,700	866,200	656,3
Depreciation & Amort.	86,500	71,200	82,900	83,300	85,600	79,700	72,400	74,7
Operating Income	201,800	288,600	257,000	340,800	256,200	251,600	19,900	219,0
Net Interest Inc./(Exp.)	(28,300)	(24,500)	(25,600)	(27,100)	(27,900)	(23,100)	(16,600)	(22,50
Income Taxes	36,300	87,500	78,400	99,300	80,800	77,600	23,300	77,3
Income from Cont Ops	96,700	...	...	...	...	...	...	...
Net Income	107,900	185,000	158,300	194,400	150,000	137,800	(41,900)	96,9
Average Shs. Outstg.	84,839	88,246	87,467	87,667	89,886	90,193	89,469	88,8
Balance Sheet								
Cash & Cash Equivalents	204,400	121,700	115,200	93,600	88,000	110,100	152,200	84,0
Total Current Assets	1,200,700	1,190,400	1,141,400	1,094,300	1,091,000	1,086,400	1,005,300	910,9
Total Assets	2,423,800	2,418,200	1,839,500	1,724,400	1,722,400	1,755,900	1,679,700	1,581,6
Total Current Liabilities	753,500	680,900	825,500	707,300	693,000	702,100	622,700	381,6
Long–Term Obligations	534,500	564,300	196,800	248,700	290,000	344,800	283,700	342,6
Net Stockholders' Equity	858,600	983,800	832,300	736,500	735,400	669,400	607,800	780,1
Net Working Capital	447,200	509,500	315,900	387,000	398,000	384,300	382,600	529,3
Shares Outstanding	81,276	86,835	84,658	85,188	88,945	88,772	88,788	88,7
Statistical Record								
Operating Profit Margin %	7.53	11.12	9.79	12.39	9.31	9.21	0.74	8.
Return on Equity %	11.26	18.80	19.01	26.39	20.39	20.58	N.M.	12.
Return on Assets %	3.98	7.65	8.60	11.27	8.70	7.84	N.M.	6.
Debt/Total Assets %	22.05	23.33	10.69	14.42	16.83	19.63	16.88	21.6
Price Range	37.87–21.00	51.98–28.38	46.60–28.50	31.19–19.25	33.81–22.13	56.38–24.50	47.19–27.00	32.69–24.
P/E Ratio	33.22–18.42	24.75–13.51	25.75–15.75	14.05–8.67	20.25–13.25	36.85–16.01	N/A	29.99–22.
Average Yield %	3.57	2.48	2.46	3.45	3.08	2.01	1.88	3.

Address: 1000 Stanley Drive, New Britain, CT 06053	Officers: John F. Lundgren – Chmn., C.E.O., J. M. Loree – Exec. V.P., C.F.O.	Investor Contact: 860–827–3833
Telephone: (860) 225–5111	Transfer Agents: EquiServe Limited Partnership, Boston, MA	Institutional Holding
Web Site: www.stanleyworks.com		No of Institutions: 250
		Shares: 55,218,112 % Held: 64.50%

STATE AUTO FINANCIAL CORP.

Exchange	Symbol	Price	52Wk Range	Yield	P/E
NMS	STFC	$25.81 (3/31/2004)	26.82-16.78	0.62	16.33

Year Price Score 151.2 *NYSE Composite Index=100 *12 Month Price Score 103.1

Interim Earnings (Per Share)

Qtr.	Mar	Jun	Sep	Dec
2000	0.35	0.32	0.20	0.34
2001	0.36	0.24	0.18	(0.26)
2002	0.33	(0.04)	0.15	0.49
2003	0.53	0.21	0.38	0.46

Interim Dividends (Per Share)

Amt	Decl	Ex	Rec	Pay
0.035Q	5/23/2003	6/11/2003	6/13/2003	6/30/2003
0.04Q	8/15/2003	9/11/2003	9/15/2003	9/30/2003
0.04Q	11/21/2003	12/17/2003	12/19/2003	12/31/2003
0.04Q	3/5/2004	3/17/2004	3/19/2004	3/31/2004

Indicated Div: $0.16 (Div. Reinv. Plan)

Valuation Analysis

Forecast P/E	12.98	Trailing P/E 16.33
Market Cap	$1.0 Billion	Book Value 515.9 Million
Price/Book	N/A	Price/Sales N/A

Dividend Achiever Status

Rank	149	10 Year Growth Rate 10.22%
Total Years of Dividend Growth		12

Business Summary: Insurance (MIC: 8.2 SIC: 6331 NAIC:524126)

State Auto Financial, through its principal insurance subsidiaries, State Auto Property and Casualty Insurance, Milbank Insurance, Farmers Casualty Insurance and State Auto Insurance, provides personal and commercial insurance. Co.'s principal lines of business include personal and commercial auto, homeowners, commercial multi-peril, workers' compensation, general liability and fire insurance. As of Dec 2003, Co. marketed its products through about 22,400 independent insurance agents associated with 3,400 agencies in 26 states and the District of Columbia. Co.'s products are marketed primarily in the central and eastern U.S., excluding New York, New Jersey and the New England States.

Recent Developments: For the year ended Dec 31 2003, net income jumped 72.0% to $63.6 million from $37.0 million the previous year. Earnings were fueled by higher net premiums written, as well as disciplined pricing and underwriting initiatives, despite absorbing a record $65.4 million in catastrophe losses. Total revenue increased 7.7% to $1.04 billion from $967.5 million in the prior year. Net premiums written grew 4.7% to $987.3 million. Earned premiums advanced 7.1% to $960.6 million versus $896.6 million a year earlier. Net investment income rose 8.3% to $64.6 million. Co. reported a combined loss and expense ratio of 98.2% compared with 102.4% the year before.

Prospects: Looking ahead, premiums will likely continue to rise, although probably not at the same pace of prior years. At the same time, Co. should benefit from increased policyholder count, reflecting the capacity-related retrenching at other companies. Moreover, Co.'s disciplined approach should allow it to recognize the benefits of its sound underwriting, pricing and claims-handling decisions. As a result of these measures, and the absence of loss reserve strengthening from Meridian business, Co. should report continued operating improvement throughout 2004.

Financial Data

(US$ in Thousands)	12/31/2003	12/31/2002	12/31/2001	12/31/2000	12/31/1999	12/31/1998	12/31/1997	12/31/1996
Earnings Per Share	1.58	0.93	0.52	1.21	1.03	0.87	0.91	0.62
Tang. Book Val. Per Share	13.70	11.89	10.22	9.95	8.22	8.06	6.14	5.14
Dividends Per Share	0.140	0.135	0.125	0.115	0.105	0.095	0.060	0.070
Dividend Payout %	9.17	14.52	24.04	9.50	10.19	10.92	6.86	11.29
Income Statement								
Total Premium Income	960,568	896,595	555,207	397,967	392,058	356,210	254,682	240,345
Other Income	81,128	70,884	68,065	64,807	48,813	45,849	34,326	33,300
Total Revenues	1,041,696	967,479	623,272	462,774	440,871	402,059	289,008	273,645
Total Indirect Exp.	291,823	264,348	167,207	119,569	111,772	104,224	74,213	67,447
Inc. Before Inc. Taxes	83,277	37,790	17,976	61,444	56,985	49,605	47,084	30,148
Income Taxes	19,655	795	(2,639)	13,730	14,169	12,108	13,125	7,546
Net Income	63,622	36,995	20,615	47,714	42,816	37,497	33,959	22,602
Average Shs. Outstg.	40,153	39,743	39,681	39,120	41,526	42,901	37,314	36,140
Balance Sheet								
Cash & Cash Equivalents	40,005	96,048	30,016	21,305	24,560	32,605	23,918	12,868
Premiums Due	14,474	23,035	15,468	9,503	10,807	22,667	12,050	9,691
Invst. Assets: Total	1,570,312	1,272,314	1,138,656	750,870	627,305	579,966	404,179	384,307
Total Assets	1,836,640	1,592,995	1,367,496	898,106	759,945	709,778	493,151	453,120
Long-Term Obligations	161,220	75,500	45,500	45,500	45,500	...	...	...
Net Stockholders' Equity	542,291	463,769	400,193	386,059	317,687	340,824	225,479	186,461
Shares Outstanding	39,559	39,001	38,937	38,554	38,321	42,027	36,684	36,272
Statistical Record								
Return on Equity %	11.73	7.97	5.15	12.35	13.47	11.00	15.06	12.12
Return on Assets %	3.46	2.32	1.50	5.31	5.63	5.28	6.88	4.98
Price Range	26.82-15.33	17.19-13.10	17.67-12.50	18.00-7.19	13.81-8.88	19.88-11.63	16.13-8.38	9.00-6.50
P/E Ratio	16.97-9.70	18.48-14.09	33.98-24.04	14.88-5.94	13.41-8.62	22.84-13.36	17.72-9.20	14.52-10.48
Average Yield %	0.66	0.84	0.58	0.99	1.16	0.59	0.56	0.90

Address: 518 East Broad Street, Columbus, OH 43215-3976	Officers: Robert H. Moone – Chmn., Pres., C.E.O., Mark A. Blackburn – Sr. V.P.	Investor Contact: (614) 464-5373
Telephone: (614) 464-5000		Institutional Holding
Web Site: www.stateauto.com		No of Institutions: 46
		Shares: 4,818,652 % Held: 12%

STATE STREET CORP.

Exchange	Symbol	Price	52Wk Range	Yield	P/E
NYS	STT	$52.13 (3/31/2004)	56.45-32.01	1.15	24.25

*7 Year Price Score 105.9 *NYSE Composite Index=100 *12 Month Price Score 107.5

Interim Earnings (Per Share)

Qtr.	Mar	Jun	Sep	Dec
2000	0.46	0.45	0.45	0.45
2001	0.36	0.50	0.51	0.53
2002	0.54	0.54	0.56	1.46
2003	0.29	(0.07)	0.60	1.33

Interim Dividends (Per Share)

Amt	Decl	Ex	Rec	P
0.14Q	6/19/2003	6/27/2003	7/1/2003	7/15/20
0.14Q	9/18/2003	9/29/2003	10/1/2003	10/15/20
0.15Q	12/18/2003	12/30/2003	1/2/2004	1/15/20
0.15Q	3/18/2004	3/30/2004	4/1/2004	4/15/20
Indicated Div: $0.60 (Div. Reinv. Plan)				

Valuation Analysis

Forecast P/E	19.92	Trailing P/E	24.25
Market Cap	$16.9 Billion	Book Value	5.7 Billion
Price/Book	3.04	Price/Sales	3.65

Dividend Achiever Status

Rank	70	10 Year Growth Rate	15.76%
Total Years of Dividend Growth	23		

Business Summary: Commercial Banking (MIC: 8.1 SIC: 6022 NAIC:522110)

State Street, is a bank holding company with $87.53 billion in assets as of Dec 31 2003, that conducts business worldwide principal through its subsidiary, State Street Bank and Trust Company. Co. has two lines of business: investment servicing and investme management. Investment Servicing includes primarily accounting, custody and other services for large pools of assets. Investme management offers index and active equity strategies, short–term investment funds and fixed income products. As of Dec 31 2003, C had $1.10 trillion in assets under management.

Recent Developments: For the year ended Dec 31 2003, net income fell 28.9% to $722.0 million from $1.01 billion the year befor Results included a net loss of $38.0 million in 2003 and a net gain of $551.0 million in 2002 related to various items. Net interest reven fell 17.3% to $810.0 million, reflecting the challenging interest rate environment. Provision for loan losses amounted to $4.0 million 2002. Total fee revenue grew 24.8% to $3.56 billion, primarily due to the Jan 2003 acquisition of the Global Securities Services busines Servicing fees rose 27.4% to $1.95 billion and management fees grew 9.9% to $533.0 million. Total operating expenses increased 27.5 to $3.62 billion.

Prospects: Co. continues to benefit from its acquisition of the Global Securities Services (GSS) business. As of Dec 31 2003, Co assets under custody were $9.40 trillion, up 51.6% year over year from $6.20 trillion, primarily due to GSS. Separately, Co.'s long–ter revenue goal is for a 12.5% real, or inflation adjusted, compound annual growth rate of revenue from 2000 through 2010. At present, th equates to approximately a 15.0% nominal compound annual growth rate. The return on stockholders'equity goal is 13.0% to 15.0% f 2004. Co. will reevaluate this goal at the end of 2004. Meanwhile, Co. announced the opening of new offices in Milan.

Financial Data

(US$ in Thousands)	12/31/2003	12/31/2002	12/31/2001	12/31/2000	12/31/1999	12/31/1998	12/31/1997	12/31/199
Earnings Per Share	2.15	3.10	1.90	1.81	1.89	1.33	1.16	0.8
Tang. Book Val. Per Share	11.64	12.91	11.87	10.08	8.30	7.19	5.96	5.
Dividends Per Share	0.540	0.460	0.390	0.330	0.290	0.250	0.210	0.1
Dividend Payout %	25.11	14.83	20.52	18.18	15.34	18.79	18.10	20.
Income Statement								
Total Interest Income	1,539,000	1,974,000	2,855,000	3,256,000	2,437,000	2,237,000	1,755,000	1,443,0
Total Interest Expense	729,000	995,000	1,830,000	2,362,000	1,656,000	1,492,000	1,114,000	892,0
Net Interest Income	810,000	979,000	1,025,000	894,000	781,000	745,000	641,000	551,0
Provision for Loan Losses	...	4,000	10,000	9,000	14,000	17,000	16,000	8,0
Non–Interest Income	3,248,000	3,121,000	2,414,000	2,278,000	2,231,000	1,708,000	1,428,000	1,176,0
Non–Interest Expense	3,622,000	2,841,000	2,867,000	2,644,000	2,336,000	2,068,000	1,734,000	1,398,0
Income Before Taxes	436,000	1,255,000	562,000	519,000	662,000	368,000	319,000	321,0
Income from Cont Ops	46,000	715,000	260,000	208,000	313,000	147,000	135,000	167,0
Net Income	722,000	1,015,000	628,000	595,000	619,000	436,000	380,000	293,0
Average Shs. Outstg.	335,326	327,477	330,492	328,088	327,502	327,854	327,578	329,2
Balance Sheet								
Cash & Due from Banks	3,376,000	1,361,000	1,651,000	1,618,000	2,930,000	1,365,000	2,411,000	1,623,0
Securities Avail. for Sale	405,000	29,055,000	21,775,000	14,744,000	15,489,000	10,072,000	10,580,000	9,642,0
Net Loans & Leases	4,960,000	4,113,000	5,283,000	5,216,000	4,245,000	6,225,000	5,479,000	4,640,0
Total Assets	87,534,000	85,794,000	69,896,000	69,298,000	60,896,000	47,082,000	37,975,000	31,524,0
Total Deposits	47,516,000	45,468,000	38,559,000	37,937,000	34,145,000	27,539,000	24,878,000	19,519,0
Long–Term Obligations	2,222,000	1,270,000	1,217,000	1,219,000	921,000	922,000	774,000	476,0
Total Liabilities	81,787,000	81,007,000	66,051,000	66,036,000	58,244,000	44,771,000	35,980,000	29,749,0
Net Stockholders' Equity	5,747,000	4,787,000	3,845,000	3,262,000	2,652,000	2,311,000	1,995,000	1,775,0
Shares Outstanding	334,474	324,927	323,670	323,422	319,180	321,390	334,446	324,6
Statistical Record								
Return on Equity %	0.80	14.93	6.76	6.37	11.80	6.36	6.76	9.
Return on Assets %	0.05	0.83	0.37	0.30	0.51	0.31	0.35	0.
Equity/Assets %	6.56	5.57	5.50	4.70	4.35	4.90	5.25	5.
Non–Int. Exp./Tot. Inc. %	66.30	52.65	50.86	44.65	46.96	48.84	50.58	50.
Price Range	53.18-31.63	57.59-32.38	62.75-38.66	66.93-31.69	47.63-27.94	36.66-24.72	31.13-15.72	17.06-10.
P/E Ratio	24.73-14.71	18.58-10.45	33.03-20.35	36.98-17.51	25.20-14.78	27.56-18.59	26.83-13.55	19.17-11.
Average Yield %	1.28	1.00	0.77	0.63	0.78	0.78	0.88	1.

Address: 225 Franklin Street, Boston, MA 02110	Officers: David A. Spina – Chmn., C.E.O, John R. Towers – Vice Chmn.	Investor Contact:617–664–3477
Telephone: (617) 786–3000	Transfer Agents:EquiServe Trust Company, N.A., Providence, RI	Institutional Holding No of Institutions: 5
Web Site: www.statestreet.com		Shares: 4,778,310 % Held: –

STEPAN CO.

Exchange	Symbol	Price	52Wk Range	Yield	P/E
NYS	SCL	$22.84 (3/31/2004)	26.20-21.70	3.37	50.76

Year Price Score 101.0 *NYSE Composite Index=100 *12 Month Price Score 92.9

Interim Earnings (Per Share)

Qtr.	Mar	Jun	Sep	Dec
2000	0.41	0.64	0.61	(0.19)
2001	0.36	0.61	0.44	0.18
2002	0.45	0.84	0.58	0.18
2003	0.23	0.49	0.12	(0.39)

Interim Dividends (Per Share)

Amt	Decl	Ex	Rec	Pay
0.19Q	4/29/2003	5/28/2003	5/30/2003	6/13/2003
0.19Q	8/12/2003	8/27/2003	8/29/2003	9/15/2003
0.193Q	11/10/2003	11/25/2003	11/28/2003	12/15/2003
0.193Q	2/10/2004	2/25/2004	2/27/2004	3/15/2004

Indicated Div: $0.77

Valuation Analysis

Forecast P/E N/A	Trailing P/E 50.76
Market Cap $202.4 Million	Book Value 147.5 Million
Price/Book 1.33	Price/Sales 0.26

Dividend Achiever Status

Rank 226 10 Year Growth Rate 6.53%
Total Years of Dividend Growth 37

Business Summary: Chemicals (MIC: 11.1 SIC: 2843 NAIC:325613)

Stepan Company produces specialty and intermediate chemicals. Co. operates in three segments: surfactants, polymers, and specialty products. Surfactants are a principal ingredient in cleaning products such as detergents, shampoos, lotions, toothpastes and cosmetics. Other applications include lubricating ingredients and emulsifiers for agricultural products, plastics and composites. Polymer products include phthalic anhydride, polyols and polyurethane foam systems, which are used in plastics, building materials and refrigeration industries, as well as for coating adhesive, sealant and elastomer applications. Specialty products include chemicals used in food, flavoring and pharmaceuticals.

Recent Developments: For the year ended Dec 31 2003, net income declined 75.6% to $4.9 million versus $20.1 million in the previous year. Earnings were adversely affected by lower North American surfactant sales volume and increased operating expenses. Net sales increased 4.9% to $784.9 million from $748.5 million a year earlier. Surfactant sales rose 3.4% to $620.1 million, primarily due to currency translation gains from strengthening European currencies. Polymer sales climbed 12.4% to $139.8 million, due to passing recent raw material cost increases to customers, as well as higher sales volume and currency translation gains. Gross profit fell 15.3% to $103.7 million from $122.5 million the year before.

Prospects: Efforts to replace recent surfactant volume losses have progressed slower than anticipated. Consequently, Co. is taking aggressive actions to reduce costs including a headcount reduction and a 2004 salary freeze. In 2004, Co. intends to focus its efforts on growing its surfactant business in agricultural, emulsion and polymerization and oilfield markets, as well as achieving further growth in fabric softeners and personal care specialties including new products for soap bars. Separately, Co. has entered into a joint venture agreement with Sinopec, Jinling Petrochemical Corporation in Nanjing, China to manufacture aromatic polyester polyols for the domestic Chinese market.

Financial Data

(US$ in Thousands)	12/31/2003	12/31/2002	12/31/2001	12/31/2000	12/31/1999	12/31/1998	12/31/1997	12/31/1996
Earnings Per Share	0.45	2.05	1.59	1.47	2.08	2.12	1.86	1.71
Cash Flow Per Share	5.01	4.69	5.28	5.22	4.76	5.32	5.73	6.57
Tang. Book Val. Per Share	14.31	13.98	15.40	15.46	14.28	13.24	12.16	11.37
Dividends Per Share	0.760	0.730	0.700	0.660	0.610	0.560	0.510	0.470
Dividend Payout %	169.44	35.97	44.49	45.06	29.44	26.53	27.55	27.92
Income Statement								
Total Revenues	784,855	748,539	711,517	698,937	666,784	610,451	581,949	536,635
Total Indirect Exp.	93,943	88,596	76,004	79,998	79,167	66,172	59,801	55,829
Depreciation & Amort.	41,426	40,117	39,972	39,277	39,452	37,347	35,281	32,138
Operating Income	9,796	33,930	31,225	32,028	41,778	45,423	44,370	40,386
Net Interest Inc./(Exp.)	(8,061)	(7,388)	(7,168)	(8,328)	(8,376)	(7,453)	(7,595)	(7,243)
Income Taxes	360	10,139	9,774	9,395	12,700	15,312	14,464	13,194
Equity Earns/Minority Int.	2,170	3,577	1,869	703	1,427	796	(1,901)	(882)
Net Income	4,911	20,129	16,152	15,008	22,119	23,454	20,410	19,067
Average Shs. Outstg.	9,086	9,802	10,133	10,236	10,632	11,043	10,959	10,002
Balance Sheet								
Cash & Cash Equivalents	4,235	3,188	4,224	3,536	3,969	983	5,507	4,778
Total Current Assets	204,460	185,112	185,194	177,213	166,660	149,758	146,482	153,698
Total Assets	464,217	439,667	435,488	415,049	414,576	404,361	374,936	381,012
Total Current Liabilities	132,939	105,017	109,730	108,341	98,045	87,944	82,693	83,376
Long-Term Obligations	92,004	104,304	109,588	96,466	107,420	107,708	94,898	102,567
Net Stockholders' Equity	162,067	158,829	159,729	154,176	155,064	147,984	137,598	131,615
Net Working Capital	71,521	80,095	75,464	68,872	68,615	61,814	63,789	70,322
Shares Outstanding	8,933	8,880	9,420	9,024	9,487	9,693	9,692	9,817
Statistical Record								
Operating Profit Margin %	1.24	4.53	4.38	4.58	6.26	7.44	7.62	7.52
Return on Equity %	3.03	12.67	10.11	9.73	14.27	15.84	14.83	14.48
Return on Assets %	1.05	4.57	3.70	3.61	5.33	5.80	5.44	5.00
Debt/Total Assets %	19.81	23.72	25.16	23.24	25.91	26.63	25.31	26.91
Price Range	26.80-21.55	29.21-23.55	26.38-17.80	25.00-18.50	26.63-22.25	32.13-23.13	32.25-18.00	20.50-16.00
P/E Ratio	59.56-47.89	14.25-11.49	16.59-11.19	17.01-12.59	12.80-10.70	15.15-10.91	17.34-9.68	11.99-9.36
Average Yield %	3.11	2.75	3.02	3.06	2.52	1.97	2.20	2.54

Address: Edens &Winnetka Road, Northfield, IL 60093	**Officers:** F. Quinn Stepan – Chmn., C.E.O., F. Quinn Stepan – Pres., C.O.O.	**Investor Contact:**847–501–2164
Telephone: (847) 446–7500	**Transfer Agents:**Computershare Investor Services, LLC, Chicago, IL	**Institutional Holding**
Web Site: www.stepan.com		**No of Institutions:** 43
		Shares: 3,082,934 **% Held:** 34.30%

249

STERLING BANCSHARES, INC.

Exchange	Symbol	Price	52Wk Range	Yield	P/E
NMS	SBIB	$13.39 (3/31/2004)	14.22-11.12	1.49	12.17

***7 Year Price Score 120.0** *NYSE Composite Index=100 ***12 Month Price Score 92.1**

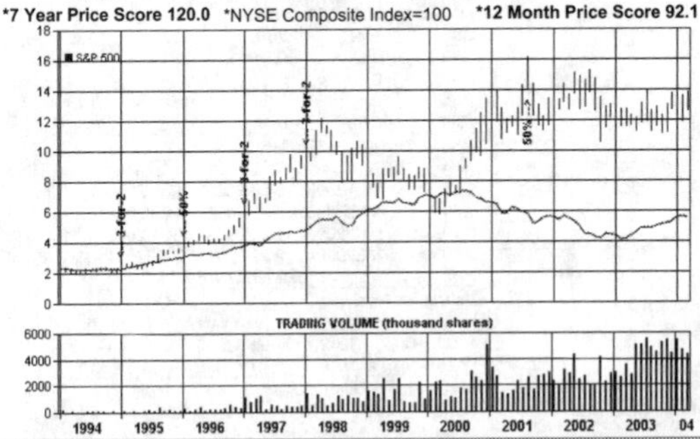

Interim Earnings (Per Share)

Qtr.	Mar	Jun	Sep	Dec
2000	0.15	0.16	0.17	0.18
2001	0.16	0.19	0.18	0.18
2002	0.19	0.21	0.18	0.24
2003	0.21	0.14	0.17	0.58

Interim Dividends (Per Share)

Amt	Decl	Ex	Rec	Pa
0.045Q	4/28/2003	5/7/2003	5/9/2003	5/23/200
0.045Q	7/29/2003	8/6/2003	8/8/2003	8/22/200
0.045Q	10/27/2003	11/5/2003	11/7/2003	11/21/200
0.05Q	1/26/2004	2/4/2004	2/6/2004	2/20/200

Indicated Div: $0.20

Valuation Analysis

Forecast P/E	N/A	Trailing P/E	12.17
Market Cap	$587.6 Million	Book Value	287.1 Million
Price/Book	N/A	Price/Sales	N/A

Dividend Achiever Status

Rank	47	**10 Year Growth Rate**	17.61%
Total Years of Dividend Growth			10

Business Summary: Commercial Banking (MIC: 8.1 SIC: 6022 NAIC:522110)

Sterling Bancshares is a bank holding company that provides commercial and retail banking services primarily in the Houston, Dallas an San Antonio metropolitan areas through the banking offices of Sterling Bank. Co.'s commercial and consumer banking services includ demand, savings and time deposits; commercial, real estate and consumer loans; merchant credit card services; letters of credit; and cas and asset management services. In addition, Co. facilitates sales of brokerage, mutual fund, alternative financing and insurance product through third party vendors. As of Dec 31 2003, Co. had total assets of $3.20 billion and deposits of $2.42 billion.

Recent Developments: For the year ended Dec 31 2003, income from continuing operations was $28.4 million compared with income of $33.2 million the year before. Earnings for 2003 and 2002 included gains of $20.8 million and $3.4 million, respectively, from discontinued operations. Net interest income declined 1.7% to $144.6 million from $147.1 million the previous year, primarily due to the decrease in yields on Co.'s loans, securities and deposits, partially offset by the increased volumes of loans and securities. Provision for credit losses was $17.7 million versus $11.7 million in 2002. Total noninterest income climbed 11.7% to $33.1 million, while total noninterest expense rose 1.3% to $117.6 million.

Prospects: The 2003 divestiture of Sterling Capital Mortgage has provided Co. with greater ability to focus on growing its core bank operations. In line with this focus, Co. completed the integration of the acquired assets of South Texas Capital Group, a privately held bank holding company that operates three banking offices in San Antonio, TX, in Jan 2004. The integration expands Co.'s franchise in the Sa Antonio market to eight offices and is part of Co.'s strategy to grow within the greater Houston, Dallas, and San Antonio, TX area. Looking ahead, Co. will continue to seek further opportunities to expand its presence in these key markets.

Financial Data

(US$ in Thousands)	12/31/2003	12/31/2002	12/31/2001	12/31/2000	12/31/1999	12/31/1998	12/31/1997	12/31/199
Earnings Per Share	0.64	0.82	0.71	0.66	0.54	0.47	0.40	0.3
Tang. Book Val. Per Share	5.09	3.67	3.26	3.89	3.28	2.94	2.52	3.2
Dividends Per Share	0.180	0.160	0.140	0.130	0.120	0.100	0.090	0.08
Dividend Payout %	28.12	19.51	20.66	19.99	22.22	22.53	24.04	21.7
Income Statement								
Total Interest Income	171,383	176,391	173,053	156,430	123,621	103,031	79,268	53,41
Total Interest Expense	26,769	29,719	50,052	58,109	35,132	29,681	24,785	16,72
Net Interest Income	144,614	146,672	123,001	98,321	88,489	73,350	54,483	36,68
Provision for Loan Losses	17,698	14,018	11,684	9,100	8,643	5,892	2,945	2,11
Non-Interest Income	29,561	94,510	66,171	39,567	29,268	20,086	9,419	7,64
Non-Interest Expense	117,603	172,352	130,677	89,927	78,026	62,344	41,618	27,13
Income Before Taxes	38,874	54,812	46,811	38,861	31,088	25,200	19,339	15,08
Eqty Earns/Minority Int.	6,188	6,758	6,989	3,420	3,020	3,467	1,839	31
Income from Cont Ops	24,837	36,673	...	...	...	16,809	12,763	10,60
Net Income	49,110	36,551	30,401	26,580	21,423	17,304	13,083	10,65
Average Shs. Outstg.	44,648	44,756	43,044	39,832	39,505	36,484	32,407	27,76
Balance Sheet								
Cash & Due from Banks	...	...	...	...	...	...	110,479	78,44
Securities Avail. for Sale	522,936	251,165	276,804	238,117	399,961	123,328	97,088	4,17
Net Loans & Leases	2,126,317	1,882,944	1,643,861	1,213,288	1,111,390	851,790	660,541	450,12
Total Assets	3,204,405	3,582,745	2,778,090	1,925,131	1,959,480	1,416,312	1,182,877	790,07
Total Deposits	2,418,369	2,532,902	2,268,980	1,577,735	1,415,551	1,251,685	1,022,220	717,41
Long-Term Obligations	46,533	...	...	...	...	...	...	.
Total Liabilities	2,831,809	3,253,418	2,503,221	1,737,247	1,796,187	1,276,053	1,074,143	730,66
Net Stockholders' Equity	212,596	169,327	159,869	130,384	105,793	82,759	51,234	59,40
Shares Outstanding	44,642	43,982	43,769	39,345	39,045	35,814	30,960	17,92
Statistical Record								
Return on Equity %	8.48	14.70	13.98	16.70	15.92	15.07	15.95	17.8
Return on Assets %	0.77	1.02	1.09	1.38	1.09	1.18	1.07	1.3
Equity/Assets %	9.13	6.95	7.82	8.26	6.86	7.87	6.76	7.5
Non-Int. Exp./Tot. Inc. %	57.51	63.62	54.62	45.88	51.03	50.43	46.75	44.2
Price Range	14.00-11.12	15.30-10.60	16.15-10.83	13.42-5.81	10.04-6.83	12.17-7.96	9.78-5.43	5.59-3.3
P/E Ratio	21.88-17.38	18.66-12.93	22.74-15.26	20.33-8.81	18.60-12.65	25.89-16.93	24.44-13.56	14.72-8.7
Average Yield %	1.46	1.21	1.12	1.54	1.46	0.99	1.19	1.8

Address: 2550 North Loop West, Houston, TX 77092
Telephone: (713) 466-8300
Web Site: N/A

Officers: George Martinez - Chmn., J. Downey Bridgwater - Pres., C.E.O.

Investor Contact: (888) 577-7242
Institutional Holding
No of Institutions: 4
Shares: 132,464 **% Held:** -

STERLING FINANCIAL CORP. (PA)

*7 Year Price Score 125.4 *NYSE Composite Index=100 *12 Month Price Score 99.3

Interim Earnings (Per Share)

Qtr.	Mar	Jun	Sep	Dec
2000	0.24	0.27	0.12	0.21
2001	0.24	0.26	0.25	0.28
2002	0.27	0.28	0.29	0.33
2003	0.31	0.32	0.35	0.37

Interim Dividends (Per Share)

Amt	Decl	Ex	Rec	Pay
0.144Q	8/26/2003	9/11/2003	9/15/2003	10/1/2003
0.144Q	11/18/2003	12/11/2003	12/15/2003	1/2/2004
25%	1/27/2004	2/23/2004	2/6/2004	2/20/2004
0.15Q	2/24/2004	3/11/2004	3/15/2004	4/1/2004
		Indicated Div: $0.60		

Valuation Analysis

Forecast P/E	14.67	Trailing P/E	19.04
Market Cap	$433.9 Million	Book Value	220.0 Million
Price/Book	2.24	Price/Sales	2.78

Dividend Achiever Status

Rank	179	10 Year Growth Rate	8.94%
Total Years of Dividend Growth		16	

Business Summary: Commercial Banking (MIC: 8.1 SIC: 6021 NAIC:522110)

Sterling Financial is a multi-bank financial holding company with $2.34 billion of assets as of Dec 31 2003. Co. provides a broad range of financial services to individuals and businesses through its banking and nonbanking subsidiaries, including personal and business banking, leasing, insurance and wealth management. As of Dec 31 2003, Co. operated 57 branch banking offices in south central Pennsylvania and northern Maryland through its subsidiary banks, Bank of Lancaster County, N.A., Bank of Hanover and Trust Company, and First National Bank of North East.

Recent Developments: For the year ended Dec 31 2003, net income climbed 17.4% to $29.1 million from $24.7 million in the corresponding prior-year period. Earnings for 2003 included securities gains of $511,000, while earnings for 2002 included securities losses of $460,000. Net interest income advanced 14.6% to $85.9 million from $74.9 million the previous year. Provision for loan losses totaled $3.7 million, up 76.5% compared with $2.1 million a year earlier. Non-interest income grew 10.9% to $49.7 million from $44.8 million the year before. Non-interest expense rose 7.7% to $92.6 million from $85.9 million in 2002.

Prospects: On Jan 13 2004, Co. announced that it has entered into a definitive agreement to acquire StoudtAdvisors, a Lancaster, PA-based employee benefits consulting and brokerage firm. Co. anticipates the acquisition will be completed early in the second quarter of 2004 and should be accretive to earnings in the first full year of operation. Terms of the deal were not disclosed. Meanwhile, results are benefiting from strong fee-based revenue growth, which is being fueled by higher mortgage banking income. Earnings are also being positively affected by increased trust and investment services revenues due to improved conditions in the equity markets.

Financial Data

(US$ in Thousands)	12/31/2003	12/31/2002	12/31/2001	12/31/2000	12/31/1999	12/31/1998	12/31/1997	12/31/1996
Earnings Per Share	1.35	1.17	1.03	0.84	0.94	0.91	0.81	0.76
Tang. Book Val. Per Share	8.49	8.44	7.78	7.10	6.45	6.46	5.86	5.42
Dividends Per Share	0.550	0.520	0.490	0.470	0.450	0.410	0.390	0.330
Dividend Payout %	40.88	44.21	47.53	56.43	47.56	45.27	48.21	43.42
Income Statement								
Total Interest Income	127,074	123,591	115,916	113,319	67,714	60,066	56,499	52,558
Total Interest Expense	41,156	48,617	57,274	58,501	29,797	27,925	25,326	22,823
Net Interest Income	85,918	74,974	58,642	54,818	37,917	32,141	31,173	29,735
Provision for Loan Losses	3,697	2,095	1,217	605	420	896	1,129	580
Non-Interest Income	49,721	44,806	43,925	37,508	29,497	14,187	11,930	10,572
Non-Interest Expense	92,568	85,922	75,172	70,203	48,831	30,188	28,082	26,769
Income Before Taxes	39,374	31,763	26,178	21,518	18,163	15,244	13,892	12,958
Net Income	29,059	24,745	20,334	16,567	13,239	11,601	10,401	9,811
Average Shs. Outstg.	21,448	21,028	19,656	19,619	13,960	12,652	12,727	12,786
Balance Sheet								
Cash & Due from Banks	64,996	82,208	68,926	61,287	47,674	34,089	34,242	31,339
Securities Avail. for Sale	540,049	551,696	490,955	435,296	207,183	177,878	121,474	79,375
Net Loans & Leases	1,481,369	1,283,075	1,087,102	1,021,499	654,834	526,591	503,907	466,032
Total Assets	2,343,517	2,156,309	1,861,439	1,726,138	1,059,374	919,264	845,488	764,072
Total Deposits	1,778,587	1,702,302	1,535,649	1,420,300	892,432	781,383	718,661	647,036
Long-Term Obligations	195,762	155,478	121,093	113,850	34,291	...	...	...
Total Liabilities	2,123,506	1,959,476	1,709,328	1,586,791	969,356	837,951	771,501	694,893
Net Stockholders' Equity	220,011	196,833	152,111	139,347	90,018	81,313	73,987	69,179
Shares Outstanding	21,717	21,125	19,549	19,603	13,955	12,578	12,612	12,755
Statistical Record								
Return on Equity %	13.20	12.57	13.36	11.88	14.70	14.26	14.05	14.18
Return on Assets %	1.23	1.14	1.09	0.95	1.24	1.26	1.23	1.28
Equity/Assets %	9.38	9.12	8.17	8.07	8.49	8.84	8.75	9.05
Non-Int. Exp./Tot. Inc. %	52.35	51.02	47.02	46.54	50.23	40.65	41.03	42.40
Price Range	23.54–17.38	21.44–14.40	16.19–9.68	19.84–9.04	23.17–15.87	26.50–15.24	15.60–12.19	13.93–11.64
P/E Ratio	17.44–12.88	18.32–12.31	15.72–9.40	23.62–10.76	24.65–16.89	29.12–16.75	19.26–15.05	18.33–15.32
Average Yield %	2.72	2.88	3.60	4.10	2.47	2.07	3.08	2.62

Address: 101 North Pointe Boulevard, Lancaster, PA 17601-4133 Telephone: (717) 581-6030 Web Site: www.sterlingfi.com	Officers: John E. Stefan – Chmn., J. Roger Moyer – Pres., C.E.O.	Investor Contact:717-735-5602 Institutional Holding No of Institutions: 12 Shares: 219,830 % Held: –

STRYKER CORP.

Exchange	Symbol	Price	52Wk Range	Yield	P/E
NYS	SYK	$88.53 (3/31/2004)	92.77–63.45	0.16	39.70

*7 Year Price Score N/A *NYSE Composite Index=100 *12 Month Price Score 101.1

Interim Earnings (Per Share)

Qtr.	Mar	Jun	Sep	Dec
2000	0.26	0.26	0.25	0.33
2001	0.32	0.32	0.30	0.40
2002	0.40	0.42	0.36	0.52
2003	0.51	0.53	0.53	0.66

Interim Dividends (Per Share)

Amt	Decl	Ex	Rec	Pa
0.08A	12/15/2000	12/27/2000	12/29/2000	1/31/200
0.10A	12/21/2001	12/27/2001	12/31/2001	1/31/200
0.12A	12/3/2002	12/27/2002	12/31/2002	1/31/200
0.14A	12/2/2003	12/29/2003	12/31/2003	1/30/200

Indicated Div: $0.14

Valuation Analysis

Forecast P/E	29.26	Trailing P/E	39.70
Market Cap	$17.5 Billion	Book Value	2.2 Billion
Price/Book	7.85	Price/Sales	4.67

Dividend Achiever Status

Rank	18	10 Year Growth Rate	23.11%
Total Years of Dividend Growth			11

Business Summary: Medical Instruments &Equipment (MIC: 9.6 SIC: 3841 NAIC:339112)

Stryker develops, manufactures and markets specialty surgical and medical products. Operations are divided into two reportable busines segments: Orthopaedic Implants and MedSurg Equipment. The Orthopaedic Implants segment includes orthopaedic reconstructive (hip knee and shoulder), trauma and spinal implants, bone cement and the bone growth factor osteogenic protein–1. The MedSurg Equipme segment includes powered surgical instruments, endoscopic products, hospital beds and stretchers and micro implant and surgica navigation systems. Co. also provides outpatient physical and occupational rehabilitative services in the U.S.

Recent Developments: For the year ended Dec 31 2003, net income grew 31.2% to $453.5 million from $345.6 million in the pric year. Results for 2002 included restructuring and acquisition–related charges of $17.2 million. Net sales increased 20.4% to $3.63 billio Sales of Orthopaedic Implants climbed 22.8% to $2.09 billion from $1.70 billion a year earlier, reflecting higher shipments c reconstructive trauma and spinal implants. Sales of MedSurg Equipment increased 18.5% to $1.31 billion, due to higher shipments c powered surgical instruments, endoscopic products, hospital beds and stretchers and micro implant and surgical navigation systems. Sale from Physical therapy services rose 10.7% to $223.0 million.

Prospects: In response to the underlying growth rates in orthopaedic procedures, Co. announced that it would construct manufacturin facilities in Portage, MI over the next two years. Specifically, Co. expects to construct an additional 200,000 square–foot manufacturin facility and make renovations to Stryker Instruments' existing 250,000 square–foot facility. Additionally, a new 400,000 square–foo manufacturing facility will be constructed at Stryker Medical. For 2004, Co. expects net sales growth of about 16.0%, reflecting stron shipments of Orthopaedic Implants and MedSurg Equipment, favorable foreign currency rates and higher physical therapy revenue. C expects net income per share of $2.68.

Financial Data

(US$ in Thousands)	12/31/2003	12/31/2002	12/31/2001	12/31/2000	12/31/1999	12/31/1998	12/31/1997	12/31/1996
Earnings Per Share	2.23	1.70	1.34	1.10	0.10	0.20	0.64	0.5
Cash Flow Per Share	3.18	2.47	2.30	1.64	1.43	0.78	0.46	1.0
Tang. Book Val. Per Share	5.95	2.84	1.29	0.07	N.M	N.M	2.94	2.5
Dividends Per Share	0.120	0.100	0.080	0.060	0.060	0.050	0.050	0.02
Dividend Payout %	5.38	5.88	5.97	5.90	60.00	27.50	7.81	3.7
Income Statement								
Total Revenues	3,625,300	3,011,600	2,602,300	2,289,400	2,103,700	1,103,208	980,135	910,06
Total Indirect Exp.	1,641,600	1,352,900	1,166,500	1,041,500	966,400	575,509	398,395	444,60
Depreciation & Amort.	90,800	57,800	76,800	69,400	67,800	37,596	33,264	34,65
Operating Income	716,700	576,400	510,400	467,400	181,500	55,626	183,974	31,31
Net Interest Inc./(Exp.)	(22,600)	(40,300)	(67,900)	(96,600)	(122,600)	...	...	...
Income Taxes	199,000	161,100	133,900	113,900	10,440	20,390	70,000	61,65
Eqty Earns/Minority Int.	(45,400)	(28,900)	(38,400)	(34,700)	(33,900)	...	870	5,66
Income from Cont Ops	...	346,600	271,800	...	...	...	...	(17,728
Net Income	453,500	345,600	267,000	221,000	19,400	39,570	125,320	104,46
Average Shs. Outstg.	203,400	203,800	203,000	201,100	198,600	196,260	196,264	193,67
Balance Sheet								
Cash & Cash Equivalents	65,900	37,800	50,100	54,000	83,500	142,209	351,068	367,57
Total Current Assets	1,397,600	1,151,300	993,100	997,000	1,110,400	1,311,843	756,408	753,53
Total Assets	3,159,100	2,815,500	2,423,600	2,430,800	2,580,500	2,885,852	985,075	993,50
Total Current Liabilities	850,500	707,500	533,400	617,400	669,600	699,455	303,011	251,74
Long–Term Obligations	18,800	491,000	720,900	876,500	1,181,100	1,487,971	4,449	89,50
Net Stockholders' Equity	2,154,800	1,498,200	1,056,500	854,900	671,500	652,075	612,775	530,36
Net Working Capital	547,100	443,800	459,700	379,600	440,800	612,388	453,597	501,79
Shares Outstanding	199,700	198,100	196,700	195,900	194,400	193,080	192,118	193,57
Statistical Record								
Operating Profit Margin %	19.76	19.13	19.61	20.41	8.62	5.04	18.77	3.4
Return on Equity %	21.04	23.13	25.73	25.85	2.88	6.06	20.45	N.M
Return on Assets %	14.35	12.31	11.21	9.09	0.75	1.37	12.72	N.M
Debt/Total Assets %	0.59	17.43	29.74	36.05	45.77	51.56	0.45	9.0
Price Range	85.01–60.24	67.23–45.44	61.51–44.11	54.00–25.50	35.84–22.38	27.53–15.53	22.31–17.91	..
P/E Ratio	38.12–27.01	39.55–26.73	45.90–32.92	49.09–23.18	358.4–223.8	137.7–77.66	34.86–27.98	
Average Yield %	0.17	0.17	0.15	0.15	0.21	0.25	0.25	N/A

Address: 2725 Fairfield Road, Kalamazoo, MI 49002 Telephone: (269) 385–2600 Web Site: www.strykercorp.com	Officers: John W. Brown – Chmn., C.E.O., Stephen P. MacMillan – Pres., C.O.O. Transfer Agents:National City Bank, Cleveland, OH	Investor Contact:616–385–2600 Institutional Holding No of Institutions: 32 Shares: 276,883,031 % Held: –

SUNTRUST BANKS, INC.

Exchange	Symbol	Price	52Wk Range	Yield	P/E
NYS	STI	$69.71 (3/31/2004)	76.41–51.56	2.87	14.74

Year Price Score 98.1 *NYSE Composite Index=100 *12 Month Price Score 102.8

Interim Earnings (Per Share)

Qtr.	Mar	Jun	Sep	Dec
2000	1.04	1.05	1.10	1.11
2001	1.14	1.25	1.15	1.16
2002	1.06	1.20	1.20	1.20
2003	1.17	1.17	1.18	1.21

Interim Dividends (Per Share)

Amt	Decl	Ex	Rec	Pay
0.45Q	4/15/2003	5/28/2003	5/30/2003	6/13/2003
0.45Q	8/12/2003	8/27/2003	8/29/2003	9/15/2003
0.45Q	11/11/2003	11/26/2003	12/1/2003	12/15/2003
0.50Q	2/10/2004	2/26/2004	3/1/2004	3/15/2004

Indicated Div: $2.00 (Div. Reinv. Plan)

Valuation Analysis

Forecast P/E	12.49	Trailing P/E	14.74
Market Cap	$19.9 Billion	Book Value	9.7 Billion
Price/Book	2.07	Price/Sales	2.85

Dividend Achiever Status

Rank	120	10 Year Growth Rate	11.99%
Total Years of Dividend Growth			18

Business Summary: Commercial Banking (MIC: 8.1 SIC: 6021 NAIC:522110)

SunTrust Banks, through its primary subsidiary, SunTrust Bank, provides deposit, credit, trust and investment services to a broad range of retail, business and institutional clients. Other subsidiaries provide mortgage banking, credit–related insurance, asset management, brokerage and capital market services. Co. operates 1,201 traditional and in–store branches and 2,225 ATMs located in Florida, Georgia, Maryland, Tennessee, Virginia and the District of Columbia. In addition, Co. provides customers with a full range of technology–based banking channels including Internet, personal computer and telephone banking. At Dec 31 2003, Co. had total assets of $125.39 billion.

Recent Developments: For the twelve months ended Dec 31 2003, net income totaled $1.33 billion, essentially unchanged compared with the corresponding prior–year period. Results for 2002 included a pre–tax merger–related charge of $16.0 million. Net interest income climbed 2.4% to $3.32 billion from $3.24 billion the previous year. Provision for loan losses fell 33.3% to $313.6 million from $469.8 million a year earlier. Total non–interest income grew 1.5% to $2.30 billion from $2.27 billion in 2002, while total non–interest expense increased 5.6% to $3.40 billion from $3.22 billion the prior year. Total assets amounted to $125.39 billion as of Dec 31 2003, up 6.9% versus $117.32 billion on Dec 31 2002.

Prospects: Results are being positively affected by higher net interest income and continued solid fee income growth, partially offset by weak commercial loan demand. Meanwhile, non–interest income growth is being fueled by increases in service charges on deposit accounts, higher investment banking and trading income, and increased mortgage servicing income. Separately, higher non–interest expenses are resulting from the consolidation of certain affordable housing partnerships and the integration of Lighthouse Financial, which was completed in January 2004. Looking ahead, Co. expects mid– to high–single digit percentage growth in loans during 2004, including a gradual increase in corporate lending.

Financial Data

(US$ in Thousands)	12/31/2003	12/31/2002	12/31/2001	12/31/2000	12/31/1999	12/31/1998	12/31/1997	12/31/1996
Earnings Per Share	4.73	4.66	4.70	4.30	3.50	3.04	3.13	2.76
Tang. Book Val. Per Share	28.42	26.55	26.66	25.07	23.24	22.98	23.37	20.87
Dividends Per Share	1.800	1.720	1.600	1.480	1.380	1.000	0.920	0.820
Dividend Payout %	38.05	36.90	34.04	34.41	39.42	32.89	29.55	29.71
Income Statement								
Total Interest Income	4,768,842	5,135,197	6,279,574	6,845,419	5,960,208	5,675,900	3,650,739	3,246,042
Total Interest Expense	1,448,539	1,891,488	3,026,974	3,736,981	2,814,752	2,746,779	1,756,373	1,461,832
Net Interest Income	3,320,303	3,243,709	3,252,600	3,108,438	3,145,456	2,929,121	1,894,366	1,784,210
Provision for Loan Losses	313,550	469,792	275,165	133,974	170,437	214,602	117,043	115,916
Non–Interest Income	2,303,001	2,391,675	2,155,823	1,773,625	1,660,031	1,716,173	934,238	817,989
Non–Interest Expense	3,400,616	3,342,268	3,113,538	2,828,533	2,939,393	2,932,386	1,685,595	1,583,083
Income Before Taxes	1,909,138	1,823,324	2,019,720	1,919,556	1,695,657	1,498,306	1,025,966	903,200
Income from Cont Ops	...	...	1,369,219	...	1,123,952	...	...	...
Net Income	1,332,297	1,331,809	1,375,537	1,294,100	1,326,600	971,017	667,253	616,615
Average Shs. Outstg.	281,434	286,052	291,584	300,956	317,079	319,711	213,480	223,486
Balance Sheet								
Cash & Due from Banks	3,931,653	4,455,776	4,229,074	4,110,489	3,909,687	4,289,889	2,991,263	3,037,309
Securities Avail. for Sale	26,051,796	25,162,956	20,999,993	19,752,165	18,576,844	17,798,708	178,434	80,377
Net Loans & Leases	79,790,399	72,237,821	68,092,163	71,365,273	65,131,508	60,596,089	39,383,675	34,678,322
Total Assets	125,393,153	117,322,523	104,740,644	103,496,380	95,389,968	93,169,932	57,982,736	52,468,249
Total Deposits	81,189,519	79,706,628	67,536,422	69,533,337	60,100,529	59,033,283	38,197,528	36,890,389
Long–Term Obligations	15,313,922	10,229,820	11,010,580	7,895,430	4,967,346	4,757,869	3,171,832	1,565,341
Total Liabilities	115,661,987	108,553,027	96,381,076	95,257,172	87,763,106	84,991,288	52,783,354	47,588,269
Net Stockholders' Equity	9,731,166	8,769,496	8,359,568	8,239,208	7,626,862	8,178,644	5,199,382	4,879,980
Shares Outstanding	281,923	270,843	283,040	296,266	293,543	321,124	209,909	220,469
Statistical Record								
Return on Equity %	13.69	15.18	16.37	15.70	14.73	11.87	12.83	12.63
Return on Assets %	1.06	1.13	1.30	1.25	1.17	1.04	1.15	1.17
Equity/Assets %	7.76	7.47	7.98	7.96	7.99	8.77	8.96	9.30
Non–Int. Exp./Tot. Inc. %	48.08	44.40	36.91	32.81	38.57	39.66	36.76	38.95
Price Range	71.55–51.56	70.00–51.79	71.81–58.10	68.81–42.56	79.81–62.25	87.44–54.94	74.94–44.38	51.75–32.25
P/E Ratio	15.13–10.90	15.02–11.11	15.28–12.36	16.00–9.90	22.80–17.79	28.76–18.07	23.94–14.18	18.75–11.68
Average Yield %	2.96	2.71	2.48	2.80	2.01	1.38	1.56	2.10

Address: 303 Peachtree Street, NE, Atlanta, GA 30308	**Officers:** L. Phillip Humann – Chmn., Pres., C.E.O., John W. Spiegal – Vice–Chmn., C.F.O.	**Investor Contact:**404–658–4879
Telephone: (404) 588–7711	**Transfer Agents:**SunTrust Bank Atlanta, Atlanta, GA	**Institutional Holding**
Web Site: www.suntrust.com		**No of Institutions:** 469
		Shares: 136,966,850 **% Held:** 48.90%

SUPERIOR INDUSTRIES INTERNATIONAL, INC.

Exchange	Symbol	Price	52Wk Range	Yield	P/E
NYS	SUP	$35.44 (3/31/2004)	45.91–34.20	1.55	12.98

*7 Year Price Score 126.2 *NYSE Composite Index=100 *12 Month Price Score 94.7

Interim Earnings (Per Share)

Qtr.	Mar	Jun	Sep	Dec
2000	0.70	0.83	0.66	0.85
2001	0.61	0.51	0.41	0.57
2002	0.65	0.78	0.65	0.83
2003	0.83	0.66	0.40	0.84

Interim Dividends (Per Share)

Amt	Decl	Ex	Rec	Pa
0.138Q	5/9/2003	7/1/2003	7/3/2003	7/18/200
0.138Q	7/28/2003	10/1/2003	10/3/2003	10/17/200
0.138Q	11/5/2003	1/7/2004	1/9/2004	1/23/200
0.138Q	3/23/2004	4/6/2004	4/9/2004	4/23/200

Indicated Div: $0.55 (Div. Reinv. Plan)

Valuation Analysis

Forecast P/E	12.31	Trailing P/E	12.98
Market Cap	$934.4 Million	Book Value	592.2 Million
Price/Book	1.97	Price/Sales	1.39

Dividend Achiever Status

Rank	53	10 Year Growth Rate	16.92%
Total Years of Dividend Growth			18

Business Summary: Automotive (MIC: 15.1 SIC: 3714 NAIC:336399)

Superior Industries International designs and manufactures automotive parts and accessories for original equipment manufacture (OEMs). Co. supplies cast and forged aluminum wheels to automobile and light truck manufacturers, with wheel manufacturing faciliti in the U.S., Mexico and Hungary. The OEM cast aluminum road wheels, Co.'s primary product, are sold to General Motors and For which together accounted for 85.0% of 2003 sales, as well as to DaimlerChrysler, Audi, BMW, Isuzu, Jaguar, Land Rover, Mazda, M Rover, Mitsubishi, Nissan, Subaru, Toyota and Volkswagen. Co. also manufactures aluminum suspension and underbody components.

Recent Developments: For the year ended Dec 31 2003, net income decreased 5.8% to $73.7 million compared with $78.3 million th previous year. Results for 2002 included start–up and pre–production costs of $8.5 million. Net sales advanced 7.4% to $840.3 millic from $782.6 million a year earlier, due to a 3.0% increase in unit shipments and 3.0% higher average aluminum wheel selling price Gross profit fell 11.8% to $123.8 million, or 14.7% of net sales, from $140.3 million, or 17.9% of net sales, the year before. The declin in gross margin reflects the inclusion of costs associated with Co.'s aluminum suspension and underbody parts business, and decreases certain high–volume, high–profit specialty wheels.

Prospects: Co.'s original equipment manufacturer customers continue to demand higher wheel volumes at increasingly competitiv prices. To meet these requirements, Co. is focused on a long–term strategy to realize efficiency and productivity gains throug automation, implementation of best practices, and employee training and development. Co. expects earnings for the first quarter of 200 to be approximately $0.50 per diluted share. The impact of lower pricing due to the intense global competitive environment in Co. specific product group, and certain operating problems that are undergoing focused improvement programs at several of its expande plants, are the main causes for this lower outlook.

Financial Data

(US$ in Thousands)	12/31/2003	12/31/2002	12/31/2001	12/31/2000	12/31/1999	12/31/1998	12/31/1997	12/31/199
Earnings Per Share	2.73	2.91	2.10	3.04	2.62	1.88	1.96	1.6
Cash Flow Per Share	2.83	3.56	2.24	3.64	3.21	2.86	2.64	3.3
Tang. Book Val. Per Share	22.12	19.96	17.30	15.45	13.34	11.42	10.30	8.8
Dividends Per Share	0.520	0.470	0.420	0.380	0.340	0.300	0.260	0.22
Dividend Payout %	19.23	16.15	20.00	12.50	12.97	15.95	13.26	13.5
Income Statement								
Total Revenues	840,349	782,599	643,395	644,899	571,782	539,431	549,131	504,24
Total Indirect Exp.	22,902	30,843	29,249	20,716	20,310	19,758	19,986	19,93
Depreciation & Amort.	33,577	32,605	28,388	26,920	28,523	26,698	26,917	27,33
Operating Income	100,889	109,467	76,106	121,505	105,208	80,346	88,184	81,78
Net Interest Inc./(Exp.)	2,727	3,519	4,048	7,323	5,451	4,287	2,170	(32(
Income Taxes	39,695	42,134	28,835	42,573	37,710	28,482	30,819	27,22
Eqty Earns/Minority Int.	8,655	6,260	3,941	...	...	...	...	
Net Income	73,720	78,250	55,354	79,937	70,808	52,319	55,389	46,85
Average Shs. Outstg.	27,033	26,907	26,361	26,255	27,056	27,818	28,221	28,79
Balance Sheet								
Cash & Cash Equivalents	156,847	155,184	106,839	93,503	108,081	86,566	73,693	42,10
Total Current Assets	388,510	368,941	280,271	245,579	263,740	235,886	199,846	164,08
Total Assets	703,205	645,796	540,838	491,664	460,468	427,430	382,679	357,59
Total Current Liabilities	83,621	97,123	71,137	75,022	86,847	91,111	65,415	76,3(
Long–Term Obligations	...	...	...	...	340	673	1,344	1,94
Net Stockholders' Equity	592,206	530,431	448,741	399,319	353,086	312,034	287,416	251,1
Net Working Capital	304,889	271,818	209,134	170,557	176,893	144,775	134,431	87,7
Shares Outstanding	26,768	26,573	25,932	25,840	26,454	27,312	27,902	28,32
Statistical Record								
Operating Profit Margin %	12.00	13.98	11.82	18.84	18.40	14.89	16.05	16.2
Return on Equity %	12.44	14.75	12.33	20.01	20.05	16.76	19.27	18.6
Return on Assets %	10.48	12.11	10.23	16.25	15.37	12.24	14.47	13.
Debt/Total Assets %	...	...	...	...	0.07	0.15	0.35	0.5
Price Range	45.91–33.89	53.12–36.20	44.62–29.40	35.31–23.50	29.06–22.81	33.50–20.19	29.38–22.50	28.25–22.7
P/E Ratio	16.82–12.41	18.25–12.44	21.25–14.00	11.62–7.73	11.09–8.71	17.82–10.74	14.99–11.48	17.33–13.9
Average Yield %	1.26	1.06	1.13	1.28	1.29	1.10	1.01	0.8

Address: 7800 Woodley Avenue, Van Nuys, CA 91406	Officers: Louis L. Borick – Chmn., C.E.O., Steven J. Borick – Pres., C.O.O.	Institutional Holding No of Institutions: 10
Telephone: (818) 781–4973	Transfer Agents:Registrar and Transfer Company, Cranford, NJ	Shares: 11,573,062 % Held: –
Web Site: www.supind.com		

SUPERVALU INC.

Exchange	Symbol	Price	52Wk Range	Yield	P/E
NYS	SVU	$30.54 (3/31/2004)	30.54-15.50	1.90	16.60

Year Price Score 103.5 *NYSE Composite Index=100 *12 Month Price Score 112.4

Interim Earnings (Per Share)

Qtr.	Jun	Sep	Dec	Feb
2000–01	0.53	0.43	0.36	(0.70)
2001–02	0.45	0.39	0.44	0.25
2002–03	0.57	0.44	0.43	0.47
2003–04	0.55	0.46	0.36	...

Interim Dividends (Per Share)

Amt	Decl	Ex	Rec	Pay
0.143Q	4/9/2003	5/29/2003	6/2/2003	6/16/2003
0.145Q	8/13/2003	8/28/2003	9/2/2003	9/15/2003
0.145Q	10/3/2003	11/26/2003	12/1/2003	12/15/2003
0.145Q	2/11/2004	2/26/2004	3/1/2004	3/15/2004

Indicated Div: $0.58 (Div. Reinv. Plan)

Valuation Analysis

Forecast P/E	10.78	Trailing P/E	N/A
Market Cap	$4.1 Billion	Book Value	N/A
Price/Book	N/A	Price/Sales	N/A

Dividend Achiever Status

Rank	279	10 Year Growth Rate 3.31%
Total Years of Dividend Growth	31	

Business Summary: Retail - Food &Beverage (MIC: 5.3 SIC: 5141 NAIC:424410)

Supervalu is a major food retailer and distributor to independently-owned retail food stores. As of Jul 10 2003, Co. operated 1,170 Save-A-Lot limited assortment stores, including 794 licensed Save-A-Lot locations, 279 Co.-owned stores and 97 Deals-Nothing Over A Dollar general merchandise stores; 266 regional supermarkets under the Cub Foods, Shop 'n Save, Shoppers Food Warehouse, bigg's, Farm Fresh, Scott's Foods, and Hornbacher's banners. Additionally, Co. is the primary supplier to approximately 2,500 retail grocery stores, as well as 29 of Co.'s franchised Cub Foods locations and its 266 regional supermarkets, while serving as a secondary supplier to about 1,400 stores.

Recent Developments: For the 12 weeks ended Nov 29 2003, net earnings declined 14.9% to $48.6 million compared with $57.1 million in the corresponding period the year before. Results for 2003 included after-tax restructuring and other charges of $4.5 million. Net sales climbed 4.1% to $4.74 billion from $4.55 billion a year earlier. Retail food net sales grew 6.5% to $2.42 billion from $2.27 billion in 2002, while food distribution net sales rose 1.7% to $2.32 billion from $2.28 billion in the prior-year period. Operating earnings totaled $127.4 million, down 0.8% compared with $128.5 million the previous year. Earnings before income taxes slipped 1.3% to $89.5 million from $90.7 million the year before.

Prospects: During the third quarter of fiscal 2004, Co. announced the sale of its operations in Denver, CO that included nine retail stores and a distribution warehouse building. The sale is strategically in line with Co.'s plan to divest underperforming operations. Separately, Co. projects full-year fiscal 2004 earnings per share in the range of $2.04 to $2.10 and earnings per share for the fourth quarter of $0.67 to $0.73. Looking ahead to fiscal 2005, comparable store sales are projected to increase 1.0% to 2.0% based on a recovering economy, planned in-market store expansion, and a modest inflationary environment.

Financial Data

(US$ in Thousands)	9 Mos	6 Mos	3 Mos	02/22/2003	02/23/2002	02/24/2001	02/26/2000	02/27/1999
Earnings Per Share	1.38	1.02	0.55	1.91	1.53	0.62	1.87	1.57
Cash Flow Per Share	3.53	3.39	1.60	4.25	5.87	4.90	2.62	4.59
Tang. Book Val. Per Share	4.30	3.95	3.61	3.23	2.90	1.63	1.58	6.09
Dividends Per Share	0.573	0.570	0.568	0.565	0.550	0.540	0.530	0.520
Dividend Payout %	41.48	55.88	103.18	29.58	36.27	87.90	28.60	33.43
Income Statement								
Total Revenues	15,165,920	10,426,937	5,836,287	19,160,368	20,908,522	23,194,279	20,339,079	17,420,507
Total Indirect Exp.	1,662,235	1,144,047	638,916	2,023,028	2,084,071	2,213,523	1,481,275	1,382,212
Depreciation & Amort.	...	...	...	297,069	340,750	343,779	277,062	233,523
Operating Income	421,389	293,947	161,830	569,943	516,477	345,192	582,846	418,168
Net Interest Inc./(Exp.)	(115,266)	(77,371)	(44,428)	(161,939)	(172,774)	(190,835)	(135,392)	(101,907)
Income Taxes	121,605	80,674	43,732	150,962	138,168	72,392	204,513	124,923
Net Income	184,518	135,902	73,670	257,042	205,535	81,965	242,941	191,338
Average Shs. Outstg.	133,848	133,790	134,118	134,877	133,978	132,829	130,090	121,961
Balance Sheet								
Cash & Cash Equivalents	52,274	205,327	71,777	29,188	12,171	10,396	10,920	7,608
Total Current Assets	1,962,064	1,952,292	1,768,264	1,647,366	1,604,027	2,091,676	2,177,639	1,582,527
Total Assets	6,117,381	6,145,737	6,007,591	5,896,245	5,824,782	6,407,172	6,495,353	4,265,949
Total Current Liabilities	1,954,291	1,697,285	1,571,194	1,525,307	1,701,489	2,341,170	2,509,620	1,521,907
Long-Term Obligations	1,624,852	1,978,592	2,018,390	2,019,658	1,875,873	2,008,474	1,953,741	1,246,269
Net Stockholders' Equity	2,142,161	2,111,531	2,065,534	2,009,240	1,916,693	1,793,495	1,821,479	1,305,639
Net Working Capital	7,773	255,007	197,070	122,059	(97,462)	(249,494)	(331,981)	60,620
Shares Outstanding	134,399	134,088	133,804	133,688	132,889	132,374	134,662	120,109
Statistical Record								
Operating Profit Margin %	2.77	2.81	2.77	2.97	2.47	1.48	2.86	2.40
Return on Equity %	8.61	6.43	3.56	12.79	10.72	4.57	13.33	14.65
Return on Assets %	3.01	2.21	1.22	4.35	3.52	1.27	3.74	4.48
Debt/Total Assets %	26.56	32.19	33.59	34.25	32.20	31.34	30.07	29.21
Price Range	26.24-12.60	24.91-12.60	22.64-12.60	30.50-14.32	24.68-12.80	22.50-11.75	26.13-16.19	28.75-20.31
P/E Ratio	19.01-9.13	24.42-12.35	41.16-22.91	15.97-7.50	16.13-8.37	36.29-18.95	13.97-8.66	18.31-12.94
Average Yield %	2.72	2.96	3.40	2.60	2.88	3.22	2.47	2.16

Address: 11840 Valley View Road, Eden Prairie, MN 55344 **Telephone:** (952) 828-4000 **Web Site:** www.supervalu.com	**Officers:** Jeffrey Noddle – Chmn., Pres., C.E.O., Pamela K. Knous – Exec. V.P., C.F.O. **Transfer Agents:** Wells Fargo Shareowner Services, St. Paul, MN	**Investor Contact:**952-828-4000 **Institutional Holding** **No of Institutions:** 13 **Shares:** 370,545 **% Held:** –

SUSQUEHANNA BANCSHARES, INC

Exchange	Symbol	Price	52Wk Range	Yield	P/E
NMS	SUSQ	$25.68 (3/31/2004)	27.80–21.00	3.43	16.46

*7 Year Price Score 123.0 *NYSE Composite Index=100 ***12 Month Price Score 96.3**

Interim Earnings (Per Share)

Qtr.	Mar	Jun	Sep	Dec
2000	0.34	0.35	0.36	0.35
2001	0.32	0.36	0.36	0.37
2002	0.37	0.39	0.40	0.39
2003	0.40	0.41	0.40	0.35

Interim Dividends (Per Share)

Amt	Decl	Ex	Rec	P
0.21Q	4/16/2003	4/28/2003	4/30/2003	5/20/20
0.22Q	7/16/2003	7/28/2003	7/30/2003	8/20/20
0.22Q	10/15/2003	10/28/2003	10/30/2003	11/20/20
0.22Q	1/21/2004	1/29/2004	2/2/2004	2/20/20
Indicated Div: $0.88 (Div. Reinv. Plan)				

Valuation Analysis

Forecast P/E	15.76	Trailing P/E	16.46
Market Cap	$1.0 Billion	Book Value	547.4 Million
Price/Book	1.87	Price/Sales	2.64

Dividend Achiever Status

Rank	207	10 Year Growth Rate	7.69%
Total Years of Dividend Growth			33

Business Summary: Commercial Banking (MIC: 8.1 SIC: 6021 NAIC:522110)

Susquehanna Bancshares is a financial holding company that provides a wide range of retail and commercial banking and financial servic through its subsidiaries in the mid-Atlantic region. Co. operates eight commercial banks, a trust and investment company, an ass management company, a property and casualty insurance brokerage company and a vehicle company. Co.'s depository institution subsidia ies provide commercial and retail banking services in Pennsylvania, Maryland, and New Jersey. As of Dec 31 2003, Co. had total assets $5.95 billion, net loans and leases of $4.22 billion and total deposits of $4.13 billion.

Recent Developments: For the year ended Dec 31 2003, net income climbed 1.1% to $62.4 million compared with $61.7 million 2002. Results for 2003 and 2002 included gains on the sale of loans and leases of $9.7 million and $4.6 million, and net gains on securiti of $2.1 million and $3.4 million, respectively. Net interest income slipped 0.1% to $187.0 million versus $187.2 million the year befo Provision for loan and lease losses declined 4.1% to $10.2 million from $10.7 million a year earlier. Total non-interest income rose 8.1% $101.8 million from $94.2 million and total non-interest expense climbed 4.3% to $189.4 million from $181.7 million the year before.

Prospects: The definitive merger agreement that was signed in December 2003 between Co. and Patriot Bank, a $1.00 billion financia holding company with 20 offices in the Greater Delaware Valley region of Pennsylvania, is on track. The transaction will enhance Co presence in the high-growth counties of Berks, Chester, Lehigh, Montgomery and Northampton, PA. The acquisition is expected to completed in the second quarter of 2004. Meanwhile, Farmers First Bank, a subsidiary of Co., is building a 33,000 square-foot, three-stor building in Lancaster, PA. The relocation of Farmers' headquarters will allow it to better fuel its growth. The new building is expected be completed in the fall of 2004.

Financial Data

(US$ in Thousands)	12/31/2003	12/31/2002	12/31/2001	12/31/2000	12/31/1999	12/31/1998	12/31/1997	12/31/199
Earnings Per Share	1.56	1.55	1.41	1.40	1.17	1.26	1.20	1.
Tang. Book Val. Per Share	12.13	11.95	12.54	11.56	10.92	10.90	10.24	9.
Dividends Per Share	0.860	0.810	0.770	0.700	0.620	0.570	0.540	0.5
Dividend Payout %	55.12	52.25	54.60	50.00	52.99	45.23	45.55	51.
Income Statement								
Total Interest Income	286,020	316,713	341,295	353,416	299,770	292,766	264,100	231,8
Total Interest Expense	99,014	129,473	169,051	188,464	138,848	138,576	118,447	103,1
Net Interest Income	187,006	187,240	172,244	164,952	160,922	154,190	145,653	128,6
Provision for Loan Losses	10,222	10,664	7,310	3,726	7,200	5,247	4,557	4,5
Non-Interest Income	101,750	94,150	84,166	74,010	39,979	30,921	23,754	21,3
Non-Interest Expense	189,430	181,663	167,763	155,581	131,882	113,206	106,028	100,8
Income Before Taxes	89,104	89,063	81,337	79,655	61,879	66,658	58,822	44,6
Net Income	62,373	61,721	55,716	54,962	43,397	45,574	40,202	29,9
Average Shs. Outstg.	40,037	39,932	39,593	39,365	37,137	36,179	33,495	29,6
Balance Sheet								
Cash & Due from Banks	176,240	156,320	149,233	129,101	144,548	105,263	97,341	98,5
Securities Avail. for Sale	1,062,844	1,174,866	1,107,878	941,320	896,647	949,101	615,426	550,1
Net Loans & Leases	4,220,600	3,791,282	3,481,800	3,396,423	2,957,919	2,738,379	2,535,063	2,141,1
Total Assets	5,953,100	5,544,647	5,051,092	4,792,856	4,310,606	4,064,827	3,524,887	3,038,4
Total Deposits	4,134,467	3,831,344	3,484,331	3,249,013	3,180,520	3,124,332	2,851,217	2,493,5
Long-Term Obligations	743,850	723,166	675,580	467,954	467,414	370,160	181,888	115,3
Total Liabilities	5,405,725	5,010,821	4,557,556	4,339,419	3,906,216	3,673,631	3,178,149	2,745,7
Net Stockholders' Equity	547,382	533,855	493,536	453,437	404,390	391,196	346,738	292,6
Shares Outstanding	39,861	39,638	39,344	39,221	37,022	35,857	33,832	29,6
Statistical Record								
Return on Equity %	11.39	11.56	11.28	12.12	10.73	11.64	11.59	10.
Return on Assets %	1.04	1.11	1.10	1.14	1.00	1.12	1.14	0.
Equity/Assets %	9.19	9.62	9.77	9.46	9.38	9.62	9.83	9.
Non–Int. Exp./Tot. Inc. %	48.85	44.21	39.43	36.39	38.81	34.97	36.83	39.
Price Range	27.80-20.20	25.97-18.41	22.80-15.75	17.50-12.25	20.69-15.03	26.00-16.38	25.50-14.56	15.89-11.
P/E Ratio	17.82-12.95	16.75-11.88	16.17-11.17	12.50-8.75	17.68-12.85	20.63-13.00	21.25-12.13	15.73-11.
Average Yield %	3.60	3.60	4.00	4.97	3.50	2.51	2.97	4.

Address: 26 North Cedar St., Lititz, PA 17543	Officers: William J. Reuter – Chmn., Pres., C.E.O., Gregory A. Duncan – Exec. V.P., C.O.O.	Investor Contact: (717) 625–6260
Telephone: (717) 626–4721		Institutional Holding
Web Site: www.susqbanc.com		No of Institutions: 113
		Shares: 13,144,976 % Held: 33.20%

SWS GROUP, INC.

Exchange	Symbol	Price	52Wk Range	Yield	P/E
NYS	SWS	$17.91 (3/31/2004)	22.44–14.45	2.23	77.87

Year Price Score N/A *NYSE Composite Index=100* ***12 Month Price Score 94.8**

Interim Earnings (Per Share)

Qtr.	Sep	Dec	Mar	Jun
2000–01	0.46	0.30	0.20	0.30
2001–02	0.11	0.08	0.06	(0.67)
2002–03	(0.02)	0.05	(0.04)	0.15
2003–04	0.07	0.25	...	

Interim Dividends (Per Share)

Amt	Decl	Ex	Rec	Pay
0.10Q	5/22/2003	6/12/2003	6/16/2003	7/1/2003
0.10Q	8/21/2003	9/11/2003	9/15/2003	10/1/2003
0.10Q	11/13/2003	12/11/2003	12/15/2003	1/2/2004
0.10Q	2/18/2004	3/11/2004	3/15/2004	4/1/2004

Indicated Div: $0.40

Valuation Analysis

Forecast P/E	N/A	Trailing P/E	77.87
Market Cap	$303.5 Million	Book Value	251.2 Million
Price/Book	1.34	Price/Sales	1.29

Dividend Achiever Status

Rank	10	10 Year Growth Rate	26.20%
Total Years of Dividend Growth	11		

Business Summary: Finance Intermediaries &Services (MIC: 8.7 SIC: 6211 NAIC:523110)

SWS Group is a full-service securities and banking firm delivering a range of investment, commercial banking and related financial services to its clients, which include individual and institutional investors, broker/dealers, corporations, governmental entities and financial intermediaries. Co. provides clearing services to 227 correspondent broker/dealers and over 400 independent registered representatives, as well as full-service and limited on-line brokerage services to individual investors. Also, Co. offers full-service, traditional and Internet banking through First Savings Bank, FSB, in Arlington, TX, and asset management services through SWS Capital Corporation.

Recent Developments: For the three months ended Dec 31 2003, net income surged to $4.3 million compared with $849,000 in the corresponding year-earlier period. Results for 2003 included an after-tax charge of $2.2 million to establish a reserve for fraudulent mortgages that were purchased by Co.'s First Savings Bank subsidiary. Total revenues improved 8.5% to $72.0 million from $66.4 million the previous year, primarily due to an increase in commission revenue, coupled with an increase in net gains on principal transactions resulting from higher fixed income trading profits.

Prospects: Co. is encouraged by the operating performance of its retail brokerage business, which is being driven by the recent expansion of that business and improved market conditions. In addition to increased commission revenue, margin balances are growing significantly, reflecting an upswing in investor confidence. Additionally, Co. is benefiting from its diverse product lines as fixed income sales and trading are showing improvement. Meanwhile, Co. will continue to focus on growing its business lines and expanding revenue sources. During the fourth quarter of 2003, Co. completed the sale of half of its ownership interest in Archipelago, an electronic stock exchange.

Financial Data

(US$ in Thousands)	6 Mos	3 Mos	06/27/2003	06/28/2002	06/29/2001	06/30/2000	06/25/1999	06/26/1998
Earnings Per Share	0.43	0.23	0.14	(0.42)	1.26	5.35	2.00	1.59
Tang. Book Val. Per Share	14.46	14.30	14.28	14.80	17.36	16.65	20.19	10.68
Dividends Per Share	0.400	0.400	0.400	0.380	0.310	0.250	0.200	0.160
Dividend Payout %	93.02	173.91	285.71	N.M.	24.72	4.68	9.98	10.14
Income Statement								
Total Interest Income	48,142	24,403	97,304	125,119	249,427	265,664	147,006	143,121
Total Interest Expense	16,592	8,169	39,885	65,807	171,578	178,084	99,951	100,704
Net Interest Income	31,550	16,234	57,419	59,312	77,849	87,580	47,055	42,417
Non–Interest Income	87,646	39,367	166,177	207,031	221,275	323,422	190,264	142,637
Non–Interest Expense	110,323	53,491	218,581	273,728	262,722	273,097	196,799	153,156
Income Before Taxes	8,873	2,110	5,015	(7,385)	36,402	137,905	40,520	31,898
Eqty Earns/Minority Int.	(521)	(300)	(1,551)	(1,151)	(2,384)	(793)	...	...
Income from Cont Ops	...	...	2,423	...	22,213	...	...	...
Net Income	5,539	1,283	2,868	(7,184)	19,339	94,234	26,219	20,630
Average Shs. Outstg.	17,228	17,206	16,997	17,215	17,500	17,603	13,022	12,939
Balance Sheet								
Securities Avail. for Sale	10,551	8,640	5,599	3,932	9,687	46,283	172,928	...
Net Loans & Leases	380,944	362,350	366,008	345,538	319,949	247,958	...	...
Total Assets	4,614,371	4,671,812	4,092,084	3,363,653	3,784,751	5,229,035	4,293,274	3,220,106
Total Deposits	529,792	632,757	528,515	265,370	336,281	265,804	...	...
Long–Term Obligations	29,138	27,096	57,169	167,253	122,045	100,368	50,000	...
Total Liabilities	4,359,746	4,420,613	3,842,311	3,108,368	3,485,318	4,937,895	4,030,990	3,094,639
Net Stockholders' Equity	254,625	251,199	249,773	255,285	299,439	291,140	262,284	125,467
Shares Outstanding	17,051	17,020	16,957	17,240	17,247	17,481	12,986	11,745
Statistical Record								
Return on Equity %	2.17	0.51	0.97	N.M.	7.41	32.36	9.99	16.44
Return on Assets %	0.12	0.02	0.05	N.M.	0.58	1.80	0.61	0.64
Equity/Assets %	5.51	5.37	6.10	7.58	7.91	5.56	6.10	3.89
Non–Int. Exp./Tot. Inc. %	81.24	83.88	82.95	82.41	55.81	46.35	58.35	53.59
Price Range	22.44–17.65	22.44–18.83	21.14–9.97	26.83–15.48	33.52–14.82	53.91–15.29	62.92–11.93	21.38–15.12
P/E Ratio	70.13–55.16	320.6–269.0	151.0–71.21	N/A	26.61–11.76	10.08–2.86	31.46–5.96	13.44–9.51
Average Yield %	1.99	1.97	2.78	1.89	1.35	0.87	0.89	0.88

Address: 1201 Elm Street, Dallas, TX 75270	Officers: Don A. Buchholz – Chmn., William D. Felder – Pres.	Institutional Holding
Telephone: (214) 859–1800		No of Institutions: 26
Web Site:		Shares: 118,959 % Held: –
www.southwestsecurities.com		

SYNOVUS FINANCIAL CORP.

Exchange	Symbol	Price	52Wk Range	Yield	P/E
NYS	SNV	$24.45 (3/31/2004)	29.04–17.31	2.84	19.10

*7 Year Price Score 105.3 *NYSE Composite Index=100 *12 Month Price Score 110.2

Interim Earnings (Per Share)

Qtr.	Mar	Jun	Sep	Dec
2000	0.22	0.22	0.23	0.25
2001	0.25	0.26	0.27	0.27
2002	0.28	0.29	0.31	0.33
2003	0.30	0.32	0.33	0.33

Interim Dividends (Per Share)

Amt	Decl	Ex	Rec	P
0.165Q	6/10/2003	6/18/2003	6/20/2003	7/1/200
0.165Q	8/20/2003	9/17/2003	9/19/2003	10/1/200
0.165Q	11/20/2003	12/17/2003	12/19/2003	1/2/200
0.173Q	2/26/2004	3/17/2004	3/19/2004	4/1/200

Indicated Div: $0.6932 (Div. Reinv. Plan)

Valuation Analysis

Forecast P/E	18.41	Trailing P/E	19.10
Market Cap	$7.2 Billion	Book Value	2.2 Billion
Price/Book	3.89	Price/Sales	3.59

Dividend Achiever Status

Rank	35	10 Year Growth Rate	19.67%
Total Years of Dividend Growth		27

Business Summary: Commercial Banking (MIC: 8.1 SIC: 6021 NAIC:522110)

Synovus Financial, with assets of $21.63 billion as of Dec 31 2003, is a registered bank holding company. Co. provides financial servic including commercial and retail banking, financial management, insurance, mortgage and leasing services through affiliate banks a other offices in Georgia, Alabama, South Carolina, Florida and Tennessee. Co. also owns 81.0% of Total System Services, Inc.®(TSYS which provides electronic payment processing services including consumer, debit, commercial, retail and stored value card processin and related services, as well as student loan processing.

Recent Developments: For the twelve months ended Dec 31 2003, net income increased 6.5% to $388.9 million from $365.3 milli in the corresponding period of the prior year. Results for 2002 included a pre–tax charge of $8.4 million related to an impairment loss a private equity investment. Net interest income grew 6.3% to $763.1 million from $717.5 million the year before. Provision for loa losses climbed 9.9% to $71.8 million from $65.3 million the previous year. Total non–interest income was up 10.9% to $1.37 billio while total non–interest expense rose 9.4% to $1.42 billion. Total assets were $21.63 billion, up 13.6% compared with $19.04 billion t prior year.

Prospects: On Feb 2 2004, Co. announced that it has completed its acquisition of Peoples Florida Banking Corporation, state–chartered commercial bank with four offices in the Tampa, FL area and assets of $255.6 million. Meanwhile, on Feb 19 2004, C announced plans to consolidate three of its affiliate banks in the Atlanta, GA area under the Bank of North Georgia charter. Th consolidation will help expand the products and services offered at these locations and will provide customers with greater lendin capacity. Looking ahead, Co anticipates full–year 2004 earnings per share growth in the range of 8.0% to 10.0%, helped by expected loa growth of between 10.0% and 12.0% during the year.

Financial Data

(US$ in Thousands)	12/31/2003	12/31/2002	12/31/2001	12/31/2000	12/31/1999	12/31/1998	12/31/1997	12/31/199
Earnings Per Share	1.28	1.21	1.05	0.92	0.80	0.70	0.62	0.5
Tang. Book Val. Per Share	6.49	6.39	5.75	4.97	4.34	3.96	3.43	2.9
Dividends Per Share	0.640	0.570	0.490	0.420	0.340	0.270	0.220	0.18
Dividend Payout %	50.19	47.10	46.90	45.65	42.91	39.99	36.91	33.9
Income Statement								
Total Interest Income	1,061,492	1,055,040	1,130,888	1,097,805	888,007	769,248	725,673	663,30
Total Interest Expense	298,428	337,536	501,097	535,473	374,713	328,722	313,284	288,42
Net Interest Income	763,064	717,504	629,791	562,332	513,294	440,526	412,389	374,87
Provision for Loan Losses	71,777	65,327	51,673	44,341	34,007	26,660	32,296	31,76
Non–Interest Income	1,366,838	1,240,539	935,975	832,732	738,563	560,674	489,269	425,5
Non–Interest Expense	1,422,143	1,299,470	1,005,963	923,274	856,549	673,648	601,293	541,58
Income Before Taxes	609,010	569,597	488,271	410,954	348,113	290,333	258,926	219,48
Income from Cont Ops	386,434	371,064	309,894	261,776	224,105	185,809	165,259	139,78
Net Income	388,925	365,347	311,616	262,557	225,307	187,108	165,236	139,60
Average Shs. Outstg.	304,928	301,197	295,850	286,882	283,355	269,151	265,665	261,29
Balance Sheet								
Cash & Due from Banks	696,030	741,092	648,179	558,054	466,543	348,365	388,134	404,95
Securities Avail. for Sale	2,529,257	2,237,725	2,088,287	1,807,039	1,716,678	1,514,054	1,325,036	1,276,08
Net Loans & Leases	16,238,855	14,264,068	12,247,148	10,604,020	8,940,681	7,301,170	6,506,822	5,970,54
Total Assets	21,632,629	19,036,246	16,657,947	14,908,092	12,547,001	10,498,009	9,260,331	8,612,34
Total Deposits	15,941,609	13,928,834	12,146,198	11,161,710	9,440,087	8,542,798	7,707,927	7,203,03
Long–Term Obligations	1,575,777	1,336,200	1,052,943	840,859	318,620	127,015	7,188	97,28
Total Liabilities	19,387,590	16,995,393	14,963,001	13,490,921	11,320,332	9,426,408	8,237,689	7,828,59
Net Stockholders' Equity	2,245,039	2,040,853	1,694,946	1,417,171	1,226,669	1,070,601	903,656	783,7
Shares Outstanding	302,090	300,397	294,673	284,642	282,014	270,218	262,808	261,77
Statistical Record								
Return on Equity %	17.21	18.18	18.28	18.47	18.26	17.35	18.28	17.8
Return on Assets %	1.78	1.94	1.86	1.75	1.78	1.76	1.78	1.6
Equity/Assets %	10.37	10.72	10.17	9.50	9.77	10.19	9.75	9.1
Non–Int. Exp./Tot. Inc. %	58.50	56.74	48.63	47.80	52.62	50.60	49.49	49.7
Price Range	29.04–17.31	31.74–16.81	34.45–23.02	27.19–14.50	25.00–17.50	25.83–18.06	22.21–13.11	14.83–7.9
P/E Ratio	22.69–13.52	26.23–13.89	32.81–21.92	29.55–15.76	31.25–21.88	36.90–25.80	35.82–21.15	27.99–15.0
Average Yield %	2.79	2.32	1.75	2.15	1.63	1.21	1.30	1.6

Address: 901 Front Avenue, Columbus, GA 31902	Officers: James D. Yancey – Chmn., Pres., C.O.O., Richard E. Anthony – Pres.	Investor Contact:706–649–5220
Telephone: (706) 649–2401	Transfer Agents:State Street Bank and Trust Company, Boston, MA	Institutional Holding No of Institutions: 26
Web Site: www.synovus.com		Shares: 4,023,382 % Held: –

SYSCO CORP.

Exchange	Symbol	Price	52Wk Range	Yield	P/E
NYS	SYY	$39.05 (3/31/2004)	40.90-26.00	1.33	30.51

*7 Year Price Score 150.9   ***NYSE Composite Index=100**   ***12 Month Price Score 103.8**

Interim Earnings (Per Share)

Qtr.	Sep	Dec	Mar	Jun
2000-01	0.43	0.21	0.21	0.03
2001-02	0.24	0.24	0.23	0.30
2002-03	0.28	0.28	0.26	0.36
2003-04	0.32	0.34	...	...

Interim Dividends (Per Share)

Amt	Decl	Ex	Rec	Pay
0.11Q	5/9/2003	7/1/2003	7/3/2003	7/25/2003
0.11Q	9/12/2003	10/1/2003	10/3/2003	10/24/2003
0.13Q	11/7/2003	12/30/2003	1/2/2004	1/23/2004
0.13Q	2/13/2004	3/31/2004	4/2/2004	4/23/2004

Indicated Div: $0.52 (Div. Reinv. Plan)

Valuation Analysis

Forecast P/E	21.03	Trailing P/E	N/A
Market Cap	$25.9 Billion	Book Value	N/A
Price/Book	N/A	Price/Sales	N/A

Dividend Achiever Status

Rank	34	10 Year Growth Rate	20.18%
Total Years of Dividend Growth		27

Business Summary: Retail - Food &Beverage (MIC: 5.3 SIC: 5141 NAIC:424410)

Sysco, acting through its subsidiaries and divisions, is a distributor of food and food related products to the foodservice or "food-prepared-away-from-home" industry. Co. provides its products and services to restaurants, healthcare and educational facilities, lodging establishments and other foodservice customers. Co.'s Broadline companies segment distributes food products and non-food products to both Co.'s traditional and chain restaurant customers. SYGMA companies distribute food products and non-food products to some of Co.'s chain restaurant customer locations.

Recent Developments: For the 13 weeks ended Dec 27 2003, net earnings totaled $222.0 million, up 20.3% compared with $184.6 million in the corresponding prior-year period. Sales climbed 10.8% to $7.04 billion from $6.35 billion a year earlier. Broadline sales increased 8.7% to $5.68 billion from $5.23 billion in 2002, while sales for SYGMA, Co.'s chain restaurant distribution subsidiary, advanced 21.6% to $863.5 million from $710.3 million the previous year. Cost of sales was $5.67 billion, or 80.6% of sales, versus $5.10 billion, or 80.3% of total sales, the year before. Earnings before income taxes climbed 20.8% to $360.9 million from $298.9 million the prior year.

Prospects: Results are being positively affected by Co.'s efforts to reduce costs and improve productivity, partially offset by lower gross margins stemming from increased sales of meat products and growth of Co.'s multi-unit business. Meanwhile, sales and earnings growth is being fueled by Co.'s ongoing efforts to expand its operations. Co. plans to open a new broadline distribution "fold-out" facility, or foodservice distribution center, in Post Falls, ID. The facility is expected to be operational by 2005. In addition, Co. has new fold-out facilities in Fargo, ND and Oxnard, CA under construction and anticipates capital expenditures of approximately $490.0 million during the current fiscal year.

Financial Data

(US$ in Thousands)	6 Mos	3 Mos	06/28/2003	06/29/2002	06/30/2001	07/01/2000	07/03/1999	06/27/1998
Earnings Per Share	0.65	0.32	1.18	1.01	0.88	0.68	0.54	0.47
Cash Flow Per Share	0.55	0.28	2.07	1.61	1.43	1.05	0.86	0.52
Tang. Book Val. Per Share	1.86	1.81	1.68	1.85	2.07	1.89	1.70	1.56
Dividends Per Share	0.440	0.420	0.400	0.320	0.260	0.220	0.190	0.160
Dividend Payout %	67.69	131.25	33.89	31.68	29.54	32.35	35.18	34.21
Income Statement								
Total Revenues	14,170,801	7,134,281	26,140,337	23,350,504	21,784,497	19,303,268	17,422,815	15,327,536
Total Indirect Exp.	2,021,189	1,024,336	3,836,507	3,467,379	3,232,827	2,843,755	2,547,266	2,236,932
Depreciation & Amort.	138,679	69,679	273,142	278,251	248,240	220,661	205,005	181,234
Operating Income	726,446	356,178	1,324,274	1,160,962	1,038,532	809,962	667,689	590,968
Net Interest Inc./(Exp.)	(35,007)	(18,631)	(72,234)	(62,897)	(71,776)	(70,832)	(72,839)	(58,422)
Income Taxes	269,682	130,719	482,099	421,083	369,746	283,979	231,616	207,672
Income from Cont Ops	...	...	...	...	...	453,629	...	324,821
Net Income	430,792	208,811	778,288	679,787	596,909	445,588	362,271	296,768
Average Shs. Outstg.	660,127	657,274	661,535	673,445	667,949	669,555	673,594	686,880
Balance Sheet								
Cash & Cash Equivalents	232,595	221,544	337,447	230,439	135,743	159,128	149,303	110,288
Total Current Assets	3,738,789	3,776,173	3,629,534	3,185,289	2,984,882	2,733,215	2,408,767	2,180,067
Total Assets	7,305,577	7,214,194	6,936,521	5,989,753	5,468,521	4,813,955	4,096,582	3,780,189
Total Current Liabilities	2,734,868	2,790,506	2,701,109	2,239,357	2,089,895	1,782,935	1,427,540	1,324,190
Long-Term Obligations	1,395,981	1,195,282	1,249,467	1,176,307	961,421	1,023,642	997,717	867,017
Net Stockholders' Equity	2,365,824	2,324,594	2,197,531	2,132,519	2,147,520	1,761,568	1,427,196	1,356,589
Net Working Capital	...	985,667	928,405	945,932	894,987	950,280	981,227	855,877
Shares Outstanding	642,204	644,779	643,657	653,540	665,137	662,969	659,344	670,018
Statistical Record								
Operating Profit Margin %	5.12	4.99	5.06	4.97	4.76	4.19	3.83	3.85
Return on Equity %	18.20	8.98	35.41	31.87	27.79	25.75	25.38	23.94
Return on Assets %	5.89	2.89	11.22	11.34	10.91	9.42	8.84	8.59
Debt/Total Assets %	19.10	16.56	18.01	19.63	17.58	21.26	24.35	22.93
Price Range	36.84-28.75	33.99-28.75	32.34-21.81	30.15-22.22	30.03-19.59	21.69-13.63	15.75-10.09	13.16-8.61
P/E Ratio	56.68-44.23	106.22-89.84	27.41-18.48	29.85-22.00	34.13-22.27	31.89-20.04	29.17-18.69	27.99-18.32
Average Yield %	1.34	1.36	1.39	1.17	1.02	1.23	1.42	1.47

Address: 1390 Enclave Parkway, Houston, TX 77077-2099 Telephone: (281) 584-1390 Web Site: www.sysco.com	Officers: Richard J. Schnieders - Chmn., C.E.O., Thomas E. Lankford - Pres., C.O.O. Transfer Agents:EquiServe Trust Company, N.A., Providence, RI	Investor Contact:281-584-1458 Institutional Holding No of Institutions: 14 Shares: 1,927,072 % Held: -

T ROWE PRICE GROUP INC.

Exchange	Symbol	Price	52Wk Range	Yield	P/E
NMS	TROW	$53.83 (3/31/2004)	55.78-27.27	1.41	30.41

*7 Year Price Score 107.5   *NYSE Composite Index=100   *12 Month Price Score 107.5

Interim Earnings (Per Share)

Qtr.	Mar	Jun	Sep	Dec
2000	0.58	0.54	0.53	0.43
2001	0.38	0.40	0.39	0.35
2002	0.41	0.40	0.34	0.37
2003	0.31	0.42	0.51	0.53

Interim Dividends (Per Share)

Amt	Decl	Ex	Rec	Pay
0.17Q	6/5/2003	6/18/2003	6/20/2003	7/7/2003
0.17Q	9/4/2003	9/24/2003	9/26/2003	10/10/2003
0.19Q	12/11/2003	12/23/2003	12/26/2003	1/9/2004
0.19Q	3/9/2004	3/19/2004	3/23/2004	4/6/2004

Indicated Div: $0.76

Valuation Analysis

Forecast P/E	N/A	Trailing P/E	30.41
Market Cap	$6.6 Billion	Book Value	1.3 Billion
Price/Book	4.38	Price/Sales	5.83

Dividend Achiever Status

Rank	31	10 Year Growth Rate	20.54%
Total Years of Dividend Growth			17

Business Summary: Wealth Management (MIC: 8.8 SIC: 6282 NAIC:523930)

T. Rowe Price Group is a financial services holding company with total assets under management of $190.00 billion as of Dec 31 2003. Through its subsidiaries, Co. is engaged in providing investment advisory services to individual and institutional investors through the sponsored T. Rowe Price mutual funds and other investment portfolios. Co.'s assets under management are sourced approximately 20.0% to 30.0% from each of the following: individual U.S. investors, U.S. defined contribution retirement plans, third–party distributors in the U.S. and internationally, and institutional investors in the U.S. and foreign countries.

Recent Developments: For the year ended Dec 31 2003, net income climbed 17.1% to $227.5 million compared with $194.3 million in 2002. Net revenues grew 7.8% to $995.6 million from $923.5 million a year earlier. Net operating income advanced 13.9% to $365.0 million versus $320.5 million the year before. Net non–operating income was $476,000 versus a loss of $10.9 million in 2002. Assets under management jumped 35.1% to $190.00 billion. The improvement in assets under management was primarily attributed to improving financial market valuations and income added in excess of $36.00 billion during 2003, and net investor inflows that contributed more than $13.00 billion.

Prospects: Co. is cautiously optimistic with regard to its outlook for 2004, based on improving conditions in the U.S. economy, continued low interest rates and renewed investor interest in the equity markets. However, concern still exists given the geopolitical uncertainty that is present on several fronts, which could have an effect on business activity. Meanwhile, Co.'s earnings and cash flow remain strong and should continue to provide Co. with considerable financial flexibility. At the beginning of 2004, Co. held cash and liquid investment holdings of nearly $400.0 million and no outstanding debt.

Financial Data

(US$ in Thousands)	12/31/2003	12/31/2002	12/31/2001	12/31/2000	12/31/1999	12/31/1998	12/31/1997	12/31/1996
Earnings Per Share	1.77	1.52	1.52	2.08	1.85	1.34	1.13	0.79
Cash Flow Per Share	2.31	2.10	2.25	2.49	2.29	1.78	1.54	1.13
Tang. Book Val. Per Share	5.40	3.81	3.34	2.41	6.41	5.11	4.11	3.00
Dividends Per Share	0.680	0.640	0.600	0.520	0.400	0.340	0.260	0.210
Dividend Payout %	38.41	42.10	39.47	25.00	21.62	25.37	23.00	26.58
Income Statement								
Total Revenues	998,855	925,829	1,027,496	1,212,327	1,036,379	886,142	754,957	586,070
Total Indirect Exp.	630,527	602,991	709,599	763,856	621,609	573,328	490,198	398,599
Depreciation & Amort.	45,289	50,578	28,921	11,879	32,628	32,615	29,034	18,062
Operating Income	365,040	320,511	330,589	458,192	414,770	312,814	264,759	187,471
Net Interest Inc./(Exp.)	(1,699)	(2,634)	(12,692)	(9,721)	...	...	...	...
Income Taxes	138,020	115,350	135,078	174,818	155,166	118,676	101,208	72,608
Eqty Earns/Minority Int.	...	...	357	(14,345)	(20,200)	(19,998)	(19,154)	(16,410)
Net Income	227,487	194,254	195,868	269,029	239,404	174,140	144,397	98,453
Average Shs. Outstg.	128,289	127,706	129,045	129,600	129,200	129,952	128,073	123,884
Balance Sheet								
Cash & Cash Equivalents	236,533	111,418	79,741	80,526	358,472	283,838	200,409	114,551
Total Current Assets	357,828	208,205	183,742	211,567	480,109	384,540	287,204	187,790
Total Assets	1,546,577	1,370,433	1,313,115	1,469,459	998,039	796,784	646,067	478,834
Total Current Liabilities	121,221	99,402	105,979	154,819	149,919	129,814	109,557	95,000
Long–Term Obligations	...	55,889	103,889	312,277	17,716	...	...	...
Net Stockholders' Equity	1,329,080	1,133,840	1,077,825	991,065	770,184	614,304	486,673	345,666
Net Working Capital	236,607	108,803	77,763	56,748	330,190	254,726	177,647	92,790
Shares Outstanding	122,648	122,648	123,088	122,439	120,107	120,183	118,195	115,146
Statistical Record								
Operating Profit Margin %	36.54	34.61	32.17	37.79	40.02	35.30	35.06	31.98
Return on Equity %	17.11	17.13	18.17	27.14	31.08	28.34	29.67	28.48
Return on Assets %	14.70	14.17	14.91	18.30	23.98	21.85	22.35	20.56
Debt/Total Assets %	...	4.07	7.91	21.25	1.77	...	...	...
Price Range	47.41-24.30	41.99-21.45	42.69-25.70	48.63-30.19	40.88-26.44	42.44-22.75	36.75-18.56	22.75-10.81
P/E Ratio	26.79-13.73	27.63-14.11	28.08-16.91	23.38-14.51	22.09-14.29	31.67-16.98	32.52-16.43	28.80-13.69
Average Yield %	1.89	1.98	1.73	1.29	1.16	1.00	0.98	1.41

Address: 100 East Pratt Street, Baltimore, MD 21202 **Telephone:** (410) 345–2000 **Web Site:** www.troweprice.com	**Officers:** George A. Roche – Chmn., Pres., Interim C.F.O., James S. Riepe – Vice–Chmn., V.P.	**Investor Contact:** 410–345–2124 **Institutional Holding** **No of Institutions:** 283 **Shares:** 70,267,878 **% Held:** 57.6

TANGER FACTORY OUTLET CENTERS, INC.

Exchange	Symbol	Price	52Wk Range	Yield	P/E
NYS	SKT	$45.32 (3/31/2004)	45.32–30.76	5.43	40.11

*7 Year Price Score 134.1 *NYSE Composite Index=100 *12 Month Price Score 107.1

Interim Earnings (Per Share)

Qtr.	Mar	Jun	Sep	Dec
2000	0.28	(0.25)	0.26	0.02
2001	0.06	0.12	0.17	0.35
2002	0.12	0.13	0.20	0.35
2003	0.19	0.26	0.33	0.39

Interim Dividends (Per Share)

Amt	Decl	Ex	Rec	Pay
0.615Q	4/10/2003	4/28/2003	4/30/2003	5/15/2003
0.615Q	7/10/2003	7/29/2003	7/31/2003	8/15/2003
0.615Q	10/9/2003	10/29/2003	10/31/2003	11/14/2003
0.615Q	1/15/2004	1/28/2004	1/30/2004	2/16/2004

Indicated Div: $2.46 (Div. Reinv. Plan)

Valuation Analysis

Forecast P/E	10.12	Trailing P/E 40.11
Market Cap	$363.9 Million	Book Value 90.7 Million
Price/Book	4.19	Price/Sales 3.16

Dividend Achiever Status

Rank	61	10 Year Growth Rate 16.47%
Total Years of Dividend Growth	10	

Business Summary: Property, Real Estate &Development (MIC: 8.3 SIC: 6798 NAIC:525930)

Tanger Factory Outlet Centers is a fully-integrated, self-administered and self-managed real estate investment trust, focusing exclusively on developing, acquiring, owning, operating and managing factory outlet centers. As of Dec 31 2003, Co. had ownership interests in or management responsibilities for 40 centers with a total gross leasable area of approximately 9.3 million square feet. These centers were approximately 96.0% occupied, contained over 2,000 stores and represented over 400 store brands. Co.'s factory outlet centers and other assets are held by, and all of its operations are conducted by, Tanger Properties Limited Partnership.

Recent Developments: For the year ended Dec 31 2003, income totaled $12.9 million, before a $16,000 charge from discontinued operations, compared with income of $8.4 million, before a gain of $2.6 million from discontinued operations, the previous year. Total revenues climbed 10.1% to $122.0 million from $110.8 million a year earlier. Revenues from base rentals increased 9.3% to $81.0 million from $74.1 million the year before, while revenues from expense reimbursements advanced 14.4% to $34.2 million from $29.9 million the prior year. Operating income was $43.1 million, up 11.1% versus $38.8 million in 2002.

Prospects: Top-line results are being positively affected by Co.'s efforts to expand its operations. In December 2003, Co. acquired a 1/3 interest in nine outlet centers totaling approximately 3.3 million square feet through a joint venture agreement with an affiliate of Blackstone Real Estate Advisors. Meanwhile, Co. is underway with a 79,000 square-foot expansion at its outlet center in Myrtle Beach, SC. Co. expects to complete the expansion with stores opening during the summer of 2004. Looking ahead, Co. is targeting full-year 2004 earnings of between $0.62 and $0.72 per share. In addition, Co. estimates funds from operations to range from $3.68 to $3.76 per share for 2004.

Financial Data

(US$ in Thousands)	12/31/2003	12/31/2002	12/31/2001	12/31/2000	12/31/1999	12/31/1998	12/31/1997	12/31/1996
Earnings Per Share	1.17	0.80	0.70	0.31	1.77	1.28	1.54	1.46
Tang. Book Val. Per Share	12.91	10.00	9.63	11.47	13.68	14.43	17.39	16.75
Dividends Per Share	2.450	2.440	2.430	2.420	2.410	2.350	2.170	2.060
Dividend Payout %	210.04	305.93	348.21	783.06	136.44	183.59	140.90	141.09
Income Statement								
Rental Income	84,229	79,313	78,089	74,710	72,321	69,274	59,444	52,613
Total Income	121,972	113,167	111,068	108,821	104,016	97,766	85,271	75,500
Total Indirect Exp.	78,920	130,985	131,710	124,137	111,185	104,685	84,523	73,480
Depreciation	29,124	28,754	28,572	26,218	24,824	22,154	18,439	16,458
Interest Expense	26,486	56,920	60,268	55,130	48,478	44,056	33,670	27,996
Eqty Earns/Minority Int.	(3,701)	(2,014)	(2,136)	(956)	(5,374)	(3,944)	(4,756)	(4,425)
Income from Cont Ops	12,865	8,628	7,356	11,293	11,696	11,165	...	11,593
Net Income	12,849	11,007	7,112	4,312	15,588	11,827	12,827	11,191
Average Shs. Outstg.	10,283	8,514	7,948	7,922	7,872	8,009	7,140	6,402
Balance Sheet								
Cash & Cash Equivalents	9,836	1,072	515	634	503	6,330	3,607	2,585
Total Assets	987,437	477,675	476,272	487,408	490,069	471,795	416,014	332,138
Long–Term Obligations	540,319	345,005	358,195	346,843	329,647	302,485	229,050	178,004
Total Liabilities	820,019	387,040	399,901	396,531	382,305	357,756	279,365	221,481
Net Stockholders' Equity	167,418	90,635	76,371	90,877	107,764	114,039	136,649	110,657
Shares Outstanding	12,960	9,061	7,929	7,918	7,876	7,897	7,854	6,603
Statistical Record								
Net Inc.+Depr./Assets %	4.24	8.23	7.49	6.30	8.25	7.20	7.52	8.32
Return on Equity %	7.68	9.51	9.63	12.42	10.85	9.79	9.38	10.47
Return on Assets %	1.30	1.80	1.54	2.31	2.38	2.36	3.08	3.49
Price Range	42.36-28.85	31.20-20.85	23.31-19.81	24.88-18.50	26.44-18.81	31.75-18.94	30.94-23.75	27.13-22.88
P/E Ratio	36.21-24.66	39.00-26.06	33.30-28.30	80.24-59.68	14.94-10.63	24.80-14.79	20.09-15.42	18.58-15.67
Average Yield %	7.14	8.99	11.24	11.16	10.47	8.55	7.87	8.46

Address: 3200 Northline Avenue, Greensboro, NC 27408 **Telephone:** (336) 292–3010 **Web Site:** www.tangeroutlet.com	**Officers:** Stanley K. Tanger – Chmn., C.E.O., Steven B. Tanger – Pres., C.O.O.	**Investor Contact:** (336) 292–3010 **Institutional Holding** **No of Institutions:** 12 **Shares:** 379,669 **% Held:** –

TARGET CORP

Exchange	Symbol	Price	52Wk Range	Yield	P/E
NYS	TGT	$45.04 (3/31/2004)	45.63–29.15	0.62	22.41

*7 Year Price Score 121.9 *NYSE Composite Index=100 *12 Month Price Score 97.8

Interim Earnings (Per Share)

Qtr.	Apr	Jul	Oct	Jan
2000–01	0.26	0.28	0.24	0.60
2001–02	0.28	0.30	0.20	0.73
2002–03	0.38	0.38	0.30	0.75
2003–04	0.38	0.39	0.33	0.91

Interim Dividends (Per Share)

Amt	Decl	Ex	Rec	Pay
0.07Q	6/12/2003	8/18/2003	8/20/2003	9/10/2003
0.07Q	9/11/2003	11/18/2003	11/20/2003	12/10/2003
0.07Q	1/15/2004	2/18/2004	2/20/2004	3/10/2004
0.07Q	4/11/2004	5/18/2004	5/20/2004	6/10/2004

Indicated Div: $0.28 (Div. Reinv. Plan)

Valuation Analysis

Forecast P/E	17.20	Trailing P/E	22.41
Market Cap	$40.9 Billion	Book Value	10.3 Billion
Price/Book	3.34	Price/Sales	0.73

Dividend Achiever Status

Rank	216	10 Year Growth Rate	6.91%
Total Years of Dividend Growth			32

Business Summary: Retail – General (MIC: 5.2 SIC: 5331 NAIC:452990)

Target is a diversified general merchandise retailer. As of Aug 14 2003, Co. operated 1,519 stores in 47 states including 1,191 Target stores, 266 Mervyn's stores and 62 Marshall Field's stores. Target is a national discount store chain offering low prices with stores selling hardlines and fashion softgoods; Mervyn's is a moderate–priced department store chain specializing in active and casual apparel and home softlines. Marshall Field's (including stores formerly named Dayton's and Hudson's) is a full–service, full–line department store chain offering moderate to better merchandise.

Recent Developments: For the twelve months ended Jan 31 2004, net earnings totaled $1.84 billion, up 11.4% compared with $1.65 billion a year earlier. Total revenues climbed 9.7% to $48.16 billion from $43.92 billion the previous year. Revenues from Target stores advanced 12.0% to $41.35 billion from $36.92 billion the year before. Revenues from Mervyn's slipped 6.9% to $3.55 billion from $3.82 billion the prior year, while revenues from Marshall Field's slid 4.0% to $2.58 billion from $2.69 billion a year earlier. Total comparable–store sales increased 2.9% year over year, driven by comparable–store sales growth of 4.4% at Target stores. Earnings before income taxes rose 10.6% to $2.96 billion.

Prospects: On Mar 10 2004, Co. announced that it is considering strategic alternatives for its Mervyn's and Marshall Field's department store operations. The alternatives include the possible sale of one or both of these businesses to existing retailers or other qualified buyers. The sale of Mervyn's, which operates 266 stores and generated revenues of $3.60 billion in 2003, and Marshall Field's, which operates 62 stores and reported revenues of $2.60 billion in 2003, would help Co. focus on growing its chain of discount stores. Looking ahead, Co. anticipates first–quarter 2004 earnings per share of $0.45, and full–year 2004 earnings of approximately $2.27 per share.

Financial Data

(US$ in Millions)	9 Mos	6 Mos	3 Mos	02/01/2003	02/02/2002	02/03/2001	01/29/2000	01/30/1999
Earnings Per Share	1.10	0.77	0.38	1.81	1.51	1.38	1.27	1.02
Cash Flow Per Share	0.92	0.61	(0.26)	1.73	2.18	2.08	2.41	1.99
Tang. Book Val. Per Share	11.26	11.02	10.71	10.37	8.68	7.15	6.42	6.12
Dividends Per Share	0.250	0.240	0.240	0.240	0.220	0.210	0.200	0.180
Dividend Payout %	22.72	31.16	63.15	13.25	14.56	15.21	15.74	17.64
Income Statement								
Total Revenues	32,592	21,306	10,322	43,917	39,888	36,903	33,702	30,951
Total Indirect Exp.	9,155	5,858	2,853	11,393	9,962	9,130	8,344	6,363
Depreciation & Amort.	976	646	317	1,212	1,079	940	854	780
Operating Income	2,051	1,439	705	3,264	2,680	2,478	2,329	1,954
Net Interest Inc./(Exp.)	(429)	(298)	(142)	(588)	(464)	(425)	(393)	(398)
Income Taxes	613	434	214	1,022	842	789	751	594
Income from Cont Ops	...	...	...	...	1,374	...	1,185	962
Net Income	1,009	707	349	1,654	1,368	1,264	1,144	935
Average Shs. Outstg.	917	916	915	914	909	913	931	934
Balance Sheet								
Cash & Cash Equivalents	495	429	452	758	499	2,297	2,057	1,911
Total Current Assets	13,284	11,973	11,992	11,935	9,648	7,304	6,483	6,005
Total Assets	31,424	29,634	29,172	28,603	24,154	19,490	17,143	15,666
Total Current Liabilities	8,596	6,961	6,801	7,523	7,054	6,301	5,850	5,057
Long–Term Obligations	11,003	11,088	11,118	10,186	8,088	5,634	4,521	4,452
Net Stockholders' Equity	10,265	10,044	9,760	9,443	7,860	6,519	5,862	5,311
Net Working Capital	4,688	5,012	5,191	4,412	2,594	1,003	633	948
Shares Outstanding	911	910	910	909	905	911	911	823
Statistical Record								
Operating Profit Margin %	6.29	6.75	6.83	7.43	6.71	6.71	6.91	6.31
Return on Equity %	9.82	7.03	3.57	17.51	17.48	19.38	20.21	18.11
Return on Assets %	3.21	2.38	1.19	5.78	5.68	6.48	6.91	6.14
Debt/Total Assets %	35.01	37.41	38.11	35.61	33.48	28.90	26.37	28.41
Price Range	41.54–26.06	39.82–26.06	33.44–26.06	45.72–26.15	44.41–26.68	38.63–22.75	37.88–27.63	31.88–16.88
P/E Ratio	37.76–23.69	51.71–33.84	88.00–68.58	25.26–14.45	29.41–17.67	27.99–16.49	29.82–21.75	31.25–16.54
Average Yield %	0.71	0.72	0.81	0.66	0.60	0.69	0.62	0.80

Address: 1000 Nicollet Mall, Minneapolis, MN 55403 **Telephone:** (612) 304–6073 **Web Site:** www.target.com	**Officers:** Robert J. Ulrich – Chmn., C.E.O., Gerald L. Storch – Vice–Chmn. **Transfer Agents:**EquiServe, Jersey City, NJ	**Investor Contact:**612–370–6736 **Institutional Holding** **No of Institutions:** 7 **Shares:** 869,205 **% Held:** –

TCF FINANCIAL CORP.

Exchange	Symbol	Price	52Wk Range	Yield	P/E
NYS	TCB	$51.07 (3/31/2004)	53.56–37.08	2.94	16.74

*7 Year Price Score 130.0 *NYSE Composite Index=100 *12 Month Price Score 104.4

Interim Earnings (Per Share)

Qtr.	Mar	Jun	Sep	Dec
2000	0.51	0.59	0.59	0.66
2001	0.62	0.67	0.69	0.72
2002	0.75	0.78	0.80	0.82
2003	0.83	0.85	0.51	0.86

Interim Dividends (Per Share)

Amt	Decl	Ex	Rec	Pay
0.325Q	4/21/2003	4/30/2003	5/2/2003	5/30/2003
0.325Q	7/21/2003	7/30/2003	8/1/2003	8/29/2003
0.325Q	10/20/2003	11/5/2003	11/7/2003	11/28/2003
0.375Q	1/15/2004	2/4/2004	2/6/2004	2/27/2004

Indicated Div: $1.50

Valuation Analysis

Forecast P/E	13.14	Trailing P/E	16.74
Market Cap	$3.8 Billion	Book Value	920.9 Million
Price/Book	3.97	Price/Sales	3.31

Dividend Achiever Status

Rank	22	10 Year Growth Rate	22.43%
Total Years of Dividend Growth		12

Business Summary: Commercial Banking (MIC: 8.1 SIC: 6021 NAIC:522110)

TCF Financial, with $11.32 billion in assets as of Dec 31 2003, is the holding company for two national banks. As of Dec 31 2003, Co. operated more than 400 banking offices, including 240 full-service supermarket branches, in Illinois, Indiana, Michigan, Minnesota, Wisconsin and Colorado. Co.'s primary focus is lower- and middle-income customers and small- to medium-sized businesses in its markets. Co.'s branches are typically open 12 hours a day, seven days a week and on holidays. Co.'s products include commercial, consumer and residential mortgage loans and deposit and equipment finance, discount brokerage and investment and insurance sales products.

Recent Developments: For the year ended Dec 31 2003, net income slid 7.3% to $215.9 million versus $232.9 million the year before. Results for 2003 and 2002 included net gains gains of $32.8 million and $13.5 million, primarily on sales of securities available for sale. Results for 2003 also included losses of $44.3 million on the termination of debt. Net interest income slid 3.6% to $481.1 million, while net interest margin declined to 4.54% from 4.71% in 2002, primarily due to low interest rates and the prepayment and refinancing of higher-yielding assets. Provision for credit losses fell 43.1% to $12.5 million. Non-interest income slid 0.1% to $419.3 million. Non-interest expense rose 3.9% to $560.1 million.

Prospects: Results are being negatively affected by very low interest rates, which are causing a high level of prepayments in Co.'s residential loans and mortgage-backed securities portfolio. Also, loan yields are decreasing faster than Co. can reduce its costs of funds, lowering its net interest margin. During 2003, Co. prepaid $954.0 million of high cost fixed-rate borrowings to restructure its balance sheet and reduce its cost of funds in future periods. Separately, Co.'s credit quality remains strong. Additionally, the focus on opening new branches will continue in 2004, with the planned opening of 28 branches, including 22 new traditional branches and six new supermarket branches.

Financial Data

(US$ in Thousands)	12/31/2003	12/31/2002	12/31/2001	12/31/2000	12/31/1999	12/31/1998	12/31/1997	12/31/1996
Earnings Per Share	3.05	3.15	2.70	2.35	2.00	1.76	1.69	1.21
Tang. Book Val. Per Share	10.18	10.30	9.90	9.28	7.77	7.74	7.93	7.35
Dividends Per Share	1.300	1.150	1.000	0.820	0.720	0.610	0.460	0.350
Dividend Payout %	42.62	36.50	37.03	35.10	36.25	34.80	27.73	28.92
Income Statement								
Total Interest Income	641,519	733,363	826,609	826,681	752,101	748,894	682,614	582,861
Total Interest Expense	160,374	234,138	345,387	388,145	327,888	323,160	289,018	242,721
Net Interest Income	481,145	499,225	481,222	438,536	424,213	425,734	393,596	340,140
Provision for Loan Losses	12,532	22,006	20,878	14,772	16,923	23,280	17,795	19,820
Non–Interest Income	463,624	416,880	351,625	312,384	288,909	256,174	200,839	145,094
Non–Interest Expense	560,109	538,369	501,996	462,528	452,798	428,700	361,562	341,070
Income Before Taxes	327,783	357,692	329,834	302,838	273,091	265,249	240,907	137,047
Net Income	215,878	232,931	207,322	186,245	166,039	156,179	145,061	85,663
Average Shs. Outstg.	70,770	73,940	76,842	79,388	83,071	88,916	86,134	70,684
Balance Sheet								
Cash & Due from Banks	370,054	416,397	386,700	392,007	429,262	420,477	297,010	238,670
Securities Avail. for Sale	1,533,288	2,426,794	1,584,661	1,403,888	1,521,661	1,677,919	1,430,192	1,003,464
Net Loans & Leases	8,271,159	8,044,120	8,169,174	8,480,030	7,839,988	7,061,165	6,986,605	4,925,213
Total Assets	11,319,015	12,202,069	11,358,715	11,197,462	10,661,716	10,164,594	9,744,660	7,090,862
Total Deposits	7,611,749	7,709,988	7,098,958	6,891,824	6,584,835	6,715,146	6,907,310	4,977,630
Long–Term Obligations	1,536,413	2,268,244	2,303,166	2,098,925	2,073,888	2,093,766	1,614,708	1,200,086
Total Liabilities	10,398,157	11,225,049	10,441,682	10,287,242	9,852,734	9,319,092	8,790,980	6,541,356
Net Stockholders' Equity	920,858	977,020	917,033	910,220	808,982	845,502	953,680	549,642
Shares Outstanding	70,476	73,855	76,931	80,289	81,941	85,569	92,822	69,514
Statistical Record								
Return on Equity %	23.44	23.84	22.60	20.46	20.52	18.47	15.21	15.58
Return on Assets %	1.90	1.90	1.82	1.66	1.55	1.53	1.48	1.20
Equity/Assets %	8.13	8.00	8.07	8.12	7.58	8.31	9.78	7.75
Non–Int. Exp./Tot. Inc. %	50.68	46.80	42.60	40.60	43.49	42.65	40.92	46.85
Price Range	53.56–37.05	54.39–35.21	50.70–33.70	45.31–18.50	30.25–22.00	36.75–16.56	34.13–19.31	22.50–15.00
P/E Ratio	17.56–12.15	17.27–11.18	18.78–12.48	19.28–7.87	15.13–11.00	20.88–9.41	20.19–11.43	18.60–12.40
Average Yield %	2.91	2.43	2.36	2.77	2.65	2.13	1.83	1.92

Address: 200 Lake Street East, Wayzata, MN 55391–1693 Telephone: (612) 661–6500 Web Site: www.tcfexpress.com	Officers: William A. Cooper – Chmn., C.E.O., Lynn A. Nagorske – Pres., C.O.O. Transfer Agents: EquiServe Trust Company, N.A., Providence, RI	Investor Contact: (952) 745–2755 Institutional Holding No of Institutions: 16 Shares: 3,774,944 % Held: –

TELEFLEX INCORPORATED

Exchange	Symbol	Price	52Wk Range	Yield	P/E
NYS	TFX	$49.23 (3/31/2004)	54.82-35.62	1.63	18.03

*7 Year Price Score 108.2 *NYSE Composite Index=100 *12 Month Price Score 96.5

Interim Earnings (Per Share)

Qtr.	Mar	Jun	Sep	Dec
2000	0.70	0.76	0.56	0.81
2001	0.77	0.79	0.56	0.74
2002	0.77	0.84	0.66	0.88
2003	0.74	0.80	0.45	0.74

Interim Dividends (Per Share)

Amt	Decl	Ex	Rec	Pay
0.20Q	4/25/2003	5/21/2003	5/26/2003	6/16/2003
0.20Q	8/4/2003	8/21/2003	8/25/2003	9/15/2003
0.20Q	11/4/2003	11/21/2003	11/25/2003	12/15/2003
0.20Q	2/9/2004	2/23/2004	2/25/2004	3/15/2004

Indicated Div: $0.80 (Div. Reinv. Plan)

Valuation Analysis

Forecast P/E	15.04	Trailing P/E	18.03
Market Cap	$1.9 Billion	Book Value	1.1 Billion
Price/Book	1.81	Price/Sales	0.84

Dividend Achiever Status

Rank	102	10 Year Growth Rate	13.24%
Total Years of Dividend Growth		26

Business Summary: Medical Instruments &Equipment (MIC: 9.6 SIC: 3841 NAIC:339112)

Teleflex operates in three segments. Commercial Products designs and manufactures proprietary mechanical and electrical/electronic controls for the automotive market; mechanical, electrical and hydraulic controls, and electronics for the marine market; and proprietary products for fluid transfer and industrial applications. Medical Products manufactures and distributes a broad range of invasive disposable and reusable devices for selected medical care markets. Aerospace Products designs and manufactures cargo handling systems and containers for aviation, and provide surface treatments, repair services and manufactured components for the aerospace and turbine engine markets.

Recent Developments: For the year ended Dec 28 2003, net income declined 12.9% to $109.1 million compared with $125.3 million in 2002. Results for 2003 and 2002 included gains from asset sales and net insurance proceeds of $3.1 million and $10.1 million respectively. Revenues climbed 9.9% to $2.28 billion from $2.08 billion the previous year. Sales of commercial products grew 12.3% to $1.22 billion, while sales of medical products rose 19.2% to $534.7 million. However, sales of aerospace products slipped 2.5% to $528. million due to the weaker performance in industrial gas turbine services, pricing pressures and an adverse product mix. Operating profit decreased to $177.8 million.

Prospects: Co. expects earnings per share for full-year 2004 in the range of $3.10 to $3.20. Moreover, earnings for the first quarter of 2004 should be in line with the first quarter of 2002, with expected accelerated earnings growth in subsequent quarters. Meanwhile, the Aerospace segment should continue to benefit from cost-reduction efforts and improved performance in the industrial gas turbine services product line. The Commercial segment is expected to benefit due to new global program introductions in the automotive and other markets. Operating profit in the Medical segment is expected to increase as Co. realizes benefits from acquisitions.

Financial Data
(US$ in Thousands)

	12/28/2003	12/29/2002	12/30/2001	12/31/2000	12/26/1999	12/27/1998	12/28/1997	12/29/1996
Earnings Per Share	2.73	3.15	2.86	2.83	2.47	2.15	1.86	1.5
Cash Flow Per Share	5.63	5.04	4.79	4.90	3.48	3.42	2.14	1.9
Tang. Book Val. Per Share	19.41	16.60	19.98	18.00	15.84	14.20	12.49	11.2
Dividends Per Share	0.780	0.710	0.660	0.580	0.500	0.440	0.380	0.34
Dividend Payout %	28.57	22.53	23.07	20.49	20.44	20.69	20.83	21.5
Income Statement								
Total Revenues	2,282,435	2,076,229	1,905,004	1,764,482	1,601,069	1,437,578	1,145,773	931,18
Total Indirect Exp.	416,892	394,900	404,061	352,852	320,166	300,214	259,023	218,09
Depreciation & Amort.	104,352	95,117	92,401	77,417	67,389	60,105	47,940	38,75
Operating Income	177,828	172,488	159,695	158,214	142,756	124,760	106,405	86,77
Net Interest Inc./(Exp.)	(26,337)	(25,023)	(28,465)	(20,787)	(17,732)	(17,054)	(14,435)	(13,87(
Income Taxes	42,388	47,222	47,384	48,990	47,536	42,210	36,333	29,61
Net Income	109,103	125,266	112,311	109,224	95,220	82,550	70,072	57,16
Average Shs. Outstg.	39,942	39,786	39,280	38,633	38,525	38,425	37,661	36,19
Balance Sheet								
Cash & Cash Equivalents	56,580	44,494	46,900	45,139	29,040	66,689	30,702	68,6
Total Current Assets	1,006,187	837,895	747,477	662,038	604,940	616,942	566,477	466,02
Total Assets	2,110,613	1,813,384	1,635,020	1,401,288	1,263,444	1,215,917	1,079,165	857,85
Total Current Liabilities	612,671	498,483	495,426	383,872	329,412	311,479	294,907	196,6(
Long-Term Obligations	229,882	240,123	228,180	220,557	246,191	275,581	237,562	195,94
Net Stockholders' Equity	1,062,302	912,281	778,143	690,422	602,564	534,450	463,753	409,17
Net Working Capital	393,516	339,412	252,051	278,166	275,528	305,463	271,570	269,35
Shares Outstanding	39,795	39,398	38,932	38,344	38,018	37,615	37,118	36,22
Statistical Record								
Operating Profit Margin %	7.79	8.30	8.38	8.96	8.91	8.67	9.28	9.3
Return on Equity %	10.27	13.73	14.43	15.81	15.80	15.44	15.10	13.9
Return on Assets %	5.16	6.90	6.86	7.79	7.53	6.78	6.49	6.(
Debt/Total Assets %	10.89	13.24	13.95	15.73	19.48	22.66	22.01	22.8
Price Range	49.95-34.24	58.57-40.92	50.98-35.71	44.69-26.94	50.38-29.69	45.50-30.00	39.38-23.38	26.00-19.1
P/E Ratio	18.30-12.54	18.59-12.99	17.83-12.49	15.79-9.52	20.39-12.02	21.16-13.95	21.17-12.57	16.46-12.
Average Yield %	1.83	1.44	1.49	1.67	1.23	1.13	1.21	1.4

Address: 630 West Germantown Pike, Plymouth Meeting, PA 19462	Officers: Lennox K. Black – Chmn., John J. Sickler – Vice-Chmn.	Investor Contact:610-834-6362
Telephone: (610) 834-6301	Transfer Agents:American Stock Transfer &Trust	Institutional Holding
Web Site: www.teleflex.com	Company, New York, NY	No of Institutions: 35
		Shares: 633,895 % Held: –

TELEPHONE AND DATA SYSTEMS, INC.

Exchange	Symbol	Price	52Wk Range	Yield	P/E
ASE	TDS	$70.87 (3/31/2004)	74.43–42.01	0.93	196.86

*7 Year Price Score 75.7   *NYSE Composite Index=100   *12 Month Price Score 107.7

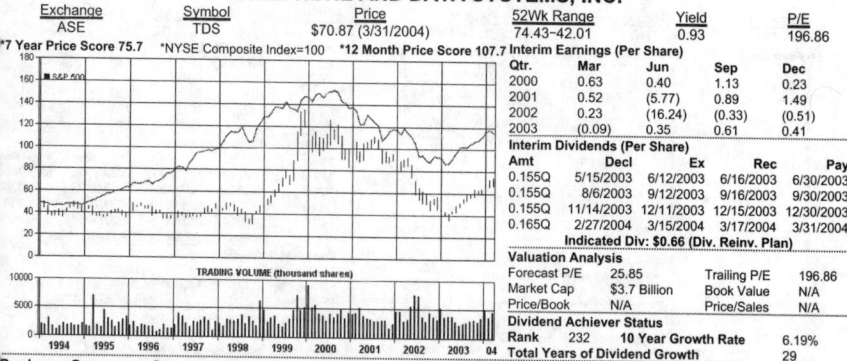

Interim Earnings (Per Share)

Qtr.	Mar	Jun	Sep	Dec
2000	0.63	0.40	1.13	0.23
2001	0.52	(5.77)	0.89	1.49
2002	0.23	(16.24)	(0.33)	(0.51)
2003	(0.09)	0.35	0.61	0.41

Interim Dividends (Per Share)

Amt	Decl	Ex	Rec	Pay
0.155Q	5/15/2003	6/12/2003	6/16/2003	6/30/2003
0.155Q	8/6/2003	9/12/2003	9/16/2003	9/30/2003
0.155Q	11/14/2003	12/11/2003	12/15/2003	12/30/2003
0.165Q	2/27/2004	3/15/2004	3/17/2004	3/31/2004

Indicated Div: $0.66 (Div. Reinv. Plan)

Valuation Analysis

Forecast P/E	25.85	Trailing P/E	196.86
Market Cap	$3.7 Billion	Book Value	N/A
Price/Book	N/A	Price/Sales	N/A

Dividend Achiever Status

Rank	232	10 Year Growth Rate	6.19%
Total Years of Dividend Growth		29	

Business Summary: Communications (MIC: 10.1 SIC: 4812 NAIC:517212)

Telephone and Data Systems is a diversified telecommunications service company with wireless telephone and wireline telephone operations. At Dec 31 2003, Co. served approximately 5.5 million customers in 36 states, including 4.4 million wireless customers and 1.1 million wireline telephone equivalent access lines. Co. conducts substantially all of its wireless operations through its 82.1%–owned subsidiary, United States Cellular Corporation. Co. conducts its wireline telephone operations through its wholly owned subsidiary, TDS Telecommunications Corporation.

Recent Developments: For the year ended Dec 31 2003, income from continuing operations was $74.9 million compared with a loss of $987.7 million a year earlier. Results for 2003 and 2002 included losses on marketable equity securities and other investments of $10.2 million and $1.89 billion, respectively. Results for 2003 also included a loss of $52.8 million on assets held for sale and impairment of assets. Total operating revenues advanced 14.9% to $3.45 billion, reflecting growth in wireless customers and equivalent access lines. However, operating income slid 18.3% to $315.5 million due mainly to costs associated with the acquisition of the Chicago market and increased marketing and depreciation expenses.

Prospects: Co.'s near–term outlook remains mixed. For the quarter ended Dec 31 2003, U.S. Cellular reported net wireless customer additions of 141,000, an improvement from 66,000 in the prior quarter but down from 160,000 a year earlier. Also, average monthly revenue per unit declined to $47.80 from $49.05 in the prior quarter and $47.91 the year before. On the plus side, postpay churn, or the rate of customers moving between carriers, was 1.4% versus 1.6% last quarter and 1.8% the previous year, despite continued competition and the availability of wireless local number portability. Meanwhile, TDS Telecom's top line should continue to benefit from digital subscriber line and long distance growth.

Financial Data

(US$ in Thousands)	12/31/2003	12/31/2002	12/31/2001	12/31/2000	12/31/1999	12/31/1998	12/31/1997	12/31/1996
Earnings Per Share	1.28	(16.85)	(2.87)	2.39	5.02	1.03	(0.19)	2.08
Cash Flow Per Share	15.90	13.53	9.30	12.45	7.64	5.84	3.42	4.85
Tang. Book Val. Per Share	15.66	14.78	37.29	47.16	21.70	11.85	7.54	9.19
Dividends Per Share	0.620	0.580	0.540	0.610	0.450	0.430	0.410	0.300
Dividend Payout %	48.43	N.M.	N.M.	25.73	9.06	42.23	N.M.	14.42
Income Statement								
Total Revenues	3,445,216	2,985,366	2,588,542	2,326,856	1,963,098	1,805,725	1,471,533	1,214,636
Total Indirect Exp.	1,946,787	...	1,263	10,258	12,927	34,207	...	...
Depreciation & Amort.	595,732	510,445	2,526	20,516	25,854	22,790	301,556	231,583
Operating Income	315,544	386,355	436,155	420,066	370,393	(20,904)	(3,702)	154,098
Net Interest Inc./(Exp.)	(171,391)	(132,224)	(103,710)	(100,559)	(99,984)	(126,360)	(89,744)	(42,853)
Income Taxes	79,892	(577,000)	(44,908)	149,481	228,176	69,297	28,559	123,646
Eqty Earns/Minority Int.	(23,612)	(9,068)	(42,419)	(61,683)	(12,927)	(11,395)	...	...
Income from Cont Ops	74,888	(987,717)	(168,248)	145,527	314,151	...	...	...
Net Income	61,490	(984,371)	(198,055)	2,237,002	229,961	64,408	(9,549)	128,139
Average Shs. Outstg.	57,875	58,644	58,661	60,636	62,736	60,982	60,211	60,732
Balance Sheet								
Cash & Cash Equivalents	937,651	1,298,936	140,744	102,635	115,993	60,424	75,567	119,297
Total Current Assets	1,504,946	1,948,012	674,356	527,100	508,008	405,439	408,284	346,070
Total Assets	10,171,238	9,602,028	8,046,792	8,634,609	5,375,828	5,527,545	4,971,601	4,200,969
Total Current Liabilities	696,945	1,167,166	816,216	984,411	369,672	623,379	905,885	509,267
Long–Term Obligations	1,994,913	1,641,624	1,507,764	1,172,987	1,279,877	1,553,096	1,264,218	982,232
Net Stockholders' Equity	3,108,019	3,059,577	3,526,366	3,943,894	2,492,106	2,263,893	1,999,106	2,060,941
Net Working Capital	808,001	780,846	(141,860)	(457,311)	138,336	(217,940)	(497,601)	(163,197)
Shares Outstanding	62,722	58,678	58,569	58,688	61,133	61,177	60,585	61,154
Statistical Record								
Operating Profit Margin %	9.15	12.94	16.84	18.05	18.86	N.M.	N.M.	12.68
Return on Equity %	2.40	N.M	N.M	3.68	12.60	2.84	N.M.	6.21
Return on Assets %	0.73	N.M.	N.M.	1.68	5.84	1.16	N.M.	3.05
Debt/Total Assets %	19.61	17.09	18.73	13.58	23.80	28.09	25.42	23.38
Price Range	63.92–35.96	91.90–44.45	111.2–87.00	126.4–82.95	135.4–44.44	49.69–31.06	48.50–34.63	48.75–35.00
P/E Ratio	49.94–28.09	N/A	N/A	52.88–34.71	26.97–8.85	48.24–30.16	N/A	23.44–16.83
Average Yield %	1.21	0.85	0.55	0.57	0.58	1.02	1.02	0.71

Address: 30 North Lasalle Street, Chicago, IL 60602	Officers: Walter C.D. Carlson – Chmn., LeRoy T. Carlson – Pres., C.E.O.	Investor Contact: (312) 630–1900
Telephone: (312) 630–1900		Institutional Holding
Web Site: www.teldta.com		No of Institutions: 1
		Shares: 1,364 % Held: —

TENNANT CO.

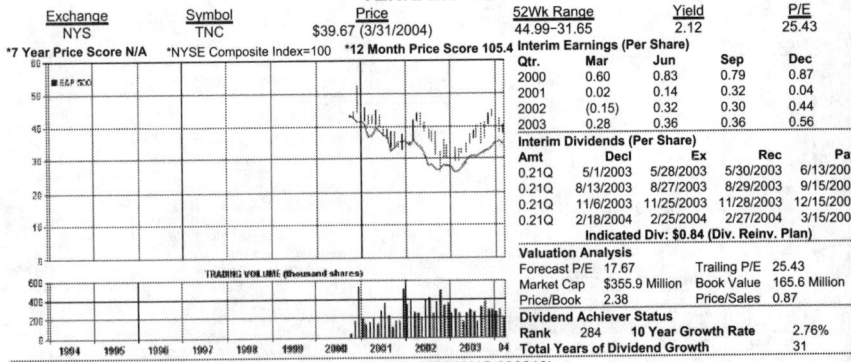

Exchange NYS	**Symbol** TNC	**Price** $39.67 (3/31/2004)	**52Wk Range** 44.99-31.65		**Yield** 2.12		**P/E** 25.43

*7 Year Price Score N/A   *NYSE Composite Index=100   *12 Month Price Score 105.4

Interim Earnings (Per Share)

Qtr.	Mar	Jun	Sep	Dec
2000	0.60	0.83	0.79	0.87
2001	0.02	0.14	0.32	0.04
2002	(0.15)	0.32	0.30	0.44
2003	0.28	0.36	0.36	0.56

Interim Dividends (Per Share)

Amt	Decl	Ex	Rec	Pay
0.21Q	5/1/2003	5/28/2003	5/30/2003	6/13/2003
0.21Q	8/13/2003	8/27/2003	8/29/2003	9/15/2003
0.21Q	11/6/2003	11/25/2003	11/28/2003	12/15/2003
0.21Q	2/18/2004	2/25/2004	2/27/2004	3/15/2004

Indicated Div: $0.84 (Div. Reinv. Plan)

Valuation Analysis

Forecast P/E	17.67	Trailing P/E	25.43
Market Cap	$355.9 Million	Book Value	165.6 Million
Price/Book	2.38	Price/Sales	0.87

Dividend Achiever Status

Rank	284	10 Year Growth Rate	2.76%
Total Years of Dividend Growth			31

Business Summary: Purpose Machinery (MIC: 11.13 SIC: 3589 NAIC:333319)

Tennant is a manufacturer of nonresidential floor maintenance and outdoor cleaning equipment, floor coatings and related offerings. Co.'s products include scrubbers, sweepers, extractors, buffers and other specialized floor cleaning equipment and supplies, plus an array of industrial floor coatings. Co. has manufacturing operations in Holland, Michigan and United Kingdom, The Netherlands. Co. sells its products directly in ten countries and through distributors in 50 others.

Recent Developments: For the year ended Dec 31 2003, net income climbed 71.3% to $14.2 million from $8.3 million the previous year. Results for 2002 included restructuring charges of $4.0 million. Net sales grew 7.0% to $454.0 million, primarily due to foreign currency gains. In North America, sales rose 2.5% to $319.7 million due to the addition of previously deferred revenues of $6.4 million resulting from the amendment of a contract with a third–party lessor. European sales climbed 20.5% to $88.8 million, while other international sales grew 17.9% to $45.5 million. Operating income increased 45.6% to $22.7 million.

Prospects: Co.'s prospects appear to be mixed. While the North American industrial economy appears to be growing, the impact on orders for Co.'s industrial cleaning equipment has typically lagged the onset of recovery by one to two quarters. In addition, budget constraints continue to dampen demand for cleaning equipment in the North American public sector. Conversely, Co.'s expanded sales and service coverage in Europe is resulting in solid volume growth. Co.'s January 2004 acquisition of Walter–Broadley should build on this growth, doubling its revenue base in the U.K. and tripling the number of service representatives. For 2004, Co. expects net earnings per share of $1.55 to $1.85.

Financial Data
(US$ in Thousands)

	12/31/2003	12/31/2002	12/31/2001	12/31/2000	12/31/1999	12/31/1998	12/31/1997	12/31/1996
Earnings Per Share	1.56	0.91	0.52	3.09	2.15	2.67	2.41	2.10
Cash Flow Per Share	3.36	2.12	3.70	4.25	4.19	4.51	4.17	4.44
Tang. Book Val. Per Share	16.43	15.18	15.17	15.16	13.06	12.67	12.12	11.14
Dividends Per Share	0.840	0.820	0.800	0.970	0.760	0.730	0.720	0.510
Dividend Payout %	53.84	90.10	153.84	31.39	35.34	27.34	29.87	24.29
Income Statement								
Total Revenues	453,962	424,183	422,970	454,044	429,407	389,388	372,428	344,433
Total Indirect Exp.	159,002	154,247	134,546	139,665	142,747	128,450	120,948	110,745
Depreciation & Amort.	13,879	16,947	18,507	18,391	18,667	17,550	17,468	16,387
Operating Income	22,675	15,576	13,416	43,524	31,262	37,349	36,088	31,631
Net Interest Inc./(Exp.)	608	510	340	807	(1,097)	1,479	2,678	1,768
Income Taxes	8,328	6,633	8,945	15,794	10,893	13,767	13,425	11,302
Net Income	14,155	8,265	4,804	28,250	19,693	25,325	24,205	21,027
Average Shs. Outstg.	9,064	9,048	9,203	9,135	9,140	9,500	10,032	10,021
Balance Sheet								
Cash & Cash Equivalents	24,587	16,356	23,783	21,512	14,928	17,693	16,279	9,881
Total Current Assets	176,370	162,901	152,387	171,628	165,093	150,868	143,105	126,481
Total Assets	258,873	256,237	246,619	263,285	257,533	239,098	233,870	219,180
Total Current Liabilities	59,507	70,349	55,648	67,255	74,999	60,809	57,149	7,898
Long–Term Obligations	6,295	5,000	10,000	10,000	16,003	23,038	20,678	21,824
Net Stockholders' Equity	165,616	154,145	154,328	154,948	135,915	131,267	134,086	128,866
Net Working Capital	116,863	92,552	96,739	104,373	90,094	90,059	85,956	118,583
Shares Outstanding	8,994	8,981	9,036	9,052	8,989	9,123	9,699	9,965
Statistical Record								
Operating Profit Margin %	4.99	3.67	3.17	9.58	7.28	9.59	9.68	9.18
Return on Equity %	8.54	5.36	3.11	18.23	14.48	19.29	18.05	16.31
Return on Assets %	5.46	3.22	1.94	10.72	7.64	10.59	10.34	9.59
Debt/Total Assets %	2.43	1.95	4.05	3.79	6.21	9.63	8.84	9.95
Price Range	44.99-29.28	44.00-26.62	48.88-32.90	52.31-43.06	...	...	...	...
P/E Ratio	28.84-18.77	48.35-29.25	93.99-63.27	16.93-13.94	...	...	...	...
Average Yield %	2.30	2.24	2.01	2.13	N/A	N/A	N/A	N/A

Address: 701 North Lilac Drive, Minneapolis, MN 55440
Telephone: (763) 540-1208
Web Site: www.tennantco.com

Officers: Janet M. Dolan – Pres., C.E.O., Eric A. Blanchard – V.P., Gen. Couns., Sec.
Transfer Agents: Wells Fargo Bank Minnesota, N.A., St. Paul, MN

Investor Contact: 763–540–1553
Institutional Holding
No of Institutions: 4
Shares: 7,296   **% Held:** –

TEPPCO PARTNERS, L.P.

Exchange	Symbol	Price	52Wk Range	Yield	P/E
NYS	TPP	$41.97 (3/31/2004)	41.97-30.35	6.19	24.98

7 Year Price Score 127.8 *NYSE Composite Index=100 **12 Month Price Score 102.3**

TRADING VOLUME (thousand shares)

Interim Earnings (Per Share)

Qtr.	Mar	Jun	Sep	Dec
2000	0.60	0.35	0.41	0.53
2001	0.55	0.89	0.35	0.39
2002	0.46	0.39	0.48	0.46
2003	0.43	0.43	0.36	0.30

Interim Dividends (Per Share)

Amt	Decl	Ex	Rec	Pay
0.625Q	3/27/2003	4/28/2003	4/30/2003	5/9/2003
0.625Q	7/16/2003	7/29/2003	7/31/2003	8/8/2003
0.65Q	10/17/2003	10/29/2003	10/31/2003	11/7/2003
0.65Q	1/16/2004	1/28/2004	1/30/2004	2/6/2004

Indicated Div: $2.60

Valuation Analysis

Forecast P/E	21.37	Trailing P/E	24.98
Market Cap	$2.1 Billion	Book Value	1.1 Billion
Price/Book	1.80	Price/Sales	0.50

Dividend Achiever Status

Rank	187	10 Year Growth Rate	8.46%
Total Years of Dividend Growth			11

Business Summary: Oil and Gas (MIC: 14.2 SIC: 4613 NAIC:486910)

TEPPCO Partners operates through three segments. The downstream segment includes transportation and storage of refined products, liquefied petroleum gases and petrochemicals. The upstream segment includes gathering, transportation, marketing and storage of crude oil, and distribution of lubrication oils and specialty chemicals. The midstream segment includes natural gas gathering services, fractionation of natural gas liquids (NGLs) and transportation of NGLs. Texas Eastern Products Pipeline Co., a subsidiary of Duke Energy Field Services (DEFS), serves as the general partner of TPP. Certain assets of the midstream segment are managed and operated by DEFS under an agreement with Co.

Recent Developments: For the year ended Dec 31 2003, net income was $125.8 million compared with $117.9 million a year earlier. Results for 2003 included a $3.9 million gain on the sale of assets. Total operating revenues rose 31.3% to $4.26 billion. Co. noted that capacity resulting from its investment in Centennial Pipeline and other system improvements allowed for higher refined products and liquefied petroleum gas deliveries, while capacity expansions on the Jonah system resulted in increased natural gas gathering volumes. Also, higher utilization across several crude oil systems, combined with the Nov 1 2003 acquisition of the Genesis Pipeline Texas, L.P. assets, resulted in increased crude oil deliveries.

Prospects: Co.'s near-term prospects appear moderately positive. For full-year 2004, Co. expects earnings in the range of $1.55 to $1.85 per unit, which reflects the full year effect of its acquisition of the crude supply and transportation assets from Genesis Crude Oil L.P. and Genesis Pipeline Texas L.P. and completion of several organic growth projects in 2004. Co. anticipates that total capital expenditures for 2004 will be about $140.0 million, including $112.0 million for revenue generating and facility improvement projects and $28.0 million for maintenance capital.

Financial Data

(US$ in Thousands)	12/31/2003	12/31/2002	12/31/2001	12/31/2000	12/31/1999	12/31/1998	12/31/1997	12/31/1996
Earnings Per Share	1.52	1.79	2.18	1.89	1.91	1.61	1.95	1.89
Cash Flow Per Share	4.00	4.77	4.30	3.21	2.28	1.24	...	2.96
Tang. Book Val. Per Share	N.M	N.M	N.M	N.M	N.M	N.M	...	...
Dividends Per Share	2.500	2.350	2.150	2.000	1.850	1.750	1.550	1.450
Dividend Payout %	164.47	131.28	98.62	105.82	96.85	108.69	79.48	76.71
Income Statement								
Total Revenues	4,255,832	3,242,163	3,556,413	3,087,941	1,934,883	429,638	222,093	216,025
Total Indirect Exp.	4,059,476	3,071,916	3,405,424	2,979,044	1,834,793	349,672	130,543	128,591
Depreciation & Amort.	100,728	86,032	45,899	35,163	32,656	26,938	23,772	23,409
Operating Income	192,408	170,247	150,989	108,025	100,090	79,966	91,550	87,434
Net Interest Inc./(Exp.)	(84,250)	(66,192)	(62,057)	(44,423)	(29,430)	(28,989)	(32,229)	(33,534)
Eqty Earns/Minority Int.	16,863	11,980	16,598	11,425	(736)	(544)	(625)	(598)
Income from Cont Ops	...	...	...	...	...	53,341	...	...
Net Income	125,769	117,862	109,131	77,376	72,120	(19,426)	61,300	58,648
Average Shs. Outstg.	59,765	49,202	39,258	33,594	45,058	74,933	29,000	57,456
Balance Sheet								
Cash & Cash Equivalents	29,469	30,968	25,479	27,096	32,593	47,423	43,961	34,047
Total Current Assets	452,818	360,567	283,480	363,397	263,009	188,576	91,159	98,743
Total Assets	2,940,992	2,770,642	2,065,348	1,622,810	1,041,373	914,969	673,909	671,241
Total Current Liabilities	475,591	366,783	668,842	358,271	243,492	148,225	53,875	47,553
Long-Term Obligations	1,339,650	1,377,692	730,472	835,784	455,753	427,722	309,512	326,512
Net Stockholders' Equity	1,109,321	891,842	543,181	315,057	229,767	227,186	302,967	290,311
Net Working Capital	(22,773)	(6,216)	(385,362)	5,126	19,517	40,351	37,284	51,190
Shares Outstanding	62,998	53,809	40,500	32,700	29,000	29,000	29,000	29,000
Statistical Record								
Operating Profit Margin %	4.52	5.25	4.24	3.49	5.17	18.61	41.22	40.47
Return on Equity %	11.33	13.21	20.09	24.55	31.38	23.47	20.23	20.20
Return on Assets %	4.27	4.25	5.28	4.76	6.92	5.82	9.09	8.73
Debt/Total Assets %	45.55	49.72	35.36	51.50	43.76	46.74	45.92	48.64
Price Range	41.15-27.75	33.00-26.10	35.90-24.75	26.63-19.31	27.94-18.00	30.50-24.25	27.88-20.13	21.00-17.31
P/E Ratio	27.07-18.26	18.44-14.58	16.47-11.35	14.09-10.22	14.63-9.42	18.94-15.06	14.29-10.32	11.11-9.16
Average Yield %	7.26	7.80	7.32	8.72	7.79	6.35	6.56	7.61

Address: 2929 Allen Pkwy, Houston, TX 77252-2521	**Officers:** Jim W. Mogg – Chmn., Barry R. Pearl – Pres., C.E.O., C.O.O.	**Investor Contact:** (800) 659-0059
Telephone: (713) 759-3636	**Transfer Agents:** ChaseMellon Shareholder Services, L.L.C., Ridgefield Park, NJ	**Institutional Holding** No of Institutions: 3
Web Site: www.teppco.com		Shares: 258 % Held: –

TOOTSIE ROLL INDUSTRIES INC

Exchange	Symbol	Price	52Wk Range	Yield	P/E
NYS	TR	$36.56 (3/31/2004)	37.61-27.91	0.77	29.02

*7 Year Price Score 95.6 *NYSE Composite Index=100 *12 Month Price Score 102.2

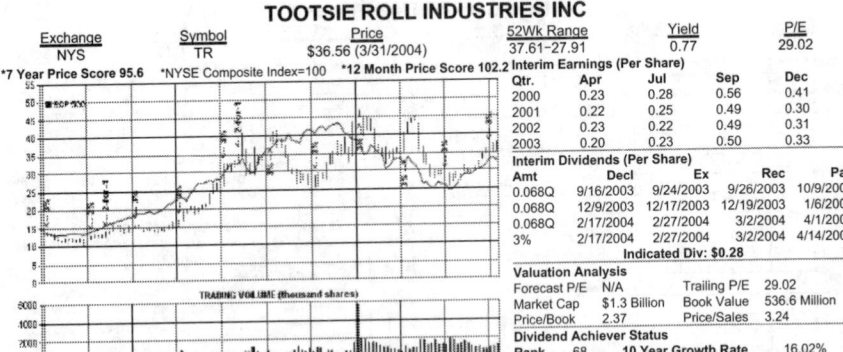

Interim Earnings (Per Share)

Qtr.	Apr	Jul	Sep	Dec
2000	0.23	0.28	0.56	0.41
2001	0.22	0.25	0.49	0.30
2002	0.23	0.22	0.49	0.31
2003	0.20	0.23	0.50	0.33

Interim Dividends (Per Share)

Amt	Decl	Ex	Rec	Pay
0.068Q	9/16/2003	9/24/2003	9/26/2003	10/9/2003
0.068Q	12/9/2003	12/17/2003	12/19/2003	1/6/2004
0.068Q	2/17/2004	2/27/2004	3/2/2004	4/1/2004
3%	2/17/2004	2/27/2004	3/2/2004	4/14/2004

Indicated Div: $0.28

Valuation Analysis

Forecast P/E	N/A	Trailing P/E	29.02
Market Cap	$1.3 Billion	Book Value	536.6 Million
Price/Book	2.37	Price/Sales	3.24

Dividend Achiever Status

Rank	68	10 Year Growth Rate	16.02%
Total Years of Dividend Growth			40

Business Summary: Food (MIC: 4.1 SIC: 2064 NAIC:311340)

Tootsie Roll Industries is engaged in the manufacture and sale of candy. The majority of Co.'s products are sold under the following registered trademarks: *Tootsie Roll, Tootsie Roll Pops, Caramel Apple Pops, Child's Play, Charms, Blow Pop, Blue Razz, Cella's* chocolate covered cherries, *Mason Dots, Mason Crows, Junior Mints, Charleston Chew, Sugar Daddy, Sugar Babies, Andes* and *Fluffy Stuff* cotton candy. Co. has manufacturing facilities in Illinois, New York, Tennessee, Massachusetts, Wisconsin, Maryland and Mexico.

Recent Developments: For the year ended Dec 31 2003, net income declined 2.1% to $65.0 million from $66.4 million the previous year. Sales slipped slightly to $392.7 million from $393.2 million a year earlier, reflecting sluggish U.S. economic conditions in the first half of 2003 as well as lower sales in Mexico. This decrease was partially offset by successful marketing and promotional programs, particularly Co.'s Halloween 2003 sales promotion. Selective price increases also added to sales during the year, but these gains were partially offset by increased trade promotions and discounts. Gross profit was essentially unchanged at $170.1 million. Operating earnings fell 3.0% to $92.4 million.

Prospects: Co.'s near-term prospects appear to be mixed. On one hand, Co.'s core brands should continue to benefit from selected price increases and an improving retail spending environment. Conversely, Co. noted that it is continuing to experience margin pressures from higher costs for major ingredients. For instance, Cocoa prices remain high coming into the year due to a disruption in the supply of beans coming from the Ivory Coast, the world's largest producer. Similarly, soybean oil prices increased toward the end of the year due to poor yields in the soybean crop. In response, Co. will remain committed to minimizing costs, and will re-examine its operations in search of operational improvements.

Financial Data
(US$ in Thousands)

	12/31/2003	12/31/2002	12/31/2001	12/31/2000	12/31/1999	12/31/1998	12/31/1997	12/31/1996
Earnings Per Share	1.26	1.25	1.26	1.48	1.41	1.36	2.50	0.8
Cash Flow Per Share	1.61	1.34	1.57	1.67	1.45	1.57	2.81	1.32
Tang. Book Val. Per Share	8.18	7.79	7.53	6.68	6.91	6.26	10.81	3.79
Dividends Per Share	0.268	0.260	0.250	0.230	0.190	0.150	0.120	0.100
Dividend Payout %	21.27	20.80	19.84	15.54	13.48	11.03	4.80	12.35
Income Statement								
Total Revenues	392,656	393,185	423,496	427,054	396,750	388,659	375,594	340,909
Total Indirect Exp.	77,756	75,751	112,895	109,225	99,670	99,777	97,194	90,888
Depreciation & Amort.	13,913	12,354	3,778	3,420	2,706	2,706	2,706	2,706
Operating Income	92,353	96,669	93,944	110,729	104,519	101,265	90,087	71,532
Net Interest Inc./(Exp.)	4,292	5,244	6,200	6,770	6,996	6,178	5,281	2,389
Income Taxes	32,933	34,300	35,100	42,071	40,137	38,537	34,679	27,891
Net Income	65,014	66,388	65,687	75,737	71,310	67,526	60,682	47,207
Average Shs. Outstg.	51,784	53,078	51,964	50,917	50,443	49,492	24,248	57,842
Balance Sheet								
Cash & Cash Equivalents	171,045	146,244	175,161	132,487	159,506	163,920	142,280	144,157
Total Current Assets	243,705	224,948	246,096	203,211	224,532	228,539	206,961	201,513
Total Assets	665,297	646,080	618,676	562,442	529,416	487,423	436,742	391,456
Total Current Liabilities	62,887	63,096	57,846	57,446	56,109	53,384	53,606	48,186
Long-Term Obligations	7,500	7,500	7,500	7,500	7,500	7,500	7,500	7,500
Net Stockholders' Equity	536,581	526,740	508,461	458,696	430,646	396,457	351,163	312,881
Net Working Capital	180,818	161,852	188,250	145,765	168,423	175,155	153,355	153,329
Shares Outstanding	51,171	52,480	51,917	50,496	49,966	49,271	24,099	57,842
Statistical Record								
Operating Profit Margin %	23.52	24.58	22.18	25.92	26.34	26.05	23.98	20.98
Return on Equity %	12.11	12.60	12.91	16.51	16.55	17.03	17.28	15.05
Return on Assets %	9.77	10.27	10.61	13.46	13.46	13.85	13.89	12.05
Debt/Total Assets %	1.12	1.16	1.21	1.33	1.41	1.53	1.71	1.9
Price Range	35.86-25.73	45.22-27.82	46.76-32.10	43.76-25.71	41.54-26.49	40.76-24.99	27.17-15.35	16.36-13.8
P/E Ratio	28.46-20.42	36.17-22.25	37.11-25.48	29.56-17.37	29.46-18.79	29.97-18.38	10.87-6.14	20.20-17.1
Average Yield %	0.87	0.73	0.64	0.71	0.56	0.46	0.59	0.6

Address: 7401 South Cicero Avenue, Chicago, IL 60629 **Telephone:** (773) 838-3400 **Web Site:** www.tootsie.com	**Officers:** Melvin J. Gordon - Chmn., C.E.O., Ellen R. Gordon - Pres., C.O.O. **Transfer Agents:** Mellon Investor Services, L.L.C., Ridgefield Park, NJ	**Investor Contact:** 800-851-9677 **Institutional Holding** **No of Institutions:** 143 **Shares:** 12,300,560 **% Held:** 22.80%

TRANSATLANTIC HOLDINGS, INC.

Exchange	Symbol	Price	52Wk Range	Yield	P/E
NYS	TRH	$87.21 (3/31/2004)	87.46-66.15	0.50	15.16

*7 Year Price Score 117.8 *NYSE Composite Index=100 *12 Month Price Score 99.0

Interim Earnings (Per Share)

Qtr.	Mar	Jun	Sep	Dec
2000	1.07	0.97	1.02	0.97
2001	0.96	0.76	(1.49)	0.13
2002	1.00	1.16	1.16	(0.11)
2003	1.19	1.43	1.53	1.60

Interim Dividends (Per Share)

Amt	Decl	Ex	Rec	Pay
0.11Q	5/15/2003	9/3/2003	9/5/2003	9/12/2003
0.11Q	9/18/2003	11/25/2003	11/28/2003	12/12/2003
0.11Q	12/4/2003	3/3/2004	3/5/2004	3/19/2004
0.11Q	3/25/2004	6/2/2004	6/4/2004	6/18/2004

Indicated Div: $0.44

Valuation Analysis

Forecast P/E	13.91	Trailing P/E	21.59
Market Cap	$4.6 Billion	Book Value	2.3 Billion
Price/Book	1.63	Price/Sales	1.16

Dividend Achiever Status

Rank	105	10 Year Growth Rate	12.93%
Total Years of Dividend Growth			13

Business Summary: Insurance (MIC: 8.2 SIC: 6331 NAIC:524126)

Transatlantic Holdings, through its wholly-owned subsidiaries Transatlantic Reinsurance Company, Trans Re Zurich and Putnam Reinsurance Company, offers reinsurance capacity for a full range of property and casualty products on a treaty and facultative basis, directly and through brokers, to insurance and reinsurance companies, in both the domestic and international markets. Co.'s principal lines of reinsurance include auto liability, other liability, accident and health, medical malpractice, marine and aviation, and surety and credit in the casualty lines, and fire and allied in the property lines.

Recent Developments: For the twelve months ended Dec 31 2003, net income jumped 79.3% to $303.6 million compared with $169.3 million in the prior-year period. Total revenues advanced 32.0% to $3.45 billion from $2.62 billion the previous year. Revenues included realized net capital gains of $9.9 million in 2003 and realized net capital losses of $6.0 million in 2002. Net premiums written increased 33.6% to $3.34 billion from $2.50 billion the year before. Net premiums earned climbed 33.8% to $3.17 billion from $2.37 billion a year earlier. Total expenses were $3.07 billion, up 26.3% versus $2.43 billion the prior year.

Prospects: Earnings are being positively affected by strong growth in net premiums written, driven by rate increases, along with increased coverage provided and favorable foreign currency exchange rates. Domestic net premiums written are benefiting from overall improved market conditions, with significant increases in specialty casualty, principally directors' and officers' liability, medical malpractice and other professional liability, property and ocean marine and aviation lines. Meanwhile, higher international net premiums written are being fueled by property, specialty casualty and auto liability lines. Looking ahead, Co. anticipates worldwide market conditions to remain strong in 2004.

Financial Data

(US$ in Thousands)	9 Mos	6 Mos	3 Mos	12/31/2002	12/31/2001	12/31/2000	12/31/1999	12/31/1998
Earnings Per Share	4.15	2.62	1.19	3.21	0.36	4.03	3.58	4.73
Tang. Book Val. Per Share	...	...	39.71	38.78	35.32	35.58	31.53	30.96
Dividends Per Share	0.410	0.400	0.390	0.390	0.370	0.340	0.310	0.280
Dividend Payout %	9.87	15.26	33.27	12.21	103.33	8.59	8.75	5.91
Income Statement								
Total Premium Income	2,318,589	1,454,930	692,167	2,369,452	1,790,339	1,631,536	1,484,634	1,380,570
Net Investment Income	201,584	133,095	64,614	252,026	240,083	234,485	230,739	222,000
Other Income	6,770	1,269	538	(5,951)	(240)	0.00	0.00	0.00
Total Revenues	2,526,943	1,589,294	757,319	2,615,527	2,030,182	1,866,021	1,715,373	1,602,570
Total Indirect Exp.	656,109	418,181	218,944	662,579	526,962	373,566	250,972	140,029
Inc. Before Inc. Taxes	281,033	175,602	79,208	188,320	(34,107)	267,982	236,097	323,351
Income Taxes	62,247	37,596	16,380	19,002	(52,999)	56,344	48,735	75,828
Net Income	218,786	138,006	62,828	169,318	18,892	211,638	187,362	247,523
Average Shs. Outstg.	52,734	52,715	52,689	52,755	52,736	52,476	52,323	52,297
Balance Sheet								
Cash & Cash Equivalents	...	...	139,029	487,861	559,534	157,337	109,952	95,641
Premiums Due	...	...	1,198,155	1,167,802	1,254,216	778,501	777,086	658,027
Invst. Assets: Total	...	...	5,519,439	5,460,128	4,880,217	4,261,980	4,229,445	4,258,244
Total Assets	...	...	7,839,762	7,286,525	6,741,303	5,522,672	5,480,198	5,253,249
Net Stockholders' Equity	...	...	2,080,236	2,030,767	1,846,010	1,856,365	1,642,517	1,610,139
Shares Outstanding	52,414	52,413	52,382	52,360	52,255	52,160	52,091	52,000
Statistical Record								
Return on Equity %	...	...	3.02	8.33	1.02	11.40	11.40	15.37
Return on Assets %	...	...	0.80	2.32	0.28	3.83	3.41	4.71
Price Range	73.30-61.48	71.45-61.48	69.70-61.48	91.00-60.55	92.00-63.18	70.58-45.96	53.42-46.12	62.92-46.37
P/E Ratio	17.66-14.81	27.27-23.47	58.57-51.66	28.35-18.86	255.6-175.5	17.51-11.40	14.92-12.88	13.30-9.80
Average Yield %	0.60	0.60	0.59	0.51	0.48	0.60	0.62	0.54

Address: 80 Pine Street, New York, NY 10005
Telephone: (212) 770-2000
Web Site: www.transre.com

Officers: M. R. Greenberg – Chmn., Robert F. Orlich – Pres., C.E.O.
Transfer Agents: American Stock Transfer & Trust Company, New York, NY

Investor Contact: 212-770-2040
Institutional Holding
No of Institutions: 6
Shares: 118,096 % Held: –

TRUSTMARK CORP.

Exchange	Symbol	Price	52Wk Range	Yield	P/E
NMS	TRMK	$29.02 (3/31/2004)	30.60-23.80	2.62	14.51

*7 Year Price Score 124.7 *NYSE Composite Index=100 *12 Month Price Score 99.1

Interim Earnings (Per Share)

Qtr.	Mar	Jun	Sep	Dec
2000	0.37	0.39	0.37	0.40
2001	0.40	0.41	0.45	0.46
2002	0.48	0.50	0.49	0.47
2003	0.41	0.53	0.55	0.51

Interim Dividends (Per Share)

Amt	Decl	Ex	Rec	Pay
0.165Q	4/15/2003	5/28/2003	6/1/2003	6/15/2003
0.165Q	7/15/2003	8/27/2003	9/1/2003	9/15/2003
0.19Q	10/21/2003	11/26/2003	12/1/2003	12/15/2003
0.19Q	1/20/2004	2/26/2004	3/1/2004	3/15/2004

Indicated Div: $0.76 (Div. Reinv. Plan)

Valuation Analysis

Forecast P/E	13.39	Trailing P/E 14.51
Market Cap	$1.8 Billion	Book Value 689.6 Million
Price/Book	2.53	Price/Sales 3.37

Dividend Achiever Status

Rank	100	10 Year Growth Rate 13.68%
Total Years of Dividend Growth		30

Business Summary: Commercial Banking (MIC: 8.1 SIC: 6021 NAIC:522110)

Trustmark is the holding company for Trustmark National Bank, along with its wholly-owned subsidiaries Trustmark Securities, Inc, Trustmark Investment Advisors, Inc. and The Bottrell Insurance Agency, Inc. Co. also provides banking services through it wholly-owned subsidiary, Somerville Bank & Trust Company. Co. provides a full range of financial products and services to individual and small-business customers through 144 offices in Mississippi, Tennessee and Florida. Co. also provides trust and fiduciary services, brokerage services, insurance services, as well as credit card and mortgage services. In addition, Co. operates a proprietary mutual fund family, The Performance Funds.

Recent Developments: For the year ended Dec 31 2003, net income totaled $118.5 million, down 2.2% compared with $121.1 million in the prior year. Earnings for 2003 and 2002 included pre-tax gains on the sale of loans of $15.9 million and $9.4 million and securit gains of $12.2 million and $13.6 million, respectively. Net interest income slipped 7.7% to $269.8 million from $292.2 million the year before. Provision for loan losses declined 30.7% to $9.8 million from $14.1 million the previous year. Total non-interest income climbe 11.0% to $157.5 million from $141.9 million in 2002, while total non-interest expense rose 1.0% to $236.1 million from $233.8 million year earlier.

Prospects: Results should benefit from Co.'s efforts to expand its operations into new markets. On Mar 12 2004, Co. announced that has completed its acquisition of five branches of Allied Houston Bank, which reported approximately $145.0 million in loans and tota deposits of $160.0 million, for a $10.0 million deposit premium. The acquisition will expand Co.'s operations into Texas with branche located in the Houston market. Meanwhile, earnings are being negatively affected by sharply lower interest rates and increased salary an benefits expenses, partially offset by increased mortgage refinancing activity and higher service charge income on deposit accounts.

Financial Data

(US$ in Thousands)	12/31/2003	12/31/2002	12/31/2001	12/31/2000	12/31/1999	12/31/1998	12/31/1997	12/31/1996
Earnings Per Share	2.00	1.94	1.72	1.53	1.36	1.14	0.98	0.9
Tang. Book Val. Per Share	8.96	9.25	8.92	8.69	8.38	8.29	7.60	6.9
Dividends Per Share	0.680	0.610	0.550	0.510	0.440	0.350	0.290	0.25
Dividend Payout %	34.25	31.70	32.26	33.33	32.35	30.92	29.84	26.8
Income Statement								
Total Interest Income	359,388	405,952	477,820	488,759	448,509	420,100	376,892	358,06
Total Interest Expense	89,558	113,766	209,242	255,196	205,079	191,900	172,887	164,00
Net Interest Income	269,830	292,186	268,578	233,563	243,430	228,200	204,005	194,05
Provision for Loan Losses	9,771	14,107	13,200	10,401	9,072	7,771	4,682	5,78
Non-Interest Income	157,543	141,870	131,990	124,540	101,943	89,060	75,555	66,97
Non-Interest Expense	236,120	233,841	215,941	189,377	187,071	180,391	167,915	157,81
Income Before Taxes	181,482	186,108	171,427	158,325	149,230	129,098	106,963	97,43
Income from Cont Ops	...	...	...	104,201	...	...	...	...
Net Income	118,530	121,140	111,281	101,737	97,994	83,314	71,064	65,13
Average Shs. Outstg.	59,244	62,416	64,876	67,928	71,921	72,946	72,785	69,82
Balance Sheet								
Cash & Due from Banks	333,096	357,427	328,779	298,651	279,957	312,527	292,555	337,09
Securities Avail. for Sale	1,933,993	1,262,570	1,061,495	1,120,633	783,220	776,049	610,570	528,04
Net Loans & Leases	4,845,776	4,542,595	4,448,832	4,078,083	3,949,085	3,636,168	2,919,555	2,571,57
Total Assets	7,914,321	7,138,706	6,886,988	6,886,988	6,743,404	6,355,190	5,545,158	5,193,68
Total Deposits	5,089,459	4,686,296	4,613,365	4,058,418	3,924,796	3,946,397	3,818,949	3,597,43
Long-Term Obligations	531,035	475,000	225,000	250,000	...	...	...	...
Total Liabilities	7,224,748	6,459,172	6,494,895	6,257,347	6,087,648	5,703,314	4,951,533	4,669,50
Net Stockholders' Equity	689,573	679,534	685,444	629,641	655,756	651,876	593,625	524,18
Shares Outstanding	58,246	60,516	63,705	64,755	70,423	72,531	72,740	69,82
Statistical Record								
Return on Equity %	17.18	17.82	16.23	16.54	14.94	12.78	11.97	12.4
Return on Assets %	1.49	1.69	1.54	1.51	1.45	1.31	1.28	1.2
Equity/Assets %	8.71	9.51	9.54	9.14	9.72	10.25	10.70	10.0
Non-Int. Exp./Tot. Inc. %	45.67	42.68	35.41	30.87	33.98	35.42	37.11	37.1
Price Range	29.82-22.74	26.90-20.49	24.70-19.56	21.61-15.31	24.06-18.38	25.75-15.38	23.50-12.13	14.00-9.8
P/E Ratio	14.91-11.37	13.87-10.56	14.36-11.37	14.12-10.01	17.69-13.51	22.59-13.49	23.98-12.37	15.05-10.6
Average Yield %	2.60	2.51	2.46	2.72	1.99	1.66	1.98	2.3

Address: 248 East Capitol Street, Jackson, MS 39201 Telephone: (601) 208-5111 Web Site: www.trustmark.com	Officers: Richard G. Hickson - Chmn., Pres., C.E.O., Louis E. Greer - Chief Acctg. Officer	Investor Contact: (601) 949-6898 Institutional Holding No of Institutions: 17 Shares: 3,537,235 % Held: -

UGI CORP.

Exchange	Symbol	Price	52Wk Range	Yield	P/E
NYS	UGI	$32.92 (3/31/2004)	34.90-28.93	3.46	14.38

*7 Year Price Score 164.2 *NYSE Composite Index=100 *12 Month Price Score 94.6

Interim Earnings (Per Share)

Qtr.	Dec	Mar	Jun	Sep
2000-01	0.66	1.11	(0.10)	(0.41)
2001-02	0.58	1.28	0.09	(0.15)
2002-03	0.86	1.62	(0.05)	(0.14)
2003-04	0.88	...	...	...

Interim Dividends (Per Share)

Amt	Decl	Ex	Rec	Pay
0.285Q	4/29/2003	5/28/2003	5/30/2003	7/1/2003
0.285Q	7/29/2003	8/27/2003	8/29/2003	10/1/2003
0.285Q	10/28/2003	11/25/2003	11/28/2003	1/1/2004
0.285Q	1/27/2004	2/25/2004	2/27/2004	4/1/2004

Indicated Div: $1.14 (Div. Reinv. Plan)

Valuation Analysis

Forecast P/E	13.44	Trailing P/E	14.38
Market Cap	$907.5 Million	Book Value	569.8 Million
Price/Book	2.17	Price/Sales	0.41

Dividend Achiever Status

Rank	287
10 Year Growth Rate	2.53%
Total Years of Dividend Growth	16

Business Summary: Gas Utilities (MIC: 7.4 SIC: 4924 NAIC:221210)

UGI is a holding company that operates propane distribution, gas and electric utility, energy marketing and related businesses through subsidiaries. Co.'s majority-owned subsidiary AmeriGas Partners, L.P. conducts a retail propane distribution business. UGI Utilities, Inc. owns and operates a natural gas distribution utility and an electricity distribution utility in eastern Pennsylvania. UGI Enterprises, Inc., conducts domestic and international energy-related businesses through subsidiaries. Additionally, Enterprises owns FLAGA GmbH, which is engaged in the distribution of propane in Austria, the Czech Republic, and Slovakia.

Recent Developments: For the quarter ended Dec 31 2003, net income increased 5.7% to $38.8 million from $36.7 million in the prior-year quarter. Results benefited from Co.'s acquisitions in gas marketing, electric generation and domestic propane distribution, partially offset by the impact of milder weather. Revenues increased 20.8% to $893.7 million. By segment, net income for AmeriGas propane rose 1.6% to $12.9 million. Gas utility net income fell 13.6% to $15.2 million, while electric utility net income dropped 17.2% to $2.4 million. Net income for energy services climbed 60.9% to $3.7 million, while net income for international propane jumped to $4.8 million from $1.2 million a year earlier.

Prospects: On Jan 19 2004, a subsidiary of Co. agreed to acquire the remaining outstanding 81.5% interests of AGZ Holding, the parent On Jan 19 2004, a subsidiary of Co. agreed to acquire the remaining outstanding 81.5% interests of AGZ Holding, the parent company of Antargaz, one of the four largest retail distributors of propane and butane in France. The acquisition provides Co. with a favorable market, strong cash flow characteristics and should enlarge its platform for growth in Europe. Co. expects the transaction to be accretive to earnings per share in fiscal year 2005. Assuming the closure of Antargaz, Co. intends to increase the annual dividend rate to $1.25 per share, effective with the July 2004 dividend payment. Co. also raised its fiscal 2004 earnings per share guidance to a range of $2.10 to $2.20.

Financial Data
US$ in Thousands

	3 Mos	09/30/2003	09/30/2002	09/30/2001	09/30/2000	09/30/1999	09/30/1998	09/30/1997
Earnings Per Share	2.31	2.29	1.80	1.26	1.09	1.16	0.81	1.04
Cash Flow Per Share	0.30	5.76	5.90	4.95	3.24	2.95	3.59	3.46
Tang. Book Val. Per Share	N.M	N.M	N.M	N.M	N.M	N.M	N.M	N.M
Dividends Per Share	1.130	1.120	1.070	1.040	1.000	0.970	0.960	0.950
Dividend Payout %	48.92	48.90	59.72	82.23	92.22	83.90	118.44	91.35
Income Statement								
Total Revenues	893,700	3,026,100	2,213,700	2,468,100	1,761,700	1,383,600	1,439,700	1,642,000
Total Indirect Exp.	183,100	719,700	668,100	597,900	522,000	510,500	500,100	480,700
Costs & Expenses	785,400	2,723,800	1,961,100	2,240,700	1,570,500	1,207,700	1,269,500	1,442,100
Depreciation & Amort.	27,500	103,000	93,500	105,200	97,500	89,700	87,800	86,100
Operating Income	108,300	302,300	252,600	227,400	191,200	175,900	170,200	199,900
Net Interest Inc./(Exp.)	(26,700)	(109,200)	(109,100)	(104,800)	(98,500)	(84,600)	(84,400)	(83,100)
Income Taxes	24,300	61,100	46,900	45,400	40,100	43,200	34,400	43,600
Eqty Earns/Minority Int.	4,200	5,300	8,500	...	...	...	...	...
Income from Cont Ops	...	98,500	...	52,000	...	...	...	...
Net Income	38,800	98,900	75,500	56,500	44,700	55,700	40,300	52,100
Average Shs. Outstg.	43,947	43,236	41,907	41,059	40,882	48,024	49,684	49,698
Balance Sheet								
Net Property	1,360,300	1,336,800	1,271,900	1,268,000	1,073,200	1,084,100	999,000	987,200
Total Assets	3,027,000	2,781,700	2,614,400	2,550,200	2,278,800	2,135,900	2,074,600	2,151,700
Long-Term Obligations	1,161,600	1,158,500	1,127,000	1,196,900	1,029,700	989,600	890,800	844,800
Net Stockholders' Equity	608,600	569,800	297,300	235,600	227,200	229,200	347,100	343,900
Shares Outstanding	42,906	42,699	41,551	40,944	40,490	40,905	49,234	49,798
Statistical Record								
Operating Profit Margin %	12.11	9.98	11.41	9.21	10.85	12.71	11.82	12.17
Net Inc./Net Property %	2.85	7.39	5.93	4.45	4.16	5.13	4.03	5.27
Net Inc./Tot. Capital %	1.92	5.01	4.59	3.45	3.08	3.94	2.85	3.79
Return on Equity %	6.37	17.28	23.79	20.34	18.08	22.35	10.97	13.85
Accum. Depr./Gross Prop. %	37.82	37.59	36.16	33.73	35.04	32.20	31.78	29.34
Price Range	34.05-28.93	34.90-23.47	24.43-17.73	19.39-14.46	16.17-12.17	16.79-10.62	19.87-13.87	18.58-14.00
P/E Ratio	38.69-32.88	15.24-10.25	13.57-9.85	15.39-11.47	14.83-11.16	14.48-9.16	24.54-17.13	17.87-13.46
Average Yield %	3.54	3.88	5.20	6.18	6.95	6.82	5.45	6.01

Address: 460 North Gulph Road, King of Prussia, PA 19406 **Telephone:** (610) 337-1000 **Web Site:** www.ugicorp.com	**Officers:** Lon R. Greenberg – Chmn., Pres., C.E.O., Anthony J. Mendicino – Sr. V.P., Fin., C.F.O. **Transfer Agents:** Mellon Investor Services, LLC	**Investor Contact:** (610) 337-1000 **Institutional Holding** No of Institutions: 2 Shares: 74,400 % Held: –

UNITED BANKSHARES, INC.

Exchange	Symbol	Price	52Wk Range	Yield	P/E
NMS	UBSI	$30.50 (3/31/2004)	31.53-28.00	3.28	16.49

*7 Year Price Score 119.8   *NYSE Composite Index=100   *12 Month Price Score 92.3

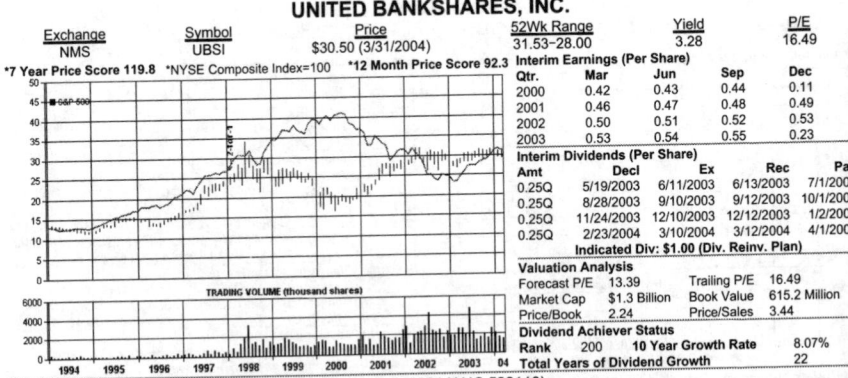

Interim Earnings (Per Share)

Qtr.	Mar	Jun	Sep	Dec
2000	0.42	0.43	0.44	0.11
2001	0.46	0.47	0.48	0.49
2002	0.50	0.51	0.52	0.53
2003	0.53	0.54	0.55	0.23

Interim Dividends (Per Share)

Amt	Decl	Ex	Rec	Pay
0.25Q	5/19/2003	6/11/2003	6/13/2003	7/1/2003
0.25Q	8/28/2003	9/10/2003	9/12/2003	10/1/2003
0.25Q	11/24/2003	12/10/2003	12/12/2003	1/2/2004
0.25Q	2/23/2004	3/10/2004	3/12/2004	4/1/2004

Indicated Div: $1.00 (Div. Reinv. Plan)

Valuation Analysis

Forecast P/E	13.39	Trailing P/E	16.49
Market Cap	$1.3 Billion	Book Value	615.2 Million
Price/Book	2.24	Price/Sales	3.44

Dividend Achiever Status

Rank	200	10 Year Growth Rate	8.07%
Total Years of Dividend Growth		22

Business Summary: Commercial Banking (MIC: 8.1 SIC: 6021 NAIC:522110)
United Bankshares is a bank holding company with assets of $6.38 billion as of Dec 31 2003. Co., through its subsidiaries, United National Bank and United Bank, engages primarily in community banking and mortgage banking and additionally offers most types of business permitted by law and regulation. Included among the banking services offered are the acceptance of deposits in checking, savings, and money market accounts; the making of personal and student loans; and the making of real estate loans. Co. also owns nonbank subsidiaries that engage in mortgage banking and asset management. As of Dec 31 2003, Co. operated 91 offices in West Virginia, Virginia, Maryland, Ohio, and Washington.

Recent Developments: For the year ended Dec 31 2003, net income slipped 11.4% to $78.8 million from $88.9 million in the prior year. Earnings included a gain of $1.8 million in 2003 and a loss of $6.3 million in 2002 on security transactions. Earnings for 2003 also included debt prepayment penalties of $16.7 million.Total interest income declined 12.4% to $297.5 million, while total interest expense fell 21.4% to $104.2 million. Net interest income slid 6.6% to $193.4 million. Provision for loan losses declined 5.8% to $7.5 million. Total non-interest income advanced 40.6% to $103.3 million, primarily due to increased mortgage-banking income. Total non-interest expense rose 22.6% to $176.7 million.

Prospects: Although mortgage origination and sale activity will likely decline in 2004, Co. expects to see a related decline in mortgage banking expenses. Additionally, during the fourth quarter of 2003, Co. prepaid certain Federal Home Loan Bank long-term advances in light of the low interest rate environment and significant liquidity arising from its mortgage banking subsidiary's reduced originations. The prepayment of these borrowings should improve Co.'s net interest margin and enhance future earnings. Meanwhile, Co. continues to benefit from the acquisition of Sequoia Bancshares of Bethesda, MD, which expanded Co.'s presence in the Northern Virginia, Washington, D.C. and suburban Maryland market.

Financial Data

(US$ in Thousands)	12/31/2003	12/31/2002	12/31/2001	12/31/2000	12/31/1999	12/31/1998	12/31/1997	12/31/1996
Earnings Per Share	1.85	2.06	1.90	1.40	1.61	1.02	1.35	1.00
Tang. Book Val. Per Share	10.19	10.73	11.79	10.31	9.31	9.74	9.32	8.56
Dividends Per Share	1.00	0.930	0.890	0.840	0.810	0.720	0.660	0.610
Dividend Payout %	54.05	45.14	46.84	60.00	50.31	70.58	48.88	61.00
Income Statement								
Total Interest Income	297,508	339,478	360,610	377,847	354,665	325,647	190,252	172,358
Total Interest Expense	104,151	132,557	175,507	197,766	174,402	155,354	84,499	73,185
Net Interest Income	193,357	206,921	185,103	180,081	180,263	170,293	105,753	99,173
Provision for Loan Losses	7,475	7,937	12,833	15,745	8,800	12,156	3,100	2,611
Non-Interest Income	103,316	73,479	62,205	33,786	51,078	41,752	19,732	14,189
Non-Interest Expense	176,678	144,130	115,745	110,422	117,519	137,964	59,949	63,549
Income Before Taxes	112,520	128,333	118,730	87,700	105,022	61,925	62,436	47,203
Net Income	78,765	88,933	79,991	58,976	70,248	44,402	40,939	30,517
Average Shs. Outstg.	42,620	43,113	42,064	42,260	43,722	43,461	30,272	30,506
Balance Sheet								
Cash & Due from Banks	217,229	162,261	156,058	142,801	131,091	124,591	80,447	86,323
Securities Avail. for Sale	1,266,635	1,022,314	1,147,280	865,266	1,207,363	565,165	273,868	161,622
Net Loans & Leases	4,045,587	3,525,774	3,454,926	3,151,962	3,130,497	2,613,202	2,028,693	1,823,844
Total Assets	6,378,999	5,792,019	5,631,775	4,904,547	5,069,160	4,567,899	2,699,790	2,326,877
Total Deposits	4,182,372	3,900,848	3,787,793	3,391,449	3,260,985	3,493,058	2,106,047	1,827,558
Long-Term Obligations	858,174	679,712	736,455	706,512	953,347	345,867	142,695	132,637
Total Liabilities	5,763,808	5,250,480	5,125,246	4,473,677	4,673,230	4,146,368	2,420,352	2,068,364
Net Stockholders' Equity	615,191	541,539	506,529	430,870	395,930	421,531	279,438	258,512
Shares Outstanding	43,689	42,031	42,926	41,765	42,487	43,256	29,968	30,186
Statistical Record								
Return on Equity %	12.80	16.42	15.79	13.68	17.74	10.53	14.65	11.8
Return on Assets %	1.23	1.53	1.42	1.20	1.38	0.97	1.51	1.3
Equity/Assets %	9.64	9.34	8.99	8.78	7.81	9.22	10.35	11.1
Non-Int. Exp./Tot. Inc. %	44.07	34.90	27.37	26.82	28.96	37.55	28.54	34.0
Price Range	31.53-26.97	32.01-26.24	28.86-20.19	23.88-16.44	27.25-22.81	34.13-21.50	24.19-16.13	16.50-13.1
P/E Ratio	17.04-14.58	15.54-12.74	15.19-10.63	17.05-11.74	16.93-14.17	33.46-21.08	17.92-11.94	16.50-13.1
Average Yield %	3.38	3.16	3.57	4.25	3.23	2.74	3.29	4.2

Address: 300 United Center, Charleston, WV 25301 **Telephone:** (304) 424-8800 **Web Site:** www.ubsi-wv.com	**Officers:** Richard M. Adams – Chmn., C.E.O., Steven E. Wilson – C.F.O., Chief Acctg. Officer	**Investor Contact:** (304) 424-8704 **Institutional Holding** No of Institutions: 15 Shares: 2,460,051 % Held: –

UNITED DOMINION REALTY TRUST, INC.

Exchange	Symbol	Price	52Wk Range	Yield	P/E
NYS	UDR	$19.62 (3/31/2004)	19.65–16.11	5.96	392.40

7 Year Price Score 130.3 *NYSE Composite Index=100 *12 Month Price Score 95.5

Interim Earnings (Per Share)

Qtr.	Mar	Jun	Sep	Dec
2000	0.09	0.06	0.11	0.15
2001	(0.03)	0.20	0.07	0.03
2002	0.07	0.07	0.03	0.04
2003	0.05	0.01	(0.06)	0.05

Interim Dividends (Per Share)

Amt	Decl	Ex	Rec	Pay
0.285Q	6/12/2003	7/16/2003	7/18/2003	7/31/2003
0.285Q	9/25/2003	10/15/2003	10/17/2003	10/31/2003
0.285Q	12/5/2003	1/14/2004	1/16/2004	2/2/2004
0.293Q	3/18/2004	4/14/2004	4/16/2004	4/30/2004

Indicated Div: $1.17

Valuation Analysis

Forecast P/E	11.88	Trailing P/E	392.40
Market Cap	$2.1 Billion	Book Value	690.3 Million
Price/Book	3.39	Price/Sales	3.87

Dividend Achiever Status

Rank	252	10 Year Growth Rate	5.08%
Total Years of Dividend Growth		18	

Business Summary: Property, Real Estate &Development (MIC: 8.3 SIC: 6798 NAIC:525930)

United Dominion Realty Trust is a self–administered real estate investment trust that owns, develops, acquires, renovates, and manages middle–market apartment communities nationwide. At Dec 31 2003, Co.'s apartment portfolio included 264 communities located in 55 markets, with a total of 76,244 completed apartment homes. In addition, Co. had three apartment communities under development. Co. focuses on the broad middle–market segment of the apartment that generally consists of young professionals, blue–collar families, single parent households, older singles, immigrants, non–related parties and families renting while waiting to purchase a home.

Recent Developments: For the year ended Dec 31 2003, Co. reported income of $51.6 million, before income from discontinued operations of $18.8 million, compared with income of $12.6 million, before income from discontinued operations of $40.7 million, in the prior year. Results for 2003 included an impairment charge of $1.4 million, while results for 2002 included a charge of $35.5 million for the early retirement of debt. Total revenues increased 3.4% to $604.4 million from $584.6 million the previous year. Rental income rose 1.5% to $603.4 million, while non–property income fell 40.9% to $1.1 million. Funds from operations amounted to $207.6 million, up 23.0% from $168.8 million a year earlier.

Prospects: Going forward, Co. should benefit from 25.0% of its portfolio being repositioned, which has significantly improved the quality of its assets. In addition, Co. is well positioned to take advantage of any improvement in the job market. Co. noted that its top markets are projected to see above–average job growth in 2004. Separately, Co. is estimating that recurring capital expenditures for 2004 will be $470.00 per apartment home. Co. is targeting funds from operations in the range of $1.48 to $1.60 per diluted share and earnings per share in the range of $0.40 to $0.75 for the full–year 2004.

Financial Data

(US$ in Thousands)	12/31/2003	12/31/2002	12/31/2001	12/31/2000	12/31/1999	12/31/1998	12/31/1997	12/31/1996
Earnings Per Share	0.05	0.21	0.27	0.41	0.54	0.49	0.60	0.49
Tang. Book Val. Per Share	7.28	6.48	7.10	7.91	8.58	9.10	9.00	9.09
Dividends Per Share	1.130	1.100	1.070	1.060	1.050	1.040	0.990	0.940
Dividend Payout %	N.M.	525.00	399.07	260.36	195.83	212.24	166.25	191.84
Income Statement								
Rental Income	603,367	594,314	618,590	616,825	618,749	478,718	386,672	242,112
Total Income	604,435	596,120	623,183	622,151	620,691	482,100	387,795	243,819
Total Indirect Exp.	187,088	175,608	187,897	176,805	159,302	128,963	87,247	71,765
Depreciation	165,070	156,265	155,327	157,361	126,152	103,233	78,772	48,709
Interest Expense	117,185	130,956	144,379	156,040	153,748	106,238	79,004	50,843
Equity Earns/Minority Int.	(982)	(2,914)	(4,192)	(4,386)	(5,679)	(1,541)	(278)	(58)
Income from Cont Ops	51,603	50,058	65,299	75,784	92,695	72,470	70,199	38,014
Net Income	70,404	53,229	61,828	76,615	93,622	72,332	70,149	37,991
Average Shs. Outstg.	115,648	106,952	101,037	103,208	103,639	100,062	87,339	57,482
Balance Sheet								
Cash & Cash Equivalents	12,364	14,925	31,471	55,248	64,647	76,886	17,580	13,452
Total Real Estate Inv.	3,409,883	3,165,870	3,212,213	3,252,103	3,204,684	3,362,582	2,080,932	1,834,321
Total Assets	3,543,643	3,276,136	3,348,091	3,453,957	3,688,317	3,762,940	2,313,725	1,966,904
Long–Term Obligations	2,132,037	2,057,640	2,064,197	1,992,330	2,127,305	2,117,749	1,156,226	1,044,835
Total Liabilities	2,616,771	2,585,265	2,615,766	2,645,271	2,805,977	2,818,819	1,510,368	1,221,525
Net Stockholders' Equity	1,163,436	1,001,271	1,042,725	1,218,892	1,310,212	1,374,121	1,058,357	850,379
Shares Outstanding	127,295	106,605	103,133	102,219	102,740	103,639	89,168	81,983
Statistical Record								
Inc.+Depr./Assets %	6.60	6.30	6.60	6.80	5.90	4.70	4.70	4.40
Return on Equity %	4.43	4.99	6.26	6.21	7.07	5.27	6.63	4.47
Return on Assets %	1.45	1.52	1.95	2.19	2.51	1.92	3.03	1.93
Price Range	19.37–15.22	16.70–13.95	14.72–10.75	11.75–9.44	11.94–9.31	14.75–10.06	16.00–13.50	15.75–13.25
P/E Ratio	387.4–304.4	79.52–66.43	54.52–39.81	28.66–23.02	22.11–17.25	30.10–20.54	26.67–22.50	32.14–27.04
Average Yield %	6.52	7.16	8.04	10.14	9.79	8.11	6.77	6.49

Address: 1745 Shea Center Dr., Highlands Ranch, CO 80129 **Telephone:** (720) 283–6120 **Web Site:** www.udrt.com	**Officers:** Robert C. Larson – Chmn., James D. Klingbeil – Vice–Chmn. **Transfer Agents:**ChaseMellon Shareholder Services, L.L.C., Pittisburg, PA	**Institutional Holding** **No of Institutions:** 24 **Shares:** 2,623,165 **% Held:** –

UNITED MOBILE HOMES INC

Exchange	Symbol	Price	52Wk Range	Yield	P/E
ASE	UMH	$16.11 (3/31/2004)	17.50-14.05	5.77	16.11

*7 Year Price Score 135.0 *NYSE Composite Index=100 *12 Month Price Score 100.9

Interim Earnings (Per Share)

Qtr.	Mar	Jun	Sep	Dec
2000	0.20	0.17	0.18	0.16
2001	0.19	0.21	0.23	0.11
2002	0.24	0.20	0.19	0.22
2003	0.23	0.25	0.29	0.25

Interim Dividends (Per Share)

Amt	Decl	Ex	Rec	Pay
0.225Q	3/15/2003	5/13/2003	5/15/2003	6/16/2003
0.228Q	6/19/2003	8/13/2003	8/15/2003	9/15/2003
0.23Q	10/1/2003	11/13/2003	11/17/2003	12/15/2003
0.233Q	1/14/2004	2/12/2004	2/17/2004	3/15/2004

Indicated Div: $0.93 (Div. Reinv. Plan)

Valuation Analysis

Forecast P/E	N/A	Trailing P/E	16.11
Market Cap	$122.9 Million	Book Value	36.4 Million
Price/Book	3.25	Price/Sales	3.73

Dividend Achiever Status

Rank 142   10 Year Growth Rate   10.78%
Total Years of Dividend Growth   13

Business Summary: Property, Real Estate &Development (MIC: 8.3 SIC: 6798 NAIC:525930)

United Mobile Homes, a real estate investment trust (REIT), is engaged in the ownership and operation of manufactured home communities located in New Jersey, New York, Ohio, Pennsylvania and Tennessee. As of Dec 31 2003, Co. owned 26 manufactured home communities containing 6,129 sites. Co.'s primary business is leasing manufactured home spaces on a month-to-month basis to private manufactured home owners. Co. also leases manufactured homes to residents, and through its wholly-owned taxable REIT subsidiary, sells homes to residents and prospective residents of its communities.

Recent Developments: For the year ended Dec 31 2003, net income rose 24.8% to $8.1 million compared with $6.5 million a year earlier. Total revenues grew 14.8% to $33.8 million, mainly due to the acquisition of a new community in 2003 and rental increases to residents. Rental and related income rose 4.0% to $21.0 million, while sales of manufactured homes climbed 22.0% to $6.8 million. Revenues for 2003 and 2002 included interest and dividend income of $3.3 million and $2.9 million, and net gains on securities available for sales transactions of $2.7 million and $794,950, respectively. Funds from operations were $11.0 million versus $9.3 million in 2002 and included a gain of $661,000 on the sale of land.

Prospects: On Mar 3 2004, Co. announced the $3.5 million acquisition of Bishop's Mobile Home Court and Whispering Pines Community, in Somerset Township, PA. Bishop's Mobile Home Court is an existing family community consisting of 124 lots, which is located next to Whispering Pines Community, a 55-and-older community consisting of 15 existing home sites and 60 acres to expand. Meanwhile, despite a slight drop in occupancy of about 1.0% from 87.0% in 2002, Co.'s near-term prospects appear solid, reflecting the aforementioned acquisition as well as its ability to obtain annual rent increases. Co. noted that during 2003, it was able to obtain an average rent increase of approximately 4.0%.

Financial Data

(US$ in Thousands)	12/31/2003	12/31/2002	12/31/2001	12/31/2000	12/31/1999	12/31/1998	12/31/1997	12/31/1996
Earnings Per Share	1.02	0.85	0.74	0.71	0.63	0.60	0.63	0.6
Tang. Book Val. Per Share	4.78	3.87	3.70	3.08	2.92	3.20	3.03	2.5
Dividends Per Share	0.900	0.860	0.800	0.758	0.750	0.730	0.700	0.60
Dividend Payout %	88.72	101.76	108.44	106.76	119.04	122.91	111.11	98.3
Income Statement								
Total Income	33,791	29,424	26,882	20,645	18,807	17,193	15,664	14,62
Total Indirect Exp.	13,244	12,775	11,195	9,809	8,362	6,907	5,762	6,39
Depreciation	3,018	2,923	2,772	2,708	2,530	2,509	2,159	2,00
Interest Expense	6,381	6,629	5,652	5,250	4,211	3,011	2,247	2,87
Net Income	8,127	6,512	5,550	5,189	4,556	4,202	4,197	3,73
Average Shs. Outstg.	7,942	7,677	7,496	7,341	7,267	7,060	6,679	6,07
Balance Sheet								
Cash & Cash Equivalents	34,341	35,124	27,486	16,894	13,519	8,585	3,739	2,63
Ttl Real Estate Inv.	40,842	39,866	40,681	38,418	39,193	36,252	35,293	27,72
Total Assets	94,310	89,027	80,335	62,946	58,575	50,047	43,599	35,87
Long-Term Obligations	44,223	43,322	38,652	32,056	30,419	21,412	20,111	17,35
Total Liabilities	55,210	59,290	52,370	40,106	37,184	26,834	22,769	19,44
Net Stockholders' Equity	39,100	29,736	27,965	22,839	21,391	23,213	20,831	16,42
Shares Outstanding	8,164	7,671	7,542	7,394	7,312	7,246	6,865	6,43
Statistical Record								
Net Inc.+Depr./Assets %	11.81	10.60	10.40	12.50	12.10	13.40	14.60	16.0
Return on Equity %	20.78	21.89	19.84	22.72	21.29	18.10	20.14	22.7
Return on Assets %	8.61	7.31	6.90	8.24	7.77	8.39	9.62	10.3
Price Range	17.50-12.86	13.75-11.80	12.40-9.63	9.88-7.06	10.75-8.00	12.50-9.69	13.50-11.13	13.63-9.6
P/E Ratio	17.16-12.61	16.18-13.88	16.76-13.01	13.91-9.95	17.06-12.70	20.83-16.15	21.43-17.66	22.34-15.7
Average Yield %	5.94	6.72	7.31	8.81	8.12	6.69	5.88	5.2

Address: Juniper Business Plaza, Freehold, NJ 07728 Telephone: (732) 577-9997 Web Site: www.umh.com	Officers: Eugene W. Landy – Chmn., Samuel A. Landy -- Pres.	Institutional Holding No of Institutions: 15 Shares: 3,157,403 % Held: –

UNITED TECHNOLOGIES CORP.

Exchange	Symbol	Price	52Wk Range	Yield	P/E
NYS	UTX	$86.30 (3/31/2004)	97.50–58.75	1.62	18.40

Year Price Score 124.0 *NYSE Composite Index=100 *12 Month Price Score 108.3

Interim Earnings (Per Share)

Qtr.	Mar	Jun	Sep	Dec
2000	0.74	1.00	0.98	0.83
2001	0.86	1.16	1.12	0.69
2002	0.92	1.23	1.21	1.06
2003	1.00	1.26	1.27	1.16

Interim Dividends (Per Share)

Amt	Decl	Ex	Rec	Pay
0.27Q	4/9/2003	5/14/2003	5/16/2003	6/10/2003
0.27Q	6/11/2003	8/20/2003	8/22/2003	9/10/2003
0.35Q	9/10/2003	11/12/2003	11/14/2003	12/10/2003
0.35Q	2/3/2004	2/18/2004	2/20/2004	3/10/2004

Indicated Div: $1.40 (Div. Reinv. Plan)

Valuation Analysis

Forecast P/E	15.81	Trailing P/E	N/A
Market Cap	$40.7 Billion	Book Value	N/A
Price/Book	N/A	Price/Sales	N/A

Dividend Achiever Status

Rank	163	10 Year Growth Rate 9.69%
Total Years of Dividend Growth		10

Business Summary: Aviation (MIC: 1.1 SIC: 3724 NAIC:336412)

United Technologies provides high technology products and services to the building systems and aerospace industries. Co.'s products include Otis elevators, escalators and automated people movers; Carrier HVAC systems and equipment, refrigeration equipment, aftermarket service and components; Chubb electronic security, fire detection and suppression, monitoring and rapid response systems and security personnel services; Pratt & Whitney commercial, general aviation and military aircraft engines, parts, service, industrial gas turbines and space propulsion; Flight Systems aerospace products and aftermarket services and commercial/military helicopters, aftermarket helicopter and aircraft parts.

Recent Developments: For the year ended Dec 31 2003, net income rose 5.6% to $2.36 billion from $2.24 billion the previous year. Results included restructuring and related charges of $182.0 million and $321.0 million in 2003 and 2002, respectively. Revenues increased 10.0% to $31.03 billion from $28.21 billion a year earlier. Revenues at Carrier grew 5.4% to $9.25 billion, while revenues at Otis climbed 16.4% to $7.93 billion. Revenues in the Flight Systems segment were up 2.5% to $5.71 billion, while revenues at Pratt & Whitney slipped 1.8% to $7.51 billion. Results also included $1.14 billion in revenues from Chubb plc, which was acquired in July 2003. Operating profit rose 5.1% to $3.85 billion.

Prospects: Earnings are being positively affected by strong operating profitability at Otis and Carrier, along with improved results from Co.'s military aerospace operations, partially offset by continued weak conditions in the commercial aviation industry. Meanwhile, bottom-line results are benefiting from the July 2003 acquisition of Chubb plc, as well as favorable foreign currency exchange rates. Looking ahead, Co. is targeting full-year 2004 earnings in the range of $5.00 and $5.30 per share and revenues of about $34.00 billion. Separately, on Mar 15 2004, Co. announced that it has entered into a definitive agreement to acquire Linde AG's refrigeration division for approximately $305.0 million.

Financial Data
($ in Millions)

	12/31/2003	12/31/2002	12/31/2001	12/31/2000	12/31/1999	12/31/1998	12/31/1997	12/31/1996
Earnings Per Share	4.69	4.42	3.83	3.55	1.65	2.52	2.10	1.71
Cash Flow Per Share	5.71	5.64	5.70	5.17	4.55	5.07	4.19	4.01
Tang. Book Val. Per Share	4.62	2.92	3.31	1.89	3.11	5.84	7.84	7.61
Dividends Per Share	1.130	0.980	0.900	0.820	0.760	0.690	0.620	0.550
Dividend Payout %	24.20	22.17	23.49	23.23	46.06	27.52	29.45	32.06
Income Statement								
Total Revenues	31,034	28,212	27,897	26,583	24,127	25,715	24,713	23,512
Total Indirect Exp.	4,681	4,394	4,577	4,473	4,425	4,272	4,102	3,994
Depreciation & Amort.	799	727	905	859	844	854	848	853
Operating Income	3,845	3,657	3,233	3,140	1,517	2,167	1,959	1,781
Net Interest Inc./(Exp.)	(375)	(381)	(426)	(382)	(260)	(204)	(195)	(221)
Income Taxes	941	887	755	853	325	623	573	523
Minority Earns/Minority Int.	(168)	(153)	(114)	(97)	(91)	(85)	(119)	(131)
Income from Cont Ops	...	...	...	...	841	...	...	...
Net Income	2,361	2,236	1,938	1,808	1,531	1,255	1,072	906
Average Shs. Outstg.	502	505	505	508	506	494	508	526
Balance Sheet								
Cash & Cash Equivalents	1,623	2,080	1,558	748	957	550	755	1,127
Total Current Assets	12,364	11,751	11,263	10,662	10,627	9,355	9,248	9,611
Total Assets	34,648	29,090	26,969	25,364	24,366	18,375	16,719	16,745
Total Current Liabilities	10,295	7,903	8,371	9,344	9,215	7,735	7,311	7,390
Long-Term Obligations	4,257	4,632	4,237	3,476	3,086	1,575	1,275	1,437
Net Stockholders' Equity	11,707	8,355	8,369	7,662	7,117	4,378	4,574	4,306
Working Capital	2,069	3,848	2,892	1,318	1,412	1,620	1,937	2,221
Shares Outstanding	514	469	472	470	474	450	458	476
Statistical Record								
Operating Profit Margin %	12.38	12.96	11.58	11.81	6.28	8.42	7.92	7.57
Return on Equity %	20.16	26.76	23.15	23.59	11.81	28.66	23.43	21.04
Return on Assets %	6.81	7.68	7.18	7.12	3.45	6.82	6.41	5.41
Debt/Total Assets %	12.28	15.92	15.71	13.70	12.66	8.57	7.62	8.58
Price Range	95.54–54.15	77.25–49.19	87.21–41.64	79.75–48.06	74.81–52.31	55.88–34.25	43.63–32.81	35.06–22.78
P/E Ratio	20.37–11.55	17.48–11.13	22.77–10.87	22.46–13.54	45.34–31.70	22.17–13.59	20.77–15.63	20.50–13.32
Average Yield %	1.55	1.50	1.26	1.29	1.32	1.21	1.53	1.92

Address: United Technologies Building, Hartford, CT 06103	**Officers:** George David – Chmn., Pres., C.E.O., Stephen F. Page – Vice-Chmn., C.F.O.	**Investor Contact:**800–881–1914
Telephone: (860) 728–7000	**Transfer Agents:**EquiServe Trust Company, N.A. of Providence, RI	**Institutional Holding** **No of Institutions:** 6
Web Site: www.utc.com		**Shares:** 86,988 **% Held:** –

UNIVERSAL CORP.

*7 Year Price Score 122.1 *NYSE Composite Index=100 *12 Month Price Score 93.6

Interim Earnings (Per Share)

Qtr.	Sep	Dec	Mar	Jun
2000–01	0.89	1.01	1.31	0.87
2001–02	1.04	1.09	1.26	0.61
2002–03	1.09	1.04	0.94	1.27
2003–04	1.37	1.48	...	

Interim Dividends (Per Share)

Amt	Decl	Ex	Rec	P
0.36Q	2/6/2003	4/10/2003	4/14/2003	5/12/20
0.36Q	5/1/2003	7/10/2003	7/14/2003	8/11/20
0.39Q	12/4/2003	1/9/2004	1/13/2004	2/9/20
0.39Q	2/5/2004	4/7/2004	4/12/2004	5/10/20

Indicated Div: $1.56 (Div. Reinv. Plan)

Valuation Analysis

Forecast P/E	N/A	Trailing P/E	10.04
Market Cap	$1.3 Billion	Book Value	683.6 Million
Price/Book	1.60	Price/Sales	0.38

Dividend Achiever Status

Rank	253	10 Year Growth Rate	5.05%
Total Years of Dividend Growth			33

Business Summary: Trusts &Holding Entities (MIC: 8.9 SIC: 6719 NAIC:551112)

Universal is a holding company. Through its primary subsidiaries, Co. is a major independent leaf tobacco merchant and has operations
agri–products and the distribution of lumber and building products. Co.'s tobacco business includes the selecting, buying, shippin
processing, packing, storing, and financing of leaf tobacco for sale to manufacturers of tobacco products. Co.'s agri–products busine
involves selecting, buying and processing a number of products, including tea, rubber, sunflower seeds, nuts, dried fruit, and canned a
frozen foods. Co. is also engaged in lumber and building products distribution and processing in the Netherlands, Belgium, and oth
countries in Europe.

Recent Developments: For the quarter ended Dec 31 2003, net income rose 39.7% to $37.4 million compared with $26.7 millior
year earlier. Sales and other operating revenues advanced 13.0% to $801.0 million. Co.'s results benefited from higher sales and operati
profit from across its three business segments. Co. noted that its tobacco segment, which posted a 3.7% gain in revenues to $473.0 milli
and 35.6% increase in operating profit to $70.5 million, reflected the benefit of a one–time shift in the allocation of fixed facto
overhead associated with the change in Co.'s fiscal year end to March 31. Excluding the effect of this change, tobacco operating pro
would have risen about 24.1% to $64.5 million.

Prospects: Co.'s near–term outlook appears solid, reflecting increased leaf demand from growth in international cigarette sales. C
noted that demand for U.S. leaf continues to fall due to non–competitive prices. However, Co. expects that its U.S. tobacco operatio
will benefit from new processing business from the Kentucky burley pool, which has moved some of its processing business out
Kentucky for the first time. Additionally, despite weakness in sales volumes due to the lingering recession in the Netherlands and oth
European markets, Co.'s lumber and building product segment's results should continue to be aided by the strong euro.

Financial Data

(US$ in Thousands)	6 Mos	3 Mos	06/30/2003	06/30/2002	06/30/2001	06/30/2000	06/30/1999	06/30/199
Earnings Per Share	2.85	1.37	4.34	4.00	4.08	3.77	3.80	3.
Cash Flow Per Share	4.25	2.09	(1.75)	6.38	5.83	5.88	9.93	3.
Tang. Book Val. Per Share	22.04	20.66	19.55	17.64	15.76	13.04	12.47	11.
Dividends Per Share	1.440	1.420	1.400	1.320	1.260	1.220	1.160	1.0
Dividend Payout %	50.52	103.64	32.25	33.00	30.88	32.36	30.52	27.
Income Statement								
Total Revenues	1,587,612	786,601	2,636,776	2,500,078	3,017,579	3,401,969	4,004,903	4,287,2
Total Indirect Exp.	163,560	79,939	330,336	292,844	292,522	364,088	355,928	335,2
Depreciation & Amort.	28,000	12,684	53,504	54,987	56,399	52,022	52,762	51,0
Operating Income	136,151	59,654	207,815	200,507	238,782	233,924	254,556	278,3
Net Interest Inc./(Exp.)	(23,274)	(11,076)	(45,270)	(47,831)	(61,576)	(56,869)	(56,837)	(63,97
Income Taxes	41,318	18,847	53,094	59,821	66,336	68,221	75,963	98,6
Eqty Earns/Minority Int.	236	4,697	1,143	13,807	1,799	4,971	5,520	8,7
Net Income	71,795	34,428	110,594	106,662	112,669	113,805	127,276	141,2
Average Shs. Outstg.	25,150	25,135	25,499	26,680	27,645	30,205	33,477	35,3
Balance Sheet								
Cash & Cash Equivalents	135,793	57,183	44,659	58,003	109,540	61,395	92,784	79,8
Total Current Assets	1,469,142	1,503,072	1,374,997	1,105,037	1,132,646	1,088,150	1,170,325	1,430,2
Total Assets	2,379,952	2,395,170	2,243,074	1,844,415	1,782,373	1,748,104	1,823,123	2,056,7
Total Current Liabilities	729,856	952,352	824,281	673,421	581,765	883,234	898,500	1,101,5
Long–Term Obligations	775,358	609,939	614,994	435,592	515,349	223,262	221,545	263,1
Net Stockholders' Equity	683,643	648,800	620,278	587,995	552,129	497,779	539,036	547,8
Net Working Capital	...	550,720	550,716	431,606	550,881	204,916	271,825	328,7
Shares Outstanding	24,983	24,983	24,920	26,224	27,184	28,146	32,090	34,8
Statistical Record								
Operating Profit Margin %	8.57	7.58	7.88	8.02	7.91	6.87	6.35	6.
Return on Equity %	10.50	5.30	17.82	18.13	20.40	22.86	23.61	25.
Return on Assets %	3.01	1.43	4.93	5.78	6.32	6.51	6.98	6.
Debt/Total Assets %	32.57	25.46	27.41	23.61	28.91	12.77	12.15	12.
Price Range	44.28–40.78	43.85–41.20	43.01–31.81	43.05–31.74	41.30–20.63	31.00–13.56	38.75–23.88	48.50–31.
P/E Ratio	15.54–14.31	32.01–30.07	9.91–7.33	10.76–7.94	10.12–5.06	8.22–3.60	10.20–6.28	12.16–7.
Average Yield %	3.36	3.34	3.73	3.48	3.91	5.28	3.64	2

UNIVERSAL HEALTH REALTY INCOME TRUST

Exchange	Symbol	Price	52Wk Range	Yield	P/E
NYS	UHT	$33.70 (3/31/2004)	33.70-25.95	5.85	16.28

Year Price Score 128.9 *NYSE Composite Index=100 *12 Month Price Score 95.9

TRADING VOLUME (thousand shares)

Interim Earnings (Per Share)

Qtr.	Mar	Jun	Sep	Dec
2000	0.44	0.42	0.43	0.52
2001	0.46	0.44	0.42	0.42
2002	0.53	0.44	0.43	0.44
2003	0.48	0.45	0.45	0.69

Interim Dividends (Per Share)

Amt	Decl	Ex	Rec	Pay
0.49Q	6/2/2003	6/12/2003	6/16/2003	6/30/2003
0.49Q	9/4/2003	9/12/2003	9/16/2003	9/30/2003
0.495Q	12/2/2003	12/15/2003	12/17/2003	12/31/2003
0.495Q	3/10/2004	3/17/2004	3/19/2004	3/31/2004

Indicated Div: $1.97

Valuation Analysis

Forecast P/E	N/A	Trailing P/E	16.28
Market Cap	$299.0 Million	Book Value	152.2 Million
Price/Book	2.35	Price/Sales	12.64

Dividend Achiever Status

Rank	294	10 Year Growth Rate	1.68%
Total Years of Dividend Growth		16	

Business Summary: Property, Real Estate &Development (MIC: 8.3 SIC: 6798 NAIC:525930)

Universal Health Realty Income Trust is an organized Maryland real estate investment trust (REIT). As of Dec 31 2003, Co. had investments in 44 facilities located in 15 states consisting of investments in healthcare and human service related facilities including acute care hospitals, behavioral healthcare facilities, rehabilitation hospitals, sub–acute care facilities, surgery centers, pre–school and childcare centers and medical office buildings. Six of Co.'s hospital facilities and three medical office buildings are leased to subsidiaries of Universal Health Services, Inc. (UHS). As of Dec 31 2003, UHS owned 6.6% of Co.'s outstanding shares.

Recent Developments: For the year ended Dec 31 2003, net income increased 13.0% to $24.4 million from $21.6 million the previous year. Results for 2003 and 2002 included a pre–tax gain of $10,000 and pre–tax loss of $217,000, respectively, from derivatives. Total revenues slipped to $28.3 million from $28.4 million the year before. Base rental revenues declined 2.1% to $23.8 million from $24.3 million, while bonus rental revenues advanced 9.4% to $4.6 million from $4.2 million a year earlier. Funds from operations climbed 4.7% to $30.1 million from $28.8 million the prior year.

Prospects: Co. is experiencing lower revenues due to a decrease in base rentals from Universal Health Services' (UHS) facilities, reflecting the 2003 lease renewal at Chalmette Medical Center at a lower annual base rental rate. In addition, Co.'s revenues continue to be negatively affected by lower base rental and tenant reimbursements due to increased vacancy rates at three medical office buildings. Meanwhile, during the fourth quarter of 2003, a LLC in which Co. owns a 95.0% interest, completed the acquisition of a 60,000 square–foot medical office building in Las Vegas, NV. Also, Co. purchased an 85.0% interest in a LLC that owns a 27,000 square–foot medical office building in Apache Junction, AZ.

Financial Data

(US$ in Thousands)	12/31/2003	12/31/2002	12/31/2001	12/31/2000	12/31/1999	12/31/1998	12/31/1997	12/31/1996
Earnings Per Share	2.07	1.84	1.74	1.81	1.56	1.76	1.56	1.58
Tang. Book Val. Per Share	12.96	12.72	12.84	11.05	11.08	11.31	11.46	11.61
Dividends Per Share	1.960	1.920	1.875	1.84	1.810	1.755	1.750	1.695
Dividend Payout %	94.69	104.35	107.76	101.66	116.03	99.72	109.29	107.28
Income Statement								
Rental Income	28,313	28,429	27,574	27,315	23,584	23,123	22,180	21,172
Interest Income	...	...	...	...	281	111	584	751
Total Income	28,313	28,429	27,574	27,315	23,865	23,234	22,764	21,923
Total Indirect Exp.	9,375	9,109	8,956	8,614	6,860	6,944	6,299	5,829
Depreciation	4,536	4,431	4,401	4,461	3,857	3,879	3,775	3,636
Interest Expense	2,497	2,403	3,896	6,114	4,004	3,490	2,943	2,565
Equity Earns/Minority Int.	7,974	4,923	3,610	1,774	2,554	1,537	445	629
Net Income	24,425	21,623	18,349	16,256	13,972	14,337	13,967	14,158
Average Shs. Outstg.	11,779	11,750	10,536	9,003	8,977	8,974	8,967	8,960
Balance Sheet								
Cash & Cash Equivalents	628	598	629	294	852	572	1,238	137
Net Real Estate Inv.	130,789	134,886	139,215	143,108	141,367	129,838	133,486	139,434
Total Assets	194,291	185,117	187,904	183,658	178,821	169,406	146,755	148,566
Long–Term Obligations	...	...	1,446	1,359	1,289	1,216	1,147	1,082
Total Liabilities	42,093	36,255	37,870	84,401	79,146	68,058	44,063	44,584
Net Stockholders' Equity	152,198	148,862	150,034	99,257	99,675	101,348	102,692	103,982
Shares Outstanding	11,736	11,698	11,678	8,980	8,990	8,955	8,954	8,952
Statistical Record								
Net Inc.+Depr./Assets %	14.90	14.10	12.10	11.30	10.00	10.80	12.10	12.00
Return on Equity %	16.04	14.52	12.22	16.37	14.01	14.14	13.60	13.61
Return on Assets %	12.57	11.68	9.76	8.85	7.81	8.46	9.51	9.52
Price Range	30.55-25.30	28.50-22.69	25.70-18.94	19.88-14.31	20.50-14.63	22.50-18.06	22.38-18.50	20.50-17.50
P/E Ratio	14.76-12.22	15.49-12.33	14.77-10.88	10.98-7.91	13.14-9.38	12.78-10.26	14.34-11.86	12.97-11.08
Average Yield %	7.15	7.55	6.33	13.56	9.65	8.68	8.43	6.66

Address: Universal Corporate Center, King of Prussia, PA 19406–0958
Telephone: (610) 265–0688
Web Site: www.uhrit.com

Officers: Alan B. Miller – Chmn., Pres., C.E.O., Charles F. Boyle – V.P., C.F.O., Contr.
Transfer Agents: EquiServe Trust Company, N.A., Providence, R.I.

Institutional Holding
No of Institutions: 73
Shares: 3,510,095 **% Held:** 30%

UNIZAN FINANCIAL CORP

Exchange	Symbol	Price	52Wk Range	Yield	P/E
NMS	UNIZ	$24.91 (3/31/2004)	26.68-16.50	2.17	23.72

*7 Year Price Score 108.9 *NYSE Composite Index=100 *12 Month Price Score 95.1

Interim Earnings (Per Share)

Qtr.	Mar	Jun	Sep	Dec
2000	0.34	0.35	0.34	0.32
2001	0.41	0.35	0.33	0.36
2002	(0.08)	0.40	0.40	0.56
2003	0.32	0.30	0.31	0.12

Interim Dividends (Per Share)

Amt	Decl	Ex	Rec	P
0.135Q	5/23/2003	6/12/2003	6/16/2003	6/30/20
0.135Q	8/22/2003	9/12/2003	9/16/2003	9/30/20
0.135Q	11/21/2003	12/15/2003	12/17/2003	12/31/20
0.135Q	2/20/2004	3/15/2004	3/17/2004	3/31/20

Indicated Div: $0.54 (Div. Reinv. Plan)

Valuation Analysis

Forecast P/E	N/A	Trailing P/E 23.72
Market Cap	$550.0 Million	Book Value 302.5 Million
Price/Book	N/A	Price/Sales N/A

Dividend Achiever Status

Rank	172	10 Year Growth Rate 9.39%
Total Years of Dividend Growth		19

Business Summary: Commercial Banking (MIC: 8.1 SIC: 6021 NAIC:522110)

Unizan Financial is a holding company with total assets of $2.73 billion at Dec 31 2003. Through its subsidiaries, Co. offers full-servi banking through 45 banking offices in Ohio. Co.'s services include loan, deposit, trust and miscellaneous products and services, as well ATM access, safe deposit boxes, night deposits, U.S. savings bonds, traveler's checks, money orders and cashier checks, and electron and on-line banking services. Additionally, Co. offers investment and funds management services through Unizan Financial Services a Unizan Financial Advisors; consumer finance through Unizan Banc Financial Services and title insurance through Unizan Title Services

Recent Developments: For the year ended Dec 31 2003, net income dropped 12.4% to $23.2 million compared with income of $26 million, before an accounting change charge of $1.4 million, in 2002. Total interest income fell 5.4% to $138.9 million from $146 million a year earlier, reflecting the impact of low rate environment throughout 2003, partially offset by the increase in averag interest-earnings assets added from the acquisition of UNB Corp. Total interest expense decreased 5.2% to $62.1 million. Net intere income slid 5.5% to $76.7 million. Provision for loan losses fell 38.8% to $4.8 million. Total other income advanced 19.4% to $30 million, while total other expenses climbed 12.3% to $68.2 million.

Prospects: On Jan 27 2004, Co. and Huntington Bancshares Incorporated announced the signing of a definitive agreement, und which, Huntington will acquire Co. Under the terms of the agreement, Co. shareholders will receive 1.1424 shares of Huntingt common stock, on a tax-free basis, for each share of Co., which values the transaction at approximately $587.0 million. The transacti was unanimously approved by both boards and will likely close late in the second quarter of 2004, pending customary regulato approvals, as well as Co. shareholder approval.

Financial Data

(US$ in Thousands)	12/31/2003	12/31/2002	12/31/2001	12/31/2000	12/31/1999	12/31/1998	12/31/1997	12/31/199
Earnings Per Share	1.05	1.28	1.45	1.35	1.28	0.94	0.76	0.
Tang. Book Val. Per Share	8.86	8.61	7.97	7.04	6.26	6.06	6.15	5.
Dividends Per Share	0.530	0.520	0.500	0.480	0.470	0.360	0.320	0.2
Dividend Payout %	50.95	40.63	34.48	35.55	36.71	38.82	42.76	42.
Income Statement								
Total Interest Income	138,860	146,720	81,184	80,676	68,878	66,005	63,362	59,1
Total Interest Expense	62,129	65,510	38,194	42,740	31,440	30,583	30,322	27,8
Net Interest Income	76,731	81,210	42,990	37,936	37,438	35,422	33,040	31,3
Provision for Loan Losses	4,833	7,893	2,818	1,046	2,425	2,748	2,929	3,1
Non-Interest Income	30,602	25,620	15,469	12,627	14,061	10,934	7,197	6,3
Non-Interest Expense	68,169	60,693	32,349	27,704	27,487	27,018	23,505	22,1
Income Before Taxes	34,331	38,244	23,292	21,813	21,587	16,590	13,803	12,4
Income from Cont Ops	...	26,505	15,344	...	...	...	...	
Net Income	23,223	25,113	15,330	14,270	14,055	10,900	9,006	8,1
Average Shs. Outstg.	22,205	20,778	10,604	10,608	10,981	11,638	11,786	11,8
Balance Sheet								
Securities Avail. for Sale	471,775	446,301	...	...	...	...	...	
Net Loans & Leases	1,943,873	1,881,103	865,969	859,255	761,646	660,261	620,768	609,2
Total Assets	2,727,249	2,691,902	1,096,842	1,053,947	970,529	868,743	826,313	809,9
Total Deposits	1,975,792	1,931,615	819,488	827,641	764,234	685,494	649,481	600,6
Long-Term Obligations	365,472	331,911	114,818	61,188	54,332	41,571	35,650	62,6
Total Liabilities	2,424,426	2,387,612	1,011,474	978,019	899,855	797,041	749,793	738,6
Net Stockholders' Equity	302,823	304,290	85,368	75,928	70,674	71,702	76,520	71,3
Shares Outstanding	21,682	22,070	10,440	10,436	10,752	11,098	11,568	11,5
Statistical Record								
Return on Equity %	7.66	8.71	17.97	18.79	19.88	15.20	11.76	11.
Return on Assets %	0.85	0.98	1.39	1.35	1.44	1.25	1.08	1.
Equity/Assets %	11.10	11.30	7.78	7.20	7.28	8.25	9.26	8.
Non-Int. Exp./Tot. Inc. %	40.22	35.21	33.46	29.69	33.14	35.11	33.31	33.
Price Range	21.67-16.50	21.50-17.25	19.98-11.69	16.00-12.13	21.25-13.00	21.50-19.56	20.50-15.00	16.50-6.
P/E Ratio	20.64-15.71	16.80-13.48	13.78-8.06	11.85-8.98	16.60-10.16	22.87-20.81	26.97-19.74	23.91-8.
Average Yield %	2.78	2.01	3.02	3.67	2.61	1.79	1.75	2.

Address: 220 Market Avenue South, Canton, OH 44702 Telephone: (330) 438-1118 Web Site: www.unizan.com	Officers: Gary N. Fields – Chmn., Roger L. Mann – Pres., C.E.O.	Investor Contact:330-438-1118 Institutional Holding No of Institutions: 63 Shares: 748,687 % Held: –

VALLEY NATIONAL BANCORP

Exchange	Symbol	Price	52Wk Range	Yield	P/E
NYS	VLY	$27.97 (3/31/2004)	29.97–24.01	3.22	17.27

Year Price Score 130.3 *NYSE Composite Index=100 *12 Month Price Score 96.7

Interim Earnings (Per Share)

Qtr.	Mar	Jun	Sep	Dec
2000	0.31	0.31	0.31	0.33
2001	0.27	0.33	0.35	0.36
2002	0.38	0.40	0.40	0.39
2003	0.40	0.40	0.42	0.40

Interim Dividends (Per Share)

Amt	Decl	Ex	Rec	Pay
0.225Q	5/27/2003	6/4/2003	6/6/2003	7/1/2003
0.225Q	8/22/2003	9/3/2003	9/5/2003	10/1/2003
0.225Q	11/25/2003	12/3/2003	12/5/2003	1/2/2004
0.225Q	2/26/2004	3/4/2004	3/8/2004	4/1/2004

Indicated Div: $0.90

Valuation Analysis

Forecast P/E	N/A	Trailing P/E	17.27
Market Cap	$2.6 Billion	Book Value	652.8 Million
Price/Book	4.20	Price/Sales	4.67

Dividend Achiever Status

Rank	162	10 Year Growth Rate	9.72%
Total Years of Dividend Growth			12

Business Summary: Commercial Banking (MIC: 8.1 SIC: 6021 NAIC:522110)

Valley National Bancorp, with $9.88 billion in assets as of Dec 31 2003, is a bank holding company. Co.'s principal subsidiary is Valley National Bank (VNB). VNB is a national banking association, which provides a full range of commercial and retail banking services through 129 branch offices located in 83 communities serving 11 counties throughout northern New Jersey and Manhattan. These services include the following: the acceptance of demand, savings and time deposits; extension of consumer, real estate, small business administration and other commercial credits; title insurance; investment services; and full personal and corporate trust, as well as pension and fiduciary services.

Recent Developments: For the year ended Dec 31 2003, net income slid 0.8% to $153.4 million from $154.6 million the year before. Net interest income rose 1.3% to $348.6 million from $344.0 million in 2002. Provision for loan losses dropped 46.2% to $7.3 million. Total non-interest income advanced 33.2% to $108.2 million, supported by contributions from the acquisitions of Masters Insurance and NIA Title, both acquired in late 2002, and the acquisition of Glen Rauch Securities, acquired in early 2003. Total non-interest expense rose 12.5% to $216.3 million, largely due to higher expenses associated with recent acquisitions, business expansion, and investments in technology systems.

Prospects: Results continue to be negatively affected by difficult market conditions resulting from the soft U.S. economy, record low interest rates and significant refinance activity. However, Co. is positioning itself for long-term profitability by enhancing its balance sheet and daily operations through several initiatives. Such actions include expanding Co.'s customer call center to a seven day, 24 hour model, the addition of Sunday branch hours at 21 locations, a renewed emphasis on small business lending and the introduction of other new services.

Financial Data

(US$ in Thousands)	12/31/2003	12/31/2002	12/31/2001	12/31/2000	12/31/1999	12/31/1998	12/31/1997	12/31/1996
Earnings Per Share	1.62	1.57	1.31	1.26	1.25	1.20	1.38	1.21
Tang. Book Val. Per Share	6.95	6.64	6.75	6.58	7.06	6.94	7.75	7.16
Dividends Per Share	0.870	0.830	0.780	0.730	0.680	0.610	0.540	0.480
Dividend Payout %	54.23	52.97	59.26	58.01	54.84	51.15	39.09	39.67
Income Statement								
Total Interest Income	497,498	517,419	553,486	460,853	427,535	389,656	368,318	324,284
Total Interest Expense	148,922	157,723	218,653	202,756	169,177	160,104	155,977	145,522
Net Interest Income	348,576	359,696	334,833	258,097	258,358	229,552	212,341	178,762
Provision for Loan Losses	7,345	13,644	15,706	6,130	9,120	12,370	12,250	2,446
Non-Interest Income	108,197	81,238	64,476	50,883	47,252	43,073	42,315	26,279
Non-Interest Expense	216,278	207,994	188,248	141,013	137,946	134,757	123,228	101,168
Income Before Taxes	214,708	212,204	195,791	161,482	156,012	124,080	117,026	100,646
Income from Cont Ops	126,986	147,524	131,640	106,418	103,792	95,930	82,840	66,714
Net Income	153,415	154,616	135,204	106,773	106,324	97,348	84,992	67,495
Average Shs. Outstg.	94,498	98,357	102,425	84,215	84,486	80,465	61,597	55,746
Balance Sheet								
Cash & Due from Banks	218,166	243,923	311,850	186,720	161,561	175,794	148,175	162,872
Securities Avail. for Sale	1,809,932	2,140,366	2,171,695	1,035,769	1,005,419	929,073	1,017,225	950,192
Total Loans & Leases	6,107,759	5,698,401	5,268,004	4,607,679	4,499,632	3,927,982	(46,273)	(41,154)
Total Assets	9,880,740	9,134,674	8,583,765	6,425,837	6,360,394	5,541,207	1,468,323	1,509,510
Total Deposits	7,162,968	6,683,387	6,306,974	5,123,717	5,051,255	4,674,689	4,402,954	4,176,206
Long-Term Obligations	1,547,221	1,119,642	975,728	591,808	564,881	...	...	...
Total Liabilities	9,227,951	8,302,936	7,705,390	5,880,763	5,806,894	4,985,420	4,615,296	4,290,138
Net Stockholders' Equity	652,789	431,738	478,375	545,074	553,500	555,787	475,359	396,522
Shares Outstanding	93,910	95,049	100,363	82,739	78,347	79,971	61,296	55,310
Statistical Record								
Return on Equity %	19.45	23.35	19.40	19.52	18.75	17.26	17.42	16.82
Return on Assets %	1.28	1.61	1.53	1.65	1.63	1.73	5.64	4.41
Equity/Assets %	6.60	6.91	7.90	8.48	8.70	10.03	32.37	26.26
Net Int. Exp./Tot. Inc. %	35.70	34.74	30.26	27.55	29.05	31.14	30.00	28.85
Price Range	29.97–22.86	27.57–23.29	25.70–18.96	24.31–14.94	20.26–16.29	23.36–16.54	21.19–12.72	14.86–11.34
P/E Ratio	18.50–14.11	17.56–14.83	19.16–14.20	19.29–11.86	16.21–13.03	19.47–13.78	15.36–9.22	12.28–9.37
Average Yield %	3.24	3.19	3.61	3.90	3.74	3.07	3.53	3.70

Address: 1455 Valley Road, Wayne, NJ 07470	**Officers:** Gerald H. Lipkin – Chmn., Pres., C.E.O., Peter Crocitto – Exec. V.P.	**Investor Contact:** (973) 305–8800
Telephone: (973) 305–8800	**Transfer Agents:** American Stock Transfer & Trust Company, New York, NY	**Institutional Holding**
Web Site: www.valleynationalbank.com		**No of Institutions:** 9
		Shares: 346,108 **% Held:** –

279

VALSPAR CORP.

Exchange	Symbol	Price	52Wk Range	Yield	P/E
NYS	VAL	$49.23 (3/31/2004)	50.33-40.30	1.46	22.18

*7 Year Price Score 124.4 *NYSE Composite Index=100 ***12 Month Price Score 97.4**

TRADING VOLUME (thousand shares)

Interim Earnings (Per Share)

Qtr.	Jan	Apr	Jul	Oct
2000–01	0.10	0.44	0.51	0.05
2001–02	0.25	0.67	0.74	0.68
2002–03	0.30	0.62	0.77	0.48
2003–05	0.35	...	...	...

Interim Dividends (Per Share)

Amt	Decl	Ex	Rec	P
0.15Q	6/12/2003	6/27/2003	7/1/2003	7/15/20
0.15Q	8/14/2003	9/29/2003	10/1/2003	10/15/20
0.18Q	12/10/2003	12/29/2003	12/31/2003	1/15/20
0.18Q	2/25/2004	3/30/2004	4/1/2004	4/15/20

Indicated Div: $0.72 (Div. Reinv. Plan)

Valuation Analysis

Forecast P/E	16.77	Trailing P/E	22.18
Market Cap	$2.5 Billion	Book Value	897.0 Million
Price/Book	2.77	Price/Sales	1.09

Dividend Achiever Status

Rank	143	10 Year Growth Rate	10.55%
Total Years of Dividend Growth		25	

Business Summary: Chemicals (MIC: 11.1 SIC: 2851 NAIC:325510)

Valspar is a global paint and coatings manufacturer. Co. manufactures and distributes a portfolio of products, including: Industri coatings for factory application by industrial customers and original equipment manufacturers; Architectural paints, varnishes and sta for the do–it–yourself and professional markets; Packaging coatings and inks for rigid containers, particularly food and beverage ca Automotive refinish and other specialty coatings, including high performance floor coatings; and Specialty polymers, composites a colorants for use by coatings manufacturers and others, including Co.

Recent Developments: For the quarter ended Jan 30 2004, net income climbed 17.7% to $18.4 million compared with $15.6 milli in the equivalent 2003 quarter. Net sales grew 7.0% to $501.6 million from $469.0 million a year earlier, reflecting favorable fore currency exchange and continuing strength in Co.'s Paints segment and progressive improvement in its coatings segment. Gross pro increased 8.8% to $156.4 million versus $143.6 million the year before. Gross profit as a percentage of net sales was 31.2% in 2004 a 30.6% in 2003. Operating income advanced 8.4% to $40.3 million versus $37.1 million the year before.

Prospects: In January 2004, Co. acquired De Beer Lakfabrieken B.V., a manufacturer and distributor of automotive refinish coati based in The Netherlands. Co. expects De Beer to add approximately $50.0 million in annualized sales. The acquisition is also expect to be slightly accretive to earnings for the balance of 2004. Meanwhile, Co. is focused on cost reduction initiatives to counter r material cost pressures. Co. should be well positioned to take advantage of a recovery in the industrial economy and to participate consolidation opportunities as they occur.

Financial Data

(US$ in Thousands)	3 Mos	10/31/2003	10/25/2002	10/26/2001	10/27/2000	10/29/1999	10/30/1998	10/31/199
Earnings Per Share	0.35	2.17	2.34	1.10	2.00	1.87	1.63	1.
Cash Flow Per Share	(0.41)	4.81	4.18	4.23	2.16	2.90	2.56	1.
Tang. Book Val. Per Share	N.M	N.M	N.M	N.M	5.38	4.07	5.42	6.
Dividends Per Share	0.630	0.600	0.560	0.540	0.520	0.460	0.420	0.3
Dividend Payout %	180.00	27.64	23.93	49.09	26.00	24.59	25.76	24
Income Statement								
Total Revenues	501,591	2,247,926	2,126,853	1,920,970	1,483,320	1,387,677	1,155,134	1,017,2
Total Indirect Exp.	116,100	478,279	447,064	413,114	280,118	282,271	230,152	206,8
Depreciation & Amort.	14,388	4,463	4,863	29,283	10,675	39,800	30,742	25,7
Operating Income	40,252	227,503	249,605	160,922	163,935	145,011	121,742	111,9
Net Interest Inc./(Exp.)	(10,390)	(45,843)	(48,171)	(72,559)	(21,989)	(19,089)	(10,707)	(5,29
Income Taxes	11,269	68,960	78,427	39,650	55,280	52,944	46,658	43,3
Net Income	18,386	112,514	120,121	51,500	86,466	82,142	72,130	65,8
Average Shs. Outstg.	52,602	51,924	51,370	46,657	43,195	43,835	44,319	44,2
Balance Sheet								
Cash & Cash Equivalents	38,854	41,589	22,715	20,139	20,935	33,189	14,990	3,1
Total Current Assets	750,470	738,831	701,788	661,494	533,864	514,928	426,069	356,8
Total Assets	2,564,260	2,496,524	2,419,552	2,226,070	1,125,030	1,110,720	801,680	615,4
Total Current Liabilities	524,210	531,063	503,895	475,067	334,288	374,712	267,984	259,4
Long–Term Obligations	790,885	749,199	885,819	1,006,217	300,300	298,874	164,768	35,8
Net Stockholders' Equity	896,990	869,317	737,253	654,565	437,571	393,756	340,188	295,0
Net Working Capital	226,260	207,768	197,893	186,427	199,576	140,216	158,085	97,4
Shares Outstanding	51,053	50,730	50,104	49,481	42,481	42,983	43,418	43,6
Statistical Record								
Operating Profit Margin %	8.02	10.12	11.73	8.37	11.05	10.44	10.53	11
Return on Equity %	2.04	12.94	16.29	7.86	19.76	20.86	21.20	22
Return on Assets %	0.71	4.50	4.96	2.31	7.68	7.39	8.99	10
Debt/Total Assets %	30.84	30.00	36.61	45.20	26.69	26.90	20.55	5
Price Range	49.70-47.26	47.95-37.69	49.91-33.21	37.49-25.45	43.06-26.60	39.56-28.06	42.00-26.31	32.94-24
P/E Ratio	142.0-135.0	22.10-17.37	21.33-14.19	34.08-23.14	21.53-10.30	21.16-15.01	25.77-16.14	22.11-16
Average Yield %	1.30	1.37	1.33	1.69	1.55	1.33	1.20	1.

Address: 1101 Third Street South, Minneapolis, MN 55415 **Telephone:** (612) 332–7371 **Web Site:** www.valspar.com	**Officers:** Richard M. Rompala – Chmn., C.E.O., Steven L. Erdahl – Exec. V.P., **Transfer Agents:**Mellon Investor Services LLC, Ridgefield Park, NJ	**Investor Contact:**612–332–7371 **Institutional Holding** **No of Institutions:** 3 **Shares:** 101,532 **% Held:** –

VECTREN CORP

Exchange	Symbol	Price	52Wk Range	Yield	P/E
NYS	VVC	$24.67 (3/31/2004)	26.00–21.35	4.62	15.71

7 Year Price Score 94.4   *NYSE Composite Index=100   *12 Month Price Score 92.1

TRADING VOLUME (thousand shares)

1994 1995 1996 1997 1998 1999 2000 2001 2002 2003 04

Interim Earnings (Per Share)

Qtr.	Mar	Jun	Sep	Dec
2000	0.36	0.13	0.25	0.43
2001	0.61	(0.15)	0.07	0.48
2002	0.67	0.21	0.21	0.59
2003	0.82	0.06	0.10	0.59

Interim Dividends (Per Share)

Amt	Decl	Ex	Rec	Pay
0.275Q	4/23/2003	5/13/2003	5/15/2003	6/2/2003
0.275Q	7/22/2003	8/13/2003	8/15/2003	9/2/2003
0.285Q	10/31/2003	11/12/2003	11/14/2003	12/1/2003
0.285Q	1/28/2004	2/11/2004	2/13/2004	3/1/2004

Indicated Div: $1.14

Valuation Analysis

Forecast P/E	13.24	Trailing P/E	15.71
Market Cap	$1.7 Billion	Book Value	1.1 Billion
Price/Book	1.53	Price/Sales	0.95

Dividend Achiever Status

Rank	268	10 Year Growth Rate	3.96%
Total Years of Dividend Growth			28

Business Summary: Electricity (MIC: 7.1 SIC: 4932 NAIC:221210)

Vectren is an energy and applied technology holding company. At Dec 31 2003, Co. supplied natural gas service to 972,230 Indiana and Ohio customers, including 887,891 residential, 80,292 commercial, and 4,047 industrial and other customers. In addition, at Dec 31 2003, Co. supplied electric service to 135,098 Indiana customers, including 117,868 residential, 17,054 commercial, and 176 industrial and other customers. Co. is also involved in nonregulated activities in four primary business areas: Energy Marketing and Services, Coal Mining, Utility Infrastructure Services, and Broadband.

Recent Developments: For the year ended Dec 31 2003, net income declined 2.4% to $111.2 million compared with $114.0 million in 2002. The decline in earnings was primarily due to the Utility Group's results, which decreased $11.5 million, partially offset by increased earnings of $8.6 million from the non–regulated group. Total operating revenues grew 4.2% to $1.59 billion from $1.52 billion a year earlier. Gas utility operating revenues increased 22.5% to $1.11 billion. Electric utility operating revenues climbed 2.1% to $335.7 million. Energy services and other operating revenues dropped 51.4% to $139.7 million. Operating income declined 5.1% to $199.4 million.

Prospects: On Mar 19 2003, Co.'s subsidiary, Vectren Energy Delivery of Indiana – North, filed a petition with the Indiana Utility Regulatory Commission to adjust its base rates and charges for its gas distribution business. Providing it is approved, Vectren North will increase its base rates by about $47.0 million to cover the ongoing cost of operating, maintaining and expanding distribution and storage used to serve more than 525,000 customers. Meanwhile, Co. is targeting earnings growth of approximately 5.0% for 2004 and even greater improvement in 2005, reflecting Co.'s anticipation of rate relief in its gas distribution operations and continued growth in unregulated contributions.

Financial Data

(US$ in Thousands)	12/31/2003	12/31/2002	12/31/2001	12/31/2000	12/31/1999	12/31/1998
Earnings Per Share	1.57	1.68	1.01	1.17	1.48	1.40
Cash Flow Per Share	2.50	4.30	2.74	0.66	2.42	2.93
Tang. Book Val. Per Share	11.46	9.83	9.68	8.68	11.57	...
Dividends Per Share	1.110	1.070	1.030	0.740	...	...
Dividend Payout %	70.70	63.69	101.98	63.24	...	...
Income Statement						
Total Revenues	1,587,700	1,804,300	2,170,000	1,648,690	1,068,417	997,706
Total Indirect Exp.	419,400	394,500	435,900	384,407	306,530	290,745
Costs & Expenses	1,388,300	1,593,000	2,030,400	1,517,769	907,645	849,169
Depreciation & Amort.	128,700	119,600	123,700	105,661	86,998	81,558
Operating Income	199,400	211,300	139,600	130,921	160,772	148,537
Net Interest Inc./(Exp.)	(66,500)	(68,100)	(82,600)	(57,133)	(42,862)	(40,301)
Income Taxes	37,700	38,900	18,600	34,223	45,708	42,328
Equity Earns/Minority Int.	12,100	8,600	13,500	16,550	10,722	11,682
Income from Cont Ops	...	...	67,400	...	...	...
Net Income	111,200	114,000	63,600	72,040	90,748	86,600
Average Shs. Outstg.	70,800	67,900	66,900	61,380	61,430	61,578
Balance Sheet						
Net Property	2,226,000	1,876,100	1,776,700	1,659,238	1,400,807	...
Total Assets	3,353,400	2,926,500	2,856,800	2,888,189	1,940,025	...
Long–Term Obligations	1,072,800	954,200	1,014,000	631,954	486,726	...
Net Stockholders' Equity	1,071,500	869,600	848,100	723,608	701,564	...
Shares Outstanding	75,600	67,900	67,700	61,419	61,305	...
Statistical Record						
Operating Profit Margin %	12.55	11.71	6.43	7.94	15.04	14.88
Net Inc./Net Property %	4.99	6.07	3.57	4.34	6.47	...
Net Inc./Tot. Capital %	4.67	5.63	3.07	4.51	6.42	...
Return on Equity %	10.37	13.10	7.94	9.84	12.78	...
Accum. Depr./Gross Prop. %	38.36	45.73	45.06	44.21	43.56	...
Price Range	26.00–20.01	25.87–18.69	24.19–19.90	26.50–15.75	35.88–22.56	36.56–27.31
P/E Ratio	16.56–12.75	15.40–11.13	23.95–19.70	22.65–13.46	24.24–15.24	26.12–19.51
Average Yield %	4.81	4.49	4.70	3.54	N/A	N/A

Address: 20 N.W. Fourth Street, Evansville, IN 47708	**Officers:** Niel C. Ellerbrook – Chmn., Pres., C.E.O., Jerome A. Benkert – Exec. V.P., C.F.O.	**Investor Contact:**800–227–8625
Telephone: (812) 491–4000	**Transfer Agents:**National City Bank, Cleveland, OH	**Institutional Holding**
Web Site: www.vectren.com		**No of Institutions:** 4
		Shares: 2,340 **% Held:** –

VF CORP.

Exchange	Symbol	Price	52Wk Range	Yield	P/E
NYS	VFC	$46.70 (3/31/2004)	46.89–33.91	2.23	12.94

*7 Year Price Score 101.7 ***NYSE Composite Index=100** ***12 Month Price Score 97.2**

Interim Earnings (Per Share)

Qtr.	Mar	Jun	Sep	Dec
2000	0.68	0.69	0.86	0.04
2001	0.67	0.60	0.90	(0.98)
2002–03	0.69	0.79	1.15	0.61
2003–04	0.83	0.68	1.14	0.96

Interim Dividends (Per Share)

Amt	Decl	Ex	Rec	Pa
0.25Q	4/22/2003	6/6/2003	6/10/2003	6/20/200
0.25Q	7/22/2003	9/5/2003	9/9/2003	9/19/200
0.26Q	10/23/2003	12/5/2003	12/9/2003	12/19/200
0.26Q	2/11/2004	3/5/2004	3/9/2004	3/19/200

Indicated Div: $1.04 (Div. Reinv. Plan)

Valuation Analysis

Forecast P/E	10.51	Trailing P/E	12.94
Market Cap	$5.1 Billion	Book Value	2.0 Billion
Price/Book	2.33	Price/Sales	0.89

Dividend Achiever Status

Rank	248	10 Year Growth Rate	5.17%
Total Years of Dividend Growth			31

Business Summary: Apparel (MIC: 4.4 SIC: 2329 NAIC:315228)

VF designs, manufactures and markets branded jeanswear, sportswear, intimate apparel, occupational apparel, knitwear, outdoor appare and equipment, and other apparel. Co. manages its business through over 25 marketing units that support specific brands. Marketing unit with similar products have been grouped together into four reportable segments: consumer apparel, occupational apparel, outdoor appare and equipment, and all other. Co.'s principal brands include: Lee®, Rustler®, Wrangler®, Riders®, Vanity Fair®, Vassarette®, Bestform® Lily of France®, Lee Sport®, Healthtex®, JanSport®, Eastpak®, Red Kap®, Nautica® and The North Face®.

Recent Developments: For the year ended Jan 3 2004, net income rose 9.2% to $397.9 million compared with income of $364. million, before an accounting change charge of $527.3 million, in 2002. Results benefited from favorable foreign currency translations ar from contributions from Co.'s newer businesses, Nautica® and The North Face®. Results for 2003 excluded a gain from discontinue operations of $8.3 million. Net sales rose 2.4% to $5.21 billion from $5.08 billion in the prior year. The addition of Nautica Enterprises, In contributed $249.0 million in net sales to year-end results. Operating income climbed 3.7% to $644.9 million compared with $621.9 millio the year before.

Prospects: Looking ahead, Co. currently projects a 5.0% increase in both earnings and sales for full-year 2004. Sales growth will driven primarily from the acquisition of Nautica®, which is expected to contribute about $550.0 million to full-year 2004 sales and at le $0.16 per share to earnings per share. Co.'s outdoor businesses are also expected to report double-digit sales growth. Total jeanswear sal are expected to be about flat with levels in 2003, with low-single digit sales increases expected in both global intimate apparel a imagewear. In addition, Co. expects sales will reflect the exit of its playwear business, which contributed about $141.0 million to sales 2003.

Financial Data

(US$ in Thousands)	01/03/2004	01/04/2003	12/29/2001	12/30/2000	01/01/2000	01/02/1999	01/03/1998	01/04/199
Earnings Per Share	3.61	3.24	1.19	2.27	2.99	3.10	2.70	2.2
Cash Flow Per Share	4.92	5.74	5.97	3.78	3.46	3.46	3.50	5.5
Tang. Book Val. Per Share	8.61	10.91	9.97	12.55	10.08	9.33	8.68	8.5
Dividends Per Share	1.010	0.970	0.930	0.890	0.850	0.810	0.770	0.73
Dividend Payout %	27.97	29.93	78.15	39.20	28.42	26.12	28.51	32.1
Income Statement								
Total Revenues	5,207,459	5,083,523	5,518,805	5,747,879	5,551,616	5,478,807	5,222,246	5,137,17
Total Indirect Exp.	1,268,576	1,207,591	1,372,725	1,395,435	1,241,864	1,207,922	1,176,562	1,121,72
Depreciation & Amort.	118,376	107,398	168,972	173,422	167,432	161,385	156,252	160,57
Operating Income	644,889	621,924	347,246	509,993	652,632	684,169	605,073	557,28
Net Interest Inc./(Exp.)	(49,912)	(63,928)	(86,515)	(81,032)	(62,490)	(55,871)	(25,877)	(49,38
Income Taxes	200,573	197,300	124,971	164,417	229,334	243,292	234,938	208,88
Income from Cont Ops	...	364,428	...	267,116	...	...	...	
Net Income	397,933	(154,543)	137,830	260,334	366,242	388,306	350,942	299,52
Average Shs. Outstg.	110,323	112,336	114,764	117,218	122,258	124,995	129,720	127,29
Balance Sheet								
Cash & Cash Equivalents	514,785	496,367	332,049	118,891	79,861	63,208	124,094	270,62
Total Current Assets	2,208,531	2,074,540	2,031,420	2,110,096	1,877,416	1,848,152	1,601,466	1,706,32
Total Assets	4,245,552	3,503,151	4,103,016	4,358,156	4,026,514	3,836,646	3,322,782	3,449,53
Total Current Liabilities	871,857	874,844	813,833	1,006,200	1,113,473	1,033,006	765,908	766,26
Long–Term Obligations	956,383	602,287	904,035	905,031	517,834	521,657	516,226	519,05
Net Stockholders' Equity	1,921,320	1,620,946	2,067,165	2,143,330	2,112,274	2,011,964	1,810,428	1,902,79
Net Working Capital	1,336,674	1,199,696	1,217,587	1,103,896	763,943	815,146	835,558	940,05
Shares Outstanding	108,170	108,525	109,998	86,807	116,204	119,466	121,225	127,81
Statistical Record								
Operating Profit Margin %	12.38	12.23	6.29	8.87	11.75	12.48	11.58	10.8
Return on Equity %	20.39	21.98	6.52	12.18	16.92	18.79	18.79	15.2
Return on Assets %	9.37	10.40	3.35	6.12	9.09	10.12	10.56	8.0
Debt/Total Assets %	22.52	17.19	22.03	20.76	12.86	13.59	15.53	15.0
Price Range	44.05–32.85	45.33–32.09	41.99–28.61	36.56–22.00	54.25–28.00	53.81–34.00	47.88–32.63	34.94–24.3
P/E Ratio	12.20–9.10	13.99–9.90	35.29–24.04	16.11–9.69	18.14–9.36	17.36–10.97	17.73–12.08	15.39–10.7
Average Yield %	2.64	2.43	2.56	3.38	2.13	1.73	1.89	2.4

Address: 105 Corporate Center Boulevard, Greensboro, NC 27408	**Officers:** Mackey J. nald – Chmn., Pres., C.E.O., Robert K. Shearer – V.P., Fin., C.F.O.	**Investor Contact:**ations,
Telephone: (336) 424–6000	**Transfer Agents:** First Chicago Trust Company of New York, Jersey City, NJ	**Institutional Holding**
Web Site: www.vfc.com		**No of Institutions:** 53
		Shares: 499,036,355 **% Held:** –

VULCAN MATERIALS CO.

Exchange	Symbol	Price	52Wk Range	Yield	P/E
NYS	VMC	$47.44 (3/31/2004)	50.12–30.77	2.19	21.76

*7 Year Price Score 98.6   *NYSE Composite Index=100   *12 Month Price Score 105.5

Interim Earnings (Per Share)

Qtr.	Mar	Jun	Sep	Dec
2000	0.23	0.75	0.85	0.33
2001	0.06	0.78	0.90	0.43
2002	0.11	0.64	0.75	0.36
2003	0.01	0.65	0.91	0.61

Interim Dividends (Per Share)

Amt	Decl	Ex	Rec	Pay
0.245Q	5/9/2003	5/21/2003	5/23/2003	6/10/2003
0.245Q	7/11/2003	8/25/2003	8/27/2003	9/10/2003
0.245Q	10/10/2003	11/24/2003	11/26/2003	12/10/2003
0.26Q	2/13/2004	2/25/2004	2/27/2004	3/10/2004

Indicated Div: $1.04 (Div. Reinv. Plan)

Valuation Analysis

Forecast P/E	17.67	Trailing P/E	21.76
Market Cap	$4.8 Billion	Book Value	1.8 Billion
Price/Book	2.70	Price/Sales	1.68

Dividend Achiever Status

Rank	180	10 Year Growth Rate	8.84%
Total Years of Dividend Growth	11

Business Summary: Earth &Rock Mining (MIC: 14.5 SIC: 1422 NAIC:212312)

Vulcan Materials and its subsidiaries are engaged in the production, distribution and sale of construction materials and industrial and specialty chemical, including chloralkali. Co.'s construction materials business consists of the production and sale of construction aggregates and other construction materials and related services. Construction aggregates include crushed stone, sand and gravel, rock asphalt, recrushed concrete, and are employed in virtually all types of construction, including highway construction and maintenance. Other Construction Materials products and services include asphalt mix and related products and ready–mixed concrete.

Recent Developments: For the year ended Dec 31 2003, Co. reported earnings from continuing operations of $223.5 million, compared with income of $196.7 million the year before. Earnings for 2003 and 2002 excluded losses on discontinued operations of $9.7 million and $6.2 million, and accounting change charges of $18.8 million and $20.5 million, respectively. Total revenues rose 9.2% to $2.89 billion from $2.65 billion a year earlier. On a segment basis, Construction Materials sales rose 5.4% to $2.09 billion, led by higher aggregates shipments in most markets. Chemicals sales were $531.9 million, up 25.2% from the year before, supported by higher sales prices for caustic soda and chlorine.

Prospects: Co. should continue to benefit from higher demand and shipments in the construction materials markets. Co. anticipates the pace of residential construction in 2004 to be level with 2003, while highway construction is projected to increase modestly. Additionally, Co. anticipates aggregates shipments and pricing in its markets to improve, with construction material earnings ranging from $415.0 million to $445.0 million. Meanwhile, Co.'s chemicals segment should benefit from additional improvements in plant operating performance. Looking ahead, earnings per share from continuing operations are projected to range from $2.45 and $2.65 in 2004.

Financial Data

(US$ in Thousands)	12/31/2003	12/31/2002	12/31/2001	12/31/2000	12/31/1999	12/31/1998	12/31/1997	12/31/1996
Earnings Per Share	2.18	1.86	2.17	2.16	2.35	2.50	2.03	1.78
Cash Flow Per Share	5.05	4.50	4.97	4.09	3.94	3.54	3.36	3.27
Tang. Book Val. Per Share	12.01	11.04	10.02	9.00	8.62	11.46	9.81	8.42
Dividends Per Share	0.980	0.940	0.900	0.840	0.780	0.690	0.620	0.560
Dividend Payout %	44.95	50.53	41.47	38.88	33.19	27.73	30.82	31.46
Income Statement								
Total Revenues	2,892,186	2,796,577	3,019,990	2,491,744	2,355,778	1,776,434	1,678,581	1,568,945
Total Indirect Exp.	202,458	248,328	279,032	243,198	228,357	206,807	195,558	179,015
Depreciation & Amort.	277,091	267,676	278,209	232,365	207,108	137,792	120,624	112,600
Operating Income	353,116	292,664	370,422	340,489	358,094	342,863	283,570	274,488
Net Interest Inc./(Exp.)	(49,592)	(51,469)	(56,836)	(43,409)	(44,246)	(128)	(3,724)	(5,457)
Income Taxes	87,971	67,247	101,373	92,345	111,868	118,936	91,356	96,985
Income from Cont Ops	223,454	190,413	...	...	...	...	...	...
Net Income	194,952	169,876	222,024	219,893	239,693	255,908	209,145	188,595
Average Shs. Outstg.	102,710	102,515	102,497	102,012	102,190	102,177	102,849	105,519
Balance Sheet								
Cash & Cash Equivalents	421,663	170,728	100,802	55,276	52,834	180,568	128,566	50,816
Total Current Assets	1,050,242	789,688	729,952	694,504	624,724	576,381	487,132	394,045
Total Assets	3,636,860	3,448,221	3,398,224	3,228,574	2,839,493	1,658,611	1,449,246	1,320,645
Total Current Liabilities	542,952	297,709	344,945	572,231	386,642	211,462	207,697	194,654
Long–Term Obligations	607,654	857,757	906,299	685,361	698,862	76,533	81,931	85,535
Net Stockholders' Equity	1,802,836	1,696,986	1,604,274	1,471,496	1,323,653	1,153,700	991,497	883,664
Net Working Capital	507,290	491,979	385,457	122,273	238,082	364,919	279,435	199,391
Shares Outstanding	101,811	101,557	101,320	101,043	100,734	100,596	101,061	104,913
Statistical Record								
Operating Profit Margin %	12.20	10.46	12.26	13.66	15.20	19.30	16.89	17.49
Return on Equity %	12.39	11.22	13.88	14.94	18.10	22.18	21.09	21.34
Return on Assets %	6.14	5.52	6.55	6.81	8.44	15.42	14.43	14.28
Debt/Total Assets %	16.70	24.87	26.66	21.22	24.61	4.61	5.65	6.47
Price Range	48.25–29.06	49.55–32.37	55.10–38.15	48.50–36.69	50.50–34.88	44.06–31.62	34.44–18.46	21.58–17.83
P/E Ratio	22.13–13.33	26.64–17.40	25.39–17.58	22.45–16.98	21.49–14.84	17.62–12.65	16.96–9.09	12.13–10.02
Average Yield %	2.56	2.23	1.91	1.95	1.81	1.86	2.38	2.87

Address: 1200 Urban Center Drive, Birmingham, AL 35242	**Officers:** Donald M. James – Chmn., C.E.O., Mark E. Tomkins – Sr. V.P., C.F.O., Treas.	**Investor Contact:** 205–298–3220
Telephone: (205) 298–3000	**Transfer Agents:** The Bank of New York., New York, New York	**Institutional Holding** **No of Institutions:** 255
Web Site: www.vulcanmaterials.com		**Shares:** 70,289,533 **% Held:** 68.90%

WALGREEN CO.

Exchange	Symbol	Price	52Wk Range	Yield	P/E
NYS	WAG	$32.95 (3/31/2004)	37.15–29.05	0.52	28.16

*7 Year Price Score 114.1 *NYSE Composite Index=100 ***12 Month Price Score 101.0**

Interim Earnings (Per Share)

Qtr.	Nov	Feb	May	Aug
2000–01	0.15	0.29	0.21	0.21
2001–02	0.18	0.32	0.25	0.24
2002–03	0.22	0.36	0.29	0.27
2003–04	0.25	...	...	...

Interim Dividends (Per Share)

Amt	Decl	Ex	Rec	Pa
0.038Q	4/9/2003	5/19/2003	5/21/2003	6/12/200
0.043Q	7/9/2003	8/18/2003	8/20/2003	9/12/200
0.043Q	10/8/2003	11/13/2003	11/17/2003	12/12/200
0.043Q	1/14/2004	2/17/2004	2/19/2004	3/12/200

Indicated Div: $0.1725 (Div. Reinv. Plan)

Valuation Analysis

Forecast P/E	24.96	Trailing P/E	28.16
Market Cap	$33.8 Billion	Book Value	7.4 Billion
Price/Book	4.26	Price/Sales	0.93

Dividend Achiever Status

Rank	210	10 Year Growth Rate	7.60%
Total Years of Dividend Growth			28

Business Summary: Retail – Miscellaneous (MIC: 5.11 SIC: 5912 NAIC:446110)

Walgreen is engaged in the operation of retail drugstores. Co.'s drugstores are engaged in the retail sale of prescription ar non–prescription drugs and carry additional product lines such as general merchandise, cosmetics, toiletries, household items, food ar beverages. Customer prescription purchases can be made at the drugstores as well as through the mail, by telephone and on the Interne The total number of stores at Aug 31 2003 was 4,224 stores located in 44 states and Puerto Rico. In addition, Co. operates three ma service facilities.

Recent Developments: For the three months ended Feb 29 2004, net earnings climbed 16.9% to $433.5 million from $370.9 millio in the corresponding prior–year period. Results for 2004 and 2003 included after–tax gains of $7.9 million and $200,000, respectively from litigation settlements. Net sales totaled $9.78 billion, up 15.8% compared with $8.45 billion the previous year. Comparable–sto sales increased 11.5% year over year. Prescription sales, which accounted for approximately 60.0% of sales in the second quarter of fisc 2004, advanced 19.0%. Prescription sales in comparable stores rose 15.5%. Earnings before income taxes increased 16.4% to $693 million from $595.8 million the year before.

Prospects: Results are being positively affected by stronger demand for prescription drugs and increased customer traffic leve partially offset by a decline in the number of new generic prescription drug introductions. Meanwhile, results should continue to bene from Co.'s ongoing store expansion program. During the first half of the current fiscal year, Co. has opened 109 net new stores. C anticipates a fiscal 2004 net increase of about 365 stores after closing and relocations. In May 2004, a new distribution center in Southe California is expected to be operational, which will help support Co.'s aggressive growth in this region.

Financial Data
(US$ in Thousands)

	3 Mos	08/31/2003	08/31/2002	08/31/2001	08/31/2000	08/31/1999	08/31/1998	08/31/199
Earnings Per Share	0.25	1.14	0.99	0.86	0.76	0.62	0.53	0.4
Cash Flow Per Share	0.12	1.44	1.42	0.69	0.95	0.61	0.56	0.6
Tang. Book Val. Per Share	7.19	7.02	6.07	5.10	4.18	3.47	2.85	2.4
Dividends Per Share	0.150	0.149	0.144	0.139	0.134	0.129	0.123	0.1
Dividend Payout %	62.25	13.04	14.52	16.13	17.59	20.76	23.13	26.
Income Statement								
Total Revenues	8,720,800	32,505,400	28,681,100	24,623,000	21,206,900	17,838,800	15,307,000	13,363,00
Total Indirect Exp.	1,895,100	6,950,900	5,980,800	5,175,800	4,516,900	3,844,800	3,332,000	2,973,00
Depreciation & Amort.	...	346,100	307,300	269,200	230,100	210,100	189,000	164,00
Operating Income	405,000	1,848,300	1,624,200	1,398,300	1,224,100	1,015,400	835,000	708,00
Net Interest Inc./(Exp.)	2,800	10,800	6,900	2,300	5,700	11,900	5,000	4,00
Income Taxes	152,900	713,000	618,100	537,100	486,400	403,200	340,000	276,00
Income from Cont Ops	...	...	...	...	...	...	537,000	
Net Income	254,900	1,175,700	1,019,000	885,600	776,900	624,000	511,000	436,00
Average Shs. Outstg.	1,032,200	1,031,580	1,032,270	1,028,946	1,019,888	1,014,281	1,005,692	996,6
Balance Sheet								
Cash & Cash Equivalents	868,100	1,017,100	449,900	16,900	12,800	141,800	144,000	73,00
Total Current Assets	6,937,100	6,358,100	5,166,500	4,393,900	3,550,100	3,221,700	2,623,000	2,326,00
Total Assets	12,097,000	11,405,900	9,878,800	8,833,800	7,103,700	5,906,700	4,902,000	4,207,00
Total Current Liabilities	3,883,200	3,420,500	2,955,200	3,011,600	2,303,700	1,923,800	1,580,000	1,439,00
Net Stockholders' Equity	7,374,500	7,195,700	6,230,200	5,207,200	4,234,000	3,484,300	2,849,000	2,373,00
Net Working Capital	3,053,900	2,937,600	2,211,300	1,382,300	1,246,400	1,297,900	1,043,000	887,00
Shares Outstanding	1,024,532	1,024,908	1,024,908	1,019,425	1,010,818	1,004,022	996,488	987,58
Statistical Record								
Operating Profit Margin %	4.64	5.68	5.66	5.67	5.77	5.69	5.45	5.2
Return on Equity %	3.45	16.33	16.35	17.00	18.34	17.91	18.84	18.3
Return on Assets %	2.10	10.30	10.31	10.02	10.93	10.56	10.95	10.
Price Range	36.81–30.57	35.96–27.35	40.24–30.98	45.63–31.43	35.25–22.75	33.06–19.25	24.47–12.81	14.81–8.2
P/E Ratio	147.2–122.3	31.54–23.99	40.65–31.29	53.05–36.55	46.38–29.93	53.33–31.05	46.17–24.17	33.66–18.
Average Yield %	0.45	0.45	0.39	0.33	0.46	0.45	0.68	0.9

Address: 200 Wilmot Road, Deerfield, IL 60015 **Telephone:** (847) 940–2500 **Web Site:** www.walgreens.com	**Officers:** David W. Bernauer – Chmn., C.E.O., Jeffrey A. Rein – Pres., C.O.O. **Transfer Agents:**Computershare Investor Services, Chicago, IL	**Investor Contact:**847–914–2972 **Institutional Holding** **No of Institutions:** 37 **Shares:** 1,634,938 **% Held:** –

WAL-MART STORES, INC.

Exchange	Symbol	Price	52Wk Range	Yield	P/E
NYS	WMT	$59.69 (3/31/2004)	61.05–50.74	0.87	29.55

Year Price Score 125.0 *NYSE Composite Index=100 *12 Month Price Score 90.0

Interim Earnings (Per Share)

Qtr.	Apr	Jul	Oct	Jan
2000–01	0.30	0.36	0.31	0.43
2001–02	0.30	0.36	0.33	0.50
2002–03	0.37	0.46	0.41	0.57
2003–04	0.41	0.52	0.46	0.63

Interim Dividends (Per Share)

Amt	Decl	Ex	Rec	Pay
0.13Q	3/2/2004	3/17/2004	3/19/2004	4/5/2004
0.13Q	3/2/2004	5/19/2004	5/21/2004	6/7/2004
0.13Q	3/2/2004	8/18/2004	8/20/2004	9/7/2004
0.13Q	3/2/2004	12/15/2004	12/17/2004	1/3/2005

Indicated Div: $0.52 (Div. Reinv. Plan)

Valuation Analysis

Forecast P/E	24.97	Trailing P/E	29.55
Market Cap	$263.5 Billion	Book Value	N/A
Price/Book	N/A	Price/Sales	N/A

Dividend Achiever Status

Rank	39	10 Year Growth Rate	18.75%
Total Years of Dividend Growth			22

Business Summary: Retail – General (MIC: 5.2 SIC: 5331 NAIC:452990)

Wal–Mart Stores operated 1,508 discount department stores, 1,356 Supercenters, 528 Sam's Clubs and 53 Neighborhood Markets in the U.S. as of Jul 31 2003. Co. also operated 610 Wal–Mart stores in Mexico, 260 in the U.K., 213 in Canada, 92 in Germany, 52 in Puerto Rico, 24 in Brazil, 15 in South Korea, and eleven in Argentina. Co. also operated 28 stores in China under joint venture agreements. Co.'s Supercenters combine food, general merchandise, and services including pharmacy, dry cleaning, portrait studios, photo finishing, hair salons, and optical shops. In addition, Co. owns a 35.0% interest in Seiyu, Ltd., which operates over 400 stores throughout Japan.

Recent Developments: For the twelve months ended Jan 31 2004, income from continuing operations climbed 13.3% to $8.86 billion versus income from continuing operations of $7.82 billion a year earlier. Net sales increased 11.6% to $256.33 billion from $229.62 billion the year before. Total U.S. comparable-store sales were up 4.1% year over year, reflecting a 3.9% same-store increase at Wal–Mart stores and a 5.3% comparable-store gain for Sam's Club locations. Cost of sales totaled $198.75 billion, or 77.5% of net sales, compared with $178.30 billion, or 77.7% of net sales, the previous year. Income before income taxes climbed 14.8% to $14.19 billion from $12.37 billion the prior year.

Prospects: Sales and earnings growth should benefit from Co.'s efforts to expand internationally. On Mar 1 2004, Co. announced that it has acquired Bompreco, an operator of 118 hypermarkets, supermarkets and mini markets in Brazil with annual sales of about $1.13 billion, for about $300.0 million from Royal Ahold N.V. The acquisition expands Co.'s operations into northeastern Brazil. Separately, inventory levels are in good shape heading into the spring selling season following markdowns on apparel that helped spur sales in late winter. Looking ahead, Co. is targeting first-quarter 2004 earnings of between $0.48 and $0.50 per share, and full-year 2004 earnings in the range of $2.34 to $2.38 per share.

Financial Data

(US$ in Thousands)	9 Mos	6 Mos	3 Mos	01/31/2003	01/31/2002	01/31/2001	01/31/2000	01/31/1999
Earnings Per Share	1.40	0.94	0.41	1.81	1.49	1.40	1.25	0.99
Cash Flow Per Share	1.75	1.43	0.60	2.81	2.28	2.14	1.83	1.69
Tang. Book Val. Per Share	7.56	7.55	7.05	6.78	5.95	4.98	3.68	4.17
Dividends Per Share	0.340	0.330	0.310	0.300	0.280	0.240	0.200	0.150
Dividend Payout %	24.64	35.10	76.82	16.57	18.79	17.14	16.00	15.65
Income Statement								
Total Revenues	183,491,000	120,455,000	57,224,000	246,525,000	219,812,000	193,295,000	166,809,000	139,208,000
Total Indirect Exp.	32,704,000	21,360,000	10,216,000	41,043,000	36,173,000	31,550,000	27,040,000	22,363,000
Depreciation & Amort.	2,813,000	1,842,000	888,000	3,432,000	3,290,000	2,868,000	2,375,000	1,872,000
Operating Income	10,279,000	6,879,000	3,090,000	13,644,000	12,077,000	11,490,000	10,105,000	8,120,000
Net Interest Inc./(Exp.)	(631,000)	(425,000)	(212,000)	(925,000)	(1,326,000)	(1,374,000)	(1,022,000)	(797,000)
Income Taxes	3,377,000	2,259,000	1,006,000	4,487,000	3,897,000	3,692,000	3,338,000	2,740,000
Eqty Earns/Minority Int.	(131,000)	(83,000)	(42,000)	(193,000)	(183,000)	(129,000)	(170,000)	(153,000)
Income from Cont Ops	6,140,000	4,112,000	1,830,000	...	...	...	5,575,000	...
Net Income	6,333,000	4,305,000	1,861,000	8,039,000	6,671,000	6,295,000	5,377,000	4,430,000
Average Shs. Outstg.	4,385,000	4,392,000	4,395,000	4,446,000	4,481,000	4,484,000	4,474,000	4,485,000
Balance Sheet								
Cash & Cash Equivalents	3,312,000	4,472,000	2,468,000	2,758,000	2,161,000	2,054,000	1,856,000	1,879,000
Total Current Assets	36,790,000	32,153,000	31,348,000	30,483,000	28,246,000	26,555,000	24,356,000	21,132,000
Total Assets	104,821,000	98,786,000	96,473,000	94,685,000	83,451,000	78,130,000	70,349,000	49,996,000
Total Current Liabilities	39,225,000	32,833,000	32,222,000	32,617,000	27,282,000	28,949,000	25,803,000	16,762,000
Long-Term Obligations	19,948,000	20,207,000	20,939,000	19,608,000	18,732,000	15,655,000	16,674,000	9,607,000
Net Stockholders' Equity	42,172,000	42,594,000	40,200,000	39,337,000	35,102,000	31,343,000	25,834,000	21,112,000
Net Working Capital	2,435,000	680,000	(874,000)	(2,134,000)	964,000	(2,394,000)	(1,447,000)	4,370,000
Shares Outstanding	4,327,781	4,369,200	4,378,918	4,395,000	4,453,000	4,470,000	4,457,000	4,448,000
Statistical Record								
Operating Profit Margin %	5.60	5.71	5.39	5.53	5.49	5.94	6.05	5.83
Return on Equity %	14.55	9.65	4.55	20.43	19.00	20.08	21.58	20.98
Return on Assets %	5.85	4.16	1.89	8.49	7.99	8.05	7.92	8.86
Debt/Total Assets %	19.03	20.45	21.70	20.70	22.44	20.03	23.70	19.21
Price Range	60.08–46.74	57.32–46.74	56.58–46.74	63.75–44.60	59.98–44.00	63.56–43.25	69.75–40.19	43.00–20.41
P/E Ratio	42.91–33.39	60.98–49.72	138.0–114.0	35.22–24.64	40.26–29.53	45.40–30.89	55.80–32.15	43.43–20.61
Average Yield %	0.62	0.62	0.61	0.55	0.53	0.45	0.40	0.49

Address: 702 S.W. Eighth Street,
Bentonville, AR 72716
Telephone: (479) 273–4000
Web Site: www.wal–mart.com

Officers: S. Robson Walton – Chmn., Thomas M. Coughlin – Vice–Chmn., Exec. V.P.
Transfer Agents: EquiServe Trust Company, N.A., Providence, RI

Institutional Holding
No of Institutions: 9
Shares: 3,970,827   % Held: –

WASHINGTON FEDERAL INC.

Exchange	Symbol	Price	52Wk Range	Yield	P/E
NMS	WFSL	$25.53 (3/31/2004)	26.36–19.15	3.13	14.07

*7 Year Price Score 128.0   *NYSE Composite Index=100   *12 Month Price Score 103.3

Interim Earnings (Per Share)

Qtr.	Dec	Mar	Jun	Sep
2000–01	0.35	0.35	0.38	0.38
2001–02	0.45	0.46	0.46	0.48
2002–03	0.52	0.49	0.47	0.40
2003–04	0.46	...	...	...

Interim Dividends (Per Share)

Amt	Decl	Ex	Rec	P
0.20Q	9/22/2003	10/1/2003	10/3/2003	10/17/20
0.20Q	12/22/2003	1/7/2004	1/9/2004	1/23/20
10%	1/21/2004	2/4/2004	2/6/2004	2/20/20
0.20Q	3/22/2004	3/31/2004	4/2/2004	4/16/20
		Indicated Div: $0.80		

Valuation Analysis

Forecast P/E	11.97	Trailing P/E	14.07
Market Cap	$1.6 Billion	Book Value	1.1 Billion
Price/Book	1.90	Price/Sales	4.55

Dividend Achiever Status

Rank	190	10 Year Growth Rate	8.43%
Total Years of Dividend Growth			20

Business Summary: Other Depository Banking (MIC: 8.5 SIC: 6035 NAIC:522120)

Washington Federal is a non–diversified unitary savings and loan holding company with total assets of $7,535,975,000, as of Sept. 3 2003. Co. conducts its operations through its federally insured savings and loan association subsidiary, Washington Federal Savings a Loan Association. Co.'s business consists primarily of attracting savings deposits from the general public and investing these funds loans secured by first mortgage liens on single–family dwellings, including loans for the construction of such dwellings, and loans multi–family dwellings. Co. operates 119 offices located in eight states in the western United States.

Recent Developments: For the three months ended Dec 31 2003, net income declined 11.6% to $32.8 million compared with $37 million in the corresponding year-earlier period. Co. attributed the decrease in earnings primarily to continued margin compression caus mainly by a changing asset mix that included more short-term assets as well as lower yielding loans. Net interest income fell 14.2% to $58 million from $68.4 million the previous year. Provision for loan losses amounted to nil versus $1.3 million the year before. Other incom increased 24.2% to $2.7 million from $2.2 million last year, primarily as a result of net gains of $536,000 on the sale of securities.

Prospects: Recent favorable asset quality indicator trends reinforce Co.'s near-term outlook. For example, for the quarter ende Dec 31 2003, nonperforming assets amounted to $24.8 million or 0.33% of total assets versus $33.6 million, or 0.46% of total assets t previous year. Also, delinquencies on permanent loans fell to $24.5 million from $29.1 million a year earlier. However, Co. noted that wea economic conditions, including unemployment that is higher than the national average, continue in its primary markets. Separately, Co previous decision to invest cautiously given historically lower interest rates and raise short-term assets could pay off in 2004 if interest rat increase meaningfully.

Financial Data

(US$ in Thousands)	3 Mos	09/30/2003	09/30/2002	09/30/2001	09/30/2000	09/30/1999	09/30/1998	09/30/199
Earnings Per Share	1.82	1.88	1.85	1.46	1.36	1.40	1.31	1..
Tang. Book Val. Per Share	14.17	12.71	12.03	11.97	9.40	8.84	9.47	7.1
Dividends Per Share	0.780	0.770	0.730	0.690	0.650	0.590	0.540	0.4
Dividend Payout %	42.86	40.97	39.39	47.41	48.00	42.79	41.53	39..
Income Statement								
Total Interest Income	102,682	450,185	507,317	536,410	498,027	455,577	460,604	459,0(
Total Interest Expense	44,056	194,884	234,941	320,120	299,511	244,490	252,233	257,4
Net Interest Income	58,626	255,301	272,376	216,290	198,516	211,087	208,371	201,5(
Provision for Loan Losses	...	1,500	7,000	1,850	...	684	740	8
Non–Interest Income	2,723	15,017	8,088	9,736	10,377	12,665	11,032	5,0
Non–Interest Expense	10,779	44,059	51,228	49,113	46,646	46,101	45,116	44,3(
Income Before Taxes	50,695	224,565	222,354	175,464	163,179	177,081	173,785	163,3
Net Income	32,822	145,544	143,954	113,614	105,679	114,286	111,836	105,0(
Average Shs. Outstg.	71,931	77,255	77,575	77,507	77,473	81,706	85,144	84,1(
Balance Sheet								
Securities Avail. for Sale	741,309	1,608,372	1,837,552	2,159,792	2,356,928	2,339,834	1,528,376	1,344,2
Net Loans & Leases	4,666,904	4,606,726	4,292,003	4,207,769	4,949,235	4,378,728	4,143,525	4,190,7
Total Assets	7,544,844	7,535,975	7,392,441	7,026,743	6,719,841	6,163,503	5,637,011	5,719,5(
Total Deposits	4,524,690	4,520,051	4,452,250	4,251,113	3,375,036	3,291,637	3,071,175	2,905,3
Long–Term Obligations	1,750,000	1,650,000	1,650,000	1,637,500	1,209,000	1,454,000	1,356,500	1,601,0(
Total Liabilities	6,474,644	6,480,379	6,431,723	6,152,734	5,960,676	5,413,480	4,869,839	5,001,8
Net Stockholders' Equity	1,070,200	1,055,596	960,718	874,009	759,165	750,023	767,172	717,7
Shares Outstanding	71,281	78,290	76,884	70,012	76,310	79,401	75,322	84,1(
Statistical Record								
Return on Equity %	3.06	13.78	14.98	12.99	13.92	15.23	14.57	14.
Return on Assets %	0.43	1.93	1.94	1.61	1.57	1.85	1.98	1.
Equity/Assets %	14.18	14.00	12.99	12.43	11.29	12.16	13.60	12..
Non–Int. Exp./Tot. Inc. %	10.22	9.47	9.93	8.99	9.17	9.84	9.56	9.
Price Range	26.29–22.91	24.01–17.07	22.65–16.53	20.77–13.53	16.22–10.20	17.46–14.09	18.80–13.82	16.79–11..
P/E Ratio	57.15–49.80	12.77–9.08	12.24–8.93	14.22–9.27	11.93–7.50	12.47–10.06	14.35–10.55	13.54–9..
Average Yield %	3.13	3.73	3.63	3.78	4.99	3.75	3.16	3.

Address: 425 Pike Street, Seattle, WA 98101	Officers: Guy C. Pinkerton – Chmn., Roy M. Whitehead – Vice Chmn., Pres., C.E.O.	Investor Contact: (206) 624–7930
Telephone: (206) 624–7930		Institutional Holding
Web Site: www.washingtonfederal.com		No of Institutions: 13
		Shares: 480,672 % Held: –

WASHINGTON MUTUAL INC.

Exchange	Symbol	Price	52Wk Range	Yield	P/E
NYS	WM	$42.71 (3/31/2004)	46.55-35.68	3.93	10.37

Year Price Score N/A *NYSE Composite Index=100 *12 Month Price Score 99.0

Interim Earnings (Per Share)

Qtr.	Mar	Jun	Sep	Dec
2000	0.55	0.61	0.57	0.63
2001	0.76	0.91	0.85	0.63
2002	0.98	1.01	1.01	1.05
2003	1.07	1.10	1.11	0.84

Interim Dividends (Per Share)

Amt	Decl	Ex	Rec	Pay
0.30Q	4/15/2003	4/28/2003	4/30/2003	5/15/2003
0.40Q	7/15/2003	7/29/2003	7/31/2003	8/15/2003
0.41Q	10/21/2003	10/29/2003	10/31/2003	11/14/2003
0.42Q	1/20/2004	1/28/2004	1/30/2004	2/13/2004

Indicated Div: $1.68 (Div. Reinv. Plan)

Valuation Analysis

Forecast P/E	8.72	Trailing P/E	10.37
Market Cap	$40.4 Billion	Book Value	19.7 Billion
Price/Book	1.83	Price/Sales	2.45

Dividend Achiever Status

Rank	32	10 Year Growth Rate	20.29%
Total Years of Dividend Growth			14

Business Summary: Other Depository Banking (MIC: 8.5 SIC: 6036 NAIC:522120)

Washington Mutual is a holding company for both banking and nonbanking subsidiaries. Co.'s primary banking subsidiaries are Washington Mutual Bank, FA, Washington Mutual Bank and Washington Mutual Bank fsb. These organizations provide consumer banking, mortgage lending, commercial banking, consumer finance and financial services. Co. operates in two segments: consumer group, which offers products and services to consumers and manages activities and operations affecting consumers; and commercial group, which offers a full array of commercial banking products and services. As of Dec 31 2003, Co. and its subsidiaries had assets of 275.18 billion and operated more than 2,400 offices nationwide.

Recent Developments: For the year ended Dec 31 2003, income from continuing operations remained relatively stable at $3.79 billion versus 2002. Earnings for 2003 and 2002 included net nonrecurring gains from various items of $3.43 billion and $2.52 billion, and excluded gains from discontinued operations of $87.0 million and $72.0 million, respectively. Net interest income slipped 6.2% to 7.63 billion due to the sale of certain available for sale securities and the slowing mortgage refinance market. Provision for loan and lease losses dropped 89.6% to $42.0 million. Total non-interest income advanced 30.9% to $5.85 billion, while total non-interest expense grew 19.7% to $7.41 billion.

Prospects: Co. plans to open approximately 250 new retail banking stores in 2004. Additionally, in Dec 2003, Co. announced its cost leadership initiative to cut approximately $1.00 billion from its annualized fourth-quarter 2003 noninterest expense run rate by June 2005. Under this initiative, Co. eliminated the equivalent of 4,500 full-time positions in its home lending support operations during the last four months of 2003, and reduced 2,900 full-time equivalent personnel in the first quarter of 2004. Looking ahead, diluted earnings per share for 2004 is expected to range from $4.30 to $4.80.

Financial Data

(US$ in Thousands)	12/31/2003	12/31/2002	12/31/2001	12/31/2000	12/31/1999	12/31/1998	12/31/1997	12/31/1996
Earnings Per Share	4.12	4.05	3.15	2.36	2.10	1.70	0.82	0.37
Tang. Book Val. Per Share	7.87	9.02	6.29	9.95	8.40	8.84	7.97	7.97
Dividends Per Share	1.400	1.060	0.890	0.760	0.650	0.540	0.470	0.400
Dividend Payout %	33.98	26.17	28.46	32.20	31.01	32.03	56.98	105.87
Income Statement								
Total Interest Income	12,163,000	14,247,000	15,065,000	13,783,000	12,062,198	11,221,468	6,810,964	3,149,236
Total Interest Expense	4,534,000	5,906,000	8,189,000	9,472,000	7,610,408	6,929,743	4,154,491	1,958,229
Net Interest Income	7,629,000	8,341,000	6,876,000	4,311,000	4,451,790	4,291,725	2,656,473	1,191,007
Provision for Loan Losses	42,000	595,000	575,000	185,000	167,076	161,968	207,139	201,512
Non-Interest Income	5,850,000	4,790,000	2,627,000	1,984,000	1,508,997	1,577,019	750,892	259,264
Non-Interest Expense	7,408,000	6,382,000	4,617,000	3,126,000	2,909,551	3,337,319	2,299,100	1,025,304
Income Before Taxes	2,760,000	3,538,000	4,311,000	2,984,000	2,884,160	2,369,457	901,126	223,455
Eqty Earns/Minority Int.	...	...	...	...	...	...	...	(13,570)
Income from Cont Ops	3,793,000	...	2,732,000	...	...	...	...	...
Net Income	3,880,000	3,896,000	3,114,000	1,899,000	1,817,064	1,486,932	481,778	114,278
Average Shs. Outstg.	921,757	960,152	864,700	804,694	861,829	867,843	555,851	254,562
Balance Sheet								
Securities Avail. for Sale	74,795,000	43,972,000	58,349,000	42,159,000	82,391,631	65,355,712	21,585,393	9,112,921
Net Loans & Leases	174,394,000	145,875,000	131,587,000	118,612,000	112,703,721	106,544,357	66,454,441	30,103,386
Total Assets	275,178,000	268,298,000	242,506,000	194,716,000	186,513,630	165,493,281	96,981,099	44,551,925
Total Deposits	153,181,000	155,516,000	107,182,000	79,574,000	81,129,768	85,492,141	50,986,017	24,080,141
Long-Term Obligations	63,813,000	66,529,000	73,758,000	67,785,000	63,297,250	45,198,121	22,991,325	7,918,478
Total Liabilities	255,436,000	248,164,000	228,341,000	184,550,000	177,460,951	156,148,881	91,672,028	42,154,037
Net Stockholders' Equity	19,742,000	20,134,000	13,961,000	10,166,000	9,052,679	9,344,400	5,309,071	2,397,888
Shares Outstanding	880,985	944,046	873,089	809,783	857,383	890,112	579,510	283,819
Statistical Record								
Return on Equity %	19.21	19.35	19.42	18.67	20.07	15.91	9.07	4.76
Return on Assets %	1.38	1.45	1.12	0.97	0.97	0.89	0.49	0.25
Equity/Assets %	7.17	7.50	5.79	5.22	4.85	5.64	5.47	5.38
Non-Int. Exp./Tot. Inc. %	41.12	33.52	26.09	19.82	21.43	26.07	30.40	30.08
Price Range	46.55-32.98	39.45-28.41	42.69-28.56	37.25-14.50	30.17-16.75	26.08-21.87	...	...
P/E Ratio	11.30-8.00	9.74-7.01	13.55-9.07	15.78-6.14	14.37-7.98	15.34-12.87	...	...
Average Yield %	3.57	3.00	2.54	3.50	2.73	2.28	N/A	N/A

Address: 1201 Third Avenue, Seattle, WA 98101	**Officers:** Kerry K. Killinger - Chmn., Pres., C.E.O., William A. Longbrake - Vice-Chmn.	**Investor Contact:** 206-461-3186
Telephone: (206) 461-2000	**Transfer Agents:** Mellon Investor Services, L.L.C., Ridgefield Park, NJ	**Institutional Holding**
Web Site: www.wamu.com		**No of Institutions:** 21
		Shares: 1,421,530 **% Held:** -

WASHINGTON REAL ESTATE INVESTMENT TRUST

Exchange	Symbol	Price	52Wk Range	Yield	P/E
NYS	WRE	$32.45 (3/31/2004)	32.45–26.14	4.59	28.72

*7 Year Price Score 134.8 *NYSE Composite Index=100 *12 Month Price Score 97.2

Interim Earnings (Per Share)

Qtr.	Mar	Jun	Sep	Dec
2000	0.31	0.28	0.36	0.18
2001	0.30	0.33	0.43	0.19
2002	0.32	0.30	0.30	0.30
2003	0.28	0.29	0.28	0.28

Interim Dividends (Per Share)

Amt	Decl	Ex	Rec	Pa
0.373Q	5/12/2003	6/12/2003	6/16/2003	6/30/200
0.373Q	8/7/2003	9/12/2003	9/16/2003	9/30/200
0.373Q	11/19/2003	12/15/2003	12/17/2003	12/31/200
0.373Q	2/19/2004	3/15/2004	3/17/2004	3/31/200

Indicated Div: $1.49 (Div. Reinv. Plan)

Valuation Analysis

Forecast P/E	14.48	Trailing P/E	28.72
Market Cap	$1.3 Billion	Book Value	378.7 Million
Price/Book	3.10	Price/Sales	7.18

Dividend Achiever Status

Rank	250	10 Year Growth Rate	5.15%
Total Years of Dividend Growth			42

Business Summary: Property, Real Estate &Development (MIC: 8.3 SIC: 6798 NAIC:525930)

Washington Real Estate Investment Trust is a self–administered qualified equity real estate investment trust. Co.'s business consists of th ownership and operation of income–producing real estate properties principally in the Greater Washington, D.C.–Baltimore, MD are Upon the purchase of a property, Co. begins a program of improving the real estate to increase the value and to improve the operation with the goals of generating higher rental income and reducing expenses. As of Mar 12 2003, Co. owned a diversified portfolio of 6 properties consisting of 11 retail centers, 29 office buildings, nine multifamily buildings and 18 industrial/flex properties.

Recent Developments: For the year ended Dec 31 2003, Co. reported net income of $44.9 million compared with income of $48. million, before income from discontinued operations of $3.8 million, the year before. Total revenue increased 6.7% to $163.8 millic from $153.6 million the previous year. The increase in revenue was due primarily to the increase in rent from properties acquired in 200 and 2002, combined with an increase in minimum base rent for Co.'s core properties. Real estate rental revenue grew 6.9% to $163 million. Funds from operations increased 4.4% to $80.6 million from $77.2 million a year earlier. As of Dec 31 2003, Co.'s propertie were 89.5% occupied versus 90.1% occupied on Dec 31 2002.

Prospects: Going forward, Co. is likely to benefit from increased spending by the Federal government. During the past twelve month the Federal government has escalated its issuance of defense, intelligence, security, and healthcare contracts. This has resulted in sever large office space lease transactions throughout the region, and should have a positive impact on the industrial and multifamily rent markets, which have also been soft over the last two years. Separately, on Mar 12 2003, Co. acquired 8880 Gorman Road in Laurel, M for $11.5 million. The property is 100% occupied by a single tenant and is anticipated to produce a first year return on investment c 8.8%.

Financial Data

(US$ in Thousands)	12/31/2003	12/31/2002	12/31/2001	12/31/2000	12/31/1999	12/31/1998	12/31/1997	12/31/199
Earnings Per Share	1.13	1.22	1.25	1.13	1.24	1.15	0.90	0.8
Tang. Book Val. Per Share	9.10	8.32	8.33	7.23	7.19	7.10	7.06	6.
Dividends Per Share	1.47	1.39	1.310	1.230	1.150	1.380	1.07	1.0
Dividend Payout %	128.31	85.04	104.80	108.84	93.34	120.00	88.88	117.0
Income Statement								
Rental Income	163,405	152,929	148,424	134,732	118,975	103,597	79,429	65,54
Total Income	163,819	153,609	148,424	134,732	118,975	103,597	79,429	65,54
Total Indirect Exp.	115,671	103,178	47,050	43,397	33,061	28,969	21,051	16,07
Depreciation	35,755	29,200	53,470	45,446	39,180	30,798	21,822	15,56
Interest Expense	60,080	55,698	27,071	25,531	22,271	17,106	9,691	5,47
Eqty Earns/Minority Int.	...	...	(32,835)	(30,256)	(25,763)	(21,957)	(15,154)	(10,879
Income from Cont Ops	...	48,080	48,057	41,572	36,392	34,300	...	
Net Income	44,887	51,836	52,353	45,139	44,301	41,064	30,136	27,96
Average Shs. Outstg.	39,600	39,281	37,951	35,872	35,700	35,700	33,400	31,80
Balance Sheet								
Cash & Cash Equivalents	5,486	13,076	26,441	6,426	4,716	4,595	7,908	1,67
Ttl Real Estate Inv.	878,794	706,790	651,961	597,607	578,296	530,573	448,300	305,94
Total Assets	927,129	755,997	707,935	632,047	608,480	558,707	468,571	318,48
Long–Term Obligations	517,182	351,951	359,726	351,260	297,038	238,912	107,461	107,59
Total Liabilities	548,381	429,820	384,328	373,391	351,291	304,974	216,483	122,86
Net Stockholders' Equity	378,748	326,177	323,607	258,656	257,189	253,733	252,088	195,62
Shares Outstanding	41,607	39,168	38,829	35,740	35,721	35,692	35,678	31,80
Statistical Record								
Net Inc.+Depr./Assets %	8.70	10.20	11.20	10.70	10.50	10.10	8.80	11.2
Return on Equity %	11.85	14.74	14.85	16.07	14.14	13.51	11.95	14.2
Return on Assets %	4.84	6.35	6.78	6.57	5.98	6.13	6.43	8.
Price Range	31.04–24.10	30.15–21.96	25.45–21.27	25.00–14.31	18.63–14.00	18.63–15.56	19.38–15.88	17.50–15.2
P/E Ratio	27.47–21.33	24.71–18.00	20.36–17.02	22.12–12.67	15.02–11.29	16.20–13.53	21.53–17.64	19.89–17.3
Average Yield %	5.25	3.94	5.59	6.89	7.07	8.11	4.67	6.4

Address: 6110 Executive Boulevard, Rockville, MD 20852–3927 **Telephone:** (301) 984–9400 **Web Site:** www.writ.com	**Officers:** Edmund B. Cronin – Chmn., Pres., C.E.O., George F. McKenzie – Exec. V.P., Real Estate **Transfer Agents:**EquiServe Trust Company N.A., Providence, RI	**Institutional Holding** **No of Institutions:** 32 **Shares:** 1,200,667 **% Held:** –

WEBSTER FINANCIAL CORP.

Exchange	Symbol	Price	52Wk Range	Yield	P/E
NYS	WBS	$50.71 (3/31/2004)	51.65-35.11	1.66	14.41

Year Price Score 132.1 *NYSE Composite Index=100 *12 Month Price Score 103.6

Interim Earnings (Per Share)

Qtr.	Mar	Jun	Sep	Dec
2000	0.61	0.66	0.64	0.64
2001	0.54	0.69	0.70	0.75
2002	0.80	0.82	0.84	0.85
2003	0.86	0.88	0.89	0.89

Interim Dividends (Per Share)

Amt	Decl	Ex	Rec	Pay
0.21Q	4/22/2003	5/1/2003	5/5/2003	5/19/2003
0.21Q	7/22/2003	7/31/2003	8/4/2003	8/18/2003
0.21Q	10/20/2003	10/30/2003	11/3/2003	11/17/2003
0.21Q	1/27/2004	2/5/2004	2/9/2004	2/23/2004

Indicated Div: $0.84

Valuation Analysis

Forecast P/E	10.89	Trailing P/E	14.41
Market Cap	$2.4 Billion	Book Value	1.2 Billion
Price/Book	1.81	Price/Sales	2.36

Dividend Achiever Status

Rank	109	10 Year Growth Rate	12.69%
Total Years of Dividend Growth			11

Business Summary: Other Depository Banking (MIC: 8.5 SIC: 6035 NAIC:522120)

Webster Financial is a holding company with $14.57 billion in assets as of Dec 31 2003. Through its subsidiaries, Co. is engaged in providing financial services to individuals, families and businesses, primarily in Connecticut and equipment financing, asset-based lending, mortgage origination and financial advisory services to public and private companies throughout the U.S. Co. provides business and consumer banking, mortgage origination and lending, trust and investment services and insurance services through 119 banking and other offices, 233 ATMs and its Internet website.

Recent Developments: For the year ended Dec 31 2003, net income grew 2.0% to $163.2 million compared with income of $160.0 million, before an accounting change charge of $7.3 million, in 2002. Total interest income dropped 4.8% to $658.7 million. Total interest expense fell 14.4% to $245.2 million versus $286.3 million the year before. Net interest income climbed 1.9% to $413.5 million. Total noninterest income advanced 25.3% to $232.5 million from $185.6 million the year before due to the growth of deposit and loan service fees, insurance revenues and net gains on sales of loans and loan servicing. Total noninterest expense grew 15.1% to $378.0 million.

Prospects: On Dec 18 2003, Co. announced a definitive agreement to acquire Phoenix National Trust Company, a wholly-owned subsidiary of the Phoenix Companies, Inc. The transaction's closing is subject to receipt of regulatory approval and other customary closing conditions and is expected to close in the second quarter of 2004. Upon completion of the transaction, Phoenix will become part of Webster Financial Advisors, the investment and trust division of Webster Bank. Phoenix offers trust, custody and other financial services. Separately, subsequent to year end, Co. sold its interest in Duff & Phelps, LLC.

Financial Data

(US$ in Thousands)	12/31/2003	12/31/2002	12/31/2001	12/31/2000	12/31/1999	12/31/1998	12/31/1997	12/31/1996
Earnings Per Share	3.52	3.31	2.68	2.55	2.10	1.83	1.22	1.39
Tang. Book Val. Per Share	17.76	16.17	13.96	11.52	10.98	12.76	12.20	10.21
Dividends Per Share	0.820	0.740	0.670	0.620	0.470	0.430	0.390	0.340
Dividend Payout %	23.29	22.35	25.00	24.31	22.38	23.49	31.96	24.37
Income Statement								
Total Interest Income	658,718	692,034	757,235	738,911	645,792	622,453	445,848	265,534
Total Interest Expense	245,199	286,306	389,756	412,395	342,279	377,018	253,923	149,745
Net Interest Income	413,519	405,728	367,479	326,516	303,513	245,435	191,925	115,789
Provision for Loan Losses	25,000	29,000	14,400	11,800	9,000	6,800	15,835	4,000
Non-Interest Income	232,483	185,572	162,098	128,821	92,630	74,163	35,990	25,530
Non-Interest Expense	377,982	328,323	308,932	267,130	244,461	197,789	158,547	97,249
Income Before Taxes	243,020	233,977	206,245	176,407	142,682	115,009	53,533	40,070
Income from Cont Ops	...	160,012	136,815	...	...	...	...	...
Net Income	163,248	152,732	133,188	118,291	95,350	70,465	33,798	25,608
Average Shs. Outstg.	46,362	48,392	42,742	46,427	45,393	38,571	27,656	18,326
Balance Sheet								
Cash & Due from Banks	209,234	266,463	218,908	265,035	245,783	173,863	122,267	85,163
Securities Avail. for Sale	4,128,255	4,119,245	3,999,133	3,143,327	2,700,585	2,969,822	2,290,254	573,616
Net Loans & Leases	9,091,135	7,795,835	6,869,911	6,819,209	6,022,236	4,993,509	3,824,602	2,525,543
Total Assets	14,568,690	13,468,004	11,857,382	11,249,508	9,931,744	9,033,917	7,019,621	3,917,600
Total Deposits	8,372,135	7,606,122	7,066,471	6,941,522	6,191,091	5,651,273	4,365,756	3,095,876
Long-Term Obligations	3,044,255	2,289,029	2,531,179	2,380,074	1,714,441	1,774,560	1,071,620	407,734
Total Liabilities	13,406,218	12,301,714	10,691,338	10,159,557	9,096,500	8,279,461	6,487,858	3,711,304
Net Stockholders' Equity	1,143,318	904,626	846,890	690,797	436,090	355,302	232,609	206,296
Shares Outstanding	46,276	45,625	49,149	48,939	45,243	37,327	27,306	15,852
Statistical Record								
Return on Equity %	14.15	15.45	13.59	13.28	14.99	12.69	8.84	12.41
Return on Assets %	1.12	1.18	1.15	1.05	0.96	0.78	0.48	0.65
Equity/Assets %	7.91	7.68	8.48	7.91	6.40	6.14	5.44	5.26
Non-Int. Exp./Tot. Inc. %	42.41	37.41	33.60	30.78	33.10	28.39	32.90	33.41
Price Range	46.50-33.93	39.96-30.65	37.06-26.44	29.63-20.13	32.00-21.88	36.25-18.88	33.38-17.56	19.09-13.38
P/E Ratio	13.21-9.64	12.07-9.26	13.83-9.86	11.62-7.89	15.24-10.42	19.81-10.31	27.36-14.40	13.74-9.62
Average Yield %	2.11	2.11	2.09	2.15	2.68	1.70	1.45	1.62	2.19

Address: Webster Plaza, Waterbury, CT 06702	Officers: James C. Smith – Chmn., C.E.O., William T. Bromage – Pres., C.O.O.	Investor Contact:203–578–2318
Telephone: (203) 753–2921	Transfer Agents:American Stock Transfer &Trust Co, New York, NY	Institutional Holding No of Institutions: 4
Web Site: www.websteronline.com		Shares: 118,322 % Held: –

WEINGARTEN REALTY INVESTORS

Exchange	Symbol	Price	52Wk Range	Yield	P/E
NYS	WRI	$34.60 (3/31/2004)	34.60–26.33	7.20	20.00

*7 Year Price Score 136.7 *NYSE Composite Index=100 *12 Month Price Score 95.3

Interim Earnings (Per Share)

Qtr.	Mar	Jun	Sep	Dec
2000	0.36	0.37	0.36	0.37
2001	0.45	0.43	0.46	0.50
2002	0.45	0.45	0.45	0.40
2003	0.46	0.40	0.47	0.41

Interim Dividends (Per Share)

Amt	Decl	Ex	Rec	Pa
0.585Q	8/11/2003	8/28/2003	9/2/2003	9/15/200
0.585Q	10/27/2003	11/26/2003	12/1/2003	12/15/200
0.623Q	2/23/2004	3/3/2004	3/5/2004	3/15/200
50%	2/23/2004	3/31/2004	3/16/2004	3/30/200
		Indicated Div: $2.49		

Valuation Analysis

Forecast P/E	12.36	Trailing P/E	20.00
Market Cap	$1.8 Billion	Book Value	923.5 Million
Price/Book	2.54	Price/Sales	5.84

Dividend Achiever Status

Rank	256	10 Year Growth Rate	4.97%
Total Years of Dividend Growth	15		

Business Summary: Property, Real Estate &Development (MIC: 8.3 SIC: 6798 NAIC:525930)

Weingarten Realty Investors is a self-administered and self-managed real estate investment trust that acquires, develops and manages re
estate, primarily anchored neighborhood and community shopping centers and, to a lesser extent, industrial properties. As of Dec 31 200.
Co. owned or operated under long-term leases interests in 327 developed income-producing real estate projects. Co. owned 266 shoppir
centers located in the Houston metropolitan area and in other parts of Texas and in California, Louisiana, Arizona, Nevada, Arkansas, Ne
Mexico, Oklahoma, Tennessee, Kansas, Colorado, Missouri, Illinois, Florida, North Carolina, Utah, Georgia, Mississippi and Maine.

Recent Developments: For the year ended Dec 31 2003, income was $109.8 million, before a gain of $6.5 million from discontinue
operations, compared with income of $109.6 million, before a gain of $22.2 million from discontinued operations, the previous year
Results for 2003 and 2002 included pre-tax gains of $6.8 million and $19.7 million, respectively, on the sale of properties. Total revenue
advanced 15.4% to $419.2 million from $363.1 million a year earlier. The increase in revenues was largely attributed 15.0% growth i
rental income. Operating income slipped 1.7% to $107.1 million versus $108.9 million the year before. Funds from operations rose 10.6%
to $184.0 million from $174.0 million in 2002.

Prospects: Among Co.'s goals for 2004 are the investment of approximately $400.0 million through its acquisitions program and the
Among Co.'s goals for 2004 are the investment of approximately $400.0 million through its acquisitions program and the investment o
between $50.0 million and $75.0 million for new development properties. Co. is cautiously optimistic that, through these efforts, as we
as the growth of its existing portfolio through increased occupancy and rental rates, it will produce funds from operations of $2.47 ar
$2.51 per diluted share, on a post split basis, during 2004. Meanwhile, Co.'s portfolio of neighborhood and community shopping center
remains extremely stable and it expects the upward trend in occupancy to continue throughout 2004.

Financial Data

(US$ in Thousands)	12/31/2003	12/31/2002	12/31/2001	12/31/2000	12/31/1999	12/31/1998	12/31/1997	12/31/199¢
Earnings Per Share	1.74	1.75	1.84	1.46	1.90	1.38	1.36	1.3
Tang. Book Val. Per Share	15.04	17.91	17.87	15.59	16.12	13.32	9.75	10.(
Dividends Per Share	2.340	2.220	2.100	2.00	1.890	1.780	1.700	1.6!
Dividend Payout %	134.48	126.85	114.49	136.98	99.29	128.84	124.87	122.2
Income Statement								
Rental Income	410,490	359,044	309,457	264,552	225,244	194,624	169,041	145,3C
Interest Income	1,594	1,054	1,167	5,638	1,888	...	2,487	3,14
Total Income	419,160	365,410	314,892	273,374	225,450	194,969	174,512	151,12
Total Indirect Exp.	338,701	265,725	225,775	191,991	151,819	140,836	117,852	98,6(
Depreciation	94,108	78,481	68,316	58,518	49,612	41,946	37,976	33,7(
Interest Expense	177,742	131,726	108,946	91,090	66,372	67,308	44,220	37,74
Eqty Earns/Minority Int.	2,020	490	5,072	(8,041)	2,616	1,920	...	
Income from Cont Ops	109,781	110,611	...	...	93,917	60,179	...	
Net Income	116,280	131,867	108,542	79,001	96,130	60,365	54,966	53,9:
Average Shs. Outstg.	54,383	53,360	48,369	40,396	40,335	40,303	40,116	39,8;
Balance Sheet								
Cash & Cash Equivalents	20,255	27,420	12,434	14,825	5,842	16,623	15,099	13,97
Total Assets	2,923,794	2,423,889	2,095,747	1,646,011	1,309,396	1,107,043	946,793	831,0S
Long–Term Obligations	1,810,706	1,330,369	1,070,835	869,627	594,185	516,366	507,366	389,22
Total Liabilities	2,102,231	1,490,476	1,174,675	1,016,144	663,494	573,864	556,807	430,0S
Net Stockholders' Equity	821,563	933,413	921,072	629,867	645,902	533,179	389,986	400,9S
Shares Outstanding	54,592	52,076	51,520	40,381	40,042	40,009	39,990	39,8(
Statistical Record								
Net Inc.+Depr./Assets %	7.19	7.80	8.40	8.40	11.10	9.40	9.80	10.6
Return on Equity %	13.36	11.85	11.78	12.54	14.54	11.28	14.09	13.4
Return on Assets %	3.75	4.56	5.17	4.79	7.17	5.43	5.80	6.4
Price Range	30.70–23.80	25.76–20.57	22.40–17.80	19.89–15.42	20.28–16.61	20.61–16.25	20.11–17.39	18.06–15.3
P/E Ratio	17.64–13.68	14.72–11.75	12.17–9.68	13.62–10.56	10.67–8.74	14.94–11.78	14.79–12.79	13.37–11.4
Average Yield %	8.38	9.39	10.45	11.20	10.58	9.35	9.05	9.7

Address: 2600 Citadel Plaza Drive, Houston, TX 77292–4133 Telephone: (713) 866–6000 Web Site: www.weingarten.com	Officers: Stanford Alexander – Chmn., Martin Debrovner – Vice–Chmn. Transfer Agents:Mellon Investor Services, LLC, Ridgefield Park, NJ	Investor Contact: (713) 866–6050 Institutional Holding No of Institutions: 7 Shares: 423,186 % Held: –

WELLS FARGO & CO.

Exchange	Symbol	Price	52Wk Range	Yield	P/E
NYS	WFC	$56.67 (3/31/2004)	58.94-46.24	3.18	15.53

*7 Year Price Score 122.1 *NYSE Composite Index=100 *12 Month Price Score 100.4

Interim Earnings (Per Share)

Qtr.	Mar	Jun	Sep	Dec
2000	0.61	0.63	0.64	0.45
2001	0.67	(0.05)	0.67	0.68
2002	0.80	0.82	0.84	0.86
2003	0.88	0.90	0.92	0.95

Interim Dividends (Per Share)

Amt	Decl	Ex	Rec	Pay
0.30Q	4/22/2003	5/7/2003	5/9/2003	6/1/2003
0.45Q	7/22/2003	8/6/2003	8/8/2003	9/1/2003
0.45Q	10/27/2003	11/5/2003	11/7/2003	12/1/2003
0.45Q	1/27/2004	2/4/2004	2/6/2004	3/1/2004

Indicated Div: $1.80

Valuation Analysis

Forecast P/E	N/A	Trailing P/E	15.53
Market Cap	$95.9 Billion	Book Value	34.5 Billion
Price/Book	2.89	Price/Sales	3.14

Dividend Achiever Status

Rank	58	10 Year Growth Rate	16.71%
Total Years of Dividend Growth			16

Business Summary: Commercial Banking (MIC: 8.1 SIC: 6021 NAIC:522110)

Wells Fargo is the fifth largest bank holding company in the U.S., based on total assets of $387.80 billion as of Dec 31 2003. Through its subsidiaries, Co. engages in banking and a variety of related financial services businesses. Retail, commercial and corporate banking services are provided through banking stores in 23 states. Other financial services are engaged in various businesses, principally wholesale banking, mortgage banking, consumer finance, equipment leasing, agricultural finance, commercial finance, securities brokerage and investment banking, insurance agency services, computer services, trust services, mortgage–backed securities servicing and venture capital investment.

Recent Developments: For the year ended Dec 31 2003, net income improved 8.6% to $6.20 billion from $5.70 billion, before an accounting change charge of $276.0 million, the year before. Results included net gains of $55.0 million in 2003 and net losses of $327.0 million in 2002 from equity investments. Results also included net losses of $42.0 million in 2003 and net gains of $241.0 million in 2002, primarily on debt securities available for sale. Net interest income climbed 10.5% to $16.01 billion due to strong growth in loans and deposits. Provision for loan losses rose 2.3% to $1.72 billion. Total non–interest income grew 15.0% to $12.38 billion, while total non–interest expense rose 16.9% to $17.19 billion.

Prospects: On Nov 3 2003, Co. completed its acquisition of Pacific Northwest Bancorp, significantly increasing its presence in western and central Washington. The transaction includes 57 banking locations and $2.90 billion in assets. Additionally, Pacific Northwest contributed approximately $1.10 billion in average loans and about $1.20 billion in average core deposits to Co. at the end of 2003.The integration of Pacific Northwest is expected to be complete during the second quarter of 2004. Meanwhile, Co. continues to tightly manage expense to ensure that savings are realized and that costs are aligned with business levels.

Financial Data

(US$ in Thousands)	12/31/2003	12/31/2002	12/31/2001	12/31/2000	12/31/1999	12/31/1998	12/31/1997	12/31/1996
Earnings Per Share	3.65	3.32	1.97	2.33	2.23	1.17	1.75	1.53
Tang. Book Val. Per Share	14.19	11.67	9.79	9.17	7.91	6.76	9.00	7.96
Dividends Per Share	1.500	1.100	1.000	0.900	0.780	0.700	0.610	0.520
Dividend Payout %	41.09	33.13	50.76	38.62	35.20	59.82	35.14	34.20
Income Statement								
Total Interest Income	19,418,000	18,832,000	19,201,000	18,725,000	14,375,000	14,055,000	6,697,400	6,318,300
Total Interest Expense	3,411,000	3,977,000	6,741,000	7,860,000	5,020,000	5,065,000	2,664,000	2,617,000
Net Interest Income	16,007,000	14,855,000	12,460,000	10,865,000	9,355,000	8,990,000	4,033,400	3,701,300
Provision for Loan Losses	1,722,000	1,733,000	1,780,000	1,329,000	1,045,000	1,545,000	524,700	394,700
Non–Interest Income	12,382,000	9,641,000	7,690,000	8,843,000	7,420,000	6,427,000	2,962,300	2,564,600
Non–Interest Expense	17,190,000	13,909,000	12,891,000	11,830,000	9,782,000	10,579,000	4,421,300	4,089,700
Income Before Taxes	9,477,000	8,854,000	5,479,000	6,549,000	5,948,000	3,293,000	2,049,700	1,781,500
Income from Cont Ops	...	5,710,000	...	...	...	...	...	...
Net Income	6,202,000	5,434,000	3,423,000	4,026,000	3,747,000	1,950,000	1,351,000	1,153,900
Average Shs. Outstg.	1,697,500	1,718,000	1,726,900	1,718,400	1,665,200	1,641,800	750,059	741,342
Balance Sheet								
Cash & Due from Banks	15,547,000	17,820,000	16,968,000	16,978,000	13,250,000	12,731,000	4,912,100	4,856,600
Securities Avail. for Sale	32,953,000	27,947,000	40,308,000	38,655,000	38,518,000	31,997,000	18,470,800	16,433,600
Net Loans & Leases	249,182,000	192,772,000	168,738,000	157,405,000	116,294,000	104,860,000	41,287,700	38,340,200
Total Assets	387,798,000	349,259,000	307,569,000	272,426,000	218,102,000	202,475,000	88,540,200	80,175,400
Total Deposits	247,527,000	216,916,000	187,266,000	169,559,000	132,708,000	136,788,000	55,457,100	50,130,200
Long–Term Obligations	63,642,000	7,459,903	36,095,000	32,046,000	23,375,000	19,709,000	12,766,700	13,082,200
Total Liabilities	353,329,000	279,040,903	280,355,000	245,938,000	195,971,000	181,716,000	81,518,000	74,111,200
Net Stockholders' Equity	34,469,000	30,358,000	27,214,000	26,488,000	22,131,000	20,759,000	7,022,200	6,064,200
Shares Outstanding	1,698,109	1,685,906	1,695,494	1,714,645	1,626,849	1,644,057	758,619	737,406
Statistical Record								
Return on Equity %	17.99	18.80	12.57	15.19	16.93	9.39	19.23	19.02
Return on Assets %	1.59	1.63	1.11	1.47	1.71	0.96	1.52	1.43
Equity/Assets %	8.88	8.69	8.84	9.72	10.14	10.25	7.93	7.56
Non–Int. Exp./Tot. Inc. %	54.05	48.84	47.93	42.91	44.88	51.65	45.77	46.04
Price Range	58.94-44.15	53.21-42.63	53.94-38.85	55.75-31.94	49.25-32.75	43.44-29.75	38.88-21.63	23.38-15.50
P/E Ratio	16.15-12.10	16.03-12.84	27.38-19.72	23.93-13.71	22.09-14.69	37.13-25.43	22.21-12.36	15.28-10.13
Average Yield %	2.97	2.26	2.17	2.11	1.92	1.86	2.12	2.76

Address: 420 Montgomery Street, San Francisco, CA 94104
Telephone: (800) 292–9932
Web Site: www.wellsfargo.com

Officers: Richard M. Kovacevich – Chmn., Pres., C.E.O., Howard I. Atkins – Exec. V.P., C.F.O.
Transfer Agents: Wells Fargo Shareowners Services, St. Paul, MN

Investor Contact: (415) 396–0523
Institutional Holding
No of Institutions: 23
Shares: 7,026,576 **% Held:** –

WESBANCO, INC.

Interim Earnings (Per Share)

Qtr.	Mar	Jun	Sep	Dec
2000	0.35	0.35	0.34	0.37
2001	0.40	0.40	0.39	0.41
2002	0.42	0.41	0.43	0.44
2003	0.44	0.38	0.49	0.49

Interim Dividends (Per Share)

Amt	Decl	Ex	Rec	Pay
0.24Q	5/21/2003	6/4/2003	6/6/2003	7/1/2003
0.24Q	8/26/2003	9/3/2003	9/5/2003	10/1/2003
0.24Q	11/19/2003	12/3/2003	12/5/2003	1/2/2004
0.25Q	2/19/2004	3/4/2004	3/8/2004	4/1/2004

Indicated Div: $1.00 (Div. Reinv. Plan)

Valuation Analysis

Forecast P/E	14.23	Trailing P/E	16.86
Market Cap	$629.9 Million	Book Value	318.4 Million
Price/Book	1.78	Price/Sales	2.85

Dividend Achiever Status

Rank	225	10 Year Growth Rate	6.54%
Total Years of Dividend Growth	18		

Business Summary: Commercial Banking (MIC: 8.1 SIC: 6021 NAIC:522110)

WesBanco is a bank holding company. Through its subsidiary, WesBanco Bank, Inc., Co. offers a range of financial services including retail banking, corporate banking, personal and corporate trust services, brokerage, mortgage banking and insurance through 72 offices located in West Virginia, central and eastern Ohio and western Pennsylvania. Co. also offers services through its non-banking affiliates. WesBanco Insurance Services is a multi-line insurance agency specializing in property, casualty and life insurance. WesBanco Securities is a full service broker-dealer. Co. also serves as investment adviser to a family of mutual funds under the name WesMark Funds.

Recent Developments: For the year ended Dec 31 2003, net income climbed 3.7% to $36.1 million compared with $34.8 million in 2002. Results for 2003 and 2002 included net securities gains of $2.8 million and $1.9 million, and merger-related expenses of $256,000 and $2.5 million, respectively. Net interest income slipped 0.6% to $103.0 million from $103.6 million the year before. Provision for loan losses climbed 2.7% to $9.6 million. Total non-interest income rose 19.3% to $33.2 million, reflecting growth in deposit activity fees increases in ATM and debit card interchange income, bank-owned life insurance income and net security gains. Total non-interest expense climbed 6.7% to $81.8 million.

Prospects: Co. is experiencing growth in commercial and mortgage lending due to its increased focus on new business development particularly in newer markets in southwestern Pennsylvania and Columbus, OH. This trend is expected to continue into 2004. Also, Co. is focusing on lower cost transaction accounts and continues to conservatively price its certificates of deposit to further reduce its funding costs. Meanwhile, pension expense for 2004 is anticipated to be approximately $2.3 million, which is consistent with results in 2003. In addition, Co. expects the effective tax rate will be approximately 19.5% in 2004.

Financial Data

(US$ in Thousands)	12/31/2003	12/31/2002	12/31/2001	12/31/2000	12/31/1999	12/31/1998	12/31/1997	12/31/1996
Earnings Per Share	1.80	1.70	1.60	1.41	1.37	1.36	1.40	1.38
Tang. Book Val. Per Share	13.20	13.01	14.46	12.31	13.62	14.35	15.58	14.41
Dividends Per Share	0.950	0.930	0.910	0.890	0.870	0.830	0.770	0.700
Dividend Payout %	53.05	54.70	57.18	63.12	63.50	61.02	55.23	50.47
Income Statement								
Total Interest Income	165,516	176,155	163,939	163,079	155,861	162,718	124,530	112,938
Total Interest Expense	62,512	72,555	76,354	79,552	69,231	73,925	55,774	48,218
Net Interest Income	103,004	103,600	87,585	83,527	86,630	88,793	68,756	64,720
Provision for Loan Losses	9,612	9,359	5,995	3,225	4,295	4,392	4,314	4,336
Non–Interest Income	33,230	27,852	24,588	23,376	24,581	25,715	14,693	12,273
Non–Interest Expense	81,810	76,647	64,894	64,483	67,813	68,308	48,704	43,152
Income Before Taxes	44,812	45,446	41,284	39,195	39,103	41,808	30,431	29,505
Net Income	36,130	34,826	29,002	26,924	27,638	28,313	22,274	21,161
Average Shs. Outstg.	20,056	20,459	18,123	19,092	20,229	20,867	15,867	15,253
Balance Sheet								
Cash & Due from Banks	88,021	80,101	81,563	72,796	67,166	62,989	56,446	58,828
Securities Avail. for Sale	766,883	694,735	517,517	350,287	354,675	465,705	342,510	276,201
Net Loans & Leases	1,905,562	1,791,081	1,513,387	1,568,231	1,493,941	1,344,640	1,005,747	1,010,842
Total Assets	3,445,006	3,297,231	2,474,454	2,310,137	2,269,726	2,242,712	1,789,295	1,677,771
Total Deposits	2,482,082	2,399,926	1,913,843	1,870,361	1,814,001	1,787,642	1,414,254	1,342,820
Long–Term Obligations	217,754	175,634	172,242	159,317	41,588	22,194	...	...
Total Liabilities	3,126,570	2,972,060	2,216,263	2,051,631	2,000,062	1,946,229	1,539,745	1,450,239
Net Stockholders' Equity	318,436	325,171	258,201	258,506	269,664	296,483	249,550	227,532
Shares Outstanding	19,741	20,461	17,854	20,996	19,789	20,660	16,015	15,783
Statistical Record								
Return on Equity %	11.34	10.71	11.23	10.41	10.24	9.54	8.92	9.30
Return on Assets %	1.04	1.05	1.17	1.16	1.21	1.26	1.24	1.26
Equity/Assets %	9.24	9.86	10.43	11.19	11.88	13.21	13.94	13.56
Non–Int. Exp./Tot. Inc. %	41.16	37.57	34.42	34.58	37.58	36.25	34.98	34.46
Price Range	28.74–21.99	25.86–19.42	26.10–17.69	26.00–19.13	30.25–21.69	31.00–23.38	31.25–21.33	21.67–17.17
P/E Ratio	15.97–12.22	15.21–11.42	16.31–11.05	18.44–13.56	22.08–15.83	22.79–17.19	22.32–15.24	15.70–12.44
Average Yield %	3.81	4.00	4.19	3.91	3.11	3.02	2.98	3.78

WESCO FINANCIAL CORP.

Exchange	Symbol	Price	52Wk Range	Yield	P/E
ASE	WSC	$387.00 (3/31/2004)	397.5–290.5	0.36	36.89

*7 Year Price Score 107.0 *NYSE Composite Index=100 *12 Month Price Score 97.5

Interim Earnings (Per Share)

Qtr.	Mar	Jun	Sep	Dec
2000	18.64	41.87	62.24	6.81
2001	2.78	2.12	1.57	0.91
2002	2.03	2.09	2.12	1.16
2003	1.76	6.45	1.00	1.28

Interim Dividends (Per Share)

Amt	Decl	Ex	Rec	Pay
0.335Q	7/17/2003	8/4/2003	8/6/2003	9/4/2003
0.335Q	9/18/2003	11/3/2003	11/5/2003	12/3/2003
0.345Q	12/10/2003	2/2/2004	2/4/2004	3/3/2004
0.345Q	3/11/2004	5/3/2004	5/5/2004	6/2/2004

Indicated Div: $1.38

Valuation Analysis

Forecast P/E	N/A	Trailing P/E	N/A
Market Cap	$2.8 Billion	Book Value	N/A
Price/Book	N/A	Price/Sales	N/A

Dividend Achiever Status

Rank	272	10 Year Growth Rate	3.61%
Total Years of Dividend Growth			32

Business Summary: Engineering Services (MIC: 12.1 SIC: 5051 NAIC:423510)

Wesco Financial is engaged in three principal businesses: the insurance business, through Wesco-Financial Insurance Company, which engages in the property and casualty insurance business, and The Kansas Bankers Surety Company, which provides specialized insurance coverages for banks; the furniture rental business, through CORT Business Services Corporation, a provider of rental furniture, accessories and related services; and the steel service center business, through Precision Steel Warehouse, Inc. Co.'s operations also include, through MS Property Company, the ownership and management of commercial real estate property, and the development and liquidation of foreclosed real estate.

Recent Developments: For the year ended Dec 31 2003, net income totaled $74.7 million, up 41.7% compared with $52.7 million in the corresponding prior-year period. Results for 2003 included a pre-tax realized investment gain of $53.5 million. Total revenues, including the aforementioned investment gain, climbed 6.7% to $614.3 million from $575.7 million the previous year. Furniture rental segment revenues slipped 7.3% to $360.1 million from $388.6 million, while revenues in the industrial segment slid 5.0% to $46.1 million from $48.6 million a year earlier. Insurance segment premiums earned advanced 65.0% to $106.7 million from $64.6 million in 2002.

Prospects: Sales and rentals of furniture are being hampered by unfavorable economic conditions. Meanwhile, sales for the industrial segment are being hurt by the prolonged downturn in domestic manufacturing activity and a shift by many manufacturers from domestic to overseas production, along with increased competitive pressures and a trend towards smaller-sized orders. However, a shortage of raw materials from domestic mills since the beginning of 2004 is boosting sales and earnings at Precision Steel. Separately, results are benefiting from underwriting gains at Wesco-Financial Insurance Company, primarily stemming from reduced aviation losses.

Financial Data

(US$ in Thousands)	12/31/2003	12/31/2002	12/31/2001	12/31/2000	12/31/1999	12/31/1998	12/31/1997	12/31/1996
Earnings Per Share	10.49	7.40	7.38	129.56	7.60	10.08	14.30	4.30
Cash Flow Per Share	17.29	26.47	23.11	N/A	3.29	1.85	4.90	3.47
Tang. Book Val. Per Share	254.44	237.64	231.45	241.15	262.20	308.20	243.56	171.36
Dividends Per Share	1.340	1.300	1.260	1.220	1.180	1.140	1.100	1.060
Dividend Payout %	12.77	17.57	17.07	0.94	15.53	11.31	7.69	24.65
Income Statement								
Total Revenues	614,317	575,677	561,079	1,823,964	145,706	176,179	219,051	108,019
Total Indirect Exp.	278,090	288,353	284,188	234,296	10,265	11,156	9,393	10,849
Depreciation & Amort.	44,114	51,914	7,476	6,342	1,995	2,068	2,056	1,672
Operating Income	109,005	82,911	85,497	1,423,627	77,347	105,322	156,088	42,852
Net Interest Inc./(Exp.)	(749)	(1,994)	(4,169)	(5,235)	(2,549)	(3,016)	(3,320)	(3,352)
Income Taxes	34,852	28,199	28,792	495,922	20,655	30,503	50,959	8,881
Eqty Earns/Minority Int.	1,307	...	...	...	...	...	...	...
Income from Cont Ops	73,404	...	...	...	...	...	...	...
Net Income	74,711	52,718	52,536	922,470	54,143	71,803	101,809	30,619
Average Shs. Outstg.	7,119	7,119	7,119	7,119	7,119	7,120	7,120	7,120
Balance Sheet								
Cash & Cash Equivalents	1,807,096	976,580	788,046	987,747	2,281,214	3,098,629	2,235,535	1,556,048
Total Current Assets	2,030,963	1,231,485	1,044,503	1,271,038	2,281,214	3,098,629	2,242,683	1,563,988
Total Assets	2,538,395	2,406,975	2,319,693	2,460,915	2,652,195	3,228,406	2,588,112	1,818,405
Total Current Liabilities	296,172	272,086	262,459	339,056	707,345	920,035	733,488	468,370
Long–Term Obligations	12,679	32,481	33,649	56,035	3,635	33,635	33,635	37,162
Net Stockholders' Equity	2,078,190	1,958,162	1,912,397	1,977,034	1,895,372	2,223,756	1,764,292	1,251,015
Net Working Capital	1,734,791	959,399	782,044	931,982	1,573,869	2,178,594	1,509,195	1,095,618
Shares Outstanding	7,119	7,119	7,119	7,119	7,119	7,120	7,120	7,120
Statistical Record								
Operating Profit Margin %	17.74	14.40	15.23	78.05	53.08	59.78	71.25	39.67
Return on Equity %	3.53	2.69	2.74	46.65	2.85	3.22	5.77	2.44
Return on Assets %	2.89	2.19	2.26	37.48	2.04	2.22	3.93	1.68
Debt/Total Assets %	0.49	1.34	1.45	2.27	0.13	1.04	1.29	2.04
Price Range	370.0–286.0	334.0–298.0	347.9–273.0	290.0–205.0	354.8–241.5	391.0–284.0	339.5–180.0	190.0–155.0
P/E Ratio	35.27–27.26	45.14–40.27	47.14–36.99	2.24–1.58	46.68–31.78	38.79–28.17	23.74–12.59	44.19–36.05
Average Yield %	0.42	0.42	0.41	0.50	0.38	0.33	0.40	0.61

Address: 301 East Colorado Boulevard, Pasadena, CA 91101–1901	Officers: Charles T. Munger – Chmn., C.E.O., Robert H. Bird – Pres.	Institutional Holding
Telephone: (626) 585-6700		No of Institutions: 1
Web Site: N/A		Shares: 60,000 % Held: –

WEST PHARMACEUTICAL SERVICES, INC.

Exchange	Symbol	Price	52Wk Range	Yield	P/E
NYS	WST	$37.40 (3/31/2004)	37.91–20.00	2.25	17.08

*7 Year Price Score 95.1   *NYSE Composite Index=100   *12 Month Price Score 115.4

Interim Earnings (Per Share)

Qtr.	Mar	Jun	Sep	Dec
2000	0.35	0.35	0.32	(0.91)
2001	0.38	0.22	0.41	0.36
2002	0.45	0.37	(0.16)	0.23
2003	0.26	0.48	0.28	1.17

Interim Dividends (Per Share)

Amt	Decl	Ex	Rec	Pay
0.20Q	6/17/2003	7/21/2003	7/23/2003	8/6/2003
0.21Q	8/12/2003	10/20/2003	10/22/2003	11/5/2003
0.21Q	10/28/2003	1/16/2004	1/21/2004	2/4/2004
0.21Q	3/25/2004	4/19/2004	4/21/2004	5/5/2004

Indicated Div: $0.84 (Div. Reinv. Plan)

Valuation Analysis

Forecast P/E	14.50	Trailing P/E	17.08
Market Cap	$540.9 Million	Book Value	257.6 Million
Price/Book	1.93	Price/Sales	1.01

Dividend Achiever Status

Rank	214	10 Year Growth Rate	7.05%
Total Years of Dividend Growth	11		

TRADING VOLUME (thousand shares)

Business Summary: Rubber Products (MIC: 11.6 SIC: 3069 NAIC:326299)

West Pharmaceutical Services provides closure systems and components, primarily for use with parenterally administered drugs, and conducts research and development of proprietary drug formulation and delivery technology for nasal and targeted oral delivery of drugs. Operations are divided into two segments. The pharmaceutical systems segment designs, manufactures and sells stoppers, closures, medical device components and assemblies made from elastomers, metals and plastics and provides contract laboratory services for testing drug packaging. The drug delivery systems segment identifies and develops products using Co.'s proprietary drug delivery technology.

Recent Developments: For the year ended Dec 31 2003, net income was $31.9 million versus income of $12.8 million, before income from discontinued operations of $5.6 million, in the prior year. Results for 2003 included a gain of $17.3 million from an insurance settlement. Results for 2003 and 2002 included restructuring and impairment charges of $7.0 million and $9.9 million, respectively. Net sales grew 16.9% to $490.7 million, reflecting strong demand for Co.'s closure and medical device components in the Pharmaceutical Systems Division and demand for Phase I clinical testing services in the Drug Delivery business during the last two quarters of 2003. Gross margin improved to 31.8% from 28.0% the year before.

Prospects: Co. finalized an insurance claim for $66.0 million associated with the January 2003 explosion and fire at its Kinston, NC plant. Co. recently began construction on a new rubber compression-molding facility, and expects that full production capacity will return to normal levels by September 2004. Looking ahead, Co. expects sales growth in its Pharmaceutical Systems division to moderate in the first half of 2004. However, growth should begin to accelerate in the fourth quarter of 2004 as a number of new products come to market. In the Drug Delivery division, Co. expects a substantial improvement in the operating results due to anticipated licensing revenue and cost containment programs.

Financial Data (US$ in Thousands)	12/31/2003	12/31/2002	12/31/2001	12/31/2000	12/31/1999	12/31/1998	12/31/1997	12/31/1996
Earnings Per Share	2.19	0.89	1.37	0.11	2.57	0.40	2.68	1.00
Cash Flow Per Share	4.75	3.16	2.16	3.37	4.61	4.30	4.08	3.86
Tang. Book Val. Per Share	14.29	10.84	10.05	10.64	11.23	11.24	13.64	11.78
Dividends Per Share	0.810	0.770	0.730	0.690	0.650	0.610	0.570	0.530
Dividend Payout %	36.98	86.51	53.28	627.27	25.29	152.50	21.26	53.00
Income Statement								
Total Revenues	490,700	419,700	396,900	430,100	469,100	449,700	452,500	458,800
Total Indirect Exp.	101,900	89,300	73,300	87,900	76,200	97,700	68,000	92,500
Depreciation & Amort.	33,000	33,000	32,000	37,000	35,700	32,300	31,900	30,700
Operating Income	54,500	26,700	41,300	15,200	66,900	35,000	63,000	32,700
Net Interest Inc./(Exp.)	(7,500)	(9,500)	(12,000)	(10,400)	(7,900)	(4,500)	(3,600)	(6,900)
Income Taxes	16,700	4,100	8,600	1,500	18,400	21,200	13,300	10,800
Eqty Earns/Minority Int.	1,600	(300)	400	1,000	600	100	300	1,400
Income from Cont Ops	...	12,800	19,600	...	...	...	...	...
Net Income	31,900	18,400	(5,200)	1,600	38,700	6,700	44,400	16,400
Average Shs. Outstg.	14,546	14,434	14,348	14,409	15,048	16,504	16,572	16,418
Balance Sheet								
Cash & Cash Equivalents	37,800	33,200	42,100	42,700	45,300	31,300	52,300	27,300
Total Current Assets	216,700	161,300	158,500	173,100	184,700	159,700	170,700	156,700
Total Assets	623,600	536,800	511,300	557,400	551,800	505,600	477,900	477,400
Total Current Liabilities	118,900	87,700	75,300	79,300	104,000	104,200	58,000	65,600
Long–Term Obligations	167,000	159,200	184,300	195,800	141,500	105,000	87,400	95,500
Net Stockholders' Equity	257,600	201,500	176,800	204,800	231,200	230,100	277,700	252,000
Net Working Capital	97,800	73,600	83,200	93,800	80,700	55,500	112,700	91,100
Shares Outstanding	14,632	14,480	14,344	14,310	14,664	15,026	16,568	16,383
Statistical Record								
Operating Profit Margin %	11.10	6.36	10.40	3.53	14.26	7.78	13.92	7.12
Return on Equity %	12.38	6.35	11.08	0.78	16.73	2.91	15.98	6.50
Return on Assets %	5.11	2.38	3.83	0.28	7.01	1.32	9.29	3.43
Debt/Total Assets %	26.77	29.65	36.04	35.12	25.64	20.76	18.28	20.00
Price Range	35.60-17.00	32.09-16.55	28.05-22.90	31.69-19.88	40.25-30.88	35.69-25.81	34.94-27.13	30.00-22.25
P/E Ratio	16.26-7.76	36.06-18.60	20.47-16.72	288.1-180.7	15.66-12.01	89.22-64.53	13.04-10.12	30.00-22.25
Average Yield %	3.06	3.01	2.86	2.86	1.83	2.04	1.91	2.10

Address: 101 Gordon Drive, Lionville, PA 19341–0645	Officers: Donald E. Morel – Chmn., Pres., C.E.O., William J. Federici – V.P., C.F.O.	Investor Contact: (610) 594–3346 Institutional Holding
Telephone: (610) 594–2900 Web Site: www.westpharma.com	Transfer Agents: American Stock Transfer and Trust Company, New York, NY	No of Institutions: 80 Shares: 10,221,481 % Held: 70.70%

WESTAMERICA BANCORPORATION

Exchange	Symbol	Price	52Wk Range	Yield	P/E
NMS	WABC	$50.46 (3/31/2004)	53.28–39.65	2.06	17.71

*7 Year Price Score 130.1 *NYSE Composite Index=100 *12 Month Price Score 103.2

Interim Earnings (Per Share)

Qtr.	Mar	Jun	Sep	Dec
2000	0.52	0.54	0.55	0.55
2001	0.56	0.58	0.60	0.62
2002	0.63	0.57	0.67	0.68
2003	0.69	0.71	0.72	0.73

Interim Dividends (Per Share)

Amt	Decl	Ex	Rec	Pay
0.24Q	4/24/2003	4/30/2003	5/2/2003	5/16/2003
0.26Q	7/24/2003	7/30/2003	8/1/2003	8/15/2003
0.26Q	10/23/2003	10/29/2003	10/31/2003	11/14/2003
0.26Q	1/22/2004	1/29/2004	2/2/2004	2/13/2004

Indicated Div: $1.04 (Div. Reinv. Plan)

Valuation Analysis

Forecast P/E	14.45	Trailing P/E	17.71
Market Cap	$1.7 Billion	Book Value	340.4 Million
Price/Book	4.82	Price/Sales	6.16

Dividend Achiever Status

Rank	41	10 Year Growth Rate	18.49%
Total Years of Dividend Growth			14

Business Summary: Commercial Banking (MIC: 8.1 SIC: 6021 NAIC:522110)

Westamerica Bancorp is a bank holding company that provides a full range of banking services to individual and corporate customers in northern and central California through its subsidiary bank, Westamerica Bank. Co. is a regional community bank with 88 branches serving 22 California counties. At Dec 31 2003, Co. had total assets of $4.58 billion and total deposits of $3.46 billion. Co.'s focus is on serving the needs of small businesses. In addition, Co. also owns Community Banker Services Corporation, which is engaged in providing Co. and its subsidiaries data processing services and other support functions.

Recent Developments: For the year ended Dec 31 2003, net income advanced 9.1% to $95.1 million versus $87.1 million in the previous year. Results for 2003 included a loss on extinguishment of debt of $2.2 million. Net interest income slipped 1.1% to $196.3 million from $198.5 million a year earlier. Total interest income decreased 6.0% to $223.5 million, while total interest expense fell 30.6% to $27.2 million. Provision for loan losses declined 8.3% to $3.3 million. Non–interest income climbed 17.4% to $42.9 million from $36.6 million the year before, reflecting higher service charges on deposit accounts. Non–interest expense slipped 1.6% to $101.7 million. Low–cost deposit accounts grew 7.0% in 2003.

Prospects: Low interest rates and reduced commercial loan demand continue to pressure Co.'s net interest margin. However, Co.'s non–interest income is benefiting from gains from investment securities and increased services charges on deposit accounts, mortgage banking income, and debit card fees. Meanwhile, earnings continue to be favorably affected by expense controls and Co.'s higher–than–average percentage of low–cost demand deposits. As the economy strengthens, lower costs and expenses should drive improved results. Going forward, Co. will continue to seek acquisitions in an effort to expand its market share.

Financial Data
(US$ in Thousands)

	12/31/2003	12/31/2002	12/31/2001	12/31/2000	12/31/1999	12/31/1998	12/31/1997	12/31/1996
Earnings Per Share	2.85	2.55	2.36	2.16	1.94	1.73	1.10	1.31
Tang. Book Val. Per Share	10.54	10.22	9.18	9.31	8.09	9.25	9.51	8.44
Dividends Per Share	1.000	0.900	0.820	0.740	0.660	0.520	0.360	0.290
Dividend Payout %	35.08	35.29	34.74	34.25	34.02	30.05	32.72	22.14
Income Statement								
Total Interest Income	223,493	237,633	257,056	269,516	257,656	266,820	270,670	174,265
Total Interest Expense	27,197	39,182	68,887	88,614	78,456	86,665	88,054	60,917
Net Interest Income	196,296	198,451	188,169	180,902	179,200	180,155	182,616	113,348
Provision for Loan Losses	3,300	3,600	3,600	3,675	4,780	5,180	7,645	4,575
Non–Interest Income	42,916	36,551	42,655	41,130	40,174	37,805	37,013	22,043
Non–Interest Expense	101,703	103,323	102,651	100,198	100,133	101,408	137,878	75,627
Income Before Taxes	134,209	128,079	124,573	118,159	114,461	111,372	74,106	55,189
Net Income	95,063	87,138	84,279	79,779	76,088	73,396	48,116	37,740
Average Shs. Outstg.	33,369	34,225	35,748	36,936	39,194	42,524	43,827	28,839
Balance Sheet								
Cash & Due from Banks	189,628	222,577	179,182	286,482	255,738	229,734	250,824	149,429
Securities Avail. for Sale	1,414,445	948,481	949,504	921,525	982,587	987,911	1,003,484	696,860
Net Loans & Leases	2,269,420	2,440,411	2,432,371	2,429,880	2,269,272	2,246,593	2,211,307	1,409,318
Total Assets	4,576,385	4,224,867	3,927,967	4,031,381	3,893,187	3,844,298	3,848,444	2,548,487
Total Deposits	3,463,991	3,294,065	3,234,635	3,236,744	3,065,344	3,189,005	3,078,501	2,081,396
Long–Term Obligations	129,643	194,607	27,821	31,036	41,500	47,500	52,500	42,500
Total Liabilities	4,236,014	3,883,368	3,613,608	3,693,634	3,592,595	3,475,702	3,441,292	2,309,541
Net Stockholders' Equity	340,371	341,499	314,359	337,747	300,592	368,596	407,152	238,946
Shares Outstanding	32,287	33,411	34,220	36,251	37,125	39,828	42,799	28,305
Statistical Record								
Return on Equity %	27.92	25.51	26.80	23.62	25.31	19.91	11.81	15.79
Return on Assets %	2.07	2.06	2.14	1.97	1.95	1.90	1.25	1.48
Equity/Assets %	7.43	8.08	8.00	8.37	7.72	9.58	10.57	9.37
Non–Int. Exp./Tot. Inc. %	38.17	37.68	34.24	32.25	33.62	33.28	44.81	38.52
Price Range	53.28–38.70	45.67–35.57	42.00–32.55	43.75–21.00	37.50–26.63	37.00–24.25	34.67–18.96	19.58–14.42
P/E Ratio	18.69–13.58	17.91–13.95	17.80–13.79	20.25–9.72	19.33–13.72	21.39–14.02	31.52–17.23	14.95–11.01
Average Yield %	2.26	2.19	2.16	2.54	2.00	1.62	1.42	1.78

Address: 1108 Fifth Avenue, San Rafael, CA 94901 Telephone: (707) 863–6000 Web Site: www.westamerica.com	Officers: David L. Payne – Chmn., Pres., C.E.O., Jennifer J. Finger – Sr. V.P., C.F.O.	Investor Contact: (707) 863–6992 Institutional Holding No of Institutions: 25 Shares: 1,057,005 % Held: –

WEYCO GROUP, INC

Exchange	Symbol	Price	52Wk Range	Yield	P/E
NMS	WEYS	$37.00 (3/31/2004)	38.34–27.72	1.08	12.71

*7 Year Price Score 164.5 ***NYSE Composite Index=100** ***12 Month Price Score 92.6**

Interim Earnings (Per Share)

Qtr.	Mar	Jun	Sep	Dec
2000	0.48	0.38	0.38	0.48
2001	0.39	0.28	0.41	0.56
2002	0.40	0.28	0.78	0.83
2003	0.80	0.60	0.59	0.92

Interim Dividends (Per Share)

Amt	Decl	Ex	Rec	Pay
50%	7/30/2003	10/2/2003	8/29/2003	10/1/2003
0.10Q	7/30/2003	8/27/2003	8/29/2003	10/1/2003
0.10Q	11/3/2003	11/26/2003	12/1/2003	1/2/2004
0.10Q	1/26/2004	3/4/2004	3/8/2004	4/1/2004

Indicated Div: $0.40

Valuation Analysis

Forecast P/E	N/A	Trailing P/E	12.71
Market Cap	$105.5 Million	Book Value	98.8 Million
Price/Book	1.48	Price/Sales	0.68

Dividend Achiever Status

Rank	201	10 Year Growth Rate	8.06%
Total Years of Dividend Growth		23

TRADING VOLUME (thousand shares)

Business Summary: Leather and Leather Products (MIC: 4.5 SIC: 3143 NAIC:316213)

Weyco Group is engaged in the distribution of men's footwear. Co.'s products consist of both mid-priced leather dress shoes and lower-priced casual footwear. These shoes are sold under various brand names. The principal brands of shoes sold are Florsheim, Nunn Bush, Nunn Bush NXXT, Brass Boot, Stacy Adams and SAO by Stacy Adams. Co.'s wholesale division markets footwear through more than 10,000 shoe, clothing and department stores across the U.S. As of Dec 31 2003, the retail division consisted of 30 Company-operated stores in the U.S and three retail stores in Europe.

Recent Developments: For the year ended Dec 31 2003, net income advanced 29.9% to $17.1 million from $13.2 million the previous year. Net sales grew 19.1% to $215.8 million from $181.2 million in the prior year. The increase in sales was primarily due to the inclusion of the Florsheim brand for a full year versus about seven months in 2002. Wholesale sales grew 14.5% to $187.3 million. Retail sales climbed 56.6% to $24.9 million, while licensing revenues jumped to $3.6 million compared with $1.7 million in 2002. Gross profit rose 29.3% to $76.4 million. Selling, general and administrative expenses grew 30.4% to $49.2 million. Operating profit was $27.3 million, up 27.4% from $21.4 million a year earlier.

Prospects: Co. is encouraged with the growth opportunities of its brands as it heads into 2004. For instance, within the Florsheim brand, Co. has worked through the excess inventory that it acquired, pruned back the distribution, and retooled the product line to broaden the brand's appeal to a more modern consumer. The Comfort-Gel construction continues to be well received by retail customers. Meanwhile, the casual streetwear market in which SAO by Stacy Adams competes remains challenging, as preferences of consumers has shifted more toward athletic shoes. Despite this setback, Co. believes that the SAO business is stabilizing and its new designs for Fall 2004 will been well received.

Financial Data
(US$ in Thousands)

	12/31/2003	12/31/2002	12/31/2001	12/31/2000	12/31/1999	12/31/1998	12/31/1997	12/31/1996
Earnings Per Share	2.91	2.29	1.64	1.72	1.70	1.38	1.25	1.10
Cash Flow Per Share	4.47	2.48	1.72	1.89	0.40	1.34	1.57	1.64
Tang. Book Val. Per Share	15.62	13.01	13.08	11.97	10.85	9.81	9.30	8.27
Dividends Per Share	0.360	0.330	0.300	0.280	0.250	0.220	0.200	0.190
Dividend Payout %	12.60	14.53	18.69	16.21	14.90	16.42	16.13	17.27
Income Statement								
Total Revenues	215,761	181,200	131,693	148,155	133,498	127,074	127,029	129,314
Total Indirect Exp.	49,184	37,732	24,231	24,586	22,538	22,311	22,674	23,176
Depreciation & Amort.	2,510	2,231	1,609	1,490	1,242	626	821	1,045
Operating Income	27,261	21,406	13,354	15,972	15,223	13,801	12,646	11,664
Net Interest Inc./(Exp.)	(846)	(436)	726	479	831	1,419	1,475	...
Income Taxes	9,555	7,800	5,200	5,850	5,900	5,450	5,065	4,718
Net Income	17,135	13,188	9,501	10,622	11,058	9,805	9,068	8,072
Average Shs. Outstg.	5,878	5,753	5,792	6,162	6,507	7,096	7,237	7,305
Balance Sheet								
Cash & Cash Equivalents	13,298	9,400	20,118	11,210	8,704	13,094	10,684	15,017
Total Current Assets	90,605	95,544	61,720	51,670	53,093	48,051	42,912	47,813
Total Assets	151,186	146,235	97,954	91,943	95,919	92,782	82,204	73,077
Total Current Liabilities	44,254	20,233	20,911	17,758	26,253	26,387	14,643	13,973
Long–Term Obligations	...	37,802	...	...	...	...	...	...
Net Stockholders' Equity	98,846	84,784	73,592	71,345	67,751	65,148	66,677	59,104
Net Working Capital	46,351	75,311	40,810	33,912	26,840	21,664	28,269	33,840
Shares Outstanding	5,630	5,683	5,623	5,959	6,241	6,635	7,162	7,143
Statistical Record								
Operating Profit Margin %	12.63	11.81	10.14	10.78	11.40	10.86	9.95	9.02
Return on Equity %	17.33	15.55	12.91	14.88	16.32	15.04	13.60	13.65
Return on Assets %	11.33	9.01	9.69	11.55	11.52	10.56	11.03	11.04
Debt/Total Assets %	...	25.85	...	...	...	...	...	...
Price Range	38.34–20.83	27.33–16.90	17.33–15.33	17.75–15.00	17.42–14.42	19.00–14.17	21.33–8.94	9.28–8.33
P/E Ratio	13.18–7.16	11.93–7.38	10.57–9.35	10.32–8.72	10.25–8.48	13.77–10.27	17.07–7.16	8.43–7.58
Average Yield %	1.17	1.47	1.86	1.71	1.56	1.32	1.41	2.17

Address: 333 West Estabrook Boulevard, Milwaukee, WI 53201 **Telephone:** (414) 908–1600 **Web Site:** www.stacyadams.com	**Officers:** Thomas W. Florsheim – Chmn., C.E.O., John W. Florsheim – Pres., C.O.O.	**Investor Contact:** (414) 908–1600 **Institutional Holding** **No of Institutions:** 8 **Shares:** 73,700 **% Held:** –

WGL HOLDINGS, INC.

Exchange	Symbol	Price	52Wk Range	Yield	P/E
NYS	WGL	$30.10 (3/31/2004)	30.10–25.37	4.32	14.68

7 Year Price Score 104.0   *NYSE Composite Index=100   *12 Month Price Score 91.4

Interim Earnings (Per Share)

Qtr.	Dec	Mar	Jun	Sep
2000–01	1.08	1.44	(0.15)	(0.62)
2001–02	0.62	0.94	(0.29)	(0.47)
2002–03	1.06	1.66	(0.05)	(0.37)
2003–04	0.81	...	...	...

Interim Dividends (Per Share)

Amt	Decl	Ex	Rec	Pay
0.32Q	6/25/2003	7/8/2003	7/10/2003	8/1/2003
0.32Q	9/24/2003	10/8/2003	10/10/2003	11/1/2003
0.32Q	12/19/2003	1/7/2004	1/9/2004	2/1/2004
0.325Q	3/2/2004	4/6/2004	4/9/2004	5/1/2004

Indicated Div: $1.30 (Div. Reinv. Plan)

Valuation Analysis

Forecast P/E	14.68	Trailing P/E	14.68
Market Cap	$1.5 Billion	Book Value	870.9 Million
Price/Book	1.56	Price/Sales	0.65

Dividend Achiever Status

Rank	295	10 Year Growth Rate	1.65%
Total Years of Dividend Growth			27

Business Summary: Gas Utilities (MIC: 7.4 SIC: 4924 NAIC:221210)

WGL Holdings through its subsidiaries, engages in the sale and distribution of natural gas and other energy–related products and services. Washington Gas Light Company is a regulated natural gas utility serving over 960,000 customers in Washington D.C., Virginia and Maryland as of Jul 30 2003. Hampshire Gas Company is a regulated natural gas storage business, serving Washington Gas Light Company. Washington Gas Energy Services, Inc. sells natural gas and electricity to the Washington D.C. area as well as Baltimore, Maryland and Richmond, Virginia. Washington Gas Energy Systems, Inc. designs cost–saving energy systems for the commercial and government markets.

Recent Developments: For the three months ended Dec 31 2003, net income decreased 23.4% to $39.5 million compared with $51.6 million in the corresponding quarter of the previous year. The decreased earnings was largely attributed to lower gas deliveries to firm customers and additional depreciation expenses due to the Virginia rate order. Operating revenues inched up to $375.3 million from $375.0 million in the year–earlier period. Utility net revenues declined 5.7% to $162.8 million from $172.7 million the year before. Utility operating income dropped 21.0% to $47.7 million from $60.4 million in the prior–year quarter.

Prospects: Co.'s regulated utility continues to benefit from operational efficiencies from process improvements, customer growth and rate relief. Also, results from Co.'s retail energy–marketing business is benefiting from higher gross margin from the sales of both natural gas and electricity. Looking ahead, Co. expects earnings to range from $1.45 to $1.55 per share for the second quarter of 2004 and from $1.72 to $1.82 per share for the full year 2004. This estimate includes projected fiscal 2004 earnings from Co.'s unregulated businesses to e in the range of $0.02 to $0.04 per share.

Financial Data

(US$ in Thousands)	3 Mos	09/30/2003	09/30/2002	09/30/2001	09/30/2000	09/30/1999	09/30/1998	09/30/1997
Earnings Per Share	0.81	2.30	0.80	1.75	1.79	1.47	1.54	1.85
Cash Flow Per Share	0.46	2.94	4.22	1.69	1.90	3.32	2.78	3.54
Tang. Book Val. Per Share	17.32	16.83	15.78	16.23	15.31	14.71	13.82	13.47
Dividends Per Share	1.270	1.270	1.260	1.250	1.230	1.210	1.190	1.170
Dividend Payout %	157.71	55.43	158.12	71.42	68.71	82.31	77.27	63.24
Income Statement								
Total Revenues	585,289	2,064,248	1,569,969	1,933,024	1,247,954	1,112,214	1,040,618	1,055,754
Total Indirect Exp.	265,150	923,395	789,371	634,723	339,663	255,363	124,053	122,640
Costs & Expenses	519,136	1,905,012	1,484,008	1,792,980	1,119,009	1,004,457	938,639	940,479
Depreciation & Amort.	50,410	83,549	72,921	68,754	65,514	59,940	54,875	51,363
Operating Income	52,384	159,236	85,961	140,044	128,945	107,757	101,979	115,275
Net Interest Inc./(Exp.)	(11,591)	(46,381)	(45,877)	(50,000)	(43,736)	(36,971)	(37,719)	(34,142)
Income Taxes	...	68,801	30,427	59,372	49,263	42,519	38,006	47,864
Net Income	39,543	113,662	40,441	83,765	84,574	68,768	68,629	82,019
Average Shs. Outstg.	48,812	48,756	48,563	47,120	46,473	45,984	43,691	43,706
Balance Sheet								
Net Property	1,876,280	1,874,923	1,606,843	1,519,747	1,460,280	1,402,742	1,319,501	1,217,137
Total Assets	2,659,952	2,436,052	2,113,664	2,081,113	1,939,840	1,766,724	1,682,433	1,552,032
Long–Term Obligations	637,610	636,650	667,951	584,370	559,576	506,084	428,641	431,575
Net Stockholders' Equity	814,567	846,391	794,576	816,426	739,669	712,454	636,179	617,465
Shares Outstanding	48,641	48,611	48,564	48,542	46,469	46,473	43,955	43,700
Statistical Record								
Operating Profit Margin %	8.95	7.71	5.47	7.24	10.33	9.68	9.79	10.91
Net Inc./Net Property %	2.10	6.06	2.51	5.51	5.79	4.90	5.20	6.73
Net Inc./Tot. Capital %	2.26	6.60	2.41	5.20	5.75	5.00	5.67	6.91
Return on Equity %	4.73	13.42	5.08	10.25	11.43	9.65	10.78	13.28
Accum. Depr./Gross Prop. %	27.37	26.87	35.25	35.06	34.37	33.64	33.78	34.08
Price Range	28.32–26.27	28.64–22.38	29.45–20.16	31.44–25.19	29.25–22.63	28.50–21.50	30.94–23.44	26.13–21.25
P/E Ratio	34.96–32.43	12.45–9.73	36.81–25.20	17.96–14.39	16.34–12.64	19.39–14.63	20.09–15.22	14.12–11.49
Average Yield %	4.64	4.95	4.80	4.55	4.72	4.76	4.50	4.98

Address: 1100 H Street, N.W., Washington, DC 20080 **Telephone:** (703) 750–2000 **Web Site:** www.washgas.com	**Officers:** James H. DeGraffenreidt – Chmn., C.E.O., Terry D. McCallister – Pres., C.O.O. **Transfer Agents:** The Riggs National Bank, Washington, D.C.	**Investor Contact:** 202–624–6410 **Institutional Holding** **No of Institutions:** 6 **Shares:** 24,921 **% Held:** –

WHITNEY HOLDING CORP.

Exchange	Symbol	Price	52Wk Range	Yield	P/E
NMS	WTNY	$41.74 (3/31/2004)	43.27-31.67	3.16	17.11

*7 Year Price Score 120.2   *NYSE Composite Index=100   *12 Month Price Score 101.4

Interim Earnings (Per Share)

Qtr.	Mar	Jun	Sep	Dec
2000	0.48	0.48	0.50	0.50
2001	0.46	0.46	0.48	0.50
2002	0.36	0.59	0.60	0.83
2003	0.58	0.59	0.68	0.59

Interim Dividends (Per Share)

Amt	Decl	Ex	Rec	Pa
0.30Q	5/28/2003	6/12/2003	6/16/2003	7/1/200
0.30Q	8/27/2003	9/11/2003	9/15/2003	10/1/200
0.33Q	11/19/2003	12/11/2003	12/15/2003	1/2/200
0.33Q	2/18/2004	3/11/2004	3/15/2004	4/1/200

Indicated Div: $1.32 (Div. Reinv. Plan)

Valuation Analysis

Forecast P/E	14.35	Trailing P/E	17.11
Market Cap	$1.7 Billion	Book Value	840.3 Million
Price/Book	1.93	Price/Sales	3.81

Dividend Achiever Status

Rank	51	10 Year Growth Rate	17.25%
Total Years of Dividend Growth			10

Business Summary: Commercial Banking (MIC: 8.1 SIC: 6021 NAIC:522110)

Whitney Holding, through its principal banking subsidiary, Whitney National Bank, serves the five-state Gulf Coast region stretching from Houston, TX, across southern Louisiana and the coastal region of Mississippi, to central and south Alabama, and into the panhandle o Florida. Co. serves commercial, small business and retail customers, and offers a range of transaction and savings deposit products and cash management services, secured and unsecured loan products, including revolving credit facilities, and letters of credit and similar financial guarantees. Co. also provides trust and investment management services to retirement benefit plans, corporations and individuals.

Recent Developments: For the year ended Dec 31 2003, net income rose 3.4% to $98.5 million compared with $95.3 million in 2002 Results for 2003 and 2002 included securities transaction gains of $863,000 and $411,000, respectively. Net interest income slipped 0.2% to $294.6 million from $295.2 million in the prior year. Results for 2003 included a $3.5 million negative provision for loan losses versu a provision of $7.5 million in 2002. Total non-interest income rose 5.1% to $89.5 million compared with $85.2 million the previous yea Total non-interest expense climbed 5.2% to $242.9 million versus $230.9 million the year before.

Prospects: On Mar 19 2004, Co. signed a definitive agreement to acquire Madison Bancshares, the parent company of Madison Bank which has approximately $200.0 million in total assets in three locations in Pinellas and Pasco counties in the Tampa Bay, FL area. A fourt location is under construction and is expected to open in June 2004. Under the agreement, shareholders of Madison Bancshares will receiv $29.89 in cash and/or Co. common stock for each share held. The transaction will allow Co. to enter into the Tampa Bay, FL market that h in excess of $36.00 billion in deposits. A presence in this market is strategically in line with Co.'s market territory and expansion strategy

Financial Data

(US$ in Thousands)	12/31/2003	12/31/2002	12/31/2001	12/31/2000	12/31/1999	12/31/1998	12/31/1997	12/31/199
Earnings Per Share	2.44	2.38	1.90	1.96	1.80	1.49	1.66	1.5
Tang. Book Val. Per Share	18.48	17.53	15.48	15.30	15.46	15.98	15.34	15.0
Dividends Per Share	1.200	1.070	0.990	0.940	0.860	0.780	0.720	0.62
Dividend Payout %	49.18	45.23	52.63	47.95	47.77	52.67	43.59	41.5
Income Statement								
Total Interest Income	338,069	370,909	441,145	417,687	349,813	336,113	291,409	241,70
Total Interest Expense	43,509	75,701	161,349	170,574	124,065	122,981	106,947	89,89
Net Interest Income	294,560	295,208	279,796	247,113	225,748	213,132	184,462	151,81
Provision for Loan Losses	(3,500)	7,500	19,500	10,000	6,000	73	(2,812)	(5,00
Non–Interest Income	89,504	85,185	91,209	71,625	66,663	60,771	51,035	37,32
Non–Interest Expense	242,923	230,926	239,104	208,903	194,163	195,993	159,630	134,39
Income Before Taxes	143,486	141,967	112,401	99,835	92,248	77,837	78,679	59,73
Income from Cont Ops	97,387	...	...	...	...	...	...	...
Net Income	98,542	95,323	75,820	67,020	62,420	52,679	52,218	40,62
Average Shs. Outstg.	40,396	40,121	39,836	34,256	34,636	35,250	31,299	26,97
Balance Sheet								
Cash & Due from Banks	270,387	326,124	271,512	256,825	230,690	214,963	221,318	221,09
Securities Avail. for Sale	2,090,870	1,773,591	1,440,527	456,758	206,932	105,361	103,253	146,97
Net Loans & Leases	4,823,135	4,389,297	4,482,905	4,245,501	3,628,581	3,230,299	2,604,773	2,025,56
Total Assets	7,754,982	7,097,881	7,243,650	6,242,076	5,454,388	5,211,919	4,312,987	3,774,50
Total Deposits	6,158,582	5,782,879	5,950,160	4,960,177	4,309,398	4,256,662	3,510,723	2,861,88
Total Liabilities	6,914,669	6,297,398	6,525,762	5,619,116	4,897,285	4,650,958	3,834,259	3,369,85
Net Stockholders' Equity	840,313	800,483	717,888	622,960	557,103	560,961	478,728	404,65
Shares Outstanding	40,447	40,067	39,667	35,027	33,861	35,089	31,206	26,92
Statistical Record								
Return on Equity %	11.58	11.90	10.56	10.75	11.20	9.39	10.90	10.0
Return on Assets %	1.25	1.34	1.04	1.07	1.14	1.01	1.21	1.0
Equity/Assets %	10.83	11.27	9.91	9.98	10.21	10.76	11.09	10.7
Non–Int. Exp./Tot. Inc. %	56.81	50.63	44.91	42.69	46.62	49.38	46.61	48.
Price Range	40.99-31.62	38.52-27.98	32.56-24.00	27.79-21.00	27.83-21.46	42.25-23.83	39.83-23.17	23.92-19.0
P/E Ratio	16.80-12.96	16.18-11.76	17.14-12.63	14.18-10.71	15.46-11.92	28.36-16.00	24.00-13.96	15.94-13.
Average Yield %	3.46	3.27	3.55	4.00	3.45	2.38	2.54	2.9

Address: 228 St. Charles Avenue, New Orleans, LA 70130 **Telephone:** (504) 586-7272 **Web Site:** www.whitneybank.com	**Officers:** William L. Marks – Chmn., C.E.O., R. King Milling – Pres.	**Investor Contact:** (504) 552-4591 **Institutional Holding** **No of Institutions:** 15 **Shares:** 13,709 **% Held:** –

WILEY (JOHN) & SONS INC.

Exchange	Symbol	Price	52Wk Range	Yield	P/E
NYS	JW A	$29.93 (3/31/2004)	29.93–22.06	0.87	21.53

*Year Price Score 135.1 *NYSE Composite Index=100 *12 Month Price Score 91.0

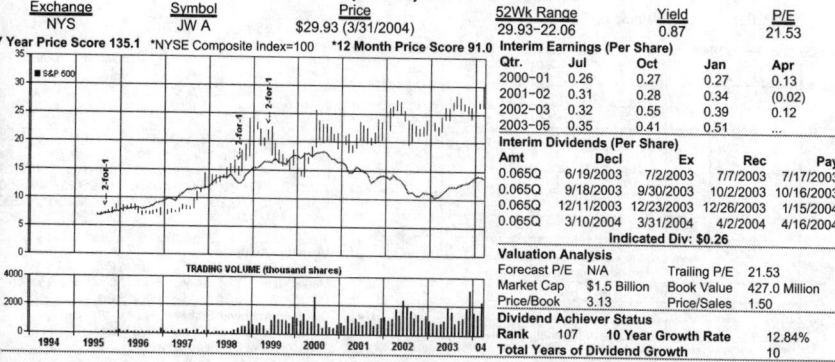

Interim Earnings (Per Share)

Qtr.	Jul	Oct	Jan	Apr
2000–01	0.26	0.27	0.27	0.13
2001–02	0.31	0.28	0.34	(0.02)
2002–03	0.32	0.55	0.39	0.12
2003–05	0.35	0.41	0.51	...

Interim Dividends (Per Share)

Amt	Decl	Ex	Rec	Pay
0.065Q	6/19/2003	7/2/2003	7/7/2003	7/17/2003
0.065Q	9/18/2003	9/30/2003	10/2/2003	10/16/2003
0.065Q	12/11/2003	12/23/2003	12/26/2003	1/15/2004
0.065Q	3/10/2004	3/31/2004	4/2/2004	4/16/2004

Indicated Div: $0.26

Valuation Analysis

Forecast P/E	N/A	Trailing P/E	21.53
Market Cap	$1.5 Billion	Book Value	427.0 Million
Price/Book	3.13	Price/Sales	1.50

Dividend Achiever Status

Rank	107	10 Year Growth Rate	12.84%
Total Years of Dividend Growth		10

Business Summary: Non–Media Publishing (MIC: 13.3 SIC: 2731 NAIC:511130)

John Wiley & Sons develops, publishes and markets textbooks, reference works, consumer books, periodicals, including journals and other subscription-based products and electronic media products, to colleges and universities, libraries, bookstores, professional groups, industrial organizations, government agencies and individuals in the U.S. and abroad. In addition, Co. imports, adapts, markets and distributes books from other publishers. Co. also develops and markets computer software and electronic databases for educational use and professional research and training.

Recent Developments: For the third quarter ended Jan 31 2004, net income grew 29.4% to $31.3 million compared with $24.2 million in the equivalent 2002 quarter. Revenues climbed 9.6% to $242.4 million from $221.2 million a year earlier. The improvement in earnings and revenues was primarily driven by Scientific, Technical and Medical journals, Professional/Trade books, and Higher Education textbooks and educational materials. In addition, Co.'s results were boosted by the positive effects of operations, the resolution of certain tax matters and favorable foreign exchange rates. Operating income advanced 19.0% to $43.9 million versus $36.9 million the year before.

Prospects: Although market conditions remain challenging, Co. is seeing growing momentum across its core businesses with recent sales notably higher for its scientific, technical and medical journals, professional/trade books and higher education textbooks and educational materials. Consequently, Co. expects fiscal 2004 revenue growth to approach the high end of its 4.0% to 6.0% guidance, and earnings per share to reach the high end of its mid to high single digit guidance. These projections exclude unusual items and a tax benefit recorded in the third quarter, and are based on nine months results and expectations for the fourth quarter of fiscal 2004.

Financial Data

(US$ in Thousands)	9 Mos	6 Mos	3 Mos	04/30/2003	04/30/2002	04/30/2001	04/30/2000	04/30/1999
Earnings Per Share	1.27	0.75	0.35	1.38	0.91	0.93	0.81	0.60
Cash Flow Per Share	2.81	(0.0084)	(0.23)	2.68	2.22	2.06	2.03	1.77
Dividends Per Share	0.240	0.230	0.210	0.200	0.180	0.160	0.140	0.120
Dividend Payout %	19.29	30.66	61.42	14.49	19.78	17.20	17.59	21.25
Income Statement								
Total Revenues	690,897	448,540	219,660	853,971	734,396	613,790	594,815	508,435
Total Indirect Exp.	344,732	228,204	114,373	442,320	391,125	318,966	310,872	270,798
Depreciation & Amort.	7,382	4,865	2,330	9,620	17,662	17,496	16,447	9,445
Operating Income	113,895	70,045	33,178	120,261	87,763	95,424	89,004	63,654
Net Interest Inc./(Exp.)	(3,092)	(1,872)	(1,260)	(7,964)	(7,480)	(8,025)	(8,390)	(7,322)
Income Taxes	32,011	20,725	10,118	25,284	23,802	31,309	30,243	22,336
Net Income	78,792	47,448	21,800	87,275	57,316	58,918	52,388	39,709
Average Shs. Outstg.	61,800	63,091	62,964	63,086	63,094	63,300	64,825	66,513
Balance Sheet								
Cash & Cash Equivalents	93,051	10,756	8,085	33,241	39,705	52,947	42,299	148,970
Total Current Assets	363,881	300,050	265,923	283,844	275,259	189,535	177,111	255,970
Total Assets	1,045,539	974,588	938,942	955,972	896,145	588,002	569,337	528,552
Total Current Liabilities	330,385	284,020	277,181	323,265	320,393	246,761	254,050	195,100
Long–Term Obligations	200,000	200,000	200,000	200,000	235,000	65,000	95,000	125,000
Net Stockholders' Equity	426,994	399,412	372,866	344,004	276,650	220,023	172,738	162,212
Net Working Capital	...	...	(11,258)	(39,421)	(45,134)	(57,226)	(76,939)	60,870
Shares Outstanding	62,042	62,140	62,172	61,630	61,701	60,734	60,712	62,382
Statistical Record								
Operating Profit Margin %	16.48	15.61	15.10	14.08	11.95	15.54	14.96	12.51
Return on Equity %	18.45	11.87	5.84	25.37	20.71	26.77	30.32	24.47
Return on Assets %	7.53	4.86	2.32	9.12	6.39	10.02	9.20	7.51
Debt/Total Assets %	19.12	20.52	21.30	20.92	26.22	11.05	16.68	23.64
Price Range	28.26–24.07	28.26–24.07	27.21–24.07	27.30–19.61	27.46–18.65	25.69–17.56	22.75–13.88	24.16–13.31
P/E Ratio	22.25–18.95	37.68–32.09	77.74–68.77	19.78–14.21	30.18–20.49	27.62–18.88	28.09–17.13	40.26–22.19
Average Yield %	0.92	0.88	0.82	0.87	0.80	0.77	0.81	0.68

Address: 111 River Street, Hoboken, 07030	**Officers:** Peter Booth Wiley – Chmn., William J. Pesce – Pres., C.E.O.	**Investor Contact:** (201) 748–6000
Telephone: (201) 748–6000	**Transfer Agents:** Registrar and Transfer Company, Cranford, NJ	**Institutional Holding**
Web Site: www.wiley.com		**No of Institutions:** 10
		Shares: 359,105 **% Held:** –

WILMINGTON TRUST CORP. (DE)

Exchange	Symbol	Price	52Wk Range	Yield	P/E
NYS	WL	$37.37 (3/31/2004)	38.30–26.65	2.89	19.31

*7 Year Price Score N/A   *NYSE Composite Index=100   *12 Month Price Score 101.8

TRADING VOLUME (thousand shares)

Interim Earnings (Per Share)

Qtr.	Mar	Jun	Sep	Dec
2000	0.47	0.47	0.47	0.44
2001	0.46	0.47	0.47	0.48
2002	0.48	0.52	0.52	0.49
2003	0.44	0.49	0.52	0.57

Interim Dividends (Per Share)

Amt	Decl	Ex	Rec	Pa
0.27Q	4/17/2003	4/29/2003	5/1/2003	5/15/200
0.27Q	7/18/2003	7/30/2003	8/1/2003	8/15/200
0.27Q	10/17/2003	10/30/2003	11/3/2003	11/17/200
0.27Q	1/16/2004	1/29/2004	2/2/2004	2/16/200

Indicated Div: $1.08

Valuation Analysis

Forecast P/E	14.85	Trailing P/E	19.31
Market Cap	$2.5 Billion	Book Value	783.6 Million
Price/Book	2.59	Price/Sales	3.21

Dividend Achiever Status

Rank	198	10 Year Growth Rate	8.13%
Total Years of Dividend Growth		22

Business Summary: Commercial Banking (MIC: 8.1 SIC: 6022 NAIC:522110)
Wilmington Trust, with assets of $8.82 billion as of Dec 31 2003, is a financial services holding company with offices in California, Delaware, Florida, Georgia, Maryland, Nevada, New York, Pennsylvania, Tennessee, the Cayman and Channel Islands, Dublin, London and Milan. Co. provides wealth management and specialized corporate services to clients throughout the United States and in more than 5 other countries, and commercial banking services throughout the Delaware Valley region. In addition, Co. is authorized to do business in Luxembourg and the Netherlands.

Recent Developments: For the year ended Dec 31 2003, net income rose 0.9% to $134.4 million compared with $133.2 million the year before. Net interest income improved 0.2% to $277.1 million from $276.5 million a year earlier. Net interest margin was down 42 basis points to 3.60% as a result of the effects of the continued low interest rate environment and Co.'s asset sensitivity. Provision for loan losses declined 1.8% to $21.6 million compared with $22.0 million in 2002. Non-interest income was up 0.8% to $264.2 million. Non-interest expense increased slightly to $312.0 million from $309.9 million a year earlier. Expense growth was limited by Co.'s continued emphasis on controlling costs.

Prospects:
During the fourth quarter of 2003, Co. reported very strong business development in all of its businesses. If that trend of growth continues, and if the economy and the equity markets continue to move in a positive direction, Co. expects to see continued growth in loan balances and advisory income. However, expenses will increase as Co. continues to invest in its business. Salary and employment-related expenses will rise as Co. adds to its staff. In addition, several large multiyear insurance policies will renew in 2004, and Co. anticipates a considerable increase in annual insurance expense, which currently is in the $1.5 million range.

Financial Data

(US$ in Thousands)	12/31/2003	12/31/2002	12/31/2001	12/31/2000	12/31/1999	12/31/1998	12/31/1997	12/31/199
Earnings Per Share	2.02	2.01	1.88	1.85	1.60	1.67	1.54	1.4
Tang. Book Val. Per Share	8.07	7.30	7.25	6.48	5.17	6.07	7.51	6.8
Dividends Per Share	1.060	1.000	0.940	0.880	0.820	0.760	0.700	0.64
Dividend Payout %	52.72	49.75	50.13	47.83	51.40	45.80	45.77	45.3
Income Statement								
Total Interest Income	368,800	392,871	468,798	530,454	462,176	456,939	430,639	402,85
Total Interest Expense	91,700	116,341	209,985	275,315	216,263	219,242	200,623	188,62
Net Interest Income	277,100	276,530	258,813	255,139	245,913	237,697	230,016	214,22
Provision for Loan Losses	21,600	22,013	19,850	21,900	17,500	20,000	21,500	16,00
Non-Interest Income	264,200	262,159	228,003	216,210	191,453	183,917	157,542	138,23
Non-Interest Expense	312,000	309,892	276,917	264,682	258,204	230,066	207,671	192,33
Income Before Taxes	206,000	205,531	181,854	177,280	161,662	171,548	158,387	144,11
Eqty Earns/Minority Int.	(1,100)	(625)	...	...	...	...	...	
Income from Cont Ops	...	...	124,040	...	...	...	...	
Net Income	134,400	133,157	125,170	120,939	107,297	114,325	106,044	97,27
Average Shs. Outstg.	66,536	66,301	65,942	65,360	66,766	68,550	68,932	68,79
Balance Sheet								
Cash & Due from Banks	210,200	248,850	210,104	223,819	225,145	204,579	239,392	231,23
Securities Avail. for Sale	1,875,200	1,343,899	1,264,848	1,440,065	1,686,267	1,298,741	1,316,403	798,51
Net Loans & Leases	6,135,400	5,939,947	5,407,175	5,111,670	4,743,154	4,247,727	3,930,130	3,717,12
Total Assets	8,820,200	8,131,275	7,518,462	7,321,616	7,201,944	6,300,565	6,122,351	5,564,40
Total Deposits	6,577,200	6,337,093	5,590,785	5,286,016	5,369,484	4,536,763	4,169,030	3,913,69
Long-Term Obligations	407,100	160,500	160,500	168,000	168,000	168,000	43,000	43,00
Total Liabilities	8,019,400	7,390,006	6,835,932	6,729,716	6,703,713	5,754,356	5,619,344	5,099,69
Net Stockholders' Equity	800,800	741,269	682,530	591,900	498,231	546,209	503,007	464,71
Shares Outstanding	66,063	65,627	65,400	64,786	64,705	66,658	66,956	67,78
Statistical Record								
Return on Equity %	16.57	17.79	16.97	19.16	21.53	20.93	21.08	20.9
Return on Assets %	1.50	1.62	1.54	1.54	1.48	1.81	1.73	1.7
Equity/Assets %	9.07	9.11	9.07	8.08	6.91	8.66	8.21	8.3
Non-Int. Exp./Tot. Inc. %	49.28	47.30	39.74	35.44	39.50	35.89	35.30	35.5
Price Range	36.21-26.35	34.58-25.30	33.42-25.65	31.56-20.75	30.94-23.00	...	...	
P/E Ratio	17.93-13.04	17.20-12.59	17.78-13.64	17.06-11.22	19.34-14.38	...	...	
Average Yield %	3.45	3.21	3.12	3.56	2.98	N/A	N/A	N,

Address: Rodney Square North, Wilmington, DE 19890-0001 **Telephone:** (302) 651-1000 **Web Site:** www.wilmingtontrust.com	**Officers:** Ted T. Cecala – Chmn., C.E.O., Robert V. A. Harra – Pres., C.O.O., Treas. **Transfer Agents:** Wells Fargo Shareowner Services, St. Paul, MN	**Investor Contact:** (302) 651-8069 **Institutional Holding** **No of Institutions:** 11 **Shares:** 469,986 **% Held:** –

WOLVERINE WORLD WIDE, INC.

Exchange	Symbol	Price	52Wk Range	Yield	P/E
NYS	WWW	$24.13 (3/31/2004)	24.33-16.26	1.08	22.55

7 Year Price Score 112.4   *NSYE Composite Index=100   *12 Month Price Score 98.3

Interim Earnings (Per Share)

Qtr.	Mar	Jun	Sep	Dec
2000	0.12	0.18	(0.37)	0.33
2001	0.14	0.21	0.34	0.38
2002	0.15	0.21	0.37	0.42
2003-04	0.18	0.23	0.40	0.46

Interim Dividends (Per Share)

Amt	Decl	Ex	Rec	Pay
0.055Q	4/30/2003	6/27/2003	7/1/2003	8/1/2003
0.055Q	7/10/2003	9/29/2003	10/1/2003	11/3/2003
0.055Q	12/9/2003	12/30/2003	1/2/2004	2/2/2004
0.065Q	2/19/2004	3/30/2004	4/1/2004	5/3/2004

Indicated Div: $0.26

Valuation Analysis

Forecast P/E	14.22	Trailing P/E	22.55
Market Cap	$1.1 Billion	Book Value	395.0 Million
Price/Book	2.28	Price/Sales	1.04

Dividend Achiever Status

Rank	29	10 Year Growth Rate	20.85%
Total Years of Dividend Growth		10

Business Summary: Leather and Leather Products (MIC: 4.5 SIC: 3149 NAIC:316219)

Wolverine World Wide is a designer, manufacturer and marketer of a broad line of casual shoes, rugged outdoor and work footwear, and constructed slippers and moccasins. The products are marketed throughout the world under brand names including *Bates®, CAT®, Coleman®, Harley–Davidson®, Hush Puppies®, HyTest®, Merrell®, Sebago®, Stanley®* and *Wolverine®*. Co.'s footwear is distributed domestically through 64 Co.-owned retail stores and to numerous accounts including department stores, footwear chains, catalogs, specialty retailers, mass merchants and Internet retailers as of Jan 3 2004. Co.'s products are distributed worldwide in over 140 markets through licensees and distributors.

Recent Developments: For the year ended Jan 3 2004, net earnings advanced 7.9% to $51.7 million compared with $47.9 million a year earlier. Revenues increased 7.5% to $888.9 million from $827.1 million the previous year. Co. attributed the higher revenues to increases in unit volume, changes in product mix and changes in selling price for its Branded Footwear operations. Gross margin amounted to $326.6 million, or 36.7% of total revenue, versus $294.2 million, or 35.6% of total revenue, the year before. Gross margin benefited from an increased sales mix of Co.'s lifestyle product offerings, fewer required markdowns on slow moving inventories and favorable foreign exchange rate changes.

Prospects: Co.'s near–term outlook appears favorable, reflecting solid new order growth, improving margins and reduced inventory markdowns. For instance, as of Mar 13 2004, Co. had a backlog of footwear orders of approximately $274.0 million, 17.6% higher than the year before. Co.'s increased order backlog is being driven by its growing lifestyle and sandal businesses, solid work boot and military contract demand as well as the November 2003 addition of the Sebago business. Accordingly, Co. continues to expect revenue for full–year fiscal 2004 will range between $945.0 million and $965.0 million. Also, Co. has increased its earning per share estimates by $0.03 to a range of $1.37 to $1.43.

Financial Data

(US$ in Thousands)	01/03/2004	12/28/2002	12/29/2001	12/30/2000	01/01/2000	01/02/1999	01/03/1998	12/28/1996
Earnings Per Share	1.27	1.15	1.07	0.26	0.78	0.97	0.96	1.00
Cash Flow Per Share	2.50	2.11	1.27	1.69	1.13	(0.10)	(0.0052)	0.34
Tang. Book Val. Per Share	9.83	8.38	8.64	7.77	7.64	6.87	6.19	5.46
Dividends Per Share	0.210	0.170	0.150	0.130	0.110	0.100	0.080	0.060
Dividend Payout %	16.53	15.21	14.48	51.92	15.06	10.74	8.63	6.89
Income Statement								
Total Revenues	888,926	827,106	720,066	701,291	665,576	669,329	665,125	511,029
Total Indirect Exp.	257,600	230,086	195,662	218,771	168,672	157,961	149,827	110,682
Depreciation & Amort.	17,947	16,860	17,621	17,695	14,881	13,036	9,151	7,147
Operating Income	74,462	70,608	68,116	15,111	50,249	61,921	58,909	46,718
Net Interest Inc./(Exp.)	(5,474)	(6,466)	(6,742)	(9,909)	(10,346)	(7,279)	(4,610)	(1,595)
Income Taxes	23,262	23,599	23,307	4,325	17,166	20,157	19,542	14,811
Eqty Earns/Minority Int.	(170)	(143)	...	...	...	...	...	...
Net Income	51,716	47,912	45,240	10,690	32,380	41,651	41,539	32,856
Average Shs. Outstg.	40,720	41,793	42,448	41,795	41,486	42,952	43,464	43,017
Balance Sheet								
Cash & Cash Equivalents	55,356	27,078	35,820	8,434	1,446	6,203	5,768	8,534
Total Current Assets	386,636	363,345	374,802	325,086	349,301	340,978	303,861	264,628
Total Assets	578,981	531,994	543,678	494,568	534,395	521,478	449,663	361,598
Total Current Liabilities	85,766	80,177	74,521	54,004	48,539	51,268	64,895	69,810
Long-Term Obligations	43,903	57,885	75,818	87,878	134,831	157,089	89,847	41,233
Net Stockholders' Equity	430,054	369,097	374,152	337,238	332,015	300,320	282,430	239,292
Net Working Capital	300,870	283,168	300,281	271,082	300,762	289,710	238,966	194,818
Shares Outstanding	39,453	39,970	41,555	41,552	41,300	40,765	42,553	41,698
Statistical Record								
Operating Profit Margin %	8.37	8.53	9.45	2.15	7.54	9.25	8.85	9.14
Return on Equity %	12.02	12.98	12.09	3.16	9.74	13.86	14.70	13.73
Return on Assets %	8.93	9.00	8.32	2.16	6.05	7.98	9.23	9.08
Debt/Total Assets %	7.58	10.88	13.94	17.76	25.23	30.12	19.98	11.40
Price Range	21.28-14.39	19.24-12.90	19.20-12.56	16.56-8.63	14.00-9.00	30.50-8.44	30.38-19.08	19.33-10.89
P/E Ratio	16.76-11.33	16.73-11.22	17.94-11.74	63.70-33.17	17.95-11.54	31.44-8.70	31.64-19.88	19.33-10.89
Average Yield %	1.13	1.05	0.94	1.18	0.98	0.51	0.33	0.40

Address: 9341 Courtland Drive, Rockford, MI 49351	**Officers:** Geoffrey B. Bloom – Chmn., Timothy J. ODonovan – Pres., C.E.O.	**Investor Contact:** (616) 866–5589
Telephone: (616) 866–5500		**Institutional Holding**
Web Site: www.wolverineworldwide.com		**No of Institutions:** –
		Shares: – **% Held:** –

WPS RESOURCES CORP.

Exchange	Symbol	Price	52Wk Range	Yield	P/E
NYS	WPS	$47.80 (3/31/2004)	48.86-38.55	4.56	14.75

*7 Year Price Score 125.0 *NYSE Composite Index=100 *12 Month Price Score 97.2

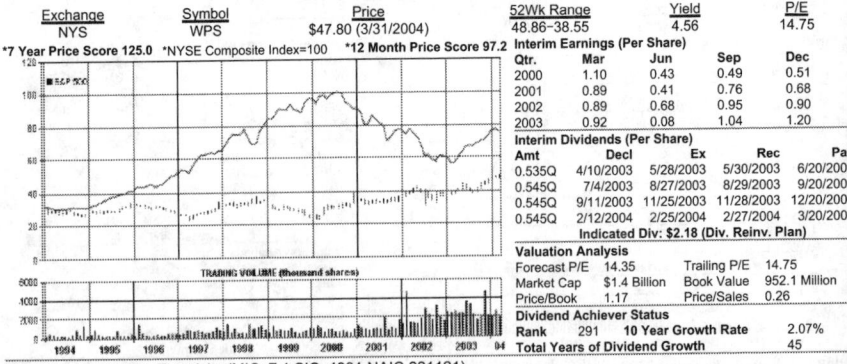

Interim Earnings (Per Share)

Qtr.	Mar	Jun	Sep	Dec
2000	1.10	0.43	0.49	0.51
2001	0.89	0.41	0.76	0.68
2002	0.89	0.68	0.95	0.90
2003	0.92	0.08	1.04	1.20

Interim Dividends (Per Share)

Amt	Decl	Ex	Rec	Pa
0.535Q	4/10/2003	5/28/2003	5/30/2003	6/20/200
0.545Q	7/4/2003	8/27/2003	8/29/2003	9/20/200
0.545Q	9/11/2003	11/25/2003	11/28/2003	12/20/200
0.545Q	2/12/2004	2/25/2004	2/27/2004	3/20/200

Indicated Div: $2.18 (Div. Reinv. Plan)

Valuation Analysis

Forecast P/E	14.35	Trailing P/E	14.75
Market Cap	$1.4 Billion	Book Value	952.1 Million
Price/Book	1.17	Price/Sales	0.26

Dividend Achiever Status

Rank	291	10 Year Growth Rate	2.07%
Total Years of Dividend Growth			45

Business Summary: Electricity (MIC: 7.1 SIC: 4931 NAIC:221121)

WPS Resources operates as a holding company with both regulated utility and non-regulated business units serving an 11,000 squar mile service territory in northeastern Wisconsin and an adjacent portion of the Upper Peninsula of Michigan. Co.'s principa wholly-owned subsidiaries are: Wisconsin Public Service Corporation (WPSC), a regulated electric and gas utility in Wisconsin an Michigan; Upper Peninsula Power Company, a regulated electric utility in Michigan; and WPS Energy Service, Inc. and WPS Powe Development, Inc., both non-regulated subsidiaries. As of Dec 31 2002, WPSC served 407,696 electric retail and 295,816 gas reta. customers.

Recent Developments: For the quarter ended Sep 30 2003, net income was $34.1 million compared with $30.5 million in th equivalent period a year earlier. The increase in net income was largely due to lower maintenance and interest expense. Total revenue surged to $1.01 billion from $377.1 million the year before, reflecting a change in accounting for revenues of WPS Energy Service Nonregulated revenues jumped to $742.8 million from $129.4 million as a result of the change in accounting noted above. Utilit revenues improved 8.8% to $269.5 million primarily due to increased retail and wholesale electric rates for Co.'s Wisconsin an Michigan customers.

Prospects: Co. continues to seek balanced growth within its utility and nonregulated businesses. However, more emphasis is bein placed on regulated growth, which should reduce exposure to the risks of the nonregulated markets. Looking ahead, Co.s' long-terr earnings per share growth rate target is 6.0% to 8.0% on an average annualized basis. Co.'s target for 2003 earnings per share is betwee $2.75 and $2.95, but Co. may be at the lower end of the range given its delayed rate case order in Wisconsin. Meanwhile, Co. agreed t sell its Sunbury Generating Station to Duquesne Power, L.P. The sale price is anticipated to be about $120.0 million for the plan inventory and related equipment.

Financial Data

(US$ in Thousands)	12/31/2003	12/31/2002	12/31/2001	12/31/2000	12/31/1999	12/31/1998	12/31/1997	12/31/1996
Earnings Per Share	3.24	3.42	2.74	2.53	2.24	1.76	2.25	2.0
Cash Flow Per Share	1.87	6.11	5.04	5.32	4.31	4.13	5.99	4.8
Tang. Book Val. Per Share	27.39	24.43	22.72	20.21	19.97	19.47	19.99	19.5
Dividends Per Share	2.160	2.120	2.080	2.040	2.000	1.960	1.920	1.88
Dividend Payout %	66.66	61.98	75.91	80.63	89.28	111.36	85.33	94.0
Income Statement								
Total Revenues	4,321,300	2,674,900	2,675,500	1,951,574	1,098,540	1,063,736	878,340	858,25
Total Indirect Exp.	182,200	138,100	122,800	133,641	115,562	118,176	103,989	92,04
Costs & Expenses	4,190,600	2,523,800	2,568,200	1,838,744	978,803	963,692	778,251	759,91
Operating Income	130,700	151,100	107,300	112,830	119,737	100,044	100,089	98,34
Net Interest Inc./(Exp.)	...	(58,100)	(55,800)	(50,780)	(32,768)	(28,637)	(26,403)	(25,00
Income Taxes	33,700	24,800	4,800	6,005	29,741	23,445	29,270	24,35
Eqty Earns/Minority Int.	...	...	...	...	...	611	797	34
Income from Cont Ops	110,600	...	...	...	62,670	...	...	
Net Income	97,800	112,500	80,700	70,104	59,565	49,763	56,853	50,86
Average Shs. Outstg.	33,200	31,700	28,300	26,463	26,644	26,511	23,873	23,89
Balance Sheet								
Net Property	1,828,700	1,610,200	1,463,600	1,198,324	1,150,902	1,010,158	886,360	892,85
Total Assets	4,292,300	3,207,900	2,870,000	2,816,142	1,816,548	1,510,387	1,299,602	1,330,66
Long-Term Obligations	871,900	824,400	727,800	72,955	73,585	343,037	304,008	305,78
Net Stockholders' Equity	1,054,300	833,900	767,000	593,945	587,493	568,390	529,023	518,72
Shares Outstanding	36,621	32,040	31,496	26,851	26,851	26,551	23,897	23,89
Statistical Record								
Operating Profit Margin %	3.02	5.64	4.01	5.78	10.89	9.40	11.39	11.4
Net Inc./Net Property %	5.34	6.98	5.51	5.85	5.17	4.92	6.41	5.6
Net Inc./Tot. Capital %	4.87	6.49	5.15	9.13	7.71	4.81	5.92	5.3
Return on Equity %	10.49	13.49	10.52	11.80	10.66	8.75	10.74	9.8
Accum. Depr./Gross Prop. %	40.60	49.84	51.29	53.59	53.24	54.88	54.33	52.
Price Range	46.77-37.12	42.45-31.52	36.55-31.82	38.69-22.81	35.50-24.63	37.25-30.25	34.19-23.50	34.13-28.2
P/E Ratio	14.44-11.46	12.41-9.22	13.34-11.61	15.29-9.02	15.85-10.99	21.16-17.19	15.19-10.44	17.06-14.
Average Yield %	5.27	5.55	6.08	6.89	6.74	5.88	6.89	5.9

Address: 700 North Adams Street, Green Bay, WI 54307-9001 Telephone: (920) 433-4901 Web Site: www.wpsr.com	Officers: Larry L. Weyers – Chmn., Pres., C.E.O., Thomas P. Meinz – Sr. V.P., Public Affairs Transfer Agents:American Stock Transfer &Trust Company New York NY	Investor Contact:920-433-1857 Institutional Holding No of Institutions: 7 Shares: 327,449 % Held: –

WRIGLEY (WILLIAM) JR. CO.

Exchange	Symbol	Price	52Wk Range	Yield	P/E
NYS	WWY	$59.12 (3/31/2004)	59.63–52.58	1.59	29.86

7 Year Price Score 125.5 *NYSE Composite Index=100 *12 Month Price Score 89.4

Interim Earnings (Per Share)

Qtr.	Mar	Jun	Sep	Dec
2000	0.32	0.40	0.37	0.36
2001	0.36	0.44	0.41	0.40
2002	0.38	0.49	0.44	0.47
2003	0.43	0.56	0.50	0.49

Interim Dividends (Per Share)

Amt	Decl	Ex	Rec	Pay
0.22Q	5/21/2003	7/11/2003	7/15/2003	8/1/2003
0.22Q	8/20/2003	10/10/2003	10/15/2003	11/3/2003
0.22Q	10/20/2003	1/13/2004	1/15/2004	2/2/2004
0.235Q	1/28/2004	4/13/2004	4/15/2004	5/3/2004

Indicated Div: $0.94

Valuation Analysis

Forecast P/E	24.95	Trailing P/E	29.86
Market Cap	$10.8 Billion	Book Value	1.8 Billion
Price/Book	5.61	Price/Sales	3.33

Dividend Achiever Status

Rank	182	10 Year Growth Rate	8.72%
Total Years of Dividend Growth		23

Business Summary: Food (MIC: 4.1 SIC: 2067 NAIC:311340)

William Wrigley Jr. is a manufacturer and marketer of chewing gum and other confectionery products, both in the U.S. and abroad. Co. has manufacturing facilities in four factories in the U.S. and 11 factories in other countries. Two domestic wholly–owned associated companies, L.A. Dreyfus Company and Northwestern Flavors, LLC, manufacture products other than chewing gum or confectionery products. Co.'s brands are sold in over 150 countries and territories. Brand names include *Doublemint®, Wrigley's Spearmint®, Big Red®, Juicy Fruit®, Winterfresh®, Extra®, Freedent®, Hubba Bubba®, Orbit®, Excel®, Eclipse®, Airwaves®, Alpine®, Cool Air®,* and *P.K.*

Recent Developments: For the year ended Dec 31 2003, net income advanced 11.1% to $445.9 million compared with $401.5 million in 2002. Net sales increased 11.8% to $3.07 billion from $2.75 billion the year before, reflecting a 6.0% sales gain in the Americas driven by an increase in shipments and positive mix, including higher sales of *Orbit®* in the U.S. and *Juicy Fruit®* pellet products in the U.S. and Canada. International net sales grew by 16.0% due to favorable currency translation, overall growth in volume and selected selling price increases. Strong shipments across Europe were partially offset by slightly lower shipments in Asia resulting from the impact of the severe acute respiratory syndrome crisis.

Prospects: On Mar 2 2004, Co. introduced *Eclipse Mints®*, the newest entry into the projected $554.0 million mint category. In addition, this is Co.'s first mint product released in the U.S. Co. will kick off the launch of *Eclipse Mints®* with "Conversations," an integrated–marketing campaign. On Jan 8 2004, Co. signed a purchase agreement with Agrolimen, a privately–held Spanish food conglomerate, for certain confectionery businesses of its Joyco Group for $272.0 million. The transaction includes Joyco's operations in China, France, India, Italy, Poland and Spain, as well as Cafosa, its chewing and bubble gum base business. New brands will include *Boomer®* bubble gum and *Pim Pom®* lollipops.

Financial Data

(US$ in Thousands)	12/31/2003	12/31/2002	12/31/2001	12/31/2000	12/31/1999	12/31/1998	12/31/1997	12/31/1996
Earnings Per Share	1.98	1.78	1.61	1.45	1.33	1.31	1.17	0.99
Cash Flow Per Share	2.86	1.66	1.73	1.97	1.54	1.39	1.26	1.23
Tang. Book Val. Per Share	8.09	6.76	5.67	4.87	4.97	4.98	4.24	3.86
Dividends Per Share	0.860	0.800	0.740	0.700	0.660	0.650	0.580	0.510
Dividend Payout %	43.68	45.22	46.27	48.27	50.00	49.42	50.00	56.52
Income Statement								
Total Revenues	3,069,088	2,746,318	2,429,646	2,145,706	2,079,238	2,023,355	1,954,174	1,850,601
Total Indirect Exp.	1,142,991	1,011,029	919,236	778,197	779,168	723,094	711,610	695,345
Depreciation & Amort.	120,040	85,568	68,326	57,880	61,225	55,774	50,439	47,288
Operating Income	649,362	585,074	513,356	463,243	445,139	441,494	395,198	360,209
Net Interest Inc./(Exp.)	...	...	...	...	(709)	(615)	(958)	(1,097)
Income Taxes	205,647	181,896	164,380	150,370	136,247	136,378	122,614	128,840
Net Income	445,894	401,525	362,986	328,942	308,183	304,501	271,626	230,272
Average Shs. Outstg.	224,963	225,145	225,349	227,036	231,722	231,928	231,928	231,966
Balance Sheet								
Cash & Cash Equivalents	527,726	304,897	333,235	329,900	306,914	351,684	327,355	300,563
Total Current Assets	1,290,591	1,006,292	913,843	828,715	803,746	843,172	797,673	729,424
Total Assets	2,520,410	2,108,296	1,765,648	1,574,740	1,547,745	1,520,855	1,343,126	1,233,543
Total Current Liabilities	464,794	386,087	332,324	288,210	251,825	218,626	225,816	218,152
Net Stockholders' Equity	1,820,821	1,522,576	1,276,197	1,132,897	1,138,775	1,157,032	985,379	897,431
Net Working Capital	825,797	620,205	581,519	540,505	551,921	624,546	571,857	511,272
Shares Outstanding	224,860	225,056	224,950	232,442	228,992	232,220	231,938	231,940
Statistical Record								
Operating Profit Margin %	21.15	21.30	21.12	21.58	21.40	21.81	20.22	19.46
Return on Equity %	24.48	26.37	28.44	29.03	27.06	26.31	27.56	25.65
Return on Assets %	17.69	19.04	20.55	20.88	19.91	20.02	20.22	18.66
Price Range	58.11–51.18	58.35–44.52	52.92–43.34	47.91–30.31	50.00–33.66	51.66–36.56	40.81–27.63	31.00–24.31
P/E Ratio	29.35–25.85	32.78–25.01	32.87–26.92	33.04–20.91	37.59–25.31	39.43–27.91	34.88–23.61	31.31–24.56
Average Yield %	1.55	1.50	1.53	1.80	1.57	1.53	1.73	1.82

Address: 410 North Michigan Avenue, Chicago, IL 60611 Telephone: (312) 644–2121 Web Site: www.wrigley.com	Officers: William Wrigley – Chmn., Pres., C.E.O., Dushan Petrovich – Sr. V.P., Chief Admin. Officer Transfer Agents: EquiServe Trust Company, N.A., Providence, RI	Investor Contact: 800–874–0474 Institutional Holding No of Institutions: 8 Shares: 9,414,934 % Held: –

AGF MANAGEMENT LTD

Exchange	Symbol	Price	52Wk Range	Yield	P/E
TSX	AGF B	C$18.85 (3/31/2004)	19.17–12.11	2.33	20.27

*7 Year Price Score 99.9 ***NYSE Composite Index=100** ***12 Month Price Score 105.1**

TRADING VOLUME (thousand shares)

Interim Earnings (Per Share) Can$

Qtr.	Feb	May	Aug	Nov
1999–00	0.26	0.30	0.33	0.18
2000–01	0.68	0.63	0.28	0.18
2001–02	0.37	0.40	0.34	0.19
2002–03	0.30	0.21	0.23	(0.27)

Interim Dividends (Per Share) Can$

Amt	Decl	Ex	Rec	Pa
0.075Q	6/25/2003	7/4/2003	7/8/2003	7/18/200
0.08Q	9/24/2003	10/2/2003	10/6/2003	10/16/200
0.08Q	12/9/2003	12/17/2003	12/19/2003	1/7/200
0.11Q	3/31/2004	4/8/2004	4/13/2004	4/23/200

Indicated Div: Can$0.44

Valuation Analysis

Forecast P/E	N/A	Trailing P/E	20.27
Market Cap	$80.8 Million	Book Value	N/A
Price/Book	N/A	Price/Sales	N/A

Dividend Achiever Status

Rank	10	5 Year Growth Rate 17.81%
Total Years of Dividend Growth		7

Business Summary: Wealth Management (MIC: 8.8 SIC: 6282 NAIC:523930)

AGF Management is an investment management company with offices across Canada and subsidiaries around the world. Co. serves mo than 1.0 million investors and manages about C$31.00 billion in total assets. Co.'s products and services include a diversified family more than 50 mutual funds, AGF Harmony tailored investment program, AGF Private Investment Management and AGF Trust GIC loans and mortgages. In addition to offices across Canada, Co. has international operations in London, Dublin, Singapore, Tokyo a Beijing. Moreover, Co. has diversified revenue streams from complementary businesses including Unisen, Smith & Williamson a Investmaster Group.

Recent Developments: For the year ended Nov 30 2003, net income dropped 63.2% to C$44.0 million compared with C$119.8 milli in 2002. Results for 2003 and 2002 included integration costs of C$5.4 million and C$6.5 million, and the write-down of short-term investments of C$643,000 and C$1.4 million, respectively. Results for 2003 also included a gain on the sale of investment of C$12.8 million, while results for 2002 included a non-controlling interest share of loss of subsidiary of C$83,000. Revenue was C$566.1 million down 10.2% from C$630.1 million in the prior year. Provision for loan losses jumped 38.1% to C$2.0 million versus C$1.4 million the year before.

Prospects: Co. has taken steps to improve its mutual fund sales performance and maintain redemption levels. Merging funds and streamlining external investment managers will help to focus sales of products that have the best potential for growth. Meanwhile, th trend of outsourcing should present market opportunities for Unisen, Co.'s third-party administrative services and transfer agency. In 2004, Unisen will focus on revenue growth through new client acquisition and by providing additional services to existing customers. Unisen is also expected to achieve further cost synergies once the migration of all third-party unitholder record-keeping clients into Unitrax is completed in mid-2004.

Financial Data

(Can$ in Thousands)	9 Mos	6 Mos	3 Mos	11/30/2002	11/30/2001	11/30/2000	11/30/1999	11/30/199
Earnings Per Share	0.75	0.52	0.30	1.30	1.77	1.07	0.76	0.
Dividends Per Share	0.280	0.270	0.260	0.250	0.220	0.180	0.150	0.1
Dividend Payout %	37.33	51.92	86.66	19.61	12.42	16.82	19.73	21.
Income Statement								
Total Revenues	446,926	299,528	158,711	654,103	639,994	508,681	356,703	288,8
Total Indirect Exp.	327,150	217,725	110,660	464,515	463,727	349,368	242,846	195,1
Depreciation & Amort.	116,014	76,606	38,688	147,181	165,645	92,224	70,276	52,7
Operating Income	96,583	66,214	40,265	164,765	151,153	147,839	103,034	82,8
Income Taxes	26,809	18,211	11,893	43,645	(14,867)	59,987	41,324	34,0
Eqty Earns/Minority Int.	...	...	...	(83)	(481)	(36)	...	
Net Income	69,774	48,003	28,372	119,839	163,754	87,888	61,710	48,7
Balance Sheet								
Cash & Cash Equivalents	27,121	24,202	23,938	28,385	23,466	94,876	56,231	53,2
Total Current Assets	84,200	90,251	83,817	84,296	79,508	127,227	85,622	76,0
Total Assets	1,927,679	1,987,741	1,988,267	1,974,920	1,508,473	1,250,636	628,821	526,1
Total Current Liabilities	79,847	74,699	74,029	102,220	118,954	224,412	44,360	40,9
Long–Term Obligations	150,447	194,929	214,887	225,403	165,481	278,051	72,048	81,4
Net Stockholders' Equity	942,569	927,415	912,492	887,566	764,707	472,048	284,244	233,3
Net Working Capital	...	...	9,788	(17,924)	(39,446)	(97,185)	41,262	35,0
Shares Outstanding	92,572	92,284	91,611	91,100	89,338	83,046	78,044	77,0
Statistical Record								
Operating Profit Margin %	21.61	22.10	25.37	25.18	23.61	29.06	28.88	28.
Return on Equity %	7.40	5.17	3.10	13.50	21.41	18.61	21.71	20.
Return on Assets %	3.61	2.41	1.42	6.06	10.85	7.02	9.81	9.
Debt/Total Assets %	7.80	9.80	10.80	11.41	10.97	22.23	11.45	15.
Price Range	17.13–12.11	16.00–12.11	16.00–13.21	28.18–11.75	28.90–18.20	28.20–10.50	14.00–9.03	14.05–6.
P/E Ratio	22.84–16.15	30.77–23.29	53.33–44.03	21.68–9.04	16.33–10.28	26.36–9.81	18.42–11.88	23.81–11.
Average Yield %	1.92	1.94	1.76	1.23	0.88	0.95	1.31	1.

Address: P.O. Box 50, Toronto, ON M5K 1E9 Telephone: (416) 367–1900 Web Site: www.agf.com	Officers: C. Warren Goldring – Chmn., W. Robert Farquharson – Vice–Chmn., Chief Investment. Off.	Institutional Holding No of Institutions: 2 Shares: 4,230,500 % Held: 4.70

ATCO LTD.

Exchange	Symbol	Price	52Wk Range	Yield	P/E
TSX	ACO X	C$53.00 (3/31/2004)	54.00–41.15	2.64	13.05

7 Year Price Score 116.2 *NYSE Composite Index=100 **12 Month Price Score 92.1**

Interim Earnings (Per Share) Can$

Qtr.	Mar	Jun	Sep	Dec
2000	1.31	0.68	0.74	1.02
2001	1.40	0.75	0.81	1.16
2002	2.57	0.72	0.87	1.23
2003	1.51	0.67	0.75	1.42

Interim Dividends (Per Share) Can$

Amt	Decl	Ex	Rec	Pay
0.32Q	4/25/2003	6/12/2003	6/16/2003	6/30/2003
0.32Q	7/24/2003	9/11/2003	9/15/2003	9/30/2003
0.32Q	10/21/2003	12/10/2003	12/12/2003	12/31/2003
0.35Q	2/26/2004	3/15/2004	3/17/2004	3/31/2004

Indicated Div: Can$1.40

Valuation Analysis

Forecast P/E	9.95	Trailing P/E	13.05
Market Cap	$1.4 Billion	Book Value	N/A
Price/Book	N/A	Price/Sales	N/A

Dividend Achiever Status

Rank	15	5 Year Growth Rate	13.49%
Total Years of Dividend Growth			10

Business Summary: Electricity (MIC: 7.1 SIC: 4911 NAIC:221122)

Atco is a management holding company. Through subsidiaries, Co. operates the following groups: The Power Generation segment includes the supply of electricity. The Logistics & Energy unit includes transportation and supply of natural gas. The Utilities unit includes natural gas, electricity and water services and engineering, procurement and construction services. The Industrial group includes the manufacture and sale of transportable workforce shelters and space rentals products. The Technologies group includes information systems and services, sale of fuel byproducts and manufacture of wood preservation products

Recent Developments: For the year ended Dec 31 2003, net earnings declined 19.5% to C$131.2 million compared with C$163.0 million in 2002. Earnings were hampered by the weak performances of ATCO Pipelines, ATCO Frontec, ATCO Structures, and ATCO Noise Management. Results for 2002 included a gain on the sale of Viking-Kinsella property of C$110.1 million. Revenues rose 22.9% to $3.93 billion from C$3.20 billion in the prior year, primarily due to the increased price of natural gas and electricity purchased by ATCO Gas and ATCO Electric, and higher natural gas prices on gas sales by ATCO Midstream.

Prospects: Going forward, Co. should continue to benefit from revenue growth due to higher natural gas prices and increasing business activity in several of Co.'s businesses. However, Co.'s ATCO Pipelines, ATCO Frontec, ATCO Structures and ATCO Noise management subsidiaries may continue to suffer from weak economic conditions. Moreover, expenses may continue to rise due to increased natural gas supply and purchased power costs and higher operations and maintenance expenses. Nevertheless, cash flow from operations continues to be strong, rising 5.4% to C$573.6 million at Dec 31 2003 versus the prior year.

Financial Data

(Can$ in Thousands)	12/31/2003	12/31/2002	12/31/2001	12/31/2000	12/31/1999	12/31/1998	12/31/1997	12/31/1996
Earnings Per Share	4.35	5.39	4.12	3.75	3.32	2.96	2.68	2.41
Cash Flow Per Share	17.08	12.22	...	...	...	...	...	...
Dividends Per Share	1.250	1.130	1.010	0.890	0.770	0.650	0.530	0.410
Dividend Payout %	28.73	20.96	24.51	23.73	23.19	21.96	19.78	17.01
Income Statement								
Total Revenues	3,929,700	3,196,300	3,754,300	3,076,000	2,374,800	2,071,400	2,045,100	1,937,300
Total Indirect Exp.	3,309,300	2,610,500	3,165,400	2,480,700	1,828,800	1,552,500	1,550,100	1,434,500
Costs & Expenses	3,508,200	2,799,700	3,368,500	2,680,600	2,014,200	1,728,000	1,719,800	1,619,000
Depreciation & Amort.	284,700	257,100	257,500	253,500	241,000	211,000	202,800	195,100
Operating Income	421,500	396,600	385,800	395,400	360,600	343,400	325,300	318,300
Income Taxes	159,800	196,700	174,800	193,100	180,800	187,300	173,200	175,900
Minority Earns/Minority Int.	158,000	165,000	131,000	126,100	111,200	102,000	100,300	91,800
Income from Cont Ops	...	...	...	...	...	...	...	73,300
Net Income	131,200	163,000	124,400	112,700	100,700	88,900	81,200	80,100
Average Shs. Outstg.	30,172	30,257	29,731	29,723	29,931	30,044	30,261	30,468
Balance Sheet								
Net Property	5,128,400	4,949,200	4,590,800	4,168,200	3,976,600	3,898,400	3,639,400	3,509,100
Total Assets	6,591,200	6,403,300	5,833,500	5,815,600	4,934,900	4,793,700	4,405,100	4,241,600
Long–Term Obligations	2,789,800	2,892,400	2,658,000	2,468,800	2,226,900	2,106,000	1,844,700	1,793,000
Net Stockholders' Equity	1,133,600	1,044,800	911,600	822,300	744,200	681,400	613,000	567,700
Shares Outstanding	29,796	29,816	29,733	29,722	29,791	30,048	30,026	30,475
Statistical Record								
Operating Profit Margin %	10.72	12.40	10.27	12.85	15.18	16.57	15.90	16.43
Return on Equity %	11.57	15.60	13.64	13.70	13.53	13.04	13.24	14.10
Accum. Depr./Gross Prop. %	33.84	33.20	33.13	33.84	33.08	31.83	31.49	30.20
Price Range	49.75–41.15	54.95–41.00	53.00–42.25	47.75–28.40	43.75–32.70	39.00–30.25	34.00–23.60	24.00–17.75
P/E Ratio	11.44–9.46	10.19–7.61	12.86–10.25	12.73–7.57	13.18–9.85	13.18–10.22	12.69–8.81	9.96–7.37
Average Yield %	2.73	2.32	2.13	2.55	1.94	1.85	1.87	2.05

Address: 1400 909–11th Avenue SW, Calgary, AB T2R 1N6 Telephone: (403) 292–7500 Web Site: www.atco.com	Officers: Ronald D. Southern – Chmn., William L. Britton Q.C. – Vice-Chmn.	Investor Contact:800–387–0825 Institutional Holding No of Institutions: 1 Shares: 40,100 % Held: –

BANK OF MONTREAL

Exchange	Symbol	Price	52Wk Range	Yield	P/E
TSX	BMO	C$54.23 (3/31/2004)	58.77–39.63	2.95	14.70

*7 Year Price Score 131.7 *NYSE Composite Index=100 *12 Month Price Score 105.1

TRADING VOLUME (thousand shares)

Interim Earnings (Per Share) Can$

Qtr.	Jan	Apr	Jul	Oct
2000–01	1.45	1.10	0.83	(0.72)
2001–02	0.71	0.57	0.65	0.75
2002–03	0.75	0.77	0.95	0.97
2003–04	1.00	...	...	...

Interim Dividends (Per Share) Can$

Amt	Decl	Ex	Rec	Pa
0.33Q	7/22/2003	8/4/2003	8/6/2003	8/28/200
0.35Q	8/26/2003	11/7/2003	11/12/2003	11/27/200
0.35Q	11/25/2003	2/4/2004	2/6/2004	2/26/200
0.40Q	2/24/2004	5/5/2004	5/7/2004	5/28/200

Indicated Div: Can$1.60 (Div. Reinv. Plan)

Valuation Analysis

Forecast P/E	12.49	Trailing P/E	14.70
Market Cap	$0.00	Book Value	182.6 Billion
Price/Book	N/A	Price/Sales	N/A

Dividend Achiever Status

Rank	22	5 Year Growth Rate	8.77%
Total Years of Dividend Growth			11

Business Summary: Commercial Banking (MIC: 8.1 SIC: 6029 NAIC:522110)

Bank of Montreal offers a broad range of credit and non–credit products and services to individuals, industry, financial institutions an governments directly and through special–purpose domestic and foreign subsidiaries. Co. operates 970 bank branches in Canada; an operates internationally in 10 other countries. Through the Harris Bank group, Co., operates its own banking business in the U.S. ar provides retail banking, private client, personal trust services, corporate and investment banking. Co. also provides a full range investment dealer services through the BMO Nesbitt Burns group of companies. As of Oct 31 2003, Co.'s total assets amounted approx. C$265.5 billion.

Recent Developments: For the three months ended Jan 31 2004, net income rose 33.3% to C$532.0 million compared with C$399. million in the equivalent quarter of 2003. Net income benefited from better credit performance and Co.'s continued focus on improvin productivity. Results for included an investment securities gain of C$40.0 million in 2004 and a loss of C$16.0 million in 2003. Net interes income increased 2.0% to C$1.26 billion from C$1.23 billion the year before. Provision for credit losses plunged 90.0% to C$15.0 millio versus C$150.0 million a year earlier. Non-interest income and non-interest revenue grew 10.3% to C$2.35 billion, while non-interes expense slipped 0.8% to C$1.56 billion.

Prospects: Looking ahead to fiscal 2004, Co. anticipates that improving conditions in both the Canadian and U.S. economies shoul support growth in mortgages and facilitate a pickup in business investment and lending. Meanwhile, Co.'s financial targets for the ye include earnings per share growth of 10.0% to 15.0% and return on equity of 16.0% to 18.0%. Moreover, provision for credit losses expected to be about C$500.0 million or less. Also, Co. is looking to improve its cash productivity by 150 to 200 basis points for the yea Separately, Co. agreed to acquire Lakeland Community Bank in Lake County, IL. The acquisition should complement Co.'s existir presence in the Chicagoland area.

Financial Data

(Can$ in Millions)	3 Mos	10/31/2003	10/31/2002	10/31/2001	10/31/2000	10/31/1999	10/31/1998	10/31/199
Earnings Per Share	1.00	3.44	2.68	2.66	3.28	2.36	2.33	2.3
Dividends Per Share	1.340	1.290	1.180	1.090	0.980	0.920	0.880	0.8
Dividend Payout %	134.00	37.50	44.02	40.97	30.03	39.19	37.76	34.
Income Statement								
Total Interest Income	2,212	8,927	9,135	13,000	14,303	13,174	14,121	11,5
Total Interest Expense	955	4,028	4,306	8,501	10,099	8,895	10,097	7,4
Net Interest Income	1,242	4,899	4,829	4,499	4,204	4,279	4,024	4,0
Provision for Loan Losses	15	455	820	980	358	320	130	22
Non–Interest Expense	1,561	6,542	6,850	6,651	5,659	5,467	4,963	4,88
Income Before Taxes	787	2,577	1,903	2,070	2,914	2,182	2,179	2,1
Eqty Earns/Minority Int.	15	64	62	42	19	21	25	
Net Income	532	1,825	1,417	1,471	1,857	1,382	1,350	1,30
Average Shs. Outstg.	515	507	499	523	542	545	538	5
Balance Sheet								
Total Assets	265,394	256,494	252,864	239,409	233,396	230,615	222,590	207,8.
Total Deposits	178,069	171,551	161,838	154,290	156,697	156,874	143,983	144,2
Long–Term Obligations	2,460	2,856	3,794	4,674	4,911	4,712	4,791	3,8
Total Liabilities	252,458	244,012	240,970	228,727	221,455	219,634	211,982	198,9
Net Stockholders' Equity	12,936	12,482	11,894	10,682	11,941	10,981	10,608	8,9
Shares Outstanding	502	499	492	489	522	534	528	5
Statistical Record								
Return on Equity %	4.11	14.62	11.91	13.77	15.55	12.58	12.72	14.
Return on Assets %	0.20	0.71	0.56	0.61	0.79	0.59	0.60	0.
Equity/Assets %	4.87	4.86	4.70	4.46	5.11	4.76	4.76	4.
Non–Int. Exp./Tot. Inc. %	47.05	73.28	74.98	51.16	39.56	41.49	35.14	42.
Price Range	58.77–49.33	50.06–38.10	40.30–32.10	44.23–32.80	35.75–21.50	34.65–24.88	43.05–26.35	30.63–19.
P/E Ratio	58.77–49.33	14.55–11.08	15.04–11.98	16.63–12.33	10.90–6.55	14.68–10.54	18.48–11.31	13.26–8.
Average Yield %	2.49	3.03	3.24	2.81	3.48	3.12	2.50	3.

Address: 129 St. Jaques Street, Montreal, QC H2Y 1L6 Telephone: (514) 877-7110 Web Site: www.bmo.com	Officers: F. Anthony Comper – Chmn., C.E.O., William A. Downe – Deputy Chair, C.E.O. of BMO	Investor Contact: (416) 867-6785 Institutional Holding No of Institutions: 64 Shares: 198,759,440 % Held: 40.50

BMTC GROUP INC.

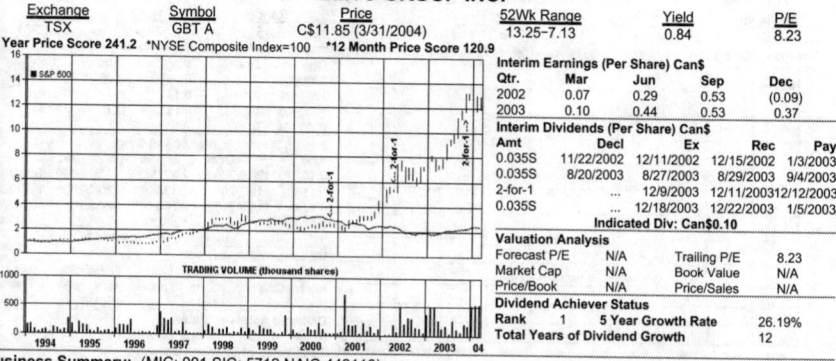

Exchange	Symbol	Price	52Wk Range	Yield	P/E
TSX	GBT A	C$11.85 (3/31/2004)	13.25-7.13	0.84	8.23

Year Price Score 241.2 *NYSE Composite Index=100 *12 Month Price Score 120.9

Interim Earnings (Per Share) Can$

Qtr.	Mar	Jun	Sep	Dec
2002	0.07	0.29	0.53	(0.09)
2003	0.10	0.44	0.53	0.37

Interim Dividends (Per Share) Can$

Amt	Decl	Ex	Rec	Pay
0.035S	11/22/2002	12/11/2002	12/15/2002	1/3/2003
0.035S	8/20/2003	8/27/2003	8/29/2003	9/4/2003
2-for-1	...	12/9/2003	12/11/2003	12/12/2003
0.035S	...	12/18/2003	12/22/2003	1/5/2004

Indicated Div: Can$0.10

Valuation Analysis

Forecast P/E	N/A	Trailing P/E	8.23
Market Cap	N/A	Book Value	N/A
Price/Book	N/A	Price/Sales	N/A

Dividend Achiever Status

Rank	1	5 Year Growth Rate	26.19%
Total Years of Dividend Growth			12

Business Summary: (MIC: 001 SIC: 5712 NAIC:442110)

BMTC Group is a holding company. Through its subsidiaries, Brault et Martineau Inc. and Ameublements Tanguay, Inc., Co. manages and operates a retail sales network of furniture and household and electronic appliances in Quebec. As of Dec 31 2002, Co.'s network was comprised of twenty stores in the Montreal, Quebec City, Laval, Ste-Therese, Ste-Foy, St-Georges, Three Rivers, Sherbrooke, Chicoutimi, Riviere-du-Loup, Rimouski and Gatineau regions in Quebec. Co.'s network also includes two distribution and administrative centers in Montreal and Quebec City.

Recent Developments: For the twelve months ended Dec 31 2003, net earnings declined 3.8% to C$37.0 million compared with C$38.4 million in 2002. Results for 2003 included an after-tax compensation charge of C$8.0 million versus an after-tax charge of C$6.3 million in 2002 due to the application of the new recommendations with respect to stock-based compensation and other stock-based payments. Revenues rose 6.6% to C$802.9 million from C$753.4 million the year before. Working capital showed a deficit of C$13.4 million, a reversal of C$33.2 million from 2002, primarily due to Co.'s share repurchases of C$54.3 million during 2003.

Prospects: Co. was able to generate solid improvement in sales for 2003, which suggests that market conditions may be strengthening. Moreover, Co. feels that backed by its solid financial position and aggressive merchandising and advertising initiatives, that it can continue to capture additional market share. Meanwhile, Co. approved changes to its supplementary retirement entitlements that were available to certain management personnel and its funding, which are set to improve retirement benefits and permit early retirement under certain conditions. As a result, Co. incurred an after-tax charge of C$1.6 million.

Financial Data
(In$ in Thousands)

	12/31/2003	12/31/2002	12/31/2001
Earnings Per Share	0.91	0.80	0.44
Cash Flow Per Share	2.96	0.73	0.66
Tang. Book Val. Per Share	2.97	3.01	2.48
Dividends Per Share	0.070	0.058	0.050
Dividend Payout %	7.69	7.14	11.36
Income Statement			
Total Revenues	802,870	807,937	642,532
Total Indirect Exp.	746,309	749,462	607,097
Depreciation & Amort.	3,875	3,927	3,389
Operating Income	55,220	57,326	34,193
Income Taxes	18,229	18,884	12,472
Net Income	36,991	38,442	21,721
Average Shs. Outstg.	40,458	47,758	49,416
Balance Sheet			
Cash & Cash Equivalents	57,487	7,875	2,815
Total Current Assets	137,142	145,329	95,008
Total Assets	264,776	260,563	206,289
Total Current Liabilities	150,584	125,490	87,020
Net Stockholders' Equity	113,233	133,808	117,599
Net Working Capital	(13,442)	19,839	7,988
Shares Outstanding	38,000	44,400	47,339
Statistical Record			
Operating Profit Margin %	6.87	7.09	5.32
Return on Equity %	32.66	28.72	18.47
Return on Assets %	13.97	14.75	10.52
Price Range	13.25-6.88	7.75-4.13	4.50-2.00
P/E Ratio	14.56-7.55	9.69-5.16	10.23-4.55
Average Yield %	0.74	0.81	1.71

Address: 8500 Place Marien, Montreal, QC H1B 5W8
Telephone: (514) 648 5757
Web Site: www.braultetmartineau.com

Officers: Yves Des Groseillers – Pres., C.E.O., Yves Des Groseillers – Chmn.

Institutional Holding
No of Institutions: 1
Shares: 116,721   % Held:

BUHLER INDUSTRIES, INC.

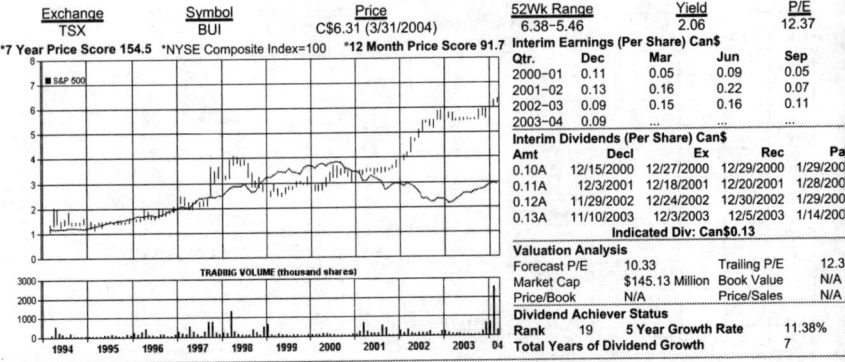

Exchange	Symbol	Price	52Wk Range	Yield	P/E
TSX	BUI	C$6.31 (3/31/2004)	6.38–5.46	2.06	12.37

*7 Year Price Score 154.5 *NYSE Composite Index=100 *12 Month Price Score 91.7

Interim Earnings (Per Share) Can$

Qtr.	Dec	Mar	Jun	Sep
2000–01	0.11	0.05	0.09	0.05
2001–02	0.13	0.16	0.22	0.07
2002–03	0.09	0.15	0.16	0.11
2003–04	0.09	...	...	...

Interim Dividends (Per Share) Can$

Amt	Decl	Ex	Rec	Pay
0.10A	12/15/2000	12/27/2000	12/29/2000	1/29/200
0.11A	12/3/2001	12/18/2001	12/20/2001	1/28/200
0.12A	11/29/2002	12/24/2002	12/30/2002	1/29/200
0.13A	11/10/2003	12/3/2003	12/5/2003	1/14/200

Indicated Div: Can$0.13

Valuation Analysis

Forecast P/E	10.33	Trailing P/E	12.3
Market Cap	$145.13 Million	Book Value	N/A
Price/Book	N/A	Price/Sales	N/A

Dividend Achiever Status

Rank	19	5 Year Growth Rate	11.38%
Total Years of Dividend Growth			7

TRADING VOLUME (thousand shares)

Business Summary: Machinery Supply Retail (MIC: 12.9 SIC: 5083 NAIC:423820)

Buhler Industries is engaged in the design, manufacturing and distributing of a wide range of agricultural equipment marketed throughout North America under five primary brand names: Buhler®, Allied®, Farm King®, Inland® and Buhler Versatile®. Co.'s products include augers, belt conveyors, box scrapers, cultivators, discs, drag harrows, front-end loaders, grain cleaners, hammermills, hay rakes, landscape rakes, mounted following harrows, mowers, rear blades, rollermills, rotary tillers, round bale carrier, round baler, snowblowers, square bale carrier, swath rollers, tractors, and wheel loaders.

Recent Developments: For the quarter ended Dec 31 2003, net income climbed 5.4% to C$2.1 million compared with C$2.0 million in the corresponding quarter of the previous year. Revenues totaled C$42.3 million, up 9.4% compared with C$38.7 million a year earlier, reflecting consistent increases in Co.'s core products. Gross profit was C$8.6 million, 20.3% of revenues, versus C$8.4 million, or 21.7% of revenues, the year before. Gross margin was down due to a weakened U.S. dollar. Operating income declined 4.5% to C$5.0 million from $5.2 million the prior year. Cash flow grew 3.7% to C$3.8 million.

Prospects: Looking ahead, revenues should continue to benefit from higher sales of Co.'s core products and new tractor dealers being added each month. However, Co. holds some concern about the possible adverse effect that the Mad Cow Disease (BSE) alarm may have on future business levels. Meanwhile, Co. expect gross profit to remain in the range of 20.0% to 22.0% as a result of the weakened U.S. dollar. Separately, Co. anticipates earnings to be affected by unfavorable exchange rate in the short term; however, long term earnings should continue to increase, provided that the U.S. dollar stabilizes and the BSE issue is resolved.

Financial Data

(Can$ in Thousands)	3 Mos	09/30/2003	09/30/2002	09/30/2001	09/30/2000	09/30/1999	09/30/1998	09/30/1997
Earnings Per Share	0.09	0.51	0.58	0.30	0.30	0.23	0.28	0.2
Dividends Per Share	0.120	0.120	0.110	0.100	0.090	0.080	0.070	0.06
Dividend Payout %	133.33	23.52	18.96	33.33	30.00	34.78	25.00	25.0
Income Statement								
Total Revenues	42,303	181,162	232,619	187,633	116,700	79,961	89,194	85,37
Total Indirect Exp.	3,598	26,712	29,947	24,462	20,076	16,967	17,183	16,20
Depreciation & Amort.	1,669	6,894	7,339	7,684	5,520	5,126	4,808	4,80
Operating Income	4,993	14,521	19,538	6,948	10,226	9,240	12,060	10,85
Net Interest Inc./(Exp.)	146	703	369	1,032	671	434	458	45
Income Taxes	541	2,647	5,134	(1,313)	2,393	3,131	5,216	4,27
Eqty Earns/Minority Int.	...	267	809	847	903	224	...	...
Net Income	2,093	11,630	13,360	7,115	7,298	5,797	7,113	6,13
Average Shs. Outstg.	...	...	...	...	24,225	24,459	24,968	25,51
Balance Sheet								
Total Current Assets	135,123	132,272	110,455	87,456	99,635	34,403	32,010	28,93
Total Assets	179,918	178,281	156,305	127,531	148,973	74,843	61,139	60,71
Total Current Liabilities	53,889	49,742	49,860	42,239	54,038	14,195	13,004	16,13
Long–Term Obligations	40,530	40,577	42,690	31,850	35,200	1,704	2,770	6,51
Net Stockholders' Equity	69,971	70,868	61,998	53,442	51,659	47,327	44,790	37,49
Net Working Capital	81,234	82,530	60,595	45,217	45,597	20,208	19,006	12,80
Shares Outstanding	23,000	23,000	23,000	23,483	24,225	24,459	24,968	24,12
Statistical Record								
Operating Profit Margin %	11.80	8.01	8.39	3.70	8.76	11.55	13.52	12.7
Return on Equity %	2.99	16.41	21.54	13.31	14.12	12.24	15.88	16.3
Return on Assets %	1.16	6.52	8.54	5.57	4.89	7.74	11.63	10.0
Debt/Total Assets %	22.52	22.76	27.31	24.97	23.62	2.27	4.53	10.7
Price Range	5.94–5.52	5.92–5.20	5.50–3.48	3.60–3.00	3.70–2.65	3.24–2.35	4.10–2.39	2.50–1.7
P/E Ratio	66.00–61.33	11.61–10.20	9.48–6.00	12.00–10.00	12.33–8.83	14.09–10.22	14.64–8.54	10.42–7.0
Average Yield %	2.09	2.16	2.47	2.91	2.94	2.90	1.99	2.8

Address: 1201 Regent Avenue West, Winnipeg, MB R2C 3B2 **Telephone:** (204) 661-8711 **Web Site:** www.buhler.com	**Officers:** John Buhler – Chmn., C.E.O., Craig P. Engel – Pres., C.O.O.	**Institutional Holding** **No of Institutions:** N/A **Shares:** N/A **% Held:** N/A

308

CANADIAN NATIONAL RAILWAY CO.

Exchange	Symbol	Price	52Wk Range	Yield	P/E
TSX	CNR	C$51.24 (3/31/2004)	55.19-42.00	1.52	20.25

*Year Price Score 137.2 *NYSE Composite Index=100 *12 Month Price Score 100.3

Interim Earnings (Per Share) Can$

Qtr.	Mar	Jun	Sep	Dec
2001	0.92	0.12	0.84	0.53
2002	0.76	0.69	0.88	(0.45)
2003	0.85	0.60	0.72	0.36

Interim Dividends (Per Share) Can$

Amt	Decl	Ex	Rec	Pay
0.25Q	7/22/2003	9/5/2003	9/9/2003	9/30/2003
0.25Q	10/21/2003	12/4/2003	12/8/2003	12/29/2003
50%	1/28/2004	3/1/2004	2/23/2004	2/27/2004
0.195Q	1/28/2004	3/4/2004	3/8/2004	3/29/2004
		Indicated Div: Can$0.78		

Valuation Analysis

Forecast P/E	12.21	Trailing P/E	20.25
Market Cap	$10.3 Billion	Book Value	N/A
Price/Book	N/A	Price/Sales	N/A

Dividend Achiever Status

Rank	14	5 Year Growth Rate	13.54%
Total Years of Dividend Growth		7

Business Summary: Rail Transport (MIC: 15.5 SIC: 4011 NAIC:482111)

Canadian National Railway is engaged in the rail transportation business. Co. spans Canada and mid-America, from the Atlantic and Pacific oceans to the Gulf of Mexico, serving the ports of Vancouver, Prince Rupert, B.C., Montreal, Halifax, New Orleans and Mobile, Alabama, and the cities of Toronto, Buffalo, Chicago, Detroit, Duluth, Minnesota/Superior, Wisconsin, Green Bay, Wisconsin, Minneapolis/St. Paul, Memphis, St. Louis and Jackson, Mississippi, with connections to all points in North America. Co.'s movement of goods includes petroleum and chemicals, grain and fertilizers, coal, metals and minerals, forest products, intermodal and automotive.

Recent Developments: For the year ended Dec 31 2003, income grew 20.8% to C$966.0 million, before an accounting credit of C$48.0 million, compared with net income of C$800.0 million in 2002. Earnings benefited from net deferred income tax recoveries of C$44.0 million in 2003 relating mainly to the resolution of matters pertaining to prior years' income taxes, partially offset by the adverse effect of the appreciation in the Canadian dollar relative to the U.S. dollar. Results for 2002 included U.S. personal injury and other claims provision charge of C$281.0 million and workforce reduction charges of C$120.0 million. Revenues fell 3.7% to C$5.88 billion. Operating income rose 21.0% to $1.78 billion.

Prospects: Co. expects that its capital expenditures in 2004 will grow slightly from C$1.04 billion in 2003 due to the acquisition of additional locomotives, and will include funds required for ongoing renewal of the basic plant and other acquisitions and investments required to improve Co.'s operating efficiency and customer service. Separately, during March 2004, Co. announced that it anticipates that its month long strike will reduce its first quarter earnings per share by between C$0.08 and C$0.10. Accordingly, earnings per share for the first quarter are expected to be about C$0.69.

Financial Data

(Can$ in Thousands)	12/31/2003	12/31/2002	12/31/2001	12/31/2000	12/31/1999	12/31/1998	12/31/1997	12/31/1996
Earnings Per Share	2.52	1.88	2.41	2.54	2.01	1.61	1.65	0.48
Cash Flow Per Share	5.15	3.85	4.08	3.70	...	...	...	...
Dividends Per Share	0.660	0.570	0.520	0.460	0.400	0.350	0.300	0.260
Dividend Payout %	26.38	30.49	21.54	18.37	19.90	21.90	18.18	54.17
Income Statement								
Total Revenues	5,884,000	6,110,000	5,652,000	5,446,000	5,261,000	4,121,000	4,352,000	4,159,000
Total Indirect Exp.	4,516,000	4,994,000	4,286,000	4,061,000	4,028,000	3,637,000	3,442,000	3,845,000
Depreciation & Amort.	472,000	499,000	463,000	412,000	400,000	316,000	200,000	194,000
Operating Income	1,368,000	1,116,000	1,366,000	1,385,000	1,233,000	418,000	807,000	229,000
Net Interest Inc./(Exp.)	317,000	353,000	312,000	295,000	308,000	242,000	118,000	120,000
Income Taxes	338,000	268,000	392,000	442,000	369,000	74,000	325,000	11,000
Equity Earns/Minority Int.	...	...	...	...	...	(63,000)	...	...
Income from Cont Ops	...	...	...	...	...	224,000	421,000	124,000
Net Income	734,000	571,000	727,000	772,000	602,000	266,000	403,000	142,000
Average Shs. Outstg.	290,700	304,200	301,500	304,200	295,950	274,500	255,300	254,700
Balance Sheet								
Cash & Cash Equivalents	130,000	25,000	53,000	19,000	307,000	262,000	365,000	106,000
Total Current Assets	1,092,000	1,163,000	1,164,000	1,125,000	1,527,000	1,038,000	1,549,000	1,161,000
Total Assets	17,150,000	18,924,000	18,788,000	15,196,000	14,757,000	11,952,000	7,075,000	6,236,000
Total Current Liabilities	1,922,000	2,134,000	1,638,000	1,903,000	1,777,000	1,380,000	1,205,000	1,337,000
Long-Term Obligations	4,175,000	5,003,000	5,764,000	3,887,000	3,961,000	3,995,000	1,640,000	1,499,000
Net Stockholders' Equity	6,480,000	6,627,000	6,361,000	5,698,000	5,506,000	5,045,000	3,417,000	2,380,000
Net Working Capital	(830,000)	(971,000)	(474,000)	(778,000)	(250,000)	(342,000)	344,000	(176,000)
Shares Outstanding	284,100	296,250	289,050	285,900	303,600	287,700	256,374	254,835
Statistical Record								
Operating Profit Margin %	23.24	18.26	24.16	25.43	23.43	10.14	18.54	5.50
Return on Equity %	11.32	8.61	11.42	13.54	10.93	5.27	11.79	5.96
Return on Assets %	4.27	3.01	3.86	5.08	4.07	2.22	5.69	2.27
Debt/Total Assets %	24.34	26.43	30.67	25.57	26.84	33.42	23.18	24.03
Price Range	54.99-39.69	56.07-38.61	52.21-28.67	32.97-22.43	36.33-23.07	31.78-21.37	26.28-15.82	18.42-15.92
P/E Ratio	21.82-15.75	29.82-20.54	21.66-11.89	12.98-8.83	18.08-11.48	19.74-13.27	15.93-9.59	38.37-33.16
Average Yield %	1.42	1.18	1.26	1.64	1.35	1.30	1.45	1.50

Address: 935 de La Gauchetiere Street West, Montreal, QC H3B 2M9 **Telephone:** (514) 399–7212 **Web Site:** www.cn.ca	**Officers:** David G.A. McLean – Chmn., E. Hunter Harrison – Pre. &, C.E.O.	**Investor Contact:**800–319–9929 **Institutional Holding** **No of Institutions:** 181 **Shares:** 110,888,621 **% Held:** 57.10%

309

CANADIAN UTILITIES LTD.

Exchange	Symbol	Price	52Wk Range	Yield	P/E
TSX	CU	C$62.50 (3/31/2004)	64.00-45.10	3.39	15.35

*7 Year Price Score 117.7 ***NYSE Composite Index=100** ***12 Month Price Score 94.9**

Interim Earnings (Per Share) Can$

Qtr.	Mar	Jun	Sep	Dec
2000	1.20	0.68	0.64	1.06
2001	1.24	0.71	0.65	1.12
2002	2.27	0.67	0.70	1.15
2003	1.34	0.69	0.68	1.36

Interim Dividends (Per Share) Can$

Amt	Decl	Ex	Rec	Pa
0.51Q	4/25/2003	5/7/2003	5/9/2003	6/1/20
0.51Q	7/24/2003	8/6/2003	8/8/2003	9/1/20
0.51Q	10/21/2003	11/5/2003	11/7/2003	12/1/20
0.53Q	1/23/2004	2/9/2004	2/11/2004	3/1/20

Indicated Div: Can$2.12

Valuation Analysis

Forecast P/E	14.74	Trailing P/E	15.35
Market Cap	$2.5 Billion	Book Value	N/A
Price/Book	N/A	Price/Sales	N/A

Dividend Achiever Status

Rank	26	5 Year Growth Rate	4.46%
Total Years of Dividend Growth			21

Business Summary: Electricity (MIC: 7.1 SIC: 4939 NAIC:221121)

Canadian Utilities operates through four business groups. Power Generation consists of ATCO Power's independent power plants and Co regulated plants in Alberta. Utilities delivers natural gas and electricity to industrial, commercial and residential customers in Alber Yukon and the Northwest Territories. Logistics and Energy Services provides project management and technical services; transmission natural gas; and natural gas gathering, processing and storage, as well as liquids extraction. Technologies provides billing and customer ca services; corporate and vacation travel services; and markets coal combustion and wood preservation products.

Recent Developments: For the year ended Dec 31 2003, net income decreased 9.5% to C$292.4 million compared with C$323 million in 2002. Earnings reflected stronger operational results in all subsidiaries except ATCO Pipelines and ATCO Frontec. Results 2002 included a gain on the sales of Viking-Kinsella property of C$110.1 million. Revenues advanced 25.8% to C$3.74 billion from C$2 billion a year earlier due to the higher price of natural gas and electricity purchased for customers on a "no margin" basis by ATCO Gas a ATCO Electric, higher natural gas prices on gas sales by ATCO Midstream and increased business activity in all subsidiaries except ATC Pipelines and ATCO Frontec.

Prospects: The sale of Co.'s retail energy operations to Direct Energy Marketing Limited is slowly progressing. In Dec 2003, the Alb Energy and Utilities Board (AEUB) issued decisions approving the transfer of the retail operations of ATCO Gas and ATCO Electric Direct Energy. Co. is reviewing AEUB's decision and certain other conditions, which must be satisfied in order to close the sale. If t transaction does not close under the expected terms, ATCO Gas and ATCO Electric will no longer arrange for the supply and sale of natu gas and electricity, but will continue to provide transportation and distribution services under AEUB approved rates that provide for t recovery of costs of service.

Financial Data

(Can$ in Thousands)	9 Mos	6 Mos	3 Mos	12/31/2002	12/31/2001	12/31/2000	12/31/1999	12/31/199
Earnings Per Share	2.71	2.03	1.34	4.79	3.72	3.58	3.16	3.
Cash Flow Per Share	6.23	3.99	1.67	5.34	11.71	5.53	6.72	4.
Dividends Per Share	2.020	2.000	1.980	1.960	1.880	1.800	1.720	1.6
Dividend Payout %	74.53	98.52	147.76	40.91	50.53	50.27	54.43	54.
Income Statement								
Total Revenues	2,792,300	2,169,700	1,372,200	2,975,900	3,500,100	2,923,100	2,207,700	1,945,7
Total Indirect Exp.	2,350,200	1,854,000	1,180,700	2,414,900	2,927,400	2,328,900	1,657,700	1,396,9
Costs & Expenses	2,493,400	1,949,500	1,228,500	2,599,000	3,126,000	2,328,900	1,657,700	1,396,9
Depreciation & Amort.	196,200	134,100	70,900	244,400	241,700	238,700	229,500	204,1
Operating Income	298,900	220,200	143,700	376,900	374,100	594,200	550,000	548,8
Net Interest Inc./(Exp.)	143,200	95,500	47,800	184,100	198,600	196,000	181,900	173,0
Income Taxes	126,000	91,000	56,700	189,900	164,000	179,400	172,100	180,5
Net Income	196,800	144,400	92,500	323,200	254,100	244,200	215,000	200,6
Average Shs. Outstg.	63,671	63,658	63,659	63,700	63,315	63,328	63,367	63,3
Balance Sheet								
Net Property	4,713,100	4,647,500	4,617,900	4,657,000	6,821,800	6,321,200	5,982,900	5,781,8
Total Assets	5,935,800	5,956,600	6,002,500	5,934,400	7,851,200	7,704,300	6,663,800	6,417,0
Long-Term Obligations	2,667,300	2,733,500	2,735,600	2,738,000	2,534,300	2,422,600	2,192,300	2,085,4
Net Stockholders' Equity	2,530,100	2,519,600	2,364,700	2,316,600	1,980,300	1,863,000	1,789,600	1,800,9
Shares Outstanding	63,425	63,385	63,412	63,412	63,317	63,305	63,349	63,3
Statistical Record								
Operating Profit Margin %	10.70	10.14	10.47	12.66	10.68	20.32	24.91	28.
Net Inc./Net Property %	4.17	3.10	2.00	6.94	3.72	3.86	3.59	3.
Net Inc./Tot. Capital %	3.78	2.74	1.81	6.40	5.63	5.70	5.40	5.
Return on Equity %	7.77	5.73	3.91	13.95	12.83	13.10	12.01	11.
Accum. Depr./Gross Prop. %	...	...	...	33.97	33.74	34.20	33.35	32.
Price Range	57.85-45.10	56.50-45.10	53.00-47.19	59.98-48.94	56.05-46.00	51.00-31.40	49.00-33.40	48.70-38.
P/E Ratio	21.35-16.64	27.83-22.22	39.55-35.22	12.52-10.22	15.07-12.37	14.25-8.77	15.51-10.57	16.23-12.
Average Yield %	3.85	3.94	3.95	3.56	3.67	4.53	3.97	3.

Address: 1400, Calgary, AB T2R 1N6	**Officers:** Ronald D. Southern – Chmn., William L.	**Investor Contact:** (800) 387-0825
Telephone: (403) 292-7500	Britton – Vice-Chmn.	**Institutional Holding**
Web Site: www.canadian-utilities.com		**No of Institutions:** 2
		Shares: 455,982 **% Held:** –

EMPIRE CO. LTD.

Exchange	Symbol	Price	52Wk Range	Yield	P/E
TSX	EMP A	C$27.81 (3/31/2004)	29.15–21.80	1.44	10.91

Year Price Score 152.1 *NYSE Composite Index=100 ***12 Month Price Score 89.5**

Interim Earnings (Per Share) Can$

Qtr.	Jul	Oct	Jan	Apr
2000–01	7.80	0.33	0.18	0.51
2001–02	0.68	0.61	0.53	0.26
2002–03	0.60	0.59	0.60	0.55
2003–04	0.64	0.56	0.80	...

Interim Dividends (Per Share) Can$

Amt	Decl	Ex	Rec	Pay
0.10Q	6/26/2003	7/11/2003	7/15/2003	7/31/2003
0.10Q	9/10/2003	10/10/2003	10/15/2003	10/31/2003
0.10Q	12/10/2003	1/13/2004	1/15/2004	1/30/2004
0.10Q	3/5/2004	4/13/2004	4/15/2004	4/30/2004

Indicated Div: Can$0.40

Valuation Analysis

Forecast P/E	10.37	Trailing P/E	10.91
Market Cap	$914.9 Million	Book Value	2.7 Billion
Price/Book	N/A	Price/Sales	N/A

Dividend Achiever Status

Rank	4	5 Year Growth Rate	22.70%
Total Years of Dividend Growth		9

Business Summary: Retail − Food &Beverage (MIC: 5.3 SIC: 5149 NAIC:424490)

Empire operates principally in three business segments: food distribution, real estate and investments & theater operations. Through its 44.4% owned subsidiary Sobeys Inc., Co. operates a national network of over 1,300 corporate and franchised stores under banners such as IGA, Sobeys and Price Chopper. Co.'s real estate operations are focused on the acquisition, development and management of a portfolio of properties primarily located in Atlantic Canada. In addition, Co. maintains a portfolio of short-term liquid equity investments and operates Empire Theatres Limited, a movie exhibitor in Atlantic Canada.

Recent Developments: For the three months ended Jan 31 2004, net earnings advanced 34.9% to C$53.0 million from C$39.3 million in the corresponding period a year earlier. Results for the recent period included an after-tax capital gain of C$8.8 million, primarily related to the sale of Delhaize Le Lion common stock. Revenue climbed 5.9% to C$2.80 billion from C$2.64 billion the previous year. Food distribution revenue grew 5.6% to C$2.74 billion from C$2.59 billion the year before, while real estate revenue increased 18.0% to C$53.0 million from C$44.9 million the prior year. Operating income totaled C$110.4 million, up 2.6% compared with C$107.6 million in fiscal 2003.

Prospects: On Feb 1, 2004, Co.'s subsidiary, Sobeys Inc., completed its acquisition of Commisso's Food Markets Limited and Commisso's Grocery Distributors Limited for about C$61.0 million in cash. Also, on Feb 1 2004, Co.'s subsidiary, Crombie Properties Limited, completed its purchase of six properties located in Southern Ontario and the Niagara Peninsula for C$42.5 million. Meanwhile, top-line growth is being fueled by increased same-store sales from Co.'s food distribution operations, along with additional sales generated by new retail square footage. Separately, real estate revenue growth is benefiting from increased occupancy levels and higher rental renewal rates.

Financial Data

(C$ in Thousands)	6 Mos	3 Mos	04/30/2003	04/30/2002	04/30/2001	04/30/2000	04/30/1999	04/30/1998
Earnings Per Share	1.20	0.64	2.34	2.08	8.82	1.12	1.76	1.15
Cash Flow Per Share	1.07	(0.07)	5.40	...	...	...	...	...
Dividends Per Share	0.340	0.330	0.300	0.200	0.170	0.140	0.130	0.120
Dividend Payout %	28.95	51.56	12.98	9.62	19.27	12.50	7.57	10.38
Income Statement								
Total Revenues	5,609,100	2,814,700	10,624,200	9,926,500	11,538,600	11,164,495	6,377,651	3,320,000
Total Indirect Exp.	78,700	38,400	143,600	118,900	117,900	121,416	103,720	70,404
Depreciation & Amort.	78,700	38,400	143,600	118,900	117,900	121,416	103,720	70,404
Operating Income	203,800	101,900	337,100	286,600	202,400	176,435	63,405	45,816
Net Interest Inc./(Exp.)	46,900	24,000	92,900	111,600	142.100	159,511	112,379	76,668
Income Taxes	57,200	30,100	120,400	104,800	148,600	80,543	10,218	32,884
Equity Earns/Minority Int.	30,300	14,900	67,800	50,000	23,200	38,295	(11,917)	7
Income from Cont Ops	...	...	...	137,200	...	...	...	...
Net Income	79,100	42,300	153,900	195,900	580,000	86,812	134,950	87,782
Average Shs. Outstg.	65,504	65,503	65,781	65,700	65,626	75,572	75,004	73,900
Balance Sheet								
Cash & Cash Equivalents	95,100	253,400	316,800	782,400	556,700	68,090	97,031	184,656
Total Current Assets	1,027,000	1,109,200	1,182,800	1,563,700	1,585,400	1,121,643	1,009,819	486,778
Total Assets	4,474,100	4,515,600	4,516,100	4,312,600	4,254,300	4,171,087	4,023,498	1,907,233
Total Current Liabilities	1,288,700	1,369,800	1,387,500	1,360,800	1,498,700	1,855,772	1,587,151	659,240
Long-Term Obligations	897,100	914,500	923,100	975,000	1,108,300	1,323,700	1,392,435	616,571
Net Stockholders' Equity	1,496,500	1,464,600	1,427,100	1,290,600	1,115,000	602,768	737,682	558,339
Net Working Capital	(261,700)	(260,600)	(204,700)	202,900	86,700	(734,129)	(577,332)	(172,462)
Shares Outstanding	65,804	65,794	65,758	66,607	65,657	65,549	78,266	73,969
Statistical Record								
Operating Profit Margin %	3.63	3.62	3.17	2.88	1.75	1.58	0.99	1.38
Return on Equity %	5.28	2.88	10.78	15.17	52.01	14.40	18.29	15.72
Return on Assets %	1.76	0.93	3.40	4.54	13.63	2.08	3.35	4.60
Debt/Total Assets %	20.05	20.25	20.44	22.60	26.05	31.73	34.60	32.32
Price Range	27.55–23.10	27.55–23.10	33.25–21.80	31.25–15.75	18.13–13.95	16.98–12.33	16.35–12.50	14.20–7.80
P/E Ratio	22.96–19.25	43.05–36.09	14.21–9.32	15.02–7.57	2.05–1.58	15.16–11.00	9.29–7.10	12.35–6.78
Average Yield %	1.31	1.28	1.09	0.99	0.73	1.19	0.93	1.19

Address: 115 King Street, Stellarton, NS B0K 1S0	**Officers:** Donald R. Sobey − Chmn., Paul D. Sobey − Pres., C.E.O.	
Telephone: (902) 755−4440		**Institutional Holding**
Web Site: www.empireco.ca		No of Institutions: 1
		Shares: 72,500 % Held: −

ENBRIDGE INC

Exchange	Symbol	Price	52Wk Range	Yield	P/E
TSX	ENB	C$53.30 (3/31/2004)	54.95–42.90	3.43	13.33

*7 Year Price Score 132.4 *NYSE Composite Index=100 *12 Month Price Score 99.4

Interim Earnings (Per Share) Can$

Qtr.	Mar	Jun	Sep	Dec
2000	0.55	1.27	0.28	0.44
2001	0.53	1.69	0.37	0.01
2002	0.65	1.25	(0.03)	0.19
2003	0.63	2.68	0.53	0.16

Interim Dividends (Per Share) Can$

Amt	Decl	Ex	Rec	Pa
0.415Q	5/7/2003	5/19/2003	5/21/2003	6/1/200
0.415Q	7/30/2003	8/13/2003	8/15/2003	9/1/200
0.415Q	10/30/2003	11/12/2003	11/14/2003	12/1/200
0.458Q	1/27/2004	2/11/2004	2/13/2004	3/1/200

Indicated Div: Can$1.83 (Div. Reinv. Plan)

Valuation Analysis

Forecast P/E	17.12	Trailing P/E	13.33
Market Cap	$8.3 Billion	Book Value	4.9 Billion
Price/Book	N/A	Price/Sales	N/A

Dividend Achiever Status

Rank	23	5 Year Growth Rate	8.19%
Total Years of Dividend Growth			8

Business Summary: Oil and Gas (MIC: 14.2 SIC: 4619 NAIC:486990)

Enbridge is engaged in the transportation and distribution of energy. Co. operates common carrier and feeder pipelines that transpo crude oil and other liquid hydrocarbons in Canada, as well as transmission pipelines that transport natural gas. Co. also has gas utili operations, which serve residential, commercial, industrial and transportation customers, primarily in central and eastern Ontario, ar natural gas distribution activities in Quebec, New Brunswick and New York. In addition, Co. has investments in energy transportatic and related energy projects outside of Canada and the U.S.

Recent Developments: For the year ended Dec 31 2003, net earnings totaled C$700.8 million compared with income of C$367.8 million, before a C$242.3 gain from discontinued operations, a year earlier. Results for 2003 included a C$239.9 million gain from the sale of assets to Enbridge Income Fund, while results for 2002 included a C$122.7 million charge for the writedown of the assets of Enbridge Midcoast Energy. Revenues increased 6.8% to C$4.86 billion from C$4.55 billion the previous year. Gas sales rose 2.5% to C$3.06 billion, while transportation revenues grew 20.4% to C$1.56 billion. Energy services revenues slid 11.5% to C$233.0 million. Operating income advanced 46.4% to C$891.4 million.

Prospects: Results are being positively affected by crude oil pipeline expansion and increased demand for natural gas due to colder than-normal weather. Operating performance is also benefiting from higher ownership interest in the Alliance Pipeline, as well as higher earnings from additional equity earnings from Enbridge Energy Partners, L.P. and CLH of Spain. Going forward, Co. is focused on expanding its core pipeline, gas distribution and services, and international operations through organic growth and acquisition of strategi assets. Looking ahead, Co. is projecting earnings of between $3.00 and $3.10 per share for 2004.

Financial Data

(Can$ in Thousands)	9 Mos	6 Mos	3 Mos	12/31/2002	12/31/2001	12/31/2000	12/31/1999	12/31/1998
Earnings Per Share	3.84	3.31	0.63	2.06	2.60	2.54	1.91	1.6
Cash Flow Per Share	0.87	2.53	0.19	5.62	0.84	1.71	...	
Dividends Per Share	1.620	1.590	1.550	1.520	1.400	1.270	1.190	1.12
Dividend Payout %	42.31	48.03	246.82	73.78	53.84	50.00	62.30	67.8
Income Statement								
Total Revenues	4,001,000	2,932,900	1,045,800	4,547,500	4,050,100	2,945,000	2,687,700	2,341,70
Total Indirect Exp.	3,211,800	2,326,400	888,600	3,938,700	3,334,400	2,290,300	2,108,500	1,849,0
Depreciation & Amort.	334,000	226,600	98,000	403,900	392,500	453,500	383,800	309,0
Operating Income	789,200	606,500	157,200	608,800	715,700	654,700	579,200	492,7
Net Interest Inc./(Exp.)	337,100	228,600	101,100	422,000	437,100	427,700	380,600	312,9
Income Taxes	181,400	157,300	3,200	102,100	66,700	1,900	87,500	95,3
Income from Cont Ops	...	...	...	367,800	437,600	...	...	
Net Income	665,100	566,000	112,500	610,100	482,900	410,100	299,800	240,9
Average Shs. Outstg.	...	164,800	164,600	162,000	158,800	154,469	150,995	145,44
Balance Sheet								
Cash & Cash Equivalents	...	...	42,400	40,700	74,000	67,000	53,600	124,90
Total Current Assets	...	...	1,744,300	1,442,000	2,281,700	1,334,300	1,107,200	1,094,00
Total Assets	...	...	13,081,400	12,987,400	13,127,700	10,568,200	9,208,200	8,347,2
Total Current Liabilities	...	...	1,916,200	1,716,500	3,200,300	1,259,900	910,500	1,286,7
Long–Term Obligations	...	...	6,041,600	6,040,300	5,922,800	5,592,700	5,284,800	4,502,3
Net Stockholders' Equity	...	...	3,797,900	3,832,400	3,032,100	2,763,400	2,500,600	2,061,4
Net Working Capital	241,000	335,400	(171,900)	(274,500)	(918,600)	74,400	196,700	(192,70
Shares Outstanding	171,536	171,049	170,009	169,700	162,900	161,846	156,308	155,71
Statistical Record								
Operating Profit Margin %	19.72	20.67	15.03	13.38	17.67	22.23	21.55	21.0
Return on Equity %	...	...	2.96	15.91	15.92	14.99	11.98	11.6
Return on Assets %	...	...	0.85	4.69	3.67	3.92	3.25	2.8
Debt/Total Assets %	...	...	46.18	46.50	45.11	52.92	57.39	53.9
Price Range	51.70–41.08	49.25–41.08	44.15–41.08	49.25–41.20	45.25–41.20	45.25–34.05	43.70–24.10	36.20–28.65	35.63–29.0
P/E Ratio	13.46–10.70	14.88–12.41	70.08–65.21	23.91–20.00	17.40–13.10	17.20–9.49	18.95–15.00	21.59–17.5
Average Yield %	3.51	3.60	3.64	3.37	3.44	3.87	3.64	3.4

Address: 3000, 425–1st Street S.W., Calgary, AB T2P 3L8 Telephone: (403) 231–3900 Web Site: www.enbridge.com	Officers: Patrick D. Daniel – Pres., C.E.O., Dan C. Tutcher – Group V.P.,	Investor Contact:800–481–2804 Institutional Holding No of Institutions: 37 Shares: 37,759,463 % Held: 23%

GREAT-WEST LIFECO INC.

Exchange	Symbol	Price	52Wk Range	Yield	P/E
TSX	GWO	C$50.75 (3/31/2004)	51.98-36.80	2.54	17.44

Year Price Score 142.6 *NYSE Composite Index=100 *12 Month Price Score 96.0

Interim Earnings (Per Share) Can$

Qtr.	Mar	Jun	Sep	Dec
2001	0.43	0.09	0.32	0.52
2002	0.58	0.63	0.64	0.64
2003	0.68	0.70	0.73	0.80

Interim Dividends (Per Share) Can$

Amt	Decl	Ex	Rec	Pay
0.27Q	1/30/2003	3/13/2003	3/17/2003	3/31/2003
0.27Q	5/2/2003	6/12/2003	6/16/2003	6/30/2003
0.293Q	7/30/2003	8/28/2003	9/2/2003	9/30/2003
0.323Q	1/29/2004	3/1/2004	3/3/2004	3/31/2004

Indicated Div: Can$1.29

Valuation Analysis

Forecast P/E	13.82	Trailing P/E	17.44
Market Cap	$9.5 Billion	Book Value	N/A
Price/Book	N/A	Price/Sales	N/A

Dividend Achiever Status

Rank	7	5 Year Growth Rate	20.65%
Total Years of Dividend Growth	11	

Business Summary: Insurance (MIC: 8.2 SIC: 6311 NAIC:524113)

Great-West Lifeco is a financial services holding company with interests in the life insurance, health insurance, retirement savings, and insurance businesses. Co. has operations in Canada and internationally through The Great-West Life Assurance Company, London Life Insurance and The Canada Life Assurance Company, and in the United States through Great-West Life & Annuity Insurance and The Canada Life Assurance Company. As of Dec 31 2003, Co. had assets under administration of $112.10 billion in its Canada/Europe segment and $47.10 billion in its United States segment.

Recent Developments: For the year ended Dec 31 2003, net income grew 28.5% to C$1.24 billion from C$962.0 million in 2002. Results for 2003 included a C$20.0 million after-tax restructuring charge. Total income amounted to C$13.43 billion compared with $16.63 billion the previous year, reflecting initial ceded premiums of C$5.37 billion in 2003 related to the reinsurance of certain blocks of individual, non-participating life insurance. Net investment income climbed 24.5% to C$4.53 billion from C$3.64 billion the year before. Premium income increased 11.2% to C$12.44 billion from C$11.19 billion a year earlier.

Prospects: Results are being positively affected by the acquisition of Canada Life Financial, which was completed on July 10 2003. Separately, on Jan 14 2004, Co. announced that it has entered into an agreement to sell the U.S. business group of its indirect subsidiary, The Canada Life Assurance Company, to Jefferson-Pilot. This business, which consists of group life, disability and dental insurance with approximately $340.0 million in annual premiums, should allow Co. to continue to focus on growing its core healthcare and retirement services businesses.

Financial Data

(Can$ in Thousands)	9 Mos	6 Mos	3 Mos	12/31/2002	12/31/2001	12/31/2000	12/31/1999	12/31/1998
Earnings Per Share	2.14	1.39	0.68	2.49	1.36	1.72	1.43	1.17
Dividends Per Share	1.080	1.035	0.990	0.945	0.780	0.650	0.530	2.755
Dividend Payout %	50.47	74.45	145.59	38.33	57.35	37.79	37.06	235.47
Income Statement								
Total Premium Income	8,682,000	5,618,000	2,949,000	11,187,000	10,477,000	9,976,000	8,526,000	9,237,000
Total Revenues	7,750,000	8,301,000	4,330,000	16,632,000	16,048,000	15,266,000	13,328,000	13,756,000
Total Indirect Exp.	2,175,000	1,227,000	630,000	2,613,000	2,761,000	2,639,000	2,274,000	2,134,000
Inc. Before Inc. Taxes	1,313,000	784,000	378,000	1,426,000	1,053,000	1,253,000	1,118,000	942,000
Income Taxes	376,000	221,000	106,000	430,000	397,000	451,000	366,000	361,000
Equity Earns/Minority Int.	72,000	37,000	13,000	34,000	44,000	63,000	123,000	108,000
Net Income	865,000	526,000	259,000	962,000	546,000	674,000	569,000	473,000
Average Shs. Outstg.	394,737	369,836	370,254	372,607	377,364	373,548	373,890	373,000
Balance Sheet								
Cash & Cash Equivalents	8,113,000	5,812,000	5,757,000	912,000	837,000	740,000	732,000	759,000
Premiums Due	...	...	352,000	305,000	410,000	606,000	496,000	378,000
Invst. Assets: Total	59,389,000	35,328,000	36,515,000	36,612,000	35,232,000	32,671,000	32,312,000	32,698,000
Total Assets	99,083,000	57,705,000	59,533,000	60,071,000	59,159,000	55,754,000	53,256,000	54,725,000
Long-Term Obligations	2,999,000	1,547,000	1,568,000	1,012,000	1,075,000	1,032,000	690,000	601,000
Net Stockholders' Equity	8,518,000	4,525,000	4,626,000	4,707,570	4,397,100	4,182,365	3,789,000	3,547,000
Shares Outstanding	448,074	365,463	365,926	366,376	369,459	372,404	374,380	373,000
Statistical Record								
Return on Revenues %	11.16	6.33	5.98	5.78	3.40	4.41	4.26	3.43
Return on Equity %	10.15	11.62	5.59	20.43	12.41	16.11	15.01	13.33
Return on Assets %	0.87	0.91	0.43	1.60	0.92	1.20	1.06	0.86
Price Range	42.30-35.02	42.30-35.02	38.99-35.02	39.80-32.49	40.04-30.95	42.00-16.75	31.00-17.80	27.00-18.00
P/E Ratio	19.77-16.36	30.43-25.19	57.34-51.50	15.98-13.05	29.44-22.76	24.42-9.74	21.68-12.45	23.08-15.38
Average Yield %	3.21	2.68	2.67	2.64	2.20	2.21	2.17	12.24

Address: 100 Osborne Street North, Winnipeg, MB R3C 3A5 **Telephone:** (204) 946-1190 **Web Site:** www.greatwestlifeco.com	**Officers:** Robert Gratton - Chmn., Raymond L. McFeetors - Co-Pres., C.E.O.	**Investor Contact:** (204) 946-7341 **Institutional Holding** **No of Institutions:** 1 **Shares:** 1,797,496 **% Held:** -

313

IMPERIAL OIL LTD.

Exchange	Symbol	Price	52Wk Range	Yield	P/E
TSX	IMO	C$58.87 (3/31/2004)	64.00-43.45	1.49	13.02

*7 Year Price Score 138.6 ***NYSE Composite Index=100** ***12 Month Price Score 98.6**

Interim Earnings (Per Share) Can$

Qtr.	Mar	Jun	Sep	Dec
2001	0.96	1.04	0.61	0.55
2002	0.29	0.81	0.91	1.18
2003	1.42	1.38	1.01	0.71

Interim Dividends (Per Share) Can$

Amt	Decl	Ex	Rec	Pa
0.22Q	5/20/2003	6/2/2003	6/4/2003	7/1/200
0.22Q	8/13/2003	8/28/2003	9/2/2003	10/1/200
0.22Q	11/20/2003	12/1/2003	12/3/2003	1/1/200
0.22Q	2/18/2004	3/1/2004	3/3/2004	4/1/200

Indicated Div: Can$0.88 (Div. Reinv. Plan)

Valuation Analysis

Forecast P/E	15.70	Trailing P/E	13.02
Market Cap	$22.3 Billion	Book Value	8.9 Billion
Price/Book	1.48	Price/Sales	0.68

Dividend Achiever Status

Rank	27	10 Year Growth Rate	3.14%
Total Years of Dividend Growth		9

Business Summary: Oil and Gas (MIC: 14.2 SIC: 1311 NAIC:211111)

Imperial Oil is an integrated oil company. Co.'s operations are conducted in three main segments: natural resources include th exploration for, and production of, crude oil and natural gas; petroleum products consist of the transportation, refining and blending o crude oil and refined products; and chemicals consist of the manufacturing and marketing of various petrochemicals.In Canada, Co. is major producer of crude oil and natural gas, and a refiner and marketer of petroleum products. Co. is also a supplier of petrochemicals.A of Dec 31 2003, proved reserves of crude oil and natural gas were 1,670 million barrels and 1,023 billion cubic feet, respectively.

Recent Developments: For the year ended Dec 31 2003, net income climbed 37.4% to C$1.68 billion compared with C$1.22 billio the previous year. Results for 2003 included an C$87.0 million financing gain, while results for 2002 included financing costs of C$32. million. Total revenues advanced 12.7% to C$19.21 billion from C$17.04 billion a year earlier. Expenses from purchases of crude oil an products grew 14.0% to C$11.58 billion from C$10.16 billion the prior year. Earnings before income taxes increased 31.1% to C$2.3 billion from C$1.80 billion the year before.

Prospects: Earnings are being positively affected by higher prices for natural gas and crude oil due to a combination of supply concern and increased demand worldwide. In addition, results are benefiting from improved margins for petroleum products, partially offset b unfavorable foreign currency exchange rates. Separately, Co. anticipates total capital and exploration expenditures in 2004 c approximately C$1.50 billion, which will be financed primarily from internally generated funds. These expenditures will be used mainl for growth and productivity improvements.

Financial Data

(Can$ in Millions)	12/31/2003	12/31/2002	12/31/2001	12/31/2000	12/31/1999	12/31/1998	12/31/1997	12/31/1996
Earnings Per Share	4.52	3.19	3.16	3.40	1.35	1.26	1.83	1.4
Cash Flow Per Share	5.89	4.42	5.10	5.01	3.42	1.95	...	.
Dividends Per Share	0.860	0.840	0.810	0.780	0.740	0.730	0.730	0.66
Dividend Payout %	19.02	26.33	25.63	22.94	54.81	57.94	39.89	44.3
Income Statement								
Total Revenues	19,208	17,042	17,245	18,053	10,348	9,145	11,122	10,50
Total Indirect Exp.	5,353	5,074	5,076	4,799	4,533	4,456	4,627	4,59
Depreciation & Amort.	750	703	716	724	667	647	685	71
Operating Income	2,362	1,781	1,897	2,321	1,032	747	1,527	93
Income Taxes	680	571	653	901	450	193	680	14
Net Income	1,682	1,210	1,244	1,420	582	554	847	78
Average Shs. Outstg.	372	378	393	417	431	438	462	52
Balance Sheet								
Cash & Cash Equivalents	448	766	872	1,020	674	463	770	58
Total Current Assets	2,628	2,980	2,685	3,476	2,388	2,037	2,428	2,20
Total Assets	12,361	11,868	10,761	11,222	9,687	9,429	10,060	10,52
Total Current Liabilities	3,390	2,743	3,027	3,417	2,239	1,938	2,158	2,37
Long-Term Obligations	859	1,466	906	928	1,239	1,312	1,506	1,54
Net Stockholders' Equity	5,778	5,212	4,429	4,321	4,438	4,180	4,383	4,56
Net Working Capital	(762)	237	(342)	59	149	99	270	(172
Shares Outstanding	362	378	379	398	431	431	447	47
Statistical Record								
Operating Profit Margin %	12.29	10.45	11.00	12.85	9.97	8.16	13.72	8.8
Return on Equity %	29.11	23.21	28.08	32.86	13.11	13.25	19.32	17.2
Return on Assets %	13.60	10.19	11.56	12.65	6.00	5.87	8.41	7.4
Debt/Total Assets %	6.94	12.35	8.41	8.26	12.79	13.91	14.97	14.6
Price Range	58.22-43.45	49.30-39.50	45.65-34.75	42.25-26.85	35.70-22.00	30.67-21.15	30.67-20.00	21.50-16.0
P/E Ratio	12.88-9.61	15.45-12.38	14.45-11.00	12.43-7.90	26.44-16.30	24.34-16.79	16.76-10.93	14.43-10.7
Average Yield %	1.78	1.89	1.98	2.22	2.53	2.81	3.01	3.5

Address: 111 St. Clair Avenue West, Toronto, ON M5W 1K3 **Telephone:** (416) 968-8145 **Web Site:** www.imperialoil.ca	**Officers:** T. J. Hearn – Chmn., Pres., C.E.O., B. J. Fischer – Sr. V.P., Products & Chemicals Div.	**Investor Contact:** 416 968 8145 **Institutional Holding** **No of Institutions:** 101 **Shares:** 48,371,486 **% Held:** 12.80%

INVESTORS GROUP INC.

Exchange	Symbol	Price	52Wk Range	Yield	P/E
TSX	IGI	C$35.75 (3/31/2004)	36.12-24.39	3.08	17.70

7 Year Price Score 125.3 *NYSE Composite Index=100* **12 Month Price Score 98.4**

Interim Earnings (Per Share) Can$

Qtr.	Mar	Jun	Sep	Dec
2000	0.25	0.34	0.36	0.40
2001	0.30	0.10	0.31	0.33
2002	0.44	0.49	0.47	0.44
2003	0.45	0.48	0.58	0.51

Interim Dividends (Per Share) Can$

Amt	Decl	Ex	Rec	Pay
0.24Q	4/28/2003	6/25/2003	6/27/2003	7/28/2003
0.255Q	7/31/2003	9/26/2003	9/30/2003	10/30/2003
0.255Q	10/30/2003	12/29/2003	12/31/2003	1/30/2004
0.275Q	1/30/2004	3/25/2004	3/29/2004	4/30/2004

Indicated Div: Can$1.10

Valuation Analysis

Forecast P/E	14.92	Trailing P/E	17.70
Market Cap	$9.4 Billion	Book Value	N/A
Price/Book	N/A	Price/Sales	N/A

Dividend Achiever Status

Rank	5	5 Year Growth Rate	21.67%
Total Years of Dividend Growth			12

Business Summary: Wealth Management (MIC: 8.8 SIC: 6282 NAIC:523930)

Investors Group provides personal wealth creation and financial planning services. Co. offers financial planning, a family of mutual funds and a comprehensive range of other investment products and financial services, including registered retirement savings plans, registered retirement income funds, deferred profit sharing plans, life and disability insurance, guaranteed investment certificates and mortgages. Co. serves over 1.0 million clients through its network of over 3,300 consultants, working out of 100 financial planning centers across Canada.

Recent Developments: For the year ended Dec 31 2003, net income was C$559.8 million versus income of C$509.9 million, before income from discontinued operations of C$1.8 million, in the prior year. Results for 2003 included a dilution gain of C$14.8 million resulting from the reduction in Co.'s percentage ownership of Great-West Lifeco Inc, a restructuring gain of C$24.8 million and a non-cash income tax charge of C$24.8 million. Total fee and net investment income declined 3.4% to C$1.87 billion. Management fees fell 6.1% to C$1.30 billion. Administration declined 2.9% to C$286.8 million, while distribution dropped 4.7% to C$131.5 million. Net investment income and other fees climbed 26.3% to C$159.8 million.

Prospects: Co. begins 2004 with growing momentum. For example, efforts to strengthen its position in financial planning, such as product and service enhancements and improved support for consultants, are triggering increasing sales of mutual funds for Co.'s Investors Group Inc. During the fourth quarter, mutual fund sales were C$997.0 million versus C$965.0 million a year ago and mutual fund net redemptions were C$92.0 million compared with net redemptions of C$439.0 million a year earlier. Meanwhile, global economic improvements and strong financial markets helped Mackenzie to add C$5.28 billion in gross sales for the year.

Financial Data

(Can$ in Thousands)	9 Mos	6 Mos	3 Mos	12/31/2002	12/31/2001	12/31/2000	12/31/1999	12/31/1998
Earnings Per Share	1.52	0.94	0.45	1.84	1.04	1.35	1.12	0.89
Cash Flow Per Share	1.38	0.68	0.25	1.34	...	...	...	...
Dividends Per Share	0.930	0.890	0.860	0.820	0.700	0.580	0.460	0.360
Dividend Payout %	60.94	95.21	190.26	44.66	66.85	42.96	41.07	40.45
Income Statement								
Total Revenues	1,389,411	915,035	454,884	1,940,036	1,784,165	1,197,108	1,014,720	929,481
Total Indirect Exp.	722,521	483,123	246,161	1,032,852	1,112,521	690,875	600,582	605,310
Depreciation & Amort.	164,213	110,691	56,242	230,856	...	...	...	...
Operating Income	605,136	389,460	187,792	827,670	598,449	506,233	414,138	324,171
Income Taxes	199,912	130,013	62,870	317,401	252,994	222,208	178,525	135,827
Eqty Earns/Minority Int.	...	...	...	321	492	...	...	...
Income from Cont Ops	...	...	...	509,948	...	...	...	...
Net Income	420,044	259,447	124,922	511,759	272,994	284,025	235,613	188,344
Average Shs. Outstg.	265,099	264,982	264,992	264,873	247,932	210,012	210,854	211,396
Balance Sheet								
Cash & Cash Equivalents	966,067	1,016,901	1,046,279	927,708	1,102,480	1,132,344	948,267	939,584
Total Current Assets	1,581,633	1,583,790	1,628,221	1,476,677	1,757,574	1,348,126	1,257,180	1,287,742
Total Assets	6,246,323	6,126,390	6,161,860	5,986,952	6,122,468	1,985,212	1,811,958	1,798,944
Total Current Liabilities	714,045	737,617	759,045	709,012	671,248	218,980	306,809	371,628
Long-Term Obligations	1,409,580	1,409,580	1,484,580	1,386,365	1,362,268	168,435	171,220	262,382
Net Stockholders' Equity	3,161,912	3,073,096	3,003,884	2,949,955	2,678,244	1,096,285	966,867	850,928
Net Working Capital	867,588	846,173	869,176	767,665	1,086,326	1,129,146	950,371	916,114
Shares Outstanding	263,972	263,938	263,845	263,845	263,081	209,742	210,453	211,283
Statistical Record								
Operating Profit Margin %	43.55	42.56	41.28	42.66	33.54	42.28	40.81	34.87
Return on Equity %	13.28	8.44	4.15	17.34	10.19	25.90	24.36	22.13
Return on Assets %	6.72	4.23	2.02	8.54	4.45	14.30	13.00	10.46
Debt/Total Assets %	22.56	23.00	24.09	23.15	22.25	8.48	9.44	14.58
Price Range	29.50-23.60	29.00-23.60	28.17-23.60	32.59-21.90	26.75-18.20	27.85-13.90	26.40-17.15	28.00-17.50
P/E Ratio	19.41-15.53	30.85-25.11	62.60-52.44	17.71-11.90	25.72-17.50	20.63-10.30	23.57-15.31	31.46-19.66
Average Yield %	3.45	3.39	3.34	3.00	3.13	2.90	2.26	1.55

Address: One Canada Centre, Winnipeg, MB R3C 3B6	Officers: Robert Gratton – Chmn., R. Jeffrey Orr – Pres., C.E.O.	Investor Contact:204-956-8532
Telephone: (204) 943-0361		Institutional Holding
Web Site: www.investorsgroup.com		No of Institutions: 4
		Shares: 6,640,892 % Held: 2.52%

JEAN COUTU GROUP (PJC) INC.

Exchange	Symbol	Price	52Wk Range	Yield	P/E
TSX	PJC A	C$17.10 (3/31/2004)	17.75–13.54	0.70	22.8

*7 Year Price Score 153.9   *NYSE Composite Index=100   *12 Month Price Score 93.4

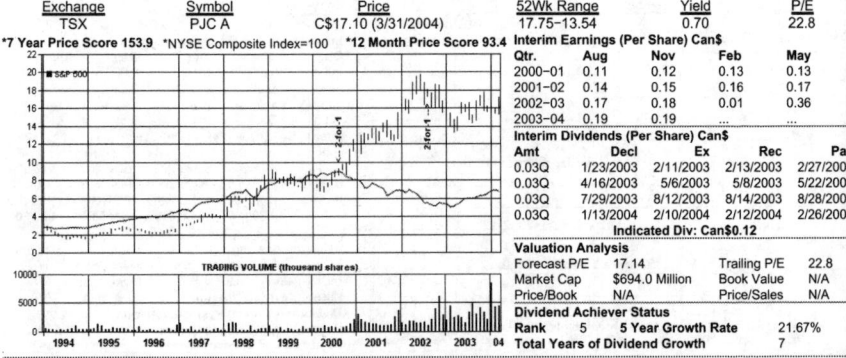

Interim Earnings (Per Share) Can$

Qtr.	Aug	Nov	Feb	May
2000–01	0.11	0.12	0.13	0.13
2001–02	0.14	0.15	0.16	0.17
2002–03	0.17	0.18	0.01	0.36
2003–04	0.19	0.19	...	...

Interim Dividends (Per Share) Can$

Amt	Decl	Ex	Rec	Pay
0.03Q	1/23/2003	2/11/2003	2/13/2003	2/27/200:
0.03Q	4/16/2003	5/6/2003	5/8/2003	5/22/200:
0.03Q	7/29/2003	8/12/2003	8/14/2003	8/28/200:
0.03Q	1/13/2004	2/10/2004	2/12/2004	2/26/200

Indicated Div: Can$0.12

Valuation Analysis

Forecast P/E	17.14	Trailing P/E 22.8
Market Cap	$694.0 Million	Book Value N/A
Price/Book	N/A	Price/Sales N/A

Dividend Achiever Status

Rank	5 5 Year Growth Rate	21.67%
Total Years of Dividend Growth		7

Business Summary: Retail – Miscellaneous (MIC: 5.11 SIC: 5912 NAIC:446110)

Jean Coutu Group is engaged in the distribution and retail sales of pharmaceutical and para-pharmaceutical products. Co.'s franchise network is based mainly in Quebec. As of Nov 30 2003, Co.'s Canadian network was comprised of 275 PJC outlets, 42 PJC Clinic and 2 PJC Santé Beauté, all franchised, in Quebec, New Brunswick and Ontario. In the U.S., Co. also owns and operates 332 Brooks Pharmac outlets in six northeastern states.

Recent Developments: For the quarter ended Nov 30 2003, net income rose 5.5% to C$44.2 million from C$41.9 million in the comparable prior–year period. Net revenues slid 1.8% to C$1.01 billion. On a geographic basis, the revenues of Co.'s Canadia operations advanced 16.1% to C$426.2 million, while revenues from Co.'s American operations improved 4.2% to C$440.8 million Moreover, the Canadian franchise network recorded retail sales of C$637.2 million, an increase of 6.8%. The American corporate pharmacy network reported retail sales of C$439.2 million, up 4.4% from the year before. In terms of comparable stores, the Canadian network's total sales were up 6.5%, while total sales in the U.S. rose by 4.4%.

Prospects: Results reflect solid performances from both of Co.'s American and Canadian networks, which are benefiting from stron retail sales, particularly prescription sales. However, earnings are being negatively affected by the devaluation of the American dollar Separately, during the second quarter of fiscal 2004, Co. opened one new pharmacy in Canada. Additionally, two outlets were enlarge and two others were renovated to feature the new Jean Coutu concept. In the United States, two corporate stores were relocated and five others were remodeled or expanded.

Financial Data

(Can$ in Thousands)	6 Mos	3 Mos	05/31/2003	05/31/2002	05/31/2001	05/31/2000	05/31/1999	05/31/1998
Earnings Per Share	0.39	0.19	0.72	0.62	0.49	0.40	0.35	0.3(
Cash Flow Per Share	0.66	0.10	0.93	...	...	...	...	...
Dividends Per Share	0.120	0.120	0.120	0.090	0.080	0.055	0.050	0.04(
Dividend Payout %	30.76	63.15	16.66	15.32	16.32	13.75	14.18	13.3:
Income Statement								
Total Revenues	2,006,943	992,267	4,052,173	3,481,277	2,924,844	2,577,727	2,289,370	1,940,07
Total Indirect Exp.	1,869,620	923,277	3,791,690	3,255,542	2,748,217	2,429,318	2,153,033	1,827,63
Depreciation & Amort.	25,711	12,893	56,293	43,541	47,348	45,993	40,455	33,83
Operating Income	127,714	63,738	234,995	209,592	163,170	133,535	119,457	98,37
Income Taxes	39,701	19,957	71,373	69,713	57,229	47,344	45,150	35,13
Net Income	88,013	43,781	163,622	139,879	105,941	86,191	74,307	63,23
Average Shs. Outstg.	227,935	227,848	227,690	227,267	216,513	211,182	211,035	210,66
Balance Sheet								
Cash & Cash Equivalents	434	...	...	...	163,771	19,400	5,861	12,79:
Total Current Assets	799,166	820,838	799,260	778,441	698,162	538,527	444,822	422,91
Total Assets	1,738,024	1,775,117	1,723,567	1,661,605	1,230,805	1,032,671	920,101	851,20
Total Current Liabilities	422,782	437,176	425,233	383,109	266,641	296,155	241,555	317,65
Long–Term Obligations	236,558	258,944	262,981	324,083	124,552	141,700	162,579	82,12
Net Stockholders' Equity	1,064,503	1,065,497	1,019,869	946,059	831,927	588,578	509,465	446,73:
Net Working Capital	...	383,662	374,027	395,332	431,521	242,372	203,267	105,26
Shares Outstanding	226,923	226,747	209,676	225,717	224,759	211,229	211,167	210,78
Statistical Record								
Operating Profit Margin %	6.36	6.42	5.79	6.02	5.57	5.18	5.21	5.0
Return on Equity %	8.26	4.10	16.04	14.78	12.73	14.64	14.58	14.1
Return on Assets %	5.06	2.46	9.49	8.41	8.60	8.34	8.07	7.4:
Debt/Total Assets %	13.61	14.58	15.25	19.50	10.11	13.72	17.66	9.6
Price Range	17.75–14.41	16.58–14.41	19.75–13.25	19.60–12.10	13.75–7.50	9.03–6.75	9.55–4.75	6.30–3.4
P/E Ratio	45.51–36.95	87.26–75.84	27.43–18.40	31.61–19.51	28.06–15.31	22.56–16.88	27.29–13.57	21.00–11.5
Average Yield %	0.74	0.77	0.73	0.60	0.75	0.65	0.69	0.8

Address: 530 Beriault Street, Longueuil, QC J4G 1S8 **Telephone:** (450) 646–9760 **Web Site:** www.jeancoutu.com; www.brooks–rx.com	**Officers:** Jean Coutu – Chmn., C.E.O., Francois J. Coutu – Pres., C.E.O.	**Investor Contact:** (514) 842–1433 **Institutional Holding** **No of Institutions:** 3 **Shares:** 2,108,100 **% Held:** –

LEON'S FURNITURE LTD.

Exchange	Symbol	Price	52Wk Range	Yield	P/E
TSX	LNF	C$30.25 (3/31/2004)	31.00–25.50	1.85	15.59

Year Price Score 127.9 *NYSE Composite Index=100 *12 Month Price Score 89.3

Interim Earnings (Per Share) Can$

Qtr.	Mar	Jun	Sep	Dec
2001	0.27	0.31	0.49	0.72
2002	0.34	0.35	0.53	0.71
2003	0.23	0.35	0.57	0.82

Interim Dividends (Per Share) Can$

Amt	Decl	Ex	Rec	Pay
0.12Q	5/8/2003	6/2/2003	6/4/2003	7/4/2003
0.12Q	8/21/2003	9/22/2003	9/24/2003	10/24/2003
0.14Q	11/26/2003	12/12/2003	12/16/2003	1/16/2004
0.14Q	2/19/2004	3/3/2004	3/5/2004	4/6/2004

Indicated Div: Can$0.56

Valuation Analysis

Forecast P/E	N/A	Trailing P/E	15.59
Market Cap	$608.7 Million	Book Value	N/A
Price/Book	N/A	Price/Sales	N/A

Dividend Achiever Status

Rank	18	5 Year Growth Rate	12.20%
Total Years of Dividend Growth			7

Business Summary: Chemicals (MIC: 11.1 SIC: 2599 NAIC:337127)

Leon's Furniture is a manufacturer and retailer of furniture and other home furnishings and accessories. Co. sells products through a network of retail stores and corporate–owned franchises located throughout Canada, including Quebec, Ontario, Manitoba, Alberta, Saskatchewan and the Atlantic Provinces. Co.'s product selection includes dining room furniture, bedroom suites, occasional tables, chests, desks, kitchen appliances, washers and dryers, vacuums, and home entertainment. These product lines cover all major design categories including European traditional, contemporary/transitional, American traditional and country/casual designs.

Recent Developments: For the year ended Dec 31 2003, net income rose 0.9% to C$38.9 million from C$38.5 million the previous year. Earnings reflected improved sales growth, higher interest income and a decrease in Co.'s effective corporate tax rate, partially offset by higher operating costs. Sales increased 1.5% to C$456.4 million from C$449.7 million in the prior year. Cost of sales, operating, administrative and selling expenses grew 2.3% to C$388.9 million. Interest income climbed 27.9% to C$3.4 million. Income before income taxes amounted to C$61.0 million, down 4.3% from C$63.7 million a year earlier.

Prospects: Near–term prospects are encouraging as Co. is beginning to see the benefits of a more aggressive marketing campaign. Co. noted that despite the recent harsh weather conditions, sales managed to increase during the first few weeks of 2004. Separately, Co. is moving forward with its expansion plans. For 2004, significant renovations will be completed in Co.'s Burlington and Ottawa stores and started in its Windsor, Ontario; Halifax, Nova Scotia; and Kitchener, Ontario stores. Co. also plans to open new warehouse showrooms in South Edmonton, Alberta; Hamilton, Ontario; and Quebec City, Quebec. Meanwhile, land has been secured for a new store in Saskatoon, Saskatchewan.

Financial Data

(Can$ in Thousands)	9 Mos	6 Mos	3 Mos	12/31/2002	12/31/2001	12/31/2000	12/31/1999	12/31/1998
Earnings Per Share	1.12	0.55	0.23	1.93	1.79	1.78	1.73	1.27
Cash Flow Per Share	2.04	0.88	0.32	1.81	1.64	...	...	...
Dividends Per Share	0.480	0.480	0.980	0.960	0.400	1.130	0.810	0.270
Dividend Payout %	42.85	87.27	426.08	49.74	22.34	63.48	46.82	21.25
Income Statement								
Total Revenues	319,198	197,924	91,892	449,693	425,687	402,236	370,825	336,895
Total Indirect Exp.	286,186	182,044	85,673	138,074	131,610	122,124	109,782	103,363
Depreciation & Amort.	7,200	4,626	2,247	8,552	7,742	6,933	6,401	5,649
Operating Income	33,012	15,880	6,219	50,354	45,632	45,314	43,398	34,144
Net Interest Inc./(Exp.)	2,659	1,476	661	2,650	4,178	5,041	4,675	4,440
Income Taxes	13,103	6,320	2,313	25,211	26,522	27,301	27,880	21,530
Net Income	22,568	11,036	4,567	38,520	36,323	36,700	36,166	27,314
Average Shs. Outstg.	20,234	20,253	20,280	19,956	20,265	20,575	20,920	20,684
Balance Sheet								
Cash & Cash Equivalents	94,880	87,002	84,010	86,014	99,282	103,369	108,124	101,085
Total Current Assets	169,373	162,562	154,576	179,845	171,906	167,145	168,556	156,584
Total Assets	317,335	305,202	296,838	320,439	295,675	280,656	268,581	245,270
Total Current Liabilities	79,570	69,019	62,602	87,605	77,414	78,232	90,232	81,325
Net Stockholders' Equity	237,395	235,813	233,866	232,635	218,122	202,345	178,313	163,917
Net Working Capital	89,803	93,543	91,974	92,240	94,492	88,913	78,324	75,259
Shares Outstanding	...	19,312	19,490	19,490	19,631	20,228	20,268	20,122
Statistical Record								
Operating Profit Margin %	10.34	8.02	6.76	11.19	10.71	11.26	11.70	10.13
Return on Equity %	9.50	4.67	1.95	16.55	16.65	18.13	20.28	16.66
Return on Assets %	7.11	3.61	1.53	12.02	12.28	13.07	13.46	11.13
Price Range	31.00–25.50	31.00–25.50	31.00–26.00	34.50–22.20	25.00–19.00	24.25–18.50	24.70–17.00	22.00–16.50
P/E Ratio	27.68–22.77	56.36–46.36	134.8–113.0	17.88–11.50	13.97–10.61	13.62–10.39	14.28–9.83	17.32–12.99
Average Yield %	1.72	1.74	3.42	3.22	1.82	5.60	4.06	1.40

Address: 45 Gordon MacKay Road, Weston, ON M9L 2R8 **Telephone:** (413) 243–7880 **Web Site:** www.leons.ca	**Officers:** Anthony T. Leon – Chmn., Mark J. Leon – V. Chmn., C.E.O.	**Investor Contact:** (416) 243–7880 **Institutional Holding** **No of Institutions:** 1 **Shares:** 18,800 **% Held:** –

LOBLAW COS. LTD.

Exchange	Symbol	Price	52Wk Range	Yield	P/E
TSX	L	C$62.60 (3/31/2004)	68.20–53.18	1.21	20.52

*7 Year Price Score 142.2 *NYSE Composite Index=100 *12 Month Price Score 95.2

Interim Earnings (Per Share) Can$

Qtr.	Mar	Jun	Oct	Dec
2000	0.28	0.34	0.41	0.67
2001	0.34	0.41	0.50	0.78
2002	0.46	0.53	0.68	0.95
2003	0.55	0.65	0.79	1.06

Interim Dividends (Per Share) Can$

Amt	Decl	Ex	Rec	Pa
0.15Q	4/30/2003	6/11/2003	6/15/2003	7/1/200
0.15Q	8/27/2003	9/11/2003	9/15/2003	10/1/200
0.15Q	11/25/2003	12/11/2003	12/15/2003	12/30/200
0.19Q	2/12/2004	3/11/2004	3/15/2004	4/1/200

Indicated Div: Can$0.76

Valuation Analysis

Forecast P/E	19.57	Trailing P/E	20.52
Market Cap	$17.3 Billion	Book Value	N/A
Price/Book	N/A	Price/Sales	N/A

Dividend Achiever Status

Rank	2	5 Year Growth Rate	24.57%
Total Years of Dividend Growth			10

Business Summary: Retail − General (MIC: 5.2 SIC: 5399 NAIC:452910)

Loblaw Companies is Canada's largest food distributor, with operations across the country. Co. sells a complete line of traditional grocer and other household products. Co.'s food labels include *President's Choice*, *President's Choice Organic*, *Club Pack* and *no name*. Co operates stores under various banners including Atlantic SaveEasy, Atlantic Superstore, Dominion, Extra Foods, Fortinos, Loblaws Lucky Dollar Foods, Maxi, No Frills, Provigo, The Real Canadian Superstore, The Real Canadian Wholesale Club, Shop Easy Food SuperValu, Valu−mart, Your Independent Grocer, Zehrs Markets and Cash and Carry.

Recent Developments: For the fifty−three weeks ended Jan 3 2004, net income increased 16.1% to C$845.0 million from C$728. million in the fifty−two weeks ended Dec 28 2002. Sales grew 9.3% to C$25.22 billion from C$23.08 billion the previous year. Operatin income rose 12.6% to C$1.47 billion. Operating margin improved to 5.8% versus 5.6% a year earlier, reflecting a favorable sales mi cost control and operating efficiencies, reduced product costs from buying synergies and reduced net stock−based compensation cost These improvements were partially offset by a C$25.0 million charge relating to a voluntary early retirement offer, lower selling price and higher defined benefit pension plan costs.

Prospects: As part of a long−term labor strategy to establish a competitive framework for its Real Canadian Superstore concept Ontario, 541 employees in Ontario received a voluntary early retirement offer during the fourth quarter. Subsequently, an additional 9 employees have accepted the voluntary early retirement offer. As a result, Co. expects to incur an additional charge of C$2.0 million the first quarter of 2004. Going forward, sales and earnings growth rates are expected to remain solid in 2004, supported by th continuation of Co.'s capital investment program, good cash flow generation and a strong financial position.

Financial Data

(Can$ in Thousands)	9 Mos	6 Mos	3 Mos	12/28/2002	12/30/2001	12/30/2000	01/01/2000	01/02/1999
Earnings Per Share	1.99	1.20	0.55	2.62	2.03	1.70	1.37	1.0
Cash Flow Per Share	1.72	0.57	(0.65)	3.53	...	...	...	.
Dividends Per Share	0.570	0.510	0.480	0.460	0.400	0.310	0.220	0.20
Dividend Payout %	28.64	42.50	87.27	17.55	19.70	18.23	16.06	18.8
Income Statement								
Total Revenues	18,847,000	11,174,000	5,376,000	23,082,000	21,486,000	20,121,000	18,783,000	12,497,00
Total Indirect Exp.	17,863,000	10,587,000	5,106,000	354,000	315,000	283,000	273,000	183,00
Depreciation & Amort.	299,000	177,000	86,000	354,000	315,000	283,000	273,000	183,00
Operating Income	984,000	587,000	270,000	1,303,000	1,136,000	976,000	811,000	529,00
Net Interest Inc./(Exp.)	144,000	82,000	38,000	161,000	158,000	143,000	112,000	68,00
Income Taxes	289,000	172,000	81,000	414,000	372,000	317,000	280,000	199,00
Net Income	551,000	333,000	151,000	728,000	563,000	473,000	376,000	261,00
Average Shs. Outstg.	277,100	277,200	275,900	277,900	276,247	276,003	275,076	246,52
Balance Sheet								
Cash & Cash Equivalents	1,159,000	1,092,000	1,198,000	1,127,000	1,001,000	1,050,000	726,000	672,00
Total Current Assets	3,768,000	3,596,000	3,575,000	3,526,000	3,086,000	2,916,000	2,415,000	2,249,00
Total Assets	12,010,000	11,525,000	11,261,000	11,110,000	10,008,000	9,025,000	7,979,000	7,105,00
Total Current Liabilities	3,291,000	3,058,000	3,083,000	3,154,000	2,796,000	3,207,000	2,812,000	2,956,00
Long−Term Obligations	3,861,000	3,811,000	3,617,000	3,420,000	3,333,000	2,377,000	1,979,000	1,364,00
Net Stockholders' Equity	4,510,000	4,334,000	4,194,000	4,124,000	3,569,000	3,124,000	2,904,000	2,595,00
Net Working Capital	477,000	538,000	492,000	372,000	290,000	(291,000)	(397,000)	(707,00
Shares Outstanding	275,300	275,300	275,318	276,018	276,252	276,245	274,910	274,42
Statistical Record								
Operating Profit Margin %	5.22	5.25	5.02	5.64	5.28	4.85	4.31	4.2
Return on Equity %	12.21	7.68	3.60	17.65	15.77	15.14	12.94	10.0
Return on Assets %	4.58	2.88	1.34	6.55	5.62	5.24	4.71	3.6
Debt/Total Assets %	32.14	33.06	32.11	30.78	33.30	26.33	24.80	19.
Price Range	64.94–51.95	62.90–51.95	57.00–51.95	63.81–50.50	54.05–46.10	54.50–30.30	41.25–33.00	37.50–24.5
P/E Ratio	32.63–26.11	52.42–43.29	103.6–94.45	24.35–19.27	26.63–22.71	32.06–17.82	30.11–24.09	35.38–23.1
Average Yield %	0.98	0.91	0.88	0.80	0.79	0.74	0.59	0.6

Address: 22 St. Clair Avenue East, Toronto, ON M4T 2S7 Telephone: (416) 922−8500 Web Site: www.loblaw.com	Officers: W. Galen Weston − Chmn., John A. Lederer − Pres.	Institutional Holding No of Institutions: 3 Shares: 8,130,291 % Held: 2.95

MELCOR DEVELOPMENTS LTD.

Exchange	Symbol	Price	52Wk Range	Yield	P/E
TSX	MRD	C$47.75 (3/31/2004)	48.50-37.00	2.30	8.15

7 Year Price Score N/A *NYSE Composite Index=100 *12 Month Price Score 100.7

Interim Earnings (Per Share) Can$

Qtr.	Mar	Jun	Sep	Dec
2000	0.09	...	...	3.39
2001	0.19	1.17	1.47	2.38
2002	1.70	1.08	1.65	2.98
2003	1.18	0.71	2.07	1.90

Interim Dividends (Per Share) Can$

Amt	Decl	Ex	Rec	Pay
0.50S	4/26/2002	6/12/2002	6/15/2002	6/28/2002
0.50S	10/24/2002	12/11/2002	12/13/2002	12/27/2002
0.55S	4/24/2003	6/11/2003	6/15/2003	6/30/2003
0.55S	12/28/2003	12/10/2003	12/13/2003	12/30/2003
			Indicated Div: Can$1.10	

Valuation Analysis

Forecast P/E	N/A	Trailing P/E	8.15
Market Cap	$145.7 Million	Book Value	N/A
Price/Book	N/A	Price/Sales	N/A

Dividend Achiever Status

Rank	17	5 Year Growth Rate	12.89%
Total Years of Dividend Growth	8		

Business Summary: Property, Real Estate &Development (MIC: 8.3 SIC: 6552 NAIC:237210)

Melcor Developments is a real estate development company. Co. conducts business through four divisions. The Community Development division is engaged in the acquisition of land for development and sale for residential communities, multi–family sites and commercial sites. Co.'s development is concentrated in Alberta in the regions of Calgary, Edmonton, Red Deer and Lethbridge and the greater Tuscon, AZ area. The Property Development division develops income producing properties, which once completed and 75.0% leased, are transferred to the Investment Property division, which holds the properties as long–term investments. The Golf Courses division owns two public 18–hole golf courses.

Recent Developments: For the year ended Dec 31 2003, net earnings declined 20.3% to C$18.4 million compared with C$23.1 million the previous year. Results for 2003 and 2002 included gains on the sale of investment properties of C$1.6 million and C$1.0 million, respectively. Gross profit decreased 22.0% to C$33.5 million from C$42.9 million the year before. Growth in assets in 2003 amounted to C$20.0 million, or 9.0% over the end of 2002. During the year, Co. acquired 820 acres of land for about C$26.1 million in Edmonton, Calgary and Red Deer. Co. also acquired a 68,000 square foot suburban office building in Edmonton and commenced a commercial development known as "Leduc Common".

Prospects: Co.'s near term outlook continues to be positive as general real estate market conditions remain relatively strong. Furthermore, there continues to be a significant increase in capital assets over the past nine months that relate to the acquisition and development of commercial properties in Co.'s Investment Property Division. Meanwhile, the Community Development division has significant plan registrations activity and has significant presales related to those registrations. Accordingly, Co is confident that it will meet or exceed its business objectives going forward.

Financial Data

(Can$ in Thousands)	12/31/2003	12/31/2002	12/31/2001	12/31/2000	12/31/1999	12/31/1998	12/31/1997	12/31/1996
Earnings Per Share	5.86	7.41	5.21	3.48	2.50	3.08	2.64	1.19
Cash Flow Per Share	5.91	9.00	5.75	...	...	...	...	...
Dividends Per Share	1.100	1	0.900	0.800	0.700	0.600	0.500	0.400
Dividend Payout %	18.77	13.49	17.27	22.99	28.00	19.48	18.93	33.61
Income Statement								
Total Revenues	80,035	110,565	82,607	61,221	46,563	57,661	50,589	33,964
Total Indirect Exp.	7,584	8,062	6,838	5,822	5,041	5,234	4,499	3,438
Depreciation & Amort.	1,091	906	832	...	...	...	...	...
Operating Income	23,534	33,343	23,392	16,665	12,454	16,276	14,885	6,879
Net Interest Inc./(Exp.)	26	186	349	389	382	148	(799)	(931)
Income Taxes	9,095	12,974	8,871	7,663	6,345	7,863	6,925	3,075
Income from Cont Ops	...	...	...	...	...	9,750	8,581	3,994
Net Income	18,406	23,089	15,971	10,630	7,767	9,659	8,502	3,854
Average Shs. Outstg.	3,139	3,115	3,065	...	...	...	...	...
Balance Sheet								
Cash & Cash Equivalents	5,080	7,105	1,325	1,181	8,404	11,544	12,080	1,905
Total Current Assets	54,320	67,113	47,941	38,088	40,739	47,618	37,622	22,310
Total Assets	251,806	231,795	177,218	158,786	153,350	153,590	128,042	111,229
Total Current Liabilities	9,839	16,410	11,116	7,439	7,109	8,937	7,634	4,200
Long–Term Obligations	74,862	61,539	41,503	37,033	40,479	35,792	26,683	21,567
Net Stockholders' Equity	140,737	126,511	106,718	92,885	85,577	80,963	73,499	67,336
Net Working Capital	44,481	50,703	36,825	30,649	33,630	38,681	29,988	18,110
Shares Outstanding	3,082	3,052	3,045	3,038	3,104	3,134	3,183	3,215
Statistical Record								
Operating Profit Margin %	29.40	30.15	28.31	27.22	26.74	28.22	29.42	20.25
Return on Equity %	13.07	18.25	14.96	11.44	9.07	11.93	11.56	5.72
Return on Assets %	7.30	9.96	9.01	6.69	5.06	6.28	6.64	3.46
Debt/Total Assets %	29.73	26.54	23.41	23.32	26.39	23.30	20.83	19.38
Price Range	48.00-37.00	42.00-26.50	28.50-20.00	20.25-17.00	19.75-16.05	21.25-15.50	18.00-14.25	14.90-10.00
P/E Ratio	8.19-6.31	5.67-3.58	5.47-3.84	5.82-4.89	7.90-6.42	6.90-5.03	6.82-5.40	12.52-8.40
Average Yield %	2.73	2.86	3.72	4.40	3.94	3.30	3.12	3.43

Address: 900 – 10310 Jasper Avenue, Edmonton, AB T5J 1Y8 Telephone: (780) 423–6931 Web Site: www.melcor.ca	Officers: Timothy C. Melton – Exec. Chmn., Ralph B. Young – Pres., C.E.O.	Institutional Holding No of Institutions: Shares: % Held:

METRO INC

Exchange	Symbol	Price	52Wk Range	Yield	P/E
TSX	MRU A	C$21.95 (3/31/2004)	22.25–17.10	1.55	12.91

*7 Year Price Score 153.8 *NYSE Composite Index=100 *12 Month Price Score 96.4

TRADING VOLUME (thousand shares)

Interim Earnings (Per Share) Can$

Qtr.	Dec	Mar	Jun	Sep
2000–01	0.24	0.30	0.37	0.27
2001–02	0.29	0.30	0.45	0.37
2002–03	0.35	0.37	0.53	0.42
2003–04	0.38	...	...	...

Interim Dividends (Per Share) Can$

Amt	Decl	Ex	Rec	Pa
0.07Q	4/15/2003	5/8/2003	5/12/2003	6/2/200
0.07Q	8/6/2003	8/14/2003	8/18/2003	9/2/200
0.07Q	9/30/2003	11/6/2003	11/10/2003	12/1/200
0.085Q	1/27/2004	2/6/2004	2/10/2004	3/3/200
	Indicated Div: Can $0.34			

Valuation Analysis

Forecast P/E	10.77	Trailing P/E	12.91
Market Cap	$2.2 Billion	Book Value	N/A
Price/Book	N/A	Price/Sales	N/A

Dividend Achiever Status

Rank	8	5 Year Growth Rate	20.55%
Total Years of Dividend Growth		8	

Business Summary: Retail – Food &Beverage (MIC: 5.3 SIC: 5141 NAIC:424410)

Metro is a major Canadian food retailer and distributor with operations concentrated in Quebec and Ontario. Co. is the secon largest food retailer in Quebec, where it also holds a substantial position in the food services industry. In addition, Co. is active i the distribution of pharmaceutical products and as the franchisor of Brunet drugstores and Clini–Plus pharmacies. In Ontario, with i Loeb and Super C banners, Co. ranks second in the supermarket segment in Ottawa and northeastern regions of the Province. In 2003, th floor space of Co.'s food retail network totalled more than 9.6 million square feet.

Recent Developments: For the twelve weeks ended Dec 20 2003, net earnings advanced 6.5% to C$37.6 million compared with C$35.3 million in the corresponding prior-year period. Total sales increased 3.0% to C$1.35 billion from C$1.31 billion a year earlier. Foo distribution segment sales grew 2.8% to C$1.24 billion, primarily due to ongoing investment in Co.'s retail network, new merchandising strategies and the acquisition of Alexandre Gaudet Ltee, a grocery distributor of small surface stores. Pharmaceutical distribution segmen sales climbed 5.6% to C$106.0 million, reflecting an increase in the number of Brunet drugstores and Clini–Plus pharmacies. Operating income rose 5.1% to C$56.1 million.

Prospects: Going forward, Co. expects to benefit from its merchandising programs and its consumer–focused products and service Meanwhile, Co. will continue with its investment program in the retail network with the objective of investing more than C$450.0 millio over the next three years to build, expand and remodel stores. Specifically, Co. intends to open new Super C stores in bot Quebec and Ontario and will further support its expansion in the Ontario market by building, expanding and renovating Loel supermarkets. Co. will also intensify the development of its McMahon Distributeur pharmaceutique inc. subsidiary, particularly in its ro as franchisor of the Brunet and Clini–Plus banners.

Financial Data

(Can$ in Thousands)	3 Mos	09/27/2003	09/28/2002	09/29/2001	09/30/2000	09/25/1999	09/26/1998	09/27/1997
Earnings Per Share	0.38	1.67	1.41	1.18	0.93	0.72	0.72	0.6
Cash Flow Per Share	0.58	1.97	2.21	...	...	...	...	
Dividends Per Share	0.280	0.260	0.210	0.170	0.140	0.120	0.100	0.07
Dividend Payout %	73.68	15.86	14.89	14.61	15.59	17.24	14.13	11.9
Income Statement								
Total Revenues	1,348,500	5,567,300	5,146,800	4,868,900	4,657,500	3,995,500	3,653,000	3,432,30
Total Indirect Exp.	1,292,400	64,900	57,600	61,400	52,500	44,300	39,700	39,20
Depreciation & Amort.	15,900	64,900	57,600	61,400	52,500	44,300	39,700	39,20
Operating Income	56,100	249,500	224,500	189,200	167,000	143,000	130,200	115,40
Net Interest Inc./(Exp.)	1,300	2,800	3,000	5,200	9,200	5,900	4,900	5,30
Income Taxes	17,200	80,400	77,800	61,200	60,500	45,700	41,900	43,90
Net Income	37,600	166,300	143,700	122,800	97,300	76,400	65,400	66,20
Average Shs. Outstg.	98,800	99,800	101,900	100,200	100,400	101,800	101,800	102,40
Balance Sheet								
Cash & Cash Equivalents	...	...	...	...	...	...	400	700	2,40
Total Current Assets	665,900	647,800	556,600	504,500	421,800	382,800	350,500	328,10
Total Assets	1,565,100	1,507,100	1,329,100	1,186,000	1,059,700	996,200	787,500	725,50
Total Current Liabilities	702,400	678,700	568,100	492,100	447,600	425,000	366,400	323,50
Long–Term Obligations	8,200	8,800	25,000	55,300	88,600	144,200	48,600	94,60
Net Stockholders' Equity	784,200	751,900	644,200	558,000	461,700	392,300	342,600	296,20
Net Working Capital	(36,500)	(30,900)	(11,500)	12,400	(25,800)	(42,200)	(15,900)	4,60
Shares Outstanding	97,965	97,812	99,486	100,166	100,416	100,707	101,552	102,08
Statistical Record								
Operating Profit Margin %	4.16	4.48	4.36	3.88	3.58	3.57	3.56	3.3
Return on Equity %	4.79	22.11	22.30	22.00	21.07	19.47	19.08	22.3
Return on Assets %	2.40	11.03	10.81	10.35	9.18	7.66	8.30	9.1
Debt/Total Assets %	0.52	0.58	1.88	4.66	8.36	14.47	6.17	13.0
Price Range	21.33–18.75	20.00–16.10	22.20–16.95	18.50–9.25	9.85–7.48	11.50–8.63	11.00–7.33	8.50–4.6
P/E Ratio	56.13–49.34	11.98–9.64	15.74–12.02	15.68–7.84	10.59–8.04	15.97–11.98	15.28–10.17	13.49–7.3
Average Yield %	1.39	1.41	1.08	1.37	1.57	1.22	1.15	1.0

Address: 11011 Maurice–Duplessis Blvd., Montreal, QC H1C 1V6 Telephone: (514) 643–1055 Web Site: www.metro.ca	Officers: Maurice Jodoin – Chmn., Paul Gobeil – Vice–Chmn.	Investor Contact: (514) 643–1055 Institutional Holding No of Institutions: 1 Shares: 583,700 % Held: –

NATIONAL BANK OF CANADA

Exchange	Symbol	Price	52Wk Range	Yield	P/E
TSX	NA	C$45.81 (3/31/2004)	46.53–32.61	2.88	13.20

7 Year Price Score 142.0 *NYSE Composite Index=100 *12 Month Price Score 103.0

Interim Earnings (Per Share) Can$

Qtr.	Jan	Apr	Jul	Oct
2000-01	0.71	0.72	0.86	0.81
2001-02	0.11	0.62	0.13	0.73
2002-03	0.88	0.72	0.87	0.86
2003-05	1.02	...	...	...

Interim Dividends (Per Share) Can$

Amt	Decl	Ex	Rec	Pay
0.28Q	5/29/2003	6/24/2003	6/26/2003	8/1/2003
0.28Q	8/28/2003	9/23/2003	9/25/2003	11/1/2003
0.33Q	12/4/2003	12/23/2003	12/29/2003	2/1/2004
0.33Q	3/4/2004	3/23/2004	3/25/2004	5/1/2004

Indicated Div: Can$1.32

Valuation Analysis

Forecast P/E	10.83	Trailing P/E	13.20
Market Cap	$7.9 Billion	Book Value	53.7 Billion
Price/Book	N/A	Price/Sales	N/A

Dividend Achiever Status

Rank	20	5 Year Growth Rate	10.35%
Total Years of Dividend Growth		8	

Business Summary: Commercial Banking (MIC: 8.1 SIC: 6021 NAIC:522110)

National Bank of Canada is an integrated financial group. Co.'s Personal and Commercial segment comprises the branch network, intermediary services, credit cards, insurance, real estate and commercial banking services. Co.'s Wealth Management segment provides full-service retail brokerage, discount brokerage, mutual funds, trust services and portfolio management. Co.'s Financial Markets segment consists of corporate financing and lending, treasury operations, which include asset and liability management, and corporate brokerage. In addition, Co. has securitization operations. As of Oct 31 2003, Co. had assets of C$82.42 billion and total deposits of C$51.46 billion.

Recent Developments: For the first quarter ended Jan 31 2004, net income advanced 12.0% to C$186.0 million compared with C$166.0 million in the corresponding prior-year quarter. Net interest income declined 21.7% to C$278.0 million from C$355.0 million a year earlier. Interest income and dividends fell 12.9% to C$569.0 million, while interest expense decreased 2.3% to C$291.0 million. Provision for credit losses increased 7.3% to C$44.0 million from C$41.0 million the year before. Non-interest income jumped 32.3% to $635.0 million, while non-interest expense rose 5.7% to C$579.0 million.

Prospects: Co. continues to improve its offering of financial products and investment solutions. For example, National Bank Securities has introduced its Advisor Series which enables independent financial advisors to sell all of its mutual funds. Co. also continues to expand its distribution network by capitalizing on partnerships with distributors and resellers of financial products. For instance, Great-West Life and London Life representatives can now offer Co.'s financial products under their respective banners. Separately, Co. has recently strengthened its position in the cities of Saint-Hyacinthe and Rimouski, Quebec by acquiring two ScotiaMcleod branches.

Financial Data

(Can$ in Thousands)	3 Mos	10/31/2003	10/31/2002	10/31/2001	10/31/2000	10/31/1999	10/31/1998	10/31/1997
Earnings Per Share	1.02	3.33	1.59	3.10	2.52	2.21	1.67	1.84
Dividends Per Share	1.080	1.040	0.900	0.800	0.740	0.690	0.640	0.550
Dividend Payout %	105.88	31.23	56.60	25.80	29.36	31.22	38.32	29.89
Income Statement								
Total Interest Income	569,000	2,529,000	2,591,000	3,381,000	3,856,000	3,493,000	3,374,000	3,105,000
Total Interest Expense	291,000	1,205,000	1,147,000	2,043,000	2,564,000	2,211,000	2,067,000	1,786,000
Net Interest Income	278,000	1,324,000	1,444,000	1,338,000	1,292,000	1,282,000	1,307,000	1,319,000
Non-Interest Expense	579,000	2,259,000	2,040,000	1,989,000	2,184,000	1,662,000	1,653,000	1,489,000
Income Before Taxes	290,000	926,000	498,000	933,000	816,000	698,000	603,000	596,000
Eqty Earns/Minority Int.	7,000	27,000	30,000	28,000	26,000	32,000	31,000	16,000
Income from Cont Ops	...	622,000	318,000	646,000	...	...	...	...
Net Income	186,000	624,000	429,000	601,000	509,000	417,000	316,000	342,000
Average Shs. Outstg.	177,008	179,235	187,727	190,815	191,605	178,138	173,615	171,824
Balance Sheet								
Net Loans & Leases	56,408,000	56,312,000	53,679,000	56,324,000	58,332,000	56,460,000	60,674,000	60,271,000
Total Assets	80,812,000	82,423,000	74,611,000	75,763,000	75,827,000	69,801,000	70,663,000	66,235,000
Total Deposits	51,500,000	51,463,000	51,690,000	51,436,000	50,473,000	49,984,000	48,026,000	43,270,000
Long-Term Obligations	1,473,000	1,516,000	1,592,000	1,647,000	1,361,000	1,035,000	966,000	1,069,000
Total Liabilities	76,652,000	78,326,000	70,710,000	71,647,000	71,999,000	66,500,000	67,968,000	63,475,000
Net Stockholders' Equity	4,160,000	4,097,000	3,901,000	4,116,000	3,828,000	3,301,000	2,695,000	2,760,000
Shares Outstanding	173,569	174,619	182,596	190,331	189,474	188,728	171,616	170,461
Statistical Record								
Return on Equity %	4.47	14.62	10.45	12.82	12.56	12.63	11.72	12.39
Return on Assets %	0.23	0.72	0.54	0.69	0.63	0.59	0.44	0.51
Equity/Assets %	5.14	4.97	5.22	5.43	5.04	4.72	3.81	4.16
Non-Int. Exp./Tot. Inc. %	101.75	89.32	78.73	58.82	56.63	47.58	48.99	47.95
Price Range	45.00-40.17	41.19-29.39	34.93-24.12	31.00-23.00	25.25-16.40	26.25-17.15	31.25-20.05	20.35-13.00
P/E Ratio	44.12-39.38	12.37-8.83	21.97-15.17	10.00-7.42	10.02-6.51	11.88-7.76	18.71-12.01	11.06-7.07
Average Yield %	2.56	3.03	2.97	2.90	3.57	3.23	2.56	3.39

Address: National Bank Tower, Montreal, QC H3B 4L2 **Telephone:** (514) 394-5000 **Web Site:** www.nbc.ca	**Officers:** Andre Berard – Chmn., C.E.O., Real Raymond – Pres., C.E.O.	**Investor Contact:** (514) 394-6433 **Institutional Holding** **No of Institutions:** 4 **Shares:** 469,113 **% Held:** –

POWER CORP. OF CANADA

Exchange	Symbol	Price	52Wk Range	Yield	P/E
TSX	POW	C$53.80 (3/31/2004)	53.80–36.50	1.81	10.25

*7 Year Price Score 133.6 *NYSE Composite Index=100 ***12 Month Price Score 98.6**

Interim Earnings (Per Share) Can$

Qtr.	Mar	Jun	Sep	Dec
2000	0.59	1.01	0.72	0.61
2001	0.77	1.57	0.75	(0.40)
2002	0.74	0.84	0.55	0.63
2003	0.71	0.94	2.97	

Interim Dividends (Per Share) Can$

Amt	Decl	Ex	Rec	Pa
0.244Q	5/15/2003	6/5/2003	6/9/2003	6/30/200
0.244Q	8/1/2003	9/5/2003	9/9/2003	9/30/200
0.244Q	11/26/2003	12/8/2003	12/10/2003	12/31/200
0.244Q	2/20/2004	3/8/2004	3/10/2004	3/31/200

Indicated Div: Can$0.975

Valuation Analysis

Forecast P/E	12.24	Trailing P/E	10.25
Market Cap	$10.6 Billion	Book Value	N/A
Price/Book	N/A	Price/Sales	N/A

Dividend Achiever Status

Rank	12	5 Year Growth Rate	16.47%
Total Years of Dividend Growth			8

Business Summary: Other Depository Banking (MIC: 8.5 SIC: 6099 NAIC:551112)

Power Corp. of Canada is a diversified management and holding company. Co.'s principal asset is its 67.1% interest in Power Financia Corp., which holds substantial interests in the financial services industry in Canada and the U.S., as well as in Europe. Power Financia also holds a significant interest in Pargesa Holding SA through Parjointco N.V. Pargesa has interests in major media, energy, water, was services and specialty minerals companies based in Europe. Co.'s Gesca Ltee subsidiary engages in the publication of newspapers including the Montreal daily newspaper *La Presse*. Co. has interests in biotechnology and technology companies through its Powe Technology Investment Corp.

Recent Developments: For the third quarter ended Sep 30 2003, net earnings surged 423.1% to C$680.0 million from C$130. million in the prior-year quarter. Total revenues dropped 99.5% to C$26.0 million. Premiums amounted to a reversal of C$2.37 billio versus income of C$3.11 billion in 2002. Net investment income climbed 49.0% to C$1.39 billion, while fees and media income ros 5.4% to C$1.00 billion. Total expenses amounted to a credit of C$709.0 million compared with an expense of C$4.50 billion the yea before. Both revenues and expenses in 2003 were reduced by ceded premiums of C$5.43 billion related to certain blocks of insurance an annuity business being reinsured on a coinsurance/ funds withheld basis.

Prospects: Co.'s indirect subsidiary, Great–West Lifeco Inc. (Lifeco), is planning to restructure and integrate the operations of Canad Life Financial Corporation with its wholly–owned subsidiaries, The Great–West Life Assurance Company, London Life Insuranc Company and GWL&A. Lifeco expects the restructuring to be substantially completed by the end of 2004. Costs of C$450.0 million an expected to be incurred as a result, and consist primarily of the consolidation of operations and systems, compensation costs an consolidation of facilities. Separately, Co. has committed to invest up to Euro100.0 million in a new private equity fund in Europe. C owns 100.0% of the management company of this fund.

Financial Data

(Can$ in Millions)	9 Mos	6 Mos	3 Mos	12/31/2002	12/31/2001	12/31/2000	12/31/1999	12/31/1998
Earnings Per Share	4.62	0.94	0.71	2.76	2.69	2.93	2.36	1.8
Cash Flow Per Share	12.04	6.39	3.82	8.17	...	...	...	
Dividends Per Share	0.900	0.863	0.820	0.790	0.675	0.575	0.488	0.43
Dividend Payout %	19.48	91.76	115.49	28.62	25.09	19.62	20.66	23.2
Income Statement								
Total Revenues	9,469	9,443	4,877	19,017	18,360	16,906	14,739	15,05
Total Indirect Exp.	3,201	1,912	972	4,031	4,391	3,711	3,258	3,04
Depreciation & Amort.	99	47	24	131	...	...	...	
Operating Income	1,888	1,153	541	2,228	1,798	1,741	1,454	1,23
Income Taxes	565	341	149	764	663	755	547	49
Eqty Earns/Minority Int.	1,044	461	211	813	592	582	627	52
Net Income	1,067	387	167	645	618	657	533	42
Average Shs. Outstg.	226	226	225	225	225	220	...	
Balance Sheet								
Cash & Cash Equivalents	5,075	3,625	3,779	3,001	2,590	2,024	1,891	1,97
Total Current Assets	87,526	53,387	55,096	3,001	2,590	2,024	1,891	1,97
Total Assets	108,718	68,192	70,216	70,136	68,730	60,564	57,652	58,92
Total Current Liabilities	...	...	...	1,262	671	219	307	37
Long–Term Obligations	3,692	3,231	3,322	2,393	2,544	1,026	985	84
Net Stockholders' Equity	5,979	5,339	5,338	5,387	4,692	4,502	3,450	3,14
Net Working Capital	87,526	53,387	55,096	1,739	1,919	1,805	1,584	1,60
Shares Outstanding	198	198	197	197	196	195	196	19
Statistical Record								
Operating Profit Margin %	19.93	12.21	11.09	11.71	9.79	10.29	9.86	8.2
Return on Equity %	17.84	7.24	3.12	11.97	13.17	14.59	15.44	13.3
Return on Assets %	0.98	0.56	0.23	0.91	0.89	1.08	0.92	0.7
Debt/Total Assets %	3.39	4.73	4.73	3.41	3.70	1.69	1.70	1.4
Price Range	43.90–35.20	43.90–35.20	38.25–35.20	43.85–32.55	39.10–32.00	37.05–19.10	35.10–22.00	37.20–23.2
P/E Ratio	9.50–7.62	46.70–37.45	53.87–49.58	15.89–11.79	14.54–11.90	12.65–6.52	14.87–9.32	19.79–12.3
Average Yield %	2.28	2.18	2.23	2.07	1.90	2.05	1.71	1.4

Address: 751 Victoria Square, Montreal, QC H2Y 2J3 Telephone: (514) 286–7400 Web Site: www.powercorp.com	Officers: Paul Desmarais – Chmn., Co–C.E.O., Andre Desmarais – Pres., Co.–C.E.O.	Institutional Holding No of Institutions: 4 Shares: 2,655,188 % Held: –

POWER FINANCIAL CORP

Exchange	Symbol	Price	52Wk Range	Yield	P/E
TSX	PWF	C$55.50 (3/31/2004)	55.80–38.15	2.34	10.37

*7 Year Price Score 140.6   *NYSE Composite Index=100   *12 Month Price Score 99.1

Interim Earnings (Per Share) Can$

Qtr.	Mar	Jun	Sep	Dec
2000	0.50	0.55	0.57	0.56
2001	0.59	0.90	0.64	0.59
2002	0.65	0.82	0.65	0.65
2003	0.68	0.87	3.15	5.35

Interim Dividends (Per Share) Can$

Amt	Decl	Ex	Rec	Pay
0.30Q	5/14/2003	6/26/2003	6/30/2003	8/1/2003
0.30Q	8/1/2003	9/26/2003	9/30/2003	10/31/2003
0.325Q	11/26/2003	12/29/2003	12/31/2003	1/30/2004
0.325Q	4/2/2004	4/12/2004	4/14/2004	4/30/2004

Indicated Div: Can$1.30

Valuation Analysis

Forecast P/E	13.25	Trailing P/E	10.37
Market Cap	$19.3 Billion	Book Value	N/A
Price/Book	N/A	Price/Sales	N/A

Dividend Achiever Status

Rank	9	5 Year Growth Rate	19.55%
Total Years of Dividend Growth		11

Business Summary: Insurance (MIC: 8.2 SIC: 6311 NAIC:524113)

Power Financial is a diversified management and holding company. Through its respective controlling interests of 70.2% and 56.0% in Great–West Lifeco Inc. and Investors Group Inc., Co. holds substantial interests in the financial services industry in Canada and the U.S., as well as in Europe. Together with the Frere group of Belgium, Co. also holds a significant interest in Pargesa Holding SA through Parjointco N.V. The Pargesa group has substantial interests in major media, energy, water, waste services and specialty minerals companies based in Europe. Pargesa's major holdings include Bertelsmann AG, TotalFinaElf, Suez and Imerys S.A.

Recent Developments: For the quarter ended Sep 30 2003, net earnings surged 436.7% to C$1.13 billion from C$210.0 million in the 2002 quarter. Results for 2003 included a gain of C$894.0 from dilution of Great–West Lifeco interest and a C$21.0 million restructuring charge. Revenues amounted to a reversal of C$54.0 million versus revenues of C$4.92 billion a year earlier. Expenses were a credit of C$793.0 million versus expense of C$4.42 billion in 2002. Both revenues and expenses in 2003 were reduced by ceded premiums of C$5.43 billion when Lifeco subsidiaries reinsured certain blocks of insurance on a yearly renewable reinsurance basis and other insurance/annuity business on a coinsurance/funds withheld basis.

Prospects: Co.'s subsidiary, Great West Lifeco Inc. (Lifeco), is planning to restructure and integrate the operations of Canada Life Financial Corporation with its wholly–owned subsidiaries, The Great–West Life Assurance Company, London Life Insurance Company and Great West Life & Annuity Insurance Company. Lifeco expects the restructuring to be substantially completed by the end of 2004. Costs of C$450.0 million are expected to be incurred as a result, and consist primarily of the consolidation of operations and systems, compensation costs and consolidation of facilities.

Financial Data

(Can$ in Thousands)	9 Mos	6 Mos	3 Mos	12/31/2002	12/31/2001	12/31/2000	12/31/1999	12/31/1998
Earnings Per Share	4.71	1.54	0.68	2.68	2.72	2.18	2.32	1.87
Dividends Per Share	1.120	1.080	1.040	1.000	0.840	0.690	0.570	0.470
Dividend Payout %	23.77	70.12	152.94	37.31	30.88	31.65	24.57	25.13
Income Statement								
Total Premium Income	3,253,000	5,618,000	2,949,000	11,187,000	10,477,000	9,976,000	8,526,000	9,237,000
Total Revenues	9,193,000	9,247,000	4,798,000	18,620,000	17,889,000	16,531,000	14,424,000	14,767,000
Total Indirect Exp.	2,938,000	1,732,000	881,000	3,668,000	4,014,000	3,425,000	2,961,000	2,769,000
Inc. Before Inc. Taxes	2,733,000	1,178,000	541,000	2,198,000	1,953,000	1,756,000	1,704,000	1,449,000
Income Taxes	576,000	351,000	169,000	749,000	642,000	665,000	535,000	483,000
Eqty Earns/Minority Int.	393,000	203,000	123,000	461,000	284,000	305,000	335,000	288,000
Net Income	1,705,000	578,000	253,000	988,000	879,000	786,000	834,000	678,000
Average Shs. Outstg.	351,600	351,500	350,800	351,600	351,700	346,666	346,779	...
Balance Sheet								
Cash & Cash Equivalents	4,520,000	3,075,000	3,236,000	2,437,000	2,120,000	1,831,000	1,622,000	1,670,000
Invst. Assets: Total	83,091,000	50,358,000	51,952,000	52,677,000	52,004,000	49,083,000	48,578,000	50,300,000
Total Assets	106,892,000	66,372,000	68,406,000	68,319,000	67,069,000	59,354,000	56,647,000	58,033,000
Long–Term Obligations	3,612,000	3,151,000	3,242,000	2,313,000	2,437,000	1,026,000	985,000	837,000
Net Stockholders' Equity	7,974,000	6,939,000	7,117,000	6,855,000	5,828,000	4,963,000	3,912,550	4,172,000
Shares Outstanding	348,416	348,416	348,396	346,856	346,701	347,053	346,836	346,580
Statistical Record								
Return on Revenues %	18.54	6.25	5.27	5.30	4.91	4.75	5.78	4.59
Return on Equity %	21.38	8.32	3.55	14.41	15.08	15.83	21.31	16.25
Return on Assets %	1.59	0.87	0.36	1.44	1.31	1.32	1.47	1.16
Price Range	45.90–36.30	45.60–36.30	39.39–36.30	43.25–31.85	38.60–31.00	35.20–19.10	35.40–21.00	36.90–22.88
P/E Ratio	9.75–7.71	29.61–23.57	57.93–53.38	16.14–11.88	14.19–11.40	16.15–8.76	15.26–9.05	19.73–12.23
Average Yield %	2.72	2.70	2.74	2.65	2.47	2.54	2.10	1.59

Address: 751 Victoria Square, Montreal, QC H2Y 2J3 **Telephone:** (514) 286–7430 **Web Site:** www.powerfinancial.com	**Officers:** Paul Desmarais – Chmn., Andre Desmarais – Dep. Chmn.	**Institutional Holding** No of Institutions: 3 **Shares:** 9,002,325 **% Held:** 3%

QUEBECOR WORLD INC.

Exchange	Symbol	Price	52Wk Range	Yield	P/E
NYS	IQW	$18.41 (3/31/2004)	27.45-20.89	2.14	N/A

*7 Year Price Score 84.6   *NYSE Composite Index=100   *12 Month Price Score 78.2

Interim Earnings (Per Share)

Qtr.	Mar	Jun	Sep	Dec
2000	0.35	0.51	0.68	0.40
2001	0.38	0.51	0.57	...
2002	0.28	0.40	0.64	0.44
2003	0.12	(0.51)	0.38	(0.48)

Interim Dividends (Per Share)

Amt	Decl	Ex	Rec	Pay
0.13Q	4/24/2003	5/14/2003	5/16/2003	6/2/200:
0.13Q	7/24/2003	8/13/2003	8/15/2003	9/1/200:
0.13Q	10/23/2003	11/12/2003	11/14/2003	12/1/200
0.13Q	2/6/2004	2/11/2004	2/13/2004	3/1/2004

Indicated Div: $0.52

Valuation Analysis

Forecast P/E	14.07	Trailing P/E	34.15
Market Cap	$3.20	Book Value	3.4 Billion
Price/Book	N/A	Price/Sales	N/A

Dividend Achiever Status

Rank	11	5 Year Growth Rate	16.72%
Total Years of Dividend Growth			13

Business Summary: Printing (MIC: 13.4 SIC: 2759 NAIC:323113)

Quebecor World is engaged in commercial print media services. Co.'s product categories include magazines, retail inserts and circulars, books, catalogs, specialty printing and direct mail, directories, digital pre-media, logistics, mail list technologies and other services. As of Dec 31, 2003, Co. has approx. 160 printing and related facilities in the United States, Canada, France, the United Kingdom, Spain, Switzerland, Sweden, Finland, Austria, Belgium, Brazil, Chile, Argentina, Peru, Colombia, Mexico and India.

Recent Developments: For the year ended Dec 31 2003, Co. posted a net loss of $31.4 million compared with net income of $279. million a year earlier. Results for 2003 and 2002 included impairment of assets, restructuring and other charges of $98.3 million and $19.6 million, respectively. Revenues declined 1.9% to $6.39 billion from $6.27 billion the previous year. North America revenues slipped to $5.06 billion from $5.09 billion in 2002, due primarily to lower prices. In Europe, revenues rose 14.9% to $1.15 billion, aided by favorable currency translation and acquisitions. Latin America revenues declined 3.4% to $177.3 million, reflecting sharp competition and currency devaluations that offset higher volumes.

Prospects: Difficult industry and market conditions, which are resulting in significant pricing pressure, cloud Co.'s near-term outlook. In response, Co. has initiated restructuring actions across its global platforms that include workforce reductions and cost savings efforts in procurement, manufacturing and operational efficiency and financial expense. Co. noted that in total, the 2003 restructuring initiatives will involve the elimination of 2,272 employee positions, 1,769 as of Dec 31 2003 and 503 by the end of the first quarter of 2004. Co. expects these initiatives to produce annualized cost savings in excess of $90.0 million.

Financial Data
(US$ in Thousands)

	9 Mos	6 Mos	3 Mos	12/31/2002	12/31/2001	12/31/2000	12/31/1999	12/31/1998
Earnings Per Share	(0.03)	(0.39)	0.12	1.76	...	1.94	0.56	1.2
Cash Flow Per Share	0.47	0.04	(1.21)	3.53	4.03	6.24	...	:
Dividends Per Share	0.520	0.510	0.500	0.490	0.460	0.330	0.280	0.24
Dividend Payout %	N.M.	N.M.	416.66	27.84	...	17.01	50.00	18.6
Income Statement								
Total Revenues	4,624,800	3,033,800	1,531,300	6,242,000	6,320,100	6,521,077	4,952,537	3,808,15
Total Indirect Exp.	711,900	515,200	217,800	855,900	823,400	804,557	633,885	526,77
Depreciation & Amort.	249,800	166,900	87,400	335,600	337,800	345,079	285,992	239,40
Operating Income	163,500	38,500	77,800	543,200	617,800	724,803	473,245	301,88
Income Taxes	2,400	(16,100)	7,400	90,900	52,000	137,735	48,161	74,82
Eqty Earns/Minority Int.	1,400	500	400	2,800	3,200	2,353	12,701	3,19
Net Income	22,500	(37,200)	24,500	279,300	22,400	295,431	80,056	159,56
Average Shs. Outstg.	137,400	140,200	141,400	145,400	143,000	147,041	125,393	115,70
Balance Sheet								
Cash & Cash Equivalents	...	...	6,500	2,700	85,500	52,732	3,613	30
Total Current Assets	...	...	1,014,700	967,300	913,200	1,185,274	1,260,977	954,23
Total Assets	...	...	6,288,900	6,205,500	6,149,900	6,484,660	6,756,252	3,842,11
Total Current Liabilities	...	...	932,400	1,176,600	1,107,700	1,251,809	1,221,288	710,12
Long−Term Obligations	...	...	2,071,200	1,783,600	2,075,200	2,121,490	2,762,663	1,199,13
Net Stockholders' Equity	...	...	2,730,100	2,703,800	2,473,200	2,473,880	2,320,884	1,564,50
Net Working Capital	...	...	82,300	(209,300)	(194,500)	(66,535)	39,689	244,10
Shares Outstanding	131,789	139,000	141,300	141,145	140,184	146,139	159,675	127,79
Statistical Record								
Operating Profit Margin %	3.53	1.26	5.08	8.70	9.78	11.11	9.56	7.9
Return on Equity %	...	...	0.89	10.32	0.90	11.94	3.44	10.1
Return on Assets %	...	...	0.38	4.50	0.36	4.55	1.18	4.1
Debt/Total Assets %	...	...	32.93	28.74	33.74	32.71	40.89	31.2
Price Range	37.38-20.90	37.38-20.90	37.38-20.90	46.09-32.25	42.60-30.73	39.10-25.60	36.50-31.40	33.85-22.0
P/E Ratio	N/A	N/A	311.5-174.2	26.19-18.32	...	N/A	20.15-13.20	65.18-56.07	26.24-17.0
Average Yield %	1.90	1.79	1.53	1.26	1.25	0.98	0.83	0.8

Address: 612 Saint Jacques Street, Montreal, QC H3C 4M8 Telephone: (514) 877−5148 Web Site: www.quebecorworld.com	Officers: Jean Neveu − Chmn., Pierre Karl Peladeau − Vice Chmn.	Institutional Holding No of Institutions: 36 Shares: 37,799,626 % Held: 27%

ROYAL BANK OF CANADA

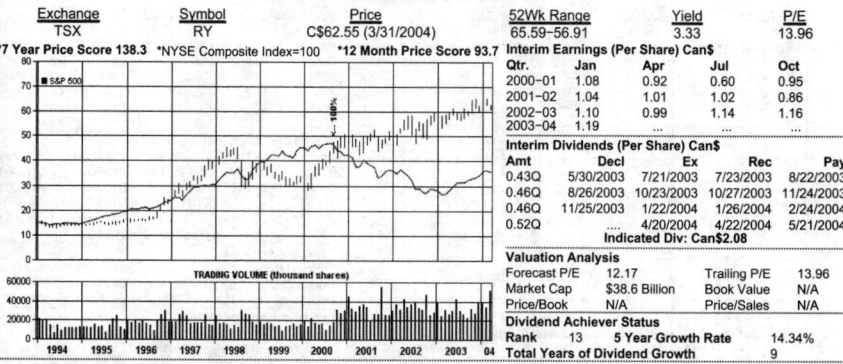

Exchange	Symbol	Price	52Wk Range	Yield	P/E
TSX	RY	C$62.55 (3/31/2004)	65.59–56.91	3.33	13.96
	NYSE				

*7 Year Price Score 138.3   *NYSE Composite Index=100   *12 Month Price Score 93.7

Interim Earnings (Per Share) Can$

Qtr.	Jan	Apr	Jul	Oct
2000–01	1.08	0.92	0.60	0.95
2001–02	1.04	1.01	1.02	0.86
2002–03	1.10	0.99	1.14	1.16
2003–04	1.19	...	...	...

Interim Dividends (Per Share) Can$

Amt	Decl	Ex	Rec	Pay
0.43Q	5/30/2003	7/21/2003	7/23/2003	8/22/2003
0.46Q	8/26/2003	10/23/2003	10/27/2003	11/24/2003
0.46Q	11/25/2003	1/22/2004	1/26/2004	2/24/2004
0.52Q	....	4/20/2004	4/22/2004	5/21/2004

Indicated Div: Can$2.08

Valuation Analysis

Forecast P/E	12.17	Trailing P/E	13.96
Market Cap	$38.6 Billion	Book Value	N/A
Price/Book	N/A	Price/Sales	N/A

Dividend Achiever Status

Rank	13	5 Year Growth Rate 14.34%
Total Years of Dividend Growth		9

Business Summary: Commercial Banking (MIC: 8.1 SIC: 6029 NAIC:522110)

Royal Bank of Canada is engaged in the personal and commercial banking (RBC Banking), wealth management (RBC Investments), insurance (RBC Insurance), corporate and investment banking (RBC Capital Markets) and transaction processing (RBC Global Services). In U.S., Co. provides mortgage origination, insurance, full–service brokerage and corporate and investment banking services through RBC Centura, RBC Mortgage, RBC Builder Finance, RBC Liberty Insurance, RBC Dain Rauscher and RBC Capital Markets. As of Oct 31 2003, Co. had total assets of C$403,033 million, deposits of C$259,145 million, 4,401 units of automated banking machines.

Recent Developments: For the quarter ended Jan 31 2004, net income rose 3.4% to C$793.0 million compared with C$767.0 million a year earlier. Net interest income fell 3.9% to C$1.65 billion, due in part to a C$60.0 million decline in the translated value of U.S. dollar-denominated net interest income and deposit spread compression in RBC Banking. Non-interest income slid 2.8% to C$2.55 billion. Co. noted that the appreciation of the Canadian dollar relative to the U.S. dollar from the first quarter of 2003 reduced the translated value of non-interest income by C$180.0 million. Recovery of credit losses amounted to C$28.0 million versus a provision for credit losses of C$200.0 million the year before.

Prospects: Co.'s near-term outlook is mixed. On one hand, a lower net interest margin due to significant growth in low interest-yielding assets such as securities, coupled with a decline in RBC Banking's net interest margin could hamper results. However, Co. should continue to benefit from improved credit quality as the North American economic recovery unfolds. Additionally, Co.'s business diversification should continue to result in higher brokerage, underwriting and mutual fund revenues as equity markets strengthen. Lastly, Co. has indicated that it is taking steps to improve returns from its banking operations in the U.S.

Financial Data

Can$ in Millions)	10/31/2003	10/31/2002	10/31/2001	10/31/2000	10/31/1999	10/31/1998	10/31/1997	10/31/1996
Earnings Per Share	4.39	3.93	3.55	3.40	2.48	2.65	2.50	2.04
Dividends Per Share	1.660	1.480	1.320	1.080	0.930	0.840	0.730	0.650
Dividend Payout %	37.81	37.65	37.18	31.76	37.50	31.88	29.20	31.86
Income Statement								
Total Interest Income	14,053	14,672	17,307	16,109	14,200	14,776	13,307	13,453
Total Interest Expense	7,411	7,514	10,810	10,830	9,083	9,712	8,307	8,563
Net Interest Income	5,921	6,093	5,378	4,588	4,357	4,489	4,620	4,450
Provision for Loan Losses	721	1,065	1,119	691	760	575	380	440
Non-Interest Income	10,776	8,562	8,155	6,680	5,491	4,985	4,279	3,021
Non-Interest Expense	11,047	9,223	8,503	6,624	6,036	5,352	5,116	4,373
Income Before Taxes	4,592	4,235	3,892	3,640	2,707	3,075	2,846	2,359
Eqty Earns/Minority Int.	127	108	107	20	8	76	77	49
Net Income	3,005	2,762	2,435	2,208	1,725	1,824	1,679	1,430
Average Shs. Outstg.	669	678	647	609	632	633	618	628
Balance Sheet								
Net Loans & Leases	249,211	242,098	246,266	228,925	211,408	212,986	201,502	179,824
Total Assets	403,033	376,956	362,483	294,054	273,298	274,399	244,774	217,950
Total Deposits	259,145	243,486	235,687	206,237	187,897	180,005	173,229	161,817
Long–Term Obligations	6,243	6,614	6,662	5,825	4,596	4,087	4,227	3,627
Total Liabilities	384,658	358,173	344,278	280,757	260,890	262,507	234,384	208,536
Net Stockholders' Equity	18,375	18,783	18,205	13,297	12,408	11,892	10,390	9,414
Shares Outstanding	656	665	674	602	617	617	616	622
Statistical Record								
Return on Equity %	16.35	14.70	13.37	16.60	13.90	15.33	16.15	15.19
Return on Assets %	0.74	0.73	0.67	0.75	0.63	0.66	0.68	0.65
Equity/Assets %	4.55	4.98	5.02	4.52	4.54	4.33	4.24	4.31
Non–Int. Exp./Tot. Inc. %	44.49	39.69	33.39	29.06	30.65	27.08	29.09	26.54
Price Range	64.90–53.70	58.70–46.56	53.02–42.75	48.30–27.75	41.88–30.15	45.65–29.10	38.00–22.15	22.15–15.00
P/E Ratio	14.78–12.23	14.94–11.85	14.94–12.04	14.21–8.16	16.89–12.16	17.23–10.98	15.20–8.86	10.86–7.35
Average Yield %	2.83	2.83	2.73	2.95	2.65	2.13	2.51	3.87

Address: 200 Bay Street, Toronto, ON M5J 2J5 **Telephone:** (416) 974–5151 **Web Site:** www.rbc.com	**Officers:** Elisabetta Bigsby – Sr. Exec. V.P., Human Res. & Public Affairs, Peter W. Currie – C.F.O.	**Institutional Holding** **No of Institutions:** 119 **Shares:** 160,956,931 **% Held:** 24%

TERASEN INC

Exchange	Symbol	Price	52Wk Range	Yield	P/E
TSX	TER	C$48.82 (3/31/2004)	49.85–37.00	3.20	19.30

*7 Year Price Score 134.4   *NYSE Composite Index=100   *12 Month Price Score 98.9

Interim Earnings (Per Share) Can$

Qtr.	Mar	Jun	Sep	Dec
2000	1.60	0.22	(0.33)	1.33
2001	1.58	(0.08)	(0.58)	1.27
2002	1.69	0.03	(0.44)	1.15
2003	...	0.16	(0.15)	2.52

Interim Dividends (Per Share) Can$

Amt	Decl	Ex	Rec	Pay
0.39Q	4/25/2003	5/14/2003	5/16/2003	5/31/2003
0.39Q	7/31/2003	8/14/2003	8/18/2003	8/31/2003
0.39Q	...	11/14/2003	11/18/2003	11/30/2003
0.39Q	...	2/23/2004	2/25/2004	2/29/2004

Indicated Div: Can$1.56

Valuation Analysis

Forecast P/E	N/A	Trailing P/E	19.30
Market Cap	$2.4 Billion	Book Value	N/A
Price/Book	N/A	Price/Sales	N/A

Dividend Achiever Status

Rank	24	5 Year Growth Rate	7.02%
Total Years of Dividend Growth		7

Business Summary: Gas Utilities (MIC: 7.4 SIC: 4925 NAIC:221210)

Terasen is a provider of energy transportation and utility asset management services. Co. operates in two primary business segments. Natural gas distribution operations involve the transmission and distribution of natural gas for residential, commercial, institutional and industrial customers in British Columbia. Petroleum transportation operations are carried out through Terasen Pipelines (Trans Mountain) Inc., Terasen Pipelines (Corridor) Inc., and Express Pipeline Ltd and Express US Holdings LP. Co. maintains a one–third ownership interest in the Express System. Co.'s other activities include non–regulated energy and utility businesses.

Recent Developments: For the year ended Dec 31 2003, net earnings increased 23.9% to C$139.4 million compared with C$112.5 million a year earlier. Revenues rose 9.9% to C$1.88 billion from C$1.71 billion the previous year. Co.'s improved results were fueled by sharply higher petroleum transportation earnings, reflecting strong throughput volumes on the Trans Mountain pipeline, the January 2003 acquisition of a one–third interest in the Express Pipeline System, and the commencement of commercial shipping on the Corridor Pipeline in May 2003. Natural gas distribution segment profit grew 6.9% to C$98.8 million, while petroleum transportation earnings jumped 91.8% to C$56.2 million versus C$29.3 million last year.

Prospects: Co.'s outlook is enhanced by the growing need for natural gas and petroleum transportation in North America. For instance Co. has indicated that it will continue to pursue the construction of additional gas transportation capacity and the installation of a liquefied natural gas storage facility on Vancouver Island. In petroleum transportation, Co. intends to make investments in the expansion of the Express and Trans Mountain pipeline systems. Co. also plans to pursue opportunities related to the development of the Bison pipeline and the TMX project for the eventual looping of the Trans Mountain pipeline. Accordingly, for full–year 2004, Co. is targeting earnings per share growth of 6.0%.

Financial Data

(Can$ in Thousands)	12/31/2003	12/31/2002	12/31/2001	12/31/2000	12/31/1999	12/31/1998	12/31/1997	12/31/1996
Earnings Per Share	2.53	2.43	2.19	2.82	2.12	1.85	1.27	2.53
Cash Flow Per Share	5.14	7.29	...	...	...	...	...	...
Dividends Per Share	1.530	1.410	1.300	1.220	1.160	1.090	0.970	0.900
Dividend Payout %	60.47	58.02	59.36	43.43	54.72	58.92	76.38	35.57
Income Statement								
Total Revenues	1,876,600	1,707,200	1,666,300	1,305,600	1,040,600	925,000	933,900	901,400
Total Indirect Exp.	516,900	471,000	367,900	333,600	318,000	326,300	314,700	307,100
Costs & Expenses	1,510,200	1,370,700	1,371,100	1,049,000	784,200	664,500	689,900	670,100
Depreciation & Amort.	133,400	115,600	95,100	86,200	82,600	84,600	77,900	78,400
Operating Income	366,400	336,500	295,200	256,600	256,400	260,500	244,000	231,300
Net Interest Inc./(Exp.)	176,000	160,800	148,300	117,500	121,600	121,800	114,700	126,500
Income Taxes	59,000	63,200	55,900	8,900	48,900	62,900	49,600	32,100
Eqty Earns/Minority Int.	...	...	...	4,000	4,700	4,600	5,800	3,900
Net Income	139,400	112,500	91,000	112,700	81,200	71,200	50,800	105,600
Average Shs. Outstg.	52,400	43,600	38,300	38,300	38,300	38,500	40,100	41,800
Balance Sheet								
Net Property	3,882,400	3,779,200	3,079,900	2,727,600	2,154,700	2,168,600	2,116,100	2,062,600
Total Assets	4,915,100	4,522,400	3,705,700	3,513,100	2,450,500	2,466,100	2,388,100	2,427,100
Long–Term Obligations	2,301,100	2,123,400	1,928,000	1,561,900	1,001,800	906,700	993,300	1,033,900
Net Stockholders' Equity	1,429,600	1,365,600	840,100	809,500	626,300	590,000	588,200	630,700
Shares Outstanding	52,077	51,681	38,343	38,326	38,279	38,266	39,093	41,26
Statistical Record								
Operating Profit Margin %	19.52	19.71	17.71	19.65	24.63	28.16	26.12	25.64
Return on Equity %	9.28	7.74	10.83	13.92	12.96	12.06	8.63	16.7
Accum. Depr./Gross Prop. %	18.96	17.79	...	...	...	...	...	...
Price Range	48.00–36.35	42.50–32.64	36.40–29.75	33.45–21.50	31.00–21.00	33.95–27.00	27.95–20.25	20.90–15.00
P/E Ratio	18.97–14.37	17.49–13.43	16.62–13.58	11.86–7.62	14.62–9.91	18.35–14.59	22.01–15.94	8.26–5.9
Average Yield %	3.62	3.68	3.92	4.44	4.14	3.60	4.02	5.1

Address: 1111 West Georgia Street, Vancouver, BC V6E 4M4 Telephone: (604) 443–6559 Web Site: www.bcgas.com	Officers: John M. Reid – Pres., C.E.O., Richard T. Ballantyne	Investor Contact:604–443–6559 Institutional Holding No of Institutions: 2 Shares: 912,400 % Held: 1.76

THOMSON CORP.

Exchange	Symbol	Price	52Wk Range	Yield	P/E
NYS	TOC	$30.86 (3/31/2004)	47.74-38.34	1.82	23.56

7 Year Price Score 97.6   *NYSE Composite Index=100   *12 Month Price Score 94.5

Interim Earnings (Per Share)

Qtr.	Mar	Jun	Sep	Dec
2001	0.24	0.18	0.23	0.40
2002	(0.05)	0.14	0.39	0.44
2003	0.10	0.16	0.45	0.60

Interim Dividends (Per Share)

Amt	Decl	Ex	Rec	Pay
0.18Q	5/1/2003	5/20/2003	5/22/2003	6/16/2003
0.18Q	7/31/2003	8/19/2003	8/21/2003	9/15/2003
0.185Q	10/30/2003	11/18/2003	11/20/2003	12/15/2003
0.185Q	2/12/2004	2/20/2004	2/24/2004	3/15/2004

Indicated Div: $0.74

Valuation Analysis

Forecast P/E	24.50	Trailing P/E	23.56
Market Cap	$26.3 Billion	Book Value	N/A
Price/Book	N/A	Price/Sales	N/A

Dividend Achiever Status

Rank	16	5 Year Growth Rate	12.94%
Total Years of Dividend Growth	9		

Business Summary: Non-Media Publishing (MIC: 13.3 SIC: 2731 NAIC:511130)

Thomson is engaged in the provision of value-added information, software tools and applications to users in the fields of law, tax, accounting, financial services, higher education, reference information, corporate training and assessment, scientific research and healthcare. Co. organizes its operations into four market groups that are structured on the basis of the customers they serve: Thomson Legal & Regulatory, Thomson Learning, Thomson Financial and Thomson Scientific & Healthcare

Recent Developments: For the year ended Dec 31 2003, income was $844.0 million, before a gain of $23.0 million from discontinued operations, compared with income of $548.0 million, before a gain of $57.0 million from discontinued operations, in the previous year. Results for 2002 included a pre-tax restructuring charge of $6.0 million. Revenues climbed 2.2% to $7.61 billion from $7.44 billion the year before. The growth in revenues was due to favorable currency translation and contributions from acquired businesses. Operating income rose 4.8% to $1.19 billion versus $1.14 billion in 2002.

Prospects: For 2004, Co. expects revenue growth to accelerate from the 2.0% level achieved in 2003, but remain below its long term growth target of 7.0% to 9.0%. Revenues should benefit from continued high growth rates in Co.'s strategic businesses, contributions from acquisitions and the anticipated improved performance of Thomson Financial, which has been hampered by depressed market conditions over the last two years. Meanwhile, Co. will continue to focus on improving its already strong cash flow position, which approached the $1.00 billion level in 2003.

Financial Data

(US$ in Millions)	12/31/2003	12/31/2002	12/31/2001	12/31/2000	12/31/1999	12/31/1998	12/31/1997	12/31/1996
Earnings Per Share	1.31	0.92	1.05	0.92	0.66	0.77	0.91	0.95
Cash Flow Per Share	2.52	2.63	...	...	...	...	...	...
Dividends Per Share	1.150	0.705	0.700	0.680	0.650	0.620	0.590	0.550
Dividend Payout %	88.01	76.63	66.66	74.45	98.48	80.52	64.84	57.89
Income Statement								
Total Revenues	7,606	7,756	7,237	6,514	5,752	6,269	8,766	7,723
Total Indirect Exp.	6,415	6,526	6,371	5,723	4,947	5,357	7,807	6,941
Depreciation & Amort.	873	830	920	743	602	644	667	554
Operating Income	1,191	1,230	866	791	805	912	959	782
Net Interest Inc./(Exp.)	252	291	236	204	186	252	293	277
Income Taxes	(156)	(192)	(168)	15	105	109	101	93
Eqty Earns/Minority Int.	(13)	(101)	(50)	...	...	...	...	...
Income from Cont Ops	1,169	1,091	1,070	569	333	502	...	...
Net Income	1,179	999	1,112	1,221	456	1,846	579	581
Average Shs. Outstg.	654	641	628	623	618	612	607	599
Balance Sheet								
Cash & Cash Equivalents	683	709	532	337	329	307	606	375
Total Current Assets	3,044	3,019	2,763	2,528	2,200	2,092	2,680	2,225
Total Assets	18,680	18,542	18,402	15,699	12,558	12,447	13,333	13,173
Total Current Liabilities	3,145	3,202	3,830	2,965	2,477	2,073	2,872	2,393
Long-Term Obligations	3,684	3,487	3,651	2,321	1,909	2,408	4,006	4,594
Net Stockholders' Equity	9,200	8,954	8,220	7,818	6,996	6,745	4,946	4,647
Net Working Capital	(101)	(183)	(1,067)	(437)	(277)	19	(192)	(168)
Shares Outstanding	654	651	630	625	621	616	610	604
Statistical Record								
Operating Profit Margin %	15.65	15.85	11.96	12.14	13.99	14.54	10.93	10.12
Return on Equity %	9.42	6.86	8.32	7.66	6.24	7.44	11.70	12.50
Return on Assets %	4.64	3.31	3.71	3.81	3.47	4.03	4.34	4.41
Debt/Total Assets %	19.72	18.80	19.84	14.78	15.20	19.34	30.04	34.87
Price Range	47.08-37.59	56.70-36.25	57.85-42.70	62.40-38.00	51.00-35.75	45.60-29.05	39.65-26.60	31.05-18.63
P/E Ratio	35.94-28.69	61.63-39.40	55.10-40.67	67.83-41.30	77.27-54.17	59.22-37.73	43.57-29.23	32.68-19.61
Average Yield %	2.75	1.52	1.37	1.30	1.56	1.56	1.84	2.38

Address: Toronto Dominion Bank Tower, Toronto, ON M5K 1A1	Officers: Richard J. Harrington – Pres., C.E.O., Robert D. Daleo – Exec. V.P., C.F.O.	Investor Contact:203-328-9470
Telephone: (416) 360-8700		Institutional Holding
Web Site: www.thomson.com		No of Institutions: 43
		Shares: 26,707,452 % Held: 4.10%

TOROMONT INDUSTRIES LTD.

*7 Year Price Score 134.8   *NYSE Composite Index=100   *12 Month Price Score 108.4

Interim Earnings (Per Share) Can$

Qtr.	Mar	Jun	Sep	Dec
2000	0.07	0.11	0.14	0.22
2001	0.09	0.23	0.12	0.26
2002	0.03	0.17	0.13	0.31
2003	0.07	0.21	0.26	0.40

Interim Dividends (Per Share) Can$

Amt	Decl	Ex	Rec	Pa
0.055Q	8/13/2003	9/15/2003	9/17/2003	10/1/200
0.055Q	10/28/2003	12/15/2003	12/17/2003	1/2/200
0.065Q	2/18/2004	3/16/2004	3/18/2004	4/1/200
100%	2/18/2004	4/1/2004	4/5/2004	4/14/200

Indicated Div: Can$0.26

Valuation Analysis

Forecast P/E	15.00	Trailing P/E	20.3
Market Cap	$1.1 Billion	Book Value	N/A
Price/Book	N/A	Price/Sales	N/A

Dividend Achiever Status

Rank 21 5 Year Growth Rate	10.30%
Total Years of Dividend Growth	14

Business Summary: Purpose Machinery (MIC: 11.13 SIC: 3585 NAIC:333415)

Toromont Industries operates in two segments, the Equipment Group and the Compression Group. The Equipment Group sells, rents an services a broad range of construction equipment and industrial engines through Co.'s Caterpillar dealership and Battlefield operation The Compression Group is engaged in manufacturing, encompassing the design, installation and servicing of industrial and recreation refrigeration, carbon dioxide compression, process systems, fuel gas compression and natural gas compression. The Compression Grou operates through Toromont Process Systems Toromont Energy Systems Inc., CIMCO Refrigeration, and Aero Tech Manufacturing.

Recent Developments: For the year ended Dec 31 2003, net income advanced 45.6% to C$60.2 million compared with C$41.4 million the previous year. Revenues jumped 20.7% to C$1.30 billion from C$1.08 billion the year before. Equipment Group revenues climbed 10.0% to C$835.3 million from C$759.7 million, while Compression Group revenues soared 46.3% to C$464.1 million from C$317.3 million a year earlier. Gross profit improved 24.7% to C$271.0 million from C$217.3 million the previous year. Operating income increased 36.5% to C$102.1 million versus C$74.8 million the prior year.

Prospects: Although the North American economic outlook for 2004 is positive, activity in Canada is expected to continue to be influenced by foreign exchange fluctuations. The improved balance in Co.'s products and markets combined with favorable exposure to after market activity should allow Co. to weather the negative impact of any short-term weaknesses in any particular industry. Product support business should benefit from the higher installed base in both operating groups, with record activity levels expected in 2004. Overall, Co. appears well positioned to continue to implement its operating and financial strategies.

Financial Data

(Can$ in Thousands)	12/31/2003	12/31/2002	12/31/2001	12/31/2000	12/31/1999	12/31/1998	12/31/1997	12/31/199
Earnings Per Share	0.94	0.64	0.70	0.54	0.52	0.46	0.41	0.3
Cash Flow Per Share	1.35	1.11	...	...	...	...	...	...
Dividends Per Share	0.200	0.170	0.160	0.150	0.130	0.120	0.090	0.0
Dividend Payout %	21.27	27.73	23.75	28.70	26.19	26.63	22.45	20.
Income Statement								
Total Revenues	1,299,389	1,076,930	911,005	800,464	723,937	683,482	684,716	542,4
Total Indirect Exp.	168,852	142,455	122,914	103,439	91,935	89,491	92,711	73,9
Depreciation & Amort.	39,423	36,652	...	...	...	...	...	...
Operating Income	102,127	74,829	65,129	59,676	53,770	52,204	46,105	35,2
Net Interest Inc./(Exp.)	13,276	11,366	11,962	10,995	8,366	1,910	2,424	5,2
Income Taxes	31,289	26,318	28,342	23,534	23,487	28,121	43,244	13,1
Eqty Earns/Minority Int.	...	...	...	...	...	...	878	5,0
Income from Cont Ops	...	...	...	...	...	...	59,955	16,8
Net Income	60,230	41,375	43,700	32,345	32,057	38,188	60,833	21,9
Average Shs. Outstg.	64,243	64,866	62,107	57,906	78,688	58,860	58,548	58,4
Balance Sheet								
Cash & Cash Equivalents	...	34,442	35,025	55,450	78,837	28,582	55,954	21,4
Total Current Assets	508,477	483,007	444,268	427,985	385,931	336,242	348,859	249,2
Total Assets	856,176	771,902	720,702	613,787	528,050	442,972	434,341	318,2
Total Current Liabilities	304,900	269,785	226,136	234,579	194,190	190,992	210,651	153,0
Long−Term Obligations	159,694	156,479	171,970	157,187	120,000	60,000	60,000	60,8
Net Stockholders' Equity	376,837	335,316	314,248	218,213	203,062	183,596	155,821	100,3
Net Working Capital	203,577	213,222	218,132	193,406	191,741	145,250	138,208	96,2
Shares Outstanding	63,563	63,455	64,194	57,951	58,576	58,916	58,796	58,5
Statistical Record								
Operating Profit Margin %	7.85	6.94	7.14	7.45	7.42	7.63	6.73	6.
Return on Equity %	15.98	12.33	13.90	14.82	15.78	20.80	39.04	21.
Return on Assets %	7.03	5.36	6.06	5.26	6.07	8.62	14.00	6.
Debt/Total Assets %	18.65	20.27	23.86	25.60	22.72	13.54	13.81	19.
Price Range	33.24−19.84	26.00−18.65	25.82−15.25	20.75−13.85	19.10−13.75	23.00−14.33	18.38−12.73	13.50−7.
P/E Ratio	35.36−21.11	40.63−29.14	36.89−21.79	38.43−25.65	36.73−26.44	50.00−31.14	44.82−31.04	37.50−20.
Average Yield %	0.79	0.79	0.80	0.88	0.78	0.67	0.61	0.

Address: 3131 Highway 7 West, Concord, ON L4K 1B7 Telephone: (416) 667−5511 Web Site: www.toromont.com	Officers: Robert M. Ogilvie − Exec. Chmn., Hugo T. Sorensen − Pres., C.E.O.	Institutional Holding No of Institutions: 1 Shares: 139,300 % Held: −

WEST FRASER TIMBER CO., LTD.

Exchange	Symbol	Price	52Wk Range	Yield	P/E
TSX	WFT	C$40.00 (3/31/2004)	42.25-30.01	1.40	34.48

7 Year Price Score 114.2 *NYSE Composite Index=100 *12 Month Price Score 90.6

Interim Earnings (Per Share) Can$

Qtr.	Mar	Jun	Sep	Dec
2000	1.10	1.12	0.64	0.56
2001	(0.09)	1.74	0.82	0.73
2002	0.70	1.90	0.11	0.76
2003	0.29	(0.14)	0.09	0.92

Interim Dividends (Per Share) Can$

Amt	Decl	Ex	Rec	Pay
0.14Q	6/17/2003	6/25/2003	6/27/2003	7/11/2003
0.14Q	9/16/2003	9/24/2003	9/26/2003	10/10/2003
0.14Q	12/9/2003	12/18/2003	12/22/2003	1/9/2004
0.14Q	2/17/2004	3/24/2004	3/26/2004	4/9/2004

Indicated Div: Can$0.56

Valuation Analysis

Forecast P/E	N/A	Trailing P/E	34.48
Market Cap	$1.3 Billion	Book Value	N/A
Price/Book	N/A	Price/Sales	N/A

Dividend Achiever Status

Rank	25	5 Year Growth Rate 4.55%
Total Years of Dividend Growth		11

Business Summary: Wood Products (MIC: 11.9 SIC: 2411 NAIC:113310)

West Fraser Timber is an integrated forest products company producing lumber, wood chips, fiberboard, plywood, pulp, linerboard, kraft paper and newsprint. Co. conducts its operations through its subsidiary companies and joint ventures owned directly or indirectly by the Co.'s principal operating subsidiary West Fraser Mills. Most of the forest products manufactured by Co. are sold outside Canada as commodities. Co. operates its facilities in Quesnel and Kitimat in British Columbia; Whitecourt, Edmonton, Slave Lake in Alberta; and West Monroe, LA.

Recent Developments: For the year ended Dec 31 2003, net income was C$43.1 million compared with income of C$129.0 million, before a gain of C$8.5 million from discontinued operations, in the previous year. Results for 2002 included a pre-tax credit of C$25.0 million for recovery of prior year export duties. Net sales declined 7.6% to C$1.51 billion. Sales from the lumber segment decreased 7.5% to C$860.7 from C$930.8 million, while panels segment sales fell 8.3% to C$198.8 million from C$216.7 million in 2002. Pulp and paper segment sales decreased 7.4% to C$448.6 from C$484.7 million the year before. Operating income dropped 95.7% to C$9.0 million versus C$208.9 million the prior year.

Prospects: Co. is seeing signs of improvement in its lumber segment, which should benefit from increases in housing starts in the U.S. Specifically, lumber prices are notably higher, and production and shipments remained strong through the end of 2003. However, Co. continues to experience unfavorable results in its panel operations due to weak medium-density fiberboard prices, partially offset by stronger plywood prices. Meanwhile, the pulp and newsprint businesses continue to produce solid results, which should help offset negative results at Co.'s Kitimat linerboard and kraft paper plant.

Financial Data
(Can$ in Thousands)

	9 Mos	6 Mos	3 Mos	12/31/2002	12/31/2001	12/31/2000	12/31/1999	12/31/1998
Earnings Per Share	0.24	0.15	0.29	3.47	3.20	3.42	3.92	0.04
Cash Flow Per Share	3.44	(0.05)	(1.41)	4.57	...	...	...	...
Dividends Per Share	0.530	0.520	0.500	0.490	0.460	0.450	0.440	0.430
Dividend Payout %	222.72	347.87	175.54	14.32	14.46	13.40	11.36	N.M.
Income Statement								
Total Revenues	1,146,700	764,400	385,400	1,632,239	1,562,306	2,309,440	2,204,115	1,863,399
Total Indirect Exp.	161,300	104,500	56,400	179,605	193,773	196,433	192,898	207,318
Depreciation & Amort.	106,400	71,900	38,900	135,434	123,279	136,961	125,142	127,774
Operating Income	(22,800)	(30,800)	2,200	208,869	187,229	278,822	321,408	118,899
Net Interest Inc./(Exp.)	13,000	8,600	4,800	...	...	...	...	61,223
Income Taxes	(13,300)	(15,300)	(2,500)	56,208	34,519	80,509	107,174	21,653
Income from Cont Ops	...	...	...	129,039	108,840	...	...	...
Net Income	8,800	5,700	10,900	137,560	126,488	131,458	147,421	5,625
Average Shs. Outstg.	37,065	37,177	37,264	37,130	33,497	36,707	35,976	35,094
Balance Sheet								
Cash & Cash Equivalents	231,700	122,800	118,200	192,916	270,057	...	97,504	...
Total Current Assets	676,200	639,700	726,800	693,351	759,015	757,665	793,549	634,611
Total Assets	2,052,700	2,033,400	2,127,200	2,115,671	2,352,586	2,453,452	2,264,920	2,108,930
Total Current Liabilities	212,200	177,600	226,300	212,225	471,224	443,322	449,830	310,067
Long-Term Obligations	293,600	293,300	322,900	337,745	359,589	570,633	589,878	718,449
Net Stockholders' Equity	1,285,800	1,287,700	1,298,000	1,291,762	1,203,410	1,127,331	1,026,273	897,631
Net Working Capital	464,500	462,100	500,500	481,126	287,791	314,343	343,719	324,544
Shares Outstanding	36,853	36,848	3,361	36,831	33,396	36,716	36,700	35,174
Statistical Record								
Operating Profit Margin %	N.M.	N.M.	0.57	12.79	11.98	12.07	14.58	6.38
Return on Equity %	0.68	0.44	0.83	10.64	10.51	11.66	14.36	0.62
Return on Assets %	0.42	0.28	0.51	6.50	5.37	5.35	6.50	0.26
Debt/Total Assets %	14.30	14.42	15.17	15.96	15.28	23.25	26.04	34.06
Price Range	39.05-30.01	39.05-30.01	39.05-31.36	40.00-26.36	31.78-21.07	31.82-17.36	33.06-23.97	33.06-16.53
P/E Ratio	162.7-125.0	260.3-200.1	134.7-108.2	11.53-7.60	9.93-6.59	9.30-5.07	8.43-6.11	826.4-413.2
Average Yield %	1.57	1.55	1.45	1.44	1.67	1.73	1.51	1.63

Address: 1000-1100 Melville Street, Vancouver, BC V6E 4A6	Officers: Henry H. Ketcham - Chmn., Pres., C.E.O., D. Wayne Clogg - V.P., Woodlands	Investor Contact: (604) 895-2700
Telephone: (604) 895-2700		Institutional Holding
Web Site: www.westfraser.com		No of Institutions: 1
		Shares: 225,000 % Held: -

WESTON (GEORGE) LIMITED

Exchange	Symbol	Price	52Wk Range	Yield	P/E
TSX	WN	C$98.12 (3/31/2004)	108.0–89.88	1.47	16.98

*7 Year Price Score 140.9   ***NYSE Composite Index=100**   ***12 Month Price Score 90.6**

Interim Earnings (Per Share) Can$

Qtr.	Mar	Jun	Sep	Dec
2000	0.55	0.78	0.90	1.41
2001	0.56	0.94	1.08	1.79
2002	0.79	1.17	1.36	1.70
2003	0.96	1.42	1.54	1.86

Interim Dividends (Per Share) Can$

Amt	Decl	Ex	Rec	Pa
0.30Q	5/7/2003	6/11/2003	6/15/2003	7/1/200
0.30Q	8/28/2003	9/11/2003	9/15/2003	10/1/200
0.30Q	11/21/2003	12/11/2003	12/15/2003	1/1/200
0.36Q	2/16/2004	3/11/2004	3/15/2004	4/1/200

Indicated Div: Can$1.44

Valuation Analysis

Forecast P/E	17.38	Trailing P/E	16.98
Market Cap	$12.9 Billion	Book Value	N/A
Price/Book	N/A	Price/Sales	N/A

Dividend Achiever Status

Rank	3	5 Year Growth Rate	24.36%
Total Years of Dividend Growth		8

Business Summary: Food (MIC: 4.1 SIC: 2051 NAIC:311812)

George Weston is engaged in food processing and food distribution. Co. operates three operating segments: Weston Foods, Foo Distribution and Fisheries. The Weston Foods segment is primarily engaged in the baking and dairy industries within North America. T Food Distribution segment, which is operated by Loblaw Companies Limited, a large food distributor in Canada, concentrates on fo retailing while increasing its offering of non-food products and services. The Fisheries segment is primarily engaged in the hatchin growing and processing of fresh farmed salmon in North America and Chile.

Recent Developments: For the year ended Dec 31 2003, net earnings advanced 14.8% to C$792.0 million compared with C$690 million the previous year. Results for 2003 included pre-tax restructuring and other charges of C$60.0 million. Sales climbed 6.1% t C$29.20 billion from C$27.45 billion a year earlier. Food Distribution segment sales jumped 9.3% to C$25.22 billion from C$23.08 billic in 2002. However, Weston Foods segment sales declined 5.6% to C$4.52 billion from C$4.79 billion, while Fisheries segment sal decreased 13.2% to C$190.0 million from C$219.0 million the prior year. Operating income rose 8.0% to C$1.81 billion versus C$1.● billion the year before.

Prospects: Going forward, Co.'s Food Distribution segment should be well-positioned to increase its food and general merchandi market share across all divisions. In addition, Co.'s Weston Foods segment will continue to focus on strengthening its competitive positi as its realigns its customer base and improves its manufacturing and distribution assets. However, Fisheries may continue to experier operating losses, although at a reduced rate compared with 2003. Meanwhile, Co.continues to expect favorable overall sales and earnir growth in 2004 and beyond.

Financial Data

(Can$ in Millions)	9 Mos	6 Mos	3 Mos	12/31/2002	12/31/2001	12/31/2000	12/31/1999	12/31/199
Earnings Per Share	3.92	2.38	0.96	5.02	4.37	3.64	2.67	5.●
Cash Flow Per Share	4.73	1.83	(1.86)	9.97	...	...	...	
Dividends Per Share	1.140	1.020	0.960	0.920	0.800	0.620	0.420	0.3
Dividend Payout %	29.08	42.85	100.00	18.32	18.30	17.03	15.73	7.
Income Statement								
Total Revenues	21,921	13,153	6,399	27,446	24,661	22,344	20,851	14,7
Total Indirect Exp.	20,643	12,380	6,057	507	431	368	357	2
Depreciation & Amort.	419	253	124	507	431	368	357	2
Operating Income	1,278	773	342	1,678	1,440	1,189	969	6
Net Interest Inc./(Exp.)	188	110	53	238	221	171	136	1
Income Taxes	338	208	97	469	435	310	301	2
Eqty Earns/Minority Int.	212	128	58	281	212	175	139	
Income from Cont Ops	...	...	...	...	...	...	...	6
Net Income	540	327	134	690	582	481	351	7
Average Shs. Outstg.	132	132	132	132	132	132	131	
Balance Sheet								
Cash & Cash Equivalents	1,907	1,518	1,590	1,555	1,261	1,270	1,011	7
Total Current Assets	5,245	4,751	4,848	4,705	5,060	3,733	3,170	2,9
Total Assets	17,529	17,069	16,939	16,663	16,277	11,421	10,049	9,0
Total Current Liabilities	4,597	4,354	4,523	4,427	5,653	3,906	3,317	3,3
Long−Term Obligations	5,735	5,686	5,491	5,391	4,908	2,986	2,584	1,9
Net Stockholders' Equity	4,627	4,477	4,466	4,382	3,626	2,904	2,618	2,3
Net Working Capital	648	397	325	278	(593)	(173)	(147)	(4]
Shares Outstanding	132	132	132	132	131	131	131	
Statistical Record								
Operating Profit Margin %	5.83	5.87	5.34	6.11	5.83	5.32	4.64	4.
Return on Equity %	11.67	7.30	3.00	15.74	16.05	16.56	13.40	32
Return on Assets %	3.08	1.91	0.79	4.14	3.57	4.21	3.49	8.
Debt/Total Assets %	32.71	33.31	32.41	32.35	30.15	26.14	25.71	21
Price Range	108.0–89.88	107.0–89.88	94.60–90.25	130.7–90.01	105.5–77.00	86.85–45.00	65.50–47.50	59.35–37
P/E Ratio	27.55–22.93	44.96–37.76	98.54–94.01	26.03–17.93	24.14–17.62	23.86–12.36	24.53–17.79	11.75–7
Average Yield %	1.16	1.08	1.04	0.84	0.86	0.97	0.74	0●

Address: 22 St. Clair Avenue East, Toronto, ON M4T 2S7 **Telephone:** (416) 922−2500 **Web Site:** www.weston.ca	**Officers:** W. Galen Weston − Chmn., Donald G. Reid − Sr. V.P.	**Institutional Holding** **No of Institutions:** 4 **Shares:** 1,494,478 **% Held:** −